FRED PRYOR

~~740 HARVMAP~~ 535 GRADYVILLE

~~610-544-7720~~ 610-558-4523

Human Beliefs and Values

Human Beliefs and Values

A cross-cultural sourcebook based on the 1999-2002 values surveys

Edited by

RONALD INGLEHART, MIGUEL BASÁÑEZ,
JAIME DÍEZ-MEDRANO,
LOEK HALMAN *and* RUUD LUIJKX

siglo veintiuno editores, s.a. de c.v.
CERRO DEL AGUA 248, DELEGACIÓN COYOACÁN, 04310, MÉXICO, D.F.

siglo xxi editores, argentina, s.a.
LAVALLE 1634, 11 A, C1048AAN, BUENOS AIRES, ARGENTINA

Cover design: Bi Puranen and Peter Welander
1st edition: 2004

ISBN 968-23-2502-1

Contents

List of tables

SECTION B: ENVIRONMENT

SECTION C: WORK

SECTION D: FAMILY

SECTION E: POLITICS AND SOCIETY

25 28

SECTION F: RELIGION AND MORALE

32 28

**SECTION G:
NATIONAL IDENTITY**

Foreword

Romano Prodi,
President of the European Commission

Each day, the geographical, economic and political boundaries that once divided the world into isolated compartments, crumble a little more. One example of this trend is the fact that, as this book is being published in 2004, the European Union is bringing the peoples of ten new countries into closer economic, social and political interaction with the peoples of the 15 countries that already are members. Countries that once seemed immensely distant from each other can be contacted almost instantly today. But the cultural diversity among the peoples of the world (and even within the 25-nation European Union) remains great, as this book demonstrates. What people believe and value, and what they want out of life, varies from country to country.

The growing globalization of the world makes it increasingly important to understand this cultural diversity. People with widely varying beliefs and values can live together and work together productively, but for this to happen, it is crucial to understand and appreciate their distinctive worldviews.

This book provides the reader with rich insight into the basic values and attitudes of the peoples of more than 80 societies on all six inhabited continents. It examines what people believe and value concerning politics, economics, religion, sexual behavior, gender roles, family values, communal identities, civic engagement and ethical concerns, and such issues as environmental protection, scientific progress and technological development and human happiness.

I recently pointed out the need for scientific measurements of basic cultural values that would make it possible to compare the cultural values of Europeans with those of other countries. These surveys represent a major step in that direction. They provide data from representative samples of the publics of societies containing 85 percent of the world's population and covering the full range of variation, from the richest countries on earth to some of the poorest, and examining societies that were historically shaped by a wide variety of religious, political and cultural traditions. These surveys were carried out in 36 European countries, including all 25 members of the European Union. They also cover 45 additional countries, making it possible to interpret the beliefs and values of any given society in a genuinely global context. In this broader global context, we find evidence of a "European culture," reflecting relatively similar beliefs shared by European publics—but we also find that certain basic values are widely shared by publics throughout the world. Thus, in every country surveyed, most people consider the family to be the most important aspect of their lives; and the desire for freedom and human liberty is universal.

This sourcebook enables the reader to compare the responses to hundreds of questions across societies from all over the world. It also enables the reader to examine the differences between the responses of men and women in each society; and to examine differences between the worldviews of older and younger generations; it enables one to quickly and conveniently examine differences linked with education and income, and to examine the changes that took place from 1990 to 2000.

Human Beliefs and Values is a valuable tool for understanding how social, political, economic and cultural attitudes differ from one society to another—and how they are changing, with economic and technological development. It provides a wealth of data that will be useful to social scientists, journalists, business executives and policy-makers working in an increasingly global context.

Acknowledgements

This sourcebook reflects the combined efforts of a network of social scientists in more than 80 societies, on all six inhabited continents. For creating and sharing this dataset, we owe a large debt of gratitude to the following people who carried out the World Values Survey and European Values Study: Anthony M. Abela, Atanas Atanasov, Abdel-Hamid Abdel-Latif, Q.K. Ahmad, Ali Aliev, Rasa Alishauskene, Helmut Anheier, Wil Arts, Jose Arocena, Soo Young Auh, Taghi Azadarmaki, Ljiljana Bacevic, Miguel Basanez, Olga Balakireva, Josip Baloban, Nilufur Banu, Kosta Barjaba, Elena Bashkirova, Abdallah Bedaida, Jorge Benitez, Jaak Billiet, Alan Black, Ammar Boukhedir, Fares al-Braizat, Augustin Canzani, Marita Carballo, Henrique Carlos de O. de Castro, Pi-Chao Chen, Pavel Campeanu, Pradeep Chhibber, Mark F. Chingono, Hei-yuan Chiu, Margit Cleveland, Andrew P. Davidson, Juan Díez Nicolas, Jaime Díez Medrano, Herman De Dijn, Karel Dobbelaere, Pieter Drenth, Javier Elzo, Yilmaz Esmer, Pol Estgen, Tony Fahey, Nadjematul Faizah, Georgy Fotev, Aikaterini Gari, James Georgas, Chris Geppaart, Renzo Gubert, Linda Luz Guerrero, Peter Gundelach, Jacques Hagenaars, Loek Halman, Sang-Jin Han, Mustafa Hamarneh, Stephen Harding, Mari Harris, Bernadette C. Hayes, Camilo Herrera, Virginia Hodgkinson, Nadra Muhammed Hosen, Ronald Inglehart, Simon Hug, Kenji Iijima, Ljubov Ishimova, Wolfgang Jagodzinski, Aleksandra Jasinska-Kania, Fridrik Jonsson, Stanislovas Juknevicius, Jan Kerkhofs , Johann Kinghorn, Joanna Konieczna, Zuzana Kusá, Michel Legrand, Noah Lewin-Epstein, Ola Listhaug, Hans-Dieter Klingemann, Hennie Kotze, Marta Lagos, Bernard Lategan, Carlos Lemoine, Jin-yun Liu, Ruud Luijkx, Brina Malnar, Mahar Mangahas, Mario Marinov, Mira Marody, Kostas Mylonas, Felipe Miranda, Robert Mattes, Carlos Matheus, Mansoor Moaddel, Jose Molina, Rafael Mendizabal, Alejandro Moreno, Gaspar K. Munishi, Elone Nwabuzor, Neil Nevitte, Nhu-Ngoc Ong, Stefan Olafsson, Francisco Andrés Orizo, Abdullah al-Otaiby, Merab Pachulia, Dragomir Pantic, Juhani Pehkonen, Paul Perry, Thorleif Pettersson, Pham Minh Hac, Pham Thanh Nghi, Gevork Pogosian, Lucien Pop, Tony Proudian, Bi Puranen, Ladislav Rabusic, Alice Ramos, Angel Rivera-Ortiz, Catalina Romero, David Rotman, Andrus Saar, Rajab Sattarov, Pascal Sciarini, Sandeep Shastri, Shen Mingming, Renata Siemienska, Jose Simeon, Richard Sinnott, John Sudarsky, Tan Ern Ser, Toru Takahashi, Farooq Tanwir, Jean-Francois Tchernia, Kareem Tejumola, Larissa Titarenko, Miklos Tomka, Jose Torregrosa, Alfredo Torres, Niko Tos, Jorge Vala, Andrei Vardomatskii, Manuel Villaverde Cabral, Malina Voicu, Alan Webster, Friedrich Welsch, Christian Welzel, Toru Takahashi, Seiko Yamazaki, Ephraim Yuchtman-Yaar, Brigita Zepa, Josefina Zaiter, Catalin Zamfir, and Paul Zulehner.

This project would not have been possible without the encouragement and generosity of many sponsors. We have been fortunate to have the support of many countries' national social science research councils and a number of charitable trusts and foundations, companies, church organizations, and private individuals, which worked to make our enterprise a success. It would be impossible to mention all organizations, enterprises, and individuals who have contributed to the project, not only because they are too numerous, but also because some of them prefer to be anonymous. Therefore we can only express our appreciation in a general way for their help in enabling us to conduct these surveys. Most of these surveys were supported by sources within the given country, but where such funding was not available, support for surveys and for central coordination was provided by the National Science Foundation, the Ford Foundation, the Bank of Sweden Tercentenary Foundation, the Swedish Agency for International Development, the Fondation Meditel, the Volkswagen Foundation, the Berlin Social Science Research Center, and the BBVA Foundation.

The World Values Surveys grew out of a study launched by the European Values Systems Study Group (EVSSG) under the leadership of Jan Kerkhofs and Ruud de Moor, with a steering committee consisting of Heinz Maier-Leibnitz, Karl Foster, Jacques Rabier, Pierre Delooz, and Mark Abrams, and a technical group consisting of Gordon Heald, Meryl James, Elisabeth Noelle-Neumann, Renate Köcher, Jean Stoetzel, Helene Riffault, Juan Linz, and Stephen Harding. In 1981, the EVSSG carried out surveys in ten West European societies; it evoked such widespread interest that it was replicated in 16 additional countries. Findings from these surveys suggested that predictable cultural changes were taking place: many variables showing large intergenerational differences, and were strongly correlated with Postmaterialist values. To monitor changes, successive waves of surveys were carried out in 1990-91, 1995-96 and 1999-2001, with input from participants from all six inhabited continents. An additional wave of surveys is scheduled for 2005. These surveys are coordinated by the World Values Survey Association, based in Stockholm, and the European Values Study group, at Tilburg University, The Netherlands.

The data from the World Values Surveys were assembled and processed at the ISR in Ann Arbor by Karen Long, Gabriela Catterberg and Zhengxu Wang. They were then cleaned and documented at JD Systems in Madrid by Miluka Galán-Moreno, Pilar Bustos and Mari Cruz Carbajo, under the direction of Jaime Díez-Medrano. Cleaning, documenting and distributing the data from the European Values Study was done in collaboration with Hermann Duelmer, Evelyn Brislinger and Wolfgang Zenk-Moeltgen, at the Zentralarchiv (Cologne), and Helga van Gelder, Cor van der Meer, and Berry Feith from the Netherlands Institute for Scientific Information Services (NIWI) in Amsterdam (see also Halman, 2001). We are indebted to these people, and to Josette Gevers, Carla Janssen, Marit Beijers, Godelief Mars, Helmine Roodenburg, Kim Colaris, Eefje Strijbosch, Maike van Damme, Jorn van der Zanden, and Jolanda van Sluijs from Tilburg University, who assisted in processing the data. We are grateful to the data archive of the Zentralarchiv für Empirische Sozialforschung at the University of Cologne, and to the Work & Organization Research Centre of the Faculty of Social and Behavioral Sciences at Tilburg University for supporting the European Values Study project in numerous ways. Juan Balderas and Dolores de los Rios of Global Quality Research in Mexico City developed a program that produced the hundreds of tables in this book and checked for accuracy and spelling. Ruud Luijkx (Tilburg University, The Netherlands) and Jaime

Díez Medrano (JD Systems and ASEP in Madrid), constructed an integrated data file containing the 1999-2001 European Values Study and World Values Surveys. The results of their efforts are presented in this book and the attached CD-ROM.

For more information about the World Values Survey, see the WVS web site http://www.worldvaluessurvey.org. For more information about the European Values Study, see the EVS website http://www.europeanvalues.nl and http://www.gesis.org/za

The Editors,
Ronald Inglehart, Miguel Basáñez, Jaime Díez-Medrano,
Loek Halman *and* Ruud Luijkx

Introduction

Ronald Inglehart, Loek Halman and Christian Welzel

This book gives insight into the basic values and attitudes of the peoples of more than 80 societies around the world. Using data from the World Values Survey and European Values Study Surveys, it examines standardized cross-cultural measures of human values and goals concerning politics, economics, religion, sexual behavior, gender roles, family values, communal identities, civic engagement and ethical concerns, and such issues as environmental protection, scientific progress and technological development and human happiness. For information about the origins of the Values Surveys and how they are organized, see Harding, Phillips and Fogarty, 1986; Barker, Halman and Vloet, 1992; Ester, Halman and de Moor, 1994; Inglehart, Basáñez and Moreno, 1998; Halman, 2001. Further information including some recent publications, a list of more than 300 earlier publications, news about conferences, and other information, can be found on the World Values Survey web site, http://www.worldvaluessurvey.org and the European Values Study website, http://www.europeanvalues.nl.

These surveys cover a broader range of variation than has ever before been available for analyzing the belief systems of mass publics. They provide data from representative national samples of the publics of 81 societies containing 85 percent of the world's population and covering the full range of variation, from societies with per capita incomes below $300 per year, to societies with per capita incomes of more than $35,000 per year; from long-established democracies to authoritarian states; and from societies with market economies to societies that are in the process of emerging from state-run economies. They cover societies that were historically shaped by a wide variety of religious and cultural traditions, from Christian to Islamic to Confucian to Hindu; and from societies whose culture emphasizes social conformity and group-obligations, to societies where the main emphasis is on human emancipation and self-expression.

The 1999-2001 Values Surveys were carried out in Albania, Algeria, Argentina, Austria, Bangladesh, Belarus, Belgium, Bosnia, Britain, Bulgaria, Canada, Chile, China, Croatia, Czech Republic, Denmark, Egypt, Estonia, Finland, France, Germany, Greece, Hungary, Iceland, India, Indonesia, Iran, Ireland, Israel, Italy, Japan, Jordan, Latvia, Lithuania, Luxembourg, Macedonia, Malta, Moldova, Montenegro, Morocco, Northern Ireland, Netherlands, Nigeria, Pakistan, Peru, Philippines, Poland, Portugal, Puerto Rico, Romania, Russia, South Africa, South Korea, Serbia, Singapore, Slovakia, Slovenia, Spain, Sweden, Tanzania, Turkey, the U.S., Uganda, Ukraine, Venezuela, Vietnam and Zimbabwe. In order to broaden the range of comparisons, this sourcebook also presents data from the following countries that were not surveyed in the 1999-2001 wave, but were included in the 1995 wave of the World Values Surveys: Armenia, Australia, Azerbaijan, Brazil, Colombia, Dominican Republic, El Salvador, Georgia, New Zealand, Norway, Switzerland, Taiwan and Uruguay.

This sourcebook enables the reader to compare the responses to hundreds of questions across societies from all over the world covering the full spectrum of economic, political, and cultural variation. It also enables the reader to examine the differences between the responses of men and women in each society; and to examine generational differences; and differences linked with education and income, and according to whether the respondent has "Materialist," "Mixed," or "Postmaterialist" values (these categories are explained below). And it makes it possible to examine the changes that took place from 1990 to 2000, for the countries that were surveyed at both times. Finally, we show the relative ranking of each society, in response to each question.

In order to present this material concisely, the responses to each question are dichotomized, with only the percentage ranking "high" being shown (missing data is excluded from the percentage base). For example, one of the first tables presented in our data section shows the responses to the question, "How important is religion in your life?" This table A006 is reproduced here to illustrate the overall pattern. As the reader will note, only the percentage saying that religion is "very important" is shown here. The first column in this table shows the name of a given country. The next set of columns compares the results from 1990 with the results from 2000 survey. Reading down one finds that in the 2000 survey in Albania, 28 percent of the public rated religion as "very important": the remaining 72 percent rated it as either "fairly important," "not very important," or "not at all important." In the 1990 Survey, Albania was not included and data is not available ("na")

The table doesn't show the breakdown among the other three categories. If the reader wishes to examine these details (or to run any number of additional cross-tabulations) is invited to use the CD ROM included with this book, which contains the raw data for all of the variables presented here, and a number of additional ones. This book shows only one response category for each variable. This sacrifice of detail brings a huge gain in conciseness: if we were to report every response category for every variable, it would be necessary to expand the hundreds of pages of tables and figures presented here into several thousand pages (this book sums up the results of more than 100,000 cross-tabulations).

This mode of presentation facilitates cross-cultural comparisons. One can simply scan down the columns in each table in order to compare the proportions in each country that consider religion "very important." The countries are listed alphabetically in each table, but they are also ranked from the highest-ranking country to the lowest-ranking country on the given variable, in the right-hand column of each table. When we scan down this column of our sample table A006, we find that Indonesia tops the list, with fully 98 percent of the public saying that religion was very important in their lives—while, at the other extreme, in China only three percent of the public considered religion to be very important in their lives. This illustrates one of the most striking findings from the Values Surveys: there is enormous cross-cultural variation in people's beliefs and values. This finding appears repeatedly throughout this book: what people believe and what they want out of life varies immensely from one society to another. To assume that everyone sees the world as you, yourself, see it, would be extremely misleading.

A006) RELIGION IMPORTANT

For each of the following aspects, indicate how important it is in your life: religion.

(WVS: V9; EVS: V6)

Very important (%)

Country	Wave		Gender		Age			Education			Income			Values		
	1990	2000	Male	Female	16-29	30-49	50+	Lower	Middle	Upper	Lower	Middle	Upper	Mat	Mixed	Postm.
Albania	na	**20**	24	32	23	24	38	35	24	21	30	27	27	29	26	32
Algeria	na	**92**	91	92	89	92	96	94	90	92	91	91	91	90	92	93
Argentina	40	**47**	39	53	36	45	58	51	40	41	54	50	36	53	48	38
Armenia	na	**27**	20	33	23	28	31	32	26	25	23	30	27	23	31	23
Australia	na	**23**	19	28	16	22	31	27	21	23	29	23	16	23	25	19
Austria	25	**20**	16	24	7	17	30	23	16	21	28	20	17	22	20	20
Azerbaijan	na	**30**	26	34	32	27	36	36	28	33	29	34	28	28	32	54
Bangladesh	na	**88**	88	88	84	89	94	92	82	83	91	85	90	93	85	79
Belarus	12	**12**	7	17	7	8	22	21	9	7	16	12	6	14	10	7
Belgium	15	**18**	14	22	11	11	27	25	16	17	28	20	9	17	18	18
Bosnia and Herz.	na	**34**	31	37	37	32	35	38	33	34	40	31	34	30	35	32
Brazil	57	**65**	60	69	59	68	69	65	65	61	70	65	59	67	65	58
Bulgaria	12	**17**	12	21	15	13	21	22	13	14	23	15	12	14	18	15
Canada	31	**30**	22	38	19	28	40	39	28	27	37	32	22	31	33	24
Chile	51	**47**	40	53	41	44	55	56	42	41	55	40	43	50	48	36
China	1	**3**	2	4	2	4	1	2	3	5	3	2	3	2	3	na
Colombia	na	**49**	43	55	43	50	59	53	50	42	51	53	43	48	47	47
Croatia	na	**26**	18	33	20	24	32	31	23	23	33	27	21	31	27	15
Czech Republic	11	**7**	6	8	5	3	12	8	6	9	9	6	5	8	7	10
Denmark	9	**8**	7	9	6	5	12	7	3	10	11	6	5	3	9	5
Dominican Rep.	na	**51**	45	56	55	46	46	59	54	50	55	50	42	54	51	55
Egypt	na	**97**	97	98	97	97	99	97	98	99	98	96	98	97	97	98
El Salvador	na	**87**	84	89	84	89	89	88	87	86	88	87	81	na	na	na
Estonia	5	**6**	4	7	3	3	9	8	5	4	9	6	4	5	5	na
Finland	15	**14**	11	17	7	9	21	15	11	16	18	14	10	12	14	17
France	14	**11**	9	13	6	9	16	13	8	9	15	10	8	12	11	8
Georgia	na	**49**	42	56	57	50	40	51	47	56	51	47	49	47	50	63
Germany	16	**9**	5	12	8	7	12	10	8	7	7	12	10	7	11	8
Great Britain	16	**13**	10	15	9	9	19	10	13	16	11	13	11	na	na	na
Greece	na	**33**	28	36	25	34	48	60	40	22	42	29	29	37	33	26
Hungary	23	**20**	14	25	10	13	32	22	14	18	24	21	16	23	16	5
Iceland	24	**19**	16	22	6	19	31	24	16	15	25	18	12	20	19	19
India	49	**57**	55	59	54	57	60	61	55	50	61	59	54	64	51	49
Indonesia	na	**98**	98	98	98	98	98	98	98	99	98	98	99	98	98	100
Iran	na	**80**	78	83	78	82	86	87	80	72	82	82	75	88	76	71
Ireland	48	**32**	25	39	6	25	59	50	24	20	51	29	20	31	34	26
Israel	na	**na**	na	na	na	na	na	na	na	na	na	na	na	na	na	na
Italy	34	**33**	24	41	20	29	44	39	27	31	41	30	27	43	32	27
Japan	6	**7**	6	9	1	8	10	10	8	4	9	7	7	7	7	9
Jordan	na	**96**	94	98	96	96	97	97	96	94	96	97	96	96	96	93
Korea, South	26	**23**	19	28	21	23	27	36	23	22	22	23	24	23	24	22
Latvia	7	**11**	6	14	6	5	17	20	8	9	15	10	5	11	10	6
Lithuania	16	**14**	7	21	7	6	27	31	7	13	27	14	9	17	14	9
Luxembourg	na	**16**	14	17	9	12	23	20	12	15	19	17	12	15	15	14
Macedonia	na	**48**	45	51	51	49	43	60	43	37	53	44	45	45	48	58
Malta	na	**66**	58	74	44	65	82	82	61	53	75	68	53	73	64	53
Mexico	34	**68**	60	75	59	70	77	75	60	57	70	67	61	70	67	62
Moldova	na	**35**	29	40	24	32	48	54	31	24	48	31	30	41	30	32
Montenegro	na	**19**	18	20	16	18	23	23	18	15	19	14	21	18	20	18
Morocco	na	**94**	93	96	93	95	98	96	91	85	97	94	91	97	93	88
Netherlands	19	**17**	14	19	10	11	26	20	14	16	22	16	11	23	15	17
New Zealand	na	**19**	16	22	19	15	23	19	20	19	24	20	12	23	18	15
Nigeria	85	**93**	92	94	93	92	96	93	93	92	93	93	93	93	93	93
Northern Ireland	34	**28**	25	30	18	20	40	32	22	28	27	30	24	30	27	28
Norway	15	**12**	9	15	11	10	16	12	10	14	na	na	na	7	13	13
Pakistan	na	**82**	79	85	78	85	81	88	76	71	87	81	76	85	77	75
Peru	na	**53**	48	57	46	56	60	57	54	47	53	53	50	55	52	51
Philippines	na	**87**	85	89	88	86	88	90	87	84	88	87	85	87	87	87
Poland	53	**45**	38	51	45	37	54	51	40	29	51	41	37	51	42	42
Portugal	17	**27**	21	33	13	24	38	33	16	14	43	27	21	31	27	13
Puerto Rico	na	**76**	70	78	60	74	84	91	76	72	80	77	71	76	76	73
Romania	42	**51**	40	62	37	45	64	68	47	30	65	55	38	59	45	32
Russian Fed.	12	**12**	7	16	8	10	17	23	11	10	16	11	9	14	10	11
Serbia	na	**29**	26	32	28	26	33	34	27	28	38	29	24	31	28	24
Singapore	na	**36**	34	38	33	38	38	38	35	34	45	37	31	42	34	32
Slovakia	na	**27**	19	35	16	20	44	41	21	24	39	26	21	30	25	26
Slovenia	17	**12**	10	14	5	10	20	23	9	7	16	16	5	13	11	15
South Africa	66	**70**	59	83	68	69	77	72	67	69	71	73	66	74	68	66
Spain	21	**19**	12	25	7	14	29	24	12	14	24	16	15	27	16	11
Sweden	10	**11**	8	14	9	9	14	11	9	14	13	10	8	14	10	11
Switzerland	24	**15**	12	18	9	13	20	21	13	16	22	17	9	20	15	10
Taiwan	na	**13**	11	14	4	14	16	17	14	9	13	12	10	11	13	11
Tanzania	na	**85**	82	89	85	85	84	87	85	80	85	87	81	86	87	92
Turkey	61	**81**	79	83	78	81	86	89	77	51	89	79	63	87	82	68
Uganda	na	**74**	69	78	71	75	82	70	76	66	78	60	80	71	72	86
Ukraine	na	**22**	13	29	15	19	28	40	19	18	25	18	21	24	18	29
United States	53	**57**	49	66	48	58	65	64	58	54	61	57	53	60	58	53
Uruguay	na	**23**	15	29	16	19	30	26	19	19	25	21	23	25	23	19
Venezuela	na	**64**	60	68	59	66	70	67	64	61	63	65	62	63	65	61
Vietnam	na	**10**	8	12	8	11	10	14	6	3	9	7	13	8	11	4
Zimbabwe	na	**78**	67	87	76	80	78	79	77	60	75	80	79	73	81	85
Total	27	**40**	36	44	42	39	41	47	36	38	46	40	36	44	39	33

RANKING	
Country	2000
Indonesia	98
Egypt	97
Jordan	96
Morocco	94
Nigeria	93
Algeria	92
Bangladesh	88
El Salvador	87
Philippines	87
Tanzania	85
Pakistan	82
Turkey	81
Iran	80
Zimbabwe	78
Puerto Rico	76
Uganda	74
South Africa	70
Mexico	68
Malta	66
Brazil	65
Venezuela	64
United States	57
India	57
Peru	53
Dominican Rep.	51
Romania	51
Georgia	49
Colombia	49
Macedonia	48
Chile	47
Argentina	47
Poland	45
Singapore	36
Moldova	35
Bosnia and Herz.	34
Italy	33
Greece	33
Ireland	32
Canada	30
Azerbaijan	30
Serbia	29
Northern Ireland	28
Portugal	27
Slovakia	27
Armenia	27
Croatia	26
Australia	23
Korea, South	23
Uruguay	23
Ukraine	22
Austria	20
Hungary	20
Montenegro	19
New Zealand	19
Iceland	19
Spain	19
Belgium	18
Netherlands	17
Bulgaria	17
Luxembourg	16
Switzerland	15
Lithuania	14
Finland	14
Taiwan	13
Great Britain	13
Slovenia	12
Belarus	12
Norway	12
Russian Fed.	12
France	11
Latvia	11
Sweden	11
Vietnam	10
Germany	9
Denmark	8
Czech Republic	7
Japan	7
Estonia	6
China	3
Total	40

In our sample table, for example, the publics of the poorest societies tend to place the greatest emphasis on religion. But it is also clear that societies with an Islamic cultural heritage are particularly likely to attach great importance to religion. Thus, Indonesia, Egypt, Jordan, Morocco, Nigeria, Algeria and Bangladesh rank highest in the importance they place on religion. All of them except Nigeria have overwhelmingly Islamic populations, and about half of the Nigerian public is Islamic.

This book mainly focuses on the results from the 2000 wave of surveys, but it also permits the reader to examine changes that took place from 1990 to 2000, for those countries that were surveyed at both times. The second set of columns in this table compares the results from 1990 with the results from 2000. The Values Surveys have expanded their coverage steadily from one wave to the next, so data are available for a considerably larger number of societies in 2000 than in 1990. Nevertheless, time series data are available for a sizeable number of countries, making it possible to examine trends. In the present case, we find that the percentage saying that religion was very important in their lives, increased in about as many countries as it declined—but the pattern varies strikingly according to level of economic development. Emphasis on religion declined in most of the advanced industrial societies, such as Austria, Canada, France, Germany, South Korea, Poland, Spain and the United Kingdom. But it increased in most of the developing countries such as Bangladesh, Brazil, India, Mexico, Nigeria and South Africa (there was also a slight increase in the U.S.). But the developing countries have much higher population growth rates than the advanced industrial societies. Consequently, although secularization seems to be taking place in most rich countries, the number of religious people seems to be increasing in the world as a whole.

The third set of columns in our sample table A006 compares the responses given by women and men. It reveals an interesting point: despite trends toward gender equality in many aspects of life, women remain more religious than men. In every one of the 80 societies for which we have data, women are at least as likely as men to say that religion is very important in their lives—and in most countries they place more emphasis on religion. We do not find a single society in which men place more emphasis on religion than women.

The age differences shown in the next set of columns of this table are also interesting. Although everyone has heard anecdotes to the effect that people get more religious as they age, we find no support for this claim. It is true in some countries but not in others. Overall, the young are about as likely to say that religion is very important in their lives, as are the old. Indeed, in some societies, the younger respondents attach more importance to religion than the older ones (for examples, see the Dominican Republic, Georgia, Macedonia and Tanzania); and in many other societies, strong emphasis on religion is virtually universal, being about as strong among the young as among the old (see Egypt, Indonesia, Jordan, Morocco, Nigeria and the Philippines). We do find large differences between younger and older generations in the importance attached to religion in some countries—with those aged 50 and over being two to four times as likely to say that religion is very important in their lives than it is to those under 30 years of age. But this pattern in mainly found in advanced industrial societies such as Austria, Belgium, Canada, France, Iceland, Italy, the Netherlands, Slovenia, Spain, the United Kingdom and the United States. This suggests that an intergenerational shift toward a more secular outlook is occurring in these societies. But there is no universal tendency for the old to be more religious than the young.

The more educated and the higher income groups tend to place less emphasis on religion than the less educated and lower income groups, as our sample table indicates. But this pattern mainly applies to advanced industrial societies. In less affluent societies, the more educated and upper income groups are as likely—and sometimes even likelier—to say that religion is very important in their lives, as are the poor and less educated (see Algeria, Brazil, Egypt, El Salvador, Georgia, Indonesia, Jordan, Nigeria and South Africa).

There is evidence of an intergenerational shift from Materialist to Postmaterialist value priorities in advanced industrial societies, as a result of rising levels of existential security (this evidence is discussed below). Because Postmaterialists take survival for granted, they are less likely to rely on religion for reassurance in the face of insecurity. On the whole, Postmaterialists place significantly less emphasis on religion than do Materialists—but this applies mainly to postindustrial societies. In low-income societies, Postmaterialists generally are a very small minority, and their numbers may be too small to provide reliable figures.

Most of the findings will seem intuitively plausible to the reader. For example, these tables show that religion tends to be considered much more important by the publics of low-income societies than by those of economically highly developed societies. These findings support the secularization thesis—and though this thesis is hotly debated, it is widely known, so the finding may not seem surprising. Nevertheless, there are some striking deviant cases, with the peoples of both the United States and Ireland showing a much more religious outlook than their economic levels would predict.

We will not pursue our interpretation of this table any farther (for a more detailed discussion of religious attitudes around the world, see Norris and Inglehart, 2004, forthcoming). This discussion is simply intended to illustrate some of the many possible types of cross-cultural comparisons that this sourcebook facilitates. The reader will find a good deal of fascinating material in the hundreds of tables presented in the data section below. An almost unlimited number of additional analyses can be carried out using the data on the attached CD-ROM.

The breakdowns presented in this sourcebook were chosen because they capture some of the most important and most theoretically interesting bases of variation. They reflect the concerns of modernization theory, a body of social thought that has been influential throughout the past two centuries. Modernization theory has been controversial since its inception, and the Values Surveys provide a massive body of new evidence with which to test its claims. As the reader will note, we consistently observe large and systematic differences between the values and attitudes found in rich and poor societies. Economic development seems to make a great deal of difference in what people value and believe. But, although we very often find strong and statistically significant relations between levels of economic development and beliefs and values, these relationships are almost never monotonic: we almost always find deviant cases, sometimes dramatic ones. Though economic development tends to push socio-cultural change in a predictable direction, each society remains unique. This reflects the fact that cultural variation reflects the entire historical experience of given peoples, including political, social, technological, geographic, and other factors and not just economic influences (Inglehart and Baker, 2000; Arts and Halman, 2004).

Implications of Modernization Theory and Human Development

The central claim of modernization theory is that economic, cultural, and political change tend to go together in a coherent pattern, with modern societies showing fundamentally different characteristics from those of pre-modern societies. The two most influential proponents of modernization theory, Karl Marx and Max Weber, agreed on this point. They disagreed profoundly on why economic, cultural, and political changes go together. For Marx and his disciples, they are linked because economic and technological change determines political and cultural changes. For Weber and his disciples, they are linked because culture helps shape economic and political life.

Modernization theory gave rise to heated debate that stimulated influential subsequent work by Deutsch, Lerner, Inkeles and Smith, Bell, Toffler, Nolan and Lenski and many others. Still more recent work analyzing evidence from the Values Surveys, suggests that the central claim of modernization theory is largely correct: economic change, cultural change, and political change are closely linked (Inglehart, 1997, Inglehart and Baker, 2000). More specifically, Welzel (2003), Welzel, Inglehart and Klingemann (2003) and Inglehart and Welzel (2004) demonstrate that the common theme underlying all these economic, cultural and political changes is "human choice," which tends to grow as people gain more material and intellectual resources, place more emphasis on self-expression and obtain democratic rights. Economic prosperity, rising emphasis on self-expression values and the strengthening of democracy, form a coherent syndrome of Human Development. Though we cannot predict exactly what will happen in a given society at a given time, major trends in Human Development are predictable in broad outline. When given processes of change reshape one aspect of this syndrome, other aspects are likely to emerge in the long run. Growing human choice in economic, cultural, and political aspects of life tend to go together.

While conceding an important role to cultural factors, modernization theorists such as Bell (1973) viewed changes in the structure of the work force as the leading cause of cultural change. For Bell, the crucial milestone in the coming of "Postindustrial society" is reached when a majority of the work force is employed in the tertiary sector of the economy, producing neither raw materials, nor manufactured goods, but offering services. This is paralleled by a massive expansion of formal education, driven by the need for an increasingly skilled and specialized work force. Other writers such as Lerner (1958) and Inkeles and Smith (1974) and Inkeles (1983) emphasized the importance of mass communications and formal education as key factors shaping a "modern" worldview. Still others, such as Ember and Ember (1994) and Nolan and Lenski (1998) see the key factor as the individualizing trend in postmodern service economies, based on the fact that service professions require individual judgment, self-reliance, initiative and intellectual creativity—factors linked with human autonomy and choice. And Inglehart (1971, 1977, 1990, 1997), Welzel (2003), and Inglehart and Welzel (2004, forthcoming) emphasize the role of economic security in reducing existential constraints on human choice, giving rise to emancipative values that emphasize human self-expression.

Though any simplistic linear version of modernization theory has long since been refuted, we do find strong empirical evidence that some scenarios of social change are far more probable than others. The Values Surveys show coherent and far-reaching cultural patterns that are closely linked with economic development. In the long term, across many societies, once given processes are set in motion, certain important changes seem likely to happen. Industrialization, for example, tends to bring increasing urbanization, growing occupational specialization and higher levels of formal education in any society that undertakes it. These are core elements of a trajectory called "Modernization."

This trajectory also tends to bring less obvious but equally important long term consequences, such as a shift from traditional religious values toward rational-bureaucratic norms; an increasing emphasis on economic achievement; rising levels of mass political participation and major changes in the types of issues that are most salient in the politics of the respective types of societies.

The modernization trajectory is linked with many other cultural changes. As this sourcebook shows, a wide range of cultural values are closely linked with a given society's level of economic development. For example, the sharply contrasting gender roles that characterize all preindustrial societies tend to give way to increasingly similar gender roles in advanced industrial societies.

The Postmodern Shift

Economic development is linked with social change—but the process is not linear. Though a specific modernization syndrome becomes increasingly probable when societies move from an agrarian mode to an industrial mode, no trend goes on in the same direction forever. It eventually reaches a point of diminishing returns. Modernization is no exception. In the past few decades, advanced industrial societies have reached an inflection point where they begin moving on a new trajectory that Inglehart (1997) describes as "Postmodernization." Inglehart and Welzel (2004, forthcoming) find that this stage brings a pervasive shift in value orientations linked with increasing emphasis on human choice in all aspects of people's lives—including mate selection, gender roles, child rearing goals, working habits, religious orientations, consumer patterns, civic action and voting behavior.

The process of economic development leads to two successive trajectories, Modernization and Postmodernization. Both of them are linked with economic development but Postmodernization represents a later stage of development that emphasizes very different beliefs from those that characterize Modernization. These belief systems are not mere consequences of economic change, but shape socioeconomic conditions as well as being shaped by them, in reciprocal fashion. At the heart of the postmodern shift lies a change of value orientations linked with increasing emphasis on human choice and self-expression. This reflects a change in which authority shifts from religious to secular institutions and ideologies, but authority remains external to the individual. At the peak of modernity, rational science has almost the same absolute authority as religion in pre-modernity. Postmodernity erodes the absoluteness of all kinds of external authority, whether religious or secular: authority becomes internalized.

Why Is the Postmodern Shift Occurring?

This is not the first major cultural shift in human history. The transition from agrarian society to industrial society was facilitated by a Modernization shift, from a worldview shaped by a steady-state economy, which discourages social mobility and emphasized tradition, inherited status, communal obligations, and absolute religious norms— to a worldview that encourages economic achievement, individualism and innovation, with increasingly secular and flexible social norms. Today, some of these trends have reached their limits in advanced industrial society, where change is taking a new direction.

This change of direction reflects the principle of diminishing marginal utility. Industrialization and modernization required breaking the cultural constraints on accumulation that are found in any steady-state economy. In West European history, this was achieved by what Weber described as the rise of the Protestant Ethic. If it had occurred two centuries earlier, it might have died out. In the environment of its time, it found a niche: technological developments were making rapid economic growth possible and the Calvinist worldview complemented these developments beautifully. These elements created a cultural-economic syndrome that accelerated the rise of capitalism and eventually, the industrial revolution. Once this had occurred, economic accumulation (for individuals) and economic growth (for societies) became top priorities for an increasing part of the world's population, and are still the central goals for much of humanity. Economic growth came to be equated with progress and was seen as the hallmark of a successful society. But eventually, diminishing returns from economic growth lead to a Postmodern shift.

Advanced industrial societies are now changing their basic value systems in a number of related ways. Growing material wealth reduces the basic existential constraints on human choice. The rise of a knowledge-based economy makes people intellectually independent, widening the areas in which people have to rely on their own choices. In that sense, the broadening of human choice is the most pervasive undercurrent of postmodern society.

In postmodern society, the emphasis on economic achievement as the top priority is now giving way to an increasing emphasis on the quality of life. In a major part of the world, the disciplined, self-denying and achievement-oriented norms of industrial society are yielding, leaving an increasingly broad latitude for individual choice of life styles and individual self-expression. The shift from "Materialist" values, emphasizing economic and physical security, to "Postmaterialist" values, emphasizing individual self-expression and quality life concerns, is the most amply documented aspect of this change, but it is only one component of a much broader syndrome of cultural change.

The theory of an intergenerational shift from Materialist to Postmaterialist value priorities is based on two key hypotheses (Inglehart, 1977):

1. A Scarcity Hypothesis. An individual's priorities reflect the socioeconomic environment: one places the greatest subjective value on those things that are in relatively short supply.

2. A Socialization Hypothesis. The relationship between socioeconomic environment and value priorities is not one of immediate adjustment: a substantial time lag is involved because, to a large extent, one's basic values reflect the conditions that prevailed during one's preadult years. This gives rise to substantial differences between the values of older and younger generations—so that cultural change largely takes place as one generation replaces another in the adult population.

The recent economic history of advanced industrial societies has significant implications in the light of the scarcity hypothesis. For these societies are a striking exception to the prevailing historical pattern: they still contain poor people, but most of their population does not live under conditions of hunger and economic insecurity. This has led to a gradual shift in which needs for belonging, esteem, and intellectual and esthetic satisfaction became more prominent. Other things being equal, we would expect prolonged periods of high prosperity to encourage the spread of Postmaterialist values; economic problems, stagnation and welfare state retrenchment would have the opposite effect, re-strengthening Materialist values.

The socialization hypothesis implies that neither an individual's values nor those of a society as a whole will change overnight. For the most part, fundamental value change takes place as younger birth cohorts replace older ones in the adult population of a society. Consequently, after a long period of rising economic and physical security, one should find substantial differences between the value priorities of older and younger groups: they have been shaped by different experiences in their formative years.

Materialist/Postmaterialist values have been measured in every wave of the Values Surveys. Materialist priorities are tapped by emphasis on such goals as economic growth, fighting rising prices, maintaining order and fighting crime; while Postmaterialist values are reflected when top priority is given to such goals as giving people more say on the job or in government decisions, or protecting freedom of speech or moving toward a less impersonal, more humane society. Analyses by Abramson and Inglehart (1995) indicate that these items tap a meaningful and comparable dimension across virtually all types of societies.

The shift toward Postmaterialist values is only one aspect of a much broader Postmodern trend toward values that emphasize human choice and emancipation. This shift from survival values towards self-expression values involves changing political, religious, sexual, and other norms. The rise of Postmodern values manifests itself in a gradual intergenerational shift, as younger, more Postmaterialist birth cohorts replace older, more Materialist ones in the adult population. The orientations that are linked with this Postmodern shift are characterized by their age-related differences and their linkages with Materialist/Postmaterialist values, both of which are shown in the following tables.

Changing Moral Orientations, Gender Roles, and Sexual Norms

Postmaterialist values developed in the environment of the historically unprecedented economic growth and the welfare states that emerged after World War II. And they are part of a Postmodern shift that is reshaping the political outlook, religious orientations, gender roles, and sexual norms of advanced industrial society.

The Postmodern shift involves an intergenerational change in a wide variety of basic social norms, from cultural norms linked with ensuring survival of the species, to norms linked with the pursuit of individual well being. For example, Postmaterialists and the young are markedly more tolerant of homosexuality than are Materialists and the old. This is part of a pervasive pattern. Postmaterialists have been shaped by security during their formative years, and are far more permissive than Materialists in their attitudes toward abortion, divorce, extramarital affairs, prostitution, and euthanasia. Materialists, conversely, tend to adhere to the traditional societal norms that favor child-bearing, but only within the traditional two-parent family—and that heavily stigmatized sexual activity outside that setting.

Traditional gender role norms from East Asia to the Islamic world to Western society discouraged women from taking jobs outside the home. Virtually all preindustrial societies emphasized child-bearing and child-rearing as the central goal of any woman, her most important function in life, and her greatest source of satisfaction. In recent years, this perspective has been increasingly called into question, as growing numbers of women postpone having children or forego them completely in order to devote themselves to careers outside the home. The sharply differentiated gender roles that characterize virtually all preindustrial societies, give way to increasingly similar gender roles in advanced industrial society.

As Table C001 in the data section demonstrates, we find enormous differences in attitudes toward equal employment opportunity for women. In Egypt, 90 percent of the public agrees that men have more right to a job than women, while in Sweden only 2 percent agree. The publics of rich countries are much more supportive of gender equality than the publics of low-income societies. Outside of advanced industrial societies, much of the world still takes it for granted that practically everyone lives in a traditional family, with a male as their principal provider. People who see the world from this perspective are willing to accord men preferential employment opportunities. Thus in Africa, Asia, and above all, the Islamic countries, pluralities or even absolute majorities of the public feel that men have more right to a job than women. In Catholic Europe and Latin America, by contrast, solid pluralities of the public feel that men do not have more right to a job than women; in the U.S., Canada, and Northern Europe, support for gender equality is overwhelming: less than one in five agree that men have more right to a job than women.

The differences linked with Materialist/Postmaterialist values are also strong: Materialists are more than twice as likely as Postmaterialists to feel that men have more right to a job than women. The more educated, and the upper income groups are also more supportive of gender equality than the less educated and lower income groups. The overall picture strongly suggests that economic development is conducive to increasing support for gender equality (see Inglehart and Norris, 2003).

Not surprisingly, women are more likely to favor equal employment opportunity than are men—the only surprising finding is the fact that the overall gender gap amounts to only 6 percentage points. Across these societies, 38 percent of the men feel that their sex has more right to a job, while only 32 percent of the women agree. But we find relatively large gender differences in the less developed societies. In the ten richest societies, on the other hand, there is a broad consensus favoring equal rights, and a gender gap of only two points.

Changing Values and Changing Political Cleavages

The pervasive cultural changes linked with Postmodernization have brought about a gradual shift in the issues underlying political cleavages in advanced industrial society.

The political agenda is moving it away from an emphasis on economic growth at any price, toward increasing concern for its environmental costs. The shift toward Postmodern values has also brought a shift from political cleavages based on social class conflict toward cleavages based on cultural issues and quality of life concerns. Economic conflicts are likely to remain important. But, while in the past they dominated the scene to such a degree that many influential thinkers accepted the Marxist view that economics was virtually the whole story, this now seems much less plausible. Today, economic conflicts are increasingly sharing the stage with new issues that were almost invisible a generation ago: in advanced industrial societies, environmental protection, abortion, ethnic conflicts, women's issues, and gay and lesbian emancipation are heated issues today—while the classic Marxist prescription, nationalization of industry, is virtually a forgotten cause.

As a result, a new dimension of political conflict has become increasingly salient. It reflects a polarization between modern and postmodern issue preferences. This new dimension is distinct from the traditional Left-Right conflict over ownership of the means of production and distribution of income. A new Postmodern political cleavage pits culturally conservative, often xenophobic parties, disproportionately supported by Materialists; against change-oriented parties, often emphasizing environmental protection, and disproportionately supported by Postmaterialists.

A Cultural Map of the World

Figure 1 below shows where each of the 81 societies examined here falls on the two main dimensions of cross-cultural variation just discussed, which are linked with the processes of "Modernization" and "Postmodernization" respectively (for a detailed discussion of these dimensions and how they were derived, see Inglehart and Baker, 2000; for a similar type of analysis applied to the European context, see Hagenaars, Halman and Moors, 2003).

These two broad dimensions reflect a large number of the key values examined in the Values Surveys. Since hundreds of questions were asked in these surveys, it would not be feasible to compare the values of each public on each topic separately. Figure 1 compares the orientations of these publics on two important dimensions that sum up the cross-national variation on scores of narrower values. These two dimensions tap:

1. Traditional authority vs. Secular-Rational authority. This dimension is based on a large number of items that reflect emphasis on obedience to traditional authority (usually religious authority), and adherence to family and communal obligations, and norms of sharing; or, on the other hand, a secular worldview in which authority is legitimated by rational-legal norms, linked with an emphasis on economic accumulation and individual achievement.

2. Survival values vs. Self-Expression values. This reflects the fact that in postindustrial society, historically unprecedented levels of wealth and the emergence of the welfare states have given rise to a shift from scarcity norms, emphasizing hard work and self-denial, to postmodern values emphasizing the quality of life, emancipation of women and sexual minorities and related Postmaterialist priorities such as emphasis on self-expression.

The two respective phases of modernization—industrialization, and the emergence of the knowledge society— each give rise to a major dimension of cross-cultural variation. This makes it possible to locate any society in the world on a two-dimensional map of cross-cultural variation. Figure 1 show this map. The Traditional/Secular-rational values dimension constitutes the vertical axis: as one moves from south to north, one moves from societies that emphasize Traditional values to those that emphasize Secular-rational values. The Survival/Self-expression values dimension constitutes the horizontal axis: as one moves from left to right, one moves from societies that emphasize Survival values to those that emphasize Self-expression values.

Figure 1 sums up an immense amount of information. It reflects the responses to scores of questions, given by over 200,000 respondents in 80 societies. There is a great

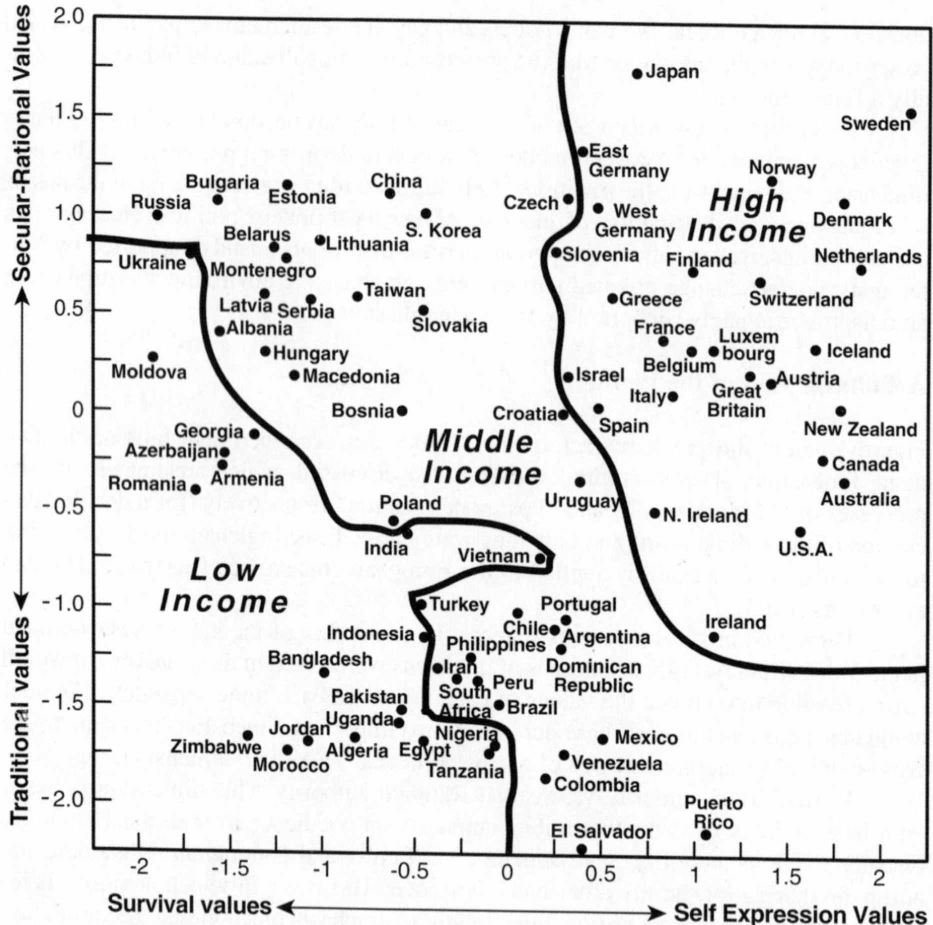

Figure 1. Cultural map of 81 societies, with economic zones superimposed. Cultural locations reflect each society's factor scores on two major dimensions of cross-cultural variation. Economic zones are from World Bank, World Development Indicators, 2002.

Source: R. Inglehart and C. Welzel. 2004. *Modernization, Cultural Change and Democracy: The Human Development Sequence.* (forthcoming).

deal of constraint among cultural systems. The first two dimensions that emerge from the principal components factor analysis depicted in Figure 1 account for over half of the cross-national variation among ten key variables. Additional dimensions explain relatively small amounts of variance. And these dimensions are robust, showing little change if we drop some of the items, even high-loading ones.

The Traditional/Secular-rational values dimension reflects the contrast between societies in which religion is very important and those in which it is not— but deference to the authority of God, Fatherland and Family are all closely linked. In traditional societies, a main goal in most people's lives is to make their parents proud; they idealize large families, and have large numbers of children. They also have high levels of national pride, favor more respect for authority, and reject divorce, abortion, euthanasia, and suicide. Societies with secular-rational values have the opposite preferences on all of these topics.

The Survival/Self-expression dimension taps a syndrome of tolerance, trust, subjective well-being, political activism and self-expression that emerges in postindustrial societies with high levels of existential security. People in societies shaped by insecurity tend to emphasize economic and physical security above all, and feel threatened by foreigners, by ethnic diversity and by cultural change— which leads to intolerance of gays and other outgroups, insistence on traditional gender roles and an authoritarian political outlook. Societies that emphasize survival values show relatively low levels of subjective well-being, report relatively poor health, are low on interpersonal trust, relatively intolerant of outgroups, and low on support for gender equality. They emphasize economic and physical security more than autonomy and self-expression, have relatively high levels of faith in science and technology, are relatively low on environmental activism, and relatively favorable to authoritarian government. Societies high on Self-expression values tend to have the opposite preferences on all of these topics.

Each individual's score on the Traditional/Secular-rational values dimension and on the Survival/Self-expression dimension is included as a variable on the accompanying CD ROM (they appear near the end of the file, with the names "Tradrat5" [factor score on Traditional/Secular-rational values] and "SurvSelf" [factor score on Survival/Self-expression values]).[1] Each person's score on Materialist/Postmaterialist values is also available.

Economic development and cultural change

As modernization theory implies, these two major dimensions of cross-cultural variation are strongly linked with a society's level of economic development. As Figure 1 demonstrates, the value systems of richer countries differ dramatically and systematically from those of poorer countries. All of the "High Income" societies (as defined by the World Bank), rank relatively high on both dimensions, falling into a zone near the upper right-hand corner. Conversely, all of the "Low Income" societies, without a single exception, fall into a cluster at the lower left of Figure 1. All of the Middle Income societies fall into an intermediate cultural-economic zone. One rarely finds such a striking and consistent correspondence between an objective independent variable such as GNP per capita, and subjective values and attitudes as is found here. Economic development seems to push societies in a predictable common direction, regardless of their cultural heritage.

[1] If one of the ten questions used to construct them was not asked in a given country, these dimensions can not be constructed for that sample. The individual-level scores are not directly equivalent to the national-level scores shown on Figures 1 and 2. If one wishes to plot given groups on these maps, the individual-level scores can be converted into a close approximation of the national-level scores by multiplying Tradrat5 by 1.56 and by multiplying Survself by 1.76.

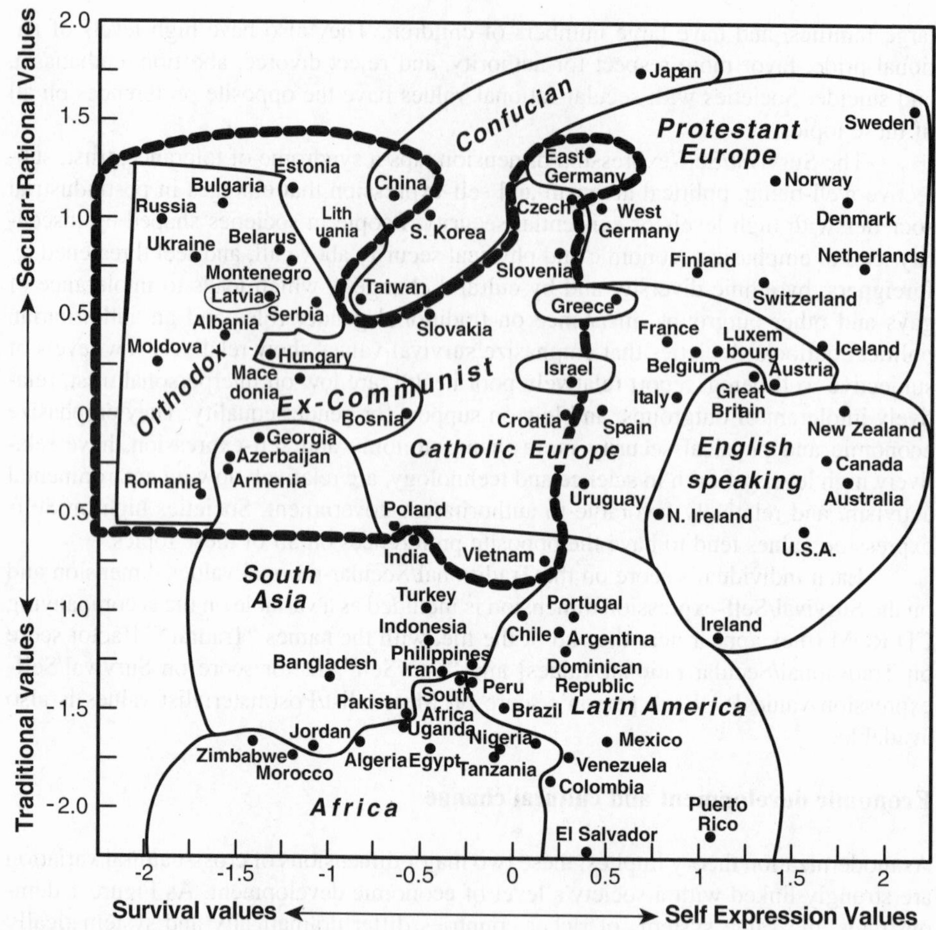

Figure 2. Cultural map of 81 societies, with cultural zones superimposed. Cultural locations reflect each society's factor scores on two major dimensions of cross-cultural variation.

Source: R. Inglehart and C. Welzel. 2004. *Modernization, Cultural Change and Democracy: The Human Development Sequence.* (forthcoming).

The persistence of Cultural Traditions

Figure 2 shows the location of these same 81 societies on our two main dimensions of cross-cultural variation. But this time, instead of showing their economic zones, we show how they fall into coherent cultural-historical zones. The boundaries around groups of countries in this figure are drawn using Huntington's (1993, 1996) cultural zones as a guide. This cultural map resembles an earlier one by Inglehart (1997:334-337) based on the 1990-1991 Values Surveys. Although Figure 2 is based on a factor analysis that uses less than half as many variables and almost twice as many societies as were analyzed by Inglehart (1997), the locations of the respective societies are strikingly similar to those on the cultural maps he generated from earlier surveys. The same cultural zones appear, in similar locations, but some of them now contain many more societies. The similarity between this map and the earlier ones reflects the fact that these two key dimensions of cross-cultural variation are robust.

The maps show consistent cultural clusters based on religion. For example, the historically Protestant societies tend to rank higher on the Survival/Self-expression dimension than the historically Roman Catholic societies. Conversely, all of the former communist societies rank relatively low on the Survival/Self-expression dimension. The historically Orthodox societies form a coherent cluster within the broader ex-communist zone—except for Greece, an Orthodox society that did not experience communist rule, and ranks substantially higher on Self-expression values than the other communist societies. The Islamic societies fall into two clusters: a larger group containing the mainline Islamic societies (Indonesia, Iran, Bangladesh, Pakistan, Turkey, Morroco, Algeria, Jordan and Egypt) constitutes a relatively compact group in the Southwest quadrant of the map; while the Islamic societies that experienced communist rule (Azerbaijan and Albania) are much more secular than the rest of the Islamic societies. Differences in levels of economic development have important influences on prevailing worldviews, as Figure 1 demonstrated, but historical cultural influences persist. The classic version of modernization theory must be supplemented by taking into account the persistence of cultural factors.

This is evident even within European context, where a rich variety of cultures exist. This variety reflects the distinctive religious, cultural, economic and social heritage of each society. Countries and their populations have remained unique in many ways and nation states remain important sources of differences in people's attitudes, values, beliefs and behaviors (Arts and Halman, 1999; 2004 forthcoming; Hagenaars, Halman & Moors, 2003)

The influence of colonial ties is apparent in the existence of a Latin American cultural zone. The Philippines could also be placed in this zone, reflecting the fact that despite their geographical remoteness, the Philippines and Latin America share the imprint of Hispanic colonial rule and the Roman Catholic Church. Former colonial ties also help account for the existence of an English-speaking zone containing Britain and the other English-speaking societies. All seven of the English-speaking societies included in this study show relatively similar cultural characteristics. Geographically, Australia and New Zealand are half-way around the world, but culturally they are neighbors of Great Britain and Canada. The impact of colonization seems especially strong when reinforced by massive immigration from the colonial society—thus, Spain, Portugal, Italy, Uruguay, Chile and Argentina are all relatively near each other on the border between Catholic Europe and Latin America: the populations of Uruguay, Chile and Argentina are largely descended from immigrants from Spain and Italy.

These maps indicate that the U.S. is not a prototype of cultural modernization for other societies to follow, as some postwar modernization writers assumed. In fact, the U.S. is a deviant case, having a much more traditional value system than any other advanced industrial society. On the traditional/secular dimension, the U.S. ranks far below other rich societies, with levels of religiosity and national pride comparable to those found in some developing societies. The phenomenon of American Exceptionalism has been discussed by Lipset (1990, 1996), Baker (2004) and others. The U.S. does rank among the most advanced societies along the Survival/Self-Expression dimension, but even here, she does not lead the world. The Swedes, the Dutch and the Australians are closer to the cutting edge of cultural change than the Americans.

Religious traditions have an enduring impact on the contemporary value systems of these societies, as Weber, Huntington and others have argued. But a society's culture reflects its entire historical heritage, including its colonial history. We have already noted the existence of Latin American and English-speaking cultural zones. The impact of another type of colonial empire is also evident. A central historical event of the 20th century was the rise and fall of a communist empire that once ruled a third of the world's population. Communism has left a clear imprint on the value systems of those who lived under it. All of the societies that experienced communist rule, fall into a larger cluster in the upper-left quadrant of the map. East Germany remains culturally close to West Germany despite four decades of communist rule, but her value system has been drawn toward the communist zone. And although China is a member of the Confucian zone, she also falls within a broad communist-influenced zone.

The ex-communist societies tend to emphasize secular-rational, rather than traditional-religious authority. This is far from surprising. Their people have lived for decades under regimes that systematically repressed religion, and in which it was natural to consider the state important because it dominated economic life, cultural life, and even one's chances of survival. Thus, almost all of the ex-communist societies fall into the upper left-hand quadrant: these societies are characterized by (1) survival values, and (2) a strong emphasis on state authority, rather than traditional authority. Poland is an exception, distinguished from the other socialist societies by her relatively strong traditional-religious values. Adherence to the Catholic church has been a mainstay of the Polish struggle for independence from Russia since 1792. The church continued to play a vital role in this struggle throughout the 1980s, revitalizing religion in the national culture.

The most secular societies in the world are Japan, China, Germany, Sweden and Norway. This seems to reflect a combination of three historic factors: (1) The relatively secular-bureaucratic Confucian tradition; (2) the secularizing impact of communism; and (3) the secularizing impact of affluent postindustrial societies when they are accompanied by an advanced welfare state.

China and the other Confucian-influenced societies have had predominantly secular cultural systems for many centuries; and bureaucratic authority developed within the Confucian system long before it reached the West. Thus China and the Confucian-influenced societies of East Asia have had one major component of modern culture for a very long time. Until recently, they lacked the emphasis on science and technology, and the esteem for economic achievement that are its other main components; but their secular, bureaucratic heritage may have facilitated rapid economic development once these were attained. China's traditional low emphasis on religion and high emphasis on the state was almost certainly accentuated by four decades of socialism. Japan, another Confucian-influenced society, and both East and West Germany are also characterized by relatively strong emphasis on secular-rational authority.

Institutional Determinism?

As we have seen, the historically Protestant countries of both Northern Europe and North America tend to cluster together to form one large group; similarly, the historically Roman Catholic countries of Western Europe, Latin America, Eastern Europe, Sub-Saharan Africa, the Islamic world, South and East Asia tend to cluster together, forming another broad but reasonably cohesive cluster. Despite the enormous recent changes linked with economic and social modernization, and despite the tremendous sociopolitical changes brought by communist domination of five of these societies throughout the Cold War, the historically Catholic societies still manifest cultural values that are relatively similar to each other in global perspective—as do the historically Protestant societies.

If institutional determinism is taken to mean simply that a society's institutions are among the factors that help shape its culture, the claim is undoubtedly correct. But institutional determinism is often pushed to a much more extreme claim than this: it is taken to mean that institutions alone determine a society's cultural values, so one needn't really take cultural factors into account: if one changes the institutions, the culture automatically changes accordingly. If one examines the evidence more closely, it is clear that this position is untenable.

The former West German and East German regions of Germany were still independent states when they were first surveyed, and they were sampled separately even after reunification, to examine the degree to which they continue to display distinctive cultures. Though West Germany falls into the upper right-hand quadrant of Figures 1 and 2, with the other West European societies, and East Germany is somewhat more secular and lower on Self-expression values, the two societies are relatively close to each other on the two main cultural dimensions. This is significant. From 1945 to 1990, the communist regime made a massive effort to reshape East German culture to support a Marxist and atheistic authoritarian regime; while the Western powers launched an equally massive effort, continued by the West German authorities, to remake political culture to support a market-oriented Western liberal democracy. The evidence indicates that 45 years under radically different regimes had some impact: in 1999, the two societies were still rather distinct. But even more impressive is the fact that, in global perspective, the basic cultural values of the two societies were still relatively similar. This natural experiment indicates that, even when it makes a conscious and concerted effort to do so, the ability of a regime to reshape its underlying culture is limited. Though they can reshape it to a limited extent, institutions do not determine culture. After 45 years under diametrically opposite political and economic institutions, East Germany and West Germany remained more similar to each other than the United States and Canada.

There are tremendous cultural differences between Protestant and Catholic societies, but for the most part they do not reflect the direct influence of the Catholic and Protestant churches today. For the direct influence of the church today is very slight in many of these countries. Though church attendance remains relatively high in Poland and Ireland (and the United States, to a lesser degree), it has fallen drastically in most of the historically Catholic countries of both Western and Eastern Europe; and it has fallen even more drastically in most of the historically Protestant societies—to the point where some observers now speak of the Nordic countries as post-Christian societies. Traditionally Catholic and Protestant societies still show very distinct values—even among segments of the population who have no contact whatever with the church. But these values persist as part of the cultural heritage of the given nations, and not through the direct influence of the religious institutions.

This point becomes vividly evident when we examine the value systems of such societies as The Netherlands and Germany—both of which were historically predominantly Protestant societies, but (through the effects of different birth rates and different rates of religious erosion) now have about as many practicing Catholics as Protestants. Despite these changes in their religious makeup today, both The Netherlands and Germany show typically Protestant value systems. Furthermore, the Catholics and Protestants within these societies do not have markedly different value systems: the Dutch Catholics are more Dutch than Catholic in most of their social norms, and have very distinctive values from those of Catholics in traditionally Catholic societies.

There is a remarkable degree of coherence. As we have seen, all of the high-income societies rank relatively high on both of our two major dimensions of cross-cultural variation, and all of the low-income societies rank relatively low on both dimensions. Furthermore, the 80 societies fall into compact and historically meaningful clusters, such as Protestant Europe, Catholic Europe, Latin America, the ex-communist zone, sub-Saharan Africa or the Confucian zone. As the reader examines the following tables, he or she will find that again and again, across scores of variables, the societies that are located near each other on Figures 1 and 2 show relatively similar values and beliefs; while those that are far apart on this figure show dissimilar values and beliefs.

The foregoing provides only a brief overview of the complex but coherent pattern of cross-national differences revealed in the Values Surveys. The tables in the data section enable one to delve into the rich body of evidence provided by these surveys in much greater detail, and to explore the implications of cross-cultural variations and their linkages with economic development and education; one can also explore the extent to which men and women have different beliefs and values; the intergenerational differences or life cycle differences linked with age groups, and the many cultural differences linked with Materialist/Postmaterialist values.

Human beliefs and values are not just an epiphenomenon that is shaped by a society's economic infrastructure. The fact that the Values Surveys cover more than 80 societies, makes it possible to carry out statistically significant cross-level analyses, examining the impact of individual-level values and beliefs on societal-level phenomena such as fertility rates or political institutions. The results indicate that cultural factors play a major role in shaping the societal-level characteristics of given societies.

Moreover, an analysis of the empirical linkages between culture and democracy demonstrates that democracies have strikingly different political cultures from authoritarian societies. Almost without exception, stable democracies rank high on self-expression values, and authoritarian societies rank low on them. These linkages persist when we control for economic level and social structure: a pro-democratic political culture seems to play an important role in sustaining democratic institutions over the long term (Inglehart, 1997).

Welzel (2002), Welzel, Inglehart and Klingemann (2003), and Inglehart and Welzel (2004) have demonstrated that economic development, rising self-expression values, and democratic institutions are so closely linked with each other that these three phenomena reflect a common underlying dimension—human development—to which each of these three components contributes in improving people's ability to exert autonomous choices. These three components occur in a specific causal sequence in which economic development tends to give rise to self-expression values, which in turn tend to promote democracy. Thus, self-expression values were a decisive factor in the Third Wave of Democratization, influencing significantly to which extent formerly non-democratic societies changed into full-fledged democracies. Self-expression values help to strengthen democracy in a number of ways: for example, they lower elite corruption, fuel "good governance" and have a strong tendency to promote gender equality.

The evidence suggests that the remarkably strong linkage found between political culture and democracy is more a matter of culture contributing to democracy, than of democracy determining culture. With economic development, cultural patterns tend to emerge that are increasingly supportive of democracy.

This Introduction is followed by the tables section, which is the heart of this book: it presents hundreds of data tables, interspersed with graphs that place these detailed tables in their broader context. Next, is a section that discusses survey methodology and cross-cultural comparisons, followed by the technical section, which provides information about the dates of fieldwork, sample sizes, data cleaning and archiving procedures, and the people who conducted the surveys in the respective countries. The English-language version of the questionnaires used in the 1999-2001 Values Surveys appears next, providing the exact text of the questions asked in the surveys. The variable numbers from these questionnaires (WVS and EVS) appear near the upper right-hand corner of each table. The text of the questionnaires used in each country can be found in the CD ROM at the back of this book. Finally, the appendix lists variables on the CD ROM, but not in the Source Book, and the Index section helps finding tables easier by a variety of entries.

The authors hope that this sourcebook will be a useful tool to anyone concerned with the role of human values and beliefs in contemporary society. Those who wish to carry out more detailed analyses can analyze the original data, which is provided on the CD ROM that accompanies this sourcebook.

REFERENCES

Arts, Wil and Loek Halman 1999. "New Directions in Quantitative Comparative Sociology." International Journal of Comparative Sociology XL: 1-12.

Arts, Wil and Loek Halman 2004. "European Values at the Turn of the Millennium: An Introduction." In Wil Arts and Loek Halman (Eds.) *European Values at the End of the Millennium*. Leiden and Boston: Brill.

Arts, Wil and Loek Halman. 2004. "European Value Change in the Second Age of Modernity." In Wil Arts and Loek Halman (Eds.) *European Values at the End of the Millennium*. Leiden and Boston: Brill.

Baker, Wayne E. 2004. *America's Crisis of Values: Perceptions and Realities*. Princeton: Princeton University Press.

Barker, David, Loek Halman and Astrid Vloet 1992. *The European Values Study 1981-1990: Summary Report*. London: Gordon Cook Foundation.Basanez, Miguel. 1993. "Protestant and Catholic Ethics: An Empirical Comparison." Paper presented at conference on Changing Political and Social Values, Complutense University, Madrid, September 27-October 1.

Ester, Peter, Loek Halman and Ruud de Moor (Eds.). 1994. *The Individualizing Society. Value Change in Europe and North America*. Tilburg: Tilburg University Press.

Hagenaars, Jacques, Loek Halman and Guy Moors. 2003. "Exploring Europe's Basic Values Map." In Wil Arts, Jacques Hagenaars and Loek Halman (Eds.), *The Cultural Diversity of European Unity: Findings, Explanations and Reflections from the European Values Study*. Leiden and Boston: Brill. Pp. 23-58.

Halman, Loek. 2001. *The European Values Study: A Third Wave*. Tilburg: EVS, WORC, Tilburg University.

Harding, Stephen, David Phillips with Michael Fogerty. 1986. *Contrasting Values in Western Europe: Unity, Diversity and Change*. London: MacMillan.

Inglehart, Ronald. 1997. *Modernization and Postmodernization: Cultural, Economic and Political Change in 43 Societies*. Princeton: Princeton University Press.

Inglehart, Ronald and Wayne E. Baker. 2000. "Modernization, Cultural Change, and the Persistence of Traditional Values," *American Sociological Review* 65 (February): 19-51.

Inglehart, Ronald, Miguel Basáñez and Alejandro Moreno 1998. *Human Values and Beliefs*. Ann Arbor: The University of Michigan Press.

Inglehart, Ronald and Pippa Norris. 2003. *Rising Tide: Gender Equality and Cultural Change around the World.* New York and Cambridge: Cambridge University Press.

Inglehart, Ronald and Christian Welzel. 2004. *Modernization, Cultural Change and Democracy: The Human Development Sequence*. New York: Cambridge University Press.

Lipset, Seymour Martin. 1990. "American Exceptionalism Reaffirmed." *Toqueville Review* 10.

Lipset, Seymour Martin. 1996. *American Exceptionalism.* New York: Norton.

Norris, Pippa and Ronald Inglehart. 2004. *Sacred and Secular: Religion and Politics around the World.* New York: Cambridge University Press.

Welzel, Christian. 2002. *Fluchtpunk Humanentwicklung: Die Grundlagen der Demokratie und die Ursachen ihrer Ausbreitung*. Opladen: Westdeustcher Verlag.

Welzel, Christian, Ronald Inglehart and Hans-Dieter Klingemann. 2003. "The Theory of Human Development: A Cross-Cultural Analysis. *European Journal of Political Research*, 42 (April).

Tables and figures

TABLE OF FREQUENCIES

Each cell shows the actual number of respondents ("n") in a given country (row) by each breakdown (column).

In some cases the number of respondents is small. When analyzing those cases, the specific "n" must be taken into account.

	Wave		Gender		Age			Education			Income			Values		
Country	1990	2000	Male	Female	16-29	30-49	50+	Lower	Middle	Upper	Lower	Middle	Upper	Mat	Mixed	Postm.
Albania	na	**1000**	495	505	258	448	294	425	411	164	355	304	332	436	467	39
Algeria	na	**1282**	650	632	547	477	258	307	555	415	445	303	289	454	642	119
Argentina	1002	**1280**	597	683	394	457	429	757	402	121	381	514	385	235	683	325
Armenia	na	**2000**	940	1060	771	748	481	168	1415	417	786	638	449	891	964	107
Australia	na	**2048**	995	1053	577	792	679	526	810	680	686	623	508	158	1152	704
Austria	1460	**1522**	659	863	260	588	674	789	544	189	335	445	434	118	920	420
Azerbaijan	na	**2002**	981	1021	731	937	333	112	1251	639	531	717	490	1205	681	68
Bangladesh	na	**1499**	828	671	606	745	142	794	403	289	426	619	434	578	799	76
Belarus	1015	**1000**	449	551	274	382	344	270	583	147	351	447	194	461	415	56
Belgium	2792	**1912**	886	1026	363	766	776	402	834	647	415	545	581	371	1022	426
Bosnia and Herz.	na	**1200**	573	627	356	486	358	204	753	243	253	612	276	364	744	53
Brazil	1782	**1149**	572	577	451	474	224	507	500	142	425	275	401	351	656	134
Bulgaria	1034	**1000**	428	572	158	362	480	268	457	275	328	270	345	415	469	29
Canada	1730	**1931**	780	1151	374	785	764	514	906	499	604	562	548	161	1181	544
Chile	1500	**1200**	566	634	331	513	356	435	552	211	466	404	279	330	645	202
China	1000	**1000**	494	506	194	572	234	418	539	43	375	345	234	424	405	32
Colombia	na	**6025**	3071	2954	2188	2833	992	2323	2231	1411	2089	2121	1700	835	2010	485
Croatia	na	**1003**	428	575	318	424	261	143	637	223	150	418	403	132	601	216
Czech Republic	1396	**1908**	913	995	384	632	886	887	752	264	557	656	509	453	1193	184
Denmark	1030	**1023**	504	519	209	415	399	540	146	271	301	405	202	80	708	151
Dominican Rep.	na	**417**	170	245	260	141	11	32	101	277	130	123	85	77	250	66
Egypt	na	**3000**	1540	1460	1020	1320	656	1516	927	555	934	702	1042	1285	1484	164
El Salvador	na	**1254**	591	663	481	472	301	665	345	242	313	522	213	0	0	0
Estonia	1008	**1005**	464	541	266	343	396	292	524	189	208	314	362	385	534	26
Finland	588	**1038**	503	533	287	406	324	549	330	134	312	295	319	256	625	109
France	1002	**1615**	806	809	320	684	611	935	324	356	386	528	378	431	863	278
Georgia	na	**2008**	901	1107	643	768	597	294	1300	414	892	479	588	930	978	75
Germany	1336	**2036**	877	1159	326	753	955	923	876	214	768	548	238	597	1078	291
Great Britain	1484	**1000**	437	562	232	393	346	397	399	135	246	215	225	0	0	0
Greece	na	**1142**	475	664	479	438	194	101	472	567	305	341	313	203	693	180
Hungary	999	**1000**	474	526	198	379	421	591	297	109	192	407	367	468	455	22
Iceland	702	**968**	483	485	259	407	302	396	371	188	269	344	290	204	644	99
India	2500	**2002**	1137	865	543	957	494	1040	487	466	416	749	818	778	850	45
Indonesia	na	**1004**	500	500	181	423	396	247	412	334	357	392	138	383	534	28
Iran	na	**2532**	1361	1171	1276	793	463	765	998	661	852	546	849	639	1012	246
Ireland	1000	**1012**	465	544	184	388	414	198	491	312	272	285	309	193	652	127
Israel	na	**1199**	540	659	413	418	360	255	559	378	330	316	317	186	899	43
Italy	2018	**2000**	959	1041	445	738	817	873	829	298	527	474	512	267	1086	537
Japan	1011	**1362**	633	729	249	514	599	142	855	319	467	391	399	225	829	128
Jordan	na	**1223**	595	628	486	515	222	623	329	269	422	425	286	495	621	72
Korea, South	1251	**1200**	604	596	314	619	267	56	681	463	456	321	423	556	572	68
Latvia	903	**1013**	461	552	185	373	455	234	597	174	459	209	286	341	589	47
Lithuania	1000	**1018**	511	507	249	412	357	166	591	261	189	252	407	245	628	60
Luxembourg	na	**1211**	581	630	387	475	349	418	550	201	211	231	180	209	672	178
Macedonia	na	**1055**	548	507	270	459	326	350	507	198	388	374	260	360	589	49
Malta	na	**1002**	483	519	220	361	421	300	597	105	240	232	245	350	574	74
Mexico	1531	**1535**	748	787	557	639	334	717	524	288	373	397	442	365	842	210
Moldova	na	**1008**	440	568	272	400	336	239	495	273	252	329	342	461	410	53
Montenegro	na	**1060**	525	530	248	412	398	428	440	187	235	261	332	492	460	62
Morocco	na	**2264**	1113	1150	1088	904	269	1738	366	160	334	469	583	851	1127	156
Netherlands	1017	**1003**	491	510	134	486	382	308	351	344	289	363	282	113	658	220
New Zealand	na	**1201**	539	653	181	496	502	468	271	413	340	367	381	107	628	235
Nigeria	1001	**2022**	1032	990	1096	782	144	769	775	470	733	663	542	715	1126	173
Northern Ireland	304	**1000**	468	532	166	351	448	475	354	166	308	221	199	249	534	152
Norway	1239	**1127**	549	578	269	481	377	339	428	354	0	0	0	152	843	126
Pakistan	na	**2000**	1041	959	678	972	350	1083	626	289	601	792	477	1153	806	12
Peru	na	**1501**	733	768	605	635	261	318	707	472	641	514	346	307	941	216
Philippines	na	**1200**	600	600	402	528	270	362	465	372	317	489	386	472	647	74
Poland	938	**1095**	495	600	169	472	454	615	322	156	461	443	165	407	565	74
Portugal	1185	**1000**	386	614	223	303	474	523	376	101	144	295	237	335	523	105
Puerto Rico	na	**720**	255	458	146	250	319	71	219	421	194	266	226	85	457	157
Romania	1103	**1146**	557	589	244	424	478	410	527	201	334	297	428	480	508	75
Russian Fed.	1961	**2500**	1037	1463	457	1026	1017	334	1645	521	847	732	763	1278	1075	36
Serbia	na	**1200**	571	624	228	462	510	414	508	271	381	286	355	573	529	71
Singapore	na	**1512**	722	790	694	589	229	549	814	148	475	537	416	409	978	112
Slovakia	na	**1331**	647	684	337	536	458	377	837	117	364	409	459	557	614	50
Slovenia	1035	**1006**	459	547	258	389	357	278	574	151	260	213	175	160	638	152
South Africa	2736	**3000**	1500	1500	1071	1243	685	1691	1168	141	921	639	992	1154	1587	196
Spain	4147	**2409**	1172	1237	575	836	998	1237	810	360	599	635	430	576	1286	387
Sweden	1047	**1015**	505	510	240	382	393	226	481	308	363	324	286	63	703	218
Switzerland	1400	**1212**	609	603	253	515	436	255	842	111	290	328	349	188	770	193
Taiwan	na	**780**	381	399	121	473	186	291	176	311	244	217	260	352	344	37
Tanzania	na	**1171**	648	509	395	534	217	620	358	173	462	380	223	369	696	24
Turkey	1030	**4607**	2305	2302	1803	2048	752	2516	1385	470	1721	1827	831	1001	2558	865
Uganda	na	**1002**	502	500	540	409	53	250	674	71	217	128	205	318	577	103
Ukraine	na	**1195**	437	758	242	485	468	164	733	297	461	387	319	500	552	37
United States	1839	**1200**	508	692	306	524	370	236	356	604	429	401	299	114	771	295
Uruguay	na	**1000**	410	590	218	347	435	563	268	168	290	311	330	162	525	252
Venezuela	na	**1200**	605	595	496	470	234	306	636	258	321	301	383	296	722	171
Vietnam	na	**995**	489	506	226	469	298	534	380	67	199	413	361	195	608	84
Zimbabwe	na	**1002**	501	501	469	364	169	583	413	6	349	312	177	403	527	55
Total	56056	118519	56888	61573	35324	48421	34479	43434	49734	24329	35549	36184	31823	33927	61203	12820

RANKING	
Country	2000
Colombia	6025
Turkey	4607
Egypt	3000
South Africa	3000
Iran	2532
Russian Fed.	2500
Spain	2409
Morocco	2264
Australia	2048
Germany	2036
Nigeria	2022
Georgia	2008
Azerbaijan	2002
India	2002
Armenia	2000
Italy	2000
Pakistan	2000
Canada	1931
Belgium	1912
Czech Republic	1908
France	1615
Mexico	1535
Austria	1522
Singapore	1512
Peru	1501
Bangladesh	1499
Japan	1362
Slovakia	1331
Algeria	1282
Argentina	1280
El Salvador	1254
Jordan	1223
Switzerland	1212
Luxembourg	1211
New Zealand	1201
Bosnia and Herz.	1200
Chile	1200
Korea, South	1200
Philippines	1200
Serbia	1200
United States	1200
Venezuela	1200
Israel	1199
Ukraine	1195
Tanzania	1171
Brazil	1149
Romania	1146
Greece	1142
Norway	1127
Poland	1095
Montenegro	1060
Macedonia	1055
Finland	1038
Denmark	1023
Lithuania	1018
Sweden	1015
Latvia	1013
Ireland	1012
Moldova	1008
Slovenia	1006
Estonia	1005
Indonesia	1004
Croatia	1003
Netherlands	1003
Malta	1002
Uganda	1002
Zimbabwe	1002
Albania	1000
Belarus	1000
Bulgaria	1000
China	1000
Great Britain	1000
Hungary	1000
Northern Ireland	1000
Portugal	1000
Uruguay	1000
Vietnam	995
Iceland	968
Taiwan	780
Puerto Rico	720
Dominican Rep.	417
Total	118519

TABLE OF PERCENTAGES

Each cell shows the actual percentage in a given country (row) by each breakdown (column).

In some cases the number of respondents is small. When analyzing those cases, the specific "n" must be taken into account.

Country	Wave		Gender		Age			Education			Income			Values			RANKING	
	1990	2000	Male	Female	16-29	30-49	50+	Lower	Middle	Upper	Lower	Middle	Upper	Mat	Mixed	Postm.	Country	2000
Albania			50	51	26	45	29	43	41	16	36	31	34	46	50	4		
Algeria			51	49	43	37	20	24	44	33	43	29	28	37	53	10		
Argentina			47	53	31	36	34	59	31	10	30	40	30	19	55	26		
Armenia			47	53	39	37	24	8	71	21	42	34	24	45	49	6		
Australia			49	51	28	39	33	26	40	34	38	34	28	8	57	35		
Austria			43	57	17	39	44	52	36	12	28	37	36	8	63	29		
Azerbaijan			49	51	37	47	17	6	63	32	31	41	28	62	35	4		
Bangladesh			55	45	41	50	10	53	27	19	29	42	29	40	55	5		
Belarus			45	55	27	38	34	27	58	15	35	45	20	50	45	6		
Belgium			46	54	19	40	41	21	44	34	27	35	38	20	56	23		
Bosnia and Herz.			48	52	30	41	30	17	63	20	22	54	24	31	64	5		
Brazil			50	50	39	41	20	44	44	12	39	25	36	31	58	12		
Bulgaria			43	57	16	36	48	27	46	28	35	29	37	46	51	3		
Canada			40	60	19	41	40	27	47	26	35	33	32	9	63	29		
Chile			47	53	28	43	30	36	46	18	41	35	24	28	55	17		
China			49	51	19	57	23	42	54	4	39	36	25	49	47	4		
Colombia			51	49	36	47	17	39	37	24	35	36	29	25	60	15		
Croatia			43	57	32	42	26	14	64	22	15	43	42	14	63	23		
Czech Republic			48	52	20	33	47	47	40	14	32	38	30	25	65	10		
Denmark			49	51	20	41	39	56	15	28	33	45	22	9	75	16		
Dominican Rep.			41	59	63	34	3	8	25	68	39	36	25	20	64	17		
Egypt			51	49	34	44	22	51	31	19	35	26	39	44	51	6		
El Salvador			47	53	38	38	24	53	28	19	30	50	20	0	0	0		
Estonia			46	54	27	34	39	29	52	19	24	36	41	41	57	3		
Finland			49	51	28	40	32	54	33	13	34	32	34	26	63	11		
France			50	50	20	42	38	58	20	22	30	41	29	27	55	18		
Georgia			45	55	32	38	30	15	65	21	46	25	30	47	49	4		
Germany			43	57	16	37	47	46	44	11	49	35	15	30	55	15		
Great Britain			44	56	24	41	36	43	43	15	36	31	33	0	0	0		
Greece			42	58	43	39	18	9	41	50	32	36	33	19	64	17		
Hungary			47	53	20	38	42	59	30	11	20	42	38	50	48	2		
Iceland			50	50	27	42	31	42	39	20	30	38	32	22	68	11		
India			57	43	27	48	25	52	24	23	21	38	41	47	51	3		
Indonesia			50	50	18	42	40	25	42	34	40	44	16	41	57	3		
Iran			54	46	50	31	18	32	41	27	38	24	38	34	53	13		
Ireland			46	54	19	39	42	20	49	31	31	33	36	20	67	13		
Israel			45	55	35	35	30	21	47	32	34	33	33	17	80	4		
Italy			48	52	22	37	41	44	41	15	35	31	34	14	58	28		
Japan			47	54	18	38	44	11	65	24	37	31	32	19	70	11		
Jordan			49	51	40	42	18	51	27	22	37	38	25	42	52	6		
Korea, South			50	50	26	52	22	5	57	39	38	27	35	47	48	6		
Latvia			46	55	18	37	45	23	59	17	48	22	30	35	60	5		
Lithuania			50	50	25	41	35	16	58	26	22	30	48	26	67	6		
Luxembourg			48	52	32	39	29	36	47	17	34	37	29	20	64	17		
Macedonia			52	48	26	44	31	33	48	19	38	37	25	36	59	5		
Malta			48	52	22	36	42	30	60	11	34	32	34	35	58	7		
Mexico			49	51	36	42	22	47	34	19	31	33	37	26	59	15		
Moldova			44	56	27	40	33	24	49	27	27	36	37	50	44	6		
Montenegro			50	50	23	39	38	41	42	18	28	32	40	49	45	6		
Morocco			49	51	48	40	12	77	16	7	24	34	42	40	53	7		
Netherlands			49	51	13	49	38	31	35	34	31	39	30	11	66	22		
New Zealand			45	55	15	42	43	41	24	36	31	34	35	11	65	24		
Nigeria			51	49	54	39	7	38	39	23	38	34	28	36	56	9		
Northern Ireland			47	53	17	36	46	48	36	17	42	30	27	27	57	16		
Norway			49	51	24	43	34	30	38	32	0	0	0	14	75	11		
Pakistan			52	48	34	49	18	54	31	15	32	42	26	59	41	1		
Peru			49	51	40	42	17	21	47	32	43	34	23	21	64	15		
Philippines			50	50	34	44	23	30	39	31	27	41	32	40	54	6		
Poland			45	55	15	43	42	56	30	14	43	41	15	39	54	7		
Portugal			39	61	22	30	47	52	38	10	21	44	35	35	54	11		
Puerto Rico			36	64	20	35	45	10	31	59	28	39	33	12	65	23		
Romania			49	51	21	37	42	36	46	18	32	28	40	45	48	7		
Russian Fed.			42	59	18	41	41	13	66	21	36	31	33	54	45	2		
Serbia			48	52	19	39	43	35	43	23	37	28	35	49	45	6		
Singapore			48	52	46	39	15	36	54	10	33	38	29	27	65	8		
Slovakia			49	51	25	40	34	28	63	9	30	33	37	46	50	4		
Slovenia			46	54	26	39	36	28	57	15	40	33	27	17	67	16		
South Africa			50	50	36	41	23	56	39	5	36	25	39	39	54	7		
Spain			49	51	24	35	41	51	34	15	36	38	26	26	57	17		
Sweden			50	50	24	38	39	22	47	30	37	33	29	6	71	22		
Switzerland			50	50	21	43	36	21	70	9	30	34	36	16	67	17		
Taiwan			49	51	16	61	24	37	23	40	34	30	36	48	47	5		
Tanzania			56	44	35	47	19	54	31	15	43	36	21	34	64	2		
Turkey			50	50	39	45	16	58	32	11	39	42	19	23	58	20		
Uganda			50	50	54	41	5	25	68	7	40	23	37	32	58	10		
Ukraine			37	63	20	41	39	14	61	25	40	33	27	46	51	3		
United States			42	58	26	44	31	20	30	51	38	36	27	10	65	25		
Uruguay			41	59	22	35	44	56	27	17	31	33	35	17	56	27		
Venezuela			50	50	41	39	20	26	53	22	32	30	38	25	61	14		
Vietnam			49	51	23	47	30	54	39	7	21	42	37	22	69	10		
Zimbabwe			50	50	47	36	17	58	41	1	42	37	21	41	54	6		
Total			48	52	30	41	29	37	42	21	34	35	31	31	57	12		

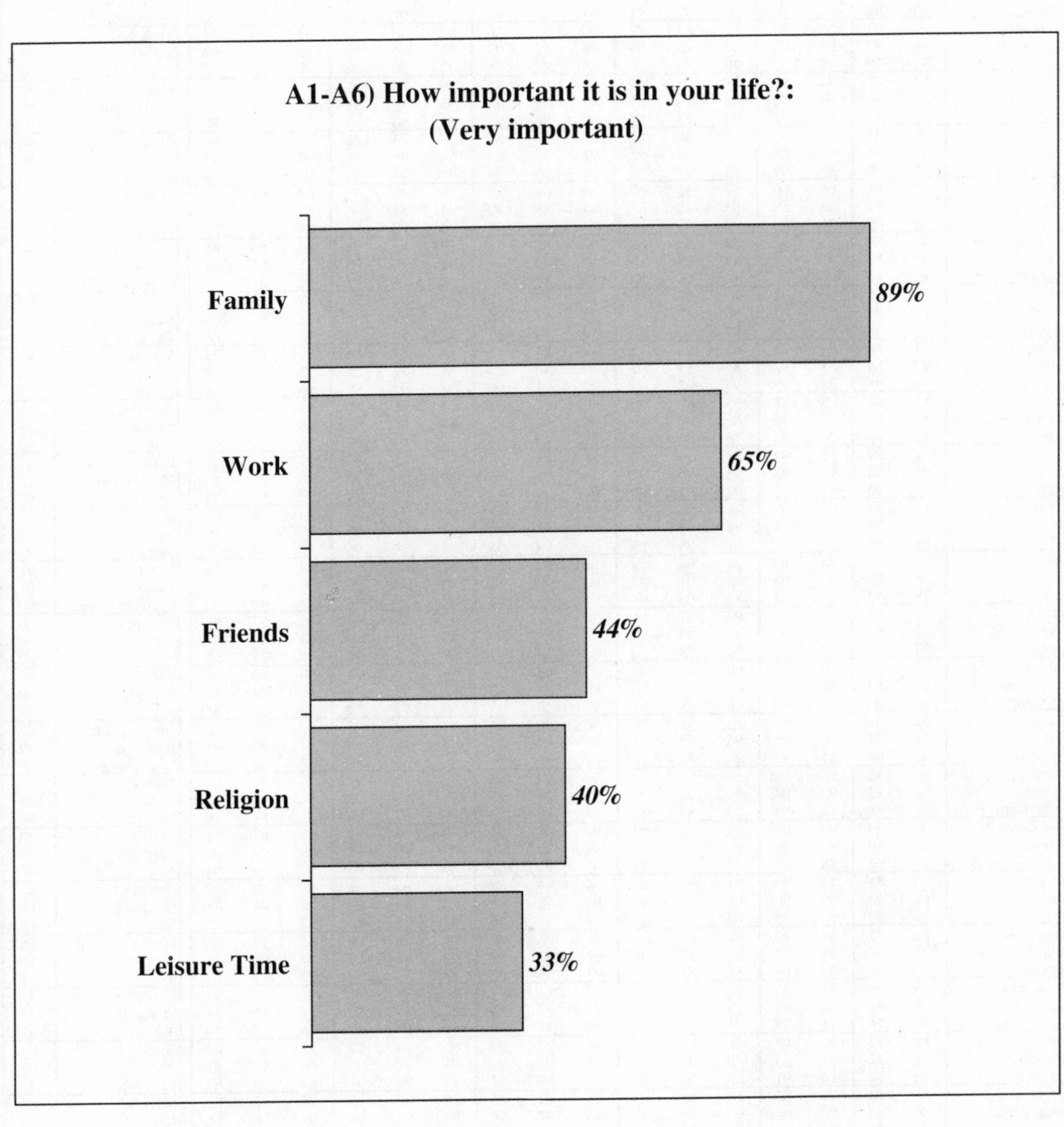
A1-A6) How important it is in your life?:
(Very important)
Family
89%
Work
65%
Friends
44%
Religion
40%
Leisure Time
33%

A001) FAMILY IMPORTANT

For each of the following aspects, indicate how important it is in your life: family.

Very important (%)

(WVS: V4; EVS: V2)

Country	Wave		Gender		Age			Education			Income			Values		
	1990	2000	Male	Female	16-29	30-49	50+	Lower	Middle	Upper	Lower	Middle	Upper	Mat	Mixed	Postm.
Albania	na	**96**	94	98	92	97	99	94	97	98	97	95	97	97	96	97
Algeria	na	**95**	94	95	95	94	96	95	94	95	94	96	94	94	95	98
Argentina	91	**90**	88	92	86	93	92	90	91	93	90	91	90	87	92	90
Armenia	na	**86**	85	88	80	91	88	83	86	88	89	86	85	85	88	84
Australia	na	**90**	87	94	87	93	91	90	92	89	89	92	91	89	91	89
Austria	86	**89**	85	93	80	92	91	91	88	85	83	92	91	87	89	90
Azerbaijan	na	**85**	86	84	82	87	87	90	84	86	85	86	86	86	86	84
Bangladesh	na	**97**	96	98	97	96	99	98	97	93	97	96	97	99	95	97
Belarus	77	**79**	74	82	79	83	74	69	82	83	77	80	78	79	80	77
Belgium	84	**87**	84	91	87	90	85	82	88	91	79	88	92	88	87	88
Bosnia and Herz.	na	**99**	99	99	98	99	99	97	99	100	98	99	99	99	99	98
Brazil	91	**93**	92	93	92	93	92	90	94	96	91	96	93	92	93	96
Bulgaria	76	**83**	80	86	75	86	84	85	81	85	78	83	86	84	80	96
Canada	92	**94**	92	96	88	96	95	91	95	94	92	95	95	94	95	91
Chile	86	**96**	96	97	98	97	95	96	96	98	95	97	97	96	97	96
China	62	**61**	61	60	57	62	60	56	64	67	56	60	70	63	62	63
Colombia	na	**86**	86	86	83	88	87	84	85	90	83	86	90	84	87	89
Croatia	na	**79**	74	83	79	81	76	78	79	79	74	80	83	84	75	87
Czech Republic	86	**85**	78	91	80	86	86	82	87	91	79	86	88	82	86	85
Denmark	88	**87**	81	93	80	89	88	86	85	90	81	90	93	81	87	91
Dominican Rep.	na	**86**	86	86	86	88	82	87	84	87	83	86	92	82	87	86
Egypt	na	**96**	96	97	95	98	96	96	97	97	96	96	98	97	96	95
El Salvador	na	**97**	97	97	96	97	98	96	97	98	95	97	100	na	na	na
Estonia	69	**68**	59	75	61	72	68	59	73	69	62	70	74	68	70	66
Finland	84	**80**	77	84	80	85	76	77	84	85	72	83	86	79	81	81
France	82	**88**	83	92	83	85	92	90	86	83	87	87	88	91	88	82
Georgia	na	**95**	95	95	93	97	94	95	94	96	93	97	95	95	95	91
Germany	85	**81**	78	83	65	87	82	80	81	88	74	86	85	83	81	80
Great Britain	89	**89**	85	93	87	90	89	91	90	85	89	88	91	na	na	na
Greece	na	**83**	78	86	78	84	89	87	80	84	78	82	86	85	84	79
Hungary	89	**89**	85	92	85	90	90	88	88	92	82	91	90	91	87	92
Iceland	91	**94**	91	98	93	96	92	94	94	96	89	96	98	98	94	89
India	77	**93**	93	93	92	93	92	93	91	94	91	92	94	93	92	98
Indonesia	na	**99**	99	99	100	99	99	98	99	99	99	99	99	99	99	100
Iran	na	**95**	95	94	94	95	94	94	96	94	94	95	95	97	93	94
Ireland	91	**92**	91	92	91	95	89	88	93	95	87	91	96	87	93	93
Israel	na	**na**	na	na	na	na	na	na	na	na	na	na	na	na	na	na
Italy	88	**90**	87	93	86	91	92	91	90	88	90	90	90	90	91	88
Japan	78	**93**	93	92	84	95	94	91	93	92	92	95	93	91	93	92
Jordan	na	**97**	98	96	97	97	96	96	97	98	97	97	96	96	97	98
Korea, South	93	**90**	90	90	83	93	90	93	89	89	88	91	90	91	89	87
Latvia	73	**72**	69	75	64	79	70	65	73	77	69	75	76	74	72	62
Lithuania	65	**66**	60	70	60	76	60	57	68	72	56	66	75	69	66	51
Luxembourg	na	**88**	86	89	83	89	90	87	88	88	82	85	89	90	88	82
Macedonia	na	**98**	98	99	98	99	97	97	98	99	98	97	99	98	99	100
Malta	na	**95**	93	97	92	98	96	96	96	93	95	98	94	97	95	92
Mexico	85	**97**	96	97	96	98	96	96	99	97	93	98	99	97	97	99
Moldova	na	**86**	85	87	86	88	84	82	85	90	86	85	88	87	85	89
Montenegro	na	**92**	89	96	86	93	95	94	90	93	96	93	92	95	91	86
Morocco	na	**93**	92	94	94	92	93	93	94	95	89	95	92	94	93	94
Netherlands	82	**80**	76	83	70	83	82	81	80	78	70	83	84	81	81	76
New Zealand	na	**93**	90	95	89	93	94	93	93	92	90	96	93	88	94	94
Nigeria	94	**99**	99	99	98	100	99	99	99	100	99	99	99	99	99	99
Northern Ireland	94	**90**	88	93	87	91	91	91	91	89	89	92	95	92	90	91
Norway	88	**88**	84	92	83	92	85	84	91	88	na	na	na	83	89	87
Pakistan	na	**93**	90	96	91	93	95	94	92	88	94	92	93	91	94	100
Peru	na	**83**	82	83	80	83	87	81	81	86	82	82	84	82	83	79
Philippines	na	**99**	99	99	98	98	100	99	98	99	99	99	98	98	99	100
Poland	91	**92**	92	92	92	92	91	90	96	91	92	92	93	92	92	91
Portugal	65	**84**	83	85	86	85	83	84	83	90	73	85	92	83	87	83
Puerto Rico	na	**96**	97	95	94	96	97	97	93	97	93	95	98	96	95	97
Romania	83	**85**	83	87	76	89	86	82	87	88	82	85	90	87	85	81
Russian Fed.	79	**76**	73	79	73	83	70	63	77	79	69	80	80	76	77	70
Serbia	na	**92**	90	95	88	92	94	93	92	90	93	94	92	92	93	89
Singapore	na	**92**	91	93	90	94	92	91	92	94	91	91	93	92	92	91
Slovakia	na	**88**	84	91	82	90	88	85	89	91	82	90	91	87	89	83
Slovenia	81	**82**	77	87	76	85	84	79	82	88	78	87	85	78	82	87
South Africa	90	**95**	96	94	96	95	93	94	97	99	93	98	96	94	96	96
Spain	82	**86**	83	89	76	87	91	89	83	81	87	86	86	89	86	78
Sweden	87	**90**	83	96	79	93	93	93	87	91	83	92	95	85	91	87
Switzerland	88	**81**	78	84	72	83	85	88	79	84	76	85	82	86	82	78
Taiwan	na	**78**	78	78	79	83	65	68	82	86	76	77	84	79	80	76
Tanzania	na	**93**	93	92	90	94	95	93	93	92	93	94	93	96	92	92
Turkey	87	**97**	97	98	97	98	97	98	97	96	97	98	97	98	98	96
Uganda	na	**91**	88	94	91	90	95	87	93	89	85	85	93	90	91	97
Ukraine	na	**82**	76	88	73	87	83	80	83	81	82	83	82	83	81	87
United States	92	**95**	94	97	94	95	97	94	97	95	93	97	98	96	97	91
Uruguay	na	**91**	91	91	84	95	92	90	94	93	87	95	93	88	92	93
Venezuela	na	**98**	98	98	97	97	100	96	98	98	98	97	99	98	98	98
Vietnam	na	**82**	83	81	80	84	81	79	86	85	82	78	87	68	87	83
Zimbabwe	na	**97**	97	97	96	98	100	97	97	100	98	98	98	98	97	97
Total	83	**89**	87	91	87	91	88	88	89	90	87	90	91	89	89	88

RANKING	
Country	**2000**
Nigeria	99
Bosnia and Herz.	99
Indonesia	99
Philippines	99
Macedonia	98
Venezuela	98
Zimbabwe	97
Turkey	97
El Salvador	97
Mexico	97
Bangladesh	97
Jordan	97
Chile	96
Egypt	96
Albania	96
Puerto Rico	96
United States	95
Malta	95
South Africa	95
Algeria	95
Georgia	95
Iran	95
Iceland	94
Canada	94
Morocco	93
Brazil	93
Japan	93
New Zealand	93
Tanzania	93
India	93
Pakistan	93
Montenegro	92
Serbia	92
Poland	92
Singapore	92
Ireland	92
Uruguay	91
Uganda	91
Northern Ireland	90
Argentina	90
Australia	90
Italy	90
Korea, South	90
Sweden	90
Austria	89
Great Britain	89
Hungary	89
Luxembourg	88
Norway	88
France	88
Slovakia	88
Belgium	87
Denmark	87
Armenia	86
Colombia	86
Moldova	86
Spain	86
Dominican Rep.	86
Azerbaijan	85
Romania	85
Czech Republic	85
Portugal	84
Bulgaria	83
Greece	83
Peru	83
Vietnam	82
Slovenia	82
Ukraine	82
Switzerland	81
Germany	81
Finland	80
Netherlands	80
Croatia	79
Belarus	79
Taiwan	78
Russian Fed.	76
Latvia	72
Estonia	68
Lithuania	66
China	61
Total	89

A002) FRIENDS IMPORTANT

For each of the following aspects, indicate how important it is in your life: friends.

Very important (%)

(WVS: V5; EVS: V3)

Country	Wave		Gender		Age			Education			Income			Values		
	1990	2000	Male	Female	16-29	30-49	50+	Lower	Middle	Upper	Lower	Middle	Upper	Mat	Mixed	Postm.
Albania	na	**32**	36	28	34	28	37	30	31	43	29	29	38	32	32	26
Algeria	na	**36**	41	31	40	35	28	29	38	39	34	34	38	35	36	40
Argentina	51	**50**	50	50	52	47	53	45	57	60	49	49	54	44	50	55
Armenia	na	**45**	52	38	48	44	40	41	44	49	49	43	40	40	49	45
Australia	na	**63**	60	66	61	63	64	62	61	66	63	62	64	58	63	65
Austria	35	**44**	40	47	62	39	39	42	45	46	43	40	47	49	41	47
Azerbaijan	na	**35**	39	32	48	29	27	27	32	43	32	34	40	32	40	54
Bangladesh	na	**32**	37	26	31	33	37	32	30	34	32	29	37	33	33	24
Belarus	37	**27**	30	24	40	26	18	17	31	29	29	25	30	22	31	45
Belgium	46	**48**	46	50	64	45	44	40	47	57	45	44	51	41	49	53
Bosnia and Herz.	na	**71**	72	69	74	70	69	68	70	75	74	72	67	67	72	74
Brazil	57	**58**	56	60	50	61	65	58	54	67	59	53	59	59	56	63
Bulgaria	38	**37**	43	32	51	39	29	29	42	41	34	39	35	33	39	52
Canada	51	**60**	58	63	66	57	61	59	60	63	54	62	64	59	60	61
Chile	19	**29**	29	30	36	27	26	20	30	49	23	30	38	26	29	37
China	22	**20**	21	19	26	20	16	17	21	49	15	23	26	19	23	25
Colombia	na	**34**	34	34	32	33	38	31	34	37	31	35	36	29	30	30
Croatia	na	**36**	36	37	43	34	35	37	36	38	36	32	44	35	35	42
Czech Republic	27	**27**	25	29	39	21	25	26	27	29	27	27	26	23	27	35
Denmark	53	**55**	49	61	69	49	54	56	58	53	61	53	50	55	56	55
Dominican Rep.	na	**36**	38	34	37	31	46	23	36	36	36	34	35	34	36	39
Egypt	na	**37**	43	31	43	35	34	31	42	47	38	35	37	32	42	47
El Salvador	na	**65**	64	66	64	61	71	64	65	66	64	63	71	na	na	na
Estonia	23	**26**	26	26	43	21	22	28	27	22	24	25	28	22	28	42
Finland	43	**51**	47	56	72	48	44	49	58	43	54	55	41	52	50	59
France	41	**50**	50	49	61	47	47	45	54	59	49	46	54	42	51	58
Georgia	na	**74**	80	69	80	74	66	70	73	79	69	73	81	71	76	80
Germany	34	**48**	48	49	58	49	43	41	54	54	40	50	50	48	48	52
Great Britain	48	**58**	56	60	67	52	58	57	57	60	51	61	56	na	na	na
Greece	na	**42**	41	43	54	33	35	26	37	50	35	41	50	41	41	49
Hungary	28	**34**	37	31	47	25	34	34	31	37	35	33	34	33	36	30
Iceland	49	**48**	43	52	62	40	46	48	50	43	50	47	46	45	48	51
India	30	**40**	46	32	43	40	37	33	45	50	39	39	41	41	42	53
Indonesia	na	**56**	63	49	63	61	48	46	56	64	55	59	52	56	58	57
Iran	na	**30**	30	29	33	29	23	25	32	32	26	28	33	27	32	25
Ireland	55	**61**	57	65	68	57	59	57	60	70	55	59	65	61	60	66
Israel	na	**na**	na	na	na	na	na	na	na	na	na	na	na	na	na	na
Italy	38	**36**	37	34	51	35	28	28	42	41	32	36	40	28	34	43
Japan	34	**48**	45	51	66	49	40	39	48	54	48	46	49	41	48	62
Jordan	na	**47**	52	43	50	44	49	47	43	54	43	53	46	48	46	55
Korea, South	52	**45**	46	43	60	41	36	42	42	49	46	43	45	42	46	57
Latvia	16	**25**	22	27	28	21	26	24	24	27	28	24	21	25	24	26
Lithuania	19	**17**	19	16	28	16	11	8	20	24	13	13	17	19	16	13
Luxembourg	na	**47**	46	47	60	46	39	41	46	58	41	42	47	45	45	51
Macedonia	na	**50**	51	48	53	44	54	47	50	52	47	49	54	43	54	58
Malta	na	**32**	33	31	38	27	33	29	32	40	29	30	31	31	33	28
Mexico	25	**38**	37	40	39	34	45	36	38	49	38	37	39	44	36	39
Moldova	na	**35**	43	28	41	31	35	29	39	35	30	34	43	35	37	34
Montenegro	na	**43**	46	40	52	42	39	36	47	51	34	36	49	39	46	50
Morocco	na	**42**	46	38	47	41	32	40	44	59	30	42	45	43	42	39
Netherlands	63	**60**	52	69	74	57	57	56	60	66	62	58	59	55	61	60
New Zealand	na	**55**	48	61	59	51	58	54	54	58	55	53	58	51	56	59
Nigeria	53	**64**	67	60	66	61	60	64	65	61	67	61	63	62	65	62
Northern Ireland	53	**65**	65	66	70	60	68	67	66	62	65	65	55	71	64	65
Norway	68	**59**	51	67	67	61	52	55	59	63	na	na	na	54	59	66
Pakistan	na	**20**	20	19	26	15	19	19	19	23	21	18	18	21	18	na
Peru	na	**25**	24	26	26	22	27	25	24	26	26	21	28	25	23	33
Philippines	na	**37**	38	35	38	32	45	39	33	40	33	36	42	37	37	40
Poland	23	**27**	26	29	35	22	29	28	27	26	28	29	25	26	27	28
Portugal	20	**30**	35	27	39	26	30	26	39	43	17	30	37	28	32	36
Puerto Rico	na	**33**	30	34	27	29	37	46	32	30	37	33	28	29	35	30
Romania	25	**26**	30	23	36	22	25	24	29	24	26	26	26	25	26	27
Russian Fed.	29	**27**	28	27	36	27	23	16	28	33	24	29	29	25	30	32
Serbia	na	**58**	61	54	65	58	54	54	58	63	56	58	56	55	60	62
Singapore	na	**40**	42	37	47	35	27	33	43	46	29	39	47	28	43	49
Slovakia	na	**34**	35	32	45	31	28	31	34	40	33	28	37	32	37	38
Slovenia	38	**42**	41	43	54	32	43	42	43	35	43	41	43	43	41	45
South Africa	23	**34**	36	32	38	31	36	31	39	37	31	29	44	31	35	51
Spain	45	**43**	45	42	50	41	41	41	44	51	40	43	48	43	43	45
Sweden	69	**71**	66	75	81	70	65	61	73	76	74	68	69	67	70	75
Switzerland	52	**59**	54	63	75	57	51	55	60	54	59	59	63	50	58	68
Taiwan	na	**29**	28	30	37	28	28	24	37	30	27	25	34	29	31	27
Tanzania	na	**32**	35	29	29	33	34	32	33	29	35	30	33	27	34	39
Turkey	55	**74**	74	73	73	75	73	72	75	80	72	74	78	73	75	73
Uganda	na	**75**	79	71	76	74	76	77	74	76	77	71	81	70	77	80
Ukraine	na	**39**	40	38	45	39	36	31	40	42	33	38	48	40	39	47
United States	54	**64**	61	68	59	62	72	58	64	67	59	66	68	62	64	65
Uruguay	na	**58**	59	58	59	56	60	53	64	68	53	59	62	59	56	62
Venezuela	na	**53**	52	53	52	49	62	58	49	54	51	52	55	52	53	51
Vietnam	na	**21**	24	18	23	20	22	17	28	19	22	19	23	14	26	22
Zimbabwe	na	**35**	34	36	36	34	34	33	38	48	38	32	33	37	33	35
Total	40	44	44	43	49	41	42	40	44	48	42	42	45	39	45	51

RANKING	
Country	2000
Uganda	75
Georgia	74
Turkey	74
Sweden	71
Bosnia and Herz.	71
Northern Ireland	65
El Salvador	65
United States	64
Nigeria	64
Australia	63
Ireland	61
Netherlands	60
Canada	60
Norway	59
Switzerland	59
Great Britain	58
Uruguay	58
Brazil	58
Serbia	58
Indonesia	56
New Zealand	55
Denmark	55
Venezuela	53
Finland	51
Argentina	50
France	50
Macedonia	50
Belgium	48
Japan	48
Germany	48
Iceland	48
Jordan	47
Luxembourg	47
Korea, South	45
Armenia	45
Austria	44
Spain	43
Montenegro	43
Greece	42
Morocco	42
Slovenia	42
India	40
Singapore	40
Ukraine	39
Mexico	38
Egypt	37
Bulgaria	37
Philippines	37
Croatia	36
Algeria	36
Dominican Rep.	36
Italy	36
Moldova	35
Azerbaijan	35
Zimbabwe	35
South Africa	34
Hungary	34
Slovakia	34
Colombia	34
Puerto Rico	33
Albania	32
Bangladesh	32
Malta	32
Tanzania	32
Portugal	30
Iran	30
Chile	29
Taiwan	29
Poland	27
Russian Fed.	27
Belarus	27
Czech Republic	27
Estonia	26
Romania	26
Latvia	25
Peru	25
Vietnam	21
China	20
Pakistan	20
Lithuania	17
Total	44

A003) LEISURE TIME

For each of the following aspects, indicate how important it is in your life: leisure.

Very important (%)

(WVS: V6; EVS: V4)

Country	Wave		Gender		Age			Education			Income			Values		
	1990	2000	Male	Female	16-29	30-49	50+	Lower	Middle	Upper	Lower	Middle	Upper	Mat	Mixed	Postm.
Albania	na	**14**	16	12	23	12	9	11	14	22	10	16	16	10	19	5
Algeria	na	**24**	25	24	31	22	13	16	27	26	29	20	23	25	24	24
Argentina	40	**36**	37	35	38	38	32	36	36	35	34	35	38	33	35	38
Armenia	na	**24**	25	22	26	24	19	17	24	26	22	26	20	20	27	22
Australia	na	**45**	45	45	41	50	43	41	46	46	40	45	51	44	43	48
Austria	37	**39**	41	38	54	37	34	39	41	34	33	41	41	46	38	39
Azerbaijan	na	**30**	28	32	40	26	22	21	26	40	24	27	39	28	34	30
Bangladesh	na	**23**	25	22	23	24	25	21	26	27	20	23	28	22	24	30
Belarus	37	**25**	29	22	35	25	18	18	28	27	26	26	23	23	26	30
Belgium	41	**40**	39	40	44	41	36	34	40	44	37	39	42	37	40	43
Bosnia and Herz.	na	**44**	44	44	49	44	37	39	44	46	44	43	44	41	44	43
Brazil	52	**54**	54	54	54	56	52	56	52	57	54	51	56	53	54	58
Bulgaria	36	**23**	26	20	31	28	15	14	28	28	16	23	26	20	26	29
Canada	42	**38**	38	39	36	39	38	37	38	40	30	37	43	31	38	42
Chile	33	**54**	57	51	58	55	49	49	55	63	55	51	57	49	56	58
China	14	**7**	8	6	10	6	8	6	7	23	5	8	11	7	7	22
Colombia	na	**40**	39	40	38	42	38	33	41	49	33	43	45	33	34	39
Croatia	na	**25**	27	22	41	21	18	25	23	28	15	22	33	16	24	36
Czech Republic	30	**21**	22	21	27	19	19	23	20	17	19	23	20	25	20	22
Denmark	48	**45**	46	43	46	47	41	46	43	44	43	47	42	46	45	53
Dominican Rep.	na	**31**	31	31	34	24	50	36	35	29	32	30	32	35	33	23
Egypt	na	**9**	11	8	12	8	8	7	10	14	9	9	10	7	10	15
El Salvador	na	**62**	62	62	61	60	67	62	62	62	62	63	63	na	na	na
Estonia	25	**19**	18	20	33	15	14	19	20	16	14	17	21	14	21	23
Finland	47	**39**	43	36	50	42	30	38	42	37	38	40	38	39	37	46
France	31	**37**	39	35	46	39	30	33	39	46	32	36	43	34	35	46
Georgia	na	**36**	39	34	45	37	26	36	35	40	33	38	40	34	38	44
Germany	36	**32**	34	31	44	33	26	27	37	34	26	31	33	31	32	37
Great Britain	45	**51**	57	45	54	54	49	50	52	48	42	53	60	na	na	na
Greece	na	**43**	44	41	53	38	30	29	38	49	41	40	46	38	42	53
Hungary	32	**31**	36	27	44	32	24	30	35	29	27	33	33	27	37	20
Iceland	36	**34**	32	36	32	34	35	35	31	35	34	34	33	33	34	38
India	17	**29**	31	26	30	28	29	25	30	36	26	27	32	27	30	31
Indonesia	na	**17**	18	16	25	19	11	11	16	24	18	17	15	18	18	21
Iran	na	**30**	27	33	34	29	21	24	29	36	25	29	32	26	31	37
Ireland	32	**41**	42	39	43	41	38	35	42	46	33	44	45	44	39	43
Israel	na	**na**	na	na	na	na	na	na	na	na	na	na	na	na	na	na
Italy	33	**29**	31	28	42	32	20	23	35	33	25	27	33	24	28	34
Japan	24	**44**	40	48	61	47	34	33	44	51	40	43	46	46	44	47
Jordan	na	**17**	16	19	19	19	11	13	17	27	13	19	21	15	19	24
Korea, South	25	**24**	23	24	31	22	20	27	20	29	24	20	27	21	25	41
Latvia	21	**17**	18	16	18	16	17	15	17	17	16	20	16	18	16	15
Lithuania	17	**16**	15	16	22	15	11	11	17	17	12	15	15	16	15	18
Luxembourg	na	**38**	43	33	46	39	31	36	38	37	35	37	35	36	35	45
Macedonia	na	**42**	44	39	44	44	37	34	43	51	40	44	43	36	45	39
Malta	na	**50**	54	46	56	49	46	42	53	49	49	49	50	44	54	41
Mexico	28	**51**	50	51	47	53	53	49	52	55	51	54	50	51	54	49
Moldova	na	**25**	26	24	30	22	24	20	28	25	21	23	32	23	28	35
Montenegro	na	**25**	25	24	36	24	18	17	29	32	16	15	33	23	24	34
Morocco	na	**40**	41	39	44	39	32	37	50	51	31	40	41	38	43	41
Netherlands	51	**53**	50	57	59	52	51	56	54	50	54	52	53	54	53	54
New Zealand	na	**45**	45	45	48	48	41	44	47	45	39	42	55	50	47	47
Nigeria	68	**52**	53	50	55	50	36	48	53	57	51	52	53	50	52	57
Northern Ireland	31	**46**	51	42	57	43	42	43	51	46	46	40	44	51	43	50
Norway	42	**39**	43	35	36	44	35	34	39	43	na	na	na	33	41	37
Pakistan	na	**5**	7	3	7	4	4	4	6	6	5	5	7	5	5	na
Peru	na	**23**	23	23	22	24	24	22	23	23	23	24	22	27	22	21
Philippines	na	**15**	17	14	15	15	16	14	16	15	17	12	18	16	15	10
Poland	35	**25**	24	26	29	27	19	22	28	30	22	27	25	21	27	28
Portugal	16	**20**	22	19	25	22	16	15	27	38	11	18	25	18	20	30
Puerto Rico	na	**53**	51	53	50	57	50	48	46	57	47	53	55	52	53	53
Romania	25	**24**	25	23	33	26	17	17	28	26	17	22	30	22	24	21
Russian Fed.	29	**20**	22	18	28	20	14	12	20	23	18	18	22	18	21	28
Serbia	na	**31**	33	29	41	36	22	25	35	34	27	31	32	29	32	39
Singapore	na	**26**	25	28	28	25	26	26	26	29	24	25	30	22	27	38
Slovakia	na	**32**	33	31	45	31	24	26	35	37	28	30	34	29	36	36
Slovenia	28	**33**	31	34	44	31	26	29	34	32	27	34	34	29	31	40
South Africa	29	**36**	41	30	41	33	30	30	43	46	25	32	50	32	38	41
Spain	38	**35**	38	33	46	38	26	29	38	47	28	37	43	32	35	41
Sweden	55	**54**	50	58	57	54	53	55	54	53	54	53	57	55	53	58
Switzerland	47	**46**	48	43	60	48	34	42	48	40	43	47	47	43	47	46
Taiwan	na	**26**	26	26	32	27	19	20	27	31	21	24	31	25	27	43
Tanzania	na	**12**	11	12	10	11	16	11	12	13	13	10	13	9	13	17
Turkey	24	**43**	41	45	47	40	39	40	46	49	40	44	50	42	44	44
Uganda	na	**45**	44	46	49	41	40	39	48	42	38	39	51	40	43	65
Ukraine	na	**25**	25	25	31	24	22	16	26	28	22	26	28	23	27	35
United States	43	**43**	41	44	43	43	43	46	39	43	40	42	48	49	41	43
Uruguay	na	**47**	50	46	47	51	45	46	49	52	44	48	48	47	44	54
Venezuela	na	**66**	66	65	64	68	65	65	65	70	60	64	70	64	66	67
Vietnam	na	**7**	8	6	6	7	9	6	8	11	6	7	7	5	9	6
Zimbabwe	na	**28**	25	29	28	29	25	27	28	38	30	27	28	30	26	29
Total	35	33	34	33	38	33	29	30	34	37	30	32	36	28	34	41

RANKING	
Country	2000
Venezuela	66
El Salvador	62
Brazil	54
Sweden	54
Chile	54
Netherlands	53
Puerto Rico	53
Nigeria	52
Great Britain	51
Mexico	51
Malta	50
Uruguay	47
Northern Ireland	46
Switzerland	46
New Zealand	45
Australia	45
Uganda	45
Denmark	45
Japan	44
Bosnia and Herz.	44
Greece	43
Turkey	43
United States	43
Macedonia	42
Ireland	41
Morocco	40
Colombia	40
Belgium	40
Austria	39
Finland	39
Norway	39
Canada	38
Luxembourg	38
France	37
Georgia	36
Argentina	36
South Africa	36
Spain	35
Iceland	34
Slovenia	33
Slovakia	32
Germany	32
Dominican Rep.	31
Hungary	31
Serbia	31
Azerbaijan	30
Iran	30
Italy	29
India	29
Zimbabwe	28
Singapore	26
Taiwan	26
Belarus	25
Ukraine	25
Moldova	25
Poland	25
Croatia	25
Montenegro	25
Algeria	24
Korea, South	24
Armenia	24
Romania	24
Bangladesh	23
Peru	23
Bulgaria	23
Czech Republic	21
Portugal	20
Russian Fed.	20
Estonia	19
Jordan	17
Indonesia	17
Latvia	17
Lithuania	16
Philippines	15
Albania	14
Tanzania	12
Egypt	9
China	7
Vietnam	7
Pakistan	5
Total	33

A004) POLITICS IMPORTANT

For each of the following aspects, indicate how important it is in your life: politics.

Very / Rather important (%) (WVS: V7; EVS: V5)

	Wave		Gender		Age			Education			Income			Values		
Country	1990	2000	Male	Female	16-29	30-49	50+	Lower	Middle	Upper	Lower	Middle	Upper	Mat	Mixed	Postm.
Albania	na	**32**	42	21	19	34	39	28	32	39	28	32	35	31	32	37
Algeria	na	**52**	56	48	48	56	53	42	48	64	49	56	52	45	57	61
Argentina	31	**24**	24	24	21	23	28	18	29	42	18	23	30	18	24	29
Armenia	na	**50**	60	42	43	55	54	49	48	57	47	52	52	47	56	27
Australia	na	**50**	51	49	36	52	60	40	46	62	48	50	55	44	48	55
Austria	35	**41**	46	37	36	41	44	35	43	60	38	39	47	29	38	52
Azerbaijan	na	**37**	44	31	36	37	39	32	33	47	34	40	40	30	49	57
Bangladesh	na	**51**	62	36	50	50	59	48	50	59	39	52	59	46	54	55
Belarus	37	**30**	38	23	29	30	29	20	32	38	26	29	37	27	32	48
Belgium	26	**32**	36	27	26	34	32	19	29	45	24	31	41	20	30	51
Bosnia and Herz.	na	**36**	43	29	29	35	44	32	34	45	37	35	38	32	37	33
Brazil	42	**51**	51	52	52	51	52	43	53	76	47	54	55	43	52	71
Bulgaria	46	**31**	34	29	27	35	31	23	33	42	27	37	33	25	38	44
Canada	48	**41**	41	40	29	41	47	37	36	53	36	38	47	32	38	48
Chile	31	**31**	36	26	30	33	29	21	34	41	24	35	36	27	30	39
China	59	**68**	72	63	70	65	72	64	70	67	68	68	65	68	70	75
Colombia	na	**32**	35	30	31	33	34	32	27	41	33	28	38	30	38	35
Croatia	na	**29**	37	23	24	28	35	23	31	41	24	24	37	29	29	32
Czech Republic	36	**31**	33	30	23	29	38	26	35	46	33	32	30	21	34	45
Denmark	43	**42**	43	40	33	41	47	34	44	55	41	40	50	25	41	60
Dominican Rep.	na	**39**	39	39	38	41	50	50	32	40	45	34	37	39	39	34
Egypt	na	**50**	55	45	47	49	56	43	53	65	46	50	56	46	54	56
El Salvador	na	**38**	42	35	44	34	34	29	43	55	30	37	50	na	na	na
Estonia	42	**21**	26	16	13	17	29	19	18	32	23	20	22	15	24	20
Finland	26	**20**	21	19	18	17	23	20	17	29	19	19	22	13	21	31
France	33	**35**	40	31	31	32	42	28	40	52	29	34	46	22	36	53
Georgia	na	**47**	51	43	34	50	56	38	47	52	50	46	43	46	47	53
Germany	57	**39**	44	36	35	40	41	28	45	70	28	38	44	33	40	49
Great Britain	43	**34**	38	31	28	32	41	28	34	54	25	34	38	na	na	na
Greece	na	**36**	43	32	33	36	43	36	32	41	30	40	41	38	35	45
Hungary	26	**18**	19	18	12	19	22	15	21	32	15	20	19	14	22	30
Iceland	26	**36**	34	38	33	36	39	32	34	49	35	33	42	27	37	48
India	40	**40**	50	26	41	40	40	32	44	52	36	37	46	43	45	38
Indonesia	na	**39**	47	31	52	37	36	28	40	47	33	42	42	37	41	62
Iran	na	**44**	47	41	49	45	30	30	43	59	40	44	49	31	51	59
Ireland	28	**32**	37	27	27	31	37	28	30	43	26	34	37	28	32	41
Israel	na	**na**	na	na	na	na	na	na	na	na	na	na	na	na	na	na
Italy	31	**34**	40	28	34	34	34	27	37	46	28	35	39	25	32	43
Japan	54	**68**	70	67	44	64	82	77	68	65	72	67	69	68	69	74
Jordan	na	**47**	46	48	48	50	40	34	55	63	37	51	56	40	51	66
Korea, South	71	**51**	52	51	44	52	58	53	52	50	53	47	53	50	53	54
Latvia	44	**24**	27	21	15	17	33	20	21	35	24	26	23	23	23	32
Lithuania	51	**41**	44	38	30	38	50	38	39	56	38	44	43	33	45	38
Luxembourg	na	**41**	43	40	32	44	44	30	44	54	40	42	46	35	42	50
Macedonia	na	**36**	42	31	26	38	43	36	35	41	35	34	42	38	37	37
Malta	na	**38**	42	34	25	36	48	42	37	31	41	36	38	37	38	36
Mexico	41	**46**	48	44	46	46	47	41	48	65	42	49	54	44	48	51
Moldova	na	**36**	40	32	28	41	37	28	34	48	33	38	40	31	42	46
Montenegro	na	**28**	37	19	22	29	31	23	31	33	32	24	32	26	30	41
Morocco	na	**25**	30	20	28	25	16	19	42	63	27	27	29	15	31	47
Netherlands	53	**57**	56	56	49	56	61	50	54	66	55	56	60	46	56	64
New Zealand	na	**42**	40	44	29	43	46	42	42	43	47	38	43	42	39	52
Nigeria	39	**52**	58	45	53	52	46	51	52	53	51	53	51	48	54	57
Northern Ireland	28	**36**	46	26	30	35	39	37	31	42	29	35	40	30	36	53
Norway	50	**45**	45	45	35	51	44	35	44	56	na	na	na	27	47	56
Pakistan	na	**14**	24	3	13	14	17	14	15	14	12	18	13	15	12	25
Peru	na	**44**	47	41	47	42	42	37	43	51	42	42	50	35	47	46
Philippines	na	**55**	57	53	60	52	54	57	53	55	54	52	61	54	56	57
Poland	42	**30**	32	29	27	28	35	28	30	39	29	32	31	25	32	45
Portugal	22	**27**	32	22	33	26	24	26	26	36	15	27	31	21	27	39
Puerto Rico	na	**40**	36	41	31	40	43	41	35	42	37	43	40	35	41	38
Romania	21	**25**	31	20	16	28	28	20	26	32	23	24	28	22	29	24
Russian Fed.	37	**38**	43	34	29	38	44	31	35	52	33	38	43	35	42	49
Serbia	na	**25**	30	20	24	25	25	18	26	31	21	23	33	19	30	31
Singapore	na	**47**	51	43	51	45	36	44	49	44	41	48	46	39	49	57
Slovakia	na	**29**	35	24	24	31	31	23	31	40	29	27	32	22	35	51
Slovenia	25	**15**	18	12	10	10	23	13	16	12	15	16	12	13	16	13
South Africa	59	**50**	55	45	47	55	46	51	50	40	55	53	43	46	54	55
Spain	22	**22**	25	19	18	25	22	18	22	35	17	23	29	18	21	32
Sweden	45	**55**	52	58	50	55	58	47	51	67	51	53	63	53	51	69
Switzerland	41	**38**	41	36	29	37	45	30	38	61	35	36	44	28	40	42
Taiwan	na	**44**	47	41	37	47	40	37	52	46	42	43	47	40	50	54
Tanzania	na	**71**	71	71	65	71	82	76	64	69	72	70	73	73	71	63
Turkey	28	**40**	43	38	41	40	38	35	45	58	34	42	54	36	40	51
Uganda	na	**55**	69	43	52	59	57	54	54	75	62	56	62	53	55	62
Ukraine	na	**38**	43	34	32	38	41	28	37	48	34	39	44	34	41	64
United States	52	**57**	56	57	52	53	66	53	53	61	55	59	58	60	56	60
Uruguay	na	**36**	39	34	32	38	37	30	43	52	31	34	45	29	38	41
Venezuela	na	**34**	37	32	36	31	38	29	36	38	34	29	38	35	34	36
Vietnam	na	**78**	83	74	68	80	83	75	82	88	79	72	85	73	85	80
Zimbabwe	na	**42**	43	41	41	43	42	46	36	15	53	38	36	40	41	59
Total	39	**39**	43	36	37	40	41	34	40	49	38	39	43	34	41	48

RANKING	
Country	**2000**
Vietnam	78
Tanzania	71
Japan	68
China	68
United States	57
Netherlands	57
Uganda	55
Philippines	55
Sweden	55
Algeria	52
Nigeria	52
Brazil	51
Korea, South	51
Bangladesh	51
Armenia	50
South Africa	50
Egypt	50
Australia	50
Jordan	47
Singapore	47
Georgia	47
Mexico	46
Norway	45
Iran	44
Taiwan	44
Peru	44
New Zealand	42
Zimbabwe	42
Denmark	42
Austria	41
Luxembourg	41
Lithuania	41
Canada	41
India	40
Turkey	40
Puerto Rico	40
Germany	39
Dominican Rep.	39
Indonesia	39
Switzerland	38
Russian Fed.	38
El Salvador	38
Ukraine	38
Malta	38
Azerbaijan	37
Greece	36
Macedonia	36
Uruguay	36
Iceland	36
Moldova	36
Bosnia and Herz.	36
Northern Ireland	36
France	35
Venezuela	34
Great Britain	34
Italy	34
Colombia	32
Ireland	32
Belgium	32
Albania	32
Czech Republic	31
Bulgaria	31
Chile	31
Poland	30
Belarus	30
Croatia	29
Slovakia	29
Montenegro	28
Portugal	27
Romania	25
Morocco	25
Serbia	25
Argentina	24
Latvia	24
Spain	22
Estonia	21
Finland	20
Hungary	18
Slovenia	15
Pakistan	14
Total	39

A005) WORK IMPORTANT

For each of the following aspects, indicate how important it is in your life: work.

Very important (%)

(WVS: V8; EVS: V1)

Country	Wave		Gender		Age			Education			Income			Values		
	1990	2000	Male	Female	16-29	30-49	50+	Lower	Middle	Upper	Lower	Middle	Upper	Mat	Mixed	Postm.
Albania	na	**82**	85	80	75	89	79	78	86	87	80	84	84	84	81	92
Algeria	na	**93**	95	91	92	94	92	92	93	93	91	95	92	93	93	93
Argentina	76	**74**	76	72	69	80	73	78	67	75	75	76	70	75	73	73
Armenia	na	**67**	73	62	60	74	67	67	66	72	69	65	68	63	71	62
Australia	na	**51**	55	47	51	55	48	53	51	51	49	52	55	48	53	50
Austria	62	**66**	68	64	61	67	67	67	65	63	66	69	65	74	68	60
Azerbaijan	na	**54**	61	47	53	57	50	53	51	60	57	56	53	51	60	71
Bangladesh	na	**92**	93	91	89	93	96	93	91	91	93	91	93	94	89	92
Belarus	55	**49**	49	48	48	55	42	37	53	54	45	53	43	47	52	61
Belgium	58	**63**	65	61	59	63	65	64	64	61	64	65	62	62	65	57
Bosnia and Herz.	na	**75**	79	71	76	83	63	56	78	80	70	75	79	74	75	72
Brazil	82	**84**	86	83	85	85	80	82	86	84	85	85	83	82	85	89
Bulgaria	57	**62**	63	60	58	68	58	58	62	68	55	66	65	62	64	48
Canada	59	**52**	55	49	48	58	49	57	53	47	55	55	50	59	52	51
Chile	75	**76**	79	73	74	79	73	79	78	64	84	71	71	81	78	63
China	64	**50**	54	46	51	51	47	48	50	61	54	48	48	52	49	56
Colombia	na	**72**	75	69	69	74	72	68	73	76	68	74	75	68	68	70
Croatia	na	**48**	52	45	45	52	46	47	48	51	40	50	54	58	47	47
Czech Republic	56	**53**	54	52	42	54	58	55	50	52	52	57	50	52	54	47
Denmark	51	**40**	45	34	39	37	43	38	42	42	42	36	44	39	41	38
Dominican Rep.	na	**66**	71	63	67	65	73	62	74	64	64	66	63	62	68	67
Egypt	na	**72**	88	55	70	75	70	67	76	78	72	74	73	69	74	77
El Salvador	na	**95**	95	95	93	97	96	95	95	96	97	95	96	na	na	na
Estonia	32	**51**	53	50	42	58	51	45	53	58	51	51	52	50	53	61
Finland	54	**52**	50	54	42	55	55	55	49	48	51	51	57	54	53	48
France	61	**69**	69	69	69	65	73	74	68	57	71	71	64	77	70	54
Georgia	na	**58**	65	53	49	69	55	58	56	67	60	60	56	60	57	57
Germany	61	**45**	54	38	43	51	39	37	48	67	37	48	46	37	49	46
Great Britain	51	**42**	51	33	44	45	36	43	43	37	39	49	46	na	na	na
Greece	na	**59**	58	60	57	59	62	56	56	62	57	58	64	61	60	58
Hungary	59	**57**	58	56	53	60	56	57	57	57	55	58	57	55	60	59
Iceland	56	**54**	58	50	39	56	65	57	50	56	55	53	57	53	55	51
India	86	**78**	81	73	79	80	73	74	83	81	76	79	78	81	79	84
Indonesia	na	**89**	94	84	87	90	89	87	90	90	91	88	88	88	90	93
Iran	na	**79**	82	75	80	80	74	74	80	82	79	79	78	77	80	76
Ireland	65	**51**	61	42	56	54	44	47	54	51	40	52	58	52	50	56
Israel	na	**na**	na	na	na	na	na	na	na	na	na	na	na	na	na	na
Italy	62	**62**	66	57	57	61	65	65	60	58	65	62	58	67	61	61
Japan	41	**49**	54	45	39	50	53	64	48	46	52	50	48	50	48	45
Jordan	na	**65**	86	45	70	63	59	61	64	75	63	69	68	61	70	68
Korea, South	69	**62**	66	58	61	63	63	55	62	64	64	61	62	61	64	63
Latvia	33	**70**	71	69	55	73	73	66	71	70	70	72	69	70	71	60
Lithuania	42	**54**	57	52	58	66	40	32	61	67	47	47	66	53	56	51
Luxembourg	na	**53**	54	51	53	53	51	58	49	52	56	53	53	57	55	42
Macedonia	na	**76**	79	74	68	84	73	72	78	79	75	76	79	76	79	56
Malta	na	**76**	81	71	75	79	73	70	79	69	72	77	77	72	78	70
Mexico	67	**87**	90	84	83	90	86	87	86	89	82	90	88	89	86	89
Moldova	na	**43**	45	41	47	44	39	35	41	54	41	40	54	40	48	38
Montenegro	na	**59**	62	55	59	62	54	55	59	64	57	58	68	63	59	36
Morocco	na	**89**	94	85	92	89	83	88	94	91	88	92	89	89	91	91
Netherlands	49	**48**	53	43	56	48	45	48	48	48	44	52	48	48	49	47
New Zealand	na	**45**	50	41	35	46	48	50	46	38	47	42	48	51	45	40
Nigeria	94	**89**	90	87	88	90	87	86	91	89	91	88	88	88	89	92
Northern Ireland	57	**42**	47	38	47	51	33	37	48	44	31	48	47	40	41	52
Norway	73	**59**	62	56	54	61	60	56	60	60	na	na	na	55	60	60
Pakistan	na	**61**	67	54	55	63	67	59	62	64	62	61	59	63	58	42
Peru	na	**69**	71	66	66	70	72	75	66	69	70	68	67	70	69	67
Philippines	na	**93**	95	92	95	95	89	93	94	94	93	95	92	93	94	96
Poland	70	**78**	82	75	81	80	74	77	79	79	81	78	73	77	77	83
Portugal	35	**58**	60	57	62	61	53	58	59	56	46	59	68	51	63	63
Puerto Rico	na	**74**	78	73	72	79	71	73	71	76	70	75	77	69	76	73
Romania	69	**71**	72	69	59	73	75	67	71	78	67	76	73	72	71	73
Russian Fed.	46	**59**	61	56	57	71	45	37	60	65	52	61	63	58	60	74
Serbia	na	**55**	59	51	47	62	52	45	60	60	55	56	58	51	60	54
Singapore	na	**53**	60	46	43	63	57	57	54	37	60	56	46	53	52	56
Slovakia	na	**62**	64	60	58	67	57	54	64	71	58	63	67	62	64	49
Slovenia	73	**62**	59	64	49	61	71	66	60	62	69	58	58	69	61	55
South Africa	79	**80**	84	76	82	83	67	83	77	72	83	85	72	83	79	76
Spain	66	**59**	60	59	59	63	57	59	61	58	58	60	63	60	59	60
Sweden	67	**54**	51	58	54	56	53	47	54	61	51	56	57	58	55	51
Switzerland	52	**47**	51	44	44	52	45	44	48	52	41	52	53	42	48	47
Taiwan	na	**45**	51	38	37	51	35	45	42	46	45	47	45	46	46	41
Tanzania	na	**96**	95	96	96	97	94	95	97	98	94	97	98	97	96	100
Turkey	59	**75**	82	67	77	76	63	71	81	80	73	75	77	73	75	80
Uganda	na	**79**	82	75	76	86	66	80	78	79	84	80	89	76	81	76
Ukraine	na	**62**	66	59	63	76	48	31	66	67	57	63	67	57	66	76
United States	62	**54**	58	50	60	55	46	65	57	48	59	53	48	48	56	50
Uruguay	na	**71**	70	72	64	75	71	71	71	73	69	72	73	69	72	67
Venezuela	na	**93**	94	91	93	94	91	91	94	91	90	92	94	93	93	92
Vietnam	na	**57**	61	53	60	59	51	54	61	60	57	49	65	48	65	60
Zimbabwe	na	**90**	90	90	89	91	92	91	89	92	90	92	92	87	92	92
Total	60	**65**	69	62	66	68	61	65	65	65	65	66	66	66	66	61

RANKING	
Country	2000
Tanzania	96
El Salvador	95
Philippines	93
Algeria	93
Venezuela	93
Bangladesh	92
Zimbabwe	90
Morocco	89
Indonesia	89
Nigeria	89
Mexico	87
Brazil	84
Albania	82
South Africa	80
Iran	79
Uganda	79
Poland	78
India	78
Macedonia	76
Chile	76
Malta	76
Bosnia and Herz.	75
Turkey	75
Puerto Rico	74
Argentina	74
Egypt	72
Colombia	72
Uruguay	71
Romania	71
Latvia	70
France	69
Peru	69
Armenia	67
Austria	66
Dominican Rep.	66
Jordan	65
Belgium	63
Korea, South	62
Ukraine	62
Italy	62
Slovenia	62
Bulgaria	62
Slovakia	62
Pakistan	61
Spain	59
Greece	59
Norway	59
Russian Fed.	59
Montenegro	59
Georgia	58
Portugal	58
Hungary	57
Vietnam	57
Serbia	55
Iceland	54
Sweden	54
Lithuania	54
Azerbaijan	54
United States	54
Czech Republic	53
Luxembourg	53
Singapore	53
Canada	52
Finland	52
Estonia	51
Australia	51
Ireland	51
China	50
Japan	49
Belarus	49
Croatia	48
Netherlands	48
Switzerland	47
New Zealand	45
Germany	45
Taiwan	45
Moldova	43
Northern Ireland	42
Great Britain	42
Denmark	40
Total	65

A006) RELIGION IMPORTANT

For each of the following aspects, indicate how important it is in your life: religion.

(WVS: V9; EVS: V6)

Very important (%)

Country	Wave		Gender		Age			Education			Income			Values		
	1990	2000	Male	Female	16-29	30-49	50+	Lower	Middle	Upper	Lower	Middle	Upper	Mat	Mixed	Postm.
Albania	na	**20**	24	32	23	24	38	35	24	21	30	27	27	29	26	32
Algeria	na	**92**	91	92	89	92	96	94	90	92	91	91	91	90	92	93
Argentina	40	**47**	39	53	36	45	58	51	40	41	54	50	36	53	48	38
Armenia	na	**27**	20	33	23	28	31	32	26	25	23	30	27	23	31	23
Australia	na	**23**	19	28	16	22	31	27	21	23	29	23	16	23	25	19
Austria	25	**20**	16	24	7	17	30	23	16	21	28	20	17	22	20	20
Azerbaijan	na	**30**	26	34	32	27	36	36	28	33	29	34	28	28	32	54
Bangladesh	na	**88**	88	88	84	89	94	92	82	83	91	85	90	93	85	79
Belarus	12	**12**	7	17	7	8	22	21	9	7	16	12	6	14	10	7
Belgium	15	**18**	14	22	11	11	27	25	16	17	28	20	9	17	18	18
Bosnia and Herz.	na	**34**	31	37	37	32	35	38	33	34	40	31	34	30	35	32
Brazil	57	**65**	60	69	59	68	69	65	65	61	70	65	59	67	65	58
Bulgaria	12	**17**	12	21	15	13	21	22	13	14	23	15	12	14	18	15
Canada	31	**30**	22	38	19	28	40	39	28	27	37	32	22	31	33	24
Chile	51	**47**	40	53	41	44	55	56	42	41	55	40	43	50	48	36
China	1	**3**	2	4	2	4	1	2	3	5	3	2	3	2	3	na
Colombia	na	**49**	43	55	43	50	59	53	50	42	51	53	43	48	47	47
Croatia	na	**26**	18	33	20	24	32	31	23	23	33	27	21	31	27	15
Czech Republic	11	**7**	6	8	5	3	12	8	6	9	9	6	5	8	7	10
Denmark	9	**8**	7	9	6	5	12	7	3	10	11	6	5	3	9	5
Dominican Rep.	na	**51**	45	56	55	46	46	59	54	50	55	50	42	54	51	55
Egypt	na	**97**	97	98	97	97	99	97	98	99	98	96	98	97	97	98
El Salvador	na	**87**	84	89	84	89	89	88	87	86	88	87	81	na	na	na
Estonia	5	**6**	4	7	3	3	9	8	5	4	9	6	4	5	5	na
Finland	15	**14**	11	17	7	9	21	15	11	16	18	14	10	12	14	17
France	14	**11**	9	13	6	9	16	13	8	9	15	10	8	12	11	8
Georgia	na	**49**	42	56	57	50	40	51	47	56	51	47	49	47	50	63
Germany	16	**9**	5	12	8	7	12	10	8	7	7	12	10	7	11	8
Great Britain	16	**13**	10	15	9	9	19	10	13	16	11	13	11	na	na	na
Greece	na	**33**	28	36	25	34	48	60	40	22	42	29	29	37	33	26
Hungary	23	**20**	14	25	10	13	32	22	14	18	24	21	16	23	16	5
Iceland	24	**19**	16	22	6	19	31	24	16	15	25	18	12	20	19	19
India	49	**57**	55	59	54	57	60	61	55	50	61	59	54	64	51	49
Indonesia	na	**98**	98	98	98	98	98	98	98	99	98	98	99	98	98	100
Iran	na	**80**	78	83	78	82	86	87	80	72	82	82	75	88	76	71
Ireland	48	**32**	25	39	6	25	59	50	24	20	51	29	20	31	34	26
Israel	na	**na**	na	na	na	na	na	na	na	na	na	na	na	na	na	na
Italy	34	**33**	24	41	20	29	44	39	27	31	41	30	27	43	32	27
Japan	6	**7**	6	9	1	8	10	10	8	4	9	7	7	7	7	9
Jordan	na	**96**	94	98	96	96	97	97	96	94	96	97	96	96	96	93
Korea, South	26	**23**	19	28	21	23	27	36	23	22	22	23	24	23	24	22
Latvia	7	**11**	6	14	6	5	17	20	8	9	15	10	5	11	10	6
Lithuania	16	**14**	7	21	7	6	27	31	7	13	27	14	9	17	14	9
Luxembourg	na	**16**	14	17	9	12	23	20	12	15	19	17	12	15	15	14
Macedonia	na	**48**	45	51	51	49	43	60	43	37	53	44	45	45	48	58
Malta	na	**66**	58	74	44	65	82	82	61	53	75	68	53	73	64	53
Mexico	34	**68**	60	75	59	70	77	75	60	57	70	67	61	70	67	62
Moldova	na	**35**	29	40	24	32	48	54	31	24	48	31	30	41	30	32
Montenegro	na	**19**	18	20	16	18	23	23	18	15	19	14	21	18	20	18
Morocco	na	**94**	93	96	93	95	98	96	91	85	97	94	91	97	93	88
Netherlands	19	**17**	14	19	10	11	26	20	14	16	22	16	11	23	15	17
New Zealand	na	**19**	16	22	19	15	23	19	20	19	24	20	12	23	18	15
Nigeria	85	**93**	92	94	93	92	96	93	93	92	93	93	93	93	93	93
Northern Ireland	34	**28**	25	30	18	20	40	32	22	28	27	30	24	30	27	28
Norway	15	**12**	9	15	11	10	16	12	10	14	na	na	na	7	13	13
Pakistan	na	**82**	79	85	78	85	81	88	76	71	87	81	76	85	77	75
Peru	na	**53**	48	57	46	56	60	57	54	47	53	53	50	55	52	51
Philippines	na	**87**	85	89	88	86	88	90	87	84	88	87	85	87	87	87
Poland	53	**45**	38	51	45	37	54	51	40	29	51	41	37	51	42	42
Portugal	17	**27**	21	33	13	24	38	33	16	14	43	27	21	31	27	13
Puerto Rico	na	**76**	70	78	60	74	84	91	76	72	80	77	71	76	76	73
Romania	42	**51**	40	62	37	45	64	68	47	30	65	55	38	59	45	32
Russian Fed.	12	**12**	7	16	8	10	17	23	11	10	16	11	9	14	10	11
Serbia	na	**29**	26	32	28	26	33	34	27	28	38	29	24	31	28	24
Singapore	na	**36**	34	38	33	38	38	38	35	34	45	37	31	42	34	32
Slovakia	na	**27**	19	35	16	20	44	41	21	24	39	26	21	30	25	26
Slovenia	17	**12**	10	14	5	10	20	23	9	7	16	16	5	13	11	15
South Africa	66	**70**	59	83	68	69	77	72	67	69	71	73	66	74	68	66
Spain	21	**19**	12	25	7	14	29	24	12	14	24	16	15	27	16	11
Sweden	10	**11**	8	14	9	9	14	11	9	14	13	10	8	14	10	11
Switzerland	24	**15**	12	18	9	13	20	21	13	16	22	17	9	20	15	10
Taiwan	na	**13**	11	14	4	14	16	17	14	9	13	12	10	11	13	11
Tanzania	na	**85**	82	89	85	85	84	87	85	80	85	87	81	86	87	92
Turkey	61	**81**	79	83	78	81	86	89	77	51	89	79	63	87	82	68
Uganda	na	**74**	69	78	71	75	82	70	76	66	78	60	80	71	72	86
Ukraine	na	**22**	13	29	15	19	28	40	19	18	25	18	21	24	18	29
United States	53	**57**	49	66	48	58	65	64	58	54	61	57	53	60	58	53
Uruguay	na	**23**	15	29	16	19	30	26	19	19	25	21	23	25	23	19
Venezuela	na	**64**	60	68	59	66	70	67	64	61	63	65	62	63	65	61
Vietnam	na	**10**	8	12	8	11	10	14	6	3	9	7	13	8	11	4
Zimbabwe	na	**78**	67	87	76	80	78	79	77	60	75	80	79	73	81	85
Total	27	**40**	36	44	42	39	41	47	36	38	46	40	36	44	39	33

RANKING	
Country	**2000**
Indonesia	98
Egypt	97
Jordan	96
Morocco	94
Nigeria	93
Algeria	92
Bangladesh	88
El Salvador	87
Philippines	87
Tanzania	85
Pakistan	82
Turkey	81
Iran	80
Zimbabwe	78
Puerto Rico	76
Uganda	74
South Africa	70
Mexico	68
Malta	66
Brazil	65
Venezuela	64
United States	57
India	57
Peru	53
Dominican Rep.	51
Romania	51
Georgia	49
Colombia	49
Macedonia	48
Chile	47
Argentina	47
Poland	45
Singapore	36
Moldova	35
Bosnia and Herz.	34
Italy	33
Greece	33
Ireland	32
Canada	30
Azerbaijan	30
Serbia	29
Northern Ireland	28
Portugal	27
Slovakia	27
Armenia	27
Croatia	26
Australia	23
Korea, South	23
Uruguay	23
Ukraine	22
Austria	20
Hungary	20
Montenegro	19
New Zealand	19
Iceland	19
Spain	19
Belgium	18
Netherlands	17
Bulgaria	17
Luxembourg	16
Switzerland	15
Lithuania	14
Finland	14
Taiwan	13
Great Britain	13
Slovenia	12
Belarus	12
Norway	12
Russian Fed.	12
France	11
Latvia	11
Sweden	11
Vietnam	10
Germany	9
Denmark	8
Czech Republic	7
Japan	7
Estonia	6
China	3
Total	40

A007) SERVICE TO OTHERS

For each of the following aspects, indicate how important it is in your life: service to others.

Very important (%)

(WVS: V10)

Country	Wave		Gender		Age			Education			Income			Values		
	1990	2000	Male	Female	16-29	30-49	50+	Lower	Middle	Upper	Lower	Middle	Upper	Mat	Mixed	Postm.
Albania	na	**20**	19	21	18	21	20	19	18	25	17	20	22	21	20	9
Algeria	na	**45**	46	43	47	42	45	41	46	47	49	41	39	46	44	43
Argentina	na	**57**	50	63	52	55	62	59	55	48	60	56	54	55	58	55
Armenia	na	**na**	na	na	na	na	na	na	na	na	na	na	na	na	na	na
Australia	na	**na**	na	na	na	na	na	na	na	na	na	na	na	na	na	na
Austria	na	**na**	na	na	na	na	na	na	na	na	na	na	na	na	na	na
Azerbaijan	na	**na**	na	na	na	na	na	na	na	na	na	na	na	na	na	na
Bangladesh	na	**47**	50	43	45	45	61	51	42	45	42	42	57	49	47	34
Belarus	na	**na**	na	na	na	na	na	na	na	na	na	na	na	na	na	na
Belgium	na	**na**	na	na	na	na	na	na	na	na	na	na	na	na	na	na
Bosnia and Herz.	na	**18**	17	18	14	16	23	18	16	21	20	17	15	14	19	21
Brazil	na	**na**	na	na	na	na	na	na	na	na	na	na	na	na	na	na
Bulgaria	na	**na**	na	na	na	na	na	na	na	na	na	na	na	na	na	na
Canada	na	**42**	38	47	37	42	46	47	42	39	48	44	37	38	44	41
Chile	na	**53**	49	58	53	52	57	56	49	60	60	46	54	49	58	48
China	na	**16**	14	17	16	17	11	17	14	21	16	15	15	15	14	19
Colombia	na	**na**	na	na	na	na	na	na	na	na	na	na	na	na	na	na
Croatia	na	**na**	na	na	na	na	na	na	na	na	na	na	na	na	na	na
Czech Republic	na	**na**	na	na	na	na	na	na	na	na	na	na	na	na	na	na
Denmark	na	**na**	na	na	na	na	na	na	na	na	na	na	na	na	na	na
Dominican Rep.	na	**na**	na	na	na	na	na	na	na	na	na	na	na	na	na	na
Egypt	na	**62**	60	64	60	63	63	60	63	66	63	65	63	63	63	60
El Salvador	na	**na**	na	na	na	na	na	na	na	na	na	na	na	na	na	na
Estonia	na	**na**	na	na	na	na	na	na	na	na	na	na	na	na	na	na
Finland	na	**na**	na	na	na	na	na	na	na	na	na	na	na	na	na	na
France	na	**na**	na	na	na	na	na	na	na	na	na	na	na	na	na	na
Georgia	na	**na**	na	na	na	na	na	na	na	na	na	na	na	na	na	na
Germany	na	**na**	na	na	na	na	na	na	na	na	na	na	na	na	na	na
Great Britain	na	**na**	na	na	na	na	na	na	na	na	na	na	na	na	na	na
Greece	na	**na**	na	na	na	na	na	na	na	na	na	na	na	na	na	na
Hungary	na	**na**	na	na	na	na	na	na	na	na	na	na	na	na	na	na
Iceland	na	**na**	na	na	na	na	na	na	na	na	na	na	na	na	na	na
India	na	**47**	48	44	46	47	45	44	49	49	44	48	47	50	45	53
Indonesia	na	**36**	40	33	38	41	31	30	34	45	32	41	36	35	39	52
Iran	na	**62**	60	65	58	65	69	63	62	58	63	64	59	67	59	58
Ireland	na	**na**	na	na	na	na	na	na	na	na	na	na	na	na	na	na
Israel	na	**na**	na	na	na	na	na	na	na	na	na	na	na	na	na	na
Italy	na	**na**	na	na	na	na	na	na	na	na	na	na	na	na	na	na
Japan	na	**9**	7	10	5	6	13	15	9	5	10	8	7	5	8	12
Jordan	na	**67**	64	70	60	73	70	69	68	63	68	66	69	71	66	67
Korea, South	na	**11**	10	12	8	11	14	18	12	9	12	12	9	9	12	15
Latvia	na	**na**	na	na	na	na	na	na	na	na	na	na	na	na	na	na
Lithuania	na	**na**	na	na	na	na	na	na	na	na	na	na	na	na	na	na
Luxembourg	na	**na**	na	na	na	na	na	na	na	na	na	na	na	na	na	na
Macedonia	na	**15**	17	12	11	14	19	16	15	12	18	11	16	13	16	15
Malta	na	**na**	na	na	na	na	na	na	na	na	na	na	na	na	na	na
Mexico	na	**64**	60	67	58	65	69	66	59	66	62	65	63	65	65	66
Moldova	na	**32**	30	34	32	30	36	35	33	28	34	31	35	32	34	28
Montenegro	na	**13**	13	14	12	11	16	12	13	15	11	9	15	14	13	12
Morocco	na	**72**	72	72	72	73	70	72	73	66	65	64	75	75	72	62
Netherlands	na	**na**	na	na	na	na	na	na	na	na	na	na	na	na	na	na
New Zealand	na	**na**	na	na	na	na	na	na	na	na	na	na	na	na	na	na
Nigeria	na	**62**	64	60	62	62	63	59	64	65	60	62	65	62	62	65
Northern Ireland	na	**na**	na	na	na	na	na	na	na	na	na	na	na	na	na	na
Norway	na	**na**	na	na	na	na	na	na	na	na	na	na	na	na	na	na
Pakistan	na	**33**	34	33	31	35	34	37	30	26	36	33	29	32	35	42
Peru	na	**49**	46	52	46	51	53	52	50	47	50	48	51	51	49	52
Philippines	na	**58**	60	55	52	59	63	56	57	60	55	56	62	56	58	65
Poland	na	**na**	na	na	na	na	na	na	na	na	na	na	na	na	na	na
Portugal	na	**na**	na	na	na	na	na	na	na	na	na	na	na	na	na	na
Puerto Rico	na	**78**	73	80	66	77	84	93	75	77	87	74	76	79	79	76
Romania	na	**na**	na	na	na	na	na	na	na	na	na	na	na	na	na	na
Russian Fed.	na	**na**	na	na	na	na	na	na	na	na	na	na	na	na	na	na
Serbia	na	**38**	36	39	33	39	40	35	40	39	42	41	36	33	42	53
Singapore	na	**16**	16	16	16	15	17	15	17	15	17	15	18	14	16	19
Slovakia	na	**na**	na	na	na	na	na	na	na	na	na	na	na	na	na	na
Slovenia	na	**na**	na	na	na	na	na	na	na	na	na	na	na	na	na	na
South Africa	na	**49**	45	54	53	48	46	44	56	67	42	55	52	49	51	47
Spain	na	**30**	27	34	25	28	35	32	28	27	34	26	31	36	28	25
Sweden	na	**37**	29	46	40	37	36	31	36	45	40	32	37	46	35	42
Switzerland	na	**na**	na	na	na	na	na	na	na	na	na	na	na	na	na	na
Taiwan	na	**na**	na	na	na	na	na	na	na	na	na	na	na	na	na	na
Tanzania	na	**59**	58	59	58	57	64	63	54	55	66	57	52	62	58	58
Turkey	na	**na**	na	na	na	na	na	na	na	na	na	na	na	na	na	na
Uganda	na	**48**	50	46	50	48	39	45	50	41	53	44	54	45	49	54
Ukraine	na	**na**	na	na	na	na	na	na	na	na	na	na	na	na	na	na
United States	na	**51**	43	60	42	52	59	54	51	51	54	53	46	48	51	52
Uruguay	na	**na**	na	na	na	na	na	na	na	na	na	na	na	na	na	na
Venezuela	na	**68**	64	72	64	69	73	69	66	69	67	65	70	62	69	74
Vietnam	na	**16**	17	15	15	16	17	13	20	19	22	16	13	14	18	17
Zimbabwe	na	**62**	59	65	67	63	50	61	64	92	60	64	67	61	62	76
Total	na	**43**	42	45	44	42	43	46	40	45	44	41	43	42	44	48

RANKING	
Country	2000
Puerto Rico	78
Morocco	72
Venezuela	68
Jordan	67
Mexico	64
Iran	62
Zimbabwe	62
Nigeria	62
Egypt	62
Tanzania	59
Philippines	58
Argentina	57
Chile	53
United States	51
Peru	49
South Africa	49
Uganda	48
Bangladesh	47
India	47
Algeria	45
Canada	42
Serbia	38
Sweden	37
Indonesia	36
Pakistan	33
Moldova	32
Spain	30
Bosnia and Herz.	18
Vietnam	16
Singapore	16
China	16
Macedonia	15
Montenegro	13
Korea, South	11
Japan	9
Total	43

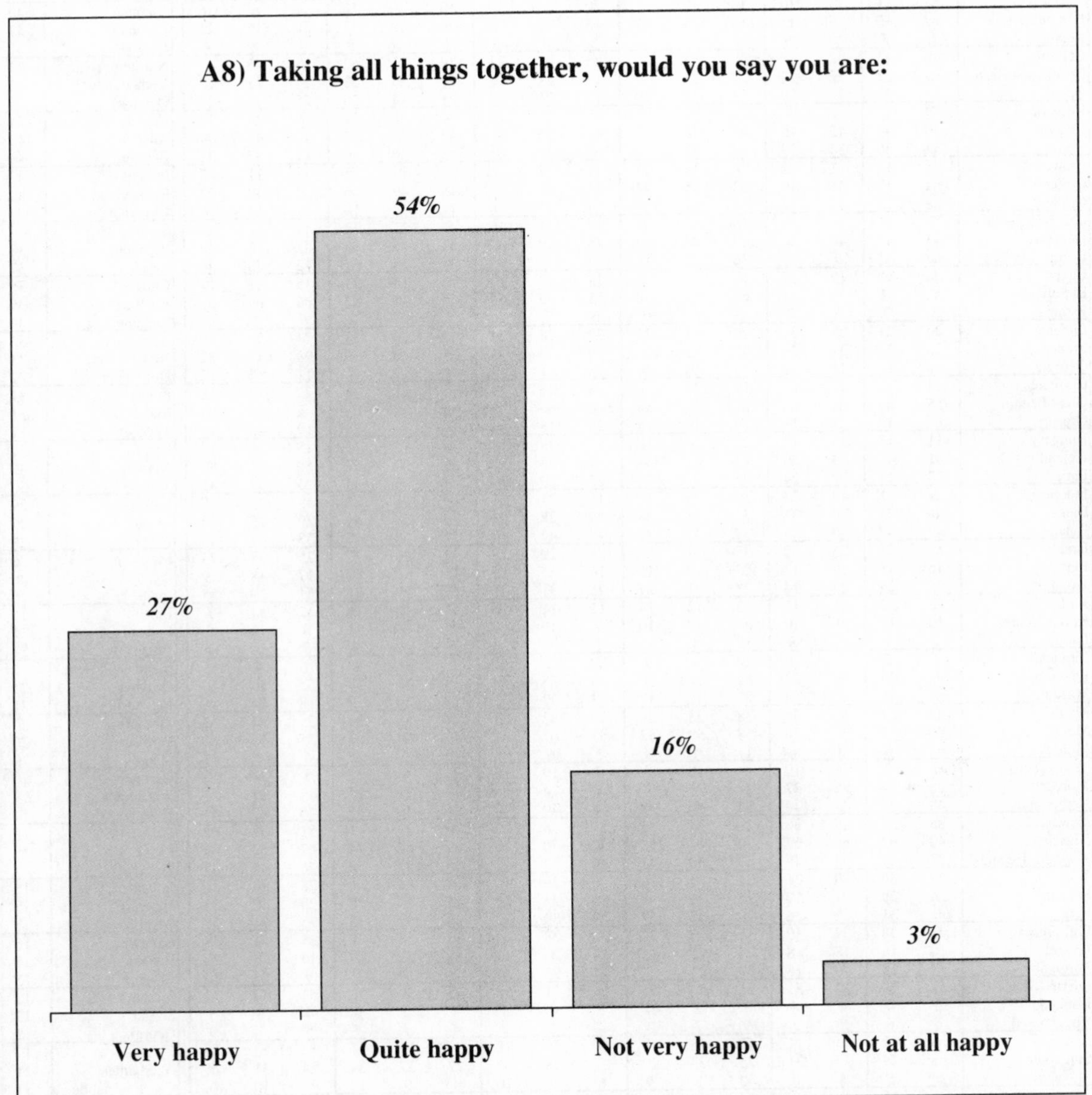
A8) Taking all things together, would you say you are:
54%
27%
16%
3%
Very happy
Quite happy
Not very happy
Not at all happy

A008) FEELING OF HAPPINESS

Taking all things together, would you say you are:

Very happy (%)

(WVS: V11)

Country	Wave 1990	Wave 2000	Gender Male	Gender Female	Age 16-29	Age 30-49	Age 50+	Education Lower	Education Middle	Education Upper	Income Lower	Income Middle	Income Upper	Values Mat	Values Mixed	Values Postm.
Albania	na	**10**	10	10	11	11	7	6	9	20	7	9	14	8	11	13
Algeria	na	**17**	14	19	16	18	15	14	18	18	15	15	21	18	15	23
Argentina	33	**33**	31	35	39	33	28	30	37	37	31	33	37	28	35	33
Armenia	na	**6**	6	6	6	7	5	5	6	9	7	4	9	7	6	4
Australia	na	**43**	40	46	43	44	42	41	47	40	38	44	45	46	44	41
Austria	30	**36**	35	37	45	36	31	36	37	34	29	32	44	33	37	34
Azerbaijan	na	**11**	13	10	15	10	7	20	11	10	10	9	16	11	12	16
Bangladesh	na	**15**	15	15	15	13	22	13	17	18	6	12	27	14	15	11
Belarus	6	**5**	4	6	8	4	4	3	7	5	4	6	8	4	8	4
Belgium	40	**43**	42	44	48	43	40	35	44	48	29	43	52	37	45	42
Bosnia and Herz.	na	**22**	22	22	28	21	17	17	21	28	17	20	32	22	22	15
Brazil	21	**22**	24	20	23	23	19	23	21	20	21	19	26	25	21	21
Bulgaria	7	**8**	8	8	17	7	5	2	11	13	4	9	11	7	9	13
Canada	30	**44**	43	46	43	42	47	49	43	41	40	45	46	44	44	44
Chile	33	**36**	34	39	44	32	36	33	36	43	33	36	40	41	35	32
China	28	**12**	11	12	9	13	11	12	12	5	8	14	15	11	11	13
Colombia	na	**47**	45	49	52	45	44	44	51	44	45	49	46	50	49	52
Croatia	na	**13**	14	12	21	11	10	14	11	18	11	14	14	11	14	14
Czech Republic	5	**11**	9	13	16	11	8	10	11	16	8	11	13	11	11	13
Denmark	43	**45**	46	44	47	46	43	45	40	48	37	49	55	43	46	46
Dominican Rep.	na	**32**	28	35	36	27	18	32	31	33	38	25	37	42	28	34
Egypt	na	**18**	19	17	18	18	18	15	22	20	16	18	21	16	21	19
El Salvador	na	**56**	58	54	61	53	52	51	60	63	45	57	67	na	na	na
Estonia	3	**7**	6	7	9	7	5	6	7	8	5	7	7	6	7	na
Finland	20	**24**	25	24	29	23	23	22	26	29	17	26	33	24	23	30
France	25	**31**	31	32	41	32	26	30	36	31	25	30	39	28	33	32
Georgia	na	**12**	11	12	16	10	9	13	11	13	9	12	14	11	12	12
Germany	14	**20**	16	22	19	21	18	13	23	29	15	21	26	22	19	18
Great Britain	38	**na**	na	na	na	na	na	na	na	na	na	na	na	na	na	na
Greece	na	**19**	21	18	19	19	18	25	18	19	19	13	24	19	20	15
Hungary	11	**17**	16	18	25	16	13	17	18	16	12	16	23	15	19	13
Iceland	41	**47**	44	50	43	51	44	43	48	52	33	50	57	50	47	37
India	24	**26**	27	24	25	27	23	22	29	30	24	19	33	23	33	42
Indonesia	na	**21**	18	24	19	25	17	17	21	24	17	23	25	19	23	25
Iran	na	**25**	20	31	27	23	24	24	28	23	20	24	31	29	25	22
Ireland	44	**42**	40	45	34	47	42	45	42	40	32	48	46	38	43	43
Israel	na	**28**	25	30	35	24	22	24	29	28	22	26	27	25	28	23
Italy	16	**18**	19	18	25	19	15	16	21	18	15	17	22	17	18	19
Japan	18	**29**	22	34	28	31	27	25	31	27	27	29	31	31	29	25
Jordan	na	**13**	11	15	13	13	14	12	11	16	14	10	16	12	14	5
Korea, South	10	**10**	9	10	9	10	10	7	10	9	8	9	11	9	10	9
Latvia	2	**7**	5	8	12	4	7	7	6	8	6	7	9	7	7	4
Lithuania	4	**5**	6	4	10	4	2	2	5	9	2	6	6	1	4	25
Luxembourg	na	**36**	39	33	34	36	36	34	35	39	36	37	39	38	35	40
Macedonia	na	**19**	20	18	27	16	17	13	22	25	12	20	29	18	21	18
Malta	na	**31**	32	31	38	28	29	29	33	28	28	35	34	25	34	33
Mexico	26	**57**	58	56	58	59	52	53	62	61	49	64	61	55	58	64
Moldova	na	**6**	6	6	11	4	4	5	6	7	4	5	9	6	7	11
Montenegro	na	**9**	7	10	8	10	8	7	10	10	5	8	12	8	9	13
Morocco	na	**26**	26	27	27	26	25	27	24	28	17	21	26	27	27	25
Netherlands	48	**46**	44	48	55	49	38	44	49	44	34	46	55	46	47	44
New Zealand	na	**33**	29	36	27	34	35	31	38	32	30	27	41	31	32	32
Nigeria	40	**67**	66	67	70	64	58	62	70	70	61	67	74	67	67	69
Northern Ireland	37	**47**	45	48	47	50	47	41	52	52	35	52	58	46	49	47
Norway	29	**30**	29	31	34	31	26	26	29	36	na	na	na	28	30	31
Pakistan	na	**20**	21	19	27	19	8	16	23	26	15	20	26	20	20	25
Peru	na	**31**	29	32	33	31	27	29	30	33	28	33	33	25	31	38
Philippines	na	**38**	37	40	45	37	32	35	38	42	30	38	47	35	41	38
Poland	10	**18**	18	18	27	17	13	17	20	13	12	20	23	16	18	25
Portugal	13	**18**	19	18	30	21	8	14	25	27	4	19	24	9	23	20
Puerto Rico	na	**54**	57	51	55	53	53	51	51	56	46	59	56	52	54	52
Romania	6	**4**	4	4	5	2	4	5	4	1	7	2	2	4	3	3
Russian Fed.	6	**6**	7	5	9	7	3	4	6	7	4	7	7	5	7	9
Serbia	na	**12**	13	11	12	13	12	9	15	12	9	11	17	12	13	16
Singapore	na	**29**	27	31	25	33	29	27	28	38	27	27	34	24	31	25
Slovakia	na	**8**	8	8	12	8	5	6	9	10	4	9	10	6	10	6
Slovenia	9	**16**	16	15	20	17	11	11	18	16	11	19	21	12	17	17
South Africa	24	**39**	35	43	39	36	45	35	43	37	31	37	49	39	40	25
Spain	20	**20**	21	19	23	20	18	19	22	21	16	20	21	21	20	18
Sweden	41	**37**	33	40	35	36	38	44	33	37	27	41	44	41	37	34
Switzerland	36	**40**	37	43	44	38	40	40	41	35	35	41	41	41	41	37
Taiwan	na	**30**	26	33	28	33	22	25	37	30	22	31	36	31	32	28
Tanzania	na	**57**	57	58	66	50	58	57	60	48	59	53	55	52	60	67
Turkey	29	**31**	26	36	30	31	32	34	27	27	31	31	31	32	32	27
Uganda	na	**26**	26	26	29	24	25	22	27	35	32	28	31	21	27	37
Ukraine	na	**6**	7	6	10	6	4	2	6	10	3	5	10	4	7	14
United States	41	**39**	37	42	38	36	44	42	36	41	35	41	43	37	39	40
Uruguay	na	**21**	17	24	24	20	20	20	22	21	16	19	28	19	21	19
Venezuela	na	**57**	57	57	59	55	56	50	58	62	49	56	64	52	59	57
Vietnam	na	**49**	49	50	46	53	47	47	54	43	42	50	52	52	51	49
Zimbabwe	na	**20**	18	22	25	16	15	18	24	10	17	21	24	19	20	27
Total	23	27	26	27	30	26	23	25	26	30	22	27	30	21	28	31

RANKING Country	2000
Nigeria	67
Tanzania	57
Mexico	57
Venezuela	57
El Salvador	56
Puerto Rico	54
Vietnam	49
Colombia	47
Iceland	47
Northern Ireland	47
Netherlands	46
Denmark	45
Canada	44
Australia	43
Belgium	43
Ireland	42
Switzerland	40
United States	39
South Africa	39
Philippines	38
Sweden	37
Chile	36
Austria	36
Luxembourg	36
Argentina	33
New Zealand	33
Dominican Rep.	32
France	31
Malta	31
Turkey	31
Peru	31
Norway	30
Taiwan	30
Singapore	29
Japan	29
Israel	28
Morocco	26
Uganda	26
India	26
Iran	25
Finland	24
Brazil	22
Bosnia and Herz.	22
Uruguay	21
Indonesia	21
Zimbabwe	20
Pakistan	20
Spain	20
Germany	20
Macedonia	19
Greece	19
Italy	18
Egypt	18
Portugal	18
Poland	18
Hungary	17
Algeria	17
Slovenia	16
Bangladesh	15
Croatia	13
Jordan	13
Serbia	12
Georgia	12
China	12
Azerbaijan	11
Czech Republic	11
Korea, South	10
Montenegro	9
Slovakia	8
Bulgaria	8
Estonia	7
Latvia	7
Armenia	6
Moldova	6
Russian Fed.	6
Ukraine	6
Belarus	5
Lithuania	5
Romania	4
Total	27

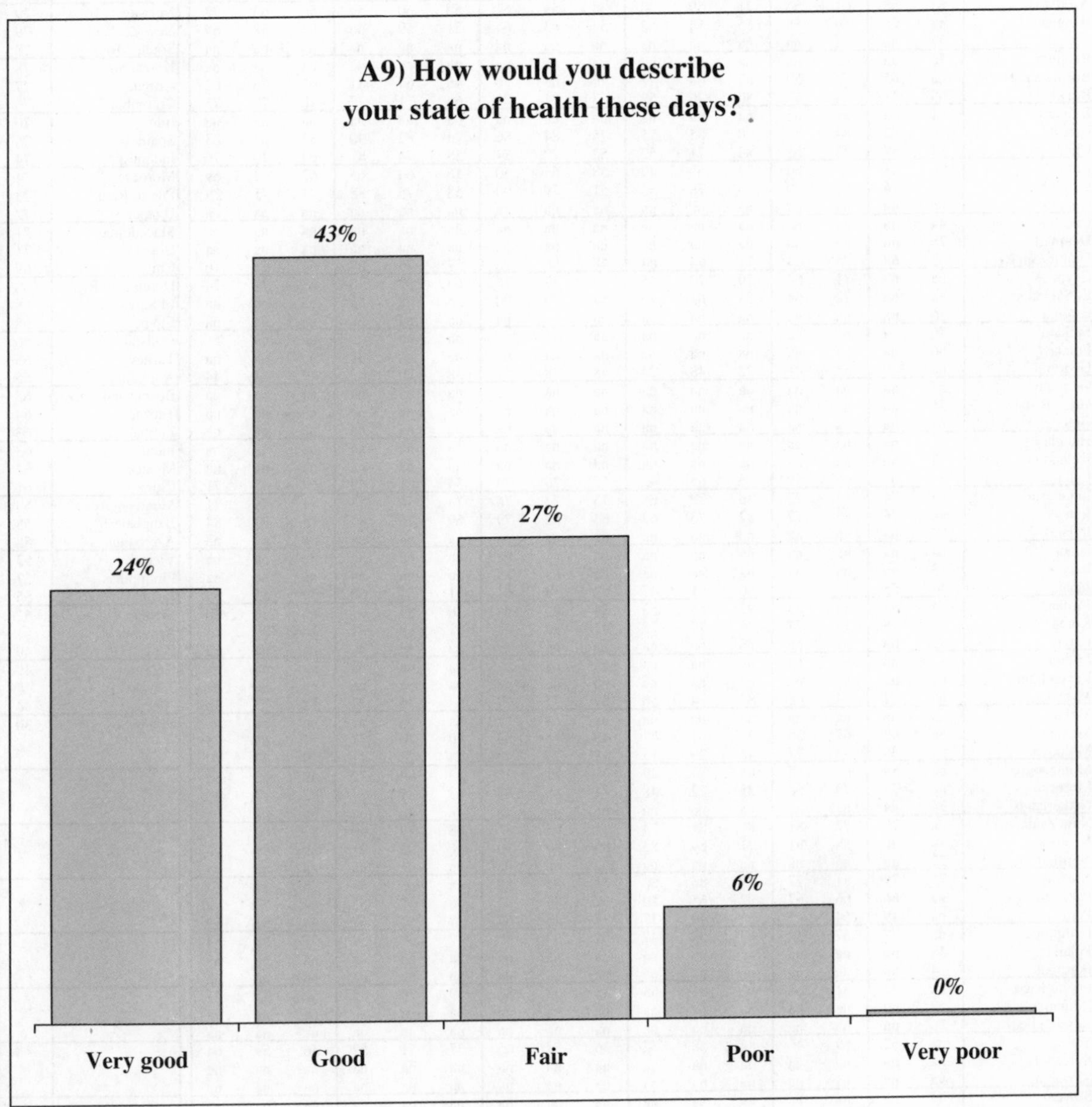
A9) How would you describe your state of health these days?
24%
43%
27%
6%
0%
Very good
Good
Fair
Poor
Very poor

A009) STATE OF HEALTH

All in all, how would you describe your state of health these days? Would you say it is…

Very good / Good (%)

(WVS: V12)

Country	Wave		Gender		Age			Education			Income			Values		
	1990	2000	Male	Female	16-29	30-49	50+	Lower	Middle	Upper	Lower	Middle	Upper	Mat	Mixed	Postm.
Albania	na	**75**	76	74	87	83	52	64	81	89	65	78	83	70	79	90
Algeria	na	**44**	45	42	47	48	28	33	45	50	37	45	51	39	48	45
Argentina	60	**65**	67	63	71	68	56	60	72	75	58	64	73	59	65	68
Armenia	na	**51**	54	48	70	45	28	39	51	53	62	44	39	51	49	66
Australia	na	**80**	79	80	83	85	70	70	81	87	70	82	89	76	80	80
Austria	62	**na**	na	na	na	na	na	na	na	na	na	na	na	na	na	na
Azerbaijan	na	**58**	61	56	71	59	30	34	59	61	56	60	59	56	63	57
Bangladesh	na	**58**	59	58	65	54	52	54	63	64	51	59	66	57	58	69
Belarus	27	**na**	na	na	na	na	na	na	na	na	na	na	na	na	na	na
Belgium	72	**na**	na	na	na	na	na	na	na	na	na	na	na	na	na	na
Bosnia and Herz.	na	**65**	70	59	82	65	47	46	68	70	46	64	81	62	66	62
Brazil	69	**71**	74	67	80	70	52	63	75	80	64	71	77	70	70	75
Bulgaria	51	**na**	na	na	na	na	na	na	na	na	na	na	na	na	na	na
Canada	80	**82**	84	80	90	85	75	75	84	86	74	82	90	83	82	83
Chile	54	**69**	73	65	82	71	52	52	77	84	58	74	81	64	70	76
China	56	**61**	63	60	74	62	49	58	65	50	56	64	65	62	62	69
Colombia	na	**76**	81	70	85	78	53	51	79	90	58	75	88	71	75	79
Croatia	na	**na**	na	na	na	na	na	na	na	na	na	na	na	na	na	na
Czech Republic	44	**na**	na	na	na	na	na	na	na	na	na	na	na	na	na	na
Denmark	78	**na**	na	na	na	na	na	na	na	na	na	na	na	na	na	na
Dominican Rep.	na	**68**	75	64	71	64	64	48	56	76	57	75	87	61	68	76
Egypt	na	**68**	71	64	79	70	45	59	77	76	63	67	70	63	71	74
El Salvador	na	**68**	72	64	83	63	49	54	79	90	56	68	85	na	na	na
Estonia	36	**na**	na	na	na	na	na	na	na	na	na	na	na	na	na	na
Finland	76	**na**	na	na	na	na	na	na	na	na	na	na	na	na	na	na
France	66	**na**	na	na	na	na	na	na	na	na	na	na	na	na	na	na
Georgia	na	**49**	58	41	72	48	24	48	48	51	38	50	62	45	53	44
Germany	55	**na**	na	na	na	na	na	na	na	na	na	na	na	na	na	na
Great Britain	75	**na**	na	na	na	na	na	na	na	na	na	na	na	na	na	na
Greece	na	**na**	na	na	na	na	na	na	na	na	na	na	na	na	na	na
Hungary	31	**na**	na	na	na	na	na	na	na	na	na	na	na	na	na	na
Iceland	74	**na**	na	na	na	na	na	na	na	na	na	na	na	na	na	na
India	63	**63**	66	59	75	65	45	52	70	79	54	61	69	64	67	71
Indonesia	na	**74**	77	72	76	79	68	73	73	76	73	76	73	71	76	71
Iran	na	**76**	75	77	82	73	62	64	82	79	69	76	83	75	77	84
Ireland	82	**na**	na	na	na	na	na	na	na	na	na	na	na	na	na	na
Israel	na	**na**	na	na	na	na	na	na	na	na	na	na	na	na	na	na
Italy	55	**na**	na	na	na	na	na	na	na	na	na	na	na	na	na	na
Japan	44	**55**	55	54	60	61	47	52	54	61	51	54	60	59	55	54
Jordan	na	**83**	84	83	92	85	63	74	90	94	78	83	91	80	88	80
Korea, South	na	**78**	78	77	76	79	75	43	80	78	71	82	81	76	80	74
Latvia	32	**na**	na	na	na	na	na	na	na	na	na	na	na	na	na	na
Lithuania	43	**na**	na	na	na	na	na	na	na	na	na	na	na	na	na	na
Luxembourg	na	**na**	na	na	na	na	na	na	na	na	na	na	na	na	na	na
Macedonia	na	**71**	74	68	85	74	56	59	77	77	63	76	77	72	73	68
Malta	na	**na**	na	na	na	na	na	na	na	na	na	na	na	na	na	na
Mexico	69	**62**	67	56	73	61	47	49	75	84	50	70	71	57	64	74
Moldova	na	**30**	34	27	48	29	15	18	29	43	24	28	41	29	33	29
Montenegro	na	**59**	63	55	85	71	29	39	71	78	43	60	72	49	67	82
Morocco	na	**74**	79	68	85	72	48	71	85	84	63	81	77	72	77	82
Netherlands	74	**na**	na	na	na	na	na	na	na	na	na	na	na	na	na	na
New Zealand	na	**79**	77	81	86	81	74	71	83	86	68	79	90	83	80	83
Nigeria	78	**90**	88	91	91	89	83	89	89	90	86	93	91	89	89	93
Northern Ireland	77	**na**	na	na	na	na	na	na	na	na	na	na	na	na	na	na
Norway	75	**79**	81	77	87	86	66	66	83	88	na	na	na	75	80	83
Pakistan	na	**66**	66	67	92	65	20	52	83	84	46	67	85	64	70	100
Peru	na	**49**	54	45	55	49	37	33	45	67	37	52	67	44	51	52
Philippines	na	**57**	57	58	63	58	47	51	54	69	47	63	59	57	58	54
Poland	38	**na**	na	na	na	na	na	na	na	na	na	na	na	na	na	na
Portugal	44	**na**	na	na	na	na	na	na	na	na	na	na	na	na	na	na
Puerto Rico	na	**73**	81	68	93	81	58	45	62	83	59	76	85	62	75	71
Romania	47	**na**	na	na	na	na	na	na	na	na	na	na	na	na	na	na
Russian Fed.	26	**na**	na	na	na	na	na	na	na	na	na	na	na	na	na	na
Serbia	na	**52**	59	46	84	58	32	36	58	65	37	51	62	46	59	64
Singapore	na	**na**	na	na	na	na	na	na	na	na	na	na	na	na	na	na
Slovakia	na	**na**	na	na	na	na	na	na	na	na	na	na	na	na	na	na
Slovenia	43	**na**	na	na	na	na	na	na	na	na	na	na	na	na	na	na
South Africa	68	**78**	83	72	82	81	60	72	85	94	73	76	86	78	79	77
Spain	57	**76**	80	72	94	84	57	67	87	88	52	80	83	67	78	86
Sweden	80	**na**	na	na	na	na	na	na	na	na	na	na	na	na	na	na
Switzerland	81	**85**	85	85	94	91	73	76	88	85	72	89	92	82	84	91
Taiwan	na	**48**	52	43	60	51	32	36	49	57	43	51	53	48	49	62
Tanzania	na	**64**	64	64	65	68	52	58	68	77	59	64	73	63	64	79
Turkey	60	**65**	68	62	73	65	49	61	71	67	63	66	72	63	65	70
Uganda	na	**72**	75	70	75	72	57	59	76	89	69	77	84	69	74	73
Ukraine	na	**na**	na	na	na	na	na	na	na	na	na	na	na	na	na	na
United States	79	**84**	86	82	84	87	80	81	82	86	77	88	91	85	84	83
Uruguay	na	**77**	82	73	93	83	65	70	85	91	66	84	84	63	78	85
Venezuela	na	**na**	na	na	na	na	na	na	na	na	na	na	na	na	na	na
Vietnam	na	**57**	62	53	74	62	38	54	61	66	52	56	62	61	58	56
Zimbabwe	na	**63**	65	62	74	60	44	56	73	60	57	59	75	60	66	66
Total	59	**67**	70	64	77	69	52	58	69	75	58	68	74	62	69	74

RANKING	
Country	**2000**
Nigeria	90
Switzerland	85
United States	84
Jordan	83
Canada	82
Australia	80
Norway	79
New Zealand	79
South Africa	78
Korea, South	78
Uruguay	77
Colombia	76
Iran	76
Spain	76
Indonesia	74
Morocco	74
Puerto Rico	73
Uganda	72
Macedonia	71
Brazil	71
Chile	69
Dominican Rep.	68
El Salvador	68
Egypt	68
Pakistan	66
Turkey	65
Argentina	65
Bosnia and Herz.	65
Tanzania	64
Zimbabwe	63
India	63
Mexico	62
China	61
Montenegro	59
Bangladesh	58
Azerbaijan	58
Vietnam	57
Philippines	57
Japan	55
Serbia	52
Armenia	51
Peru	49
Georgia	49
Taiwan	48
Algeria	44
Moldova	30
Total	67

A25) With which of these two statements do you tend to agree?

82%

18%

One must always love and respect our parents

One does not have the duty to respect and love parents who have not earned it

A025) RESPECT PARENTS

With which of these two statements do you tend to agree? A. Regardless of what the qualities and faults of one's parents are, One must always love and respect them (%)

(WVS: V13; EVS: V162)

Country	Wave		Gender		Age			Education			Income			Values		
	1990	2000	Male	Female	16-29	30-49	50+	Lower	Middle	Upper	Lower	Middle	Upper	Mat	Mixed	Postm.
Albania	na	**87**	86	88	84	88	88	84	88	89	85	85	91	88	86	87
Algeria	na	**93**	92	94	93	91	97	95	93	92	93	94	91	93	93	91
Argentina	75	**88**	88	88	83	89	92	90	86	79	91	88	85	93	90	81
Armenia	na	**93**	95	91	91	93	94	95	93	91	92	94	92	95	92	80
Australia	na	**74**	75	73	72	72	79	82	76	65	78	72	69	83	77	67
Austria	75	**65**	61	69	60	59	73	73	60	46	73	68	60	72	68	55
Azerbaijan	na	**92**	92	91	89	93	94	94	92	91	91	93	91	92	90	88
Bangladesh	na	**90**	90	90	90	90	92	91	90	88	93	89	89	90	90	85
Belarus	83	**71**	73	69	69	68	77	77	71	59	76	69	67	73	71	62
Belgium	77	**65**	65	65	57	60	74	75	66	56	72	68	58	71	65	58
Bosnia and Herz.	na	**91**	91	91	88	93	92	93	92	87	92	90	92	94	90	93
Brazil	90	**93**	93	93	92	92	96	95	92	87	96	95	89	96	93	85
Bulgaria	83	**82**	81	83	77	80	86	90	81	70	86	82	75	86	78	71
Canada	69	**78**	77	78	73	76	82	85	78	70	83	79	71	84	80	71
Chile	88	**87**	87	87	84	87	91	87	89	84	89	84	89	89	86	86
China	75	**95**	95	94	89	96	96	96	93	93	94	96	93	94	94	90
Colombia	na	**91**	90	92	91	91	93	91	92	90	92	91	90	91	91	89
Croatia	na	**72**	72	71	59	71	81	83	65	60	81	71	67	72	75	58
Czech Republic	67	**74**	73	75	63	73	80	77	70	73	80	73	68	77	74	64
Denmark	47	**na**	na	na	na	na	na	na	na	na	na	na	na	na	na	na
Dominican Rep.	na	**86**	82	88	85	87	82	81	85	87	87	86	78	86	87	83
Egypt	na	**95**	95	95	94	95	96	95	95	95	95	96	96	96	95	93
El Salvador	na	**94**	93	94	94	94	93	94	93	93	93	94	93	na	na	na
Estonia	62	**72**	69	75	68	71	75	72	72	71	77	72	67	77	69	65
Finland	40	**63**	65	62	59	59	71	67	60	55	63	62	65	63	65	59
France	77	**75**	75	74	71	71	80	80	68	67	77	80	69	84	76	58
Georgia	na	**91**	92	91	89	91	95	92	91	92	91	91	91	92	91	93
Germany	76	**53**	52	54	46	49	61	62	46	44	60	53	45	58	54	44
Great Britain	68	**65**	65	65	66	60	69	78	57	60	70	63	56	na	na	na
Greece	na	**69**	69	69	59	75	81	84	74	63	73	68	69	79	69	58
Hungary	81	**83**	81	85	79	79	89	86	73	81	87	80	83	85	81	72
Iceland	61	**61**	63	59	55	59	68	68	60	48	55	67	57	70	59	50
India	84	**89**	89	89	90	88	89	91	88	85	90	93	85	91	85	88
Indonesia	na	**90**	88	92	88	91	90	90	89	92	89	89	93	90	90	96
Iran	na	**89**	89	90	89	89	90	90	87	91	90	88	88	94	87	84
Ireland	78	**71**	73	69	68	67	78	81	69	59	80	71	63	76	72	57
Israel	na	**na**	na	na	na	na	na	na	na	na	na	na	na	na	na	na
Italy	84	**79**	79	80	67	80	86	86	75	71	86	80	76	88	80	72
Japan	79	**72**	72	71	55	71	78	81	72	65	76	74	66	72	70	69
Jordan	na	**94**	93	95	94	94	94	96	94	90	96	92	94	95	93	92
Korea, South	94	**92**	93	92	87	93	97	96	93	91	91	94	93	93	93	84
Latvia	72	**77**	78	77	72	82	75	79	77	76	78	79	74	75	79	74
Lithuania	80	**83**	81	85	79	83	85	84	83	82	82	87	79	80	83	91
Luxembourg	na	**59**	63	55	52	54	69	70	56	46	62	63	45	67	60	40
Macedonia	na	**91**	91	91	89	89	96	95	89	89	92	89	93	89	92	92
Malta	na	**91**	91	92	85	90	96	97	90	81	93	95	87	95	90	84
Mexico	78	**90**	90	90	90	91	89	90	91	87	88	91	91	92	91	89
Moldova	na	**90**	88	93	87	92	92	92	91	88	93	90	89	89	92	85
Montenegro	na	**87**	85	89	80	86	93	92	86	80	94	91	81	91	86	77
Morocco	na	**97**	97	98	97	98	98	98	96	94	97	98	96	99	97	91
Netherlands	38	**32**	33	31	24	27	41	45	30	21	39	31	24	51	32	20
New Zealand	na	**62**	64	61	62	56	68	69	62	55	69	64	52	65	60	55
Nigeria	87	**94**	94	95	93	95	97	96	94	94	95	95	92	95	94	89
Northern Ireland	80	**78**	79	77	75	73	84	84	74	71	80	78	79	87	79	62
Norway	45	**52**	53	51	44	48	63	61	53	42	na	na	na	60	52	41
Pakistan	na	**94**	94	95	94	94	97	95	93	96	95	94	94	95	94	100
Peru	na	**91**	91	91	89	92	90	89	90	93	90	91	92	89	91	94
Philippines	na	**94**	92	95	95	93	94	92	94	95	94	95	92	95	93	92
Poland	84	**87**	85	88	82	88	87	89	87	76	88	86	84	88	86	81
Portugal	77	**83**	81	84	79	80	87	83	83	82	86	81	84	84	84	80
Puerto Rico	na	**98**	98	97	95	96	100	97	98	97	98	98	96	98	97	97
Romania	83	**84**	82	85	76	81	90	92	83	69	91	86	78	86	82	68
Russian Fed.	76	**84**	84	85	79	85	86	84	85	82	84	85	84	85	84	83
Serbia	na	**87**	86	88	81	83	93	90	87	83	89	87	85	90	84	88
Singapore	na	**93**	92	94	94	93	93	94	94	91	93	94	93	94	94	87
Slovakia	na	**74**	70	77	64	73	82	80	70	74	77	74	71	75	73	61
Slovenia	82	**78**	77	79	72	75	86	90	77	63	84	85	65	86	77	72
South Africa	87	**91**	91	91	90	92	88	90	92	90	86	94	94	93	89	92
Spain	80	**83**	82	85	74	81	91	90	78	73	87	86	77	89	86	68
Sweden	51	**44**	50	38	33	43	51	59	43	33	49	45	36	65	45	35
Switzerland	70	**66**	68	65	58	64	75	76	65	55	73	72	56	70	69	57
Taiwan	na	**93**	91	95	91	94	94	94	90	94	93	95	91	93	93	94
Tanzania	na	**91**	90	91	91	89	95	90	92	90	90	90	93	91	91	96
Turkey	83	**86**	85	87	83	87	89	92	81	69	91	85	74	89	87	78
Uganda	na	**90**	91	89	90	90	89	85	91	96	85	94	93	94	91	75
Ukraine	na	**86**	84	87	84	83	90	93	85	85	88	83	84	85	87	89
United States	75	**77**	77	78	77	78	77	82	81	73	80	79	74	81	79	72
Uruguay	na	**78**	75	80	69	75	84	82	74	65	77	79	78	84	77	74
Venezuela	na	**94**	93	95	93	95	94	94	95	93	95	92	95	94	94	93
Vietnam	na	**99**	99	99	100	99	99	99	100	100	99	99	100	100	99	100
Zimbabwe	na	**96**	97	96	95	97	98	96	97	100	97	96	97	98	95	99
Total	74	**82**	82	82	81	82	84	86	81	77	85	83	80	87	81	71

RANKING	
Country	2000
Vietnam	99
Puerto Rico	98
Morocco	97
Zimbabwe	96
Egypt	95
China	95
Pakistan	94
Nigeria	94
Venezuela	94
Jordan	94
Philippines	94
El Salvador	94
Singapore	93
Taiwan	93
Algeria	93
Armenia	93
Brazil	93
Korea, South	92
Azerbaijan	92
Georgia	91
Bosnia and Herz.	91
Malta	91
Colombia	91
Macedonia	91
South Africa	91
Peru	91
Tanzania	91
Moldova	90
Mexico	90
Bangladesh	90
Uganda	90
Indonesia	90
Iran	89
India	89
Argentina	88
Chile	87
Montenegro	87
Serbia	87
Poland	87
Turkey	86
Dominican Rep.	86
Ukraine	86
Russian Fed.	84
Romania	84
Spain	83
Hungary	83
Lithuania	83
Portugal	83
Bulgaria	82
Italy	79
Slovenia	78
Northern Ireland	78
Uruguay	78
Canada	78
United States	77
Latvia	77
France	75
Australia	74
Czech Republic	74
Slovakia	74
Estonia	72
Japan	72
Croatia	72
Belarus	71
Ireland	71
Greece	69
Switzerland	66
Belgium	65
Great Britain	65
Austria	65
Finland	63
New Zealand	62
Iceland	61
Luxembourg	59
Germany	53
Norway	52
Sweden	44
Netherlands	32
Total	82

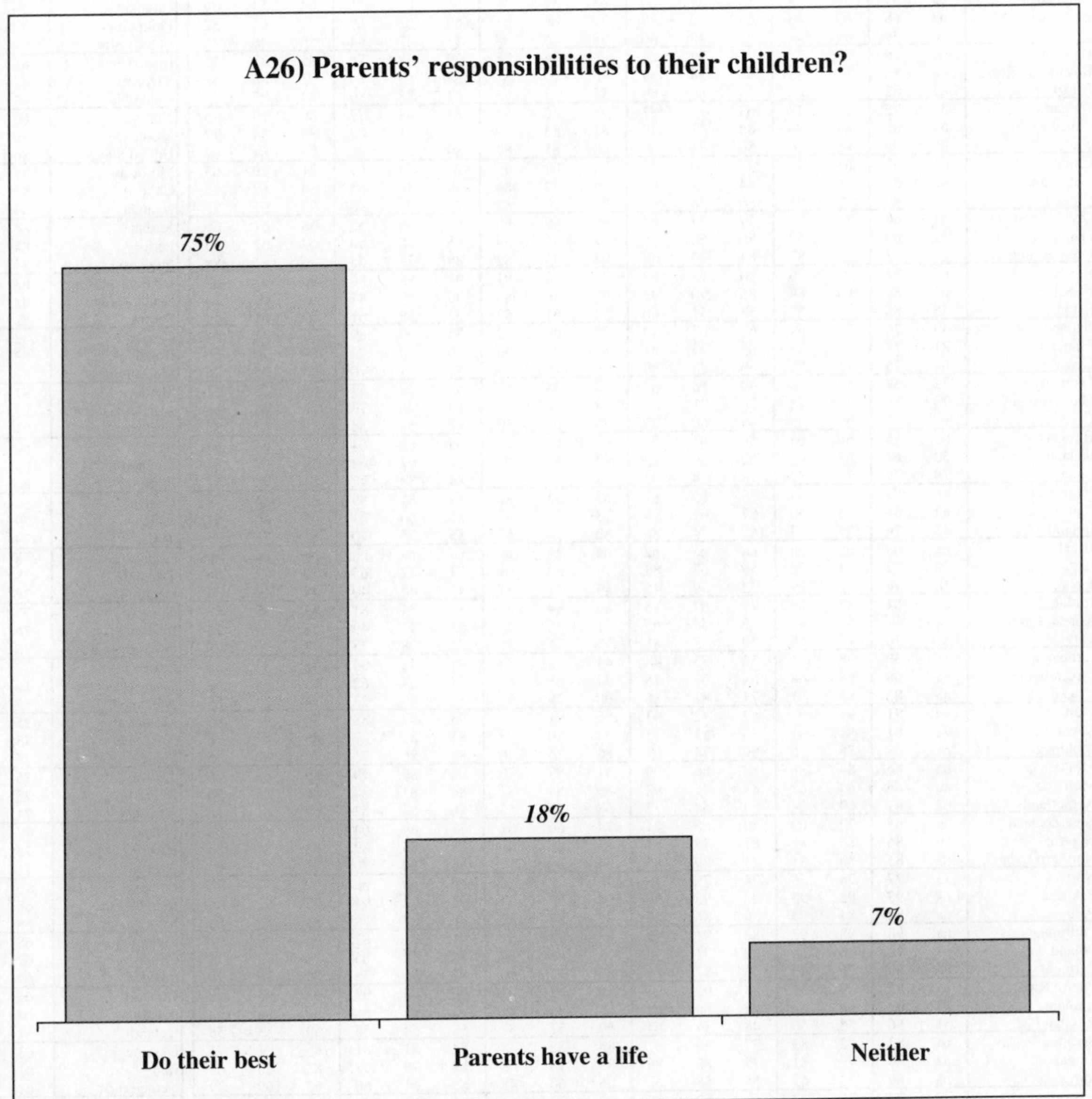
A26) Parents' responsibilities to their children?
75%
18%
7%
Do their best
Parents have a life
Neither

A026) PARENTS RESPONSIBILITIES

Which of the following statements best describes your views about parents' responsibilities to their children?

Do their best for their children even at the expense of their own well-being (%) (WVS: V14; EVS: V163)

Country	Wave 1990	Wave 2000	Gender Male	Gender Female	Age 16-29	Age 30-49	Age 50+	Education Lower	Education Middle	Education Upper	Income Lower	Income Middle	Income Upper	Values Mat	Values Mixed	Values Postm.
Albania	na	**76**	75	76	68	76	82	75	76	74	75	76	76	79	74	69
Algeria	na	**78**	79	78	74	80	84	78	80	77	80	79	72	79	78	74
Argentina	79	**81**	81	80	75	82	84	84	74	80	85	80	77	85	82	73
Armenia	na	**64**	63	66	55	67	75	66	65	61	63	66	67	68	62	57
Australia	na	**75**	75	75	73	76	77	81	75	70	77	75	74	76	77	72
Austria	61	**71**	72	69	68	67	76	75	68	61	81	76	61	78	71	66
Azerbaijan	na	**59**	55	63	58	59	60	63	59	58	65	59	56	64	53	39
Bangladesh	na	**68**	69	68	64	70	79	72	66	61	69	68	69	74	65	52
Belarus	46	**49**	49	48	39	45	60	60	46	38	53	47	44	55	46	29
Belgium	64	**78**	77	79	75	75	81	83	76	76	79	79	76	85	77	72
Bosnia and Herz.	na	**88**	87	89	88	88	89	90	90	83	88	89	86	91	88	83
Brazil	81	**82**	83	80	74	86	89	87	78	75	83	83	80	84	82	78
Bulgaria	58	**75**	72	77	63	72	82	87	72	58	83	68	72	80	70	45
Canada	67	**82**	84	80	86	83	79	83	83	79	85	81	82	85	84	77
Chile	80	**85**	85	86	86	84	87	88	85	80	89	80	86	87	84	87
China	61	**67**	61	74	47	70	79	78	62	33	71	69	61	71	60	63
Colombia	na	**87**	88	86	84	88	91	88	89	84	86	89	85	84	89	85
Croatia	na	**90**	90	91	86	88	96	93	90	83	92	91	90	95	91	88
Czech Republic	41	**60**	60	59	59	57	62	60	59	60	68	59	55	58	61	66
Denmark	52	**60**	61	60	58	56	65	61	56	59	63	58	60	63	62	55
Dominican Rep.	na	**83**	83	83	84	79	100	94	83	82	85	79	85	86	81	88
Egypt	na	**94**	92	96	90	95	98	96	92	91	95	95	94	96	93	87
El Salvador	na	**89**	89	89	85	90	93	90	89	86	90	89	87	na	na	na
Estonia	55	**58**	57	59	58	51	66	58	61	52	57	59	61	57	61	49
Finland	49	**70**	70	69	67	67	73	72	66	72	74	69	69	73	71	61
France	81	**75**	77	73	67	73	81	80	71	66	76	80	73	82	76	66
Georgia	na	**76**	75	76	69	78	80	79	76	71	81	74	70	77	75	76
Germany	72	**59**	59	58	49	55	67	62	54	62	59	59	57	65	58	51
Great Britain	74	**76**	74	78	70	71	83	78	74	74	83	76	73	na	na	na
Greece	na	**57**	59	55	44	60	79	73	61	50	61	58	54	58	57	52
Hungary	62	**65**	66	65	56	63	73	67	62	61	63	66	64	67	65	54
Iceland	50	**64**	67	61	62	66	63	63	65	64	61	67	63	59	67	57
India	78	**79**	77	82	78	78	83	84	79	67	84	84	72	84	74	64
Indonesia	na	**84**	84	84	76	85	87	87	83	84	81	85	89	82	86	78
Iran	na	**61**	63	59	57	61	73	73	56	54	65	60	61	63	60	51
Ireland	73	**76**	75	77	69	74	86	82	76	67	85	75	70	81	75	73
Israel	na	**na**	na	na	na	na	na	na	na	na	na	na	na	na	na	na
Italy	79	**72**	72	72	56	67	83	79	67	61	77	72	65	79	72	68
Japan	40	**40**	42	39	32	39	45	44	41	37	42	40	40	47	40	34
Jordan	na	**84**	85	83	79	87	88	86	84	79	87	84	81	82	86	78
Korea, South	38	**51**	55	47	32	54	65	71	56	41	55	47	49	55	50	24
Latvia	51	**76**	77	75	70	73	81	79	76	71	76	78	75	77	76	78
Lithuania	38	**39**	38	41	32	35	48	44	38	34	45	42	34	46	37	23
Luxembourg	na	**68**	68	68	64	63	75	74	66	61	74	68	62	75	68	59
Macedonia	na	**82**	83	81	77	81	86	90	79	73	88	80	73	76	84	85
Malta	na	**91**	91	92	87	92	93	95	91	83	95	92	88	95	91	83
Mexico	74	**81**	81	81	76	83	85	84	80	71	82	82	77	85	81	76
Moldova	na	**75**	75	76	69	74	83	80	76	70	81	76	71	71	80	65
Montenegro	na	**86**	84	88	80	86	90	91	83	79	92	87	79	89	83	76
Morocco	na	**85**	84	87	83	86	92	86	84	81	86	83	84	86	85	76
Netherlands	62	**61**	69	54	53	54	73	68	59	57	66	64	53	69	61	58
New Zealand	na	**68**	70	67	60	66	74	74	66	61	71	69	64	74	68	64
Nigeria	89	**86**	86	87	87	85	87	83	88	88	83	88	89	88	86	83
Northern Ireland	82	**81**	80	81	73	79	85	84	80	71	86	80	70	91	80	69
Norway	73	**77**	78	76	74	78	78	76	79	75	na	na	na	79	77	74
Pakistan	na	**93**	92	95	93	93	96	94	92	94	93	92	94	93	93	100
Peru	na	**84**	84	84	80	86	87	87	84	82	88	82	79	82	85	85
Philippines	na	**90**	88	92	88	91	90	88	92	89	91	91	87	90	90	91
Poland	63	**72**	76	68	62	71	78	78	67	58	74	72	65	70	72	71
Portugal	84	**80**	76	83	73	77	86	83	77	60	87	75	78	86	76	70
Puerto Rico	na	**92**	89	93	89	92	93	90	92	92	90	94	92	91	93	90
Romania	85	**na**	na	na	na	na	na	na	na	na	na	na	na	na	na	na
Russian Fed.	51	**56**	56	56	48	54	64	59	57	52	58	54	56	59	53	58
Serbia	na	**82**	82	83	77	79	87	86	82	78	84	81	81	85	81	71
Singapore	na	**80**	79	81	77	83	85	89	78	68	84	79	78	83	80	69
Slovakia	na	**60**	57	63	55	58	67	65	60	48	63	61	60	62	60	39
Slovenia	72	**74**	76	72	63	73	82	82	73	61	80	74	64	84	72	71
South Africa	88	**82**	80	85	83	81	83	83	81	76	82	88	77	80	85	78
Spain	75	**80**	79	82	68	78	91	88	74	68	87	80	75	89	80	68
Sweden	63	**67**	71	64	75	66	64	65	69	67	69	66	68	68	67	67
Switzerland	69	**59**	59	59	49	57	67	67	56	61	57	63	55	65	61	48
Taiwan	na	**75**	75	76	50	79	82	83	79	65	84	77	66	77	72	78
Tanzania	na	**78**	79	76	74	79	82	79	75	80	75	79	80	81	77	71
Turkey	67	**79**	78	80	75	80	85	85	75	61	85	78	66	82	79	71
Uganda	na	**84**	84	84	83	87	82	79	86	90	78	85	93	86	87	70
Ukraine	na	**63**	62	63	54	60	69	70	64	55	67	61	61	62	63	63
United States	75	**86**	86	85	91	83	84	82	89	85	87	85	87	87	85	86
Uruguay	na	**80**	78	81	75	77	84	83	77	68	83	79	77	86	80	74
Venezuela	na	**91**	91	90	89	92	93	93	93	83	94	92	89	87	92	92
Vietnam	na	**88**	86	89	80	88	93	89	87	81	86	89	86	87	88	76
Zimbabwe	na	**91**	92	90	92	92	87	90	93	100	90	91	94	92	90	93
Total	65	75	75	75	71	74	79	80	73	70	77	75	72	77	74	70

RANKING

Country	2000
Egypt	94
Pakistan	93
Puerto Rico	92
Malta	91
Zimbabwe	91
Venezuela	91
Croatia	90
Philippines	90
El Salvador	89
Bosnia and Herz.	88
Vietnam	88
Colombia	87
Nigeria	86
Montenegro	86
United States	86
Morocco	85
Chile	85
Uganda	84
Jordan	84
Peru	84
Indonesia	84
Dominican Rep.	83
South Africa	82
Serbia	82
Canada	82
Brazil	82
Macedonia	82
Mexico	81
Argentina	81
Northern Ireland	81
Spain	80
Singapore	80
Portugal	80
Uruguay	80
India	79
Turkey	79
Algeria	78
Tanzania	78
Belgium	78
Norway	77
Ireland	76
Great Britain	76
Latvia	76
Georgia	76
Albania	76
Moldova	75
Australia	75
France	75
Taiwan	75
Bulgaria	75
Slovenia	74
Poland	72
Italy	72
Austria	71
Finland	70
Bangladesh	68
New Zealand	68
Luxembourg	68
China	67
Sweden	67
Hungary	65
Armenia	64
Iceland	64
Ukraine	63
Iran	61
Netherlands	61
Slovakia	60
Denmark	60
Czech Republic	60
Azerbaijan	59
Switzerland	59
Germany	59
Estonia	58
Greece	57
Russian Fed.	56
Korea, South	51
Belarus	49
Japan	40
Lithuania	39
Total	75

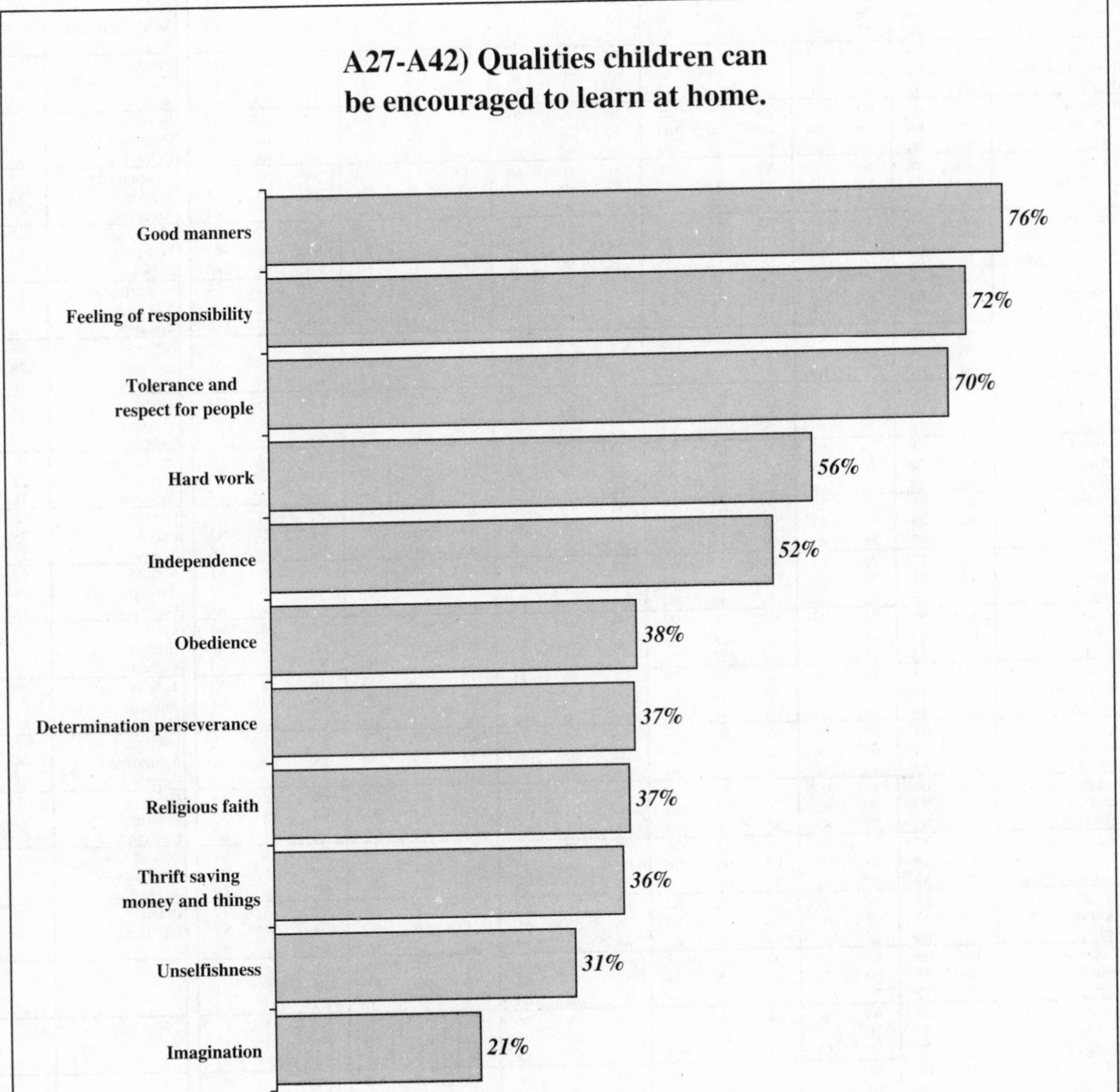
A27-A42) Qualities children can be encouraged to learn at home.
Good manners
76%
Feeling of responsibility
72%
Tolerance and respect for people
70%
Hard work
56%
Independence
52%
Obedience
38%
Determination perseverance
37%
Religious faith
37%
Thrift saving money and things
36%
Unselfishness
31%
Imagination
21%

A027_1) CHILD QUALITIES: GOOD MANNERS

Here is a list of qualities which children can be encouraged to learn at home.
Which, if any, do you consider to be especially important?
Good manners (%)

(WVS: IV15; EVS: V164)

Country	Wave		Gender		Age			Education			Income			Values		
	1990	2000	Male	Female	16-29	30-49	50+	Lower	Middle	Upper	Lower	Middle	Upper	Mat	Mixed	Postm.
Albania	na	**na**	na	na	na	na	na	na	na	na	na	na	na	na	na	na
Algeria	na	**83**	83	83	81	84	85	82	84	82	83	86	81	84	82	80
Argentina	78	**83**	83	83	82	81	85	89	76	69	90	83	75	88	85	73
Armenia	na	**76**	71	80	74	77	79	74	78	72	77	75	79	79	73	75
Australia	na	**80**	81	80	80	78	84	90	84	68	86	80	73	91	84	73
Austria	78	**78**	78	78	76	76	81	86	72	64	77	79	78	89	83	66
Azerbaijan	na	**53**	49	57	56	51	52	38	50	62	44	47	67	53	53	53
Bangladesh	na	**na**	na	na	na	na	na	na	na	na	na	na	na	na	na	na
Belarus	71	**60**	53	66	67	62	53	51	63	67	60	59	65	58	66	59
Belgium	72	**78**	77	79	79	76	79	87	81	67	83	80	73	88	81	58
Bosnia and Herz.	na	**na**	na	na	na	na	na	na	na	na	na	na	na	na	na	na
Brazil	77	**52**	56	49	57	51	47	52	56	40	56	52	51	55	53	45
Bulgaria	72	**69**	69	70	72	69	69	66	73	67	66	77	68	69	72	52
Canada	75	**na**	na	na	na	na	na	na	na	na	na	na	na	na	na	na
Chile	90	**na**	na	na	na	na	na	na	na	na	na	na	na	na	na	na
China	53	**na**	na	na	na	na	na	na	na	na	na	na	na	na	na	na
Colombia	na	**84**	84	85	85	83	87	87	88	72	88	86	77	88	85	84
Croatia	na	**97**	97	97	95	98	97	99	96	95	98	97	97	99	97	94
Czech Republic	86	**87**	86	87	83	87	89	89	86	83	89	87	85	89	87	79
Denmark	66	**72**	71	74	71	67	79	84	61	54	75	74	61	84	76	47
Dominican Rep.	na	**85**	84	85	84	87	55	94	90	81	90	81	80	88	84	80
Egypt	na	**78**	79	77	78	77	79	78	79	78	78	81	77	79	78	71
El Salvador	na	**82**	83	82	82	82	82	82	85	78	83	84	80	na	na	na
Estonia	74	**78**	76	80	78	77	80	83	78	73	80	78	77	80	77	84
Finland	82	**90**	88	92	80	90	95	93	87	82	90	89	89	91	91	84
France	53	**69**	69	69	70	65	71	75	64	57	72	72	60	79	69	51
Georgia	na	**61**	57	65	62	63	58	61	60	65	59	60	67	64	59	67
Germany	67	**64**	64	63	51	61	72	69	59	58	66	65	62	73	64	44
Great Britain	89	**92**	90	94	87	94	93	94	92	87	94	91	94	na	na	na
Greece	na	**76**	75	77	75	76	81	87	79	72	75	78	75	81	77	65
Hungary	77	**71**	74	69	71	67	76	73	71	64	77	68	71	74	69	80
Iceland	90	**74**	76	73	75	70	80	82	76	56	76	78	67	81	76	50
India	94	**na**	na	na	na	na	na	na	na	na	na	na	na	na	na	na
Indonesia	na	**85**	86	86	79	85	89	94	85	80	86	84	83	87	84	86
Iran	na	**89**	89	89	88	89	91	91	90	84	89	87	90	91	89	83
Ireland	75	**87**	86	89	92	83	89	92	88	78	89	90	82	92	86	86
Israel	na	**77**	79	75	74	75	82	88	77	68	83	78	69	78	76	81
Italy	79	**75**	75	74	76	70	79	83	73	56	80	77	67	86	76	67
Japan	83	**na**	na	na	na	na	na	na	na	na	na	na	na	na	na	na
Jordan	na	**95**	96	94	93	96	97	98	91	95	96	96	94	97	94	94
Korea, South	93	**na**	na	na	na	na	na	na	na	na	na	na	na	na	na	na
Latvia	53	**72**	71	72	68	67	77	81	71	60	76	71	68	73	71	64
Lithuania	35	**34**	29	38	42	37	24	27	34	41	29	24	44	36	32	38
Luxembourg	na	**83**	86	81	85	81	85	93	82	68	87	82	75	89	87	64
Macedonia	na	**na**	na	na	na	na	na	na	na	na	na	na	na	na	na	na
Malta	na	**82**	79	84	82	80	83	81	84	73	86	77	77	85	81	72
Mexico	73	**na**	na	na	na	na	na	na	na	na	na	na	na	na	na	na
Moldova	na	**na**	na	na	na	na	na	na	na	na	na	na	na	na	na	na
Montenegro	na	**na**	na	na	na	na	na	na	na	na	na	na	na	na	na	na
Morocco	na	**91**	89	92	89	91	94	91	91	91	93	93	88	94	88	80
Netherlands	80	**81**	78	83	83	76	85	94	81	67	83	82	75	92	84	66
New Zealand	na	**77**	77	76	76	77	76	83	78	68	77	80	74	79	78	69
Nigeria	97	**95**	95	94	95	95	90	95	95	93	94	95	96	95	95	93
Northern Ireland	95	**89**	89	89	91	88	89	89	91	84	92	92	84	90	88	88
Norway	77	**75**	72	77	73	72	80	83	76	65	na	na	na	84	78	47
Pakistan	na	**67**	65	69	55	71	80	76	59	51	73	66	62	69	64	83
Peru	na	**na**	na	na	na	na	na	na	na	na	na	na	na	na	na	na
Philippines	na	**na**	na	na	na	na	na	na	na	na	na	na	na	na	na	na
Poland	na	**58**	60	56	66	56	54	57	58	58	53	63	58	58	58	51
Portugal	82	**77**	76	77	72	77	79	79	76	63	75	78	76	80	77	63
Puerto Rico	na	**na**	na	na	na	na	na	na	na	na	na	na	na	na	na	na
Romania	92	**80**	79	81	85	84	74	67	86	91	68	81	88	80	83	76
Russian Fed.	57	**58**	57	59	65	60	53	51	58	62	56	61	59	59	58	62
Serbia	na	**na**	na	na	na	na	na	na	na	na	na	na	na	na	na	na
Singapore	na	**na**	na	na	na	na	na	na	na	na	na	na	na	na	na	na
Slovakia	na	**73**	70	75	65	74	77	74	73	67	72	74	72	76	70	67
Slovenia	89	**78**	77	78	76	74	83	91	77	56	88	76	65	84	77	70
South Africa	81	**na**	na	na	na	na	na	na	na	na	na	na	na	na	na	na
Spain	80	**86**	85	88	84	84	90	90	85	81	90	85	83	92	88	76
Sweden	78	**70**	70	71	69	66	75	84	72	57	73	71	64	83	77	47
Switzerland	59	**66**	67	66	67	62	72	80	65	48	68	68	63	77	69	56
Taiwan	na	**70**	67	72	73	70	68	63	69	76	68	68	77	71	69	70
Tanzania	na	**na**	na	na	na	na	na	na	na	na	na	na	na	na	na	na
Turkey	92	**93**	93	93	91	94	98	97	91	78	97	94	83	94	94	90
Uganda	na	**na**	na	na	na	na	na	na	na	na	na	na	na	na	na	na
Ukraine	na	**56**	52	59	58	57	54	47	56	60	53	57	58	57	58	45
United States	76	**na**	na	na	na	na	na	na	na	na	na	na	na	na	na	na
Uruguay	na	**81**	81	81	74	78	86	88	75	55	86	78	77	87	86	64
Venezuela	na	**na**	na	na	na	na	na	na	na	na	na	na	na	na	na	na
Vietnam	na	**na**	na	na	na	na	na	na	na	na	na	na	na	na	na	na
Zimbabwe	na	**na**	na	na	na	na	na	na	na	na	na	na	na	na	na	na
Total	76	76	75	76	76	75	77	80	74	71	77	76	74	76	77	67

RANKING	
Country	**2000**
Croatia	97
Jordan	95
Nigeria	95
Turkey	93
Great Britain	92
Morocco	91
Finland	90
Northern Ireland	89
Iran	89
Ireland	87
Czech Republic	87
Spain	86
Indonesia	85
Dominican Rep.	85
Colombia	84
Luxembourg	83
Algeria	83
Argentina	83
El Salvador	82
Malta	82
Uruguay	81
Netherlands	81
Australia	80
Romania	80
Egypt	78
Estonia	78
Belgium	78
Austria	78
Slovenia	78
Israel	77
New Zealand	77
Portugal	77
Armenia	76
Greece	76
Italy	75
Norway	75
Iceland	74
Slovakia	73
Denmark	72
Latvia	72
Hungary	71
Sweden	70
Taiwan	70
Bulgaria	69
France	69
Pakistan	67
Switzerland	66
Germany	64
Georgia	61
Belarus	60
Russian Fed.	58
Poland	58
Ukraine	56
Azerbaijan	53
Brazil	52
Lithuania	34
Total	76

A029) CHILD QUALITIES: INDEPENDENCE

Here is a list of qualities that children can be encouraged to learn at home.

Which, if any, do you consider to be especially important?

(WVS: V15; EVS: V165)

Independence (%)

Country	Wave		Gender		Age			Education			Income			Values		
	1990	2000	Male	Female	16-29	30-49	50+	Lower	Middle	Upper	Lower	Middle	Upper	Mat	Mixed	Postm.
Albania	na	**57**	59	56	67	55	52	49	62	65	57	60	55	53	61	69
Algeria	na	**26**	27	24	24	29	24	24	24	29	27	22	29	25	25	30
Argentina	43	**36**	31	41	39	37	33	29	43	62	28	33	50	27	33	50
Armenia	na	**32**	37	27	36	34	23	28	30	40	37	31	25	26	36	44
Australia	na	**53**	47	59	53	57	48	46	52	60	46	55	59	33	52	59
Austria	63	**71**	66	74	83	74	60	63	76	81	58	70	77	54	68	82
Azerbaijan	na	**60**	62	58	63	59	54	50	59	62	60	62	57	60	60	65
Bangladesh	na	**78**	81	74	75	80	81	75	80	82	76	78	79	77	79	72
Belarus	31	**32**	39	25	39	34	23	24	35	34	27	32	38	27	35	54
Belgium	36	**41**	42	40	45	45	35	28	41	50	34	38	48	33	39	54
Bosnia and Herz.	na	**56**	58	55	61	58	50	47	55	69	51	56	61	53	58	53
Brazil	27	**20**	18	22	21	19	18	16	20	32	16	18	26	15	19	39
Bulgaria	62	**42**	48	37	49	52	31	34	45	53	33	46	47	35	48	67
Canada	44	**62**	60	64	59	68	58	55	64	66	58	60	69	50	62	68
Chile	31	**53**	54	52	58	57	42	46	57	58	49	54	56	54	50	60
China	84	**74**	77	71	78	77	63	61	84	88	66	75	87	78	77	91
Colombia	na	**27**	26	28	26	29	25	18	25	45	19	25	40	21	26	31
Croatia	na	**85**	85	86	90	89	79	83	86	89	86	83	88	81	85	92
Czech Republic	21	**69**	70	68	68	74	66	67	70	73	66	68	74	61	71	74
Denmark	81	**81**	76	85	78	83	80	77	83	91	78	80	92	75	81	91
Dominican Rep.	na	**40**	36	42	39	43	36	9	32	46	34	42	47	34	38	52
Egypt	na	**73**	72	73	76	72	69	69	77	75	72	73	73	70	74	76
El Salvador	na	**36**	36	35	36	38	32	30	38	47	31	37	47	na	na	na
Estonia	43	**22**	21	22	28	24	17	17	22	29	18	14	27	16	26	39
Finland	57	**58**	56	59	61	64	50	53	65	62	53	62	61	57	57	62
France	27	**29**	29	29	36	36	20	21	41	41	26	30	35	13	29	53
Georgia	na	**51**	54	48	56	52	44	47	50	57	46	52	58	50	51	64
Germany	67	**70**	70	71	83	74	62	62	78	77	62	68	77	63	72	80
Great Britain	43	**53**	52	55	58	59	43	47	57	56	45	60	62	na	na	na
Greece	na	**58**	55	61	64	60	39	39	50	69	51	56	65	52	57	69
Hungary	70	**71**	72	70	73	79	62	66	77	84	67	72	73	66	75	76
Iceland	89	**76**	72	80	82	81	66	71	77	86	73	75	82	73	77	86
India	30	**56**	59	53	60	56	53	51	58	65	48	54	62	49	64	84
Indonesia	na	**76**	73	80	75	78	76	75	77	78	77	76	78	76	77	71
Iran	na	**53**	53	53	59	49	45	43	54	64	51	49	58	45	57	66
Ireland	43	**51**	51	50	49	59	42	46	51	56	45	50	57	49	50	52
Israel	na	**69**	67	70	67	72	67	64	66	76	60	66	81	74	68	70
Italy	31	**41**	41	41	49	48	31	32	45	56	36	40	46	35	39	49
Japan	65	**82**	83	81	79	84	81	74	82	85	81	82	83	83	81	91
Jordan	na	**22**	26	19	23	22	20	19	24	28	19	24	25	21	23	31
Korea, South	54	**77**	78	77	76	79	74	68	77	79	77	79	76	77	78	74
Latvia	73	**51**	51	51	51	58	45	33	54	64	46	47	57	48	51	70
Lithuania	81	**77**	79	75	81	83	68	62	82	83	74	79	82	74	79	85
Luxembourg	na	**49**	47	51	56	53	40	42	51	54	46	44	58	49	45	62
Macedonia	na	**59**	57	60	59	62	53	43	64	74	50	59	71	56	61	56
Malta	na	**31**	33	28	37	33	24	23	33	37	23	31	39	26	32	40
Mexico	47	**42**	39	45	45	45	33	38	44	60	39	44	52	39	44	55
Moldova	na	**56**	60	52	59	58	51	47	56	65	50	60	61	51	61	66
Montenegro	na	**59**	62	56	66	63	51	47	64	75	52	61	65	57	61	66
Morocco	na	**34**	37	32	39	34	22	32	41	47	36	38	40	30	38	48
Netherlands	51	**53**	50	57	57	57	48	45	50	65	53	54	57	52	48	70
New Zealand	na	**54**	47	59	49	60	50	51	51	59	44	54	63	54	51	64
Nigeria	16	**26**	28	23	26	26	24	24	26	28	26	25	28	22	27	41
Northern Ireland	37	**51**	47	54	52	53	48	48	52	58	53	46	56	47	50	58
Norway	86	**89**	85	92	89	93	83	84	89	93	na	na	na	84	89	94
Pakistan	na	**13**	16	9	21	11	1	4	18	33	4	13	22	11	15	8
Peru	na	**39**	37	40	39	40	33	33	40	41	36	38	45	33	40	38
Philippines	na	**66**	66	65	61	67	69	68	65	64	70	64	64	66	66	65
Poland	na	**22**	25	20	22	24	21	22	22	26	21	22	27	18	25	22
Portugal	24	**22**	25	20	31	21	18	18	29	44	22	20	29	13	28	31
Puerto Rico	na	**51**	51	52	61	56	43	48	42	57	45	52	55	54	49	58
Romania	24	**30**	33	27	40	36	19	18	36	37	20	29	37	26	33	49
Russian Fed.	29	**31**	36	26	40	32	24	21	30	39	27	26	38	27	33	60
Serbia	na	**61**	59	63	71	67	51	46	64	79	52	63	70	52	68	85
Singapore	na	**75**	74	76	75	77	69	76	74	73	72	76	74	75	74	80
Slovakia	na	**61**	64	59	67	64	53	50	66	70	54	61	66	60	63	70
Slovenia	33	**70**	69	71	73	75	63	65	72	76	67	72	71	73	70	74
South Africa	16	**63**	65	60	67	62	52	57	68	80	54	68	68	59	65	66
Spain	37	**39**	42	37	49	45	29	32	43	55	29	41	46	28	41	53
Sweden	36	**69**	60	77	66	75	65	58	69	77	65	65	78	55	66	82
Switzerland	42	**42**	41	44	54	44	35	33	44	47	40	41	45	35	39	60
Taiwan	na	**66**	67	65	79	69	50	52	64	81	58	66	77	64	71	68
Tanzania	na	**42**	45	38	43	41	44	39	45	49	40	39	53	37	46	42
Turkey	19	**71**	71	71	67	73	77	73	68	66	76	70	63	77	70	67
Uganda	na	**31**	30	33	29	34	29	30	32	26	29	29	29	35	30	28
Ukraine	na	**32**	37	28	41	32	27	20	30	43	28	33	36	27	38	41
United States	52	**61**	57	66	62	63	58	65	60	60	62	60	60	66	60	63
Uruguay	na	**49**	48	50	51	60	40	38	61	76	36	54	58	36	48	68
Venezuela	na	**45**	45	45	46	45	42	35	44	58	39	48	47	46	45	42
Vietnam	na	**56**	59	53	49	57	60	56	55	69	48	56	62	59	56	62
Zimbabwe	na	**26**	29	24	29	25	21	22	32	18	25	25	28	25	27	27
Total	47	**52**	52	51	53	55	46	45	53	60	47	51	57	46	53	62

RANKING

Country	2000
Norway	89
Croatia	85
Japan	82
Denmark	81
Bangladesh	78
Korea, South	77
Lithuania	77
Iceland	76
Indonesia	76
Singapore	75
China	74
Egypt	73
Turkey	71
Hungary	71
Austria	71
Germany	70
Slovenia	70
Czech Republic	69
Sweden	69
Israel	69
Taiwan	66
Philippines	66
South Africa	63
Canada	62
Slovakia	61
United States	61
Serbia	61
Azerbaijan	60
Montenegro	59
Macedonia	59
Greece	58
Finland	58
Albania	57
Bosnia and Herz.	56
India	56
Vietnam	56
Moldova	56
New Zealand	54
Netherlands	53
Great Britain	53
Iran	53
Australia	53
Chile	53
Puerto Rico	51
Latvia	51
Georgia	51
Northern Ireland	51
Ireland	51
Uruguay	49
Luxembourg	49
Venezuela	45
Switzerland	42
Mexico	42
Bulgaria	42
Tanzania	42
Italy	41
Belgium	41
Dominican Rep.	40
Spain	39
Peru	39
Argentina	36
El Salvador	36
Morocco	34
Armenia	32
Ukraine	32
Belarus	32
Uganda	31
Russian Fed.	31
Malta	31
Romania	30
France	29
Colombia	27
Zimbabwe	26
Nigeria	26
Algeria	26
Portugal	22
Jordan	22
Poland	22
Estonia	22
Brazil	20
Pakistan	13
Total	52

A030) CHILD QUALITIES: HARD WORK

Here is a list of qualities that children can be encouraged to learn at home.
Which, if any, do you consider to be especially important?
Hard work (%)

(WVS: V16; EVS: V166)

Country	Wave		Gender		Age			Education			Income			Values		
	1990	2000	Male	Female	16-29	30-49	50+	Lower	Middle	Upper	Lower	Middle	Upper	Mat	Mixed	Postm.
Albania	na	**64**	63	64	54	65	70	72	61	50	65	64	62	67	61	51
Algeria	na	**67**	69	65	68	69	62	59	69	70	68	70	65	66	69	67
Argentina	53	**57**	58	56	50	54	66	63	46	52	67	54	50	67	55	52
Armenia	na	**84**	85	82	80	86	85	83	84	82	82	88	83	87	81	79
Australia	na	**36**	42	30	34	34	40	42	35	34	34	37	36	38	38	31
Austria	14	**10**	12	8	8	9	12	12	9	5	15	8	10	15	10	7
Azerbaijan	na	**77**	76	79	73	78	84	78	76	79	76	75	77	78	76	68
Bangladesh	na	**59**	62	56	55	63	55	61	54	60	55	65	54	58	61	53
Belarus	80	**92**	91	93	86	92	96	96	90	91	94	91	90	92	93	88
Belgium	36	**38**	39	37	36	33	43	48	36	33	44	39	30	42	37	30
Bosnia and Herz.	na	**54**	55	53	47	53	62	61	56	42	59	52	55	55	53	45
Brazil	52	**47**	49	46	45	46	55	58	41	34	55	47	41	53	48	33
Bulgaria	91	**86**	84	88	74	84	94	94	84	77	93	85	80	88	84	83
Canada	35	**53**	61	45	53	50	55	55	51	54	48	51	57	55	53	50
Chile	12	**26**	27	25	19	23	36	33	22	20	25	24	30	31	26	17
China	65	**86**	86	85	81	89	82	84	87	88	83	88	89	90	86	88
Colombia	na	**18**	20	16	18	17	19	23	13	18	19	16	18	24	20	18
Croatia	na	**95**	95	95	92	95	97	98	93	91	98	94	94	97	95	94
Czech Republic	85	**73**	73	73	59	72	82	76	71	73	79	74	68	80	73	62
Denmark	2	**2**	3	1	2	2	2	3	3	1	2	2	1	1	2	1
Dominican Rep.	na	**50**	51	49	49	51	55	56	52	48	48	46	52	49	50	53
Egypt	na	**38**	44	33	36	40	41	39	38	39	38	39	37	35	41	40
El Salvador	na	**38**	38	39	35	38	44	47	29	27	50	35	30	na	na	na
Estonia	92	**82**	79	85	65	82	92	85	81	80	86	88	77	86	82	52
Finland	6	**12**	14	10	11	8	16	14	9	10	12	15	11	20	9	8
France	53	**50**	54	47	41	46	59	57	42	41	52	52	44	59	52	35
Georgia	na	**82**	81	83	72	85	89	86	80	84	83	79	82	84	80	77
Germany	16	**23**	28	18	11	18	32	30	16	21	28	23	21	29	21	19
Great Britain	29	**39**	45	33	40	38	40	38	40	39	41	39	40	na	na	na
Greece	na	**31**	30	32	27	30	44	27	29	34	27	32	33	38	30	32
Hungary	70	**71**	72	69	61	70	78	76	62	60	70	72	69	77	67	43
Iceland	78	**44**	50	39	37	41	56	49	41	41	47	41	44	48	45	30
India	67	**85**	85	85	86	84	86	87	79	86	83	84	86	86	84	82
Indonesia	na	**66**	73	60	61	66	71	73	68	62	63	69	68	68	65	79
Iran	na	**62**	63	61	61	63	64	63	62	61	64	60	61	66	61	60
Ireland	28	**37**	41	33	35	33	44	42	32	38	36	40	36	42	36	31
Israel	na	**24**	31	19	27	20	26	26	22	25	24	26	26	24	24	16
Italy	27	**36**	38	35	29	29	46	46	29	28	45	33	29	46	37	30
Japan	31	**27**	30	24	13	22	37	32	25	28	27	24	32	35	27	13
Jordan	na	**45**	49	41	41	46	51	47	41	44	47	45	41	45	45	43
Korea, South	64	**72**	76	67	68	70	79	68	72	71	73	72	70	74	71	63
Latvia	91	**85**	82	87	75	82	91	86	84	87	87	89	83	89	85	60
Lithuania	92	**86**	89	85	78	85	94	92	85	84	92	91	85	86	88	88
Luxembourg	na	**58**	60	56	50	53	68	65	55	51	68	58	44	72	58	42
Macedonia	na	**37**	39	35	33	38	38	51	28	35	37	41	29	36	36	50
Malta	na	**42**	42	42	31	41	51	60	35	38	52	38	38	47	39	43
Mexico	23	**30**	33	28	25	28	41	37	22	21	37	27	22	38	25	24
Moldova	na	**87**	87	88	81	89	91	92	88	82	90	86	86	89	87	85
Montenegro	na	**82**	82	83	69	83	90	87	79	79	87	79	83	85	81	79
Morocco	na	**70**	72	68	69	69	74	71	63	68	76	68	68	69	69	73
Netherlands	13	**14**	17	12	18	11	17	21	13	10	19	11	13	28	15	8
New Zealand	na	**37**	46	30	41	34	38	39	40	33	33	38	39	41	37	33
Nigeria	82	**80**	79	81	81	79	79	81	79	82	80	81	79	81	80	80
Northern Ireland	29	**41**	45	37	42	37	43	45	38	37	44	42	34	42	42	36
Norway	7	**11**	14	8	8	8	16	12	11	9	na	na	na	12	12	5
Pakistan	na	**56**	56	56	52	57	63	60	54	45	60	57	52	57	55	67
Peru	na	**59**	62	57	58	59	64	63	63	52	63	57	56	65	58	61
Philippines	na	**74**	75	73	71	76	74	78	72	72	76	71	75	77	73	67
Poland	na	**86**	88	84	81	86	88	88	84	77	89	85	81	89	85	85
Portugal	67	**69**	68	70	62	64	78	74	62	52	83	63	63	78	65	65
Puerto Rico	na	**52**	54	50	54	52	51	59	51	51	56	47	53	65	51	48
Romania	71	**82**	82	82	72	81	88	89	80	72	85	86	77	86	81	63
Russian Fed.	93	**91**	89	92	82	92	95	97	90	89	93	91	88	92	89	85
Serbia	na	**75**	77	73	63	73	81	80	76	65	75	82	73	79	73	59
Singapore	na	**64**	68	60	56	67	81	73	60	54	69	64	58	67	62	63
Slovakia	na	**75**	73	77	65	75	83	81	73	70	80	74	74	77	76	63
Slovenia	32	**29**	30	29	21	23	42	36	26	29	35	25	22	29	30	26
South Africa	30	**75**	74	77	75	75	76	76	74	79	77	79	69	73	76	81
Spain	48	**45**	45	45	43	42	49	51	36	43	42	54	46	54	44	37
Sweden	5	**4**	5	3	4	4	4	3	4	3	4	3	4	7	4	3
Switzerland	36	**40**	39	40	32	36	48	48	38	31	43	38	36	52	39	32
Taiwan	na	**42**	43	40	26	36	66	58	34	31	55	39	34	46	36	43
Tanzania	na	**83**	85	81	81	82	91	85	80	84	85	80	85	84	83	88
Turkey	73	**74**	75	73	69	76	81	80	68	60	80	72	63	79	74	66
Uganda	na	**86**	85	86	84	86	90	87	85	85	83	85	85	87	84	89
Ukraine	na	**89**	88	89	80	93	90	91	89	86	92	88	86	91	88	73
United States	49	**61**	68	53	68	58	58	65	61	59	60	60	62	66	59	62
Uruguay	na	**29**	30	28	31	25	31	30	28	24	27	33	27	29	32	20
Venezuela	na	**27**	29	24	27	25	30	31	26	22	28	26	28	37	24	22
Vietnam	na	**75**	73	78	74	73	80	79	70	76	78	77	73	80	76	64
Zimbabwe	na	**85**	85	86	84	85	88	87	83	82	86	88	81	87	85	74
Total	48	56	58	54	53	55	60	60	56	50	59	57	55	67	54	42

RANKING	
Country	2000
Croatia	95
Belarus	92
Russian Fed.	91
Ukraine	89
Moldova	87
Lithuania	86
Bulgaria	86
China	86
Poland	86
Uganda	86
Zimbabwe	85
India	85
Latvia	85
Armenia	84
Tanzania	83
Montenegro	82
Estonia	82
Georgia	82
Romania	82
Nigeria	80
Azerbaijan	77
Vietnam	75
South Africa	75
Slovakia	75
Serbia	75
Philippines	74
Turkey	74
Czech Republic	73
Korea, South	72
Hungary	71
Morocco	70
Portugal	69
Algeria	67
Indonesia	66
Singapore	64
Albania	64
Iran	62
United States	61
Peru	59
Bangladesh	59
Luxembourg	58
Argentina	57
Pakistan	56
Bosnia and Herz.	54
Canada	53
Puerto Rico	52
France	50
Dominican Rep.	50
Brazil	47
Spain	45
Jordan	45
Iceland	44
Malta	42
Taiwan	42
Northern Ireland	41
Switzerland	40
Great Britain	39
El Salvador	38
Egypt	38
Belgium	38
New Zealand	37
Ireland	37
Macedonia	37
Italy	36
Australia	36
Greece	31
Mexico	30
Slovenia	29
Uruguay	29
Japan	27
Venezuela	27
Chile	26
Israel	24
Germany	23
Colombia	18
Netherlands	14
Finland	12
Norway	11
Austria	10
Sweden	4
Denmark	2
Total	56

A032) CHILD QUALITIES: FEELING OF RESPONSIBILITY

Here is a list of qualities that children can be encouraged to learn at home.

Which, if any, do you consider to be especially important?

(WVS: V17; EVS: V167)

Feeling of responsibility (%)

Country	Wave		Gender		Age			Education			Income			Values		
	1990	2000	Male	Female	16-29	30-49	50+	Lower	Middle	Upper	Lower	Middle	Upper	Mat	Mixed	Postm.
Albania	na	**68**	71	66	67	68	70	64	68	79	69	67	68	69	67	72
Algeria	na	**58**	55	62	62	58	51	51	57	64	60	58	59	54	60	61
Argentina	80	**77**	77	77	77	78	76	72	85	81	73	75	82	71	77	83
Armenia	na	**69**	67	70	67	70	70	63	67	77	70	67	70	68	69	66
Australia	na	**66**	65	67	58	71	69	63	63	73	64	67	69	67	63	71
Austria	85	**86**	86	86	86	90	83	82	91	88	79	88	87	78	86	89
Azerbaijan	na	**66**	66	65	69	65	61	55	65	69	65	64	69	66	66	65
Bangladesh	na	**53**	54	53	51	55	52	56	50	52	59	50	54	53	54	47
Belarus	82	**77**	77	76	75	81	73	69	79	85	72	79	80	74	81	79
Belgium	72	**80**	80	80	78	83	79	74	80	86	76	78	84	75	81	86
Bosnia and Herz.	na	**74**	72	75	75	74	73	65	76	76	68	75	74	75	73	64
Brazil	72	**65**	64	65	67	65	58	54	70	85	56	66	72	58	66	75
Bulgaria	68	**76**	74	77	81	75	73	73	76	80	74	75	77	77	77	66
Canada	75	**77**	74	80	69	76	83	75	79	76	77	78	77	79	77	77
Chile	88	**84**	85	84	86	86	80	78	88	88	80	85	90	85	82	90
China	67	**64**	65	62	72	63	59	56	69	74	58	62	73	65	69	66
Colombia	na	**77**	79	75	75	80	74	70	77	88	73	75	85	74	75	77
Croatia	na	**94**	93	95	96	95	91	93	94	95	96	92	94	91	94	98
Czech Republic	65	**66**	65	66	63	69	65	61	69	76	59	67	69	61	67	70
Denmark	86	**81**	82	81	76	79	86	79	82	87	80	82	85	75	82	87
Dominican Rep.	na	**84**	85	85	85	83	100	81	81	87	82	86	88	81	85	89
Egypt	na	**51**	50	51	53	51	49	49	50	58	49	47	54	47	54	59
El Salvador	na	**67**	70	64	68	65	69	60	72	79	59	69	76	na	na	na
Estonia	76	**79**	77	80	82	79	77	76	80	79	71	81	84	76	80	80
Finland	83	**86**	86	87	86	88	84	83	89	91	83	88	87	86	86	84
France	72	**74**	70	77	70	74	75	72	74	77	74	73	78	70	75	77
Georgia	na	**68**	66	69	64	71	68	68	66	73	65	70	69	70	66	59
Germany	84	**84**	84	84	83	88	80	78	89	87	79	82	85	80	85	89
Great Britain	48	**56**	55	58	50	61	55	57	55	57	55	62	59	na	na	na
Greece	na	**83**	82	84	86	82	77	66	82	87	76	85	85	78	84	87
Hungary	66	**73**	74	73	73	78	69	71	80	71	71	74	76	69	76	100
Iceland	94	**81**	78	84	79	81	83	81	78	88	79	80	84	80	81	87
India	60	**68**	69	66	70	68	65	65	66	76	64	62	75	61	76	82
Indonesia	na	**82**	83	81	80	85	80	79	84	82	83	82	80	79	84	71
Iran	na	**72**	72	72	73	73	66	66	71	79	73	73	71	70	74	76
Ireland	61	**53**	56	51	49	56	52	51	54	57	50	52	57	60	51	50
Israel	na	**66**	62	68	63	69	64	49	69	72	54	63	74	70	66	58
Italy	82	**82**	80	83	84	82	80	77	84	88	78	83	83	73	84	83
Japan	84	**91**	91	91	92	90	91	90	91	92	91	89	93	91	92	85
Jordan	na	**65**	65	66	67	65	63	62	64	73	66	62	69	65	66	57
Korea, South	91	**92**	92	93	94	92	90	89	92	94	94	91	92	92	93	87
Latvia	75	**74**	76	73	75	75	74	71	75	78	70	74	82	73	75	79
Lithuania	72	**77**	77	76	81	80	70	68	79	83	73	76	79	75	79	70
Luxembourg	na	**78**	75	82	76	80	79	78	78	84	72	78	80	75	79	84
Macedonia	na	**74**	76	73	75	72	76	62	80	81	72	73	82	74	76	62
Malta	na	**77**	77	76	82	79	70	70	77	90	66	79	82	74	78	82
Mexico	77	**77**	78	75	77	79	73	72	83	85	66	83	84	75	79	86
Moldova	na	**83**	82	84	81	86	80	77	82	88	80	85	82	85	81	86
Montenegro	na	**68**	68	68	69	69	66	61	69	80	63	74	68	63	73	71
Morocco	na	**63**	65	61	65	63	59	62	66	72	58	67	60	61	65	66
Netherlands	85	**87**	86	89	86	88	87	80	91	90	82	88	94	75	88	91
New Zealand	na	**59**	57	61	53	62	58	58	58	60	57	59	63	53	58	61
Nigeria	36	**33**	34	32	34	32	31	32	33	36	35	31	33	30	35	33
Northern Ireland	38	**54**	54	53	45	53	58	54	49	61	51	47	53	52	53	56
Norway	90	**92**	91	94	91	93	93	91	92	94	na	na	na	91	93	90
Pakistan	na	**50**	49	52	49	51	51	53	48	45	54	49	46	51	49	50
Peru	na	**79**	79	79	78	81	77	77	78	82	76	82	80	76	78	86
Philippines	na	**65**	66	63	70	61	65	57	63	77	61	66	68	62	65	78
Poland	na	**73**	73	73	69	77	71	67	77	89	70	74	78	74	73	76
Portugal	77	**60**	59	61	74	59	53	55	67	84	43	53	66	52	64	69
Puerto Rico	na	**74**	75	74	76	76	72	65	71	77	68	75	80	69	75	76
Romania	56	**62**	64	60	69	67	53	46	69	77	52	58	73	56	68	85
Russian Fed.	70	**76**	76	75	78	77	73	70	75	82	69	78	81	75	78	82
Serbia	na	**72**	73	71	72	74	70	63	73	83	67	72	76	69	75	78
Singapore	na	**84**	82	85	80	87	87	83	84	84	83	83	85	79	86	85
Slovakia	na	**67**	67	66	68	70	63	59	69	81	59	67	74	64	70	68
Slovenia	71	**76**	76	76	76	78	74	67	77	90	67	76	87	70	78	79
South Africa	45	**59**	61	58	59	58	64	58	61	68	56	51	72	64	57	53
Spain	75	**83**	82	83	86	84	80	80	84	86	82	81	85	81	82	89
Sweden	89	**87**	86	88	83	88	88	87	85	90	85	87	90	75	88	85
Switzerland	77	**80**	81	80	82	80	80	78	80	87	81	77	83	72	82	84
Taiwan	na	**81**	82	80	86	83	72	71	84	89	75	84	86	80	84	81
Tanzania	na	**41**	43	40	34	44	50	41	39	53	39	39	56	42	42	38
Turkey	66	**63**	64	61	67	62	55	53	73	82	51	69	79	60	63	72
Uganda	na	**52**	55	51	54	53	45	51	53	52	51	56	57	52	54	46
Ukraine	na	**75**	74	76	78	75	74	68	76	77	74	74	78	73	77	90
United States	72	**72**	70	74	66	71	78	72	70	73	71	71	75	72	71	74
Uruguay	na	**81**	82	81	76	85	81	78	86	85	74	85	87	74	82	86
Venezuela	na	**88**	86	90	88	88	86	82	88	94	84	89	88	86	87	93
Vietnam	na	**70**	74	66	70	70	71	68	74	73	69	73	68	72	71	75
Zimbabwe	na	**48**	51	45	50	45	48	44	53	57	45	45	57	47	48	55
Total	73	**72**	72	72	71	73	72	66	74	79	68	72	76	68	74	78

RANKING	
Country	2000
Croatia	94
Korea, South	92
Norway	92
Japan	91
Venezuela	88
Netherlands	87
Sweden	87
Finland	86
Austria	86
Dominican Rep.	84
Chile	84
Germany	84
Singapore	84
Greece	83
Moldova	83
Spain	83
Indonesia	82
Italy	82
Uruguay	81
Denmark	81
Taiwan	81
Iceland	81
Switzerland	80
Belgium	80
Peru	79
Estonia	79
Luxembourg	78
Canada	77
Colombia	77
Belarus	77
Mexico	77
Argentina	77
Lithuania	77
Malta	77
Slovenia	76
Russian Fed.	76
Bulgaria	76
Ukraine	75
Puerto Rico	74
Latvia	74
Macedonia	74
Bosnia and Herz.	74
France	74
Hungary	73
Poland	73
Iran	72
United States	72
Serbia	72
Vietnam	70
Armenia	69
Albania	68
Montenegro	68
Georgia	68
India	68
El Salvador	67
Slovakia	67
Australia	66
Czech Republic	66
Azerbaijan	66
Israel	66
Jordan	65
Philippines	65
Brazil	65
China	64
Morocco	63
Turkey	63
Romania	62
Portugal	60
South Africa	59
New Zealand	59
Algeria	58
Great Britain	56
Northern Ireland	54
Bangladesh	53
Ireland	53
Uganda	52
Egypt	51
Pakistan	50
Zimbabwe	48
Tanzania	41
Nigeria	33
Total	72

A034) CHILD QUALITIES: IMAGINATION

Here is a list of qualities that children can be encouraged to learn at home.

Which, if any, do you consider to be especially important?

Imagination (%)

(WVS: V18; EVS: V168)

Country	Wave		Gender		Age			Education			Income			Values		
	1990	2000	Male	Female	16-29	30-49	50+	Lower	Middle	Upper	Lower	Middle	Upper	Mat	Mixed	Postm.
Albania	na	**29**	31	27	34	32	21	26	27	42	22	31	34	28	31	26
Algeria	na	**12**	13	12	14	10	11	9	13	13	15	15	7	12	12	14
Argentina	31	**24**	25	22	31	22	18	21	25	34	20	24	27	22	24	24
Armenia	na	**16**	16	16	17	16	13	14	14	22	20	14	9	12	19	14
Australia	na	**26**	27	26	30	31	18	18	24	37	24	28	31	15	25	31
Austria	24	**24**	26	22	31	30	14	14	28	51	16	24	29	10	19	38
Azerbaijan	na	**14**	14	14	15	14	12	10	14	15	13	17	12	11	19	19
Bangladesh	na	**36**	35	36	41	33	25	32	37	43	28	41	35	29	40	45
Belarus	7	**10**	12	9	15	9	7	6	11	16	9	9	15	9	9	25
Belgium	18	**23**	26	21	30	25	18	12	22	33	19	22	27	13	21	36
Bosnia and Herz.	na	**27**	28	26	26	31	22	19	26	37	27	27	26	26	27	30
Brazil	12	**8**	10	6	8	9	4	7	8	10	9	6	9	7	8	10
Bulgaria	16	**19**	24	16	27	24	12	13	21	27	14	22	23	16	23	31
Canada	23	**33**	36	31	46	36	22	23	33	42	28	32	39	22	29	43
Chile	32	**36**	38	34	42	38	26	27	38	47	30	36	44	31	30	60
China	27	**35**	39	32	43	38	22	28	40	49	33	35	39	36	40	47
Colombia	na	**19**	22	16	19	20	16	15	18	27	15	18	24	16	19	20
Croatia	na	**72**	71	73	74	76	66	69	73	76	75	71	71	73	70	79
Czech Republic	7	**7**	8	6	9	7	5	6	7	12	5	9	7	4	7	14
Denmark	37	**37**	39	35	43	42	28	27	50	51	34	36	50	22	35	58
Dominican Rep.	na	**13**	16	10	12	14	na	13	12	13	7	15	18	9	14	12
Egypt	na	**15**	17	13	17	15	13	14	18	16	14	16	16	16	15	17
El Salvador	na	**10**	13	8	12	9	10	9	12	14	8	10	15	na	na	na
Estonia	13	**11**	15	7	19	12	6	9	10	15	7	10	12	8	12	20
Finland	26	**28**	26	30	39	30	21	23	32	40	31	23	30	19	29	38
France	23	**18**	21	16	20	24	13	13	24	28	18	16	22	9	16	39
Georgia	na	**10**	12	9	14	9	8	7	11	11	10	10	11	9	11	16
Germany	28	**30**	27	32	46	35	17	19	38	39	26	29	29	20	28	48
Great Britain	18	**38**	41	36	44	45	30	30	44	53	35	46	41	na	na	na
Greece	na	**22**	24	21	26	20	18	10	18	28	20	22	22	14	20	36
Hungary	9	**11**	14	8	13	14	7	7	16	18	8	9	13	9	12	32
Iceland	49	**18**	19	18	23	21	10	13	18	31	15	17	23	7	19	36
India	22	**28**	28	28	32	27	27	25	28	35	25	23	34	26	33	31
Indonesia	na	**29**	33	25	20	32	30	29	31	26	33	28	28	27	30	25
Iran	na	**11**	11	11	12	11	8	9	11	13	10	12	12	7	12	13
Ireland	14	**26**	27	24	34	29	17	17	28	36	19	20	37	24	25	30
Israel	na	**23**	24	22	28	21	19	13	21	32	20	21	30	21	23	30
Italy	15	**13**	14	12	16	14	9	9	14	19	12	13	15	9	11	18
Japan	24	**35**	41	29	52	38	25	31	32	43	33	36	33	27	35	50
Jordan	na	**5**	6	5	7	5	3	5	7	6	5	6	5	3	6	15
Korea, South	6	**33**	36	30	33	34	33	21	30	39	34	32	33	29	37	37
Latvia	11	**7**	8	6	10	8	5	4	8	10	7	6	9	5	7	13
Lithuania	6	**5**	5	5	11	4	1	2	5	9	4	3	7	6	4	12
Luxembourg	na	**25**	28	22	26	30	20	20	26	35	23	23	37	19	22	41
Macedonia	na	**13**	12	14	17	14	8	6	17	16	10	16	15	15	13	17
Malta	na	**7**	9	5	9	7	5	4	7	10	4	6	9	5	7	14
Mexico	31	**24**	25	24	29	23	21	22	25	34	25	22	25	25	26	22
Moldova	na	**26**	29	24	34	26	21	18	27	33	27	27	28	24	28	42
Montenegro	na	**12**	12	11	22	12	6	6	13	22	6	11	15	8	15	21
Morocco	na	**9**	10	8	11	9	5	8	13	12	7	8	12	8	10	15
Netherlands	24	**32**	34	30	34	40	22	19	29	47	30	35	35	18	28	49
New Zealand	na	**28**	29	27	45	33	16	19	28	37	19	31	36	18	26	40
Nigeria	6	**11**	11	11	10	13	10	11	11	11	13	8	11	11	10	18
Northern Ireland	14	**31**	32	30	34	39	23	24	34	46	32	36	34	25	30	43
Norway	31	**37**	33	40	47	42	22	26	38	46	na	na	na	25	36	60
Pakistan	na	**7**	7	7	13	6	2	5	10	12	5	7	9	6	9	na
Peru	na	**23**	26	20	24	23	21	24	22	24	22	25	22	21	23	25
Philippines	na	**14**	15	12	12	14	14	14	13	14	11	14	17	12	15	13
Poland	na	**13**	16	11	21	12	9	11	14	18	12	13	16	9	16	13
Portugal	20	**15**	16	14	17	18	12	13	18	24	12	16	18	11	16	20
Puerto Rico	na	**19**	24	16	18	21	18	24	18	18	19	18	19	19	18	19
Romania	17	**14**	17	10	17	18	8	8	15	20	7	16	18	13	15	18
Russian Fed.	11	**7**	7	7	11	8	3	3	7	10	6	6	9	6	8	11
Serbia	na	**10**	12	9	12	14	6	6	11	16	9	8	13	9	11	25
Singapore	na	**14**	14	13	15	13	8	13	12	22	11	12	17	8	15	21
Slovakia	na	**3**	3	2	3	3	2	2	3	4	3	3	2	2	2	13
Slovenia	10	**12**	16	9	16	12	10	8	12	21	8	11	22	7	13	15
South Africa	8	**20**	21	19	22	18	21	22	17	30	22	22	16	18	20	22
Spain	34	**29**	32	27	39	32	21	22	33	43	25	26	36	21	29	45
Sweden	40	**40**	41	40	49	45	31	29	44	44	41	37	43	31	36	54
Switzerland	30	**23**	27	19	27	26	17	14	23	41	18	20	31	15	20	36
Taiwan	na	**15**	19	12	15	16	13	12	14	19	17	11	16	15	17	16
Tanzania	na	**61**	64	58	54	68	61	57	61	76	58	63	70	63	62	54
Turkey	23	**22**	26	19	24	22	18	17	26	43	19	23	31	18	22	30
Uganda	na	**11**	16	7	12	10	10	12	11	10	15	10	12	9	11	21
Ukraine	na	**11**	10	11	13	13	8	7	11	11	10	13	10	9	12	6
United States	27	**30**	33	28	36	30	25	24	25	35	30	30	31	17	29	36
Uruguay	na	**31**	33	30	36	37	24	23	42	45	23	34	38	26	29	40
Venezuela	na	**24**	26	22	23	22	28	20	24	28	18	24	26	24	23	28
Vietnam	na	**20**	22	19	24	20	17	19	21	22	16	23	21	11	23	19
Zimbabwe	na	**11**	13	10	10	11	13	11	12	na	10	11	13	9	13	12
Total	21	21	23	19	23	23	16	17	21	27	19	21	23	16	22	32

RANKING	
Country	2000
Croatia	72
Tanzania	61
Sweden	40
Great Britain	38
Denmark	37
Norway	37
Chile	36
Bangladesh	36
China	35
Japan	35
Korea, South	33
Canada	33
Netherlands	32
Northern Ireland	31
Uruguay	31
United States	30
Germany	30
Spain	29
Albania	29
Indonesia	29
Finland	28
India	28
New Zealand	28
Bosnia and Herz.	27
Australia	26
Moldova	26
Ireland	26
Luxembourg	25
Mexico	24
Austria	24
Venezuela	24
Argentina	24
Switzerland	23
Belgium	23
Peru	23
Israel	23
Turkey	22
Greece	22
Vietnam	20
South Africa	20
Bulgaria	19
Colombia	19
Puerto Rico	19
France	18
Iceland	18
Armenia	16
Egypt	15
Portugal	15
Taiwan	15
Azerbaijan	14
Philippines	14
Romania	14
Singapore	14
Macedonia	13
Poland	13
Dominican Rep.	13
Italy	13
Slovenia	12
Algeria	12
Montenegro	12
Uganda	11
Zimbabwe	11
Iran	11
Nigeria	11
Ukraine	11
Estonia	11
Hungary	11
El Salvador	10
Serbia	10
Belarus	10
Georgia	10
Morocco	9
Brazil	8
Pakistan	7
Latvia	7
Russian Fed.	7
Czech Republic	7
Malta	7
Jordan	5
Lithuania	5
Slovakia	3
Total	21

A035) CHILD QUALITIES: TOLERANCE AND RESPECT FOR OTHER PEOPLE

Here is a list of qualities that children can be encouraged to learn at home.

Which, if any, do you consider to be especially important?

Tolerance and respect for other people (%)

(WVS: V19; EVS: V169)

Country	Wave		Gender		Age			Education			Income			Values		
	1990	2000	Male	Female	16-29	30-49	50+	Lower	Middle	Upper	Lower	Middle	Upper	Mat	Mixed	Postm.
Albania	na	**80**	77	83	83	80	78	79	80	84	82	78	80	81	82	69
Algeria	na	**54**	52	56	56	53	52	57	54	52	57	53	51	52	56	50
Argentina	78	**70**	69	72	67	74	70	70	70	73	69	70	72	67	69	76
Armenia	na	**48**	45	52	45	48	55	51	49	45	46	50	54	49	49	36
Australia	na	**81**	78	83	76	83	82	77	81	84	80	80	83	76	81	83
Austria	66	**71**	70	73	71	79	65	65	76	86	61	75	77	55	69	82
Azerbaijan	na	**59**	59	59	58	59	61	68	63	50	66	58	55	61	58	50
Bangladesh	na	**71**	70	72	70	71	75	70	73	70	73	68	74	76	67	76
Belarus	80	**72**	69	75	69	72	75	73	71	74	71	74	70	74	71	68
Belgium	69	**83**	80	86	80	84	83	79	82	87	80	83	85	81	85	87
Bosnia and Herz.	na	**72**	71	72	72	73	70	70	72	72	74	71	70	69	73	76
Brazil	66	**59**	54	65	61	58	59	57	60	65	58	61	60	57	60	66
Bulgaria	52	**59**	58	60	56	62	59	58	60	60	51	62	65	59	62	57
Canada	80	**81**	78	83	81	80	81	79	79	84	78	80	83	76	80	84
Chile	79	**76**	73	78	74	80	72	75	77	75	75	76	79	78	75	75
China	62	**73**	76	70	75	74	67	62	81	79	67	76	78	73	77	72
Colombia	na	**68**	67	70	68	69	68	64	67	77	66	68	73	62	67	69
Croatia	na	**93**	91	96	95	94	91	93	94	92	95	92	95	91	93	96
Czech Republic	64	**63**	57	68	65	65	61	60	66	70	62	66	62	53	65	67
Denmark	81	**87**	85	90	87	91	84	85	90	91	84	89	93	84	87	93
Dominican Rep.	na	**68**	64	70	67	67	82	75	66	68	72	64	67	70	67	71
Egypt	na	**65**	63	66	64	64	66	67	64	61	68	64	63	66	63	67
El Salvador	na	**59**	58	59	59	59	59	58	61	57	54	59	60	na	na	na
Estonia	70	**71**	68	74	69	75	69	64	74	77	71	70	74	69	73	84
Finland	79	**83**	78	87	83	84	81	80	87	87	81	80	85	74	86	84
France	78	**85**	83	87	85	87	84	84	86	87	85	86	85	85	85	87
Georgia	na	**54**	51	57	51	54	58	58	54	52	56	59	48	53	56	49
Germany	74	**73**	71	75	77	76	68	66	77	86	66	71	79	69	72	83
Great Britain	79	**84**	81	86	78	85	88	85	84	85	83	83	85	na	na	na
Greece	na	**53**	52	53	52	50	56	63	53	50	54	52	49	53	55	44
Hungary	62	**66**	61	69	67	66	64	61	72	79	60	67	68	64	66	70
Iceland	93	**84**	81	88	86	84	83	80	87	90	78	89	87	82	85	89
India	59	**63**	63	64	62	65	62	61	61	71	54	64	67	59	70	76
Indonesia	na	**63**	63	63	60	62	66	64	65	60	66	61	60	58	65	61
Iran	na	**59**	57	61	57	63	57	58	61	56	60	57	58	54	60	59
Ireland	76	**75**	76	74	74	78	73	71	75	82	71	75	76	73	74	81
Israel	na	**82**	79	85	81	84	81	82	82	81	79	80	83	87	81	93
Italy	66	**75**	72	78	78	78	71	68	80	82	71	76	79	64	76	80
Japan	60	**71**	69	74	76	72	69	66	72	72	70	72	73	67	74	75
Jordan	na	**67**	67	68	65	69	69	72	66	60	69	69	61	68	68	57
Korea, South	55	**65**	63	67	75	65	53	61	62	69	58	70	68	63	64	85
Latvia	70	**70**	68	71	62	71	71	69	69	73	70	69	70	69	70	68
Lithuania	57	**58**	52	62	58	61	54	53	58	67	56	68	58	53	60	68
Luxembourg	na	**78**	77	80	78	80	76	73	79	86	70	83	86	71	81	83
Macedonia	na	**75**	74	77	75	80	70	75	75	78	73	73	81	76	75	69
Malta	na	**61**	62	60	59	62	61	58	61	67	60	60	61	56	64	67
Mexico	64	**71**	70	71	74	70	67	66	76	79	64	74	76	69	73	78
Moldova	na	**78**	77	79	75	82	76	80	76	80	79	77	77	79	77	74
Montenegro	na	**57**	58	57	60	56	57	52	60	62	56	59	58	57	58	61
Morocco	na	**65**	63	67	64	63	71	66	63	63	69	67	56	66	66	59
Netherlands	87	**91**	88	94	92	92	90	88	93	93	88	93	92	87	92	92
New Zealand	na	**78**	74	81	80	78	77	75	79	80	75	80	80	78	80	78
Nigeria	75	**59**	59	59	59	60	58	53	61	66	59	59	60	61	58	57
Northern Ireland	80	**75**	73	77	66	75	80	75	75	75	76	78	79	71	80	69
Norway	64	**66**	61	70	65	71	61	54	65	79	na	na	na	44	67	87
Pakistan	na	**53**	54	52	59	51	45	42	64	72	42	52	70	49	59	67
Peru	na	**73**	72	73	73	73	72	70	73	74	71	74	75	69	74	73
Philippines	na	**60**	59	62	56	62	63	58	59	64	59	63	57	60	60	64
Poland	na	**80**	79	81	84	82	76	76	84	89	78	81	84	76	81	91
Portugal	69	**65**	65	66	77	65	59	64	68	73	49	63	65	65	65	70
Puerto Rico	na	**61**	55	64	63	64	57	51	61	63	55	61	66	57	61	63
Romania	56	**58**	56	60	58	60	57	56	59	62	56	62	58	58	58	63
Russian Fed.	70	**67**	64	70	63	66	70	69	66	69	68	67	67	68	68	64
Serbia	na	**65**	64	65	71	68	59	48	71	79	56	66	74	57	71	79
Singapore	na	**70**	71	69	70	72	63	63	70	86	66	70	75	69	70	71
Slovakia	na	**57**	55	59	60	60	51	50	59	65	54	55	63	50	61	70
Slovenia	75	**70**	67	73	70	72	68	68	71	72	68	73	75	68	71	68
South Africa	61	**74**	74	74	72	77	71	74	73	87	73	71	81	71	77	72
Spain	71	**80**	80	80	84	82	75	76	82	86	78	80	82	74	82	84
Sweden	91	**93**	90	95	92	93	93	89	92	96	90	91	97	94	92	93
Switzerland	77	**79**	76	83	78	83	76	72	82	79	76	83	83	75	78	87
Taiwan	na	**59**	61	58	72	61	48	51	63	65	53	61	64	60	61	62
Tanzania	na	**84**	84	84	85	82	84	87	81	79	87	83	82	85	83	75
Turkey	69	**63**	61	64	63	62	62	61	62	66	62	63	64	59	62	66
Uganda	na	**57**	59	55	59	56	52	51	59	61	48	52	64	52	61	53
Ukraine	na	**66**	65	66	60	70	65	67	67	62	66	63	68	64	66	79
United States	71	**80**	77	82	78	78	84	77	81	80	78	77	84	82	80	78
Uruguay	na	**70**	71	69	67	73	68	69	69	73	68	72	69	58	73	71
Venezuela	na	**80**	76	83	78	81	80	77	80	82	76	80	85	73	81	86
Vietnam	na	**68**	72	64	68	72	63	67	70	67	69	69	68	55	74	68
Zimbabwe	na	**78**	76	80	79	78	78	78	79	86	79	76	82	78	78	79
Total	71	70	68	72	69	71	70	68	71	72	68	71	72	66	72	76

RANKING	
Country	2000
Croatia	93
Sweden	93
Netherlands	91
Denmark	87
France	85
Iceland	84
Tanzania	84
Great Britain	84
Belgium	83
Finland	83
Israel	82
Australia	81
Canada	81
Poland	80
Albania	80
Spain	80
Venezuela	80
United States	80
Switzerland	79
Zimbabwe	78
Luxembourg	78
Moldova	78
New Zealand	78
Chile	76
Macedonia	75
Ireland	75
Italy	75
Northern Ireland	75
South Africa	74
Germany	73
China	73
Peru	73
Belarus	72
Bosnia and Herz.	72
Austria	71
Estonia	71
Japan	71
Bangladesh	71
Mexico	71
Argentina	70
Slovenia	70
Singapore	70
Uruguay	70
Latvia	70
Colombia	68
Vietnam	68
Dominican Rep.	68
Jordan	67
Russian Fed.	67
Norway	66
Hungary	66
Ukraine	66
Portugal	65
Morocco	65
Korea, South	65
Egypt	65
Serbia	65
India	63
Czech Republic	63
Indonesia	63
Turkey	63
Malta	61
Puerto Rico	61
Philippines	60
Brazil	59
Bulgaria	59
Taiwan	59
Azerbaijan	59
Nigeria	59
Iran	59
El Salvador	59
Romania	58
Lithuania	58
Montenegro	57
Slovakia	57
Uganda	57
Georgia	54
Algeria	54
Pakistan	53
Greece	53
Armenia	48
Total	70

A038) CHILD QUALITIES: THRIFT SAVING MONEY AND THINGS

Here is a list of qualities that children can be encouraged to learn at home.
Which, if any, do you consider to be especially important?
Thrift saving money and things (%)

(WVS: V20; EVS: V170)

Country	Wave		Gender		Age			Education			Income			Values		
	1990	2000	Male	Female	16-29	30-49	50+	Lower	Middle	Upper	Lower	Middle	Upper	Mat	Mixed	Postm.
Albania	na	**55**	53	57	43	60	58	61	54	42	57	57	51	59	51	39
Algeria	na	**18**	17	19	18	16	21	18	16	20	20	18	17	20	16	19
Argentina	15	**15**	16	14	14	13	19	16	14	11	17	15	13	19	15	11
Armenia	na	**38**	38	39	36	37	44	44	40	30	35	41	41	46	30	42
Australia	na	**19**	19	19	19	16	23	24	19	14	22	18	15	29	21	14
Austria	55	**48**	45	50	35	40	61	63	39	16	61	46	41	68	54	30
Azerbaijan	na	**59**	59	60	56	62	60	68	61	55	65	58	57	66	50	47
Bangladesh	na	**57**	52	64	57	58	54	59	58	53	66	57	51	57	57	63
Belarus	53	**46**	46	46	41	43	54	60	44	28	51	44	42	51	43	27
Belgium	36	**43**	41	46	44	37	49	57	44	33	50	46	34	55	45	27
Bosnia and Herz.	na	**37**	39	36	35	37	39	44	38	30	35	38	35	40	36	30
Brazil	29	**39**	39	38	33	38	52	46	34	30	41	39	36	42	38	31
Bulgaria	39	**39**	38	41	31	32	49	48	37	27	49	36	34	44	34	26
Canada	21	**27**	26	28	18	23	37	38	27	18	33	26	22	39	29	20
Chile	29	**34**	34	35	31	32	41	42	32	28	37	31	35	37	36	24
China	56	**57**	58	57	57	55	64	62	56	33	59	62	49	60	55	53
Colombia	na	**25**	27	24	24	25	26	30	25	19	29	24	22	33	28	26
Croatia	na	**85**	83	87	77	87	88	88	83	84	91	82	87	91	86	81
Czech Republic	48	**32**	31	32	32	28	36	35	31	18	38	32	28	47	27	19
Denmark	19	**10**	10	10	3	5	18	15	3	2	14	9	5	22	10	2
Dominican Rep.	na	**11**	12	11	10	11	36	22	17	8	8	14	12	18	11	8
Egypt	na	**8**	9	7	9	9	6	9	8	5	9	7	7	7	9	9
El Salvador	na	**30**	29	31	27	30	33	33	29	22	29	31	25	na	na	na
Estonia	35	**45**	44	45	40	43	49	46	47	37	49	46	42	52	40	30
Finland	38	**23**	23	23	12	17	33	27	18	15	24	21	20	31	21	16
France	36	**38**	36	39	35	32	45	45	30	25	40	40	29	49	38	20
Georgia	na	**32**	32	32	25	33	37	32	35	23	34	32	29	35	31	23
Germany	58	**37**	38	36	24	33	48	48	29	25	46	41	33	47	37	24
Great Britain	26	**33**	33	33	24	31	38	37	27	32	35	36	30	na	na	na
Greece	na	**30**	31	29	30	30	33	40	33	25	33	30	30	35	30	27
Hungary	49	**42**	42	41	34	36	51	49	29	26	47	41	38	47	37	17
Iceland	69	**21**	22	19	15	17	30	28	18	11	29	16	18	27	19	15
India	24	**62**	61	63	60	63	61	66	63	52	58	65	62	67	59	42
Indonesia	na	**52**	54	50	39	50	60	56	55	46	59	49	53	50	53	43
Iran	na	**30**	33	25	28	28	37	31	28	32	31	28	30	28	29	24
Ireland	22	**21**	25	18	16	18	29	32	18	12	33	23	14	25	21	14
Israel	na	**20**	20	19	18	18	24	29	19	15	26	21	15	17	20	21
Italy	29	**35**	34	35	28	28	44	45	29	20	45	35	24	55	36	22
Japan	40	**48**	41	55	45	48	49	64	49	38	52	50	42	48	47	36
Jordan	na	**19**	18	21	17	21	21	21	17	18	19	21	19	21	19	14
Korea, South	53	**68**	64	71	62	68	73	75	73	59	70	66	66	71	66	52
Latvia	46	**45**	44	46	44	43	48	53	43	44	44	54	41	48	45	38
Lithuania	37	**42**	43	42	36	39	50	53	41	28	40	48	40	49	43	20
Luxembourg	na	**49**	47	50	49	44	54	58	45	39	61	57	32	59	50	32
Macedonia	na	**40**	38	42	33	41	43	45	39	31	43	39	36	40	41	36
Malta	na	**54**	54	54	46	52	60	69	51	31	62	55	45	57	53	40
Mexico	33	**39**	41	38	37	42	39	45	33	26	42	41	32	46	38	34
Moldova	na	**42**	40	44	47	39	41	43	40	45	41	37	47	47	40	25
Montenegro	na	**38**	35	42	24	37	49	53	31	24	50	30	36	45	34	19
Morocco	na	**37**	38	35	37	37	36	37	35	30	38	33	38	38	38	29
Netherlands	28	**22**	20	23	19	15	29	38	17	11	28	20	13	33	21	18
New Zealand	na	**25**	26	24	16	22	31	32	28	15	29	24	20	25	26	18
Nigeria	8	**10**	10	10	11	10	6	9	12	9	10	10	10	7	12	15
Northern Ireland	25	**26**	25	27	25	20	30	30	22	21	29	22	22	29	25	23
Norway	22	**13**	14	12	6	8	25	21	12	7	na	na	na	26	12	7
Pakistan	na	**56**	55	56	54	57	56	65	47	38	68	56	36	59	50	50
Peru	na	**24**	24	23	18	27	28	31	22	21	27	22	19	27	23	22
Philippines	na	**45**	45	46	43	46	47	45	47	44	45	45	46	47	45	37
Poland	na	**38**	37	40	30	36	46	44	33	26	43	36	31	43	37	23
Portugal	31	**36**	30	41	23	34	45	43	22	15	49	40	35	40	36	18
Puerto Rico	na	**24**	24	24	19	24	26	32	25	21	28	21	25	28	23	25
Romania	37	**31**	33	28	28	27	36	36	28	29	33	35	28	35	29	18
Russian Fed.	61	**51**	49	53	46	50	56	60	54	37	55	55	45	56	48	34
Serbia	na	**31**	30	31	16	27	40	45	27	17	40	26	25	38	26	13
Singapore	na	**44**	43	44	38	46	58	51	42	35	51	46	37	51	42	30
Slovakia	na	**39**	38	39	37	36	44	47	37	21	43	43	32	46	33	22
Slovenia	58	**35**	38	33	31	30	44	42	36	23	40	35	23	43	34	32
South Africa	17	**37**	37	37	43	34	31	38	38	25	41	41	28	39	36	39
Spain	18	**32**	32	32	27	29	38	37	29	23	37	32	31	41	32	20
Sweden	48	**31**	32	29	20	24	44	48	26	24	33	32	26	56	32	19
Switzerland	42	**35**	35	35	28	32	43	45	34	26	39	37	29	47	38	21
Taiwan	na	**49**	48	50	41	47	61	60	47	41	51	53	43	48	50	32
Tanzania	na	**54**	55	52	51	53	62	58	46	56	57	52	60	56	53	54
Turkey	36	**29**	28	30	27	31	29	31	28	24	28	30	29	36	30	21
Uganda	na	**11**	13	9	12	9	12	13	9	19	12	8	11	9	10	15
Ukraine	na	**50**	49	52	42	52	54	64	51	42	54	51	46	52	52	27
United States	29	**23**	24	22	20	23	25	29	24	20	25	25	17	28	25	17
Uruguay	na	**27**	27	27	24	24	30	32	20	17	28	29	24	31	28	20
Venezuela	na	**39**	40	38	37	42	39	39	40	36	45	39	36	40	39	36
Vietnam	na	**48**	49	48	37	49	57	51	50	22	64	44	45	49	47	39
Zimbabwe	na	**21**	20	21	20	21	22	23	17	22	21	25	13	22	20	14
Total	37	36	36	36	31	35	42	41	36	27	40	37	33	43	35	24

RANKING	
Country	2000
Croatia	85
Korea, South	68
India	62
Azerbaijan	59
Bangladesh	57
China	57
Pakistan	56
Albania	55
Malta	54
Tanzania	54
Indonesia	52
Russian Fed.	51
Ukraine	50
Taiwan	49
Luxembourg	49
Vietnam	48
Japan	48
Austria	48
Belarus	46
Philippines	45
Latvia	45
Estonia	45
Singapore	44
Belgium	43
Lithuania	42
Moldova	42
Hungary	42
Macedonia	40
Mexico	39
Bulgaria	39
Venezuela	39
Brazil	39
Slovakia	39
Poland	38
Montenegro	38
Armenia	38
France	38
Bosnia and Herz.	37
South Africa	37
Germany	37
Morocco	37
Portugal	36
Slovenia	35
Switzerland	35
Italy	35
Chile	34
Great Britain	33
Spain	32
Georgia	32
Czech Republic	32
Serbia	31
Romania	31
Sweden	31
Greece	30
El Salvador	30
Iran	30
Turkey	29
Canada	27
Uruguay	27
Northern Ireland	26
Colombia	25
New Zealand	25
Puerto Rico	24
Peru	24
United States	23
Finland	23
Netherlands	22
Ireland	21
Iceland	21
Zimbabwe	21
Israel	20
Jordan	19
Australia	19
Algeria	18
Argentina	15
Norway	13
Dominican Rep.	11
Uganda	11
Nigeria	10
Denmark	10
Egypt	8
Total	36

A039) CHILD QUALITIES: DETERMINATION PERSEVERANCE

Here is a list of qualities that children can be encouraged to learn at home.
Which, if any, do you consider to be especially important?

Determination, perseverance (%) (WVS: V21; EVS: V171)

Country	Wave		Gender		Age			Education			Income			Values		
	1990	2000	Male	Female	16-29	30-49	50+	Lower	Middle	Upper	Lower	Middle	Upper	Mat	Mixed	Postm.
Albania	na	**53**	53	53	58	53	49	47	56	59	51	53	56	51	55	51
Algeria	na	**18**	17	18	18	17	18	17	15	22	19	15	18	16	18	22
Argentina	29	**22**	25	20	23	26	17	15	31	37	14	23	29	18	20	31
Armenia	na	**57**	64	51	57	61	51	49	56	66	60	57	54	56	57	69
Australia	na	**36**	38	35	41	38	30	26	33	49	29	39	47	33	35	40
Austria	39	**36**	36	35	32	40	33	29	38	53	29	36	41	30	35	38
Azerbaijan	na	**47**	51	43	51	47	38	41	49	44	44	49	46	45	49	52
Bangladesh	na	**36**	36	36	39	34	35	34	37	39	31	40	34	33	38	53
Belarus	40	**49**	59	42	54	51	44	42	50	60	44	53	53	48	49	61
Belgium	39	**44**	47	41	42	49	40	34	44	50	36	40	52	36	45	53
Bosnia and Herz.	na	**46**	48	45	50	47	41	40	45	55	38	47	50	40	49	47
Brazil	26	**35**	36	33	37	36	26	25	40	51	27	28	47	24	37	52
Bulgaria	41	**56**	58	54	66	58	50	44	61	65	48	48	67	56	57	64
Canada	38	**48**	50	46	53	52	41	33	49	60	45	48	54	44	46	53
Chile	31	**44**	45	42	43	46	41	34	46	57	32	48	58	37	44	54
China	45	**16**	15	17	21	15	14	12	18	35	12	16	23	18	17	16
Colombia	na	**20**	23	17	20	20	17	16	20	35	15	21	28	16	20	26
Croatia	na	**93**	93	93	95	95	90	93	93	93	96	91	93	86	95	96
Czech Republic	42	**29**	32	26	38	32	21	24	33	35	22	27	38	26	29	36
Denmark	30	**32**	32	32	33	34	29	28	35	40	30	30	39	19	33	35
Dominican Rep.	na	**27**	28	27	25	32	36	6	19	33	19	28	40	18	30	29
Egypt	na	**9**	10	8	10	9	9	8	9	12	9	10	9	7	11	9
El Salvador	na	**14**	15	13	19	12	9	9	14	28	7	14	22	na	na	na
Estonia	51	**50**	54	46	58	54	41	47	48	59	42	44	56	43	54	73
Finland	38	**50**	52	49	54	49	49	50	50	52	51	49	51	49	53	41
France	39	**38**	42	35	41	41	34	31	44	52	30	39	50	30	39	52
Georgia	na	**37**	43	32	40	35	34	35	37	36	34	39	39	34	39	48
Germany	54	**47**	51	44	46	47	46	41	49	62	41	48	55	49	43	53
Great Britain	31	**41**	42	39	48	41	35	34	46	49	31	47	50	na	na	na
Greece	na	**54**	57	52	61	53	42	41	53	58	51	53	59	55	54	58
Hungary	12	**29**	30	28	37	35	17	22	38	46	27	26	32	24	33	36
Iceland	75	**29**	28	31	26	33	27	22	31	41	25	29	34	22	30	42
India	28	**46**	48	45	51	46	43	40	50	56	36	46	52	45	50	47
Indonesia	na	**44**	47	41	34	42	50	44	47	40	47	43	44	39	47	25
Iran	na	**28**	29	28	31	27	24	21	29	36	25	33	30	27	27	32
Ireland	26	**28**	29	27	30	30	23	16	32	40	22	24	33	26	29	22
Israel	na	**31**	32	30	35	30	26	24	32	33	29	31	35	24	33	26
Italy	27	**34**	35	33	36	37	31	28	37	45	28	37	39	31	34	38
Japan	59	**69**	69	69	75	67	68	70	70	67	70	72	65	64	70	66
Jordan	na	**17**	18	16	22	15	11	10	21	25	14	15	22	15	17	29
Korea, South	31	**42**	46	39	49	41	38	46	43	41	46	37	43	42	42	46
Latvia	40	**36**	41	32	41	41	30	27	37	47	31	35	43	33	36	47
Lithuania	34	**35**	40	31	44	40	25	21	39	43	23	35	39	30	37	43
Luxembourg	na	**39**	37	41	38	45	33	28	44	49	31	39	52	31	38	54
Macedonia	na	**43**	44	41	37	46	43	31	46	54	38	41	53	45	45	29
Malta	na	**17**	19	15	29	15	11	8	18	36	8	17	26	12	18	31
Mexico	37	**33**	38	29	34	34	31	24	43	51	24	32	45	31	33	45
Moldova	na	**33**	34	33	35	35	30	32	30	41	32	33	39	36	29	43
Montenegro	na	**44**	47	41	52	43	40	33	47	63	37	44	51	39	49	55
Morocco	na	**16**	17	16	17	17	11	14	23	28	13	18	15	16	18	13
Netherlands	30	**35**	38	31	27	37	37	27	36	40	25	34	43	24	34	40
New Zealand	na	**39**	39	39	50	41	34	32	36	50	35	39	46	36	39	50
Nigeria	21	**23**	23	22	22	23	29	18	26	27	21	22	25	26	21	23
Northern Ireland	18	**34**	33	35	33	35	33	33	31	42	36	33	34	34	31	44
Norway	33	**36**	40	31	34	38	33	31	36	39	na	na	na	24	36	44
Pakistan	na	**29**	29	30	37	29	17	17	42	48	17	31	45	26	35	25
Peru	na	**34**	36	31	34	34	31	31	30	41	30	33	41	27	35	36
Philippines	na	**37**	37	37	42	36	33	31	40	41	35	40	35	37	37	39
Poland	na	**35**	34	35	37	36	32	30	39	45	34	35	39	27	38	53
Portugal	23	**24**	29	21	37	27	15	19	33	41	12	22	34	20	26	28
Puerto Rico	na	**24**	31	20	27	23	23	24	23	24	22	23	26	22	22	27
Romania	40	**19**	23	15	25	22	12	8	21	33	10	14	27	14	23	26
Russian Fed.	40	**41**	48	34	51	44	30	23	40	50	32	39	49	37	44	55
Serbia	na	**41**	42	39	52	45	32	32	41	53	33	45	45	38	42	47
Singapore	na	**40**	42	38	48	33	30	31	45	44	30	38	50	34	41	52
Slovakia	na	**25**	29	21	29	27	20	17	27	39	19	26	27	20	28	40
Slovenia	42	**54**	57	52	59	58	45	44	55	69	42	51	66	49	54	63
South Africa	28	**42**	40	45	42	43	41	36	47	69	39	42	47	40	43	48
Spain	22	**29**	31	27	30	34	24	26	31	35	25	29	34	25	29	36
Sweden	33	**29**	29	30	22	33	30	22	27	38	25	29	35	17	28	34
Switzerland	na	**48**	49	47	54	48	44	37	50	51	36	48	55	43	48	51
Taiwan	na	**34**	37	32	38	38	23	24	38	42	28	32	44	29	41	38
Tanzania	na	**57**	57	57	56	58	56	58	54	58	57	56	66	62	56	54
Turkey	20	**21**	21	21	22	20	20	16	25	36	15	23	29	18	20	28
Uganda	na	**35**	44	28	39	29	42	32	37	28	32	43	38	36	36	31
Ukraine	na	**46**	50	43	58	50	36	28	46	58	41	53	46	42	49	57
United States	36	**45**	50	41	52	46	40	40	42	49	44	45	50	28	47	48
Uruguay	na	**42**	41	42	44	45	38	33	53	57	38	41	49	35	41	52
Venezuela	na	**45**	49	41	42	48	45	41	45	49	41	40	50	41	45	50
Vietnam	na	**50**	50	49	54	50	47	47	53	55	45	47	55	48	52	51
Zimbabwe	na	**35**	34	36	33	37	36	34	36	38	35	34	42	37	33	41
Total	36	37	39	35	39	39	34	30	40	44	33	37	43	34	38	43

RANKING	
Country	2000
Croatia	93
Japan	69
Armenia	57
Tanzania	57
Bulgaria	56
Greece	54
Slovenia	54
Albania	53
Finland	50
Estonia	50
Vietnam	50
Belarus	49
Canada	48
Switzerland	48
Azerbaijan	47
Germany	47
India	46
Ukraine	46
Bosnia and Herz.	46
United States	45
Venezuela	45
Montenegro	44
Belgium	44
Chile	44
Indonesia	44
Macedonia	43
Korea, South	42
South Africa	42
Uruguay	42
Russian Fed.	41
Great Britain	41
Serbia	41
Singapore	40
New Zealand	39
Luxembourg	39
France	38
Philippines	37
Georgia	37
Australia	36
Latvia	36
Bangladesh	36
Austria	36
Norway	36
Uganda	35
Lithuania	35
Zimbabwe	35
Poland	35
Brazil	35
Netherlands	35
Taiwan	34
Italy	34
Northern Ireland	34
Peru	34
Moldova	33
Mexico	33
Denmark	32
Israel	31
Pakistan	29
Sweden	29
Iceland	29
Spain	29
Czech Republic	29
Hungary	29
Iran	28
Ireland	28
Dominican Rep.	27
Slovakia	25
Portugal	24
Puerto Rico	24
Nigeria	23
Argentina	22
Turkey	21
Colombia	20
Romania	19
Algeria	18
Malta	17
Jordan	17
China	16
Morocco	16
El Salvador	14
Egypt	9
Total	37

A040) CHILD QUALITIES: RELIGIOUS FAITH

Here is a list of qualities that children can be encouraged to learn at home.

Which, if any, do you consider to be especially important?

Religious faith (%)

(WVS: V22; EVS: V172)

Country	Wave		Gender		Age			Education			Income			Values		
	1990	2000	Male	Female	16-29	30-49	50+	Lower	Middle	Upper	Lower	Middle	Upper	Mat	Mixed	Postm.
Albania	na	**36**	32	41	32	33	46	42	33	30	35	41	34	36	35	41
Algeria	na	**77**	76	78	76	77	78	77	74	80	78	79	73	75	78	76
Argentina	28	**44**	39	48	37	47	46	44	42	43	47	46	37	43	48	35
Armenia	na	**12**	9	15	11	11	16	16	13	10	10	16	11	8	16	10
Australia	na	**21**	20	23	16	20	28	25	20	20	26	22	14	27	23	16
Austria	23	**20**	20	21	13	19	26	21	20	21	23	21	17	24	21	19
Azerbaijan	na	**19**	18	20	19	17	24	29	18	18	20	23	14	16	20	34
Bangladesh	na	**70**	70	71	71	67	80	72	72	62	77	67	68	77	66	53
Belarus	6	**12**	7	16	6	8	22	23	8	8	18	10	6	16	8	7
Belgium	16	**14**	13	15	13	11	16	17	12	13	16	13	11	15	14	12
Bosnia and Herz.	na	**25**	22	27	27	23	24	29	24	24	25	26	21	21	25	30
Brazil	46	**57**	53	60	50	61	61	58	56	56	58	60	54	59	56	52
Bulgaria	11	**15**	14	16	8	12	21	21	12	12	22	12	11	16	14	11
Canada	31	**31**	26	36	20	30	38	41	29	25	36	33	23	37	33	26
Chile	54	**40**	35	45	32	42	46	46	38	34	48	35	37	37	43	36
China	1	**na**	na	na	na	na	na	na	na	na	na	na	na	na	na	na
Colombia	na	**42**	38	47	40	42	48	47	42	34	48	39	39	48	47	44
Croatia	na	**84**	80	87	78	85	87	89	82	72	89	83	81	91	83	81
Czech Republic	15	**7**	6	7	6	4	9	8	5	7	9	6	4	10	5	6
Denmark	9	**8**	7	10	5	5	13	8	7	7	9	6	8	9	8	6
Dominican Rep.	na	**59**	59	60	62	53	64	66	61	58	61	63	49	62	58	62
Egypt	na	**87**	85	90	84	88	91	88	85	89	88	87	89	89	86	87
El Salvador	na	**67**	65	69	67	66	69	66	68	69	69	65	63	na	na	na
Estonia	3	**6**	5	7	4	5	9	9	5	6	10	6	4	6	6	4
Finland	13	**16**	14	17	11	11	22	20	11	12	18	15	14	13	16	21
France	13	**8**	7	8	6	7	10	8	6	8	9	9	6	9	9	4
Georgia	na	**31**	28	34	35	33	24	32	30	34	31	32	29	29	32	39
Germany	16	**14**	11	15	12	12	16	15	13	9	14	13	14	10	15	16
Great Britain	19	**18**	20	17	12	16	23	15	21	21	17	23	20	na	na	na
Greece	na	**39**	37	40	32	39	53	60	47	28	45	41	32	48	40	28
Hungary	24	**19**	14	24	11	14	28	22	12	17	20	20	16	21	17	na
Iceland	50	**11**	10	11	4	11	16	12	8	12	11	11	8	13	10	7
India	29	**47**	44	51	44	46	51	54	45	31	50	50	43	50	40	27
Indonesia	na	**93**	92	94	92	94	93	92	94	93	94	94	98	92	93	96
Iran	na	**71**	69	73	69	72	74	77	68	67	73	72	67	79	68	58
Ireland	57	**38**	34	42	20	36	55	50	32	32	48	36	32	50	36	30
Israel	na	**29**	27	31	29	33	25	46	29	19	38	31	17	25	29	28
Italy	37	**31**	28	35	21	31	38	36	28	26	41	30	26	44	32	24
Japan	7	**7**	6	7	2	7	8	9	7	3	6	7	7	6	7	6
Jordan	na	**84**	81	87	83	85	84	84	84	84	86	82	84	83	86	75
Korea, South	19	**21**	19	24	16	22	25	21	22	20	18	20	25	21	21	21
Latvia	9	**12**	8	15	10	11	14	15	11	11	15	10	10	11	12	11
Lithuania	21	**22**	20	24	14	12	38	42	15	18	34	19	18	30	19	15
Luxembourg	na	**17**	18	17	13	13	26	24	11	20	23	16	16	17	19	15
Macedonia	na	**27**	27	27	34	26	23	40	21	20	29	25	24	26	27	38
Malta	na	**56**	51	62	45	54	67	67	52	54	58	57	53	59	56	47
Mexico	40	**53**	48	58	45	54	63	57	50	46	58	51	51	56	54	48
Moldova	na	**43**	41	44	37	45	44	51	43	34	55	36	38	42	46	31
Montenegro	na	**22**	20	24	16	22	25	28	20	12	27	18	20	24	19	21
Morocco	na	**78**	77	80	74	80	87	80	72	69	88	82	66	80	77	73
Netherlands	13	**9**	8	10	7	7	13	13	9	7	14	8	6	18	9	5
New Zealand	na	**16**	14	17	16	13	18	14	17	17	19	16	13	19	17	13
Nigeria	74	**68**	66	69	67	69	67	73	65	63	68	68	67	67	69	61
Northern Ireland	44	**40**	39	41	34	34	48	44	34	42	42	35	34	41	40	39
Norway	14	**12**	10	13	9	11	15	12	11	13	na	na	na	11	12	11
Pakistan	na	**86**	86	87	80	87	95	93	79	76	93	87	79	88	84	75
Peru	na	**56**	51	60	50	58	63	60	60	45	57	59	49	59	56	50
Philippines	na	**59**	55	64	63	58	57	58	60	61	55	62	60	58	60	70
Poland	na	**43**	40	45	39	39	50	51	36	24	46	41	36	53	36	40
Portugal	25	**25**	22	27	14	26	30	28	18	17	31	30	21	28	24	17
Puerto Rico	na	**69**	61	73	57	72	72	63	70	69	69	67	71	66	69	68
Romania	43	**59**	49	69	48	53	71	75	54	42	70	62	49	66	55	36
Russian Fed.	8	**9**	6	11	4	7	13	16	8	7	12	7	6	9	8	5
Serbia	na	**21**	20	21	22	18	23	27	19	16	24	18	17	22	20	13
Singapore	na	**30**	31	29	31	31	26	28	31	30	36	33	27	37	28	26
Slovakia	na	**33**	25	40	24	29	46	46	28	25	43	32	28	36	31	26
Slovenia	21	**18**	18	18	16	16	21	29	14	13	24	17	10	18	17	16
South Africa	50	**61**	55	69	60	61	69	62	61	50	62	62	62	70	58	49
Spain	23	**20**	15	25	12	14	30	26	13	15	27	18	16	30	18	10
Sweden	6	**5**	4	6	4	5	6	6	4	6	5	5	4	2	6	3
Switzerland	24	**21**	17	24	14	20	26	27	19	19	25	27	12	22	20	18
Taiwan	na	**9**	9	9	5	9	9	10	11	6	8	10	7	9	9	8
Tanzania	na	**75**	75	76	78	73	77	71	80	81	74	74	82	77	76	88
Turkey	44	**47**	45	49	45	46	55	57	37	20	57	43	30	49	48	36
Uganda	na	**69**	61	76	68	69	70	66	69	75	63	65	65	69	69	64
Ukraine	na	**18**	15	21	10	20	20	33	16	16	21	15	16	18	17	28
United States	55	**52**	43	61	40	55	58	45	57	53	50	53	54	57	53	49
Uruguay	na	**17**	11	22	12	16	21	19	15	16	19	14	20	20	17	17
Venezuela	na	**45**	41	48	46	44	44	48	45	38	51	48	39	45	47	35
Vietnam	na	**8**	7	9	8	9	8	11	5	5	6	5	12	6	9	7
Zimbabwe	na	**74**	68	79	74	76	70	72	77	90	67	77	74	72	74	86
Total	26	37	34	39	38	36	36	42	33	34	41	37	33	40	36	30

RANKING	
Country	2000
Indonesia	93
Egypt	87
Pakistan	86
Jordan	84
Croatia	84
Morocco	78
Algeria	77
Tanzania	75
Zimbabwe	74
Iran	71
Bangladesh	70
Puerto Rico	69
Uganda	69
Nigeria	68
El Salvador	67
South Africa	61
Philippines	59
Dominican Rep.	59
Romania	59
Brazil	57
Malta	56
Peru	56
Mexico	53
United States	52
Turkey	47
India	47
Venezuela	45
Argentina	44
Poland	43
Moldova	43
Colombia	42
Chile	40
Northern Ireland	40
Greece	39
Ireland	38
Albania	36
Slovakia	33
Italy	31
Georgia	31
Canada	31
Singapore	30
Israel	29
Macedonia	27
Bosnia and Herz.	25
Portugal	25
Lithuania	22
Montenegro	22
Australia	21
Korea, South	21
Serbia	21
Switzerland	21
Austria	20
Spain	20
Hungary	19
Azerbaijan	19
Great Britain	18
Ukraine	18
Slovenia	18
Luxembourg	17
Uruguay	17
Finland	16
New Zealand	16
Bulgaria	15
Belgium	14
Germany	14
Armenia	12
Belarus	12
Latvia	12
Norway	12
Iceland	11
Netherlands	9
Taiwan	9
Russian Fed.	9
Denmark	8
Vietnam	8
France	8
Czech Republic	7
Japan	7
Estonia	6
Sweden	5
Total	37

A041) CHILD QUALITIES: UNSELFISHNESS

Here is a list of qualities that children can be encouraged to learn at home.

Which, if any, do you consider to be especially important?

Unselfishness (%)

(WVS: V23; EVS: V173)

Country	Wave		Gender		Age			Education			Income			Values		
	1990	2000	Male	Female	16-29	30-49	50+	Lower	Middle	Upper	Lower	Middle	Upper	Mat	Mixed	Postm.
Albania	na	**12**	14	10	14	11	11	12	12	11	12	12	12	10	15	3
Algeria	na	**17**	18	15	17	16	17	16	19	14	19	17	15	15	16	29
Argentina	5	**13**	14	11	8	16	14	11	15	14	10	14	14	10	13	15
Armenia	na	**31**	32	29	30	34	26	26	32	29	30	28	35	31	31	18
Australia	na	**40**	38	42	42	40	38	39	41	39	37	40	39	39	40	41
Austria	7	**5**	7	4	7	4	6	5	6	3	6	6	5	7	5	6
Azerbaijan	na	**17**	18	15	17	16	18	24	18	13	19	17	14	16	18	16
Bangladesh	na	**16**	17	14	18	14	14	13	18	19	11	15	21	16	15	21
Belarus	27	**17**	16	18	19	18	15	13	19	18	18	17	17	16	18	14
Belgium	27	**29**	29	29	29	28	30	22	27	37	29	28	28	20	29	41
Bosnia and Herz.	na	**38**	38	37	40	38	35	31	39	40	36	38	36	35	39	34
Brazil	28	**32**	28	37	34	33	28	25	38	37	28	39	34	29	33	39
Bulgaria	22	**14**	13	15	17	15	13	10	16	19	12	16	16	16	13	16
Canada	42	**45**	45	45	50	44	44	44	46	44	45	47	46	46	46	45
Chile	8	**34**	33	35	37	35	30	32	34	40	33	32	40	29	35	39
China	31	**37**	37	37	38	40	29	33	40	35	37	37	39	40	38	41
Colombia	na	**37**	36	39	40	35	37	44	38	25	45	37	28	43	41	39
Croatia	na	**90**	88	91	92	91	87	87	91	90	87	91	90	85	90	93
Czech Republic	38	**37**	37	37	41	37	34	37	37	36	31	38	39	31	39	40
Denmark	50	**56**	54	58	63	59	49	56	57	54	53	59	52	66	54	64
Dominican Rep.	na	**12**	18	9	13	11	18	19	13	11	15	12	8	13	9	20
Egypt	na	**22**	20	24	22	22	20	21	22	24	20	21	25	22	22	22
El Salvador	na	**28**	27	29	28	29	27	29	26	27	30	28	24	na	na	na
Estonia	25	**17**	17	17	14	16	18	16	16	20	16	16	18	18	15	11
Finland	21	**21**	23	19	27	22	16	13	30	33	19	24	21	15	22	28
France	40	**40**	37	44	43	42	38	37	42	49	43	38	42	38	38	50
Georgia	na	**20**	20	19	20	19	20	15	20	21	19	23	18	19	20	19
Germany	9	**7**	8	7	7	7	8	8	7	5	9	8	7	10	7	5
Great Britain	57	**60**	61	59	59	63	57	55	62	69	53	63	62	na	na	na
Greece	na	**26**	24	27	26	28	24	23	30	23	31	23	24	19	26	29
Hungary	26	**21**	24	19	26	20	20	17	28	34	17	21	24	19	25	37
Iceland	75	**35**	33	36	42	34	30	34	39	29	36	36	35	36	34	39
India	32	**37**	37	36	40	37	33	35	41	37	34	37	38	37	38	29
Indonesia	na	**47**	49	46	40	46	52	48	52	42	52	45	47	41	51	39
Iran	na	**29**	31	26	31	27	28	26	28	33	28	29	30	28	28	28
Ireland	53	**49**	50	49	54	52	44	40	55	51	45	51	51	47	49	51
Israel	na	**49**	47	51	52	50	44	42	50	52	48	48	51	49	49	47
Italy	39	**41**	39	44	47	46	34	34	45	53	39	41	48	31	39	53
Japan	44	**53**	55	51	51	58	50	43	53	61	50	55	57	58	53	59
Jordan	na	**32**	30	34	33	32	28	31	34	32	30	31	34	29	33	45
Korea, South	11	**15**	14	16	16	15	12	14	13	17	14	15	15	13	15	25
Latvia	16	**12**	10	13	15	11	11	8	12	14	12	10	13	9	13	19
Lithuania	33	**29**	28	29	29	29	28	26	30	25	31	34	25	21	30	34
Luxembourg	na	**26**	23	29	25	27	24	29	21	29	27	29	28	25	25	27
Macedonia	na	**47**	48	46	49	49	43	44	47	52	44	50	47	47	46	72
Malta	na	**46**	48	44	51	50	39	44	47	44	46	44	51	44	46	55
Mexico	11	**50**	47	52	55	49	42	49	53	40	50	53	52	46	56	47
Moldova	na	**12**	15	8	13	10	13	12	12	11	10	13	12	11	14	11
Montenegro	na	**40**	40	40	44	40	37	35	43	42	46	40	36	39	41	44
Morocco	na	**10**	10	10	9	11	9	10	11	13	5	9	15	8	11	15
Netherlands	22	**28**	32	24	34	29	24	19	33	30	25	30	29	27	29	28
New Zealand	na	**33**	33	32	35	33	32	31	34	34	32	32	35	33	32	36
Nigeria	17	**23**	24	23	24	21	28	27	22	20	25	24	21	24	23	21
Northern Ireland	49	**50**	50	51	50	54	47	49	51	51	56	57	50	42	55	46
Norway	10	**11**	13	9	15	11	10	7	10	18	na	na	na	7	11	18
Pakistan	na	**38**	39	38	42	39	30	32	43	54	29	39	49	36	42	42
Peru	na	**50**	49	52	55	49	43	52	47	54	52	52	45	45	51	55
Philippines	na	**39**	39	40	41	36	44	47	41	29	43	37	39	39	40	36
Poland	na	**12**	11	14	17	13	8	7	17	24	9	13	16	12	12	15
Portugal	28	**40**	39	41	44	38	40	39	41	46	38	40	44	39	39	50
Puerto Rico	na	**28**	35	25	40	23	27	27	25	31	26	26	33	28	29	27
Romania	20	**7**	8	6	13	6	4	2	8	12	4	7	8	7	7	10
Russian Fed.	24	**21**	21	20	19	20	22	18	21	21	23	20	19	20	22	19
Serbia	na	**34**	35	35	39	35	32	29	38	36	30	34	40	33	37	34
Singapore	na	**30**	30	29	35	26	22	26	31	35	23	29	33	26	31	32
Slovakia	na	**19**	19	19	23	20	13	13	20	28	17	19	21	17	19	29
Slovenia	33	**38**	34	41	37	40	35	29	40	44	34	38	49	38	37	40
South Africa	20	**29**	30	29	28	29	31	28	30	47	28	30	28	31	29	22
Spain	12	**12**	12	12	11	10	14	14	10	10	10	14	14	14	12	9
Sweden	29	**33**	35	31	48	35	21	22	36	36	35	31	31	28	31	41
Switzerland	37	**30**	29	31	28	29	32	23	31	38	30	28	32	26	30	36
Taiwan	na	**21**	22	21	20	22	21	20	21	24	23	19	22	26	19	19
Tanzania	na	**46**	46	46	44	48	46	42	49	53	42	46	57	45	48	33
Turkey	28	**22**	21	23	25	21	15	17	27	31	19	22	30	20	22	25
Uganda	na	**31**	23	39	30	31	39	39	28	31	26	35	28	33	31	29
Ukraine	na	**15**	14	17	13	16	17	15	14	19	18	16	11	13	17	24
United States	37	**39**	38	40	40	38	39	40	41	37	38	42	38	40	38	42
Uruguay	na	**55**	57	53	58	51	56	57	51	53	56	54	55	56	55	58
Venezuela	na	**53**	51	55	56	51	51	61	51	48	58	52	50	51	54	51
Vietnam	na	**39**	39	39	45	40	33	34	45	51	40	44	35	48	38	42
Zimbabwe	na	**33**	33	33	30	37	33	33	33	53	28	37	36	30	36	28
Total	28	**31**	31	31	32	31	29	29	32	32	30	32	32	27	32	36

RANKING

Country	2000
Croatia	90
Great Britain	60
Denmark	56
Uruguay	55
Japan	53
Venezuela	53
Peru	50
Northern Ireland	50
Mexico	50
Ireland	49
Israel	49
Indonesia	47
Macedonia	47
Malta	46
Tanzania	46
Canada	45
Italy	41
France	40
Portugal	40
Montenegro	40
Australia	40
Philippines	39
Vietnam	39
United States	39
Pakistan	38
Bosnia and Herz.	38
Slovenia	38
Colombia	37
China	37
Czech Republic	37
India	37
Iceland	35
Serbia	34
Chile	34
Zimbabwe	33
New Zealand	33
Sweden	33
Brazil	32
Jordan	32
Uganda	31
Armenia	31
Switzerland	30
Singapore	30
South Africa	29
Belgium	29
Iran	29
Lithuania	29
Puerto Rico	28
Netherlands	28
El Salvador	28
Greece	26
Luxembourg	26
Nigeria	23
Turkey	22
Egypt	22
Taiwan	21
Hungary	21
Finland	21
Russian Fed.	21
Georgia	20
Slovakia	19
Belarus	17
Azerbaijan	17
Algeria	17
Estonia	17
Bangladesh	16
Ukraine	15
Korea, South	15
Bulgaria	14
Argentina	13
Dominican Rep.	12
Poland	12
Albania	12
Spain	12
Latvia	12
Moldova	12
Norway	11
Morocco	10
Germany	7
Romania	7
Austria	5
Total	31

A042) CHILD QUALITIES: OBEDIENCE

Here is a list of qualities that children can be encouraged to learn at home.
Which, if any, do you consider to be especially important?
Obedience (%)

(WVS: V24; EVS: V174)

Country	Wave		Gender		Age			Education			Income			Values		
	1990	2000	Male	Female	16-29	30-49	50+	Lower	Middle	Upper	Lower	Middle	Upper	Mat	Mixed	Postm.
Albania	na	**54**	55	53	54	54	54	53	54	57	52	52	57	50	55	77
Algeria	na	**56**	54	58	57	54	59	62	56	53	56	54	56	58	54	61
Argentina	32	**37**	37	38	44	36	32	43	32	20	41	39	30	45	40	24
Armenia	na	**18**	15	21	16	18	22	24	19	11	15	15	25	22	15	13
Australia	na	**29**	30	28	35	25	28	33	34	20	32	28	24	38	32	24
Austria	25	**17**	18	16	18	12	21	23	13	5	25	17	12	37	18	8
Azerbaijan	na	**25**	25	25	19	27	31	33	24	24	21	26	26	23	29	21
Bangladesh	na	**19**	21	18	20	17	27	17	21	24	18	17	24	20	18	17
Belarus	23	**34**	32	36	31	29	42	46	32	20	41	32	26	39	29	18
Belgium	37	**43**	43	43	49	38	45	57	46	28	47	47	35	54	44	23
Bosnia and Herz.	na	**44**	42	45	40	44	47	55	46	28	48	47	35	48	41	38
Brazil	41	**59**	61	58	61	58	56	65	58	40	67	63	48	68	60	34
Bulgaria	19	**16**	15	17	9	13	21	24	12	9	21	15	13	17	15	13
Canada	28	**30**	30	29	31	29	30	42	30	19	38	30	23	37	33	22
Chile	52	**55**	51	58	55	55	55	58	54	51	60	55	45	64	54	40
China	9	**15**	14	16	9	16	16	22	11	2	19	14	11	14	14	13
Colombia	na	**43**	42	44	47	39	45	51	44	27	53	42	31	47	48	44
Croatia	na	**86**	84	88	84	87	86	89	87	77	94	84	84	92	87	80
Czech Republic	28	**17**	19	16	17	16	19	23	12	6	22	16	14	26	15	13
Denmark	20	**14**	16	13	14	13	17	20	7	7	20	14	7	25	15	6
Dominican Rep.	na	**51**	51	50	49	53	64	63	57	47	65	52	37	53	54	35
Egypt	na	**53**	51	56	52	53	56	58	52	43	56	57	49	59	49	45
El Salvador	na	**62**	62	63	62	64	61	68	61	50	71	63	53	na	na	na
Estonia	19	**29**	31	27	28	24	33	38	26	19	32	33	23	35	24	15
Finland	25	**30**	33	28	27	31	30	37	22	18	31	33	26	39	29	16
France	53	**36**	37	34	34	34	37	44	29	20	36	38	29	48	36	17
Georgia	na	**23**	22	24	22	21	26	23	26	13	28	19	19	23	23	16
Germany	24	**12**	11	12	7	10	16	17	8	4	18	14	7	19	11	3
Great Britain	39	**49**	48	51	44	47	54	59	44	39	55	57	42	na	na	na
Greece	na	**11**	13	9	9	12	14	25	12	7	15	10	11	11	12	7
Hungary	45	**33**	32	35	30	30	39	40	22	23	41	33	29	38	30	9
Iceland	68	**17**	19	16	21	20	11	19	20	9	18	21	15	26	17	3
India	56	**56**	54	58	57	55	56	58	58	50	57	56	55	59	50	53
Indonesia	na	**53**	57	49	44	54	57	59	56	47	57	51	54	51	53	46
Iran	na	**41**	42	41	42	40	42	43	39	40	43	41	44	41	39	44
Ireland	35	**47**	45	50	48	44	50	54	46	39	57	49	39	46	48	44
Israel	na	**16**	18	15	17	15	18	23	18	10	22	22	6	19	16	16
Italy	34	**28**	29	27	24	25	33	38	22	15	38	25	19	44	29	18
Japan	10	**4**	3	5	5	4	5	5	5	3	5	4	3	4	5	2
Jordan	na	**46**	45	47	48	44	48	49	51	36	49	46	44	53	42	40
Korea, South	18	**13**	14	13	8	12	21	23	14	10	15	14	11	15	12	9
Latvia	15	**20**	22	19	28	17	20	35	18	9	21	22	18	22	20	19
Lithuania	25	**20**	18	21	12	18	27	29	18	11	29	13	13	23	19	10
Luxembourg	na	**26**	27	26	27	23	29	38	24	10	43	27	16	34	27	14
Macedonia	na	**11**	12	11	14	10	11	16	9	8	15	10	8	11	10	29
Malta	na	**41**	39	43	42	38	44	38	46	24	48	42	33	42	42	30
Mexico	45	**60**	56	63	62	57	60	61	60	49	64	60	54	63	61	51
Moldova	na	**41**	43	40	36	40	47	50	42	32	45	37	42	42	40	38
Montenegro	na	**47**	42	51	37	46	54	62	41	25	54	45	41	53	39	37
Morocco	na	**53**	49	57	49	52	64	56	43	31	58	51	51	55	51	43
Netherlands	33	**26**	26	26	27	24	26	38	26	14	29	25	21	29	29	13
New Zealand	na	**22**	21	22	21	22	22	25	24	17	25	22	18	29	24	13
Nigeria	71	**73**	71	75	72	72	76	78	71	66	70	76	72	77	71	67
Northern Ireland	56	**58**	59	56	65	50	60	61	58	47	58	58	56	60	61	45
Norway	31	**26**	28	24	24	25	29	39	29	10	na	na	na	42	26	6
Pakistan	na	**44**	44	45	38	44	59	54	37	27	55	44	30	48	39	33
Peru	na	**61**	61	61	61	61	63	71	61	54	66	62	50	65	60	59
Philippines	na	**44**	45	44	42	46	44	47	46	39	47	46	40	46	45	36
Poland	na	**33**	32	33	29	31	37	40	28	14	38	30	26	36	31	25
Portugal	45	**39**	36	41	30	38	45	41	37	25	43	45	28	46	33	43
Puerto Rico	na	**56**	52	58	56	56	56	51	58	56	56	57	55	54	55	61
Romania	20	**19**	17	21	14	15	25	30	16	5	28	21	11	24	15	7
Russian Fed.	26	**34**	31	36	29	30	42	49	36	19	43	35	23	37	30	6
Serbia	na	**32**	32	33	28	27	39	50	29	13	40	30	25	41	25	11
Singapore	na	**47**	43	51	46	47	51	51	48	34	52	46	42	48	48	33
Slovakia	na	**26**	28	25	27	23	30	34	24	14	32	28	21	29	24	20
Slovenia	40	**25**	27	24	24	24	28	36	24	9	33	23	16	23	26	20
South Africa	42	**52**	53	50	51	51	59	57	46	41	55	55	45	53	53	44
Spain	42	**49**	48	50	43	47	54	54	47	37	54	52	39	55	51	35
Sweden	25	**13**	15	11	11	10	17	22	13	6	15	16	7	24	14	4
Switzerland	20	**24**	25	23	21	25	25	33	24	7	25	30	17	38	24	13
Taiwan	na	**33**	30	36	25	32	42	49	33	19	40	36	22	35	30	22
Tanzania	na	**76**	77	76	77	76	78	78	76	71	77	74	78	77	77	79
Turkey	31	**42**	40	44	41	41	46	49	36	21	50	38	30	45	42	35
Uganda	na	**72**	68	75	73	69	78	74	71	69	71	61	74	75	72	61
Ukraine	na	**35**	32	38	30	36	38	44	37	27	40	32	33	41	30	32
United States	39	**32**	32	32	33	34	29	35	37	28	36	33	25	43	34	24
Uruguay	na	**29**	29	29	28	27	30	34	23	14	31	24	31	40	27	26
Venezuela	na	**51**	52	50	54	49	51	60	51	41	58	52	47	51	52	52
Vietnam	na	**56**	52	60	57	54	59	59	51	54	57	57	54	71	49	58
Zimbabwe	na	**68**	63	73	67	70	69	70	66	53	72	67	61	67	69	64
Total	33	**38**	37	38	39	36	38	46	35	28	42	38	32	42	36	28

RANKING	
Country	2000
Croatia	86
Tanzania	76
Nigeria	73
Uganda	72
Zimbabwe	68
El Salvador	62
Peru	61
Mexico	60
Brazil	59
Northern Ireland	58
Algeria	56
Vietnam	56
Puerto Rico	56
India	56
Chile	55
Albania	54
Egypt	53
Indonesia	53
Morocco	53
South Africa	52
Venezuela	51
Dominican Rep.	51
Great Britain	49
Spain	49
Ireland	47
Singapore	47
Montenegro	47
Jordan	46
Pakistan	44
Philippines	44
Bosnia and Herz.	44
Belgium	43
Colombia	43
Turkey	42
Iran	41
Moldova	41
Malta	41
Portugal	39
Argentina	37
France	36
Ukraine	35
Belarus	34
Russian Fed.	34
Hungary	33
Taiwan	33
Poland	33
Serbia	32
United States	32
Finland	30
Canada	30
Australia	29
Uruguay	29
Estonia	29
Italy	28
Slovakia	26
Luxembourg	26
Norway	26
Netherlands	26
Slovenia	25
Azerbaijan	25
Switzerland	24
Georgia	23
New Zealand	22
Latvia	20
Lithuania	20
Bangladesh	19
Romania	19
Armenia	18
Iceland	17
Czech Republic	17
Austria	17
Israel	16
Bulgaria	16
China	15
Denmark	14
Korea, South	13
Sweden	13
Germany	12
Macedonia	11
Greece	11
Japan	4
Total	38

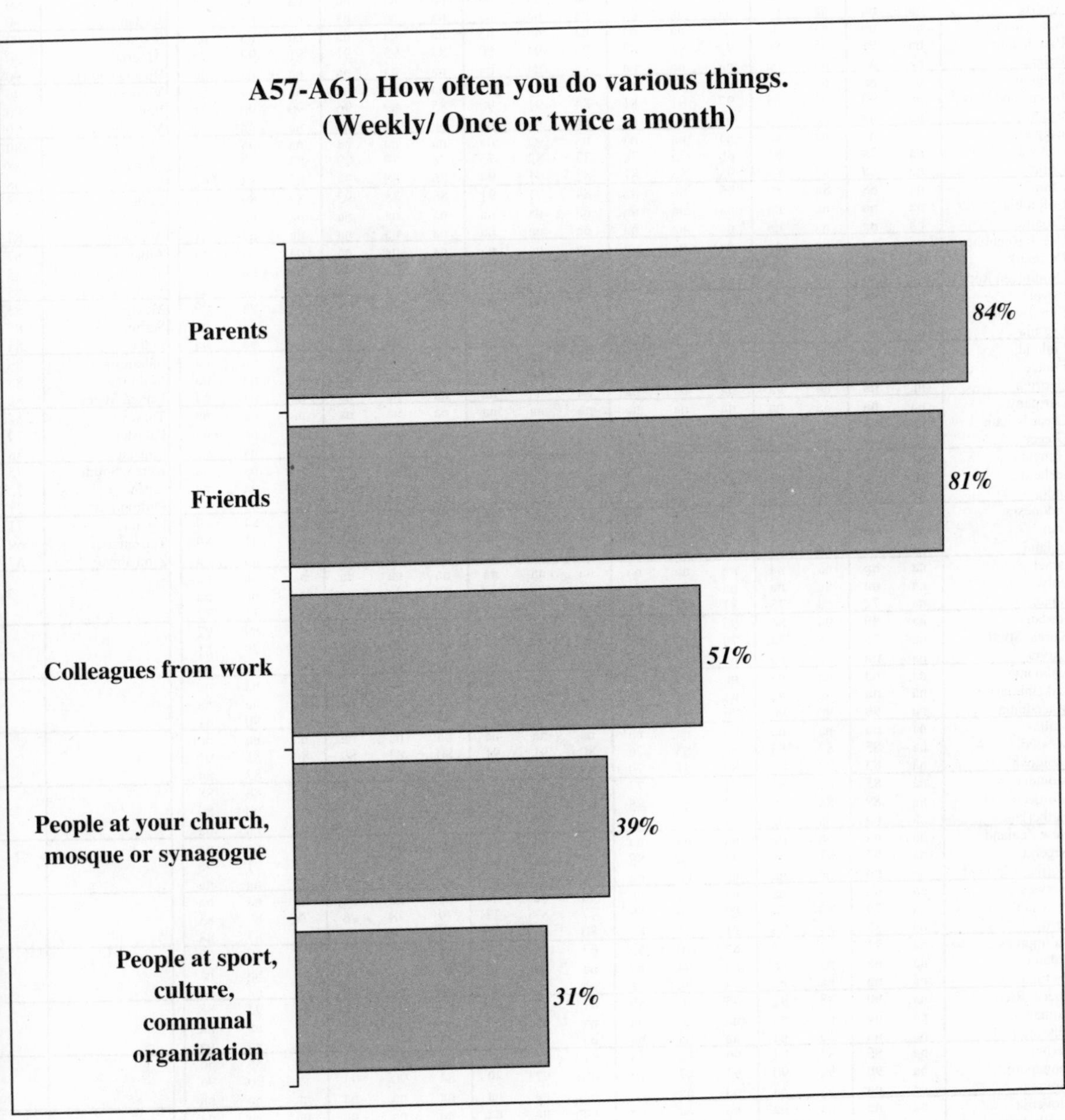
A57-A61) How often you do various things.
(Weekly/ Once or twice a month)
Parents
84%
Friends
81%
Colleagues from work
51%
People at your church, mosque or synagogue
39%
People at sport, culture, communal organization
31%

A057) SPEND TIME WITH THE PARENTS

I'm going to ask how of often you do various things? Spend time with parents or other relatives.

Weekly / Once or twice a month (%)

(WVS: V27)

Country	Wave		Gender		Age			Education			Income			Values		
	1990	2000	Male	Female	16-29	30-49	50+	Lower	Middle	Upper	Lower	Middle	Upper	Mat	Mixed	Postm.
Albania	na	**87**	87	87	95	88	78	88	86	86	88	87	86	87	88	82
Algeria	na	**90**	90	89	94	88	84	86	90	92	90	87	91	90	89	93
Argentina	na	**87**	86	88	92	86	84	85	90	91	86	87	88	86	87	87
Armenia	na	**na**	na	na	na	na	na	na	na	na	na	na	na	na	na	na
Australia	na	**na**	na	na	na	na	na	na	na	na	na	na	na	na	na	na
Austria	na	**na**	na	na	na	na	na	na	na	na	na	na	na	na	na	na
Azerbaijan	na	**na**	na	na	na	na	na	na	na	na	na	na	na	na	na	na
Bangladesh	na	**91**	95	86	93	91	87	90	94	90	87	95	91	91	92	95
Belarus	na	**na**	na	na	na	na	na	na	na	na	na	na	na	na	na	na
Belgium	na	**na**	na	na	na	na	na	na	na	na	na	na	na	na	na	na
Bosnia and Herz.	na	**90**	91	88	97	91	81	84	91	90	85	89	96	90	90	91
Brazil	na	**na**	na	na	na	na	na	na	na	na	na	na	na	na	na	na
Bulgaria	na	**na**	na	na	na	na	na	na	na	na	na	na	na	na	na	na
Canada	na	**78**	75	81	86	75	78	77	82	73	78	79	79	87	79	74
Chile	na	**88**	87	89	95	88	81	82	91	94	86	88	94	85	88	92
China	na	**88**	88	89	95	88	83	84	91	91	86	88	92	89	89	97
Colombia	na	**na**	na	na	na	na	na	na	na	na	na	na	na	na	na	na
Croatia	na	**na**	na	na	na	na	na	na	na	na	na	na	na	na	na	na
Czech Republic	na	**na**	na	na	na	na	na	na	na	na	na	na	na	na	na	na
Denmark	na	**na**	na	na	na	na	na	na	na	na	na	na	na	na	na	na
Dominican Rep.	na	**na**	na	na	na	na	na	na	na	na	na	na	na	na	na	na
Egypt	na	**98**	98	98	99	98	96	97	99	99	97	98	99	98	98	99
El Salvador	na	**na**	na	na	na	na	na	na	na	na	na	na	na	na	na	na
Estonia	na	**na**	na	na	na	na	na	na	na	na	na	na	na	na	na	na
Finland	na	**na**	na	na	na	na	na	na	na	na	na	na	na	na	na	na
France	na	**na**	na	na	na	na	na	na	na	na	na	na	na	na	na	na
Georgia	na	**na**	na	na	na	na	na	na	na	na	na	na	na	na	na	na
Germany	na	**na**	na	na	na	na	na	na	na	na	na	na	na	na	na	na
Great Britain	na	**na**	na	na	na	na	na	na	na	na	na	na	na	na	na	na
Greece	na	**na**	na	na	na	na	na	na	na	na	na	na	na	na	na	na
Hungary	na	**na**	na	na	na	na	na	na	na	na	na	na	na	na	na	na
Iceland	na	**na**	na	na	na	na	na	na	na	na	na	na	na	na	na	na
India	na	**83**	86	79	88	86	74	81	85	86	79	84	85	82	85	84
Indonesia	na	**83**	83	84	90	84	80	81	83	86	78	87	87	81	84	89
Iran	na	**90**	90	90	92	89	84	87	90	90	89	90	91	89	91	89
Ireland	na	**na**	na	na	na	na	na	na	na	na	na	na	na	na	na	na
Israel	na	**na**	na	na	na	na	na	na	na	na	na	na	na	na	na	na
Italy	na	**na**	na	na	na	na	na	na	na	na	na	na	na	na	na	na
Japan	na	**72**	69	75	81	77	64	66	72	74	69	74	71	74	71	72
Jordan	na	**90**	94	86	95	90	80	87	90	95	87	92	90	91	89	92
Korea, South	na	**75**	75	74	79	75	68	50	75	77	65	80	81	70	79	81
Latvia	na	**na**	na	na	na	na	na	na	na	na	na	na	na	na	na	na
Lithuania	na	**na**	na	na	na	na	na	na	na	na	na	na	na	na	na	na
Luxembourg	na	**na**	na	na	na	na	na	na	na	na	na	na	na	na	na	na
Macedonia	na	**90**	90	90	96	91	83	87	90	94	84	93	93	91	90	81
Malta	na	**na**	na	na	na	na	na	na	na	na	na	na	na	na	na	na
Mexico	na	**85**	87	83	93	83	76	80	91	91	80	83	89	84	85	91
Moldova	na	**83**	82	83	89	81	79	83	85	77	79	82	85	82	83	84
Montenegro	na	**85**	89	82	94	88	77	78	90	93	92	84	85	83	88	88
Morocco	na	**89**	88	89	92	86	85	87	94	92	82	89	86	88	90	89
Netherlands	na	**na**	na	na	na	na	na	na	na	na	na	na	na	na	na	na
New Zealand	na	**na**	na	na	na	na	na	na	na	na	na	na	na	na	na	na
Nigeria	na	**92**	93	91	94	90	88	91	92	93	91	93	91	93	91	90
Northern Ireland	na	**na**	na	na	na	na	na	na	na	na	na	na	na	na	na	na
Norway	na	**na**	na	na	na	na	na	na	na	na	na	na	na	na	na	na
Pakistan	na	**79**	83	74	89	78	59	77	81	77	79	78	76	78	80	83
Peru	na	**87**	89	86	91	85	85	80	88	91	83	89	94	86	87	88
Philippines	na	**71**	71	71	85	70	53	63	72	78	65	72	74	73	69	69
Poland	na	**na**	na	na	na	na	na	na	na	na	na	na	na	na	na	na
Portugal	na	**na**	na	na	na	na	na	na	na	na	na	na	na	na	na	na
Puerto Rico	na	**90**	88	92	95	90	89	87	87	93	86	92	92	86	92	87
Romania	na	**na**	na	na	na	na	na	na	na	na	na	na	na	na	na	na
Russian Fed.	na	**na**	na	na	na	na	na	na	na	na	na	na	na	na	na	na
Serbia	na	**85**	85	84	96	86	78	81	84	90	80	85	88	85	85	86
Singapore	na	**90**	90	90	97	87	76	86	92	89	84	90	94	89	90	96
Slovakia	na	**na**	na	na	na	na	na	na	na	na	na	na	na	na	na	na
Slovenia	na	**na**	na	na	na	na	na	na	na	na	na	na	na	na	na	na
South Africa	na	**85**	84	86	92	82	75	83	88	86	82	87	87	83	85	87
Spain	na	**88**	88	88	95	89	83	86	90	93	81	88	92	88	87	91
Sweden	na	**na**	na	na	na	na	na	na	na	na	na	na	na	na	na	na
Switzerland	na	**na**	na	na	na	na	na	na	na	na	na	na	na	na	na	na
Taiwan	na	**na**	na	na	na	na	na	na	na	na	na	na	na	na	na	na
Tanzania	na	**69**	68	71	76	64	70	72	71	54	73	66	62	70	68	71
Turkey	na	**82**	81	83	87	81	73	83	81	79	83	81	81	83	81	81
Uganda	na	**71**	79	63	81	63	50	56	76	80	64	78	71	71	69	77
Ukraine	na	**na**	na	na	na	na	na	na	na	na	na	na	na	na	na	na
United States	na	**82**	81	84	90	78	82	86	85	79	81	81	84	85	82	81
Uruguay	na	**na**	na	na	na	na	na	na	na	na	na	na	na	na	na	na
Venezuela	na	**93**	92	94	95	92	92	91	95	91	93	94	94	95	93	93
Vietnam	na	**90**	89	90	95	91	83	88	92	87	87	89	91	84	91	93
Zimbabwe	na	**67**	75	61	78	57	62	63	75	40	67	70	67	66	70	66
Total	na	**84**	85	84	91	83	78	82	86	86	82	85	87	84	85	85

RANKING	
Country	2000
Egypt	98
Venezuela	93
Nigeria	92
Bangladesh	91
Puerto Rico	90
Jordan	90
Singapore	90
Algeria	90
Bosnia and Herz.	90
Vietnam	90
Iran	90
Macedonia	90
Morocco	89
China	88
Spain	88
Chile	88
Peru	87
Argentina	87
Albania	87
Montenegro	85
South Africa	85
Mexico	85
Serbia	85
India	83
Indonesia	83
Moldova	83
United States	82
Turkey	82
Pakistan	79
Canada	78
Korea, South	75
Japan	72
Philippines	71
Uganda	71
Tanzania	69
Zimbabwe	67
Total	84

A058) SPEND TIME WITH FRIENDS

I'm going to ask how of often you do various things? Spend time with friends.

Weekly / Once or twice a month (%) (WVS: V28; EVS: V48)

Country	Wave		Gender		Age			Education			Income			Values		
	1990	2000	Male	Female	16-29	30-49	50+	Lower	Middle	Upper	Lower	Middle	Upper	Mat	Mixed	Postm.
Albania	na	**69**	79	59	76	66	66	63	70	80	65	68	72	65	71	69
Algeria	na	**81**	90	72	88	78	73	68	83	88	79	84	85	76	84	85
Argentina	na	**75**	80	72	87	74	66	69	83	86	68	73	85	68	76	82
Armenia	na	**na**	na	na	na	na	na	na	na	na	na	na	na	na	na	na
Australia	na	**na**	na	na	na	na	na	na	na	na	na	na	na	na	na	na
Austria	na	**88**	90	86	99	90	81	83	93	93	82	88	92	79	88	92
Azerbaijan	na	**na**	na	na	na	na	na	na	na	na	na	na	na	na	na	na
Bangladesh	na	**84**	92	74	84	84	84	81	86	90	81	84	88	84	85	72
Belarus	na	**81**	84	78	91	81	72	75	82	84	78	79	88	77	83	86
Belgium	na	**81**	82	80	95	84	72	69	83	87	75	81	86	79	82	84
Bosnia and Herz.	na	**97**	98	96	98	98	95	94	98	97	96	96	99	97	97	96
Brazil	na	**na**	na	na	na	na	na	na	na	na	na	na	na	na	na	na
Bulgaria	na	**83**	84	81	95	87	73	78	84	89	75	83	90	79	85	93
Canada	na	**90**	89	91	96	89	88	84	91	93	89	92	91	89	90	92
Chile	na	**59**	65	53	78	58	41	45	63	75	54	58	69	53	58	69
China	na	**61**	58	65	70	63	49	58	64	64	53	64	71	61	64	63
Colombia	na	**na**	na	na	na	na	na	na	na	na	na	na	na	na	na	na
Croatia	na	**90**	95	86	98	92	84	88	92	94	89	89	93	86	91	96
Czech Republic	na	**81**	81	81	95	85	70	80	82	81	74	82	87	77	82	84
Denmark	na	**91**	90	92	100	93	84	88	98	92	88	90	97	90	90	93
Dominican Rep.	na	**na**	na	na	na	na	na	na	na	na	na	na	na	na	na	na
Egypt	na	**86**	92	80	92	85	80	82	91	92	86	87	86	82	89	93
El Salvador	na	**na**	na	na	na	na	na	na	na	na	na	na	na	na	na	na
Estonia	na	**77**	75	80	96	81	63	71	80	81	74	71	82	74	78	92
Finland	na	**88**	87	89	98	89	82	88	90	86	90	89	84	91	87	88
France	na	**87**	87	86	98	86	82	83	89	93	85	85	90	86	86	90
Georgia	na	**na**	na	na	na	na	na	na	na	na	na	na	na	na	na	na
Germany	na	**86**	85	87	94	86	82	82	90	89	80	90	87	87	85	88
Great Britain	na	**93**	93	93	98	92	90	89	94	97	90	91	94	na	na	na
Greece	na	**92**	92	92	99	90	79	80	90	95	89	94	92	89	92	95
Hungary	na	**66**	71	62	88	68	52	61	77	77	60	64	73	63	69	79
Iceland	na	**89**	87	92	99	91	80	88	90	94	88	89	92	87	89	96
India	na	**72**	79	62	77	73	64	67	71	83	76	69	72	74	77	69
Indonesia	na	**97**	98	97	99	98	97	97	97	99	98	99	99	98	98	93
Iran	na	**74**	77	70	81	70	62	66	77	78	70	77	73	72	75	77
Ireland	na	**93**	93	94	99	91	92	91	95	94	91	91	96	94	93	94
Israel	na	**na**	na	na	na	na	na	na	na	na	na	na	na	na	na	na
Italy	na	**82**	87	77	95	85	72	73	88	93	74	85	88	73	82	88
Japan	na	**66**	62	70	80	63	63	65	66	67	63	65	69	61	67	67
Jordan	na	**78**	88	68	80	76	77	78	78	77	78	78	75	76	80	81
Korea, South	na	**78**	81	75	93	74	71	63	78	81	74	79	82	74	81	88
Latvia	na	**72**	76	68	91	74	62	63	73	79	69	67	79	66	75	83
Lithuania	na	**72**	75	69	94	73	54	47	80	77	67	66	76	69	73	70
Luxembourg	na	**88**	89	87	94	89	81	85	90	88	87	88	87	87	87	90
Macedonia	na	**91**	93	89	96	91	88	87	93	96	87	92	96	91	91	98
Malta	na	**61**	66	56	77	57	54	50	64	75	55	58	67	57	63	67
Mexico	na	**64**	72	57	72	63	55	57	72	80	59	66	73	66	64	69
Moldova	na	**75**	79	71	88	72	67	71	76	75	67	71	82	71	79	71
Montenegro	na	**92**	93	90	96	94	87	87	94	97	92	91	94	92	91	89
Morocco	na	**80**	85	75	86	79	66	77	89	95	71	85	84	77	82	93
Netherlands	na	**92**	91	93	99	95	85	86	94	95	90	91	97	83	94	93
New Zealand	na	**na**	na	na	na	na	na	na	na	na	na	na	na	na	na	na
Nigeria	na	**96**	98	94	97	95	90	94	97	97	96	97	96	96	96	97
Northern Ireland	na	**93**	93	93	99	93	89	90	95	96	90	94	96	93	92	95
Norway	na	**na**	na	na	na	na	na	na	na	na	na	na	na	na	na	na
Pakistan	na	**69**	73	65	74	65	73	65	73	79	67	70	67	69	70	50
Peru	na	**79**	85	74	88	75	70	70	77	88	72	84	86	73	81	82
Philippines	na	**79**	84	75	85	78	74	78	78	83	76	80	83	80	79	84
Poland	na	**67**	70	65	89	70	51	62	73	75	59	73	72	62	70	67
Portugal	na	**78**	82	75	89	74	75	73	89	84	63	78	83	72	81	90
Puerto Rico	na	**70**	77	66	81	71	64	58	68	73	63	73	73	68	72	66
Romania	na	**61**	68	53	91	60	44	51	64	70	49	61	67	57	63	73
Russian Fed.	na	**66**	71	62	88	70	48	48	67	75	60	65	73	62	72	61
Serbia	na	**92**	94	90	97	93	88	89	93	96	89	92	94	89	94	94
Singapore	na	**82**	87	78	95	71	67	77	86	82	77	81	86	77	84	90
Slovakia	na	**80**	81	78	90	78	74	78	80	82	78	79	80	78	82	88
Slovenia	na	**83**	87	80	95	84	74	75	86	88	79	81	91	79	84	88
South Africa	na	**82**	84	80	87	80	73	77	88	92	76	89	84	80	84	76
Spain	na	**86**	91	82	96	89	78	80	93	92	81	87	88	84	87	93
Sweden	na	**95**	94	96	98	95	92	92	96	95	95	95	95	88	95	97
Switzerland	na	**na**	na	na	na	na	na	na	na	na	na	na	na	na	na	na
Taiwan	na	**na**	na	na	na	na	na	na	na	na	na	na	na	na	na	na
Tanzania	na	**85**	87	82	91	83	80	81	88	91	83	84	86	83	85	100
Turkey	na	**92**	93	91	93	92	88	91	91	96	91	92	94	91	92	92
Uganda	na	**96**	98	94	98	95	94	93	97	100	96	95	99	95	97	94
Ukraine	na	**72**	77	67	91	73	59	61	71	79	66	71	79	69	75	76
United States	na	**92**	92	93	96	91	91	91	91	94	89	94	94	93	91	94
Uruguay	na	**na**	na	na	na	na	na	na	na	na	na	na	na	na	na	na
Venezuela	na	**77**	82	73	83	79	63	71	77	85	74	80	80	77	77	79
Vietnam	na	**72**	77	67	80	71	66	66	79	78	66	69	79	63	76	64
Zimbabwe	na	**87**	90	85	88	86	85	87	87	100	89	87	88	87	89	80
Total	na	**81**	84	78	90	81	73	76	83	87	77	81	84	77	83	86

RANKING	
Country	2000
Indonesia	97
Bosnia and Herz.	97
Nigeria	96
Uganda	96
Sweden	95
Ireland	93
Northern Ireland	93
Great Britain	93
United States	92
Netherlands	92
Greece	92
Serbia	92
Montenegro	92
Turkey	92
Macedonia	91
Denmark	91
Croatia	90
Canada	90
Iceland	89
Finland	88
Austria	88
Luxembourg	88
Zimbabwe	87
France	87
Spain	86
Egypt	86
Germany	86
Tanzania	85
Bangladesh	84
Slovenia	83
Bulgaria	83
Italy	82
Singapore	82
South Africa	82
Algeria	81
Belgium	81
Czech Republic	81
Belarus	81
Morocco	80
Slovakia	80
Peru	79
Philippines	79
Korea, South	78
Portugal	78
Jordan	78
Estonia	77
Venezuela	77
Argentina	75
Moldova	75
Iran	74
India	72
Vietnam	72
Latvia	72
Lithuania	72
Ukraine	72
Puerto Rico	70
Pakistan	69
Albania	69
Poland	67
Hungary	66
Japan	66
Russian Fed.	66
Mexico	64
China	61
Malta	61
Romania	61
Chile	59
Total	81

A059) SPEND TIME WITH COLLEAGUES FROM WORK

I'm going to ask how of often you do various things? Spend time socially with colleagues from work or your profession

Weekly / Once or twice a month (%) (WVS: V29; EVS: V49)

Country	Wave		Gender		Age			Education			Income			Values		
	1990	2000	Male	Female	16-29	30-49	50+	Lower	Middle	Upper	Lower	Middle	Upper	Mat	Mixed	Postm.
Albania	na	**57**	69	45	63	61	45	50	57	74	54	59	58	51	61	71
Algeria	na	**54**	64	43	52	58	50	41	60	55	52	55	57	50	57	52
Argentina	na	**37**	50	26	46	40	27	33	42	48	32	35	46	29	38	45
Armenia	na	**na**	na	na	na	na	na	na	na	na	na	na	na	na	na	na
Australia	na	**na**	na	na	na	na	na	na	na	na	na	na	na	na	na	na
Austria	na	**36**	45	28	54	44	19	34	37	42	26	35	43	26	37	38
Azerbaijan	na	**na**	na	na	na	na	na	na	na	na	na	na	na	na	na	na
Bangladesh	na	**62**	74	45	50	68	72	61	60	66	67	61	58	64	60	56
Belarus	na	**56**	65	49	70	58	41	42	61	61	50	58	65	49	60	81
Belgium	na	**35**	34	35	54	33	23	24	32	42	33	33	35	30	35	36
Bosnia and Herz.	na	**51**	57	44	50	65	33	29	53	62	30	55	59	53	48	53
Brazil	na	**na**	na	na	na	na	na	na	na	na	na	na	na	na	na	na
Bulgaria	na	**57**	63	52	76	71	34	38	61	73	35	64	71	53	63	52
Canada	na	**42**	47	36	58	45	29	31	41	51	34	42	48	44	39	46
Chile	na	**34**	38	31	49	29	29	25	36	49	34	31	38	27	36	40
China	na	**73**	76	69	73	77	62	69	75	84	69	76	78	75	74	75
Colombia	na	**na**	na	na	na	na	na	na	na	na	na	na	na	na	na	na
Croatia	na	**53**	62	42	71	54	38	37	58	65	44	54	54	36	55	63
Czech Republic	na	**41**	45	36	58	44	28	39	41	48	33	39	49	35	42	51
Denmark	na	**37**	38	36	56	37	24	32	42	42	37	35	40	44	36	41
Dominican Rep.	na	**na**	na	na	na	na	na	na	na	na	na	na	na	na	na	na
Egypt	na	**70**	76	49	66	75	64	63	75	76	68	75	73	68	73	71
El Salvador	na	**na**	na	na	na	na	na	na	na	na	na	na	na	na	na	na
Estonia	na	**42**	40	43	61	43	25	40	43	41	43	37	43	40	43	50
Finland	na	**47**	50	45	68	50	33	44	50	51	52	45	48	45	49	44
France	na	**31**	36	27	50	32	21	25	37	41	28	30	32	21	31	46
Georgia	na	**na**	na	na	na	na	na	na	na	na	na	na	na	na	na	na
Germany	na	**38**	40	37	53	43	23	30	45	42	27	43	48	38	39	38
Great Britain	na	**43**	49	37	72	41	24	31	49	57	34	39	54	na	na	na
Greece	na	**56**	56	56	68	51	44	41	53	61	49	57	63	62	55	57
Hungary	na	**na**	na	na	na	na	na	na	na	na	na	na	na	na	na	na
Iceland	na	**40**	41	38	59	36	26	40	41	37	41	37	40	37	40	40
India	na	**62**	71	49	64	65	53	59	64	66	66	60	61	66	66	73
Indonesia	na	**85**	89	82	88	89	81	83	85	89	86	85	89	85	86	93
Iran	na	**50**	60	37	49	53	47	47	47	60	47	53	48	41	55	47
Ireland	na	**53**	59	45	75	47	38	36	57	65	39	48	60	51	53	51
Israel	na	**na**	na	na	na	na	na	na	na	na	na	na	na	na	na	na
Italy	na	**39**	47	30	55	40	27	31	41	51	32	41	46	30	38	45
Japan	na	**46**	52	41	60	46	41	42	44	54	39	49	53	47	47	47
Jordan	na	**36**	63	10	36	42	22	31	36	47	31	43	36	33	39	39
Korea, South	na	**64**	70	58	79	60	54	21	62	71	58	69	66	58	68	76
Latvia	na	**na**	na	na	na	na	na	na	na	na	na	na	na	na	na	na
Lithuania	na	**28**	32	24	41	31	14	13	31	35	17	20	37	19	31	39
Luxembourg	na	**na**	na	na	na	na	na	na	na	na	na	na	na	na	na	na
Macedonia	na	**59**	66	51	65	63	46	41	65	75	45	61	74	55	62	71
Malta	na	**24**	26	21	42	19	11	8	27	31	18	14	33	22	25	24
Mexico	na	**45**	56	35	54	42	36	35	54	64	41	46	56	44	47	48
Moldova	na	**50**	52	48	60	54	37	36	52	60	45	46	59	45	55	57
Montenegro	na	**65**	74	55	82	72	46	44	75	85	58	67	76	59	71	66
Morocco	na	**50**	63	37	50	53	41	49	51	64	50	60	50	45	57	47
Netherlands	na	**45**	45	45	67	45	29	33	45	55	46	43	49	35	47	43
New Zealand	na	**na**	na	na	na	na	na	na	na	na	na	na	na	na	na	na
Nigeria	na	**86**	90	82	85	88	79	84	85	91	86	87	85	85	86	90
Northern Ireland	na	**35**	37	33	54	39	22	26	39	48	25	29	47	23	41	35
Norway	na	**na**	na	na	na	na	na	na	na	na	na	na	na	na	na	na
Pakistan	na	**31**	56	4	25	31	44	38	24	23	36	35	18	36	25	27
Peru	na	**64**	74	54	66	63	59	59	60	72	59	66	70	54	65	71
Philippines	na	**57**	70	44	53	63	52	57	56	59	55	56	60	54	59	60
Poland	na	**na**	na	na	na	na	na	na	na	na	na	na	na	na	na	na
Portugal	na	**53**	66	40	76	55	36	43	71	73	20	54	71	43	60	67
Puerto Rico	na	**39**	48	34	51	45	30	22	36	43	35	40	42	31	42	37
Romania	na	**51**	59	39	72	45	32	58	49	53	48	54	50	52	50	56
Russian Fed.	na	**37**	45	30	56	41	18	20	37	44	30	35	43	33	42	44
Serbia	na	**62**	70	55	77	70	48	47	67	75	49	67	72	57	68	69
Singapore	na	**51**	58	44	53	54	36	35	56	70	37	51	61	45	54	43
Slovakia	na	**na**	na	na	na	na	na	na	na	na	na	na	na	na	na	na
Slovenia	na	**50**	61	40	71	54	29	32	57	53	42	47	57	37	51	61
South Africa	na	**46**	55	37	42	57	28	44	48	63	40	49	56	40	50	55
Spain	na	**47**	56	37	67	52	28	35	57	63	33	50	57	40	46	63
Sweden	na	**54**	56	51	66	50	51	44	56	56	59	54	50	39	51	65
Switzerland	na	**na**	na	na	na	na	na	na	na	na	na	na	na	na	na	na
Taiwan	na	**na**	na	na	na	na	na	na	na	na	na	na	na	na	na	na
Tanzania	na	**77**	79	73	71	80	79	73	76	90	72	81	89	72	78	88
Turkey	na	**52**	73	27	55	55	39	43	62	80	47	54	64	49	54	60
Uganda	na	**61**	75	48	56	70	48	55	62	75	76	67	73	57	62	66
Ukraine	na	**44**	54	35	61	51	25	20	44	53	32	43	59	38	48	50
United States	na	**54**	59	49	66	52	46	56	52	54	49	59	54	50	54	56
Uruguay	na	**na**	na	na	na	na	na	na	na	na	na	na	na	na	na	na
Venezuela	na	**51**	58	43	58	50	37	39	49	67	49	51	54	47	51	55
Vietnam	na	**72**	76	69	78	78	59	67	78	78	68	72	76	61	77	70
Zimbabwe	na	**52**	60	45	46	59	53	49	56	100	57	54	58	51	53	54
Total	na	**51**	59	43	59	54	37	44	53	58	47	52	55	49	52	52

RANKING

Country	2000
Nigeria	86
Indonesia	85
Tanzania	77
China	73
Vietnam	72
Egypt	70
Montenegro	65
Peru	64
Korea, South	64
Serbia	62
India	62
Bangladesh	62
Uganda	61
Macedonia	59
Bulgaria	57
Philippines	57
Albania	57
Belarus	56
Greece	56
United States	54
Sweden	54
Algeria	54
Portugal	53
Croatia	53
Ireland	53
Turkey	52
Zimbabwe	52
Romania	51
Singapore	51
Bosnia and Herz.	51
Venezuela	51
Morocco	50
Slovenia	50
Moldova	50
Iran	50
Finland	47
Spain	47
Japan	46
South Africa	46
Netherlands	45
Mexico	45
Ukraine	44
Great Britain	43
Estonia	42
Canada	42
Czech Republic	41
Iceland	40
Puerto Rico	39
Italy	39
Germany	38
Argentina	37
Denmark	37
Russian Fed.	37
Austria	36
Jordan	36
Northern Ireland	35
Belgium	35
Chile	34
France	31
Pakistan	31
Lithuania	28
Malta	24
Total	51

A060) SPEND TIME WITH PEOPLE AT YOUR CHURCH, MOSQUE OR SYNAGOGUE

I'm going to ask how of often you do various things? Spend time with people at your church, mosque or synagogue

(WVS: V30; EVS: V50)

Weekly / Once or twice a month (%)

Country	Wave		Gender		Age			Education			Income			Values		
	1990	2000	Male	Female	16-29	30-49	50+	Lower	Middle	Upper	Lower	Middle	Upper	Mat	Mixed	Postm.
Albania	na	**28**	24	31	22	25	37	32	25	22	31	27	25	26	28	20
Algeria	na	**40**	57	21	36	36	55	44	38	37	40	39	42	36	43	38
Argentina	na	**32**	22	40	22	35	39	35	27	30	37	32	27	31	34	27
Armenia	na	**na**	na	na	na	na	na	na	na	na	na	na	na	na	na	na
Australia	na	**na**	na	na	na	na	na	na	na	na	na	na	na	na	na	na
Austria	na	**26**	26	26	19	29	27	25	24	33	23	28	27	19	27	27
Azerbaijan	na	**na**	na	na	na	na	na	na	na	na	na	na	na	na	na	na
Bangladesh	na	**61**	90	24	49	67	81	54	66	74	49	65	68	57	65	60
Belarus	na	**32**	23	39	29	25	44	46	29	20	40	31	20	33	33	21
Belgium	na	**21**	20	22	20	17	26	22	20	23	29	24	15	18	22	20
Bosnia and Herz.	na	**33**	31	34	35	32	32	40	31	31	34	32	31	29	34	30
Brazil	na	**na**	na	na	na	na	na	na	na	na	na	na	na	na	na	na
Bulgaria	na	**13**	13	13	9	11	16	19	9	12	17	15	6	13	13	14
Canada	na	**29**	25	33	16	27	39	35	24	31	31	32	22	28	32	23
Chile	na	**33**	28	38	25	31	44	36	31	31	40	30	28	31	37	25
China	na	**43**	46	40	50	46	30	30	53	49	32	49	51	43	49	56
Colombia	na	**na**	na	na	na	na	na	na	na	na	na	na	na	na	na	na
Croatia	na	**52**	43	61	47	53	55	61	48	50	60	53	49	61	52	47
Czech Republic	na	**12**	10	14	11	7	16	14	9	12	16	11	7	14	11	14
Denmark	na	**9**	7	11	5	8	12	8	5	12	12	6	8	5	9	5
Dominican Rep.	na	**na**	na	na	na	na	na	na	na	na	na	na	na	na	na	na
Egypt	na	**57**	78	35	51	57	67	53	58	68	54	56	63	54	60	63
El Salvador	na	**na**	na	na	na	na	na	na	na	na	na	na	na	na	na	na
Estonia	na	**24**	22	26	20	16	32	30	19	24	31	23	26	28	23	na
Finland	na	**23**	19	27	16	21	30	25	21	24	28	23	19	18	25	28
France	na	**9**	7	10	6	7	11	9	8	9	10	9	8	9	9	6
Georgia	na	**na**	na	na	na	na	na	na	na	na	na	na	na	na	na	na
Germany	na	**30**	25	33	24	23	39	33	26	34	31	32	28	21	32	37
Great Britain	na	**20**	17	23	12	17	27	16	19	26	17	20	25	na	na	na
Greece	na	**23**	22	24	18	22	36	38	26	19	27	22	22	22	25	18
Hungary	na	**na**	na	na	na	na	na	na	na	na	na	na	na	na	na	na
Iceland	na	**11**	10	11	8	11	12	13	8	11	12	11	8	13	10	8
India	na	**61**	60	62	57	62	63	61	61	62	55	59	65	60	62	67
Indonesia	na	**90**	94	86	86	91	91	91	91	89	89	92	89	90	90	89
Iran	na	**49**	53	45	46	48	62	59	46	43	50	56	44	48	50	37
Ireland	na	**44**	39	48	25	40	61	54	37	40	59	38	37	42	44	39
Israel	na	**na**	na	na	na	na	na	na	na	na	na	na	na	na	na	na
Italy	na	**24**	18	31	18	22	30	28	21	22	29	21	22	33	24	21
Japan	na	**9**	7	11	3	9	11	10	11	5	10	9	9	8	9	10
Jordan	na	**46**	79	13	37	44	66	48	44	42	43	53	41	46	47	38
Korea, South	na	**33**	28	38	26	35	36	32	35	30	29	34	37	33	33	39
Latvia	na	**na**	na	na	na	na	na	na	na	na	na	na	na	na	na	na
Lithuania	na	**15**	8	21	11	6	25	26	11	10	20	16	9	15	13	23
Luxembourg	na	**na**	na	na	na	na	na	na	na	na	na	na	na	na	na	na
Macedonia	na	**24**	29	19	22	25	24	33	20	20	25	25	21	22	25	29
Malta	na	**60**	53	66	45	59	71	75	54	54	64	60	58	67	57	55
Mexico	na	**56**	53	58	51	57	61	61	49	50	62	56	52	58	58	49
Moldova	na	**36**	26	45	25	30	52	53	32	28	43	38	30	40	30	37
Montenegro	na	**16**	17	16	14	17	17	17	15	19	19	14	14	16	16	20
Morocco	na	**35**	53	19	26	37	57	38	25	24	39	39	33	35	36	37
Netherlands	na	**20**	19	21	15	12	32	25	18	18	23	21	14	28	20	17
New Zealand	na	**na**	na	na	na	na	na	na	na	na	na	na	na	na	na	na
Nigeria	na	**92**	94	90	92	92	89	88	95	93	91	93	92	90	94	92
Northern Ireland	na	**39**	38	39	31	28	52	42	32	43	35	38	42	42	41	33
Norway	na	**na**	na	na	na	na	na	na	na	na	na	na	na	na	na	na
Pakistan	na	**55**	83	18	57	51	64	51	58	64	50	63	49	60	51	42
Peru	na	**58**	51	65	50	64	65	64	62	48	62	59	50	59	58	57
Philippines	na	**64**	61	67	61	65	65	60	64	68	62	66	63	60	66	69
Poland	na	**na**	na	na	na	na	na	na	na	na	na	na	na	na	na	na
Portugal	na	**46**	40	51	36	43	54	50	37	37	58	45	41	51	44	34
Puerto Rico	na	**65**	60	67	53	56	77	81	64	62	69	67	59	60	67	61
Romania	na	**30**	24	36	18	23	42	47	23	15	38	32	21	35	24	22
Russian Fed.	na	**8**	4	12	6	5	13	16	7	9	12	7	6	9	7	9
Serbia	na	**21**	17	25	22	18	22	25	16	23	25	19	21	20	22	19
Singapore	na	**36**	34	39	35	38	37	35	37	39	39	35	38	38	37	27
Slovakia	na	**na**	na	na	na	na	na	na	na	na	na	na	na	na	na	na
Slovenia	na	**24**	23	24	20	20	30	31	23	12	29	24	15	27	23	21
South Africa	na	**66**	57	76	62	66	76	68	63	64	71	66	59	69	64	64
Spain	na	**29**	20	38	15	23	43	36	22	23	38	27	25	40	28	16
Sweden	na	**21**	18	23	17	20	24	24	20	20	23	20	17	31	20	21
Switzerland	na	**na**	na	na	na	na	na	na	na	na	na	na	na	na	na	na
Taiwan	na	**na**	na	na	na	na	na	na	na	na	na	na	na	na	na	na
Tanzania	na	**83**	83	84	83	83	84	84	84	81	83	86	79	85	83	88
Turkey	na	**na**	na	na	na	na	na	na	na	na	na	na	na	na	na	na
Uganda	na	**77**	86	70	77	77	83	72	79	84	81	78	82	76	78	82
Ukraine	na	**16**	8	23	11	13	22	38	14	8	16	16	16	17	13	22
United States	na	**52**	45	59	42	52	61	53	51	53	52	53	50	62	52	48
Uruguay	na	**na**	na	na	na	na	na	na	na	na	na	na	na	na	na	na
Venezuela	na	**37**	32	42	31	39	45	42	34	37	43	39	33	40	36	34
Vietnam	na	**18**	14	21	17	16	21	21	13	15	19	14	20	12	19	19
Zimbabwe	na	**82**	70	92	82	84	77	83	80	52	76	87	84	80	82	92
Total	na	**39**	39	38	38	38	41	42	36	38	41	40	36	42	39	34

RANKING

Country	2000
Nigeria	92
Indonesia	90
Tanzania	83
Zimbabwe	82
Uganda	77
South Africa	66
Puerto Rico	65
Philippines	64
Bangladesh	61
India	61
Malta	60
Peru	58
Egypt	57
Mexico	56
Pakistan	55
Croatia	52
United States	52
Iran	49
Portugal	46
Jordan	46
Ireland	44
China	43
Algeria	40
Northern Ireland	39
Venezuela	37
Singapore	36
Moldova	36
Morocco	35
Korea, South	33
Chile	33
Bosnia and Herz.	33
Belarus	32
Argentina	32
Romania	30
Germany	30
Spain	29
Canada	29
Albania	28
Austria	26
Estonia	24
Italy	24
Macedonia	24
Slovenia	24
Finland	23
Greece	23
Belgium	21
Sweden	21
Serbia	21
Netherlands	20
Great Britain	20
Vietnam	18
Ukraine	16
Montenegro	16
Lithuania	15
Bulgaria	13
Czech Republic	12
Iceland	11
Japan	9
Denmark	9
France	9
Russian Fed.	8
Total	39

A061) SPEND TIME WITH PEOPLE AT SPORT, CULTURE, COMMUNAL ORGANIZATION

I'm going to ask how of often you do various things?

Spend time socially with people at sports clubs or voluntary or service organization

Weekly / Once or twice a month (%)

(WVS: V31; EVS: V51)

Country	Wave		Gender		Age			Education			Income			Values		
	1990	2000	Male	Female	16-29	30-49	50+	Lower	Middle	Upper	Lower	Middle	Upper	Mat	Mixed	Postm.
Albania	na	**20**	28	13	29	19	14	17	21	28	20	25	17	18	22	26
Algeria	na	**24**	32	15	29	22	15	14	25	30	22	19	29	18	29	18
Argentina	na	**24**	29	19	24	26	21	20	28	33	21	21	30	21	23	27
Armenia	na	**na**	na	na	na	na	na	na	na	na	na	na	na	na	na	na
Australia	na	**na**	na	na	na	na	na	na	na	na	na	na	na	na	na	na
Austria	na	**42**	50	34	48	45	36	34	49	51	36	43	45	31	43	44
Azerbaijan	na	**na**	na	na	na	na	na	na	na	na	na	na	na	na	na	na
Bangladesh	na	**31**	45	15	27	34	38	24	37	44	21	30	45	31	33	25
Belarus	na	**18**	24	14	33	15	8	6	21	24	11	20	25	15	20	33
Belgium	na	**50**	55	45	56	51	47	41	51	55	37	49	57	45	51	55
Bosnia and Herz.	na	**20**	28	14	30	20	11	8	19	35	13	21	23	14	22	35
Brazil	na	**na**	na	na	na	na	na	na	na	na	na	na	na	na	na	na
Bulgaria	na	**24**	29	18	39	29	13	10	25	38	13	29	29	19	29	22
Canada	na	**39**	40	38	39	41	37	32	40	44	35	38	43	42	38	40
Chile	na	**25**	28	22	29	24	22	21	27	26	25	25	24	23	27	23
China	na	**5**	4	6	6	5	3	3	6	7	2	7	6	5	6	6
Colombia	na	**na**	na	na	na	na	na	na	na	na	na	na	na	na	na	na
Croatia	na	**40**	52	26	52	39	32	30	42	53	31	41	40	30	39	54
Czech Republic	na	**30**	38	23	45	30	23	28	30	40	25	29	36	28	30	43
Denmark	na	**59**	61	56	61	60	55	55	64	62	54	59	64	54	60	57
Dominican Rep.	na	**na**	na	na	na	na	na	na	na	na	na	na	na	na	na	na
Egypt	na	**18**	24	10	20	18	14	8	23	33	11	14	24	12	22	29
El Salvador	na	**na**	na	na	na	na	na	na	na	na	na	na	na	na	na	na
Estonia	na	**34**	36	32	58	29	23	28	34	42	24	32	40	26	38	50
Finland	na	**36**	38	35	42	41	28	32	44	36	33	40	38	36	36	39
France	na	**34**	36	32	41	30	33	30	30	45	32	36	37	30	34	40
Georgia	na	**na**	na	na	na	na	na	na	na	na	na	na	na	na	na	na
Germany	na	**57**	61	55	63	59	53	50	63	68	42	61	68	51	59	62
Great Britain	na	**39**	42	36	39	38	41	35	41	44	34	33	47	na	na	na
Greece	na	**30**	33	27	30	30	28	19	31	30	27	29	34	32	29	28
Hungary	na	**na**	na	na	na	na	na	na	na	na	na	na	na	na	na	na
Iceland	na	**36**	38	33	38	36	33	33	39	36	26	43	39	32	37	35
India	na	**25**	30	17	31	23	21	20	22	35	26	20	28	21	29	25
Indonesia	na	**57**	67	48	59	61	53	48	60	62	58	59	59	57	58	75
Iran	na	**18**	20	16	19	17	17	15	18	21	15	20	19	14	19	16
Ireland	na	**50**	54	45	58	46	48	41	52	60	45	49	57	51	48	54
Israel	na	**na**	na	na	na	na	na	na	na	na	na	na	na	na	na	na
Italy	na	**31**	38	25	43	31	24	22	36	42	23	34	39	25	30	36
Japan	na	**25**	25	26	14	20	35	26	25	26	24	27	27	28	24	31
Jordan	na	**8**	13	3	13	5	4	3	10	14	5	7	13	6	8	17
Korea, South	na	**20**	20	19	16	20	23	14	20	20	17	21	21	17	22	23
Latvia	na	**na**	na	na	na	na	na	na	na	na	na	na	na	na	na	na
Lithuania	na	**15**	16	14	31	13	4	4	17	23	9	13	17	15	14	20
Luxembourg	na	**na**	na	na	na	na	na	na	na	na	na	na	na	na	na	na
Macedonia	na	**17**	24	11	24	20	8	11	19	25	14	20	18	18	16	31
Malta	na	**46**	52	40	46	45	48	44	47	45	41	53	56	45	47	45
Mexico	na	**27**	32	23	30	28	22	23	31	40	25	27	37	26	27	39
Moldova	na	**15**	18	12	23	14	9	8	15	21	12	14	19	11	18	19
Montenegro	na	**26**	36	16	50	26	10	11	33	41	17	22	31	17	33	41
Morocco	na	**14**	18	10	20	12	4	9	30	36	8	21	15	11	16	23
Netherlands	na	**57**	60	54	63	54	57	50	59	60	58	60	53	51	57	60
New Zealand	na	**na**	na	na	na	na	na	na	na	na	na	na	na	na	na	na
Nigeria	na	**53**	62	43	57	50	32	45	55	62	50	51	59	48	55	56
Northern Ireland	na	**34**	41	28	39	29	37	29	36	46	30	34	41	34	35	37
Norway	na	**na**	na	na	na	na	na	na	na	na	na	na	na	na	na	na
Pakistan	na	**20**	23	16	15	22	21	22	16	22	21	19	20	22	18	8
Peru	na	**39**	48	30	41	40	31	28	39	46	34	40	46	29	41	44
Philippines	na	**33**	42	23	35	31	32	25	31	44	29	30	41	33	34	23
Poland	na	**na**	na	na	na	na	na	na	na	na	na	na	na	na	na	na
Portugal	na	**28**	41	16	34	28	25	22	38	45	15	28	40	21	34	33
Puerto Rico	na	**22**	29	18	27	21	21	20	19	24	21	22	23	24	20	27
Romania	na	**11**	14	8	21	7	8	5	10	17	5	4	17	7	13	14
Russian Fed.	na	**13**	16	10	29	10	5	6	12	19	10	11	15	10	15	20
Serbia	na	**25**	39	12	41	28	15	11	30	37	16	27	32	19	30	41
Singapore	na	**25**	31	19	34	19	10	18	27	37	18	23	31	18	27	30
Slovakia	na	**na**	na	na	na	na	na	na	na	na	na	na	na	na	na	na
Slovenia	na	**34**	44	25	51	32	23	17	39	42	21	34	46	28	34	39
South Africa	na	**38**	43	32	43	37	29	34	42	50	34	41	42	32	41	56
Spain	na	**25**	30	19	32	25	19	16	33	36	21	23	33	21	25	32
Sweden	na	**46**	47	44	57	49	37	42	50	43	41	50	48	43	46	47
Switzerland	na	**na**	na	na	na	na	na	na	na	na	na	na	na	na	na	na
Taiwan	na	**na**	na	na	na	na	na	na	na	na	na	na	na	na	na	na
Tanzania	na	**49**	52	45	52	47	49	47	51	50	48	49	46	45	51	50
Turkey	na	**15**	20	8	17	13	11	7	23	29	6	19	24	12	15	20
Uganda	na	**56**	73	40	61	54	36	43	60	70	56	60	67	52	55	67
Ukraine	na	**14**	18	11	29	13	6	6	12	23	8	15	20	9	17	35
United States	na	**48**	51	45	51	48	46	50	44	49	44	46	53	47	47	50
Uruguay	na	**na**	na	na	na	na	na	na	na	na	na	na	na	na	na	na
Venezuela	na	**31**	44	18	39	29	18	22	33	38	30	30	35	28	31	41
Vietnam	na	**30**	37	23	39	27	29	28	31	39	25	27	37	29	30	36
Zimbabwe	na	**31**	37	27	34	32	24	26	38	32	27	31	42	30	34	24
Total	na	**31**	37	25	36	30	27	25	33	38	27	31	35	25	33	39

RANKING	
Country	2000
Denmark	59
Germany	57
Indonesia	57
Netherlands	57
Uganda	56
Nigeria	53
Belgium	50
Ireland	50
Tanzania	49
United States	48
Malta	46
Sweden	46
Austria	42
Croatia	40
Canada	39
Peru	39
Great Britain	39
South Africa	38
Finland	36
Iceland	36
Northern Ireland	34
Estonia	34
Slovenia	34
France	34
Philippines	33
Bangladesh	31
Zimbabwe	31
Italy	31
Venezuela	31
Czech Republic	30
Vietnam	30
Greece	30
Portugal	28
Mexico	27
Montenegro	26
Japan	25
Singapore	25
Serbia	25
Chile	25
India	25
Spain	25
Bulgaria	24
Algeria	24
Argentina	24
Puerto Rico	22
Albania	20
Bosnia and Herz.	20
Pakistan	20
Korea, South	20
Belarus	18
Iran	18
Egypt	18
Macedonia	17
Moldova	15
Lithuania	15
Turkey	15
Morocco	14
Ukraine	14
Russian Fed.	13
Romania	11
Jordan	8
China	5
Total	31

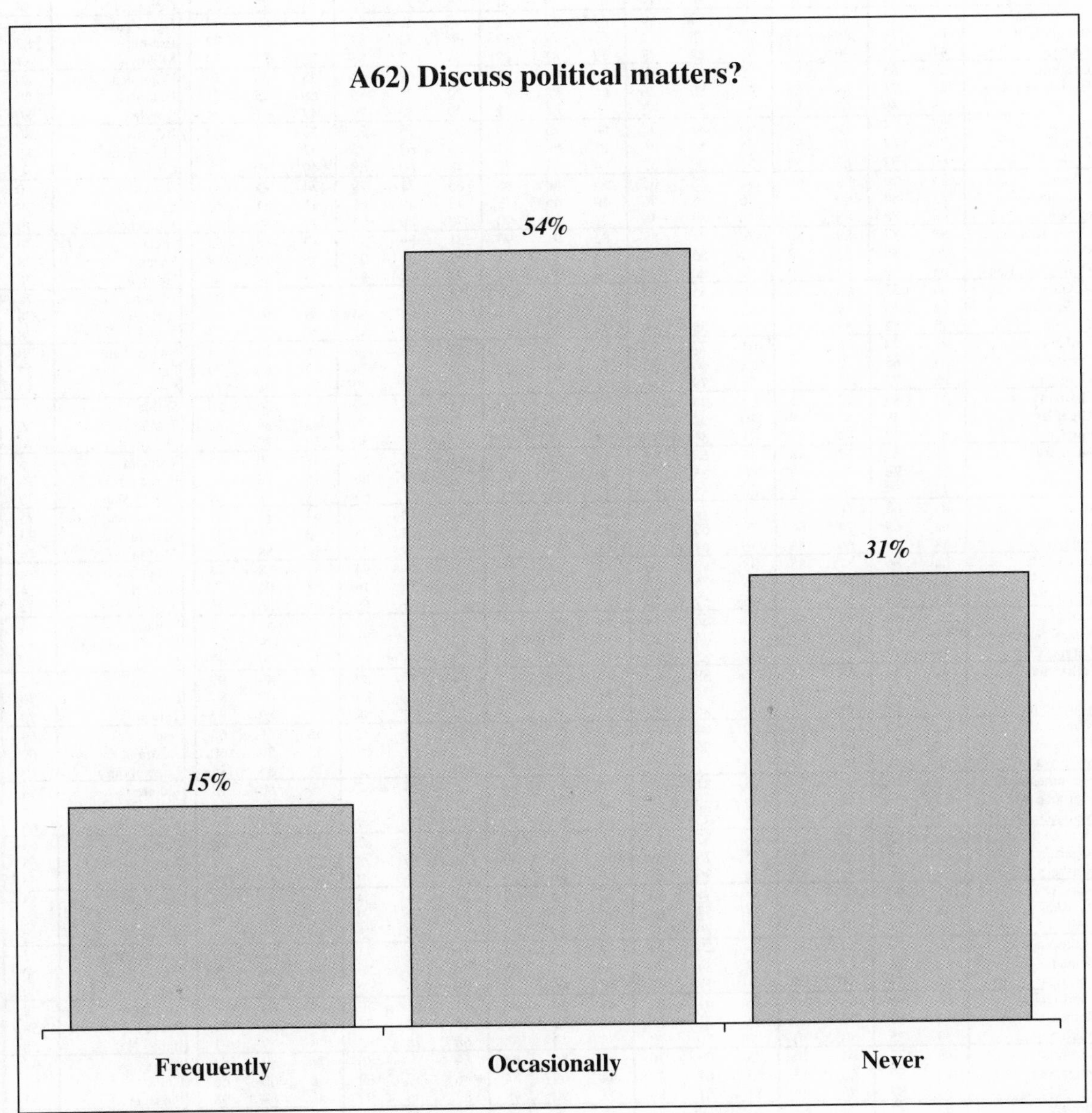
A62) Discuss political matters?
15%
54%
31%
Frequently
Occasionally
Never

A062) HOW OFTEN DISCUSSES POLITICAL MATTERS

When you get together with your friends, would you say you discuss political matters frequently, occasionally or never?

Frequently / Occasionally (%)

(WVS: V32; EVS: V7)

Country	Wave		Gender		Age			Education			Income			Values		
	1990	2000	Male	Female	16-29	30-49	50+	Lower	Middle	Upper	Lower	Middle	Upper	Mat	Mixed	Postm.
Albania	na	78	89	66	71	81	79	72	82	84	72	82	80	74	81	80
Algeria	na	74	80	68	74	77	68	57	75	84	68	80	81	66	79	86
Argentina	67	51	56	47	46	55	52	41	62	74	40	49	66	35	52	62
Armenia	na	78	83	73	72	82	79	69	77	84	78	78	79	76	80	67
Australia	na	69	72	67	56	75	75	57	65	84	64	69	83	64	67	75
Austria	69	74	79	70	63	80	74	66	79	91	66	76	80	54	73	82
Azerbaijan	na	53	61	44	51	54	50	47	47	64	47	56	59	46	63	77
Bangladesh	na	74	89	55	72	75	72	67	78	87	66	74	82	71	77	72
Belarus	91	80	86	75	78	83	78	72	82	89	74	83	83	78	83	93
Belgium	53	63	69	57	53	71	60	43	61	81	53	61	73	48	63	79
Bosnia and Herz.	na	73	80	66	61	80	76	68	72	79	70	72	79	68	75	71
Brazil	55	58	63	53	57	58	62	46	64	82	49	56	70	43	61	84
Bulgaria	88	74	79	69	64	82	72	68	75	80	71	75	78	73	77	66
Canada	75	64	70	58	58	65	66	51	60	81	54	62	75	57	62	70
Chile	60	57	62	52	58	60	52	44	61	72	48	60	68	49	57	72
China	89	70	80	60	82	68	65	55	80	88	63	71	79	74	75	87
Colombia	na	54	60	47	46	58	56	40	46	73	42	49	68	45	51	63
Croatia	na	80	85	75	76	83	78	71	84	90	72	80	84	77	80	82
Czech Republic	90	87	89	86	79	91	88	83	91	96	81	89	90	83	88	92
Denmark	79	80	82	78	77	85	77	72	87	94	72	83	94	66	79	94
Dominican Rep.	na	80	83	79	81	80	100	56	76	84	78	84	81	73	80	91
Egypt	na	57	56	59	60	55	59	58	57	57	58	58	57	57	58	62
El Salvador	na	38	49	28	42	35	37	23	45	72	19	44	64	na	na	na
Estonia	95	82	85	79	70	88	83	72	85	91	75	82	87	81	84	89
Finland	82	74	76	72	61	77	77	73	73	78	65	74	81	70	76	74
France	65	65	72	58	52	66	70	56	69	83	55	67	78	52	66	79
Georgia	na	73	74	71	58	79	80	67	72	77	74	75	70	70	74	77
Germany	94	84	92	78	82	86	83	75	90	96	74	87	90	80	86	86
Great Britain	66	49	57	40	40	52	51	39	50	74	42	48	58	na	na	na
Greece	na	79	84	75	71	86	83	69	74	85	71	82	82	75	79	82
Hungary	76	54	61	48	45	65	49	47	62	79	44	57	58	48	60	65
Iceland	78	78	79	77	66	85	79	70	81	92	70	79	86	75	78	88
India	73	58	74	36	60	57	56	42	66	81	52	51	67	58	68	69
Indonesia	na	68	78	59	81	71	60	44	69	86	63	72	73	64	73	100
Iran	na	69	74	64	76	69	51	52	70	86	65	70	74	62	75	82
Ireland	58	60	66	53	56	61	62	52	57	78	49	59	73	58	58	67
Israel	na	86	87	85	83	89	86	73	88	91	79	87	94	89	88	79
Italy	58	68	77	59	65	75	62	54	75	85	56	71	76	53	66	77
Japan	66	65	73	57	45	57	79	63	63	71	65	64	68	65	66	75
Jordan	na	50	57	44	54	53	38	36	60	69	38	56	59	41	57	65
Korea, South	88	75	82	67	70	74	80	57	75	76	72	77	75	70	79	77
Latvia	96	77	77	78	69	82	77	58	81	91	72	76	85	75	79	87
Lithuania	94	85	88	83	81	89	85	73	89	92	80	88	89	80	89	97
Luxembourg	na	69	72	66	54	74	73	53	76	82	56	72	83	65	68	81
Macedonia	na	80	89	71	72	86	78	73	82	89	76	80	88	79	82	77
Malta	na	62	69	56	60	64	63	57	63	71	57	67	72	58	65	65
Mexico	74	55	64	47	57	56	51	46	63	79	51	58	67	55	59	60
Moldova	na	81	85	78	76	87	80	72	83	87	80	82	82	78	85	86
Montenegro	na	79	90	67	75	81	79	72	81	89	86	78	82	79	80	78
Morocco	na	32	41	23	40	29	17	24	58	76	31	38	35	20	40	64
Netherlands	74	80	82	77	78	83	77	65	83	90	75	82	87	72	79	85
New Zealand	na	83	86	81	68	82	89	80	80	89	83	81	87	72	85	86
Nigeria	63	74	83	65	75	75	69	68	76	83	71	76	78	72	75	79
Northern Ireland	56	66	73	60	56	70	69	64	66	74	56	71	77	65	67	73
Norway	89	86	88	84	83	91	83	80	86	92	na	na	na	76	87	94
Pakistan	na	57	68	44	54	57	61	56	56	63	57	57	59	55	60	58
Peru	na	77	84	70	77	79	72	64	75	88	71	78	88	74	77	85
Philippines	na	76	79	74	73	79	74	74	73	84	76	76	77	75	77	79
Poland	83	76	83	71	72	84	70	68	83	95	70	80	80	68	82	79
Portugal	53	51	63	40	61	57	40	42	66	79	26	50	69	41	56	61
Puerto Rico	na	60	68	56	56	61	61	49	52	66	47	63	70	62	60	62
Romania	66	62	74	51	61	71	55	42	69	87	45	62	78	58	67	81
Russian Fed.	83	75	80	70	70	80	72	58	74	88	68	76	82	73	79	71
Serbia	na	77	84	70	73	79	76	65	80	87	69	79	86	71	82	84
Singapore	na	59	66	53	63	61	43	44	63	84	46	59	69	56	60	66
Slovakia	na	87	90	84	81	91	85	78	90	96	82	86	92	83	89	98
Slovenia	82	72	78	67	64	79	71	58	76	86	68	80	80	68	73	78
South Africa	70	62	71	51	55	69	59	58	66	79	61	63	65	53	67	75
Spain	50	55	64	46	57	63	47	44	61	78	45	58	65	47	56	71
Sweden	79	80	80	80	77	80	82	72	77	91	78	79	85	65	79	90
Switzerland	86	78	83	72	69	80	80	66	79	93	69	79	83	62	81	80
Taiwan	na	70	78	62	83	76	45	46	72	91	56	70	88	66	79	76
Tanzania	na	79	82	74	78	79	83	73	84	88	70	82	89	75	81	91
Turkey	56	54	67	41	55	54	51	43	65	83	43	59	72	47	55	66
Uganda	na	78	84	73	73	84	78	71	79	91	80	87	84	80	77	79
Ukraine	na	78	81	75	73	84	75	63	77	88	76	79	81	75	82	89
United States	72	75	78	71	65	76	80	61	70	83	66	77	82	73	74	77
Uruguay	na	53	61	47	55	58	48	42	65	77	45	51	65	45	55	57
Venezuela	na	56	62	50	54	59	55	41	57	71	44	55	69	54	55	64
Vietnam	na	75	82	68	76	76	74	69	83	83	66	75	81	70	80	76
Zimbabwe	na	48	60	37	44	54	47	47	48	100	49	47	57	43	52	50
Total	75	69	75	63	65	72	69	57	72	82	63	70	76	64	72	77

RANKING	
Country	2000
Czech Republic	87
Slovakia	87
Israel	86
Norway	86
Lithuania	85
Germany	84
New Zealand	83
Estonia	82
Moldova	81
Dominican Rep.	80
Denmark	80
Sweden	80
Belarus	80
Macedonia	80
Croatia	80
Netherlands	80
Tanzania	79
Montenegro	79
Greece	79
Iceland	78
Uganda	78
Ukraine	78
Armenia	78
Albania	78
Switzerland	78
Latvia	77
Peru	77
Serbia	77
Poland	76
Philippines	76
Vietnam	75
Russian Fed.	75
United States	75
Korea, South	75
Nigeria	74
Austria	74
Bangladesh	74
Bulgaria	74
Algeria	74
Finland	74
Bosnia and Herz.	73
Georgia	73
Slovenia	72
China	70
Taiwan	70
Iran	69
Australia	69
Luxembourg	69
Indonesia	68
Italy	68
Northern Ireland	66
France	65
Japan	65
Canada	64
Belgium	63
Malta	62
Romania	62
South Africa	62
Puerto Rico	60
Ireland	60
Singapore	59
Brazil	58
India	58
Egypt	57
Chile	57
Pakistan	57
Venezuela	56
Spain	55
Mexico	55
Colombia	54
Hungary	54
Turkey	54
Uruguay	53
Azerbaijan	53
Argentina	51
Portugal	51
Jordan	50
Great Britain	49
Zimbabwe	48
El Salvador	38
Morocco	32
Total	69

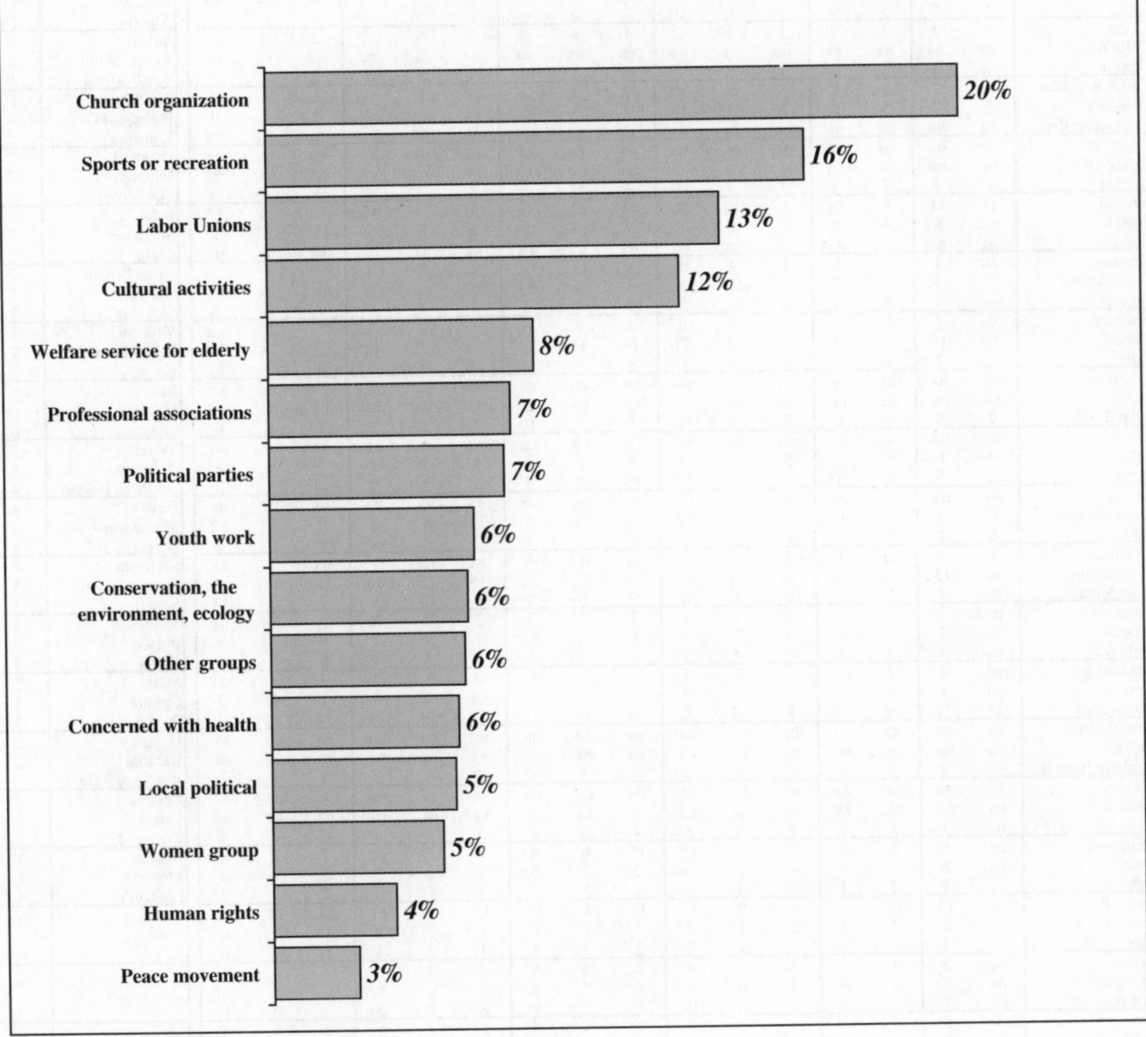
A64-A79) Voluntary organizations
do you belong to? (Belong)
Church organization
20%
Sports or recreation
16%
Labor Unions
13%
Cultural activities
12%
Welfare service for elderly
8%
Professional associations
7%
Political parties
7%
Youth work
6%
Conservation, the environment, ecology
6%
Other groups
6%
Concerned with health
6%
Local political
5%
Women group
5%
Human rights
4%
Peace movement
3%

A064) BELONG SOCIAL WELFARE SERVICE FOR ELDERLY

Please look carefully at the following list of voluntary organizations and activities and say...which, if any, do you belong to? Social welfare services for elderly, handicapped or deprived people

Belong (%)

(WVS: V39; EVS: V12)

Country	Wave		Gender		Age			Education			Income			Values		
	1990	2000	Male	Female	16-29	30-49	50+	Lower	Middle	Upper	Lower	Middle	Upper	Mat	Mixed	Postm.
Albania	na	**14**	14	14	9	13	18	11	14	19	14	11	16	12	17	5
Algeria	na	**11**	11	10	12	12	7	7	10	15	9	11	13	9	12	15
Argentina	2	**5**	4	5	2	4	9	5	5	4	5	5	5	5	5	4
Armenia	na	**na**	na	na	na	na	na	na	na	na	na	na	na	na	na	na
Australia	na	**na**	na	na	na	na	na	na	na	na	na	na	na	na	na	na
Austria	6	**7**	4	9	2	6	9	8	6	6	7	8	5	3	7	6
Azerbaijan	na	**na**	na	na	na	na	na	na	na	na	na	na	na	na	na	na
Bangladesh	na	**17**	22	11	15	19	20	14	19	25	5	21	24	15	20	11
Belarus	na	**2**	1	2	na	1	2	1	2	1	2	1	2	2	1	na
Belgium	12	**13**	10	15	10	10	16	12	11	15	16	13	11	11	12	14
Bosnia and Herz.	na	**2**	1	2	1	1	3	2	1	2	1	2	1	2	1	4
Brazil	10	**na**	na	na	na	na	na	na	na	na	na	na	na	na	na	na
Bulgaria	4	**1**	2	1	2	1	1	na	2	3	1	1	2	1	1	na
Canada	8	**13**	10	16	7	11	20	16	11	15	17	13	11	14	14	13
Chile	5	**7**	5	9	5	6	10	7	6	9	8	5	7	7	6	7
China	4	**3**	3	3	3	3	2	1	4	7	1	6	2	2	4	6
Colombia	na	**na**	na	na	na	na	na	na	na	na	na	na	na	na	na	na
Croatia	na	**2**	3	2	1	3	2	3	1	4	1	3	2	2	2	1
Czech Republic	na	**7**	5	8	3	5	10	7	6	7	9	6	5	9	6	5
Denmark	6	**7**	5	8	2	3	13	7	3	6	11	5	2	5	7	4
Dominican Rep.	na	**na**	na	na	na	na	na	na	na	na	na	na	na	na	na	na
Egypt	na	**na**	na	na	na	na	na	na	na	na	na	na	na	na	na	na
El Salvador	na	**na**	na	na	na	na	na	na	na	na	na	na	na	na	na	na
Estonia	2	**3**	2	5	3	3	4	4	2	5	4	3	4	3	3	na
Finland	11	**11**	8	14	5	10	16	11	11	16	10	15	12	10	13	12
France	7	**6**	4	7	2	5	8	4	5	9	6	6	7	5	6	7
Georgia	na	**na**	na	na	na	na	na	na	na	na	na	na	na	na	na	na
Germany	10	**4**	2	5	2	4	5	3	5	1	4	3	4	3	4	5
Great Britain	7	**7**	6	7	3	5	8	5	4	13	10	6	6	na	na	na
Greece	na	**7**	6	7	6	6	9	9	7	6	4	7	7	8	6	5
Hungary	2	**2**	1	2	1	3	2	1	2	6	1	2	3	1	3	na
Iceland	16	**17**	16	19	5	18	27	16	18	19	13	20	18	17	18	17
India	na	**7**	9	5	8	6	8	6	6	12	10	5	8	4	11	11
Indonesia	na	**na**	na	na	na	na	na	na	na	na	na	na	na	na	na	na
Iran	na	**na**	na	na	na	na	na	na	na	na	na	na	na	na	na	na
Ireland	7	**6**	4	8	5	3	10	5	5	10	8	4	7	7	6	6
Israel	na	**na**	na	na	na	na	na	na	na	na	na	na	na	na	na	na
Italy	4	**6**	5	7	5	6	7	6	7	8	5	7	7	7	6	6
Japan	2	**9**	9	10	2	4	17	18	9	8	12	8	9	14	8	10
Jordan	na	**na**	na	na	na	na	na	na	na	na	na	na	na	na	na	na
Korea, South	6	**9**	10	9	5	11	12	14	11	7	11	8	9	9	10	12
Latvia	2	**2**	2	1	na	2	2	1	1	3	2	2	na	1	2	4
Lithuania	1	**1**	na	1	2	na	na	na	1	1	na	na	1	na	1	na
Luxembourg	na	**15**	12	17	10	14	19	13	13	22	15	15	15	13	15	17
Macedonia	na	**7**	7	8	6	8	6	9	6	9	4	10	8	7	7	14
Malta	na	**2**	2	3	1	2	4	3	2	3	2	2	3	3	3	na
Mexico	5	**7**	6	8	4	7	11	8	6	9	7	9	7	9	7	7
Moldova	na	**4**	3	4	4	4	3	3	3	5	2	5	4	4	5	2
Montenegro	na	**4**	4	4	5	5	3	1	6	8	1	5	7	4	5	5
Morocco	na	**1**	1	1	1	1	2	1	2	3	na	1	6	1	2	2
Netherlands	15	**21**	19	24	8	17	32	23	19	21	22	19	22	21	22	18
New Zealand	na	**na**	na	na	na	na	na	na	na	na	na	na	na	na	na	na
Nigeria	na	**na**	na	na	na	na	na	na	na	na	na	na	na	na	na	na
Northern Ireland	9	**4**	3	5	2	4	6	4	3	8	3	5	7	4	5	3
Norway	11	**na**	na	na	na	na	na	na	na	na	na	na	na	na	na	na
Pakistan	na	**na**	na	na	na	na	na	na	na	na	na	na	na	na	na	na
Peru	na	**4**	3	5	2	4	8	4	3	6	3	4	6	4	4	4
Philippines	na	**8**	8	8	5	8	13	11	6	8	7	7	10	7	8	11
Poland	na	**3**	2	4	4	1	4	2	5	6	3	3	3	2	4	2
Portugal	5	**2**	2	3	3	2	2	1	3	10	1	1	3	2	2	2
Puerto Rico	na	**12**	10	13	8	9	17	11	8	15	13	13	11	24	11	11
Romania	2	**2**	2	2	2	1	2	1	2	2	1	2	2	1	2	0
Russian Fed.	2	**2**	1	2	na	2	1	2	2	1	1	2	1	1	1	6
Serbia	na	**3**	4	3	3	4	3	2	4	6	2	3	5	2	4	6
Singapore	na	**7**	6	8	8	6	7	6	8	8	7	8	6	5	7	10
Slovakia	na	**7**	5	8	4	6	10	6	7	9	8	7	5	7	6	6
Slovenia	1	**5**	4	6	4	3	9	7	5	5	8	5	5	8	4	5
South Africa	na	**9**	8	9	5	9	16	4	13	19	4	10	12	9	9	6
Spain	3	**3**	3	3	2	3	4	3	3	5	4	3	2	4	3	4
Sweden	8	**21**	16	25	12	21	26	18	19	26	21	15	27	14	19	28
Switzerland	9	**na**	na	na	na	na	na	na	na	na	na	na	na	na	na	na
Taiwan	na	**na**	na	na	na	na	na	na	na	na	na	na	na	na	na	na
Tanzania	na	**27**	27	27	27	26	28	28	24	28	28	28	22	24	29	25
Turkey	na	**0**	na	na	na	na	na	na	na	2	na	na	1	1	na	na
Uganda	na	**12**	15	10	11	12	19	15	11	14	19	14	12	10	13	13
Ukraine	na	**2**	2	2	1	3	2	2	2	3	2	2	2	2	2	na
United States	9	**17**	14	20	14	14	23	15	16	18	18	16	16	19	16	20
Uruguay	na	**na**	na	na	na	na	na	na	na	na	na	na	na	na	na	na
Venezuela	na	**7**	7	6	4	9	8	7	6	8	8	6	6	7	6	8
Vietnam	na	**26**	27	25	14	25	38	28	24	30	22	22	33	25	29	20
Zimbabwe	na	**9**	7	10	6	9	14	9	8	na	7	7	12	9	9	8
Total	6	**8**	7	8	6	7	10	7	7	10	8	8	8	6	8	9

RANKING	
Country	2000
Tanzania	27
Vietnam	26
Netherlands	21
Sweden	21
Iceland	17
Bangladesh	17
United States	17
Luxembourg	15
Albania	14
Canada	13
Belgium	13
Puerto Rico	12
Uganda	12
Finland	11
Algeria	11
Japan	9
Korea, South	9
South Africa	9
Zimbabwe	9
Philippines	8
Romania	2
Denmark	7
Mexico	7
Macedonia	7
India	7
Singapore	7
Chile	7
Great Britain	7
Austria	7
Slovakia	7
Venezuela	7
Czech Republic	7
Greece	7
Italy	6
Ireland	6
France	6
Slovenia	5
Argentina	5
Northern Ireland	4
Peru	4
Montenegro	4
Germany	4
Moldova	4
Estonia	3
Serbia	3
Spain	3
Poland	3
China	3
Malta	2
Croatia	2
Portugal	2
Hungary	2
Ukraine	2
Bosnia and Herz.	2
Belarus	2
Latvia	2
Russian Fed.	2
Bulgaria	1
Morocco	1
Lithuania	1
Turkey	0
Total	8

A065) BELONG CHURCH ORGANIZATION

Please look carefully at the following list of voluntary organizations and activities and say...which, if any, do you belong to?. Religious or church organizations.

Belong (%) (WVS: V40; EVS: V13)

	Wave		Gender		Age			Education			Income			Values		
Country	1990	2000	Male	Female	16-29	30-49	50+	Lower	Middle	Upper	Lower	Middle	Upper	Mat	Mixed	Postm.
Albania	na	**20**	16	24	19	18	25	24	18	17	22	22	18	21	20	18
Algeria	na	**7**	9	5	8	5	9	7	6	9	5	8	8	6	8	12
Argentina	7	**16**	9	21	10	16	21	17	14	13	18	16	12	14	16	14
Armenia	na	**na**	na	na	na	na	na	na	na	na	na	na	na	na	na	na
Australia	na	**na**	na	na	na	na	na	na	na	na	na	na	na	na	na	na
Austria	16	**26**	27	24	23	28	25	20	29	38	20	25	32	21	25	29
Azerbaijan	na	**na**	na	na	na	na	na	na	na	na	na	na	na	na	na	na
Bangladesh	na	**43**	60	23	35	47	59	38	52	45	33	47	47	43	45	36
Belarus	na	**2**	1	4	1	2	4	4	2	2	3	2	1	3	2	2
Belgium	12	**12**	10	14	6	11	16	12	9	16	14	14	11	11	12	12
Bosnia and Herz.	na	**8**	7	9	6	7	12	16	6	6	13	6	8	8	8	8
Brazil	22	**na**	na	na	na	na	na	na	na	na	na	na	na	na	na	na
Bulgaria	2	**2**	1	3	2	1	3	4	1	1	4	1	1	2	2	2
Canada	25	**30**	26	33	20	26	39	31	26	35	29	30	26	27	33	22
Chile	18	**21**	16	25	16	20	27	23	19	21	25	19	17	22	21	16
China	1	**4**	3	5	3	4	3	2	5	5	3	3	5	3	4	na
Colombia	na	**na**	na	na	na	na	na	na	na	na	na	na	na	na	na	na
Croatia	na	**13**	15	12	11	10	18	14	12	14	7	16	13	11	14	11
Czech Republic	na	**7**	6	7	6	4	9	7	5	10	8	7	4	8	6	9
Denmark	7	**12**	9	14	10	14	11	10	12	14	10	12	14	8	14	7
Dominican Rep.	na	**na**	na	na	na	na	na	na	na	na	na	na	na	na	na	na
Egypt	na	**na**	na	na	na	na	na	na	na	na	na	na	na	na	na	na
El Salvador	na	**na**	na	na	na	na	na	na	na	na	na	na	na	na	na	na
Estonia	4	**7**	5	9	4	6	11	9	6	8	10	8	6	7	7	na
Finland	18	**51**	46	55	46	49	55	51	47	63	54	52	45	43	55	52
France	6	**4**	4	5	2	5	5	3	5	7	4	6	5	5	4	5
Georgia	na	**na**	na	na	na	na	na	na	na	na	na	na	na	na	na	na
Germany	20	**14**	11	16	13	12	16	14	14	13	11	17	17	11	14	16
Great Britain	16	**5**	5	5	3	3	7	4	3	10	8	4	4	na	na	na
Greece	na	**7**	6	7	5	7	10	17	6	5	9	6	5	10	6	4
Hungary	11	**12**	12	13	9	14	13	13	9	15	11	13	13	13	10	17
Iceland	50	**71**	74	68	66	68	79	73	72	67	73	71	70	71	73	58
India	na	**18**	20	15	14	19	19	16	19	20	18	15	21	14	23	18
Indonesia	na	**na**	na	na	na	na	na	na	na	na	na	na	na	na	na	na
Iran	na	**na**	na	na	na	na	na	na	na	na	na	na	na	na	na	na
Ireland	14	**16**	14	18	8	13	26	19	12	20	20	12	18	14	17	16
Israel	na	**na**	na	na	na	na	na	na	na	na	na	na	na	na	na	na
Italy	8	**10**	7	13	9	9	12	9	11	12	10	12	10	11	10	10
Japan	7	**11**	10	11	4	11	13	7	13	8	12	10	10	8	11	12
Jordan	na	**na**	na	na	na	na	na	na	na	na	na	na	na	na	na	na
Korea, South	39	**42**	35	50	38	44	43	45	46	37	39	40	48	41	42	47
Latvia	3	**5**	3	7	7	4	6	8	4	6	7	5	3	4	6	6
Lithuania	3	**6**	4	7	4	3	9	12	4	2	6	8	3	3	6	9
Luxembourg	na	**10**	10	10	4	7	17	7	10	14	10	9	11	7	10	14
Macedonia	na	**11**	12	10	12	12	8	16	8	8	9	12	8	12	10	15
Malta	na	**14**	12	17	9	10	22	17	12	21	16	16	12	13	15	19
Mexico	14	**23**	19	27	18	23	30	25	19	28	24	27	23	26	24	20
Moldova	na	**14**	9	19	13	11	19	16	14	13	12	14	15	18	12	9
Montenegro	na	**3**	4	2	3	3	4	3	4	4	3	3	3	3	4	3
Morocco	na	**1**	1	1	na	1	1	1	na	3	na	1	2	na	1	1
Netherlands	33	**35**	34	36	25	27	47	35	37	32	32	37	32	50	34	30
New Zealand	na	**na**	na	na	na	na	na	na	na	na	na	na	na	na	na	na
Nigeria	na	**na**	na	na	na	na	na	na	na	na	na	na	na	na	na	na
Northern Ireland	25	**24**	20	27	18	19	30	25	19	32	19	24	31	25	26	14
Norway	11	**na**	na	na	na	na	na	na	na	na	na	na	na	na	na	na
Pakistan	na	**na**	na	na	na	na	na	na	na	na	na	na	na	na	na	na
Peru	na	**25**	20	31	24	25	32	28	27	22	24	26	28	25	25	26
Philippines	na	**31**	29	33	26	31	36	29	27	39	31	31	30	30	33	20
Poland	na	**6**	6	6	9	4	6	5	7	6	7	5	6	6	5	8
Portugal	11	**6**	4	7	5	8	5	6	4	9	7	6	5	5	6	7
Puerto Rico	na	**42**	38	43	31	35	51	56	39	41	52	41	35	58	41	36
Romania	5	**4**	4	5	4	3	6	4	5	3	7	3	4	4	5	7
Russian Fed.	1	**2**	1	4	1	2	4	3	2	2	3	2	1	2	3	2
Serbia	na	**3**	4	2	1	3	3	3	3	3	2	3	4	2	3	6
Singapore	na	**20**	20	20	19	22	17	14	21	32	16	18	26	19	20	18
Slovakia	na	**17**	12	21	10	13	26	25	13	11	23	16	14	18	16	13
Slovenia	3	**7**	7	6	9	5	7	8	7	5	7	10	5	5	7	9
South Africa	na	**54**	46	65	49	54	70	55	54	51	52	62	50	57	54	41
Spain	4	**7**	5	8	4	6	9	7	5	9	7	7	8	7	6	7
Sweden	10	**72**	68	75	72	70	73	74	70	73	70	71	74	62	73	69
Switzerland	11	**na**	na	na	na	na	na	na	na	na	na	na	na	na	na	na
Taiwan	na	**na**	na	na	na	na	na	na	na	na	na	na	na	na	na	na
Tanzania	na	**57**	55	60	55	59	59	57	58	59	57	65	55	58	56	71
Turkey	na	**1**	1	na	1	na	1	na	1	2	na	1	1	na	1	na
Uganda	na	**42**	52	32	39	47	37	39	43	40	47	39	45	46	41	32
Ukraine	na	**4**	3	5	3	4	5	7	4	3	5	3	5	3	5	5
United States	49	**57**	52	63	42	61	65	47	57	62	50	60	65	67	59	51
Uruguay	na	**na**	na	na	na	na	na	na	na	na	na	na	na	na	na	na
Venezuela	na	**23**	22	24	16	25	34	29	19	26	24	26	21	29	22	16
Vietnam	na	**11**	8	13	9	10	12	13	7	6	7	9	13	6	13	5
Zimbabwe	na	**76**	63	87	78	77	70	75	78	60	70	79	81	72	78	88
Total	14	**20**	19	22	19	20	22	21	19	23	21	21	20	19	22	21

RANKING	
Country	**2000**
Zimbabwe	76
Sweden	72
Iceland	71
United States	57
Tanzania	57
South Africa	54
Finland	51
Bangladesh	43
Korea, South	42
Uganda	42
Puerto Rico	42
Netherlands	35
Philippines	31
Canada	30
Austria	26
Peru	25
Northern Ireland	24
Mexico	23
Venezuela	23
Chile	21
Albania	20
Singapore	20
Romania	4
India	18
Slovakia	17
Ireland	16
Argentina	16
Malta	14
Moldova	14
Denmark	12
Germany	14
Croatia	13
Hungary	12
Belgium	12
Macedonia	11
Japan	11
Vietnam	11
Italy	10
Luxembourg	10
Bosnia and Herz.	8
Estonia	7
Algeria	7
Greece	7
Czech Republic	7
Slovenia	7
Spain	7
Poland	6
Portugal	6
Lithuania	6
Latvia	5
Great Britain	5
France	4
Ukraine	4
China	4
Montenegro	3
Serbia	3
Belarus	2
Russian Fed.	2
Bulgaria	2
Morocco	1
Turkey	1
Total	20

A066) BELONG CULTURAL ACTIVITIES

Please look carefully at the following list of voluntary organizations and activities and say...which, if any, do you belong to?. Education, arts, music or cultural activities.

Belong (%)

(WVS: V41; EVS: V14)

Country	Wave		Gender		Age			Education			Income			Values		
	1990	2000	Male	Female	16-29	30-49	50+	Lower	Middle	Upper	Lower	Middle	Upper	Mat	Mixed	Postm.
Albania	na	**14**	16	12	24	12	7	8	16	21	13	15	13	11	16	26
Algeria	na	**12**	13	10	14	11	10	5	11	18	12	10	15	8	13	17
Argentina	6	**9**	7	11	14	10	4	3	13	33	5	9	14	3	8	17
Armenia	na	**na**	na	na	na	na	na	na	na	na	na	na	na	na	na	na
Australia	na	**na**	na	na	na	na	na	na	na	na	na	na	na	na	na	na
Austria	8	**14**	15	12	12	14	14	8	15	29	9	13	18	7	12	18
Azerbaijan	na	**na**	na	na	na	na	na	na	na	na	na	na	na	na	na	na
Bangladesh	na	**30**	36	21	32	28	27	19	41	44	20	33	33	30	30	22
Belarus	na	**3**	2	3	4	2	2	na	3	6	3	2	5	2	3	2
Belgium	17	**21**	23	19	23	22	19	6	20	34	15	18	30	14	20	31
Bosnia and Herz.	na	**4**	4	5	7	2	4	1	3	12	2	4	6	5	4	8
Brazil	5	**na**	na	na	na	na	na	na	na	na	na	na	na	na	na	na
Bulgaria	4	**4**	4	4	7	6	1	1	3	12	2	5	5	2	5	10
Canada	18	**21**	18	24	25	24	17	9	19	38	15	20	29	20	21	24
Chile	9	**9**	8	10	14	7	8	3	8	24	4	9	17	8	9	11
China	7	**2**	2	3	4	2	2	na	3	19	1	2	4	1	2	19
Colombia	na	**na**	na	na	na	na	na	na	na	na	na	na	na	na	na	na
Croatia	na	**6**	6	6	13	5	2	3	5	17	3	6	7	1	7	7
Czech Republic	na	**10**	11	9	17	10	7	7	10	24	6	10	13	6	11	18
Denmark	13	**17**	16	17	17	16	17	10	22	28	13	17	23	9	17	23
Dominican Rep.	na	**na**	na	na	na	na	na	na	na	na	na	na	na	na	na	na
Egypt	na	**na**	na	na	na	na	na	na	na	na	na	na	na	na	na	na
El Salvador	na	**na**	na	na	na	na	na	na	na	na	na	na	na	na	na	na
Estonia	11	**8**	7	8	11	7	6	4	8	14	3	7	11	4	11	15
Finland	20	**16**	12	18	21	14	15	8	21	33	19	13	15	13	15	26
France	9	**8**	7	8	8	9	7	4	8	18	6	9	11	6	7	14
Georgia	na	**na**	na	na	na	na	na	na	na	na	na	na	na	na	na	na
Germany	9	**8**	8	8	6	9	8	5	9	18	5	7	11	7	7	12
Great Britain	10	**10**	8	11	12	11	7	2	10	28	8	6	17	na	na	na
Greece	na	**21**	19	22	22	21	16	6	19	25	14	23	25	23	19	23
Hungary	3	**3**	3	4	3	4	4	1	4	17	2	4	4	1	5	16
Iceland	14	**16**	12	19	10	19	16	11	12	31	11	16	19	11	16	22
India	na	**15**	17	11	18	15	12	10	15	26	14	11	19	9	24	31
Indonesia	na	**na**	na	na	na	na	na	na	na	na	na	na	na	na	na	na
Iran	na	**na**	na	na	na	na	na	na	na	na	na	na	na	na	na	na
Ireland	10	**10**	10	11	10	11	9	6	9	21	6	10	16	8	10	17
Israel	na	**na**	na	na	na	na	na	na	na	na	na	na	na	na	na	na
Italy	4	**10**	10	10	14	10	8	4	12	23	7	10	14	6	9	14
Japan	6	**11**	12	10	6	9	15	15	9	15	10	9	15	13	11	14
Jordan	na	**na**	na	na	na	na	na	na	na	na	na	na	na	na	na	na
Korea, South	11	**19**	18	20	32	16	11	4	15	27	15	20	23	16	19	43
Latvia	7	**4**	3	4	6	4	3	1	4	6	3	4	4	2	5	2
Lithuania	7	**2**	2	2	3	3	1	1	2	7	1	2	3	1	2	3
Luxembourg	na	**18**	17	18	15	19	18	12	18	28	13	12	23	14	17	21
Macedonia	na	**12**	13	11	19	12	6	6	13	20	7	12	17	9	12	26
Malta	na	**5**	6	3	4	4	6	3	5	6	3	6	6	5	5	5
Mexico	12	**8**	8	8	9	7	6	4	8	25	4	8	14	6	8	13
Moldova	na	**12**	10	14	18	13	8	2	10	26	7	12	18	10	13	25
Montenegro	na	**9**	10	8	23	7	3	2	13	19	5	10	14	6	14	8
Morocco	na	**3**	4	3	3	5	1	1	8	20	1	3	15	2	5	6
Netherlands	36	**45**	41	50	45	48	43	29	43	64	42	45	48	24	45	56
New Zealand	na	**na**	na	na	na	na	na	na	na	na	na	na	na	na	na	na
Nigeria	na	**na**	na	na	na	na	na	na	na	na	na	na	na	na	na	na
Northern Ireland	11	**8**	9	7	9	8	7	4	8	18	6	5	15	7	10	4
Norway	14	**na**	na	na	na	na	na	na	na	na	na	na	na	na	na	na
Pakistan	na	**na**	na	na	na	na	na	na	na	na	na	na	na	na	na	na
Peru	na	**13**	15	11	14	13	9	9	10	21	9	14	19	9	13	18
Philippines	na	**5**	5	6	7	4	7	2	4	12	3	4	9	4	7	7
Poland	na	**2**	4	1	5	2	1	1	3	7	1	3	5	1	3	1
Portugal	8	**3**	4	2	5	4	2	2	4	14	na	2	4	2	4	3
Puerto Rico	na	**13**	17	11	17	14	11	4	7	18	9	12	20	18	11	19
Romania	2	**3**	3	2	5	3	1	0	3	5	0	2	5	2	3	4
Russian Fed.	5	**1**	1	2	2	1	1	na	1	2	1	2	2	1	1	6
Serbia	na	**3**	3	3	6	3	1	1	4	3	2	3	3	3	3	3
Singapore	na	**14**	12	16	24	6	4	13	13	21	8	12	18	9	15	19
Slovakia	na	**7**	6	8	10	6	6	3	8	14	5	7	9	5	9	10
Slovenia	3	**9**	10	9	14	9	6	5	8	23	3	12	16	4	10	13
South Africa	na	**17**	18	16	23	15	9	12	22	45	10	24	21	23	15	7
Spain	6	**7**	7	7	10	8	4	4	6	17	5	7	12	6	5	14
Sweden	13	**26**	24	29	32	21	28	16	21	43	27	22	30	16	23	39
Switzerland	7	**na**	na	na	na	na	na	na	na	na	na	na	na	na	na	na
Taiwan	na	**na**	na	na	na	na	na	na	na	na	na	na	na	na	na	na
Tanzania	na	**28**	26	30	34	27	20	23	34	38	27	32	27	22	32	29
Turkey	na	**1**	2	1	1	1	na	na	1	6	na	1	4	na	2	1
Uganda	na	**21**	29	15	33	11	7	11	27	8	19	22	23	19	24	17
Ukraine	na	**3**	2	4	5	4	2	1	2	8	3	2	5	3	4	2
United States	20	**37**	38	37	48	35	32	23	29	48	29	37	49	30	35	45
Uruguay	na	**na**	na	na	na	na	na	na	na	na	na	na	na	na	na	na
Venezuela	na	**18**	18	17	21	17	12	10	15	34	14	17	23	17	18	20
Vietnam	na	**17**	17	18	21	19	13	14	21	27	13	14	24	16	20	14
Zimbabwe	na	**7**	10	5	9	6	3	3	12	39	3	6	18	6	8	8
Total	10	**12**	12	12	16	12	9	7	12	24	9	12	16	8	13	19

RANKING	
Country	2000
Netherlands	45
United States	37
Bangladesh	30
Tanzania	28
Sweden	26
Canada	21
Uganda	21
Greece	21
Belgium	21
Denmark	17
Korea, South	19
Venezuela	18
Luxembourg	18
Vietnam	17
South Africa	17
Finland	16
Iceland	16
India	15
Singapore	14
Albania	14
Austria	14
Puerto Rico	13
Peru	13
Moldova	12
Algeria	12
Romania	3
Macedonia	12
Japan	11
Czech Republic	10
Ireland	10
Italy	10
Great Britain	10
Slovenia	9
Argentina	9
Montenegro	9
Chile	9
Germany	8
France	8
Estonia	8
Mexico	8
Northern Ireland	8
Zimbabwe	7
Slovakia	7
Spain	7
Croatia	6
Philippines	5
Malta	5
Bosnia and Herz.	4
Bulgaria	4
Latvia	4
Hungary	3
Morocco	3
Portugal	3
Ukraine	3
Serbia	3
Belarus	3
China	2
Poland	2
Lithuania	2
Russian Fed.	1
Turkey	1
Total	12

A067) BELONG LABOR UNIONS

Please look carefully at the following list of voluntary organizations and activities and say...which, if any, do you belong to? Labor unions.

(WVS: V42; EVS: V15)

Belong (%)

Country	Wave		Gender		Age			Education			Income			Values		
	1990	2000	Male	Female	16-29	30-49	50+	Lower	Middle	Upper	Lower	Middle	Upper	Mat	Mixed	Postm.
Albania	na	**9**	12	7	7	12	8	6	10	17	9	9	11	9	9	26
Algeria	na	**na**	na	na	na	na	na	na	na	na	na	na	na	na	na	na
Argentina	1	**3**	4	1	2	2	3	2	2	6	2	3	3	2	2	3
Armenia	na	**na**	na	na	na	na	na	na	na	na	na	na	na	na	na	na
Australia	na	**na**	na	na	na	na	na	na	na	na	na	na	na	na	na	na
Austria	19	**20**	25	16	16	24	18	20	19	24	14	23	25	16	21	20
Azerbaijan	na	**na**	na	na	na	na	na	na	na	na	na	na	na	na	na	na
Bangladesh	na	**15**	22	6	11	18	17	12	21	14	12	17	15	13	17	12
Belarus	na	**44**	45	42	48	57	24	25	49	53	41	47	40	39	48	45
Belgium	16	**18**	23	13	16	25	13	15	18	19	11	22	23	20	19	16
Bosnia and Herz.	na	**7**	8	6	3	11	5	4	7	8	3	8	10	6	7	8
Brazil	6	**na**	na	na	na	na	na	na	na	na	na	na	na	na	na	na
Bulgaria	19	**7**	7	6	3	13	3	2	7	13	3	10	9	3	11	8
Canada	12	**14**	19	10	11	18	13	10	15	17	7	16	21	19	13	17
Chile	6	**3**	5	1	1	4	3	3	3	3	2	3	5	1	4	2
China	2	**7**	9	5	3	9	6	1	11	21	1	8	15	10	6	9
Colombia	na	**na**	na	na	na	na	na	na	na	na	na	na	na	na	na	na
Croatia	na	**11**	15	7	6	17	7	5	15	14	5	13	11	12	11	10
Czech Republic	na	**11**	12	9	6	13	11	11	10	13	7	12	13	12	11	8
Denmark	49	**54**	57	52	47	69	43	53	57	59	34	72	64	49	55	62
Dominican Rep.	na	**na**	na	na	na	na	na	na	na	na	na	na	na	na	na	na
Egypt	na	**na**	na	na	na	na	na	na	na	na	na	na	na	na	na	na
El Salvador	na	**na**	na	na	na	na	na	na	na	na	na	na	na	na	na	na
Estonia	59	**5**	6	4	3	7	4	2	5	9	2	6	6	4	5	8
Finland	36	**35**	36	34	25	51	27	32	34	49	22	38	47	37	35	31
France	5	**4**	5	3	na	5	5	3	3	8	1	6	7	1	4	8
Georgia	na	**na**	na	na	na	na	na	na	na	na	na	na	na	na	na	na
Germany	56	**7**	10	5	4	9	7	6	8	8	4	9	13	6	8	7
Great Britain	14	**8**	9	7	4	11	8	7	9	12	7	8	16	na	na	na
Greece	na	**8**	10	7	5	11	10	6	8	10	5	10	12	9	8	10
Hungary	32	**7**	8	6	3	9	8	5	8	14	6	7	8	6	8	5
Iceland	60	**60**	61	58	68	55	59	65	61	47	61	62	58	59	62	50
India	na	**8**	11	5	7	10	7	8	9	8	11	8	7	6	10	18
Indonesia	na	**na**	na	na	na	na	na	na	na	na	na	na	na	na	na	na
Iran	na	**na**	na	na	na	na	na	na	na	na	na	na	na	na	na	na
Ireland	9	**10**	15	6	9	12	9	7	8	20	4	12	16	8	10	12
Israel	na	**na**	na	na	na	na	na	na	na	na	na	na	na	na	na	na
Italy	6	**6**	8	5	3	8	6	5	6	9	3	6	10	4	7	6
Japan	7	**7**	10	4	6	9	4	4	6	9	3	8	10	7	8	4
Jordan	na	**na**	na	na	na	na	na	na	na	na	na	na	na	na	na	na
Korea, South	7	**6**	8	3	5	6	6	2	6	6	6	7	4	5	7	7
Latvia	52	**11**	9	13	9	18	7	3	11	23	6	12	20	13	12	2
Lithuania	43	**2**	3	1	2	3	1	1	2	3	1	1	4	1	2	3
Luxembourg	na	**12**	16	9	5	15	14	11	14	13	10	13	15	10	14	13
Macedonia	na	**6**	8	4	2	10	4	3	8	7	6	7	5	6	6	6
Malta	na	**9**	14	4	12	10	6	2	12	12	3	9	19	7	10	9
Mexico	4	**6**	9	3	3	8	6	4	6	15	4	7	8	6	6	7
Moldova	na	**15**	14	15	14	16	13	4	12	29	12	17	17	12	18	22
Montenegro	na	**16**	20	11	10	26	10	4	23	27	9	16	24	13	19	21
Morocco	na	**1**	1	1	na	1	1	na	2	6	na	1	4	na	1	3
Netherlands	17	**22**	28	17	15	24	25	24	20	24	20	27	22	22	20	30
New Zealand	na	**na**	na	na	na	na	na	na	na	na	na	na	na	na	na	na
Nigeria	na	**na**	na	na	na	na	na	na	na	na	na	na	na	na	na	na
Northern Ireland	12	**7**	9	4	6	7	6	5	7	11	3	11	10	5	8	4
Norway	42	**na**	na	na	na	na	na	na	na	na	na	na	na	na	na	na
Pakistan	na	**na**	na	na	na	na	na	na	na	na	na	na	na	na	na	na
Peru	na	**5**	6	3	3	6	5	3	6	4	4	6	3	4	5	6
Philippines	na	**4**	6	2	3	5	5	4	4	5	5	4	4	5	4	5
Poland	na	**10**	12	8	5	15	8	7	14	17	6	13	12	8	11	17
Portugal	5	**2**	2	1	na	4	1	1	2	5	na	2	3	1	2	3
Puerto Rico	na	**4**	6	4	3	6	4	3	3	6	1	5	8	2	3	9
Romania	20	**9**	11	7	8	16	4	1	11	22	1	7	18	8	10	19
Russian Fed.	62	**24**	25	23	20	35	13	9	24	32	17	27	29	24	25	18
Serbia	na	**14**	16	11	4	24	9	5	17	20	8	15	20	12	16	18
Singapore	na	**4**	5	3	2	6	6	4	4	8	5	3	6	6	4	2
Slovakia	na	**16**	17	15	10	22	13	9	18	24	9	18	21	14	17	25
Slovenia	19	**17**	17	17	12	30	7	13	18	21	17	24	24	20	17	13
South Africa	na	**10**	13	6	4	16	5	9	11	4	4	15	14	10	10	8
Spain	4	**4**	6	2	3	6	3	2	4	7	2	4	8	2	4	8
Sweden	59	**64**	60	68	52	75	61	58	61	73	58	68	70	59	63	69
Switzerland	6	**na**	na	na	na	na	na	na	na	na	na	na	na	na	na	na
Taiwan	na	**na**	na	na	na	na	na	na	na	na	na	na	na	na	na	na
Tanzania	na	**29**	27	30	21	37	23	22	30	51	20	39	37	28	28	46
Turkey	na	**2**	3	1	2	2	1	1	2	4	na	2	3	1	2	3
Uganda	na	**7**	11	3	7	7	8	9	6	4	9	4	7	8	6	11
Ukraine	na	**21**	22	20	19	28	16	5	20	33	15	24	26	23	22	20
United States	9	**14**	19	8	12	15	14	15	14	13	10	17	17	17	13	14
Uruguay	na	**na**	na	na	na	na	na	na	na	na	na	na	na	na	na	na
Venezuela	na	**3**	4	2	2	4	4	2	3	4	4	3	3	3	3	3
Vietnam	na	**11**	12	11	8	15	9	6	15	31	8	11	13	10	13	12
Zimbabwe	na	**3**	5	2	4	4	na	3	4	na	2	4	5	3	4	4
Total	23	13	16	11	10	17	11	10	14	18	10	16	17	11	14	15

RANKING	
Country	2000
Denmark	54
Sweden	64
Iceland	60
Belarus	44
Romania	9
Finland	35
Tanzania	29
Russian Fed.	24
Netherlands	22
Ukraine	21
Austria	20
Belgium	18
Slovenia	17
Slovakia	16
Montenegro	16
Bangladesh	15
Moldova	15
Canada	14
United States	14
Serbia	14
Luxembourg	12
Latvia	11
Vietnam	11
Croatia	11
Czech Republic	11
Poland	10
Ireland	10
South Africa	10
Albania	9
Malta	9
Greece	8
Great Britain	8
India	8
Germany	7
Hungary	7
China	7
Bosnia and Herz.	7
Uganda	7
Bulgaria	7
Japan	7
Northern Ireland	7
Italy	6
Macedonia	6
Mexico	6
Korea, South	6
Estonia	5
Peru	5
Puerto Rico	4
Singapore	4
France	4
Philippines	4
Spain	4
Zimbabwe	3
Chile	3
Venezuela	3
Argentina	3
Lithuania	2
Portugal	2
Turkey	2
Morocco	1
Total	13

A068) BELONG POLITICAL PARTIES

Please look carefully at the following list of voluntary organizations and activities and say...which, if any, do you belong to? Political parties or groups.

Belong (%)

(WVS: V43; EVS: V16)

Country	Wave 1990	Wave 2000	Gender Male	Gender Female	Age 16-29	Age 30-49	Age 50+	Education Lower	Education Middle	Education Upper	Income Lower	Income Middle	Income Upper	Values Mat	Values Mixed	Values Postm.
Albania	na	**15**	22	7	10	15	17	12	16	17	17	13	14	13	17	8
Algeria	na	**6**	8	3	3	6	10	6	3	8	5	4	7	5	6	8
Argentina	2	**5**	5	4	4	5	4	3	7	8	4	4	7	1	5	7
Armenia	na	**na**	na	na	na	na	na	na	na	na	na	na	na	na	na	na
Australia	na	**na**	na	na	na	na	na	na	na	na	na	na	na	na	na	na
Austria	12	**12**	15	8	7	13	13	13	8	19	9	13	15	5	12	11
Azerbaijan	na	**na**	na	na	na	na	na	na	na	na	na	na	na	na	na	na
Bangladesh	na	**24**	36	9	22	24	29	17	29	34	24	21	26	22	25	25
Belarus	na	**1**	2	na	na	1	na	na	1	2	1	1	na	na	1	na
Belgium	6	**7**	9	5	5	6	9	4	7	10	5	7	8	3	7	10
Bosnia and Herz.	na	**7**	11	4	7	7	7	4	6	12	6	6	11	6	8	4
Brazil	5	**na**	na	na	na	na	na	na	na	na	na	na	na	na	na	na
Bulgaria	11	**4**	6	3	4	4	4	2	4	9	3	5	5	2	5	5
Canada	7	**6**	9	4	4	6	8	4	4	13	5	4	10	2	5	9
Chile	5	**2**	4	1	2	4	1	1	3	4	2	2	5	1	2	5
China	35	**8**	12	5	9	7	11	4	8	49	4	8	16	9	9	25
Colombia	na	**na**	na	na	na	na	na	na	na	na	na	na	na	na	na	na
Croatia	na	**4**	6	2	2	4	4	1	5	11	3	3	6	3	4	6
Czech Republic	na	**4**	5	2	2	2	6	4	3	7	4	4	3	3	4	3
Denmark	7	**7**	8	5	5	7	8	6	7	8	5	6	9	8	6	11
Dominican Rep.	na	**na**	na	na	na	na	na	na	na	na	na	na	na	na	na	na
Egypt	na	**na**	na	na	na	na	na	na	na	na	na	na	na	na	na	na
El Salvador	na	**na**	na	na	na	na	na	na	na	na	na	na	na	na	na	na
Estonia	8	**2**	3	1	1	1	3	1	1	3	na	1	3	1	2	na
Finland	14	**7**	10	5	3	5	11	6	10	8	4	8	11	5	8	6
France	3	**2**	2	2	1	2	2	1	2	5	1	2	3	na	1	6
Georgia	na	**na**	na	na	na	na	na	na	na	na	na	na	na	na	na	na
Germany	11	**3**	4	2	1	3	4	2	3	10	2	3	4	1	3	4
Great Britain	6	**3**	3	2	2	2	3	1	2	5	2	3	3	na	na	na
Greece	na	**8**	11	6	6	9	11	6	9	8	4	11	11	8	8	10
Hungary	2	**2**	2	1	1	1	3	1	2	6	1	2	3	1	3	na
Iceland	15	**19**	22	17	14	17	26	17	21	19	18	17	23	21	19	18
India	na	**11**	16	5	11	12	10	9	14	14	10	11	13	13	13	13
Indonesia	na	**na**	na	na	na	na	na	na	na	na	na	na	na	na	na	na
Iran	na	**na**	na	na	na	na	na	na	na	na	na	na	na	na	na	na
Ireland	4	**4**	7	2	4	3	6	5	3	6	5	4	6	3	5	3
Israel	na	**na**	na	na	na	na	na	na	na	na	na	na	na	na	na	na
Italy	5	**4**	6	2	2	5	5	3	4	8	3	5	5	2	3	7
Japan	2	**4**	5	2	na	3	5	5	3	4	3	2	6	4	3	6
Jordan	na	**na**	na	na	na	na	na	na	na	na	na	na	na	na	na	na
Korea, South	5	**3**	4	2	2	3	3	na	2	4	3	3	2	3	2	4
Latvia	18	**2**	2	2	1	1	3	1	2	2	3	1	1	2	2	4
Lithuania	7	**1**	2	1	1	1	1	na	1	6	1	1	2	na	2	4
Luxembourg	na	**6**	8	5	2	6	9	4	8	7	5	6	8	7	6	10
Macedonia	na	**12**	15	8	12	14	8	9	12	17	9	15	10	11	12	17
Malta	na	**6**	9	3	3	6	8	6	6	5	7	5	7	5	6	5
Mexico	5	**4**	6	2	3	4	4	3	3	10	4	4	5	3	4	5
Moldova	na	**5**	7	4	4	6	5	2	4	11	3	6	6	5	6	9
Montenegro	na	**20**	28	11	18	24	17	9	26	30	17	22	25	17	23	31
Morocco	na	**1**	2	1	1	1	1	1	1	6	1	2	4	1	1	2
Netherlands	8	**9**	11	8	3	7	15	8	7	14	8	6	14	8	8	14
New Zealand	na	**na**	na	na	na	na	na	na	na	na	na	na	na	na	na	na
Nigeria	na	**na**	na	na	na	na	na	na	na	na	na	na	na	na	na	na
Northern Ireland	2	**2**	3	2	2	3	3	2	1	6	1	5	3	1	3	3
Norway	14	**na**	na	na	na	na	na	na	na	na	na	na	na	na	na	na
Pakistan	na	**na**	na	na	na	na	na	na	na	na	na	na	na	na	na	na
Peru	na	**5**	7	3	4	5	6	2	4	8	3	5	8	4	5	7
Philippines	na	**4**	6	2	1	5	5	4	3	7	3	4	6	3	5	4
Poland	na	**1**	1	na	na	na	2	na	1	2	1	1	na	na	1	1
Portugal	5	**1**	1	1	1	na	1	1	1	2	na	1	2	na	1	2
Puerto Rico	na	**6**	8	6	6	8	5	1	2	9	3	6	11	5	5	11
Romania	3	**2**	4	1	2	3	1	0	2	6	1	2	3	2	3	5
Russian Fed.	11	**1**	1	1	1	1	1	na	1	2	na	1	1	1	1	3
Serbia	na	**6**	9	3	6	8	4	2	7	10	5	6	8	4	8	13
Singapore	na	**0**	na	na	na	na	1	na	na	2	na	na	1	1	na	na
Slovakia	na	**7**	9	4	3	7	9	1	9	12	4	7	8	4	9	15
Slovenia	3	**3**	4	2	2	3	4	3	4	1	2	5	5	3	3	3
South Africa	na	**12**	17	6	9	16	9	13	10	14	13	13	13	12	12	12
Spain	2	**2**	3	1	1	2	1	1	2	4	1	1	3	1	1	4
Sweden	10	**11**	12	10	5	8	16	12	9	12	8	15	8	11	9	14
Switzerland	9	**na**	na	na	na	na	na	na	na	na	na	na	na	na	na	na
Taiwan	na	**na**	na	na	na	na	na	na	na	na	na	na	na	na	na	na
Tanzania	na	**26**	27	25	21	24	42	31	20	22	32	22	26	26	26	33
Turkey	na	**4**	6	2	3	5	2	3	4	6	3	4	4	2	3	7
Uganda	na	**9**	14	5	8	9	17	5	10	18	11	12	12	10	10	7
Ukraine	na	**2**	4	1	1	4	2	1	2	4	2	3	3	1	4	na
United States	14	**19**	22	17	13	17	27	8	15	26	13	24	23	23	17	24
Uruguay	na	**na**	na	na	na	na	na	na	na	na	na	na	na	na	na	na
Venezuela	na	**4**	6	2	4	5	3	1	4	7	3	4	5	5	4	4
Vietnam	na	**29**	34	24	28	28	30	22	35	52	23	25	36	19	35	24
Zimbabwe	na	**7**	10	5	5	8	10	7	7	na	8	8	6	8	5	15
Total	8	7	9	5	6	7	8	6	6	10	6	7	9	6	7	9

RANKING

Country	2000
Vietnam	29
Tanzania	26
Bangladesh	24
Montenegro	20
United States	19
Iceland	19
Albania	15
South Africa	12
Austria	12
Macedonia	12
India	11
Sweden	11
Romania	2
Netherlands	9
Uganda	9
China	8
Denmark	7
Greece	8
Belgium	7
Bosnia and Herz.	7
Finland	7
Zimbabwe	7
Slovakia	7
Canada	6
Puerto Rico	6
Luxembourg	6
Malta	6
Serbia	6
Algeria	6
Moldova	5
Peru	5
Argentina	5
Ireland	4
Italy	4
Philippines	4
Bulgaria	4
Mexico	4
Venezuela	4
Croatia	4
Czech Republic	4
Japan	4
Turkey	4
Slovenia	3
Germany	3
Korea, South	3
Great Britain	3
Chile	2
Northern Ireland	2
Ukraine	2
France	2
Latvia	2
Hungary	2
Spain	2
Estonia	2
Lithuania	1
Morocco	1
Portugal	1
Belarus	1
Poland	1
Russian Fed.	1
Singapore	0
Total	7

A069) BELONG LOCAL COMMUNITY ACTIONS

Please look carefully at the following list of voluntary organizations and activities and say...which, if any, do you belong to?

Local community action on issues like poverty, employment, housing, racial equality

Belong (%) (WVS: V44; EVS: V17)

Country	Wave		Gender		Age			Education			Income			Values		
	1990	2000	Male	Female	16-29	30-49	50+	Lower	Middle	Upper	Lower	Middle	Upper	Mat	Mixed	Postm.
Albania	na	**12**	13	10	11	11	12	9	12	15	12	8	15	12	12	8
Algeria	na	**6**	8	4	6	4	7	5	5	8	4	6	7	5	6	5
Argentina	1	**3**	2	5	4	2	4	2	5	5	3	3	5	3	4	3
Armenia	na	**na**	na	na	na	na	na	na	na	na	na	na	na	na	na	na
Australia	na	**na**	na	na	na	na	na	na	na	na	na	na	na	na	na	na
Austria	2	**3**	2	3	na	4	3	2	2	6	3	2	4	2	3	3
Azerbaijan	na	**na**	na	na	na	na	na	na	na	na	na	na	na	na	na	na
Bangladesh	na	**26**	32	19	22	28	30	22	30	34	14	30	32	25	27	22
Belarus	na	**0**	na	na	na	na	na	na	na	na	na	na	na	na	na	na
Belgium	5	**5**	5	5	4	5	6	2	4	8	6	5	6	2	4	8
Bosnia and Herz.	na	**1**	1	1	1	1	1	na	1	2	na	1	1	1	1	2
Brazil	8	**na**	na	na	na	na	na	na	na	na	na	na	na	na	na	na
Bulgaria	2	**1**	1	1	3	1	na	1	2	2	1	2	1	1	2	2
Canada	5	**8**	8	8	5	8	10	6	7	13	7	7	9	5	8	9
Chile	4	**5**	4	5	4	4	6	5	4	5	4	4	6	5	4	8
China	1	**2**	2	1	3	1	1	1	2	5	1	2	2	1	3	3
Colombia	na	**na**	na	na	na	na	na	na	na	na	na	na	na	na	na	na
Croatia	na	**2**	3	1	2	1	2	1	3	2	na	2	3	2	1	3
Czech Republic	na	**3**	3	3	4	4	3	4	3	4	4	3	4	4	3	5
Denmark	5	**6**	7	5	3	7	7	5	6	9	8	5	6	4	6	8
Dominican Rep.	na	**na**	na	na	na	na	na	na	na	na	na	na	na	na	na	na
Egypt	na	**na**	na	na	na	na	na	na	na	na	na	na	na	na	na	na
El Salvador	na	**na**	na	na	na	na	na	na	na	na	na	na	na	na	na	na
Estonia	5	**2**	2	2	na	2	3	3	2	1	2	2	2	2	2	na
Finland	3	**3**	2	3	1	4	3	2	4	3	5	2	2	4	2	3
France	3	**2**	2	3	na	2	4	2	1	5	1	2	5	2	2	5
Georgia	na	**na**	na	na	na	na	na	na	na	na	na	na	na	na	na	na
Germany	3	**1**	1	na	na	1	1	1	1	1	1	1	1	na	1	2
Great Britain	4	**4**	4	4	4	4	3	4	3	5	4	5	5	na	na	na
Greece	na	**4**	4	5	3	4	6	5	5	4	3	5	4	3	4	7
Hungary	1	**1**	1	1	na	1	2	1	1	2	1	1	2	na	2	na
Iceland	2	**3**	3	2	2	2	4	2	2	4	3	3	2	2	2	6
India	na	**6**	7	5	6	6	6	5	6	9	6	5	7	4	9	4
Indonesia	na	**na**	na	na	na	na	na	na	na	na	na	na	na	na	na	na
Iran	na	**na**	na	na	na	na	na	na	na	na	na	na	na	na	na	na
Ireland	3	**6**	6	6	3	6	8	5	5	8	6	7	6	5	5	7
Israel	na	**na**	na	na	na	na	na	na	na	na	na	na	na	na	na	na
Italy	2	**2**	2	3	2	3	2	1	3	5	2	3	3	3	2	2
Japan	0	**1**	2	1	na	1	2	1	1	2	1	1	2	1	1	3
Jordan	na	**na**	na	na	na	na	na	na	na	na	na	na	na	na	na	na
Korea, South	13	**7**	10	4	5	6	11	7	8	6	8	5	7	5	9	6
Latvia	5	**1**	1	1	na	1	1	na	1	2	1	1	1	na	1	na
Lithuania	2	**1**	1	1	1	1	1	na	1	1	na	1	1	na	1	1
Luxembourg	na	**6**	6	5	5	5	8	4	5	10	4	6	9	4	6	6
Macedonia	na	**6**	5	6	5	7	5	6	5	6	4	7	6	4	6	12
Malta	na	**3**	4	2	1	3	4	1	3	3	2	3	4	2	3	3
Mexico	4	**5**	5	5	3	5	7	5	4	6	4	8	5	6	5	4
Moldova	na	**3**	2	3	2	3	2	1	3	3	1	2	3	2	3	4
Montenegro	na	**1**	1	na	na	na	1	1	1	1	na	1	1	1	1	na
Morocco	na	**1**	1	1	1	1	na	1	1	2	na	1	3	na	2	1
Netherlands	5	**7**	6	8	5	8	7	6	6	9	5	8	8	5	7	8
New Zealand	na	**na**	na	na	na	na	na	na	na	na	na	na	na	na	na	na
Nigeria	na	**na**	na	na	na	na	na	na	na	na	na	na	na	na	na	na
Northern Ireland	2	**3**	3	4	2	4	3	4	2	4	4	3	5	2	4	4
Norway	3	**na**	na	na	na	na	na	na	na	na	na	na	na	na	na	na
Pakistan	na	**na**	na	na	na	na	na	na	na	na	na	na	na	na	na	na
Peru	na	**7**	7	7	3	9	9	5	7	6	5	8	7	6	7	7
Philippines	na	**7**	9	5	6	6	9	6	5	9	6	6	9	5	8	7
Poland	na	**2**	3	1	1	2	2	1	2	5	2	2	2	na	2	6
Portugal	2	**1**	1	1	2	1	1	na	1	8	na	na	1	1	1	2
Puerto Rico	na	**9**	10	8	5	10	10	6	5	12	8	6	14	5	9	12
Romania	1	**1**	1	1	2	0	1	0	1	1	0	1	1	0	2	0
Russian Fed.	3	**1**	1	1	1	1	1	1	1	2	1	1	1	1	1	na
Serbia	na	**1**	1	na	1	na	1	1	1	na	1	1	na	1	na	1
Singapore	na	**2**	2	3	1	3	4	3	2	2	2	3	2	3	2	4
Slovakia	na	**8**	10	6	6	8	10	6	8	13	8	7	9	7	10	8
Slovenia	6	**9**	10	9	4	8	16	10	9	10	9	15	7	10	10	7
South Africa	na	**9**	10	7	5	9	16	9	7	19	8	9	10	12	7	8
Spain	1	**2**	2	2	2	2	2	1	2	5	2	2	4	1	1	6
Sweden	2	**9**	10	9	7	9	11	10	8	12	13	8	8	11	8	15
Switzerland	3	**na**	na	na	na	na	na	na	na	na	na	na	na	na	na	na
Taiwan	na	**na**	na	na	na	na	na	na	na	na	na	na	na	na	na	na
Tanzania	na	**24**	23	24	22	24	23	22	25	27	21	25	29	20	25	25
Turkey	na	**0**	na	na	na	na	na	na	na	1	na	na	1	na	na	na
Uganda	na	**10**	17	3	10	10	7	8	10	17	12	8	13	11	9	11
Ukraine	na	**2**	2	2	1	2	2	1	1	4	1	2	3	1	3	3
United States	5	**13**	12	14	12	11	16	10	12	15	10	14	15	15	10	19
Uruguay	na	**na**	na	na	na	na	na	na	na	na	na	na	na	na	na	na
Venezuela	na	**10**	12	8	8	11	12	10	10	11	10	11	13	8	11	10
Vietnam	na	**26**	29	24	17	29	29	26	26	27	21	23	33	24	30	26
Zimbabwe	na	**5**	5	4	5	3	6	4	5	na	4	4	8	4	5	1
Total	3	5	6	5	5	6	5	5	5	7	5	6	7	4	6	7

RANKING	
Country	2000
Vietnam	26
Bangladesh	26
Tanzania	24
United States	13
Albania	12
Venezuela	10
Uganda	10
Sweden	9
Slovenia	9
Puerto Rico	9
South Africa	9
Canada	8
Slovakia	8
Denmark	6
Korea, South	7
Netherlands	7
Philippines	7
Peru	7
India	6
Algeria	6
Luxembourg	6
Ireland	6
Macedonia	6
Belgium	5
Mexico	5
Chile	5
Zimbabwe	5
Greece	4
Romania	1
Great Britain	4
Argentina	3
Northern Ireland	3
Czech Republic	3
Finland	3
Austria	3
Malta	3
Moldova	3
Iceland	3
Italy	2
Singapore	2
France	2
Spain	2
Estonia	2
Ukraine	2
Poland	2
Croatia	2
China	2
Bulgaria	1
Japan	1
Bosnia and Herz.	1
Hungary	1
Portugal	1
Morocco	1
Germany	1
Russian Fed.	1
Latvia	1
Montenegro	1
Lithuania	1
Serbia	1
Turkey	0
Belarus	0
Total	5

A070) BELONG THIRD WORLD DEVELOPMENT / HUMAN RIGHTS

Please look carefully at the following list of voluntary organizations and activities and say...which, if any, do you belong to? Third world development / human rights.

Belong (%) (WVS: V45; EVS: V18)

Country	Wave		Gender		Age			Education			Income			Values		
	1990	2000	Male	Female	16-29	30-49	50+	Lower	Middle	Upper	Lower	Middle	Upper	Mat	Mixed	Postm.
Albania	na	**6**	6	7	7	7	5	4	7	10	6	5	8	6	8	5
Algeria	na	**3**	4	3	4	3	2	1	3	5	3	4	3	2	4	3
Argentina	0	**1**	1	1	1	na	1	na	1	1	1	na	1	na	1	1
Armenia	na	**na**	na	na	na	na	na	na	na	na	na	na	na	na	na	na
Australia	na	**na**	na	na	na	na	na	na	na	na	na	na	na	na	na	na
Austria	2	**3**	3	4	4	2	4	2	3	9	2	3	4	na	3	6
Azerbaijan	na	**na**	na	na	na	na	na	na	na	na	na	na	na	na	na	na
Bangladesh	na	**11**	16	5	8	12	16	8	12	18	6	11	16	9	13	5
Belarus	na	**1**	1	1	na	1	na	na	1	1	na	1	1	na	1	2
Belgium	7	**10**	9	10	8	10	10	3	7	18	10	7	11	5	7	17
Bosnia and Herz.	na	**0**	na	na	na	na	1	na	na	na	na	na	na	na	na	na
Brazil	1	**na**	na	na	na	na	na	na	na	na	na	na	na	na	na	na
Bulgaria	2	**0**	na	1	na	1	na	1	na	1	1	1	na	na	na	na
Canada	5	**5**	5	5	3	5	6	3	4	9	4	6	6	2	6	5
Chile	1	**2**	2	2	2	2	2	1	3	2	1	2	4	2	2	2
China	1	**0**	na	na	1	na	na	na	1	na	na	1	na	na	1	3
Colombia	na	**na**	na	na	na	na	na	na	na	na	na	na	na	na	na	na
Croatia	na	**1**	1	na	na	1	na	na	1	1	na	1	1	na	1	1
Czech Republic	na	**1**	1	1	1	1	1	1	1	2	1	1	1	1	1	2
Denmark	3	**4**	3	5	5	4	4	1	7	9	4	3	7	3	3	11
Dominican Rep.	na	**na**	na	na	na	na	na	na	na	na	na	na	na	na	na	na
Egypt	na	**na**	na	na	na	na	na	na	na	na	na	na	na	na	na	na
El Salvador	na	**na**	na	na	na	na	na	na	na	na	na	na	na	na	na	na
Estonia	1	**0**	na	na	na	na	na	na	na	na	na	na	na	na	na	na
Finland	6	**6**	5	8	5	7	7	5	5	15	7	4	9	4	7	8
France	3	**1**	1	2	1	1	2	na	1	5	1	2	3	na	1	4
Georgia	na	**na**	na	na	na	na	na	na	na	na	na	na	na	na	na	na
Germany	1	**1**	1	1	na	1	1	na	1	2	na	1	1	na	na	2
Great Britain	2	**3**	2	3	3	2	2	1	4	3	2	2	4	na	na	na
Greece	na	**5**	4	6	7	4	3	1	5	6	4	6	5	5	5	6
Hungary	0	**0**	1	na	na	na	1	na	na	1	1	1	na	na	1	1
Iceland	3	**8**	6	9	5	9	9	5	7	15	5	11	7	4	8	15
India	na	**3**	3	2	3	3	3	3	2	4	5	2	3	3	4	4
Indonesia	na	**na**	na	na	na	na	na	na	na	na	na	na	na	na	na	na
Iran	na	**na**	na	na	na	na	na	na	na	na	na	na	na	na	na	na
Ireland	2	**2**	2	3	na	3	4	1	2	6	2	3	3	1	2	7
Israel	na	**na**	na	na	na	na	na	na	na	na	na	na	na	na	na	na
Italy	1	**3**	3	3	4	2	3	2	3	5	3	3	3	2	3	4
Japan	0	**2**	2	2	1	1	3	1	1	3	2	1	2	2	2	3
Jordan	na	**na**	na	na	na	na	na	na	na	na	na	na	na	na	na	na
Korea, South	2	**2**	3	2	3	1	4	2	2	3	4	2	1	2	2	7
Latvia	1	**1**	1	1	1	1	na	na	1	1	na	1	1	na	1	na
Lithuania	1	**0**	na	na	na	na	na	na	na	na	na	na	na	na	na	na
Luxembourg	na	**12**	9	14	6	15	12	8	10	22	10	9	18	8	10	18
Macedonia	na	**3**	3	4	3	5	2	4	1	7	1	5	4	3	4	10
Malta	na	**0**	1	na	1	na	na	na	na	1	na	1	na	na	na	na
Mexico	1	**3**	3	2	1	3	3	2	3	3	2	2	3	3	2	2
Moldova	na	**2**	3	2	4	2	1	1	2	4	1	2	4	2	3	5
Montenegro	na	**1**	1	1	na	2	1	na	2	2	1	1	2	na	2	3
Morocco	na	**0**	na	na	na	na	na	na	na	2	na	na	1	na	na	na
Netherlands	14	**24**	20	27	14	27	26	14	23	33	15	25	33	7	25	28
New Zealand	na	**na**	na	na	na	na	na	na	na	na	na	na	na	na	na	na
Nigeria	na	**na**	na	na	na	na	na	na	na	na	na	na	na	na	na	na
Northern Ireland	3	**2**	2	3	na	4	2	1	1	7	2	2	4	2	3	1
Norway	5	**na**	na	na	na	na	na	na	na	na	na	na	na	na	na	na
Pakistan	na	**na**	na	na	na	na	na	na	na	na	na	na	na	na	na	na
Peru	na	**2**	2	3	1	3	4	3	1	4	2	2	3	1	2	4
Philippines	na	**5**	7	2	4	5	6	5	3	6	3	4	7	3	6	2
Poland	na	**0**	1	na	1	na	na	na	1	1	na	na	2	na	1	1
Portugal	1	**1**	1	1	1	1	1	na	1	5	na	na	1	na	1	3
Puerto Rico	na	**5**	4	5	6	5	4	4	3	6	4	3	7	1	4	6
Romania	0	**1**	1	0	0	0	1	0	0	2	0	0	1	0	1	1
Russian Fed.	0	**0**	na	na	na	na	na	na	na	na	na	na	na	na	na	na
Serbia	na	**1**	1	1	1	1	na	na	1	1	na	1	1	1	na	1
Singapore	na	**1**	na	1	na	1	na	1	na	1	na	1	1	na	1	2
Slovakia	na	**0**	na	na	na	na	na	na	na	1	na	na	na	na	na	na
Slovenia	0	**1**	1	na	na	1	1	1	1	1	1	1	1	1	1	1
South Africa	na	**4**	5	2	3	5	2	4	4	2	2	7	4	4	3	7
Spain	1	**3**	2	3	3	3	2	2	2	8	2	3	4	2	2	5
Sweden	9	**15**	12	18	13	17	15	7	12	27	13	12	22	8	12	26
Switzerland	na	**na**	na	na	na	na	na	na	na	na	na	na	na	na	na	na
Taiwan	na	**na**	na	na	na	na	na	na	na	na	na	na	na	na	na	na
Tanzania	na	**19**	18	20	22	17	14	17	21	19	18	20	19	16	20	21
Turkey	na	**0**	na	na	na	na	na	na	1	na	na	na	na	na	na	na
Uganda	na	**5**	10	1	8	3	1	6	4	10	5	6	10	5	5	5
Ukraine	na	**1**	1	1	2	na	na	na	1	1	1	1	na	na	1	3
United States	2	**6**	5	6	6	4	7	4	6	6	3	5	8	6	5	7
Uruguay	na	**na**	na	na	na	na	na	na	na	na	na	na	na	na	na	na
Venezuela	na	**9**	11	7	8	10	10	6	8	14	9	8	9	8	9	10
Vietnam	na	**2**	2	1	na	2	2	1	2	na	1	2	2	1	2	1
Zimbabwe	na	**2**	2	2	2	1	1	1	3	na	1	1	4	2	2	2
Total	2	**4**	4	4	3	4	3	3	3	7	3	4	5	2	4	6

RANKING	
Country	2000
Netherlands	24
Tanzania	19
Sweden	15
Luxembourg	12
Bangladesh	11
Belgium	10
Venezuela	9
Iceland	8
Albania	6
Finland	6
United States	6
Canada	5
Greece	5
Uganda	5
Denmark	4
Philippines	5
Puerto Rico	5
South Africa	4
Austria	3
Macedonia	3
Algeria	3
Italy	3
India	3
Romania	1
Great Britain	3
Spain	3
Mexico	3
Ireland	2
Moldova	2
Peru	2
Korea, South	2
Northern Ireland	2
Chile	2
Japan	2
Zimbabwe	2
Vietnam	2
France	1
Montenegro	1
Portugal	1
Slovenia	1
Croatia	1
Czech Republic	1
Ukraine	1
Belarus	1
Germany	1
Latvia	1
Argentina	1
Singapore	1
Serbia	1
Bulgaria	0
China	0
Poland	0
Bosnia and Herz.	0
Hungary	0
Malta	0
Lithuania	0
Turkey	0
Estonia	0
Morocco	0
Russian Fed.	0
Slovakia	0
Total	4

A071) BELONG CONSERVATION, THE ENVIRONMENT, ECOLOGY, ANIMAL RIGHTS

Please look carefully at the following list of voluntary organizations and activities and say...which, if any, do you belong to? Conservation, environment, animal rights groups.

Belong (%)

(WVS: V46; EVS: V19)

Country	Wave		Gender		Age			Education			Income			Values		
	1990	2000	Male	Female	16-29	30-49	50+	Lower	Middle	Upper	Lower	Middle	Upper	Mat	Mixed	Postm.
Albania	na	**10**	11	10	9	10	12	9	10	17	11	7	14	9	12	8
Algeria	na	**4**	5	4	4	6	2	2	5	6	4	4	5	4	5	5
Argentina	0	**2**	3	2	3	2	2	2	3	4	1	3	3	1	2	3
Armenia	na	**na**	na	na	na	na	na	na	na	na	na	na	na	na	na	na
Australia	na	**na**	na	na	na	na	na	na	na	na	na	na	na	na	na	na
Austria	3	**9**	8	10	10	9	9	6	11	15	7	9	12	2	10	10
Azerbaijan	na	**na**	na	na	na	na	na	na	na	na	na	na	na	na	na	na
Bangladesh	na	**20**	24	16	19	20	25	15	27	27	9	22	29	18	22	22
Belarus	na	**1**	2	1	2	1	na	na	2	1	na	1	2	1	1	2
Belgium	8	**12**	12	12	13	11	12	5	13	15	10	10	14	9	11	15
Bosnia and Herz.	na	**2**	2	2	2	2	1	1	2	5	1	2	4	1	2	4
Brazil	3	**na**	na	na	na	na	na	na	na	na	na	na	na	na	na	na
Bulgaria	4	**1**	1	2	3	2	na	1	1	3	1	2	2	1	2	2
Canada	8	**9**	11	8	8	8	11	5	8	14	6	11	11	5	8	12
Chile	2	**3**	3	3	3	3	3	1	3	6	1	4	6	2	3	4
China	1	**1**	2	1	2	1	na	1	2	5	1	1	2	1	1	3
Colombia	na	**na**	na	na	na	na	na	na	na	na	na	na	na	na	na	na
Croatia	na	**2**	4	1	4	2	1	na	3	7	na	1	5	na	3	2
Czech Republic	na	**7**	7	6	7	6	7	6	8	8	7	7	6	7	7	6
Denmark	13	**13**	10	16	9	12	17	10	16	18	10	13	19	4	13	20
Dominican Rep.	na	**na**	na	na	na	na	na	na	na	na	na	na	na	na	na	na
Egypt	na	**na**	na	na	na	na	na	na	na	na	na	na	na	na	na	na
El Salvador	na	**na**	na	na	na	na	na	na	na	na	na	na	na	na	na	na
Estonia	3	**2**	2	2	1	2	2	2	1	3	1	1	3	2	2	8
Finland	5	**5**	4	6	5	7	3	3	6	10	3	3	9	3	6	7
France	2	**2**	2	3	1	2	3	2	2	3	2	2	2	1	3	3
Georgia	na	**na**	na	na	na	na	na	na	na	na	na	na	na	na	na	na
Germany	4	**3**	3	3	2	4	2	2	3	7	1	2	7	2	3	4
Great Britain	6	**2**	1	2	2	1	1	1	2	1	2	1	2	na	na	na
Greece	na	**11**	10	12	15	8	8	4	9	14	11	9	14	10	11	10
Hungary	1	**2**	1	2	2	1	2	1	2	4	1	2	2	1	2	9
Iceland	5	**5**	6	3	1	7	5	4	2	11	3	6	4	2	5	11
India	na	**7**	9	5	8	7	7	5	6	12	8	5	8	4	11	22
Indonesia	na	**na**	na	na	na	na	na	na	na	na	na	na	na	na	na	na
Iran	na	**na**	na	na	na	na	na	na	na	na	na	na	na	na	na	na
Ireland	2	**3**	3	3	4	2	3	na	2	8	2	2	4	2	2	6
Israel	na	**na**	na	na	na	na	na	na	na	na	na	na	na	na	na	na
Italy	3	**4**	3	4	5	4	3	1	5	7	4	3	4	2	3	6
Japan	1	**3**	4	3	1	3	5	4	3	3	3	3	4	2	3	6
Jordan	na	**na**	na	na	na	na	na	na	na	na	na	na	na	na	na	na
Korea, South	2	**6**	8	4	4	7	8	4	7	5	8	6	4	3	8	10
Latvia	4	**1**	1	1	1	na	1	na	1	2	na	1	1	na	1	na
Lithuania	2	**1**	1	1	2	1	na	na	1	1	na	na	na	na	1	2
Luxembourg	na	**11**	8	15	10	13	10	8	11	18	9	6	16	9	11	15
Macedonia	na	**5**	5	5	5	6	3	4	4	9	3	5	7	4	5	9
Malta	na	**2**	2	2	3	2	2	1	2	5	na	3	3	2	2	6
Mexico	3	**5**	5	4	4	5	5	4	5	6	5	4	7	5	4	6
Moldova	na	**5**	4	5	5	5	4	3	5	7	3	5	6	6	3	6
Montenegro	na	**4**	6	3	4	5	3	1	5	12	3	5	6	4	5	2
Morocco	na	**1**	1	1	na	na	1	na	1	4	na	1	1	na	1	1
Netherlands	24	**44**	40	47	28	47	49	38	41	53	35	48	50	35	43	49
New Zealand	na	**na**	na	na	na	na	na	na	na	na	na	na	na	na	na	na
Nigeria	na	**na**	na	na	na	na	na	na	na	na	na	na	na	na	na	na
Northern Ireland	2	**1**	2	1	na	2	1	1	1	3	1	na	3	na	2	1
Norway	4	**na**	na	na	na	na	na	na	na	na	na	na	na	na	na	na
Pakistan	na	**na**	na	na	na	na	na	na	na	na	na	na	na	na	na	na
Peru	na	**3**	4	2	3	3	5	3	3	4	3	3	4	2	3	5
Philippines	na	**8**	10	7	6	8	11	10	8	7	5	5	15	6	10	9
Poland	na	**1**	2	1	1	1	1	1	2	2	1	1	3	na	2	na
Portugal	1	**1**	1	na	1	na	1	na	1	3	na	na	1	na	na	3
Puerto Rico	na	**4**	3	4	6	5	2	3	1	6	3	3	5	4	4	3
Romania	1	**1**	2	0	1	1	1	0	1	3	0	1	2	0	2	1
Russian Fed.	2	**1**	1	1	1	1	1	na	na	2	na	1	1	1	1	3
Serbia	na	**1**	1	na	1	1	1	1	1	na	1	na	1	1	1	na
Singapore	na	**1**	na	2	1	1	na	1	1	na	2	1	1	1	1	na
Slovakia	na	**3**	3	2	3	2	3	2	2	5	2	3	3	2	3	na
Slovenia	2	**3**	6	1	3	4	3	3	3	5	2	6	5	3	4	2
South Africa	na	**4**	4	4	3	5	3	3	5	10	2	6	4	3	4	9
Spain	1	**2**	2	2	4	2	1	1	2	7	1	2	3	1	1	6
Sweden	11	**11**	11	12	11	13	10	7	10	17	8	13	14	7	11	15
Switzerland	11	**na**	na	na	na	na	na	na	na	na	na	na	na	na	na	na
Taiwan	na	**na**	na	na	na	na	na	na	na	na	na	na	na	na	na	na
Tanzania	na	**20**	20	20	24	19	14	15	26	26	17	25	21	16	22	25
Turkey	na	**0**	na	na	na	na	na	na	na	na	na	na	na	na	na	na
Uganda	na	**10**	19	2	13	7	11	10	11	5	14	16	17	7	13	6
Ukraine	na	**1**	1	na	na	1	1	1	na	1	1	na	2	1	1	na
United States	9	**16**	14	17	13	15	19	13	12	19	9	20	18	15	14	21
Uruguay	na	**na**	na	na	na	na	na	na	na	na	na	na	na	na	na	na
Venezuela	na	**12**	15	9	13	13	9	8	9	24	8	11	15	11	12	15
Vietnam	na	**8**	9	6	8	9	6	7	7	13	6	8	9	6	9	11
Zimbabwe	na	**2**	4	1	3	1	4	1	4	na	1	2	6	2	3	1
Total	5	6	6	5	6	6	5	4	5	10	5	6	7	4	7	9

RANKING	
Country	2000
Netherlands	44
Bangladesh	20
Tanzania	20
United States	16
Denmark	13
Venezuela	12
Belgium	12
Sweden	11
Greece	11
Luxembourg	11
Albania	10
Uganda	10
Austria	9
Canada	9
Philippines	8
Vietnam	8
India	7
Czech Republic	7
Korea, South	6
Macedonia	5
Finland	5
Romania	1
Iceland	5
Moldova	5
Mexico	5
Algeria	4
Montenegro	4
South Africa	4
Italy	4
Puerto Rico	4
Slovenia	3
Japan	3
Peru	3
Chile	3
Ireland	3
Germany	3
Slovakia	3
Zimbabwe	2
France	2
Argentina	2
Croatia	2
Spain	2
Malta	2
Bosnia and Herz.	2
Estonia	2
Hungary	2
Great Britain	2
Bulgaria	1
China	1
Poland	1
Northern Ireland	1
Belarus	1
Singapore	1
Serbia	1
Latvia	1
Lithuania	1
Russian Fed.	1
Ukraine	1
Morocco	1
Portugal	1
Turkey	0
Total	6

A072) BELONG PROFESSIONAL ASSOCIATIONS

Please look carefully at the following list of voluntary organizations and activities and say...which, if any, do you belong to? Professional associations.

Belong (%)

(WVS: V47; EVS: V20)

Country	Wave		Gender		Age			Education			Income			Values		
	1990	2000	Male	Female	16-29	30-49	50+	Lower	Middle	Upper	Lower	Middle	Upper	Mat	Mixed	Postm.
Albania	na	**11**	15	7	8	14	8	6	12	22	9	13	11	10	11	13
Algeria	na	**9**	10	8	8	9	9	4	11	10	9	9	9	10	8	8
Argentina	3	**2**	2	1	1	2	2	na	1	13	1	1	4	na	2	4
Armenia	na	**na**	na	na	na	na	na	na	na	na	na	na	na	na	na	na
Australia	na	**na**	na	na	na	na	na	na	na	na	na	na	na	na	na	na
Austria	6	**7**	10	5	4	9	7	5	6	21	5	6	12	5	8	8
Azerbaijan	na	**na**	na	na	na	na	na	na	na	na	na	na	na	na	na	na
Bangladesh	na	**21**	28	11	17	24	19	15	24	32	17	20	24	21	21	18
Belarus	na	**1**	1	na	na	1	na	na	1	na	na	1	1	1	1	na
Belgium	7	**9**	11	7	7	12	8	4	8	15	5	8	13	4	10	11
Bosnia and Herz.	na	**2**	3	2	2	3	2	na	2	6	1	2	6	3	2	4
Brazil	5	**na**	na	na	na	na	na	na	na	na	na	na	na	na	na	na
Bulgaria	5	**3**	4	2	1	6	1	na	2	8	1	3	5	2	4	na
Canada	16	**18**	22	14	13	22	16	4	11	41	7	14	33	14	15	25
Chile	3	**4**	4	3	2	5	2	na	2	13	na	3	10	2	4	6
China	26	**1**	2	1	3	1	na	na	2	7	na	1	3	1	2	na
Colombia	na	**na**	na	na	na	na	na	na	na	na	na	na	na	na	na	na
Croatia	na	**3**	4	3	2	4	3	2	2	10	na	3	6	2	4	2
Czech Republic	na	**6**	7	5	4	7	6	3	7	18	3	4	12	4	6	13
Denmark	12	**11**	13	9	4	12	13	7	10	19	6	14	16	5	10	20
Dominican Rep.	na	**na**	na	na	na	na	na	na	na	na	na	na	na	na	na	na
Egypt	na	**na**	na	na	na	na	na	na	na	na	na	na	na	na	na	na
El Salvador	na	**na**	na	na	na	na	na	na	na	na	na	na	na	na	na	na
Estonia	4	**4**	3	4	2	7	2	2	2	10	1	2	8	3	4	7
Finland	15	**6**	9	4	6	8	5	3	7	15	6	4	9	3	7	7
France	5	**3**	4	2	1	6	2	2	3	7	1	4	5	1	3	7
Georgia	na	**na**	na	na	na	na	na	na	na	na	na	na	na	na	na	na
Germany	6	**4**	7	3	4	6	3	2	5	12	1	4	6	1	6	6
Great Britain	11	**2**	2	2	na	3	1	na	2	5	1	na	5	na	na	na
Greece	na	**14**	18	12	8	20	17	5	12	18	8	16	22	15	15	13
Hungary	6	**4**	4	4	2	6	2	2	3	17	2	4	5	3	5	8
Iceland	15	**19**	20	18	9	25	20	7	16	50	9	19	30	12	21	24
India	na	**9**	11	7	8	11	8	6	12	15	7	6	13	7	14	4
Indonesia	na	**na**	na	na	na	na	na	na	na	na	na	na	na	na	na	na
Iran	na	**na**	na	na	na	na	na	na	na	na	na	na	na	na	na	na
Ireland	5	**8**	10	5	11	9	4	1	3	31	2	4	18	7	8	6
Israel	na	**na**	na	na	na	na	na	na	na	na	na	na	na	na	na	na
Italy	4	**7**	10	4	5	9	7	4	5	23	4	5	13	3	8	9
Japan	4	**5**	7	3	2	3	8	6	5	6	4	4	8	5	5	9
Jordan	na	**na**	na	na	na	na	na	na	na	na	na	na	na	na	na	na
Korea, South	13	**9**	13	5	11	8	8	2	5	16	7	8	11	6	11	12
Latvia	6	**1**	na	2	na	2	1	na	1	5	1	2	2	2	1	2
Lithuania	3	**1**	1	na	1	1	1	na	na	2	na	na	1	na	1	3
Luxembourg	na	**6**	8	5	5	7	6	3	7	11	3	4	10	8	5	9
Macedonia	na	**7**	8	6	5	9	5	3	6	14	5	8	9	7	6	9
Malta	na	**3**	5	2	4	4	2	na	2	18	na	1	8	1	4	9
Mexico	3	**3**	4	2	3	3	2	1	1	16	1	2	6	2	3	6
Moldova	na	**7**	7	8	7	9	6	4	7	12	3	8	10	8	7	8
Montenegro	na	**6**	7	5	4	6	6	2	6	14	2	7	8	3	8	8
Morocco	na	**3**	3	2	2	4	2	2	1	10	1	4	8	1	4	7
Netherlands	12	**16**	21	12	13	20	15	4	15	30	10	15	28	5	16	23
New Zealand	na	**na**	na	na	na	na	na	na	na	na	na	na	na	na	na	na
Nigeria	na	**na**	na	na	na	na	na	na	na	na	na	na	na	na	na	na
Northern Ireland	7	**4**	6	3	3	5	5	2	2	15	3	2	12	3	6	2
Norway	16	**na**	na	na	na	na	na	na	na	na	na	na	na	na	na	na
Pakistan	na	**na**	na	na	na	na	na	na	na	na	na	na	na	na	na	na
Peru	na	**6**	8	4	5	6	8	2	3	13	3	6	10	5	6	6
Philippines	na	**4**	4	4	3	4	6	1	1	12	2	4	7	3	5	3
Poland	na	**4**	5	4	3	5	4	2	6	14	3	5	7	3	5	7
Portugal	4	**1**	2	1	2	2	1	na	2	7	na	1	2	1	1	na
Puerto Rico	na	**11**	12	10	9	14	9	3	4	15	4	11	17	7	11	11
Romania	2	**2**	2	2	2	2	2	0	1	7	0	0	4	0	3	7
Russian Fed.	2	**1**	1	1	2	1	1	na	1	2	1	1	1	1	1	na
Serbia	na	**3**	3	2	2	3	3	na	2	7	1	3	3	2	3	6
Singapore	na	**4**	6	3	3	6	3	na	2	25	na	2	11	6	4	6
Slovakia	na	**5**	6	4	4	6	4	1	4	26	3	3	8	3	6	10
Slovenia	6	**7**	9	5	2	11	5	2	5	21	3	9	13	4	7	7
South Africa	na	**6**	8	2	2	8	6	1	9	35	na	6	13	6	6	2
Spain	2	**2**	3	2	1	4	2	1	1	9	1	2	5	1	2	4
Sweden	12	**15**	14	15	8	17	16	9	8	30	10	14	21	12	13	18
Switzerland	14	**na**	na	na	na	na	na	na	na	na	na	na	na	na	na	na
Taiwan	na	**na**	na	na	na	na	na	na	na	na	na	na	na	na	na	na
Tanzania	na	**23**	23	23	22	24	21	14	26	49	15	30	31	18	26	38
Turkey	na	**1**	2	na	1	1	2	1	1	7	na	1	4	na	2	1
Uganda	na	**9**	14	5	8	11	6	4	12	10	7	12	18	8	10	10
Ukraine	na	**2**	2	2	3	1	3	1	1	5	1	2	3	1	2	3
United States	15	**28**	33	23	23	30	30	10	19	40	15	30	44	26	28	30
Uruguay	na	**na**	na	na	na	na	na	na	na	na	na	na	na	na	na	na
Venezuela	na	**9**	11	7	8	12	7	3	7	22	5	9	13	9	9	9
Vietnam	na	**13**	16	11	9	16	12	11	16	15	11	13	16	11	15	12
Zimbabwe	na	**4**	7	2	3	5	5	2	6	78	1	3	15	4	5	3
Total	8	7	9	5	6	9	6	4	6	17	4	7	12	5	8	10

RANKING	
Country	2000
United States	28
Tanzania	23
Bangladesh	21
Iceland	19
Canada	18
Netherlands	16
Sweden	15
Greece	14
Vietnam	13
Denmark	11
Albania	11
Puerto Rico	11
Venezuela	9
India	9
Belgium	9
Uganda	9
Korea, South	9
Algeria	9
Romania	2
Ireland	8
Austria	7
Moldova	7
Italy	7
Slovenia	7
Macedonia	7
Luxembourg	6
Finland	6
Czech Republic	6
Peru	6
Montenegro	6
South Africa	6
Slovakia	5
Japan	5
Germany	4
Singapore	4
Poland	4
Northern Ireland	4
Zimbabwe	4
Philippines	4
Estonia	4
Hungary	4
Chile	4
Croatia	3
France	3
Malta	3
Mexico	3
Morocco	3
Bulgaria	3
Serbia	3
Bosnia and Herz.	2
Spain	2
Ukraine	2
Argentina	2
Great Britain	2
Latvia	1
China	1
Portugal	1
Turkey	1
Russian Fed.	1
Belarus	1
Lithuania	1
Total	7

A073) BELONG YOUTH WORK

Please look carefully at the following list of voluntary organizations and activities and say...which, if any, do you belong to? Youth work (e.g. scouts, guides, youth clubs etc.).

(WVS: V48; EVS: V21)

Belong (%)

Country	Wave		Gender		Age			Education			Income			Values		
	1990	2000	Male	Female	16-29	30-49	50+	Lower	Middle	Upper	Lower	Middle	Upper	Mat	Mixed	Postm.
Albania	na	12	15	9	33	6	3	10	12	18	13	12	11	10	14	18
Algeria	na	10	13	7	15	7	4	2	10	15	11	8	11	4	13	9
Argentina	2	3	2	3	5	2	2	2	4	5	2	2	5	1	4	2
Armenia	na	na	na	na	na	na	na	na	na	na	na	na	na	na	na	na
Australia	na	na	na	na	na	na	na	na	na	na	na	na	na	na	na	na
Austria	3	3	2	4	5	4	2	2	4	8	2	3	3	2	3	6
Azerbaijan	na	na	na	na	na	na	na	na	na	na	na	na	na	na	na	na
Bangladesh	na	12	17	6	14	11	10	6	17	23	11	11	15	11	13	13
Belarus	na	1	1	na	2	na	1	na	1	2	na	1	1	na	1	na
Belgium	8	8	9	7	18	9	3	3	9	10	4	6	12	6	8	12
Bosnia and Herz.	na	2	3	2	6	1	na	1	2	4	1	3	2	2	2	4
Brazil	4	na	na	na	na	na	na	na	na	na	na	na	na	na	na	na
Bulgaria	2	1	2	1	3	2	na	1	1	4	1	1	2	1	2	na
Canada	10	11	10	12	12	14	7	6	11	15	7	12	14	4	12	10
Chile	6	5	6	4	10	4	1	1	6	8	4	5	5	4	5	7
China	9	1	1	1	5	na	na	na	2	7	1	1	1	1	2	3
Colombia	na	na	na	na	na	na	na	na	na	na	na	na	na	na	na	na
Croatia	na	2	2	3	7	1	na	1	2	5	1	1	5	na	3	3
Czech Republic	na	7	7	7	9	9	4	6	7	14	5	7	8	5	7	10
Denmark	5	7	8	5	8	8	5	5	10	9	5	7	10	4	7	9
Dominican Rep.	na	na	na	na	na	na	na	na	na	na	na	na	na	na	na	na
Egypt	na	na	na	na	na	na	na	na	na	na	na	na	na	na	na	na
El Salvador	na	na	na	na	na	na	na	na	na	na	na	na	na	na	na	na
Estonia	3	2	3	2	5	1	2	1	2	5	1	1	4	1	3	4
Finland	5	7	7	8	11	9	4	3	12	13	5	7	10	8	7	7
France	3	2	2	2	3	2	1	2	1	5	2	3	1	2	2	2
Georgia	na	na	na	na	na	na	na	na	na	na	na	na	na	na	na	na
Germany	3	2	1	3	2	3	1	1	3	2	1	2	2	na	2	4
Great Britain	4	6	4	7	5	8	4	6	5	7	5	6	9	na	na	na
Greece	na	6	7	4	6	5	5	2	4	7	4	6	6	10	4	4
Hungary	2	1	1	1	1	na	1	na	na	4	1	1	1	na	2	na
Iceland	8	7	7	7	7	9	5	6	9	5	6	9	7	6	8	3
India	na	6	8	4	10	6	3	5	4	11	8	4	7	3	10	9
Indonesia	na	na	na	na	na	na	na	na	na	na	na	na	na	na	na	na
Iran	na	na	na	na	na	na	na	na	na	na	na	na	na	na	na	na
Ireland	6	7	8	7	10	8	4	3	9	10	5	7	10	5	8	8
Israel	na	na	na	na	na	na	na	na	na	na	na	na	na	na	na	na
Italy	3	4	4	5	7	5	3	2	7	6	3	5	4	2	4	6
Japan	1	2	3	2	1	2	2	na	2	3	1	2	4	2	2	2
Jordan	na	na	na	na	na	na	na	na	na	na	na	na	na	na	na	na
Korea, South	7	4	6	3	5	4	5	2	4	6	3	4	6	3	6	6
Latvia	2	1	1	1	3	na	na	na	1	na	na	1	1	na	1	na
Lithuania	5	2	1	3	6	na	na	1	2	2	1	1	2	1	2	1
Luxembourg	na	9	10	8	17	6	6	6	8	13	5	10	11	8	8	15
Macedonia	na	5	6	4	13	4	1	3	6	7	3	4	9	4	6	10
Malta	na	2	3	2	4	2	2	1	3	5	1	3	3	1	3	1
Mexico	4	4	5	4	6	4	2	3	5	10	3	3	7	4	5	6
Moldova	na	6	5	6	13	3	2	2	6	9	2	4	10	4	5	15
Montenegro	na	3	3	2	9	2	na	1	4	4	3	5	1	1	4	5
Morocco	na	1	1	1	2	1	1	1	4	3	1	1	4	1	1	3
Netherlands	7	7	6	7	14	7	2	3	9	7	7	6	5	3	8	4
New Zealand	na	na	na	na	na	na	na	na	na	na	na	na	na	na	na	na
Nigeria	na	na	na	na	na	na	na	na	na	na	na	na	na	na	na	na
Northern Ireland	11	6	6	6	10	7	3	4	7	10	3	6	9	4	7	7
Norway	6	na	na	na	na	na	na	na	na	na	na	na	na	na	na	na
Pakistan	na	na	na	na	na	na	na	na	na	na	na	na	na	na	na	na
Peru	na	6	7	5	10	3	3	6	5	7	4	7	6	4	6	7
Philippines	na	8	9	6	11	6	4	4	8	12	6	5	13	5	9	7
Poland	na	2	2	1	2	1	2	1	2	3	2	1	3	1	2	3
Portugal	3	1	2	1	2	1	1	1	3	1	1	1	3	1	2	2
Puerto Rico	na	9	12	8	10	12	8	4	6	12	7	11	11	6	9	13
Romania	1	1	1	1	2	0	0	0	1	1	0	1	1	1	0	3
Russian Fed.	3	1	1	1	3	na	na	na	1	1	na	1	1	1	1	na
Serbia	na	1	1	1	5	1	na	1	1	3	1	na	2	1	2	1
Singapore	na	8	8	8	15	2	1	11	7	8	7	9	8	5	9	12
Slovakia	na	7	6	7	11	6	5	4	7	12	3	7	8	5	8	11
Slovenia	2	5	6	3	8	4	2	1	5	8	4	5	9	3	5	6
South Africa	na	10	10	11	17	6	6	7	14	17	6	14	13	12	10	7
Spain	2	2	2	2	4	2	1	1	3	5	2	1	4	1	1	5
Sweden	9	7	8	6	10	9	3	6	8	6	6	5	11	4	7	9
Switzerland	4	na	na	na	na	na	na	na	na	na	na	na	na	na	na	na
Taiwan	na	na	na	na	na	na	na	na	na	na	na	na	na	na	na	na
Tanzania	na	18	18	18	26	17	10	17	22	16	20	20	14	15	21	13
Turkey	na	1	1	na	1	na	na	na	1	4	na	na	2	na	1	1
Uganda	na	21	27	16	35	8	7	14	25	13	21	25	21	19	21	26
Ukraine	na	1	2	1	3	1	na	na	1	4	1	1	2	na	2	na
United States	13	26	24	28	26	33	18	19	28	28	19	27	37	30	26	24
Uruguay	na	na	na	na	na	na	na	na	na	na	na	na	na	na	na	na
Venezuela	na	8	11	5	11	8	5	3	9	13	8	8	10	9	8	10
Vietnam	na	16	19	12	37	12	5	11	21	24	13	17	16	14	17	14
Zimbabwe	na	6	8	3	8	2	4	2	11	na	4	6	9	4	6	7
Total	5	6	7	5	11	5	3	4	6	9	5	6	7	4	7	8

RANKING

Country	2000
United States	26
Uganda	21
Tanzania	18
Vietnam	16
Albania	12
Bangladesh	12
Canada	11
South Africa	10
Algeria	10
Puerto Rico	9
Luxembourg	9
Venezuela	8
Singapore	8
Belgium	8
Denmark	7
Philippines	8
Finland	7
Ireland	7
Czech Republic	7
Iceland	7
Sweden	7
Slovakia	7
Netherlands	7
India	6
Northern Ireland	6
Peru	6
Great Britain	6
Moldova	6
Greece	6
Zimbabwe	6
Macedonia	5
Chile	5
Slovenia	5
Korea, South	4
Italy	4
Mexico	4
Austria	3
Romania	1
Argentina	3
Montenegro	3
Estonia	2
Malta	2
Croatia	2
Bosnia and Herz.	2
Japan	2
France	2
Spain	2
Germany	2
Lithuania	2
Poland	2
Bulgaria	1
Morocco	1
Ukraine	1
Serbia	1
Portugal	1
China	1
Hungary	1
Belarus	1
Latvia	1
Russian Fed.	1
Turkey	1
Total	6

A074) BELONG SPORTS OR RECREATION

Please look carefully at the following list of voluntary organizations and activities and say...which, if any, do you belong to? Sports or recreation.

Belong (%)

(WVS: V49; EVS: V22)

Country	Wave		Gender		Age			Education			Income			Values		
	1990	2000	Male	Female	16-29	30-49	50+	Lower	Middle	Upper	Lower	Middle	Upper	Mat	Mixed	Postm.
Albania	na	**11**	18	4	24	8	3	7	12	16	7	12	12	7	14	15
Algeria	na	**14**	20	9	22	11	5	4	18	17	14	14	18	13	16	11
Argentina	5	**8**	11	5	9	9	5	6	10	11	4	7	11	6	8	9
Armenia	na	**na**	na	na	na	na	na	na	na	na	na	na	na	na	na	na
Australia	na	**na**	na	na	na	na	na	na	na	na	na	na	na	na	na	na
Austria	17	**23**	30	16	30	25	17	17	31	23	16	23	28	14	24	24
Azerbaijan	na	**na**	na	na	na	na	na	na	na	na	na	na	na	na	na	na
Bangladesh	na	**25**	33	15	29	23	22	12	36	45	20	27	27	23	27	22
Belarus	na	**2**	3	1	5	1	1	na	3	3	1	2	4	2	2	na
Belgium	20	**26**	31	21	40	31	14	13	27	34	18	21	37	22	28	28
Bosnia and Herz.	na	**11**	19	5	23	10	3	4	11	19	5	10	16	8	12	17
Brazil	8	**na**	na	na	na	na	na	na	na	na	na	na	na	na	na	na
Bulgaria	4	**5**	8	2	11	5	2	1	6	9	2	7	5	3	7	2
Canada	23	**28**	32	23	34	32	19	16	28	37	17	27	36	22	28	28
Chile	12	**15**	23	8	25	14	7	9	17	21	10	18	20	12	16	18
China	4	**3**	3	4	6	3	na	1	5	7	2	2	6	4	4	3
Colombia	na	**na**	na	na	na	na	na	na	na	na	na	na	na	na	na	na
Croatia	na	**12**	21	4	22	12	5	5	16	19	5	10	18	11	10	21
Czech Republic	na	**23**	30	16	35	25	14	20	24	30	14	24	28	19	25	27
Denmark	34	**33**	37	29	40	38	24	29	45	37	22	39	41	28	34	35
Dominican Rep.	na	**na**	na	na	na	na	na	na	na	na	na	na	na	na	na	na
Egypt	na	**na**	na	na	na	na	na	na	na	na	na	na	na	na	na	na
El Salvador	na	**na**	na	na	na	na	na	na	na	na	na	na	na	na	na	na
Estonia	14	**9**	12	6	22	7	4	8	10	9	3	7	12	6	12	7
Finland	23	**26**	33	20	29	33	17	20	36	27	16	28	35	25	27	23
France	16	**17**	20	13	21	18	12	12	19	26	11	18	23	12	16	24
Georgia	na	**na**	na	na	na	na	na	na	na	na	na	na	na	na	na	na
Germany	21	**28**	32	26	41	33	18	18	37	32	15	28	42	26	28	35
Great Britain	18	**3**	3	3	2	5	1	2	3	5	2	3	5	na	na	na
Greece	na	**15**	22	10	20	13	9	7	18	15	14	16	18	15	14	18
Hungary	4	**4**	5	3	9	3	2	2	6	12	1	4	6	2	5	5
Iceland	30	**34**	39	29	38	38	25	29	38	39	25	36	43	26	38	32
India	na	**11**	15	7	14	11	8	8	10	18	13	9	12	7	17	24
Indonesia	na	**na**	na	na	na	na	na	na	na	na	na	na	na	na	na	na
Iran	na	**na**	na	na	na	na	na	na	na	na	na	na	na	na	na	na
Ireland	24	**28**	37	19	41	28	18	17	28	45	12	30	41	32	27	31
Israel	na	**na**	na	na	na	na	na	na	na	na	na	na	na	na	na	na
Italy	10	**12**	16	8	16	14	6	7	14	18	8	10	18	10	12	11
Japan	9	**14**	16	13	9	15	16	13	15	13	13	17	14	18	13	18
Jordan	na	**na**	na	na	na	na	na	na	na	na	na	na	na	na	na	na
Korea, South	17	**25**	29	21	26	26	20	2	21	33	22	23	28	21	28	31
Latvia	9	**7**	10	4	18	7	3	4	6	13	4	4	12	5	8	13
Lithuania	8	**4**	4	3	10	2	na	na	5	5	1	3	4	4	4	2
Luxembourg	na	**26**	30	22	35	30	16	18	30	30	15	28	33	24	27	27
Macedonia	na	**13**	19	7	19	15	6	6	15	20	9	13	19	11	14	26
Malta	na	**9**	17	2	14	10	5	4	11	16	4	10	20	7	10	16
Mexico	8	**9**	13	5	15	7	4	4	13	24	5	9	17	7	10	14
Moldova	na	**6**	7	4	14	3	2	1	5	9	3	5	9	5	6	7
Montenegro	na	**11**	18	5	24	12	3	4	16	18	9	9	16	7	16	16
Morocco	na	**5**	7	3	9	3	1	4	12	11	3	5	9	4	6	7
Netherlands	43	**51**	54	49	63	54	42	41	55	57	40	54	60	41	53	53
New Zealand	na	**na**	na	na	na	na	na	na	na	na	na	na	na	na	na	na
Nigeria	na	**na**	na	na	na	na	na	na	na	na	na	na	na	na	na	na
Northern Ireland	17	**14**	19	10	23	13	11	7	16	29	11	14	22	9	16	18
Norway	33	**na**	na	na	na	na	na	na	na	na	na	na	na	na	na	na
Pakistan	na	**na**	na	na	na	na	na	na	na	na	na	na	na	na	na	na
Peru	na	**11**	18	6	15	10	7	7	11	16	9	12	14	8	12	15
Philippines	na	**12**	19	6	19	10	8	7	12	19	8	10	20	10	15	10
Poland	na	**3**	5	1	5	3	2	2	4	8	2	2	7	2	4	4
Portugal	14	**9**	16	3	11	12	6	6	14	16	1	9	19	6	10	12
Puerto Rico	na	**8**	13	6	15	8	5	4	5	11	6	7	13	7	8	9
Romania	3	**2**	3	1	5	2	1	0	2	4	0	1	4	1	3	4
Russian Fed.	5	**4**	6	3	11	3	1	na	4	8	3	3	6	2	6	8
Serbia	na	**8**	14	3	13	9	5	4	10	12	5	8	11	7	10	11
Singapore	na	**15**	22	9	21	12	5	9	17	24	8	14	22	10	16	26
Slovakia	na	**18**	30	7	23	20	11	12	20	18	13	18	20	15	20	21
Slovenia	8	**17**	25	10	25	19	9	6	20	28	7	17	31	16	17	16
South Africa	na	**24**	33	14	34	21	8	19	29	47	16	27	32	20	24	44
Spain	6	**8**	11	5	14	8	4	4	12	11	4	7	14	5	8	12
Sweden	32	**37**	40	34	42	44	27	29	40	39	27	39	49	33	36	44
Switzerland	na	**na**	na	na	na	na	na	na	na	na	na	na	na	na	na	na
Taiwan	na	**na**	na	na	na	na	na	na	na	na	na	na	na	na	na	na
Tanzania	na	**29**	32	26	36	28	19	23	38	33	25	34	28	27	30	42
Turkey	na	**1**	1	na	na	1	na	na	1	2	na	1	1	na	1	1
Uganda	na	**24**	39	10	32	18	9	15	28	22	24	30	29	20	25	31
Ukraine	na	**2**	3	1	3	3	na	na	2	4	1	2	5	2	2	2
United States	20	**36**	45	27	43	41	24	28	39	38	25	38	51	33	37	35
Uruguay	na	**na**	na	na	na	na	na	na	na	na	na	na	na	na	na	na
Venezuela	na	**21**	32	10	28	18	11	10	22	32	15	20	30	20	21	28
Vietnam	na	**19**	26	12	24	19	15	14	23	36	18	14	25	13	23	18
Zimbabwe	na	**8**	16	1	13	5	2	4	15	10	5	7	18	7	9	8
Total	16	**16**	21	11	22	16	10	11	17	22	11	16	21	11	18	22

RANKING	
Country	2000
Netherlands	51
Denmark	33
Sweden	37
United States	36
Iceland	34
Tanzania	29
Germany	28
Ireland	28
Canada	28
Luxembourg	26
Belgium	26
Finland	26
Bangladesh	25
Korea, South	25
Uganda	24
South Africa	24
Czech Republic	23
Austria	23
Venezuela	21
Vietnam	19
Slovakia	18
Slovenia	17
France	17
Greece	15
Singapore	15
Chile	15
Algeria	14
Northern Ireland	14
Japan	14
Macedonia	13
Philippines	12
Croatia	12
Italy	12
Peru	11
Bosnia and Herz.	11
Montenegro	11
India	11
Albania	11
Malta	9
Romania	2
Estonia	9
Portugal	9
Mexico	9
Zimbabwe	8
Puerto Rico	8
Serbia	8
Spain	8
Argentina	8
Latvia	7
Moldova	6
Morocco	5
Bulgaria	5
Russian Fed.	4
Hungary	4
Lithuania	4
China	3
Poland	3
Great Britain	3
Belarus	2
Ukraine	2
Turkey	1
Total	16

A075) BELONG WOMEN'S GROUP

Please look carefully at the following list of voluntary organizations and activities and say...which, if any, do you belong to?

Women's groups.

Belong (%)

(WVS: V50; EVS: V23)

Country	Wave		Gender		Age			Education			Income			Values		
	1990	2000	Male	Female	16-29	30-49	50+	Lower	Middle	Upper	Lower	Middle	Upper	Mat	Mixed	Postm.
Albania	na	14	2	25	10	16	14	14	14	12	14	16	12	12	15	10
Algeria	na	4	1	8	4	5	4	3	5	4	4	4	7	4	5	3
Argentina	1	1	na	1	1	1	1	na	2	1	1	1	1	1	1	1
Armenia	na	na	na	na	na	na	na	na	na	na	na	na	na	na	na	na
Australia	na	na	na	na	na	na	na	na	na	na	na	na	na	na	na	na
Austria	4	4	na	8	2	4	5	5	3	5	4	4	4	2	4	5
Azerbaijan	na	na	na	na	na	na	na	na	na	na	na	na	na	na	na	na
Bangladesh	na	14	11	19	14	15	14	15	13	15	11	17	13	15	15	9
Belarus	na	0	na	1	na	1	na	na	1	1	na	1	1	na	1	na
Belgium	9	10	2	16	2	8	15	13	7	9	13	9	8	13	9	7
Bosnia and Herz.	na	3	1	5	2	4	2	2	3	2	1	3	4	2	3	8
Brazil	2	na	na	na	na	na	na	na	na	na	na	na	na	na	na	na
Bulgaria	2	1	na	2	1	2	1	na	2	1	1	2	1	1	1	na
Canada	7	8	2	14	5	7	11	7	8	10	8	7	9	8	8	9
Chile	3	5	na	10	4	6	7	6	5	5	6	5	5	7	5	5
China	3	3	1	6	3	4	2	1	5	5	1	4	6	3	4	3
Colombia	na	na	na	na	na	na	na	na	na	na	na	na	na	na	na	na
Croatia	na	2	1	4	na	5	na	5	1	1	2	2	3	3	2	2
Czech Republic	na	3	1	4	1	2	3	3	3	1	4	2	2	5	2	4
Denmark	2	2	0	4	0	3	3	2	2	3	3	2	1	1	2	3
Dominican Rep.	na	na	na	na	na	na	na	na	na	na	na	na	na	na	na	na
Egypt	na	na	na	na	na	na	na	na	na	na	na	na	na	na	na	na
El Salvador	na	na	na	na	na	na	na	na	na	na	na	na	na	na	na	na
Estonia	2	2	na	4	1	4	2	2	2	4	3	3	1	1	3	na
Finland	3	4	na	8	1	4	7	6	4	2	6	4	5	4	5	3
France	1	0	na	1	1	na	na	na	na	1	1	na	1	1	na	1
Georgia	na	na	na	na	na	na	na	na	na	na	na	na	na	na	na	na
Germany	7	4	na	6	na	5	4	3	4	5	3	4	5	5	3	5
Great Britain	5	2	1	3	2	1	3	2	1	2	2	2	1	na	na	na
Greece	na	4	2	6	1	5	8	2	6	3	1	7	4	5	3	6
Hungary	1	0	na	na	1	1	na	na	na	2	na	na	1	na	na	na
Iceland	7	6	1	11	2	4	11	6	4	10	6	6	6	6	6	5
India	na	6	4	9	7	6	5	6	5	7	6	5	7	4	8	7
Indonesia	na	na	na	na	na	na	na	na	na	na	na	na	na	na	na	na
Iran	na	na	na	na	na	na	na	na	na	na	na	na	na	na	na	na
Ireland	5	4	1	8	3	3	7	5	4	5	5	6	4	4	4	6
Israel	na	na	na	na	na	na	na	na	na	na	na	na	na	na	na	na
Italy	0	0	na	1	na	na	na	na	1	na	1	1	na	1	na	na
Japan	3	4	1	7	na	2	7	5	5	1	4	4	4	3	4	4
Jordan	na	na	na	na	na	na	na	na	na	na	na	na	na	na	na	na
Korea, South	3	4	1	7	3	4	3	na	4	4	3	5	3	4	3	4
Latvia	1	0	na	1	na	na	1	na	1	na	1	na	na	na	na	2
Lithuania	3	0	na	1	na	1	na	na	na	1	na	na	1	na	na	na
Luxembourg	na	6	5	7	4	7	6	6	6	6	7	5	5	4	6	7
Macedonia	na	6	2	10	5	8	5	6	5	10	3	7	9	6	6	2
Malta	na	1	na	2	na	na	3	3	1	na	1	na	1	1	1	2
Mexico	2	3	1	5	3	4	3	3	3	4	4	3	3	3	3	4
Moldova	na	3	1	4	3	3	2	1	3	4	na	3	4	2	3	na
Montenegro	na	3	na	6	2	6	2	1	5	7	2	3	5	4	4	na
Morocco	na	2	na	3	2	2	1	1	1	6	1	3	3	1	2	1
Netherlands	8	5	1	8	2	3	8	5	4	5	4	4	5	7	4	6
New Zealand	na	na	na	na	na	na	na	na	na	na	na	na	na	na	na	na
Nigeria	na	na	na	na	na	na	na	na	na	na	na	na	na	na	na	na
Northern Ireland	5	4	1	7	1	3	5	5	3	4	4	3	6	4	4	4
Norway	3	na	na	na	na	na	na	na	na	na	na	na	na	na	na	na
Pakistan	na	na	na	na	na	na	na	na	na	na	na	na	na	na	na	na
Peru	na	6	1	11	4	8	5	9	6	4	8	6	4	5	7	4
Philippines	na	10	2	19	7	12	11	11	10	10	9	10	12	9	11	16
Poland	na	1	1	2	1	2	1	1	1	2	2	na	2	1	2	na
Portugal	0	na	na	na	na	na	na	na	na	na	na	na	na	na	na	na
Puerto Rico	na	3	4	2	4	2	3	1	1	4	3	1	5	2	2	5
Romania	1	0	0	1	1	0	0	0	0	1	1	0	1	0	1	1
Russian Fed.	2	1	na	1	na	1	na	na	1	na	1	na	na	1	na	na
Serbia	na	0	na	1	na	1	na	na	na	1	na	1	1	na	na	1
Singapore	na	1	na	2	1	2	2	1	1	2	1	1	2	2	1	2
Slovakia	na	7	1	12	2	7	11	8	7	3	9	6	7	7	8	2
Slovenia	0	2	2	2	1	1	3	3	2	2	2	3	2	1	2	1
South Africa	na	9	1	19	3	12	15	8	11	10	7	15	7	9	9	11
Spain	1	2	1	3	1	2	2	2	2	3	2	2	3	2	2	4
Sweden	3	4	na	7	na	3	6	3	2	6	3	2	5	5	2	5
Switzerland	na	na	na	na	na	na	na	na	na	na	na	na	na	na	na	na
Taiwan	na	na	na	na	na	na	na	na	na	na	na	na	na	na	na	na
Tanzania	na	24	10	41	22	28	18	24	20	30	24	25	22	23	23	33
Turkey	na	0	na	1	na	na	na	na	na	2	na	na	1	na	na	1
Uganda	na	16	1	29	10	23	15	25	13	4	17	14	16	19	14	12
Ukraine	na	1	na	2	1	2	na	na	1	2	na	1	2	na	1	2
United States	8	14	3	26	8	14	20	12	14	15	14	12	15	21	14	12
Uruguay	na	na	na	na	na	na	na	na	na	na	na	na	na	na	na	na
Venezuela	na	5	4	7	5	5	5	6	4	7	6	5	6	7	4	5
Vietnam	na	29	5	51	22	36	22	30	29	18	27	28	31	30	30	30
Zimbabwe	na	10	1	19	6	13	17	12	8	na	7	9	12	11	10	9
Total	3	5	1	8	4	6	5	5	5	5	5	5	5	5	5	5

RANKING

Country	2000
Vietnam	29
Tanzania	24
Uganda	16
Bangladesh	14
United States	14
Albania	14
Philippines	10
Zimbabwe	10
Belgium	10
South Africa	9
Canada	8
Slovakia	7
Peru	6
Macedonia	6
Luxembourg	6
Iceland	6
India	6
Chile	5
Venezuela	5
Netherlands	5
Algeria	4
Finland	4
Ireland	4
Austria	4
Greece	4
Northern Ireland	4
Japan	4
Germany	4
Korea, South	4
Sweden	4
China	3
Montenegro	3
Mexico	3
Puerto Rico	3
Bosnia and Herz.	3
Moldova	3
Czech Republic	3
Denmark	2
Croatia	2
Estonia	2
Spain	2
Romania	0
Slovenia	2
Great Britain	2
Morocco	2
Poland	1
Singapore	1
Malta	1
Bulgaria	1
Argentina	1
Ukraine	1
Russian Fed.	1
Belarus	0
France	0
Italy	0
Serbia	0
Hungary	0
Latvia	0
Lithuania	0
Turkey	0
Total	5

A076) BELONG PEACE MOVEMENT

Please look carefully at the following list of voluntary organizations and activities and say...which, if any, do you belong to? Peace movement.

Belong (%)

(WVS: V51; EVS: V24)

Country	Wave		Gender		Age			Education			Income			Values		
	1990	2000	Male	Female	16-29	30-49	50+	Lower	Middle	Upper	Lower	Middle	Upper	Mat	Mixed	Postm.
Albania	na	**7**	8	7	7	7	8	4	9	12	8	6	8	6	9	8
Algeria	na	**na**	na	na	na	na	na	na	na	na	na	na	na	na	na	na
Argentina	0	**na**	na	na	na	na	na	na	na	na	na	na	na	na	na	na
Armenia	na	**na**	na	na	na	na	na	na	na	na	na	na	na	na	na	na
Australia	na	**na**	na	na	na	na	na	na	na	na	na	na	na	na	na	na
Austria	1	**1**	1	1	1	1	1	1	1	1	2	1	1	2	1	1
Azerbaijan	na	**na**	na	na	na	na	na	na	na	na	na	na	na	na	na	na
Bangladesh	na	**23**	30	15	22	22	35	20	27	28	12	26	29	21	25	21
Belarus	na	**0**	na	na	na	na	na	na	na	na	na	na	na	na	na	na
Belgium	2	**2**	2	2	2	3	2	2	2	2	1	2	2	1	2	2
Bosnia and Herz.	na	**0**	na	na	na	na	na	1	na	na	na	na	na	na	na	na
Brazil	2	**na**	na	na	na	na	na	na	na	na	na	na	na	na	na	na
Bulgaria	1	**1**	na	1	na	2	na	1	na	2	1	1	na	na	1	2
Canada	2	**2**	2	2	na	3	3	3	2	3	2	2	3	2	2	2
Chile	1	**2**	2	2	1	2	2	1	2	3	1	2	2	2	2	na
China	1	**1**	1	1	1	1	1	na	1	5	1	1	1	1	1	3
Colombia	na	**na**	na	na	na	na	na	na	na	na	na	na	na	na	na	na
Croatia	na	**1**	1	1	1	1	2	1	1	1	1	2	1	na	1	1
Czech Republic	na	**1**	1	2	1	1	2	1	2	na	2	1	1	1	1	3
Denmark	2	**1**	1	1	0	1	1	1	1	1	1	1	0	0	1	2
Dominican Rep.	na	**na**	na	na	na	na	na	na	na	na	na	na	na	na	na	na
Egypt	na	**na**	na	na	na	na	na	na	na	na	na	na	na	na	na	na
El Salvador	na	**na**	na	na	na	na	na	na	na	na	na	na	na	na	na	na
Estonia	1	**0**	na	na	na	na	na	na	na	na	na	na	1	na	na	na
Finland	2	**1**	2	1	2	1	2	1	1	2	1	2	2	na	1	5
France	1	**1**	na	1	na	na	1	na	na	1	1	na	na	1	1	na
Georgia	na	**na**	na	na	na	na	na	na	na	na	na	na	na	na	na	na
Germany	2	**0**	na	na	na	na	na	na	na	na	na	na	na	na	na	na
Great Britain	1	**1**	1	na	1	1	na	1	na	1	1	1	1	na	na	na
Greece	na	**4**	5	4	4	4	4	4	5	3	4	5	3	5	4	5
Hungary	1	**0**	1	na	1	na	na	na	na	1	na	na	na	na	na	na
Iceland	1	**1**	1	2	na	1	2	1	1	2	2	1	1	na	1	4
India	na	**5**	6	4	5	5	3	5	4	6	8	4	4	2	8	9
Indonesia	na	**na**	na	na	na	na	na	na	na	na	na	na	na	na	na	na
Iran	na	**na**	na	na	na	na	na	na	na	na	na	na	na	na	na	na
Ireland	1	**2**	2	2	2	1	3	2	2	2	2	2	1	1	2	4
Israel	na	**na**	na	na	na	na	na	na	na	na	na	na	na	na	na	na
Italy	1	**1**	1	2	1	2	1	1	2	2	1	2	1	1	1	2
Japan	1	**2**	2	2	na	1	3	4	2	2	3	1	2	2	1	4
Jordan	na	**na**	na	na	na	na	na	na	na	na	na	na	na	na	na	na
Korea, South	2	**2**	2	1	2	2	3	na	2	1	2	3	1	1	3	na
Latvia	1	**0**	na	na	na	na	na	na	na	na	na	na	na	na	na	na
Lithuania	1	**0**	na	na	na	na	na	na	na	na	na	na	na	na	na	na
Luxembourg	na	**2**	3	2	2	2	3	1	2	5	1	na	4	2	3	2
Macedonia	na	**5**	5	6	7	6	3	5	5	8	3	6	8	4	6	9
Malta	na	**0**	na	na	na	na	na	na	na	na	1	na	na	na	na	na
Mexico	1	**3**	4	3	2	3	4	4	3	2	4	3	3	3	3	4
Moldova	na	**2**	2	2	3	2	2	1	3	3	1	3	3	2	3	na
Montenegro	na	**1**	1	na	na	na	2	1	1	1	2	1	na	1	na	na
Morocco	na	**0**	na	na	na	1	na	na	1	3	na	na	2	na	1	na
Netherlands	3	**3**	2	4	1	1	6	2	3	3	3	2	4	1	2	6
New Zealand	na	**na**	na	na	na	na	na	na	na	na	na	na	na	na	na	na
Nigeria	na	**na**	na	na	na	na	na	na	na	na	na	na	na	na	na	na
Northern Ireland	1	**2**	2	3	3	4	1	2	2	5	1	3	5	1	2	5
Norway	2	**na**	na	na	na	na	na	na	na	na	na	na	na	na	na	na
Pakistan	na	**na**	na	na	na	na	na	na	na	na	na	na	na	na	na	na
Peru	na	**1**	1	1	1	1	1	2	1	1	1	1	1	na	1	1
Philippines	na	**11**	16	7	7	13	14	12	10	13	9	11	14	11	12	8
Poland	na	**1**	1	na	1	na	1	na	1	na	1	na	2	na	1	na
Portugal	1	**1**	1	na	na	1	1	na	1	1	na	1	1	na	na	1
Puerto Rico	na	**1**	2	1	3	na	1	1	na	2	2	na	2	na	1	3
Romania	0	**0**	0	0	0	0	0	0	0	0	0	0	0	0	0	0
Russian Fed.	1	**0**	na	na	na	na	na	na	na	na	na	na	na	na	na	na
Serbia	na	**na**	na	na	na	na	na	na	na	na	na	na	na	na	na	na
Singapore	na	**1**	1	1	1	1	na	1	1	na	3	na	na	1	1	na
Slovakia	na	**0**	1	na	na	na	1	na	na	2	1	1	na	na	na	2
Slovenia	0	**1**	1	1	1	na	1	2	1	na	1	1	1	2	na	1
South Africa	na	**6**	5	8	7	5	8	6	6	3	6	9	3	8	5	8
Spain	1	**1**	1	1	1	2	1	na	1	4	1	1	2	1	1	3
Sweden	3	**2**	1	2	1	2	1	2	1	3	1	1	2	3	1	3
Switzerland	na	**na**	na	na	na	na	na	na	na	na	na	na	na	na	na	na
Taiwan	na	**na**	na	na	na	na	na	na	na	na	na	na	na	na	na	na
Tanzania	na	**5**	5	6	5	5	4	5	5	7	6	4	5	4	5	8
Turkey	na	**0**	na	na	na	na	na	na	na	na	na	na	na	na	na	na
Uganda	na	**10**	16	4	10	10	8	11	8	20	15	9	13	9	10	12
Ukraine	na	**0**	na	na	na	na	na	na	na	na	na	na	na	na	na	na
United States	2	**5**	5	4	6	3	6	4	4	5	4	4	5	5	4	4
Uruguay	na	**na**	na	na	na	na	na	na	na	na	na	na	na	na	na	na
Venezuela	na	**6**	8	4	5	7	5	4	6	7	7	5	5	6	6	5
Vietnam	na	**9**	9	10	9	10	9	8	10	15	8	10	9	9	10	13
Zimbabwe	na	**3**	3	3	4	2	3	2	4	14	1	4	8	2	5	2
Total	1	**3**	3	2	3	3	2	2	2	3	2	3	3	2	3	3

RANKING	
Country	2000
Bangladesh	23
Philippines	11
Uganda	10
Vietnam	9
Albania	7
South Africa	6
Venezuela	6
Macedonia	5
Tanzania	5
India	5
United States	5
Greece	4
Zimbabwe	3
Mexico	3
Netherlands	3
Luxembourg	2
Moldova	2
Northern Ireland	2
Canada	2
Belgium	2
Japan	2
Korea, South	2
Ireland	2
Chile	2
Sweden	2
Finland	1
Italy	1
Czech Republic	1
Puerto Rico	1
Croatia	1
Iceland	1
Spain	1
Austria	1
China	1
Denmark	1
Peru	1
Singapore	1
Slovenia	1
Montenegro	1
Bulgaria	1
Poland	1
Portugal	1
Great Britain	1
France	1
Morocco	0
Romania	0
Bosnia and Herz.	0
Hungary	0
Slovakia	0
Estonia	0
Germany	0
Latvia	0
Lithuania	0
Malta	0
Belarus	0
Russian Fed.	0
Turkey	0
Ukraine	0
Total	3

A077) BELONG GROUPS CONCERNED WITH HEALTH

Please look carefully at the following list of voluntary organizations and activities and say...which, if any, do you belong to?

Voluntary organizations concerned with health.

(WVS: V52; EVS: V25)

Belong (%)

Country	Wave		Gender		Age			Education			Income			Values		
	1990	2000	Male	Female	16-29	30-49	50+	Lower	Middle	Upper	Lower	Middle	Upper	Mat	Mixed	Postm.
Albania	na	**13**	12	14	10	14	14	11	14	15	14	12	13	14	13	5
Algeria	na	**na**	na	na	na	na	na	na	na	na	na	na	na	na	na	na
Argentina	2	**2**	1	4	2	3	2	1	4	6	4	1	3	na	3	3
Armenia	na	**na**	na	na	na	na	na	na	na	na	na	na	na	na	na	na
Australia	na	**na**	na	na	na	na	na	na	na	na	na	na	na	na	na	na
Austria	3	**9**	9	8	8	8	9	7	10	12	8	9	9	10	9	9
Azerbaijan	na	**na**	na	na	na	na	na	na	na	na	na	na	na	na	na	na
Bangladesh	na	**22**	26	17	21	22	25	16	28	30	10	25	29	20	24	18
Belarus	na	**1**	1	1	1	1	1	na	1	1	na	1	1	1	1	na
Belgium	4	**6**	5	6	6	4	6	4	5	7	5	7	6	5	5	7
Bosnia and Herz.	na	**3**	3	2	3	3	2	1	2	5	2	2	5	2	3	na
Brazil	3	**na**	na	na	na	na	na	na	na	na	na	na	na	na	na	na
Bulgaria	2	**1**	1	1	2	1	1	1	1	3	1	1	1	1	1	na
Canada	9	**11**	10	12	7	11	14	9	11	14	9	11	13	9	10	14
Chile	3	**3**	2	4	3	3	4	2	3	6	2	3	7	4	3	3
China	2	**3**	2	3	4	2	2	1	4	7	2	3	5	4	2	6
Colombia	na	**na**	na	na	na	na	na	na	na	na	na	na	na	na	na	na
Croatia	na	**3**	4	2	2	5	2	2	4	6	1	3	5	4	2	4
Czech Republic	na	**6**	4	8	4	6	7	5	6	8	8	6	5	7	6	4
Denmark	6	**4**	4	4	2	4	5	2	8	6	4	3	5	4	4	3
Dominican Rep.	na	**na**	na	na	na	na	na	na	na	na	na	na	na	na	na	na
Egypt	na	**na**	na	na	na	na	na	na	na	na	na	na	na	na	na	na
El Salvador	na	**na**	na	na	na	na	na	na	na	na	na	na	na	na	na	na
Estonia	2	**1**	1	na	na	1	1	1	1	1	1	na	2	1	1	na
Finland	7	**10**	8	12	4	7	16	9	11	14	10	9	11	11	10	8
France	3	**3**	2	3	3	2	3	3	2	2	4	3	2	2	3	3
Georgia	na	**na**	na	na	na	na	na	na	na	na	na	na	na	na	na	na
Germany	5	**3**	3	2	2	2	4	2	3	3	2	2	4	2	3	3
Great Britain	4	**3**	2	4	3	1	5	2	3	5	4	2	4	na	na	na
Greece	na	**5**	4	5	5	4	6	3	5	5	3	4	6	5	4	7
Hungary	4	**2**	1	3	1	4	1	2	1	5	3	2	2	2	2	9
Iceland	5	**3**	3	3	2	3	5	3	2	5	3	2	3	1	4	2
India	na	**8**	8	7	8	8	7	5	9	12	7	6	10	6	11	16
Indonesia	na	**na**	na	na	na	na	na	na	na	na	na	na	na	na	na	na
Iran	na	**na**	na	na	na	na	na	na	na	na	na	na	na	na	na	na
Ireland	3	**4**	3	5	2	6	4	2	3	9	5	3	6	3	4	3
Israel	na	**na**	na	na	na	na	na	na	na	na	na	na	na	na	na	na
Italy	3	**5**	4	6	5	6	4	3	5	8	4	6	6	4	4	6
Japan	1	**3**	2	4	na	1	6	5	3	3	3	3	4	3	3	7
Jordan	na	**na**	na	na	na	na	na	na	na	na	na	na	na	na	na	na
Korea, South	15	**10**	12	8	7	10	12	na	12	9	9	8	11	9	11	4
Latvia	2	**1**	na	2	1	1	1	na	1	1	1	1	1	1	1	na
Lithuania	1	**2**	1	3	4	2	1	1	2	4	2	2	2	2	2	3
Luxembourg	na	**8**	7	9	6	7	10	7	8	9	8	6	7	5	8	10
Macedonia	na	**8**	7	9	6	10	6	6	8	12	6	9	8	5	9	17
Malta	na	**1**	1	1	2	1	1	1	1	2	na	1	2	1	1	3
Mexico	2	**6**	5	7	5	7	6	6	7	8	6	6	8	7	7	5
Moldova	na	**3**	2	3	3	3	2	1	2	6	1	3	3	2	3	6
Montenegro	na	**3**	3	2	2	3	2	1	3	4	1	2	3	2	2	2
Morocco	na	**1**	1	1	1	1	na	na	2	4	na	1	3	na	1	1
Netherlands	20	**9**	7	11	4	6	14	10	7	9	8	7	11	7	10	6
New Zealand	na	**na**	na	na	na	na	na	na	na	na	na	na	na	na	na	na
Nigeria	na	**na**	na	na	na	na	na	na	na	na	na	na	na	na	na	na
Northern Ireland	3	**4**	3	5	3	3	6	3	3	11	4	3	7	6	5	na
Norway	12	**na**	na	na	na	na	na	na	na	na	na	na	na	na	na	na
Pakistan	na	**na**	na	na	na	na	na	na	na	na	na	na	na	na	na	na
Peru	na	**5**	4	6	5	5	5	3	5	5	4	5	6	3	5	7
Philippines	na	**9**	11	8	8	9	11	10	6	13	8	8	12	7	11	10
Poland	na	**1**	2	1	na	1	2	na	2	5	2	1	1	1	2	3
Portugal	3	**2**	3	2	1	4	2	3	1	2	na	5	2	2	2	2
Puerto Rico	na	**5**	4	6	3	7	4	6	2	6	5	4	7	5	5	5
Romania	1	**1**	0	2	2	1	0	0	1	3	0	1	2	0	1	3
Russian Fed.	1	**1**	na	1	1	1	na	na	1	2	1	na	1	1	1	na
Serbia	na	**1**	2	1	1	2	1	1	2	2	1	2	1	2	1	1
Singapore	na	**4**	3	4	4	4	1	4	3	5	3	3	4	2	4	1
Slovakia	na	**4**	4	5	4	5	5	3	4	11	4	4	5	4	5	8
Slovenia	1	**3**	3	3	3	2	4	3	2	6	2	3	5	1	3	4
South Africa	na	**6**	3	9	7	5	7	4	9	3	3	11	4	7	5	2
Spain	1	**2**	3	2	2	3	3	1	3	5	3	2	4	2	3	2
Sweden	2	**7**	5	8	3	6	9	6	6	8	8	4	9	11	5	8
Switzerland	na	**na**	na	na	na	na	na	na	na	na	na	na	na	na	na	na
Taiwan	na	**na**	na	na	na	na	na	na	na	na	na	na	na	na	na	na
Tanzania	na	**19**	16	24	20	19	16	17	20	25	19	22	17	16	21	13
Turkey	na	**0**	na	na	na	1	1	na	na	2	na	na	1	1	na	na
Uganda	na	**12**	15	9	12	13	8	7	14	18	10	15	18	12	12	12
Ukraine	na	**1**	1	1	1	2	1	2	1	3	1	1	2	1	2	na
United States	8	**17**	14	19	13	17	20	13	15	19	15	17	18	22	16	16
Uruguay	na	**na**	na	na	na	na	na	na	na	na	na	na	na	na	na	na
Venezuela	na	**10**	11	9	8	12	9	6	9	16	9	10	12	6	11	10
Vietnam	na	**15**	16	14	11	15	18	13	17	22	13	14	17	15	17	14
Zimbabwe	na	**5**	5	4	5	4	6	3	7	14	3	5	10	3	6	7
Total	4	**6**	5	6	5	6	6	4	5	8	5	6	7	5	6	6

RANKING

Country	2000
Bangladesh	22
Tanzania	19
United States	17
Vietnam	15
Albania	13
Uganda	12
Canada	11
Finland	10
Korea, South	10
Venezuela	10
Philippines	9
Netherlands	9
Austria	9
Macedonia	8
Luxembourg	8
India	8
Sweden	7
Mexico	6
Czech Republic	6
South Africa	6
Belgium	6
Puerto Rico	5
Peru	5
Zimbabwe	5
Denmark	4
Greece	5
Italy	5
Slovakia	4
Romania	1
Northern Ireland	4
Ireland	4
Singapore	4
Chile	3
Croatia	3
Japan	3
Iceland	3
Great Britain	3
Slovenia	3
Moldova	3
China	3
Bosnia and Herz.	3
France	3
Germany	3
Montenegro	3
Argentina	2
Spain	2
Portugal	2
Hungary	2
Lithuania	2
Poland	1
Ukraine	1
Serbia	1
Bulgaria	1
Malta	1
Latvia	1
Belarus	1
Estonia	1
Russian Fed.	1
Morocco	1
Turkey	0
Total	6

A079) BELONG OTHER GROUPS

Please look carefully at the following list of voluntary organizations and activities and say...which, if any, do you belong to? Other groups.

Belong (%)

(WVS: V53; EVS: V26)

Country	Wave		Gender		Age			Education			Income			Values		
	1990	2000	Male	Female	16-29	30-49	50+	Lower	Middle	Upper	Lower	Middle	Upper	Mat	Mixed	Postm.
Albania	na	**5**	5	6	7	4	5	4	7	4	7	5	5	4	6	10
Algeria	na	**na**	na	na	na	na	na	na	na	na	na	na	na	na	na	na
Argentina	3	**4**	4	4	4	3	5	3	5	4	4	3	6	2	4	7
Armenia	na	**na**	na	na	na	na	na	na	na	na	na	na	na	na	na	na
Australia	na	**na**	na	na	na	na	na	na	na	na	na	na	na	na	na	na
Austria	6	**9**	10	8	6	9	11	9	9	10	9	7	11	13	9	8
Azerbaijan	na	**na**	na	na	na	na	na	na	na	na	na	na	na	na	na	na
Bangladesh	na	**2**	2	1	2	2	1	1	1	5	1	2	2	1	2	1
Belarus	na	**1**	2	na	2	na	1	na	1	1	na	1	1	1	1	na
Belgium	5	**11**	12	9	7	10	13	11	10	12	10	10	13	11	11	12
Bosnia and Herz.	na	**3**	5	2	1	3	5	2	3	6	3	3	4	2	4	2
Brazil	0	**na**	na	na	na	na	na	na	na	na	na	na	na	na	na	na
Bulgaria	3	**2**	2	2	3	2	1	1	2	2	2	1	1	1	2	na
Canada	13	**11**	12	10	8	12	11	8	13	11	11	10	13	8	10	13
Chile	4	**1**	2	1	1	1	3	1	1	2	1	1	2	1	2	1
China	2	**na**	na	na	na	na	na	na	na	na	na	na	na	na	na	na
Colombia	na	**na**	na	na	na	na	na	na	na	na	na	na	na	na	na	na
Croatia	na	**5**	9	1	4	5	4	2	6	5	3	5	4	2	5	3
Czech Republic	na	**9**	12	6	6	8	11	9	8	13	10	9	8	8	9	4
Denmark	11	**14**	15	14	11	12	19	13	11	17	17	12	15	15	15	10
Dominican Rep.	na	**na**	na	na	na	na	na	na	na	na	na	na	na	na	na	na
Egypt	na	**na**	na	na	na	na	na	na	na	na	na	na	na	na	na	na
El Salvador	na	**na**	na	na	na	na	na	na	na	na	na	na	na	na	na	na
Estonia	4	**5**	6	4	3	6	5	3	6	5	3	4	7	4	5	12
Finland	9	**13**	12	14	6	11	18	11	14	19	13	13	14	12	14	8
France	5	**7**	8	6	5	6	9	6	6	9	6	8	9	6	7	8
Georgia	na	**na**	na	na	na	na	na	na	na	na	na	na	na	na	na	na
Germany	8	**4**	5	3	3	3	5	4	4	4	6	3	3	3	4	5
Great Britain	8	**5**	5	5	2	5	6	4	5	7	4	4	8	na	na	na
Greece	na	**7**	7	6	8	4	8	7	7	7	6	8	7	4	7	10
Hungary	2	**3**	3	3	3	1	4	3	2	3	3	3	1	3	2	na
Iceland	10	**3**	1	5	1	3	4	2	2	6	2	3	3	3	3	2
India	na	**7**	8	5	6	7	7	5	8	9	4	6	9	4	10	13
Indonesia	na	**na**	na	na	na	na	na	na	na	na	na	na	na	na	na	na
Iran	na	**na**	na	na	na	na	na	na	na	na	na	na	na	na	na	na
Ireland	2	**5**	7	4	5	6	6	4	6	8	7	5	4	5	6	6
Israel	na	**na**	na	na	na	na	na	na	na	na	na	na	na	na	na	na
Italy	2	**3**	3	2	2	3	2	2	3	3	3	2	4	2	3	3
Japan	5	**7**	8	6	2	5	11	9	7	6	7	8	7	6	6	16
Jordan	na	**na**	na	na	na	na	na	na	na	na	na	na	na	na	na	na
Korea, South	4	**na**	na	na	na	na	na	na	na	na	na	na	na	na	na	na
Latvia	4	**5**	6	4	8	4	5	4	5	8	5	5	5	4	5	13
Lithuania	2	**2**	2	2	2	4	1	na	2	6	2	2	3	1	3	4
Luxembourg	na	**4**	5	4	6	3	4	5	4	4	6	4	5	6	5	2
Macedonia	na	**8**	9	7	12	7	5	9	8	6	6	10	6	6	9	10
Malta	na	**3**	4	3	3	4	3	3	3	4	4	4	4	3	4	1
Mexico	2	**1**	2	1	1	1	1	1	1	1	1	2	1	2	1	2
Moldova	na	**3**	3	2	4	3	2	na	4	4	2	3	4	3	3	4
Montenegro	na	**4**	5	4	5	4	5	3	5	6	5	5	4	4	5	5
Morocco	na	**1**	1	1	1	1	na	na	1	3	1	na	2	na	1	1
Netherlands	9	**9**	11	8	7	8	11	8	9	11	8	11	9	14	8	11
New Zealand	na	**na**	na	na	na	na	na	na	na	na	na	na	na	na	na	na
Nigeria	na	**na**	na	na	na	na	na	na	na	na	na	na	na	na	na	na
Northern Ireland	7	**7**	6	7	6	7	7	7	8	6	5	10	4	9	6	7
Norway	19	**na**	na	na	na	na	na	na	na	na	na	na	na	na	na	na
Pakistan	na	**na**	na	na	na	na	na	na	na	na	na	na	na	na	na	na
Peru	na	**0**	na	na	na	na	na	na	na	na	na	na	1	na	na	na
Philippines	na	**4**	5	4	4	4	5	4	4	4	3	5	5	4	5	2
Poland	na	**3**	4	2	2	3	3	2	3	4	4	2	2	2	3	4
Portugal	3	**3**	4	2	3	3	4	3	4	4	3	3	3	1	4	7
Puerto Rico	na	**5**	8	4	7	3	5	3	4	6	4	5	6	8	4	6
Romania	2	**2**	2	2	3	2	2	1	2	5	1	1	4	1	3	7
Russian Fed.	2	**1**	2	1	2	1	1	na	1	2	1	2	1	1	1	na
Serbia	na	**4**	5	3	4	4	3	3	3	5	2	4	5	4	3	1
Singapore	na	**4**	4	3	3	4	5	4	3	5	5	3	4	5	3	4
Slovakia	na	**8**	9	6	6	7	10	7	8	8	10	8	7	7	7	13
Slovenia	5	**10**	15	6	11	7	12	10	10	11	9	9	7	11	9	12
South Africa	na	**9**	11	8	11	8	10	9	10	6	10	10	10	10	10	5
Spain	4	**2**	2	2	2	2	2	2	2	4	3	1	3	2	2	3
Sweden	19	**25**	28	22	21	24	29	25	21	31	24	25	27	27	25	25
Switzerland	na	**na**	na	na	na	na	na	na	na	na	na	na	na	na	na	na
Taiwan	na	**na**	na	na	na	na	na	na	na	na	na	na	na	na	na	na
Tanzania	na	**18**	17	19	19	18	17	14	20	24	15	20	19	16	19	29
Turkey	na	**2**	2	1	2	1	3	na	3	4	na	2	4	2	2	2
Uganda	na	**7**	9	4	7	6	6	6	7	9	5	5	5	7	7	2
Ukraine	na	**2**	3	1	2	2	2	na	2	4	2	2	3	1	3	3
United States	10	**22**	26	17	22	19	26	17	20	25	20	20	28	16	23	21
Uruguay	na	**na**	na	na	na	na	na	na	na	na	na	na	na	na	na	na
Venezuela	na	**1**	1	na	1	1	na	1	1	1	1	na	1	1	1	1
Vietnam	na	**4**	5	2	2	3	6	3	5	2	4	3	4	4	4	4
Zimbabwe	na	**1**	2	1	1	2	3	1	2	na	2	1	3	2	1	3
Total	6	**6**	7	5	5	5	7	5	5	8	6	6	6	4	6	7

RANKING	
Country	2000
Sweden	25
United States	22
Tanzania	18
Denmark	14
Finland	13
Canada	11
Belgium	11
Slovenia	10
South Africa	9
Romania	2
Austria	9
Netherlands	9
Czech Republic	9
Slovakia	8
Macedonia	8
France	7
Japan	7
Northern Ireland	7
Greece	7
India	7
Uganda	7
Ireland	5
Albania	5
Latvia	5
Great Britain	5
Puerto Rico	5
Estonia	5
Croatia	5
Luxembourg	4
Montenegro	4
Philippines	4
Argentina	4
Germany	4
Singapore	4
Vietnam	4
Serbia	4
Malta	3
Portugal	3
Bosnia and Herz.	3
Iceland	3
Moldova	3
Poland	3
Hungary	3
Italy	3
Lithuania	2
Spain	2
Ukraine	2
Bulgaria	2
Bangladesh	2
Turkey	2
Chile	1
Zimbabwe	1
Russian Fed.	1
Mexico	1
Belarus	1
Venezuela	1
Morocco	1
Peru	0
Total	6

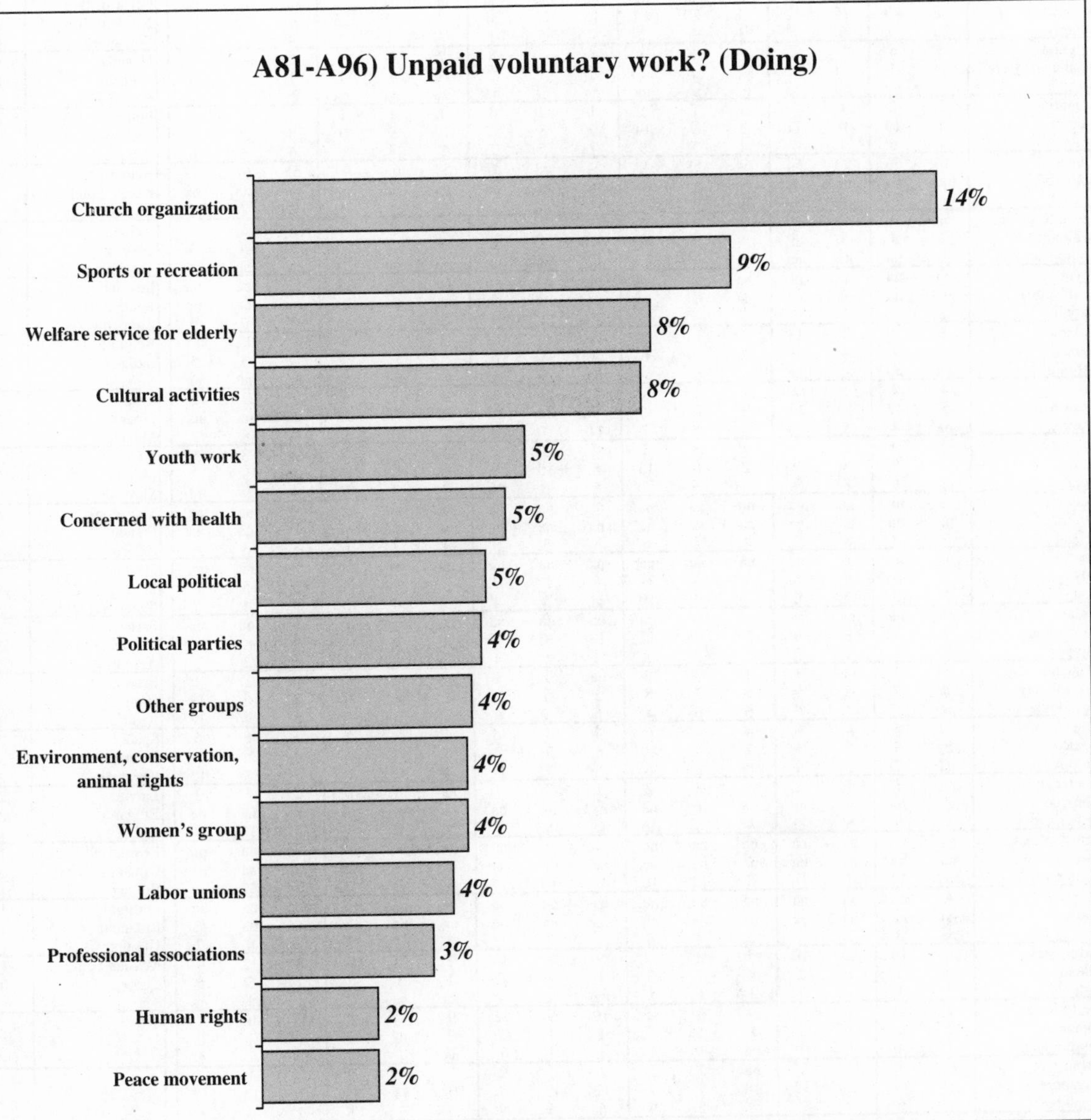
A81-A96) Unpaid voluntary work? (Doing)
Church organization
14%
Sports or recreation
9%
Welfare service for elderly
8%
Cultural activities
8%
Youth work
5%
Concerned with health
5%
Local political
5%
Political parties
4%
Other groups
4%
Environment, conservation, animal rights
4%
Women's group
4%
Labor unions
4%
Professional associations
3%
Human rights
2%
Peace movement
2%

A081) UNPAID WORK SOCIAL WELFARE SERVICE FOR ELDERLY

And for which, if any, are you currently doing unpaid voluntary work? Social welfare services for elderly, handicapped or deprived people.

Belong (%)

(WVS: V54; EVS: V30)

Country	Wave		Gender		Age			Education			Income			Values		
	1990	2000	Male	Female	16-29	30-49	50+	Lower	Middle	Upper	Lower	Middle	Upper	Mat	Mixed	Postm.
Albania	na	**11**	10	11	7	12	12	9	11	13	12	11	10	11	12	3
Algeria	na	**19**	21	17	21	20	13	12	20	23	15	21	21	16	20	28
Argentina	2	**3**	2	3	2	3	4	2	4	2	2	3	3	1	3	3
Armenia	na	**na**	na	na	na	na	na	na	na	na	na	na	na	na	na	na
Australia	na	**na**	na	na	na	na	na	na	na	na	na	na	na	na	na	na
Austria	3	**2**	1	3	1	2	4	3	2	2	4	2	1	3	3	2
Azerbaijan	na	**na**	na	na	na	na	na	na	na	na	na	na	na	na	na	na
Bangladesh	na	**19**	25	12	18	20	19	15	21	31	8	23	25	15	23	15
Belarus	na	**4**	3	5	3	6	3	4	5	1	4	4	5	4	5	5
Belgium	6	**6**	5	8	5	5	8	8	5	8	7	8	5	5	6	7
Bosnia and Herz.	na	**1**	na	2	1	1	1	2	1	2	na	1	1	1	1	4
Brazil	6	**na**	na	na	na	na	na	na	na	na	na	na	na	na	na	na
Bulgaria	2	**2**	1	2	2	2	1	1	2	3	1	1	2	1	2	5
Canada	6	**10**	9	11	3	9	14	9	8	12	10	9	10	6	10	11
Chile	4	**6**	4	7	4	5	9	7	5	7	7	4	6	6	5	6
China	16	**56**	58	54	64	58	45	51	62	37	58	63	44	55	61	69
Colombia	na	**na**	na	na	na	na	na	na	na	na	na	na	na	na	na	na
Croatia	na	**1**	na	2	1	1	2	2	na	2	1	1	1	2	1	1
Czech Republic	na	**3**	2	5	3	3	4	3	3	6	5	3	3	5	3	1
Denmark	2	**4**	3	5	1	2	8	4	1	6	7	3	1	1	4	3
Dominican Rep.	na	**na**	na	na	na	na	na	na	na	na	na	na	na	na	na	na
Egypt	na	**na**	na	na	na	na	na	na	na	na	na	na	na	na	na	na
El Salvador	na	**na**	na	na	na	na	na	na	na	na	na	na	na	na	na	na
Estonia	1	**3**	2	3	3	4	2	2	3	4	2	3	4	3	2	9
Finland	8	**10**	7	13	4	10	14	8	11	18	9	17	8	7	12	13
France	5	**4**	3	6	2	3	6	4	3	6	5	4	5	3	5	5
Georgia	na	**na**	na	na	na	na	na	na	na	na	na	na	na	na	na	na
Germany	4	**2**	1	2	1	2	3	1	3	1	2	2	1	1	3	2
Great Britain	5	**13**	10	17	8	14	17	9	14	22	12	12	22	na	na	na
Greece	na	**8**	5	10	8	8	7	11	7	8	6	10	9	9	8	9
Hungary	2	**3**	2	3	4	3	2	2	2	7	3	2	3	2	3	1
Iceland	10	**9**	8	9	2	9	15	8	10	9	6	11	11	8	9	7
India	na	**6**	8	4	5	6	8	5	6	10	7	4	8	4	9	11
Indonesia	na	**na**	na	na	na	na	na	na	na	na	na	na	na	na	na	na
Iran	na	**na**	na	na	na	na	na	na	na	na	na	na	na	na	na	na
Ireland	7	**4**	3	5	4	2	6	3	3	8	4	2	6	4	3	6
Israel	na	**na**	na	na	na	na	na	na	na	na	na	na	na	na	na	na
Italy	3	**5**	4	6	3	5	6	5	5	7	5	7	4	5	5	6
Japan	2	**5**	5	6	2	2	10	11	5	4	7	4	5	9	4	7
Jordan	na	**na**	na	na	na	na	na	na	na	na	na	na	na	na	na	na
Korea, South	7	**9**	9	9	7	9	12	13	10	7	10	7	10	9	10	9
Latvia	4	**2**	1	2	1	3	2	2	1	4	2	2	2	1	2	2
Lithuania	1	**1**	na	1	1	na	na	na	1	1	na	na	1	na	1	1
Luxembourg	na	**7**	5	9	6	7	8	5	6	14	8	8	10	8	6	12
Macedonia	na	**5**	4	6	5	6	4	6	4	6	3	6	6	5	4	12
Malta	na	**5**	4	6	4	4	6	4	4	11	4	3	8	3	6	6
Mexico	3	**5**	5	6	2	5	10	6	3	7	6	6	5	8	5	4
Moldova	na	**7**	5	9	8	8	6	5	7	11	4	10	8	6	8	12
Montenegro	na	**3**	5	2	5	3	2	1	3	7	na	3	6	2	5	3
Morocco	na	**na**	na	na	na	na	na	na	na	na	na	na	na	na	na	na
Netherlands	9	**9**	8	11	4	6	16	11	8	9	9	9	9	8	10	8
New Zealand	na	**na**	na	na	na	na	na	na	na	na	na	na	na	na	na	na
Nigeria	na	**na**	na	na	na	na	na	na	na	na	na	na	na	na	na	na
Northern Ireland	5	**12**	7	18	6	12	16	12	10	17	5	14	16	15	12	10
Norway	4	**na**	na	na	na	na	na	na	na	na	na	na	na	na	na	na
Pakistan	na	**na**	na	na	na	na	na	na	na	na	na	na	na	na	na	na
Peru	na	**3**	2	4	2	4	6	3	2	5	2	4	5	3	4	2
Philippines	na	**10**	10	10	9	9	14	9	9	13	7	11	12	8	12	4
Poland	na	**2**	2	2	4	1	3	1	2	7	1	3	2	1	3	5
Portugal	3	**1**	1	1	1	1	1	na	2	4	na	na	1	1	1	na
Puerto Rico	na	**11**	8	12	9	6	15	10	9	12	9	14	8	19	10	7
Romania	2	**1**	1	1	1	1	1	1	1	1	0	1	2	1	1	0
Russian Fed.	1	**1**	1	1	na	1	1	1	1	1	na	1	1	na	1	6
Serbia	na	**1**	2	1	na	2	2	1	1	2	1	na	2	2	1	1
Singapore	na	**12**	11	12	18	5	7	12	12	7	10	14	11	7	13	17
Slovakia	na	**6**	4	8	4	5	9	6	6	8	6	7	5	7	6	6
Slovenia	1	**5**	4	6	4	3	8	5	5	4	7	4	3	5	4	7
South Africa	na	**7**	5	9	5	7	12	4	11	7	3	10	9	9	7	1
Spain	4	**2**	3	2	2	2	3	2	2	5	3	3	2	2	2	3
Sweden	3	**9**	7	12	4	7	14	9	9	10	8	6	13	10	8	12
Switzerland	na	**na**	na	na	na	na	na	na	na	na	na	na	na	na	na	na
Taiwan	na	**na**	na	na	na	na	na	na	na	na	na	na	na	na	na	na
Tanzania	na	**25**	24	25	25	24	24	25	21	31	27	24	24	19	27	33
Turkey	na	**0**	1	na	na	1	na	na	1	2	na	na	1	1	na	1
Uganda	na	**11**	13	10	11	12	15	14	10	10	18	11	12	9	13	12
Ukraine	na	**1**	1	1	na	1	1	na	1	1	1	1	1	na	1	na
United States	6	**14**	11	17	11	11	20	9	14	16	14	13	15	16	13	16
Uruguay	na	**na**	na	na	na	na	na	na	na	na	na	na	na	na	na	na
Venezuela	na	**na**	na	na	na	na	na	na	na	na	na	na	na	na	na	na
Vietnam	na	**28**	29	28	20	26	39	30	26	33	25	26	34	28	31	21
Zimbabwe	na	**7**	6	7	4	9	9	7	6	na	6	6	11	6	7	4
Total	4	**8**	7	8	7	8	8	7	8	9	8	8	8	7	8	7

RANKING	
Country	2000
China	56
Vietnam	28
Tanzania	25
Bangladesh	19
Algeria	19
United States	14
Great Britain	13
Northern Ireland	12
Singapore	12
Uganda	11
Albania	11
Puerto Rico	11
Finland	10
Philippines	10
Canada	10
Netherlands	9
Korea, South	9
Sweden	9
Iceland	9
Greece	8
Moldova	7
Luxembourg	7
South Africa	7
Zimbabwe	7
Belgium	6
India	6
Slovakia	6
Chile	6
Japan	5
Mexico	5
Italy	5
Malta	5
Slovenia	5
Macedonia	5
France	4
Belarus	4
Denmark	4
Ireland	4
Czech Republic	3
Peru	3
Montenegro	3
Argentina	3
Estonia	3
Hungary	3
Austria	2
Spain	2
Poland	2
Germany	2
Latvia	2
Bulgaria	2
Serbia	1
Bosnia and Herz.	1
Croatia	1
Romania	1
Portugal	1
Lithuania	1
Ukraine	1
Russian Fed.	1
Turkey	0
Total	8

A082) UNPAID WORK CHURCH ORGANIZATION

And for which, if any, are you currently doing unpaid voluntary work? Religious or church organizations.

(WVS: V55; EVS: V31)

Belong (%)

Country	Wave		Gender		Age			Education			Income			Values		
	1990	2000	Male	Female	16-29	30-49	50+	Lower	Middle	Upper	Lower	Middle	Upper	Mat	Mixed	Postm.
Albania	na	**15**	12	18	14	13	19	18	13	10	18	15	11	15	14	10
Algeria	na	**14**	18	9	18	11	11	10	13	17	14	15	11	10	15	19
Argentina	5	**9**	6	12	5	9	13	9	9	11	10	9	9	6	10	10
Armenia	na	**na**	na	na	na	na	na	na	na	na	na	na	na	na	na	na
Australia	na	**na**	na	na	na	na	na	na	na	na	na	na	na	na	na	na
Austria	6	**7**	7	7	5	8	7	4	11	9	7	7	8	2	7	10
Azerbaijan	na	**na**	na	na	na	na	na	na	na	na	na	na	na	na	na	na
Bangladesh	na	**40**	57	20	34	43	54	35	48	45	32	44	44	38	44	30
Belarus	na	**7**	4	9	7	7	6	8	7	5	6	7	7	6	8	na
Belgium	7	**6**	5	7	3	5	8	5	4	10	7	6	6	5	6	5
Bosnia and Herz.	na	**5**	4	5	3	5	5	7	4	3	8	3	4	4	5	6
Brazil	13	**na**	na	na	na	na	na	na	na	na	na	na	na	na	na	na
Bulgaria	2	**2**	2	2	1	1	3	3	1	2	3	1	2	2	2	9
Canada	16	**18**	16	21	9	19	24	16	16	24	17	22	16	16	21	13
Chile	12	**17**	13	20	13	15	22	20	14	16	21	14	15	18	17	12
China	2	**4**	4	5	4	5	3	3	5	5	4	4	5	4	4	6
Colombia	na	**na**	na	na	na	na	na	na	na	na	na	na	na	na	na	na
Croatia	na	**5**	5	6	4	5	7	4	6	7	3	6	7	6	5	6
Czech Republic	na	**3**	3	2	3	2	4	3	3	5	3	3	2	3	2	4
Denmark	2	**3**	2	4	1	4	4	3	2	5	4	2	5	1	3	3
Dominican Rep.	na	**na**	na	na	na	na	na	na	na	na	na	na	na	na	na	na
Egypt	na	**na**	na	na	na	na	na	na	na	na	na	na	na	na	na	na
El Salvador	na	**na**	na	na	na	na	na	na	na	na	na	na	na	na	na	na
Estonia	1	**3**	3	3	3	1	4	4	3	2	4	3	3	2	3	4
Finland	7	**11**	8	14	8	8	17	11	11	16	11	14	9	9	12	11
France	5	**3**	3	4	2	4	3	2	4	5	3	4	3	3	3	4
Georgia	na	**na**	na	na	na	na	na	na	na	na	na	na	na	na	na	na
Germany	9	**6**	4	7	5	5	7	5	6	9	3	8	9	4	6	7
Great Britain	6	**6**	6	7	2	7	8	5	6	12	5	4	12	na	na	na
Greece	na	**6**	6	7	4	7	10	14	6	5	8	7	5	8	6	4
Hungary	3	**6**	6	5	4	6	6	6	5	7	7	7	4	6	6	8
Iceland	4	**5**	5	5	1	6	6	4	4	7	5	5	3	5	5	4
India	na	**14**	17	11	10	15	17	13	17	14	14	11	17	10	19	9
Indonesia	na	**na**	na	na	na	na	na	na	na	na	na	na	na	na	na	na
Iran	na	**na**	na	na	na	na	na	na	na	na	na	na	na	na	na	na
Ireland	7	**8**	6	10	5	5	12	7	6	14	8	6	9	7	8	10
Israel	na	**na**	na	na	na	na	na	na	na	na	na	na	na	na	na	na
Italy	6	**7**	6	8	6	7	7	5	8	8	5	8	8	6	7	7
Japan	3	**3**	3	3	1	2	5	4	4	2	4	4	3	2	3	3
Jordan	na	**na**	na	na	na	na	na	na	na	na	na	na	na	na	na	na
Korea, South	7	**27**	23	31	24	28	27	27	30	23	25	24	31	25	28	29
Latvia	3	**4**	2	5	4	3	5	4	3	7	5	4	2	4	4	na
Lithuania	3	**5**	3	6	4	2	7	10	3	2	4	7	3	2	5	9
Luxembourg	na	**6**	6	7	4	5	10	5	6	10	6	6	9	4	6	9
Macedonia	na	**9**	9	8	10	10	5	13	6	7	7	9	8	10	7	12
Malta	na	**13**	10	15	7	9	20	14	11	20	13	14	12	9	15	16
Mexico	10	**20**	17	23	15	20	26	21	17	19	21	23	19	21	21	17
Moldova	na	**16**	11	20	15	13	20	17	16	14	10	16	18	20	13	11
Montenegro	na	**2**	2	2	1	2	2	1	3	2	2	3	1	1	3	2
Morocco	na	**na**	na	na	na	na	na	na	na	na	na	na	na	na	na	na
Netherlands	10	**11**	11	11	4	9	18	13	10	11	11	12	11	12	11	11
New Zealand	na	**na**	na	na	na	na	na	na	na	na	na	na	na	na	na	na
Nigeria	na	**na**	na	na	na	na	na	na	na	na	na	na	na	na	na	na
Northern Ireland	10	**43**	44	42	30	32	55	50	30	49	50	36	43	50	48	18
Norway	6	**na**	na	na	na	na	na	na	na	na	na	na	na	na	na	na
Pakistan	na	**na**	na	na	na	na	na	na	na	na	na	na	na	na	na	na
Peru	na	**20**	16	24	19	20	26	20	22	17	19	20	24	20	21	19
Philippines	na	**30**	28	32	24	29	39	29	26	36	30	30	29	29	31	25
Poland	na	**4**	4	4	7	2	4	3	4	6	3	4	5	3	3	8
Portugal	6	**3**	3	3	2	3	2	2	3	8	1	3	3	2	3	1
Puerto Rico	na	**31**	26	33	23	24	40	42	29	30	37	32	24	42	29	31
Romania	4	**4**	3	4	2	3	5	4	4	2	6	2	3	3	4	5
Russian Fed.	1	**1**	na	1	1	1	na	1	na	1	na	1	na	na	1	na
Serbia	na	**1**	1	1	1	1	2	1	1	1	1	2	1	1	1	na
Singapore	na	**12**	12	12	13	12	10	8	12	23	10	12	16	12	12	8
Slovakia	na	**13**	9	17	7	10	22	22	9	9	19	13	10	15	12	9
Slovenia	2	**5**	5	4	4	3	6	5	4	3	7	4	3	4	5	5
South Africa	na	**37**	30	47	31	38	51	36	38	48	36	44	33	39	38	24
Spain	7	**4**	3	5	2	4	6	4	4	5	4	5	5	4	4	5
Sweden	3	**23**	20	27	26	20	26	24	21	27	24	20	25	16	24	23
Switzerland	na	**na**	na	na	na	na	na	na	na	na	na	na	na	na	na	na
Taiwan	na	**na**	na	na	na	na	na	na	na	na	na	na	na	na	na	na
Tanzania	na	**62**	60	65	58	65	64	64	56	67	66	71	53	62	63	67
Turkey	na	**1**	1	na	1	1	1	na	1	2	na	1	1	na	1	na
Uganda	na	**39**	48	31	36	43	37	36	40	34	43	37	41	43	38	31
Ukraine	na	**2**	2	3	3	2	3	3	2	2	2	2	3	2	2	7
United States	29	**38**	34	42	29	43	39	27	36	43	29	39	50	47	40	30
Uruguay	na	**na**	na	na	na	na	na	na	na	na	na	na	na	na	na	na
Venezuela	na	**na**	na	na	na	na	na	na	na	na	na	na	na	na	na	na
Vietnam	na	**10**	9	11	8	10	9	12	6	5	7	8	12	5	12	5
Zimbabwe	na	**54**	42	65	52	58	50	54	55	52	49	55	66	51	56	59
Total	7	**14**	13	14	13	14	14	14	12	15	14	14	13	13	14	13

RANKING	
Country	2000
Tanzania	62
Zimbabwe	54
Northern Ireland	43
Bangladesh	40
Uganda	39
United States	38
South Africa	37
Puerto Rico	31
Philippines	30
Korea, South	27
Sweden	23
Peru	20
Mexico	20
Canada	18
Chile	17
Moldova	16
Albania	15
India	14
Algeria	14
Slovakia	13
Malta	13
Singapore	12
Netherlands	11
Finland	11
Vietnam	10
Argentina	9
Macedonia	9
Ireland	8
Austria	7
Belarus	7
Italy	7
Luxembourg	6
Great Britain	6
Greece	6
Belgium	6
Germany	6
Hungary	6
Croatia	5
Iceland	5
Bosnia and Herz.	5
Lithuania	5
Slovenia	5
China	4
Spain	4
Romania	4
Latvia	4
Poland	4
Japan	3
France	3
Denmark	3
Estonia	3
Czech Republic	3
Portugal	3
Ukraine	2
Bulgaria	2
Montenegro	2
Serbia	1
Turkey	1
Russian Fed.	1
Total	14

A083) UNPAID WORK CULTURAL ACTIVITIES

And for which, if any, are you currently doing unpaid voluntary work? Education, arts, music or cultural activities.

Belong (%)

(WVS: V56; EVS: V32)

Country	Wave		Gender		Age			Education			Income			Values		
	1990	2000	Male	Female	16-29	30-49	50+	Lower	Middle	Upper	Lower	Middle	Upper	Mat	Mixed	Postm.
Albania	na	**10**	11	9	16	10	5	5	13	14	11	11	7	10	11	13
Algeria	na	**12**	13	10	14	10	11	6	12	17	13	11	13	10	12	16
Argentina	4	**4**	3	4	5	4	2	2	5	14	1	4	6	2	3	7
Armenia	na	**na**	na	na	na	na	na	na	na	na	na	na	na	na	na	na
Australia	na	**na**	na	na	na	na	na	na	na	na	na	na	na	na	na	na
Austria	4	**7**	9	5	7	7	6	4	8	15	4	7	9	4	6	10
Azerbaijan	na	**na**	na	na	na	na	na	na	na	na	na	na	na	na	na	na
Bangladesh	na	**29**	37	18	30	29	24	18	39	44	19	31	34	27	31	24
Belarus	na	**3**	3	3	6	3	2	na	4	7	4	3	4	1	5	3
Belgium	7	**10**	11	10	10	12	8	3	9	18	7	9	15	6	10	14
Bosnia and Herz.	na	**3**	2	3	4	2	3	na	2	7	1	3	3	4	2	4
Brazil	3	**na**	na	na	na	na	na	na	na	na	na	na	na	na	na	na
Bulgaria	3	**3**	4	2	4	4	1	na	1	11	1	4	3	1	4	7
Canada	9	**11**	10	13	8	13	11	4	10	19	7	10	15	11	11	12
Chile	6	**7**	6	8	12	4	7	3	7	16	3	8	12	5	8	7
China	8	**16**	16	16	20	16	14	12	18	40	15	17	19	14	20	38
Colombia	na	**na**	na	na	na	na	na	na	na	na	na	na	na	na	na	na
Croatia	na	**3**	3	3	7	3	na	1	2	9	2	2	4	na	3	3
Czech Republic	na	**6**	7	5	10	6	4	4	6	15	3	6	8	4	6	8
Denmark	5	**5**	6	5	5	6	5	3	8	10	4	5	7	0	5	11
Dominican Rep.	na	**na**	na	na	na	na	na	na	na	na	na	na	na	na	na	na
Egypt	na	**na**	na	na	na	na	na	na	na	na	na	na	na	na	na	na
El Salvador	na	**na**	na	na	na	na	na	na	na	na	na	na	na	na	na	na
Estonia	7	**6**	6	6	10	5	4	4	6	9	3	4	9	3	7	13
Finland	9	**7**	6	8	8	7	6	4	9	15	9	4	8	6	6	15
France	5	**5**	5	5	6	6	4	3	5	10	4	5	7	3	5	9
Georgia	na	**na**	na	na	na	na	na	na	na	na	na	na	na	na	na	na
Germany	4	**3**	3	2	1	3	3	2	3	5	2	3	3	2	3	4
Great Britain	3	**3**	2	4	5	3	1	1	3	7	3	2	4	na	na	na
Greece	na	**14**	13	15	14	16	10	7	12	17	10	16	16	19	12	18
Hungary	2	**3**	3	3	3	4	3	1	3	16	1	3	4	2	5	11
Iceland	5	**6**	5	7	5	8	4	4	4	15	2	8	6	3	6	7
India	na	**12**	14	8	13	12	10	7	11	22	12	8	15	8	18	27
Indonesia	na	**na**	na	na	na	na	na	na	na	na	na	na	na	na	na	na
Iran	na	**na**	na	na	na	na	na	na	na	na	na	na	na	na	na	na
Ireland	4	**5**	5	5	4	5	5	2	5	8	2	7	7	4	4	9
Israel	na	**na**	na	na	na	na	na	na	na	na	na	na	na	na	na	na
Italy	3	**6**	7	6	10	6	4	3	7	14	4	7	8	3	5	10
Japan	3	**4**	5	3	3	4	5	6	3	5	4	4	6	5	4	3
Jordan	na	**na**	na	na	na	na	na	na	na	na	na	na	na	na	na	na
Korea, South	3	**9**	8	9	13	7	7	4	7	11	8	9	9	7	10	12
Latvia	5	**5**	4	5	5	6	4	2	4	9	4	4	5	3	6	2
Lithuania	6	**2**	1	2	2	3	1	1	1	7	na	2	2	1	2	3
Luxembourg	na	**9**	8	10	10	7	9	5	9	13	4	7	14	8	9	12
Macedonia	na	**7**	7	8	13	7	3	4	8	13	3	7	12	5	9	8
Malta	na	**4**	6	2	4	2	5	2	4	7	3	4	5	2	4	7
Mexico	5	**5**	5	5	7	5	4	3	6	14	3	6	9	5	5	10
Moldova	na	**9**	8	10	12	10	6	2	8	17	6	9	12	7	9	26
Montenegro	na	**3**	2	3	5	2	2	1	3	5	1	4	4	1	4	5
Morocco	na	**na**	na	na	na	na	na	na	na	na	na	na	na	na	na	na
Netherlands	11	**16**	15	17	13	21	12	9	13	26	13	16	18	9	15	22
New Zealand	na	**na**	na	na	na	na	na	na	na	na	na	na	na	na	na	na
Nigeria	na	**na**	na	na	na	na	na	na	na	na	na	na	na	na	na	na
Northern Ireland	3	**10**	9	11	10	16	6	3	12	15	3	7	15	8	11	7
Norway	5	**na**	na	na	na	na	na	na	na	na	na	na	na	na	na	na
Pakistan	na	**na**	na	na	na	na	na	na	na	na	na	na	na	na	na	na
Peru	na	**10**	11	9	10	10	8	7	8	14	6	10	15	7	10	12
Philippines	na	**4**	4	4	4	3	5	2	2	10	2	4	6	2	5	2
Poland	na	**2**	2	2	3	2	1	1	1	8	na	3	3	1	2	1
Portugal	4	**2**	4	1	3	3	1	2	3	9	na	2	2	2	3	3
Puerto Rico	na	**8**	9	7	9	10	6	3	4	11	4	9	11	9	6	12
Romania	2	**2**	2	1	4	2	0	0	3	2	0	2	3	1	2	4
Russian Fed.	3	**0**	na	1	1	na	na	na	na	1	na	1	na	na	na	na
Serbia	na	**1**	1	1	2	1	na	na	1	1	na	1	1	1	na	3
Singapore	na	**6**	5	8	11	3	3	4	7	12	3	6	8	4	7	13
Slovakia	na	**6**	5	6	8	5	5	3	6	10	4	6	7	4	7	6
Slovenia	3	**7**	8	6	9	6	5	4	6	15	3	8	13	3	8	8
South Africa	na	**7**	9	5	9	7	4	5	9	26	5	8	10	8	7	4
Spain	4	**3**	3	3	5	3	2	1	3	9	2	2	7	2	2	8
Sweden	3	**11**	11	11	19	7	12	7	9	18	11	11	12	6	10	18
Switzerland	na	**na**	na	na	na	na	na	na	na	na	na	na	na	na	na	na
Taiwan	na	**na**	na	na	na	na	na	na	na	na	na	na	na	na	na	na
Tanzania	na	**26**	25	26	29	26	18	22	28	34	23	28	29	21	28	29
Turkey	na	**1**	2	1	1	1	na	na	2	6	na	1	4	na	2	2
Uganda	na	**16**	22	11	26	7	5	8	21	7	15	17	14	14	17	17
Ukraine	na	**2**	1	2	3	2	2	1	1	4	1	2	3	1	3	2
United States	10	**20**	18	22	23	18	19	9	19	25	14	19	27	20	19	22
Uruguay	na	**na**	na	na	na	na	na	na	na	na	na	na	na	na	na	na
Venezuela	na	**na**	na	na	na	na	na	na	na	na	na	na	na	na	na	na
Vietnam	na	**16**	15	16	22	16	11	14	18	22	12	13	21	15	18	16
Zimbabwe	na	**4**	6	2	5	4	2	2	7	9	1	4	10	4	4	6
Total	5	**8**	8	7	10	8	5	5	7	14	6	8	10	6	8	11

RANKING	
Country	2000
Bangladesh	29
Tanzania	26
United States	20
China	16
Uganda	16
Netherlands	16
Vietnam	16
Greece	14
Algeria	12
India	12
Sweden	11
Canada	11
Belgium	10
Albania	10
Peru	10
Northern Ireland	10
Moldova	9
Luxembourg	9
Korea, South	9
Puerto Rico	8
South Africa	7
Macedonia	7
Chile	7
Finland	7
Austria	7
Slovenia	7
Singapore	6
Italy	6
Czech Republic	6
Iceland	6
Estonia	6
Slovakia	6
Mexico	5
Denmark	5
France	5
Ireland	5
Latvia	5
Zimbabwe	4
Philippines	4
Japan	4
Argentina	4
Malta	4
Belarus	3
Hungary	3
Spain	3
Croatia	3
Germany	3
Great Britain	3
Bosnia and Herz.	3
Bulgaria	3
Montenegro	3
Portugal	2
Romania	2
Poland	2
Ukraine	2
Lithuania	2
Turkey	1
Serbia	1
Russian Fed.	0
Total	8

A084) UNPAID WORK LABOR UNIONS

And for which, if any, are you currently doing unpaid voluntary work? Labor unions / Trade unions.

(WVS: V57; EVS: V33)

Belong (%)

Country	Wave		Gender		Age			Education			Income			Values		
	1990	2000	Male	Female	16-29	30-49	50+	Lower	Middle	Upper	Lower	Middle	Upper	Mat	Mixed	Postm.
Albania	na	**4**	6	3	2	5	5	4	4	5	6	4	4	5	5	3
Algeria	na	**na**	na	na	na	na	na	na	na	na	na	na	na	na	na	na
Argentina	1	**1**	2	na	na	1	1	1	na	2	na	1	1	1	1	1
Armenia	na	**na**	na	na	na	na	na	na	na	na	na	na	na	na	na	na
Australia	na	**na**	na	na	na	na	na	na	na	na	na	na	na	na	na	na
Austria	2	**2**	4	1	2	3	1	3	1	3	1	3	3	1	2	2
Azerbaijan	na	**na**	na	na	na	na	na	na	na	na	na	na	na	na	na	na
Bangladesh	na	**14**	21	6	10	17	17	12	18	15	11	16	14	11	17	12
Belarus	na	**9**	9	9	10	12	5	3	11	11	7	10	9	6	10	23
Belgium	2	**3**	4	2	1	3	3	2	2	4	1	2	4	2	3	3
Bosnia and Herz.	na	**2**	2	2	1	3	2	2	2	3	2	2	3	2	2	4
Brazil	2	**na**	na	na	na	na	na	na	na	na	na	na	na	na	na	na
Bulgaria	5	**3**	4	3	1	6	2	1	3	9	1	4	5	2	6	na
Canada	4	**3**	5	2	2	4	3	na	4	6	2	3	7	6	3	5
Chile	2	**2**	4	1	1	3	2	2	3	2	2	2	5	1	4	1
China	1	**7**	10	5	6	7	9	3	10	14	3	10	11	8	8	9
Colombia	na	**na**	na	na	na	na	na	na	na	na	na	na	na	na	na	na
Croatia	na	**4**	5	2	2	6	3	1	5	5	2	3	5	6	4	2
Czech Republic	na	**3**	3	3	1	3	4	2	4	3	2	4	4	3	3	2
Denmark	3	**4**	4	3	1	7	3	3	5	4	1	5	7	3	3	7
Dominican Rep.	na	**na**	na	na	na	na	na	na	na	na	na	na	na	na	na	na
Egypt	na	**na**	na	na	na	na	na	na	na	na	na	na	na	na	na	na
El Salvador	na	**na**	na	na	na	na	na	na	na	na	na	na	na	na	na	na
Estonia	11	**1**	1	na	1	1	na	na	1	1	na	1	1	1	na	na
Finland	8	**6**	6	5	2	10	4	6	5	9	2	7	9	5	6	7
France	2	**1**	2	1	na	2	2	1	1	2	na	2	2	1	2	1
Georgia	na	**na**	na	na	na	na	na	na	na	na	na	na	na	na	na	na
Germany	10	**0**	1	na	1	na	na	1	na	2	na	1	1	1	na	na
Great Britain	1	**2**	2	2	na	3	3	2	2	5	3	3	2	na	na	na
Greece	na	**5**	6	3	3	6	4	5	4	5	3	6	5	5	4	4
Hungary	5	**1**	2	1	1	1	2	1	1	5	1	2	1	1	2	na
Iceland	3	**3**	4	2	2	5	2	3	2	6	2	4	4	2	3	7
India	na	**7**	8	4	5	8	6	7	7	6	11	6	6	5	9	13
Indonesia	na	**na**	na	na	na	na	na	na	na	na	na	na	na	na	na	na
Iran	na	**na**	na	na	na	na	na	na	na	na	na	na	na	na	na	na
Ireland	1	**2**	3	1	1	2	1	1	1	5	1	1	3	1	2	1
Israel	na	**na**	na	na	na	na	na	na	na	na	na	na	na	na	na	na
Italy	3	**2**	3	2	1	3	2	2	2	3	1	2	3	2	3	2
Japan	1	**1**	1	na	na	na	1	1	1	na	na	1	1	1	1	1
Jordan	na	**na**	na	na	na	na	na	na	na	na	na	na	na	na	na	na
Korea, South	1	**2**	4	1	1	2	6	4	3	2	2	4	2	1	3	3
Latvia	9	**2**	2	3	3	3	1	na	1	9	1	3	4	2	3	na
Lithuania	9	**1**	1	1	2	2	na	na	2	2	1	1	2	1	2	1
Luxembourg	na	**3**	4	2	3	3	3	3	3	3	3	4	4	2	3	2
Macedonia	na	**2**	3	1	na	3	2	na	3	na	1	2	1	2	2	na
Malta	na	**2**	3	1	3	1	2	na	2	4	na	2	5	1	3	5
Mexico	2	**2**	3	1	2	2	3	2	3	5	2	3	3	3	2	2
Moldova	na	**8**	8	8	9	8	7	1	7	16	6	9	9	8	7	21
Montenegro	na	**1**	2	1	na	2	1	1	1	3	1	1	2	na	2	3
Morocco	na	**na**	na	na	na	na	na	na	na	na	na	na	na	na	na	na
Netherlands	1	**2**	3	1	1	2	3	2	1	3	2	3	3	2	2	2
New Zealand	na	**na**	na	na	na	na	na	na	na	na	na	na	na	na	na	na
Nigeria	na	**na**	na	na	na	na	na	na	na	na	na	na	na	na	na	na
Northern Ireland	2	**6**	6	5	11	4	5	5	6	6	9	9	5	7	7	2
Norway	6	**na**	na	na	na	na	na	na	na	na	na	na	na	na	na	na
Pakistan	na	**na**	na	na	na	na	na	na	na	na	na	na	na	na	na	na
Peru	na	**3**	4	2	1	4	4	1	4	2	2	4	2	3	3	3
Philippines	na	**3**	5	2	2	4	4	5	3	3	4	2	4	3	4	1
Poland	na	**2**	3	2	1	4	2	2	3	3	1	2	4	2	2	3
Portugal	1	**0**	1	na	na	1	na	na	1	1	na	1	na	na	1	na
Puerto Rico	na	**2**	3	2	2	2	2	3	1	3	1	3	2	1	2	3
Romania	14	**6**	8	4	5	11	2	1	7	14	1	4	11	4	7	13
Russian Fed.	9	**4**	4	3	4	5	2	na	3	7	2	4	5	4	4	7
Serbia	na	**2**	2	2	na	4	1	1	2	4	1	1	4	3	1	1
Singapore	na	**1**	1	1	na	2	na	1	1	1	1	1	1	1	1	1
Slovakia	na	**6**	6	6	5	9	3	2	7	8	4	6	8	6	5	10
Slovenia	2	**3**	4	3	2	5	2	3	3	7	4	3	5	4	3	4
South Africa	na	**5**	7	3	2	8	2	4	6	na	1	8	8	5	5	7
Spain	1	**1**	2	1	na	2	1	1	1	3	1	1	4	na	1	3
Sweden	6	**10**	11	10	8	11	11	8	10	12	9	10	13	10	9	13
Switzerland	na	**na**	na	na	na	na	na	na	na	na	na	na	na	na	na	na
Taiwan	na	**na**	na	na	na	na	na	na	na	na	na	na	na	na	na	na
Tanzania	na	**21**	21	20	14	27	16	15	22	39	14	29	27	19	21	33
Turkey	na	**1**	2	na	1	1	1	na	1	3	na	1	2	1	1	2
Uganda	na	**4**	6	2	5	4	1	5	4	2	4	3	4	5	3	5
Ukraine	na	**4**	4	4	4	5	4	1	4	7	2	5	5	3	5	5
United States	2	**3**	5	2	3	3	4	2	3	4	2	4	4	1	4	3
Uruguay	na	**na**	na	na	na	na	na	na	na	na	na	na	na	na	na	na
Venezuela	na	**na**	na	na	na	na	na	na	na	na	na	na	na	na	na	na
Vietnam	na	**10**	10	10	8	13	6	6	13	24	8	11	10	9	11	10
Zimbabwe	na	**1**	2	na	1	1	1	1	2	na	1	1	2	na	2	na
Total	4	**4**	5	3	3	5	3	3	4	5	3	4	5	4	4	4

RANKING	
Country	2000
Tanzania	21
Bangladesh	14
Sweden	10
Vietnam	10
Belarus	9
Moldova	8
China	7
India	7
Romania	6
Finland	6
Slovakia	6
Northern Ireland	6
South Africa	5
Greece	5
Albania	4
Denmark	4
Uganda	4
Ukraine	4
Croatia	4
Russian Fed.	4
Bulgaria	3
Canada	3
Philippines	3
Slovenia	3
United States	3
Iceland	3
Luxembourg	3
Czech Republic	3
Peru	3
Belgium	3
Chile	2
Korea, South	2
Latvia	2
Mexico	2
Great Britain	2
Italy	2
Poland	2
Netherlands	2
Puerto Rico	2
Austria	2
Malta	2
Bosnia and Herz.	2
Serbia	2
Ireland	2
Macedonia	2
France	1
Hungary	1
Lithuania	1
Spain	1
Montenegro	1
Singapore	1
Zimbabwe	1
Turkey	1
Argentina	1
Japan	1
Estonia	1
Germany	0
Portugal	0
Total	4

A085) UNPAID WORK POLITICAL PARTIES

And for which, if any, are you currently doing unpaid voluntary work? Political parties or groups.

Belong (%)

(WVS: V58; EVS: V34)

Country	Wave		Gender		Age			Education			Income			Values		
	1990	2000	Male	Female	16-29	30-49	50+	Lower	Middle	Upper	Lower	Middle	Upper	Mat	Mixed	Postm.
Albania	na	**11**	18	5	6	13	13	9	13	13	15	10	9	12	12	5
Algeria	na	**6**	8	4	4	7	9	5	4	8	6	4	7	4	7	8
Argentina	1	**3**	4	2	2	4	3	2	4	5	3	3	4	1	3	5
Armenia	na	**na**	na	na	na	na	na	na	na	na	na	na	na	na	na	na
Australia	na	**na**	na	na	na	na	na	na	na	na	na	na	na	na	na	na
Austria	3	**3**	5	2	2	4	3	4	2	5	1	5	4	na	3	5
Azerbaijan	na	**na**	na	na	na	na	na	na	na	na	na	na	na	na	na	na
Bangladesh	na	**23**	34	9	21	24	25	16	30	32	24	21	24	20	25	26
Belarus	na	**1**	2	1	1	3	na	na	2	4	1	2	na	1	2	3
Belgium	2	**3**	4	2	3	3	3	2	2	5	2	2	4	1	3	5
Bosnia and Herz.	na	**3**	5	1	4	4	2	1	3	5	3	3	5	3	3	2
Brazil	2	**na**	na	na	na	na	na	na	na	na	na	na	na	na	na	na
Bulgaria	5	**3**	5	2	2	3	4	2	3	7	2	4	3	2	4	8
Canada	4	**3**	4	2	2	2	4	1	2	6	2	2	4	3	2	3
Chile	2	**2**	3	1	2	2	1	1	2	3	2	1	3	1	2	4
China	26	**10**	12	8	12	9	10	7	11	28	8	10	13	9	12	25
Colombia	na	**na**	na	na	na	na	na	na	na	na	na	na	na	na	na	na
Croatia	na	**2**	3	1	2	1	3	na	2	4	1	1	3	na	1	4
Czech Republic	na	**2**	3	1	1	2	3	2	1	6	2	3	1	2	2	3
Denmark	2	**3**	3	2	3	2	3	2	2	3	1	2	3	0	3	5
Dominican Rep.	na	**na**	na	na	na	na	na	na	na	na	na	na	na	na	na	na
Egypt	na	**na**	na	na	na	na	na	na	na	na	na	na	na	na	na	na
El Salvador	na	**na**	na	na	na	na	na	na	na	na	na	na	na	na	na	na
Estonia	4	**2**	2	1	2	1	2	1	2	2	na	1	2	1	2	na
Finland	7	**4**	7	1	1	3	6	4	3	7	2	4	7	2	4	5
France	2	**1**	1	1	1	1	1	1	1	2	1	na	1	na	na	4
Georgia	na	**na**	na	na	na	na	na	na	na	na	na	na	na	na	na	na
Germany	6	**1**	1	1	na	1	1	na	1	4	1	1	1	na	1	2
Great Britain	2	**1**	2	1	1	2	1	1	1	2	1	2	2	na	na	na
Greece	na	**5**	7	4	4	6	6	2	6	6	4	7	7	4	5	8
Hungary	1	**1**	2	1	2	1	1	1	1	4	1	1	1	2	1	na
Iceland	4	**3**	4	3	3	4	3	2	4	5	3	4	4	3	3	7
India	na	**8**	12	3	9	9	7	6	12	9	9	8	8	10	9	13
Indonesia	na	**na**	na	na	na	na	na	na	na	na	na	na	na	na	na	na
Iran	na	**na**	na	na	na	na	na	na	na	na	na	na	na	na	na	na
Ireland	2	**2**	3	1	1	1	3	1	1	3	1	1	3	1	2	1
Israel	na	**na**	na	na	na	na	na	na	na	na	na	na	na	na	na	na
Italy	4	**2**	4	1	2	2	3	2	2	5	1	3	3	1	2	4
Japan	1	**1**	2	1	na	1	2	3	1	1	1	1	3	1	1	2
Jordan	na	**na**	na	na	na	na	na	na	na	na	na	na	na	na	na	na
Korea, South	2	**2**	3	1	1	2	3	2	2	2	3	2	1	3	2	4
Latvia	6	**1**	1	1	1	1	1	na	1	1	1	1	1	1	1	4
Lithuania	4	**1**	2	1	2	1	1	na	1	6	1	1	2	na	1	4
Luxembourg	na	**3**	3	3	2	3	3	2	3	4	3	3	4	3	3	4
Macedonia	na	**8**	11	5	9	10	5	7	8	10	6	10	8	8	8	13
Malta	na	**4**	6	3	3	4	6	4	4	4	3	4	6	3	5	5
Mexico	3	**4**	5	2	3	3	4	3	3	8	3	3	4	3	4	4
Moldova	na	**5**	6	4	4	6	5	2	4	9	5	5	5	5	6	9
Montenegro	na	**3**	4	2	3	3	2	1	4	5	na	3	5	1	4	10
Morocco	na	**na**	na	na	na	na	na	na	na	na	na	na	na	na	na	na
Netherlands	2	**3**	3	2	2	2	4	2	2	4	2	2	4	3	3	3
New Zealand	na	**na**	na	na	na	na	na	na	na	na	na	na	na	na	na	na
Nigeria	na	**na**	na	na	na	na	na	na	na	na	na	na	na	na	na	na
Northern Ireland	1	**4**	6	3	4	5	4	7	2	4	1	9	3	na	5	6
Norway	4	**na**	na	na	na	na	na	na	na	na	na	na	na	na	na	na
Pakistan	na	**na**	na	na	na	na	na	na	na	na	na	na	na	na	na	na
Peru	na	**3**	5	2	3	4	5	1	3	6	2	4	6	4	3	6
Philippines	na	**4**	5	3	3	5	4	4	3	6	4	4	3	1	6	3
Poland	na	**1**	1	na	na	na	1	na	1	2	1	1	na	na	1	1
Portugal	3	**1**	1	na	na	1	1	na	1	2	na	na	2	na	1	1
Puerto Rico	na	**4**	6	3	4	5	3	4	2	6	2	5	6	4	4	7
Romania	2	**2**	3	1	1	3	1	0	1	6	1	2	2	1	2	5
Russian Fed.	5	**0**	1	na	na	na	na	na	na	1	na	na	1	na	na	3
Serbia	na	**1**	2	1	1	2	1	1	1	3	1	1	2	1	2	3
Singapore	na	**0**	na	na	na	na	1	na	na	1	na	na	1	1	na	na
Slovakia	na	**5**	6	3	3	4	7	1	7	5	3	6	5	3	6	11
Slovenia	1	**1**	2	1	2	1	1	1	1	1	na	2	3	na	1	2
South Africa	na	**6**	9	3	4	8	4	6	6	7	8	6	5	6	7	5
Spain	1	**1**	2	na	1	2	1	1	2	3	1	1	2	1	1	4
Sweden	4	**4**	6	3	1	4	7	6	3	4	3	6	3	7	4	6
Switzerland	na	**na**	na	na	na	na	na	na	na	na	na	na	na	na	na	na
Taiwan	na	**na**	na	na	na	na	na	na	na	na	na	na	na	na	na	na
Tanzania	na	**21**	22	20	18	22	28	27	15	14	27	20	15	20	22	29
Turkey	na	**3**	5	1	3	3	2	2	3	6	2	3	4	2	2	6
Uganda	na	**6**	9	4	8	5	3	4	6	12	8	8	7	5	7	5
Ukraine	na	**1**	2	1	na	3	1	1	1	3	1	1	2	1	2	na
United States	5	**7**	9	5	8	4	11	3	6	9	6	7	9	8	6	10
Uruguay	na	**na**	na	na	na	na	na	na	na	na	na	na	na	na	na	na
Venezuela	na	**na**	na	na	na	na	na	na	na	na	na	na	na	na	na	na
Vietnam	na	**24**	29	19	23	23	27	19	30	36	21	19	31	14	29	20
Zimbabwe	na	**5**	7	3	3	4	9	5	4	na	6	5	3	5	4	10
Total	4	**4**	6	3	4	5	4	4	4	6	4	5	5	4	5	5

RANKING	
Country	**2000**
Vietnam	24
Bangladesh	23
Tanzania	21
Albania	11
China	10
India	8
Macedonia	8
United States	7
South Africa	6
Uganda	6
Algeria	6
Greece	5
Moldova	5
Slovakia	5
Zimbabwe	5
Sweden	4
Malta	4
Northern Ireland	4
Puerto Rico	4
Philippines	4
Finland	4
Mexico	4
Iceland	3
Austria	3
Peru	3
Argentina	3
Bosnia and Herz.	3
Bulgaria	3
Denmark	3
Turkey	3
Montenegro	3
Belgium	3
Luxembourg	3
Canada	3
Netherlands	3
Italy	2
Korea, South	2
Czech Republic	2
Romania	2
Chile	2
Ireland	2
Croatia	2
Estonia	2
Great Britain	1
Belarus	1
Lithuania	1
Slovenia	1
Spain	1
Ukraine	1
Serbia	1
Hungary	1
Japan	1
Germany	1
Latvia	1
France	1
Poland	1
Portugal	1
Russian Fed.	0
Singapore	0
Total	4

A086) UNPAID WORK LOCAL POLITICAL

And for which, if any, are you currently doing unpaid voluntary work? Local community action on issues like poverty, employment, housing, racial equality.

(WVS: V59; EVS: V35)

Belong (%)

	Wave		Gender		Age			Education			Income			Values		
Country	1990	2000	Male	Female	16-29	30-49	50+	Lower	Middle	Upper	Lower	Middle	Upper	Mat	Mixed	Postm.
Albania	na	**8**	9	7	7	9	7	9	7	6	11	6	6	9	7	3
Algeria	na	**7**	9	5	8	6	8	5	7	9	7	8	6	7	7	11
Argentina	1	**3**	2	3	3	2	3	2	4	4	2	2	5	2	3	3
Armenia	na	**na**	na	na	na	na	na	na	na	na	na	na	na	na	na	na
Australia	na	**na**	na	na	na	na	na	na	na	na	na	na	na	na	na	na
Austria	1	**1**	1	1	na	2	1	1	1	2	1	1	2	na	1	1
Azerbaijan	na	**na**	na	na	na	na	na	na	na	na	na	na	na	na	na	na
Bangladesh	na	**24**	31	17	21	25	30	21	27	31	14	28	30	23	26	22
Belarus	na	**2**	2	1	1	2	2	1	2	1	1	2	na	1	2	5
Belgium	3	**3**	3	2	2	2	3	1	2	5	4	2	3	2	2	3
Bosnia and Herz.	na	**1**	1	1	1	2	1	1	1	2	na	2	1	2	1	2
Brazil	4	**na**	na	na	na	na	na	na	na	na	na	na	na	na	na	na
Bulgaria	2	**1**	1	1	2	1	na	na	1	2	1	1	2	1	1	na
Canada	4	**5**	5	5	3	5	6	4	4	8	4	4	7	3	5	6
Chile	3	**4**	3	4	4	3	4	5	3	4	4	3	4	3	3	7
China	5	**14**	15	13	12	16	11	12	15	16	13	17	14	12	18	28
Colombia	na	**na**	na	na	na	na	na	na	na	na	na	na	na	na	na	na
Croatia	na	**1**	1	1	1	na	2	1	1	1	na	1	2	2	1	2
Czech Republic	na	**2**	2	2	2	2	2	2	3	2	3	2	2	3	2	3
Denmark	2	**3**	4	3	1	4	3	2	2	5	4	2	4	0	3	5
Dominican Rep.	na	**na**	na	na	na	na	na	na	na	na	na	na	na	na	na	na
Egypt	na	**na**	na	na	na	na	na	na	na	na	na	na	na	na	na	na
El Salvador	na	**na**	na	na	na	na	na	na	na	na	na	na	na	na	na	na
Estonia	4	**2**	2	2	2	2	2	2	2	2	1	2	2	2	1	4
Finland	3	**2**	2	3	1	3	2	3	3	1	4	2	2	3	3	1
France	3	**2**	2	2	na	1	2	2	1	2	1	1	3	1	2	3
Georgia	na	**na**	na	na	na	na	na	na	na	na	na	na	na	na	na	na
Germany	1	**0**	1	na	na	na	1	na	1	na	1	na	1	na	1	1
Great Britain	1	**2**	2	2	1	3	1	1	2	2	2	2	3	na	na	na
Greece	na	**7**	6	7	7	7	7	7	7	6	7	7	6	5	7	10
Hungary	2	**1**	2	1	na	2	1	1	na	4	1	1	3	na	3	na
Iceland	1	**1**	na	1	na	1	1	1	na	1	na	1	1	1	1	1
India	na	**5**	7	4	5	5	5	4	5	8	6	4	6	5	7	2
Indonesia	na	**na**	na	na	na	na	na	na	na	na	na	na	na	na	na	na
Iran	na	**na**	na	na	na	na	na	na	na	na	na	na	na	na	na	na
Ireland	3	**4**	3	4	2	3	5	4	3	4	2	8	3	3	3	8
Israel	na	**na**	na	na	na	na	na	na	na	na	na	na	na	na	na	na
Italy	1	**2**	2	2	2	2	2	1	2	5	2	2	3	2	2	2
Japan	1	**0**	1	na	na	na	1	1	na	1	na	na	1	na	na	2
Jordan	na	**na**	na	na	na	na	na	na	na	na	na	na	na	na	na	na
Korea, South	3	**7**	9	5	6	6	11	5	8	6	7	8	7	6	8	7
Latvia	8	**2**	1	2	2	2	2	na	2	4	2	2	2	2	2	2
Lithuania	2	**1**	1	1	1	1	na	na	1	1	na	1	1	na	1	1
Luxembourg	na	**3**	4	3	3	2	4	2	3	4	5	1	3	3	3	6
Macedonia	na	**3**	3	4	3	4	3	4	3	4	2	4	4	2	4	6
Malta	na	**4**	5	3	3	3	5	2	4	6	3	3	6	2	4	7
Mexico	3	**4**	5	4	3	4	6	5	3	5	4	7	4	5	4	4
Moldova	na	**3**	3	3	4	3	2	1	4	3	1	3	4	3	3	4
Montenegro	na	**0**	na	na	1	na	na	na	na	1	na	na	na	na	na	na
Morocco	na	**na**	na	na	na	na	na	na	na	na	na	na	na	na	na	na
Netherlands	3	**4**	4	4	3	4	4	2	4	6	2	5	5	2	4	6
New Zealand	na	**na**	na	na	na	na	na	na	na	na	na	na	na	na	na	na
Nigeria	na	**na**	na	na	na	na	na	na	na	na	na	na	na	na	na	na
Northern Ireland	2	**5**	3	7	na	8	4	9	3	2	13	5	3	4	4	11
Norway	1	**na**	na	na	na	na	na	na	na	na	na	na	na	na	na	na
Pakistan	na	**na**	na	na	na	na	na	na	na	na	na	na	na	na	na	na
Peru	na	**4**	4	4	2	5	7	4	5	4	4	5	4	5	4	5
Philippines	na	**7**	8	5	6	5	9	6	5	9	5	8	7	4	8	6
Poland	na	**1**	2	1	1	1	1	na	2	5	1	2	1	na	1	7
Portugal	1	**1**	1	1	1	na	1	na	1	3	na	1	1	na	1	2
Puerto Rico	na	**4**	5	4	3	4	4	3	2	6	3	4	6	2	5	4
Romania	1	**1**	1	1	1	0	0	0	1	0	0	1	1	0	1	0
Russian Fed.	2	**1**	na	1	1	1	1	na	na	1	1	1	na	na	1	na
Serbia	na	**0**	1	na	1	na	na	na	1	na	na	1	na	na	1	na
Singapore	na	**2**	2	2	1	3	5	3	2	2	1	3	2	2	2	na
Slovakia	na	**7**	10	4	6	7	7	6	7	9	6	8	7	6	8	6
Slovenia	3	**6**	5	7	4	5	8	7	5	6	8	8	5	8	6	3
South Africa	na	**5**	6	4	3	5	9	5	5	6	4	4	8	7	4	4
Spain	1	**2**	2	2	2	2	2	1	2	4	1	2	3	1	1	5
Sweden	1	**6**	6	5	2	5	8	6	4	8	6	5	5	3	5	9
Switzerland	1	**na**	na	na	na	na	na	na	na	na	na	na	na	na	na	na
Taiwan	na	**na**	na	na	na	na	na	na	na	na	na	na	na	na	na	na
Tanzania	na	**23**	22	25	21	25	23	23	22	28	21	25	27	19	26	25
Turkey	na	**0**	na	na	na	na	na	na	na	1	na	na	1	na	na	na
Uganda	na	**6**	11	2	7	7	1	6	6	7	10	6	5	7	6	5
Ukraine	na	**1**	1	1	1	1	1	1	1	2	1	1	2	na	2	3
United States	3	**7**	7	7	6	8	8	4	7	9	6	7	9	6	6	11
Uruguay	na	**na**	na	na	na	na	na	na	na	na	na	na	na	na	na	na
Venezuela	na	**na**	na	na	na	na	na	na	na	na	na	na	na	na	na	na
Vietnam	na	**26**	27	25	20	28	27	26	27	25	20	24	31	22	30	24
Zimbabwe	na	**2**	3	1	1	2	2	2	3	na	1	1	5	2	2	na
Total	2	5	5	4	4	5	4	4	4	6	4	5	5	4	5	5

RANKING	
Country	**2000**
Vietnam	26
Bangladesh	24
Tanzania	23
China	14
Albania	8
United States	7
Algeria	7
Korea, South	7
Greece	7
Slovakia	7
Philippines	7
Uganda	6
Slovenia	6
Sweden	6
India	5
Canada	5
South Africa	5
Northern Ireland	5
Puerto Rico	4
Mexico	4
Peru	4
Netherlands	4
Chile	4
Ireland	4
Malta	4
Macedonia	3
Denmark	3
Luxembourg	3
Moldova	3
Argentina	3
Belgium	3
Finland	2
Czech Republic	2
Singapore	2
Estonia	2
Zimbabwe	2
Italy	2
Latvia	2
Spain	2
Great Britain	2
Belarus	2
France	2
Bosnia and Herz.	1
Hungary	1
Poland	1
Austria	1
Romania	1
Croatia	1
Ukraine	1
Bulgaria	1
Iceland	1
Lithuania	1
Portugal	1
Russian Fed.	1
Germany	0
Japan	0
Serbia	0
Montenegro	0
Turkey	0
Total	5

A087) UNPAID WORK HUMAN RIGHTS

And for which, if any, are you currently doing unpaid voluntary work? Third world development or human rights.

Belong (%) (WVS: V60; EVS: V36)

Country	Wave		Gender		Age			Education			Income			Values		
	1990	2000	Male	Female	16-29	30-49	50+	Lower	Middle	Upper	Lower	Middle	Upper	Mat	Mixed	Postm.
Albania	na	2	2	3	4	2	2	2	3	2	4	2	1	2	2	5
Algeria	na	6	6	6	8	4	3	3	5	8	5	5	6	5	7	4
Argentina	0	0	1	na	na	na	1	na	na	1	na	na	na	na	na	1
Armenia	na	na	na	na	na	na	na	na	na	na	na	na	na	na	na	na
Australia	na	na	na	na	na	na	na	na	na	na	na	na	na	na	na	na
Austria	1	1	1	1	na	1	1	na	1	3	na	1	1	na	1	1
Azerbaijan	na	na	na	na	na	na	na	na	na	na	na	na	na	na	na	na
Bangladesh	na	11	16	5	7	13	17	8	10	21	5	11	15	8	13	9
Belarus	na	1	2	na	1	1	1	2	1	1	1	1	3	1	2	na
Belgium	3	4	4	4	4	5	5	2	3	8	5	3	4	2	4	6
Bosnia and Herz.	na	0	1	na	na	na	1	na	na	na	na	na	na	na	na	na
Brazil	1	na	na	na	na	na	na	na	na	na	na	na	na	na	na	na
Bulgaria	1	0	na	na	na	na	na	na	na	1	na	1	na	na	na	2
Canada	3	3	2	3	1	3	3	2	2	4	3	4	1	1	3	3
Chile	1	2	2	2	1	2	2	1	3	1	1	2	3	1	2	1
China	0	5	4	5	8	4	4	3	6	5	3	6	6	4	5	16
Colombia	na	na	na	na	na	na	na	na	na	na	na	na	na	na	na	na
Croatia	na	0	na	na	1	na	na	1	na	2	na	na	1	na	na	na
Czech Republic	na	0	na	na	na	na	1	na	na	1	na	1	na	1	na	na
Denmark	1	1	1	2	1	1	2	1	2	2	1	0	3	0	1	3
Dominican Rep.	na	na	na	na	na	na	na	na	na	na	na	na	na	na	na	na
Egypt	na	na	na	na	na	na	na	na	na	na	na	na	na	na	na	na
El Salvador	na	na	na	na	na	na	na	na	na	na	na	na	na	na	na	na
Estonia	1	0	1	na	1	na	na	na	1	na	na	na	1	na	na	na
Finland	2	5	3	6	5	6	3	5	3	7	7	3	4	4	5	2
France	1	1	na	1	na	1	1	na	na	3	na	1	1	na	1	2
Georgia	na	na	na	na	na	na	na	na	na	na	na	na	na	na	na	na
Germany	0	0	na	na	na	na	na	na	na	1	na	na	na	na	na	na
Great Britain	1	4	4	5	5	5	4	1	5	9	3	2	7	na	na	na
Greece	na	6	4	7	8	5	3	4	5	7	6	6	5	4	6	8
Hungary	0	0	1	na	1	na	na	na	na	1	na	1	na	na	na	na
Iceland	0	1	1	2	1	1	2	1	1	2	1	2	na	2	1	1
India	na	2	3	1	2	2	3	2	1	4	3	2	3	1	4	4
Indonesia	na	na	na	na	na	na	na	na	na	na	na	na	na	na	na	na
Iran	na	na	na	na	na	na	na	na	na	na	na	na	na	na	na	na
Ireland	1	2	2	2	1	1	4	2	2	3	1	3	2	2	1	5
Israel	na	na	na	na	na	na	na	na	na	na	na	na	na	na	na	na
Italy	1	2	2	2	3	2	2	2	2	2	2	2	2	1	2	2
Japan	0	0	na	na	na	na	1	na	na	1	na	na	1	1	na	na
Jordan	na	na	na	na	na	na	na	na	na	na	na	na	na	na	na	na
Korea, South	2	1	2	1	2	1	3	2	1	2	2	2	1	1	2	3
Latvia	4	0	na	1	na	1	na	na	na	1	na	1	na	na	na	na
Lithuania	1	0	na	na	na	na	na	na	na	na	na	na	na	na	na	na
Luxembourg	na	5	5	6	4	5	7	5	4	10	8	5	7	6	5	10
Macedonia	na	2	2	2	2	3	1	3	1	4	1	2	3	1	3	2
Malta	na	2	1	2	2	2	1	1	2	3	na	2	3	1	2	4
Mexico	1	1	1	2	2	1	2	1	2	1	2	1	1	2	1	1
Moldova	na	2	2	3	3	2	2	na	3	2	na	2	4	2	3	2
Montenegro	na	0	1	na	1	na	na	na	na	2	na	na	1	na	1	na
Morocco	na	na	na	na	na	na	na	na	na	na	na	na	na	na	na	na
Netherlands	3	4	3	5	3	4	6	4	3	6	3	5	4	1	4	4
New Zealand	na	na	na	na	na	na	na	na	na	na	na	na	na	na	na	na
Nigeria	na	na	na	na	na	na	na	na	na	na	na	na	na	na	na	na
Northern Ireland	0	5	5	5	na	9	3	2	2	13	3	7	6	6	6	2
Norway	1	na	na	na	na	na	na	na	na	na	na	na	na	na	na	na
Pakistan	na	na	na	na	na	na	na	na	na	na	na	na	na	na	na	na
Peru	na	2	1	2	1	2	3	2	1	3	2	1	3	1	2	3
Philippines	na	5	7	4	3	6	7	8	3	6	4	4	8	4	6	7
Poland	na	0	na	na	na	na	na	na	na	1	na	na	na	na	na	1
Portugal	1	1	1	1	1	na	1	1	1	2	na	na	1	na	na	2
Puerto Rico	na	2	1	2	2	2	1	3	na	2	1	2	2	1	1	3
Romania	0	0	1	0	0	0	1	0	0	1	0	0	1	0	1	1
Russian Fed.	0	na	na	na	na	na	na	na	na	na	na	na	na	na	na	na
Serbia	na	0	na	na	na	na	na	na	na	na	na	na	na	na	na	na
Singapore	na	1	na	1	1	1	na	1	1	1	na	1	na	1	1	na
Slovakia	na	0	na	na	na	na	na	na	na	1	na	na	na	na	na	na
Slovenia	1	0	1	na	na	na	1	1	na	1	na	1	na	na	na	1
South Africa	na	1	2	1	2	1	1	1	2	1	1	2	1	1	1	2
Spain	1	1	1	2	2	1	1	1	1	5	1	1	2	1	1	3
Sweden	3	5	4	5	3	4	5	1	4	7	4	3	7	3	3	11
Switzerland	na	na	na	na	na	na	na	na	na	na	na	na	na	na	na	na
Taiwan	na	na	na	na	na	na	na	na	na	na	na	na	na	na	na	na
Tanzania	na	20	19	20	24	19	12	19	21	19	20	22	16	14	23	17
Turkey	na	0	na	na	na	na	na	na	1	na	na	na	na	na	na	na
Uganda	na	3	6	na	5	1	1	6	2	3	5	5	1	4	3	2
Ukraine	na	0	na	na	1	na	na	na	na	1	na	na	na	na	na	na
United States	1	3	3	3	4	2	3	1	4	3	2	3	4	4	3	3
Uruguay	na	na	na	na	na	na	na	na	na	na	na	na	na	na	na	na
Venezuela	na	na	na	na	na	na	na	na	na	na	na	na	na	na	na	na
Vietnam	na	1	1	1	1	2	1	1	2	5	1	1	1	2	1	2
Zimbabwe	na	1	1	na	1	1	na	na	1	na	1	na	1	1	na	na
Total	1	2	3	2	3	2	2	2	2	4	2	2	2	2	2	3

RANKING

Country	2000
Tanzania	20
Bangladesh	11
Greece	6
Algeria	6
Luxembourg	5
Philippines	5
Northern Ireland	5
China	5
Finland	5
Sweden	5
Belgium	4
Great Britain	4
Netherlands	4
Uganda	3
United States	3
Canada	3
Albania	2
India	2
Moldova	2
Macedonia	2
Italy	2
Ireland	2
Chile	2
Peru	2
Malta	2
Puerto Rico	2
Mexico	1
Spain	1
Iceland	1
Korea, South	1
Vietnam	1
South Africa	1
Belarus	1
Denmark	1
Austria	1
France	1
Portugal	1
Singapore	1
Zimbabwe	1
Croatia	0
Czech Republic	0
Slovenia	0
Montenegro	0
Argentina	0
Bosnia and Herz.	0
Estonia	0
Japan	0
Latvia	0
Bulgaria	0
Germany	0
Hungary	0
Turkey	0
Ukraine	0
Serbia	0
Lithuania	0
Poland	0
Slovakia	0
Romania	0
Total	2

A088) UNPAID WORK ENVIRONMENT, CONSERVATION, ANIMAL RIGHTS

And for which, if any, are you currently doing unpaid voluntary work? Conservation, environmental, animal rights groups.

Belong (%) (WVS: V61; EVS: V37)

	Wave		Gender		Age			Education			Income			Values		
Country	1990	2000	Male	Female	16-29	30-49	50+	Lower	Middle	Upper	Lower	Middle	Upper	Mat	Mixed	Postm.
Albania	na	**7**	8	6	5	8	7	5	7	12	6	6	9	6	8	5
Algeria	na	**6**	7	5	8	6	3	3	6	8	7	5	5	6	7	5
Argentina	0	**1**	2	1	2	1	1	1	2	3	1	2	2	1	1	2
Armenia	na	**na**	na	na	na	na	na	na	na	na	na	na	na	na	na	na
Australia	na	**na**	na	na	na	na	na	na	na	na	na	na	na	na	na	na
Austria	1	**2**	3	2	2	2	2	2	3	4	2	2	3	1	2	1
Azerbaijan	na	**na**	na	na	na	na	na	na	na	na	na	na	na	na	na	na
Bangladesh	na	**19**	25	12	18	19	25	14	25	27	8	20	30	15	22	24
Belarus	na	**4**	4	3	4	4	3	4	3	5	4	4	2	3	4	3
Belgium	3	**4**	5	3	6	3	4	2	4	5	2	4	4	3	3	4
Bosnia and Herz.	na	**2**	2	1	1	2	1	na	1	4	1	1	3	1	2	4
Brazil	1	**na**	na	na	na	na	na	na	na	na	na	na	na	na	na	na
Bulgaria	3	**1**	1	2	3	1	1	na	1	4	na	2	2	1	2	2
Canada	4	**4**	6	3	4	5	5	3	4	7	4	4	6	2	5	5
Chile	1	**2**	2	2	2	2	2	1	2	4	1	3	4	1	2	3
China	2	**28**	29	27	31	28	24	21	32	40	24	29	32	29	31	47
Colombia	na	**na**	na	na	na	na	na	na	na	na	na	na	na	na	na	na
Croatia	na	**2**	3	na	1	2	1	na	2	4	na	1	3	na	2	2
Czech Republic	na	**3**	4	2	5	3	3	3	4	5	3	3	5	5	2	4
Denmark	1	**2**	3	1	2	2	3	1	3	3	1	3	1	0	2	6
Dominican Rep.	na	**na**	na	na	na	na	na	na	na	na	na	na	na	na	na	na
Egypt	na	**na**	na	na	na	na	na	na	na	na	na	na	na	na	na	na
El Salvador	na	**na**	na	na	na	na	na	na	na	na	na	na	na	na	na	na
Estonia	2	**1**	2	na	2	1	2	1	1	3	1	na	3	1	1	9
Finland	3	**3**	2	3	5	5	na	2	3	4	3	2	4	2	3	6
France	2	**1**	1	1	na	1	1	1	1	1	1	1	1	na	2	1
Georgia	na	**na**	na	na	na	na	na	na	na	na	na	na	na	na	na	na
Germany	2	**1**	1	1	1	1	1	1	2	1	1	1	2	1	2	1
Great Britain	2	**8**	10	6	4	12	7	1	7	28	2	3	20	na	na	na
Greece	na	**10**	9	10	13	8	5	5	8	12	11	9	11	10	9	14
Hungary	1	**2**	2	2	1	2	2	1	2	6	1	2	2	1	3	4
Iceland	2	**1**	1	1	na	3	1	1	1	3	1	1	2	1	1	4
India	na	**5**	7	4	6	5	6	3	5	10	5	3	7	2	9	18
Indonesia	na	**na**	na	na	na	na	na	na	na	na	na	na	na	na	na	na
Iran	na	**na**	na	na	na	na	na	na	na	na	na	na	na	na	na	na
Ireland	1	**1**	1	1	na	1	2	na	1	3	1	1	1	na	1	2
Israel	na	**na**	na	na	na	na	na	na	na	na	na	na	na	na	na	na
Italy	1	**2**	2	2	3	2	1	1	3	2	2	1	2	1	2	2
Japan	1	**1**	2	1	na	1	2	1	1	1	2	1	2	1	2	na
Jordan	na	**na**	na	na	na	na	na	na	na	na	na	na	na	na	na	na
Korea, South	2	**5**	6	3	4	4	7	4	5	4	5	4	4	3	6	6
Latvia	5	**1**	na	1	na	1	1	na	na	2	na	2	na	na	1	na
Lithuania	2	**1**	na	1	1	na	na	na	1	1	na	na	na	na	1	2
Luxembourg	na	**5**	4	5	5	4	4	3	4	8	5	4	8	5	5	6
Macedonia	na	**3**	3	3	4	3	2	3	2	6	2	2	5	1	4	8
Malta	na	**2**	2	2	2	1	2	1	2	4	na	2	3	1	2	7
Mexico	2	**3**	3	3	3	3	3	2	3	6	3	2	4	4	3	5
Moldova	na	**4**	4	4	6	4	3	1	5	7	3	5	5	5	4	1
Montenegro	na	**3**	3	2	3	3	2	2	2	6	na	1	5	3	3	na
Morocco	na	**na**	na	na	na	na	na	na	na	na	na	na	na	na	na	na
Netherlands	3	**2**	3	2	2	3	3	2	2	4	2	2	4	1	2	4
New Zealand	na	**na**	na	na	na	na	na	na	na	na	na	na	na	na	na	na
Nigeria	na	**na**	na	na	na	na	na	na	na	na	na	na	na	na	na	na
Northern Ireland	1	**3**	2	3	na	4	3	3	1	5	5	2	3	2	3	2
Norway	1	**na**	na	na	na	na	na	na	na	na	na	na	na	na	na	na
Pakistan	na	**na**	na	na	na	na	na	na	na	na	na	na	na	na	na	na
Peru	na	**2**	3	1	1	2	4	2	2	3	2	2	4	1	2	4
Philippines	na	**9**	12	6	6	9	12	10	7	10	7	6	15	6	11	9
Poland	na	**1**	1	na	na	1	na	na	na	2	na	1	na	na	1	na
Portugal	1	**0**	1	na	na	na	1	na	na	2	na	na	1	na	na	2
Puerto Rico	na	**3**	2	3	6	3	1	1	1	4	1	3	4	2	3	2
Romania	1	**1**	1	0	0	1	1	0	1	1	0	0	1	0	1	0
Russian Fed.	1	**0**	na	1	na	na	1	na	na	1	na	1	1	1	na	na
Serbia	na	**0**	1	na	na	na	na	na	na	na	1	na	na	na	na	na
Singapore	na	**1**	1	2	2	1	na	1	1	na	2	1	1	1	1	2
Slovakia	na	**2**	3	1	3	2	2	1	2	3	2	3	2	1	3	na
Slovenia	1	**3**	5	1	2	3	3	3	3	4	na	5	5	1	4	1
South Africa	na	**2**	2	1	2	1	2	1	2	5	1	na	2	1	1	5
Spain	1	**1**	1	1	2	1	1	1	1	3	1	1	2	na	1	3
Sweden	3	**4**	3	4	3	3	5	4	3	5	3	5	4	3	4	5
Switzerland	na	**na**	na	na	na	na	na	na	na	na	na	na	na	na	na	na
Taiwan	na	**na**	na	na	na	na	na	na	na	na	na	na	na	na	na	na
Tanzania	na	**21**	21	22	26	20	16	17	24	28	20	24	22	17	23	25
Turkey	na	**0**	na	na	na	na	na	na	na	na	na	na	na	na	na	na
Uganda	na	**8**	16	1	10	5	9	8	8	6	11	14	12	6	10	3
Ukraine	na	**0**	na	na	na	na	na	1	na	na	1	na	na	na	1	na
United States	4	**9**	7	10	8	7	11	7	6	11	6	10	10	7	8	10
Uruguay	na	**na**	na	na	na	na	na	na	na	na	na	na	na	na	na	na
Venezuela	na	**na**	na	na	na	na	na	na	na	na	na	na	na	na	na	na
Vietnam	na	**8**	10	6	10	8	6	6	9	15	7	9	8	4	10	11
Zimbabwe	na	**1**	2	na	1	1	2	1	2	na	1	1	3	1	1	1
Total	2	**4**	5	3	5	4	3	3	4	6	3	4	5	3	4	4

RANKING	
Country	**2000**
China	28
Tanzania	21
Bangladesh	19
Greece	10
Philippines	9
United States	9
Uganda	8
Vietnam	8
Great Britain	8
Albania	7
Algeria	6
India	5
Korea, South	5
Luxembourg	5
Canada	4
Moldova	4
Belgium	4
Sweden	4
Belarus	4
Czech Republic	3
Macedonia	3
Mexico	3
Slovenia	3
Finland	3
Northern Ireland	3
Puerto Rico	3
Montenegro	3
Netherlands	2
Peru	2
Austria	2
Denmark	2
Chile	2
Slovakia	2
Hungary	2
Italy	2
Malta	2
Bosnia and Herz.	2
Croatia	2
South Africa	2
Argentina	1
Bulgaria	1
Iceland	1
Estonia	1
Japan	1
Singapore	1
Zimbabwe	1
Germany	1
Spain	1
Romania	1
France	1
Ireland	1
Latvia	1
Lithuania	1
Poland	1
Portugal	0
Russian Fed.	0
Ukraine	0
Serbia	0
Turkey	0
Total	4

A089) UNPAID WORK PROFESSIONAL ASSOCIATIONS

And for which, if any, are you currently doing unpaid voluntary work?. Professional associations.

Belong (%) (WVS: V62; EVS: V38)

	Wave		Gender		Age			Education			Income			Values		
Country	1990	2000	Male	Female	16-29	30-49	50+	Lower	Middle	Upper	Lower	Middle	Upper	Mat	Mixed	Postm.
Albania	na	**7**	9	5	5	10	5	5	7	14	6	10	6	7	8	na
Algeria	na	**9**	9	8	9	9	8	4	11	11	9	11	8	9	8	13
Argentina	1	**1**	1	1	na	2	1	na	1	7	na	1	2	na	1	3
Armenia	na	**na**	na	na	na	na	na	na	na	na	na	na	na	na	na	na
Australia	na	**na**	na	na	na	na	na	na	na	na	na	na	na	na	na	na
Austria	1	**2**	3	1	na	2	2	2	1	3	1	1	2	3	2	1
Azerbaijan	na	**na**	na	na	na	na	na	na	na	na	na	na	na	na	na	na
Bangladesh	na	**na**	na	na	na	na	na	na	na	na	na	na	na	na	na	na
Belarus	na	**1**	2	na	2	1	na	na	2	na	1	1	2	na	2	na
Belgium	2	**3**	4	2	3	4	2	2	2	5	2	2	5	2	3	3
Bosnia and Herz.	na	**1**	1	1	1	1	1	1	na	4	na	1	3	1	1	2
Brazil	2	**na**	na	na	na	na	na	na	na	na	na	na	na	na	na	na
Bulgaria	2	**2**	2	1	na	4	1	na	1	6	1	2	2	1	3	na
Canada	5	**6**	7	5	4	8	6	1	4	14	3	4	12	3	5	10
Chile	1	**2**	3	2	2	4	1	na	2	7	na	4	4	2	2	3
China	17	**4**	4	3	4	4	3	3	4	12	4	4	4	4	4	6
Colombia	na	**na**	na	na	na	na	na	na	na	na	na	na	na	na	na	na
Croatia	na	**2**	3	2	1	3	2	1	2	6	na	2	5	na	3	1
Czech Republic	na	**2**	3	2	2	3	2	1	2	8	2	1	4	2	2	3
Denmark	3	**4**	5	2	1	5	4	3	3	4	3	4	6	1	3	7
Dominican Rep.	na	**na**	na	na	na	na	na	na	na	na	na	na	na	na	na	na
Egypt	na	**na**	na	na	na	na	na	na	na	na	na	na	na	na	na	na
El Salvador	na	**na**	na	na	na	na	na	na	na	na	na	na	na	na	na	na
Estonia	2	**2**	2	1	2	3	na	na	1	5	na	na	4	1	2	na
Finland	7	**3**	5	1	2	4	3	2	4	5	3	3	4	2	3	2
France	3	**1**	2	1	na	2	1	1	2	2	na	2	3	1	1	2
Georgia	na	**na**	na	na	na	na	na	na	na	na	na	na	na	na	na	na
Germany	3	**1**	1	na	1	1	na	na	1	1	na	na	1	na	1	na
Great Britain	2	**8**	6	9	6	11	5	7	7	13	8	6	14	na	na	na
Greece	na	**6**	8	4	4	7	7	2	5	7	4	6	8	6	5	7
Hungary	2	**2**	2	2	1	3	2	1	1	11	2	2	2	1	3	6
Iceland	3	**3**	3	3	1	5	3	2	2	8	na	3	6	2	3	7
India	na	**6**	6	5	6	6	5	4	6	9	4	5	7	5	8	4
Indonesia	na	**na**	na	na	na	na	na	na	na	na	na	na	na	na	na	na
Iran	na	**na**	na	na	na	na	na	na	na	na	na	na	na	na	na	na
Ireland	1	**3**	4	2	4	4	1	1	1	13	na	2	8	3	4	2
Israel	na	**na**	na	na	na	na	na	na	na	na	na	na	na	na	na	na
Italy	1	**3**	5	2	1	4	4	2	2	10	2	3	6	1	3	5
Japan	1	**1**	2	na	na	1	2	1	1	2	1	2	2	2	1	1
Jordan	na	**na**	na	na	na	na	na	na	na	na	na	na	na	na	na	na
Korea, South	2	**4**	6	2	4	4	5	2	2	7	4	4	5	3	5	6
Latvia	3	**1**	na	1	1	1	na	na	na	2	na	2	1	1	na	2
Lithuania	1	**0**	1	na	na	na	na	na	na	1	na	na	1	na	na	2
Luxembourg	na	**2**	2	1	1	2	2	2	1	2	2	1	4	1	2	1
Macedonia	na	**3**	3	3	2	4	2	1	3	4	3	2	4	3	3	na
Malta	na	**2**	3	1	2	1	2	na	1	9	na	1	4	na	2	8
Mexico	1	**2**	2	1	2	1	2	1	1	7	1	2	3	1	2	3
Moldova	na	**4**	5	3	4	4	3	1	4	7	1	6	3	3	5	11
Montenegro	na	**2**	2	2	2	2	1	na	2	4	na	2	2	na	3	5
Morocco	na	**na**	na	na	na	na	na	na	na	na	na	na	na	na	na	na
Netherlands	2	**3**	5	2	1	6	2	2	3	6	2	3	6	1	3	5
New Zealand	na	**na**	na	na	na	na	na	na	na	na	na	na	na	na	na	na
Nigeria	na	**na**	na	na	na	na	na	na	na	na	na	na	na	na	na	na
Northern Ireland	1	**2**	3	2	na	4	2	na	2	6	3	na	5	1	3	2
Norway	3	**na**	na	na	na	na	na	na	na	na	na	na	na	na	na	na
Pakistan	na	**na**	na	na	na	na	na	na	na	na	na	na	na	na	na	na
Peru	na	**3**	5	2	2	4	4	1	2	7	2	4	5	3	3	4
Philippines	na	**2**	3	2	2	2	5	1	1	7	2	2	4	1	3	2
Poland	na	**1**	2	1	1	2	1	1	2	2	1	1	3	1	2	na
Portugal	1	**1**	1	na	na	1	1	na	1	4	na	1	na	1	1	na
Puerto Rico	na	**6**	6	5	3	8	5	1	2	8	2	6	9	4	7	3
Romania	2	**1**	1	1	2	1	1	0	0	4	0	0	2	0	1	5
Russian Fed.	1	**0**	na	na	na	na	na	na	na	1	na	1	na	na	na	na
Serbia	na	**1**	1	1	2	na	na	na	1	2	na	1	1	1	1	3
Singapore	na	**1**	1	na	1	1	na	na	1	3	na	na	2	1	1	1
Slovakia	na	**3**	4	2	3	4	2	1	2	16	1	1	6	2	4	8
Slovenia	2	**3**	3	2	1	4	3	2	2	9	2	3	7	1	3	3
South Africa	na	**2**	3	1	1	3	2	na	3	10	na	3	3	1	2	2
Spain	1	**1**	1	na	1	1	1	1	1	2	na	1	1	1	1	1
Sweden	3	**4**	4	4	2	5	5	2	2	10	2	5	6	2	4	6
Switzerland	na	**na**	na	na	na	na	na	na	na	na	na	na	na	na	na	na
Taiwan	na	**na**	na	na	na	na	na	na	na	na	na	na	na	na	na	na
Tanzania	na	**20**	20	21	22	21	16	13	22	43	14	26	28	17	23	29
Turkey	na	**1**	1	na	1	1	1	na	1	5	na	1	2	na	1	1
Uganda	na	**5**	7	3	5	5	4	4	5	5	5	5	6	5	4	7
Ukraine	na	**1**	1	1	1	na	1	1	na	2	na	na	1	na	1	3
United States	5	**11**	13	9	9	11	12	3	7	16	7	11	17	9	12	9
Uruguay	na	**na**	na	na	na	na	na	na	na	na	na	na	na	na	na	na
Venezuela	na	**na**	na	na	na	na	na	na	na	na	na	na	na	na	na	na
Vietnam	na	**11**	13	8	8	13	9	9	12	13	8	11	11	9	11	10
Zimbabwe	na	**2**	4	1	2	2	2	1	4	18	1	1	8	2	2	6
Total	3	3	4	3	3	4	3	2	3	7	2	3	5	2	4	4

RANKING

Country	2000
Tanzania	20
United States	11
Vietnam	11
Algeria	9
Great Britain	8
Albania	7
Canada	6
Puerto Rico	6
Greece	6
India	6
Uganda	5
Sweden	4
Korea, South	4
Denmark	4
Moldova	4
China	4
Netherlands	3
Italy	3
Peru	3
Ireland	3
Iceland	3
Slovakia	3
Belgium	3
Finland	3
Macedonia	3
Slovenia	3
Czech Republic	2
Philippines	2
Northern Ireland	2
Chile	2
Croatia	2
Zimbabwe	2
Hungary	2
South Africa	2
Bulgaria	2
Malta	2
Montenegro	2
Estonia	2
Austria	2
Luxembourg	2
Mexico	2
France	1
Japan	1
Poland	1
Bosnia and Herz.	1
Romania	1
Argentina	1
Belarus	1
Singapore	1
Spain	1
Serbia	1
Turkey	1
Germany	1
Portugal	1
Ukraine	1
Latvia	1
Russian Fed.	0
Lithuania	0
Total	3

A090) UNPAID WORK YOUTH WORK

And for which, if any, are you currently doing unpaid voluntary work? Youth work (scouts, guides, youth clubs, etc.).

(WVS: V63; EVS: V39)

Belong (%)

Country	Wave		Gender		Age			Education			Income			Values		
	1990	2000	Male	Female	16-29	30-49	50+	Lower	Middle	Upper	Lower	Middle	Upper	Mat	Mixed	Postm.
Albania	na	**9**	11	7	24	4	2	8	9	11	10	9	8	9	9	10
Algeria	na	**10**	13	7	14	9	4	2	11	15	11	9	10	6	13	11
Argentina	2	**2**	2	2	4	2	1	1	3	3	1	2	3	2	3	2
Armenia	na	**na**	na	na	na	na	na	na	na	na	na	na	na	na	na	na
Australia	na	**na**	na	na	na	na	na	na	na	na	na	na	na	na	na	na
Austria	2	**2**	1	3	3	3	1	1	3	5	1	2	2	na	2	4
Azerbaijan	na	**na**	na	na	na	na	na	na	na	na	na	na	na	na	na	na
Bangladesh	na	**14**	20	6	15	13	11	7	17	27	13	12	15	12	15	17
Belarus	na	**2**	1	2	4	1	na	na	2	2	1	3	na	1	2	3
Belgium	5	**5**	7	4	14	5	1	2	6	7	2	5	7	4	5	5
Bosnia and Herz.	na	**2**	1	2	5	na	na	1	1	3	na	2	na	1	2	4
Brazil	2	**na**	na	na	na	na	na	na	na	na	na	na	na	na	na	na
Bulgaria	1	**2**	2	1	4	1	1	na	1	4	1	2	2	1	2	2
Canada	7	**8**	7	9	8	12	5	5	8	11	6	9	10	4	10	7
Chile	4	**4**	5	3	9	3	1	1	5	8	3	4	5	3	4	5
China	10	**10**	9	11	11	10	9	9	10	16	9	11	9	8	12	9
Colombia	na	**na**	na	na	na	na	na	na	na	na	na	na	na	na	na	na
Croatia	na	**2**	2	2	4	1	na	1	1	3	1	1	4	na	2	1
Czech Republic	na	**6**	7	5	9	7	3	4	7	12	2	6	8	5	6	10
Denmark	3	**5**	6	4	6	6	4	4	8	7	3	6	8	3	5	8
Dominican Rep.	na	**na**	na	na	na	na	na	na	na	na	na	na	na	na	na	na
Egypt	na	**na**	na	na	na	na	na	na	na	na	na	na	na	na	na	na
El Salvador	na	**na**	na	na	na	na	na	na	na	na	na	na	na	na	na	na
Estonia	2	**2**	2	2	5	2	1	1	2	3	1	1	4	1	2	4
Finland	5	**6**	6	7	9	9	3	2	10	12	5	6	8	6	6	10
France	3	**2**	1	2	2	2	1	1	1	3	1	2	1	2	2	1
Georgia	na	**na**	na	na	na	na	na	na	na	na	na	na	na	na	na	na
Germany	2	**2**	na	3	3	3	na	1	2	1	1	2	2	na	2	3
Great Britain	3	**15**	21	10	17	17	10	10	15	31	10	14	23	na	na	na
Greece	na	**5**	5	5	6	4	4	4	3	6	4	5	5	8	4	4
Hungary	1	**1**	1	1	na	2	1	na	na	10	na	1	2	na	2	na
Iceland	5	**3**	4	3	3	5	2	2	3	7	2	4	5	3	4	2
India	na	**5**	7	3	7	5	3	3	5	9	8	3	6	4	7	16
Indonesia	na	**na**	na	na	na	na	na	na	na	na	na	na	na	na	na	na
Iran	na	**na**	na	na	na	na	na	na	na	na	na	na	na	na	na	na
Ireland	5	**5**	5	5	5	6	2	3	6	6	3	5	7	4	5	9
Israel	na	**na**	na	na	na	na	na	na	na	na	na	na	na	na	na	na
Italy	3	**3**	2	4	5	3	2	1	5	3	2	3	4	1	3	3
Japan	1	**1**	1	1	na	1	1	na	1	2	na	1	2	1	1	na
Jordan	na	**na**	na	na	na	na	na	na	na	na	na	na	na	na	na	na
Korea, South	3	**3**	5	2	5	3	3	4	3	4	4	2	4	2	5	3
Latvia	3	**1**	1	1	3	na	na	na	1	1	na	2	na	na	1	na
Lithuania	4	**1**	na	2	4	na	na	na	2	1	na	na	1	1	2	na
Luxembourg	na	**6**	6	6	10	4	5	5	7	7	4	6	9	6	5	11
Macedonia	na	**3**	4	3	9	2	1	2	4	4	2	3	6	2	4	6
Malta	na	**3**	3	3	6	3	2	na	3	9	1	4	6	1	5	4
Mexico	2	**4**	4	4	6	3	2	2	5	9	3	3	6	3	5	4
Moldova	na	**4**	4	4	9	2	2	1	4	6	1	3	7	3	4	9
Montenegro	na	**1**	1	1	2	1	na	na	1	2	na	1	1	na	2	2
Morocco	na	**na**	na	na	na	na	na	na	na	na	na	na	na	na	na	na
Netherlands	5	**5**	4	5	10	5	2	2	8	4	5	4	4	3	5	3
New Zealand	na	**na**	na	na	na	na	na	na	na	na	na	na	na	na	na	na
Nigeria	na	**na**	na	na	na	na	na	na	na	na	na	na	na	na	na	na
Northern Ireland	8	**15**	15	14	34	13	8	12	16	15	18	15	14	11	17	10
Norway	4	**na**	na	na	na	na	na	na	na	na	na	na	na	na	na	na
Pakistan	na	**na**	na	na	na	na	na	na	na	na	na	na	na	na	na	na
Peru	na	**5**	6	4	9	2	2	4	4	6	3	6	6	4	5	6
Philippines	na	**6**	8	5	9	5	6	4	5	12	4	5	11	5	8	9
Poland	na	**1**	1	1	3	na	na	na	1	2	1	na	2	1	1	na
Portugal	2	**1**	1	1	1	1	1	1	2	1	1	1	3	na	1	1
Puerto Rico	na	**4**	5	4	4	6	3	3	1	7	3	6	4	2	5	3
Romania	1	**1**	1	1	2	0	0	0	1	1	0	1	1	0	0	3
Russian Fed.	3	**0**	na	na	1	na	na	na	na	na	na	na	na	na	na	na
Serbia	na	**0**	na	na	1	na	na	1	na	1	na	na	na	na	1	na
Singapore	na	**8**	9	7	14	1	2	9	7	7	5	8	8	5	8	12
Slovakia	na	**6**	4	7	9	5	4	4	6	9	3	6	7	5	6	9
Slovenia	1	**4**	4	3	7	3	2	1	4	5	2	4	5	2	3	7
South Africa	na	**7**	7	7	11	4	6	6	8	7	5	9	6	8	6	8
Spain	1	**1**	1	1	3	1	na	na	2	3	1	1	2	1	1	3
Sweden	7	**5**	7	3	7	7	2	6	6	4	4	4	8	2	5	6
Switzerland	na	**na**	na	na	na	na	na	na	na	na	na	na	na	na	na	na
Taiwan	na	**na**	na	na	na	na	na	na	na	na	na	na	na	na	na	na
Tanzania	na	**20**	19	20	26	18	12	19	21	20	20	19	20	16	22	21
Turkey	na	**1**	1	na	1	na	na	na	1	4	na	na	2	na	1	1
Uganda	na	**18**	22	14	30	6	3	9	21	15	14	21	19	15	19	21
Ukraine	na	**1**	1	1	2	1	na	na	1	3	na	1	2	na	2	na
United States	10	**22**	20	24	19	28	16	13	23	25	14	22	31	27	22	21
Uruguay	na	**na**	na	na	na	na	na	na	na	na	na	na	na	na	na	na
Venezuela	na	**na**	na	na	na	na	na	na	na	na	na	na	na	na	na	na
Vietnam	na	**14**	17	11	35	10	5	10	18	25	12	16	14	14	15	17
Zimbabwe	na	**4**	7	1	6	1	2	2	7	na	3	4	8	2	5	7
Total	4	5	6	5	9	5	3	4	6	8	4	5	6	4	6	6

RANKING	
Country	2000
United States	22
Tanzania	20
Uganda	18
Great Britain	15
Northern Ireland	15
Vietnam	14
Bangladesh	14
Algeria	10
China	10
Albania	9
Canada	8
Singapore	8
South Africa	7
Finland	6
Philippines	6
Luxembourg	6
Czech Republic	6
Slovakia	6
India	5
Sweden	5
Denmark	5
Belgium	5
Ireland	5
Peru	5
Greece	5
Netherlands	5
Puerto Rico	4
Chile	4
Zimbabwe	4
Mexico	4
Moldova	4
Slovenia	4
Iceland	3
Korea, South	3
Macedonia	3
Malta	3
Italy	3
Austria	2
Argentina	2
Estonia	2
Germany	2
Bulgaria	2
Croatia	2
Bosnia and Herz.	2
Belarus	2
France	2
Hungary	1
Lithuania	1
Spain	1
Romania	1
Japan	1
Portugal	1
Ukraine	1
Montenegro	1
Latvia	1
Poland	1
Turkey	1
Russian Fed.	0
Serbia	0
Total	5

A091) UNPAID WORK SPORTS OR RECREATION

And for which, if any, are you currently doing unpaid voluntary work? Sports or recreation.

Belong (%)

(WVS: V64; EVS: V40)

Country	Wave		Gender		Age			Education			Income			Values		
	1990	2000	Male	Female	16-29	30-49	50+	Lower	Middle	Upper	Lower	Middle	Upper	Mat	Mixed	Postm.
Albania	na	8	14	2	19	6	2	6	9	12	6	10	8	6	9	13
Algeria	na	15	20	9	22	11	6	6	17	18	15	16	17	13	16	16
Argentina	2	3	4	1	3	3	2	3	2	6	1	2	4	2	3	3
Armenia	na	na	na	na	na	na	na	na	na	na	na	na	na	na	na	na
Australia	na	na	na	na	na	na	na	na	na	na	na	na	na	na	na	na
Austria	7	9	13	5	11	10	6	6	13	8	6	10	10	7	8	11
Azerbaijan	na	na	na	na	na	na	na	na	na	na	na	na	na	na	na	na
Bangladesh	na	25	33	15	28	24	20	13	35	44	21	26	27	21	28	28
Belarus	na	2	3	1	4	2	1	na	3	1	1	2	2	1	3	3
Belgium	6	9	13	4	10	12	5	3	9	11	3	7	13	7	10	7
Bosnia and Herz.	na	7	12	3	16	5	1	2	7	13	3	6	11	4	8	13
Brazil	4	na	na	na	na	na	na	na	na	na	na	na	na	na	na	na
Bulgaria	4	4	6	2	9	4	2	na	6	6	2	6	5	3	6	2
Canada	12	13	14	12	15	16	8	7	14	16	8	13	17	11	13	13
Chile	7	12	18	7	19	12	6	7	15	15	10	13	15	10	13	13
China	6	13	12	13	18	13	9	9	15	19	10	14	14	13	14	16
Colombia	na	na	na	na	na	na	na	na	na	na	na	na	na	na	na	na
Croatia	na	7	12	2	11	8	3	4	9	11	5	6	10	7	7	8
Czech Republic	na	11	16	6	16	11	7	9	12	15	7	11	13	10	11	13
Denmark	11	14	17	12	15	19	9	14	18	12	7	19	17	15	14	17
Dominican Rep.	na	na	na	na	na	na	na	na	na	na	na	na	na	na	na	na
Egypt	na	na	na	na	na	na	na	na	na	na	na	na	na	na	na	na
El Salvador	na	na	na	na	na	na	na	na	na	na	na	na	na	na	na	na
Estonia	8	4	5	2	8	3	2	2	5	4	1	3	6	3	4	4
Finland	16	17	23	12	17	23	11	14	23	16	9	18	25	17	17	17
France	6	9	12	6	7	11	8	8	7	12	4	10	12	7	9	11
Georgia	na	na	na	na	na	na	na	na	na	na	na	na	na	na	na	na
Germany	11	7	9	6	5	9	5	4	9	9	3	9	10	8	6	8
Great Britain	na	4	na	7	2	2	6	4	2	4	4	3	3	na	na	na
Greece	na	9	12	7	11	7	6	4	10	9	6	10	13	12	8	12
Hungary	2	3	4	2	6	3	1	2	4	9	2	2	4	2	3	na
Iceland	14	11	17	6	10	14	9	8	14	14	10	10	15	10	12	10
India	na	9	12	4	10	9	7	6	9	14	12	7	9	6	14	20
Indonesia	na	na	na	na	na	na	na	na	na	na	na	na	na	na	na	na
Iran	na	na	na	na	na	na	na	na	na	na	na	na	na	na	na	na
Ireland	7	14	19	8	20	14	9	7	15	23	4	15	20	16	12	19
Israel	na	na	na	na	na	na	na	na	na	na	na	na	na	na	na	na
Italy	6	6	10	3	9	8	3	4	9	6	6	5	10	5	7	6
Japan	3	3	5	2	1	3	5	4	3	3	4	4	3	4	3	4
Jordan	na	na	na	na	na	na	na	na	na	na	na	na	na	na	na	na
Korea, South	3	12	14	10	14	11	12	4	11	14	13	11	12	12	12	12
Latvia	9	6	9	4	16	7	2	4	6	11	4	3	11	5	8	7
Lithuania	7	2	4	1	6	2	na	na	3	6	1	2	3	3	2	na
Luxembourg	na	9	10	8	13	8	8	7	11	9	6	10	13	10	9	10
Macedonia	na	9	12	5	14	9	4	3	11	13	6	7	14	7	9	17
Malta	na	6	11	1	8	6	3	1	6	12	1	6	13	5	6	9
Mexico	5	7	10	4	12	5	4	3	11	15	4	8	12	6	7	12
Moldova	na	4	6	3	10	2	1	1	4	7	2	4	6	3	5	5
Montenegro	na	5	9	2	10	5	3	2	7	10	1	6	10	4	7	8
Morocco	na	na	na	na	na	na	na	na	na	na	na	na	na	na	na	na
Netherlands	8	17	22	13	27	15	15	11	21	20	12	18	21	12	19	17
New Zealand	na	na	na	na	na	na	na	na	na	na	na	na	na	na	na	na
Nigeria	na	na	na	na	na	na	na	na	na	na	na	na	na	na	na	na
Northern Ireland	6	18	19	17	36	18	13	13	18	24	5	17	20	14	18	19
Norway	14	na	na	na	na	na	na	na	na	na	na	na	na	na	na	na
Pakistan	na	na	na	na	na	na	na	na	na	na	na	na	na	na	na	na
Peru	na	8	13	4	11	7	4	5	9	10	7	9	10	6	8	11
Philippines	na	12	18	7	18	10	8	7	13	17	8	11	17	11	14	7
Poland	na	2	4	1	3	2	1	1	3	7	2	2	4	2	2	3
Portugal	6	4	9	1	5	6	2	2	9	7	1	2	11	3	5	6
Puerto Rico	na	5	9	3	9	5	3	4	3	7	5	5	7	7	5	6
Romania	3	1	2	0	3	1	1	0	1	3	0	0	2	0	2	4
Russian Fed.	3	1	1	1	4	1	1	na	1	3	1	1	2	1	2	5
Serbia	na	3	6	1	4	4	3	3	4	4	2	4	4	4	4	na
Singapore	na	6	8	4	9	5	1	4	7	10	5	5	8	4	6	14
Slovakia	na	13	23	5	17	16	8	9	15	14	10	14	15	12	15	15
Slovenia	3	9	13	5	12	10	4	3	10	13	4	11	14	9	8	9
South Africa	na	15	22	8	22	14	5	12	18	41	12	14	21	11	17	32
Spain	4	3	5	1	5	3	2	2	5	4	2	3	6	3	3	4
Sweden	17	18	20	15	18	24	12	16	19	16	11	20	24	17	17	20
Switzerland	na	na	na	na	na	na	na	na	na	na	na	na	na	na	na	na
Taiwan	na	na	na	na	na	na	na	na	na	na	na	na	na	na	na	na
Tanzania	na	31	33	27	40	28	23	28	35	30	29	35	27	26	33	42
Turkey	na	1	1	na	na	1	na	na	1	2	na	1	1	na	1	1
Uganda	na	20	34	9	28	15	6	13	24	19	21	26	25	16	22	26
Ukraine	na	1	2	na	2	1	na	na	1	1	na	na	2	1	1	na
United States	8	19	24	14	23	23	10	15	23	18	14	17	30	16	20	16
Uruguay	na	na	na	na	na	na	na	na	na	na	na	na	na	na	na	na
Venezuela	na	na	na	na	na	na	na	na	na	na	na	na	na	na	na	na
Vietnam	na	18	25	11	23	17	15	14	22	31	18	13	23	10	21	24
Zimbabwe	na	4	7	1	5	3	2	2	6	10	3	1	11	4	4	3
Total	7	9	13	6	14	10	5	7	10	12	7	10	12	8	10	11

RANKING

Country	2000
Tanzania	31
Bangladesh	25
Uganda	20
United States	19
Northern Ireland	18
Vietnam	18
Sweden	18
Netherlands	17
Finland	17
South Africa	15
Algeria	15
Denmark	14
Ireland	14
Slovakia	13
Canada	13
China	13
Philippines	12
Chile	12
Korea, South	12
Iceland	11
Czech Republic	11
Luxembourg	9
Greece	9
India	9
Austria	9
France	9
Macedonia	9
Belgium	9
Slovenia	9
Albania	8
Peru	8
Bosnia and Herz.	7
Mexico	7
Croatia	7
Germany	7
Italy	6
Latvia	6
Singapore	6
Malta	6
Montenegro	5
Puerto Rico	5
Portugal	4
Bulgaria	4
Moldova	4
Great Britain	4
Zimbabwe	4
Estonia	4
Serbia	3
Japan	3
Spain	3
Hungary	3
Argentina	3
Lithuania	2
Poland	2
Belarus	2
Russian Fed.	1
Romania	1
Ukraine	1
Turkey	1
Total	9

A092) UNPAID WORK WOMEN'S GROUP

And for which, if any, are you currently doing unpaid voluntary work? Women's groups.

(WVS: V65; EVS: V41)

Belong (%)

Country	Wave		Gender		Age			Education			Income			Values		
	1990	2000	Male	Female	16-29	30-49	50+	Lower	Middle	Upper	Lower	Middle	Upper	Mat	Mixed	Postm.
Albania	na	**9**	2	17	5	11	11	10	10	6	12	9	7	9	9	8
Algeria	na	**6**	2	9	6	6	4	2	7	6	5	6	6	6	6	7
Argentina	0	**1**	1	1	1	1	na	na	1	1	1	1	1	na	1	1
Armenia	na	**na**	na	na	na	na	na	na	na	na	na	na	na	na	na	na
Australia	na	**na**	na	na	na	na	na	na	na	na	na	na	na	na	na	na
Austria	2	**2**	na	5	1	2	3	3	3	1	2	2	2	1	2	3
Azerbaijan	na	**na**	na	na	na	na	na	na	na	na	na	na	na	na	na	na
Bangladesh	na	**13**	10	17	14	13	13	14	13	13	10	17	13	14	14	9
Belarus	na	**1**	na	2	na	2	na	na	1	4	na	2	1	na	1	5
Belgium	3	**3**	1	5	1	3	5	5	3	2	4	3	3	3	4	2
Bosnia and Herz.	na	**2**	1	3	2	3	1	1	2	1	na	2	3	2	2	6
Brazil	1	**na**	na	na	na	na	na	na	na	na	na	na	na	na	na	na
Bulgaria	1	**1**	na	2	1	2	na	na	1	1	1	2	1	1	1	na
Canada	5	**5**	1	8	1	5	6	4	4	6	5	3	5	3	5	5
Chile	2	**5**	na	8	2	5	6	6	4	2	6	4	4	5	5	4
China	3	**15**	6	24	12	16	14	15	15	14	12	18	14	15	15	19
Colombia	na	**na**	na	na	na	na	na	na	na	na	na	na	na	na	na	na
Croatia	na	**2**	1	4	na	5	na	5	1	1	2	2	3	3	3	2
Czech Republic	na	**1**	1	2	1	1	1	1	2	1	1	1	1	2	1	na
Denmark	1	**1**	0	1	0	1	1	1	1	1	1	0	0	1	1	1
Dominican Rep.	na	**na**	na	na	na	na	na	na	na	na	na	na	na	na	na	na
Egypt	na	**na**	na	na	na	na	na	na	na	na	na	na	na	na	na	na
El Salvador	na	**na**	na	na	na	na	na	na	na	na	na	na	na	na	na	na
Estonia	2	**2**	1	2	2	2	1	na	2	2	2	2	1	1	2	na
Finland	3	**3**	na	5	na	3	4	3	4	1	3	4	3	2	3	1
France	1	**0**	na	na	na	na	na	na	na	na	na	na	na	na	na	na
Georgia	na	**na**	na	na	na	na	na	na	na	na	na	na	na	na	na	na
Germany	3	**2**	na	3	na	2	2	1	3	2	1	1	4	2	1	4
Great Britain	na	**1**	1	1	2	1	1	1	2	2	1	2	1	na	na	na
Greece	na	**3**	2	4	2	3	5	2	3	3	2	3	4	3	3	3
Hungary	1	**0**	na	na	na	1	na	na	na	2	na	na	na	na	1	na
Iceland	3	**2**	na	4	na	1	5	3	2	1	2	2	2	3	2	1
India	na	**6**	4	8	6	6	5	6	4	7	6	5	6	4	8	4
Indonesia	na	**na**	na	na	na	na	na	na	na	na	na	na	na	na	na	na
Iran	na	**na**	na	na	na	na	na	na	na	na	na	na	na	na	na	na
Ireland	2	**3**	1	4	2	2	4	4	1	4	3	4	2	1	2	7
Israel	na	**na**	na	na	na	na	na	na	na	na	na	na	na	na	na	na
Italy	0	**0**	na	1	1	na	na	1	na	na	1	na	na	na	1	na
Japan	2	**1**	1	2	na	na	3	1	2	na	1	1	2	3	1	2
Jordan	na	**na**	na	na	na	na	na	na	na	na	na	na	na	na	na	na
Korea, South	2	**4**	2	6	3	5	4	4	5	3	3	5	4	4	4	4
Latvia	2	**0**	na	1	1	na	na	na	1	na	1	na	na	1	na	2
Lithuania	2	**0**	na	na	na	1	na	na	na	na	na	na	1	na	na	na
Luxembourg	na	**2**	2	3	2	3	2	3	2	2	4	1	2	4	3	1
Macedonia	na	**4**	1	7	3	5	3	4	3	6	3	4	5	3	4	2
Malta	na	**2**	1	2	1	1	3	2	1	3	1	1	2	1	1	4
Mexico	1	**3**	2	5	2	4	4	3	4	2	4	4	3	3	4	4
Moldova	na	**3**	2	4	3	3	2	1	2	4	1	3	3	3	3	na
Montenegro	na	**1**	na	2	1	2	na	na	1	4	na	2	1	na	2	na
Morocco	na	**na**	na	na	na	na	na	na	na	na	na	na	na	na	na	na
Netherlands	3	**2**	na	4	1	2	4	2	2	3	2	3	1	3	2	3
New Zealand	na	**na**	na	na	na	na	na	na	na	na	na	na	na	na	na	na
Nigeria	na	**na**	na	na	na	na	na	na	na	na	na	na	na	na	na	na
Northern Ireland	2	**5**	2	8	na	4	6	9	2	2	8	3	5	2	6	7
Norway	1	**na**	na	na	na	na	na	na	na	na	na	na	na	na	na	na
Pakistan	na	**na**	na	na	na	na	na	na	na	na	na	na	na	na	na	na
Peru	na	**5**	1	9	4	6	5	7	5	3	6	5	3	5	5	3
Philippines	na	**9**	3	15	6	9	13	12	7	9	8	8	11	7	10	15
Poland	na	**1**	na	1	1	na	1	na	na	2	1	na	1	na	1	na
Portugal	0	**0**	na	na	na	na	na	na	na	na	na	na	na	na	na	na
Puerto Rico	na	**2**	2	1	2	2	1	1	1	2	1	na	4	na	1	3
Romania	0	**0**	0	1	0	1	0	0	0	0	1	0	0	0	0	1
Russian Fed.	1	**0**	na	1	na	1	na	na	na	na	1	na	na	na	na	na
Serbia	na	**0**	na	1	na	1	na	na	na	1	na	1	1	na	na	1
Singapore	na	**1**	na	1	1	na	1	na	1	na	na	1	1	na	na	2
Slovakia	na	**5**	1	8	2	4	7	5	5	2	6	4	5	5	5	2
Slovenia	0	**1**	1	2	na	1	2	1	1	1	2	2	1	1	1	1
South Africa	na	**8**	1	15	2	10	13	8	8	6	7	11	6	9	7	9
Spain	0	**1**	na	1	1	1	1	1	1	1	1	1	1	1	1	2
Sweden	2	**2**	na	4	na	2	4	2	1	4	1	2	4	2	2	3
Switzerland	na	**na**	na	na	na	na	na	na	na	na	na	na	na	na	na	na
Taiwan	na	**na**	na	na	na	na	na	na	na	na	na	na	na	na	na	na
Tanzania	na	**23**	8	42	20	28	17	24	21	25	23	25	20	24	23	17
Turkey	na	**0**	na	1	na	na	na	na	na	2	na	na	1	na	na	1
Uganda	na	**12**	2	22	9	20	3	19	11	4	17	13	12	12	13	12
Ukraine	na	**0**	na	1	na	1	na	na	1	na	na	1	na	na	1	na
United States	5	**8**	2	15	5	9	11	7	8	9	9	7	8	13	8	6
Uruguay	na	**na**	na	na	na	na	na	na	na	na	na	na	na	na	na	na
Venezuela	na	**na**	na	na	na	na	na	na	na	na	na	na	na	na	na	na
Vietnam	na	**27**	4	49	23	32	22	29	28	13	24	29	27	31	28	21
Zimbabwe	na	**7**	1	11	3	8	12	7	6	14	4	5	9	6	7	5
Total	2	4	1	7	3	5	3	5	4	4	4	5	4	4	4	4

RANKING	
Country	2000
Vietnam	27
Tanzania	23
China	15
Bangladesh	13
Uganda	12
Albania	9
Philippines	9
United States	8
South Africa	8
Zimbabwe	7
Algeria	6
India	6
Peru	5
Northern Ireland	5
Slovakia	5
Canada	5
Chile	5
Korea, South	4
Macedonia	4
Mexico	3
Belgium	3
Greece	3
Finland	3
Ireland	3
Moldova	3
Austria	2
Luxembourg	2
Iceland	2
Netherlands	2
Croatia	2
Sweden	2
Bosnia and Herz.	2
Germany	2
Estonia	2
Malta	2
Puerto Rico	2
Slovenia	1
Great Britain	1
Japan	1
Montenegro	1
Czech Republic	1
Denmark	1
Bulgaria	1
Belarus	1
Spain	1
Argentina	1
Poland	1
Singapore	1
Italy	0
Serbia	0
Latvia	0
Russian Fed.	0
Ukraine	0
Hungary	0
Lithuania	0
Turkey	0
France	0
Portugal	0
Romania	0
Total	4

A093) UNPAID WORK PEACE MOVEMENT

And for which, if any, are you currently doing unpaid voluntary work? Peace movement.

Belong (%)

(WVS: V66; EVS: V42)

Country	Wave		Gender		Age			Education			Income			Values		
	1990	2000	Male	Female	16-29	30-49	50+	Lower	Middle	Upper	Lower	Middle	Upper	Mat	Mixed	Postm.
Albania	na	**3**	4	3	4	3	3	2	3	7	4	2	3	3	3	10
Algeria	na	**na**	na	na	na	na	na	na	na	na	na	na	na	na	na	na
Argentina	0	**0**	1	na	na	1	na	na	na	na	na	na	na	na	na	1
Armenia	na	**na**	na	na	na	na	na	na	na	na	na	na	na	na	na	na
Australia	na	**na**	na	na	na	na	na	na	na	na	na	na	na	na	na	na
Austria	0	**0**	na	na	na	na	na	na	na	1	na	na	na	na	na	na
Azerbaijan	na	**na**	na	na	na	na	na	na	na	na	na	na	na	na	na	na
Bangladesh	na	**27**	34	18	25	27	35	23	29	37	18	29	33	25	29	26
Belarus	na	**1**	1	1	1	2	na	1	1	1	1	1	na	1	1	na
Belgium	1	**1**	1	1	1	1	1	1	1	2	1	2	1	na	1	1
Bosnia and Herz.	na	**0**	na	na	na	na	na	na	na	na	na	na	na	na	na	na
Brazil	1	**na**	na	na	na	na	na	na	na	na	na	na	na	na	na	na
Bulgaria	1	**0**	na	1	na	1	na	na	na	2	1	1	na	na	1	3
Canada	2	**1**	1	1	na	1	1	1	1	1	1	1	1	1	1	2
Chile	1	**2**	2	2	2	3	2	1	2	4	1	3	4	1	3	2
China	0	**16**	18	14	17	17	12	11	20	26	12	18	19	15	19	41
Colombia	na	**na**	na	na	na	na	na	na	na	na	na	na	na	na	na	na
Croatia	na	**1**	1	na	1	na	1	na	1	1	na	1	1	na	1	na
Czech Republic	na	**0**	na	na	na	na	na	na	na	na	na	1	na	na	na	na
Denmark	0	**0**	0	0	0	0	1	1	0	0	1	0	0	0	0	1
Dominican Rep.	na	**na**	na	na	na	na	na	na	na	na	na	na	na	na	na	na
Egypt	na	**na**	na	na	na	na	na	na	na	na	na	na	na	na	na	na
El Salvador	na	**na**	na	na	na	na	na	na	na	na	na	na	na	na	na	na
Estonia	1	**0**	1	na	1	na	na	na	na	na	na	na	1	na	na	na
Finland	1	**1**	1	1	1	2	1	1	1	3	na	2	1	na	1	4
France	1	**0**	na	na	na	na	na	na	na	1	na	na	1	na	na	na
Georgia	na	**na**	na	na	na	na	na	na	na	na	na	na	na	na	na	na
Germany	1	**0**	na	na	na	na	na	na	na	na	na	na	na	na	na	na
Great Britain	na	**4**	3	6	4	2	6	2	4	6	5	2	6	na	na	na
Greece	na	**5**	5	6	7	4	4	5	6	5	6	6	5	5	5	10
Hungary	0	**0**	1	na	na	1	na	na	na	2	na	na	1	na	1	na
Iceland	0	**0**	na	na	na	na	na	na	na	na	na	na	na	na	na	na
India	na	**4**	5	3	4	5	3	4	3	5	7	4	3	2	7	4
Indonesia	na	**na**	na	na	na	na	na	na	na	na	na	na	na	na	na	na
Iran	na	**na**	na	na	na	na	na	na	na	na	na	na	na	na	na	na
Ireland	0	**1**	1	1	na	na	2	1	na	2	2	na	1	1	na	3
Israel	na	**na**	na	na	na	na	na	na	na	na	na	na	na	na	na	na
Italy	1	**1**	1	1	1	1	1	1	1	1	1	2	1	na	1	1
Japan	1	**1**	1	1	na	na	1	1	1	na	1	na	1	na	1	1
Jordan	na	**na**	na	na	na	na	na	na	na	na	na	na	na	na	na	na
Korea, South	2	**2**	2	2	2	2	3	2	2	2	2	1	2	1	2	na
Latvia	1	**0**	na	na	na	na	na	na	na	na	na	na	na	na	na	na
Lithuania	1	**0**	na	na	na	na	na	na	na	na	na	1	na	na	na	na
Luxembourg	na	**1**	2	1	2	1	2	1	1	3	1	1	2	2	1	2
Macedonia	na	**3**	3	3	3	4	2	4	2	3	2	4	3	1	3	6
Malta	na	**1**	na	1	1	1	na	na	na	2	na	na	1	na	1	2
Mexico	1	**3**	3	3	3	3	3	3	3	3	3	4	2	4	3	4
Moldova	na	**2**	2	2	2	2	2	1	3	2	1	3	2	1	3	2
Montenegro	na	**1**	na	1	1	1	na	na	1	1	na	na	1	na	1	na
Morocco	na	**na**	na	na	na	na	na	na	na	na	na	na	na	na	na	na
Netherlands	1	**1**	na	1	1	na	1	1	1	1	1	1	na	na	1	1
New Zealand	na	**na**	na	na	na	na	na	na	na	na	na	na	na	na	na	na
Nigeria	na	**na**	na	na	na	na	na	na	na	na	na	na	na	na	na	na
Northern Ireland	0	**5**	2	9	9	9	2	7	4	5	5	na	12	na	6	8
Norway	0	**na**	na	na	na	na	na	na	na	na	na	na	na	na	na	na
Pakistan	na	**na**	na	na	na	na	na	na	na	na	na	na	na	na	na	na
Peru	na	**0**	na	na	1	1	na	1	na	na	1	na	na	na	na	1
Philippines	na	**11**	15	6	8	11	14	11	8	14	8	10	13	10	11	7
Poland	na	**na**	na	na	na	na	na	na	na	na	na	na	na	na	na	na
Portugal	0	**0**	na	na	na	na	na	na	na	1	na	na	1	na	na	na
Puerto Rico	na	**1**	1	1	1	1	1	1	na	1	1	1	2	1	1	1
Romania	0	**0**	0	0	0	0	0	0	0	0	0	0	0	0	0	0
Russian Fed.	1	**na**	na	na	na	na	na	na	na	na	na	na	na	na	na	na
Serbia	na	**na**	na	na	na	na	na	na	na	na	na	na	na	na	na	na
Singapore	na	**1**	1	1	1	na	na	1	1	na	1	1	1	1	1	na
Slovakia	na	**0**	na	na	na	na	na	na	na	na	na	na	na	na	na	na
Slovenia	0	**1**	1	1	1	na	1	1	na	na	na	1	1	1	na	1
South Africa	na	**4**	3	5	3	5	2	4	4	2	4	4	3	3	4	4
Spain	1	**1**	na	1	1	1	na	na	na	2	1	na	na	na	na	2
Sweden	2	**0**	1	na	1	na	1	1	na	1	na	1	na	na	na	1
Switzerland	na	**na**	na	na	na	na	na	na	na	na	na	na	na	na	na	na
Taiwan	na	**na**	na	na	na	na	na	na	na	na	na	na	na	na	na	na
Tanzania	na	**4**	4	5	5	4	4	4	5	6	5	5	3	2	5	4
Turkey	na	**0**	na	na	na	na	na	na	na	na	na	na	na	na	na	na
Uganda	na	**6**	11	2	6	6	3	7	5	12	9	7	6	6	6	8
Ukraine	na	**na**	na	na	na	na	na	na	na	na	na	na	na	na	na	na
United States	1	**2**	2	2	3	1	3	1	2	3	2	2	2	1	2	2
Uruguay	na	**na**	na	na	na	na	na	na	na	na	na	na	na	na	na	na
Venezuela	na	**na**	na	na	na	na	na	na	na	na	na	na	na	na	na	na
Vietnam	na	**7**	8	6	8	7	6	6	7	12	6	8	6	6	7	14
Zimbabwe	na	**1**	2	na	1	1	2	na	2	14	1	1	4	1	2	na
Total	1	2	3	2	3	3	2	2	2	3	2	3	3	2	2	2

RANKING	
Country	2000
Bangladesh	27
China	16
Philippines	11
Vietnam	7
Uganda	6
Greece	5
Northern Ireland	5
Great Britain	4
Tanzania	4
India	4
South Africa	4
Albania	3
Mexico	3
Macedonia	3
Chile	2
Moldova	2
United States	2
Korea, South	2
Luxembourg	1
Finland	1
Belgium	1
Zimbabwe	1
Belarus	1
Canada	1
Puerto Rico	1
Italy	1
Ireland	1
Japan	1
Singapore	1
Croatia	1
Netherlands	1
Slovenia	1
Montenegro	1
Malta	1
Spain	1
Bulgaria	0
Estonia	0
Hungary	0
Peru	0
Sweden	0
Argentina	0
France	0
Bosnia and Herz.	0
Czech Republic	0
Austria	0
Germany	0
Iceland	0
Latvia	0
Lithuania	0
Portugal	0
Slovakia	0
Turkey	0
Denmark	0
Total	2

A094) UNPAID WORK CONCERNED WITH HEALTH

And for which, if any, are you currently doing unpaid voluntary work? Voluntary organizations concerned with health.

(WVS: V67; EVS: V43)

Belong (%)

Country	Wave		Gender		Age			Education			Income			Values		
	1990	2000	Male	Female	16-29	30-49	50+	Lower	Middle	Upper	Lower	Middle	Upper	Mat	Mixed	Postm.
Albania	na	**8**	7	9	7	8	11	9	9	6	9	10	6	10	8	3
Algeria	na	**na**	na	na	na	na	na	na	na	na	na	na	na	na	na	na
Argentina	2	**2**	1	3	1	3	2	1	3	6	3	2	2	1	2	3
Armenia	na	**na**	na	na	na	na	na	na	na	na	na	na	na	na	na	na
Australia	na	**na**	na	na	na	na	na	na	na	na	na	na	na	na	na	na
Austria	2	**3**	2	3	3	2	3	2	3	2	3	3	1	1	3	3
Azerbaijan	na	**na**	na	na	na	na	na	na	na	na	na	na	na	na	na	na
Bangladesh	na	**22**	27	16	22	22	20	16	25	33	11	25	27	19	24	22
Belarus	na	**3**	3	2	5	3	2	1	4	2	2	3	2	1	5	3
Belgium	2	**5**	5	6	4	4	6	4	4	7	4	6	5	5	5	5
Bosnia and Herz.	na	**2**	2	1	2	2	1	1	1	4	2	1	4	1	2	na
Brazil	2	**na**	na	na	na	na	na	na	na	na	na	na	na	na	na	na
Bulgaria	2	**1**	1	1	1	1	na	na	na	3	na	1	1	1	1	na
Canada	7	**8**	7	9	5	8	12	7	8	10	7	9	9	8	8	11
Chile	2	**3**	2	3	2	2	4	4	2	3	3	1	5	3	3	3
China	2	**24**	23	25	28	25	19	21	27	16	19	26	30	24	25	38
Colombia	na	**na**	na	na	na	na	na	na	na	na	na	na	na	na	na	na
Croatia	na	**2**	2	2	1	2	2	2	1	4	1	1	3	2	1	2
Czech Republic	na	**3**	2	4	2	4	3	3	3	5	3	3	3	4	3	4
Denmark	1	**1**	1	1	1	1	1	0	2	1	1	1	1	3	1	1
Dominican Rep.	na	**na**	na	na	na	na	na	na	na	na	na	na	na	na	na	na
Egypt	na	**na**	na	na	na	na	na	na	na	na	na	na	na	na	na	na
El Salvador	na	**na**	na	na	na	na	na	na	na	na	na	na	na	na	na	na
Estonia	1	**1**	na	1	1	1	na	na	1	2	na	na	1	1	na	na
Finland	4	**6**	5	7	3	5	9	5	7	8	6	6	6	7	6	3
France	2	**2**	2	2	2	1	2	2	1	1	2	2	1	1	2	1
Georgia	na	**na**	na	na	na	na	na	na	na	na	na	na	na	na	na	na
Germany	2	**1**	2	1	3	na	2	1	2	na	1	1	1	1	1	1
Great Britain	na	**10**	9	11	5	10	13	9	9	13	8	5	14	na	na	na
Greece	na	**6**	4	7	6	6	4	7	5	6	5	7	7	7	5	8
Hungary	2	**1**	1	1	na	3	1	1	1	4	1	2	1	1	1	4
Iceland	4	**2**	1	2	na	2	3	3	na	4	2	1	2	2	2	1
India	na	**7**	8	6	8	7	7	5	8	11	5	6	9	6	10	11
Indonesia	na	**na**	na	na	na	na	na	na	na	na	na	na	na	na	na	na
Iran	na	**na**	na	na	na	na	na	na	na	na	na	na	na	na	na	na
Ireland	2	**3**	2	4	1	3	4	3	2	5	3	3	4	1	3	6
Israel	na	**na**	na	na	na	na	na	na	na	na	na	na	na	na	na	na
Italy	2	**3**	3	3	3	3	3	2	3	5	3	4	4	2	3	4
Japan	1	**2**	1	2	na	na	3	3	2	1	1	2	2	2	1	5
Jordan	na	**na**	na	na	na	na	na	na	na	na	na	na	na	na	na	na
Korea, South	3	**na**	na	na	na	na	na	na	na	na	na	na	na	na	na	na
Latvia	2	**1**	na	1	na	1	1	na	na	2	1	1	na	1	1	na
Lithuania	1	**1**	na	1	na	1	na	na	1	1	na	1	1	na	na	3
Luxembourg	na	**3**	2	4	2	2	5	3	3	4	2	3	3	3	3	3
Macedonia	na	**5**	4	5	4	6	3	4	5	7	4	7	3	2	6	8
Malta	na	**2**	2	2	3	1	2	1	2	5	na	2	3	1	2	5
Mexico	1	**5**	4	6	4	7	4	5	5	7	4	7	7	6	6	3
Moldova	na	**4**	3	4	4	3	4	2	4	6	3	5	4	3	4	6
Montenegro	na	**3**	3	2	4	3	2	1	3	3	1	3	4	2	2	2
Morocco	na	**na**	na	na	na	na	na	na	na	na	na	na	na	na	na	na
Netherlands	3	**7**	5	9	3	5	11	9	6	7	7	6	8	7	8	5
New Zealand	na	**na**	na	na	na	na	na	na	na	na	na	na	na	na	na	na
Nigeria	na	**na**	na	na	na	na	na	na	na	na	na	na	na	na	na	na
Northern Ireland	2	**15**	11	19	13	11	19	15	10	24	20	11	21	25	18	na
Norway	3	**na**	na	na	na	na	na	na	na	na	na	na	na	na	na	na
Pakistan	na	**na**	na	na	na	na	na	na	na	na	na	na	na	na	na	na
Peru	na	**4**	3	4	3	4	4	2	5	4	3	4	4	2	4	6
Philippines	na	**9**	10	8	8	10	9	7	8	13	9	8	12	8	10	9
Poland	na	**1**	1	1	na	1	1	na	1	3	1	1	na	na	1	2
Portugal	2	**1**	1	1	na	2	1	1	1	1	na	2	na	na	1	2
Puerto Rico	na	**3**	3	4	na	5	3	9	na	4	3	3	5	5	3	3
Romania	0	**1**	0	1	1	1	0	0	1	1	0	1	1	0	1	1
Russian Fed.	1	**0**	na	1	na	na	na	na	na	1	na	na	na	na	na	na
Serbia	na	**0**	1	na	na	1	na	na	na	1	na	1	1	1	na	na
Singapore	na	**4**	3	6	5	4	1	4	5	2	3	4	5	2	6	1
Slovakia	na	**4**	3	4	4	4	3	1	4	9	3	3	4	3	4	9
Slovenia	1	**2**	2	2	1	2	3	2	1	6	1	2	4	1	2	3
South Africa	na	**5**	4	7	7	3	6	4	7	5	4	9	3	7	4	4
Spain	1	**2**	1	2	2	1	1	1	2	3	2	1	3	1	2	2
Sweden	1	**3**	3	3	2	3	3	3	2	3	3	na	4	3	2	6
Switzerland	na	**na**	na	na	na	na	na	na	na	na	na	na	na	na	na	na
Taiwan	na	**na**	na	na	na	na	na	na	na	na	na	na	na	na	na	na
Tanzania	na	**21**	20	23	24	20	20	19	22	29	19	23	25	16	24	25
Turkey	na	**0**	na	na	na	1	1	na	na	2	na	na	1	1	na	na
Uganda	na	**10**	12	8	10	10	6	6	10	16	8	12	14	9	9	11
Ukraine	na	**1**	1	1	na	1	1	1	na	1	1	1	1	1	1	na
United States	5	**11**	8	14	10	11	13	8	10	13	10	12	12	14	11	11
Uruguay	na	**na**	na	na	na	na	na	na	na	na	na	na	na	na	na	na
Venezuela	na	**na**	na	na	na	na	na	na	na	na	na	na	na	na	na	na
Vietnam	na	**15**	17	14	12	15	18	13	17	25	19	14	15	17	17	13
Zimbabwe	na	**3**	3	2	2	2	6	2	3	na	3	2	4	2	3	7
Total	2	5	5	5	5	5	5	4	5	6	4	5	6	4	5	5

RANKING	
Country	2000
China	24
Bangladesh	22
Tanzania	21
Vietnam	15
Northern Ireland	15
United States	11
Great Britain	10
Uganda	10
Philippines	9
Canada	8
Albania	8
India	7
Netherlands	7
Finland	6
Greece	6
Mexico	5
Belgium	5
South Africa	5
Macedonia	5
Singapore	4
Moldova	4
Peru	4
Slovakia	4
Puerto Rico	3
Czech Republic	3
Luxembourg	3
Chile	3
Italy	3
Belarus	3
Ireland	3
Zimbabwe	3
Sweden	3
Austria	3
Montenegro	3
Argentina	2
Slovenia	2
Iceland	2
Bosnia and Herz.	2
Croatia	2
France	2
Malta	2
Japan	2
Spain	2
Germany	1
Hungary	1
Denmark	1
Romania	1
Portugal	1
Bulgaria	1
Estonia	1
Poland	1
Ukraine	1
Latvia	1
Lithuania	1
Serbia	0
Russian Fed.	0
Turkey	0
Total	5

A096_1) UNPAID WORK OTHER GROUPS

And for which, if any, are you currently doing unpaid voluntary work? Other social groups.

Belong (%)

(WVS: V67B; EVS: V44)

Country	Wave		Gender		Age			Education			Income			Values		
	1990	2000	Male	Female	16-29	30-49	50+	Lower	Middle	Upper	Lower	Middle	Upper	Mat	Mixed	Postm.
Albania	na	**na**	na	na	na	na	na	na	na	na	na	na	na	na	na	na
Algeria	na	**na**	na	na	na	na	na	na	na	na	na	na	na	na	na	na
Argentina	2	**2**	2	2	2	2	2	1	3	2	1	2	3	1	1	4
Armenia	na	**na**	na	na	na	na	na	na	na	na	na	na	na	na	na	na
Australia	na	**na**	na	na	na	na	na	na	na	na	na	na	na	na	na	na
Austria	3	**4**	6	2	2	5	4	4	5	3	3	5	4	2	5	4
Azerbaijan	na	**na**	na	na	na	na	na	na	na	na	na	na	na	na	na	na
Bangladesh	na	**2**	2	2	2	2	2	1	2	4	1	2	2	2	2	3
Belarus	na	**2**	4	1	3	2	1	na	3	2	1	3	2	1	3	na
Belgium	3	**8**	9	6	5	9	8	5	7	11	5	7	11	7	8	9
Bosnia and Herz.	na	**na**	na	na	na	na	na	na	na	na	na	na	na	na	na	na
Brazil	0	**na**	na	na	na	na	na	na	na	na	na	na	na	na	na	na
Bulgaria	2	**2**	2	2	1	2	2	1	1	4	2	1	1	1	2	na
Canada	9	**8**	8	8	4	9	9	6	9	8	8	7	10	7	8	10
Chile	3	**na**	na	na	na	na	na	na	na	na	na	na	na	na	na	na
China	2	**2**	1	2	1	1	3	2	1	2	2	1	1	1	1	na
Colombia	na	**na**	na	na	na	na	na	na	na	na	na	na	na	na	na	na
Croatia	na	**3**	6	1	1	3	5	1	5	4	3	4	2	2	4	3
Czech Republic	na	**4**	7	3	4	3	6	4	4	8	4	4	5	4	5	2
Denmark	4	**7**	8	5	5	8	6	5	7	10	6	5	10	6	7	5
Dominican Rep.	na	**na**	na	na	na	na	na	na	na	na	na	na	na	na	na	na
Egypt	na	**na**	na	na	na	na	na	na	na	na	na	na	na	na	na	na
El Salvador	na	**na**	na	na	na	na	na	na	na	na	na	na	na	na	na	na
Estonia	2	**3**	4	2	3	4	2	2	3	4	2	3	4	3	3	na
Finland	7	**8**	8	8	4	8	10	8	6	11	6	10	7	9	8	4
France	4	**6**	6	6	5	5	8	6	5	7	4	7	7	6	6	5
Georgia	na	**na**	na	na	na	na	na	na	na	na	na	na	na	na	na	na
Germany	4	**3**	3	2	2	2	3	3	2	3	3	3	2	2	3	3
Great Britain	na	**na**	na	na	na	na	na	na	na	na	na	na	na	na	na	na
Greece	na	**5**	5	4	4	4	4	2	5	5	4	4	6	5	4	7
Hungary	1	**2**	3	1	2	2	2	2	1	3	2	3	1	2	2	na
Iceland	4	**2**	1	2	na	2	3	1	1	3	2	1	2	2	2	1
India	na	**5**	7	4	5	5	6	3	8	8	4	4	8	4	8	13
Indonesia	na	**na**	na	na	na	na	na	na	na	na	na	na	na	na	na	na
Iran	na	**na**	na	na	na	na	na	na	na	na	na	na	na	na	na	na
Ireland	2	**4**	4	4	4	3	5	3	4	6	5	4	4	5	5	3
Israel	na	**na**	na	na	na	na	na	na	na	na	na	na	na	na	na	na
Italy	2	**2**	2	1	1	2	1	1	2	3	2	2	2	1	2	2
Japan	4	**na**	na	na	na	na	na	na	na	na	na	na	na	na	na	na
Jordan	na	**na**	na	na	na	na	na	na	na	na	na	na	na	na	na	na
Korea, South	3	**na**	na	na	na	na	na	na	na	na	na	na	na	na	na	na
Latvia	2	**5**	7	3	7	4	5	4	4	8	5	6	4	3	6	11
Lithuania	2	**2**	2	2	2	4	1	na	3	5	2	2	3	1	3	3
Luxembourg	na	**2**	3	1	2	1	2	1	3	3	1	2	3	2	2	2
Macedonia	na	**na**	na	na	na	na	na	na	na	na	na	na	na	na	na	na
Malta	na	**2**	2	2	3	2	2	1	2	4	3	1	3	1	2	5
Mexico	1	**na**	na	na	na	na	na	na	na	na	na	na	na	na	na	na
Moldova	na	**na**	na	na	na	na	na	na	na	na	na	na	na	na	na	na
Montenegro	na	**na**	na	na	na	na	na	na	na	na	na	na	na	na	na	na
Morocco	na	**na**	na	na	na	na	na	na	na	na	na	na	na	na	na	na
Netherlands	5	**6**	8	5	5	5	9	6	6	7	5	8	6	11	5	9
New Zealand	na	**na**	na	na	na	na	na	na	na	na	na	na	na	na	na	na
Nigeria	na	**na**	na	na	na	na	na	na	na	na	na	na	na	na	na	na
Northern Ireland	2	**20**	16	23	20	25	16	23	22	13	21	23	10	26	17	22
Norway	7	**na**	na	na	na	na	na	na	na	na	na	na	na	na	na	na
Pakistan	na	**na**	na	na	na	na	na	na	na	na	na	na	na	na	na	na
Peru	na	**0**	na	na	na	na	na	na	na	na	na	na	1	na	na	na
Philippines	na	**na**	na	na	na	na	na	na	na	na	na	na	na	na	na	na
Poland	na	**2**	3	2	2	2	3	2	2	4	3	1	1	2	2	na
Portugal	2	**3**	3	2	2	2	3	3	2	3	3	3	3	1	3	4
Puerto Rico	na	**3**	4	3	4	2	3	na	2	4	2	3	4	5	2	5
Romania	2	**1**	2	1	2	1	1	1	1	4	1	1	3	1	2	5
Russian Fed.	2	**1**	1	na	1	1	na	na	1	2	1	1	1	1	1	na
Serbia	na	**na**	na	na	na	na	na	na	na	na	na	na	na	na	na	na
Singapore	na	**na**	na	na	na	na	na	na	na	na	na	na	na	na	na	na
Slovakia	na	**6**	8	4	6	6	6	3	8	6	7	7	6	6	6	7
Slovenia	3	**6**	9	3	7	5	6	7	6	4	4	6	4	8	5	8
South Africa	na	**na**	na	na	na	na	na	na	na	na	na	na	na	na	na	na
Spain	1	**2**	2	3	3	3	1	2	2	5	3	2	4	2	2	5
Sweden	9	**10**	12	8	10	11	10	10	9	12	9	10	12	8	10	11
Switzerland	na	**na**	na	na	na	na	na	na	na	na	na	na	na	na	na	na
Taiwan	na	**na**	na	na	na	na	na	na	na	na	na	na	na	na	na	na
Tanzania	na	**na**	na	na	na	na	na	na	na	na	na	na	na	na	na	na
Turkey	na	**1**	2	1	1	na	3	na	2	4	na	1	3	1	1	2
Uganda	na	**na**	na	na	na	na	na	na	na	na	na	na	na	na	na	na
Ukraine	na	**1**	2	1	na	1	1	na	1	1	1	1	1	na	2	3
United States	6	**15**	19	11	14	14	17	11	13	18	12	14	19	9	16	16
Uruguay	na	**na**	na	na	na	na	na	na	na	na	na	na	na	na	na	na
Venezuela	na	**na**	na	na	na	na	na	na	na	na	na	na	na	na	na	na
Vietnam	na	**na**	na	na	na	na	na	na	na	na	na	na	na	na	na	na
Zimbabwe	na	**na**	na	na	na	na	na	na	na	na	na	na	na	na	na	na
Total	3	**4**	5	3	4	4	5	3	4	6	4	4	5	3	5	6

RANKING	
Country	**2000**
Northern Ireland	20
United States	15
Sweden	10
Canada	8
Finland	8
Belgium	8
Denmark	7
Netherlands	6
France	6
Slovakia	6
Slovenia	6
India	5
Latvia	5
Greece	5
Czech Republic	4
Ireland	4
Austria	4
Croatia	3
Estonia	3
Puerto Rico	3
Germany	3
Portugal	3
Spain	2
Lithuania	2
Bangladesh	2
Poland	2
Argentina	2
Belarus	2
Luxembourg	2
Malta	2
Hungary	2
Bulgaria	2
Iceland	2
China	2
Italy	2
Turkey	1
Romania	1
Ukraine	1
Russian Fed.	1
Peru	0
Total	4

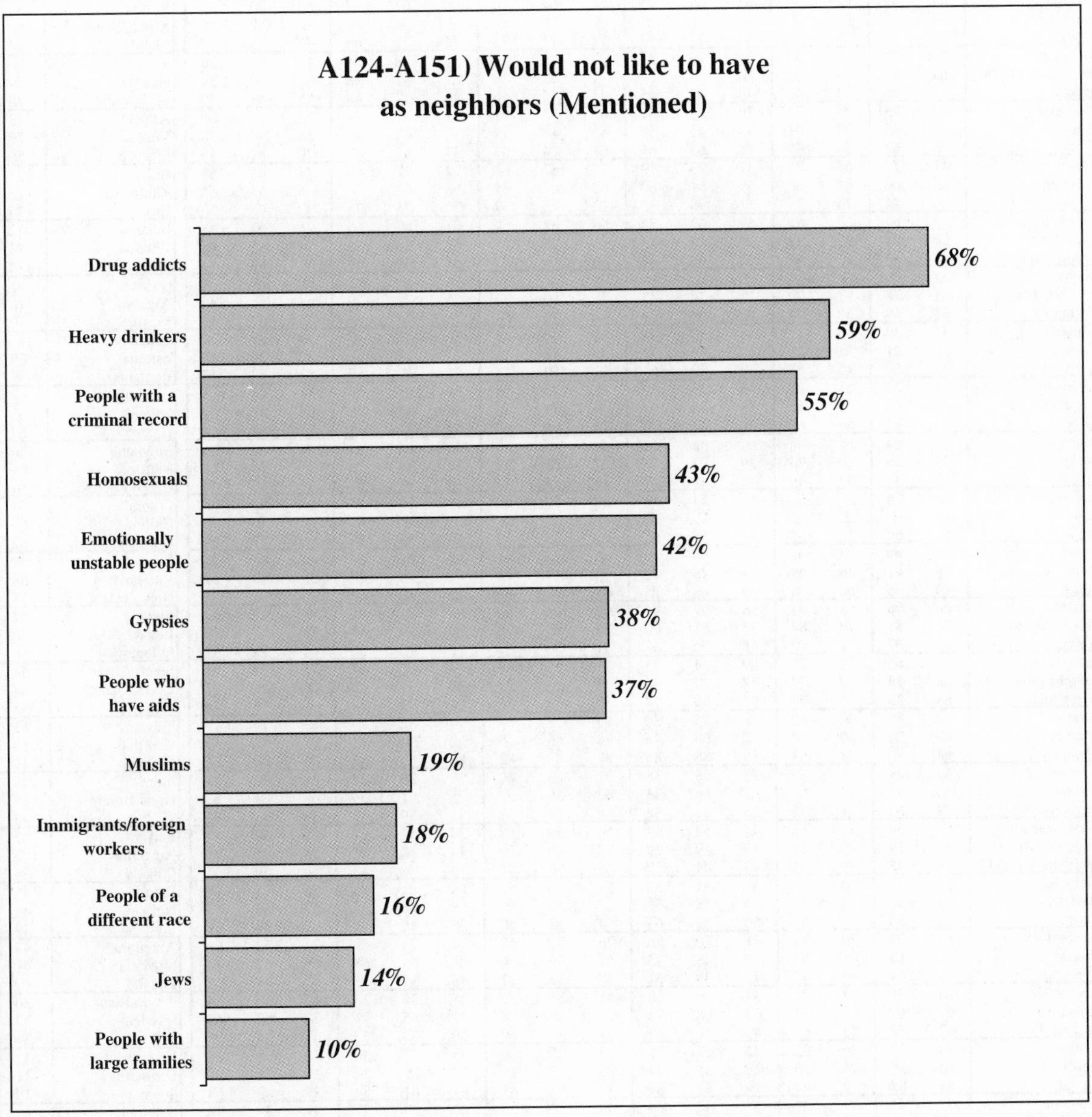

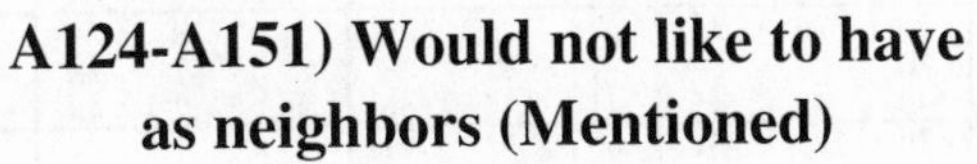

A124-A151) Would not like to have as neighbors (Mentioned)
Drug addicts
68%
Heavy drinkers
59%
People with a criminal record
55%
Homosexuals
43%
Emotionally unstable people
42%
Gypsies
38%
People who have aids
37%
Muslims
19%
Immigrants/foreign workers
18%
People of a different race
16%
Jews
14%
People with large families
10%

A124) NEIGHBORS: PEOPLE WITH A CRIMINAL RECORD

On this list are various groups of people. Could you please sort out any that you would not like to have as neighbors?

People with a criminal record (%) (WVS: V68; EVS: V52)

v Country	Wave		Gender		Age			Education			Income			Values		
	1990	2000	Male	Female	16-29	30-49	50+	Lower	Middle	Upper	Lower	Middle	Upper	Mat	Mixed	Postm.
Albania	na	**97**	97	97	97	97	98	98	97	96	98	96	97	98	96	97
Algeria	na	**70**	69	71	65	72	77	75	71	66	70	71	70	73	70	64
Argentina	41	**43**	43	44	35	42	53	46	39	43	44	42	44	49	44	38
Armenia	na	**78**	73	83	75	78	83	77	78	77	78	77	82	78	78	79
Australia	na	**45**	45	45	41	45	50	48	45	43	48	44	43	58	48	39
Austria	32	**27**	25	29	21	23	33	30	23	24	29	25	25	44	28	19
Azerbaijan	na	**69**	67	70	65	69	75	77	67	70	60	67	77	67	72	62
Bangladesh	na	**4**	3	5	4	4	3	4	2	6	2	4	4	3	4	4
Belarus	72	**72**	68	76	65	74	77	77	71	71	75	72	68	77	68	75
Belgium	28	**30**	27	33	28	26	35	37	29	26	34	30	24	40	28	20
Bosnia and Herz.	na	**88**	86	90	86	88	89	91	87	88	89	87	88	85	89	89
Brazil	52	**45**	44	46	45	45	45	41	45	56	42	47	48	45	44	49
Bulgaria	70	**75**	72	77	70	71	81	80	72	71	77	72	75	73	76	68
Canada	42	**45**	39	51	45	41	50	50	41	49	42	42	46	58	47	38
Chile	46	**63**	59	65	58	63	65	61	64	61	57	65	67	70	61	55
China	41	**71**	67	75	57	73	79	77	67	63	72	72	69	74	66	59
Colombia	na	**64**	61	66	69	61	60	68	67	57	68	67	56	66	65	64
Croatia	na	**74**	74	75	62	73	85	72	75	77	70	75	78	90	73	70
Czech Republic	72	**64**	60	67	52	62	72	66	62	60	67	64	60	71	62	58
Denmark	28	**31**	29	32	25	29	35	36	28	23	32	27	35	34	35	15
Dominican Rep.	na	**62**	62	63	63	62	64	56	58	65	64	65	69	51	63	74
Egypt	na	**3**	3	3	3	2	4	3	3	3	3	3	2	2	3	5
El Salvador	na	**78**	77	79	77	79	78	77	80	79	76	79	79	na	na	na
Estonia	63	**69**	63	74	62	68	74	68	70	68	72	76	63	73	67	69
Finland	34	**39**	36	42	34	39	43	38	40	44	36	41	40	50	39	20
France	20	**21**	21	21	17	17	27	25	18	13	22	22	19	32	20	9
Georgia	na	**50**	45	53	39	49	61	53	50	47	51	49	48	52	48	47
Germany	35	**25**	21	28	16	23	31	31	22	15	31	25	19	34	24	15
Great Britain	41	**48**	46	51	38	48	53	49	50	38	49	45	48	na	na	na
Greece	na	**67**	66	68	61	67	78	70	65	68	64	71	67	73	67	62
Hungary	77	**na**	na	na	na	na	na	na	na	na	na	na	na	na	na	na
Iceland	24	**26**	26	26	29	22	28	27	25	25	25	24	26	33	26	12
India	93	**48**	47	49	48	48	47	40	55	59	30	49	57	51	48	44
Indonesia	na	**56**	55	57	51	55	58	59	52	60	49	60	58	57	55	57
Iran	na	**1**	1	2	1	2	1	1	2	2	1	1	2	na	2	1
Ireland	52	**56**	53	59	43	56	65	61	53	52	58	55	55	58	57	48
Israel	na	**na**	na	na	na	na	na	na	na	na	na	na	na	na	na	na
Italy	48	**47**	46	49	41	46	52	53	43	46	49	46	47	58	50	39
Japan	50	**na**	na	na	na	na	na	na	na	na	na	na	na	na	na	na
Jordan	na	**96**	98	94	96	97	94	97	96	96	96	97	95	96	97	92
Korea, South	31	**81**	79	84	75	81	90	89	83	78	80	79	84	82	82	72
Latvia	63	**57**	51	62	45	50	67	51	56	67	58	56	55	61	55	57
Lithuania	69	**66**	56	75	59	64	73	71	65	63	74	65	67	75	64	51
Luxembourg	na	**30**	30	29	27	27	34	35	26	27	33	31	24	28	31	22
Macedonia	na	**76**	76	77	74	79	74	82	73	75	78	77	74	76	76	79
Malta	na	**80**	80	80	78	75	86	85	77	83	79	82	77	83	79	79
Mexico	69	**70**	69	70	67	69	74	73	66	66	72	70	67	72	72	57
Moldova	na	**83**	78	88	79	86	84	87	82	82	86	86	82	86	80	85
Montenegro	na	**29**	25	33	23	28	35	31	28	30	18	29	34	31	29	29
Morocco	na	**64**	60	68	61	64	73	66	58	52	75	61	59	68	63	55
Netherlands	28	**32**	31	33	26	31	36	36	29	32	31	30	33	43	33	25
New Zealand	na	**58**	53	61	47	54	64	56	59	58	57	53	61	58	58	50
Nigeria	80	**79**	79	78	78	79	79	77	80	80	78	78	81	75	81	79
Northern Ireland	46	**48**	44	51	46	44	52	47	50	44	49	46	43	52	50	35
Norway	37	**44**	40	48	38	41	52	51	40	41	na	na	na	55	45	27
Pakistan	na	**58**	59	56	58	58	58	57	59	58	58	58	55	57	59	58
Peru	na	**53**	53	53	50	52	63	54	55	50	58	46	54	47	54	59
Philippines	na	**72**	70	74	71	70	76	76	71	68	74	72	69	71	72	67
Poland	na	**68**	68	68	61	68	73	67	69	70	66	69	68	68	67	73
Portugal	59	**44**	43	44	40	39	51	48	39	22	58	41	35	42	44	41
Puerto Rico	na	**36**	37	37	34	36	38	44	37	35	38	36	35	41	36	34
Romania	67	**69**	67	71	65	68	72	71	68	68	71	65	71	70	69	65
Russian Fed.	63	**58**	52	62	49	56	65	61	56	60	60	58	55	61	54	55
Serbia	na	**29**	26	32	22	27	35	35	25	30	33	28	30	30	29	24
Singapore	na	**30**	26	35	23	35	44	35	27	31	32	29	30	39	28	23
Slovakia	na	**82**	79	84	79	82	84	82	82	81	81	81	84	81	83	68
Slovenia	37	**41**	42	39	33	42	44	49	38	33	47	39	27	49	39	38
South Africa	na	**54**	53	55	57	52	50	54	56	40	55	57	49	56	53	52
Spain	36	**32**	31	34	23	30	40	37	28	26	33	32	33	41	32	22
Sweden	35	**33**	34	32	28	35	35	35	34	31	34	33	31	50	35	23
Switzerland	7	**20**	18	22	23	17	22	23	19	24	24	15	23	24	21	17
Taiwan	na	**51**	49	54	37	50	64	57	45	51	53	47	54	57	48	43
Tanzania	na	**89**	88	91	91	86	93	89	90	88	87	92	89	89	89	88
Turkey	81	**80**	77	83	77	81	85	84	77	68	84	77	77	85	80	74
Uganda	na	**88**	92	84	87	87	99	88	87	94	93	89	83	86	89	92
Ukraine	na	**72**	66	77	69	69	76	69	73	72	76	66	76	76	72	60
United States	50	**54**	47	61	48	54	59	53	51	56	48	54	62	60	56	46
Uruguay	na	**70**	67	72	61	68	75	72	66	66	72	67	70	72	73	64
Venezuela	na	**77**	77	77	78	76	78	78	78	76	79	72	75	77	77	77
Vietnam	na	**49**	48	49	51	46	50	52	47	37	55	47	48	63	45	39
Zimbabwe	na	**75**	74	75	76	75	72	71	80	70	71	74	73	75	76	68
Total	49	**55**	53	58	53	55	59	56	56	54	57	56	55	61	55	44

RANKING	
Country	2000
Albania	97
Jordan	96
Tanzania	89
Uganda	88
Bosnia and Herz.	88
Moldova	83
Slovakia	82
Korea, South	81
Malta	80
Turkey	80
Nigeria	79
El Salvador	78
Armenia	78
Venezuela	77
Macedonia	76
Bulgaria	75
Zimbabwe	75
Croatia	74
Belarus	72
Ukraine	72
Philippines	72
China	71
Algeria	70
Mexico	70
Uruguay	70
Estonia	69
Romania	69
Azerbaijan	69
Poland	68
Greece	67
Lithuania	66
Morocco	64
Czech Republic	64
Colombia	64
Chile	63
Dominican Rep.	62
Pakistan	58
Russian Fed.	58
New Zealand	58
Latvia	57
Ireland	56
Indonesia	56
South Africa	54
United States	54
Peru	53
Taiwan	51
Georgia	50
Vietnam	49
India	48
Great Britain	48
Northern Ireland	48
Italy	47
Australia	45
Canada	45
Brazil	45
Norway	44
Portugal	44
Argentina	43
Slovenia	41
Finland	39
Puerto Rico	36
Sweden	33
Spain	32
Netherlands	32
Denmark	31
Singapore	30
Belgium	30
Luxembourg	30
Serbia	29
Montenegro	29
Austria	27
Iceland	26
Germany	25
France	21
Switzerland	20
Bangladesh	4
Egypt	3
Iran	1
Total	55

A125) NEIGHBORS: PEOPLE OF A DIFFERENT RACE

On this list are various groups of people. Could you please sort out any that you would not like to have as neighbors?

People of a different race (%) (WVS: V69; EVS: V53)

Country	Wave		Gender		Age			Education			Income			Values		
	1990	2000	Male	Female	16-29	30-49	50+	Lower	Middle	Upper	Lower	Middle	Upper	Mat	Mixed	Postm.
Albania	na	**30**	26	35	22	35	32	33	32	18	31	34	27	27	30	51
Algeria	na	**28**	29	27	28	26	32	35	28	24	36	22	23	28	28	29
Argentina	3	**5**	5	4	3	3	8	6	3	na	7	4	2	9	4	2
Armenia	na	**19**	16	22	17	20	23	24	20	14	15	19	27	22	18	10
Australia	na	**5**	7	3	4	4	7	7	5	3	6	5	4	6	5	5
Austria	8	**7**	7	6	4	6	9	9	4	6	8	8	5	19	7	2
Azerbaijan	na	**12**	12	13	11	12	17	18	12	12	11	14	8	13	11	12
Bangladesh	na	**72**	72	71	72	71	75	69	73	77	69	72	74	74	72	79
Belarus	17	**17**	13	19	9	15	24	26	14	11	19	16	12	20	14	5
Belgium	17	**17**	18	16	13	13	22	25	16	10	22	15	14	22	15	10
Bosnia and Herz.	na	**13**	13	13	10	15	14	15	13	12	13	15	11	14	14	6
Brazil	5	**3**	2	3	1	4	4	5	2	na	5	2	2	2	4	na
Bulgaria	39	**28**	30	27	28	29	28	32	27	23	31	31	22	34	25	12
Canada	5	**3**	4	3	2	4	5	6	2	3	5	4	2	5	4	2
Chile	11	**9**	9	9	8	9	9	8	9	11	9	9	8	8	9	8
China	12	**15**	13	16	8	14	21	18	12	9	15	14	14	12	14	16
Colombia	na	**2**	2	2	3	2	2	4	2	1	3	2	1	3	3	1
Croatia	na	**20**	18	21	16	22	19	20	21	14	18	20	20	23	21	11
Czech Republic	31	**10**	11	9	7	10	12	12	9	4	12	10	8	14	9	7
Denmark	7	**7**	9	6	4	5	11	11	5	3	9	7	4	13	9	na
Dominican Rep.	na	**19**	14	22	19	17	27	28	23	16	20	13	15	22	18	15
Egypt	na	**66**	67	65	66	66	66	65	62	74	62	66	69	63	68	70
El Salvador	na	**na**	na	na	na	na	na	na	na	na	na	na	na	na	na	na
Estonia	19	**15**	16	15	12	15	17	22	13	11	20	17	10	15	16	4
Finland	25	**12**	16	9	14	12	12	14	11	7	13	14	12	20	11	3
France	9	**9**	10	8	7	7	12	12	6	3	12	9	7	15	8	2
Georgia	na	**10**	12	7	11	8	10	10	9	9	9	9	11	8	10	15
Germany	12	**5**	4	5	2	4	7	8	3	2	7	6	3	8	3	3
Great Britain	9	**9**	9	9	7	7	10	11	7	6	7	9	7	na	na	na
Greece	na	**14**	16	13	14	10	24	23	17	11	14	14	13	14	16	8
Hungary	23	**na**	na	na	na	na	na	na	na	na	na	na	na	na	na	na
Iceland	8	**3**	4	2	2	3	5	4	3	1	5	2	3	3	3	3
India	35	**42**	42	41	42	41	43	47	41	33	51	42	37	44	38	29
Indonesia	na	**35**	34	36	31	35	37	43	38	26	39	33	29	40	33	25
Iran	na	**24**	24	25	25	26	20	19	25	29	20	28	28	22	23	28
Ireland	6	**12**	11	13	6	8	19	20	8	8	22	11	5	10	13	9
Israel	na	**na**	na	na	na	na	na	na	na	na	na	na	na	na	na	na
Italy	13	**16**	16	15	14	10	22	21	13	7	23	11	8	24	16	10
Japan	11	**na**	na	na	na	na	na	na	na	na	na	na	na	na	na	na
Jordan	na	**20**	20	20	20	19	22	25	15	16	20	22	20	23	19	13
Korea, South	58	**35**	35	34	18	34	56	61	41	23	37	33	33	39	33	15
Latvia	13	**5**	5	5	2	2	8	6	4	6	7	3	3	4	5	6
Lithuania	20	**10**	8	11	10	6	13	14	9	6	10	9	10	11	9	10
Luxembourg	na	**6**	5	7	5	5	9	9	5	4	11	5	2	10	6	3
Macedonia	na	**19**	21	17	16	20	21	21	20	13	24	17	15	19	20	12
Malta	na	**19**	16	21	11	15	27	28	16	11	23	16	14	23	16	15
Mexico	17	**15**	13	17	9	16	21	21	8	9	20	13	11	16	14	12
Moldova	na	**11**	11	11	12	11	10	13	12	8	13	11	10	10	9	18
Montenegro	na	**19**	16	22	13	18	24	26	14	14	14	18	17	18	21	18
Morocco	na	**11**	10	13	10	13	13	12	9	4	25	7	11	12	11	7
Netherlands	6	**5**	5	5	1	2	10	9	3	4	6	4	4	16	4	2
New Zealand	na	**3**	5	2	4	3	2	5	2	2	4	2	3	5	2	2
Nigeria	31	**30**	30	30	30	31	29	32	31	27	31	34	27	32	28	38
Northern Ireland	7	**11**	12	11	11	10	9	12	12	9	11	6	5	10	10	17
Norway	12	**8**	10	7	5	6	13	12	7	5	na	na	na	15	8	2
Pakistan	na	**7**	7	7	6	7	7	6	7	7	5	7	7	7	6	na
Peru	na	**11**	12	11	13	9	12	15	10	10	13	11	9	14	12	5
Philippines	na	**21**	21	22	17	23	25	27	20	17	27	17	21	22	21	20
Poland	na	**17**	16	18	7	15	26	22	13	7	20	15	17	21	16	15
Portugal	16	**8**	9	7	9	6	8	8	8	3	13	11	4	7	6	11
Puerto Rico	na	**4**	5	4	3	5	4	3	7	4	5	4	5	5	3	5
Romania	28	**24**	22	26	14	21	33	39	19	9	37	24	14	28	20	11
Russian Fed.	11	**8**	8	8	8	8	9	10	9	6	9	9	7	7	9	10
Serbia	na	**6**	5	7	4	4	10	12	3	3	8	5	5	8	4	na
Singapore	na	**5**	5	5	4	4	8	4	5	3	6	4	5	4	5	4
Slovakia	na	**17**	19	16	17	15	19	18	17	16	20	15	15	17	17	10
Slovenia	40	**12**	12	12	6	11	18	22	9	6	14	11	5	19	10	11
South Africa	na	**24**	24	23	17	28	29	24	24	21	25	23	21	24	23	23
Spain	12	**11**	10	12	5	10	16	15	7	7	12	10	12	15	11	6
Sweden	7	**3**	4	1	2	1	4	2	3	2	2	3	2	4	3	1
Switzerland	2	**9**	10	8	7	6	13	13	8	8	11	7	8	8	11	4
Taiwan	na	**17**	16	18	7	15	29	25	18	9	24	16	10	20	14	19
Tanzania	na	**17**	15	19	17	14	22	21	13	11	24	13	11	18	15	25
Turkey	34	**32**	30	33	29	31	40	43	21	5	45	24	14	38	31	21
Uganda	na	**18**	19	18	17	17	27	19	18	14	20	12	11	17	17	27
Ukraine	na	**11**	11	10	9	11	11	12	11	8	12	9	8	10	11	na
United States	9	**8**	8	8	10	7	9	10	9	7	8	7	8	10	7	8
Uruguay	na	**7**	6	8	3	8	8	8	4	8	7	7	6	4	7	8
Venezuela	na	**16**	15	16	14	16	19	18	16	11	16	17	16	19	15	11
Vietnam	na	**32**	30	34	33	34	30	32	32	36	40	31	30	41	32	35
Zimbabwe	na	**20**	20	20	21	18	20	23	15	30	20	25	19	21	19	22
Total	16	16	16	16	15	15	17	20	14	12	18	16	14	19	15	10

RANKING	
Country	2000
Bangladesh	72
Egypt	66
India	42
Indonesia	35
Korea, South	35
Vietnam	32
Turkey	32
Albania	30
Nigeria	30
Bulgaria	28
Algeria	28
Iran	24
Romania	24
South Africa	24
Philippines	21
Jordan	20
Zimbabwe	20
Croatia	20
Armenia	19
Montenegro	19
Macedonia	19
Malta	19
Dominican Rep.	19
Uganda	18
Poland	17
Taiwan	17
Slovakia	17
Tanzania	17
Belgium	17
Belarus	17
Italy	16
Venezuela	16
Estonia	15
Mexico	15
China	15
Greece	14
Bosnia and Herz.	13
Finland	12
Azerbaijan	12
Ireland	12
Slovenia	12
Morocco	11
Peru	11
Northern Ireland	11
Moldova	11
Spain	11
Ukraine	11
Czech Republic	10
Lithuania	10
Georgia	10
Chile	9
France	9
Switzerland	9
Great Britain	9
Norway	8
Russian Fed.	8
United States	8
Portugal	8
Denmark	7
Uruguay	7
Austria	7
Pakistan	7
Luxembourg	6
Serbia	6
Netherlands	5
Australia	5
Germany	5
Latvia	5
Singapore	5
Argentina	5
Puerto Rico	4
Canada	3
Iceland	3
New Zealand	3
Brazil	3
Sweden	3
Colombia	2
Total	16

A126) NEIGHBORS: HEAVY DRINKERS

On this list are various groups of people. Could you please sort out any that you would not like to have as neighbors?

Heavy drinkers (%) (WVS: V70; EVS: V55)

Country	Wave		Gender		Age			Education			Income			Values		
	1990	2000	Male	Female	16-29	30-49	50+	Lower	Middle	Upper	Lower	Middle	Upper	Mat	Mixed	Postm.
Albania	na	**81**	76	85	81	78	83	83	81	73	85	76	80	81	79	80
Algeria	na	**69**	65	73	68	72	68	71	68	70	68	70	68	75	66	67
Argentina	45	**37**	32	41	27	33	50	40	32	32	39	36	35	42	38	29
Armenia	na	**86**	82	91	81	90	90	89	87	84	86	85	92	88	85	82
Australia	na	**60**	54	65	54	59	66	62	59	59	64	57	57	66	61	57
Austria	60	**53**	49	56	43	54	57	52	52	60	50	53	56	51	56	49
Azerbaijan	na	**85**	84	87	86	84	87	84	85	87	88	86	82	86	86	79
Bangladesh	na	**4**	5	4	5	4	3	5	3	6	4	5	4	3	5	7
Belarus	82	**83**	76	89	88	79	83	78	84	89	83	85	79	80	86	88
Belgium	50	**45**	42	47	42	41	49	50	43	43	47	47	40	49	46	38
Bosnia and Herz.	na	**77**	72	83	76	79	77	80	78	75	79	77	77	79	77	83
Brazil	41	**46**	42	51	48	45	46	48	44	48	44	46	50	50	45	42
Bulgaria	73	**76**	73	78	70	74	80	77	75	74	72	76	79	75	78	82
Canada	55	**51**	45	57	52	50	52	51	50	53	54	50	49	52	51	50
Chile	52	**51**	46	55	51	53	47	47	51	59	46	53	57	55	48	53
China	58	**74**	70	78	73	73	77	71	76	77	72	72	80	73	76	75
Colombia	na	**33**	29	38	31	36	31	31	32	36	33	34	33	29	30	42
Croatia	na	**63**	58	67	51	63	70	62	63	63	61	63	65	74	64	53
Czech Republic	74	**76**	69	81	72	75	77	72	79	82	76	76	76	78	75	69
Denmark	34	**36**	36	36	33	38	36	37	39	36	38	31	42	38	38	27
Dominican Rep.	na	**55**	51	58	54	58	46	53	54	56	59	59	48	49	56	62
Egypt	na	**1**	2	1	1	1	2	1	1	2	1	1	1	1	1	1
El Salvador	na	**90**	90	90	91	91	88	88	92	93	87	91	92	na	na	na
Estonia	90	**84**	79	89	84	84	84	80	86	86	83	85	84	85	84	84
Finland	54	**51**	49	53	55	51	49	48	54	61	48	50	54	55	50	46
France	50	**47**	45	49	39	44	54	52	40	41	55	46	43	58	46	32
Georgia	na	**70**	60	77	63	71	75	73	69	69	70	73	68	72	68	52
Germany	72	**56**	51	60	56	55	58	56	55	63	53	54	57	55	58	56
Great Britain	48	**51**	47	55	36	47	64	54	50	47	55	48	51	na	na	na
Greece	na	**37**	37	38	32	38	50	54	36	35	33	43	39	42	37	34
Hungary	82	**na**	na	na	na	na	na	na	na	na	na	na	na	na	na	na
Iceland	61	**62**	62	61	67	61	59	61	64	60	63	61	65	67	62	53
India	91	**46**	44	47	45	46	44	37	52	56	31	46	53	47	47	53
Indonesia	na	**58**	57	59	58	59	57	56	55	65	50	62	67	57	58	68
Iran	na	**2**	2	1	2	1	1	1	2	2	2	1	2	na	2	2
Ireland	34	**36**	33	39	23	38	44	44	34	29	46	32	38	41	37	32
Israel	na	**na**	na	na	na	na	na	na	na	na	na	na	na	na	na	na
Italy	51	**40**	39	42	36	37	46	48	34	37	46	38	37	52	41	34
Japan	58	**na**	na	na	na	na	na	na	na	na	na	na	na	na	na	na
Jordan	na	**94**	93	94	94	94	95	95	94	91	96	95	91	95	95	81
Korea, South	17	**76**	68	83	68	77	81	86	81	67	77	71	78	80	73	62
Latvia	85	**75**	67	81	72	71	79	73	74	82	70	75	80	78	75	68
Lithuania	92	**82**	76	87	80	84	82	80	82	87	84	78	87	84	82	85
Luxembourg	na	**32**	32	32	35	26	37	39	29	27	35	29	24	36	31	30
Macedonia	na	**64**	62	66	63	68	59	73	60	58	67	64	57	62	63	69
Malta	na	**74**	70	78	64	73	81	81	70	75	73	77	72	77	72	77
Mexico	56	**56**	52	59	55	52	65	58	53	54	58	59	55	57	56	52
Moldova	na	**85**	78	91	86	82	87	88	81	88	87	86	86	87	83	85
Montenegro	na	**63**	52	74	60	62	66	66	61	61	61	60	68	67	60	65
Morocco	na	**87**	82	91	85	87	88	87	87	83	90	86	85	88	86	82
Netherlands	60	**59**	56	61	51	59	62	60	60	55	57	58	60	62	61	50
New Zealand	na	**66**	63	69	56	66	69	58	69	71	66	64	68	64	64	73
Nigeria	72	**65**	61	70	64	66	68	66	66	63	65	65	67	62	68	62
Northern Ireland	43	**51**	48	54	47	52	53	53	54	41	49	56	48	54	48	56
Norway	32	**32**	33	31	32	29	36	40	29	28	na	na	na	48	31	21
Pakistan	na	**1**	1	1	1	1	1	1	2	1	1	1	1	1	2	na
Peru	na	**52**	50	53	48	53	55	56	50	50	54	49	50	49	51	56
Philippines	na	**56**	51	61	56	52	64	57	55	56	62	58	47	59	54	53
Poland	na	**78**	75	80	74	77	80	76	78	86	75	80	79	74	80	72
Portugal	51	**38**	32	44	30	41	41	41	35	29	44	42	32	42	37	35
Puerto Rico	na	**41**	41	41	37	39	44	45	37	43	41	41	43	39	41	42
Romania	79	**77**	75	78	75	76	78	78	75	79	77	69	82	76	79	77
Russian Fed.	82	**73**	65	80	72	70	77	70	72	80	70	73	77	74	73	63
Serbia	na	**56**	49	63	52	54	60	61	51	60	55	58	57	57	55	48
Singapore	na	**64**	57	70	64	63	68	66	63	62	64	64	63	68	63	51
Slovakia	na	**80**	76	84	83	79	79	77	82	81	77	80	84	82	79	78
Slovenia	45	**69**	66	72	66	68	73	72	69	66	71	73	63	74	69	68
South Africa	na	**50**	50	49	51	49	50	46	56	30	47	50	52	55	48	37
Spain	40	**39**	39	40	32	38	45	44	34	35	41	39	42	48	38	35
Sweden	45	**33**	33	34	38	32	32	30	33	36	34	35	30	32	35	30
Switzerland	23	**47**	44	51	44	43	54	48	48	46	52	45	50	55	47	47
Taiwan	na	**81**	77	84	82	81	80	76	80	86	78	78	87	82	82	78
Tanzania	na	**79**	78	81	82	77	83	79	80	78	77	80	79	81	79	79
Turkey	87	**87**	83	91	86	88	89	91	83	76	91	86	80	90	88	81
Uganda	na	**70**	64	75	73	66	71	72	69	76	62	67	65	69	69	76
Ukraine	na	**79**	73	84	75	78	82	76	78	83	82	76	77	79	82	78
United States	60	**56**	52	60	50	58	58	61	58	53	57	54	56	57	58	50
Uruguay	na	**59**	56	61	52	56	64	60	56	58	62	54	59	69	59	56
Venezuela	na	**57**	56	59	53	58	64	58	55	62	55	53	60	54	57	63
Vietnam	na	**44**	43	45	44	42	47	44	46	37	50	42	44	62	41	42
Zimbabwe	na	**56**	50	62	57	56	56	56	57	40	53	58	56	57	56	58
Total	59	59	55	62	56	58	62	58	60	58	60	59	59	63	58	51

RANKING	
Country	2000
Jordan	94
El Salvador	90
Turkey	87
Morocco	87
Armenia	86
Azerbaijan	85
Moldova	85
Estonia	84
Belarus	83
Lithuania	82
Taiwan	81
Albania	81
Slovakia	80
Tanzania	79
Ukraine	79
Poland	78
Bosnia and Herz.	77
Romania	77
Bulgaria	76
Korea, South	76
Czech Republic	76
Latvia	75
China	74
Malta	74
Russian Fed.	73
Uganda	70
Georgia	70
Algeria	69
Slovenia	69
New Zealand	66
Nigeria	65
Singapore	64
Macedonia	64
Montenegro	63
Croatia	63
Iceland	62
Australia	60
Uruguay	59
Netherlands	59
Indonesia	58
Venezuela	57
Germany	56
Zimbabwe	56
Serbia	56
Mexico	56
Philippines	56
United States	56
Dominican Rep.	55
Austria	53
Peru	52
Northern Ireland	51
Great Britain	51
Canada	51
Finland	51
Chile	51
South Africa	50
Switzerland	47
France	47
Brazil	46
India	46
Belgium	45
Vietnam	44
Puerto Rico	41
Italy	40
Spain	39
Portugal	38
Greece	37
Argentina	37
Ireland	36
Denmark	36
Colombia	33
Sweden	33
Luxembourg	32
Norway	32
Bangladesh	4
Iran	2
Pakistan	1
Egypt	1
Total	59

A127) NEIGHBORS: EMOTIONALLY UNSTABLE PEOPLE

On this list are various groups of people. Could you please sort out any that you would not like to have as neighbors?

Emotionally unstable people (%) (WVS: V71; EVS: V58)

Country	Wave		Gender		Age			Education			Income			Values		
	1990	2000	Male	Female	16-29	30-49	50+	Lower	Middle	Upper	Lower	Middle	Upper	Mat	Mixed	Postm.
Albania	na	**61**	56	65	60	61	60	61	61	57	59	62	61	64	56	80
Algeria	na	**44**	44	44	47	44	39	39	47	45	48	41	40	50	40	46
Argentina	22	**22**	23	22	18	19	30	20	24	32	21	23	23	21	24	20
Armenia	na	**75**	74	77	74	77	75	74	75	76	79	67	81	76	74	82
Australia	na	**39**	42	37	32	40	45	39	39	40	42	38	40	50	39	37
Austria	20	**18**	19	18	28	17	15	20	17	18	19	18	19	30	19	15
Azerbaijan	na	**75**	73	77	78	73	73	72	74	77	76	79	68	77	72	74
Bangladesh	na	**28**	31	25	28	29	27	29	26	31	24	34	25	26	29	40
Belarus	63	**60**	58	61	58	64	56	54	61	63	60	60	57	59	61	54
Belgium	21	**22**	23	22	21	20	26	28	20	22	27	21	20	25	22	17
Bosnia and Herz.	na	**58**	57	59	55	59	60	60	58	55	59	58	58	59	59	59
Brazil	16	**18**	19	16	13	20	23	16	18	23	17	16	21	14	20	19
Bulgaria	53	**44**	42	46	49	45	41	41	45	48	38	46	46	44	46	37
Canada	30	**33**	33	32	29	36	32	33	32	34	33	29	33	37	35	27
Chile	28	**25**	24	26	21	28	24	25	24	30	23	25	30	27	24	27
China	46	**64**	60	67	60	65	64	62	66	65	55	68	73	63	65	56
Colombia	na	**17**	19	16	14	20	15	12	14	25	12	16	22	11	18	17
Croatia	na	**41**	43	40	42	39	43	38	44	39	44	43	39	42	41	45
Czech Republic	33	**19**	19	19	17	16	22	19	18	19	19	19	20	21	19	14
Denmark	11	**14**	14	15	15	14	14	14	15	13	18	12	14	16	14	9
Dominican Rep.	na	**52**	60	47	49	59	64	66	55	51	55	52	52	44	52	64
Egypt	na	**28**	31	25	25	29	30	31	24	26	28	30	27	27	28	27
El Salvador	na	**82**	84	80	82	81	82	81	84	79	79	85	81	na	na	na
Estonia	37	**54**	49	58	50	53	57	52	55	52	52	56	54	55	54	67
Finland	24	**29**	34	26	26	32	29	28	31	33	26	32	31	32	30	20
France	17	**22**	23	22	22	21	24	25	21	17	25	21	21	25	24	14
Georgia	na	**55**	53	56	49	56	59	61	53	56	54	58	54	61	50	49
Germany	20	**22**	21	23	19	24	22	26	21	12	24	24	25	29	20	14
Great Britain	28	**39**	41	38	27	42	44	42	37	38	33	41	42	na	na	na
Greece	na	**62**	63	61	65	58	62	60	62	62	64	63	61	67	63	53
Hungary	23	**na**	na	na	na	na	na	na	na	na	na	na	na	na	na	na
Iceland	33	**31**	36	26	40	31	23	30	34	26	31	29	33	38	31	20
India	69	**39**	38	39	39	38	39	33	41	49	30	37	45	41	39	44
Indonesia	na	**49**	46	53	53	48	49	47	46	57	46	50	53	46	53	39
Iran	na	**2**	1	2	2	2	1	1	2	2	2	na	2	1	2	2
Ireland	30	**25**	27	23	20	26	27	24	25	25	27	22	27	29	23	26
Israel	na	**na**	na	na	na	na	na	na	na	na	na	na	na	na	na	na
Italy	34	**38**	37	39	35	36	42	40	36	37	40	38	37	45	39	34
Japan	62	**na**	na	na	na	na	na	na	na	na	na	na	na	na	na	na
Jordan	na	**66**	67	64	63	67	68	68	66	60	62	68	70	70	65	50
Korea, South	17	**89**	88	90	84	89	93	89	89	88	89	86	91	90	89	78
Latvia	54	**35**	32	37	37	34	35	27	35	43	33	30	40	34	36	28
Lithuania	48	**61**	55	66	58	62	63	59	61	66	59	63	64	67	60	49
Luxembourg	na	**19**	19	19	21	17	20	19	19	21	20	20	19	24	19	16
Macedonia	na	**47**	49	46	44	48	49	44	48	53	47	49	49	49	48	46
Malta	na	**30**	26	34	28	29	32	33	28	29	25	32	27	33	29	26
Mexico	38	**34**	34	33	29	34	38	34	30	40	33	33	37	35	34	31
Moldova	na	**68**	67	70	71	69	66	68	69	68	73	68	66	68	69	73
Montenegro	na	**77**	75	80	73	78	80	79	75	78	79	77	78	83	73	69
Morocco	na	**69**	67	71	68	70	68	69	71	59	77	67	65	70	67	64
Netherlands	15	**25**	29	21	24	24	25	27	23	24	25	27	23	21	27	21
New Zealand	na	**60**	62	58	50	61	63	62	62	56	59	60	63	61	61	57
Nigeria	57	**52**	54	51	51	54	52	49	54	56	49	55	55	50	55	47
Northern Ireland	23	**35**	34	35	27	37	35	33	36	37	30	32	36	33	37	30
Norway	22	**37**	38	36	33	36	41	40	36	35	na	na	na	47	37	27
Pakistan	na	**40**	38	42	38	41	39	44	35	33	44	37	36	41	38	25
Peru	na	**38**	39	38	36	40	40	41	36	40	39	36	41	34	39	41
Philippines	na	**26**	24	27	24	23	32	26	26	25	32	25	20	23	27	22
Poland	na	**59**	57	60	61	60	55	57	59	61	57	60	61	57	60	60
Portugal	47	**28**	25	30	25	29	28	26	28	37	25	28	29	29	24	30
Puerto Rico	na	**34**	35	33	29	36	34	31	30	35	30	32	36	32	32	37
Romania	64	**53**	53	53	55	54	51	55	50	55	54	50	54	56	52	55
Russian Fed.	51	**54**	52	56	57	56	50	48	54	58	53	52	57	55	53	56
Serbia	na	**57**	55	60	61	57	56	58	55	59	58	62	53	57	58	51
Singapore	na	**58**	57	58	53	61	66	55	57	69	50	54	66	60	58	49
Slovakia	na	**22**	21	23	24	20	23	21	21	28	21	22	22	20	23	24
Slovenia	36	**30**	34	28	28	30	33	36	29	27	32	32	21	38	27	35
South Africa	na	**39**	36	42	39	38	40	37	42	41	36	41	43	39	40	33
Spain	25	**25**	25	25	21	25	27	27	22	24	24	28	28	27	26	22
Sweden	17	**17**	18	15	20	17	14	16	18	14	18	17	14	24	18	13
Switzerland	4	**17**	20	15	17	14	21	19	17	18	16	19	16	18	17	16
Taiwan	na	**73**	73	72	73	72	76	72	71	75	73	68	77	73	74	73
Tanzania	na	**5**	4	7	5	6	2	5	5	7	5	5	4	5	5	8
Turkey	72	**76**	73	79	78	75	73	77	75	72	79	72	74	76	76	72
Uganda	na	**46**	47	46	50	42	43	43	49	35	36	45	41	46	46	49
Ukraine	na	**63**	61	64	67	61	62	59	62	66	63	60	65	65	65	49
United States	43	**52**	54	49	45	53	56	49	51	53	47	52	59	51	55	46
Uruguay	na	**33**	33	33	30	31	36	33	33	32	33	31	33	37	31	36
Venezuela	na	**46**	46	46	44	46	52	44	45	52	44	43	46	48	45	49
Vietnam	na	**39**	38	39	37	36	44	40	37	36	40	36	42	55	36	39
Zimbabwe	na	**42**	44	41	45	40	40	38	48	32	38	39	53	37	46	51
Total	35	**42**	42	43	42	43	42	40	43	45	42	43	43	47	41	35

RANKING	
Country	**2000**
Korea, South	89
El Salvador	82
Montenegro	77
Turkey	76
Armenia	75
Azerbaijan	75
Taiwan	73
Morocco	69
Moldova	68
Jordan	66
China	64
Ukraine	63
Greece	62
Lithuania	61
Albania	61
New Zealand	60
Belarus	60
Poland	59
Bosnia and Herz.	58
Singapore	58
Serbia	57
Georgia	55
Russian Fed.	54
Estonia	54
Romania	53
Nigeria	52
Dominican Rep.	52
United States	52
Indonesia	49
Macedonia	47
Uganda	46
Venezuela	46
Algeria	44
Bulgaria	44
Zimbabwe	42
Croatia	41
Pakistan	40
Great Britain	39
Australia	39
South Africa	39
India	39
Vietnam	39
Peru	38
Italy	38
Norway	37
Northern Ireland	35
Latvia	35
Mexico	34
Puerto Rico	34
Uruguay	33
Canada	33
Iceland	31
Slovenia	30
Malta	30
Finland	29
Bangladesh	28
Egypt	28
Portugal	28
Philippines	26
Chile	25
Ireland	25
Spain	25
Netherlands	25
Belgium	22
France	22
Argentina	22
Slovakia	22
Germany	22
Luxembourg	19
Czech Republic	19
Austria	18
Brazil	18
Colombia	17
Switzerland	17
Sweden	17
Denmark	14
Tanzania	5
Iran	2
Total	42

A128) NEIGHBORS: MUSLIMS

On this list are various groups of people. Could you please sort out any that you would not like to have as neighbors? Minority group (1).

Muslims (%)

(WVS: V72; EVS: V59)

Country	Wave		Gender		Age			Education			Income			Values		
	1990	2000	Male	Female	16-29	30-49	50+	Lower	Middle	Upper	Lower	Middle	Upper	Mat	Mixed	Postm.
Albania	na	**30**	28	33	27	33	30	31	33	22	27	32	31	25	32	39
Algeria	na	**na**	na	na	na	na	na	na	na	na	na	na	na	na	na	na
Argentina	6	**6**	8	5	4	4	11	8	5	2	10	5	4	9	6	4
Armenia	na	**na**	na	na	na	na	na	na	na	na	na	na	na	na	na	na
Australia	na	**na**	na	na	na	na	na	na	na	na	na	na	na	na	na	na
Austria	14	**15**	16	15	11	12	21	19	12	13	20	16	12	28	17	10
Azerbaijan	na	**na**	na	na	na	na	na	na	na	na	na	na	na	na	na	na
Bangladesh	na	**na**	na	na	na	na	na	na	na	na	na	na	na	na	na	na
Belarus	24	**27**	26	27	20	25	33	36	23	23	30	25	23	29	25	14
Belgium	26	**22**	22	22	17	18	28	31	22	14	27	21	20	30	20	14
Bosnia and Herz.	na	**13**	14	12	9	15	14	14	13	11	12	15	11	13	13	6
Brazil	na	**na**	na	na	na	na	na	na	na	na	na	na	na	na	na	na
Bulgaria	41	**21**	22	20	22	22	21	18	24	21	19	26	19	23	20	16
Canada	10	**7**	8	5	5	6	9	9	6	6	9	7	5	7	7	5
Chile	12	**7**	6	9	6	8	9	7	8	7	8	9	5	10	7	4
China	12	**na**	na	na	na	na	na	na	na	na	na	na	na	na	na	na
Colombia	na	**na**	na	na	na	na	na	na	na	na	na	na	na	na	na	na
Croatia	na	**27**	30	23	27	26	27	28	27	22	25	26	28	27	27	26
Czech Republic	49	**15**	17	13	15	13	17	17	15	10	17	16	14	22	14	11
Denmark	15	**16**	19	14	12	13	23	23	12	5	20	15	13	20	19	6
Dominican Rep.	na	**na**	na	na	na	na	na	na	na	na	na	na	na	na	na	na
Egypt	na	**na**	na	na	na	na	na	na	na	na	na	na	na	na	na	na
El Salvador	na	**na**	na	na	na	na	na	na	na	na	na	na	na	na	na	na
Estonia	21	**22**	22	23	18	21	26	25	21	20	23	23	21	22	23	12
Finland	10	**19**	23	16	18	18	21	21	19	12	18	24	16	29	17	7
France	18	**16**	17	15	9	15	21	20	16	6	21	15	14	25	15	7
Georgia	na	**na**	na	na	na	na	na	na	na	na	na	na	na	na	na	na
Germany	20	**11**	12	10	8	10	14	15	8	9	16	11	9	13	11	8
Great Britain	17	**14**	14	13	9	13	17	16	13	9	9	13	11	na	na	na
Greece	na	**21**	22	21	20	17	30	35	24	16	23	19	19	21	22	19
Hungary	18	**na**	na	na	na	na	na	na	na	na	na	na	na	na	na	na
Iceland	12	**12**	14	9	10	11	14	13	13	6	15	8	12	12	13	2
India	29	**na**	na	na	na	na	na	na	na	na	na	na	na	na	na	na
Indonesia	na	**na**	na	na	na	na	na	na	na	na	na	na	na	na	na	na
Iran	na	**na**	na	na	na	na	na	na	na	na	na	na	na	na	na	na
Ireland	13	**14**	15	12	9	11	20	18	12	10	23	11	8	13	14	9
Israel	na	**na**	na	na	na	na	na	na	na	na	na	na	na	na	na	na
Italy	15	**17**	17	18	14	12	24	23	14	12	25	12	11	25	18	11
Japan	29	**na**	na	na	na	na	na	na	na	na	na	na	na	na	na	na
Jordan	na	**na**	na	na	na	na	na	na	na	na	na	na	na	na	na	na
Korea, South	21	**57**	57	58	45	59	69	68	64	46	58	57	57	61	55	43
Latvia	26	**15**	15	15	9	12	19	11	15	18	16	12	16	14	15	17
Lithuania	34	**33**	31	35	27	33	38	42	31	25	39	33	31	42	29	31
Luxembourg	na	**14**	16	13	15	13	16	18	13	9	20	11	10	19	14	10
Macedonia	na	**26**	27	26	23	26	29	31	26	18	30	23	24	26	27	14
Malta	na	**28**	23	32	21	24	36	38	25	15	31	31	18	35	24	21
Mexico	19	**17**	16	18	14	17	21	22	11	9	19	18	12	18	17	12
Moldova	na	**44**	41	47	42	44	47	45	49	37	39	48	47	46	42	46
Montenegro	na	**20**	19	21	14	20	24	27	18	11	36	20	13	24	17	13
Morocco	na	**na**	na	na	na	na	na	na	na	na	na	na	na	na	na	na
Netherlands	12	**12**	14	10	7	9	18	18	12	6	11	12	10	22	13	4
New Zealand	na	**na**	na	na	na	na	na	na	na	na	na	na	na	na	na	na
Nigeria	24	**na**	na	na	na	na	na	na	na	na	na	na	na	na	na	na
Northern Ireland	15	**16**	16	15	16	14	14	17	17	10	15	11	13	19	14	19
Norway	21	**19**	23	16	10	17	29	29	16	14	na	na	na	28	20	6
Pakistan	na	**na**	na	na	na	na	na	na	na	na	na	na	na	na	na	na
Peru	na	**14**	13	14	13	13	15	17	15	10	16	13	11	18	14	7
Philippines	na	**26**	24	28	24	26	30	34	24	20	29	26	24	24	29	18
Poland	na	**24**	22	25	11	25	30	29	21	11	25	23	24	27	23	20
Portugal	18	**8**	9	7	4	8	10	9	8	2	11	10	5	8	8	10
Puerto Rico	na	**na**	na	na	na	na	na	na	na	na	na	na	na	na	na	na
Romania	35	**31**	31	32	25	28	38	41	29	18	41	29	25	36	29	17
Russian Fed.	16	**14**	14	13	14	14	13	14	15	10	15	14	12	14	13	16
Serbia	na	**14**	12	15	14	13	14	20	11	9	18	11	10	16	12	6
Singapore	na	**na**	na	na	na	na	na	na	na	na	na	na	na	na	na	na
Slovakia	na	**25**	27	23	23	25	26	27	24	21	27	27	19	26	24	20
Slovenia	38	**23**	22	23	18	21	28	33	21	12	30	21	12	33	20	23
South Africa	na	**24**	26	21	24	23	27	23	25	36	23	21	26	24	24	23
Spain	14	**13**	11	15	9	12	17	16	11	9	14	12	18	17	14	7
Sweden	17	**9**	12	7	8	6	12	12	10	4	10	10	6	13	11	3
Switzerland	na	**19**	22	15	18	17	22	19	19	18	15	20	19	26	19	12
Taiwan	na	**19**	19	19	8	18	28	25	22	12	28	16	13	18	21	16
Tanzania	na	**13**	12	13	15	12	8	12	14	12	15	13	9	11	13	13
Turkey	55	**na**	na	na	na	na	na	na	na	na	na	na	na	na	na	na
Uganda	na	**14**	13	16	15	14	10	13	16	5	4	10	12	18	14	6
Ukraine	na	**24**	23	25	26	22	25	23	25	21	21	24	28	25	26	10
United States	14	**11**	10	11	12	10	11	15	10	10	12	9	9	16	10	10
Uruguay	na	**na**	na	na	na	na	na	na	na	na	na	na	na	na	na	na
Venezuela	na	**na**	na	na	na	na	na	na	na	na	na	na	na	na	na	na
Vietnam	na	**27**	27	28	30	26	28	29	25	28	31	29	24	37	26	33
Zimbabwe	na	**18**	18	18	20	16	16	16	20	18	14	22	19	15	18	35
Total	21	**19**	20	19	17	18	22	21	20	15	21	19	18	24	19	12

RANKING	
Country	**2000**
Korea, South	57
Moldova	44
Lithuania	33
Romania	31
Albania	30
Malta	28
Vietnam	27
Belarus	27
Croatia	27
Philippines	26
Macedonia	26
Slovakia	25
Ukraine	24
South Africa	24
Poland	24
Slovenia	23
Estonia	22
Belgium	22
Bulgaria	21
Greece	21
Montenegro	20
Finland	19
Norway	19
Taiwan	19
Switzerland	19
Zimbabwe	18
Italy	17
Mexico	17
Denmark	16
France	16
Northern Ireland	16
Austria	15
Czech Republic	15
Latvia	15
Luxembourg	14
Uganda	14
Russian Fed.	14
Ireland	14
Great Britain	14
Serbia	14
Peru	14
Spain	13
Bosnia and Herz.	13
Tanzania	13
Netherlands	12
Iceland	12
Germany	11
United States	11
Sweden	9
Portugal	8
Chile	7
Canada	7
Argentina	6
Total	19

A129) NEIGHBORS: IMMIGRANTS / FOREIGN WORKERS

On this list are various groups of people. Could you please sort out any that you would not like to have as neighbors?

Immigrants / Foreign workers (%) (WVS: V73; EVS: V60)

Country	Wave		Gender		Age			Education			Income			Values		
	1990	2000	Male	Female	16-29	30-49	50+	Lower	Middle	Upper	Lower	Middle	Upper	Mat	Mixed	Postm.
Albania	na	**17**	15	18	12	19	17	17	17	14	17	18	14	12	18	31
Algeria	na	**24**	25	22	24	21	28	30	24	19	31	22	16	23	23	24
Argentina	2	**6**	8	4	6	5	8	7	5	2	8	6	4	13	5	2
Armenia	na	**22**	23	21	23	20	22	20	22	22	18	20	29	22	21	24
Australia	na	**5**	6	3	4	4	6	6	5	3	6	4	3	3	5	4
Austria	20	**12**	13	12	11	9	16	16	9	5	18	10	9	32	13	6
Azerbaijan	na	**20**	17	23	20	19	24	30	20	18	23	23	14	21	18	15
Bangladesh	na	**67**	67	67	69	66	66	65	68	73	64	66	71	68	68	78
Belarus	17	**17**	15	19	11	17	22	25	14	14	19	17	14	17	18	9
Belgium	21	**18**	19	18	14	13	25	29	18	11	26	17	14	27	16	10
Bosnia and Herz.	na	**25**	26	24	19	27	28	25	26	21	23	28	24	25	25	21
Brazil	4	**4**	4	4	3	5	2	5	3	na	5	3	2	3	4	1
Bulgaria	34	**25**	28	22	23	23	27	28	24	21	26	27	20	29	22	17
Canada	6	**4**	4	4	3	4	6	7	4	3	6	5	3	7	4	3
Chile	12	**11**	11	11	11	10	11	12	10	12	12	11	9	12	11	8
China	13	**16**	14	18	8	16	22	22	12	7	20	14	12	13	16	19
Colombia	na	**na**	na	na	na	na	na	na	na	na	na	na	na	na	na	na
Croatia	na	**22**	25	19	24	21	21	23	22	16	21	21	23	24	23	17
Czech Republic	34	**19**	21	18	17	19	22	23	17	12	23	18	16	27	18	12
Denmark	12	**11**	10	11	7	9	14	15	6	4	13	10	7	18	12	4
Dominican Rep.	na	**18**	12	22	17	18	18	44	20	14	19	13	18	22	18	9
Egypt	na	**42**	47	38	43	40	45	40	38	55	38	41	46	37	46	48
El Salvador	na	**na**	na	na	na	na	na	na	na	na	na	na	na	na	na	na
Estonia	17	**21**	22	21	17	20	24	25	19	18	23	24	20	20	23	13
Finland	5	**13**	15	11	13	12	13	16	10	9	13	14	12	24	11	3
France	13	**12**	13	11	8	12	14	15	10	6	13	12	11	19	11	5
Georgia	na	**11**	14	9	10	10	13	11	12	8	12	14	8	11	10	21
Germany	19	**9**	10	8	8	9	9	9	8	7	12	7	7	8	10	6
Great Britain	12	**16**	17	14	11	17	18	21	13	11	14	13	17	na	na	na
Greece	na	**14**	16	12	14	10	19	19	16	11	12	15	11	14	14	11
Hungary	22	**na**	na	na	na	na	na	na	na	na	na	na	na	na	na	na
Iceland	8	**3**	4	2	2	2	5	4	3	1	4	2	3	4	3	3
India	37	**38**	40	36	40	38	37	42	35	33	45	39	35	40	35	29
Indonesia	na	**40**	41	40	41	38	42	46	43	34	44	37	41	46	39	25
Iran	na	**10**	10	10	11	9	7	7	11	12	8	12	11	10	10	15
Ireland	5	**12**	12	13	7	11	17	16	10	11	18	11	8	9	13	11
Israel	na	**na**	na	na	na	na	na	na	na	na	na	na	na	na	na	na
Italy	15	**17**	18	16	17	12	21	21	15	10	21	12	10	25	16	11
Japan	17	**na**	na	na	na	na	na	na	na	na	na	na	na	na	na	na
Jordan	na	**40**	46	34	41	41	37	40	41	39	38	41	40	43	38	38
Korea, South	53	**47**	46	48	37	46	60	63	52	37	49	48	44	52	44	32
Latvia	31	**10**	12	8	5	9	12	10	9	13	10	8	11	10	10	11
Lithuania	15	**24**	20	26	20	20	30	35	19	23	29	21	21	29	21	18
Luxembourg	na	**8**	8	9	9	7	10	11	8	4	13	8	4	7	9	5
Macedonia	na	**19**	19	18	16	19	20	20	19	14	21	19	16	16	21	8
Malta	na	**15**	14	16	8	14	21	23	14	7	18	14	10	21	13	8
Mexico	18	**14**	14	15	12	15	15	18	10	9	20	14	9	14	14	13
Moldova	na	**19**	16	21	18	20	18	16	22	16	20	18	21	14	19	33
Montenegro	na	**20**	19	21	15	20	24	26	17	15	21	17	22	26	17	10
Morocco	na	**18**	18	19	15	18	26	21	10	8	25	11	16	22	14	13
Netherlands	7	**5**	5	5	1	3	9	8	5	2	5	5	4	12	5	2
New Zealand	na	**5**	6	5	6	6	5	10	3	2	7	5	4	5	5	3
Nigeria	26	**28**	29	27	27	30	27	30	27	26	30	29	25	32	26	24
Northern Ireland	7	**18**	19	18	16	19	15	20	18	14	18	15	15	22	17	17
Norway	16	**10**	12	8	7	7	15	15	9	6	na	na	na	17	9	5
Pakistan	na	**29**	35	23	29	28	31	26	34	30	26	28	33	31	26	42
Peru	na	**11**	10	12	11	10	11	13	12	8	13	11	7	16	11	4
Philippines	na	**15**	17	14	13	15	18	20	13	14	19	13	15	15	16	14
Poland	na	**24**	23	24	14	23	29	27	20	18	25	22	26	28	22	21
Portugal	10	**3**	4	2	2	2	3	3	2	3	5	2	3	2	2	6
Puerto Rico	na	**6**	4	7	3	6	6	7	9	4	6	6	5	4	6	4
Romania	30	**21**	21	21	14	21	25	30	19	10	31	20	15	24	20	5
Russian Fed.	12	**11**	12	11	8	10	14	13	12	9	12	12	9	11	11	15
Serbia	na	**8**	7	9	4	7	10	12	6	4	11	7	5	9	7	3
Singapore	na	**26**	23	29	25	27	25	24	26	32	28	22	31	24	27	18
Slovakia	na	**23**	23	23	21	24	23	22	23	23	25	19	23	23	22	8
Slovenia	40	**16**	18	14	13	14	20	24	15	8	19	14	9	23	15	13
South Africa	na	**31**	32	29	30	33	27	31	32	22	33	34	23	30	33	22
Spain	11	**10**	8	12	5	10	14	13	7	6	12	9	12	12	11	5
Sweden	9	**3**	4	1	3	1	4	3	4	1	2	4	3	6	3	1
Switzerland	2	**10**	11	9	10	8	13	15	9	7	14	11	7	11	12	5
Taiwan	na	**27**	27	27	21	25	39	35	28	20	37	23	22	27	29	24
Tanzania	na	**18**	16	19	17	16	19	20	17	12	25	13	13	14	19	8
Turkey	28	**39**	37	41	38	39	41	49	30	18	49	35	26	42	40	29
Uganda	na	**13**	14	12	12	12	22	13	14	5	7	5	11	18	11	12
Ukraine	na	**15**	15	15	11	15	18	16	16	13	15	14	16	14	16	9
United States	10	**10**	10	10	11	10	10	13	11	8	10	10	8	13	9	10
Uruguay	na	**7**	8	7	6	7	8	9	6	3	8	9	5	6	8	5
Venezuela	na	**18**	20	16	17	16	24	21	18	14	22	17	19	20	18	15
Vietnam	na	**33**	31	35	30	33	35	34	30	37	40	31	31	36	35	33
Zimbabwe	na	**21**	21	20	21	20	20	23	17	40	20	26	20	20	20	32
Total	17	**18**	19	17	17	18	19	21	17	14	20	18	17	22	17	11

RANKING	
Country	2000
Bangladesh	67
Korea, South	47
Egypt	42
Indonesia	40
Jordan	40
Turkey	39
India	38
Vietnam	33
South Africa	31
Pakistan	29
Nigeria	28
Taiwan	27
Singapore	26
Bosnia and Herz.	25
Bulgaria	25
Lithuania	24
Algeria	24
Poland	24
Slovakia	23
Armenia	22
Croatia	22
Romania	21
Estonia	21
Zimbabwe	21
Montenegro	20
Azerbaijan	20
Czech Republic	19
Moldova	19
Macedonia	19
Belgium	18
Morocco	18
Northern Ireland	18
Venezuela	18
Dominican Rep.	18
Tanzania	18
Belarus	17
Albania	17
Italy	17
China	16
Slovenia	16
Great Britain	16
Malta	15
Philippines	15
Ukraine	15
Mexico	14
Greece	14
Finland	13
Uganda	13
Ireland	12
Austria	12
France	12
Russian Fed.	11
Georgia	11
Peru	11
Chile	11
Denmark	11
Spain	10
United States	10
Switzerland	10
Latvia	10
Norway	10
Iran	10
Germany	9
Luxembourg	8
Serbia	8
Uruguay	7
Argentina	6
Puerto Rico	6
New Zealand	5
Netherlands	5
Australia	5
Canada	4
Brazil	4
Iceland	3
Sweden	3
Portugal	3
Total	18

A130) NEIGHBORS: PEOPLE WHO HAVE AIDS

On this list are various groups of people. Could you please sort out any that you would not like to have as neighbors?

People who have AIDS (%) (WVS: V74; EVS: V61)

	Wave		Gender		Age			Education			Income			Values		
Country	1990	2000	Male	Female	16-29	30-49	50+	Lower	Middle	Upper	Lower	Middle	Upper	Mat	Mixed	Postm.
Albania	na	**70**	69	71	64	71	75	77	68	56	76	69	64	73	66	80
Algeria	na	**68**	68	69	65	71	70	73	69	64	69	72	62	71	68	65
Argentina	32	**12**	14	10	5	10	20	16	6	3	18	11	6	19	11	6
Armenia	na	**85**	84	87	78	89	90	85	87	79	82	87	92	91	81	82
Australia	na	**15**	20	11	8	13	24	22	15	10	21	14	9	19	16	12
Austria	32	**17**	20	15	13	14	23	21	14	16	22	19	14	38	16	14
Azerbaijan	na	**89**	90	88	88	90	90	90	90	88	96	92	81	90	89	82
Bangladesh	na	**6**	5	6	8	4	4	6	5	7	5	6	6	4	7	8
Belarus	73	**58**	53	61	53	55	64	63	58	48	59	58	53	61	59	32
Belgium	24	**13**	12	15	11	9	19	23	12	9	20	13	10	19	11	8
Bosnia and Herz.	na	**60**	60	59	55	62	62	66	63	45	67	61	51	64	58	57
Brazil	24	**14**	14	14	12	13	20	20	11	4	19	12	10	20	12	8
Bulgaria	63	**52**	52	52	55	42	59	61	51	39	60	50	45	55	53	49
Canada	21	**12**	13	12	7	11	17	21	10	10	17	10	9	21	13	8
Chile	41	**24**	23	25	18	24	29	28	22	21	22	26	22	31	22	15
China	76	**79**	79	79	77	82	76	75	83	77	75	82	84	81	80	84
Colombia	na	**8**	8	9	10	8	9	12	10	4	11	9	6	11	11	7
Croatia	na	**51**	51	51	41	52	56	55	50	42	48	54	48	56	51	50
Czech Republic	64	**21**	22	19	13	17	28	25	17	14	23	22	17	32	18	12
Denmark	9	**6**	6	5	3	4	10	8	3	4	9	4	4	9	7	1
Dominican Rep.	na	**30**	29	30	27	36	18	44	37	26	31	22	32	33	30	21
Egypt	na	**2**	1	2	2	1	2	2	1	3	2	2	1	1	2	2
El Salvador	na	**67**	68	67	64	66	74	79	63	40	81	65	49	na	na	na
Estonia	63	**42**	39	44	32	40	50	50	40	36	49	47	36	45	40	44
Finland	24	**21**	25	17	15	19	26	23	21	12	20	24	19	29	20	12
France	15	**9**	9	8	5	6	13	11	6	4	14	8	6	15	8	2
Georgia	na	**71**	71	71	67	73	74	75	73	63	74	73	66	74	70	57
Germany	20	**11**	11	11	5	10	15	16	8	5	14	13	9	17	10	6
Great Britain	23	**25**	26	24	19	21	31	31	22	17	28	22	20	na	na	na
Greece	na	**27**	28	26	23	25	39	46	28	23	30	26	24	36	28	15
Hungary	66	**na**	na	na	na	na	na	na	na	na	na	na	na	na	na	na
Iceland	18	**7**	8	6	4	5	13	7	8	4	10	6	4	8	7	5
India	93	**39**	38	41	42	39	38	30	50	50	23	40	47	41	43	40
Indonesia	na	**52**	52	53	53	51	53	53	48	58	48	54	58	49	55	57
Iran	na	**1**	1	na	1	1	na	na	1	1	1	na	1	na	1	2
Ireland	35	**23**	22	23	11	20	34	34	18	14	33	21	16	26	22	17
Israel	na	**na**	na	na	na	na	na	na	na	na	na	na	na	na	na	na
Italy	44	**31**	32	30	25	22	43	42	23	19	41	27	22	47	31	24
Japan	77	**na**	na	na	na	na	na	na	na	na	na	na	na	na	na	na
Jordan	na	**96**	96	96	95	97	95	96	96	95	97	95	95	97	96	91
Korea, South	4	**89**	89	90	84	90	93	95	91	86	89	89	90	92	89	71
Latvia	65	**29**	28	30	19	22	39	34	26	32	34	28	23	34	27	28
Lithuania	78	**55**	52	58	47	52	63	65	52	50	67	54	50	64	52	41
Luxembourg	na	**12**	12	12	8	13	15	18	9	8	15	10	6	12	13	8
Macedonia	na	**52**	52	52	51	52	53	62	51	38	58	52	43	45	56	53
Malta	na	**38**	35	41	29	34	49	53	34	28	47	35	28	47	34	28
Mexico	57	**34**	34	33	28	35	40	42	25	17	43	32	24	39	34	21
Moldova	na	**66**	66	66	69	65	65	65	69	61	61	62	72	69	65	58
Montenegro	na	**76**	76	76	72	75	80	79	77	68	83	81	75	82	72	60
Morocco	na	**81**	80	83	79	82	86	86	68	48	85	74	82	86	80	56
Netherlands	13	**8**	10	6	2	6	13	13	7	4	11	7	5	13	9	3
New Zealand	na	**17**	22	12	7	14	23	21	19	10	18	16	15	18	17	11
Nigeria	79	**68**	66	69	66	70	65	67	68	68	69	69	64	64	70	71
Northern Ireland	28	**31**	32	30	23	28	35	36	29	20	35	27	21	30	31	31
Norway	25	**14**	16	12	6	11	24	23	12	8	na	na	na	29	13	5
Pakistan	na	**7**	10	3	8	7	5	4	11	9	4	7	11	7	7	8
Peru	na	**29**	27	30	27	28	35	33	32	20	36	25	20	35	27	26
Philippines	na	**62**	60	64	57	61	72	70	61	54	69	62	57	63	62	60
Poland	na	**44**	46	41	23	41	59	54	32	28	48	41	39	47	41	44
Portugal	44	**27**	27	27	20	30	29	31	21	11	32	29	19	31	26	11
Puerto Rico	na	**12**	16	11	9	11	15	25	14	10	16	12	10	17	12	10
Romania	66	**47**	48	46	37	41	57	64	43	23	61	50	35	58	40	25
Russian Fed.	68	**52**	50	54	42	53	58	60	53	45	55	54	48	57	48	40
Serbia	na	**51**	48	54	37	52	57	60	51	38	58	49	47	59	46	27
Singapore	na	**35**	35	35	31	36	50	43	34	22	38	32	32	44	32	30
Slovakia	na	**45**	45	44	40	45	49	49	43	42	46	48	43	48	44	32
Slovenia	41	**33**	38	29	17	33	45	49	29	22	51	33	18	42	33	23
South Africa	na	**27**	28	25	22	28	33	28	24	32	29	25	23	26	28	19
Spain	33	**21**	20	21	13	17	28	27	15	12	26	20	20	26	22	10
Sweden	18	**7**	10	4	4	7	9	10	7	3	6	9	5	12	7	5
Switzerland	na	**12**	13	11	9	9	18	18	11	10	13	11	14	13	13	11
Taiwan	na	**72**	71	73	62	71	81	79	76	64	78	71	68	76	72	70
Tanzania	na	**33**	30	36	34	31	33	32	32	37	39	27	36	30	32	42
Turkey	89	**83**	83	83	79	85	88	90	80	55	90	81	70	90	83	73
Uganda	na	**17**	15	19	17	16	20	18	17	11	11	13	10	24	12	19
Ukraine	na	**59**	55	63	52	54	69	62	62	52	67	55	55	63	59	37
United States	28	**17**	20	14	12	15	23	18	21	14	15	17	16	25	16	14
Uruguay	na	**19**	22	17	16	15	24	24	13	8	26	17	13	29	21	12
Venezuela	na	**44**	47	40	42	43	49	52	45	29	53	39	37	50	42	38
Vietnam	na	**33**	31	36	31	33	35	35	33	18	34	35	32	46	31	25
Zimbabwe	na	**30**	29	31	34	28	26	34	26	40	33	33	28	30	30	41
Total	44	**37**	38	37	34	37	41	40	38	31	42	38	34	48	35	23

RANKING

Country	2000
Jordan	96
Korea, South	89
Azerbaijan	89
Armenia	85
Turkey	83
Morocco	81
China	79
Montenegro	76
Taiwan	72
Georgia	71
Albania	70
Algeria	68
Nigeria	68
El Salvador	67
Moldova	66
Philippines	62
Bosnia and Herz.	60
Ukraine	59
Belarus	58
Lithuania	55
Bulgaria	52
Russian Fed.	52
Macedonia	52
Indonesia	52
Serbia	51
Croatia	51
Romania	47
Slovakia	45
Poland	44
Venezuela	44
Estonia	42
India	39
Malta	38
Singapore	35
Mexico	34
Vietnam	33
Slovenia	33
Tanzania	33
Italy	31
Northern Ireland	31
Zimbabwe	30
Dominican Rep.	30
Latvia	29
Peru	29
Portugal	27
Greece	27
South Africa	27
Great Britain	25
Chile	24
Ireland	23
Finland	21
Spain	21
Czech Republic	21
Uruguay	19
Austria	17
Uganda	17
United States	17
New Zealand	17
Australia	15
Norway	14
Brazil	14
Belgium	13
Canada	12
Puerto Rico	12
Luxembourg	12
Switzerland	12
Argentina	12
Germany	11
France	9
Colombia	8
Netherlands	8
Iceland	7
Pakistan	7
Sweden	7
Denmark	6
Bangladesh	6
Egypt	2
Iran	1
Total	37

A131) NEIGHBORS: DRUG ADDICTS

On this list are various groups of people. Could you please sort out any that you would not like to have as neighbors?

(WVS: V75; EVS: V62)

Drug addicts (%)

Country	Wave		Gender		Age			Education			Income			Values		
	1990	2000	Male	Female	16-29	30-49	50+	Lower	Middle	Upper	Lower	Middle	Upper	Mat	Mixed	Postm.
Albania	na	**85**	83	86	80	84	89	89	84	74	84	85	86	87	82	87
Algeria	na	**77**	74	80	74	80	78	79	74	78	73	80	78	79	77	75
Argentina	50	**32**	35	29	25	29	42	35	28	26	35	31	30	41	31	25
Armenia	na	**93**	90	95	89	95	95	94	93	90	93	92	96	93	92	94
Australia	na	**74**	73	74	67	74	79	76	74	72	75	72	75	80	76	69
Austria	60	**53**	54	52	49	51	56	55	51	48	48	56	56	68	56	41
Azerbaijan	na	**97**	96	98	95	98	98	100	97	97	99	97	95	97	97	99
Bangladesh	na	**2**	2	2	2	2	1	2	2	3	1	2	2	1	2	3
Belarus	82	**87**	84	89	86	85	89	89	86	86	90	87	81	86	88	82
Belgium	53	**51**	50	52	50	47	56	60	51	46	56	55	45	59	53	41
Bosnia and Herz.	na	**82**	80	83	80	82	83	84	82	78	81	84	77	84	81	77
Brazil	58	**57**	55	58	52	58	62	59	54	59	54	61	57	63	56	45
Bulgaria	69	**72**	71	72	71	67	76	76	70	68	73	70	70	71	75	70
Canada	63	**64**	62	66	61	62	68	64	65	63	61	60	69	73	65	61
Chile	55	**53**	51	55	49	54	55	53	53	51	52	49	58	57	53	45
China	76	**90**	90	91	90	91	89	90	91	86	89	91	91	91	91	94
Colombia	na	**30**	31	30	28	29	38	38	31	24	36	31	26	33	28	27
Croatia	na	**69**	67	71	54	70	79	71	69	65	67	74	66	76	69	64
Czech Republic	81	**73**	72	75	71	73	75	74	72	73	74	76	71	79	73	60
Denmark	54	**60**	58	61	70	61	53	60	66	59	59	57	64	63	63	49
Dominican Rep.	na	**71**	74	69	69	76	73	56	68	74	79	73	72	66	72	71
Egypt	na	**1**	1	1	1	na	1	1	1	2	1	1	1	na	1	1
El Salvador	na	**89**	89	89	89	89	88	90	89	85	90	90	85	na	na	na
Estonia	87	**90**	87	92	87	91	90	90	91	87	88	93	90	91	89	90
Finland	68	**75**	74	77	74	80	72	74	76	77	71	76	78	80	75	71
France	44	**48**	50	46	44	43	55	54	42	37	54	46	42	59	48	33
Georgia	na	**81**	78	84	70	84	88	87	81	75	83	82	77	83	80	71
Germany	59	**59**	59	58	44	60	63	66	52	55	57	65	59	69	58	45
Great Britain	62	**72**	70	74	65	74	75	73	75	63	68	73	76	na	na	na
Greece	na	**45**	49	43	39	46	57	60	44	44	43	50	44	52	46	36
Hungary	84	**na**	na	na	na	na	na	na	na	na	na	na	na	na	na	na
Iceland	74	**76**	75	77	83	77	70	73	78	79	72	78	79	79	77	68
India	93	**44**	44	45	42	45	44	36	52	53	31	46	50	46	46	49
Indonesia	na	**60**	60	60	62	61	57	53	56	70	53	65	67	56	62	68
Iran	na	**1**	1	1	2	1	na	na	2	2	1	1	2	1	2	1
Ireland	64	**66**	65	68	57	67	71	71	64	62	67	66	70	68	67	63
Israel	na	**na**	na	na	na	na	na	na	na	na	na	na	na	na	na	na
Italy	60	**55**	55	54	46	51	63	61	49	51	55	55	56	69	55	48
Japan	91	**na**	na	na	na	na	na	na	na	na	na	na	na	na	na	na
Jordan	na	**99**	99	99	99	99	98	98	100	99	100	99	99	99	99	96
Korea, South	4	**93**	92	95	89	95	96	93	94	92	92	94	95	95	93	85
Latvia	89	**75**	71	78	71	76	75	68	76	77	75	77	75	79	75	62
Lithuania	89	**86**	85	87	83	88	87	84	87	88	89	87	86	89	85	88
Luxembourg	na	**43**	43	44	46	38	46	48	42	36	45	42	33	48	44	32
Macedonia	na	**73**	72	74	71	76	71	77	71	71	77	73	66	74	72	83
Malta	na	**71**	70	73	61	72	78	78	70	65	70	78	67	76	70	66
Mexico	69	**68**	68	68	69	65	72	70	66	60	71	67	67	68	71	57
Moldova	na	**91**	89	92	87	93	92	92	91	90	92	92	88	94	91	85
Montenegro	na	**86**	85	87	80	87	89	86	87	86	86	89	88	92	83	69
Morocco	na	**92**	90	95	91	93	94	92	93	89	94	93	90	94	91	85
Netherlands	73	**73**	74	72	71	73	75	78	72	70	75	70	76	78	76	65
New Zealand	na	**79**	79	79	69	80	82	77	81	80	76	79	84	78	80	80
Nigeria	77	**74**	73	75	74	76	70	74	74	75	74	74	75	72	76	76
Northern Ireland	59	**78**	78	79	72	80	81	81	78	71	80	81	81	85	78	69
Norway	55	**66**	67	65	68	63	67	64	63	71	na	na	na	70	67	54
Pakistan	na	**59**	61	57	58	58	63	56	62	64	55	60	61	55	65	67
Peru	na	**66**	65	67	63	70	65	68	67	65	68	65	67	67	66	69
Philippines	na	**82**	80	84	81	80	88	84	82	80	83	85	76	85	80	79
Poland	na	**69**	73	65	62	68	74	73	61	69	68	70	70	69	68	73
Portugal	61	**48**	48	48	40	48	53	53	40	35	54	48	51	55	46	32
Puerto Rico	na	**47**	53	43	46	50	45	47	46	48	45	47	49	55	44	47
Romania	76	**74**	75	73	66	76	76	75	75	69	73	73	75	77	74	64
Russian Fed.	86	**84**	82	86	80	84	86	84	84	85	83	86	84	87	82	72
Serbia	na	**70**	68	72	63	72	72	73	69	68	71	72	72	77	66	51
Singapore	na	**73**	70	75	70	74	79	72	72	76	69	72	75	77	71	67
Slovakia	na	**79**	78	81	79	81	79	74	81	85	77	80	83	80	80	73
Slovenia	47	**65**	69	62	58	65	70	69	65	60	70	66	59	69	65	63
South Africa	na	**62**	62	63	64	62	60	63	62	54	62	67	58	60	64	62
Spain	54	**53**	53	53	43	50	60	59	46	48	56	56	51	63	52	41
Sweden	65	**60**	62	59	68	62	55	54	62	62	60	63	59	59	63	50
Switzerland	32	**49**	48	50	43	45	58	52	49	45	53	47	50	61	52	36
Taiwan	na	**89**	88	89	81	90	89	87	89	90	88	89	91	90	89	95
Tanzania	na	**81**	80	84	84	79	85	84	79	78	82	85	75	84	81	83
Turkey	92	**94**	94	95	93	95	96	96	94	90	96	94	91	97	95	90
Uganda	na	**87**	87	87	86	87	89	88	85	97	85	91	83	83	89	89
Ukraine	na	**88**	88	89	89	87	90	88	88	89	89	86	90	90	88	78
United States	79	**74**	72	76	62	77	79	70	75	74	71	75	79	72	76	70
Uruguay	na	**44**	45	44	31	40	54	49	39	37	48	43	42	49	47	37
Venezuela	na	**73**	73	73	72	73	73	74	74	68	74	72	68	75	72	73
Vietnam	na	**54**	55	53	52	55	54	55	53	45	56	48	60	68	52	50
Zimbabwe	na	**64**	60	68	62	63	69	63	66	22	62	62	58	61	67	59
Total	67	**68**	67	69	65	68	70	67	69	67	69	69	67	73	68	58

RANKING	
Country	2000
Jordan	99
Azerbaijan	97
Turkey	94
Korea, South	93
Armenia	93
Morocco	92
Moldova	91
China	90
Estonia	90
El Salvador	89
Taiwan	89
Ukraine	88
Belarus	87
Uganda	87
Lithuania	86
Montenegro	86
Albania	85
Russian Fed.	84
Philippines	82
Bosnia and Herz.	82
Tanzania	81
Georgia	81
Slovakia	79
New Zealand	79
Northern Ireland	78
Algeria	77
Iceland	76
Finland	75
Latvia	75
Nigeria	74
United States	74
Australia	74
Romania	74
Czech Republic	73
Netherlands	73
Macedonia	73
Venezuela	73
Singapore	73
Great Britain	72
Bulgaria	72
Malta	71
Dominican Rep.	71
Serbia	70
Croatia	69
Poland	69
Mexico	68
Peru	66
Ireland	66
Norway	66
Slovenia	65
Canada	64
Zimbabwe	64
South Africa	62
Sweden	60
Denmark	60
Indonesia	60
Pakistan	59
Germany	59
Brazil	57
Italy	55
Vietnam	54
Austria	53
Chile	53
Spain	53
Belgium	51
Switzerland	49
Portugal	48
France	48
Puerto Rico	47
Greece	45
Uruguay	44
India	44
Luxembourg	43
Argentina	32
Colombia	30
Bangladesh	2
Iran	1
Egypt	1
Total	68

A132) NEIGHBORS: HOMOSEXUALS

On this list are various groups of people. Could you please sort out any that you would not like to have as neighbors?

Homosexuals (%)

(WVS: V76; EVS: V63)

Country	Wave		Gender		Age			Education			Income			Values		
	1990	2000	Male	Female	16-29	30-49	50+	Lower	Middle	Upper	Lower	Middle	Upper	Mat	Mixed	Postm.
Albania	na	**83**	83	83	79	84	84	87	81	76	81	83	83	85	81	82
Algeria	na	**81**	80	81	78	83	83	83	79	81	77	82	83	82	81	81
Argentina	39	**22**	26	19	16	18	32	28	13	18	30	22	15	34	22	13
Armenia	na	**83**	83	83	74	89	90	89	84	80	77	87	89	87	80	88
Australia	na	**25**	33	16	21	20	34	39	23	15	32	26	14	35	26	20
Austria	43	**25**	31	21	12	22	36	33	20	12	31	29	19	48	26	17
Azerbaijan	na	**91**	93	88	89	91	93	92	91	89	96	93	83	91	90	87
Bangladesh	na	**5**	5	5	5	5	4	5	4	6	4	7	3	1	7	1
Belarus	79	**63**	65	62	54	63	71	71	62	57	64	66	55	66	64	43
Belgium	24	**17**	20	15	16	12	23	26	17	11	24	19	12	23	15	12
Bosnia and Herz.	na	**64**	65	64	60	65	67	73	65	54	70	66	56	65	64	64
Brazil	30	**26**	31	22	25	25	32	30	25	18	27	26	26	31	25	19
Bulgaria	68	**54**	57	51	50	47	62	63	51	45	61	51	47	56	54	57
Canada	30	**17**	19	15	14	14	22	27	15	11	24	15	13	26	18	11
Chile	58	**33**	36	30	29	34	35	33	33	32	29	37	32	38	34	21
China	72	**73**	77	70	71	76	67	64	80	72	65	76	83	74	76	81
Colombia	na	**15**	18	11	16	14	15	17	16	12	15	16	13	18	15	17
Croatia	na	**53**	59	48	40	55	59	55	55	39	53	57	47	55	56	44
Czech Republic	59	**20**	22	18	12	16	27	25	14	12	25	20	14	27	18	12
Denmark	12	**8**	11	5	5	3	15	12	3	3	13	6	3	10	9	2
Dominican Rep.	na	**49**	52	47	44	57	55	50	54	48	52	50	47	44	50	50
Egypt	na	**0**	na	na	1	na	na	na	na	1	na	na	na	na	1	na
El Salvador	na	**78**	83	74	77	76	83	86	75	63	84	80	64	na	na	na
Estonia	73	**46**	47	46	38	43	54	49	47	39	50	51	41	51	44	38
Finland	25	**21**	29	15	17	19	25	26	17	11	22	28	14	30	19	15
France	24	**16**	20	12	9	14	21	20	10	9	19	16	15	26	14	6
Georgia	na	**77**	80	75	74	78	79	80	77	76	80	82	70	78	78	68
Germany	34	**13**	15	11	4	10	21	20	8	9	19	13	10	18	14	4
Great Britain	31	**24**	26	23	18	17	34	33	19	15	24	25	21	na	na	na
Greece	na	**27**	32	23	18	26	49	52	29	21	33	24	25	28	28	21
Hungary	75	**na**	na	na	na	na	na	na	na	na	na	na	na	na	na	na
Iceland	20	**8**	11	5	3	5	17	12	6	2	13	5	5	11	7	5
India	91	**29**	30	28	27	30	28	20	36	40	18	25	39	22	41	49
Indonesia	na	**55**	54	56	60	55	52	49	52	63	52	56	63	53	56	68
Iran	na	**1**	1	1	1	1	na	1	1	1	1	1	1	1	1	na
Ireland	33	**27**	29	25	16	23	40	42	21	14	36	29	19	34	27	18
Israel	na	**na**	na	na	na	na	na	na	na	na	na	na	na	na	na	na
Italy	39	**29**	31	27	24	21	39	40	22	17	36	24	23	na	na	na
Japan	69	**na**	na	na	na	na	na	na	na	na	na	na	na	38	31	19
Jordan	na	**98**	99	98	98	99	97	98	99	99	98	99	99	99	98	98
Korea, South	4	**82**	86	79	69	87	88	86	86	77	82	83	83	85	82	66
Latvia	78	**46**	49	43	35	45	51	46	44	49	50	46	39	50	44	45
Lithuania	87	**68**	70	65	56	69	74	72	68	57	77	67	66	69	68	65
Luxembourg	na	**19**	20	17	16	15	25	27	14	16	22	17	11	20	22	8
Macedonia	na	**54**	56	52	54	55	51	61	51	47	61	53	45	52	55	58
Malta	na	**40**	41	38	27	36	52	51	37	25	47	43	31	47	37	25
Mexico	60	**45**	50	40	37	44	56	53	36	30	50	44	40	49	45	33
Moldova	na	**77**	78	77	73	80	79	76	80	75	82	82	71	78	78	73
Montenegro	na	**74**	73	74	68	71	80	77	74	65	81	82	73	83	68	53
Morocco	na	**93**	93	94	92	94	96	95	91	82	97	91	94	95	92	83
Netherlands	9	**6**	9	4	6	3	9	11	6	2	9	5	3	13	6	3
New Zealand	na	**22**	33	14	19	17	29	28	27	13	27	21	17	29	23	15
Nigeria	76	**74**	73	74	74	74	70	72	74	75	73	74	74	71	76	71
Northern Ireland	48	**35**	37	34	31	33	38	38	36	26	35	32	29	42	34	33
Norway	20	**14**	20	9	6	11	25	23	12	8	na	na	na	24	14	5
Pakistan	na	**na**	na	na	na	na	na	na	na	na	na	na	na	na	na	na
Peru	na	**49**	51	48	46	51	54	55	51	42	55	47	41	51	49	47
Philippines	na	**24**	25	23	23	21	31	26	22	24	27	22	22	24	25	18
Poland	na	**55**	60	51	41	54	65	62	50	39	58	54	53	54	56	60
Portugal	50	**25**	27	23	14	27	31	28	22	11	35	24	20	29	25	16
Puerto Rico	na	**22**	28	19	15	21	26	30	26	19	25	23	18	26	21	19
Romania	75	**65**	68	62	58	65	70	70	65	57	70	64	63	68	65	55
Russian Fed.	81	**58**	59	57	55	59	59	56	59	56	57	61	56	60	57	52
Serbia	na	**49**	50	48	41	45	57	56	49	38	54	52	45	54	47	31
Singapore	na	**46**	48	44	41	48	55	47	46	41	46	46	44	50	43	46
Slovakia	na	**44**	45	43	41	42	48	46	44	37	49	47	39	46	44	35
Slovenia	43	**44**	52	38	31	41	58	58	43	25	58	47	29	60	42	38
South Africa	na	**46**	47	46	45	46	48	49	42	53	52	49	35	44	47	58
Spain	27	**16**	16	15	9	12	23	20	12	10	21	13	16	23	15	7
Sweden	18	**6**	9	3	3	5	9	12	6	2	7	7	4	14	6	4
Switzerland	na	**19**	22	15	12	15	27	24	17	20	20	22	16	25	20	10
Taiwan	na	**73**	75	71	58	73	81	81	74	65	80	73	67	74	72	78
Tanzania	na	**74**	73	76	82	69	76	77	75	63	75	80	58	77	73	83
Turkey	92	**90**	91	89	88	91	94	95	90	71	95	90	80	95	91	82
Uganda	na	**76**	81	72	79	73	73	76	76	76	71	82	69	76	77	72
Ukraine	na	**66**	67	65	56	67	70	67	67	62	66	67	65	68	66	43
United States	39	**23**	27	19	24	22	25	29	29	18	24	21	24	40	22	21
Uruguay	na	**32**	35	30	25	27	39	38	26	15	36	30	28	32	34	27
Venezuela	na	**57**	59	56	56	57	62	65	59	45	65	56	51	63	56	53
Vietnam	na	**39**	40	37	39	37	42	40	37	36	38	40	39	59	35	41
Zimbabwe	na	**67**	66	67	66	68	65	64	71	52	62	66	67	63	70	65
Total	49	**43**	46	41	42	43	46	46	45	37	48	44	40	52	42	29

RANKING	
Country	2000
Jordan	98
Morocco	93
Azerbaijan	91
Turkey	90
Armenia	83
Albania	83
Korea, South	82
Algeria	81
El Salvador	78
Moldova	77
Georgia	77
Uganda	76
Tanzania	74
Montenegro	74
Nigeria	74
China	73
Taiwan	73
Lithuania	68
Zimbabwe	67
Ukraine	66
Romania	65
Bosnia and Herz.	64
Belarus	63
Russian Fed.	58
Venezuela	57
Poland	55
Indonesia	55
Bulgaria	54
Macedonia	54
Croatia	53
Peru	49
Serbia	49
Dominican Rep.	49
Estonia	46
South Africa	46
Singapore	46
Latvia	46
Mexico	45
Slovenia	44
Slovakia	44
Malta	40
Vietnam	39
Northern Ireland	35
Chile	33
Uruguay	32
India	29
Italy	29
Ireland	27
Greece	27
Brazil	26
Austria	25
Portugal	25
Australia	25
Great Britain	24
Philippines	24
United States	23
New Zealand	22
Argentina	22
Puerto Rico	22
Finland	21
Czech Republic	20
Luxembourg	19
Switzerland	19
Belgium	17
Canada	17
France	16
Spain	16
Colombia	15
Norway	14
Germany	13
Denmark	8
Iceland	8
Netherlands	6
Sweden	6
Bangladesh	5
Iran	1
Egypt	0
Total	43

A133) NEIGHBORS: JEWS

On this list are various groups of people. Could you please sort out any that you would not like to have as neighbors?

Jews (%)

(WVS: V77; EVS: V64)

Country	Wave		Gender		Age			Education			Income			Values		
	1990	2000	Male	Female	16-29	30-49	50+	Lower	Middle	Upper	Lower	Middle	Upper	Mat	Mixed	Postm.
Albania	na	**17**	14	20	14	17	20	19	17	12	19	18	14	15	17	31
Algeria	na	**na**	na	na	na	na	na	na	na	na	na	na	na	na	na	na
Argentina	6	**6**	9	4	5	5	10	8	4	na	10	7	3	12	7	2
Armenia	na	**na**	na	na	na	na	na	na	na	na	na	na	na	na	na	na
Australia	na	**na**	na	na	na	na	na	na	na	na	na	na	na	na	na	na
Austria	11	**8**	9	8	7	6	11	11	6	4	13	9	6	23	8	5
Azerbaijan	na	**na**	na	na	na	na	na	na	na	na	na	na	na	na	na	na
Bangladesh	na	**20**	22	19	25	16	22	18	24	25	17	21	24	22	20	24
Belarus	21	**15**	16	14	16	13	17	18	14	10	15	14	15	15	15	7
Belgium	13	**13**	13	13	13	10	16	21	12	9	20	11	11	20	11	8
Bosnia and Herz.	na	**28**	26	30	26	28	30	30	29	22	29	29	26	28	28	23
Brazil	na	**na**	na	na	na	na	na	na	na	na	na	na	na	na	na	na
Bulgaria	30	**18**	18	18	21	18	17	20	19	13	21	22	13	18	19	13
Canada	6	**4**	4	4	3	3	5	8	3	1	6	3	2	7	4	3
Chile	16	**9**	8	9	8	9	10	9	9	10	9	9	8	9	9	6
China	na	**na**	na	na	na	na	na	na	na	na	na	na	na	na	na	na
Colombia	na	**na**	na	na	na	na	na	na	na	na	na	na	na	na	na	na
Croatia	na	**18**	21	16	19	17	19	18	20	11	16	20	18	19	19	16
Czech Republic	23	**4**	6	3	4	4	5	6	3	1	7	4	2	7	4	2
Denmark	3	**3**	3	2	2	2	4	4	1	1	2	3	1	4	3	1
Dominican Rep.	na	**na**	na	na	na	na	na	na	na	na	na	na	na	na	na	na
Egypt	na	**17**	17	16	18	18	12	16	21	11	17	18	13	12	20	21
El Salvador	na	**na**	na	na	na	na	na	na	na	na	na	na	na	na	na	na
Estonia	13	**11**	13	10	13	10	12	13	10	11	13	13	9	10	11	19
Finland	5	**9**	11	6	7	9	9	10	7	6	10	10	6	14	8	1
France	7	**6**	6	6	5	5	7	8	4	3	8	5	5	9	6	na
Georgia	na	**na**	na	na	na	na	na	na	na	na	na	na	na	na	na	na
Germany	8	**5**	7	4	2	5	7	7	4	3	7	5	5	6	6	3
Great Britain	7	**6**	6	6	3	5	9	8	5	6	5	3	6	na	na	na
Greece	na	**19**	21	17	17	17	24	35	20	15	20	17	18	21	19	16
Hungary	10	**na**	na	na	na	na	na	na	na	na	na	na	na	na	na	na
Iceland	7	**4**	5	3	2	3	8	5	4	1	6	2	3	7	4	1
India	53	**na**	na	na	na	na	na	na	na	na	na	na	na	na	na	na
Indonesia	na	**na**	na	na	na	na	na	na	na	na	na	na	na	na	na	na
Iran	na	**na**	na	na	na	na	na	na	na	na	na	na	na	na	na	na
Ireland	6	**11**	10	12	6	10	15	16	8	7	18	10	6	11	11	8
Israel	na	**na**	na	na	na	na	na	na	na	na	na	na	na	na	na	na
Italy	13	**13**	14	12	12	10	16	17	11	7	18	8	8	19	13	8
Japan	28	**na**	na	na	na	na	na	na	na	na	na	na	na	na	na	na
Jordan	na	**na**	na	na	na	na	na	na	na	na	na	na	na	na	na	na
Korea, South	na	**41**	44	38	24	42	58	63	48	29	46	39	37	44	40	27
Latvia	9	**5**	5	5	6	4	6	6	6	4	6	4	4	4	6	4
Lithuania	18	**23**	23	23	19	23	26	26	23	18	30	23	19	26	22	15
Luxembourg	na	**8**	8	9	9	7	9	11	7	6	11	8	5	9	8	7
Macedonia	na	**20**	19	21	21	19	21	27	17	15	23	18	17	19	21	11
Malta	na	**21**	18	23	15	20	26	28	19	10	25	18	16	26	19	13
Mexico	19	**na**	na	na	na	na	na	na	na	na	na	na	na	na	na	na
Moldova	na	**25**	24	26	26	25	24	25	30	16	26	21	28	26	23	33
Montenegro	na	**na**	na	na	na	na	na	na	na	na	na	na	na	na	na	na
Morocco	na	**na**	na	na	na	na	na	na	na	na	na	na	na	na	na	na
Netherlands	3	**2**	2	1	1	1	2	3	1	1	1	2	1	3	2	na
New Zealand	na	**na**	na	na	na	na	na	na	na	na	na	na	na	na	na	na
Nigeria	35	**na**	na	na	na	na	na	na	na	na	na	na	na	na	na	na
Northern Ireland	6	**12**	12	12	12	10	11	13	11	9	8	8	9	9	12	16
Norway	9	**na**	na	na	na	na	na	na	na	na	na	na	na	na	na	na
Pakistan	na	**na**	na	na	na	na	na	na	na	na	na	na	na	na	na	na
Peru	na	**na**	na	na	na	na	na	na	na	na	na	na	na	na	na	na
Philippines	na	**na**	na	na	na	na	na	na	na	na	na	na	na	na	na	na
Poland	na	**25**	27	24	13	25	33	31	20	11	28	23	25	27	24	29
Portugal	19	**11**	10	12	4	13	13	12	9	5	21	9	7	12	10	11
Puerto Rico	na	**na**	na	na	na	na	na	na	na	na	na	na	na	na	na	na
Romania	28	**23**	23	23	20	22	26	32	22	10	33	20	17	30	18	13
Russian Fed.	13	**11**	12	11	10	10	13	14	12	7	13	12	9	12	10	15
Serbia	na	**na**	na	na	na	na	na	na	na	na	na	na	na	na	na	na
Singapore	na	**na**	na	na	na	na	na	na	na	na	na	na	na	na	na	na
Slovakia	na	**10**	10	10	11	9	10	11	10	6	13	8	8	12	9	9
Slovenia	37	**17**	16	18	11	15	22	30	13	5	26	17	7	24	16	14
South Africa	na	**24**	25	24	25	24	24	25	23	32	26	27	20	22	26	31
Spain	12	**22**	21	22	21	21	23	23	18	27	16	28	24	26	22	18
Sweden	6	**2**	3	2	1	1	4	4	2	1	2	2	2	5	2	1
Switzerland	na	**na**	na	na	na	na	na	na	na	na	na	na	na	na	na	na
Taiwan	na	**na**	na	na	na	na	na	na	na	na	na	na	na	na	na	na
Tanzania	na	**na**	na	na	na	na	na	na	na	na	na	na	na	na	na	na
Turkey	59	**62**	58	65	61	61	68	76	49	23	78	61	33	64	65	48
Uganda	na	**22**	24	21	23	23	16	25	22	12	14	12	19	24	23	15
Ukraine	na	**10**	11	10	9	9	12	17	10	7	10	11	10	12	9	5
United States	5	**9**	9	9	11	8	8	12	9	8	10	8	9	13	8	9
Uruguay	na	**10**	9	11	8	10	12	12	7	9	11	11	9	10	11	8
Venezuela	na	**na**	na	na	na	na	na	na	na	na	na	na	na	na	na	na
Vietnam	na	**na**	na	na	na	na	na	na	na	na	na	na	na	na	na	na
Zimbabwe	na	**19**	18	21	22	17	17	20	19	na	19	23	21	15	20	39
Total	16	**14**	14	14	14	13	15	16	14	10	16	14	12	17	13	10

RANKING

Country	2000
Turkey	62
Korea, South	41
Bosnia and Herz.	28
Poland	25
Moldova	25
South Africa	24
Romania	23
Lithuania	23
Uganda	22
Spain	22
Malta	21
Bangladesh	20
Macedonia	20
Zimbabwe	19
Greece	19
Croatia	18
Bulgaria	18
Albania	17
Slovenia	17
Egypt	17
Belarus	15
Belgium	13
Italy	13
Northern Ireland	12
Russian Fed.	11
Estonia	11
Ireland	11
Portugal	11
Ukraine	10
Uruguay	10
Slovakia	10
United States	9
Chile	9
Finland	9
Austria	8
Luxembourg	8
Argentina	6
Great Britain	6
France	6
Germany	5
Latvia	5
Czech Republic	4
Iceland	4
Canada	4
Denmark	3
Sweden	2
Netherlands	2
Total	14

A140_1) NEIGHBORS: GYPSIES

On this list are various groups of people. Could you please sort out any that you would not like to have as neighbors?

Gypsies (%)

(WVS: V77H; EVS: V65)

Country	Wave		Gender		Age			Education			Income			Values		
	1990	2000	Male	Female	16-29	30-49	50+	Lower	Middle	Upper	Lower	Middle	Upper	Mat	Mixed	Postm.
Albania	na	**na**	na	na	na	na	na	na	na	na	na	na	na	na	na	na
Algeria	na	**na**	na	na	na	na	na	na	na	na	na	na	na	na	na	na
Argentina	na	**na**	na	na	na	na	na	na	na	na	na	na	na	na	na	na
Armenia	na	**na**	na	na	na	na	na	na	na	na	na	na	na	na	na	na
Australia	na	**na**	na	na	na	na	na	na	na	na	na	na	na	na	na	na
Austria	na	**25**	24	26	18	22	32	27	24	18	29	23	23	39	27	16
Azerbaijan	na	**na**	na	na	na	na	na	na	na	na	na	na	na	na	na	na
Bangladesh	na	**na**	na	na	na	na	na	na	na	na	na	na	na	na	na	na
Belarus	na	**51**	46	55	53	49	52	52	51	50	50	49	56	53	51	46
Belgium	na	**35**	33	37	33	32	39	43	36	28	41	32	34	47	35	21
Bosnia and Herz.	na	**na**	na	na	na	na	na	na	na	na	na	na	na	na	na	na
Brazil	na	**na**	na	na	na	na	na	na	na	na	na	na	na	na	na	na
Bulgaria	na	**54**	54	53	53	49	58	57	53	50	53	52	58	59	52	40
Canada	na	**na**	na	na	na	na	na	na	na	na	na	na	na	na	na	na
Chile	na	**na**	na	na	na	na	na	na	na	na	na	na	na	na	na	na
China	na	**na**	na	na	na	na	na	na	na	na	na	na	na	na	na	na
Colombia	na	**na**	na	na	na	na	na	na	na	na	na	na	na	na	na	na
Croatia	na	**39**	44	34	33	33	49	43	38	28	34	40	39	40	40	34
Czech Republic	na	**40**	39	41	38	45	36	41	39	34	40	41	38	52	37	27
Denmark	na	**15**	15	15	7	15	21	20	10	10	13	15	17	20	16	9
Dominican Rep.	na	**na**	na	na	na	na	na	na	na	na	na	na	na	na	na	na
Egypt	na	**na**	na	na	na	na	na	na	na	na	na	na	na	na	na	na
El Salvador	na	**na**	na	na	na	na	na	na	na	na	na	na	na	na	na	na
Estonia	na	**50**	47	52	49	49	51	53	51	41	51	55	46	51	48	54
Finland	na	**44**	48	41	46	45	44	47	41	42	41	48	45	53	44	28
France	na	**40**	40	39	38	34	46	44	36	32	45	38	41	50	40	23
Georgia	na	**na**	na	na	na	na	na	na	na	na	na	na	na	na	na	na
Germany	na	**32**	32	33	16	35	37	39	28	23	38	35	31	40	31	24
Great Britain	na	**37**	39	35	29	37	42	39	39	30	27	36	43	na	na	na
Greece	na	**33**	31	34	34	31	34	47	33	30	30	34	35	34	34	27
Hungary	na	**na**	na	na	na	na	na	na	na	na	na	na	na	na	na	na
Iceland	na	**9**	12	7	9	8	12	10	11	4	10	7	11	14	9	4
India	na	**na**	na	na	na	na	na	na	na	na	na	na	na	na	na	na
Indonesia	na	**na**	na	na	na	na	na	na	na	na	na	na	na	na	na	na
Iran	na	**na**	na	na	na	na	na	na	na	na	na	na	na	na	na	na
Ireland	na	**25**	26	23	16	26	31	30	23	20	29	26	25	25	27	16
Israel	na	**na**	na	na	na	na	na	na	na	na	na	na	na	na	na	na
Italy	na	**56**	53	58	53	49	63	61	50	54	55	54	55	69	56	50
Japan	na	**na**	na	na	na	na	na	na	na	na	na	na	na	na	na	na
Jordan	na	**na**	na	na	na	na	na	na	na	na	na	na	na	na	na	na
Korea, South	na	**na**	na	na	na	na	na	na	na	na	na	na	na	na	na	na
Latvia	na	**27**	26	28	40	26	23	24	25	37	24	26	30	25	28	34
Lithuania	na	**63**	57	69	60	61	68	66	63	60	71	60	63	75	58	57
Luxembourg	na	**25**	25	25	22	25	28	30	24	20	26	23	15	27	26	17
Macedonia	na	**na**	na	na	na	na	na	na	na	na	na	na	na	na	na	na
Malta	na	**30**	28	32	27	30	33	37	28	26	29	32	28	34	28	28
Mexico	na	**na**	na	na	na	na	na	na	na	na	na	na	na	na	na	na
Moldova	na	**na**	na	na	na	na	na	na	na	na	na	na	na	na	na	na
Montenegro	na	**24**	21	26	19	22	28	31	20	15	31	24	20	28	18	15
Morocco	na	**na**	na	na	na	na	na	na	na	na	na	na	na	na	na	na
Netherlands	na	**19**	19	20	14	17	25	24	19	16	14	19	23	23	22	11
New Zealand	na	**na**	na	na	na	na	na	na	na	na	na	na	na	na	na	na
Nigeria	na	**na**	na	na	na	na	na	na	na	na	na	na	na	na	na	na
Northern Ireland	na	**58**	57	60	54	57	62	59	58	58	57	61	63	65	61	39
Norway	na	**na**	na	na	na	na	na	na	na	na	na	na	na	na	na	na
Pakistan	na	**na**	na	na	na	na	na	na	na	na	na	na	na	na	na	na
Peru	na	**na**	na	na	na	na	na	na	na	na	na	na	na	na	na	na
Philippines	na	**na**	na	na	na	na	na	na	na	na	na	na	na	na	na	na
Poland	na	**39**	39	38	33	39	42	43	34	34	40	36	46	43	37	37
Portugal	na	**37**	34	39	30	36	41	41	28	25	46	37	34	44	34	28
Puerto Rico	na	**na**	na	na	na	na	na	na	na	na	na	na	na	na	na	na
Romania	na	**52**	49	54	48	49	55	57	50	43	56	48	51	53	49	49
Russian Fed.	na	**46**	39	51	53	43	43	42	46	48	43	45	48	46	44	40
Serbia	na	**12**	11	14	11	13	13	20	9	8	14	11	11	14	12	3
Singapore	na	**na**	na	na	na	na	na	na	na	na	na	na	na	na	na	na
Slovakia	na	**77**	76	78	83	76	74	75	79	77	75	76	80	77	80	61
Slovenia	na	**37**	38	36	33	34	42	42	35	33	42	34	29	46	35	31
South Africa	na	**na**	na	na	na	na	na	na	na	na	na	na	na	na	na	na
Spain	na	**28**	26	30	20	28	33	33	26	20	27	30	28	35	28	17
Sweden	na	**20**	21	19	13	21	23	22	21	16	18	20	21	27	22	12
Switzerland	na	**na**	na	na	na	na	na	na	na	na	na	na	na	na	na	na
Taiwan	na	**na**	na	na	na	na	na	na	na	na	na	na	na	na	na	na
Tanzania	na	**na**	na	na	na	na	na	na	na	na	na	na	na	na	na	na
Turkey	na	**72**	71	73	73	69	76	78	68	47	80	72	56	74	75	62
Uganda	na	**na**	na	na	na	na	na	na	na	na	na	na	na	na	na	na
Ukraine	na	**53**	52	54	60	51	51	54	52	55	50	52	57	56	52	36
United States	na	**na**	na	na	na	na	na	na	na	na	na	na	na	na	na	na
Uruguay	na	**na**	na	na	na	na	na	na	na	na	na	na	na	na	na	na
Venezuela	na	**na**	na	na	na	na	na	na	na	na	na	na	na	na	na	na
Vietnam	na	**na**	na	na	na	na	na	na	na	na	na	na	na	na	na	na
Zimbabwe	na	**na**	na	na	na	na	na	na	na	na	na	na	na	na	na	na
Total	na	**38**	37	39	36	36	41	41	38	32	38	37	39	45	36	26

RANKING	
Country	**2000**
Slovakia	77
Turkey	72
Lithuania	63
Northern Ireland	58
Italy	56
Bulgaria	54
Ukraine	53
Romania	52
Belarus	51
Estonia	50
Russian Fed.	46
Finland	44
Czech Republic	40
France	40
Croatia	39
Poland	39
Great Britain	37
Slovenia	37
Portugal	37
Belgium	35
Greece	33
Germany	32
Malta	30
Spain	28
Latvia	27
Luxembourg	25
Austria	25
Ireland	25
Montenegro	24
Sweden	20
Netherlands	19
Denmark	15
Serbia	12
Iceland	9
Total	38

A151_1) NEIGHBORS: PEOPLE WITH LARGE FAMILIES

On this list are various groups of people. Could you please sort out any that you would not like to have as neighbors?.

People with large families (%) (EVS: V57)

Country	Wave		Gender		Age			Education			Income			Values		
	1990	2000	Male	Female	16-29	30-49	50+	Lower	Middle	Upper	Lower	Middle	Upper	Mat	Mixed	Postm.
Albania	na	**na**	na	na	na	na	na	na	na	na	na	na	na	na	na	na
Algeria	na	**na**	na	na	na	na	na	na	na	na	na	na	na	na	na	na
Argentina	5	**na**	na	na	na	na	na	na	na	na	na	na	na	na	na	na
Armenia	na	**na**	na	na	na	na	na	na	na	na	na	na	na	na	na	na
Australia	na	**na**	na	na	na	na	na	na	na	na	na	na	na	na	na	na
Austria	5	**4**	5	3	4	4	5	4	5	3	7	4	2	6	5	2
Azerbaijan	na	**na**	na	na	na	na	na	na	na	na	na	na	na	na	na	na
Bangladesh	na	**na**	na	na	na	na	na	na	na	na	na	na	na	na	na	na
Belarus	16	**10**	10	11	8	13	10	9	10	13	9	11	12	11	9	14
Belgium	8	**9**	10	9	10	8	10	10	9	8	10	9	9	11	8	5
Bosnia and Herz.	na	**na**	na	na	na	na	na	na	na	na	na	na	na	na	na	na
Brazil	6	**na**	na	na	na	na	na	na	na	na	na	na	na	na	na	na
Bulgaria	24	**12**	12	12	14	13	10	11	11	15	13	13	9	12	13	4
Canada	6	**na**	na	na	na	na	na	na	na	na	na	na	na	na	na	na
Chile	14	**na**	na	na	na	na	na	na	na	na	na	na	na	na	na	na
China	19	**na**	na	na	na	na	na	na	na	na	na	na	na	na	na	na
Colombia	na	**na**	na	na	na	na	na	na	na	na	na	na	na	na	na	na
Croatia	na	**15**	17	13	18	13	15	14	17	13	16	13	18	6	16	14
Czech Republic	15	**9**	10	8	7	8	10	9	9	5	11	9	8	10	8	7
Denmark	3	**4**	4	5	6	3	5	5	3	4	7	2	3	8	5	3
Dominican Rep.	na	**na**	na	na	na	na	na	na	na	na	na	na	na	na	na	na
Egypt	na	**na**	na	na	na	na	na	na	na	na	na	na	na	na	na	na
El Salvador	na	**na**	na	na	na	na	na	na	na	na	na	na	na	na	na	na
Estonia	11	**14**	13	15	9	14	17	16	14	12	18	13	14	15	14	8
Finland	4	**8**	7	8	9	6	8	8	7	6	8	7	7	9	7	6
France	8	**10**	10	9	8	8	12	10	11	8	12	9	8	12	10	5
Georgia	na	**na**	na	na	na	na	na	na	na	na	na	na	na	na	na	na
Germany	7	**6**	7	5	5	6	7	8	5	5	7	6	7	5	7	5
Great Britain	11	**14**	15	14	8	12	21	18	10	19	14	12	13	na	na	na
Greece	na	**11**	12	10	10	9	12	10	12	10	8	10	12	9	12	8
Hungary	7	**na**	na	na	na	na	na	na	na	na	na	na	na	na	na	na
Iceland	2	**3**	3	2	4	2	3	3	3	1	4	3	1	4	2	2
India	35	**na**	na	na	na	na	na	na	na	na	na	na	na	na	na	na
Indonesia	na	**na**	na	na	na	na	na	na	na	na	na	na	na	na	na	na
Iran	na	**na**	na	na	na	na	na	na	na	na	na	na	na	na	na	na
Ireland	3	**9**	10	8	7	8	13	13	8	5	12	8	6	8	10	6
Israel	na	**na**	na	na	na	na	na	na	na	na	na	na	na	na	na	na
Italy	12	**14**	15	13	13	12	16	16	12	12	18	11	8	18	14	11
Japan	6	**na**	na	na	na	na	na	na	na	na	na	na	na	na	na	na
Jordan	na	**na**	na	na	na	na	na	na	na	na	na	na	na	na	na	na
Korea, South	79	**na**	na	na	na	na	na	na	na	na	na	na	na	na	na	na
Latvia	12	**5**	5	5	3	4	6	3	5	6	5	4	4	7	3	2
Lithuania	17	**12**	11	12	11	9	13	13	11	11	20	7	11	10	11	15
Luxembourg	na	**8**	9	8	8	8	8	8	7	10	11	8	6	6	10	5
Macedonia	na	**na**	na	na	na	na	na	na	na	na	na	na	na	na	na	na
Malta	na	**15**	17	14	14	15	17	14	16	14	15	22	13	17	15	12
Mexico	23	**na**	na	na	na	na	na	na	na	na	na	na	na	na	na	na
Moldova	na	**na**	na	na	na	na	na	na	na	na	na	na	na	na	na	na
Montenegro	na	**na**	na	na	na	na	na	na	na	na	na	na	na	na	na	na
Morocco	na	**na**	na	na	na	na	na	na	na	na	na	na	na	na	na	na
Netherlands	6	**8**	9	7	8	5	11	8	8	8	7	9	7	8	8	6
New Zealand	na	**na**	na	na	na	na	na	na	na	na	na	na	na	na	na	na
Nigeria	33	**na**	na	na	na	na	na	na	na	na	na	na	na	na	na	na
Northern Ireland	9	**14**	15	14	10	16	12	13	15	15	15	13	13	14	13	19
Norway	6	**na**	na	na	na	na	na	na	na	na	na	na	na	na	na	na
Pakistan	na	**na**	na	na	na	na	na	na	na	na	na	na	na	na	na	na
Peru	na	**na**	na	na	na	na	na	na	na	na	na	na	na	na	na	na
Philippines	na	**na**	na	na	na	na	na	na	na	na	na	na	na	na	na	na
Poland	na	**11**	11	11	10	10	13	13	10	8	10	11	13	11	11	18
Portugal	15	**5**	7	3	4	6	5	5	7	1	4	6	6	4	5	12
Puerto Rico	na	**na**	na	na	na	na	na	na	na	na	na	na	na	na	na	na
Romania	22	**14**	12	16	13	14	14	15	14	11	15	15	14	14	14	9
Russian Fed.	12	**6**	6	6	6	6	7	7	6	7	6	7	6	7	6	13
Serbia	na	**na**	na	na	na	na	na	na	na	na	na	na	na	na	na	na
Singapore	na	**na**	na	na	na	na	na	na	na	na	na	na	na	na	na	na
Slovakia	na	**10**	11	10	10	9	12	9	10	15	12	8	10	11	9	6
Slovenia	40	**9**	11	7	5	9	12	13	8	5	15	9	6	11	9	9
South Africa	na	**na**	na	na	na	na	na	na	na	na	na	na	na	na	na	na
Spain	10	**6**	5	7	4	7	6	6	5	8	5	10	6	7	7	2
Sweden	5	**4**	5	3	6	2	5	5	4	3	5	4	3	4	5	2
Switzerland	1	**na**	na	na	na	na	na	na	na	na	na	na	na	na	na	na
Taiwan	na	**na**	na	na	na	na	na	na	na	na	na	na	na	na	na	na
Tanzania	na	**na**	na	na	na	na	na	na	na	na	na	na	na	na	na	na
Turkey	41	**41**	39	42	38	41	48	44	37	34	43	41	34	36	41	43
Uganda	na	**na**	na	na	na	na	na	na	na	na	na	na	na	na	na	na
Ukraine	na	**9**	7	11	13	8	9	8	10	8	8	10	9	8	11	4
United States	8	**na**	na	na	na	na	na	na	na	na	na	na	na	na	na	na
Uruguay	na	**na**	na	na	na	na	na	na	na	na	na	na	na	na	na	na
Venezuela	na	**na**	na	na	na	na	na	na	na	na	na	na	na	na	na	na
Vietnam	na	**na**	na	na	na	na	na	na	na	na	na	na	na	na	na	na
Zimbabwe	na	**na**	na	na	na	na	na	na	na	na	na	na	na	na	na	na
Total	14	**10**	10	9	9	9	11	10	10	9	11	9	9	10	9	8

RANKING	
Country	**2000**
Turkey	41
Malta	15
Croatia	15
Northern Ireland	14
Great Britain	14
Estonia	14
Romania	14
Italy	14
Bulgaria	12
Lithuania	12
Poland	11
Greece	11
Belarus	10
Slovakia	10
France	10
Ireland	9
Ukraine	9
Slovenia	9
Belgium	9
Czech Republic	9
Luxembourg	8
Netherlands	8
Finland	8
Russian Fed.	6
Germany	6
Spain	6
Portugal	5
Latvia	5
Denmark	4
Austria	4
Sweden	4
Iceland	3
Total	10

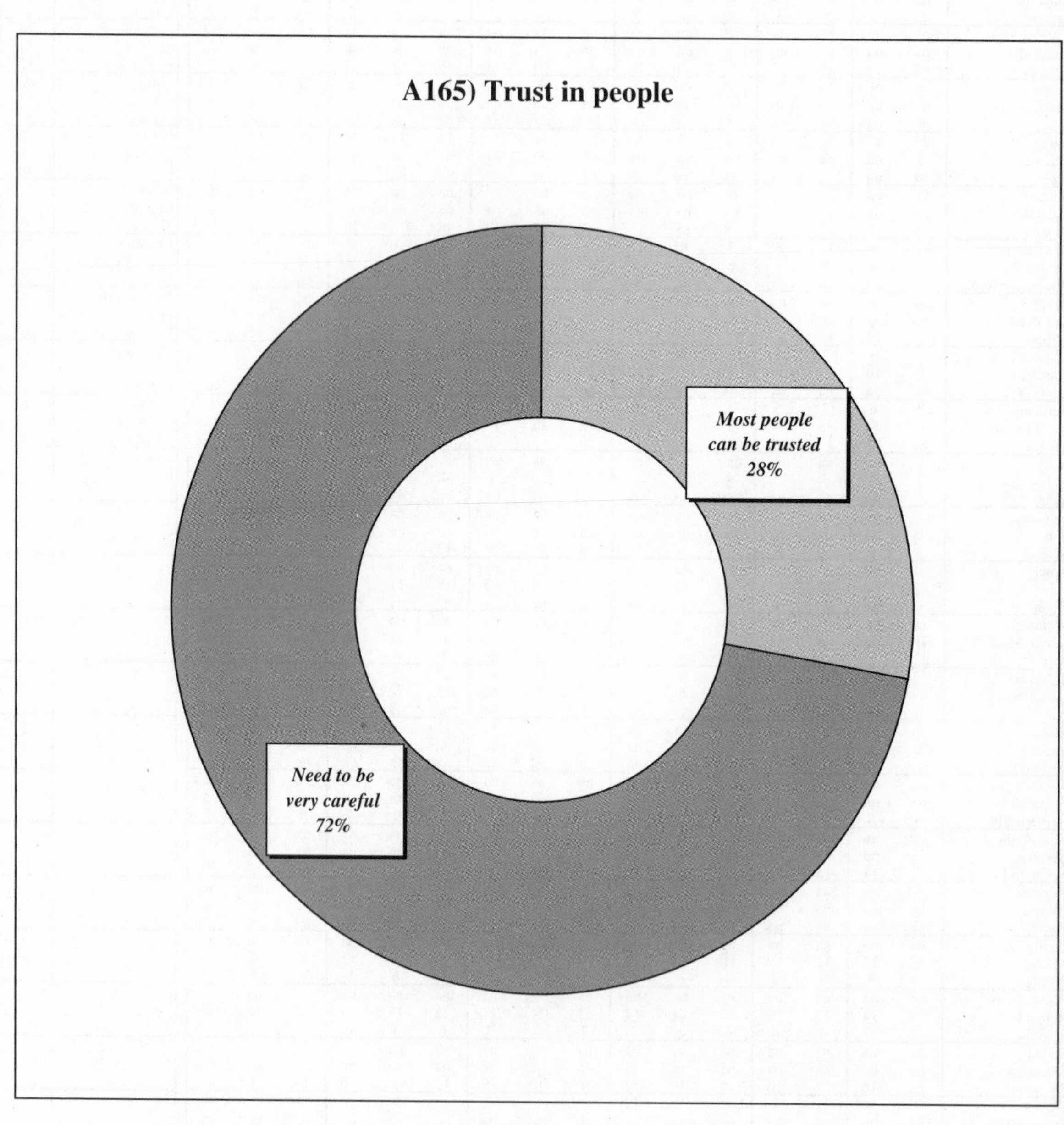
A165) Trust in people
Most people can be trusted 28%
Need to be very careful 72%

A165) MOST PEOPLE CAN BE TRUSTED

Generally speaking, would you say that most people can be trusted or that you need to be very careful in dealing with people?

Most people can be trusted (%)

(WVS: V25; EVS: V66)

Country	Wave		Gender		Age			Education			Income			Values		
	1990	2000	Male	Female	16-29	30-49	50+	Lower	Middle	Upper	Lower	Middle	Upper	Mat	Mixed	Postm.
Albania	na	**24**	24	25	25	25	24	27	23	24	24	27	22	22	24	42
Algeria	na	**11**	11	11	8	12	16	16	10	10	12	10	13	12	11	10
Argentina	23	**15**	16	15	10	18	18	14	17	21	15	14	18	15	15	17
Armenia	na	**25**	24	25	26	26	22	26	24	28	26	24	22	23	26	31
Australia	na	**40**	41	39	32	45	41	31	38	50	35	44	47	28	39	45
Austria	32	**34**	37	31	31	40	30	24	38	58	25	33	44	20	30	44
Azerbaijan	na	**21**	21	20	21	19	24	21	19	24	20	19	24	19	23	33
Bangladesh	na	**24**	24	23	22	23	31	30	17	15	23	26	21	21	25	29
Belarus	26	**42**	41	43	37	43	44	38	43	44	39	43	46	39	44	46
Belgium	33	**31**	34	28	29	34	28	18	27	47	22	28	41	21	31	46
Bosnia and Herz.	na	**16**	16	15	15	15	17	19	15	16	21	13	20	16	16	11
Brazil	7	**3**	3	2	2	4	1	2	3	5	3	2	3	2	3	6
Bulgaria	30	**27**	29	25	27	26	27	23	26	34	25	23	30	24	31	24
Canada	52	**39**	41	37	36	40	39	30	34	54	28	37	51	36	37	43
Chile	23	**23**	22	24	20	22	26	20	24	26	19	24	29	24	22	23
China	60	**55**	53	56	48	56	55	50	57	74	52	56	58	53	55	69
Colombia	na	**11**	13	9	9	12	10	9	8	17	9	9	16	10	11	11
Croatia	na	**18**	21	16	17	23	14	14	19	30	17	16	23	16	18	19
Czech Republic	28	**24**	23	25	21	24	25	20	25	40	22	23	27	16	24	39
Denmark	58	**67**	68	66	68	75	57	56	79	83	58	70	83	58	65	82
Dominican Rep.	na	**26**	25	28	26	26	55	19	17	32	22	31	25	16	29	26
Egypt	na	**38**	37	39	34	37	46	45	34	26	41	41	35	40	38	24
El Salvador	na	**15**	16	14	15	15	13	15	13	15	15	15	15	na	na	na
Estonia	28	**23**	23	22	29	18	24	19	22	33	23	17	29	19	25	27
Finland	63	**58**	56	60	61	55	59	53	63	70	53	56	62	49	60	69
France	23	**22**	22	23	23	24	21	14	27	41	18	20	35	14	20	41
Georgia	na	**19**	17	20	19	18	19	16	19	21	18	17	22	16	21	26
Germany	26	**35**	37	33	44	32	34	28	41	46	31	33	40	35	33	40
Great Britain	44	**30**	31	29	25	32	32	21	31	50	24	36	38	na	na	na
Greece	na	**24**	25	23	20	29	20	13	20	30	19	21	31	21	23	33
Hungary	25	**22**	23	21	24	21	22	16	31	35	19	18	28	19	25	18
Iceland	44	**41**	40	42	33	44	44	32	38	67	35	44	43	34	40	64
India	35	**41**	42	40	40	40	43	45	36	37	41	45	38	46	34	33
Indonesia	na	**51**	53	50	49	51	54	56	49	52	43	56	62	52	50	52
Iran	na	**65**	66	65	63	68	66	65	63	68	66	67	64	64	65	68
Ireland	47	**35**	41	30	30	39	36	33	33	45	25	36	45	28	38	34
Israel	na	**23**	22	25	24	23	22	11	21	36	18	18	33	23	24	19
Italy	34	**33**	34	31	33	36	29	21	37	55	25	33	45	15	31	44
Japan	42	**43**	42	44	45	46	40	30	42	54	36	48	47	45	42	60
Jordan	na	**28**	30	26	27	28	29	28	23	33	28	31	24	28	27	20
Korea, South	34	**27**	27	28	27	27	29	23	26	29	22	32	30	27	28	28
Latvia	19	**17**	17	17	18	18	16	13	17	23	18	14	19	14	19	16
Lithuania	31	**25**	29	21	30	26	20	21	25	33	20	23	28	22	26	24
Luxembourg	na	**26**	27	25	21	28	27	20	28	35	16	29	35	23	25	34
Macedonia	na	**14**	16	11	16	13	12	14	12	18	13	15	15	14	12	24
Malta	na	**21**	21	20	20	20	22	18	20	31	15	21	28	21	20	29
Mexico	34	**21**	23	20	22	20	23	22	18	28	23	22	21	25	19	25
Moldova	na	**15**	15	14	14	13	17	16	14	14	12	17	14	15	16	9
Montenegro	na	**34**	33	34	37	36	30	29	36	39	31	32	34	28	37	61
Morocco	na	**24**	21	26	23	22	29	25	18	23	26	17	25	24	24	23
Netherlands	56	**60**	62	58	67	63	53	38	62	79	50	58	76	43	56	78
New Zealand	na	**48**	49	48	38	51	49	43	41	61	43	50	54	53	48	53
Nigeria	23	**26**	26	25	25	26	28	28	24	24	27	25	24	24	26	35
Northern Ireland	44	**40**	42	37	30	42	44	40	38	43	38	41	42	36	38	54
Norway	65	**65**	64	67	69	74	52	46	65	84	na	na	na	49	66	80
Pakistan	na	**31**	33	29	35	32	21	31	32	27	30	28	38	28	35	55
Peru	na	**11**	11	10	10	12	9	8	9	15	9	10	15	8	11	13
Philippines	na	**8**	9	8	8	9	9	8	9	8	9	7	10	9	8	10
Poland	35	**19**	17	21	17	18	21	16	20	26	16	20	25	17	19	25
Portugal	21	**10**	12	9	9	11	10	9	12	14	7	13	12	10	10	13
Puerto Rico	na	**23**	25	21	15	21	27	13	18	27	15	25	28	24	22	24
Romania	16	**10**	11	10	11	9	10	10	9	13	9	9	12	7	13	13
Russian Fed.	38	**24**	23	24	22	24	25	21	24	25	24	23	25	22	26	25
Serbia	na	**19**	19	19	17	20	18	21	18	18	17	19	22	16	21	25
Singapore	na	**17**	19	14	20	15	10	11	18	29	11	14	23	16	17	23
Slovakia	na	**16**	16	15	16	18	13	12	17	17	11	15	19	13	17	29
Slovenia	17	**22**	23	21	21	23	21	7	23	46	13	24	34	19	22	28
South Africa	28	**12**	13	11	11	12	13	12	12	12	16	7	12	13	10	15
Spain	32	**36**	36	36	38	39	33	33	37	45	33	35	39	33	37	39
Sweden	66	**66**	66	67	67	68	65	53	63	82	63	60	80	57	62	81
Switzerland	43	**41**	40	42	35	40	45	32	41	57	37	39	47	33	39	54
Taiwan	na	**38**	39	38	56	38	29	27	40	48	33	33	48	37	38	47
Tanzania	na	**8**	9	7	6	10	7	9	5	9	11	7	7	9	6	21
Turkey	10	**16**	18	14	15	15	18	15	14	25	16	15	16	16	15	18
Uganda	na	**8**	9	7	9	6	8	7	8	9	9	11	3	7	8	8
Ukraine	na	**27**	29	26	27	28	27	24	27	29	24	31	27	27	26	27
United States	52	**36**	34	38	24	35	47	24	33	42	28	41	40	37	35	40
Uruguay	na	**22**	23	21	20	24	22	19	25	32	21	23	23	25	21	25
Venezuela	na	**16**	18	14	16	16	15	11	16	22	18	16	16	14	17	15
Vietnam	na	**41**	43	40	41	39	46	42	39	48	39	45	40	32	42	42
Zimbabwe	na	**12**	11	13	10	12	17	14	10	na	18	11	6	13	11	12
Total	35	28	29	27	25	29	29	24	27	36	25	27	31	24	28	37

RANKING

Country	2000
Denmark	67
Sweden	66
Iran	65
Norway	65
Netherlands	60
Finland	58
China	55
Indonesia	51
New Zealand	48
Japan	43
Belarus	42
Vietnam	41
Iceland	41
India	41
Switzerland	41
Australia	40
Northern Ireland	40
Canada	39
Taiwan	38
Egypt	38
Spain	36
United States	36
Ireland	35
Germany	35
Austria	34
Montenegro	34
Italy	33
Pakistan	31
Belgium	31
Great Britain	30
Jordan	28
Korea, South	27
Ukraine	27
Bulgaria	27
Dominican Rep.	26
Luxembourg	26
Nigeria	26
Lithuania	25
Armenia	25
Albania	24
Czech Republic	24
Greece	24
Russian Fed.	24
Bangladesh	24
Morocco	24
Israel	23
Chile	23
Estonia	23
Puerto Rico	23
France	22
Uruguay	22
Hungary	22
Slovenia	22
Mexico	21
Malta	21
Azerbaijan	21
Poland	19
Serbia	19
Georgia	19
Croatia	18
Latvia	17
Singapore	17
Venezuela	16
Bosnia and Herz.	16
Slovakia	16
Turkey	16
Argentina	15
Moldova	15
El Salvador	15
Macedonia	14
Zimbabwe	12
South Africa	12
Algeria	11
Colombia	11
Peru	11
Romania	10
Portugal	10
Philippines	8
Tanzania	8
Uganda	8
Brazil	3
Total	28

A168) MOST PEOPLE TRY TO BE FAIR

Do you think most people would try to take advantage of you if they got a chance, or would they try to be fair?

Try to be fair (%)

(WVS: V26)

Country	Wave		Gender		Age			Education			Income			Values		
	1990	2000	Male	Female	16-29	30-49	50+	Lower	Middle	Upper	Lower	Middle	Upper	Mat	Mixed	Postm.
Albania	na	**43**	41	44	41	43	43	44	43	39	48	41	38	43	41	51
Algeria	na	**34**	34	34	33	33	35	32	34	35	32	30	35	33	33	32
Argentina	na	**39**	38	41	39	38	41	35	44	55	38	37	45	37	38	43
Armenia	na	**na**	na	na	na	na	na	na	na	na	na	na	na	na	na	na
Australia	na	**na**	na	na	na	na	na	na	na	na	na	na	na	na	na	na
Austria	na	**na**	na	na	na	na	na	na	na	na	na	na	na	na	na	na
Azerbaijan	na	**na**	na	na	na	na	na	na	na	na	na	na	na	na	na	na
Bangladesh	na	**38**	34	44	38	39	40	48	31	26	56	32	30	48	33	19
Belarus	na	**na**	na	na	na	na	na	na	na	na	na	na	na	na	na	na
Belgium	na	**na**	na	na	na	na	na	na	na	na	na	na	na	na	na	na
Bosnia and Herz.	na	**29**	29	29	27	27	35	33	25	40	33	28	33	25	32	28
Brazil	na	**na**	na	na	na	na	na	na	na	na	na	na	na	na	na	na
Bulgaria	na	**na**	na	na	na	na	na	na	na	na	na	na	na	na	na	na
Canada	na	**67**	64	70	66	68	66	59	65	77	55	67	75	61	66	71
Chile	na	**29**	27	31	32	26	30	27	30	30	25	29	36	29	28	32
China	na	**80**	75	85	79	81	77	78	81	78	77	83	79	80	79	81
Colombia	na	**na**	na	na	na	na	na	na	na	na	na	na	na	na	na	na
Croatia	na	**na**	na	na	na	na	na	na	na	na	na	na	na	na	na	na
Czech Republic	na	**na**	na	na	na	na	na	na	na	na	na	na	na	na	na	na
Denmark	na	**na**	na	na	na	na	na	na	na	na	na	na	na	na	na	na
Dominican Rep.	na	**na**	na	na	na	na	na	na	na	na	na	na	na	na	na	na
Egypt	na	**49**	47	52	48	47	55	53	48	40	52	49	48	48	51	42
El Salvador	na	**na**	na	na	na	na	na	na	na	na	na	na	na	na	na	na
Estonia	na	**na**	na	na	na	na	na	na	na	na	na	na	na	na	na	na
Finland	na	**na**	na	na	na	na	na	na	na	na	na	na	na	na	na	na
France	na	**na**	na	na	na	na	na	na	na	na	na	na	na	na	na	na
Georgia	na	**na**	na	na	na	na	na	na	na	na	na	na	na	na	na	na
Germany	na	**na**	na	na	na	na	na	na	na	na	na	na	na	na	na	na
Great Britain	na	**na**	na	na	na	na	na	na	na	na	na	na	na	na	na	na
Greece	na	**na**	na	na	na	na	na	na	na	na	na	na	na	na	na	na
Hungary	na	**na**	na	na	na	na	na	na	na	na	na	na	na	na	na	na
Iceland	na	**na**	na	na	na	na	na	na	na	na	na	na	na	na	na	na
India	na	**41**	39	43	44	38	41	41	39	42	42	41	39	43	40	41
Indonesia	na	**67**	70	66	64	71	66	72	66	67	75	63	69	67	69	50
Iran	na	**66**	67	65	64	68	66	66	66	68	66	66	66	62	66	72
Ireland	na	**na**	na	na	na	na	na	na	na	na	na	na	na	na	na	na
Israel	na	**na**	na	na	na	na	na	na	na	na	na	na	na	na	na	na
Italy	na	**na**	na	na	na	na	na	na	na	na	na	na	na	na	na	na
Japan	na	**34**	32	36	16	28	46	41	33	30	33	36	34	37	32	32
Jordan	na	**39**	32	45	41	38	35	37	40	42	41	35	41	40	39	28
Korea, South	na	**46**	39	53	41	48	45	52	48	41	44	49	45	42	47	57
Latvia	na	**na**	na	na	na	na	na	na	na	na	na	na	na	na	na	na
Lithuania	na	**na**	na	na	na	na	na	na	na	na	na	na	na	na	na	na
Luxembourg	na	**na**	na	na	na	na	na	na	na	na	na	na	na	na	na	na
Macedonia	na	**31**	29	33	33	32	27	28	28	40	27	31	35	27	33	30
Malta	na	**na**	na	na	na	na	na	na	na	na	na	na	na	na	na	na
Mexico	na	**30**	30	31	31	30	30	29	32	31	29	30	36	33	27	38
Moldova	na	**17**	16	17	15	16	20	19	16	16	16	16	16	14	19	18
Montenegro	na	**45**	45	45	51	45	42	38	47	55	42	44	46	39	49	67
Morocco	na	**28**	25	32	29	28	29	29	26	31	14	27	39	26	30	25
Netherlands	na	**na**	na	na	na	na	na	na	na	na	na	na	na	na	na	na
New Zealand	na	**na**	na	na	na	na	na	na	na	na	na	na	na	na	na	na
Nigeria	na	**29**	28	31	30	28	25	30	29	29	26	28	35	27	29	42
Northern Ireland	na	**na**	na	na	na	na	na	na	na	na	na	na	na	na	na	na
Norway	na	**na**	na	na	na	na	na	na	na	na	na	na	na	na	na	na
Pakistan	na	**34**	36	33	39	35	22	34	36	30	33	32	39	32	37	50
Peru	na	**27**	27	27	25	29	27	26	28	26	27	26	28	32	26	26
Philippines	na	**72**	71	73	73	71	72	75	73	67	70	73	72	68	75	62
Poland	na	**na**	na	na	na	na	na	na	na	na	na	na	na	na	na	na
Portugal	na	**na**	na	na	na	na	na	na	na	na	na	na	na	na	na	na
Puerto Rico	na	**38**	34	40	35	36	40	28	34	41	22	38	51	29	39	40
Romania	na	**na**	na	na	na	na	na	na	na	na	na	na	na	na	na	na
Russian Fed.	na	**na**	na	na	na	na	na	na	na	na	na	na	na	na	na	na
Serbia	na	**48**	43	53	51	52	44	45	46	57	44	47	57	43	51	62
Singapore	na	**49**	50	48	53	46	43	46	49	58	47	49	50	47	50	46
Slovakia	na	**na**	na	na	na	na	na	na	na	na	na	na	na	na	na	na
Slovenia	na	**na**	na	na	na	na	na	na	na	na	na	na	na	na	na	na
South Africa	na	**33**	34	31	33	30	40	34	32	29	31	32	35	34	32	28
Spain	na	**50**	49	50	51	51	47	45	52	60	45	50	48	53	45	61
Sweden	na	**87**	87	88	84	89	88	84	85	94	85	88	90	84	87	89
Switzerland	na	**na**	na	na	na	na	na	na	na	na	na	na	na	na	na	na
Taiwan	na	**na**	na	na	na	na	na	na	na	na	na	na	na	na	na	na
Tanzania	na	**47**	45	50	50	46	45	53	44	34	54	47	37	48	46	70
Turkey	na	**18**	17	19	19	19	17	17	17	28	16	18	25	17	17	23
Uganda	na	**23**	20	26	24	21	26	27	22	14	24	15	21	28	21	21
Ukraine	na	**na**	na	na	na	na	na	na	na	na	na	na	na	na	na	na
United States	na	**62**	61	63	44	64	74	50	59	68	53	62	74	59	60	67
Uruguay	na	**na**	na	na	na	na	na	na	na	na	na	na	na	na	na	na
Venezuela	na	**33**	30	35	37	28	33	32	30	40	29	35	32	29	32	39
Vietnam	na	**72**	70	75	71	75	70	74	71	72	71	74	72	70	74	64
Zimbabwe	na	**33**	33	33	33	33	30	36	29	na	33	34	32	36	31	30
Total	na	**43**	42	45	41	44	46	42	43	47	42	43	46	41	44	48

RANKING	
Country	**2000**
Sweden	87
China	80
Vietnam	72
Philippines	72
Indonesia	67
Canada	67
Iran	66
United States	62
Spain	50
Egypt	49
Singapore	49
Serbia	48
Tanzania	47
Korea, South	46
Montenegro	45
Albania	43
India	41
Argentina	39
Jordan	39
Bangladesh	38
Puerto Rico	38
Pakistan	34
Algeria	34
Japan	34
Zimbabwe	33
South Africa	33
Venezuela	33
Macedonia	31
Mexico	30
Bosnia and Herz.	29
Nigeria	29
Chile	29
Morocco	28
Peru	27
Uganda	23
Turkey	18
Moldova	17
Total	43

A169) GOOD HUMAN RELATIONSHIPS

To build good human relationships, what is most important: to try to understand others' preferences or to express one's own preferences clearly?

Understand other's preferences (%)

(WVS: V38)

Country	Wave		Gender		Age			Education			Income			Values		
	1990	2000	Male	Female	16-29	30-49	50+	Lower	Middle	Upper	Lower	Middle	Upper	Mat	Mixed	Postm.
Albania	na	**51**	51	52	56	51	48	46	52	61	41	56	58	50	52	49
Algeria	na	**54**	54	55	51	53	64	62	53	52	55	57	51	54	53	60
Argentina	na	**57**	54	60	54	57	60	52	67	59	57	53	63	48	57	63
Armenia	na	**63**	61	65	64	63	61	61	62	66	66	65	57	65	63	52
Australia	na	**72**	68	75	69	74	71	64	72	77	71	72	73	70	73	69
Austria	na	**na**	na	na	na	na	na	na	na	na	na	na	na	na	na	na
Azerbaijan	na	**54**	51	57	55	54	51	57	53	56	51	46	66	54	54	49
Bangladesh	na	**54**	55	53	53	56	50	51	56	61	56	54	52	55	54	56
Belarus	na	**na**	na	na	na	na	na	na	na	na	na	na	na	na	na	na
Belgium	na	**na**	na	na	na	na	na	na	na	na	na	na	na	na	na	na
Bosnia and Herz.	na	**82**	82	82	82	81	82	82	81	83	82	81	80	83	83	78
Brazil	na	**44**	45	42	41	44	49	40	47	47	46	43	44	42	44	49
Bulgaria	na	**na**	na	na	na	na	na	na	na	na	na	na	na	na	na	na
Canada	na	**67**	66	67	62	66	70	60	65	74	58	64	75	59	65	70
Chile	na	**55**	53	56	53	54	56	55	51	62	52	56	58	55	57	45
China	na	**73**	71	75	68	75	74	72	74	79	72	71	79	76	71	79
Colombia	na	**na**	na	na	na	na	na	na	na	na	na	na	na	na	na	na
Croatia	na	**na**	na	na	na	na	na	na	na	na	na	na	na	na	na	na
Czech Republic	na	**na**	na	na	na	na	na	na	na	na	na	na	na	na	na	na
Denmark	na	**na**	na	na	na	na	na	na	na	na	na	na	na	na	na	na
Dominican Rep.	na	**72**	70	73	70	75	78	72	68	73	72	76	63	68	72	77
Egypt	na	**76**	77	75	78	76	74	75	77	78	76	74	77	76	76	72
El Salvador	na	**52**	53	51	48	53	55	46	56	61	44	55	60	na	na	na
Estonia	na	**na**	na	na	na	na	na	na	na	na	na	na	na	na	na	na
Finland	na	**na**	na	na	na	na	na	na	na	na	na	na	na	na	na	na
France	na	**na**	na	na	na	na	na	na	na	na	na	na	na	na	na	na
Georgia	na	**54**	53	55	49	56	57	51	53	60	52	56	57	55	54	47
Germany	na	**na**	na	na	na	na	na	na	na	na	na	na	na	na	na	na
Great Britain	na	**na**	na	na	na	na	na	na	na	na	na	na	na	na	na	na
Greece	na	**na**	na	na	na	na	na	na	na	na	na	na	na	na	na	na
Hungary	na	**na**	na	na	na	na	na	na	na	na	na	na	na	na	na	na
Iceland	na	**na**	na	na	na	na	na	na	na	na	na	na	na	na	na	na
India	na	**64**	64	64	64	64	65	66	61	65	67	67	61	69	60	67
Indonesia	na	**79**	79	80	80	84	74	72	83	80	78	82	79	79	80	78
Iran	na	**63**	62	64	61	66	63	63	64	61	62	64	60	61	62	61
Ireland	na	**na**	na	na	na	na	na	na	na	na	na	na	na	na	na	na
Israel	na	**na**	na	na	na	na	na	na	na	na	na	na	na	na	na	na
Italy	na	**na**	na	na	na	na	na	na	na	na	na	na	na	na	na	na
Japan	na	**81**	81	81	78	85	79	72	82	83	80	81	83	86	81	81
Jordan	na	**na**	na	na	na	na	na	na	na	na	na	na	na	na	na	na
Korea, South	na	**79**	81	77	77	80	79	67	80	78	79	79	79	78	80	74
Latvia	na	**na**	na	na	na	na	na	na	na	na	na	na	na	na	na	na
Lithuania	na	**na**	na	na	na	na	na	na	na	na	na	na	na	na	na	na
Luxembourg	na	**na**	na	na	na	na	na	na	na	na	na	na	na	na	na	na
Macedonia	na	**57**	57	57	53	56	62	55	59	55	60	57	55	57	56	68
Malta	na	**na**	na	na	na	na	na	na	na	na	na	na	na	na	na	na
Mexico	na	**46**	48	45	48	44	50	43	48	55	43	45	49	46	47	45
Moldova	na	**59**	59	58	61	56	60	58	56	64	54	59	61	58	60	53
Montenegro	na	**46**	47	46	44	43	51	51	41	49	52	51	42	48	46	34
Morocco	na	**83**	82	85	82	84	89	84	83	73	85	81	80	87	81	75
Netherlands	na	**na**	na	na	na	na	na	na	na	na	na	na	na	na	na	na
New Zealand	na	**81**	80	82	81	81	81	76	82	86	79	83	82	77	84	84
Nigeria	na	**65**	65	64	64	66	65	65	65	65	63	65	65	63	67	60
Northern Ireland	na	**na**	na	na	na	na	na	na	na	na	na	na	na	na	na	na
Norway	na	**83**	83	84	80	86	82	80	84	87	na	na	na	75	85	85
Pakistan	na	**80**	83	77	79	80	83	76	83	88	79	79	84	80	81	78
Peru	na	**61**	61	61	59	63	63	51	61	69	58	62	66	58	62	66
Philippines	na	**55**	56	54	55	53	59	55	52	60	53	57	56	57	54	55
Poland	na	**na**	na	na	na	na	na	na	na	na	na	na	na	na	na	na
Portugal	na	**na**	na	na	na	na	na	na	na	na	na	na	na	na	na	na
Puerto Rico	na	**72**	73	71	62	72	76	70	72	72	76	72	69	73	71	71
Romania	na	**na**	na	na	na	na	na	na	na	na	na	na	na	na	na	na
Russian Fed.	na	**na**	na	na	na	na	na	na	na	na	na	na	na	na	na	na
Serbia	na	**41**	39	43	41	36	45	41	43	38	39	42	43	40	43	33
Singapore	na	**na**	na	na	na	na	na	na	na	na	na	na	na	na	na	na
Slovakia	na	**na**	na	na	na	na	na	na	na	na	na	na	na	na	na	na
Slovenia	na	**na**	na	na	na	na	na	na	na	na	na	na	na	na	na	na
South Africa	na	**65**	65	65	65	66	64	62	68	80	65	65	69	65	65	66
Spain	na	**72**	69	75	70	72	72	71	72	73	72	70	75	73	70	78
Sweden	na	**68**	71	64	64	71	68	66	67	70	62	71	71	61	68	68
Switzerland	na	**na**	na	na	na	na	na	na	na	na	na	na	na	na	na	na
Taiwan	na	**74**	74	74	78	74	69	69	73	78	70	75	76	74	77	62
Tanzania	na	**65**	66	63	61	68	65	63	66	73	66	62	69	65	66	59
Turkey	na	**53**	57	50	54	52	56	52	53	60	54	52	53	54	52	52
Uganda	na	**66**	64	67	66	63	78	65	66	63	62	66	57	68	66	60
Ukraine	na	**na**	na	na	na	na	na	na	na	na	na	na	na	na	na	na
United States	na	**74**	71	76	65	74	81	61	71	80	69	77	76	70	75	74
Uruguay	na	**55**	59	52	54	54	56	50	61	63	50	49	63	53	54	60
Venezuela	na	**39**	42	36	35	42	41	37	40	39	38	35	44	42	39	35
Vietnam	na	**87**	88	86	88	88	84	86	85	96	84	88	87	93	86	69
Zimbabwe	na	**65**	62	67	65	67	62	69	60	27	74	68	58	68	64	57
Total	na	**64**	64	64	62	65	66	61	64	69	62	64	65	63	65	64

RANKING	
Country	**2000**
Vietnam	87
Morocco	83
Norway	83
Bosnia and Herz.	82
Japan	81
New Zealand	81
Pakistan	80
Indonesia	79
Korea, South	79
Egypt	76
United States	74
Taiwan	74
China	73
Dominican Rep.	72
Spain	72
Australia	72
Puerto Rico	72
Sweden	68
Canada	67
Uganda	66
South Africa	65
Zimbabwe	65
Tanzania	65
Nigeria	65
India	64
Armenia	63
Iran	63
Peru	61
Moldova	59
Argentina	57
Macedonia	57
Philippines	55
Uruguay	55
Chile	55
Algeria	54
Bangladesh	54
Georgia	54
Azerbaijan	54
Turkey	53
El Salvador	52
Albania	51
Mexico	46
Montenegro	46
Brazil	44
Serbia	41
Venezuela	39
Total	64

A170) LIFE SATISFACTION

All things considered, how satisfied are you with your life as a whole these days?

% Satisfied (7-10)

(WVS: V81; EVS: V68)

Country	Wave		Gender		Age			Education			Income			Values		
	1990	2000	Male	Female	16-29	30-49	50+	Lower	Middle	Upper	Lower	Middle	Upper	Mat	Mixed	Postm.
Albania	na	**30**	33	26	32	31	26	21	35	39	19	25	46	29	31	39
Algeria	na	**44**	39	49	42	45	44	40	45	45	37	42	55	44	43	47
Argentina	69	**69**	69	69	73	68	66	67	71	77	61	69	77	65	69	71
Armenia	na	**19**	21	18	25	17	15	26	18	21	28	14	10	16	23	16
Australia	na	**77**	76	79	75	78	79	72	79	79	70	78	86	77	77	78
Austria	64	**83**	85	81	87	84	80	79	84	91	76	81	88	73	81	89
Azerbaijan	na	**32**	34	30	39	27	30	34	30	35	22	27	46	33	30	32
Bangladesh	na	**32**	32	34	36	29	36	28	40	33	17	28	55	37	30	35
Belarus	33	**24**	25	24	34	20	22	18	26	27	16	24	40	19	27	53
Belgium	79	**79**	78	79	84	77	78	70	78	86	64	78	88	76	79	80
Bosnia and Herz.	na	**38**	38	38	46	38	30	28	37	52	25	33	61	34	40	36
Brazil	68	**63**	68	57	62	62	67	65	61	61	60	64	64	66	60	66
Bulgaria	25	**36**	39	33	51	40	25	21	40	53	21	35	49	32	40	46
Canada	84	**81**	81	81	82	79	82	79	79	87	71	82	88	78	80	83
Chile	70	**63**	62	64	65	62	63	57	62	79	56	62	76	58	66	64
China	68	**53**	52	55	54	51	58	55	53	51	46	56	61	51	54	63
Colombia	na	**85**	86	84	85	86	82	82	84	91	79	86	90	84	84	83
Croatia	na	**54**	53	55	67	54	45	49	53	69	50	53	57	46	54	57
Czech Republic	50	**67**	67	67	70	68	64	61	71	81	57	66	76	60	68	73
Denmark	86	**86**	87	84	88	88	82	83	90	88	77	89	94	86	86	91
Dominican Rep.	na	**68**	72	65	67	68	70	66	60	71	61	68	84	68	67	66
Egypt	na	**44**	43	44	44	44	43	43	44	45	44	43	43	43	45	40
El Salvador	na	**71**	73	69	76	67	69	65	76	79	63	68	84	na	na	na
Estonia	45	**44**	44	44	54	41	40	39	42	56	31	41	52	36	49	54
Finland	79	**84**	84	85	86	84	84	79	91	90	75	88	92	85	84	88
France	59	**66**	68	64	71	66	63	63	67	71	51	67	77	66	66	65
Georgia	na	**25**	26	24	31	24	20	26	24	26	17	26	35	23	27	27
Germany	59	**79**	78	79	84	78	77	76	81	79	70	81	83	82	78	78
Great Britain	74	**73**	77	69	78	74	71	75	72	76	66	73	80	na	na	na
Greece	na	**61**	62	60	57	64	63	54	58	65	52	60	69	61	61	59
Hungary	44	**37**	37	37	47	35	33	31	45	58	20	29	55	35	41	30
Iceland	85	**87**	86	88	87	91	82	82	88	96	77	90	94	89	87	82
India	53	**28**	31	24	28	28	28	22	33	35	22	21	37	28	32	33
Indonesia	na	**62**	62	62	59	66	59	53	64	68	45	69	84	59	64	71
Iran	na	**52**	48	57	53	53	49	46	52	58	41	48	63	49	54	57
Ireland	80	**85**	87	84	83	87	85	83	87	87	80	87	91	88	84	86
Israel	na	**65**	64	67	75	64	56	53	65	75	48	59	80	69	65	70
Italy	71	**70**	72	67	68	72	68	65	73	75	63	68	79	65	70	72
Japan	53	**53**	52	54	51	50	57	44	52	61	46	51	65	51	54	54
Jordan	na	**37**	33	42	39	37	35	33	33	51	28	37	50	35	39	48
Korea, South	61	**47**	46	49	44	48	49	34	47	49	36	45	61	46	48	48
Latvia	40	**33**	32	34	48	29	30	26	34	40	27	32	43	30	34	36
Lithuania	44	**33**	35	31	52	24	26	25	34	42	23	23	40	30	31	47
Luxembourg	na	**82**	83	81	81	81	84	76	85	86	76	84	89	82	80	90
Macedonia	na	**31**	30	32	38	31	25	19	35	41	16	32	53	29	33	28
Malta	na	**86**	86	86	88	87	84	82	88	86	82	88	89	84	87	88
Mexico	72	**80**	80	79	81	78	81	78	81	86	75	80	82	80	80	78
Moldova	na	**19**	19	19	26	19	14	12	19	26	8	16	29	17	21	27
Montenegro	na	**41**	40	43	43	42	39	32	45	52	24	38	54	32	51	44
Morocco	na	**38**	37	40	38	39	38	36	45	53	22	40	37	42	36	36
Netherlands	85	**90**	91	89	93	92	86	82	94	92	80	93	95	86	90	91
New Zealand	na	**77**	77	77	76	74	80	73	75	82	68	76	85	72	77	82
Nigeria	54	**64**	63	65	68	59	60	57	65	72	54	63	80	65	65	54
Northern Ireland	83	**85**	84	85	87	83	88	83	87	86	77	86	92	85	85	85
Norway	78	**79**	82	76	82	82	73	75	79	83	na	na	na	75	80	79
Pakistan	na	**10**	10	9	12	10	5	5	13	20	2	10	18	8	12	17
Peru	na	**50**	49	51	51	48	54	48	46	56	44	53	57	47	51	54
Philippines	na	**53**	53	54	57	49	57	53	49	61	40	49	72	55	53	50
Poland	57	**51**	51	50	61	48	47	46	56	59	38	54	66	47	51	62
Portugal	63	**62**	64	61	80	64	51	56	74	82	35	59	78	58	65	67
Puerto Rico	na	**85**	87	85	88	83	86	82	82	88	79	88	89	80	85	90
Romania	44	**38**	37	39	45	36	36	34	36	51	36	29	44	35	38	38
Russian Fed.	32	**27**	31	24	42	26	19	20	25	37	20	24	35	25	28	46
Serbia	na	**40**	41	39	50	40	35	30	43	48	30	41	50	34	45	51
Singapore	na	**71**	70	71	71	70	71	66	73	74	60	67	83	71	71	68
Slovakia	na	**47**	47	46	51	48	42	38	49	62	36	42	57	46	49	52
Slovenia	47	**67**	68	67	78	66	60	55	71	77	59	69	78	64	68	69
South Africa	51	**42**	45	38	37	45	46	35	50	62	21	47	66	42	44	31
Spain	66	**65**	65	65	68	66	63	61	69	71	56	69	70	63	66	70
Sweden	84	**80**	81	78	79	80	80	79	78	83	71	83	87	77	79	81
Switzerland	86	**85**	88	82	85	84	86	81	85	92	75	85	91	81	85	85
Taiwan	na	**50**	47	52	52	53	40	41	46	60	36	51	63	52	49	54
Tanzania	na	**21**	19	24	23	19	24	21	20	22	20	22	19	20	22	30
Turkey	48	**39**	33	45	41	36	41	39	36	38	34	39	50	41	38	35
Uganda	na	**36**	30	41	38	32	42	36	35	43	38	36	39	40	33	41
Ukraine	na	**25**	26	23	36	25	17	13	23	34	12	22	44	21	26	36
United States	81	**79**	79	78	79	76	83	74	77	82	72	79	90	75	79	80
Uruguay	na	**63**	62	63	63	60	65	60	64	72	53	65	70	56	65	63
Venezuela	na	**70**	73	68	71	70	69	65	69	78	59	69	77	67	71	71
Vietnam	na	**44**	45	44	41	46	45	40	50	55	29	36	62	46	48	49
Zimbabwe	na	**18**	16	20	22	16	12	16	21	39	15	18	29	19	18	16
Total	62	**56**	56	56	57	55	56	51	55	65	45	54	65	46	58	68

RANKING	
Country	2000
Netherlands	90
Iceland	87
Malta	86
Denmark	86
Ireland	85
Puerto Rico	85
Colombia	85
Switzerland	85
Northern Ireland	85
Finland	84
Austria	83
Luxembourg	82
Canada	81
Sweden	80
Mexico	80
Norway	79
United States	79
Germany	79
Belgium	79
Australia	77
New Zealand	77
Great Britain	73
El Salvador	71
Singapore	71
Venezuela	70
Italy	70
Argentina	69
Dominican Rep.	68
Slovenia	67
Czech Republic	67
France	66
Israel	65
Spain	65
Nigeria	64
Chile	63
Brazil	63
Uruguay	63
Portugal	62
Indonesia	62
Greece	61
Croatia	54
China	53
Philippines	53
Japan	53
Iran	52
Poland	51
Peru	50
Taiwan	50
Korea, South	47
Slovakia	47
Vietnam	44
Estonia	44
Algeria	44
Egypt	44
South Africa	42
Montenegro	41
Serbia	40
Turkey	39
Morocco	38
Bosnia and Herz.	38
Romania	38
Jordan	37
Hungary	37
Uganda	36
Bulgaria	36
Latvia	33
Lithuania	33
Bangladesh	32
Azerbaijan	32
Macedonia	31
Albania	30
India	28
Russian Fed.	27
Georgia	25
Ukraine	25
Belarus	24
Tanzania	21
Armenia	19
Moldova	19
Zimbabwe	18
Pakistan	10
Total	56

A173) FREEDOM FEELING

Some people feel they have completely free choice and control over their lives; while other people feel that what they do, has no real effect on what happens to them.

% Great deal (7-10)

(WVS: V82; EVS: V67)

Country	Wave		Gender		Age			Education			Income			Values		
	1990	2000	Male	Female	16-29	30-49	50+	Lower	Middle	Upper	Lower	Middle	Upper	Mat	Mixed	Postm.
Albania	na	**46**	47	44	50	49	37	42	47	53	41	45	51	45	49	44
Algeria	na	**56**	55	58	50	63	58	53	56	59	49	59	61	53	58	61
Argentina	68	**68**	68	69	72	68	65	67	71	66	64	67	73	59	70	72
Armenia	na	**36**	42	31	43	34	29	34	36	37	43	31	30	33	39	35
Australia	na	**76**	76	76	74	76	78	71	76	80	72	78	80	68	77	76
Austria	57	**70**	72	68	79	64	70	68	71	72	67	67	75	62	70	71
Azerbaijan	na	**41**	48	34	39	38	50	45	38	44	28	37	53	41	38	41
Bangladesh	na	**33**	34	30	30	32	45	31	33	37	28	25	47	42	27	22
Belarus	40	**37**	42	32	48	40	24	19	42	46	28	37	50	32	41	64
Belgium	57	**59**	60	58	66	58	56	46	61	66	49	57	70	55	58	66
Bosnia and Herz.	na	**47**	48	47	54	47	41	42	46	58	41	43	61	44	50	53
Brazil	63	**66**	73	58	69	62	68	65	68	63	66	66	65	68	64	66
Bulgaria	28	**46**	52	41	58	49	39	35	50	57	37	45	57	46	47	49
Canada	77	**77**	75	78	82	76	76	72	76	82	71	77	82	75	75	82
Chile	61	**65**	66	64	64	64	66	60	62	81	57	67	75	59	66	71
China	63	**64**	67	61	61	65	65	67	63	56	61	67	68	61	65	71
Colombia	na	**78**	82	74	79	78	75	72	76	85	69	78	84	80	77	70
Croatia	na	**60**	63	57	61	62	57	57	59	73	56	55	68	55	61	57
Czech Republic	42	**59**	63	56	65	63	54	53	64	74	51	56	69	56	59	71
Denmark	64	**72**	73	71	80	76	63	63	81	85	62	72	90	60	72	83
Dominican Rep.	na	**70**	72	69	71	70	55	53	58	75	69	70	80	65	69	76
Egypt	na	**43**	42	44	44	43	40	40	45	45	40	43	46	43	41	49
El Salvador	na	**70**	76	64	71	66	75	63	75	81	61	70	84	na	na	na
Estonia	50	**43**	42	43	53	43	36	38	41	56	33	37	47	37	47	49
Finland	79	**78**	80	76	85	83	71	70	86	92	70	79	85	76	77	85
France	45	**51**	53	49	51	50	52	50	50	53	44	51	56	50	51	52
Georgia	na	**49**	58	42	53	52	41	46	49	51	41	52	59	47	52	50
Germany	53	**73**	76	71	70	70	77	71	75	69	71	68	77	82	72	67
Great Britain	65	**67**	67	68	71	67	65	67	66	72	66	60	75	na	na	na
Greece	na	**65**	69	62	66	64	65	60	63	67	62	61	69	58	66	69
Hungary	50	**44**	48	41	54	46	37	38	56	57	32	42	54	41	49	43
Iceland	70	**81**	81	81	90	85	67	73	86	89	71	81	92	80	83	77
India	50	**22**	26	16	26	22	17	17	25	29	20	18	27	24	23	21
Indonesia	na	**67**	65	69	66	69	65	65	66	72	52	76	85	66	69	70
Iran	na	**55**	54	55	55	55	52	50	56	58	48	55	59	57	54	57
Ireland	65	**70**	70	69	77	70	63	60	72	81	57	67	82	63	70	76
Israel	na	**na**	na	na	na	na	na	na	na	na	na	na	na	na	na	na
Italy	52	**51**	56	46	68	51	41	36	60	69	41	51	62	41	50	58
Japan	29	**39**	39	39	54	40	32	30	38	48	35	38	41	34	40	47
Jordan	na	**65**	76	55	62	66	70	63	62	72	60	68	75	64	67	70
Korea, South	73	**64**	61	66	73	63	54	43	62	68	58	60	73	59	66	83
Latvia	48	**42**	45	39	52	45	34	30	45	46	38	40	46	41	40	53
Lithuania	55	**50**	50	49	61	50	41	41	51	57	45	48	54	47	48	70
Luxembourg	na	**64**	67	61	68	62	64	59	66	70	64	65	72	68	63	71
Macedonia	na	**42**	40	44	48	42	36	30	44	55	31	43	57	41	43	51
Malta	na	**75**	77	73	78	78	71	72	77	76	68	77	78	72	78	73
Mexico	70	**79**	81	78	79	79	80	77	80	87	76	81	82	79	81	80
Moldova	na	**46**	48	43	49	48	39	40	43	54	34	49	52	42	50	43
Montenegro	na	**45**	51	38	51	48	37	32	49	59	30	45	59	36	54	54
Morocco	na	**46**	51	42	46	46	47	45	54	51	38	49	44	46	48	35
Netherlands	52	**65**	70	60	75	71	53	50	68	75	58	66	75	54	66	69
New Zealand	na	**77**	76	78	81	78	74	73	79	80	67	78	84	77	77	80
Nigeria	57	**67**	68	66	68	66	66	61	69	73	62	64	79	72	65	59
Northern Ireland	75	**74**	77	72	72	75	76	73	79	70	74	75	78	79	76	65
Norway	67	**71**	69	72	79	73	61	62	71	79	na	na	na	60	71	77
Pakistan	na	**11**	13	9	7	12	15	9	14	12	7	11	15	12	10	10
Peru	na	**64**	67	61	63	64	69	65	62	68	61	66	67	61	65	71
Philippines	na	**55**	53	57	56	53	55	49	53	63	46	57	60	51	58	56
Poland	52	**48**	51	45	58	47	42	44	52	52	36	52	64	41	50	66
Portugal	52	**55**	59	50	61	54	52	49	65	70	44	53	62	49	57	70
Puerto Rico	na	**83**	80	85	83	80	84	80	78	85	80	81	85	77	85	83
Romania	49	**58**	61	54	63	61	51	46	61	67	54	56	62	57	57	60
Russian Fed.	47	**38**	45	32	49	39	29	25	36	52	27	37	49	34	41	45
Serbia	na	**44**	49	39	55	43	40	33	47	54	36	44	52	37	50	59
Singapore	na	**69**	68	69	70	67	67	66	69	75	65	64	74	63	70	75
Slovakia	na	**50**	53	48	54	51	45	42	52	65	41	48	58	44	54	64
Slovenia	44	**64**	65	63	75	66	53	48	67	80	52	67	81	55	65	68
South Africa	57	**55**	57	52	51	57	59	49	61	81	41	56	73	53	57	53
Spain	56	**58**	58	58	62	59	55	54	62	64	53	58	61	53	60	61
Sweden	74	**74**	74	74	83	77	66	63	74	82	67	75	83	62	74	77
Switzerland	66	**70**	69	72	79	69	67	68	71	72	64	63	80	70	69	70
Taiwan	na	**68**	68	69	71	70	62	63	71	71	59	68	77	66	74	65
Tanzania	na	**41**	44	37	42	38	47	45	37	35	48	43	32	41	41	42
Turkey	31	**39**	45	34	42	39	33	31	49	57	30	42	54	34	38	52
Uganda	na	**51**	52	49	50	51	56	49	52	45	44	57	48	49	52	49
Ukraine	na	**34**	38	31	47	36	25	17	34	42	24	31	50	30	39	39
United States	77	**82**	83	81	85	80	82	78	79	85	76	84	89	75	82	85
Uruguay	na	**60**	63	58	61	57	62	59	61	70	51	64	67	56	57	70
Venezuela	na	**82**	85	78	85	80	78	75	84	84	74	81	88	75	84	85
Vietnam	na	**66**	71	61	59	70	64	67	65	70	50	64	77	74	67	60
Zimbabwe	na	**44**	45	43	43	45	42	45	41	44	38	47	50	42	46	35
Total	57	**58**	60	56	61	58	55	53	58	66	51	57	65	51	60	67

RANKING	
Country	2000
Puerto Rico	83
United States	82
Venezuela	82
Iceland	81
Mexico	79
Colombia	78
Finland	78
Canada	77
New Zealand	77
Australia	76
Malta	75
Northern Ireland	74
Sweden	74
Germany	73
Denmark	72
Norway	71
Switzerland	70
El Salvador	70
Dominican Rep.	70
Austria	70
Ireland	70
Singapore	69
Argentina	68
Taiwan	68
Great Britain	67
Nigeria	67
Indonesia	67
Brazil	66
Vietnam	66
Jordan	65
Netherlands	65
Greece	65
Chile	65
China	64
Peru	64
Luxembourg	64
Korea, South	64
Slovenia	64
Uruguay	60
Croatia	60
Czech Republic	59
Belgium	59
Spain	58
Romania	58
Algeria	56
South Africa	55
Philippines	55
Portugal	55
Iran	55
France	51
Italy	51
Uganda	51
Slovakia	50
Lithuania	50
Georgia	49
Poland	48
Bosnia and Herz.	47
Bulgaria	46
Morocco	46
Albania	46
Moldova	46
Montenegro	45
Hungary	44
Serbia	44
Zimbabwe	44
Estonia	43
Egypt	43
Macedonia	42
Latvia	42
Tanzania	41
Azerbaijan	41
Turkey	39
Japan	39
Russian Fed.	38
Belarus	37
Armenia	36
Ukraine	34
Bangladesh	33
India	22
Pakistan	11
Total	58

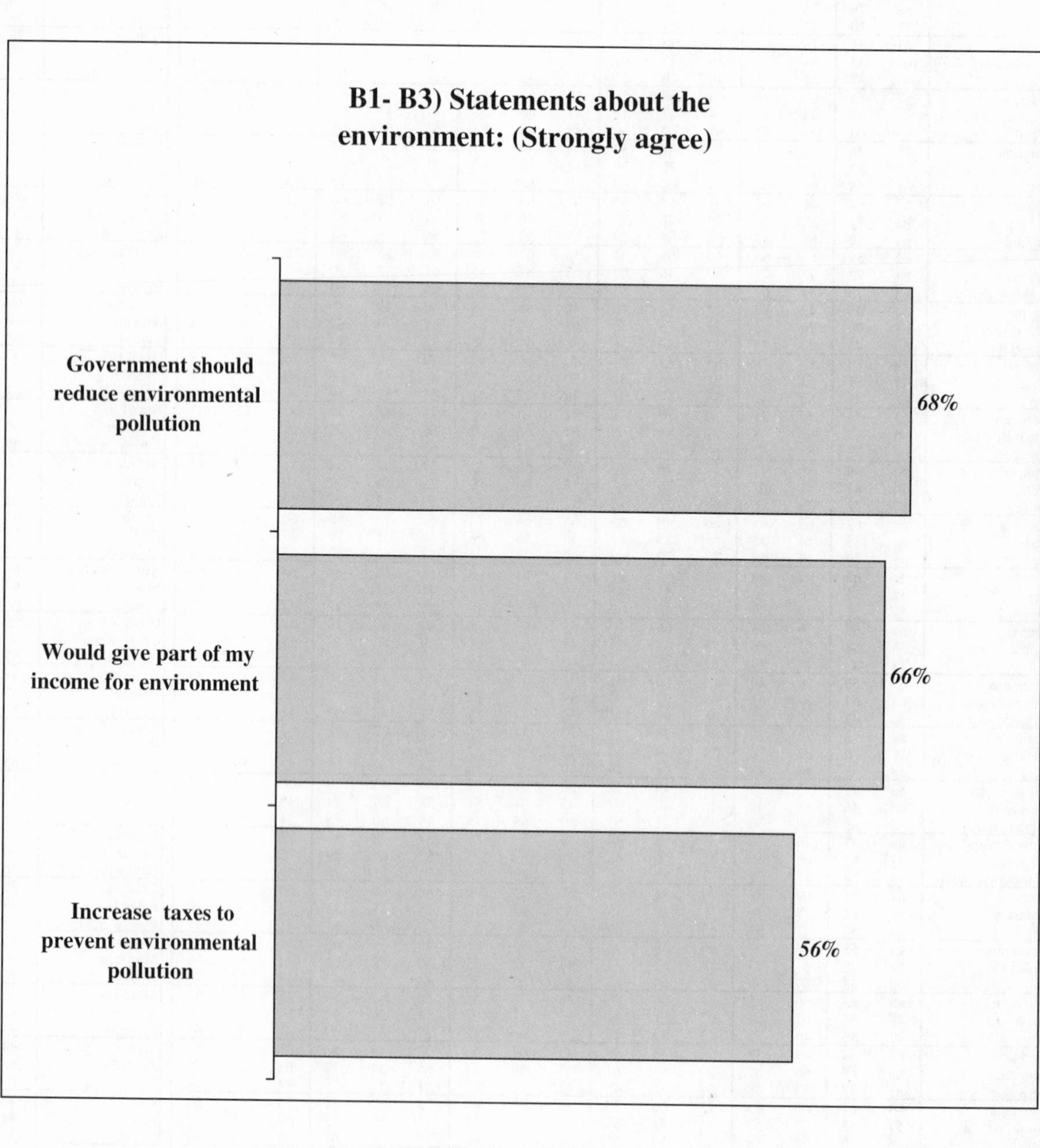

B1- B3) Statements about the environment: (Strongly agree)
Government should reduce environmental pollution
68%
Would give part of my income for environment
66%
Increase taxes to prevent environmental pollution
56%

B001) ENVIRONMENT: INCOME

I would give part of my income if I were certain that the money would be used to prevent environmental pollution

Strongly agree / Agree (%)

(WVS: V33; EVS: V8)

	Wave		Gender		Age			Education			Income			Values		
Country	1990	2000	Male	Female	16-29	30-49	50+	Lower	Middle	Upper	Lower	Middle	Upper	Mat	Mixed	Postm.
Albania	na	**70**	71	69	74	68	69	62	71	85	61	73	78	69	73	59
Algeria	na	**na**	na	na	na	na	na	na	na	na	na	na	na	na	na	na
Argentina	62	**67**	67	68	74	65	64	65	71	70	65	66	71	57	68	74
Armenia	na	**na**	na	na	na	na	na	na	na	na	na	na	na	na	na	na
Australia	na	**na**	na	na	na	na	na	na	na	na	na	na	na	na	na	na
Austria	60	**49**	50	47	52	55	41	41	54	63	38	48	58	32	46	59
Azerbaijan	na	**na**	na	na	na	na	na	na	na	na	na	na	na	na	na	na
Bangladesh	na	**80**	82	77	81	80	73	76	83	84	72	80	85	81	79	70
Belarus	80	**58**	57	58	62	60	51	48	59	70	49	63	61	54	60	71
Belgium	56	**58**	58	58	62	63	52	41	58	71	49	56	68	44	59	73
Bosnia and Herz.	na	**76**	77	74	80	73	75	69	75	84	76	74	79	64	80	89
Brazil	72	**na**	na	na	na	na	na	na	na	na	na	na	na	na	na	na
Bulgaria	83	**58**	56	59	66	69	43	34	65	78	38	61	72	44	69	74
Canada	74	**70**	68	71	79	68	67	62	71	75	66	73	72	64	69	74
Chile	84	**70**	70	70	72	69	69	62	74	75	66	73	73	67	69	77
China	78	**82**	82	82	88	81	80	74	87	88	79	82	85	82	85	90
Colombia	na	**na**	na	na	na	na	na	na	na	na	na	na	na	na	na	na
Croatia	na	**79**	77	81	83	81	74	73	81	88	79	78	78	77	78	84
Czech Republic	79	**78**	74	81	80	79	76	75	80	80	76	78	79	68	80	90
Denmark	84	**79**	75	83	81	81	75	75	78	86	78	80	82	71	78	91
Dominican Rep.	na	**na**	na	na	na	na	na	na	na	na	na	na	na	na	na	na
Egypt	na	**na**	na	na	na	na	na	na	na	na	na	na	na	na	na	na
El Salvador	na	**na**	na	na	na	na	na	na	na	na	na	na	na	na	na	na
Estonia	77	**48**	44	51	50	49	46	40	49	57	41	43	57	42	53	51
Finland	67	**53**	50	57	52	56	50	49	59	62	54	55	57	49	54	56
France	61	**46**	48	45	51	46	44	41	47	59	50	43	52	40	45	60
Georgia	na	**na**	na	na	na	na	na	na	na	na	na	na	na	na	na	na
Germany	63	**33**	33	33	40	34	29	22	39	61	24	30	42	22	35	46
Great Britain	68	**49**	46	51	53	46	49	40	53	64	46	46	55	na	na	na
Greece	na	**82**	78	86	84	82	79	81	78	86	82	83	81	78	84	82
Hungary	60	**51**	55	49	57	57	43	43	61	82	38	50	62	47	56	47
Iceland	78	**64**	55	72	62	62	67	66	59	67	65	61	65	62	63	70
India	81	**67**	69	63	70	69	60	57	70	79	60	62	74	62	73	81
Indonesia	na	**na**	na	na	na	na	na	na	na	na	na	na	na	na	na	na
Iran	na	**na**	na	na	na	na	na	na	na	na	na	na	na	na	na	na
Ireland	69	**55**	59	51	59	58	48	40	58	74	39	55	71	48	54	63
Israel	na	**na**	na	na	na	na	na	na	na	na	na	na	na	na	na	na
Italy	68	**65**	63	67	67	68	61	61	67	70	61	67	72	53	66	69
Japan	68	**70**	74	67	62	66	77	75	68	74	67	67	76	70	70	78
Jordan	na	**na**	na	na	na	na	na	na	na	na	na	na	na	na	na	na
Korea, South	84	**84**	83	84	83	85	81	62	84	86	83	86	83	79	87	90
Latvia	78	**71**	72	69	75	74	66	62	72	77	67	69	77	65	73	81
Lithuania	75	**27**	30	24	31	30	21	16	29	38	15	27	34	17	28	46
Luxembourg	na	**64**	65	63	65	63	64	56	67	70	56	65	71	69	61	71
Macedonia	na	**79**	80	78	79	82	75	70	83	83	74	78	86	79	78	89
Malta	na	**61**	60	61	68	60	56	44	64	82	47	61	73	51	65	68
Mexico	81	**78**	78	78	82	77	75	73	83	86	73	82	85	70	83	88
Moldova	na	**68**	69	67	70	74	58	55	70	75	68	68	68	63	72	72
Montenegro	na	**61**	63	58	67	63	54	48	64	80	64	58	68	57	64	74
Morocco	na	**na**	na	na	na	na	na	na	na	na	na	na	na	na	na	na
Netherlands	83	**75**	74	75	78	78	69	65	79	79	68	76	82	58	73	88
New Zealand	na	**na**	na	na	na	na	na	na	na	na	na	na	na	na	na	na
Nigeria	78	**na**	na	na	na	na	na	na	na	na	na	na	na	na	na	na
Northern Ireland	75	**46**	46	45	44	50	44	42	44	56	42	40	60	44	43	59
Norway	80	**na**	na	na	na	na	na	na	na	na	na	na	na	na	na	na
Pakistan	na	**na**	na	na	na	na	na	na	na	na	na	na	na	na	na	na
Peru	na	**81**	82	80	82	82	76	79	82	80	80	83	80	77	82	84
Philippines	na	**73**	74	72	80	68	72	67	73	79	69	75	73	68	76	71
Poland	na	**63**	67	59	70	65	55	57	67	78	49	72	69	57	64	75
Portugal	84	**57**	56	58	63	66	46	51	69	73	36	58	59	49	60	84
Puerto Rico	na	**82**	80	83	83	82	81	89	80	82	79	78	87	72	83	83
Romania	na	**52**	54	51	66	53	42	39	53	68	45	49	59	48	55	60
Russian Fed.	78	**63**	63	64	72	66	55	44	64	72	55	66	70	60	68	62
Serbia	na	**81**	81	80	81	81	80	68	83	93	74	82	87	75	84	94
Singapore	na	**60**	62	58	74	49	38	51	63	70	49	62	66	47	63	70
Slovakia	na	**57**	56	57	61	59	50	45	60	71	48	56	65	51	61	64
Slovenia	89	**82**	83	81	80	83	83	80	82	84	81	87	85	80	83	85
South Africa	na	**55**	54	57	54	58	51	55	54	70	55	54	54	50	57	68
Spain	72	**59**	59	58	65	61	52	52	64	69	51	61	64	54	59	71
Sweden	82	**79**	77	81	83	78	78	79	79	79	79	78	79	72	78	84
Switzerland	na	**na**	na	na	na	na	na	na	na	na	na	na	na	na	na	na
Taiwan	na	**na**	na	na	na	na	na	na	na	na	na	na	na	na	na	na
Tanzania	na	**84**	85	84	83	84	89	83	87	86	82	85	89	83	86	88
Turkey	87	**77**	74	79	80	74	73	73	81	81	72	76	85	79	76	79
Uganda	na	**46**	59	34	46	44	52	42	46	58	52	60	57	37	48	60
Ukraine	na	**62**	61	64	68	68	53	39	63	71	57	65	67	56	68	65
United States	74	**69**	69	70	67	68	74	69	67	71	69	71	68	67	69	72
Uruguay	na	**na**	na	na	na	na	na	na	na	na	na	na	na	na	na	na
Venezuela	na	**na**	na	na	na	na	na	na	na	na	na	na	na	na	na	na
Vietnam	na	**96**	96	97	98	95	97	95	97	97	95	99	94	97	96	98
Zimbabwe	na	**69**	71	67	71	70	60	64	75	62	65	66	79	63	72	71
Total	75	**66**	66	65	70	67	61	58	67	75	62	67	71	60	68	74

RANKING	
Country	**2000**
Vietnam	96
Tanzania	84
Korea, South	84
Greece	82
China	82
Slovenia	82
Puerto Rico	82
Peru	81
Serbia	81
Bangladesh	80
Croatia	79
Denmark	79
Sweden	79
Macedonia	79
Mexico	78
Czech Republic	78
Turkey	77
Bosnia and Herz.	76
Netherlands	75
Philippines	73
Latvia	71
Japan	70
Albania	70
Chile	70
Canada	70
United States	69
Zimbabwe	69
Moldova	68
Argentina	67
India	67
Italy	65
Luxembourg	64
Iceland	64
Russian Fed.	63
Poland	63
Ukraine	62
Malta	61
Montenegro	61
Singapore	60
Spain	59
Belgium	58
Belarus	58
Bulgaria	58
Portugal	57
Slovakia	57
South Africa	55
Ireland	55
Finland	53
Romania	52
Hungary	51
Great Britain	49
Austria	49
Estonia	48
France	46
Uganda	46
Northern Ireland	46
Germany	33
Lithuania	27
Total	66

B002) ENVIRONMENT: TAXES

I would agree to an increase in taxes if the extra money were used to prevent environmental pollution

Strongly agree / Agree (%)

(WVS: V34; EVS: V9)

	Wave		Gender		Age			Education			Income			Values		
Country	1990	2000	Male	Female	16-29	30-49	50+	Lower	Middle	Upper	Lower	Middle	Upper	Mat	Mixed	Postm.
Albania	na	**63**	65	61	68	63	57	53	65	79	55	63	71	60	65	64
Algeria	na	**na**	na	na	na	na	na	na	na	na	na	na	na	na	na	na
Argentina	50	**41**	42	41	44	42	38	40	43	46	36	42	46	34	43	45
Armenia	na	**57**	58	56	64	54	50	58	56	59	65	51	50	56	58	68
Australia	na	**69**	67	72	72	70	66	62	69	75	66	70	72	62	67	75
Austria	52	**39**	41	37	39	44	33	31	44	52	33	40	44	25	37	48
Azerbaijan	na	**55**	54	56	66	49	48	48	50	65	52	51	68	51	61	68
Bangladesh	na	**76**	79	71	76	76	73	72	79	81	74	78	74	77	75	70
Belarus	67	**46**	45	47	51	48	41	33	50	51	38	52	46	43	49	58
Belgium	41	**44**	45	42	40	47	41	31	42	56	35	46	51	31	43	60
Bosnia and Herz.	na	**70**	70	71	74	66	73	62	70	80	69	71	71	62	73	75
Brazil	71	**73**	71	75	75	71	73	76	74	59	77	76	68	75	74	65
Bulgaria	70	**45**	44	45	53	55	31	25	52	58	28	49	56	34	53	61
Canada	64	**58**	55	61	65	56	56	55	56	64	57	61	61	61	55	66
Chile	76	**62**	62	63	62	64	60	57	65	68	57	67	66	58	62	72
China	82	**74**	74	75	74	75	74	68	78	76	72	79	70	75	76	87
Colombia	na	**67**	68	67	76	66	54	59	69	71	60	68	71	62	65	76
Croatia	na	**55**	53	56	55	54	55	50	55	67	49	55	58	52	53	61
Czech Republic	67	**65**	61	69	64	69	62	61	69	73	64	64	70	57	67	75
Denmark	70	**65**	62	69	62	67	65	61	62	76	64	66	70	55	64	76
Dominican Rep.	na	**86**	83	88	88	83	82	78	87	88	83	86	93	82	86	88
Egypt	na	**na**	na	na	na	na	na	na	na	na	na	na	na	na	na	na
El Salvador	na	**84**	88	81	89	83	77	79	89	91	80	85	93	na	na	na
Estonia	59	**33**	33	34	30	34	35	27	32	48	26	30	43	28	38	35
Finland	56	**50**	47	53	51	53	46	43	59	62	48	52	55	44	53	53
France	54	**37**	37	36	41	37	34	33	33	49	35	37	43	30	36	50
Georgia	na	**69**	68	70	72	69	65	59	69	76	66	72	72	67	71	73
Germany	65	**29**	28	29	36	32	23	19	35	46	21	25	39	18	30	42
Great Britain	70	**50**	46	54	51	49	50	43	53	65	47	55	52	na	na	na
Greece	na	**65**	65	64	63	66	65	66	61	68	59	69	67	60	65	69
Hungary	35	**33**	35	32	43	34	27	30	39	38	27	31	39	31	36	48
Iceland	60	**57**	55	59	50	58	62	55	53	71	56	57	60	46	60	62
India	66	**53**	55	49	53	55	49	47	55	61	55	49	56	45	60	66
Indonesia	na	**na**	na	na	na	na	na	na	na	na	na	na	na	na	na	na
Iran	na	**na**	na	na	na	na	na	na	na	na	na	na	na	na	na	na
Ireland	51	**39**	45	33	35	43	38	33	38	51	32	38	50	34	38	50
Israel	na	**na**	na	na	na	na	na	na	na	na	na	na	na	na	na	na
Italy	54	**44**	44	43	39	47	44	40	43	55	39	45	50	37	43	48
Japan	51	**62**	66	58	50	60	69	66	58	71	59	58	73	63	62	71
Jordan	na	**na**	na	na	na	na	na	na	na	na	na	na	na	na	na	na
Korea, South	76	**57**	59	55	53	57	61	42	56	60	50	59	62	50	63	59
Latvia	64	**45**	44	47	49	43	46	46	46	42	46	43	47	42	48	50
Lithuania	66	**20**	21	19	23	21	16	11	20	34	12	19	27	13	23	27
Luxembourg	na	**56**	57	55	54	56	58	50	58	62	50	59	68	59	52	69
Macedonia	na	**64**	64	65	64	68	60	61	66	65	62	63	70	64	64	72
Malta	na	**48**	48	48	50	47	47	34	52	61	38	50	58	42	51	52
Mexico	67	**57**	55	59	59	56	55	54	60	62	50	63	63	50	61	67
Moldova	na	**38**	42	35	41	41	32	28	39	47	35	39	41	30	45	45
Montenegro	na	**61**	62	60	68	63	54	46	66	80	60	57	72	57	64	75
Morocco	na	**na**	na	na	na	na	na	na	na	na	na	na	na	na	na	na
Netherlands	69	**55**	57	53	53	59	52	46	52	67	48	59	63	36	52	74
New Zealand	na	**53**	53	53	50	52	56	47	52	62	55	54	51	47	53	62
Nigeria	59	**na**	na	na	na	na	na	na	na	na	na	na	na	na	na	na
Northern Ireland	65	**44**	45	43	36	49	45	42	43	51	45	43	57	40	41	59
Norway	73	**75**	72	79	82	73	73	71	73	83	na	na	na	70	75	87
Pakistan	na	**na**	na	na	na	na	na	na	na	na	na	na	na	na	na	na
Peru	na	**56**	57	56	55	59	54	54	58	56	52	61	56	49	57	65
Philippines	na	**64**	63	66	71	62	60	56	67	69	61	63	68	62	66	66
Poland	na	**51**	55	48	58	54	44	45	58	62	39	57	64	47	52	66
Portugal	65	**43**	43	43	47	46	37	39	52	44	37	45	42	36	45	55
Puerto Rico	na	**71**	73	70	76	70	71	69	70	73	69	71	73	67	72	73
Romania	na	**46**	47	46	57	49	37	33	46	66	37	42	56	42	49	58
Russian Fed.	66	**54**	51	57	60	56	48	39	54	61	47	56	59	50	59	54
Serbia	na	**74**	74	74	73	76	72	62	77	85	63	77	82	67	79	90
Singapore	na	**45**	46	44	56	35	33	43	46	44	40	47	47	34	49	47
Slovakia	na	**40**	38	41	43	40	37	33	40	55	36	39	43	34	43	50
Slovenia	69	**62**	63	60	64	65	57	65	58	68	63	61	69	59	61	68
South Africa	na	**45**	42	48	41	49	43	45	45	46	46	41	46	40	45	68
Spain	60	**49**	48	50	55	52	43	42	54	61	39	51	58	45	50	56
Sweden	77	**77**	75	80	83	76	76	77	78	77	77	76	80	66	77	84
Switzerland	na	**43**	40	46	52	38	43	31	43	62	47	39	45	26	41	57
Taiwan	na	**86**	85	87	85	88	81	83	84	89	81	86	90	85	87	89
Tanzania	na	**75**	75	74	72	76	79	73	76	77	72	77	80	74	76	75
Turkey	72	**56**	54	58	58	53	55	52	59	64	49	56	67	51	55	63
Uganda	na	**44**	55	35	45	43	47	39	45	57	45	61	56	37	47	56
Ukraine	na	**50**	47	52	51	52	46	29	50	58	44	51	56	44	57	42
United States	64	**61**	60	62	57	58	68	61	58	62	62	62	59	54	61	64
Uruguay	na	**58**	56	60	62	59	56	55	62	64	51	57	69	44	61	66
Venezuela	na	**na**	na	na	na	na	na	na	na	na	na	na	na	na	na	na
Vietnam	na	**91**	92	89	91	91	89	90	91	91	88	89	93	90	92	88
Zimbabwe	na	**45**	44	46	51	43	34	42	50	22	41	46	52	37	50	52
Total	63	56	56	56	59	57	52	50	56	66	53	57	60	50	57	64

RANKING	
Country	**2000**
Vietnam	91
Dominican Rep.	86
Taiwan	86
El Salvador	84
Sweden	77
Bangladesh	76
Norway	75
Tanzania	75
China	74
Serbia	74
Brazil	73
Puerto Rico	71
Bosnia and Herz.	70
Australia	69
Georgia	69
Colombia	67
Czech Republic	65
Denmark	65
Greece	65
Macedonia	64
Philippines	64
Albania	63
Chile	62
Japan	62
Slovenia	62
United States	61
Montenegro	61
Uruguay	58
Canada	58
Iceland	57
Mexico	57
Armenia	57
Korea, South	57
Peru	56
Luxembourg	56
Turkey	56
Azerbaijan	55
Netherlands	55
Croatia	55
Russian Fed.	54
New Zealand	53
India	53
Poland	51
Finland	50
Great Britain	50
Ukraine	50
Spain	49
Malta	48
Romania	46
Belarus	46
Latvia	45
Zimbabwe	45
Singapore	45
South Africa	45
Bulgaria	45
Uganda	44
Northern Ireland	44
Belgium	44
Italy	44
Switzerland	43
Portugal	43
Argentina	41
Slovakia	40
Ireland	39
Austria	39
Moldova	38
France	37
Estonia	33
Hungary	33
Germany	29
Lithuania	20
Total	56

B003) ENVIRONMENT: NO COST

Government should reduce environmental pollution, but it should not cost me any money

Strongly agree / Agree (%)

(WVS: V35; EVS: V10)

Country	Wave		Gender		Age			Education			Income			Values		
	1990	2000	Male	Female	16-29	30-49	50+	Lower	Middle	Upper	Lower	Middle	Upper	Mat	Mixed	Postm.
Albania	na	**63**	63	63	57	64	67	71	61	46	67	68	54	68	56	71
Algeria	na	**na**	na	na	na	na	na	na	na	na	na	na	na	na	na	na
Argentina	72	**86**	87	86	84	87	87	91	84	69	91	90	78	90	86	83
Armenia	na	**na**	na	na	na	na	na	na	na	na	na	na	na	na	na	na
Australia	na	**na**	na	na	na	na	na	na	na	na	na	na	na	na	na	na
Austria	61	**63**	62	65	56	56	75	73	56	48	74	62	59	73	66	55
Azerbaijan	na	**na**	na	na	na	na	na	na	na	na	na	na	na	na	na	na
Bangladesh	na	**96**	96	97	96	97	97	97	96	95	98	96	96	98	95	99
Belarus	72	**75**	73	77	65	74	85	86	73	66	79	74	71	78	76	46
Belgium	62	**63**	61	64	57	58	69	80	63	48	75	65	49	74	63	49
Bosnia and Herz.	na	**63**	62	64	63	65	60	67	65	52	62	67	53	67	59	67
Brazil	65	**na**	na	na	na	na	na	na	na	na	na	na	na	na	na	na
Bulgaria	74	**83**	83	83	80	77	89	93	82	68	92	77	79	91	76	50
Canada	52	**63**	62	64	59	61	67	72	65	51	67	63	55	68	67	53
Chile	58	**74**	73	75	71	73	77	81	72	64	84	66	67	76	77	59
China	46	**36**	35	37	21	39	42	42	32	26	41	33	34	34	35	29
Colombia	na	**na**	na	na	na	na	na	na	na	na	na	na	na	na	na	na
Croatia	na	**82**	85	80	80	84	82	90	81	69	81	85	80	87	81	83
Czech Republic	46	**55**	57	54	50	53	60	66	46	35	65	56	45	73	52	35
Denmark	29	**30**	31	29	29	23	38	33	32	21	34	28	22	45	32	13
Dominican Rep.	na	**na**	na	na	na	na	na	na	na	na	na	na	na	na	na	na
Egypt	na	**na**	na	na	na	na	na	na	na	na	na	na	na	na	na	na
El Salvador	na	**na**	na	na	na	na	na	na	na	na	na	na	na	na	na	na
Estonia	72	**88**	87	89	80	89	91	88	89	84	92	90	82	89	87	82
Finland	51	**64**	65	63	59	60	70	70	60	43	63	70	57	72	64	50
France	74	**84**	83	85	80	83	87	90	77	74	88	84	75	91	84	73
Georgia	na	**na**	na	na	na	na	na	na	na	na	na	na	na	na	na	na
Germany	48	**68**	68	68	65	63	74	75	64	50	78	70	62	85	64	53
Great Britain	56	**77**	78	76	79	76	77	88	71	57	84	77	64	na	na	na
Greece	na	**71**	72	70	67	72	76	78	75	65	76	69	63	77	69	68
Hungary	75	**86**	86	86	84	86	87	88	83	81	84	87	85	87	85	77
Iceland	28	**32**	35	29	32	32	33	40	31	20	37	33	28	45	30	23
India	52	**55**	53	58	56	54	57	54	58	54	58	55	54	61	52	29
Indonesia	na	**na**	na	na	na	na	na	na	na	na	na	na	na	na	na	na
Iran	na	**na**	na	na	na	na	na	na	na	na	na	na	na	na	na	na
Ireland	60	**70**	65	74	64	69	74	76	72	51	80	71	58	70	71	62
Israel	na	**na**	na	na	na	na	na	na	na	na	na	na	na	na	na	na
Italy	80	**81**	79	84	75	82	84	88	78	71	86	79	76	90	83	73
Japan	56	**56**	52	59	59	56	54	60	62	39	63	59	45	59	54	49
Jordan	na	**na**	na	na	na	na	na	na	na	na	na	na	na	na	na	na
Korea, South	50	**67**	63	71	66	68	65	80	69	62	70	69	61	71	63	57
Latvia	71	**87**	86	88	75	87	92	87	87	86	88	91	81	89	86	82
Lithuania	69	**89**	89	88	86	90	89	89	90	84	90	92	88	90	89	86
Luxembourg	na	**61**	61	61	67	60	58	72	56	51	76	53	43	67	61	49
Macedonia	na	**83**	82	84	80	83	84	85	83	78	85	82	81	84	82	79
Malta	na	**66**	66	65	61	66	69	79	64	40	74	64	51	72	63	53
Mexico	40	**73**	73	73	71	74	75	79	69	58	77	74	65	75	73	66
Moldova	na	**68**	69	68	61	69	74	78	68	61	69	70	64	76	62	50
Montenegro	na	**78**	77	78	75	77	80	83	76	70	72	78	75	77	79	73
Morocco	na	**na**	na	na	na	na	na	na	na	na	na	na	na	na	na	na
Netherlands	17	**23**	21	25	17	18	32	37	22	12	32	21	15	45	24	11
New Zealand	na	**na**	na	na	na	na	na	na	na	na	na	na	na	na	na	na
Nigeria	61	**na**	na	na	na	na	na	na	na	na	na	na	na	na	na	na
Northern Ireland	63	**71**	68	74	72	69	73	75	72	57	71	75	64	77	73	54
Norway	44	**na**	na	na	na	na	na	na	na	na	na	na	na	na	na	na
Pakistan	na	**na**	na	na	na	na	na	na	na	na	na	na	na	na	na	na
Peru	na	**72**	73	71	69	73	76	75	72	69	74	71	69	81	70	68
Philippines	na	**72**	73	71	71	71	76	77	72	68	75	72	69	73	72	69
Poland	na	**72**	71	74	73	68	77	78	71	54	80	68	66	76	74	49
Portugal	92	**75**	74	76	78	69	79	77	70	75	77	73	70	80	74	63
Puerto Rico	na	**66**	63	67	64	68	65	79	66	63	66	70	62	71	66	65
Romania	na	**76**	75	77	76	76	77	81	79	64	78	83	72	83	74	58
Russian Fed.	49	**80**	79	80	72	79	85	90	81	72	83	81	74	83	77	60
Serbia	na	**55**	54	56	59	53	56	64	55	43	61	56	43	60	51	44
Singapore	na	**73**	72	75	63	81	85	79	71	66	81	71	70	84	69	73
Slovakia	na	**79**	78	80	76	77	84	84	78	65	84	79	76	83	76	69
Slovenia	56	**63**	65	61	54	62	71	79	62	37	71	60	46	74	61	58
South Africa	na	**76**	76	76	74	76	81	79	75	47	74	80	78	81	73	70
Spain	76	**88**	88	89	87	87	90	92	86	81	91	91	83	90	90	80
Sweden	36	**43**	46	40	29	45	49	55	43	32	42	49	39	50	45	33
Switzerland	na	**na**	na	na	na	na	na	na	na	na	na	na	na	na	na	na
Taiwan	na	**na**	na	na	na	na	na	na	na	na	na	na	na	na	na	na
Tanzania	na	**66**	68	65	60	70	66	69	62	66	70	64	70	63	67	50
Turkey	56	**75**	75	76	75	74	77	77	76	59	78	78	67	80	75	71
Uganda	na	**60**	47	72	60	62	55	66	59	44	60	44	46	65	59	51
Ukraine	na	**81**	80	81	74	77	88	92	81	73	83	80	77	85	78	81
United States	53	**57**	56	58	58	61	50	63	67	49	59	57	53	73	57	51
Uruguay	na	**na**	na	na	na	na	na	na	na	na	na	na	na	na	na	na
Venezuela	na	**na**	na	na	na	na	na	na	na	na	na	na	na	na	na	na
Vietnam	na	**38**	34	42	37	36	41	38	38	29	48	42	27	49	35	37
Zimbabwe	na	**71**	69	73	67	73	78	77	64	48	71	73	67	77	66	69
Total	58	**68**	67	69	66	67	72	75	68	58	72	68	62	76	66	57

RANKING

Country	2000
Bangladesh	96
Lithuania	89
Spain	88
Estonia	88
Latvia	87
Argentina	86
Hungary	86
France	84
Bulgaria	83
Macedonia	83
Croatia	82
Italy	81
Ukraine	81
Russian Fed.	80
Slovakia	79
Montenegro	78
Great Britain	77
Romania	76
South Africa	76
Belarus	75
Portugal	75
Turkey	75
Chile	74
Singapore	73
Mexico	73
Poland	72
Philippines	72
Peru	72
Zimbabwe	71
Northern Ireland	71
Greece	71
Ireland	70
Moldova	68
Germany	68
Korea, South	67
Tanzania	66
Malta	66
Puerto Rico	66
Finland	64
Austria	63
Slovenia	63
Albania	63
Bosnia and Herz.	63
Canada	63
Belgium	63
Luxembourg	61
Uganda	60
United States	57
Japan	56
Czech Republic	55
India	55
Serbia	55
Sweden	43
Vietnam	38
China	36
Iceland	32
Denmark	30
Netherlands	23
Total	68

B008) ENVIRONMENTAL PROTECTION VS. ECONOMIC GROWTH

Which statement comes closer to your own point of view: protecting the environment should be given priority or economic growth and creating jobs?

Protecting the environment (%)

(WVS: V36)

Country	Wave		Gender		Age			Education			Income			Values		
	1990	2000	Male	Female	16-29	30-49	50+	Lower	Middle	Upper	Lower	Middle	Upper	Mat	Mixed	Postm.
Albania	na	**48**	50	45	54	46	45	39	49	65	41	47	55	41	54	50
Algeria	na	**34**	32	35	31	38	33	29	36	34	38	32	34	28	35	44
Argentina	na	**45**	46	44	49	47	39	41	51	51	44	43	50	37	45	50
Armenia	na	**44**	41	47	50	42	37	38	44	45	54	36	40	38	47	64
Australia	na	**63**	65	60	68	67	51	54	62	70	53	67	67	52	60	69
Austria	na	**na**	na	na	na	na	na	na	na	na	na	na	na	na	na	na
Azerbaijan	na	**50**	49	51	56	46	48	50	48	55	45	48	62	52	48	52
Bangladesh	na	**55**	55	55	54	53	70	59	50	51	45	53	66	60	52	47
Belarus	na	**na**	na	na	na	na	na	na	na	na	na	na	na	na	na	na
Belgium	na	**na**	na	na	na	na	na	na	na	na	na	na	na	na	na	na
Bosnia and Herz.	na	**42**	43	42	45	42	39	32	43	48	35	42	49	47	41	40
Brazil	na	**49**	52	46	53	48	43	47	51	50	47	52	50	51	47	55
Bulgaria	na	**na**	na	na	na	na	na	na	na	na	na	na	na	na	na	na
Canada	na	**64**	66	62	67	66	59	53	65	70	56	64	71	61	62	68
Chile	na	**50**	52	49	55	48	49	47	49	61	50	48	54	46	51	56
China	na	**61**	63	59	62	62	56	53	65	63	58	61	67	61	62	63
Colombia	na	**na**	na	na	na	na	na	na	na	na	na	na	na	na	na	na
Croatia	na	**na**	na	na	na	na	na	na	na	na	na	na	na	na	na	na
Czech Republic	na	**na**	na	na	na	na	na	na	na	na	na	na	na	na	na	na
Denmark	na	**na**	na	na	na	na	na	na	na	na	na	na	na	na	na	na
Dominican Rep.	na	**72**	67	75	70	73	90	73	74	71	80	69	64	69	71	77
Egypt	na	**52**	51	52	53	52	48	50	55	49	54	48	50	48	54	60
El Salvador	na	**85**	85	84	86	85	82	80	89	91	81	85	90	na	na	na
Estonia	na	**na**	na	na	na	na	na	na	na	na	na	na	na	na	na	na
Finland	na	**na**	na	na	na	na	na	na	na	na	na	na	na	na	na	na
France	na	**na**	na	na	na	na	na	na	na	na	na	na	na	na	na	na
Georgia	na	**64**	63	65	63	67	61	61	64	67	64	64	65	64	65	65
Germany	na	**na**	na	na	na	na	na	na	na	na	na	na	na	na	na	na
Great Britain	na	**na**	na	na	na	na	na	na	na	na	na	na	na	na	na	na
Greece	na	**na**	na	na	na	na	na	na	na	na	na	na	na	na	na	na
Hungary	na	**na**	na	na	na	na	na	na	na	na	na	na	na	na	na	na
Iceland	na	**na**	na	na	na	na	na	na	na	na	na	na	na	na	na	na
India	na	**48**	50	45	49	49	44	42	49	55	45	44	52	45	51	52
Indonesia	na	**35**	36	35	33	38	33	33	36	36	34	39	33	31	37	39
Iran	na	**46**	48	43	42	48	52	51	43	42	47	42	46	40	48	39
Ireland	na	**na**	na	na	na	na	na	na	na	na	na	na	na	na	na	na
Israel	na	**32**	33	31	37	32	25	26	32	34	30	27	33	32	30	51
Italy	na	**na**	na	na	na	na	na	na	na	na	na	na	na	na	na	na
Japan	na	**49**	51	47	48	47	51	47	48	53	44	49	57	44	50	61
Jordan	na	**54**	42	65	53	56	50	53	51	59	55	50	56	55	52	54
Korea, South	na	**53**	52	53	48	57	47	51	49	57	53	48	55	49	55	57
Latvia	na	**na**	na	na	na	na	na	na	na	na	na	na	na	na	na	na
Lithuania	na	**na**	na	na	na	na	na	na	na	na	na	na	na	na	na	na
Luxembourg	na	**na**	na	na	na	na	na	na	na	na	na	na	na	na	na	na
Macedonia	na	**48**	50	46	50	48	46	45	50	48	50	44	49	48	48	48
Malta	na	**na**	na	na	na	na	na	na	na	na	na	na	na	na	na	na
Mexico	na	**55**	54	56	59	53	54	53	55	64	58	58	52	53	55	54
Moldova	na	**58**	60	56	54	60	59	61	56	58	64	58	55	53	62	60
Montenegro	na	**35**	40	31	36	36	35	29	37	46	43	38	34	31	39	62
Morocco	na	**55**	51	60	54	54	63	57	49	44	47	46	60	53	57	52
Netherlands	na	**na**	na	na	na	na	na	na	na	na	na	na	na	na	na	na
New Zealand	na	**49**	49	49	60	62	36	34	44	70	39	51	59	43	47	67
Nigeria	na	**46**	46	47	46	46	51	50	45	42	48	45	47	45	46	50
Northern Ireland	na	**na**	na	na	na	na	na	na	na	na	na	na	na	na	na	na
Norway	na	**63**	63	63	66	66	57	56	64	68	na	na	na	54	62	79
Pakistan	na	**7**	8	7	8	8	4	1	11	22	na	4	23	2	14	70
Peru	na	**61**	63	59	63	61	56	56	59	67	57	63	65	53	64	60
Philippines	na	**63**	63	63	68	59	64	56	62	73	61	63	65	66	61	62
Poland	na	**na**	na	na	na	na	na	na	na	na	na	na	na	na	na	na
Portugal	na	**na**	na	na	na	na	na	na	na	na	na	na	na	na	na	na
Puerto Rico	na	**65**	70	63	67	68	62	46	67	67	63	67	67	59	64	72
Romania	na	**na**	na	na	na	na	na	na	na	na	na	na	na	na	na	na
Russian Fed.	na	**na**	na	na	na	na	na	na	na	na	na	na	na	na	na	na
Serbia	na	**45**	43	47	40	44	48	42	45	48	41	45	52	42	47	58
Singapore	na	**35**	36	34	43	28	27	32	37	38	31	36	39	22	39	42
Slovakia	na	**na**	na	na	na	na	na	na	na	na	na	na	na	na	na	na
Slovenia	na	**na**	na	na	na	na	na	na	na	na	na	na	na	na	na	na
South Africa	na	**36**	37	36	32	40	36	36	38	25	38	33	36	36	35	46
Spain	na	**54**	51	57	61	55	48	48	61	61	46	53	65	48	54	63
Sweden	na	**73**	70	76	76	74	70	68	74	75	72	73	75	59	71	83
Switzerland	na	**47**	45	49	50	48	44	38	49	51	47	46	50	33	46	58
Taiwan	na	**64**	60	68	74	63	61	59	61	70	60	66	68	63	64	78
Tanzania	na	**62**	60	64	60	63	60	65	59	61	61	64	62	64	61	61
Turkey	na	**67**	63	71	67	67	67	67	66	69	67	66	67	61	68	69
Uganda	na	**39**	42	35	35	38	58	39	37	48	42	31	40	37	38	48
Ukraine	na	**na**	na	na	na	na	na	na	na	na	na	na	na	na	na	na
United States	na	**61**	62	60	56	63	63	53	60	65	59	64	62	50	61	66
Uruguay	na	**61**	57	65	62	64	59	57	67	65	55	63	64	61	59	66
Venezuela	na	**70**	72	68	69	71	71	71	68	74	70	70	70	68	72	66
Vietnam	na	**61**	63	59	60	59	65	62	61	61	60	58	65	56	63	49
Zimbabwe	na	**34**	33	36	38	32	30	30	40	62	28	33	45	29	38	42
Total	na	**52**	52	53	53	53	50	48	52	59	51	52	55	46	52	61

RANKING	
Country	**2000**
El Salvador	85
Sweden	73
Dominican Rep.	72
Venezuela	70
Turkey	67
Puerto Rico	65
Taiwan	64
Georgia	64
Canada	64
Philippines	63
Norway	63
Australia	63
Tanzania	62
Uruguay	61
Vietnam	61
United States	61
Peru	61
China	61
Moldova	58
Morocco	55
Mexico	55
Bangladesh	55
Jordan	54
Spain	54
Korea, South	53
Egypt	52
Azerbaijan	50
Chile	50
Japan	49
New Zealand	49
Brazil	49
India	48
Macedonia	48
Albania	48
Switzerland	47
Nigeria	46
Iran	46
Argentina	45
Serbia	45
Armenia	44
Bosnia and Herz.	42
Uganda	39
South Africa	36
Indonesia	35
Montenegro	35
Singapore	35
Zimbabwe	34
Algeria	34
Israel	32
Pakistan	7
Total	52

B009) HUMAN & NATURE

Which statement comes closest to your own views: human beings should master nature or humans should coexist with nature?

Coexist with nature (%)

(WVS: V37)

Country	Wave		Gender		Age			Education			Income			Values		
	1990	2000	Male	Female	16-29	30-49	50+	Lower	Middle	Upper	Lower	Middle	Upper	Mat	Mixed	Postm.
Albania	na	**66**	64	68	64	66	67	64	67	67	68	66	64	68	65	63
Algeria	na	**na**	na	na	na	na	na	na	na	na	na	na	na	na	na	na
Argentina	na	**92**	91	92	92	92	91	89	96	94	90	90	96	85	92	95
Armenia	na	**78**	78	78	75	81	76	78	76	84	83	73	73	74	80	86
Australia	na	**93**	93	93	92	93	93	91	94	94	92	93	95	94	92	94
Austria	na	**na**	na	na	na	na	na	na	na	na	na	na	na	na	na	na
Azerbaijan	na	**66**	63	70	65	66	71	69	63	71	58	66	73	68	64	57
Bangladesh	na	**85**	83	86	86	83	88	85	85	82	87	81	86	87	83	84
Belarus	na	**na**	na	na	na	na	na	na	na	na	na	na	na	na	na	na
Belgium	na	**na**	na	na	na	na	na	na	na	na	na	na	na	na	na	na
Bosnia and Herz.	na	**85**	84	86	88	83	85	84	84	89	85	84	85	85	85	91
Brazil	na	**95**	96	94	97	95	91	92	98	98	93	95	97	92	96	96
Bulgaria	na	**na**	na	na	na	na	na	na	na	na	na	na	na	na	na	na
Canada	na	**92**	91	93	93	93	92	90	93	94	90	92	95	92	91	94
Chile	na	**92**	91	93	91	92	92	92	91	92	92	93	89	90	92	94
China	na	**68**	63	73	81	68	50	64	69	71	69	62	72	65	71	65
Colombia	na	**na**	na	na	na	na	na	na	na	na	na	na	na	na	na	na
Croatia	na	**na**	na	na	na	na	na	na	na	na	na	na	na	na	na	na
Czech Republic	na	**na**	na	na	na	na	na	na	na	na	na	na	na	na	na	na
Denmark	na	**na**	na	na	na	na	na	na	na	na	na	na	na	na	na	na
Dominican Rep.	na	**94**	95	93	96	90	100	91	91	95	93	94	93	88	94	98
Egypt	na	**na**	na	na	na	na	na	na	na	na	na	na	na	na	na	na
El Salvador	na	**84**	86	83	89	80	83	80	87	95	79	86	88	na	na	na
Estonia	na	**na**	na	na	na	na	na	na	na	na	na	na	na	na	na	na
Finland	na	**na**	na	na	na	na	na	na	na	na	na	na	na	na	na	na
France	na	**na**	na	na	na	na	na	na	na	na	na	na	na	na	na	na
Georgia	na	**85**	83	87	84	87	84	83	84	89	84	87	85	86	85	81
Germany	na	**na**	na	na	na	na	na	na	na	na	na	na	na	na	na	na
Great Britain	na	**na**	na	na	na	na	na	na	na	na	na	na	na	na	na	na
Greece	na	**na**	na	na	na	na	na	na	na	na	na	na	na	na	na	na
Hungary	na	**na**	na	na	na	na	na	na	na	na	na	na	na	na	na	na
Iceland	na	**na**	na	na	na	na	na	na	na	na	na	na	na	na	na	na
India	na	**83**	82	85	83	82	86	82	83	85	78	84	85	84	82	89
Indonesia	na	**na**	na	na	na	na	na	na	na	na	na	na	na	na	na	na
Iran	na	**na**	na	na	na	na	na	na	na	na	na	na	na	na	na	na
Ireland	na	**na**	na	na	na	na	na	na	na	na	na	na	na	na	na	na
Israel	na	**na**	na	na	na	na	na	na	na	na	na	na	na	na	na	na
Italy	na	**na**	na	na	na	na	na	na	na	na	na	na	na	na	na	na
Japan	na	**99**	98	99	98	100	98	99	99	97	98	100	98	98	99	99
Jordan	na	**57**	61	53	61	55	52	57	59	54	57	60	54	51	62	56
Korea, South	na	**95**	95	96	97	95	94	87	95	98	93	96	97	94	96	99
Latvia	na	**na**	na	na	na	na	na	na	na	na	na	na	na	na	na	na
Lithuania	na	**na**	na	na	na	na	na	na	na	na	na	na	na	na	na	na
Luxembourg	na	**na**	na	na	na	na	na	na	na	na	na	na	na	na	na	na
Macedonia	na	**88**	86	90	83	90	91	85	89	92	87	89	89	90	87	94
Malta	na	**na**	na	na	na	na	na	na	na	na	na	na	na	na	na	na
Mexico	na	**87**	85	88	88	88	83	86	87	89	82	86	90	89	84	91
Moldova	na	**71**	74	69	74	74	66	66	68	81	66	71	71	70	72	76
Montenegro	na	**88**	86	90	84	90	88	88	88	88	91	89	83	87	89	85
Morocco	na	**na**	na	na	na	na	na	na	na	na	na	na	na	na	na	na
Netherlands	na	**na**	na	na	na	na	na	na	na	na	na	na	na	na	na	na
New Zealand	na	**89**	89	90	92	91	87	85	92	94	85	92	93	80	91	95
Nigeria	na	**na**	na	na	na	na	na	na	na	na	na	na	na	na	na	na
Northern Ireland	na	**na**	na	na	na	na	na	na	na	na	na	na	na	na	na	na
Norway	na	**93**	93	94	91	95	94	92	93	95	na	na	na	92	93	96
Pakistan	na	**na**	na	na	na	na	na	na	na	na	na	na	na	na	na	na
Peru	na	**90**	90	90	91	88	91	90	89	91	89	89	92	87	90	92
Philippines	na	**50**	49	50	49	49	54	57	47	45	52	47	52	49	51	43
Poland	na	**na**	na	na	na	na	na	na	na	na	na	na	na	na	na	na
Portugal	na	**na**	na	na	na	na	na	na	na	na	na	na	na	na	na	na
Puerto Rico	na	**94**	93	94	95	94	93	92	94	94	96	93	93	94	94	93
Romania	na	**na**	na	na	na	na	na	na	na	na	na	na	na	na	na	na
Russian Fed.	na	**na**	na	na	na	na	na	na	na	na	na	na	na	na	na	na
Serbia	na	**94**	93	94	92	96	92	90	94	97	93	92	95	91	95	97
Singapore	na	**na**	na	na	na	na	na	na	na	na	na	na	na	na	na	na
Slovakia	na	**na**	na	na	na	na	na	na	na	na	na	na	na	na	na	na
Slovenia	na	**na**	na	na	na	na	na	na	na	na	na	na	na	na	na	na
South Africa	na	**62**	61	64	62	62	67	58	70	52	55	66	68	62	65	49
Spain	na	**92**	92	93	92	92	93	92	94	90	95	93	88	92	91	96
Sweden	na	**95**	94	97	96	95	95	94	95	96	94	96	96	96	95	95
Switzerland	na	**na**	na	na	na	na	na	na	na	na	na	na	na	na	na	na
Taiwan	na	**90**	90	89	96	90	84	86	92	91	88	92	90	90	89	86
Tanzania	na	**53**	51	56	56	52	51	47	59	65	49	52	58	54	53	42
Turkey	na	**na**	na	na	na	na	na	na	na	na	na	na	na	na	na	na
Uganda	na	**74**	82	68	74	74	76	71	75	79	70	78	73	77	73	72
Ukraine	na	**na**	na	na	na	na	na	na	na	na	na	na	na	na	na	na
United States	na	**85**	85	86	82	86	88	81	84	88	85	86	85	81	85	89
Uruguay	na	**90**	89	90	93	88	89	87	93	89	88	91	91	82	91	94
Venezuela	na	**na**	na	na	na	na	na	na	na	na	na	na	na	na	na	na
Vietnam	na	**53**	50	56	59	51	50	55	49	62	54	54	50	62	50	42
Zimbabwe	na	**61**	61	61	60	61	63	61	61	100	58	61	63	58	63	65
Total	na	**82**	81	83	81	81	83	78	82	87	80	81	83	78	82	88

RANKING	
Country	**2000**
Japan	99
Korea, South	95
Sweden	95
Brazil	95
Dominican Rep.	94
Puerto Rico	94
Serbia	94
Norway	93
Australia	93
Canada	92
Spain	92
Chile	92
Argentina	92
Uruguay	90
Taiwan	90
Peru	90
New Zealand	89
Macedonia	88
Montenegro	88
Mexico	87
United States	85
Georgia	85
Bosnia and Herz.	85
Bangladesh	85
El Salvador	84
India	83
Armenia	78
Uganda	74
Moldova	71
China	68
Azerbaijan	66
Albania	66
South Africa	62
Zimbabwe	61
Jordan	57
Tanzania	53
Vietnam	53
Philippines	50
Total	82

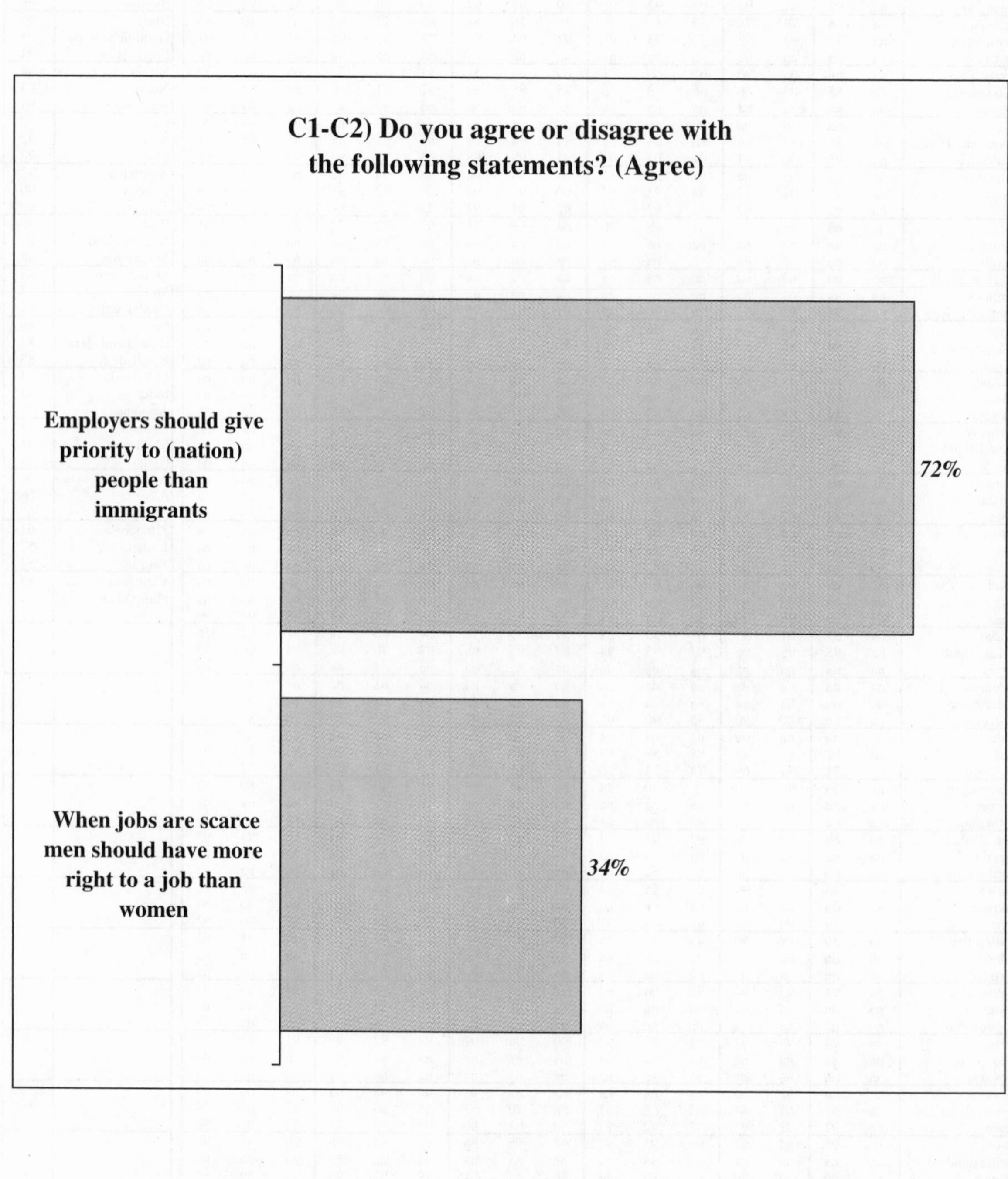
C1-C2) Do you agree or disagree with the following statements? (Agree)
Employers should give priority to (nation) people than immigrants
72%
When jobs are scarce men should have more right to a job than women
34%

C001) MEN MORE RIGHT TO A JOB

Do you agree or disagree with the following statements?

"When jobs are scarce, men should have more right to a job than women."

(WVS: V78; EVS: V99)

Agree (%)

Country	Wave 1990	Wave 2000	Gender Male	Gender Female	Age 16-29	Age 30-49	Age 50+	Education Lower	Education Middle	Education Upper	Income Lower	Income Middle	Income Upper	Values Mat	Values Mixed	Values Postm.
Albania	na	**47**	55	38	34	48	56	56	44	30	51	46	43	48	47	31
Algeria	na	**68**	80	54	69	65	69	76	67	62	68	64	67	71	66	64
Argentina	24	**26**	30	22	22	22	33	34	17	8	35	28	14	35	26	16
Armenia	na	**60**	71	50	54	64	63	63	61	54	54	61	69	68	56	38
Australia	na	**26**	27	24	12	20	44	35	27	16	35	24	16	37	27	20
Austria	50	**27**	28	26	16	22	37	35	21	14	37	28	19	35	29	18
Azerbaijan	na	**64**	70	57	66	63	61	67	64	63	67	63	63	65	62	64
Bangladesh	na	**68**	76	58	61	72	76	72	64	63	82	61	65	71	67	57
Belarus	38	**25**	31	20	21	23	31	33	24	15	26	24	25	27	23	17
Belgium	38	**25**	22	28	10	21	36	46	25	10	41	27	14	37	24	13
Bosnia and Herz.	na	**27**	31	23	23	25	32	33	27	18	34	27	20	31	24	25
Brazil	38	**36**	41	31	30	38	44	50	27	16	49	30	25	48	32	22
Bulgaria	46	**39**	45	33	33	37	44	47	40	24	48	33	34	42	36	43
Canada	19	**15**	14	15	8	11	22	28	11	9	23	14	7	25	16	9
Chile	37	**25**	31	20	22	24	30	32	23	17	29	24	22	28	24	26
China	41	**45**	47	43	27	50	48	51	43	23	45	48	42	45	43	40
Colombia	na	**29**	30	28	28	28	36	46	31	15	44	32	18	41	34	34
Croatia	na	**29**	32	27	13	34	34	38	27	11	52	28	18	27	33	16
Czech Republic	55	**18**	17	20	14	14	25	24	14	8	25	17	14	25	17	9
Denmark	11	**6**	7	5	4	2	11	9	1	2	12	5	na	14	6	1
Dominican Rep.	na	**15**	22	10	13	19	20	29	23	11	23	14	6	17	15	14
Egypt	na	**90**	93	86	86	91	92	92	87	89	90	89	91	92	88	82
El Salvador	na	**27**	28	26	26	27	29	36	23	8	44	22	12	na	na	na
Estonia	45	**14**	18	10	14	12	15	16	13	11	19	13	12	13	13	14
Finland	15	**10**	13	7	5	9	13	14	5	4	8	13	8	14	9	4
France	33	**22**	21	22	13	18	30	30	12	9	26	23	18	31	22	8
Georgia	na	**65**	74	56	64	63	67	63	67	57	67	66	60	66	63	63
Germany	31	**27**	33	22	17	22	37	38	18	17	36	30	19	35	28	13
Great Britain	34	**23**	25	21	14	17	34	35	16	8	25	21	17	na	na	na
Greece	na	**20**	28	14	13	21	35	44	25	12	27	18	19	22	21	13
Hungary	42	**25**	25	25	18	25	28	32	11	11	26	27	22	27	21	13
Iceland	6	**4**	4	3	4	3	4	6	2	1	5	2	4	7	3	1
India	49	**57**	61	52	53	59	58	62	59	46	68	61	49	65	50	41
Indonesia	na	**52**	61	43	53	52	52	62	52	47	54	49	57	54	50	57
Iran	na	**73**	80	65	69	75	80	80	69	68	76	74	68	81	70	62
Ireland	36	**15**	14	16	4	12	28	29	9	6	28	14	7	22	16	7
Israel	na	**na**	na	na	na	na	na	na	na	na	na	na	na	na	na	na
Italy	43	**27**	27	27	13	20	41	42	18	9	40	26	15	43	28	17
Japan	34	**32**	33	31	20	25	43	56	30	24	37	32	28	37	31	21
Jordan	na	**80**	87	74	78	82	84	85	82	70	84	81	77	87	78	66
Korea, South	42	**39**	44	33	14	42	60	62	43	30	41	37	38	45	35	19
Latvia	34	**20**	20	19	18	16	24	27	19	15	22	16	16	19	21	11
Lithuania	66	**24**	30	20	22	19	32	33	23	15	30	27	24	27	23	16
Luxembourg	na	**26**	30	22	18	22	36	37	23	16	34	31	17	34	28	14
Macedonia	na	**43**	46	40	40	43	45	55	41	26	51	42	33	44	40	42
Malta	na	**47**	49	46	28	46	62	68	44	14	60	53	30	52	47	30
Mexico	23	**34**	37	31	29	34	40	43	25	15	42	32	23	40	31	26
Moldova	na	**45**	46	44	43	38	55	55	46	35	56	43	37	45	42	42
Montenegro	na	**30**	43	16	22	26	39	40	26	15	35	22	28	31	28	22
Morocco	na	**83**	88	78	81	83	88	86	76	55	90	84	79	85	82	74
Netherlands	22	**12**	11	13	4	8	21	26	10	3	19	9	6	28	13	4
New Zealand	na	**13**	12	13	2	9	20	17	12	8	17	10	10	14	13	8
Nigeria	48	**60**	73	47	60	60	60	61	61	58	64	59	58	57	61	68
Northern Ireland	34	**16**	17	15	7	11	25	22	10	12	17	16	7	18	16	11
Norway	16	**14**	15	14	8	11	24	22	15	7	na	na	na	24	14	5
Pakistan	na	**67**	71	63	65	65	80	74	64	50	74	69	56	70	65	64
Peru	na	**15**	18	13	13	17	17	21	16	9	20	10	13	19	14	13
Philippines	na	**69**	72	66	61	72	75	75	71	58	74	68	66	70	69	63
Poland	55	**35**	36	34	17	32	48	47	21	18	37	34	33	41	32	28
Portugal	34	**30**	32	28	15	29	39	35	20	13	42	37	20	34	27	30
Puerto Rico	na	**21**	22	20	17	17	25	30	26	16	28	20	14	28	21	14
Romania	42	**38**	38	38	34	32	45	58	31	17	57	42	20	45	33	15
Russian Fed.	40	**36**	43	31	37	36	36	40	39	27	36	39	34	37	35	38
Serbia	na	**31**	37	27	22	29	37	46	29	15	39	29	27	37	28	17
Singapore	na	**30**	33	27	21	37	43	41	27	15	41	31	23	37	29	18
Slovakia	na	**24**	29	20	17	22	32	33	21	12	29	25	20	29	22	14
Slovenia	29	**18**	18	18	8	16	27	34	14	5	25	18	8	28	16	15
South Africa	45	**32**	43	18	30	32	38	39	23	17	38	28	27	28	34	35
Spain	31	**19**	19	19	10	14	29	27	13	9	29	17	14	28	17	8
Sweden	8	**2**	3	2	1	1	4	4	3	1	4	2	1	3	3	na
Switzerland	na	**27**	29	26	17	22	41	43	25	15	34	32	17	37	30	14
Taiwan	na	**57**	56	58	41	57	67	70	57	45	64	67	44	62	53	53
Tanzania	na	**27**	33	20	28	24	34	30	25	21	36	22	25	28	26	41
Turkey	51	**60**	67	54	55	62	67	71	50	34	72	56	41	69	60	47
Uganda	na	**41**	58	25	42	39	42	47	36	59	51	50	29	35	44	42
Ukraine	na	**31**	35	27	25	30	34	43	33	19	33	30	30	35	25	35
United States	24	**10**	11	9	7	8	14	12	10	9	12	11	6	11	12	5
Uruguay	na	**28**	33	24	27	17	37	37	15	14	37	30	16	44	28	14
Venezuela	na	**31**	36	27	30	30	36	38	33	18	38	30	29	39	31	22
Vietnam	na	**48**	54	43	45	49	50	53	45	32	56	42	51	54	48	43
Zimbabwe	na	**40**	51	31	42	35	46	43	36	30	49	41	27	42	39	42
Total	35	34	39	30	32	34	38	44	32	24	42	34	29	44	32	21

RANKING

Country	2000
Egypt	90
Morocco	83
Jordan	80
Iran	73
Philippines	69
Bangladesh	68
Algeria	68
Pakistan	67
Georgia	65
Azerbaijan	64
Turkey	60
Nigeria	60
Armenia	60
India	57
Taiwan	57
Indonesia	52
Vietnam	48
Malta	47
Albania	47
China	45
Moldova	45
Macedonia	43
Uganda	41
Zimbabwe	40
Bulgaria	39
Korea, South	39
Romania	38
Russian Fed.	36
Brazil	36
Poland	35
Mexico	34
Japan	32
South Africa	32
Venezuela	31
Serbia	31
Ukraine	31
Singapore	30
Montenegro	30
Portugal	30
Colombia	29
Croatia	29
Uruguay	28
Switzerland	27
El Salvador	27
Tanzania	27
Italy	27
Germany	27
Austria	27
Bosnia and Herz.	27
Luxembourg	26
Argentina	26
Australia	26
Chile	25
Belgium	25
Belarus	25
Hungary	25
Lithuania	24
Slovakia	24
Great Britain	23
France	22
Puerto Rico	21
Greece	20
Latvia	20
Spain	19
Czech Republic	18
Slovenia	18
Northern Ireland	16
Ireland	15
Dominican Rep.	15
Peru	15
Canada	15
Norway	14
Estonia	14
New Zealand	13
Netherlands	12
Finland	10
United States	10
Denmark	6
Iceland	4
Sweden	2
Total	34

C002) JOBS PREFERENCE TO OWN NATIONALITY

Do you agree or disagree with the following statements:

"When jobs are scarce, employers should give priority to own nationality immigrants?"

Agree (%)

(WVS: V79; EVS: V98)

Country	Wave		Gender		Age			Education			Income			Values		
	1990	2000	Male	Female	16-29	30-49	50+	Lower	Middle	Upper	Lower	Middle	Upper	Mat	Mixed	Postm.
Albania	na	**80**	83	77	78	80	80	81	81	73	79	82	78	82	79	56
Algeria	na	**87**	88	87	87	87	91	92	87	85	90	90	80	88	88	81
Argentina	60	**74**	75	73	77	72	73	75	75	62	77	76	68	80	75	69
Armenia	na	**66**	68	65	66	68	64	70	67	63	62	74	67	72	64	42
Australia	na	**45**	44	46	48	42	46	55	51	30	50	45	37	47	48	40
Austria	77	**72**	73	72	58	70	82	81	66	55	80	73	68	78	78	60
Azerbaijan	na	**86**	86	86	88	83	88	95	86	83	92	85	76	86	86	86
Bangladesh	na	**92**	92	92	92	93	91	92	94	92	98	91	89	92	92	97
Belarus	56	**85**	85	85	83	82	91	91	85	76	87	84	85	88	83	80
Belgium	66	**56**	51	60	48	51	64	72	60	37	62	58	48	72	58	28
Bosnia and Herz.	na	**9**	8	11	11	8	10	15	8	9	12	8	8	9	10	8
Brazil	82	**89**	90	87	88	88	91	90	88	83	92	87	85	90	89	84
Bulgaria	87	**88**	88	88	85	86	92	91	87	86	93	87	85	92	85	81
Canada	53	**47**	45	50	38	48	52	62	47	34	56	50	39	60	49	40
Chile	83	**83**	82	84	84	81	85	83	84	80	85	82	82	86	81	83
China	65	**73**	73	72	52	76	82	80	68	61	77	72	69	74	70	53
Colombia	na	**na**	na	na	na	na	na	na	na	na	na	na	na	na	na	na
Croatia	na	**91**	92	90	87	89	95	95	88	86	93	91	88	96	91	84
Czech Republic	88	**84**	83	85	83	84	85	87	84	68	87	84	80	88	84	72
Denmark	53	**34**	34	35	28	28	45	46	24	16	40	35	19	51	37	10
Dominican Rep.	na	**46**	47	46	44	48	78	48	40	49	45	46	53	42	48	48
Egypt	na	**99**	99	98	98	99	99	99	98	98	98	99	99	99	99	96
El Salvador	na	**na**	na	na	na	na	na	na	na	na	na	na	na	na	na	na
Estonia	82	**47**	50	45	48	42	52	54	47	38	55	48	43	47	49	28
Finland	71	**65**	68	63	61	62	70	76	55	42	65	72	61	79	63	44
France	63	**54**	53	55	46	48	64	67	43	31	63	54	42	74	53	30
Georgia	na	**83**	84	81	84	83	81	82	83	81	84	83	80	83	82	85
Germany	69	**59**	62	56	47	55	68	68	54	34	70	60	52	71	59	38
Great Britain	51	**58**	58	58	58	55	60	70	56	36	65	55	51	na	na	na
Greece	na	**78**	78	79	72	83	85	89	87	70	81	78	80	85	81	62
Hungary	87	**90**	89	91	87	91	90	92	88	84	90	91	89	94	86	83
Iceland	87	**70**	71	68	65	68	77	78	72	50	78	70	62	77	72	45
India	84	**85**	85	85	85	85	86	85	87	83	81	86	85	88	83	78
Indonesia	na	**87**	90	85	90	89	85	89	88	88	86	89	89	88	88	89
Iran	na	**94**	94	94	94	94	93	93	94	94	94	94	94	94	94	93
Ireland	69	**73**	70	76	67	71	80	83	70	61	82	74	61	82	74	53
Israel	na	**na**	na	na	na	na	na	na	na	na	na	na	na	na	na	na
Italy	74	**61**	60	63	58	54	70	73	56	43	69	61	51	77	64	47
Japan	65	**61**	64	58	44	54	73	69	60	57	65	60	58	67	61	42
Jordan	na	**93**	97	89	92	93	96	93	92	93	92	96	90	94	93	86
Korea, South	72	**84**	84	83	72	85	94	91	86	80	84	83	85	89	81	68
Latvia	80	**74**	73	76	65	72	80	81	73	71	78	71	72	75	75	64
Lithuania	92	**94**	94	95	92	96	94	95	95	90	97	96	92	97	95	87
Luxembourg	na	**48**	46	50	40	41	60	51	52	35	57	50	37	58	48	36
Macedonia	na	**78**	77	79	75	80	79	81	78	75	78	78	79	80	77	86
Malta	na	**94**	92	95	93	94	94	97	94	84	93	93	93	95	93	94
Mexico	83	**80**	79	81	80	79	82	82	76	81	84	74	79	80	80	77
Moldova	na	**65**	65	66	63	64	69	70	64	63	70	67	66	67	62	59
Montenegro	na	**85**	85	85	80	84	89	91	83	76	90	83	81	89	82	80
Morocco	na	**95**	95	94	95	95	95	95	95	88	97	93	91	96	93	91
Netherlands	30	**28**	25	31	33	23	31	43	26	17	32	30	21	46	31	12
New Zealand	na	**49**	45	53	53	46	51	59	52	36	55	50	43	54	52	40
Nigeria	80	**81**	82	79	80	80	86	80	80	83	83	81	79	78	83	79
Northern Ireland	62	**75**	75	75	70	76	78	84	71	59	75	75	64	83	72	72
Norway	59	**41**	42	41	35	38	50	56	44	25	na	na	na	60	41	20
Pakistan	na	**57**	58	55	46	62	60	68	43	45	71	56	38	60	51	50
Peru	na	**73**	74	72	73	72	75	70	75	71	74	73	71	70	74	75
Philippines	na	**86**	86	86	84	88	86	84	88	86	89	84	86	89	84	81
Poland	67	**91**	90	92	87	88	96	95	86	82	94	90	85	94	89	91
Portugal	88	**63**	59	68	57	63	68	65	62	59	71	58	60	63	63	69
Puerto Rico	na	**76**	76	77	69	79	78	76	77	77	78	78	74	86	76	74
Romania	75	**74**	72	76	64	71	83	82	74	62	79	77	69	79	72	55
Russian Fed.	63	**73**	72	74	70	72	77	78	74	69	74	75	72	75	71	74
Serbia	na	**80**	80	81	78	80	82	86	78	76	86	81	76	85	78	62
Singapore	na	**82**	81	83	76	85	94	86	82	71	88	83	81	86	81	76
Slovakia	na	**88**	88	89	86	88	90	91	88	77	91	90	85	90	88	76
Slovenia	79	**76**	74	77	72	74	81	83	76	62	78	77	67	82	78	66
South Africa	74	**79**	81	78	76	82	80	79	79	86	82	71	80	82	79	78
Spain	75	**60**	59	61	53	55	70	69	53	46	64	60	57	72	60	43
Sweden	35	**11**	15	8	10	8	16	18	12	5	12	14	8	26	12	5
Switzerland	na	**60**	60	60	54	59	65	73	58	48	66	60	55	67	62	48
Taiwan	na	**91**	90	91	89	92	87	91	87	92	91	92	92	94	90	87
Tanzania	na	**71**	74	68	73	72	67	65	79	75	63	73	79	73	72	77
Turkey	75	**66**	66	66	63	68	68	69	62	60	68	65	63	72	66	55
Uganda	na	**92**	94	91	91	93	94	92	92	97	92	96	90	92	93	89
Ukraine	na	**70**	71	69	67	70	72	79	72	60	68	74	68	75	65	60
United States	51	**49**	45	54	45	52	48	60	50	45	57	44	46	56	52	40
Uruguay	na	**83**	81	85	82	85	82	84	81	80	80	85	83	88	83	82
Venezuela	na	**82**	80	83	82	80	84	81	84	76	81	83	82	85	80	81
Vietnam	na	**79**	80	79	74	81	79	78	80	81	80	78	79	82	81	77
Zimbabwe	na	**79**	81	77	80	78	77	79	78	70	83	81	68	78	77	89
Total	70	72	72	72	71	71	74	78	72	63	76	72	70	80	71	58

RANKING

Country	2000
Egypt	99
Morocco	95
Lithuania	94
Iran	94
Malta	94
Jordan	93
Bangladesh	92
Uganda	92
Croatia	91
Poland	91
Taiwan	91
Hungary	90
Brazil	89
Bulgaria	88
Slovakia	88
Algeria	87
Indonesia	87
Philippines	86
Azerbaijan	86
Belarus	85
Montenegro	85
India	85
Czech Republic	84
Korea, South	84
Chile	83
Uruguay	83
Georgia	83
Singapore	82
Venezuela	82
Nigeria	81
Serbia	80
Mexico	80
Albania	80
South Africa	79
Vietnam	79
Zimbabwe	79
Greece	78
Macedonia	78
Puerto Rico	76
Slovenia	76
Northern Ireland	75
Latvia	74
Romania	74
Argentina	74
Russian Fed.	73
Ireland	73
Peru	73
China	73
Austria	72
Tanzania	71
Ukraine	70
Iceland	70
Armenia	66
Turkey	66
Finland	65
Moldova	65
Portugal	63
Italy	61
Japan	61
Spain	60
Switzerland	60
Germany	59
Great Britain	58
Pakistan	57
Belgium	56
France	54
United States	49
New Zealand	49
Luxembourg	48
Estonia	47
Canada	47
Dominican Rep.	46
Australia	45
Norway	41
Denmark	34
Netherlands	28
Sweden	11
Bosnia and Herz.	9
Total	72

006) FINANCIAL SATISFACTION

ow satisfied are you with the financial situation of your household?

"1" = completely dissatisfied / "10" = completely satisfied)

Satisfied (7-10)

(WVS: V80)

Country	Wave		Gender		Age			Education			Income			Values		
	1990	2000	Male	Female	16-29	30-49	50+	Lower	Middle	Upper	Lower	Middle	Upper	Mat	Mixed	Postm.
lbania	na	**22**	25	19	27	21	19	14	24	37	10	18	39	20	25	23
lgeria	na	**45**	40	51	45	49	40	38	45	50	36	44	61	40	48	52
rgentina	36	**37**	39	35	46	31	35	36	38	44	26	36	49	35	37	39
rmenia	na	**13**	14	12	18	11	8	11	13	12	21	7	6	8	17	8
ustralia	na	**53**	56	50	52	49	60	52	51	57	40	51	72	49	54	54
ustria	61	**na**	na	na	na	na	na	na	na	na	na	na	na	na	na	na
zerbaijan	na	**19**	21	17	24	16	15	17	17	22	10	14	35	19	18	12
angladesh	na	**29**	28	31	34	25	31	24	36	33	14	25	51	34	26	24
elarus	27	**na**	na	na	na	na	na	na	na	na	na	na	na	na	na	na
elgium	70	**na**	na	na	na	na	na	na	na	na	na	na	na	na	na	na
osnia and Herz.	na	**25**	27	24	32	26	18	17	23	39	8	20	54	18	29	34
razil	37	**36**	41	31	35	32	46	39	31	41	30	36	40	39	34	35
ulgaria	17	**na**	na	na	na	na	na	na	na	na	na	na	na	na	na	na
anada	68	**64**	64	63	60	59	71	62	60	72	46	65	74	63	63	65
hile	41	**36**	32	40	41	33	35	27	37	53	25	34	59	34	37	36
hina	47	**39**	35	43	43	37	42	41	38	35	32	40	49	37	38	56
olombia	na	**81**	83	79	81	81	82	80	79	84	74	79	88	77	80	81
roatia	na	**na**	na	na	na	na	na	na	na	na	na	na	na	na	na	na
zech Republic	30	**na**	na	na	na	na	na	na	na	na	na	na	na	na	na	na
enmark	66	**na**	na	na	na	na	na	na	na	na	na	na	na	na	na	na
ominican Rep.	na	**47**	51	45	52	38	55	27	32	55	31	49	69	45	48	47
gypt	na	**40**	37	42	41	39	39	38	44	38	36	40	42	38	42	39
l Salvador	na	**50**	51	50	56	44	51	44	53	65	39	47	73	na	na	na
stonia	31	**na**	na	na	na	na	na	na	na	na	na	na	na	na	na	na
inland	59	**na**	na	na	na	na	na	na	na	na	na	na	na	na	na	na
rance	42	**na**	na	na	na	na	na	na	na	na	na	na	na	na	na	na
eorgia	na	**9**	10	8	14	8	6	8	9	10	5	7	16	8	9	10
ermany	43	**na**	na	na	na	na	na	na	na	na	na	na	na	na	na	na
reat Britain	56	**na**	na	na	na	na	na	na	na	na	na	na	na	na	na	na
reece	na	**na**	na	na	na	na	na	na	na	na	na	na	na	na	na	na
ungary	30	**na**	na	na	na	na	na	na	na	na	na	na	na	na	na	na
celand	53	**na**	na	na	na	na	na	na	na	na	na	na	na	na	na	na
ndia	47	**26**	28	23	26	26	26	20	28	36	19	18	36	24	32	29
ndonesia	na	**52**	53	51	45	56	51	42	52	61	31	62	80	48	55	63
ran	na	**37**	34	41	42	34	32	31	39	42	27	31	47	32	40	39
reland	59	**na**	na	na	na	na	na	na	na	na	na	na	na	na	na	na
srael	na	**na**	na	na	na	na	na	na	na	na	na	na	na	na	na	na
taly	67	**na**	na	na	na	na	na	na	na	na	na	na	na	na	na	na
apan	41	**46**	43	49	46	42	50	43	46	48	37	44	61	46	47	46
ordan	na	**27**	23	30	30	23	27	21	24	42	17	25	44	26	28	31
Korea, South	40	**40**	41	38	40	40	39	18	38	45	22	34	62	38	40	52
atvia	21	**na**	na	na	na	na	na	na	na	na	na	na	na	na	na	na
ithuania	na	**na**	na	na	na	na	na	na	na	na	na	na	na	na	na	na
uxembourg	na	**na**	na	na	na	na	na	na	na	na	na	na	na	na	na	na
Macedonia	na	**21**	20	22	26	19	18	14	20	33	7	19	45	18	23	21
Malta	na	**na**	na	na	na	na	na	na	na	na	na	na	na	na	na	na
Mexico	51	**58**	60	57	65	56	53	53	63	70	54	56	70	55	60	63
Moldova	na	**14**	13	15	22	14	8	8	15	18	4	10	25	12	14	26
Montenegro	na	**20**	20	20	17	23	17	15	23	24	8	12	34	19	22	15
Morocco	na	**27**	23	31	29	27	20	22	40	55	15	34	26	26	26	35
Netherlands	75	**na**	na	na	na	na	na	na	na	na	na	na	na	na	na	na
New Zealand	na	**53**	54	52	43	51	59	49	56	56	35	51	72	54	53	57
Nigeria	38	**54**	54	55	58	51	41	50	54	62	45	52	72	54	55	49
Northern Ireland	58	**na**	na	na	na	na	na	na	na	na	na	na	na	na	na	na
Norway	56	**60**	62	57	58	56	65	52	59	68	na	na	na	48	62	56
Pakistan	na	**5**	6	5	4	7	4	1	7	16	na	2	17	4	8	18
Peru	na	**31**	31	31	33	27	32	27	27	39	23	34	40	33	31	29
Philippines	na	**39**	38	40	43	35	43	37	37	45	27	33	59	37	40	44
Poland	30	**na**	na	na	na	na	na	na	na	na	na	na	na	na	na	na
Portugal	43	**na**	na	na	na	na	na	na	na	na	na	na	na	na	na	na
Puerto Rico	na	**69**	75	66	73	62	73	70	65	71	64	70	75	61	71	69
Romania	29	**na**	na	na	na	na	na	na	na	na	na	na	na	na	na	na
Russian Fed.	27	**na**	na	na	na	na	na	na	na	na	na	na	na	na	na	na
Serbia	na	**15**	15	14	20	15	13	11	14	22	10	12	23	13	16	21
Singapore	na	**55**	54	57	58	52	56	52	55	65	41	50	69	50	59	48
Slovakia	na	**na**	na	na	na	na	na	na	na	na	na	na	na	na	na	na
Slovenia	23	**na**	na	na	na	na	na	na	na	na	na	na	na	na	na	na
South Africa	34	**25**	25	25	19	28	33	20	31	36	10	28	37	25	24	30
Spain	48	**48**	49	47	54	48	44	43	52	59	33	51	57	41	50	51
Sweden	63	**na**	na	na	na	na	na	na	na	na	na	na	na	na	na	na
Switzerland	83	**72**	73	72	71	68	78	69	71	87	55	69	86	63	71	80
Taiwan	na	**39**	37	40	39	42	30	29	31	52	26	32	55	38	39	51
Tanzania	na	**16**	13	20	17	16	16	17	15	16	13	20	16	16	17	26
Turkey	21	**16**	15	18	23	13	13	14	20	19	8	18	38	13	17	20
Uganda	na	**28**	22	33	27	27	37	23	30	38	16	33	32	31	25	34
Ukraine	na	**na**	na	na	na	na	na	na	na	na	na	na	na	na	na	na
United States	62	**58**	63	53	54	52	70	52	57	61	43	59	78	60	58	57
Uruguay	na	**55**	53	56	56	51	58	53	58	61	44	56	67	49	58	53
Venezuela	na	**47**	49	46	46	48	49	43	44	60	35	46	57	39	51	50
Vietnam	na	**34**	35	33	29	36	36	30	38	46	20	25	53	30	40	33
Zimbabwe	na	**13**	12	13	19	8	7	8	20	9	10	10	24	10	15	16
Total	46	37	37	38	39	35	39	31	37	48	26	35	51	30	39	46

RANKING	
Country	**2000**
Colombia	81
Switzerland	72
Puerto Rico	69
Canada	64
Norway	60
Mexico	58
United States	58
Singapore	55
Uruguay	55
Nigeria	54
Australia	53
New Zealand	53
Indonesia	52
El Salvador	50
Spain	48
Venezuela	47
Dominican Rep.	47
Japan	46
Algeria	45
Egypt	40
Korea, South	40
China	39
Philippines	39
Taiwan	39
Iran	37
Argentina	37
Chile	36
Brazil	36
Vietnam	34
Peru	31
Bangladesh	29
Uganda	28
Morocco	27
Jordan	27
India	26
Bosnia and Herz.	25
South Africa	25
Albania	22
Macedonia	21
Montenegro	20
Azerbaijan	19
Turkey	16
Tanzania	16
Serbia	15
Moldova	14
Zimbabwe	13
Armenia	13
Georgia	9
Pakistan	5
Total	37

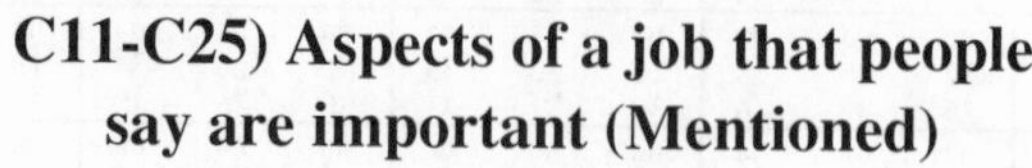

C11-C25) Aspects of a job that people say are important (Mentioned)

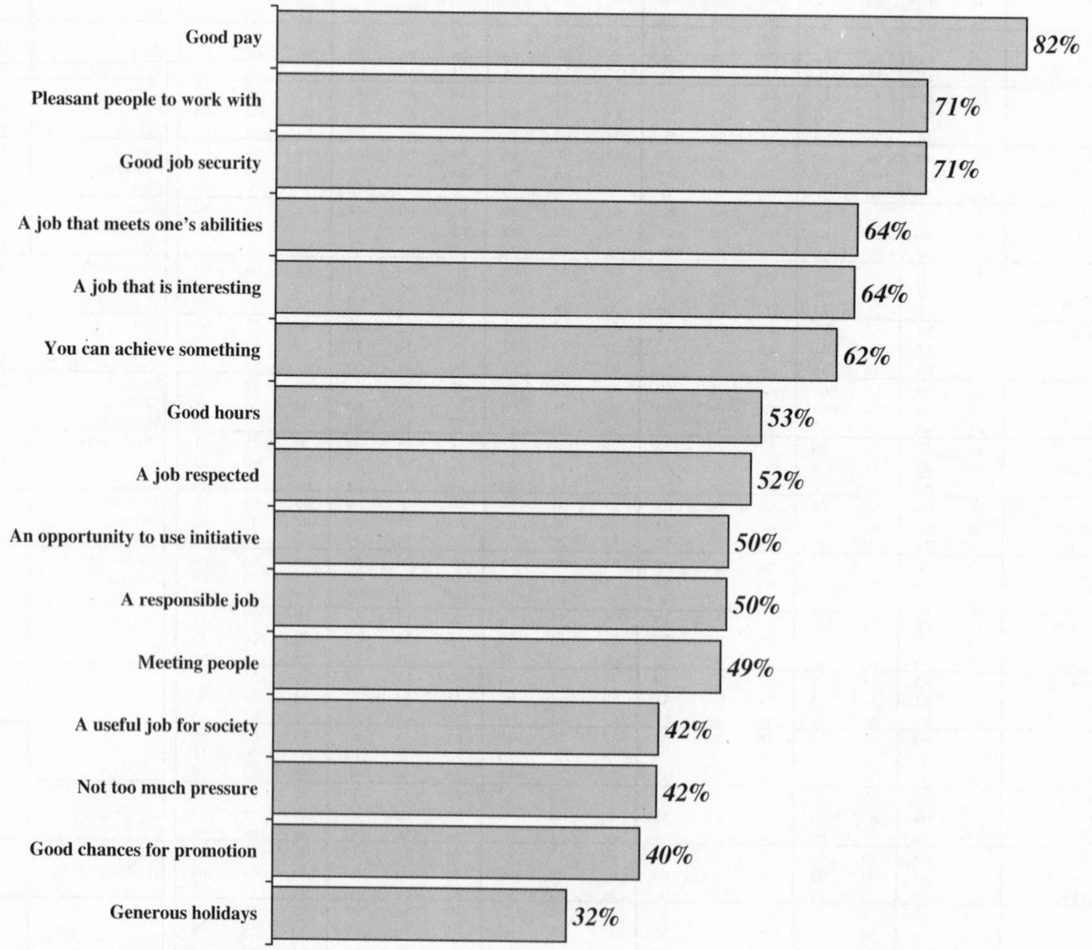

Good pay	82%
Pleasant people to work with	71%
Good job security	71%
A job that meets one's abilities	64%
A job that is interesting	64%
You can achieve something	62%
Good hours	53%
A job respected	52%
An opportunity to use initiative	50%
A responsible job	50%
Meeting people	49%
A useful job for society	42%
Not too much pressure	42%
Good chances for promotion	40%
Generous holidays	32%

C011) IMPORTANT IN A JOB: GOOD PAY

Here are some more aspects of a job that people say are important.

Please tell me which ones you personally think are important in a job?

Good pay (%) (WVS: V86; EVS: V71)

Country	Wave		Gender		Age			Education			Income			Values		
	1990	2000	Male	Female	16-29	30-49	50+	Lower	Middle	Upper	Lower	Middle	Upper	Mat	Mixed	Postm.
Albania	na	**95**	96	95	95	96	95	96	95	93	94	96	95	97	94	87
Algeria	na	**90**	90	89	91	88	92	88	92	88	91	92	90	93	89	87
Argentina	84	**75**	80	71	79	73	75	78	73	67	78	73	75	82	76	68
Armenia	na	**94**	95	93	92	97	90	89	94	94	92	94	96	96	91	92
Australia	na	**61**	66	55	68	63	51	60	60	62	57	61	66	62	61	60
Austria	60	**66**	71	62	78	68	58	67	66	61	63	70	68	76	68	60
Azerbaijan	na	**95**	97	94	95	96	93	90	95	96	96	97	95	96	96	94
Bangladesh	na	**92**	92	92	88	95	98	95	88	91	95	89	95	95	92	78
Belarus	87	**88**	92	85	93	94	78	77	92	93	87	88	91	87	90	91
Belgium	71	**73**	77	69	81	72	69	76	76	66	69	72	73	81	75	57
Bosnia and Herz.	na	**91**	90	92	92	93	88	95	91	88	90	92	90	94	90	91
Brazil	82	**56**	55	56	58	54	54	57	55	50	58	57	53	60	55	46
Bulgaria	90	**91**	92	90	91	92	90	85	94	95	88	89	95	90	94	88
Canada	76	**76**	78	74	83	77	69	72	77	76	72	75	79	87	75	74
Chile	77	**85**	87	84	84	87	84	86	86	81	86	86	83	89	86	80
China	68	**65**	66	64	63	70	54	63	67	63	66	66	64	69	69	53
Colombia	na	**66**	65	66	66	65	68	79	67	54	76	67	57	75	71	49
Croatia	na	**86**	91	82	91	84	86	87	87	82	77	86	91	94	85	86
Czech Republic	83	**74**	77	71	84	78	65	78	72	65	67	76	77	80	72	70
Denmark	55	**54**	60	48	60	58	46	54	55	55	48	56	61	55	53	56
Dominican Rep.	na	**85**	84	85	85	83	91	78	83	87	79	87	94	84	86	85
Egypt	na	**85**	85	85	82	86	89	88	81	83	86	86	83	89	81	81
El Salvador	na	**na**	na	na	na	na	na	na	na	na	na	na	na	na	na	na
Estonia	86	**89**	90	87	90	93	84	86	90	88	85	89	89	91	88	80
Finland	66	**65**	69	61	73	73	52	64	65	66	64	67	65	75	61	60
France	54	**68**	70	67	72	70	65	69	70	65	70	67	69	71	68	63
Georgia	na	**93**	94	92	90	93	95	96	92	93	92	94	93	95	91	92
Germany	71	**75**	81	71	76	78	72	77	75	65	78	78	74	84	74	62
Great Britain	69	**81**	85	77	84	87	74	83	80	82	80	83	84	na	na	na
Greece	na	**90**	88	91	94	87	84	85	89	91	89	91	89	93	90	88
Hungary	85	**90**	92	88	97	96	80	87	95	95	82	90	94	89	92	88
Iceland	86	**86**	87	85	89	88	82	84	89	85	85	88	89	89	87	78
India	87	**92**	92	92	94	93	89	91	93	93	90	92	93	94	93	93
Indonesia	na	**97**	96	98	98	97	96	94	97	99	98	98	99	96	98	96
Iran	na	**80**	82	78	78	83	83	84	79	77	82	78	81	82	80	76
Ireland	73	**89**	89	89	91	87	89	90	89	86	89	90	87	90	91	79
Israel	na	**na**	na	na	na	na	na	na	na	na	na	na	na	na	na	na
Italy	72	**85**	86	84	88	85	82	85	85	84	85	86	85	88	85	83
Japan	78	**83**	82	84	87	91	75	70	85	85	83	84	83	85	84	79
Jordan	na	**98**	98	98	97	100	96	98	98	98	99	99	97	98	98	99
Korea, South	18	**96**	94	97	98	95	94	91	95	97	94	96	97	96	95	94
Latvia	69	**75**	76	75	82	77	71	75	76	73	75	72	78	78	75	75
Lithuania	79	**93**	93	92	95	95	89	90	94	93	94	87	95	96	92	81
Luxembourg	na	**66**	67	64	74	64	62	68	65	63	70	66	70	75	67	55
Macedonia	na	**89**	89	90	92	91	86	92	90	84	91	91	85	94	88	77
Malta	na	**89**	91	88	91	90	88	91	89	90	87	89	88	87	90	91
Mexico	89	**79**	80	78	79	79	79	80	77	78	81	78	77	84	80	62
Moldova	na	**86**	85	87	84	87	87	89	82	90	85	90	87	88	83	80
Montenegro	na	**81**	81	81	86	80	78	79	81	82	86	79	81	84	78	66
Morocco	na	**98**	98	98	98	99	95	98	98	96	99	98	99	98	98	100
Netherlands	69	**72**	78	67	82	77	62	70	74	72	68	74	77	77	73	68
New Zealand	na	**79**	83	76	88	85	70	76	80	82	74	79	88	79	81	79
Nigeria	93	**97**	98	97	98	97	95	98	97	97	97	98	98	97	98	97
Northern Ireland	74	**89**	91	87	91	90	87	89	89	85	85	91	85	90	89	87
Norway	60	**58**	66	52	60	64	51	57	57	63	na	na	na	57	60	53
Pakistan	na	**na**	na	na	na	na	na	na	na	na	na	na	na	na	na	na
Peru	na	**73**	71	76	75	73	71	75	75	70	72	78	68	78	73	73
Philippines	na	**78**	80	76	75	79	80	81	75	79	75	79	80	79	78	73
Poland	na	**93**	94	92	95	94	90	96	92	84	94	91	96	96	92	85
Portugal	79	**80**	81	79	82	79	80	82	80	67	83	82	78	78	82	71
Puerto Rico	na	**77**	78	76	80	81	72	78	79	76	77	75	78	81	79	66
Romania	76	**91**	93	89	92	91	90	91	91	88	90	93	90	91	92	85
Russian Fed.	83	**90**	91	89	92	93	85	86	91	89	89	91	90	91	89	89
Serbia	na	**72**	70	74	72	74	70	79	71	66	74	73	68	76	69	61
Singapore	na	**79**	80	77	77	79	82	78	80	74	83	80	76	81	79	68
Slovakia	na	**91**	92	90	91	93	88	89	92	91	87	93	93	91	92	86
Slovenia	82	**87**	89	85	91	88	83	89	88	80	90	85	84	88	88	86
South Africa	84	**91**	93	89	89	93	91	95	87	75	94	89	89	91	92	85
Spain	75	**84**	86	83	84	84	84	86	82	81	86	84	81	88	85	77
Sweden	73	**58**	63	54	64	65	48	53	60	60	51	59	66	59	60	53
Switzerland	na	**65**	71	59	67	68	60	64	65	64	65	63	65	77	64	64
Taiwan	na	**56**	52	59	63	55	54	56	56	55	58	59	52	59	55	35
Tanzania	na	**89**	88	90	90	90	84	88	91	90	89	90	92	92	88	100
Turkey	90	**97**	97	98	97	98	97	99	96	95	98	98	95	98	98	95
Uganda	na	**93**	94	91	94	92	90	88	94	94	87	94	95	96	93	81
Ukraine	na	**89**	90	87	92	94	82	71	91	92	84	90	93	89	89	81
United States	86	**89**	90	88	93	92	81	90	91	87	89	88	89	92	91	83
Uruguay	na	**90**	91	90	90	89	91	92	88	83	91	90	89	91	92	86
Venezuela	na	**na**	na	na	na	na	na	na	na	na	na	na	na	na	na	na
Vietnam	na	**76**	75	76	81	75	73	76	78	72	74	71	81	91	76	81
Zimbabwe	na	**88**	88	89	90	85	90	89	87	70	90	88	83	92	87	76
Total	75	**82**	84	81	85	84	78	82	83	81	82	83	83	87	82	74

RANKING	
Country	2000
Morocco	98
Jordan	98
Nigeria	97
Turkey	97
Indonesia	97
Korea, South	96
Albania	95
Azerbaijan	95
Armenia	94
Poland	93
Lithuania	93
Georgia	93
Uganda	93
Bangladesh	92
India	92
Bosnia and Herz.	91
Slovakia	91
Bulgaria	91
South Africa	91
Romania	91
Uruguay	90
Algeria	90
Russian Fed.	90
Hungary	90
Greece	90
Malta	89
Macedonia	89
Ireland	89
United States	89
Northern Ireland	89
Tanzania	89
Estonia	89
Ukraine	89
Zimbabwe	88
Belarus	88
Slovenia	87
Croatia	86
Iceland	86
Moldova	86
Chile	85
Dominican Rep.	85
Egypt	85
Italy	85
Spain	84
Japan	83
Great Britain	81
Montenegro	81
Iran	80
Portugal	80
Mexico	79
New Zealand	79
Singapore	79
Philippines	78
Puerto Rico	77
Vietnam	76
Canada	76
Latvia	75
Argentina	75
Germany	75
Czech Republic	74
Peru	73
Belgium	73
Netherlands	72
Serbia	72
France	68
Austria	66
Colombia	66
Luxembourg	66
China	65
Switzerland	65
Finland	65
Australia	61
Norway	58
Sweden	58
Taiwan	56
Brazil	56
Denmark	54
Total	82

C012) IMPORTANT IN A JOB: NOT TOO MUCH PRESSURE

Here are some more aspects of a job that people say are important.

Please tell me which ones you personally think are important in a job?

Not too much pressure (%)

(WVS: V87; EVS: V73

Country	Wave		Gender		Age			Education			Income			Values		
	1990	2000	Male	Female	16-29	30-49	50+	Lower	Middle	Upper	Lower	Middle	Upper	Mat	Mixed	Postm.
Albania	na	**46**	46	45	47	44	47	42	46	54	45	44	47	46	45	56
Algeria	na	**60**	62	57	66	57	50	53	60	64	67	54	53	59	60	67
Argentina	41	**33**	33	33	37	31	31	35	29	30	33	34	31	33	35	26
Armenia	na	**53**	44	61	53	50	59	59	54	48	52	55	55	55	50	62
Australia	na	**24**	22	25	22	22	27	26	24	21	27	22	19	24	24	23
Austria	17	**18**	21	15	19	17	18	20	16	13	17	20	16	39	18	12
Azerbaijan	na	**56**	55	57	54	57	57	51	58	52	63	64	42	57	56	50
Bangladesh	na	**39**	38	41	37	42	37	45	34	30	42	36	41	39	39	40
Belarus	60	**20**	22	19	25	22	15	20	21	18	20	20	22	19	22	14
Belgium	26	**32**	31	33	28	31	34	33	33	28	32	33	31	34	32	26
Bosnia and Herz.	na	**52**	50	53	54	52	49	50	50	59	53	51	53	50	53	49
Brazil	40	**33**	31	35	32	34	33	32	33	38	34	33	31	35	32	34
Bulgaria	35	**40**	38	41	44	43	35	37	44	35	37	38	44	38	42	51
Canada	28	**28**	27	29	26	26	30	35	27	22	32	28	23	34	29	23
Chile	46	**41**	40	42	40	44	38	38	43	44	41	43	40	40	40	48
China	30	**27**	27	28	28	31	19	21	33	30	24	28	32	28	30	25
Colombia	na	**24**	24	25	24	25	23	22	26	24	23	25	24	23	27	30
Croatia	na	**63**	63	64	67	66	59	65	64	55	70	61	65	63	64	61
Czech Republic	58	**36**	35	36	41	36	33	37	35	35	32	37	38	38	35	30
Denmark	16	**14**	12	16	13	16	13	14	7	17	14	16	11	19	14	13
Dominican Rep.	na	**27**	28	27	29	23	36	63	32	21	29	24	19	35	26	20
Egypt	na	**66**	66	67	69	64	66	63	68	72	66	66	69	65	68	61
El Salvador	na	**na**	na	na	na	na	na	na	na	na	na	na	na	na	na	na
Estonia	32	**24**	21	26	30	22	23	26	25	20	25	26	20	24	24	19
Finland	20	**31**	31	31	36	34	24	33	27	28	35	29	24	31	30	28
France	8	**12**	13	10	15	12	10	12	10	11	13	9	11	11	11	13
Georgia	na	**30**	27	33	30	29	31	33	32	23	31	28	31	29	31	33
Germany	19	**24**	23	24	30	25	20	25	25	10	27	25	26	31	21	21
Great Britain	19	**28**	30	26	31	34	21	25	30	30	26	31	32	na	na	na
Greece	na	**54**	53	54	55	52	53	47	52	56	49	53	59	49	53	57
Hungary	46	**57**	57	57	67	59	49	60	57	42	52	59	59	56	59	77
Iceland	35	**32**	34	31	39	30	31	38	29	28	33	36	26	37	33	24
India	48	**54**	53	55	55	54	53	53	57	53	47	58	54	57	55	47
Indonesia	na	**85**	83	88	88	87	83	83	86	86	80	91	87	87	86	89
Iran	na	**53**	54	52	55	52	47	52	53	51	54	49	53	59	51	55
Ireland	26	**44**	42	45	39	42	48	49	40	42	49	47	36	49	42	42
Israel	na	**na**	na	na	na	na	na	na	na	na	na	na	na	na	na	na
Italy	31	**60**	58	62	65	62	57	62	61	51	64	65	55	64	60	61
Japan	42	**69**	63	75	71	73	65	59	74	63	68	71	67	72	69	69
Jordan	na	**81**	82	80	80	84	74	80	81	83	80	85	78	81	81	77
Korea, South	8	**89**	86	93	91	91	84	82	90	89	88	88	92	90	89	88
Latvia	19	**8**	11	6	12	9	6	9	9	8	5	11	12	11	7	11
Lithuania	40	**34**	33	35	37	31	35	32	35	36	36	31	35	35	35	23
Luxembourg	na	**36**	38	34	45	34	32	39	36	30	40	36	28	36	36	38
Macedonia	na	**32**	30	34	34	37	24	31	34	30	31	32	34	31	32	30
Malta	na	**68**	65	70	67	65	71	75	66	56	67	67	55	65	70	58
Mexico	47	**30**	30	30	27	31	31	33	27	21	34	23	28	31	31	27
Moldova	na	**49**	49	49	51	46	51	57	51	38	47	50	51	51	46	42
Montenegro	na	**36**	36	36	35	34	39	43	35	24	43	35	35	42	30	24
Morocco	na	**94**	93	94	94	94	92	94	94	87	96	94	90	93	95	91
Netherlands	44	**33**	28	37	31	34	33	33	36	30	37	33	28	38	33	32
New Zealand	na	**35**	35	36	32	33	40	42	32	31	37	38	30	40	34	34
Nigeria	64	**64**	64	63	64	64	58	64	62	66	65	67	59	63	65	59
Northern Ireland	20	**40**	35	45	43	45	33	39	41	41	36	39	31	37	40	43
Norway	23	**24**	23	24	25	23	24	31	22	20	na	na	na	28	23	22
Pakistan	na	**na**	na	na	na	na	na	na	na	na	na	na	na	na	na	na
Peru	na	**17**	16	17	14	20	17	20	17	14	21	14	12	19	17	14
Philippines	na	**36**	33	39	34	35	43	48	36	23	40	33	36	39	35	30
Poland	na	**63**	61	66	65	60	67	64	63	63	67	61	63	63	63	65
Portugal	41	**24**	23	26	26	28	21	23	29	24	12	27	26	23	23	30
Puerto Rico	na	**21**	17	23	21	18	23	38	22	18	22	23	19	31	21	15
Romania	37	**34**	33	34	32	33	35	43	33	15	42	34	27	38	32	19
Russian Fed.	19	**17**	16	18	19	16	18	22	18	12	19	18	15	18	17	11
Serbia	na	**23**	26	21	26	25	20	26	23	17	24	24	19	25	23	10
Singapore	na	**47**	44	50	43	47	63	55	47	24	56	45	42	52	46	40
Slovakia	na	**19**	20	17	21	18	17	21	18	13	22	18	15	22	16	21
Slovenia	48	**71**	70	73	73	73	69	76	72	62	75	74	60	69	72	72
South Africa	29	**50**	52	49	56	49	41	50	51	44	50	52	49	49	51	56
Spain	38	**39**	40	39	46	41	34	37	42	42	40	40	37	37	42	39
Sweden	48	**35**	32	38	38	38	31	37	36	31	39	36	29	40	35	32
Switzerland	na	**31**	29	33	35	29	30	34	31	23	30	28	29	35	28	37
Taiwan	na	**62**	60	65	67	61	62	62	66	61	67	64	58	63	65	57
Tanzania	na	**55**	52	58	53	54	58	52	57	63	53	58	61	51	58	46
Turkey	78	**91**	91	92	92	92	89	92	90	93	91	92	91	93	91	93
Uganda	na	**60**	64	56	63	57	56	60	61	45	51	53	62	67	58	49
Ukraine	na	**29**	23	35	33	28	28	31	30	26	29	31	29	29	31	23
United States	33	**38**	35	41	37	35	42	41	45	33	42	37	33	40	38	36
Uruguay	na	**57**	56	58	58	58	56	55	60	59	54	56	62	52	61	55
Venezuela	na	**na**	na	na	na	na	na	na	na	na	na	na	na	na	na	na
Vietnam	na	**54**	56	52	52	53	59	55	54	63	59	48	60	62	57	61
Zimbabwe	na	**27**	28	27	30	25	23	26	29	18	23	26	38	30	26	23
Total	35	**42**	42	43	45	43	39	44	42	39	43	43	41	45	42	38

RANKING	
Country	**2000**
Morocco	94
Turkey	91
Korea, South	89
Indonesia	85
Jordan	81
Slovenia	71
Japan	69
Malta	68
Egypt	66
Nigeria	64
Croatia	63
Poland	63
Taiwan	62
Italy	60
Uganda	60
Algeria	60
Uruguay	57
Hungary	57
Azerbaijan	56
Tanzania	55
Vietnam	54
India	54
Greece	54
Armenia	53
Iran	53
Bosnia and Herz.	52
South Africa	50
Moldova	49
Singapore	47
Albania	46
Ireland	44
Chile	41
Northern Ireland	40
Bulgaria	40
Spain	39
Bangladesh	39
United States	38
Philippines	36
Luxembourg	36
Montenegro	36
Czech Republic	36
New Zealand	35
Sweden	35
Lithuania	34
Romania	34
Brazil	33
Netherlands	33
Argentina	33
Iceland	32
Macedonia	32
Belgium	32
Finland	31
Switzerland	31
Georgia	30
Mexico	30
Ukraine	29
Great Britain	28
Canada	28
China	27
Dominican Rep.	27
Zimbabwe	27
Portugal	24
Colombia	24
Estonia	24
Norway	24
Germany	24
Australia	24
Serbia	23
Puerto Rico	21
Belarus	20
Slovakia	19
Austria	18
Russian Fed.	17
Peru	17
Denmark	14
France	12
Latvia	8
Total	42

C013) IMPORTANT IN A JOB: SECURITY

Here are some more aspects of a job that people say are important.
Please tell me which ones you personally think are important in a job?
Job security (%)

(WVS: V88; EVS: V74)

Country	Wave		Gender		Age			Education			Income			Values		
	1990	2000	Male	Female	16-29	30-49	50+	Lower	Middle	Upper	Lower	Middle	Upper	Mat	Mixed	Postm.
Albania	na	**81**	81	82	77	83	82	81	81	83	83	80	80	84	79	77
Algeria	na	**86**	86	87	88	86	85	82	87	88	88	86	85	89	85	87
Argentina	63	**70**	71	68	70	68	71	75	63	59	75	71	63	76	71	60
Armenia	na	**77**	76	78	70	82	82	77	78	75	78	79	76	81	76	60
Australia	na	**59**	58	59	56	59	61	62	65	48	64	59	54	65	59	56
Austria	65	**75**	77	74	73	74	78	83	72	57	76	77	75	81	80	66
Azerbaijan	na	**74**	77	72	70	76	80	72	74	76	73	77	71	74	77	72
Bangladesh	na	**97**	97	98	97	98	97	98	97	96	98	96	98	98	97	97
Belarus	37	**30**	31	28	32	30	28	24	31	35	30	29	31	28	31	21
Belgium	39	**47**	49	46	46	44	51	58	49	36	49	51	44	57	47	35
Bosnia and Herz.	na	**90**	89	91	90	91	89	91	91	88	91	92	86	93	89	89
Brazil	71	**55**	52	58	51	58	55	52	58	56	53	60	54	54	58	48
Bulgaria	57	**81**	81	81	79	77	85	81	83	75	83	80	80	83	80	68
Canada	67	**65**	64	66	63	66	65	69	69	55	68	68	61	78	68	57
Chile	69	**74**	77	71	72	77	71	75	73	73	77	73	71	79	72	71
China	44	**68**	72	64	62	72	62	62	74	40	66	75	62	75	71	53
Colombia	na	**37**	36	39	39	35	42	45	41	27	40	40	31	46	40	35
Croatia	na	**81**	80	82	78	81	83	84	81	72	83	83	78	81	83	77
Czech Republic	71	**52**	49	55	50	53	53	58	49	38	54	57	47	65	50	34
Denmark	52	**50**	52	49	43	50	54	55	46	45	50	53	48	60	52	42
Dominican Rep.	na	**66**	61	68	64	68	82	75	69	63	69	64	66	70	64	67
Egypt	na	**81**	82	79	81	80	81	79	85	79	82	80	83	82	81	77
El Salvador	na	**na**	na	na	na	na	na	na	na	na	na	na	na	na	na	na
Estonia	40	**51**	53	49	54	50	50	60	50	39	50	55	48	53	50	43
Finland	53	**68**	70	67	66	69	70	73	62	63	69	72	62	74	67	59
France	35	**46**	45	48	49	46	45	50	46	37	48	50	38	55	46	34
Georgia	na	**65**	67	63	59	68	68	67	65	63	65	64	66	71	61	45
Germany	72	**79**	82	77	79	80	78	83	79	62	79	85	80	85	79	72
Great Britain	57	**65**	70	60	61	69	63	66	64	65	61	68	65	na	na	na
Greece	na	**65**	62	68	67	63	66	68	67	63	70	62	65	62	65	71
Hungary	72	**89**	91	87	97	95	79	87	95	89	83	90	92	88	92	89
Iceland	57	**58**	59	57	63	57	56	62	60	45	58	63	53	63	60	40
India	74	**91**	92	88	94	91	87	88	93	94	89	90	92	96	93	96
Indonesia	na	**96**	96	96	96	97	96	94	97	97	98	97	99	98	97	96
Iran	na	**77**	78	76	79	78	70	72	81	77	78	72	79	80	77	81
Ireland	61	**68**	69	67	66	66	71	68	70	62	69	68	68	64	70	63
Israel	na	**na**	na	na	na	na	na	na	na	na	na	na	na	na	na	na
Italy	61	**76**	74	78	79	72	78	81	76	62	80	77	69	86	76	74
Japan	58	**80**	78	83	82	82	78	73	83	78	80	81	81	86	81	73
Jordan	na	**97**	98	95	97	97	94	96	97	98	95	98	98	97	97	95
Korea, South	35	**97**	97	97	96	97	98	100	98	96	96	96	99	99	96	93
Latvia	22	**38**	37	39	36	36	40	35	39	38	37	40	39	40	38	36
Lithuania	38	**75**	74	75	78	78	69	65	79	73	74	75	77	83	74	62
Luxembourg	na	**59**	60	58	66	57	57	67	57	51	64	61	53	62	62	52
Macedonia	na	**85**	88	83	81	88	86	86	87	81	88	85	81	87	86	75
Malta	na	**72**	70	73	71	70	74	80	69	65	75	65	66	74	72	56
Mexico	63	**65**	64	65	67	66	61	65	66	63	69	63	63	64	68	56
Moldova	na	**86**	87	86	86	87	86	90	85	85	86	85	88	86	86	82
Montenegro	na	**48**	51	45	38	48	55	55	48	33	60	40	45	59	39	40
Morocco	na	**98**	98	98	99	99	97	99	99	95	98	98	98	99	98	98
Netherlands	40	**29**	26	31	32	26	29	36	29	21	30	32	22	31	30	25
New Zealand	na	**72**	75	70	74	69	75	78	79	61	76	76	66	86	74	60
Nigeria	88	**82**	83	82	83	83	77	80	83	86	79	85	83	82	83	83
Northern Ireland	62	**76**	80	73	79	77	75	74	78	79	71	77	76	78	78	76
Norway	78	**69**	70	69	69	68	71	79	73	56	na	na	na	76	70	57
Pakistan	na	**na**	na	na	na	na	na	na	na	na	na	na	na	na	na	na
Peru	na	**47**	48	46	45	50	43	49	47	45	48	48	42	47	47	49
Philippines	na	**76**	76	76	73	77	77	74	75	79	77	78	71	78	74	70
Poland	na	**80**	80	80	73	79	84	83	77	73	86	79	68	79	81	77
Portugal	73	**64**	63	66	66	61	66	64	66	59	58	60	67	69	63	65
Puerto Rico	na	**69**	70	69	71	66	72	73	74	67	71	71	65	81	69	65
Romania	43	**87**	86	88	84	88	87	86	91	78	86	92	86	93	87	65
Russian Fed.	38	**69**	67	71	64	73	68	63	71	67	71	70	66	71	69	62
Serbia	na	**39**	43	34	33	39	41	41	43	26	43	40	36	39	41	18
Singapore	na	**66**	67	64	61	70	69	68	66	58	67	70	60	76	62	60
Slovakia	na	**72**	70	74	71	75	70	68	75	64	72	73	74	74	73	61
Slovenia	73	**88**	88	89	86	90	88	90	91	76	92	88	82	89	89	87
South Africa	68	**84**	84	84	85	85	80	84	86	72	82	92	81	87	84	80
Spain	67	**75**	76	74	74	75	76	79	71	71	78	76	71	79	77	68
Sweden	65	**51**	51	51	46	48	56	61	54	39	55	53	43	57	53	44
Switzerland	na	**64**	70	59	64	63	67	68	65	55	64	69	61	75	67	54
Taiwan	na	**75**	71	79	67	74	81	79	73	72	79	76	70	78	72	73
Tanzania	na	**79**	80	80	82	81	72	75	83	87	75	84	84	84	80	58
Turkey	83	**98**	98	98	98	98	98	98	98	94	98	99	96	98	98	97
Uganda	na	**81**	84	78	82	79	82	75	84	75	73	84	82	87	81	66
Ukraine	na	**72**	73	72	69	78	69	60	76	70	72	74	71	73	74	65
United States	72	**72**	72	72	73	74	68	72	79	68	73	73	70	80	74	63
Uruguay	na	**77**	78	75	79	79	74	78	76	67	79	73	75	79	79	73
Venezuela	na	**na**	na	na	na	na	na	na	na	na	na	na	na	na	na	na
Vietnam	na	**82**	83	81	80	84	81	78	88	91	83	78	87	87	88	87
Zimbabwe	na	**81**	82	81	79	83	84	81	82	91	79	83	83	82	81	79
Total	58	71	72	71	72	72	70	74	72	66	72	72	69	76	71	63

RANKING	
Country	2000
Morocco	98
Turkey	98
Bangladesh	97
Korea, South	97
Jordan	97
Indonesia	96
India	91
Bosnia and Herz.	90
Hungary	89
Slovenia	88
Romania	87
Algeria	86
Moldova	86
Macedonia	85
South Africa	84
Nigeria	82
Vietnam	82
Zimbabwe	81
Albania	81
Croatia	81
Uganda	81
Bulgaria	81
Egypt	81
Japan	80
Poland	80
Germany	79
Tanzania	79
Armenia	77
Iran	77
Uruguay	77
Northern Ireland	76
Italy	76
Philippines	76
Austria	75
Taiwan	75
Spain	75
Lithuania	75
Azerbaijan	74
Chile	74
Ukraine	72
New Zealand	72
Slovakia	72
United States	72
Malta	72
Argentina	70
Norway	69
Puerto Rico	69
Russian Fed.	69
Finland	68
Ireland	68
China	68
Singapore	66
Dominican Rep.	66
Greece	65
Great Britain	65
Georgia	65
Canada	65
Mexico	65
Portugal	64
Switzerland	64
Luxembourg	59
Australia	59
Iceland	58
Brazil	55
Czech Republic	52
Sweden	51
Estonia	51
Denmark	50
Montenegro	48
Belgium	47
Peru	47
France	46
Serbia	39
Latvia	38
Colombia	37
Belarus	30
Netherlands	29
Total	71

C014) IMPORTANT IN A JOB: A JOB RESPECTED

Here are some more aspects of a job that people say are important.

Please tell me which ones you personally think are important in a job?

A job respected by people in general (%)

(WVS: V89; EVS: V76)

Country	Wave		Gender		Age			Education			Income			Values		
	1990	2000	Male	Female	16-29	30-49	50+	Lower	Middle	Upper	Lower	Middle	Upper	Mat	Mixed	Postm.
Albania	na	**65**	64	65	67	63	65	61	68	67	65	66	63	68	65	67
Algeria	na	**72**	69	75	75	71	68	68	74	72	74	73	69	71	72	72
Argentina	43	**32**	33	32	28	32	36	33	29	34	34	33	30	36	33	26
Armenia	na	**70**	68	71	68	72	69	60	70	72	71	64	78	70	69	79
Australia	na	**27**	29	26	27	26	29	29	26	27	30	24	28	27	28	28
Austria	35	**36**	37	35	32	34	40	37	33	41	40	35	34	44	37	32
Azerbaijan	na	**65**	69	61	67	64	64	63	65	66	61	71	65	63	69	79
Bangladesh	na	**91**	90	93	90	91	94	90	93	92	92	89	93	93	90	92
Belarus	42	**30**	32	29	45	30	19	16	35	39	25	32	37	25	36	38
Belgium	40	**46**	44	48	39	48	48	49	44	47	47	45	46	49	47	42
Bosnia and Herz.	na	**54**	53	55	55	54	55	50	54	58	54	53	57	49	56	59
Brazil	58	**54**	50	58	51	54	59	59	51	45	60	55	47	55	56	45
Bulgaria	58	**52**	53	51	55	54	49	43	53	65	43	52	60	45	60	54
Canada	36	**36**	36	36	32	37	36	37	34	37	31	37	38	37	37	34
Chile	60	**55**	53	57	52	56	56	51	56	60	53	55	59	53	53	62
China	47	**58**	59	57	57	61	53	51	63	67	53	61	63	60	64	59
Colombia	na	**29**	29	30	30	30	28	35	29	26	30	32	26	36	27	37
Croatia	na	**51**	52	50	46	53	53	53	52	43	60	49	52	43	53	51
Czech Republic	33	**35**	35	35	33	35	36	34	35	43	37	34	36	36	35	32
Denmark	13	**11**	14	8	10	9	14	10	10	13	11	9	13	11	11	9
Dominican Rep.	na	**46**	44	47	44	50	55	59	48	44	42	43	52	46	47	39
Egypt	na	**85**	83	86	87	83	84	84	85	84	86	84	86	85	84	85
El Salvador	na	**na**	na	na	na	na	na	na	na	na	na	na	na	na	na	na
Estonia	38	**32**	26	36	31	26	38	28	31	38	32	33	31	31	32	32
Finland	24	**30**	31	29	33	31	27	28	32	34	32	27	30	30	29	32
France	17	**26**	28	24	25	25	28	27	24	25	29	24	27	27	27	21
Georgia	na	**44**	43	45	43	45	44	41	43	49	43	46	42	44	45	40
Germany	51	**43**	44	42	36	43	46	40	43	56	40	42	53	49	41	42
Great Britain	27	**25**	22	28	28	24	23	21	27	29	18	24	26	na	na	na
Greece	na	**73**	68	76	75	69	75	75	72	73	70	71	74	71	72	78
Hungary	16	**84**	84	83	90	90	74	80	90	91	73	85	89	80	90	97
Iceland	45	**51**	50	52	46	49	59	53	50	51	49	47	55	56	51	35
India	59	**77**	79	75	79	78	73	72	81	86	71	75	83	81	83	71
Indonesia	na	**87**	86	89	90	87	87	82	90	89	87	89	91	89	87	82
Iran	na	**61**	62	59	62	62	58	59	61	61	61	55	63	60	63	63
Ireland	29	**44**	43	45	33	44	52	49	39	45	49	43	44	47	44	37
Israel	na	**na**	na	na	na	na	na	na	na	na	na	na	na	na	na	na
Italy	40	**61**	60	63	57	58	67	69	57	51	68	63	55	66	63	59
Japan	26	**37**	40	35	30	30	46	45	34	40	35	34	44	40	35	38
Jordan	na	**94**	94	94	93	95	92	94	96	91	93	95	93	94	94	90
Korea, South	7	**68**	66	70	56	69	77	80	68	65	64	65	73	70	65	72
Latvia	31	**33**	33	33	24	28	41	41	29	36	33	35	32	37	31	32
Lithuania	28	**21**	22	21	28	19	19	14	23	28	18	17	23	21	22	23
Luxembourg	na	**37**	40	35	44	34	36	42	35	32	40	39	34	44	40	21
Macedonia	na	**43**	42	43	44	44	41	41	44	43	40	45	45	39	45	61
Malta	na	**74**	71	77	71	73	77	83	70	72	72	70	71	76	74	65
Mexico	54	**51**	51	52	52	51	51	53	49	48	51	49	51	51	54	47
Moldova	na	**70**	71	70	73	68	70	68	70	73	68	70	76	70	69	69
Montenegro	na	**48**	48	48	46	49	48	41	50	59	42	48	50	46	51	52
Morocco	na	**92**	92	91	93	92	87	92	91	86	85	86	95	94	93	86
Netherlands	55	**50**	51	49	47	52	50	50	47	53	45	51	56	46	51	51
New Zealand	na	**36**	37	36	30	36	39	35	37	39	35	36	37	36	37	33
Nigeria	74	**71**	70	72	72	71	63	71	70	72	70	73	69	71	72	64
Northern Ireland	20	**44**	42	45	48	39	44	41	43	51	42	35	45	41	45	47
Norway	30	**23**	19	28	17	23	29	28	23	20	na	na	na	32	22	21
Pakistan	na	**na**	na	na	na	na	na	na	na	na	na	na	na	na	na	na
Peru	na	**59**	58	60	58	58	64	65	59	54	59	61	56	59	59	61
Philippines	na	**55**	55	55	56	53	56	56	52	57	54	52	58	52	57	49
Poland	na	**67**	70	63	67	62	72	70	65	59	69	65	65	67	68	65
Portugal	59	**50**	46	53	46	50	52	50	49	45	52	50	44	49	50	50
Puerto Rico	na	**60**	57	63	63	60	59	65	59	60	60	63	57	69	60	58
Romania	55	**69**	66	71	68	70	68	68	70	68	69	72	69	71	70	57
Russian Fed.	40	**47**	45	48	45	45	50	44	45	52	45	52	45	45	48	57
Serbia	na	**32**	31	33	32	30	35	32	32	34	32	33	32	34	32	32
Singapore	na	**40**	36	44	42	40	33	37	41	43	36	39	43	38	41	35
Slovakia	na	**22**	20	23	22	21	24	19	22	31	20	21	25	20	23	28
Slovenia	59	**75**	73	76	67	76	79	85	74	59	80	76	63	75	76	73
South Africa	22	**48**	47	49	54	45	42	46	52	32	43	52	48	46	51	47
Spain	37	**48**	48	48	46	48	50	52	43	49	46	55	50	54	50	41
Sweden	43	**29**	29	28	24	30	31	28	27	32	27	29	27	27	30	27
Switzerland	na	**44**	44	45	31	43	55	47	44	43	45	45	42	39	48	42
Taiwan	na	**70**	67	72	78	69	66	63	71	75	65	66	76	73	67	65
Tanzania	na	**64**	60	70	63	67	61	63	64	72	63	66	74	63	66	58
Turkey	87	**94**	93	95	94	94	95	95	93	91	94	95	92	94	96	91
Uganda	na	**54**	58	50	59	49	49	55	54	44	46	53	54	59	54	42
Ukraine	na	**53**	50	55	49	56	52	41	53	59	52	50	57	51	57	51
United States	44	**46**	44	47	48	46	44	45	46	45	40	47	51	47	46	43
Uruguay	na	**56**	54	58	49	56	60	58	56	48	57	58	54	59	58	53
Venezuela	na	**na**	na	na	na	na	na	na	na	na	na	na	na	na	na	na
Vietnam	na	**67**	69	66	65	67	70	65	70	81	69	65	70	72	72	73
Zimbabwe	na	**39**	33	43	41	37	36	41	36	22	34	39	38	42	36	37
Total	40	**52**	52	53	54	53	51	53	51	54	52	53	54	56	53	47

RANKING	
Country	2000
Turkey	94
Jordan	94
Morocco	92
Bangladesh	91
Indonesia	87
Egypt	85
Hungary	84
India	77
Slovenia	75
Malta	74
Greece	73
Algeria	72
Nigeria	71
Moldova	70
Armenia	70
Taiwan	70
Romania	69
Korea, South	68
Vietnam	67
Poland	67
Azerbaijan	65
Albania	65
Tanzania	64
Italy	61
Iran	61
Puerto Rico	60
Peru	59
China	58
Uruguay	56
Chile	55
Philippines	55
Bosnia and Herz.	54
Brazil	54
Uganda	54
Ukraine	53
Bulgaria	52
Croatia	51
Iceland	51
Mexico	51
Netherlands	50
Portugal	50
Spain	48
South Africa	48
Montenegro	48
Russian Fed.	47
Dominican Rep.	46
Belgium	46
United States	46
Switzerland	44
Ireland	44
Georgia	44
Northern Ireland	44
Germany	43
Macedonia	43
Singapore	40
Zimbabwe	39
Luxembourg	37
Japan	37
New Zealand	36
Austria	36
Canada	36
Czech Republic	35
Latvia	33
Serbia	32
Argentina	32
Estonia	32
Belarus	30
Finland	30
Colombia	29
Sweden	29
Australia	27
France	26
Great Britain	25
Norway	23
Slovakia	22
Lithuania	21
Denmark	11
Total	52

C015) IMPORTANT IN A JOB: GOOD HOURS

Here are some more aspects of a job that people say are important.

Please tell me which ones you personally think are important in a job?

Good hours (%) (WVS: V90; EVS: V77)

Country	Wave		Gender		Age			Education			Income			Values		
	1990	2000	Male	Female	16-29	30-49	50+	Lower	Middle	Upper	Lower	Middle	Upper	Mat	Mixed	Postm.
Albania	na	**55**	53	57	64	55	48	52	59	52	54	59	52	56	56	46
Algeria	na	**51**	49	54	57	48	45	46	51	55	57	51	44	52	51	49
Argentina	44	**42**	44	41	48	41	39	45	38	40	44	45	38	44	45	33
Armenia	na	**49**	39	57	46	54	44	49	50	45	48	53	47	54	45	35
Australia	na	**35**	32	38	40	36	29	38	36	31	37	33	33	42	34	36
Austria	35	**43**	38	47	50	46	35	43	43	40	40	47	41	50	41	43
Azerbaijan	na	**55**	48	62	55	55	51	38	54	59	55	57	52	55	56	56
Bangladesh	na	**37**	37	37	38	37	30	38	37	37	34	39	39	35	38	42
Belarus	59	**54**	54	55	57	62	43	42	58	63	51	52	67	51	56	61
Belgium	40	**45**	42	47	47	45	44	49	45	41	42	43	46	50	44	39
Bosnia and Herz.	na	**59**	60	59	63	60	55	62	60	54	63	57	59	54	61	60
Brazil	46	**36**	33	38	39	34	32	40	34	24	44	34	28	43	34	26
Bulgaria	55	**62**	60	64	65	64	59	54	68	62	56	62	68	62	66	62
Canada	52	**47**	45	50	55	50	40	51	48	43	50	47	45	52	50	41
Chile	48	**52**	51	52	48	53	53	49	55	46	51	54	50	51	51	55
China	37	**33**	33	33	37	34	27	26	38	33	27	36	39	32	40	38
Colombia	na	**11**	10	13	13	9	13	14	14	5	16	12	7	17	12	8
Croatia	na	**69**	69	68	67	69	69	77	66	58	67	69	73	67	71	65
Czech Republic	59	**31**	30	32	37	34	25	34	28	27	33	33	29	36	30	23
Denmark	32	**32**	30	34	31	37	28	33	32	32	30	35	35	31	32	34
Dominican Rep.	na	**63**	57	68	64	60	82	75	63	62	67	59	60	66	66	58
Egypt	na	**69**	66	73	73	68	68	65	74	73	69	68	71	68	71	70
El Salvador	na	**na**	na	na	na	na	na	na	na	na	na	na	na	na	na	na
Estonia	58	**56**	53	59	55	62	52	56	60	48	57	61	53	59	56	29
Finland	37	**48**	48	49	56	54	39	50	45	47	52	48	43	57	44	44
France	26	**36**	35	37	41	42	28	37	34	37	36	38	34	39	35	35
Georgia	na	**26**	19	31	24	29	23	22	26	28	23	30	26	25	26	23
Germany	40	**39**	34	43	41	42	34	39	41	23	39	44	47	46	36	35
Great Britain	37	**55**	53	57	62	59	45	56	57	48	53	58	53	na	na	na
Greece	na	**52**	48	54	57	48	45	52	50	53	48	49	55	54	51	51
Hungary	60	**79**	79	79	88	87	67	75	88	84	69	79	86	75	85	89
Iceland	64	**60**	58	62	65	61	56	63	62	51	59	66	56	64	62	44
India	55	**66**	65	66	71	65	61	62	68	71	66	64	67	73	65	69
Indonesia	na	**87**	87	87	88	87	87	82	87	90	87	89	93	88	89	82
Iran	na	**55**	53	56	60	52	44	51	54	58	54	51	56	59	53	52
Ireland	46	**63**	61	64	59	62	65	67	63	55	67	68	55	67	62	61
Israel	na	**na**	na	na	na	na	na	na	na	na	na	na	na	na	na	na
Italy	39	**64**	59	68	68	64	62	66	65	57	68	65	61	64	65	64
Japan	55	**72**	62	80	77	74	67	59	75	69	71	73	72	74	72	69
Jordan	na	**92**	92	92	92	92	91	90	94	93	88	93	95	91	93	93
Korea, South	11	**83**	80	86	88	83	76	77	83	84	83	84	84	82	84	85
Latvia	34	**19**	18	19	26	18	16	18	19	18	18	17	21	20	19	21
Lithuania	54	**54**	53	55	56	54	52	47	59	43	53	55	55	63	52	46
Luxembourg	na	**52**	51	53	62	53	45	56	50	51	52	53	53	57	52	53
Macedonia	na	**48**	47	49	55	49	39	49	50	38	48	47	48	45	50	50
Malta	na	**79**	77	81	79	78	80	83	78	75	77	81	75	78	81	69
Mexico	56	**43**	39	47	43	43	43	46	40	34	44	40	41	47	45	31
Moldova	na	**57**	56	59	62	56	55	57	59	55	54	60	57	62	53	43
Montenegro	na	**46**	40	52	47	49	43	47	49	36	49	44	46	48	44	45
Morocco	na	**92**	91	92	94	92	86	92	93	86	87	91	92	92	93	86
Netherlands	47	**37**	31	42	39	37	35	41	37	32	42	34	32	41	36	36
New Zealand	na	**56**	51	59	60	60	51	56	61	53	55	61	53	59	56	52
Nigeria	80	**67**	67	67	66	70	63	67	65	70	66	69	67	68	67	65
Northern Ireland	42	**70**	69	71	74	71	67	73	72	61	69	70	63	73	71	66
Norway	32	**41**	37	45	35	46	40	45	41	38	na	na	na	47	41	42
Pakistan	na	**na**	na	na	na	na	na	na	na	na	na	na	na	na	na	na
Peru	na	**36**	33	39	38	37	32	41	40	28	40	36	30	44	35	31
Philippines	na	**46**	47	45	47	46	45	46	47	44	50	40	49	46	46	40
Poland	na	**50**	52	48	54	49	48	54	48	37	54	49	45	54	48	47
Portugal	62	**44**	38	49	44	48	41	46	44	27	34	46	40	45	41	50
Puerto Rico	na	**57**	53	59	60	56	56	63	58	56	52	57	60	65	57	54
Romania	36	**59**	57	60	65	62	53	59	64	45	59	62	58	64	58	37
Russian Fed.	46	**40**	33	46	41	43	35	36	43	33	40	42	39	40	40	45
Serbia	na	**35**	32	39	40	40	29	35	37	34	31	39	37	39	35	20
Singapore	na	**47**	43	50	42	49	56	50	49	29	55	47	43	53	45	34
Slovakia	na	**43**	39	48	46	46	38	44	45	32	42	45	43	44	44	42
Slovenia	39	**41**	38	43	24	43	50	54	38	27	54	44	25	50	41	31
South Africa	na	**68**	69	67	72	69	56	70	66	54	73	69	60	70	67	78
Spain	43	**57**	56	58	62	60	52	54	59	62	59	56	59	56	59	56
Sweden	64	**44**	44	45	40	50	42	48	46	38	49	42	41	48	46	39
Switzerland	na	**40**	37	43	45	43	33	45	38	41	41	44	38	47	37	44
Taiwan	na	**72**	69	74	65	74	70	68	77	72	75	71	71	74	71	76
Tanzania	na	**61**	58	65	62	61	57	58	64	67	58	62	67	60	63	63
Turkey	88	**93**	91	94	93	93	91	93	93	90	92	93	91	94	93	92
Uganda	na	**57**	60	54	59	54	60	52	60	41	51	60	61	58	58	50
Ukraine	na	**50**	43	55	54	51	46	44	52	48	48	48	53	50	52	37
United States	55	**66**	61	71	72	67	59	75	65	64	73	63	62	70	66	64
Uruguay	na	**49**	48	50	56	49	46	50	51	41	53	47	48	46	54	45
Venezuela	na	**na**	na	na	na	na	na	na	na	na	na	na	na	na	na	na
Vietnam	na	**63**	61	65	58	63	65	63	64	67	64	58	68	71	67	62
Zimbabwe	na	**54**	52	55	59	54	41	50	59	18	47	62	55	55	53	56
Total	48	**53**	51	56	57	55	49	55	54	51	54	54	53	57	54	49

RANKING	
Country	**2000**
Turkey	93
Jordan	92
Morocco	92
Indonesia	87
Korea, South	83
Malta	79
Hungary	79
Taiwan	72
Japan	72
Northern Ireland	70
Egypt	69
Croatia	69
South Africa	68
Nigeria	67
United States	66
India	66
Italy	64
Dominican Rep.	63
Ireland	63
Vietnam	63
Bulgaria	62
Tanzania	61
Iceland	60
Bosnia and Herz.	59
Romania	59
Moldova	57
Spain	57
Puerto Rico	57
Uganda	57
Estonia	56
New Zealand	56
Albania	55
Great Britain	55
Azerbaijan	55
Iran	55
Belarus	54
Lithuania	54
Zimbabwe	54
Luxembourg	52
Greece	52
Chile	52
Algeria	51
Poland	50
Ukraine	50
Uruguay	49
Armenia	49
Finland	48
Macedonia	48
Canada	47
Singapore	47
Philippines	46
Montenegro	46
Belgium	45
Sweden	44
Portugal	44
Slovakia	43
Mexico	43
Austria	43
Argentina	42
Norway	41
Slovenia	41
Russian Fed.	40
Switzerland	40
Germany	39
Bangladesh	37
Netherlands	37
Peru	36
France	36
Brazil	36
Serbia	35
Australia	35
China	33
Denmark	32
Czech Republic	31
Georgia	26
Latvia	19
Colombia	11
Total	53

C016) IMPORTANT IN A JOB: USE INITIATIVE

Here are some more aspects of a job that people say are important.

Please tell me which ones you personally think are important in a job?

An opportunity to use initiative (%)

(WVS: V91; EVS: V78)

Country	Wave		Gender		Age			Education			Income			Values		
	1990	2000	Male	Female	16-29	30-49	50+	Lower	Middle	Upper	Lower	Middle	Upper	Mat	Mixed	Postm.
Albania	na	40	45	35	42	42	34	29	44	57	34	37	49	37	44	44
Algeria	na	44	48	39	50	43	31	31	44	53	49	41	37	35	49	50
Argentina	55	41	42	39	35	43	44	33	45	71	35	35	54	32	38	52
Armenia	na	46	52	40	47	50	36	35	44	57	50	45	40	40	50	54
Australia	na	52	56	49	51	59	46	36	51	67	46	53	64	47	51	57
Austria	42	49	52	45	52	54	42	38	55	71	38	45	61	36	45	60
Azerbaijan	na	35	38	33	42	31	32	29	32	42	32	37	38	30	42	60
Bangladesh	na	84	85	83	82	84	91	85	82	83	86	81	86	88	81	80
Belarus	40	25	28	23	33	28	16	9	28	42	24	23	34	17	33	34
Belgium	41	49	52	47	51	49	49	36	47	62	41	45	58	41	49	57
Bosnia and Herz.	na	46	49	44	47	47	44	40	44	58	47	47	44	39	49	59
Brazil	51	45	51	39	44	45	46	39	46	62	42	40	51	36	46	59
Bulgaria	47	50	57	44	60	55	42	32	57	68	37	51	61	42	58	72
Canada	54	50	52	48	40	57	48	38	49	62	40	52	58	37	48	60
Chile	55	48	48	48	47	51	45	40	50	61	44	48	55	46	44	63
China	52	34	38	29	39	34	28	20	44	40	25	37	43	31	44	34
Colombia	na	25	29	21	24	28	19	14	23	36	18	22	34	13	26	32
Croatia	na	56	62	50	60	57	52	45	61	69	54	51	65	42	59	55
Czech Republic	55	30	33	27	35	31	26	25	33	42	26	31	32	22	31	41
Denmark	44	50	48	51	57	55	40	40	63	62	44	47	70	40	51	58
Dominican Rep.	na	63	63	62	60	67	73	56	54	67	55	67	68	55	63	74
Egypt	na	45	49	41	48	43	46	39	50	55	44	44	50	41	50	54
El Salvador	na	na	na	na	na	na	na	na	na	na	na	na	na	na	na	na
Estonia	30	35	36	34	41	35	31	21	37	53	25	33	39	24	42	49
Finland	45	48	50	47	50	54	41	41	55	62	45	50	50	44	49	51
France	38	43	43	42	46	48	36	37	47	55	37	43	51	33	45	51
Georgia	na	20	22	19	21	18	22	19	19	24	18	20	24	18	22	25
Germany	58	53	58	48	59	53	49	43	57	74	41	48	63	45	52	65
Great Britain	46	39	41	38	42	42	35	28	47	54	28	40	49	na	na	na
Greece	na	56	56	57	64	53	43	40	53	62	50	58	61	45	59	65
Hungary	37	61	65	59	73	68	48	54	74	81	47	62	70	54	70	79
Iceland	55	63	64	62	66	67	56	56	67	73	58	61	71	59	65	61
India	54	64	65	61	67	64	59	57	65	76	54	61	70	64	72	76
Indonesia	na	84	81	87	87	86	80	72	86	90	82	89	88	85	86	86
Iran	na	50	54	45	54	48	41	41	49	60	49	47	53	45	51	57
Ireland	50	59	62	55	63	58	56	49	59	75	51	61	67	55	61	55
Israel	na	na	na	na	na	na	na	na	na	na	na	na	na	na	na	na
Italy	45	65	69	60	71	65	60	57	67	77	60	62	73	51	67	70
Japan	34	50	58	43	53	48	50	44	46	64	48	46	55	44	52	60
Jordan	na	88	90	86	89	88	85	84	90	92	83	92	89	85	90	86
Korea, South	15	81	82	80	81	82	78	75	79	85	78	83	83	78	83	88
Latvia	17	14	15	13	17	13	14	11	13	23	11	13	19	13	15	23
Lithuania	29	32	34	30	47	32	21	11	37	49	20	32	37	31	31	50
Luxembourg	na	49	49	49	52	51	44	42	50	60	45	49	51	46	49	59
Macedonia	na	29	30	28	27	33	25	20	30	44	23	29	40	25	33	28
Malta	na	69	71	67	72	70	67	65	69	79	59	66	74	64	72	74
Mexico	60	42	47	38	45	44	37	34	50	64	33	45	53	38	44	56
Moldova	na	48	50	46	49	46	47	43	47	53	48	51	51	42	51	61
Montenegro	na	26	31	22	36	26	21	13	31	47	18	22	35	23	32	23
Morocco	na	89	90	88	91	90	82	87	96	94	80	87	91	88	92	90
Netherlands	64	62	63	61	72	68	51	47	69	69	53	66	71	44	64	67
New Zealand	na	73	79	68	75	76	70	66	74	79	69	74	78	66	73	80
Nigeria	82	na	na	na	na	na	na	na	na	na	na	na	na	na	na	na
Northern Ireland	38	52	55	49	59	53	45	43	53	74	42	40	57	41	55	60
Norway	45	50	52	48	53	56	39	40	51	59	na	na	na	32	51	63
Pakistan	na	na	na	na	na	na	na	na	na	na	na	na	na	na	na	na
Peru	na	40	41	40	39	42	40	36	39	46	34	43	48	36	42	41
Philippines	na	31	32	30	30	30	35	32	31	30	31	31	31	29	33	25
Poland	na	56	60	53	55	56	56	53	58	67	53	59	55	51	59	64
Portugal	55	35	35	36	44	37	29	31	40	58	26	31	36	28	40	41
Puerto Rico	na	53	59	50	51	55	53	54	48	56	46	53	59	55	53	54
Romania	38	59	65	54	68	62	52	48	61	78	50	56	71	55	63	77
Russian Fed.	29	31	34	28	37	31	26	20	29	43	25	32	35	27	34	46
Serbia	na	24	27	20	29	29	17	10	22	48	15	21	31	15	30	51
Singapore	na	44	48	41	45	49	30	31	50	59	34	45	51	39	46	45
Slovakia	na	31	31	31	33	35	25	22	33	46	28	29	36	26	33	46
Slovenia	55	78	79	78	83	82	71	69	82	83	77	78	83	75	79	86
South Africa	28	51	51	50	55	47	49	42	60	76	40	55	59	52	50	48
Spain	37	39	41	38	45	43	33	34	40	54	37	39	51	35	40	46
Sweden	71	52	53	51	52	54	50	38	55	59	46	53	58	42	50	61
Switzerland	na	61	66	57	71	60	57	53	62	76	58	53	69	47	62	71
Taiwan	na	62	66	58	64	64	56	57	66	64	62	59	67	63	63	62
Tanzania	na	61	61	61	57	64	61	56	63	74	55	66	73	60	62	63
Turkey	81	91	91	91	91	92	88	89	92	96	89	91	94	89	92	93
Uganda	na	44	48	40	49	37	43	41	45	33	37	43	32	50	42	34
Ukraine	na	42	43	42	52	43	36	25	43	52	36	41	52	37	49	62
United States	52	62	65	58	55	60	71	45	61	68	53	65	68	59	61	63
Uruguay	na	48	51	46	50	56	41	43	55	55	43	48	54	38	52	52
Venezuela	na	na	na	na	na	na	na	na	na	na	na	na	na	na	na	na
Vietnam	na	58	61	54	59	56	60	54	61	78	61	51	65	55	64	70
Zimbabwe	na	34	33	35	39	31	28	33	34	91	27	35	45	33	35	40
Total	47	50	53	47	53	52	44	44	50	61	44	50	56	44	53	59

RANKING	
Country	2000
Turkey	91
Morocco	89
Jordan	88
Bangladesh	84
Indonesia	84
Korea, South	81
Slovenia	78
New Zealand	73
Malta	69
Italy	65
India	64
Iceland	63
Dominican Rep.	63
Netherlands	62
Taiwan	62
United States	62
Hungary	61
Switzerland	61
Tanzania	61
Romania	59
Ireland	59
Vietnam	58
Greece	56
Poland	56
Croatia	56
Puerto Rico	53
Germany	53
Australia	52
Sweden	52
Northern Ireland	52
South Africa	51
Bulgaria	50
Canada	50
Iran	50
Japan	50
Denmark	50
Norway	50
Belgium	49
Luxembourg	49
Austria	49
Finland	48
Chile	48
Uruguay	48
Moldova	48
Bosnia and Herz.	46
Armenia	46
Egypt	45
Brazil	45
Singapore	44
Algeria	44
Uganda	44
France	43
Mexico	42
Ukraine	42
Argentina	41
Peru	40
Albania	40
Great Britain	39
Spain	39
Portugal	35
Azerbaijan	35
Estonia	35
Zimbabwe	34
China	34
Lithuania	32
Philippines	31
Slovakia	31
Russian Fed.	31
Czech Republic	30
Macedonia	29
Montenegro	26
Colombia	25
Belarus	25
Serbia	24
Georgia	20
Latvia	14
Total	50

C017) IMPORTANT IN A JOB: GENEROUS HOLIDAYS

Here are some more aspects of a job that people say are important.

Please tell me which ones you personally think are important in a job?

Generous holidays (%) (WVS: V92; EVS: V80)

Country	Wave		Gender		Age			Education			Income			Values		
	1990	2000	Male	Female	16-29	30-49	50+	Lower	Middle	Upper	Lower	Middle	Upper	Mat	Mixed	Postm.
Albania	na	**48**	48	49	55	49	41	44	52	51	46	50	49	46	52	33
Algeria	na	**21**	21	20	23	21	15	20	22	20	25	21	17	17	22	24
Argentina	30	**21**	26	17	25	18	20	24	15	19	22	22	19	20	23	16
Armenia	na	**31**	26	35	30	34	26	32	30	31	33	30	31	32	31	22
Australia	na	**14**	15	12	15	14	13	15	13	13	13	15	13	14	12	16
Austria	16	**20**	22	19	28	21	16	21	20	20	19	21	21	31	19	20
Azerbaijan	na	**38**	34	42	39	38	40	38	38	40	46	42	31	39	39	31
Bangladesh	na	**28**	29	27	29	29	23	29	30	25	23	34	27	23	32	36
Belarus	53	**36**	37	35	39	41	28	26	41	37	34	36	41	36	36	36
Belgium	30	**34**	34	34	34	35	33	39	34	29	33	34	34	39	34	27
Bosnia and Herz.	na	**42**	42	42	47	44	35	43	42	40	40	42	42	39	44	43
Brazil	18	**13**	12	14	12	13	17	20	8	8	21	12	8	19	11	8
Bulgaria	33	**34**	36	32	37	37	30	30	38	33	32	30	37	33	35	40
Canada	26	**26**	28	25	25	30	24	26	26	28	23	26	28	28	27	25
Chile	23	**32**	33	31	30	34	31	30	34	30	35	34	25	33	33	28
China	15	**11**	10	12	12	12	9	9	13	12	9	11	14	9	15	6
Colombia	na	**5**	5	6	6	5	6	12	5	1	11	6	2	9	7	6
Croatia	na	**48**	52	44	55	47	44	50	46	47	38	50	52	47	49	46
Czech Republic	38	**17**	19	15	23	20	11	18	16	13	14	18	20	22	15	12
Denmark	17	**16**	18	14	13	18	16	17	13	17	16	16	18	20	16	12
Dominican Rep.	na	**24**	22	24	25	22	18	34	27	21	22	19	27	21	24	26
Egypt	na	**13**	12	14	15	12	12	13	13	12	14	13	11	14	12	13
El Salvador	na	**na**	na	na	na	na	na	na	na	na	na	na	na	na	na	na
Estonia	32	**20**	19	22	24	22	17	18	21	22	20	21	17	25	17	19
Finland	20	**21**	26	16	26	25	14	22	18	20	22	23	18	26	19	15
France	15	**20**	22	18	28	22	14	19	20	23	18	17	22	20	19	22
Georgia	na	**14**	13	15	16	14	11	14	14	12	12	17	13	13	13	27
Germany	29	**24**	24	24	29	24	22	25	24	20	24	28	30	32	20	22
Great Britain	25	**39**	42	37	42	39	36	42	37	36	34	43	39	na	na	na
Greece	na	**32**	38	29	40	29	23	22	30	36	28	33	37	31	33	32
Hungary	37	**54**	55	53	59	56	49	55	52	50	47	55	59	53	56	63
Iceland	17	**18**	22	13	16	20	16	18	19	13	16	18	17	17	19	11
India	28	**56**	55	57	57	56	55	57	56	53	61	54	55	63	52	49
Indonesia	na	**30**	25	35	32	28	31	30	27	32	28	30	40	32	28	39
Iran	na	**38**	38	37	41	36	31	36	38	35	35	33	40	41	35	37
Ireland	29	**44**	45	43	39	42	50	50	42	38	48	46	42	44	44	43
Israel	na	**na**	na	na	na	na	na	na	na	na	na	na	na	na	na	na
Italy	19	**35**	35	34	37	35	33	37	33	33	35	36	34	36	36	34
Japan	52	**71**	66	75	81	78	60	54	73	73	66	73	72	69	72	70
Jordan	na	**35**	34	36	37	32	37	36	34	34	34	35	35	36	32	36
Korea, South	8	**85**	82	88	91	84	80	73	85	87	84	88	85	84	86	94
Latvia	31	**10**	10	9	12	9	10	8	9	16	7	11	13	11	9	15
Lithuania	40	**30**	29	30	32	28	30	26	32	28	30	28	31	36	29	14
Luxembourg	na	**37**	39	35	51	38	27	40	35	34	43	34	27	38	39	31
Macedonia	na	**16**	17	14	18	16	13	17	17	10	16	19	12	14	17	19
Malta	na	**36**	34	37	40	35	33	39	35	30	31	32	31	35	38	19
Mexico	33	**14**	15	13	14	13	17	18	10	10	16	13	12	18	13	8
Moldova	na	**39**	36	41	45	35	38	41	36	41	37	40	41	37	42	35
Montenegro	na	**31**	29	33	31	30	30	30	35	21	36	29	31	34	27	15
Morocco	na	**78**	75	80	79	78	73	79	76	69	65	79	80	79	79	76
Netherlands	35	**28**	26	29	31	26	27	30	26	28	32	25	24	25	28	28
New Zealand	na	**32**	34	30	37	34	29	30	33	36	32	34	33	36	32	31
Nigeria	51	**49**	47	51	51	47	42	50	49	47	50	49	48	50	49	45
Northern Ireland	27	**56**	56	55	57	56	53	57	57	52	50	53	50	52	58	58
Norway	9	**11**	12	10	10	12	10	12	9	12	na	na	na	13	10	13
Pakistan	na	**na**	na	na	na	na	na	na	na	na	na	na	na	na	na	na
Peru	na	**12**	12	11	11	12	14	19	10	9	14	12	7	12	12	8
Philippines	na	**11**	12	11	11	12	11	13	10	11	8	9	17	10	12	12
Poland	na	**31**	33	28	37	26	31	35	27	20	33	31	26	29	33	27
Portugal	47	**37**	38	37	38	40	35	38	38	31	33	39	35	35	39	36
Puerto Rico	na	**27**	27	27	26	27	27	37	30	24	23	27	28	34	28	19
Romania	35	**41**	39	42	47	41	37	44	42	29	43	40	37	46	37	31
Russian Fed.	43	**29**	27	30	26	30	29	29	30	27	30	30	28	30	28	30
Serbia	na	**18**	18	19	24	20	15	21	17	16	16	20	17	21	16	11
Singapore	na	**27**	24	30	25	28	32	31	27	15	31	28	24	32	26	18
Slovakia	na	**19**	19	18	22	19	15	19	19	12	18	18	20	20	18	17
Slovenia	29	**46**	45	47	55	48	36	52	46	35	49	46	40	43	45	53
South Africa	8	**37**	38	35	38	38	30	40	33	30	35	43	33	37	37	38
Spain	32	**37**	40	35	42	38	34	39	33	40	36	40	39	38	39	33
Sweden	35	**20**	19	20	18	20	20	19	20	18	18	24	16	21	20	16
Switzerland	na	**26**	26	26	38	26	19	25	26	29	22	26	28	25	24	32
Taiwan	na	**39**	36	42	43	39	36	35	38	43	39	42	37	42	36	32
Tanzania	na	**51**	47	56	54	50	44	47	53	60	48	51	60	49	52	54
Turkey	44	**57**	54	60	59	55	55	61	51	44	62	54	49	58	57	51
Uganda	na	**46**	49	44	49	42	50	43	47	44	39	51	37	50	45	40
Ukraine	na	**43**	40	45	44	43	42	37	44	42	43	42	45	43	45	34
United States	31	**37**	36	37	43	38	29	39	35	37	36	35	40	43	37	33
Uruguay	na	**38**	40	36	42	36	38	42	36	20	44	38	33	35	41	34
Venezuela	na	**na**	na	na	na	na	na	na	na	na	na	na	na	na	na	na
Vietnam	na	**42**	40	44	40	39	48	39	46	48	49	38	43	54	43	45
Zimbabwe	na	**39**	40	38	43	37	33	37	42	38	33	45	41	40	36	50
Total	30	32	33	32	35	33	29	34	32	31	32	33	32	34	32	29

RANKING	
Country	2000
Korea, South	85
Morocco	78
Japan	71
Turkey	57
India	56
Northern Ireland	56
Hungary	54
Tanzania	51
Nigeria	49
Albania	48
Croatia	48
Uganda	46
Slovenia	46
Ireland	44
Ukraine	43
Vietnam	42
Bosnia and Herz.	42
Romania	41
Great Britain	39
Zimbabwe	39
Taiwan	39
Moldova	39
Azerbaijan	38
Uruguay	38
Iran	38
Portugal	37
Spain	37
South Africa	37
Luxembourg	37
United States	37
Belarus	36
Malta	36
Jordan	35
Italy	35
Bulgaria	34
Belgium	34
Greece	32
New Zealand	32
Chile	32
Armenia	31
Poland	31
Montenegro	31
Indonesia	30
Lithuania	30
Russian Fed.	29
Bangladesh	28
Netherlands	28
Singapore	27
Puerto Rico	27
Canada	26
Switzerland	26
Germany	24
Dominican Rep.	24
Argentina	21
Finland	21
Algeria	21
Estonia	20
Austria	20
France	20
Sweden	20
Slovakia	19
Serbia	18
Iceland	18
Czech Republic	17
Denmark	16
Macedonia	16
Mexico	14
Australia	14
Georgia	14
Brazil	13
Egypt	13
Peru	12
Philippines	11
China	11
Norway	11
Latvia	10
Colombia	5
Total	32

C018) IMPORTANT IN A JOB: ACHIEVING

Here are some more aspects of a job that people say are important.
Please tell me which ones you personally think are important in a job?
A job in which you feel you can achieve something (%)

(WVS: V93; EVS: V82)

Country	Wave		Gender		Age			Education			Income			Values		
	1990	2000	Male	Female	16-29	30-49	50+	Lower	Middle	Upper	Lower	Middle	Upper	Mat	Mixed	Postm.
Albania	na	**51**	55	47	55	52	47	45	52	64	46	51	58	49	56	54
Algeria	na	**60**	57	63	66	59	50	50	59	69	66	58	58	56	62	71
Argentina	50	**48**	49	46	53	49	41	45	52	47	45	48	51	48	48	48
Armenia	na	**66**	68	63	69	67	58	56	65	70	71	62	69	63	68	68
Australia	na	**72**	69	74	71	74	70	63	70	81	68	72	78	67	70	76
Austria	49	**57**	59	55	63	57	52	51	62	64	51	55	63	56	55	61
Azerbaijan	na	**49**	53	46	57	45	42	39	48	53	42	51	57	47	53	63
Bangladesh	na	**88**	88	88	88	88	90	89	87	89	90	85	90	90	87	84
Belarus	42	**31**	35	28	47	29	21	14	34	51	24	34	39	22	41	36
Belgium	40	**47**	49	44	52	47	44	39	48	50	46	43	50	40	47	50
Bosnia and Herz.	na	**66**	66	67	74	64	61	55	66	75	65	66	66	62	68	77
Brazil	53	**50**	49	50	45	53	54	50	47	59	52	42	55	49	49	55
Bulgaria	42	**65**	67	62	72	68	58	50	71	78	55	64	73	60	70	82
Canada	74	**73**	70	76	72	74	72	64	72	81	66	72	77	66	72	77
Chile	58	**63**	63	64	63	67	59	59	65	69	61	63	69	60	62	75
China	38	**31**	35	27	40	29	27	24	35	44	27	33	35	27	40	47
Colombia	na	**44**	45	43	43	47	40	30	40	60	32	39	58	33	42	50
Croatia	na	**66**	69	62	73	66	61	60	70	67	68	63	68	53	68	70
Czech Republic	48	**38**	42	35	52	38	31	35	40	47	37	38	40	37	39	44
Denmark	55	**55**	52	59	57	58	52	50	55	67	49	56	70	55	54	64
Dominican Rep.	na	**67**	65	68	68	67	55	75	65	66	65	68	65	78	65	70
Egypt	na	**71**	76	65	73	70	69	65	76	79	71	66	76	67	73	82
El Salvador	na	**na**	na	na	na	na	na	na	na	na	na	na	na	na	na	na
Estonia	43	**45**	45	44	54	49	36	34	47	57	34	41	51	33	52	55
Finland	54	**56**	56	56	62	57	52	50	65	67	53	51	60	54	57	52
France	42	**50**	51	50	51	55	46	47	53	56	50	48	54	48	51	52
Georgia	na	**45**	48	43	51	45	39	42	44	51	39	47	52	44	46	49
Germany	68	**52**	54	50	59	52	48	45	55	70	46	51	60	50	51	55
Great Britain	66	**58**	58	58	62	60	55	51	62	68	52	54	66	na	na	na
Greece	na	**60**	63	58	66	56	54	50	59	63	55	60	67	61	61	62
Hungary	58	**77**	79	76	87	81	68	72	87	91	66	79	83	73	83	84
Iceland	83	**81**	80	81	79	82	80	80	81	82	76	84	82	81	82	73
India	61	**69**	71	67	73	69	64	62	72	82	61	64	77	69	77	78
Indonesia	na	**88**	86	90	91	89	86	81	88	93	89	90	89	86	90	96
Iran	na	**53**	56	48	57	51	43	43	52	63	49	48	56	51	52	60
Ireland	60	**71**	71	71	71	74	68	66	71	81	69	72	75	66	72	76
Israel	na	**na**	na	na	na	na	na	na	na	na	na	na	na	na	na	na
Italy	51	**75**	74	76	83	76	70	70	79	81	70	78	80	70	75	82
Japan	48	**70**	74	66	78	69	67	61	67	81	66	67	75	72	70	77
Jordan	na	**94**	93	94	94	95	88	92	93	97	90	96	95	93	94	97
Korea, South	24	**92**	91	92	94	92	88	88	89	96	89	94	93	90	93	97
Latvia	27	**32**	30	34	41	32	29	28	33	38	30	31	35	29	34	43
Lithuania	44	**42**	41	43	59	40	33	30	44	58	35	40	47	46	42	41
Luxembourg	na	**55**	56	54	57	55	53	53	53	64	50	56	59	51	59	61
Macedonia	na	**50**	51	49	55	53	42	34	56	64	41	53	60	44	58	47
Malta	na	**69**	73	66	76	67	67	63	70	83	56	68	74	63	72	75
Mexico	66	**53**	55	51	55	53	50	46	61	67	45	56	64	47	57	57
Moldova	na	**65**	66	64	68	65	62	61	61	74	67	66	66	62	67	68
Montenegro	na	**53**	58	48	61	52	49	42	56	72	52	52	55	51	58	50
Morocco	na	**93**	94	93	94	94	89	92	97	96	87	91	94	93	96	94
Netherlands	45	**40**	44	36	57	39	32	37	42	41	41	39	41	40	42	35
New Zealand	na	**83**	84	82	83	85	80	77	85	88	82	85	84	81	85	86
Nigeria	91	**82**	82	82	82	82	80	81	81	82	83	82	78	82	82	76
Northern Ireland	62	**67**	65	69	71	66	65	63	66	80	59	59	69	59	72	68
Norway	69	**74**	69	80	72	74	76	71	74	80	na	na	na	71	75	79
Pakistan	na	**na**	na	na	na	na	na	na	na	na	na	na	na	na	na	na
Peru	na	**47**	49	44	46	49	45	47	49	43	48	49	41	50	46	49
Philippines	na	**54**	52	55	57	54	50	50	53	60	54	52	56	52	55	51
Poland	na	**67**	69	64	67	65	68	66	67	70	64	68	72	60	71	73
Portugal	68	**48**	48	48	56	52	40	44	55	57	38	44	52	40	55	46
Puerto Rico	na	**53**	53	54	61	53	50	49	58	52	50	57	51	60	53	50
Romania	63	**74**	76	72	81	77	67	65	78	81	67	77	80	72	78	77
Russian Fed.	28	**39**	43	35	55	39	28	26	37	51	31	40	44	34	43	54
Serbia	na	**50**	53	48	60	52	45	39	50	68	40	46	66	45	55	66
Singapore	na	**61**	65	58	72	57	37	47	67	75	50	58	72	58	62	67
Slovakia	na	**36**	37	35	39	38	32	30	37	55	30	35	42	34	38	54
Slovenia	71	**90**	89	91	92	92	87	89	91	91	91	93	89	88	91	93
South Africa	na	**75**	74	76	77	75	71	70	82	81	65	76	85	74	77	70
Spain	39	**48**	50	47	55	51	42	44	51	58	45	47	55	47	49	52
Sweden	85	**72**	72	72	73	73	71	66	73	77	73	69	75	65	72	76
Switzerland	na	**56**	56	57	57	54	58	60	55	60	53	54	56	53	57	58
Taiwan	na	**69**	70	67	72	71	60	64	74	70	66	68	73	71	72	54
Tanzania	na	**68**	68	68	71	68	64	63	72	77	63	71	77	66	70	58
Turkey	86	**94**	94	94	94	94	93	93	95	94	93	94	96	92	95	94
Uganda	na	**61**	61	60	64	54	67	64	60	46	48	63	57	65	60	49
Ukraine	na	**51**	53	49	68	51	42	30	51	63	43	53	60	44	60	68
United States	71	**84**	81	86	80	85	85	81	82	86	81	85	89	82	83	84
Uruguay	na	**60**	59	60	63	62	57	58	61	65	59	62	60	53	65	56
Venezuela	na	**na**	na	na	na	na	na	na	na	na	na	na	na	na	na	na
Vietnam	na	**68**	72	64	68	67	71	64	73	87	74	65	70	73	73	77
Zimbabwe	na	**61**	62	60	65	58	57	57	67	57	55	63	67	56	64	74
Total	56	**62**	63	61	67	62	56	57	61	69	58	61	66	58	64	66

RANKING

Country	2000
Turkey	94
Jordan	94
Morocco	93
Korea, South	92
Slovenia	90
Bangladesh	88
Indonesia	88
United States	84
New Zealand	83
Nigeria	82
Iceland	81
Hungary	77
Italy	75
South Africa	75
Norway	74
Romania	74
Canada	73
Sweden	72
Australia	72
Ireland	71
Egypt	71
Japan	70
Malta	69
India	69
Taiwan	69
Vietnam	68
Tanzania	68
Dominican Rep.	67
Northern Ireland	67
Poland	67
Bosnia and Herz.	66
Armenia	66
Croatia	66
Bulgaria	65
Moldova	65
Chile	63
Singapore	61
Zimbabwe	61
Uganda	61
Algeria	60
Greece	60
Uruguay	60
Great Britain	58
Austria	57
Switzerland	56
Finland	56
Denmark	55
Luxembourg	55
Philippines	54
Puerto Rico	53
Mexico	53
Montenegro	53
Iran	53
Germany	52
Albania	51
Ukraine	51
Serbia	50
France	50
Macedonia	50
Brazil	50
Azerbaijan	49
Spain	48
Portugal	48
Argentina	48
Belgium	47
Peru	47
Georgia	45
Estonia	45
Colombia	44
Lithuania	42
Netherlands	40
Russian Fed.	39
Czech Republic	38
Slovakia	36
Latvia	32
Belarus	31
China	31
Total	62

C019) IMPORTANT IN A JOB: A RESPONSIBLE JOB

Here are some more aspects of a job that people say are important.
Please tell me which ones you personally think are important in a job?

A responsible job (%) (WVS: V94; EVS: V83)

Country	Wave		Gender		Age			Education			Income			Values		
	1990	2000	Male	Female	16-29	30-49	50+	Lower	Middle	Upper	Lower	Middle	Upper	Mat	Mixed	Postm.
Albania	na	**25**	27	24	28	24	25	19	29	33	19	26	31	22	30	18
Algeria	na	**46**	47	46	49	46	42	40	44	55	49	45	44	38	51	55
Argentina	58	**41**	42	40	36	43	43	41	40	41	44	41	38	47	42	37
Armenia	na	**43**	48	38	46	44	35	32	44	45	49	39	43	43	41	55
Australia	na	**38**	41	35	34	38	42	35	35	42	38	36	41	38	36	41
Austria	45	**49**	54	45	49	51	47	45	51	59	40	50	53	48	48	52
Azerbaijan	na	**45**	50	40	49	44	38	43	44	46	49	47	40	43	48	53
Bangladesh	na	**88**	89	87	89	87	90	86	90	91	87	86	91	89	87	88
Belarus	27	**14**	15	13	15	15	13	9	15	20	12	14	19	11	19	11
Belgium	38	**41**	46	37	43	40	42	35	38	50	39	38	44	37	42	45
Bosnia and Herz.	na	**46**	48	44	46	46	46	42	45	53	45	47	43	43	47	43
Brazil	59	**42**	46	39	40	42	47	47	38	38	46	40	40	44	42	40
Bulgaria	28	**40**	43	38	47	46	33	29	46	50	32	44	43	34	46	48
Canada	56	**43**	44	42	36	42	48	42	43	43	39	44	45	41	43	44
Chile	52	**44**	43	44	43	45	43	38	46	49	39	45	48	43	43	46
China	22	**22**	24	21	26	22	20	20	26	5	22	24	20	19	29	25
Colombia	na	**20**	22	18	19	20	22	16	19	24	18	19	22	16	17	17
Croatia	na	**44**	47	42	45	44	45	41	46	49	49	40	50	36	45	49
Czech Republic	48	**29**	31	28	26	31	29	27	30	37	26	30	32	29	29	30
Denmark	42	**48**	50	45	56	50	41	40	54	58	41	49	57	44	48	48
Dominican Rep.	na	**59**	57	61	57	62	64	69	60	57	62	51	57	64	59	55
Egypt	na	**73**	76	70	75	73	72	71	77	74	74	73	74	71	75	77
El Salvador	na	**na**	na	na	na	na	na	na	na	na	na	na	na	na	na	na
Estonia	17	**17**	19	16	22	17	16	15	17	23	16	17	18	14	20	18
Finland	30	**40**	42	39	42	41	39	37	43	50	32	44	42	37	42	33
France	53	**49**	51	47	55	49	45	48	48	53	49	47	51	48	50	50
Georgia	na	**28**	32	24	25	28	32	28	25	36	26	28	30	28	29	28
Germany	49	**55**	61	51	59	53	55	49	56	75	48	51	66	54	55	57
Great Britain	42	**37**	42	32	38	39	33	31	41	44	31	33	40	na	na	na
Greece	na	**51**	51	51	50	49	58	54	50	51	46	52	55	49	53	49
Hungary	51	**78**	81	75	84	82	70	75	83	86	67	80	83	75	83	84
Iceland	36	**39**	40	37	39	40	37	35	40	44	33	36	47	38	41	27
India	65	**73**	75	71	76	75	69	66	78	86	61	70	83	75	81	84
Indonesia	na	**95**	95	96	96	97	95	90	98	97	96	96	99	96	97	93
Iran	na	**58**	61	54	59	58	54	54	59	57	58	53	60	60	57	62
Ireland	41	**54**	55	52	54	49	58	52	54	55	55	58	53	55	56	44
Israel	na	**na**	na	na	na	na	na	na	na	na	na	na	na	na	na	na
Italy	32	**53**	59	47	56	51	52	52	53	53	52	52	57	48	53	56
Japan	48	**67**	72	63	65	65	69	63	65	74	67	65	71	71	68	66
Jordan	na	**92**	94	90	92	93	89	91	93	93	88	94	95	90	93	95
Korea, South	23	**91**	90	92	85	94	93	95	93	89	90	93	91	92	92	87
Latvia	12	**15**	16	14	20	13	15	14	14	20	12	14	20	17	14	17
Lithuania	24	**18**	21	16	26	16	15	13	19	24	18	12	19	18	18	21
Luxembourg	na	**55**	56	54	59	55	52	50	57	60	48	58	64	61	57	58
Macedonia	na	**38**	41	35	35	40	40	35	39	41	39	36	41	38	39	40
Malta	na	**60**	62	58	64	58	60	57	58	78	57	53	63	56	62	68
Mexico	57	**53**	57	49	54	51	52	48	58	58	47	54	58	54	55	52
Moldova	na	**43**	45	40	40	42	45	45	39	47	48	44	44	38	46	58
Montenegro	na	**25**	25	25	23	28	24	19	26	39	13	23	33	24	27	24
Morocco	na	**84**	86	82	84	85	81	82	90	90	73	82	87	83	86	86
Netherlands	43	**42**	49	34	48	40	40	34	46	44	43	37	49	33	43	42
New Zealand	na	**51**	56	47	49	51	52	47	53	55	47	53	53	51	52	50
Nigeria	84	**84**	82	85	83	85	81	84	83	85	84	85	81	85	84	76
Northern Ireland	35	**49**	52	47	55	51	45	44	50	60	42	40	46	41	54	54
Norway	43	**42**	41	43	46	41	41	38	40	48	na	na	na	36	43	44
Pakistan	na	**na**	na	na	na	na	na	na	na	na	na	na	na	na	na	na
Peru	na	**48**	49	47	46	51	47	53	47	48	51	46	48	48	49	44
Philippines	na	**57**	58	55	55	55	61	59	53	59	55	53	62	57	56	58
Poland	na	**53**	61	46	48	50	60	57	50	49	53	54	56	50	54	58
Portugal	54	**42**	40	44	44	44	40	42	44	44	37	47	36	43	42	40
Puerto Rico	na	**54**	55	55	50	52	59	63	58	52	58	53	51	64	55	50
Romania	28	**57**	58	56	56	60	54	53	56	64	52	57	63	57	59	53
Russian Fed.	21	**26**	28	24	26	25	27	23	25	32	23	29	28	26	27	41
Serbia	na	**18**	19	17	16	16	21	15	20	22	16	19	20	17	18	27
Singapore	na	**48**	51	44	45	51	47	45	49	49	50	46	48	48	48	42
Slovakia	na	**21**	23	20	23	21	20	15	24	28	21	19	26	19	23	28
Slovenia	53	**73**	74	72	69	74	74	76	72	68	79	73	68	74	74	70
South Africa	25	**67**	66	67	67	67	66	67	68	54	65	68	68	65	69	69
Spain	32	**39**	42	36	41	39	37	38	38	43	37	39	43	38	40	37
Sweden	72	**55**	53	56	52	56	55	51	54	59	51	56	59	57	54	55
Switzerland	na	**62**	68	56	62	64	60	55	63	69	56	58	68	51	65	62
Taiwan	na	**70**	72	69	73	69	72	70	73	69	75	68	67	72	70	76
Tanzania	na	**55**	54	56	48	59	57	51	53	72	48	58	72	50	59	67
Turkey	78	**90**	90	90	90	91	89	89	91	94	89	90	93	91	90	91
Uganda	na	**56**	58	54	62	48	61	60	56	46	46	52	45	62	55	46
Ukraine	na	**35**	36	34	31	38	35	25	36	39	31	35	41	33	39	41
United States	56	**55**	57	52	54	52	60	55	55	54	51	54	59	47	56	55
Uruguay	na	**50**	52	48	50	52	48	47	54	53	50	47	55	42	53	51
Venezuela	na	**na**	na	na	na	na	na	na	na	na	na	na	na	na	na	na
Vietnam	na	**67**	70	64	63	65	72	64	68	85	72	61	72	74	70	76
Zimbabwe	na	**41**	41	41	44	44	29	37	47	18	31	44	47	42	41	45
Total	43	**50**	52	48	52	51	47	49	48	55	48	49	52	48	52	51

RANKING	
Country	**2000**
Indonesia	95
Jordan	92
Korea, South	91
Turkey	90
Bangladesh	88
Morocco	84
Nigeria	84
Hungary	78
India	73
Egypt	73
Slovenia	73
Taiwan	70
Japan	67
South Africa	67
Vietnam	67
Switzerland	62
Malta	60
Dominican Rep.	59
Iran	58
Romania	57
Philippines	57
Uganda	56
Germany	55
Luxembourg	55
United States	55
Sweden	55
Tanzania	55
Puerto Rico	54
Ireland	54
Poland	53
Italy	53
Mexico	53
Greece	51
New Zealand	51
Uruguay	50
Northern Ireland	49
Austria	49
France	49
Peru	48
Denmark	48
Singapore	48
Algeria	46
Bosnia and Herz.	46
Azerbaijan	45
Croatia	44
Chile	44
Canada	43
Armenia	43
Moldova	43
Portugal	42
Brazil	42
Norway	42
Netherlands	42
Belgium	41
Zimbabwe	41
Argentina	41
Bulgaria	40
Finland	40
Iceland	39
Spain	39
Macedonia	38
Australia	38
Great Britain	37
Ukraine	35
Czech Republic	29
Georgia	28
Russian Fed.	26
Albania	25
Montenegro	25
China	22
Slovakia	21
Colombia	20
Lithuania	18
Serbia	18
Estonia	17
Latvia	15
Belarus	14
Total	50

C020) IMPORTANT IN A JOB: A JOB THAT IS INTERESTING

Here are some more aspects of a job that people say are important.

Please tell me which ones you personally think are important in a job?

A job that is interesting (%) (WVS: V95; EVS: V84)

Country	Wave		Gender		Age			Education			Income			Values		
	1990	2000	Male	Female	16-29	30-49	50+	Lower	Middle	Upper	Lower	Middle	Upper	Mat	Mixed	Postm.
Albania	na	**41**	45	37	51	41	33	34	42	57	37	39	48	43	42	41
Algeria	na	**57**	55	58	61	59	43	44	59	64	59	53	55	53	60	56
Argentina	51	**39**	43	37	44	40	35	38	38	57	35	37	47	37	39	41
Armenia	na	**77**	78	77	76	83	71	63	78	83	80	74	80	75	79	83
Australia	na	**74**	74	74	75	77	70	67	74	81	71	75	78	66	74	78
Austria	56	**57**	62	53	66	61	49	47	65	72	43	56	69	49	55	63
Azerbaijan	na	**81**	83	80	84	81	77	68	80	86	78	81	85	81	83	85
Bangladesh	na	**87**	88	85	88	86	89	88	85	89	91	87	84	86	88	86
Belarus	73	**58**	59	57	68	64	44	32	65	78	49	61	69	51	65	77
Belgium	47	**56**	58	54	65	55	53	49	53	66	50	55	61	51	55	63
Bosnia and Herz.	na	**71**	71	71	74	72	67	67	71	76	71	70	73	73	70	74
Brazil	46	**28**	26	29	29	26	28	28	26	32	29	22	30	31	24	34
Bulgaria	51	**64**	65	62	75	68	54	47	70	80	52	61	75	54	73	85
Canada	72	**70**	73	68	74	72	67	61	72	76	61	73	75	59	70	74
Chile	50	**58**	58	57	61	62	49	49	60	70	50	59	67	56	56	66
China	34	**18**	16	19	19	18	17	17	19	16	19	15	20	15	24	9
Colombia	na	**12**	12	13	13	12	10	8	10	18	11	9	18	8	11	17
Croatia	na	**77**	82	71	85	79	68	72	79	80	75	75	80	66	78	84
Czech Republic	69	**57**	56	57	66	58	51	51	61	71	51	56	63	51	59	65
Denmark	63	**65**	67	63	78	70	53	56	82	75	61	66	79	56	66	70
Dominican Rep.	na	**57**	54	59	56	58	64	63	48	60	52	56	68	51	58	58
Egypt	na	**47**	49	44	51	46	42	42	52	49	48	46	48	43	50	52
El Salvador	na	**na**	na	na	na	na	na	na	na	na	na	na	na	na	na	na
Estonia	68	**65**	62	68	74	67	59	57	68	73	65	63	69	65	66	57
Finland	65	**76**	76	76	86	81	68	69	85	86	74	75	79	77	76	74
France	59	**66**	66	66	72	68	60	60	70	78	62	66	68	58	67	75
Georgia	na	**65**	62	67	65	67	62	61	62	75	62	67	68	66	64	65
Germany	65	**70**	73	68	76	74	63	67	72	76	64	66	70	73	70	66
Great Britain	72	**68**	67	69	66	69	68	61	71	80	63	67	69	na	na	na
Greece	na	**69**	65	71	79	63	58	59	64	74	62	70	72	67	69	73
Hungary	51	**77**	79	75	86	83	66	72	85	89	67	78	82	74	81	94
Iceland	76	**76**	76	76	86	76	67	70	80	81	71	78	81	76	78	73
India	64	**75**	76	72	77	74	73	68	78	85	68	71	81	75	81	84
Indonesia	na	**82**	78	86	86	81	81	77	80	87	80	85	87	83	82	79
Iran	na	**57**	60	53	63	53	45	49	57	62	57	50	61	60	56	62
Ireland	70	**72**	72	72	75	72	69	65	72	83	67	74	75	71	72	71
Israel	na	**na**	na	na	na	na	na	na	na	na	na	na	na	na	na	na
Italy	56	**76**	76	75	84	74	73	71	79	79	72	77	79	69	77	79
Japan	36	**64**	65	62	81	70	51	49	64	72	60	62	66	59	64	75
Jordan	na	**88**	89	88	89	90	86	88	88	90	86	92	89	89	89	89
Korea, South	7	**79**	77	81	85	80	70	73	76	84	77	80	80	76	82	84
Latvia	60	**48**	51	46	56	50	43	37	48	61	42	51	55	48	50	43
Lithuania	64	**63**	63	64	77	70	48	44	69	76	52	63	72	60	64	77
Luxembourg	na	**64**	63	65	73	65	58	58	63	80	58	65	72	58	66	75
Macedonia	na	**52**	51	53	57	54	45	42	56	59	43	53	62	55	53	42
Malta	na	**85**	84	86	85	83	86	86	84	88	84	87	80	80	87	90
Mexico	60	**42**	44	40	44	38	46	39	43	55	40	38	49	41	43	39
Moldova	na	**75**	76	74	83	74	69	72	74	79	72	75	77	75	75	79
Montenegro	na	**58**	57	58	67	62	48	42	66	74	52	52	66	56	59	71
Morocco	na	**94**	94	94	95	95	89	94	95	94	89	89	97	95	96	92
Netherlands	60	**56**	60	51	68	63	42	36	62	68	46	58	66	35	57	65
New Zealand	na	**84**	84	84	89	84	83	80	84	89	80	85	89	89	84	88
Nigeria	83	**82**	81	82	83	80	78	83	82	80	84	81	79	84	81	78
Northern Ireland	69	**75**	76	75	79	76	72	71	77	84	68	71	76	70	79	77
Norway	64	**70**	70	70	78	77	56	59	70	81	na	na	na	55	71	82
Pakistan	na	**na**	na	na	na	na	na	na	na	na	na	na	na	na	na	na
Peru	na	**33**	34	32	35	34	26	32	32	35	31	36	33	32	33	38
Philippines	na	**45**	46	43	43	42	51	50	38	48	42	43	49	45	45	34
Poland	na	**74**	78	71	80	70	76	74	75	77	73	76	77	72	77	66
Portugal	53	**45**	39	51	49	46	42	43	50	46	41	42	43	44	43	51
Puerto Rico	na	**55**	58	53	60	53	54	49	50	59	47	56	60	58	53	60
Romania	43	**66**	67	65	74	69	60	60	71	68	62	68	70	67	67	71
Russian Fed.	67	**69**	70	69	79	69	63	56	69	78	62	72	74	67	71	80
Serbia	na	**45**	45	46	56	49	37	36	44	61	38	43	52	39	50	63
Singapore	na	**60**	62	59	66	58	46	53	66	55	53	63	65	55	62	63
Slovakia	na	**49**	49	50	56	51	43	42	52	57	44	49	54	47	52	62
Slovenia	76	**92**	93	91	95	92	88	88	94	91	92	89	94	92	91	93
South Africa	na	**65**	67	63	68	66	55	61	71	65	60	67	68	62	67	71
Spain	47	**55**	56	55	60	58	50	51	56	68	55	57	58	52	57	60
Sweden	80	**70**	71	69	79	73	61	54	74	76	69	68	74	60	69	76
Switzerland	na	**72**	74	70	82	71	68	68	73	77	72	67	76	67	72	76
Taiwan	na	**77**	79	75	83	79	69	72	79	81	78	75	78	78	80	81
Tanzania	na	**49**	48	50	46	51	48	47	47	58	46	52	57	44	52	50
Turkey	49	**49**	48	50	51	47	49	49	48	54	50	47	54	48	48	53
Uganda	na	**54**	53	54	60	44	59	54	54	45	49	41	42	54	55	47
Ukraine	na	**70**	70	70	79	73	63	48	71	82	67	70	77	67	77	72
United States	69	**82**	84	79	83	80	83	78	78	85	78	80	90	76	82	83
Uruguay	na	**50**	51	49	59	50	46	45	56	60	46	50	56	37	55	52
Venezuela	na	**na**	na	na	na	na	na	na	na	na	na	na	na	na	na	na
Vietnam	na	**59**	60	59	57	59	62	56	63	70	59	55	64	66	63	67
Zimbabwe	na	**57**	56	58	60	53	56	56	59	32	50	59	55	58	56	62
Total	60	**64**	64	63	68	64	58	57	65	72	59	63	67	61	65	68

RANKING	
Country	2000
Morocco	94
Slovenia	92
Jordan	88
Bangladesh	87
Malta	85
New Zealand	84
Indonesia	82
Nigeria	82
United States	82
Azerbaijan	81
Korea, South	79
Armenia	77
Taiwan	77
Hungary	77
Croatia	77
Iceland	76
Finland	76
Italy	76
Northern Ireland	75
Moldova	75
India	75
Poland	74
Australia	74
Switzerland	72
Ireland	72
Bosnia and Herz.	71
Canada	70
Ukraine	70
Germany	70
Norway	70
Sweden	70
Russian Fed.	69
Greece	69
Great Britain	68
Romania	66
France	66
Estonia	65
Denmark	65
South Africa	65
Georgia	65
Luxembourg	64
Japan	64
Bulgaria	64
Lithuania	63
Singapore	60
Vietnam	59
Belarus	58
Chile	58
Montenegro	58
Austria	57
Dominican Rep.	57
Zimbabwe	57
Czech Republic	57
Algeria	57
Iran	57
Belgium	56
Netherlands	56
Spain	55
Puerto Rico	55
Uganda	54
Macedonia	52
Uruguay	50
Slovakia	49
Turkey	49
Tanzania	49
Latvia	48
Egypt	47
Serbia	45
Portugal	45
Philippines	45
Mexico	42
Albania	41
Argentina	39
Peru	33
Brazil	28
China	18
Colombia	12
Total	64

C021) IMPORTANT IN A JOB: THAT MEETS ONE'S ABILITIES

Here are some more aspects of a job that people say are important.
Please tell me which ones you personally think are important in a job?

A job that meets one's abilities (%) (WVS: V96; EVS: V85)

Country	Wave		Gender		Age			Education			Income			Values		
	1990	2000	Male	Female	16-29	30-49	50+	Lower	Middle	Upper	Lower	Middle	Upper	Mat	Mixed	Postm.
Albania	na	**29**	36	23	31	30	28	24	30	43	24	28	36	24	33	36
Algeria	na	**70**	73	68	74	69	65	65	71	73	74	64	71	70	70	76
Argentina	59	**51**	49	53	46	51	56	50	53	53	49	52	52	47	51	55
Armenia	na	**66**	64	68	66	68	63	67	67	62	64	74	66	70	62	73
Australia	na	**45**	43	47	37	49	49	43	42	51	48	46	46	50	44	46
Austria	58	**59**	61	58	61	61	56	54	62	71	51	57	64	49	58	65
Azerbaijan	na	**73**	76	71	73	72	78	69	75	71	78	76	71	73	74	82
Bangladesh	na	**91**	92	89	89	92	94	90	91	91	91	91	90	93	89	91
Belarus	50	**39**	40	38	42	41	34	29	41	51	39	37	46	32	47	43
Belgium	49	**56**	57	55	63	58	52	44	54	68	50	51	63	45	57	64
Bosnia and Herz.	na	**74**	76	73	74	73	76	73	74	76	76	73	75	74	74	77
Brazil	66	**48**	46	50	43	48	56	46	49	50	50	47	48	45	51	46
Bulgaria	52	**78**	79	78	82	81	75	67	83	88	72	74	87	75	82	84
Canada	56	**52**	52	52	47	50	57	49	53	55	50	53	52	46	53	52
Chile	59	**66**	65	67	66	67	65	68	65	65	66	66	66	70	64	67
China	66	**59**	63	54	68	59	50	47	67	72	52	63	67	62	67	56
Colombia	na	**24**	23	26	23	23	28	24	23	25	24	26	21	22	20	19
Croatia	na	**74**	75	74	77	75	72	71	76	76	74	73	78	68	75	77
Czech Republic	81	**56**	59	53	62	57	52	51	59	72	52	56	60	53	56	67
Denmark	56	**54**	52	56	53	55	55	53	51	57	53	56	56	59	54	52
Dominican Rep.	na	**79**	77	81	77	82	91	94	81	77	85	80	72	82	79	80
Egypt	na	**85**	86	84	86	85	85	82	88	90	83	84	89	82	88	90
El Salvador	na	**na**	na	na	na	na	na	na	na	na	na	na	na	na	na	na
Estonia	55	**55**	55	54	52	54	57	57	54	54	53	60	51	56	55	35
Finland	45	**54**	53	56	58	60	47	50	58	64	56	53	53	60	52	51
France	43	**50**	50	50	57	51	46	46	51	60	52	48	50	44	51	58
Georgia	na	**47**	48	45	44	48	48	47	45	51	47	51	44	47	46	51
Germany	65	**54**	57	52	57	54	54	50	56	67	50	52	54	55	53	58
Great Britain	42	**39**	41	37	45	40	34	32	44	46	31	39	42	na	na	na
Greece	na	**56**	53	58	58	55	54	61	56	55	56	55	59	53	57	59
Hungary	66	**86**	88	85	93	93	76	83	93	93	78	87	92	85	90	97
Iceland	72	**65**	65	66	64	69	61	61	66	73	64	67	67	65	66	68
India	67	**77**	79	74	79	77	73	70	80	90	69	73	84	78	84	89
Indonesia	na	**93**	92	96	96	94	93	90	95	95	94	95	98	94	95	96
Iran	na	**67**	69	64	69	66	62	64	65	70	66	61	70	69	67	71
Ireland	50	**60**	60	61	48	63	67	63	58	61	64	63	57	66	60	51
Israel	na	**na**	na	na	na	na	na	na	na	na	na	na	na	na	na	na
Italy	54	**75**	76	75	76	74	76	77	74	76	78	79	73	76	76	76
Japan	71	**90**	89	91	92	91	87	85	92	89	89	89	90	94	89	91
Jordan	na	**96**	98	94	97	96	93	94	97	98	93	99	97	94	97	99
Korea, South	31	**96**	94	97	97	96	94	95	96	96	96	95	97	95	97	94
Latvia	44	**42**	42	42	38	42	43	42	42	43	43	39	43	39	44	51
Lithuania	56	**52**	53	51	52	54	49	42	54	62	47	53	53	55	53	40
Luxembourg	na	**57**	58	56	59	60	52	51	56	73	50	59	60	51	60	61
Macedonia	na	**42**	44	40	39	44	43	38	45	42	41	44	42	41	44	46
Malta	na	**93**	92	93	95	92	92	93	92	94	91	92	93	90	94	90
Mexico	65	**49**	49	48	44	50	54	49	49	46	48	51	47	50	51	40
Moldova	na	**79**	78	80	81	81	75	74	79	85	79	80	79	77	80	78
Montenegro	na	**53**	57	49	56	53	50	46	53	69	46	53	58	55	52	53
Morocco	na	**96**	96	96	97	96	94	95	99	97	92	96	95	96	97	94
Netherlands	74	**69**	73	65	79	70	63	52	77	76	64	68	80	51	70	77
New Zealand	na	**61**	60	62	62	57	65	60	62	60	67	60	55	64	59	59
Nigeria	86	**79**	78	80	79	79	79	76	80	83	78	82	77	79	79	78
Northern Ireland	41	**61**	61	61	58	64	59	58	59	72	51	55	59	53	65	64
Norway	43	**47**	41	53	48	43	52	52	46	44	na	na	na	52	46	48
Pakistan	na	**na**	na	na	na	na	na	na	na	na	na	na	na	na	na	na
Peru	na	**61**	63	60	60	60	67	61	56	68	59	63	64	58	62	64
Philippines	na	**58**	57	58	58	56	59	59	52	63	58	55	60	58	58	49
Poland	na	**66**	70	63	70	63	67	65	65	72	67	66	67	63	69	62
Portugal	57	**47**	47	46	59	46	40	42	54	61	32	40	52	38	51	52
Puerto Rico	na	**73**	69	75	73	74	72	73	68	76	70	72	79	66	75	74
Romania	52	**79**	82	77	82	84	73	72	84	85	74	83	84	83	80	76
Russian Fed.	54	**54**	54	54	56	57	50	46	54	60	53	57	53	53	56	61
Serbia	na	**40**	41	40	44	39	39	34	40	49	33	38	50	36	44	48
Singapore	na	**54**	57	51	57	56	40	43	58	68	49	56	59	55	54	48
Slovakia	na	**55**	57	54	61	55	51	44	59	70	48	54	63	49	62	79
Slovenia	61	**86**	85	88	86	88	85	87	88	80	87	90	82	84	88	88
South Africa	32	**63**	63	64	65	61	65	58	70	69	56	75	61	66	63	50
Spain	46	**60**	61	60	62	61	59	59	59	69	58	65	65	62	61	61
Sweden	53	**41**	41	41	38	40	44	43	39	43	43	39	39	39	41	40
Switzerland	na	**62**	60	65	55	62	67	59	63	67	59	65	62	66	61	68
Taiwan	na	**84**	84	83	91	84	77	77	89	87	80	85	88	86	85	70
Tanzania	na	**65**	65	66	64	68	61	63	67	75	63	65	74	62	69	67
Turkey	90	**96**	96	96	96	96	96	96	96	98	95	96	98	95	97	96
Uganda	na	**59**	57	60	63	54	57	60	59	45	49	57	50	61	61	39
Ukraine	na	**61**	64	59	67	61	58	46	62	67	59	62	66	57	67	64
United States	57	**62**	61	63	60	59	66	58	63	63	58	64	65	56	62	63
Uruguay	na	**59**	58	59	60	59	58	61	56	55	64	60	55	64	62	52
Venezuela	na	**na**	na	na	na	na	na	na	na	na	na	na	na	na	na	na
Vietnam	na	**82**	85	80	83	83	81	79	87	96	76	83	87	92	86	80
Zimbabwe	na	**55**	55	55	55	57	53	52	59	70	48	55	64	53	58	47
Total	57	**64**	64	63	66	65	61	61	64	69	62	65	66	64	65	63

RANKING	
Country	**2000**
Turkey	96
Korea, South	96
Jordan	96
Morocco	96
Indonesia	93
Malta	93
Bangladesh	91
Japan	90
Slovenia	86
Hungary	86
Egypt	85
Taiwan	84
Vietnam	82
Dominican Rep.	79
Romania	79
Moldova	79
Nigeria	79
Bulgaria	78
India	77
Italy	75
Bosnia and Herz.	74
Croatia	74
Azerbaijan	73
Puerto Rico	73
Algeria	70
Netherlands	69
Iran	67
Armenia	66
Chile	66
Poland	66
Iceland	65
Tanzania	65
South Africa	63
Switzerland	62
United States	62
Peru	61
Ukraine	61
New Zealand	61
Northern Ireland	61
Ireland	60
Spain	60
Austria	59
Uruguay	59
China	59
Uganda	59
Philippines	58
Luxembourg	57
Czech Republic	56
Greece	56
Belgium	56
Slovakia	55
Zimbabwe	55
Estonia	55
Germany	54
Denmark	54
Finland	54
Russian Fed.	54
Singapore	54
Montenegro	53
Canada	52
Lithuania	52
Argentina	51
France	50
Mexico	49
Brazil	48
Norway	47
Georgia	47
Portugal	47
Australia	45
Macedonia	42
Latvia	42
Sweden	41
Serbia	40
Belarus	39
Great Britain	39
Albania	29
Colombia	24
Total	64

C022_1) IMPORTANT IN A JOB: PLEASANT PEOPLE TO WORK WITH

Here are some more aspects of a job that people say are important.

Please tell me which ones you personally think are important in a job?

Pleasant people to work with (%)

(EVS: V72)

Country	Wave 1990	Wave 2000	Gender Male	Gender Female	Age 16-29	Age 30-49	Age 50+
Albania	na	**na**	na	na	na	na	na
Algeria	na	**na**	na	na	na	na	na
Argentina	61	**na**	na	na	na	na	na
Armenia	na	**na**	na	na	na	na	na
Australia	na	**na**	na	na	na	na	na
Austria	62	**68**	67	69	81	74	55
Azerbaijan	na	**na**	na	na	na	na	na
Bangladesh	na	**na**	na	na	na	na	na
Belarus	82	**69**	66	72	76	72	61
Belgium	68	**75**	75	74	83	75	71
Bosnia and Herz.	na	**na**	na	na	na	na	na
Brazil	58	**na**	na	na	na	na	na
Bulgaria	63	**64**	68	61	74	67	57
Canada	73	**na**	na	na	na	na	na
Chile	57	**na**	na	na	na	na	na
China	55	**na**	na	na	na	na	na
Colombia	na	**na**	na	na	na	na	na
Croatia	na	**76**	77	75	82	78	71
Czech Republic	83	**64**	61	67	70	68	58
Denmark	77	**78**	74	82	87	79	72
Dominican Rep.	na	**na**	na	na	na	na	na
Egypt	na	**na**	na	na	na	na	na
El Salvador	na	**na**	na	na	na	na	na
Estonia	77	**71**	65	76	76	71	68
Finland	64	**74**	71	77	88	75	66
France	53	**65**	63	67	72	70	57
Georgia	na	**na**	na	na	na	na	na
Germany	72	**65**	60	69	68	66	63
Great Britain	65	**73**	69	76	75	71	72
Greece	na	**76**	75	77	85	72	66
Hungary	65	**85**	86	84	94	89	76
Iceland	89	**83**	81	85	87	83	80
India	69	**na**	na	na	na	na	na
Indonesia	na	**na**	na	na	na	na	na
Iran	na	**na**	na	na	na	na	na
Ireland	64	**77**	73	80	81	75	76
Israel	na	**na**	na	na	na	na	na
Italy	50	**72**	70	73	76	73	68
Japan	78	**na**	na	na	na	na	na
Jordan	na	**na**	na	na	na	na	na
Korea, South	14	**na**	na	na	na	na	na
Latvia	55	**32**	32	32	41	32	29
Lithuania	73	**60**	59	61	72	65	46
Luxembourg	na	**74**	73	76	83	76	66
Macedonia	na	**na**	na	na	na	na	na
Malta	na	**83**	83	83	85	84	82
Mexico	69	**na**	na	na	na	na	na
Moldova	na	**na**	na	na	na	na	na
Montenegro	na	**na**	na	na	na	na	na
Morocco	na	**na**	na	na	na	na	na
Netherlands	93	**89**	89	89	95	92	83
New Zealand	na	**na**	na	na	na	na	na
Nigeria	85	**na**	na	na	na	na	na
Northern Ireland	68	**71**	64	77	78	71	67
Norway	80	**na**	na	na	na	na	na
Pakistan	na	**na**	na	na	na	na	na
Peru	na	**na**	na	na	na	na	na
Philippines	na	**na**	na	na	na	na	na
Poland	na	**74**	75	74	78	73	74
Portugal	80	**67**	63	70	74	65	64
Puerto Rico	na	**na**	na	na	na	na	na
Romania	56	**75**	74	77	80	77	72
Russian Fed.	71	**55**	53	57	59	55	53
Serbia	na	**na**	na	na	na	na	na
Singapore	na	**na**	na	na	na	na	na
Slovakia	na	**51**	47	55	58	51	46
Slovenia	82	**90**	89	91	93	90	87
South Africa	40	**na**	na	na	na	na	na
Spain	62	**66**	67	65	74	66	62
Sweden	91	**84**	80	88	92	88	76
Switzerland	na	**na**	na	na	na	na	na
Taiwan	na	**na**	na	na	na	na	na
Tanzania	na	**na**	na	na	na	na	na
Turkey	86	**97**	97	98	98	98	94
Uganda	na	**na**	na	na	na	na	na
Ukraine	na	**66**	63	68	69	66	64
United States	74	**na**	na	na	na	na	na
Uruguay	na	**na**	na	na	na	na	na
Venezuela	na	**na**	na	na	na	na	na
Vietnam	na	**na**	na	na	na	na	na
Zimbabwe	na	**na**	na	na	na	na	na
Total	69	71	70	73	78	73	66

Country	Education Lower	Education Middle	Education Upper	Income Lower	Income Middle	Income Upper	Values Mat	Values Mixed	Values Postm.
Albania	na	na	na	na	na	na	na	na	na
Algeria	na	na	na	na	na	na	na	na	na
Argentina	na	na	na	na	na	na	na	na	na
Armenia	na	na	na	na	na	na	na	na	na
Australia	na	na	na	na	na	na	na	na	na
Austria	66	70	66	58	69	73	77	65	71
Azerbaijan	na	na	na	na	na	na	na	na	na
Bangladesh	na	na	na	na	na	na	na	na	na
Belarus	51	73	85	66	69	74	66	71	73
Belgium	67	75	80	70	72	80	74	75	73
Bosnia and Herz.	na	na	na	na	na	na	na	na	na
Brazil	na	na	na	na	na	na	na	na	na
Bulgaria	50	72	74	55	63	72	58	70	80
Canada	na	na	na	na	na	na	na	na	na
Chile	na	na	na	na	na	na	na	na	na
China	na	na	na	na	na	na	na	na	na
Colombia	na	na	na	na	na	na	na	na	na
Croatia	75	76	80	74	76	79	71	77	80
Czech Republic	63	64	68	55	68	67	62	65	61
Denmark	76	81	80	77	77	81	75	79	80
Dominican Rep.	na	na	na	na	na	na	na	na	na
Egypt	na	na	na	na	na	na	na	na	na
El Salvador	na	na	na	na	na	na	na	na	na
Estonia	64	75	73	68	73	72	70	73	62
Finland	74	76	70	77	78	69	79	72	66
France	65	65	65	64	68	64	60	65	74
Georgia	na	na	na	na	na	na	na	na	na
Germany	64	66	65	61	70	67	59	66	69
Great Britain	68	74	77	70	68	78	na	na	na
Greece	68	75	79	71	76	81	74	77	78
Hungary	80	95	94	73	86	93	82	90	92
Iceland	83	85	78	82	85	81	86	83	72
India	na	na	na	na	na	na	na	na	na
Indonesia	na	na	na	na	na	na	na	na	na
Iran	na	na	na	na	na	na	na	na	na
Ireland	73	77	82	74	78	79	76	78	73
Israel	na	na	na	na	na	na	na	na	na
Italy	71	74	69	74	75	69	68	74	74
Japan	na	na	na	na	na	na	na	na	na
Jordan	na	na	na	na	na	na	na	na	na
Korea, South	na	na	na	na	na	na	na	na	na
Latvia	31	30	40	28	35	39	32	34	34
Lithuania	41	64	75	53	54	62	56	60	63
Luxembourg	73	76	70	73	77	73	73	76	75
Macedonia	na	na	na	na	na	na	na	na	na
Malta	84	83	85	79	79	85	78	86	86
Mexico	na	na	na	na	na	na	na	na	na
Moldova	na	na	na	na	na	na	na	na	na
Montenegro	na	na	na	na	na	na	na	na	na
Morocco	na	na	na	na	na	na	na	na	na
Netherlands	86	91	89	89	90	89	85	90	90
New Zealand	na	na	na	na	na	na	na	na	na
Nigeria	na	na	na	na	na	na	na	na	na
Northern Ireland	66	75	77	67	70	65	70	72	71
Norway	na	na	na	na	na	na	na	na	na
Pakistan	na	na	na	na	na	na	na	na	na
Peru	na	na	na	na	na	na	na	na	na
Philippines	na	na	na	na	na	na	na	na	na
Poland	74	76	76	75	73	77	76	73	81
Portugal	62	76	75	53	67	70	66	65	80
Puerto Rico	na	na	na	na	na	na	na	na	na
Romania	72	80	71	72	80	76	78	77	59
Russian Fed.	48	55	58	53	58	55	57	54	71
Serbia	na	na	na	na	na	na	na	na	na
Singapore	na	na	na	na	na	na	na	na	na
Slovakia	43	54	58	46	53	55	45	55	66
Slovenia	89	91	87	91	94	90	85	91	91
South Africa	na	na	na	na	na	na	na	na	na
Spain	63	67	76	64	72	75	62	69	67
Sweden	82	88	80	86	82	84	87	84	84
Switzerland	na	na	na	na	na	na	na	na	na
Taiwan	na	na	na	na	na	na	na	na	na
Tanzania	na	na	na	na	na	na	na	na	na
Turkey	98	97	95	97	98	96	97	98	96
Uganda	na	na	na	na	na	na	na	na	na
Ukraine	61	68	64	67	64	68	65	70	55
United States	na	na	na	na	na	na	na	na	na
Uruguay	na	na	na	na	na	na	na	na	na
Venezuela	na	na	na	na	na	na	na	na	na
Vietnam	na	na	na	na	na	na	na	na	na
Zimbabwe	na	na	na	na	na	na	na	na	na
Total	69	72	75	68	73	73	67	73	75

RANKING

Country	2000
Turkey	97
Slovenia	90
Netherlands	89
Hungary	85
Sweden	84
Malta	83
Iceland	83
Denmark	78
Ireland	77
Greece	76
Croatia	76
Romania	75
Belgium	75
Poland	74
Finland	74
Luxembourg	74
Great Britain	73
Italy	72
Northern Ireland	71
Estonia	71
Belarus	69
Austria	68
Portugal	67
Spain	66
Ukraine	66
Germany	65
France	65
Bulgaria	64
Czech Republic	64
Lithuania	60
Russian Fed.	55
Slovakia	51
Latvia	32
Total	71

C023_1) IMPORTANT IN A JOB: CHANCES FOR PROMOTION

Here are some more aspects of a job that people say are important.

Please tell me which ones you personally think are important in a job?

Good chances for promotion (%)

(EVS: V75)

Country	Wave		Gender		Age			Education			Income			Values		
	1990	2000	Male	Female	16-29	30-49	50+	Lower	Middle	Upper	Lower	Middle	Upper	Mat	Mixed	Postm.
Albania	na	**na**	na	na	na	na	na	na	na	na	na	na	na	na	na	na
Algeria	na	**na**	na	na	na	na	na	na	na	na	na	na	na	na	na	na
Argentina	45	**na**	na	na	na	na	na	na	na	na	na	na	na	na	na	na
Armenia	na	**na**	na	na	na	na	na	na	na	na	na	na	na	na	na	na
Australia	na	**na**	na	na	na	na	na	na	na	na	na	na	na	na	na	na
Austria	33	**36**	39	33	50	31	34	35	38	34	35	36	37	45	36	35
Azerbaijan	na	**na**	na	na	na	na	na	na	na	na	na	na	na	na	na	na
Bangladesh	na	**na**	na	na	na	na	na	na	na	na	na	na	na	na	na	na
Belarus	22	**26**	27	25	42	24	15	12	30	35	20	25	38	20	29	38
Belgium	31	**33**	35	31	44	26	33	36	33	30	28	34	33	34	33	28
Bosnia and Herz.	na	**na**	na	na	na	na	na	na	na	na	na	na	na	na	na	na
Brazil	53	**na**	na	na	na	na	na	na	na	na	na	na	na	na	na	na
Bulgaria	36	**45**	48	41	54	50	36	34	48	56	36	43	53	39	51	53
Canada	49	**na**	na	na	na	na	na	na	na	na	na	na	na	na	na	na
Chile	49	**na**	na	na	na	na	na	na	na	na	na	na	na	na	na	na
China	27	**na**	na	na	na	na	na	na	na	na	na	na	na	na	na	na
Colombia	na	**na**	na	na	na	na	na	na	na	na	na	na	na	na	na	na
Croatia	na	**60**	63	57	70	60	53	56	63	59	59	56	65	53	61	61
Czech Republic	30	**24**	24	24	32	24	21	21	27	30	21	27	27	23	24	30
Denmark	16	**17**	18	16	31	18	9	12	27	23	15	16	23	18	17	17
Dominican Rep.	na	**na**	na	na	na	na	na	na	na	na	na	na	na	na	na	na
Egypt	na	**na**	na	na	na	na	na	na	na	na	na	na	na	na	na	na
El Salvador	na	**na**	na	na	na	na	na	na	na	na	na	na	na	na	na	na
Estonia	12	**27**	29	25	45	23	20	21	27	36	20	25	30	22	30	40
Finland	30	**20**	23	16	31	18	15	17	23	25	19	18	21	19	20	18
France	25	**30**	32	28	30	32	29	32	30	26	29	34	27	31	31	26
Georgia	na	**na**	na	na	na	na	na	na	na	na	na	na	na	na	na	na
Germany	28	**37**	44	32	55	35	32	34	39	43	30	39	45	36	38	37
Great Britain	35	**36**	37	34	45	34	31	27	42	40	26	34	40	na	na	na
Greece	na	**68**	68	68	76	61	61	50	64	74	59	69	74	64	68	73
Hungary	42	**67**	68	67	81	69	57	65	76	66	53	68	76	66	71	86
Iceland	37	**44**	45	43	58	45	31	44	47	39	39	42	50	49	45	29
India	72	**na**	na	na	na	na	na	na	na	na	na	na	na	na	na	na
Indonesia	na	**na**	na	na	na	na	na	na	na	na	na	na	na	na	na	na
Iran	na	**na**	na	na	na	na	na	na	na	na	na	na	na	na	na	na
Ireland	38	**51**	52	50	58	45	51	49	51	54	49	50	55	55	52	44
Israel	na	**na**	na	na	na	na	na	na	na	na	na	na	na	na	na	na
Italy	28	**48**	51	45	51	43	50	49	48	43	47	46	48	53	48	46
Japan	23	**na**	na	na	na	na	na	na	na	na	na	na	na	na	na	na
Jordan	na	**na**	na	na	na	na	na	na	na	na	na	na	na	na	na	na
Korea, South	2	**na**	na	na	na	na	na	na	na	na	na	na	na	na	na	na
Latvia	9	**20**	20	20	37	17	16	15	20	26	16	22	24	21	20	32
Lithuania	16	**37**	39	36	55	36	26	25	40	49	31	30	44	37	38	33
Luxembourg	na	**35**	38	32	42	33	34	40	32	33	36	37	31	34	39	30
Macedonia	na	**na**	na	na	na	na	na	na	na	na	na	na	na	na	na	na
Malta	na	**62**	66	57	72	57	59	57	62	72	51	57	68	53	66	66
Mexico	61	**na**	na	na	na	na	na	na	na	na	na	na	na	na	na	na
Moldova	na	**na**	na	na	na	na	na	na	na	na	na	na	na	na	na	na
Montenegro	na	**na**	na	na	na	na	na	na	na	na	na	na	na	na	na	na
Morocco	na	**na**	na	na	na	na	na	na	na	na	na	na	na	na	na	na
Netherlands	35	**32**	36	28	48	28	27	28	38	29	28	34	32	32	35	24
New Zealand	na	**na**	na	na	na	na	na	na	na	na	na	na	na	na	na	na
Nigeria	89	**na**	na	na	na	na	na	na	na	na	na	na	na	na	na	na
Northern Ireland	41	**49**	48	50	62	45	45	43	50	61	39	44	46	47	49	54
Norway	19	**na**	na	na	na	na	na	na	na	na	na	na	na	na	na	na
Pakistan	na	**na**	na	na	na	na	na	na	na	na	na	na	na	na	na	na
Peru	na	**na**	na	na	na	na	na	na	na	na	na	na	na	na	na	na
Philippines	na	**na**	na	na	na	na	na	na	na	na	na	na	na	na	na	na
Poland	na	**50**	52	48	58	46	50	50	51	46	52	49	48	51	50	51
Portugal	57	**32**	30	34	34	36	27	30	38	30	21	31	36	31	33	32
Puerto Rico	na	**na**	na	na	na	na	na	na	na	na	na	na	na	na	na	na
Romania	30	**61**	62	60	69	65	54	52	66	67	54	65	66	60	64	68
Russian Fed.	17	**29**	33	26	45	28	22	21	28	38	24	30	34	25	33	42
Serbia	na	**na**	na	na	na	na	na	na	na	na	na	na	na	na	na	na
Singapore	na	**na**	na	na	na	na	na	na	na	na	na	na	na	na	na	na
Slovakia	na	**25**	26	24	34	24	18	17	27	35	18	23	30	22	27	41
Slovenia	62	**74**	75	72	80	71	71	76	74	69	75	73	67	71	74	74
South Africa	38	**na**	na	na	na	na	na	na	na	na	na	na	na	na	na	na
Spain	33	**44**	48	40	54	41	40	40	44	53	43	44	55	41	44	48
Sweden	41	**30**	33	27	39	30	25	20	37	27	31	29	28	33	30	28
Switzerland	na	**na**	na	na	na	na	na	na	na	na	na	na	na	na	na	na
Taiwan	na	**na**	na	na	na	na	na	na	na	na	na	na	na	na	na	na
Tanzania	na	**na**	na	na	na	na	na	na	na	na	na	na	na	na	na	na
Turkey	61	**73**	67	79	74	72	73	77	70	61	80	71	65	79	74	65
Uganda	na	**na**	na	na	na	na	na	na	na	na	na	na	na	na	na	na
Ukraine	na	**39**	39	39	46	39	35	28	40	44	35	38	48	37	44	46
United States	58	**na**	na	na	na	na	na	na	na	na	na	na	na	na	na	na
Uruguay	na	**na**	na	na	na	na	na	na	na	na	na	na	na	na	na	na
Venezuela	na	**na**	na	na	na	na	na	na	na	na	na	na	na	na	na	na
Vietnam	na	**na**	na	na	na	na	na	na	na	na	na	na	na	na	na	na
Zimbabwe	na	**na**	na	na	na	na	na	na	na	na	na	na	na	na	na	na
Total	36	**40**	42	39	52	39	35	36	43	44	36	39	44	39	42	41

RANKING	
Country	2000
Slovenia	74
Turkey	73
Greece	68
Hungary	67
Malta	62
Romania	61
Croatia	60
Ireland	51
Poland	50
Northern Ireland	49
Italy	48
Bulgaria	45
Iceland	44
Spain	44
Ukraine	39
Germany	37
Lithuania	37
Austria	36
Great Britain	36
Luxembourg	35
Belgium	33
Portugal	32
Netherlands	32
France	30
Sweden	30
Russian Fed.	29
Estonia	27
Belarus	26
Slovakia	25
Czech Republic	24
Latvia	20
Finland	20
Denmark	17
Total	40

C024_1) IMPORTANT IN A JOB: A USEFUL FOR SOCIETY

Here are some more aspects of a job that people say are important.
Please tell me which ones you personally think are important in a job?
A useful job for society (%)

(EVS: V79)

Country	Wave		Gender		Age			Education			Income			Values		
	1990	2000	Male	Female	16-29	30-49	50+	Lower	Middle	Upper	Lower	Middle	Upper	Mat	Mixed	Postm.
Albania	na	**na**	na	na	na	na	na	na	na	na	na	na	na	na	na	na
Algeria	na	**na**	na	na	na	na	na	na	na	na	na	na	na	na	na	na
Argentina	43	**na**	na	na	na	na	na	na	na	na	na	na	na	na	na	na
Armenia	na	**na**	na	na	na	na	na	na	na	na	na	na	na	na	na	na
Australia	na	**na**	na	na	na	na	na	na	na	na	na	na	na	na	na	na
Austria	35	**36**	34	38	31	35	40	34	35	43	36	35	39	26	36	38
Azerbaijan	na	**na**	na	na	na	na	na	na	na	na	na	na	na	na	na	na
Bangladesh	na	**na**	na	na	na	na	na	na	na	na	na	na	na	na	na	na
Belarus	42	**26**	26	26	29	24	26	19	27	35	28	25	26	22	30	34
Belgium	40	**41**	41	41	37	39	45	40	39	45	42	42	40	40	39	45
Bosnia and Herz.	na	**na**	na	na	na	na	na	na	na	na	na	na	na	na	na	na
Brazil	58	**na**	na	na	na	na	na	na	na	na	na	na	na	na	na	na
Bulgaria	58	**57**	56	58	55	60	55	52	57	69	51	58	62	50	65	60
Canada	36	**na**	na	na	na	na	na	na	na	na	na	na	na	na	na	na
Chile	60	**na**	na	na	na	na	na	na	na	na	na	na	na	na	na	na
China	47	**na**	na	na	na	na	na	na	na	na	na	na	na	na	na	na
Colombia	na	**na**	na	na	na	na	na	na	na	na	na	na	na	na	na	na
Croatia	na	**59**	61	57	56	62	57	61	58	56	62	62	56	55	60	58
Czech Republic	33	**32**	30	35	32	29	35	29	35	42	35	31	32	34	31	36
Denmark	13	**26**	26	26	24	24	29	23	21	33	29	24	26	26	26	30
Dominican Rep.	na	**na**	na	na	na	na	na	na	na	na	na	na	na	na	na	na
Egypt	na	**na**	na	na	na	na	na	na	na	na	na	na	na	na	na	na
El Salvador	na	**na**	na	na	na	na	na	na	na	na	na	na	na	na	na	na
Estonia	38	**27**	22	31	25	26	30	26	26	32	22	33	26	25	28	38
Finland	24	**31**	30	31	28	30	32	29	29	41	34	28	30	23	33	30
France	17	**30**	31	30	30	31	30	28	30	35	32	30	30	26	31	35
Georgia	na	**na**	na	na	na	na	na	na	na	na	na	na	na	na	na	na
Germany	51	**33**	31	35	33	32	35	29	36	43	31	32	40	34	33	36
Great Britain	27	**27**	27	28	28	29	25	21	31	36	24	26	30	na	na	na
Greece	na	**53**	50	54	52	49	62	67	49	52	47	55	52	47	53	57
Hungary	16	**74**	72	75	81	77	67	72	77	82	67	75	78	69	81	77
Iceland	45	**47**	47	46	38	42	60	46	45	53	50	44	44	46	47	44
India	59	**na**	na	na	na	na	na	na	na	na	na	na	na	na	na	na
Indonesia	na	**na**	na	na	na	na	na	na	na	na	na	na	na	na	na	na
Iran	na	**na**	na	na	na	na	na	na	na	na	na	na	na	na	na	na
Ireland	29	**41**	41	41	35	37	50	42	38	46	46	38	41	43	40	44
Israel	na	**na**	na	na	na	na	na	na	na	na	na	na	na	na	na	na
Italy	40	**66**	65	66	66	65	66	66	65	65	67	67	64	64	66	66
Japan	26	**na**	na	na	na	na	na	na	na	na	na	na	na	na	na	na
Jordan	na	**na**	na	na	na	na	na	na	na	na	na	na	na	na	na	na
Korea, South	7	**na**	na	na	na	na	na	na	na	na	na	na	na	na	na	na
Latvia	31	**29**	30	29	24	21	38	31	26	38	31	29	29	31	29	32
Lithuania	28	**29**	28	30	30	27	30	22	30	35	29	29	28	30	28	28
Luxembourg	na	**44**	46	42	41	43	47	47	42	45	48	44	48	48	45	42
Macedonia	na	**na**	na	na	na	na	na	na	na	na	na	na	na	na	na	na
Malta	na	**72**	71	73	71	71	75	78	68	78	71	73	69	69	74	71
Mexico	54	**na**	na	na	na	na	na	na	na	na	na	na	na	na	na	na
Moldova	na	**na**	na	na	na	na	na	na	na	na	na	na	na	na	na	na
Montenegro	na	**na**	na	na	na	na	na	na	na	na	na	na	na	na	na	na
Morocco	na	**na**	na	na	na	na	na	na	na	na	na	na	na	na	na	na
Netherlands	55	**39**	39	39	33	33	48	41	32	45	42	35	43	38	37	45
New Zealand	na	**na**	na	na	na	na	na	na	na	na	na	na	na	na	na	na
Nigeria	74	**na**	na	na	na	na	na	na	na	na	na	na	na	na	na	na
Northern Ireland	20	**40**	42	39	41	38	42	38	36	57	36	32	42	32	44	44
Norway	30	**na**	na	na	na	na	na	na	na	na	na	na	na	na	na	na
Pakistan	na	**na**	na	na	na	na	na	na	na	na	na	na	na	na	na	na
Peru	na	**na**	na	na	na	na	na	na	na	na	na	na	na	na	na	na
Philippines	na	**na**	na	na	na	na	na	na	na	na	na	na	na	na	na	na
Poland	na	**48**	48	48	42	43	57	51	44	50	53	46	45	51	46	46
Portugal	59	**52**	47	55	50	47	56	50	52	62	49	47	44	49	53	57
Puerto Rico	na	**na**	na	na	na	na	na	na	na	na	na	na	na	na	na	na
Romania	55	**65**	64	66	67	66	63	61	69	64	64	70	65	68	66	59
Russian Fed.	40	**22**	21	23	23	22	22	17	23	23	20	23	23	21	23	32
Serbia	na	**na**	na	na	na	na	na	na	na	na	na	na	na	na	na	na
Singapore	na	**na**	na	na	na	na	na	na	na	na	na	na	na	na	na	na
Slovakia	na	**24**	22	26	24	22	28	21	25	27	28	21	25	23	25	40
Slovenia	59	**73**	71	75	62	77	77	78	73	64	77	74	69	76	74	70
South Africa	22	**na**	na	na	na	na	na	na	na	na	na	na	na	na	na	na
Spain	37	**44**	44	44	43	45	44	43	42	49	50	45	50	43	42	53
Sweden	43	**25**	23	27	28	22	26	21	25	28	28	24	21	25	22	32
Switzerland	na	**na**	na	na	na	na	na	na	na	na	na	na	na	na	na	na
Taiwan	na	**na**	na	na	na	na	na	na	na	na	na	na	na	na	na	na
Tanzania	na	**na**	na	na	na	na	na	na	na	na	na	na	na	na	na	na
Turkey	87	**98**	98	98	98	98	97	98	98	97	98	99	96	98	99	98
Uganda	na	**na**	na	na	na	na	na	na	na	na	na	na	na	na	na	na
Ukraine	na	**31**	30	32	28	28	35	28	30	35	29	29	37	27	37	38
United States	44	**na**	na	na	na	na	na	na	na	na	na	na	na	na	na	na
Uruguay	na	**na**	na	na	na	na	na	na	na	na	na	na	na	na	na	na
Venezuela	na	**na**	na	na	na	na	na	na	na	na	na	na	na	na	na	na
Vietnam	na	**na**	na	na	na	na	na	na	na	na	na	na	na	na	na	na
Zimbabwe	na	**na**	na	na	na	na	na	na	na	na	na	na	na	na	na	na
Total	40	**42**	42	43	42	41	44	42	41	46	42	42	43	41	44	47

RANKING	
Country	2000
Turkey	98
Hungary	74
Slovenia	73
Malta	72
Italy	66
Romania	65
Croatia	59
Bulgaria	57
Greece	53
Portugal	52
Poland	48
Iceland	47
Luxembourg	44
Spain	44
Ireland	41
Belgium	41
Northern Ireland	40
Netherlands	39
Austria	36
Germany	33
Czech Republic	32
Ukraine	31
Finland	31
France	30
Latvia	29
Lithuania	29
Great Britain	27
Estonia	27
Belarus	26
Denmark	26
Sweden	25
Slovakia	24
Russian Fed.	22
Total	42

C025_1) IMPORTANT IN A JOB: MEETING PEOPLE

Here are some more aspects of a job that people say are important.
Please tell me which ones you personally think are important in a job?

(EVS: V81)

Meeting people (%)

Country	Wave		Gender		Age			Education			Income			Values		
	1990	2000	Male	Female	16-29	30-49	50+	Lower	Middle	Upper	Lower	Middle	Upper	Mat	Mixed	Postm.
Albania	na	**na**	na	na	na	na	na	na	na	na	na	na	na	na	na	na
Algeria	na	**na**	na	na	na	na	na	na	na	na	na	na	na	na	na	na
Argentina	50	**na**	na	na	na	na	na	na	na	na	na	na	na	na	na	na
Armenia	na	**na**	na	na	na	na	na	na	na	na	na	na	na	na	na	na
Australia	na	**na**	na	na	na	na	na	na	na	na	na	na	na	na	na	na
Austria	39	**47**	43	51	50	47	46	43	49	56	40	45	54	39	46	52
Azerbaijan	na	**na**	na	na	na	na	na	na	na	na	na	na	na	na	na	na
Bangladesh	na	**na**	na	na	na	na	na	na	na	na	na	na	na	na	na	na
Belarus	53	**37**	35	38	35	42	32	28	38	48	37	36	37	33	41	32
Belgium	45	**53**	49	57	58	55	49	45	50	62	48	51	57	51	52	57
Bosnia and Herz.	na	**na**	na	na	na	na	na	na	na	na	na	na	na	na	na	na
Brazil	42	**na**	na	na	na	na	na	na	na	na	na	na	na	na	na	na
Bulgaria	44	**56**	59	54	70	58	48	43	62	69	44	53	70	47	65	86
Canada	42	**na**	na	na	na	na	na	na	na	na	na	na	na	na	na	na
Chile	39	**na**	na	na	na	na	na	na	na	na	na	na	na	na	na	na
China	26	**na**	na	na	na	na	na	na	na	na	na	na	na	na	na	na
Colombia	na	**na**	na	na	na	na	na	na	na	na	na	na	na	na	na	na
Croatia	na	**62**	66	59	70	64	55	59	66	57	65	64	59	51	62	73
Czech Republic	54	**34**	28	39	40	33	32	35	32	37	33	35	34	34	35	32
Denmark	43	**46**	42	50	48	46	45	46	47	49	45	44	56	58	45	44
Dominican Rep.	na	**na**	na	na	na	na	na	na	na	na	na	na	na	na	na	na
Egypt	na	**na**	na	na	na	na	na	na	na	na	na	na	na	na	na	na
El Salvador	na	**na**	na	na	na	na	na	na	na	na	na	na	na	na	na	na
Estonia	57	**44**	37	50	47	43	44	40	48	41	42	45	44	40	48	47
Finland	30	**41**	38	43	48	43	34	37	45	46	39	46	36	43	38	42
France	39	**44**	36	50	54	46	36	41	46	47	42	41	48	40	42	52
Georgia	na	**na**	na	na	na	na	na	na	na	na	na	na	na	na	na	na
Germany	50	**52**	48	55	59	52	49	47	56	57	49	51	60	52	50	61
Great Britain	43	**42**	37	47	48	39	43	43	45	36	41	43	40	na	na	na
Greece	na	**53**	50	55	60	48	50	44	55	54	49	53	55	54	53	56
Hungary	40	**69**	69	70	77	75	60	66	77	72	65	68	75	66	74	74
Iceland	59	**54**	51	57	60	50	53	54	57	45	55	53	53	59	54	40
India	45	**na**	na	na	na	na	na	na	na	na	na	na	na	na	na	na
Indonesia	na	**na**	na	na	na	na	na	na	na	na	na	na	na	na	na	na
Iran	na	**na**	na	na	na	na	na	na	na	na	na	na	na	na	na	na
Ireland	35	**52**	50	54	53	49	55	52	52	53	55	55	51	56	52	47
Israel	na	**na**	na	na	na	na	na	na	na	na	na	na	na	na	na	na
Italy	43	**66**	64	67	71	68	61	64	67	67	67	66	67	62	65	71
Japan	48	**na**	na	na	na	na	na	na	na	na	na	na	na	na	na	na
Jordan	na	**na**	na	na	na	na	na	na	na	na	na	na	na	na	na	na
Korea, South	24	**na**	na	na	na	na	na	na	na	na	na	na	na	na	na	na
Latvia	39	**43**	36	48	37	43	45	43	41	50	44	39	45	46	43	38
Lithuania	59	**40**	33	47	47	42	34	31	43	48	36	36	45	42	40	46
Luxembourg	na	**48**	46	49	62	48	38	54	45	43	47	51	41	48	51	45
Macedonia	na	**na**	na	na	na	na	na	na	na	na	na	na	na	na	na	na
Malta	na	**59**	57	61	64	55	60	60	60	53	54	51	57	53	63	62
Mexico	47	**na**	na	na	na	na	na	na	na	na	na	na	na	na	na	na
Moldova	na	**na**	na	na	na	na	na	na	na	na	na	na	na	na	na	na
Montenegro	na	**na**	na	na	na	na	na	na	na	na	na	na	na	na	na	na
Morocco	na	**na**	na	na	na	na	na	na	na	na	na	na	na	na	na	na
Netherlands	71	**61**	56	66	67	63	56	53	62	68	56	63	66	51	62	65
New Zealand	na	**na**	na	na	na	na	na	na	na	na	na	na	na	na	na	na
Nigeria	68	**na**	na	na	na	na	na	na	na	na	na	na	na	na	na	na
Northern Ireland	16	**59**	56	61	62	60	56	58	59	59	52	53	52	56	60	62
Norway	41	**na**	na	na	na	na	na	na	na	na	na	na	na	na	na	na
Pakistan	na	**na**	na	na	na	na	na	na	na	na	na	na	na	na	na	na
Peru	na	**na**	na	na	na	na	na	na	na	na	na	na	na	na	na	na
Philippines	na	**na**	na	na	na	na	na	na	na	na	na	na	na	na	na	na
Poland	na	**52**	52	52	59	48	53	54	53	42	51	55	50	48	53	58
Portugal	53	**36**	31	40	41	38	31	34	42	36	19	39	36	33	37	38
Puerto Rico	na	**na**	na	na	na	na	na	na	na	na	na	na	na	na	na	na
Romania	27	**55**	55	55	61	58	50	53	60	48	53	58	57	60	54	49
Russian Fed.	27	**34**	30	37	34	34	34	33	34	36	34	36	34	35	35	27
Serbia	na	**na**	na	na	na	na	na	na	na	na	na	na	na	na	na	na
Singapore	na	**na**	na	na	na	na	na	na	na	na	na	na	na	na	na	na
Slovakia	na	**23**	20	27	33	20	19	16	26	31	20	23	26	19	27	35
Slovenia	56	**69**	67	72	73	70	66	71	71	62	73	68	67	68	69	72
South Africa	na	**na**	na	na	na	na	na	na	na	na	na	na	na	na	na	na
Spain	35	**38**	37	39	44	39	33	34	39	48	40	40	44	35	37	44
Sweden	64	**46**	44	48	55	44	42	40	50	43	47	44	46	42	46	47
Switzerland	na	**na**	na	na	na	na	na	na	na	na	na	na	na	na	na	na
Taiwan	na	**na**	na	na	na	na	na	na	na	na	na	na	na	na	na	na
Tanzania	na	**na**	na	na	na	na	na	na	na	na	na	na	na	na	na	na
Turkey	68	**88**	88	88	89	87	86	87	92	79	86	89	89	84	89	90
Uganda	na	**na**	na	na	na	na	na	na	na	na	na	na	na	na	na	na
Ukraine	na	**42**	38	45	43	43	40	32	42	47	40	40	46	41	46	42
United States	38	**na**	na	na	na	na	na	na	na	na	na	na	na	na	na	na
Uruguay	na	**na**	na	na	na	na	na	na	na	na	na	na	na	na	na	na
Venezuela	na	**na**	na	na	na	na	na	na	na	na	na	na	na	na	na	na
Vietnam	na	**na**	na	na	na	na	na	na	na	na	na	na	na	na	na	na
Zimbabwe	na	**na**	na	na	na	na	na	na	na	na	na	na	na	na	na	na
Total	45	**49**	46	52	55	49	46	47	50	51	47	49	51	46	51	55

RANKING

Country	2000
Turkey	88
Hungary	69
Slovenia	69
Italy	66
Croatia	62
Netherlands	61
Malta	59
Northern Ireland	59
Bulgaria	56
Romania	55
Iceland	54
Greece	53
Belgium	53
Germany	52
Ireland	52
Poland	52
Luxembourg	48
Austria	47
Denmark	46
Sweden	46
Estonia	44
France	44
Latvia	43
Great Britain	42
Ukraine	42
Finland	41
Lithuania	40
Spain	38
Belarus	37
Portugal	36
Russian Fed.	34
Czech Republic	34
Slovakia	23
Total	49

C036) WORK: NEED A JOB TO DEVELOP TALENTS

Do you agree or disagree with the following statements: "To fully develop your talents, you need to have a job?"

Strongly agree / Agree (%)

(WVS: V97; EVS: V90)

Country	Wave		Gender		Age			Education			Income			Values		
	1990	2000	Male	Female	16-29	30-49	50+	Lower	Middle	Upper	Lower	Middle	Upper	Mat	Mixed	Postm.
Albania	na	**80**	82	78	81	82	77	78	81	85	83	77	80	79	81	90
Algeria	na	**na**	na	na	na	na	na	na	na	na	na	na	na	na	na	na
Argentina	na	**89**	89	89	85	86	94	92	85	78	93	87	86	93	88	86
Armenia	na	**na**	na	na	na	na	na	na	na	na	na	na	na	na	na	na
Australia	na	**na**	na	na	na	na	na	na	na	na	na	na	na	na	na	na
Austria	na	**na**	na	na	na	na	na	na	na	na	na	na	na	na	na	na
Azerbaijan	na	**na**	na	na	na	na	na	na	na	na	na	na	na	na	na	na
Bangladesh	na	**78**	76	80	76	79	76	84	69	73	74	79	78	78	78	70
Belarus	na	**75**	76	73	71	77	76	72	74	81	76	73	75	75	75	71
Belgium	na	**51**	54	48	43	46	58	57	50	47	56	57	43	50	51	51
Bosnia and Herz.	na	**85**	85	85	88	85	83	85	85	86	85	85	84	86	86	85
Brazil	na	**na**	na	na	na	na	na	na	na	na	na	na	na	na	na	na
Bulgaria	na	**87**	86	88	79	89	90	89	87	84	92	87	82	89	85	83
Canada	na	**54**	62	47	49	52	61	63	55	46	61	58	48	59	57	47
Chile	na	**73**	78	68	69	74	74	75	74	66	78	67	74	74	73	71
China	na	**83**	83	83	81	83	84	81	84	83	82	83	83	81	84	87
Colombia	na	**na**	na	na	na	na	na	na	na	na	na	na	na	na	na	na
Croatia	na	**63**	65	62	53	61	73	60	66	61	73	59	64	70	64	56
Czech Republic	na	**80**	82	78	67	77	89	81	78	79	82	78	78	79	80	79
Denmark	na	**73**	76	71	73	67	80	78	70	65	79	69	75	80	76	63
Dominican Rep.	na	**na**	na	na	na	na	na	na	na	na	na	na	na	na	na	na
Egypt	na	**na**	na	na	na	na	na	na	na	na	na	na	na	na	na	na
El Salvador	na	**na**	na	na	na	na	na	na	na	na	na	na	na	na	na	na
Estonia	na	**80**	81	79	75	85	77	74	81	86	80	78	82	79	81	81
Finland	na	**59**	60	58	48	55	69	65	52	54	60	58	59	65	60	47
France	na	**78**	82	74	75	72	84	80	71	76	81	77	77	81	79	68
Georgia	na	**na**	na	na	na	na	na	na	na	na	na	na	na	na	na	na
Germany	na	**83**	89	78	87	78	86	82	84	81	81	82	80	83	85	78
Great Britain	na	**54**	64	44	55	51	56	57	51	54	54	57	51	na	na	na
Greece	na	**68**	70	66	59	72	79	74	65	69	72	69	66	70	71	58
Hungary	na	**82**	84	81	85	78	84	80	87	86	76	82	86	81	84	81
Iceland	na	**36**	40	32	30	31	48	41	34	27	45	33	31	38	35	36
India	na	**79**	79	80	80	80	76	79	80	78	82	80	78	78	84	77
Indonesia	na	**na**	na	na	na	na	na	na	na	na	na	na	na	na	na	na
Iran	na	**na**	na	na	na	na	na	na	na	na	na	na	na	na	na	na
Ireland	na	**60**	74	48	58	57	67	67	56	59	62	62	58	65	60	54
Israel	na	**87**	89	86	85	87	91	90	88	85	85	90	85	90	88	91
Italy	na	**73**	77	70	70	69	79	75	71	75	74	73	74	73	73	74
Japan	na	**64**	69	60	58	62	69	75	64	60	66	64	64	71	62	60
Jordan	na	**na**	na	na	na	na	na	na	na	na	na	na	na	na	na	na
Korea, South	na	**89**	90	89	90	89	89	84	88	92	86	91	92	87	92	88
Latvia	na	**85**	81	89	85	80	90	87	85	83	85	85	86	85	85	85
Lithuania	na	**71**	74	69	76	71	68	61	73	82	68	68	75	71	71	84
Luxembourg	na	**69**	75	64	68	64	76	74	70	62	76	74	64	71	72	60
Macedonia	na	**68**	70	66	68	69	67	75	66	61	73	67	62	69	65	82
Malta	na	**50**	63	37	54	47	50	46	51	53	47	52	52	50	49	54
Mexico	na	**69**	73	66	65	69	75	74	65	61	73	67	65	73	68	64
Moldova	na	**80**	80	79	76	83	78	81	79	80	85	80	77	78	83	72
Montenegro	na	**78**	82	75	73	80	81	78	79	79	84	85	75	81	78	72
Morocco	na	**97**	98	97	97	97	99	98	95	90	99	98	89	98	97	96
Netherlands	na	**38**	46	31	41	33	42	48	34	34	46	35	35	51	40	29
New Zealand	na	**na**	na	na	na	na	na	na	na	na	na	na	na	na	na	na
Nigeria	na	**na**	na	na	na	na	na	na	na	na	na	na	na	na	na	na
Northern Ireland	na	**58**	67	49	56	53	61	60	54	61	61	56	46	61	55	65
Norway	na	**na**	na	na	na	na	na	na	na	na	na	na	na	na	na	na
Pakistan	na	**na**	na	na	na	na	na	na	na	na	na	na	na	na	na	na
Peru	na	**61**	60	62	59	61	67	68	62	56	65	62	54	69	61	54
Philippines	na	**92**	94	91	91	93	93	93	92	92	93	91	94	92	93	91
Poland	na	**92**	93	91	89	90	96	93	89	96	93	93	87	91	92	92
Portugal	na	**90**	90	90	89	88	91	91	89	85	92	84	87	89	89	94
Puerto Rico	na	**50**	53	49	38	47	59	63	61	43	62	50	40	64	52	38
Romania	na	**79**	80	78	74	81	79	75	80	83	78	80	80	78	81	71
Russian Fed.	na	**81**	82	79	79	82	80	76	79	88	78	80	84	79	83	82
Serbia	na	**65**	66	65	60	64	70	67	67	61	67	68	67	66	66	55
Singapore	na	**72**	73	71	70	74	73	74	73	64	76	71	68	73	72	68
Slovakia	na	**67**	66	68	61	68	71	66	67	68	68	68	69	70	67	59
Slovenia	na	**72**	72	72	56	71	84	82	69	62	80	78	61	78	73	65
South Africa	na	**70**	72	68	72	68	72	75	64	62	79	69	58	68	71	72
Spain	na	**69**	71	68	66	65	75	73	66	67	77	67	69	72	70	66
Sweden	na	**50**	54	46	36	46	62	68	46	43	52	50	49	56	52	42
Switzerland	na	**na**	na	na	na	na	na	na	na	na	na	na	na	na	na	na
Taiwan	na	**na**	na	na	na	na	na	na	na	na	na	na	na	na	na	na
Tanzania	na	**96**	95	96	94	95	98	97	95	94	96	95	95	96	95	96
Turkey	na	**88**	91	85	86	88	97	91	84	88	93	87	83	87	89	87
Uganda	na	**67**	59	75	69	67	56	77	64	61	68	72	62	66	68	63
Ukraine	na	**80**	79	82	80	82	80	71	78	90	79	78	86	76	85	87
United States	na	**48**	55	41	53	43	50	59	46	45	50	47	46	46	48	49
Uruguay	na	**na**	na	na	na	na	na	na	na	na	na	na	na	na	na	na
Venezuela	na	**na**	na	na	na	na	na	na	na	na	na	na	na	na	na	na
Vietnam	na	**95**	95	94	95	95	93	94	95	96	93	93	96	95	97	95
Zimbabwe	na	**72**	68	75	74	68	75	74	70	40	74	75	66	71	71	89
Total	na	**72**	75	70	70	71	75	76	71	67	75	73	70	76	72	64

RANKING

Country	2000
Morocco	97
Tanzania	96
Vietnam	95
Philippines	92
Poland	92
Portugal	90
Korea, South	89
Argentina	89
Turkey	88
Israel	87
Bulgaria	87
Bosnia and Herz.	85
Latvia	85
China	83
Germany	83
Hungary	82
Russian Fed.	81
Ukraine	80
Albania	80
Estonia	80
Czech Republic	80
Moldova	80
India	79
Romania	79
Montenegro	78
France	78
Bangladesh	78
Belarus	75
Italy	73
Denmark	73
Chile	73
Zimbabwe	72
Singapore	72
Slovenia	72
Lithuania	71
South Africa	70
Spain	69
Luxembourg	69
Mexico	69
Macedonia	68
Greece	68
Slovakia	67
Uganda	67
Serbia	65
Japan	64
Croatia	63
Peru	61
Ireland	60
Finland	59
Northern Ireland	58
Canada	54
Great Britain	54
Belgium	51
Puerto Rico	50
Sweden	50
Malta	50
United States	48
Netherlands	38
Iceland	36
Total	72

C037) WORK: HUMILIATING TO RECEIVE MONEY WITHOUT WORKING FOR IT

Do you agree or disagree with the following statement: "It is humiliating to receive money without having to work for it?"

Strongly agree / Agree (%) (WVS: V98; EVS: V91)

Country	Wave		Gender		Age			Education			Income			Values		
	1990	2000	Male	Female	16-29	30-49	50+	Lower	Middle	Upper	Lower	Middle	Upper	Mat	Mixed	Postm.
Albania	na	**76**	73	79	73	74	81	77	74	81	76	78	75	79	76	67
Algeria	na	**na**	na	na	na	na	na	na	na	na	na	na	na	na	na	na
Argentina	na	**69**	65	72	61	71	74	71	67	61	73	67	67	66	69	69
Armenia	na	**na**	na	na	na	na	na	na	na	na	na	na	na	na	na	na
Australia	na	**na**	na	na	na	na	na	na	na	na	na	na	na	na	na	na
Austria	na	**na**	na	na	na	na	na	na	na	na	na	na	na	na	na	na
Azerbaijan	na	**na**	na	na	na	na	na	na	na	na	na	na	na	na	na	na
Bangladesh	na	**96**	95	97	95	97	93	96	97	94	95	96	95	97	95	93
Belarus	na	**54**	54	54	45	48	68	58	51	59	58	53	49	57	53	53
Belgium	na	**42**	43	42	33	38	51	44	45	36	47	43	38	43	43	40
Bosnia and Herz.	na	**60**	59	60	54	63	61	58	59	64	59	61	57	60	60	54
Brazil	na	**na**	na	na	na	na	na	na	na	na	na	na	na	na	na	na
Bulgaria	na	**72**	70	73	52	72	81	76	71	67	76	68	70	73	71	79
Canada	na	**48**	50	46	40	45	56	57	48	41	54	48	44	54	48	45
Chile	na	**61**	65	57	54	63	64	63	62	53	61	59	63	65	61	52
China	na	**73**	71	75	64	74	80	74	73	71	69	75	75	75	71	78
Colombia	na	**na**	na	na	na	na	na	na	na	na	na	na	na	na	na	na
Croatia	na	**67**	63	70	50	67	77	65	67	71	72	64	69	75	65	68
Czech Republic	na	**47**	44	49	37	41	57	47	48	44	51	47	46	41	48	55
Denmark	na	**37**	39	36	41	29	45	45	35	23	43	39	28	46	40	23
Dominican Rep.	na	**na**	na	na	na	na	na	na	na	na	na	na	na	na	na	na
Egypt	na	**na**	na	na	na	na	na	na	na	na	na	na	na	na	na	na
El Salvador	na	**na**	na	na	na	na	na	na	na	na	na	na	na	na	na	na
Estonia	na	**53**	50	55	40	50	63	53	52	56	55	57	50	47	57	52
Finland	na	**43**	41	45	31	38	54	48	37	35	45	40	44	46	44	33
France	na	**44**	44	44	35	37	56	48	38	40	53	42	40	45	46	37
Georgia	na	**na**	na	na	na	na	na	na	na	na	na	na	na	na	na	na
Germany	na	**38**	39	37	30	37	43	39	36	44	41	35	45	45	38	31
Great Britain	na	**39**	42	35	33	39	42	44	35	35	41	38	37	na	na	na
Greece	na	**54**	52	56	42	61	69	79	54	50	60	55	51	59	54	50
Hungary	na	**51**	50	52	37	47	63	52	49	53	56	50	50	54	48	52
Iceland	na	**42**	43	40	33	36	57	51	36	32	47	40	38	42	43	34
India	na	**81**	81	82	81	82	80	81	81	81	78	83	82	85	80	82
Indonesia	na	**na**	na	na	na	na	na	na	na	na	na	na	na	na	na	na
Iran	na	**na**	na	na	na	na	na	na	na	na	na	na	na	na	na	na
Ireland	na	**47**	54	40	41	47	51	46	47	50	42	49	52	44	46	56
Israel	na	**60**	61	59	50	64	67	68	59	55	58	58	59	68	59	67
Italy	na	**67**	67	68	55	67	75	73	63	63	76	66	63	71	68	66
Japan	na	**43**	44	41	35	36	51	53	43	36	46	39	43	46	42	38
Jordan	na	**na**	na	na	na	na	na	na	na	na	na	na	na	na	na	na
Korea, South	na	**67**	70	63	52	69	78	76	69	62	67	69	64	65	69	58
Latvia	na	**63**	62	63	44	57	74	65	60	67	65	64	59	64	63	49
Lithuania	na	**70**	66	73	60	68	79	76	68	67	76	75	67	68	71	78
Luxembourg	na	**55**	55	56	48	53	63	59	54	51	56	58	52	58	56	51
Macedonia	na	**73**	74	72	71	73	75	81	68	70	77	71	69	77	70	78
Malta	na	**64**	65	63	57	60	72	71	62	57	64	66	62	67	65	47
Mexico	na	**56**	58	55	49	57	64	59	50	59	54	55	57	56	54	61
Moldova	na	**57**	53	61	48	60	61	61	57	54	63	54	53	62	58	35
Montenegro	na	**74**	76	71	65	70	83	76	69	80	83	72	68	78	73	65
Morocco	na	**94**	95	93	93	94	97	95	91	84	97	93	92	95	94	91
Netherlands	na	**27**	28	25	26	19	35	35	26	20	32	25	20	40	26	20
New Zealand	na	**na**	na	na	na	na	na	na	na	na	na	na	na	na	na	na
Nigeria	na	**na**	na	na	na	na	na	na	na	na	na	na	na	na	na	na
Northern Ireland	na	**36**	36	36	31	34	41	40	35	28	36	38	34	41	36	34
Norway	na	**na**	na	na	na	na	na	na	na	na	na	na	na	na	na	na
Pakistan	na	**na**	na	na	na	na	na	na	na	na	na	na	na	na	na	na
Peru	na	**65**	63	66	61	67	67	62	66	65	63	68	62	66	64	70
Philippines	na	**78**	78	79	75	80	80	79	76	81	82	80	73	80	77	73
Poland	na	**64**	64	63	45	65	73	65	64	58	67	65	56	61	64	72
Portugal	na	**57**	59	55	49	55	62	59	51	56	60	52	58	59	57	52
Puerto Rico	na	**62**	59	64	50	59	70	70	62	60	63	59	62	64	61	65
Romania	na	**65**	63	67	54	64	72	67	62	68	62	67	66	64	67	54
Russian Fed.	na	**64**	61	67	47	63	76	72	61	69	66	65	63	66	62	82
Serbia	na	**72**	69	76	60	70	79	71	74	71	73	73	74	77	68	73
Singapore	na	**58**	58	58	55	60	62	58	59	57	57	60	59	57	58	60
Slovakia	na	**54**	52	55	46	52	62	55	53	54	56	51	56	54	55	47
Slovenia	na	**53**	50	56	37	49	68	64	49	49	58	54	47	64	52	47
South Africa	na	**53**	49	57	49	53	62	52	54	55	50	57	55	56	50	59
Spain	na	**44**	44	44	39	40	51	48	40	43	47	49	37	50	43	38
Sweden	na	**40**	39	41	39	33	47	49	39	33	42	41	34	41	43	30
Switzerland	na	**na**	na	na	na	na	na	na	na	na	na	na	na	na	na	na
Taiwan	na	**na**	na	na	na	na	na	na	na	na	na	na	na	na	na	na
Tanzania	na	**66**	65	68	65	65	72	63	71	70	67	64	67	69	67	57
Turkey	na	**88**	89	87	87	90	84	88	88	84	88	90	85	88	87	89
Uganda	na	**54**	57	52	48	61	57	59	51	65	64	69	59	48	57	61
Ukraine	na	**63**	61	66	45	63	75	67	62	65	67	65	60	61	64	67
United States	na	**37**	37	36	33	35	43	45	39	33	37	39	33	31	37	40
Uruguay	na	**na**	na	na	na	na	na	na	na	na	na	na	na	na	na	na
Venezuela	na	**na**	na	na	na	na	na	na	na	na	na	na	na	na	na	na
Vietnam	na	**72**	75	70	71	74	71	71	73	74	66	76	71	79	71	61
Zimbabwe	na	**64**	59	69	58	71	69	68	58	100	66	61	66	61	67	66
Total	na	58	58	58	52	58	64	62	57	54	61	59	57	63	58	52

RANKING	
Country	2000
Bangladesh	96
Morocco	94
Turkey	88
India	81
Philippines	78
Albania	76
Montenegro	74
China	73
Macedonia	73
Vietnam	72
Serbia	72
Bulgaria	72
Lithuania	70
Argentina	69
Italy	67
Croatia	67
Korea, South	67
Tanzania	66
Romania	65
Peru	65
Zimbabwe	64
Malta	64
Russian Fed.	64
Poland	64
Ukraine	63
Latvia	63
Puerto Rico	62
Chile	61
Israel	60
Bosnia and Herz.	60
Singapore	58
Moldova	57
Portugal	57
Mexico	56
Luxembourg	55
Uganda	54
Greece	54
Belarus	54
Slovakia	54
Slovenia	53
Estonia	53
South Africa	53
Hungary	51
Canada	48
Ireland	47
Czech Republic	47
Spain	44
France	44
Finland	43
Japan	43
Belgium	42
Iceland	42
Sweden	40
Great Britain	39
Germany	38
Denmark	37
United States	37
Northern Ireland	36
Netherlands	27
Total	58

C038) WORK: PEOPLE WHO DON'T WORK TURN LAZY

Do you agree or disagree with the following statements: "People who don't work turn lazy?"

Strongly agree / Agree (%)

(WVS: V99; EVS: V92)

Country	Wave		Gender		Age			Education			Income			Values		
	1990	2000	Male	Female	16-29	30-49	50+	Lower	Middle	Upper	Lower	Middle	Upper	Mat	Mixed	Postm.
Albania	na	**80**	80	80	77	78	87	81	79	83	80	81	81	82	79	82
Algeria	na	**na**	na	na	na	na	na	na	na	na	na	na	na	na	na	na
Argentina	na	**78**	77	78	76	77	80	83	74	56	84	78	71	85	80	66
Armenia	na	**na**	na	na	na	na	na	na	na	na	na	na	na	na	na	na
Australia	na	**na**	na	na	na	na	na	na	na	na	na	na	na	na	na	na
Austria	na	**na**	na	na	na	na	na	na	na	na	na	na	na	na	na	na
Azerbaijan	na	**na**	na	na	na	na	na	na	na	na	na	na	na	na	na	na
Bangladesh	na	**85**	84	86	84	85	91	84	88	85	87	82	86	89	82	81
Belarus	na	**66**	63	69	58	65	75	72	64	66	69	66	62	71	63	61
Belgium	na	**50**	53	48	47	44	57	58	53	40	54	49	50	57	53	36
Bosnia and Herz.	na	**68**	68	68	70	69	65	69	69	65	73	67	65	68	69	70
Brazil	na	**na**	na	na	na	na	na	na	na	na	na	na	na	na	na	na
Bulgaria	na	**68**	68	67	56	61	79	73	66	62	74	66	61	67	72	60
Canada	na	**53**	58	49	48	52	59	69	53	40	60	57	45	64	56	45
Chile	na	**67**	68	66	66	67	69	68	66	67	67	67	68	73	65	61
China	na	**86**	85	87	81	86	90	85	86	93	85	87	87	88	86	68
Colombia	na	**na**	na	na	na	na	na	na	na	na	na	na	na	na	na	na
Croatia	na	**68**	68	67	62	66	73	69	68	62	73	64	71	68	69	63
Czech Republic	na	**79**	77	81	68	78	86	77	82	78	78	81	77	77	81	70
Denmark	na	**65**	69	62	75	59	67	75	59	50	70	65	61	74	69	46
Dominican Rep.	na	**na**	na	na	na	na	na	na	na	na	na	na	na	na	na	na
Egypt	na	**na**	na	na	na	na	na	na	na	na	na	na	na	na	na	na
El Salvador	na	**na**	na	na	na	na	na	na	na	na	na	na	na	na	na	na
Estonia	na	**65**	65	64	64	62	67	67	62	68	60	66	68	60	69	66
Finland	na	**55**	60	51	48	56	58	59	54	43	57	57	54	63	55	39
France	na	**55**	59	50	46	48	65	61	49	42	59	55	50	62	57	38
Georgia	na	**na**	na	na	na	na	na	na	na	na	na	na	na	na	na	na
Germany	na	**50**	56	46	43	48	55	52	48	48	48	55	47	43	56	43
Great Britain	na	**43**	49	38	41	40	49	47	45	34	48	44	39	na	na	na
Greece	na	**56**	58	55	49	58	72	71	59	51	56	55	59	61	57	46
Hungary	na	**74**	73	74	71	70	78	74	72	72	68	75	74	75	74	73
Iceland	na	**17**	21	14	14	13	27	23	16	7	25	13	15	18	19	6
India	na	**85**	84	86	84	86	86	85	87	84	81	86	87	85	85	84
Indonesia	na	**na**	na	na	na	na	na	na	na	na	na	na	na	na	na	na
Iran	na	**na**	na	na	na	na	na	na	na	na	na	na	na	na	na	na
Ireland	na	**57**	62	51	51	57	62	59	58	51	58	62	58	62	57	48
Israel	na	**75**	78	73	70	75	81	85	77	66	76	75	71	75	75	76
Italy	na	**76**	77	74	71	70	84	82	72	66	81	76	71	80	78	70
Japan	na	**72**	75	70	71	68	76	76	71	74	73	71	73	75	73	65
Jordan	na	**na**	na	na	na	na	na	na	na	na	na	na	na	na	na	na
Korea, South	na	**85**	87	84	78	86	93	89	87	82	87	86	83	87	84	79
Latvia	na	**75**	74	75	63	71	83	78	74	73	76	80	72	74	75	80
Lithuania	na	**55**	51	57	43	55	63	64	51	54	58	57	53	55	53	66
Luxembourg	na	**61**	65	57	63	55	65	67	62	45	66	62	50	66	63	46
Macedonia	na	**78**	78	77	72	78	82	85	74	74	81	78	74	77	76	86
Malta	na	**74**	78	69	77	70	76	71	75	73	69	75	78	73	73	80
Mexico	na	**80**	80	80	79	78	85	82	78	78	80	79	81	79	81	76
Moldova	na	**20**	20	20	17	18	26	23	23	13	17	22	17	21	22	22
Montenegro	na	**77**	79	74	69	75	83	82	72	75	88	76	75	84	71	66
Morocco	na	**89**	90	88	88	90	90	90	87	79	91	89	81	88	90	87
Netherlands	na	**35**	37	32	30	27	45	53	30	22	41	28	33	59	35	22
New Zealand	na	**na**	na	na	na	na	na	na	na	na	na	na	na	na	na	na
Nigeria	na	**na**	na	na	na	na	na	na	na	na	na	na	na	na	na	na
Northern Ireland	na	**48**	48	48	50	42	52	52	46	41	54	49	39	52	48	41
Norway	na	**na**	na	na	na	na	na	na	na	na	na	na	na	na	na	na
Pakistan	na	**na**	na	na	na	na	na	na	na	na	na	na	na	na	na	na
Peru	na	**80**	78	82	78	81	84	78	81	80	80	81	80	80	81	81
Philippines	na	**65**	65	65	63	64	69	64	64	66	67	63	65	64	65	68
Poland	na	**78**	81	75	72	77	83	79	76	77	76	81	78	74	80	79
Portugal	na	**70**	70	70	64	69	74	72	69	58	78	66	69	76	67	63
Puerto Rico	na	**78**	79	78	70	75	84	83	80	76	79	78	75	82	78	76
Romania	na	**80**	81	80	68	82	85	85	78	77	83	83	77	83	78	72
Russian Fed.	na	**74**	73	74	67	72	80	76	72	78	73	73	75	75	72	77
Serbia	na	**77**	77	77	68	76	81	77	78	74	79	78	77	79	77	63
Singapore	na	**77**	78	76	75	81	76	77	80	66	77	79	75	80	77	68
Slovakia	na	**79**	77	81	72	77	86	81	78	79	80	76	83	79	80	80
Slovenia	na	**86**	85	87	76	85	94	90	85	79	92	89	79	93	86	80
South Africa	na	**55**	55	54	51	56	59	57	52	51	48	58	62	59	51	55
Spain	na	**63**	63	63	61	54	71	69	60	48	66	66	57	70	62	53
Sweden	na	**37**	42	31	39	36	36	39	43	25	38	41	29	44	40	23
Switzerland	na	**na**	na	na	na	na	na	na	na	na	na	na	na	na	na	na
Taiwan	na	**na**	na	na	na	na	na	na	na	na	na	na	na	na	na	na
Tanzania	na	**88**	89	86	88	86	92	89	90	78	88	89	83	91	87	83
Turkey	na	**90**	92	88	87	92	94	92	87	87	92	89	89	93	89	89
Uganda	na	**75**	74	77	74	77	74	79	72	88	81	88	77	71	78	77
Ukraine	na	**66**	65	68	60	62	74	76	63	71	67	66	68	66	68	80
United States	na	**53**	61	44	59	50	51	65	57	46	56	56	45	59	52	52
Uruguay	na	**na**	na	na	na	na	na	na	na	na	na	na	na	na	na	na
Venezuela	na	**na**	na	na	na	na	na	na	na	na	na	na	na	na	na	na
Vietnam	na	**88**	89	87	91	88	86	87	90	90	85	89	88	93	87	83
Zimbabwe	na	**69**	64	73	62	73	77	71	65	70	73	65	66	69	68	79
Total	na	**67**	69	66	64	66	71	72	67	60	70	68	66	72	68	57

RANKING

Country	2000
Turkey	90
Morocco	89
Vietnam	88
Tanzania	88
China	86
Slovenia	86
Korea, South	85
India	85
Bangladesh	85
Romania	80
Albania	80
Peru	80
Mexico	80
Czech Republic	79
Slovakia	79
Poland	78
Puerto Rico	78
Macedonia	78
Argentina	78
Singapore	77
Serbia	77
Montenegro	77
Italy	76
Uganda	75
Israel	75
Latvia	75
Hungary	74
Malta	74
Russian Fed.	74
Japan	72
Portugal	70
Zimbabwe	69
Bosnia and Herz.	68
Croatia	68
Bulgaria	68
Chile	67
Ukraine	66
Belarus	66
Denmark	65
Philippines	65
Estonia	65
Spain	63
Luxembourg	61
Ireland	57
Greece	56
Finland	55
France	55
Lithuania	55
South Africa	55
Canada	53
United States	53
Belgium	50
Germany	50
Northern Ireland	48
Great Britain	43
Sweden	37
Netherlands	35
Moldova	20
Iceland	17
Total	67

C039) WORK: IS A DUTY TOWARDS SOCIETY

Do you agree or disagree with the following statement: "Work is a duty towards society?"

(WVS: V100; EVS: V93)

Strongly agree / Agree (%)

Country	Wave		Gender		Age			Education			Income			Values		
	1990	2000	Male	Female	16-29	30-49	50+	Lower	Middle	Upper	Lower	Middle	Upper	Mat	Mixed	Postm.
Albania	na	**64**	66	61	61	61	71	63	61	70	63	60	67	65	65	55
Algeria	na	**na**	na	na	na	na	na	na	na	na	na	na	na	na	na	na
Argentina	na	**79**	78	79	69	79	88	86	68	69	87	79	71	86	80	71
Armenia	na	**na**	na	na	na	na	na	na	na	na	na	na	na	na	na	na
Australia	na	**na**	na	na	na	na	na	na	na	na	na	na	na	na	na	na
Austria	na	**na**	na	na	na	na	na	na	na	na	na	na	na	na	na	na
Azerbaijan	na	**na**	na	na	na	na	na	na	na	na	na	na	na	na	na	na
Bangladesh	na	**97**	96	97	98	96	96	96	97	99	97	96	97	98	96	95
Belarus	na	**63**	60	66	46	59	81	77	59	55	66	63	57	68	62	40
Belgium	na	**62**	65	59	55	53	73	69	63	56	65	65	60	64	64	56
Bosnia and Herz.	na	**49**	45	52	44	49	54	55	47	51	53	49	46	45	52	49
Brazil	na	**na**	na	na	na	na	na	na	na	na	na	na	na	na	na	na
Bulgaria	na	**75**	72	79	54	73	87	86	70	69	81	78	70	75	76	73
Canada	na	**65**	68	63	54	62	76	75	65	59	70	68	58	74	69	56
Chile	na	**68**	70	67	67	68	71	71	68	64	68	72	66	71	68	68
China	na	**86**	87	84	75	87	92	85	86	90	85	88	84	84	87	81
Colombia	na	**na**	na	na	na	na	na	na	na	na	na	na	na	na	na	na
Croatia	na	**61**	55	67	52	65	64	63	60	63	73	57	59	68	59	63
Czech Republic	na	**63**	59	67	52	53	77	66	60	57	70	65	56	67	64	54
Denmark	na	**70**	76	64	70	62	78	77	71	56	76	66	66	82	73	52
Dominican Rep.	na	**na**	na	na	na	na	na	na	na	na	na	na	na	na	na	na
Egypt	na	**na**	na	na	na	na	na	na	na	na	na	na	na	na	na	na
El Salvador	na	**na**	na	na	na	na	na	na	na	na	na	na	na	na	na	na
Estonia	na	**60**	58	62	45	54	74	65	59	54	60	69	53	62	60	43
Finland	na	**62**	59	64	53	50	76	66	59	52	65	60	60	63	62	53
France	na	**56**	61	52	47	45	71	62	48	48	61	57	51	64	58	43
Georgia	na	**na**	na	na	na	na	na	na	na	na	na	na	na	na	na	na
Germany	na	**64**	67	61	55	61	70	64	63	68	63	63	67	65	65	61
Great Britain	na	**49**	50	48	46	44	58	51	51	45	56	44	44	na	na	na
Greece	na	**49**	46	51	35	54	73	77	49	44	57	50	40	54	49	46
Hungary	na	**70**	68	71	67	62	79	72	67	60	63	69	74	72	68	84
Iceland	na	**59**	65	52	43	55	77	64	59	45	67	59	50	65	59	37
India	na	**82**	83	80	81	83	80	78	84	85	72	82	85	80	85	91
Indonesia	na	**na**	na	na	na	na	na	na	na	na	na	na	na	na	na	na
Iran	na	**na**	na	na	na	na	na	na	na	na	na	na	na	na	na	na
Ireland	na	**60**	64	56	49	59	72	67	57	57	66	65	55	62	60	54
Israel	na	**70**	72	68	65	70	75	78	70	65	72	73	63	74	70	76
Italy	na	**68**	69	66	54	64	79	74	62	64	72	68	66	69	69	65
Japan	na	**61**	66	56	41	52	77	74	58	61	61	62	63	69	60	59
Jordan	na	**na**	na	na	na	na	na	na	na	na	na	na	na	na	na	na
Korea, South	na	**61**	66	56	48	61	75	71	63	56	63	56	61	62	61	49
Latvia	na	**67**	65	69	49	62	79	72	68	60	71	73	60	71	66	64
Lithuania	na	**45**	41	49	34	46	52	47	46	38	43	57	40	47	44	52
Luxembourg	na	**69**	71	67	65	62	79	75	69	58	68	72	70	72	68	65
Macedonia	na	**67**	67	67	62	67	72	74	63	64	75	61	64	73	63	74
Malta	na	**88**	86	90	84	84	93	90	87	85	87	89	83	85	90	84
Mexico	na	**78**	78	78	75	78	83	81	76	72	79	79	77	80	78	76
Moldova	na	**53**	49	55	42	48	67	64	52	44	61	58	45	55	50	44
Montenegro	na	**54**	58	51	39	53	64	61	46	57	52	53	56	54	55	54
Morocco	na	**96**	96	96	95	96	98	96	94	94	96	93	96	98	96	89
Netherlands	na	**59**	62	56	60	46	71	74	56	48	65	60	48	73	60	48
New Zealand	na	**na**	na	na	na	na	na	na	na	na	na	na	na	na	na	na
Nigeria	na	**na**	na	na	na	na	na	na	na	na	na	na	na	na	na	na
Northern Ireland	na	**50**	48	53	47	44	58	56	46	46	53	48	47	57	50	43
Norway	na	**na**	na	na	na	na	na	na	na	na	na	na	na	na	na	na
Pakistan	na	**na**	na	na	na	na	na	na	na	na	na	na	na	na	na	na
Peru	na	**84**	84	85	83	85	87	86	87	80	88	85	76	86	83	89
Philippines	na	**76**	74	79	76	77	77	76	76	78	76	77	76	75	77	78
Poland	na	**73**	74	73	59	70	85	79	66	65	76	73	66	72	73	72
Portugal	na	**86**	83	89	78	87	90	90	77	80	91	82	83	88	84	90
Puerto Rico	na	**85**	86	85	74	84	92	91	88	83	88	87	80	87	87	80
Romania	na	**79**	79	80	67	75	90	88	75	75	86	80	74	82	79	63
Russian Fed.	na	**56**	53	58	36	52	72	71	53	55	60	58	51	60	52	43
Serbia	na	**65**	62	67	52	62	73	68	65	60	70	67	65	66	64	55
Singapore	na	**75**	76	74	75	75	76	77	77	59	78	80	69	76	76	64
Slovakia	na	**63**	58	68	54	61	72	66	62	61	68	61	64	64	64	61
Slovenia	na	**76**	75	77	60	74	90	86	76	61	83	83	63	85	77	70
South Africa	na	**77**	78	75	74	79	76	78	76	72	79	78	75	77	76	79
Spain	na	**63**	63	63	53	57	75	71	56	55	71	66	56	71	63	53
Sweden	na	**58**	62	55	53	53	67	71	55	53	63	56	53	67	63	41
Switzerland	na	**na**	na	na	na	na	na	na	na	na	na	na	na	na	na	na
Taiwan	na	**na**	na	na	na	na	na	na	na	na	na	na	na	na	na	na
Tanzania	na	**97**	97	97	97	97	98	97	98	98	97	98	99	98	98	100
Turkey	na	**89**	91	87	86	91	93	91	87	81	91	90	83	93	90	83
Uganda	na	**80**	83	78	81	80	82	78	82	79	82	86	84	75	84	80
Ukraine	na	**53**	47	58	27	51	70	73	50	49	58	51	49	53	55	46
United States	na	**58**	60	56	61	53	62	71	59	53	63	58	50	60	58	57
Uruguay	na	**na**	na	na	na	na	na	na	na	na	na	na	na	na	na	na
Venezuela	na	**na**	na	na	na	na	na	na	na	na	na	na	na	na	na	na
Vietnam	na	**95**	96	94	93	96	95	94	97	100	95	95	96	96	97	94
Zimbabwe	na	**85**	86	85	83	85	92	84	87	100	81	89	90	87	84	89
Total	na	**69**	69	68	63	66	76	75	66	62	72	70	65	71	69	62

RANKING

Country	2000
Tanzania	97
Bangladesh	97
Morocco	96
Vietnam	95
Turkey	89
Malta	88
Portugal	86
China	86
Zimbabwe	85
Puerto Rico	85
Peru	84
India	82
Uganda	80
Romania	79
Argentina	79
Mexico	78
South Africa	77
Philippines	76
Slovenia	76
Bulgaria	75
Singapore	75
Poland	73
Denmark	70
Hungary	70
Israel	70
Luxembourg	69
Chile	68
Italy	68
Latvia	67
Macedonia	67
Canada	65
Serbia	65
Germany	64
Albania	64
Spain	63
Belarus	63
Slovakia	63
Czech Republic	63
Belgium	62
Finland	62
Croatia	61
Korea, South	61
Japan	61
Ireland	60
Estonia	60
Netherlands	59
Iceland	59
Sweden	58
United States	58
France	56
Russian Fed.	56
Montenegro	54
Ukraine	53
Moldova	53
Northern Ireland	50
Great Britain	49
Greece	49
Bosnia and Herz.	49
Lithuania	45
Total	69

C040) WORK: PEOPLE SHOULD NOT HAVE TO WORK

Do you agree or disagree with the following statement: "People should not have to work if they don't want to?"

Strongly agree / Agree (%)

(WVS: V101; EVS: V94)

Country	Wave		Gender		Age			Education			Income			Values		
	1990	2000	Male	Female	16-29	30-49	50+	Lower	Middle	Upper	Lower	Middle	Upper	Mat	Mixed	Postm.
Albania	na	**44**	46	43	37	44	51	48	43	37	45	45	42	47	42	30
Algeria	na	**na**	na	na	na	na	na	na	na	na	na	na	na	na	na	na
Argentina	na	**20**	20	20	26	20	14	20	19	21	21	21	17	14	21	21
Armenia	na	**na**	na	na	na	na	na	na	na	na	na	na	na	na	na	na
Australia	na	**na**	na	na	na	na	na	na	na	na	na	na	na	na	na	na
Austria	na	**na**	na	na	na	na	na	na	na	na	na	na	na	na	na	na
Azerbaijan	na	**na**	na	na	na	na	na	na	na	na	na	na	na	na	na	na
Bangladesh	na	**38**	37	40	39	41	24	41	38	34	37	42	35	35	41	44
Belarus	na	**54**	57	51	61	55	45	55	55	46	51	51	62	57	49	61
Belgium	na	**30**	29	32	35	35	24	24	32	33	24	28	36	25	30	37
Bosnia and Herz.	na	**36**	34	38	38	37	34	35	37	35	42	36	32	35	37	40
Brazil	na	**na**	na	na	na	na	na	na	na	na	na	na	na	na	na	na
Bulgaria	na	**33**	36	31	50	36	23	19	39	45	27	28	44	30	36	43
Canada	na	**14**	14	15	21	16	9	10	14	17	12	14	16	11	12	18
Chile	na	**32**	31	32	31	33	30	33	31	29	34	31	27	31	32	29
China	na	**31**	31	31	30	35	23	26	33	46	30	28	36	32	30	45
Colombia	na	**na**	na	na	na	na	na	na	na	na	na	na	na	na	na	na
Croatia	na	**22**	25	19	30	16	24	18	24	27	28	21	20	17	24	18
Czech Republic	na	**32**	37	27	41	36	23	30	32	41	21	34	40	24	32	45
Denmark	na	**9**	10	9	11	11	7	8	15	10	7	12	10	6	8	16
Dominican Rep.	na	**na**	na	na	na	na	na	na	na	na	na	na	na	na	na	na
Egypt	na	**na**	na	na	na	na	na	na	na	na	na	na	na	na	na	na
El Salvador	na	**na**	na	na	na	na	na	na	na	na	na	na	na	na	na	na
Estonia	na	**33**	36	31	41	36	26	31	34	35	36	28	36	33	32	45
Finland	na	**27**	31	22	34	28	20	28	25	22	28	30	23	30	25	28
France	na	**33**	30	37	39	38	26	29	38	39	32	32	37	31	32	41
Georgia	na	**na**	na	na	na	na	na	na	na	na	na	na	na	na	na	na
Germany	na	**20**	18	21	27	19	18	22	20	8	24	20	18	22	20	18
Great Britain	na	**19**	17	21	22	18	19	21	19	17	24	15	20	na	na	na
Greece	na	**29**	30	28	32	29	22	24	28	30	27	29	33	26	29	33
Hungary	na	**26**	28	24	34	26	20	26	25	25	29	24	25	23	29	26
Iceland	na	**42**	46	37	50	39	37	40	42	43	41	41	41	41	42	44
India	na	**41**	40	42	40	42	41	44	38	38	39	46	38	41	40	36
Indonesia	na	**na**	na	na	na	na	na	na	na	na	na	na	na	na	na	na
Iran	na	**na**	na	na	na	na	na	na	na	na	na	na	na	na	na	na
Ireland	na	**28**	25	32	34	28	23	28	29	28	30	27	30	31	26	34
Israel	na	**42**	44	40	51	39	35	41	43	42	44	39	39	52	39	40
Italy	na	**24**	21	27	25	28	20	24	25	25	24	22	25	23	23	26
Japan	na	**21**	23	18	41	23	10	12	18	32	17	19	22	20	20	30
Jordan	na	**na**	na	na	na	na	na	na	na	na	na	na	na	na	na	na
Korea, South	na	**34**	28	40	41	33	27	40	32	36	33	33	36	32	36	38
Latvia	na	**34**	36	32	50	40	23	26	35	41	32	30	40	32	36	34
Lithuania	na	**38**	41	37	45	42	30	30	41	40	34	42	41	37	38	45
Luxembourg	na	**30**	35	24	36	31	25	24	29	45	30	26	39	25	29	38
Macedonia	na	**31**	33	29	42	29	23	34	31	24	35	28	27	26	33	33
Malta	na	**47**	42	52	54	51	40	44	49	44	49	46	45	49	46	48
Mexico	na	**31**	31	31	35	28	30	32	31	25	36	30	24	27	33	32
Moldova	na	**40**	45	36	49	38	36	43	41	36	42	37	45	36	48	38
Montenegro	na	**39**	39	40	50	38	35	36	43	39	42	41	39	40	39	38
Morocco	na	**48**	45	50	50	45	52	49	47	34	48	49	46	52	43	54
Netherlands	na	**20**	23	18	20	24	16	14	21	26	18	19	25	11	18	33
New Zealand	na	**na**	na	na	na	na	na	na	na	na	na	na	na	na	na	na
Nigeria	na	**na**	na	na	na	na	na	na	na	na	na	na	na	na	na	na
Northern Ireland	na	**24**	25	24	26	26	22	23	25	24	27	19	21	30	24	17
Norway	na	**na**	na	na	na	na	na	na	na	na	na	na	na	na	na	na
Pakistan	na	**na**	na	na	na	na	na	na	na	na	na	na	na	na	na	na
Peru	na	**24**	25	24	26	23	24	27	25	21	24	27	21	26	25	20
Philippines	na	**39**	39	40	35	40	44	43	39	34	38	38	41	38	39	38
Poland	na	**67**	72	61	77	66	60	67	67	64	64	68	68	59	72	68
Portugal	na	**16**	17	15	16	19	15	16	16	21	17	20	14	18	15	20
Puerto Rico	na	**28**	30	26	32	32	22	30	31	25	32	26	27	26	29	25
Romania	na	**56**	57	54	58	54	56	62	56	42	62	59	46	61	51	53
Russian Fed.	na	**36**	40	32	49	38	23	30	35	39	32	33	40	33	38	39
Serbia	na	**39**	41	37	54	42	30	34	39	46	35	41	41	33	44	52
Singapore	na	**26**	27	26	25	28	26	25	26	32	22	23	29	23	28	27
Slovakia	na	**22**	24	20	29	23	15	17	23	29	17	21	24	20	23	38
Slovenia	na	**17**	21	13	25	15	12	15	19	9	15	15	20	11	17	21
South Africa	na	**32**	31	33	33	35	22	34	29	34	33	33	27	26	34	50
Spain	na	**26**	27	24	31	27	21	23	27	32	21	28	31	22	28	28
Sweden	na	**12**	11	12	14	12	10	10	12	12	12	12	11	7	12	12
Switzerland	na	**na**	na	na	na	na	na	na	na	na	na	na	na	na	na	na
Taiwan	na	**na**	na	na	na	na	na	na	na	na	na	na	na	na	na	na
Tanzania	na	**24**	23	26	21	26	25	27	20	22	30	22	20	25	25	24
Turkey	na	**42**	41	44	44	41	39	46	37	37	50	40	32	31	44	47
Uganda	na	**32**	28	36	31	35	29	29	34	33	31	30	42	34	32	29
Ukraine	na	**39**	42	36	50	43	28	29	39	42	31	43	43	33	43	65
United States	na	**22**	24	19	31	19	18	23	22	21	21	22	23	20	22	21
Uruguay	na	**na**	na	na	na	na	na	na	na	na	na	na	na	na	na	na
Venezuela	na	**na**	na	na	na	na	na	na	na	na	na	na	na	na	na	na
Vietnam	na	**62**	63	62	60	63	63	62	62	71	59	64	62	69	64	53
Zimbabwe	na	**36**	37	36	41	34	27	36	37	na	39	37	24	42	30	56
Total	na	**32**	33	31	37	33	26	31	33	31	32	32	33	33	32	31

RANKING	
Country	2000
Poland	67
Vietnam	62
Romania	56
Belarus	54
Morocco	48
Malta	47
Albania	44
Turkey	42
Israel	42
Iceland	42
India	41
Moldova	40
Montenegro	39
Philippines	39
Serbia	39
Ukraine	39
Bangladesh	38
Lithuania	38
Bosnia and Herz.	36
Zimbabwe	36
Russian Fed.	36
Korea, South	34
Latvia	34
Bulgaria	33
France	33
Estonia	33
Uganda	32
South Africa	32
Czech Republic	32
Chile	32
China	31
Mexico	31
Macedonia	31
Belgium	30
Luxembourg	30
Greece	29
Ireland	28
Puerto Rico	28
Finland	27
Singapore	26
Spain	26
Hungary	26
Northern Ireland	24
Italy	24
Peru	24
Tanzania	24
Croatia	22
United States	22
Slovakia	22
Japan	21
Netherlands	20
Germany	20
Argentina	20
Great Britain	19
Slovenia	17
Portugal	16
Canada	14
Sweden	12
Denmark	9
Total	32

C041) WORK: SHOULD ALWAYS COME FIRST

Do you agree or disagree with the following statement: "Work should always come first, even if it means less spare time?"

(WVS: V102; EVS: V95)

Strongly agree / Agree (%)

Country	Wave		Gender		Age			Education			Income			Values		
	1990	2000	Male	Female	16-29	30-49	50+	Lower	Middle	Upper	Lower	Middle	Upper	Mat	Mixed	Postm.
Albania	na	**88**	89	87	84	87	94	90	88	84	89	87	89	92	87	78
Algeria	na	**na**	na	na	na	na	na	na	na	na	na	na	na	na	na	na
Argentina	na	**77**	78	76	69	78	84	85	68	61	82	80	69	82	79	71
Armenia	na	**na**	na	na	na	na	na	na	na	na	na	na	na	na	na	na
Australia	na	**na**	na	na	na	na	na	na	na	na	na	na	na	na	na	na
Austria	na	**na**	na	na	na	na	na	na	na	na	na	na	na	na	na	na
Azerbaijan	na	**na**	na	na	na	na	na	na	na	na	na	na	na	na	na	na
Bangladesh	na	**93**	91	94	92	93	94	92	95	92	92	90	98	93	92	90
Belarus	na	**36**	35	36	22	32	50	46	33	27	39	35	29	42	31	20
Belgium	na	**33**	33	34	19	24	48	48	33	23	45	39	24	37	35	26
Bosnia and Herz.	na	**67**	69	66	63	67	71	71	69	60	73	66	66	72	66	62
Brazil	na	**na**	na	na	na	na	na	na	na	na	na	na	na	na	na	na
Bulgaria	na	**53**	53	53	46	48	60	52	53	55	56	52	53	49	57	56
Canada	na	**45**	47	43	37	36	59	63	42	33	54	43	33	54	48	36
Chile	na	**53**	59	47	47	51	60	61	51	39	58	53	43	54	55	44
China	na	**84**	82	85	72	85	90	88	82	67	87	84	78	84	82	71
Colombia	na	**na**	na	na	na	na	na	na	na	na	na	na	na	na	na	na
Croatia	na	**54**	55	53	32	55	67	61	51	43	77	49	45	58	56	44
Czech Republic	na	**56**	55	57	40	51	68	57	55	52	64	56	49	62	54	51
Denmark	na	**49**	54	45	33	36	72	57	41	38	60	46	41	55	53	30
Dominican Rep.	na	**na**	na	na	na	na	na	na	na	na	na	na	na	na	na	na
Egypt	na	**na**	na	na	na	na	na	na	na	na	na	na	na	na	na	na
El Salvador	na	**na**	na	na	na	na	na	na	na	na	na	na	na	na	na	na
Estonia	na	**48**	48	47	34	41	61	54	44	48	50	50	46	46	50	37
Finland	na	**39**	37	40	21	28	59	47	29	28	45	36	35	44	39	29
France	na	**34**	38	31	21	23	51	43	27	18	45	34	27	45	35	16
Georgia	na	**na**	na	na	na	na	na	na	na	na	na	na	na	na	na	na
Germany	na	**47**	52	44	39	45	54	49	46	49	51	51	50	47	49	47
Great Britain	na	**26**	27	26	24	18	37	36	19	18	35	25	15	na	na	na
Greece	na	**38**	40	37	24	42	64	63	44	29	44	38	36	45	38	30
Hungary	na	**78**	75	80	69	73	87	78	77	76	78	77	77	80	77	78
Iceland	na	**34**	36	32	19	26	57	44	30	18	41	33	25	39	34	18
India	na	**72**	72	72	70	74	72	71	71	75	66	74	73	74	71	72
Indonesia	na	**na**	na	na	na	na	na	na	na	na	na	na	na	na	na	na
Iran	na	**na**	na	na	na	na	na	na	na	na	na	na	na	na	na	na
Ireland	na	**35**	38	33	25	30	50	49	30	22	50	38	26	33	36	34
Israel	na	**67**	68	67	60	66	78	84	66	58	71	71	61	69	68	65
Italy	na	**50**	53	46	35	40	66	64	41	31	65	47	39	64	50	43
Japan	na	**19**	22	17	5	10	33	44	17	13	26	17	17	23	18	10
Jordan	na	**na**	na	na	na	na	na	na	na	na	na	na	na	na	na	na
Korea, South	na	**39**	43	34	22	39	57	60	42	31	44	36	35	42	38	23
Latvia	na	**50**	49	51	28	42	66	62	48	41	56	54	39	54	50	30
Lithuania	na	**55**	56	54	40	55	67	65	53	51	64	62	49	52	57	51
Luxembourg	na	**40**	45	36	29	34	55	49	37	33	51	42	32	49	43	26
Macedonia	na	**79**	79	79	72	80	84	88	77	69	86	76	74	83	77	74
Malta	na	**45**	50	40	30	40	61	61	41	30	58	41	36	45	48	30
Mexico	na	**70**	71	68	63	70	79	78	64	49	78	68	62	75	69	56
Moldova	na	**65**	64	65	54	63	75	75	61	61	74	69	59	62	68	48
Montenegro	na	**69**	69	70	58	69	77	79	64	60	84	71	71	77	64	53
Morocco	na	**94**	95	93	93	94	96	96	88	85	96	95	91	97	92	89
Netherlands	na	**23**	25	21	13	14	38	37	18	14	31	18	19	37	23	15
New Zealand	na	**na**	na	na	na	na	na	na	na	na	na	na	na	na	na	na
Nigeria	na	**na**	na	na	na	na	na	na	na	na	na	na	na	na	na	na
Northern Ireland	na	**31**	33	29	20	24	41	38	26	22	37	34	22	37	29	27
Norway	na	**na**	na	na	na	na	na	na	na	na	na	na	na	na	na	na
Pakistan	na	**na**	na	na	na	na	na	na	na	na	na	na	na	na	na	na
Peru	na	**75**	74	75	71	77	76	80	76	68	78	75	67	80	73	78
Philippines	na	**83**	83	83	80	85	84	84	84	80	88	82	80	84	82	81
Poland	na	**62**	66	59	41	61	76	71	50	52	70	60	52	64	61	57
Portugal	na	**46**	47	46	36	46	53	53	36	24	58	50	50	43	49	40
Puerto Rico	na	**52**	58	48	39	42	66	77	63	43	68	49	44	57	56	40
Romania	na	**80**	79	81	62	80	90	86	77	78	83	83	77	85	79	63
Russian Fed.	na	**50**	53	48	36	48	62	62	50	46	53	53	45	54	48	53
Serbia	na	**66**	66	66	48	63	77	71	65	60	74	67	64	68	64	63
Singapore	na	**54**	58	50	48	54	74	59	54	39	61	56	49	55	54	53
Slovakia	na	**61**	58	64	48	60	73	66	60	50	65	61	60	65	61	47
Slovenia	na	**56**	56	55	30	52	77	71	53	37	67	56	45	70	55	48
South Africa	na	**73**	73	74	78	69	75	76	71	54	78	80	61	76	72	75
Spain	na	**50**	49	50	40	41	63	60	42	32	63	46	44	56	51	33
Sweden	na	**29**	34	24	16	23	42	46	27	18	34	29	21	45	31	18
Switzerland	na	**na**	na	na	na	na	na	na	na	na	na	na	na	na	na	na
Taiwan	na	**na**	na	na	na	na	na	na	na	na	na	na	na	na	na	na
Tanzania	na	**87**	88	86	85	87	91	87	87	85	88	84	90	86	87	96
Turkey	na	**72**	71	73	65	76	83	81	62	51	81	70	58	76	73	64
Uganda	na	**81**	86	76	77	83	89	78	81	91	80	87	84	81	80	84
Ukraine	na	**47**	48	47	27	46	60	56	47	43	52	40	49	49	47	53
United States	na	**36**	40	32	36	33	39	51	37	28	42	35	27	36	37	32
Uruguay	na	**na**	na	na	na	na	na	na	na	na	na	na	na	na	na	na
Venezuela	na	**na**	na	na	na	na	na	na	na	na	na	na	na	na	na	na
Vietnam	na	**79**	80	78	78	78	81	77	81	90	83	80	77	84	81	84
Zimbabwe	na	**86**	86	87	84	87	90	89	83	62	87	89	84	84	87	96
Total	na	56	58	55	50	54	65	66	54	45	63	57	52	63	56	43

RANKING	
Country	2000
Morocco	94
Bangladesh	93
Albania	88
Tanzania	87
Zimbabwe	86
China	84
Philippines	83
Uganda	81
Romania	80
Macedonia	79
Vietnam	79
Hungary	78
Argentina	77
Peru	75
South Africa	73
India	72
Turkey	72
Mexico	70
Montenegro	69
Bosnia and Herz.	67
Israel	67
Serbia	66
Moldova	65
Poland	62
Slovakia	61
Czech Republic	56
Slovenia	56
Lithuania	55
Singapore	54
Croatia	54
Bulgaria	53
Chile	53
Puerto Rico	52
Russian Fed.	50
Latvia	50
Italy	50
Spain	50
Denmark	49
Estonia	48
Germany	47
Ukraine	47
Portugal	46
Malta	45
Canada	45
Luxembourg	40
Finland	39
Korea, South	39
Greece	38
United States	36
Belarus	36
Ireland	35
France	34
Iceland	34
Belgium	33
Northern Ireland	31
Sweden	29
Great Britain	26
Netherlands	23
Japan	19
Total	56

C059) WORK: EFFICIENCY IS PAID MORE

Imagine two secretaries, of the same age, doing practically the same job. One finds out that the other earns considerably more than she does. The better paid secretary, however, is quicker, more efficient and more reliable at her job. In your opinion, is it fair or not fair that one secretary is paid more than the other? (% "fair") (WVS: V103; EVS: V96)

Country	Wave		Gender		Age			Education			Income			Values		
	1990	2000	Male	Female	16-29	30-49	50+	Lower	Middle	Upper	Lower	Middle	Upper	Mat	Mixed	Postm.
Albania	na	**83**	83	82	86	81	83	83	81	86	82	83	85	84	84	74
Algeria	na	**82**	81	83	81	82	84	81	81	84	82	87	81	77	85	83
Argentina	83	**60**	60	60	54	60	66	53	71	69	53	58	69	54	60	66
Armenia	na	**94**	94	94	94	96	92	88	94	97	97	94	88	94	95	92
Australia	na	**82**	83	81	80	82	84	75	82	88	79	84	85	83	81	84
Austria	90	**89**	90	88	88	88	91	87	90	93	86	89	89	82	90	88
Azerbaijan	na	**93**	93	93	94	91	95	94	93	93	92	94	94	92	94	93
Bangladesh	na	**82**	80	84	83	81	80	78	86	87	86	80	82	83	81	83
Belarus	93	**85**	85	85	87	87	82	81	86	90	82	87	88	85	85	89
Belgium	72	**70**	74	65	68	69	71	61	69	77	66	69	75	61	72	77
Bosnia and Herz.	na	**89**	90	87	90	88	88	85	88	94	86	87	94	87	90	83
Brazil	78	**77**	79	74	74	76	82	74	77	84	73	75	82	73	77	84
Bulgaria	86	**89**	91	88	85	93	88	87	89	94	87	89	93	91	89	98
Canada	82	**84**	87	80	84	82	85	79	82	91	76	84	89	78	84	83
Chile	62	**67**	69	66	69	66	68	61	68	79	62	69	73	70	66	66
China	97	**93**	95	91	90	92	97	93	93	95	91	93	96	96	90	87
Colombia	na	**82**	83	81	82	82	83	77	81	87	76	82	86	76	82	79
Croatia	na	**88**	92	84	85	90	88	80	92	95	81	89	92	87	87	93
Czech Republic	44	**96**	96	97	96	97	97	95	98	97	95	97	97	96	97	97
Denmark	76	**82**	87	78	83	83	81	79	93	83	77	82	91	74	83	79
Dominican Rep.	na	**91**	89	91	88	95	91	88	87	92	89	90	95	86	90	95
Egypt	na	**97**	96	98	97	97	96	96	98	98	97	97	97	97	97	98
El Salvador	na	**70**	72	68	66	73	72	67	66	83	61	73	82	na	na	na
Estonia	95	**85**	86	83	83	85	85	80	85	91	78	83	91	85	84	87
Finland	74	**76**	82	71	79	77	73	71	82	83	71	78	79	75	76	74
France	79	**77**	82	72	73	77	78	76	75	81	72	77	81	72	79	77
Georgia	na	**92**	91	93	92	91	93	92	91	95	91	92	94	93	90	96
Germany	96	**87**	89	85	86	87	87	86	87	93	84	84	92	86	87	89
Great Britain	79	**73**	75	71	67	72	77	66	76	85	67	69	81	na	na	na
Greece	na	**88**	87	88	87	89	88	82	87	90	88	88	88	88	88	86
Hungary	90	**83**	87	80	86	85	80	78	92	97	77	81	90	79	89	75
Iceland	75	**86**	90	82	89	87	83	81	92	89	85	84	90	86	87	81
India	78	**63**	64	61	62	63	63	58	62	71	68	60	63	65	66	56
Indonesia	na	**86**	87	86	93	87	84	80	86	92	87	87	85	88	87	61
Iran	na	**79**	81	77	79	80	81	80	80	83	81	82	77	84	80	75
Ireland	73	**65**	70	60	71	63	62	53	67	80	53	62	77	53	66	76
Israel	na	**na**	na	na	na	na	na	na	na	na	na	na	na	na	na	na
Italy	79	**78**	83	73	78	84	72	69	82	90	75	76	85	75	77	82
Japan	59	**88**	89	86	86	90	86	76	87	94	86	87	90	84	89	92
Jordan	na	**82**	81	82	81	81	85	79	84	84	81	85	83	80	83	82
Korea, South	73	**87**	87	87	82	86	94	91	89	83	86	90	87	89	86	75
Latvia	95	**81**	82	80	80	82	81	71	81	91	78	79	86	78	83	83
Lithuania	94	**82**	83	81	84	79	83	76	82	89	84	78	84	78	84	79
Luxembourg	na	**83**	84	81	81	82	84	76	85	89	83	82	86	83	82	88
Macedonia	na	**72**	72	72	76	73	67	61	74	83	67	72	78	74	72	56
Malta	na	**77**	80	75	74	76	80	77	76	82	78	78	86	78	75	86
Mexico	85	**78**	78	78	81	75	78	75	81	80	72	79	80	78	77	80
Moldova	na	**87**	90	84	90	85	86	88	87	86	88	86	90	84	91	85
Montenegro	na	**83**	82	85	86	85	80	82	84	86	90	86	84	87	81	75
Morocco	na	**95**	95	95	95	95	95	95	95	97	92	95	96	98	93	93
Netherlands	68	**76**	80	72	72	76	78	69	77	80	67	75	86	68	79	69
New Zealand	na	**90**	93	88	90	90	90	87	91	94	87	91	95	89	91	94
Nigeria	80	**77**	77	78	77	78	77	74	79	79	78	78	78	80	76	75
Northern Ireland	71	**71**	72	70	68	71	73	67	72	75	65	69	71	75	71	67
Norway	54	**54**	62	48	51	55	56	47	54	62	na	na	na	50	55	57
Pakistan	na	**na**	na	na	na	na	na	na	na	na	na	na	na	na	na	na
Peru	na	**76**	76	75	76	75	76	73	76	76	73	79	75	79	73	81
Philippines	na	**68**	70	67	71	65	71	68	68	69	68	66	72	71	67	66
Poland	na	**88**	90	86	91	88	87	85	90	94	86	91	85	85	90	87
Portugal	74	**73**	73	73	75	75	70	72	75	83	68	71	72	75	71	73
Puerto Rico	na	**77**	82	74	76	76	78	76	72	79	67	80	81	76	76	80
Romania	88	**89**	89	90	92	87	90	88	89	93	87	87	93	86	93	93
Russian Fed.	94	**93**	94	93	93	94	93	89	93	96	91	93	96	93	93	94
Serbia	na	**88**	90	86	88	89	87	80	91	93	85	85	92	85	91	91
Singapore	na	**93**	93	93	92	93	97	92	94	95	88	95	95	96	93	88
Slovakia	na	**91**	92	91	95	90	90	87	92	97	86	91	96	90	93	92
Slovenia	91	**89**	92	87	92	87	88	77	93	97	85	90	97	85	90	92
South Africa	na	**60**	59	60	60	61	56	56	61	88	51	61	67	56	61	71
Spain	75	**66**	67	64	65	65	67	63	66	74	63	62	68	66	64	65
Sweden	62	**74**	75	74	76	73	75	62	72	89	68	74	83	74	76	71
Switzerland	69	**85**	88	82	79	85	88	81	86	87	77	85	90	80	85	89
Taiwan	na	**92**	92	92	93	94	87	89	91	95	90	91	95	93	93	83
Tanzania	na	**76**	78	73	76	73	84	75	78	73	71	79	77	75	77	79
Turkey	72	**78**	77	79	79	77	79	76	77	86	76	80	81	77	79	78
Uganda	na	**76**	71	80	72	79	79	70	79	74	69	80	70	76	76	77
Ukraine	na	**92**	94	90	94	93	90	79	94	93	90	93	92	90	93	97
United States	86	**91**	92	91	88	92	93	87	90	94	89	90	96	88	92	91
Uruguay	na	**72**	74	71	70	70	75	68	79	75	70	71	75	69	73	72
Venezuela	na	**na**	na	na	na	na	na	na	na	na	na	na	na	na	na	na
Vietnam	na	**94**	94	93	94	94	93	93	94	96	94	94	93	96	93	92
Zimbabwe	na	**59**	60	59	59	59	61	57	61	100	53	60	69	55	63	59
Total	79	**81**	83	80	81	82	82	77	83	86	79	82	85	82	82	81

RANKING

Country	2000
Egypt	97
Czech Republic	96
Morocco	95
Armenia	94
Vietnam	94
Russian Fed.	93
Singapore	93
Azerbaijan	93
China	93
Taiwan	92
Georgia	92
Ukraine	92
Slovakia	91
United States	91
Dominican Rep.	91
New Zealand	90
Bulgaria	89
Romania	89
Slovenia	89
Austria	89
Bosnia and Herz.	89
Croatia	88
Poland	88
Greece	88
Serbia	88
Japan	88
Korea, South	87
Germany	87
Moldova	87
Iceland	86
Indonesia	86
Belarus	85
Switzerland	85
Estonia	85
Canada	84
Hungary	83
Montenegro	83
Albania	83
Luxembourg	83
Colombia	82
Denmark	82
Lithuania	82
Bangladesh	82
Algeria	82
Australia	82
Jordan	82
Latvia	81
Iran	79
Turkey	78
Mexico	78
Italy	78
Nigeria	77
Malta	77
Brazil	77
France	77
Puerto Rico	77
Finland	76
Tanzania	76
Uganda	76
Netherlands	76
Peru	76
Sweden	74
Portugal	73
Great Britain	73
Uruguay	72
Macedonia	72
Northern Ireland	71
El Salvador	70
Belgium	70
Philippines	68
Chile	67
Spain	66
Ireland	65
India	63
Argentina	60
South Africa	60
Zimbabwe	59
Norway	54
Total	81

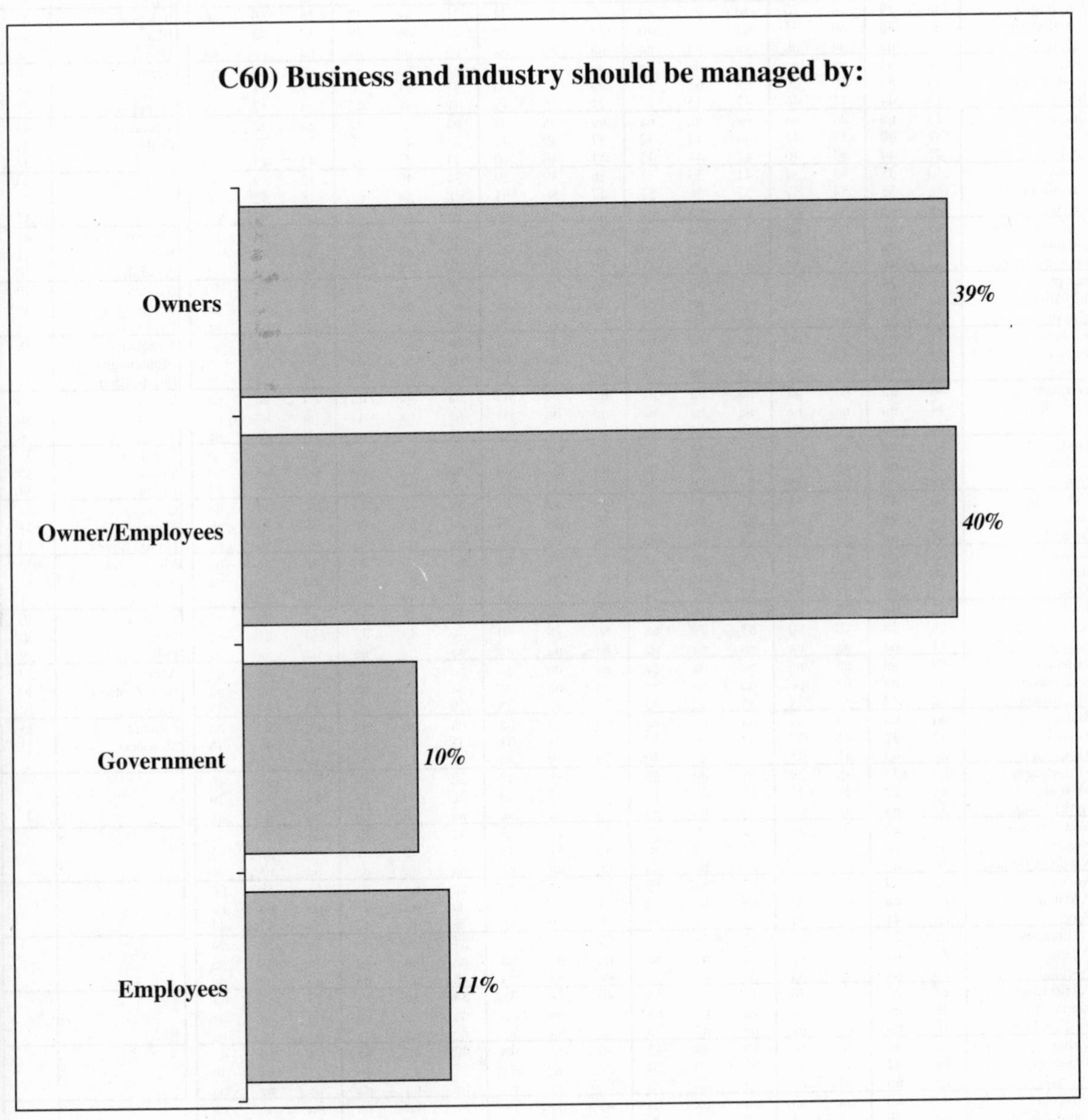
C60) Business and industry should be managed by:
Owners
39%
Owner/Employees
40%
Government
10%
Employees
11%

C060) BUSINESS MANAGEMENT: OWNERS AND EMPLOYEES

There is a lot of discussion about how business and industry should be managed. Which of these four statements comes closest to your opinion?

Owners & employees participate (%)

(WVS: V104)

Country	Wave		Gender		Age			Education			Income			Values		
	1990	2000	Male	Female	16-29	30-49	50+	Lower	Middle	Upper	Lower	Middle	Upper	Mat	Mixed	Postm.
Albania	na	25	26	23	28	25	22	23	24	32	22	28	25	21	29	19
Algeria	na	27	26	28	29	25	25	25	27	27	27	27	23	25	26	31
Argentina	47	45	45	45	44	48	43	47	43	45	49	44	44	40	44	50
Armenia	na	31	28	34	36	29	28	26	33	28	31	32	30	31	29	56
Australia	na	40	39	41	44	44	32	34	36	50	37	43	44	36	37	47
Austria	42	na	na	na	na	na	na	na	na	na	na	na	na	na	na	na
Azerbaijan	na	29	28	30	30	29	24	25	26	34	21	34	32	28	28	36
Bangladesh	na	38	39	35	41	35	40	33	41	45	23	46	38	30	43	41
Belarus	23	na	na	na	na	na	na	na	na	na	na	na	na	na	na	na
Belgium	44	na	na	na	na	na	na	na	na	na	na	na	na	na	na	na
Bosnia and Herz.	na	58	56	60	54	61	58	59	57	60	51	61	56	59	57	52
Brazil	43	44	41	46	47	45	34	41	45	48	41	48	42	34	47	49
Bulgaria	23	na	na	na	na	na	na	na	na	na	na	na	na	na	na	na
Canada	37	40	37	42	44	44	32	37	40	41	43	41	37	33	37	48
Chile	47	44	43	46	47	44	42	41	48	40	44	47	45	42	45	45
China	40	35	35	34	41	33	33	26	39	29	34	40	31	32	39	36
Colombia	na	55	54	57	57	56	51	47	56	61	48	54	61	48	52	50
Croatia	na	na	na	na	na	na	na	na	na	na	na	na	na	na	na	na
Czech Republic	43	na	na	na	na	na	na	na	na	na	na	na	na	na	na	na
Denmark	46	na	na	na	na	na	na	na	na	na	na	na	na	na	na	na
Dominican Rep.	na	46	34	54	51	39	18	19	47	48	48	48	37	45	48	41
Egypt	na	34	32	36	38	32	29	26	37	48	29	31	39	32	35	40
El Salvador	na	na	na	na	na	na	na	na	na	na	na	na	na	na	na	na
Estonia	26	na	na	na	na	na	na	na	na	na	na	na	na	na	na	na
Finland	51	na	na	na	na	na	na	na	na	na	na	na	na	na	na	na
France	61	na	na	na	na	na	na	na	na	na	na	na	na	na	na	na
Georgia	na	34	31	36	33	39	28	34	32	37	34	33	35	34	34	26
Germany	46	na	na	na	na	na	na	na	na	na	na	na	na	na	na	na
Great Britain	44	na	na	na	na	na	na	na	na	na	na	na	na	na	na	na
Greece	na	na	na	na	na	na	na	na	na	na	na	na	na	na	na	na
Hungary	47	na	na	na	na	na	na	na	na	na	na	na	na	na	na	na
Iceland	37	na	na	na	na	na	na	na	na	na	na	na	na	na	na	na
India	48	30	31	28	31	29	28	22	33	39	27	23	38	23	36	34
Indonesia	na	48	48	48	47	53	43	43	47	52	53	46	44	44	51	48
Iran	na	46	45	48	47	46	44	38	48	49	44	50	49	39	49	59
Ireland	42	na	na	na	na	na	na	na	na	na	na	na	na	na	na	na
Israel	na	na	na	na	na	na	na	na	na	na	na	na	na	na	na	na
Italy	46	na	na	na	na	na	na	na	na	na	na	na	na	na	na	na
Japan	47	54	51	57	57	52	54	55	53	54	56	49	56	52	55	54
Jordan	na	36	28	44	40	38	24	30	41	41	35	38	35	34	38	32
Korea, South	68	78	76	80	85	79	68	56	78	80	76	83	75	74	81	82
Latvia	31	na	na	na	na	na	na	na	na	na	na	na	na	na	na	na
Lithuania	19	na	na	na	na	na	na	na	na	na	na	na	na	na	na	na
Luxembourg	na	na	na	na	na	na	na	na	na	na	na	na	na	na	na	na
Macedonia	na	33	31	34	33	32	33	30	33	35	29	35	34	29	34	38
Malta	na	na	na	na	na	na	na	na	na	na	na	na	na	na	na	na
Mexico	42	41	44	37	44	39	37	38	41	51	35	41	42	38	41	46
Moldova	na	43	41	45	45	44	40	50	39	44	42	43	43	44	45	35
Montenegro	na	37	35	39	38	39	35	34	38	41	32	38	39	33	41	46
Morocco	na	22	23	21	26	21	14	18	33	46	26	30	23	18	23	39
Netherlands	57	na	na	na	na	na	na	na	na	na	na	na	na	na	na	na
New Zealand	na	29	26	31	37	29	26	27	27	33	32	28	27	31	26	38
Nigeria	31	33	34	32	33	34	30	32	31	38	35	32	31	33	33	32
Northern Ireland	36	na	na	na	na	na	na	na	na	na	na	na	na	na	na	na
Norway	62	59	57	62	62	58	59	59	61	58	na	na	na	61	58	66
Pakistan	na	na	na	na	na	na	na	na	na	na	na	na	na	na	na	na
Peru	na	41	41	41	43	39	38	35	40	45	38	39	47	37	41	44
Philippines	na	29	30	29	31	28	30	29	28	33	31	26	33	29	30	24
Poland	42	na	na	na	na	na	na	na	na	na	na	na	na	na	na	na
Portugal	36	na	na	na	na	na	na	na	na	na	na	na	na	na	na	na
Puerto Rico	na	37	34	38	40	37	35	40	34	38	34	39	37	24	35	47
Romania	33	na	na	na	na	na	na	na	na	na	na	na	na	na	na	na
Russian Fed.	18	na	na	na	na	na	na	na	na	na	na	na	na	na	na	na
Serbia	na	45	40	50	49	43	45	40	46	49	42	48	45	44	46	45
Singapore	na	42	41	43	50	39	24	37	45	47	37	43	46	37	44	50
Slovakia	na	na	na	na	na	na	na	na	na	na	na	na	na	na	na	na
Slovenia	37	na	na	na	na	na	na	na	na	na	na	na	na	na	na	na
South Africa	45	39	34	45	37	42	35	42	37	24	42	38	36	44	34	48
Spain	53	46	46	46	47	47	43	44	44	54	46	50	41	49	44	50
Sweden	65	na	na	na	na	na	na	na	na	na	na	na	na	na	na	na
Switzerland	43	43	40	47	48	43	41	43	43	46	43	51	39	39	43	51
Taiwan	na	55	54	56	63	56	46	48	55	61	54	56	59	54	55	71
Tanzania	na	31	30	31	36	31	20	26	38	33	22	35	31	28	32	38
Turkey	38	36	34	39	41	34	33	33	39	43	34	37	42	33	37	41
Uganda	na	30	33	27	33	27	24	26	32	27	31	24	38	29	30	34
Ukraine	na	na	na	na	na	na	na	na	na	na	na	na	na	na	na	na
United States	35	33	32	34	30	36	31	29	31	35	33	33	31	23	32	40
Uruguay	na	38	35	40	42	39	35	36	43	37	41	34	40	26	40	45
Venezuela	na	44	43	46	45	46	40	37	44	53	40	47	50	35	47	52
Vietnam	na	35	37	34	38	34	35	30	42	35	40	34	34	29	39	31
Zimbabwe	na	36	39	33	36	35	38	35	38	44	30	38	45	33	39	33
Total	42	40	38	41	42	40	37	35	41	45	38	41	40	36	41	45

RANKING	
Country	2000
Korea, South	78
Norway	59
Bosnia and Herz.	58
Colombia	55
Taiwan	55
Japan	54
Indonesia	48
Iran	46
Dominican Rep.	46
Spain	46
Argentina	45
Serbia	45
Venezuela	44
Chile	44
Brazil	44
Switzerland	43
Moldova	43
Singapore	42
Mexico	41
Peru	41
Australia	40
Canada	40
South Africa	39
Uruguay	38
Bangladesh	38
Montenegro	37
Puerto Rico	37
Turkey	36
Jordan	36
Zimbabwe	36
Vietnam	35
China	35
Egypt	34
Georgia	34
Nigeria	33
United States	33
Macedonia	33
Armenia	31
Tanzania	31
Uganda	30
India	30
Philippines	29
Azerbaijan	29
New Zealand	29
Algeria	27
Albania	25
Morocco	22
Total	40

C060B) BUSINESS MANAGEMENT: OWNERS ALONE

There is a lot of discussion about how business and industry should be managed.
Which of these four statements comes closest to your opinion?
Owners should run their business or appoint the managers (%)

(WVS: V104)

Country	Wave		Gender		Age			Education			Income			Values		
	1990	2000	Male	Female	16-29	30-49	50+	Lower	Middle	Upper	Lower	Middle	Upper	Mat	Mixed	Postm.
Albania	na	**53**	52	55	55	53	52	52	54	54	51	51	58	59	50	56
Algeria	na	**37**	39	36	39	38	32	31	36	43	33	37	45	37	38	38
Argentina	31	**29**	28	31	26	28	35	25	35	36	24	26	38	35	29	29
Armenia	na	**26**	32	19	30	27	16	20	23	37	32	20	21	22	29	22
Australia	na	**51**	52	49	45	48	58	52	56	43	52	47	52	54	54	44
Austria	50	**na**	na	na	na	na	na	na	na	na	na	na	na	na	na	na
Azerbaijan	na	**30**	33	27	35	29	19	19	32	27	26	26	36	28	33	33
Bangladesh	na	**43**	39	48	44	43	39	41	48	42	49	34	51	47	41	35
Belarus	9	**na**	na	na	na	na	na	na	na	na	na	na	na	na	na	na
Belgium	46	**na**	na	na	na	na	na	na	na	na	na	na	na	na	na	na
Bosnia and Herz.	na	**20**	21	18	22	20	17	17	18	25	14	18	28	20	19	23
Brazil	32	**35**	36	35	33	34	44	35	36	36	35	32	40	40	34	32
Bulgaria	38	**na**	na	na	na	na	na	na	na	na	na	na	na	na	na	na
Canada	53	**52**	53	50	47	47	59	52	50	53	43	51	56	59	54	42
Chile	24	**41**	42	40	40	41	42	40	40	46	40	39	43	47	40	33
China	22	**30**	32	29	22	34	31	37	28	21	33	25	34	39	25	4
Colombia	na	**42**	44	41	42	41	47	52	43	34	50	44	35	51	47	49
Croatia	na	**na**	na	na	na	na	na	na	na	na	na	na	na	na	na	na
Czech Republic	34	**na**	na	na	na	na	na	na	na	na	na	na	na	na	na	na
Denmark	47	**na**	na	na	na	na	na	na	na	na	na	na	na	na	na	na
Dominican Rep.	na	**44**	57	36	40	51	55	65	39	44	38	44	57	45	45	41
Egypt	na	**33**	35	30	31	33	33	34	31	32	33	32	32	34	32	27
El Salvador	na	**na**	na	na	na	na	na	na	na	na	na	na	na	na	na	na
Estonia	42	**na**	na	na	na	na	na	na	na	na	na	na	na	na	na	na
Finland	42	**na**	na	na	na	na	na	na	na	na	na	na	na	na	na	na
France	24	**na**	na	na	na	na	na	na	na	na	na	na	na	na	na	na
Georgia	na	**33**	39	28	41	30	28	32	33	34	29	31	39	34	31	38
Germany	32	**na**	na	na	na	na	na	na	na	na	na	na	na	na	na	na
Great Britain	44	**na**	na	na	na	na	na	na	na	na	na	na	na	na	na	na
Greece	na	**na**	na	na	na	na	na	na	na	na	na	na	na	na	na	na
Hungary	24	**na**	na	na	na	na	na	na	na	na	na	na	na	na	na	na
Iceland	48	**na**	na	na	na	na	na	na	na	na	na	na	na	na	na	na
India	22	**26**	26	26	24	27	27	26	23	27	25	26	26	28	25	18
Indonesia	na	**43**	43	44	50	37	47	42	44	44	38	44	52	43	44	37
Iran	na	**22**	23	20	21	22	22	24	22	21	19	18	22	24	20	12
Ireland	43	**na**	na	na	na	na	na	na	na	na	na	na	na	na	na	na
Israel	na	**na**	na	na	na	na	na	na	na	na	na	na	na	na	na	na
Italy	43	**na**	na	na	na	na	na	na	na	na	na	na	na	na	na	na
Japan	44	**39**	43	35	28	40	43	37	40	38	38	43	38	44	38	35
Jordan	na	**36**	42	29	32	35	45	41	30	32	38	29	39	39	35	25
Korea, South	23	**14**	16	12	9	13	21	20	13	15	13	12	17	16	13	4
Latvia	31	**na**	na	na	na	na	na	na	na	na	na	na	na	na	na	na
Lithuania	38	**na**	na	na	na	na	na	na	na	na	na	na	na	na	na	na
Luxembourg	na	**na**	na	na	na	na	na	na	na	na	na	na	na	na	na	na
Macedonia	na	**41**	43	40	45	45	32	46	38	42	37	43	42	43	40	50
Malta	na	**na**	na	na	na	na	na	na	na	na	na	na	na	na	na	na
Mexico	47	**45**	44	46	43	45	50	45	46	40	47	42	47	49	44	40
Moldova	na	**21**	23	20	23	25	16	13	23	26	18	16	28	20	23	27
Montenegro	na	**30**	31	30	43	31	21	20	34	41	24	30	38	28	33	24
Morocco	na	**49**	46	52	45	51	50	51	40	40	42	44	49	53	46	35
Netherlands	33	**na**	na	na	na	na	na	na	na	na	na	na	na	na	na	na
New Zealand	na	**62**	67	59	55	63	65	64	65	60	55	63	70	62	68	55
Nigeria	53	**48**	48	48	49	47	51	43	54	47	43	50	53	48	49	44
Northern Ireland	55	**na**	na	na	na	na	na	na	na	na	na	na	na	na	na	na
Norway	32	**34**	36	32	29	38	34	33	33	38	na	na	na	31	36	27
Pakistan	na	**na**	na	na	na	na	na	na	na	na	na	na	na	na	na	na
Peru	na	**35**	37	33	32	36	38	31	35	38	33	36	37	34	36	32
Philippines	na	**56**	55	57	54	60	54	55	59	54	54	60	54	59	54	56
Poland	15	**na**	na	na	na	na	na	na	na	na	na	na	na	na	na	na
Portugal	48	**na**	na	na	na	na	na	na	na	na	na	na	na	na	na	na
Puerto Rico	na	**48**	52	47	47	48	49	46	49	48	52	46	50	57	51	39
Romania	35	**na**	na	na	na	na	na	na	na	na	na	na	na	na	na	na
Russian Fed.	11	**na**	na	na	na	na	na	na	na	na	na	na	na	na	na	na
Serbia	na	**26**	32	19	28	31	20	18	27	35	20	25	29	20	28	45
Singapore	na	**49**	50	48	41	55	64	51	47	50	53	48	48	58	47	36
Slovakia	na	**na**	na	na	na	na	na	na	na	na	na	na	na	na	na	na
Slovenia	26	**na**	na	na	na	na	na	na	na	na	na	na	na	na	na	na
South Africa	40	**47**	51	43	50	43	53	42	51	71	38	48	57	44	51	28
Spain	31	**38**	36	40	34	34	44	40	38	32	40	35	42	43	39	24
Sweden	30	**na**	na	na	na	na	na	na	na	na	na	na	na	na	na	na
Switzerland	51	**46**	52	39	38	43	53	43	46	49	41	38	54	52	48	32
Taiwan	na	**30**	29	31	23	30	36	36	31	25	29	31	28	35	25	15
Tanzania	na	**26**	28	23	21	26	34	20	27	42	20	24	42	28	25	17
Turkey	27	**32**	35	30	30	33	36	35	29	29	32	34	35	37	32	27
Uganda	na	**64**	64	65	62	68	61	65	63	71	62	67	59	66	65	56
Ukraine	na	**na**	na	na	na	na	na	na	na	na	na	na	na	na	na	na
United States	57	**59**	59	59	58	56	64	59	60	58	60	57	62	70	62	49
Uruguay	na	**47**	48	46	41	45	51	50	43	43	44	47	48	64	46	32
Venezuela	na	**47**	49	45	47	46	50	51	47	43	48	44	44	57	46	33
Vietnam	na	**23**	20	26	30	23	18	24	21	27	20	22	25	25	23	26
Zimbabwe	na	**51**	49	53	50	50	55	53	48	57	55	47	47	56	47	48
Total	36	39	41	38	39	39	41	40	39	40	37	37	42	39	40	36

RANKING	
Country	2000
Uganda	64
New Zealand	62
United States	59
Philippines	56
Albania	53
Canada	52
Zimbabwe	51
Australia	51
Singapore	49
Morocco	49
Nigeria	48
Puerto Rico	48
Venezuela	47
South Africa	47
Uruguay	47
Switzerland	46
Mexico	45
Dominican Rep.	44
Bangladesh	43
Indonesia	43
Colombia	42
Macedonia	41
Chile	41
Japan	39
Spain	38
Algeria	37
Jordan	36
Brazil	35
Peru	35
Norway	34
Georgia	33
Egypt	33
Turkey	32
China	30
Montenegro	30
Taiwan	30
Azerbaijan	30
Argentina	29
Serbia	26
India	26
Armenia	26
Tanzania	26
Vietnam	23
Iran	22
Moldova	21
Bosnia and Herz.	20
Korea, South	14
Total	39

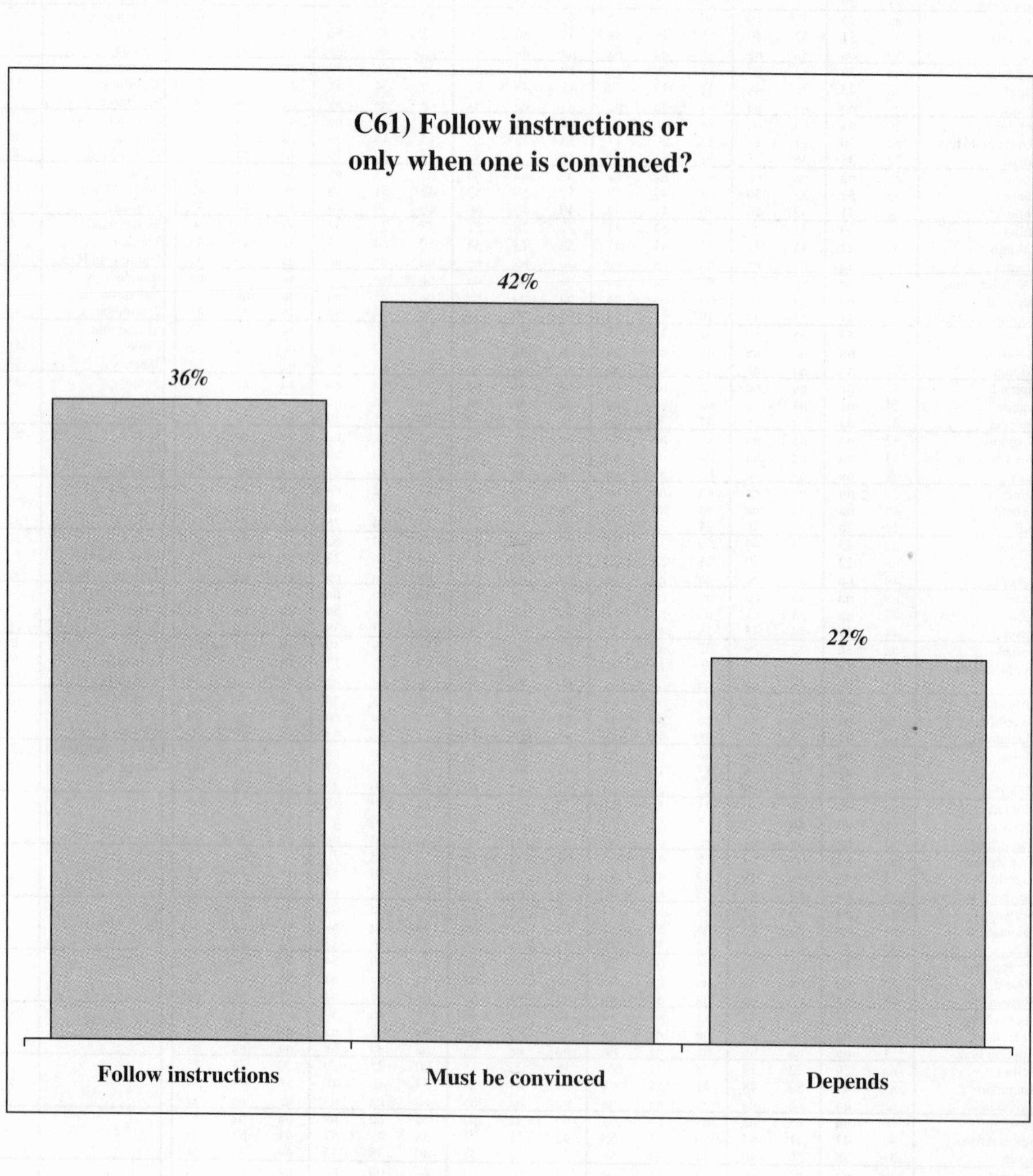
C61) Follow instructions or
only when one is convinced?
36%
42%
22%
Follow instructions
Must be convinced
Depends

C061) FOLLOWING INSTRUCTIONS: MUST BE CONVINCED

Some say that one should follow one's superior's instructions even when one does not fully agree with them. Others say that one should follow one's superior's instructions only when one is convinced that they are right.

Must be convinced first (%) (WVS: V105; EVS: V97)

Country	Wave		Gender		Age			Education			Income			Values		
	1990	2000	Male	Female	16-29	30-49	50+	Lower	Middle	Upper	Lower	Middle	Upper	Mat	Mixed	Postm.
Albania	na	**30**	27	33	26	31	31	30	29	31	33	28	28	31	29	28
Algeria	na	**45**	45	46	52	41	39	36	46	51	46	48	39	42	47	51
Argentina	50	**47**	47	48	54	47	41	45	47	60	43	47	51	39	48	52
Armenia	na	**62**	59	65	65	66	52	39	64	65	64	60	66	57	66	72
Australia	na	**41**	42	39	40	41	41	40	36	46	40	41	41	33	39	46
Austria	38	**40**	42	38	39	43	37	38	42	41	36	45	36	34	40	43
Azerbaijan	na	**46**	46	47	49	46	40	43	46	49	56	47	40	46	47	57
Bangladesh	na	**54**	56	52	60	49	60	55	53	55	57	50	58	62	50	55
Belarus	55	**38**	36	39	37	38	38	35	38	40	32	38	45	39	38	44
Belgium	43	**44**	44	44	45	46	41	42	40	51	40	44	46	42	43	50
Bosnia and Herz.	na	**38**	38	38	34	37	43	34	39	38	37	39	38	36	39	49
Brazil	78	**78**	77	78	79	78	74	70	84	85	72	84	80	72	79	86
Bulgaria	65	**46**	47	44	54	53	35	25	56	55	37	49	50	43	49	66
Canada	29	**31**	32	30	33	31	29	24	32	35	30	28	35	25	30	35
Chile	49	**35**	35	34	42	35	27	27	36	49	32	33	41	27	38	39
China	34	**67**	68	66	63	66	72	71	64	63	67	71	63	63	71	56
Colombia	na	**na**	na	na	na	na	na	na	na	na	na	na	na	na	na	na
Croatia	na	**51**	47	55	54	54	46	43	56	57	49	51	53	46	51	58
Czech Republic	51	**34**	33	35	31	33	37	36	33	29	39	33	31	37	33	36
Denmark	54	**26**	28	25	28	25	28	26	29	27	26	26	27	24	26	32
Dominican Rep.	na	**53**	47	57	55	48	55	50	52	54	59	44	57	51	53	58
Egypt	na	**43**	44	42	53	41	31	36	51	48	41	39	44	34	48	58
El Salvador	na	**32**	33	32	37	30	29	30	35	34	33	28	34	na	na	na
Estonia	44	**31**	35	27	27	29	34	30	27	41	27	35	30	24	34	36
Finland	45	**59**	59	59	60	63	56	60	59	58	61	60	61	55	60	68
France	48	**40**	43	38	36	45	38	38	42	45	36	43	46	35	41	46
Georgia	na	**11**	10	12	13	11	10	13	10	14	9	10	15	11	11	8
Germany	36	**28**	28	28	37	29	23	22	32	34	22	29	34	21	29	38
Great Britain	43	**33**	33	33	39	29	34	31	36	33	36	27	32	na	na	na
Greece	na	**32**	31	33	28	34	38	32	31	33	31	32	32	25	34	37
Hungary	59	**34**	33	35	33	36	33	33	34	37	31	34	35	29	39	48
Iceland	33	**33**	30	35	34	33	31	32	34	34	36	31	31	29	33	36
India	55	**39**	40	37	37	40	37	34	39	46	38	33	43	33	44	52
Indonesia	na	**51**	49	53	48	53	50	48	49	56	49	52	56	49	53	65
Iran	na	**59**	59	61	62	59	53	56	61	59	59	61	61	57	61	71
Ireland	41	**38**	37	39	37	36	42	40	38	34	36	37	39	31	39	45
Israel	na	**na**	na	na	na	na	na	na	na	na	na	na	na	na	na	na
Italy	46	**33**	33	33	33	32	34	31	34	37	31	34	35	25	35	33
Japan	11	**10**	12	7	9	9	10	16	9	9	9	10	10	10	10	7
Jordan	na	**72**	69	76	75	71	69	70	78	71	73	74	73	69	74	78
Korea, South	48	**51**	50	52	49	53	47	52	50	51	52	52	48	47	53	59
Latvia	45	**46**	43	50	45	44	49	42	48	49	45	50	47	46	48	45
Lithuania	33	**47**	47	46	44	56	39	32	49	58	45	43	49	38	51	49
Luxembourg	na	**32**	32	33	33	34	30	30	33	34	29	29	37	22	31	45
Macedonia	na	**44**	44	43	41	45	44	38	46	46	42	44	45	41	46	40
Malta	na	**51**	48	53	53	55	45	44	52	57	41	50	56	48	50	69
Mexico	38	**41**	41	41	46	43	30	34	47	54	37	44	49	38	42	50
Moldova	na	**54**	55	53	58	55	50	50	53	60	56	53	55	51	57	59
Montenegro	na	**40**	39	40	40	39	40	38	38	46	32	44	46	38	43	38
Morocco	na	**51**	52	50	55	49	43	46	68	70	62	60	42	44	55	66
Netherlands	48	**31**	29	32	25	32	32	32	30	30	33	30	30	38	27	38
New Zealand	na	**23**	25	22	16	21	28	21	24	23	23	22	25	23	22	28
Nigeria	49	**43**	46	40	42	43	49	41	45	42	42	46	39	44	43	38
Northern Ireland	38	**36**	40	33	41	36	34	33	39	39	32	39	44	36	34	49
Norway	34	**33**	31	35	37	34	29	36	35	29	na	na	na	41	31	38
Pakistan	na	**na**	na	na	na	na	na	na	na	na	na	na	na	na	na	na
Peru	na	**54**	56	52	55	57	47	48	56	56	55	55	53	50	55	59
Philippines	na	**49**	49	49	55	49	43	47	49	53	46	52	50	44	50	70
Poland	na	**50**	50	49	43	49	54	48	48	60	51	48	51	46	53	45
Portugal	39	**44**	43	45	50	44	41	42	51	45	39	46	48	41	40	61
Puerto Rico	na	**43**	39	45	49	46	37	34	43	45	45	38	46	42	41	45
Romania	75	**29**	30	28	29	27	31	24	32	33	26	30	30	31	30	25
Russian Fed.	56	**47**	50	44	50	50	41	31	48	50	43	47	50	43	52	31
Serbia	na	**43**	43	44	48	44	40	33	48	50	40	43	50	38	48	51
Singapore	na	**55**	55	55	62	53	35	49	58	58	51	54	59	49	56	66
Slovakia	na	**32**	33	31	31	34	30	28	33	36	29	31	33	27	35	44
Slovenia	58	**48**	48	48	40	45	57	51	48	42	54	54	43	50	47	50
South Africa	na	**44**	46	42	47	44	37	42	47	41	43	43	48	41	45	53
Spain	52	**42**	43	41	47	46	35	38	48	41	37	40	41	38	43	50
Sweden	41	**33**	31	35	36	30	35	33	35	30	40	30	30	29	31	42
Switzerland	na	**41**	42	40	44	40	40	36	41	48	43	40	43	30	41	49
Taiwan	na	**56**	59	54	61	57	52	51	57	61	51	61	57	52	59	73
Tanzania	na	**28**	28	27	25	27	33	28	27	29	29	27	30	30	27	46
Turkey	54	**55**	52	59	56	57	51	53	59	62	52	57	62	50	56	64
Uganda	na	**47**	52	42	48	49	36	48	47	40	52	53	47	49	48	39
Ukraine	na	**42**	43	42	48	47	35	30	42	50	38	42	51	41	45	60
United States	23	**20**	18	22	25	18	19	18	19	22	20	20	20	15	21	21
Uruguay	na	**15**	16	15	21	14	14	14	15	23	14	16	15	9	16	16
Venezuela	na	**57**	54	59	57	58	52	54	58	56	55	60	58	50	58	64
Vietnam	na	**40**	40	40	41	41	38	35	45	44	46	36	40	32	44	39
Zimbabwe	na	**47**	48	46	50	43	48	48	46	31	45	50	42	45	48	53
Total	45	42	42	42	45	43	38	39	43	44	41	42	43	41	43	46

RANKING

Country	2000
Brazil	78
Jordan	72
China	67
Armenia	62
Iran	59
Finland	59
Venezuela	57
Taiwan	56
Turkey	55
Singapore	55
Bangladesh	54
Peru	54
Moldova	54
Dominican Rep.	53
Croatia	51
Morocco	51
Korea, South	51
Malta	51
Indonesia	51
Poland	50
Philippines	49
Slovenia	48
Argentina	47
Zimbabwe	47
Uganda	47
Lithuania	47
Russian Fed.	47
Azerbaijan	46
Latvia	46
Bulgaria	46
Algeria	45
Portugal	44
South Africa	44
Belgium	44
Macedonia	44
Serbia	43
Egypt	43
Nigeria	43
Puerto Rico	43
Ukraine	42
Spain	42
Mexico	41
Switzerland	41
Australia	41
France	40
Vietnam	40
Austria	40
Montenegro	40
India	39
Bosnia and Herz.	38
Ireland	38
Belarus	38
Northern Ireland	36
Chile	35
Czech Republic	34
Hungary	34
Sweden	33
Italy	33
Norway	33
Great Britain	33
Iceland	33
El Salvador	32
Luxembourg	32
Greece	32
Slovakia	32
Netherlands	31
Canada	31
Estonia	31
Albania	30
Romania	29
Germany	28
Tanzania	28
Denmark	26
New Zealand	23
United States	20
Uruguay	15
Georgia	11
Japan	10
Total	42

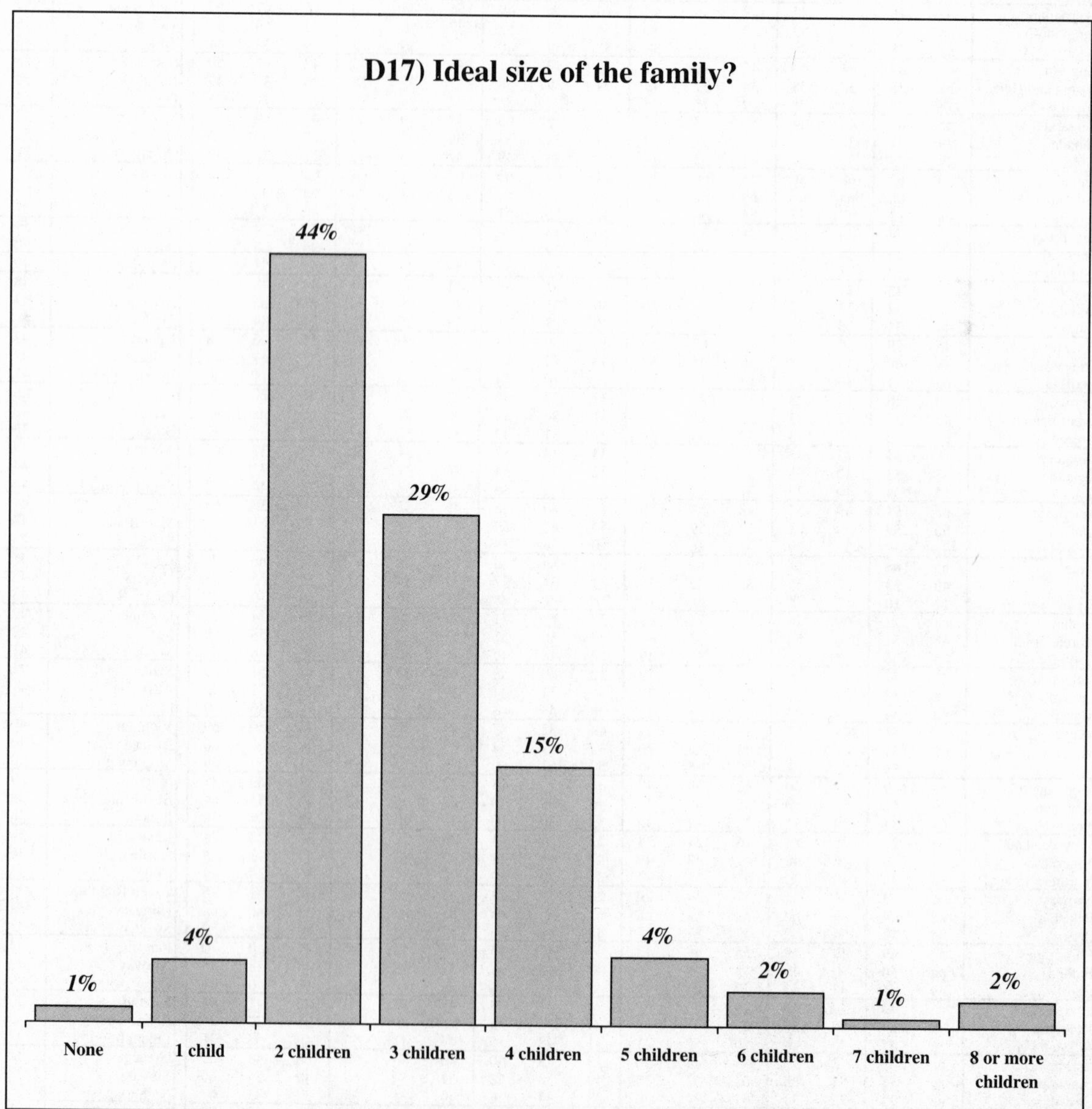
D17) Ideal size of the family?
1%
4%
44%
29%
15%
4%
2%
1%
2%
None
1 child
2 children
3 children
4 children
5 children
6 children
7 children
8 or more children

D017) IDEAL NUMBER OF CHILDREN

What do you think is the ideal size of the family? How many children, if any?

% two or fewer - codes 0 to 2 (WVS: V108)

Country	Wave		Gender		Age			Education			Income			Values		
	1990	2000	Male	Female	16-29	30-49	50+	Lower	Middle	Upper	Lower	Middle	Upper	Mat	Mixed	Postm.
Albania	na	**48**	51	45	65	49	30	41	52	54	41	49	49	46	50	33
Algeria	na	**32**	31	34	36	30	28	23	34	36	31	34	47	29	34	31
Argentina	44	**49**	51	46	55	47	44	47	51	49	45	48	52	39	48	54
Armenia	na	**42**	39	44	57	37	26	32	44	40	42	42	39	40	42	59
Australia	na	**52**	54	50	53	61	42	44	56	54	46	51	59	51	52	54
Austria	66	**na**	na	na	na	na	na	na	na	na	na	na	na	na	na	na
Azerbaijan	na	**58**	57	59	69	57	38	38	60	59	61	58	47	59	58	53
Bangladesh	na	**91**	90	91	92	90	85	91	91	89	92	89	91	92	90	92
Belarus	56	**na**	na	na	na	na	na	na	na	na	na	na	na	na	na	na
Belgium	61	**na**	na	na	na	na	na	na	na	na	na	na	na	na	na	na
Bosnia and Herz.	na	**52**	54	51	58	55	43	50	53	52	48	56	44	51	53	48
Brazil	54	**60**	58	62	71	56	49	57	62	65	60	62	64	56	61	67
Bulgaria	68	**na**	na	na	na	na	na	na	na	na	na	na	na	na	na	na
Canada	49	**56**	57	55	62	58	49	50	57	60	50	55	63	60	53	61
Chile	36	**51**	52	51	57	54	42	47	56	49	51	52	52	53	51	52
China	93	**na**	na	na	na	na	na	na	na	na	na	na	na	na	na	na
Colombia	na	**56**	55	56	68	51	46	49	58	57	51	57	55	56	54	51
Croatia	na	**na**	na	na	na	na	na	na	na	na	na	na	na	na	na	na
Czech Republic	70	**na**	na	na	na	na	na	na	na	na	na	na	na	na	na	na
Denmark	57	**na**	na	na	na	na	na	na	na	na	na	na	na	na	na	na
Dominican Rep.	na	**32**	36	30	38	23	18	14	31	34	29	35	35	27	33	37
Egypt	na	**40**	35	45	46	37	37	39	40	44	38	39	42	41	40	37
El Salvador	na	**51**	53	49	57	48	46	39	59	71	34	50	66	0	0	0
Estonia	43	**na**	na	na	na	na	na	na	na	na	na	na	na	na	na	na
Finland	50	**na**	na	na	na	na	na	na	na	na	na	na	na	na	na	na
France	49	**na**	na	na	na	na	na	na	na	na	na	na	na	na	na	na
Georgia	na	**21**	19	23	30	19	14	16	22	21	21	21	32	19	22	21
Germany	83	**na**	na	na	na	na	na	na	na	na	na	na	na	na	na	na
Great Britain	64	**na**	na	na	na	na	na	na	na	na	na	na	na	na	na	na
Greece	na	**na**	na	na	na	na	na	na	na	na	na	na	na	na	na	na
Hungary	67	**na**	na	na	na	na	na	na	na	na	na	na	na	na	na	na
Iceland	24	**na**	na	na	na	na	na	na	na	na	na	na	na	na	na	na
India	72	**73**	75	70	84	71	64	62	79	87	67	83	59	72	77	90
Indonesia	na	**35**	39	31	43	38	29	25	39	36	42	38	31	32	38	32
Iran	na	**78**	80	75	85	73	67	68	81	86	81	76	83	75	79	83
Ireland	24	**na**	na	na	na	na	na	na	na	na	na	na	na	na	na	na
Israel	na	**na**	na	na	na	na	na	na	na	na	na	na	na	na	na	na
Italy	61	**na**	na	na	na	na	na	na	na	na	na	na	na	na	na	na
Japan	38	**39**	38	40	64	42	26	22	39	46	37	41	36	34	41	34
Jordan	na	**11**	12	10	11	12	7	8	15	11	11	10	15	9	12	14
Korea, South	78	**61**	61	61	70	62	47	35	59	67	61	62	58	58	64	63
Latvia	40	**na**	na	na	na	na	na	na	na	na	na	na	na	na	na	na
Lithuania	36	**na**	na	na	na	na	na	na	na	na	na	na	na	na	na	na
Luxembourg	na	**na**	na	na	na	na	na	na	na	na	na	na	na	na	na	na
Macedonia	na	**51**	50	53	57	52	45	43	55	56	49	53	53	51	52	38
Malta	na	**na**	na	na	na	na	na	na	na	na	na	na	na	na	na	na
Mexico	50	**46**	47	46	58	41	39	39	54	59	41	49	52	45	48	50
Moldova	na	**50**	47	53	66	46	40	44	50	55	45	51	65	44	54	65
Montenegro	na	**25**	26	25	38	25	17	16	33	25	21	27	25	22	29	33
Morocco	na	**55**	54	56	62	51	42	52	68	61	50	56	55	55	54	64
Netherlands	55	**na**	na	na	na	na	na	na	na	na	na	na	na	na	na	na
New Zealand	na	**44**	42	46	40	46	44	46	46	42	41	44	48	55	46	40
Nigeria	6	**6**	6	6	7	5	4	7	7	5	7	6	6	6	6	9
Northern Ireland	42	**na**	na	na	na	na	na	na	na	na	na	na	na	na	na	na
Norway	55	**46**	53	38	53	47	39	41	51	43	0	0	0	47	46	40
Pakistan	na	**42**	37	48	51	45	16	36	52	45	40	42	45	43	42	64
Peru	na	**70**	68	72	80	65	61	72	69	71	71	70	68	70	69	76
Philippines	na	**29**	29	30	36	27	25	26	29	34	28	30	31	29	30	29
Poland	58	**na**	na	na	na	na	na	na	na	na	na	na	na	na	na	na
Portugal	68	**na**	na	na	na	na	na	na	na	na	na	na	na	na	na	na
Puerto Rico	na	**55**	55	55	70	63	42	38	55	57	52	61	62	56	54	56
Romania	70	**na**	na	na	na	na	na	na	na	na	na	na	na	na	na	na
Russian Fed.	49	**na**	na	na	na	na	na	na	na	na	na	na	na	na	na	na
Serbia	na	**47**	46	47	57	46	42	45	49	43	44	47	45	51	43	47
Singapore	na	**55**	57	53	62	54	32	49	59	52	54	57	54	49	56	65
Slovakia	na	**na**	na	na	na	na	na	na	na	na	na	na	na	na	na	na
Slovenia	65	**na**	na	na	na	na	na	na	na	na	na	na	na	na	na	na
South Africa	35	**54**	51	56	63	51	36	44	66	56	41	56	71	52	52	71
Spain	65	**69**	73	65	75	74	61	67	74	71	64	70	67	70	69	72
Sweden	58	**54**	58	50	55	56	51	52	56	53	51	50	58	48	55	53
Switzerland	55	**68**	70	66	74	71	60	64	70	59	62	69	72	64	70	65
Taiwan	na	**58**	55	61	79	59	42	48	60	67	57	52	64	57	59	68
Tanzania	na	**18**	18	19	23	17	10	14	23	23	14	22	26	15	19	25
Turkey	71	**63**	61	64	66	62	57	54	75	76	56	77	77	65	64	63
Uganda	na	**19**	17	22	28	12	2	15	21	13	13	19	0	20	20	13
Ukraine	na	**na**	na	na	na	na	na	na	na	na	na	na	na	na	na	na
United States	55	**56**	57	55	56	60	50	53	58	56	51	59	55	44	56	61
Uruguay	na	**63**	67	60	71	64	59	63	66	56	64	65	59	67	64	64
Venezuela	na	**48**	47	48	56	45	35	37	51	53	39	47	50	48	47	51
Vietnam	na	**86**	87	84	92	85	81	83	91	84	84	88	77	90	84	94
Zimbabwe	na	**15**	16	15	21	11	8	7	26	26	11	13	39	14	17	8
Total	55	**48**	49	48	54	48	41	44	51	51	44	52	51	45	49	53

RANKING	
Country	2000
Bangladesh	91
Vietnam	86
Iran	78
India	73
Peru	70
Spain	69
Switzerland	68
Turkey	63
Uruguay	63
Korea, South	61
Brazil	60
Azerbaijan	58
Taiwan	58
Canada	56
Colombia	56
United States	56
Morocco	55
Puerto Rico	55
Singapore	55
South Africa	54
Sweden	54
Australia	52
Bosnia and Herz.	52
Chile	51
El Salvador	51
Macedonia	51
Moldova	50
Argentina	49
Albania	48
Venezuela	48
Serbia	47
Mexico	46
Norway	46
New Zealand	44
Armenia	42
Pakistan	42
Egypt	40
Japan	39
Indonesia	35
Algeria	32
Dominican Rep.	32
Philippines	29
Montenegro	25
Georgia	21
Uganda	19
Tanzania	18
Zimbabwe	15
Jordan	11
Nigeria	6
Total	48

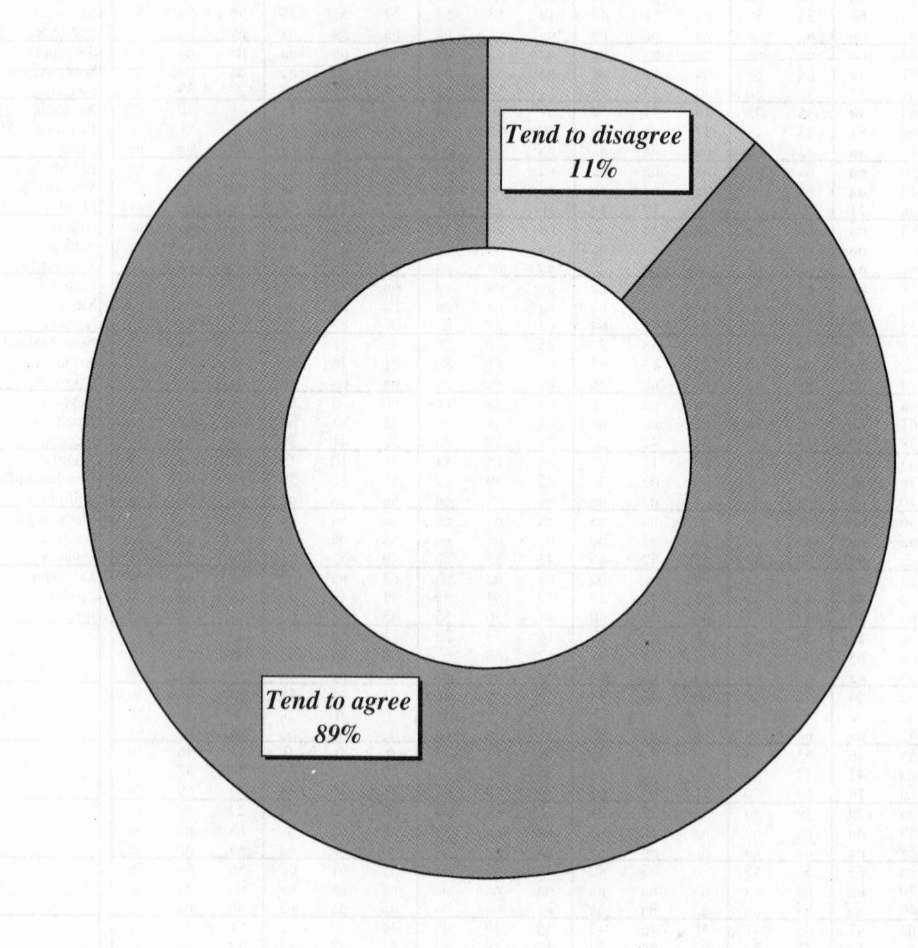
D18) A child needs a home with both a father and a mother to grow up happily?
Tend to disagree
11%
Tend to agree
89%

D018) CHILD NEEDS PARENTS

If someone says a child needs a home with both a father and a mother to grow up happily, would you tend to agree or disagree?

(WVS: V109; EVS: V148)

Tend to agree (%)

Country	Wave		Gender		Age			Education			Income			Values		
	1990	2000	Male	Female	16-29	30-49	50+	Lower	Middle	Upper	Lower	Middle	Upper	Mat	Mixed	Postm.
Albania	na	**99**	99	99	98	100	98	99	99	99	99	99	99	99	98	100
Algeria	na	**98**	97	98	97	98	98	100	98	96	98	99	96	98	98	98
Argentina	95	**91**	94	89	89	90	95	94	87	88	93	90	92	94	92	89
Armenia	na	**98**	99	97	98	98	97	98	98	99	97	99	97	99	97	100
Australia	na	**71**	80	62	60	69	82	75	69	69	72	71	71	86	72	65
Austria	94	**88**	92	84	80	87	93	92	84	84	90	87	89	95	89	83
Azerbaijan	na	**92**	91	92	95	91	86	89	92	91	98	91	92	91	94	93
Bangladesh	na	**99**	99	99	98	100	99	99	100	99	99	98	100	99	99	100
Belarus	na	**95**	95	94	94	94	96	94	95	96	94	95	94	96	92	96
Belgium	92	**81**	83	79	77	75	89	90	81	74	84	83	78	84	81	78
Bosnia and Herz.	na	**95**	97	93	93	95	95	95	95	94	96	94	94	95	94	94
Brazil	88	**87**	93	82	85	89	87	90	85	83	89	87	86	90	86	85
Bulgaria	95	**97**	96	98	95	97	99	98	96	98	98	96	97	98	96	100
Canada	78	**72**	79	64	63	69	79	81	71	65	76	74	64	79	75	64
Chile	93	**83**	85	81	81	81	89	87	83	76	87	80	79	87	85	72
China	98	**95**	94	97	92	96	97	97	94	91	96	95	95	96	95	91
Colombia	na	**86**	88	85	86	85	91	92	87	82	90	87	84	90	87	81
Croatia	na	**89**	92	87	83	92	90	93	88	81	89	88	90	95	89	84
Czech Republic	99	**86**	89	83	79	83	92	86	84	91	87	85	85	87	86	86
Denmark	73	**67**	74	60	57	62	77	76	56	52	66	70	63	84	68	45
Dominican Rep.	na	**85**	88	83	83	89	91	91	88	84	91	87	76	88	87	80
Egypt	na	**99**	98	99	98	99	99	99	98	98	99	99	99	99	98	98
El Salvador	na	**94**	96	93	92	95	96	97	93	88	97	95	88	na	na	na
Estonia	99	**96**	97	95	95	95	97	97	95	96	95	95	96	96	95	100
Finland	86	**60**	69	52	51	52	73	65	56	53	58	61	63	62	61	58
France	94	**86**	91	82	80	83	92	87	83	87	82	86	89	90	86	80
Georgia	na	**98**	98	98	97	98	99	98	97	100	98	97	98	98	98	99
Germany	97	**90**	92	89	80	90	95	94	87	90	90	92	90	97	89	82
Great Britain	74	**67**	74	60	55	61	78	72	62	66	62	65	68	na	na	na
Greece	na	**96**	95	97	95	96	99	95	97	96	94	97	97	96	97	94
Hungary	99	**95**	96	95	94	94	98	95	95	97	97	94	96	96	95	91
Iceland	79	**71**	77	65	61	68	84	74	72	62	71	72	66	74	72	60
India	97	**96**	96	95	96	96	95	96	95	96	94	95	96	98	93	98
Indonesia	na	**89**	88	89	89	93	85	87	88	91	86	91	88	88	89	86
Iran	na	**86**	86	86	84	86	90	89	85	85	89	88	85	87	86	80
Ireland	83	**66**	75	58	55	60	82	77	60	64	71	68	65	72	66	56
Israel	na	**na**	na	na	na	na	na	na	na	na	na	na	na	na	na	na
Italy	97	**92**	92	93	89	91	96	95	91	89	93	93	92	94	93	89
Japan	95	**90**	92	88	83	88	95	96	90	89	88	90	93	95	89	87
Jordan	na	**98**	97	99	97	98	99	98	98	98	98	97	99	98	98	100
Korea, South	na	**97**	97	97	93	98	99	100	97	96	98	96	97	98	97	87
Latvia	99	**93**	96	91	89	93	94	97	91	95	93	95	93	93	93	89
Lithuania	94	**80**	81	78	70	78	88	86	76	82	86	77	80	82	80	62
Luxembourg	na	**85**	86	85	79	83	92	89	84	85	87	87	81	89	85	85
Macedonia	na	**97**	97	97	98	98	95	97	97	97	96	98	97	96	98	98
Malta	na	**93**	94	92	89	92	96	96	93	88	94	96	90	95	93	82
Mexico	88	**87**	88	87	86	88	89	90	86	79	86	90	86	88	88	78
Moldova	na	**97**	97	97	96	97	98	98	96	97	98	98	96	97	97	92
Montenegro	na	**97**	98	95	94	98	97	98	96	94	97	97	98	98	96	90
Morocco	na	**98**	99	98	98	98	99	98	97	98	98	98	98	99	98	100
Netherlands	74	**66**	75	58	54	61	79	75	64	61	69	63	66	74	67	61
New Zealand	na	**76**	84	70	66	70	85	78	80	72	77	75	75	78	78	65
Nigeria	97	**97**	96	97	97	96	97	98	97	95	97	96	97	98	96	94
Northern Ireland	81	**70**	75	65	52	66	80	76	65	64	71	66	71	75	71	61
Norway	86	**85**	92	79	82	83	90	87	87	82	na	na	na	89	85	79
Pakistan	na	**98**	98	98	97	98	99	99	98	98	99	98	97	98	98	100
Peru	na	**94**	95	92	93	93	96	95	94	93	96	92	92	94	94	93
Philippines	na	**97**	97	97	97	97	95	97	96	97	97	97	96	97	96	95
Poland	98	**97**	98	96	94	98	98	98	96	94	97	97	96	97	96	98
Portugal	93	**73**	77	71	64	72	80	78	65	60	86	73	70	74	75	65
Puerto Rico	na	**76**	83	72	67	70	84	87	82	71	78	78	73	85	75	72
Romania	97	**95**	95	95	90	94	97	97	95	91	96	96	92	95	96	84
Russian Fed.	97	**95**	96	94	91	95	97	94	95	94	95	96	94	95	95	97
Serbia	na	**89**	92	87	84	90	91	93	90	84	90	90	88	92	86	90
Singapore	na	**94**	96	92	92	96	96	95	94	90	95	93	93	95	94	85
Slovakia	na	**95**	96	95	94	95	96	95	96	93	94	95	97	97	95	89
Slovenia	94	**88**	92	84	81	88	94	93	86	87	89	89	86	90	88	88
South Africa	92	**90**	92	86	84	93	93	92	87	83	92	87	89	88	91	85
Spain	91	**87**	87	86	78	84	94	93	82	75	91	86	81	93	87	75
Sweden	85	**60**	73	47	51	58	68	75	55	56	56	64	61	82	61	50
Switzerland	na	**89**	91	86	86	88	91	91	87	92	90	88	88	92	90	84
Taiwan	na	**98**	98	97	98	98	97	98	97	98	97	98	99	97	98	100
Tanzania	na	**97**	97	96	99	96	96	97	97	95	97	97	96	97	97	100
Turkey	96	**96**	96	96	96	96	97	98	95	93	98	96	94	96	96	95
Uganda	na	**96**	97	96	96	95	99	98	95	98	96	96	92	98	96	94
Ukraine	na	**97**	97	98	95	97	99	100	97	97	98	98	96	98	97	96
United States	73	**64**	72	57	61	62	71	65	62	65	63	61	70	65	65	63
Uruguay	na	**90**	91	89	88	87	93	91	87	91	90	89	91	95	91	86
Venezuela	na	**89**	91	86	87	90	91	91	88	87	90	86	90	93	87	88
Vietnam	na	**98**	97	98	96	98	98	98	97	94	97	97	99	96	98	98
Zimbabwe	na	**98**	98	98	98	98	99	99	98	100	99	97	99	99	98	98
Total	91	**89**	91	87	87	88	91	91	88	85	90	89	88	93	88	80

RANKING

Country	2000
Bangladesh	99
Albania	99
Egypt	99
Zimbabwe	98
Morocco	98
Pakistan	98
Georgia	98
Jordan	98
Armenia	98
Taiwan	98
Algeria	98
Vietnam	98
Bulgaria	97
Ukraine	97
Korea, South	97
Macedonia	97
Poland	97
Moldova	97
Tanzania	97
Montenegro	97
Nigeria	97
Philippines	97
Turkey	96
Uganda	96
Greece	96
Estonia	96
India	96
China	95
Hungary	95
Slovakia	95
Russian Fed.	95
Bosnia and Herz.	95
Romania	95
Belarus	95
El Salvador	94
Singapore	94
Peru	94
Latvia	93
Malta	93
Italy	92
Azerbaijan	92
Argentina	91
Germany	90
Japan	90
Uruguay	90
South Africa	90
Serbia	89
Croatia	89
Venezuela	89
Indonesia	89
Switzerland	89
Slovenia	88
Austria	88
Mexico	87
Brazil	87
Spain	87
Colombia	86
France	86
Czech Republic	86
Iran	86
Luxembourg	85
Dominican Rep.	85
Norway	85
Chile	83
Belgium	81
Lithuania	80
New Zealand	76
Puerto Rico	76
Portugal	73
Canada	72
Iceland	71
Australia	71
Northern Ireland	70
Denmark	67
Great Britain	67
Ireland	66
Netherlands	66
United States	64
Finland	60
Sweden	60
Total	89

D19) A woman has to have children in order to be fulfilled?

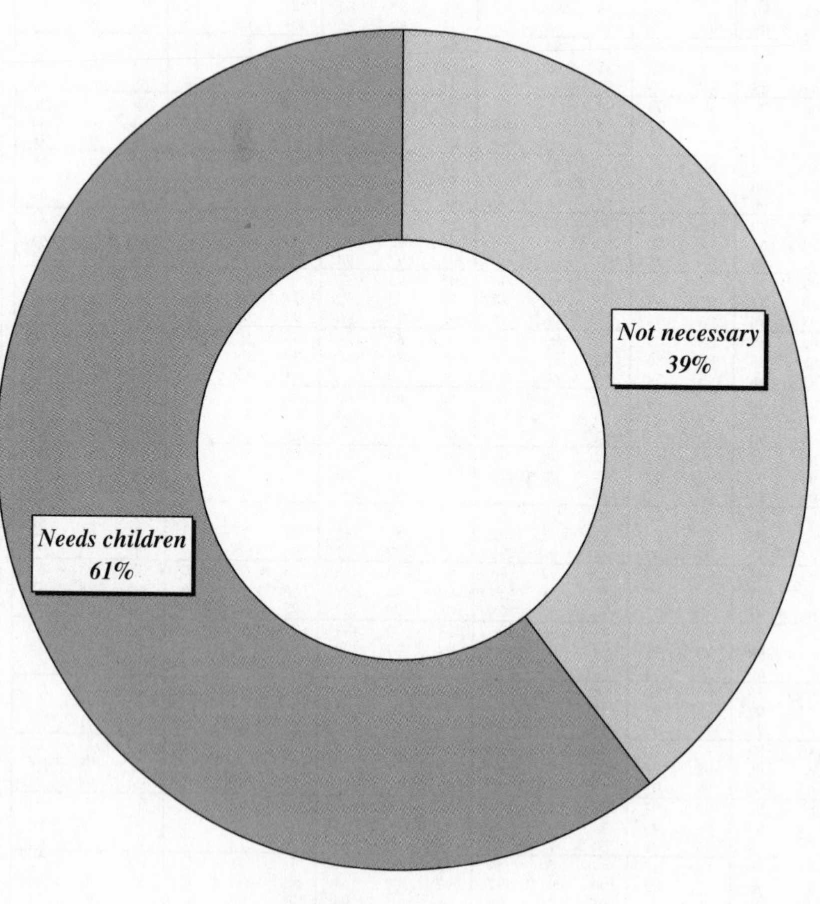

D019) WOMAN NEEDS CHILD

Do you think that a woman has to have children in order to be fulfilled or is this not necessary?

Needs children (%) (WVS: V110; EVS: V149)

Country	Wave		Gender		Age			Education			Income			Values		
	1990	2000	Male	Female	16-29	30-49	50+	Lower	Middle	Upper	Lower	Middle	Upper	Mat	Mixed	Postm.
Albania	na	**92**	92	93	91	92	94	93	92	90	92	91	94	93	92	85
Algeria	na	**81**	84	78	79	82	83	85	82	77	79	84	83	84	81	78
Argentina	60	**56**	56	56	49	58	61	61	50	44	59	55	54	61	59	45
Armenia	na	**83**	83	83	78	85	88	86	83	83	83	86	78	88	81	62
Australia	na	**20**	25	15	12	19	27	24	17	18	24	19	16	28	22	14
Austria	51	**34**	36	33	21	32	42	41	29	21	41	37	31	45	36	26
Azerbaijan	na	**61**	63	59	55	64	68	78	64	53	67	56	58	65	56	51
Bangladesh	na	**98**	98	98	97	99	99	99	99	96	99	98	98	99	98	96
Belarus	97	**77**	77	76	66	80	82	83	75	71	81	76	70	80	73	73
Belgium	46	**33**	36	31	28	27	42	42	32	29	42	35	27	32	33	34
Bosnia and Herz.	na	**87**	86	88	85	88	87	92	87	82	90	86	87	86	87	81
Brazil	56	**53**	57	50	48	55	61	57	52	44	58	51	52	56	52	53
Bulgaria	92	**76**	74	77	63	73	84	88	70	67	86	74	68	80	72	71
Canada	24	**19**	20	17	14	18	22	27	18	13	27	19	11	25	20	13
Chile	64	**65**	63	67	60	61	76	70	65	56	66	67	64	70	66	56
China	46	**37**	30	43	27	39	40	48	29	36	39	35	36	34	34	33
Colombia	na	**56**	54	59	51	57	65	70	56	47	66	58	48	61	65	54
Croatia	na	**59**	55	62	46	59	67	64	56	54	64	55	62	78	60	41
Czech Republic	87	**44**	42	46	32	40	54	47	40	42	50	44	39	49	44	38
Denmark	82	**80**	84	76	75	77	85	79	75	82	81	80	80	76	80	83
Dominican Rep.	na	**65**	66	64	62	69	82	81	71	60	74	60	59	60	67	62
Egypt	na	**88**	89	88	86	89	91	91	85	88	92	89	86	90	88	85
El Salvador	na	**69**	69	69	59	74	76	80	61	52	80	68	56	na	na	na
Estonia	91	**75**	71	78	61	74	83	74	75	78	77	77	74	78	73	73
Finland	20	**12**	12	12	8	9	18	17	7	6	13	12	10	16	10	15
France	75	**67**	69	66	61	63	73	70	62	64	67	68	65	74	67	55
Georgia	na	**81**	79	83	77	83	84	87	82	76	84	81	77	84	79	77
Germany	66	**54**	56	53	36	52	64	62	48	44	59	58	57	79	50	30
Great Britain	21	**21**	22	20	15	18	27	26	19	14	23	24	18	na	na	na
Greece	na	**75**	72	77	73	74	82	82	76	73	77	77	72	76	78	67
Hungary	96	**94**	92	96	89	94	97	94	94	93	94	94	95	94	95	97
Iceland	42	**35**	40	31	26	31	50	41	33	27	41	34	32	40	35	22
India	89	**85**	83	88	83	87	86	89	85	78	90	89	80	87	81	86
Indonesia	na	**93**	93	94	83	94	96	98	97	85	95	93	91	95	92	96
Iran	na	**49**	49	49	43	51	62	61	46	39	54	49	44	56	44	35
Ireland	26	**15**	19	12	6	14	25	26	9	12	28	14	11	19	15	11
Israel	na	**na**	na	na	na	na	na	na	na	na	na	na	na	na	na	na
Italy	67	**56**	55	58	46	51	67	65	51	47	61	55	52	71	57	46
Japan	76	**66**	70	62	40	58	79	83	66	54	71	58	70	74	62	60
Jordan	na	**91**	92	90	88	93	93	94	87	90	96	90	90	91	92	92
Korea, South	76	**92**	95	89	86	93	98	94	95	88	92	95	90	94	92	75
Latvia	96	**91**	90	91	77	93	94	88	91	93	92	93	88	92	90	86
Lithuania	89	**68**	65	71	56	69	75	76	66	67	71	68	68	73	68	50
Luxembourg	na	**38**	41	35	32	35	45	43	37	33	40	39	27	43	38	26
Macedonia	na	**70**	71	69	70	70	70	83	65	58	74	69	64	70	68	79
Malta	na	**44**	52	37	30	45	52	54	41	36	53	47	39	45	44	37
Mexico	52	**45**	45	46	33	48	59	56	33	31	55	40	37	53	41	31
Moldova	na	**79**	75	82	75	80	81	78	80	77	79	79	76	77	83	63
Montenegro	na	**78**	79	77	61	78	86	87	73	67	85	75	75	84	71	64
Morocco	na	**88**	88	87	85	89	90	91	75	76	93	82	89	90	86	84
Netherlands	9	**7**	7	7	3	3	13	12	4	5	11	5	5	14	5	8
New Zealand	na	**17**	19	16	9	16	21	20	15	16	23	13	15	22	16	11
Nigeria	87	**92**	91	92	92	93	89	90	93	91	91	92	93	93	91	93
Northern Ireland	32	**18**	21	16	9	19	23	22	17	11	24	17	17	18	20	11
Norway	23	**19**	22	17	20	16	23	22	21	15	na	na	na	27	19	8
Pakistan	na	**98**	99	98	98	98	99	99	98	96	99	98	97	99	98	100
Peru	na	**40**	39	40	32	41	54	48	39	36	44	39	32	47	38	34
Philippines	na	**87**	83	91	88	88	84	89	88	82	88	87	86	88	86	91
Poland	79	**70**	73	67	57	66	82	75	65	59	74	69	62	72	67	75
Portugal	61	**68**	64	71	51	66	79	75	57	42	78	69	56	75	65	54
Puerto Rico	na	**34**	34	34	26	29	42	43	32	34	46	31	29	48	34	29
Romania	85	**83**	81	86	71	82	90	92	80	77	90	82	81	87	81	70
Russian Fed.	92	**83**	81	86	75	83	89	88	83	83	85	84	82	86	82	72
Serbia	na	**67**	66	68	54	67	73	75	69	53	71	70	60	73	62	53
Singapore	na	**56**	55	57	45	61	83	70	49	50	64	55	51	68	53	39
Slovakia	na	**46**	44	47	37	46	52	50	44	39	53	44	43	50	44	34
Slovenia	58	**38**	37	39	25	31	55	50	34	32	46	40	33	46	37	37
South Africa	70	**45**	44	46	38	47	54	57	30	21	63	32	31	46	45	39
Spain	46	**48**	47	49	33	41	63	59	38	33	59	49	42	62	47	28
Sweden	21	**25**	29	21	22	26	26	26	27	21	24	28	24	41	25	21
Switzerland	31	**35**	41	30	27	33	43	47	33	33	37	39	34	55	34	26
Taiwan	na	**55**	51	58	40	54	66	68	52	44	59	56	48	59	49	50
Tanzania	na	**85**	85	84	80	85	93	87	83	78	85	85	81	87	84	96
Turkey	72	**75**	73	77	67	77	87	84	65	58	82	73	60	81	75	64
Uganda	na	**63**	57	69	56	69	75	67	61	68	56	67	65	66	63	58
Ukraine	na	**86**	82	89	73	87	91	89	85	86	86	87	85	88	83	83
United States	20	**15**	18	13	16	15	14	20	17	12	20	12	13	22	15	12
Uruguay	na	**59**	62	58	56	59	61	60	62	48	58	64	56	66	62	52
Venezuela	na	**54**	54	54	49	52	68	63	53	45	55	53	52	62	51	50
Vietnam	na	**86**	83	89	82	87	88	87	86	75	87	86	85	88	86	80
Zimbabwe	na	**77**	73	80	74	76	86	85	67	30	85	74	65	81	75	70
Total	61	**61**	61	60	56	61	65	67	58	53	66	62	58	72	58	43

RANKING	
Country	2000
Pakistan	98
Bangladesh	98
Hungary	94
Indonesia	93
Albania	92
Korea, South	92
Nigeria	92
Jordan	91
Latvia	91
Egypt	88
Morocco	88
Bosnia and Herz.	87
Philippines	87
Vietnam	86
Ukraine	86
India	85
Tanzania	85
Russian Fed.	83
Romania	83
Armenia	83
Algeria	81
Georgia	81
Denmark	80
Moldova	79
Montenegro	78
Zimbabwe	77
Belarus	77
Bulgaria	76
Greece	75
Turkey	75
Estonia	75
Macedonia	70
Poland	70
El Salvador	69
Lithuania	68
Portugal	68
Serbia	67
France	67
Japan	66
Chile	65
Dominican Rep.	65
Uganda	63
Azerbaijan	61
Uruguay	59
Croatia	59
Italy	56
Colombia	56
Singapore	56
Argentina	56
Taiwan	55
Germany	54
Venezuela	54
Brazil	53
Iran	49
Spain	48
Slovakia	46
Mexico	45
South Africa	45
Czech Republic	44
Malta	44
Peru	40
Slovenia	38
Luxembourg	38
China	37
Switzerland	35
Iceland	35
Puerto Rico	34
Austria	34
Belgium	33
Sweden	25
Great Britain	21
Australia	20
Norway	19
Canada	19
Northern Ireland	18
New Zealand	17
Ireland	15
United States	15
Finland	12
Netherlands	7
Total	61

D020_1) MAN NEEDS CHILDREN

Do you agree or disagree with the following statement: "A man has to have children in order to be fulfilled?"

Agree strongly / Agree (%) (EVS: V152)

	Wave		Gender		Age			Education			Income			Values		
Country	1990	2000	Male	Female	16-29	30-49	50+	Lower	Middle	Upper	Lower	Middle	Upper	Mat	Mixed	Postm.
Albania	na	**na**	na	na	na	na	na	na	na	na	na	na	na	na	na	na
Algeria	na	**na**	na	na	na	na	na	na	na	na	na	na	na	na	na	na
Argentina	na	**na**	na	na	na	na	na	na	na	na	na	na	na	na	na	na
Armenia	na	**na**	na	na	na	na	na	na	na	na	na	na	na	na	na	na
Australia	na	**na**	na	na	na	na	na	na	na	na	na	na	na	na	na	na
Austria	na	**26**	32	21	21	21	35	31	24	17	33	26	25	33	28	22
Azerbaijan	na	**na**	na	na	na	na	na	na	na	na	na	na	na	na	na	na
Bangladesh	na	**na**	na	na	na	na	na	na	na	na	na	na	na	na	na	na
Belarus	na	**77**	75	79	62	79	87	86	74	73	84	73	72	81	73	66
Belgium	na	**25**	29	22	23	22	30	27	27	23	33	28	20	23	25	29
Bosnia and Herz.	na	**na**	na	na	na	na	na	na	na	na	na	na	na	na	na	na
Brazil	na	**na**	na	na	na	na	na	na	na	na	na	na	na	na	na	na
Bulgaria	na	**54**	54	55	33	50	68	73	46	42	75	49	40	58	49	65
Canada	na	**na**	na	na	na	na	na	na	na	na	na	na	na	na	na	na
Chile	na	**na**	na	na	na	na	na	na	na	na	na	na	na	na	na	na
China	na	**na**	na	na	na	na	na	na	na	na	na	na	na	na	na	na
Colombia	na	**na**	na	na	na	na	na	na	na	na	na	na	na	na	na	na
Croatia	na	**77**	73	80	65	79	83	84	74	67	90	74	72	85	79	65
Czech Republic	na	**60**	60	60	48	56	71	65	56	51	67	58	56	66	61	43
Denmark	na	**65**	68	61	63	62	68	62	67	67	63	63	68	61	64	72
Dominican Rep.	na	**na**	na	na	na	na	na	na	na	na	na	na	na	na	na	na
Egypt	na	**na**	na	na	na	na	na	na	na	na	na	na	na	na	na	na
El Salvador	na	**na**	na	na	na	na	na	na	na	na	na	na	na	na	na	na
Estonia	na	**67**	63	70	51	65	77	68	65	71	69	70	63	70	66	53
Finland	na	**28**	29	27	26	24	32	32	24	17	30	26	27	32	27	28
France	na	**53**	56	51	48	52	56	55	46	54	53	56	55	57	54	45
Georgia	na	**na**	na	na	na	na	na	na	na	na	na	na	na	na	na	na
Germany	na	**39**	44	35	22	37	49	46	34	30	42	47	36	58	34	27
Great Britain	na	**11**	14	9	6	9	17	13	10	8	14	16	11	na	na	na
Greece	na	**48**	49	47	47	44	58	61	43	49	47	50	45	45	50	45
Hungary	na	**76**	79	73	60	76	85	79	68	75	78	76	75	82	72	51
Iceland	na	**29**	37	21	23	26	38	32	28	24	33	28	27	31	31	17
India	na	**na**	na	na	na	na	na	na	na	na	na	na	na	na	na	na
Indonesia	na	**na**	na	na	na	na	na	na	na	na	na	na	na	na	na	na
Iran	na	**na**	na	na	na	na	na	na	na	na	na	na	na	na	na	na
Ireland	na	**15**	18	13	6	16	22	23	11	11	22	15	11	17	15	17
Israel	na	**na**	na	na	na	na	na	na	na	na	na	na	na	na	na	na
Italy	na	**45**	47	42	36	39	54	52	40	36	52	45	39	56	45	37
Japan	na	**na**	na	na	na	na	na	na	na	na	na	na	na	na	na	na
Jordan	na	**na**	na	na	na	na	na	na	na	na	na	na	na	na	na	na
Korea, South	na	**na**	na	na	na	na	na	na	na	na	na	na	na	na	na	na
Latvia	na	**90**	89	90	79	91	93	93	87	94	90	90	88	89	91	82
Lithuania	na	**48**	48	47	32	45	61	57	45	43	60	41	47	51	49	38
Luxembourg	na	**30**	35	25	30	27	33	34	29	25	41	31	18	33	29	23
Macedonia	na	**na**	na	na	na	na	na	na	na	na	na	na	na	na	na	na
Malta	na	**34**	37	30	21	30	45	44	30	26	44	33	30	37	32	30
Mexico	na	**na**	na	na	na	na	na	na	na	na	na	na	na	na	na	na
Moldova	na	**na**	na	na	na	na	na	na	na	na	na	na	na	na	na	na
Montenegro	na	**na**	na	na	na	na	na	na	na	na	na	na	na	na	na	na
Morocco	na	**na**	na	na	na	na	na	na	na	na	na	na	na	na	na	na
Netherlands	na	**5**	6	4	4	3	7	8	3	4	8	3	5	11	4	4
New Zealand	na	**na**	na	na	na	na	na	na	na	na	na	na	na	na	na	na
Nigeria	na	**na**	na	na	na	na	na	na	na	na	na	na	na	na	na	na
Northern Ireland	na	**16**	18	15	6	17	21	21	13	11	21	12	13	17	17	10
Norway	na	**na**	na	na	na	na	na	na	na	na	na	na	na	na	na	na
Pakistan	na	**na**	na	na	na	na	na	na	na	na	na	na	na	na	na	na
Peru	na	**na**	na	na	na	na	na	na	na	na	na	na	na	na	na	na
Philippines	na	**na**	na	na	na	na	na	na	na	na	na	na	na	na	na	na
Poland	na	**54**	56	53	39	51	67	61	51	34	57	56	43	59	51	54
Portugal	na	**50**	46	53	34	47	62	58	36	22	64	49	44	59	45	41
Puerto Rico	na	**na**	na	na	na	na	na	na	na	na	na	na	na	na	na	na
Romania	na	**75**	77	72	60	73	84	86	71	62	83	77	71	79	72	53
Russian Fed.	na	**71**	72	70	61	70	79	77	72	65	76	70	68	73	69	63
Serbia	na	**na**	na	na	na	na	na	na	na	na	na	na	na	na	na	na
Singapore	na	**na**	na	na	na	na	na	na	na	na	na	na	na	na	na	na
Slovakia	na	**39**	39	39	34	40	42	41	39	31	46	36	39	42	38	31
Slovenia	na	**37**	42	33	26	31	52	47	35	32	43	40	33	45	35	44
South Africa	na	**na**	na	na	na	na	na	na	na	na	na	na	na	na	na	na
Spain	na	**36**	36	36	27	28	47	48	27	28	42	35	28	52	33	21
Sweden	na	**na**	na	na	na	na	na	na	na	na	na	na	na	na	na	na
Switzerland	na	**na**	na	na	na	na	na	na	na	na	na	na	na	na	na	na
Taiwan	na	**na**	na	na	na	na	na	na	na	na	na	na	na	na	na	na
Tanzania	na	**na**	na	na	na	na	na	na	na	na	na	na	na	na	na	na
Turkey	na	**63**	62	64	58	65	69	71	54	46	74	63	42	70	64	53
Uganda	na	**na**	na	na	na	na	na	na	na	na	na	na	na	na	na	na
Ukraine	na	**73**	71	75	55	75	82	84	71	73	79	70	71	75	72	69
United States	na	**na**	na	na	na	na	na	na	na	na	na	na	na	na	na	na
Uruguay	na	**na**	na	na	na	na	na	na	na	na	na	na	na	na	na	na
Venezuela	na	**na**	na	na	na	na	na	na	na	na	na	na	na	na	na	na
Vietnam	na	**na**	na	na	na	na	na	na	na	na	na	na	na	na	na	na
Zimbabwe	na	**na**	na	na	na	na	na	na	na	na	na	na	na	na	na	na
Total	na	**47**	48	46	38	45	55	52	45	42	55	49	45	58	46	36

RANKING	
Country	**2000**
Latvia	90
Belarus	77
Croatia	77
Hungary	76
Romania	75
Ukraine	73
Russian Fed.	71
Estonia	67
Denmark	65
Turkey	63
Czech Republic	60
Bulgaria	54
Poland	54
France	53
Portugal	50
Greece	48
Lithuania	48
Italy	45
Germany	39
Slovakia	39
Slovenia	37
Spain	36
Malta	34
Luxembourg	30
Iceland	29
Finland	28
Austria	26
Belgium	25
Northern Ireland	16
Ireland	15
Great Britain	11
Netherlands	5
Total	47

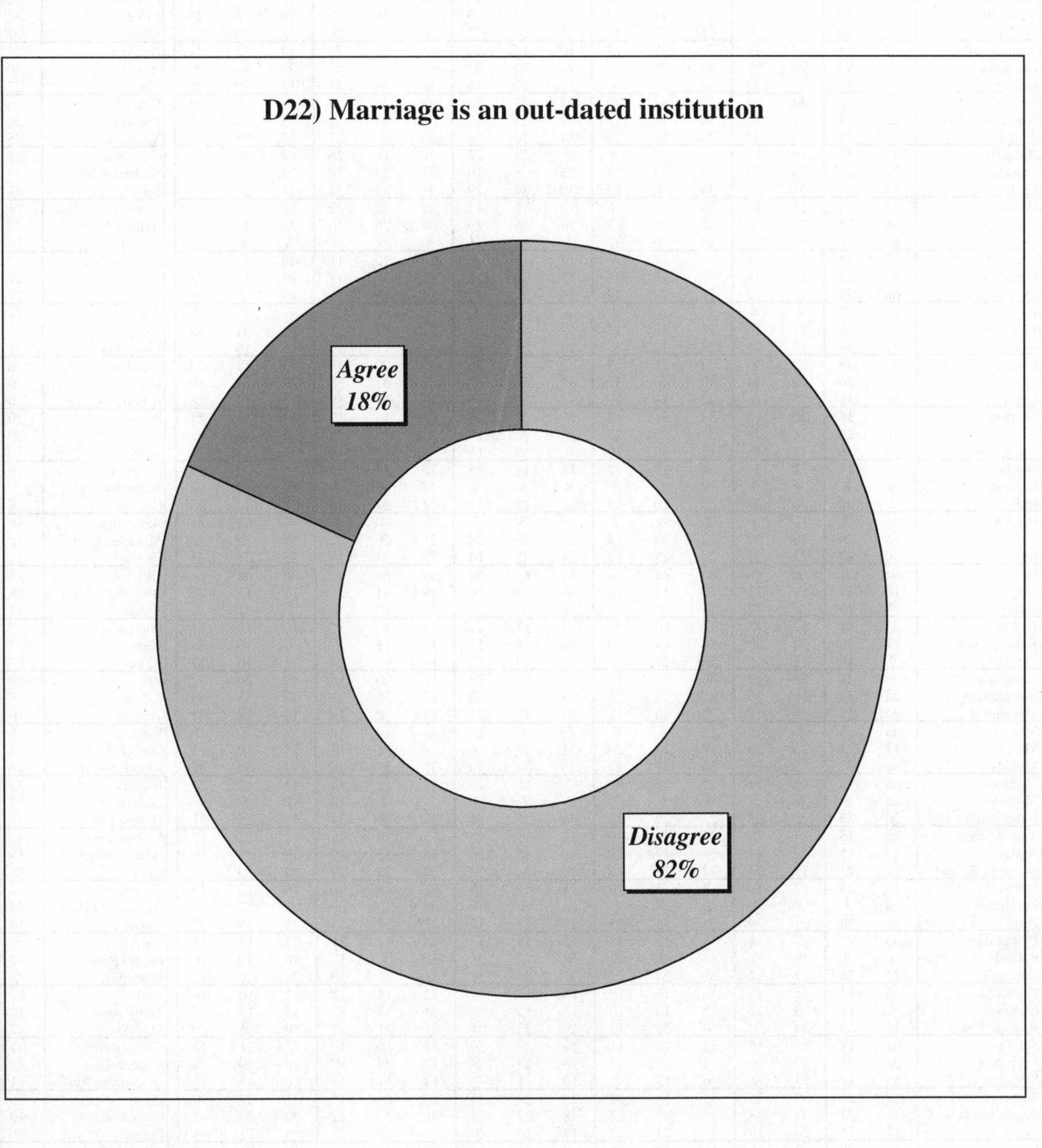
D22) Marriage is an out-dated institution
Agree
18%
Disagree
82%

D022) MARRIAGE IS AN OUT-DATED INSTITUTION

Do you agree or disagree with the following statement: "Marriage is an out-dated institution?"

Agree (%)

(WVS: V111; EVS: V150)

	Wave		Gender		Age			Education			Income			Values		
Country	1990	2000	Male	Female	16-29	30-49	50+	Lower	Middle	Upper	Lower	Middle	Upper	Mat	Mixed	Postm.
Albania	na	**9**	12	6	16	7	5	8	8	12	6	13	7	6	10	18
Algeria	na	**13**	13	13	16	10	12	13	12	13	13	12	15	13	12	13
Argentina	9	**19**	20	19	26	19	13	18	22	20	20	19	19	18	19	22
Armenia	na	**14**	15	13	17	16	8	12	15	13	14	11	18	11	17	19
Australia	na	**19**	19	18	25	18	13	19	20	16	22	16	16	18	16	23
Austria	12	**20**	20	20	26	22	15	17	24	22	20	19	20	23	19	22
Azerbaijan	na	**18**	17	19	20	19	13	10	17	22	16	19	22	14	25	24
Bangladesh	na	**95**	94	96	92	96	99	96	95	91	97	93	95	96	94	97
Belarus	16	**17**	19	15	26	18	8	10	20	16	16	18	17	15	20	25
Belgium	22	**31**	34	27	29	34	29	33	32	26	36	31	30	29	30	35
Bosnia and Herz.	na	**14**	11	16	14	16	12	12	15	12	14	15	11	13	14	16
Brazil	27	**30**	28	32	27	32	29	34	26	26	30	30	27	30	28	32
Bulgaria	11	**18**	19	17	37	22	6	9	23	22	9	19	26	14	20	26
Canada	13	**22**	25	20	29	24	16	25	24	16	27	22	18	25	21	26
Chile	15	**31**	31	32	38	36	19	30	34	29	31	33	30	25	34	35
China	15	**14**	13	16	14	14	16	18	12	12	15	15	12	13	14	21
Colombia	na	**25**	28	23	26	25	25	34	26	19	34	26	20	30	26	20
Croatia	na	**8**	8	8	15	7	6	5	9	16	4	9	9	6	8	12
Czech Republic	10	**11**	12	11	19	14	6	12	11	6	13	12	11	10	13	11
Denmark	18	**15**	16	14	17	18	11	13	20	15	15	15	17	18	14	25
Dominican Rep.	na	**11**	10	12	11	12	na	16	8	11	14	9	8	16	9	11
Egypt	na	**4**	4	4	4	4	4	4	3	7	3	4	5	3	5	5
El Salvador	na	**15**	14	16	18	13	12	17	15	9	22	15	11	na	na	na
Estonia	11	**16**	17	15	27	17	9	14	18	13	19	12	15	15	16	31
Finland	13	**18**	20	16	23	21	13	22	15	9	20	20	16	23	15	22
France	29	**36**	39	34	40	40	31	37	39	33	37	37	36	29	36	49
Georgia	na	**15**	15	16	22	14	10	12	16	15	14	15	18	13	17	28
Germany	14	**18**	20	18	32	21	11	16	22	15	23	14	17	12	19	27
Great Britain	18	**26**	28	24	37	27	18	28	26	19	35	25	18	na	na	na
Greece	na	**16**	17	15	15	19	10	9	18	15	18	13	16	9	15	26
Hungary	11	**17**	22	13	24	19	11	18	17	15	20	15	19	15	20	35
Iceland	6	**8**	9	7	12	8	5	9	9	4	14	6	7	8	8	13
India	5	**20**	20	20	20	20	18	20	22	16	22	23	15	16	24	20
Indonesia	na	**3**	4	3	4	4	2	2	5	2	3	4	1	4	3	na
Iran	na	**20**	20	20	22	20	17	20	15	26	21	20	22	18	19	27
Ireland	10	**23**	23	23	29	25	17	28	22	14	31	23	16	25	21	25
Israel	na	**na**	na	na	na	na	na	na	na	na	na	na	na	na	na	na
Italy	14	**17**	19	15	20	18	14	16	19	16	19	14	20	17	15	22
Japan	7	**10**	9	12	15	8	11	18	9	10	13	10	8	8	11	8
Jordan	na	**12**	12	13	16	10	9	13	13	11	11	10	15	13	12	11
Korea, South	na	**16**	12	20	24	14	10	18	14	17	17	13	17	14	16	24
Latvia	9	**16**	17	16	25	21	9	13	19	11	18	16	14	15	16	22
Lithuania	9	**21**	25	17	36	19	11	12	24	20	16	20	18	19	20	32
Luxembourg	na	**33**	36	30	35	38	26	33	34	30	32	35	33	28	33	43
Macedonia	na	**18**	19	17	22	20	13	19	17	21	19	18	19	18	18	27
Malta	na	**7**	8	5	11	6	4	6	8	3	4	5	8	6	7	9
Mexico	17	**21**	22	20	17	23	20	24	17	16	27	18	18	21	19	22
Moldova	na	**32**	35	28	36	32	27	30	34	30	35	27	36	34	29	32
Montenegro	na	**12**	13	11	25	12	6	7	15	20	11	11	14	11	12	22
Morocco	na	**5**	6	5	6	5	3	5	6	3	3	4	10	4	6	6
Netherlands	20	**25**	25	25	23	29	22	24	25	26	25	26	23	15	25	31
New Zealand	na	**15**	14	15	25	16	10	16	13	15	13	16	14	12	12	17
Nigeria	13	**15**	17	14	15	17	13	16	15	16	15	15	19	13	17	19
Northern Ireland	14	**23**	23	23	37	22	16	22	26	20	29	22	19	24	19	33
Norway	10	**14**	17	11	18	14	10	14	11	15	na	na	na	16	12	23
Pakistan	na	**1**	1	2	2	2	1	na	2	4	na	2	3	1	2	na
Peru	na	**20**	21	19	25	18	15	22	21	17	22	22	14	21	19	23
Philippines	na	**17**	17	18	18	19	13	15	19	17	14	17	21	21	15	15
Poland	8	**9**	10	9	12	9	8	9	10	9	10	8	12	10	10	4
Portugal	23	**26**	27	24	33	24	22	22	32	31	31	25	30	21	26	35
Puerto Rico	na	**13**	12	13	16	15	10	10	17	11	12	14	11	11	12	16
Romania	9	**13**	13	12	15	14	10	15	12	9	14	13	11	11	13	17
Russian Fed.	15	**22**	24	20	34	23	13	19	23	21	21	21	22	19	24	20
Serbia	na	**18**	17	19	25	20	13	14	20	20	18	16	17	15	21	22
Singapore	na	**21**	21	20	24	20	13	18	23	20	17	26	19	18	20	38
Slovakia	na	**12**	15	9	16	12	8	10	13	7	12	11	11	10	13	11
Slovenia	18	**27**	30	25	33	31	20	28	28	25	28	24	31	31	27	30
South Africa	13	**34**	31	38	33	37	27	38	29	17	41	37	22	32	34	45
Spain	17	**21**	24	19	33	23	13	17	25	29	18	21	23	15	21	31
Sweden	14	**20**	23	18	17	28	16	19	23	18	26	20	14	10	21	25
Switzerland	13	**24**	25	24	30	26	18	21	26	16	32	21	24	27	22	29
Taiwan	na	**16**	13	19	15	16	18	20	16	13	22	15	13	14	19	17
Tanzania	na	**8**	8	9	9	8	8	9	9	4	12	7	6	7	8	4
Turkey	11	**8**	8	8	9	8	6	6	10	13	7	7	12	7	8	10
Uganda	na	**20**	15	25	27	14	7	18	22	8	14	22	16	17	23	14
Ukraine	na	**18**	21	15	27	18	13	14	18	19	16	16	23	16	21	23
United States	8	**10**	12	9	16	9	6	15	12	7	12	10	7	12	8	14
Uruguay	na	**21**	18	23	30	24	15	19	22	28	17	24	19	17	18	27
Venezuela	na	**25**	27	23	28	24	24	25	27	22	30	30	20	23	27	22
Vietnam	na	**8**	9	8	10	8	9	11	5	9	10	7	9	6	9	11
Zimbabwe	na	**11**	9	12	13	10	9	11	11	8	13	12	10	11	11	13
Total	14	**18**	19	18	22	19	13	18	19	17	19	18	18	16	18	23

RANKING	
Country	2000
Bangladesh	95
France	36
South Africa	34
Luxembourg	33
Moldova	32
Chile	31
Belgium	31
Brazil	30
Slovenia	27
Great Britain	26
Portugal	26
Venezuela	25
Colombia	25
Netherlands	25
Switzerland	24
Northern Ireland	23
Ireland	23
Canada	22
Russian Fed.	22
Spain	21
Uruguay	21
Singapore	21
Mexico	21
Lithuania	21
Sweden	20
Iran	20
Austria	20
Peru	20
Uganda	20
India	20
Argentina	19
Australia	19
Germany	18
Azerbaijan	18
Macedonia	18
Finland	18
Ukraine	18
Bulgaria	18
Serbia	18
Philippines	17
Hungary	17
Belarus	17
Italy	17
Latvia	16
Taiwan	16
Estonia	16
Greece	16
Korea, South	16
Nigeria	15
Georgia	15
Denmark	15
El Salvador	15
New Zealand	15
China	14
Armenia	14
Bosnia and Herz.	14
Norway	14
Algeria	13
Puerto Rico	13
Romania	13
Jordan	12
Montenegro	12
Slovakia	12
Czech Republic	11
Zimbabwe	11
Dominican Rep.	11
Japan	10
United States	10
Poland	9
Albania	9
Vietnam	8
Croatia	8
Iceland	8
Tanzania	8
Turkey	8
Malta	7
Morocco	5
Egypt	4
Indonesia	3
Pakistan	1
Total	18

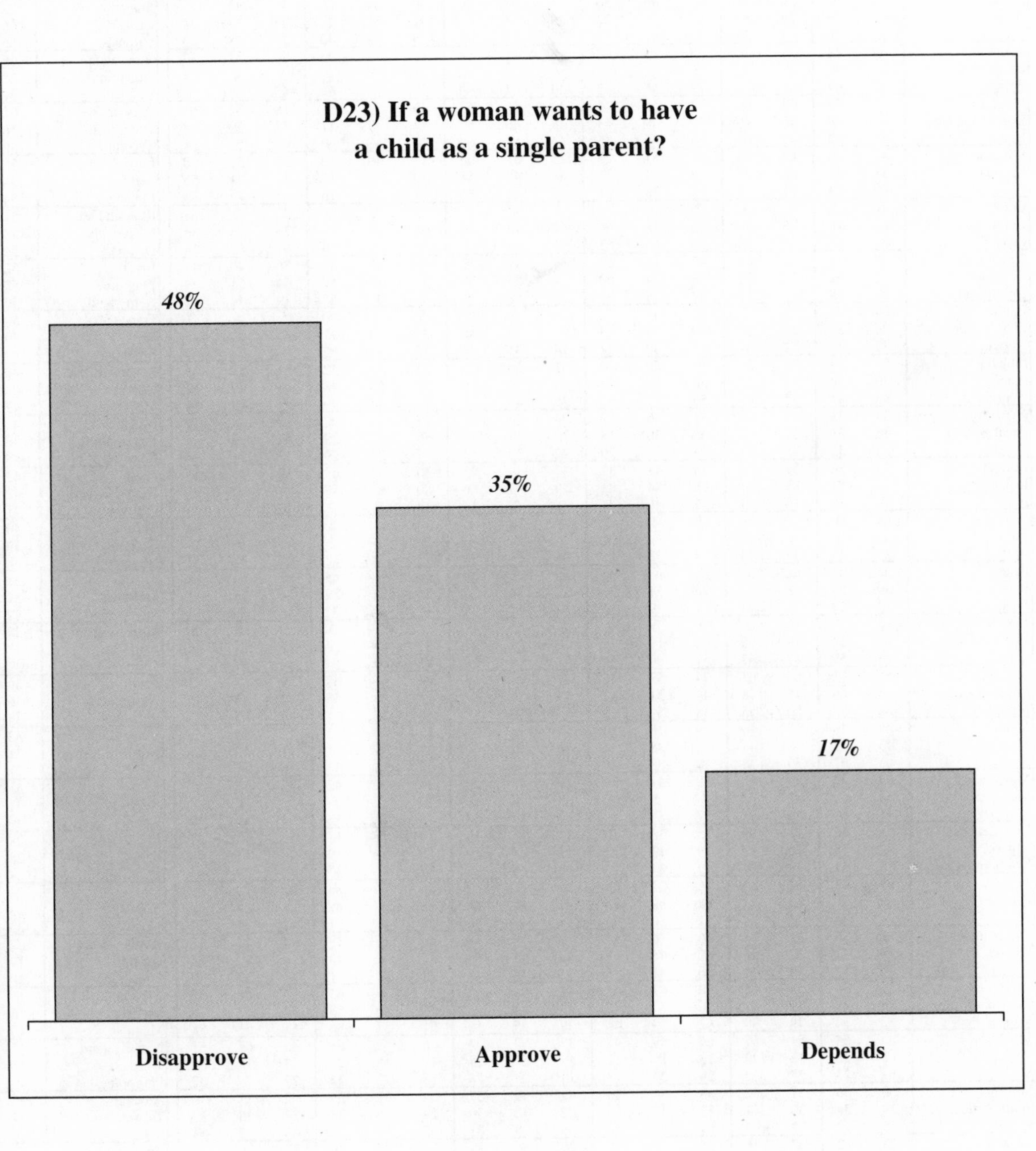
D23) If a woman wants to have
a child as a single parent?
48%
35%
17%
Disapprove
Approve
Depends

D023) WOMAN AS A SINGLE PARENT

If a woman wants to have a child as a single parent, but she doesn't want to have a stable relationship with a man, do you approve or disapprove?

Approve (%)

(WVS: V112; EVS: V151)

Country	Wave		Gender		Age			Education			Income			Values		
	1990	2000	Male	Female	16-29	30-49	50+	Lower	Middle	Upper	Lower	Middle	Upper	Mat	Mixed	Postm.
Albania	na	**12**	12	12	18	10	8	7	14	16	7	16	12	7	13	24
Algeria	na	**6**	6	7	7	4	9	8	6	6	6	4	9	5	8	5
Argentina	58	**61**	58	65	64	65	55	60	64	64	59	64	61	65	61	60
Armenia	na	**37**	36	38	35	43	30	26	36	46	40	41	26	31	43	33
Australia	na	**36**	36	37	51	36	22	29	38	41	31	37	43	27	33	44
Austria	39	**38**	42	35	42	41	34	33	43	43	35	42	40	27	38	43
Azerbaijan	na	**24**	22	26	25	25	20	16	23	28	16	23	35	20	31	37
Bangladesh	na	**4**	4	3	5	3	4	2	2	10	1	5	4	3	4	na
Belarus	47	**61**	63	59	72	65	47	49	64	69	56	63	64	55	68	67
Belgium	32	**52**	48	56	54	58	44	43	56	52	46	53	55	48	52	53
Bosnia and Herz.	na	**48**	46	49	51	49	43	35	48	57	44	47	51	44	50	48
Brazil	51	**52**	43	61	64	49	36	43	57	67	46	48	60	44	53	71
Bulgaria	47	**46**	45	48	57	61	29	25	55	65	29	49	60	38	55	50
Canada	38	**45**	46	45	52	54	31	34	48	51	40	41	56	42	41	55
Chile	60	**73**	71	75	79	78	61	68	76	76	71	74	76	67	74	85
China	6	**2**	3	1	3	1	1	3	1	5	2	2	2	1	2	na
Colombia	na	**76**	76	76	76	78	68	66	78	80	68	76	80	75	76	86
Croatia	na	**66**	63	69	70	67	63	66	67	65	66	67	66	61	65	78
Czech Republic	23	**39**	37	41	47	41	34	39	41	37	34	42	41	36	40	47
Denmark	67	**52**	52	52	53	54	50	47	57	59	53	51	57	44	51	69
Dominican Rep.	na	**48**	42	51	49	46	36	50	48	48	49	42	55	39	47	52
Egypt	na	**5**	5	5	4	6	4	5	5	5	5	5	4	5	5	3
El Salvador	na	**28**	28	29	30	30	23	23	27	46	25	29	37	na	na	na
Estonia	32	**29**	22	34	33	32	24	24	31	29	30	25	32	26	29	39
Finland	56	**54**	53	54	57	55	50	52	56	53	55	56	52	51	52	65
France	39	**50**	49	50	56	52	44	51	50	46	52	50	48	46	49	57
Georgia	na	**41**	37	45	50	41	31	36	40	48	37	41	49	39	42	54
Germany	34	**31**	29	32	44	36	19	24	36	37	27	29	29	22	33	39
Great Britain	36	**31**	31	31	42	36	18	30	29	37	39	31	29	na	na	na
Greece	na	**31**	28	33	33	34	20	22	32	31	34	29	29	27	31	38
Hungary	39	**38**	39	38	45	41	32	37	39	45	40	34	44	39	39	46
Iceland	84	**82**	82	81	78	84	82	79	83	86	80	81	87	81	80	94
India	3	**10**	10	11	12	9	9	9	7	14	14	9	9	10	11	na
Indonesia	na	**4**	4	5	7	4	3	2	4	6	3	4	5	4	5	na
Iran	na	**3**	4	3	4	3	3	3	3	4	4	2	3	3	3	4
Ireland	23	**33**	33	34	44	38	21	35	34	29	33	32	32	28	35	33
Israel	na	**na**	na	na	na	na	na	na	na	na	na	na	na	na	na	na
Italy	39	**28**	28	27	26	31	26	26	29	29	26	31	29	24	27	31
Japan	15	**23**	23	23	37	29	12	14	21	35	17	24	27	16	24	33
Jordan	na	**2**	2	3	2	2	2	2	2	3	2	2	3	2	2	5
Korea, South	na	**22**	19	25	40	19	7	4	20	27	21	20	24	17	24	46
Latvia	26	**55**	47	62	57	60	51	47	58	58	56	55	54	52	57	64
Lithuania	55	**61**	59	63	74	67	46	49	65	63	52	60	68	59	63	53
Luxembourg	na	**46**	45	46	44	51	42	43	50	43	43	41	56	42	46	53
Macedonia	na	**53**	50	55	58	59	39	47	50	68	44	53	61	49	55	65
Malta	na	**16**	17	14	20	18	10	11	17	19	11	14	17	16	15	21
Mexico	43	**47**	46	48	54	48	34	36	59	67	38	48	61	41	50	59
Moldova	na	**37**	36	38	50	38	26	28	38	44	33	33	44	36	37	47
Montenegro	na	**37**	33	41	58	41	20	19	45	60	26	39	45	32	42	53
Morocco	na	**3**	2	3	3	2	1	2	4	5	1	2	5	1	4	2
Netherlands	44	**50**	46	54	57	56	40	42	53	54	45	53	54	37	49	60
New Zealand	na	**15**	13	17	25	18	10	13	15	18	14	15	18	11	14	21
Nigeria	9	**18**	18	18	19	17	17	15	21	19	18	16	19	16	18	28
Northern Ireland	25	**31**	28	34	49	34	20	28	35	32	32	25	32	27	29	44
Norway	27	**23**	22	24	26	24	20	22	22	27	na	na	na	22	23	29
Pakistan	na	**0**	na	na	na	na	na	na	na	na	na	na	na	na	na	na
Peru	na	**49**	47	51	51	50	43	44	47	56	43	48	61	42	51	52
Philippines	na	**15**	15	14	16	14	14	13	14	18	13	13	18	14	14	17
Poland	18	**42**	37	46	42	46	37	40	46	39	42	42	40	38	42	54
Portugal	40	**37**	39	34	50	41	25	31	48	48	21	35	41	34	39	39
Puerto Rico	na	**56**	53	58	68	67	43	41	54	60	51	53	63	45	60	55
Romania	38	**49**	51	47	56	54	40	33	54	66	41	46	58	38	57	70
Russian Fed.	42	**54**	49	58	62	57	44	39	55	58	51	53	56	51	56	58
Serbia	na	**54**	51	57	60	59	47	37	57	73	46	55	65	45	63	61
Singapore	na	**18**	17	20	23	15	12	14	20	25	17	18	21	14	19	30
Slovakia	na	**23**	25	22	29	25	18	18	25	28	18	23	27	22	25	37
Slovenia	60	**56**	51	60	58	54	56	49	59	57	54	57	59	52	57	56
South Africa	19	**36**	30	44	37	41	20	32	42	39	29	46	38	34	38	37
Spain	65	**72**	72	73	84	81	58	66	79	81	65	77	79	63	75	84
Sweden	25	**32**	27	36	25	32	36	28	34	31	37	27	30	33	29	39
Switzerland	38	**37**	38	36	41	40	32	32	39	34	35	40	39	27	39	43
Taiwan	na	**11**	11	12	18	12	4	9	10	14	12	12	10	8	16	8
Tanzania	na	**15**	14	16	16	16	10	12	14	29	15	11	25	13	15	13
Turkey	7	**6**	7	6	8	6	3	2	9	20	2	6	17	3	6	13
Uganda	na	**19**	14	23	26	14	3	17	21	9	13	21	17	16	22	12
Ukraine	na	**40**	37	42	47	46	31	28	42	42	39	42	41	37	45	42
United States	38	**42**	41	42	43	45	37	52	43	37	46	43	37	47	37	52
Uruguay	na	**66**	62	68	73	70	59	61	73	68	59	70	69	57	65	76
Venezuela	na	**65**	61	68	63	69	62	58	65	71	56	67	67	67	63	71
Vietnam	na	**16**	17	15	17	18	12	18	13	20	11	19	15	10	16	12
Zimbabwe	na	**7**	6	8	9	8	3	5	10	8	7	4	14	7	8	5
Total	37	35	33	37	38	37	31	29	38	40	32	36	39	29	37	46

RANKING

Country	2000
Iceland	82
Colombia	76
Chile	73
Spain	72
Croatia	66
Uruguay	66
Venezuela	65
Argentina	61
Lithuania	61
Belarus	61
Puerto Rico	56
Slovenia	56
Latvia	55
Serbia	54
Finland	54
Russian Fed.	54
Macedonia	53
Denmark	52
Brazil	52
Belgium	52
Netherlands	50
France	50
Peru	49
Romania	49
Bosnia and Herz.	48
Dominican Rep.	48
Mexico	47
Bulgaria	46
Luxembourg	46
Canada	45
Poland	42
United States	42
Georgia	41
Ukraine	40
Czech Republic	39
Hungary	38
Austria	38
Moldova	37
Switzerland	37
Montenegro	37
Armenia	37
Portugal	37
South Africa	36
Australia	36
Ireland	33
Sweden	32
Northern Ireland	31
Great Britain	31
Greece	31
Germany	31
Estonia	29
El Salvador	28
Italy	28
Azerbaijan	24
Slovakia	23
Norway	23
Japan	23
Korea, South	22
Uganda	19
Singapore	18
Nigeria	18
Vietnam	16
Malta	16
New Zealand	15
Tanzania	15
Philippines	15
Albania	12
Taiwan	11
India	10
Zimbabwe	7
Turkey	6
Algeria	6
Egypt	5
Indonesia	4
Bangladesh	4
Iran	3
Morocco	3
Jordan	2
China	2
Pakistan	0
Total	35

D026_1) MARRIAGE HAPPINESS: LONG-TERM RELATIONSHIP

How would you feel about the following statements: "A marriage or a long-term stable relationship is necessary to be happy?"

(EVS: V153)

Agree strongly / Agree (%)

Country	Wave		Gender		Age			Education			Income			Values		
	1990	2000	Male	Female	16-29	30-49	50+	Lower	Middle	Upper	Lower	Middle	Upper	Mat	Mixed	Postm.
Albania	na	**na**	na	na	na	na	na	na	na	na	na	na	na	na	na	na
Algeria	na	**na**	na	na	na	na	na	na	na	na	na	na	na	na	na	na
Argentina	na	**na**	na	na	na	na	na	na	na	na	na	na	na	na	na	na
Armenia	na	**na**	na	na	na	na	na	na	na	na	na	na	na	na	na	na
Australia	na	**na**	na	na	na	na	na	na	na	na	na	na	na	na	na	na
Austria	na	**55**	59	51	45	47	68	62	49	46	60	56	53	68	57	48
Azerbaijan	na	**na**	na	na	na	na	na	na	na	na	na	na	na	na	na	na
Bangladesh	na	**na**	na	na	na	na	na	na	na	na	na	na	na	na	na	na
Belarus	na	**73**	73	73	65	72	80	80	70	70	74	72	73	77	70	64
Belgium	na	**55**	57	53	53	49	61	64	56	47	61	58	49	52	57	52
Bosnia and Herz.	na	**na**	na	na	na	na	na	na	na	na	na	na	na	na	na	na
Brazil	na	**na**	na	na	na	na	na	na	na	na	na	na	na	na	na	na
Bulgaria	na	**81**	79	82	65	81	89	94	74	73	90	79	75	85	78	76
Canada	na	**na**	na	na	na	na	na	na	na	na	na	na	na	na	na	na
Chile	na	**na**	na	na	na	na	na	na	na	na	na	na	na	na	na	na
China	na	**na**	na	na	na	na	na	na	na	na	na	na	na	na	na	na
Colombia	na	**na**	na	na	na	na	na	na	na	na	na	na	na	na	na	na
Croatia	na	**69**	64	73	58	69	76	77	64	65	77	69	65	72	69	66
Czech Republic	na	**69**	72	67	60	67	77	71	68	65	73	70	66	75	68	67
Denmark	na	**36**	39	32	34	28	44	42	32	24	42	35	27	51	36	24
Dominican Rep.	na	**na**	na	na	na	na	na	na	na	na	na	na	na	na	na	na
Egypt	na	**na**	na	na	na	na	na	na	na	na	na	na	na	na	na	na
El Salvador	na	**na**	na	na	na	na	na	na	na	na	na	na	na	na	na	na
Estonia	na	**75**	75	76	68	72	83	78	74	75	74	77	75	78	75	59
Finland	na	**36**	39	33	29	30	46	42	30	25	37	35	35	42	36	30
France	na	**65**	66	65	61	61	72	68	60	64	67	66	67	72	65	55
Georgia	na	**na**	na	na	na	na	na	na	na	na	na	na	na	na	na	na
Germany	na	**63**	66	61	45	60	74	70	58	55	65	68	67	81	61	48
Great Britain	na	**37**	42	33	28	28	51	42	32	31	40	39	26	na	na	na
Greece	na	**85**	84	85	87	82	84	92	81	86	87	82	86	84	84	88
Hungary	na	**90**	89	90	84	89	94	90	88	95	91	90	90	91	89	83
Iceland	na	**36**	44	27	30	32	45	41	34	26	40	33	33	41	35	28
India	na	**na**	na	na	na	na	na	na	na	na	na	na	na	na	na	na
Indonesia	na	**na**	na	na	na	na	na	na	na	na	na	na	na	na	na	na
Iran	na	**na**	na	na	na	na	na	na	na	na	na	na	na	na	na	na
Ireland	na	**37**	43	32	29	31	49	48	35	24	45	41	31	42	37	33
Israel	na	**na**	na	na	na	na	na	na	na	na	na	na	na	na	na	na
Italy	na	**63**	63	63	53	60	72	68	62	52	67	63	59	73	64	56
Japan	na	**na**	na	na	na	na	na	na	na	na	na	na	na	na	na	na
Jordan	na	**na**	na	na	na	na	na	na	na	na	na	na	na	na	na	na
Korea, South	na	**na**	na	na	na	na	na	na	na	na	na	na	na	na	na	na
Latvia	na	**82**	83	80	66	79	90	87	79	84	82	83	81	83	80	80
Lithuania	na	**71**	68	73	62	73	75	74	69	73	75	69	71	72	71	66
Luxembourg	na	**60**	59	60	58	56	64	62	60	55	59	60	48	64	58	57
Macedonia	na	**na**	na	na	na	na	na	na	na	na	na	na	na	na	na	na
Malta	na	**65**	67	62	58	64	70	72	63	57	65	64	68	73	61	54
Mexico	na	**na**	na	na	na	na	na	na	na	na	na	na	na	na	na	na
Moldova	na	**na**	na	na	na	na	na	na	na	na	na	na	na	na	na	na
Montenegro	na	**na**	na	na	na	na	na	na	na	na	na	na	na	na	na	na
Morocco	na	**na**	na	na	na	na	na	na	na	na	na	na	na	na	na	na
Netherlands	na	**21**	26	16	20	15	27	25	19	20	23	19	22	32	20	18
New Zealand	na	**na**	na	na	na	na	na	na	na	na	na	na	na	na	na	na
Nigeria	na	**na**	na	na	na	na	na	na	na	na	na	na	na	na	na	na
Northern Ireland	na	**34**	35	33	24	31	41	40	30	25	41	31	22	42	34	22
Norway	na	**na**	na	na	na	na	na	na	na	na	na	na	na	na	na	na
Pakistan	na	**na**	na	na	na	na	na	na	na	na	na	na	na	na	na	na
Peru	na	**na**	na	na	na	na	na	na	na	na	na	na	na	na	na	na
Philippines	na	**na**	na	na	na	na	na	na	na	na	na	na	na	na	na	na
Poland	na	**72**	75	69	62	69	82	76	70	60	74	73	66	72	72	63
Portugal	na	**70**	67	73	55	71	79	75	62	48	75	68	67	72	69	60
Puerto Rico	na	**na**	na	na	na	na	na	na	na	na	na	na	na	na	na	na
Romania	na	**84**	85	84	75	81	92	93	79	80	90	84	80	89	81	70
Russian Fed.	na	**74**	72	76	64	72	82	81	74	68	74	74	73	77	72	63
Serbia	na	**na**	na	na	na	na	na	na	na	na	na	na	na	na	na	na
Singapore	na	**na**	na	na	na	na	na	na	na	na	na	na	na	na	na	na
Slovakia	na	**77**	74	80	75	77	80	78	77	72	74	79	81	78	78	69
Slovenia	na	**82**	78	86	80	80	86	88	81	77	86	85	78	84	83	78
South Africa	na	**na**	na	na	na	na	na	na	na	na	na	na	na	na	na	na
Spain	na	**54**	52	55	45	48	64	66	46	41	61	56	49	65	55	40
Sweden	na	**42**	51	32	42	36	47	55	41	33	41	44	40	40	44	36
Switzerland	na	**na**	na	na	na	na	na	na	na	na	na	na	na	na	na	na
Taiwan	na	**na**	na	na	na	na	na	na	na	na	na	na	na	na	na	na
Tanzania	na	**na**	na	na	na	na	na	na	na	na	na	na	na	na	na	na
Turkey	na	**77**	77	76	74	78	80	80	75	58	83	75	69	80	75	74
Uganda	na	**na**	na	na	na	na	na	na	na	na	na	na	na	na	na	na
Ukraine	na	**78**	75	80	66	78	84	84	77	76	82	76	75	79	77	75
United States	na	**na**	na	na	na	na	na	na	na	na	na	na	na	na	na	na
Uruguay	na	**na**	na	na	na	na	na	na	na	na	na	na	na	na	na	na
Venezuela	na	**na**	na	na	na	na	na	na	na	na	na	na	na	na	na	na
Vietnam	na	**na**	na	na	na	na	na	na	na	na	na	na	na	na	na	na
Zimbabwe	na	**na**	na	na	na	na	na	na	na	na	na	na	na	na	na	na
Total	na	**62**	63	62	56	59	70	66	62	56	66	63	61	73	61	51

RANKING	
Country	2000
Hungary	90
Greece	85
Romania	84
Slovenia	82
Latvia	82
Bulgaria	81
Ukraine	78
Slovakia	77
Turkey	77
Estonia	75
Russian Fed.	74
Belarus	73
Poland	72
Lithuania	71
Portugal	70
Czech Republic	69
Croatia	69
France	65
Malta	65
Germany	63
Italy	63
Luxembourg	60
Belgium	55
Austria	55
Spain	54
Sweden	42
Ireland	37
Great Britain	37
Finland	36
Denmark	36
Iceland	36
Northern Ireland	34
Netherlands	21
Total	62

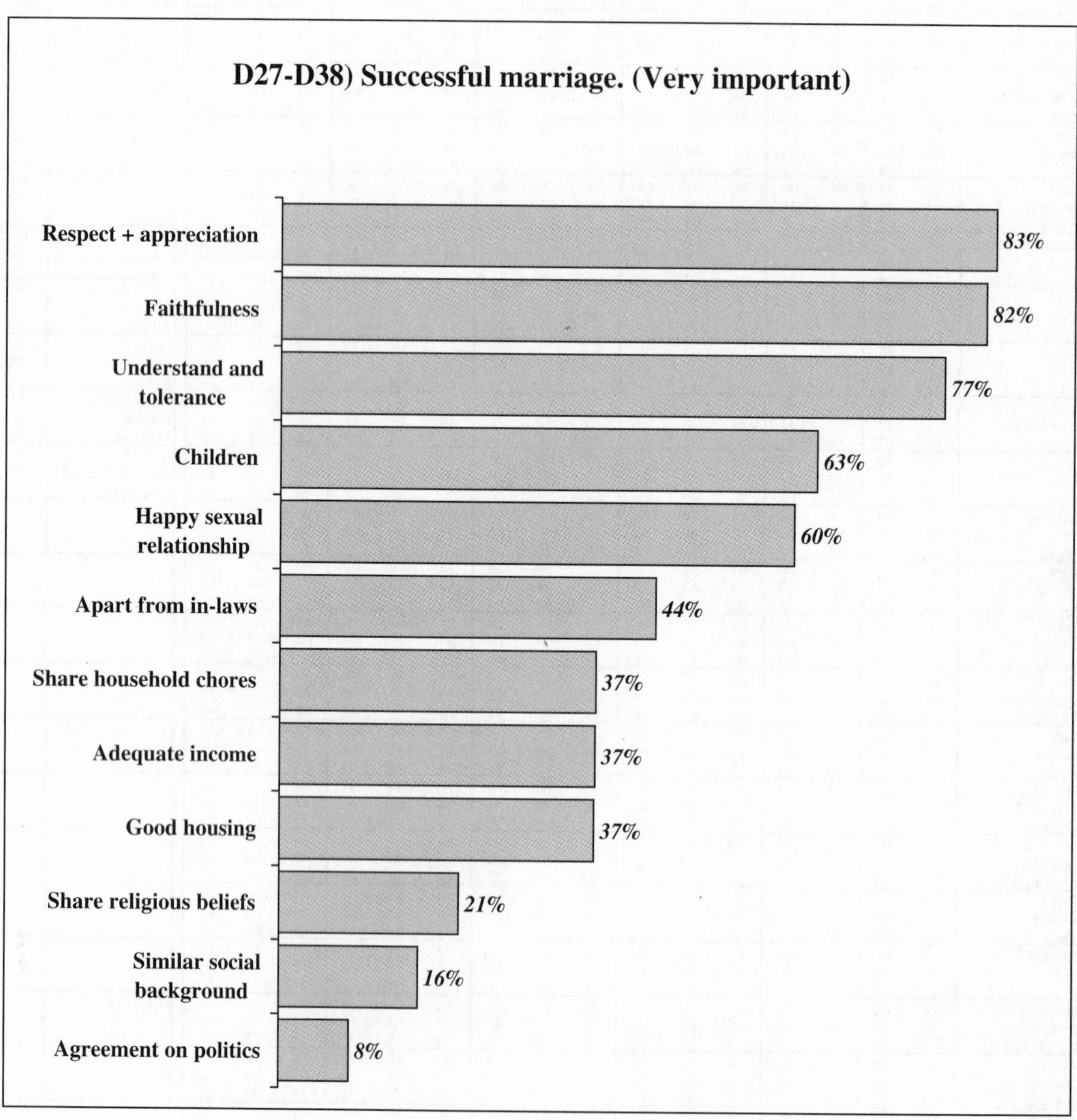
D27-D38) Successful marriage. (Very important)
Respect + appreciation
83%
Faithfulness
82%
Understand and tolerance
77%
Children
63%
Happy sexual relationship
60%
Apart from in-laws
44%
Share household chores
37%
Adequate income
37%
Good housing
37%
Share religious beliefs
21%
Similar social background
16%
Agreement on politics
8%

D027_1) MARRIAGE SUCCESS: FAITHFULNESS

Here is a list of things which some people think make for a successful marriage. Please tell me, for each one, whether you think it is...

Very important (%)

(EVS: V133)

Country	Wave		Gender		Age			Education			Income			Values		
	1990	2000	Male	Female	16-29	30-49	50+	Lower	Middle	Upper	Lower	Middle	Upper	Mat	Mixed	Postm.
Albania	na	**na**	na	na	na	na	na	na	na	na	na	na	na	na	na	na
Algeria	na	**na**	na	na	na	na	na	na	na	na	na	na	na	na	na	na
Argentina	85	**na**	na	na	na	na	na	na	na	na	na	na	na	na	na	na
Armenia	na	**na**	na	na	na	na	na	na	na	na	na	na	na	na	na	na
Australia	na	**na**	na	na	na	na	na	na	na	na	na	na	na	na	na	na
Austria	83	**86**	84	88	88	84	88	92	84	73	87	90	83	91	88	81
Azerbaijan	na	**na**	na	na	na	na	na	na	na	na	na	na	na	na	na	na
Bangladesh	na	**na**	na	na	na	na	na	na	na	na	na	na	na	na	na	na
Belarus	79	**70**	63	75	67	69	73	70	70	69	73	68	65	72	67	58
Belgium	85	**89**	88	91	93	87	89	91	90	87	87	91	88	94	88	86
Bosnia and Herz.	na	**na**	na	na	na	na	na	na	na	na	na	na	na	na	na	na
Brazil	76	**na**	na	na	na	na	na	na	na	na	na	na	na	na	na	na
Bulgaria	63	**74**	70	77	63	71	81	83	72	60	81	72	67	80	68	65
Canada	91	**na**	na	na	na	na	na	na	na	na	na	na	na	na	na	na
Chile	92	**na**	na	na	na	na	na	na	na	na	na	na	na	na	na	na
China	90	**na**	na	na	na	na	na	na	na	na	na	na	na	na	na	na
Colombia	na	**na**	na	na	na	na	na	na	na	na	na	na	na	na	na	na
Croatia	na	**72**	67	77	73	72	71	72	72	72	74	68	77	72	74	70
Czech Republic	na	**73**	71	76	78	70	73	79	68	64	76	76	68	82	72	65
Denmark	81	**84**	82	86	91	83	83	89	83	74	85	85	78	89	86	72
Dominican Rep.	na	**na**	na	na	na	na	na	na	na	na	na	na	na	na	na	na
Egypt	na	**na**	na	na	na	na	na	na	na	na	na	na	na	na	na	na
El Salvador	na	**na**	na	na	na	na	na	na	na	na	na	na	na	na	na	na
Estonia	61	**61**	57	65	57	58	67	63	61	60	64	66	58	64	59	66
Finland	75	**82**	78	85	86	81	81	82	82	79	87	79	79	80	84	76
France	74	**80**	77	83	83	78	81	85	77	72	83	80	79	88	81	70
Georgia	na	**na**	na	na	na	na	na	na	na	na	na	na	na	na	na	na
Germany	78	**85**	80	88	78	83	89	87	82	83	85	84	83	91	84	77
Great Britain	90	**90**	87	93	86	89	92	92	88	88	92	88	91	na	na	na
Greece	na	**87**	85	88	90	82	91	94	86	86	86	85	89	88	86	86
Hungary	84	**85**	80	90	85	80	90	86	85	81	80	86	88	88	84	79
Iceland	90	**96**	94	98	98	97	93	97	96	95	96	97	96	96	97	88
India	94	**na**	na	na	na	na	na	na	na	na	na	na	na	na	na	na
Indonesia	na	**na**	na	na	na	na	na	na	na	na	na	na	na	na	na	na
Iran	na	**na**	na	na	na	na	na	na	na	na	na	na	na	na	na	na
Ireland	93	**95**	95	96	94	95	97	97	94	96	95	97	95	97	96	91
Israel	na	**na**	na	na	na	na	na	na	na	na	na	na	na	na	na	na
Italy	85	**84**	80	88	85	84	84	87	85	74	85	84	80	91	84	81
Japan	73	**na**	na	na	na	na	na	na	na	na	na	na	na	na	na	na
Jordan	na	**na**	na	na	na	na	na	na	na	na	na	na	na	na	na	na
Korea, South	90	**na**	na	na	na	na	na	na	na	na	na	na	na	na	na	na
Latvia	74	**78**	72	84	75	77	81	80	79	72	80	79	76	79	78	72
Lithuania	70	**65**	55	73	62	61	70	67	64	64	74	66	62	68	64	60
Luxembourg	na	**88**	85	90	88	85	90	92	84	89	89	84	86	88	88	82
Macedonia	na	**na**	na	na	na	na	na	na	na	na	na	na	na	na	na	na
Malta	na	**97**	95	99	98	95	99	98	97	94	98	96	96	97	97	99
Mexico	81	**na**	na	na	na	na	na	na	na	na	na	na	na	na	na	na
Moldova	na	**na**	na	na	na	na	na	na	na	na	na	na	na	na	na	na
Montenegro	na	**na**	na	na	na	na	na	na	na	na	na	na	na	na	na	na
Morocco	na	**na**	na	na	na	na	na	na	na	na	na	na	na	na	na	na
Netherlands	88	**87**	87	88	90	83	90	89	90	83	84	88	89	90	88	84
New Zealand	na	**na**	na	na	na	na	na	na	na	na	na	na	na	na	na	na
Nigeria	99	**na**	na	na	na	na	na	na	na	na	na	na	na	na	na	na
Northern Ireland	94	**94**	94	94	96	91	97	94	94	93	96	95	95	97	94	87
Norway	91	**na**	na	na	na	na	na	na	na	na	na	na	na	na	na	na
Pakistan	na	**na**	na	na	na	na	na	na	na	na	na	na	na	na	na	na
Peru	na	**na**	na	na	na	na	na	na	na	na	na	na	na	na	na	na
Philippines	na	**na**	na	na	na	na	na	na	na	na	na	na	na	na	na	na
Poland	na	**87**	85	89	91	86	86	88	88	78	88	88	86	89	85	86
Portugal	77	**74**	72	76	80	71	73	73	75	78	68	73	85	71	78	75
Puerto Rico	na	**na**	na	na	na	na	na	na	na	na	na	na	na	na	na	na
Romania	77	**83**	82	83	81	82	85	81	85	81	79	86	85	86	81	80
Russian Fed.	77	**72**	68	75	63	71	78	79	73	65	75	75	65	75	70	58
Serbia	na	**na**	na	na	na	na	na	na	na	na	na	na	na	na	na	na
Singapore	na	**na**	na	na	na	na	na	na	na	na	na	na	na	na	na	na
Slovakia	na	**81**	75	86	80	81	82	81	82	71	83	81	82	83	80	71
Slovenia	80	**81**	79	83	83	79	82	85	81	71	82	87	73	81	82	80
South Africa	na	**na**	na	na	na	na	na	na	na	na	na	na	na	na	na	na
Spain	79	**80**	76	83	72	76	87	85	76	75	82	82	76	86	79	71
Sweden	89	**89**	88	89	91	87	89	93	88	86	91	88	87	91	91	82
Switzerland	81	**na**	na	na	na	na	na	na	na	na	na	na	na	na	na	na
Taiwan	na	**na**	na	na	na	na	na	na	na	na	na	na	na	na	na	na
Tanzania	na	**na**	na	na	na	na	na	na	na	na	na	na	na	na	na	na
Turkey	87	**96**	96	96	96	95	97	95	97	95	95	97	96	96	96	97
Uganda	na	**na**	na	na	na	na	na	na	na	na	na	na	na	na	na	na
Ukraine	na	**79**	74	84	71	79	85	87	81	73	86	78	74	79	79	82
United States	94	**na**	na	na	na	na	na	na	na	na	na	na	na	na	na	na
Uruguay	na	**na**	na	na	na	na	na	na	na	na	na	na	na	na	na	na
Venezuela	na	**na**	na	na	na	na	na	na	na	na	na	na	na	na	na	na
Vietnam	na	**na**	na	na	na	na	na	na	na	na	na	na	na	na	na	na
Zimbabwe	na	**na**	na	na	na	na	na	na	na	na	na	na	na	na	na	na
Total	82	**82**	79	85	82	80	84	85	81	79	84	82	80	83	82	79

RANKING	
Country	2000
Malta	97
Iceland	96
Turkey	96
Ireland	95
Northern Ireland	94
Great Britain	90
Belgium	89
Sweden	89
Luxembourg	88
Netherlands	87
Poland	87
Greece	87
Austria	86
Hungary	85
Germany	85
Denmark	84
Italy	84
Romania	83
Finland	82
Slovenia	81
Slovakia	81
France	80
Spain	80
Ukraine	79
Latvia	78
Portugal	74
Bulgaria	74
Czech Republic	73
Croatia	72
Russian Fed.	72
Belarus	70
Lithuania	65
Estonia	61
Total	82

D028_1) MARRIAGE SUCCESS: ADEQUATE INCOME

Here is a list of things which some people think make for a successful marriage. Please tell me, for each one, whether you think it is...

Very important (%)

(EVS: V134)

Country	Wave		Gender		Age			Education			Income			Values		
	1990	2000	Male	Female	16-29	30-49	50+	Lower	Middle	Upper	Lower	Middle	Upper	Mat	Mixed	Postm.
Albania	na	**na**	na	na	na	na	na	na	na	na	na	na	na	na	na	na
Algeria	na	**na**	na	na	na	na	na	na	na	na	na	na	na	na	na	na
Argentina	44	**na**	na	na	na	na	na	na	na	na	na	na	na	na	na	na
Armenia	na	**na**	na	na	na	na	na	na	na	na	na	na	na	na	na	na
Australia	na	**na**	na	na	na	na	na	na	na	na	na	na	na	na	na	na
Austria	30	**28**	29	27	25	20	37	34	24	16	32	30	22	44	31	17
Azerbaijan	na	**na**	na	na	na	na	na	na	na	na	na	na	na	na	na	na
Bangladesh	na	**na**	na	na	na	na	na	na	na	na	na	na	na	na	na	na
Belarus	66	**38**	41	36	35	43	36	40	38	38	42	37	35	41	35	40
Belgium	45	**40**	42	38	32	32	51	53	39	31	48	42	30	50	40	26
Bosnia and Herz.	na	**na**	na	na	na	na	na	na	na	na	na	na	na	na	na	na
Brazil	55	**na**	na	na	na	na	na	na	na	na	na	na	na	na	na	na
Bulgaria	45	**51**	53	50	53	52	50	50	56	45	55	47	50	56	47	53
Canada	40	**na**	na	na	na	na	na	na	na	na	na	na	na	na	na	na
Chile	67	**na**	na	na	na	na	na	na	na	na	na	na	na	na	na	na
China	31	**na**	na	na	na	na	na	na	na	na	na	na	na	na	na	na
Colombia	na	**na**	na	na	na	na	na	na	na	na	na	na	na	na	na	na
Croatia	na	**23**	26	19	20	21	27	26	22	15	27	22	22	25	22	25
Czech Republic	na	**36**	35	38	32	35	39	42	33	18	39	35	34	46	34	25
Denmark	11	**5**	6	4	4	3	7	6	3	4	6	4	3	10	4	4
Dominican Rep.	na	**na**	na	na	na	na	na	na	na	na	na	na	na	na	na	na
Egypt	na	**na**	na	na	na	na	na	na	na	na	na	na	na	na	na	na
El Salvador	na	**na**	na	na	na	na	na	na	na	na	na	na	na	na	na	na
Estonia	30	**29**	31	27	33	31	24	28	30	25	31	26	28	29	30	23
Finland	32	**17**	17	16	13	14	21	22	9	13	22	16	12	25	14	14
France	38	**36**	38	34	32	32	42	42	32	23	40	37	32	45	36	23
Georgia	na	**na**	na	na	na	na	na	na	na	na	na	na	na	na	na	na
Germany	28	**26**	29	24	23	26	29	29	25	21	29	29	26	36	26	15
Great Britain	35	**35**	36	33	33	33	35	37	33	30	38	39	32	na	na	na
Greece	na	**54**	55	54	48	59	60	73	58	47	61	53	49	57	55	53
Hungary	52	**58**	58	59	57	58	59	61	55	46	68	56	55	61	57	42
Iceland	40	**31**	33	30	16	33	41	38	26	26	33	30	31	37	29	29
India	59	**na**	na	na	na	na	na	na	na	na	na	na	na	na	na	na
Indonesia	na	**na**	na	na	na	na	na	na	na	na	na	na	na	na	na	na
Iran	na	**na**	na	na	na	na	na	na	na	na	na	na	na	na	na	na
Ireland	52	**45**	47	44	33	41	59	55	44	33	55	44	37	48	45	39
Israel	na	**na**	na	na	na	na	na	na	na	na	na	na	na	na	na	na
Italy	32	**29**	30	28	25	28	33	35	26	21	34	31	22	37	30	24
Japan	55	**na**	na	na	na	na	na	na	na	na	na	na	na	na	na	na
Jordan	na	**na**	na	na	na	na	na	na	na	na	na	na	na	na	na	na
Korea, South	34	**na**	na	na	na	na	na	na	na	na	na	na	na	na	na	na
Latvia	35	**36**	37	35	42	37	33	39	38	26	40	36	29	39	34	24
Lithuania	36	**42**	45	40	43	43	41	40	45	35	41	47	42	45	41	35
Luxembourg	na	**26**	29	22	21	22	33	34	22	19	29	29	19	31	26	16
Macedonia	na	**na**	na	na	na	na	na	na	na	na	na	na	na	na	na	na
Malta	na	**40**	44	36	37	41	40	42	40	31	40	39	38	39	40	36
Mexico	55	**na**	na	na	na	na	na	na	na	na	na	na	na	na	na	na
Moldova	na	**na**	na	na	na	na	na	na	na	na	na	na	na	na	na	na
Montenegro	na	**na**	na	na	na	na	na	na	na	na	na	na	na	na	na	na
Morocco	na	**na**	na	na	na	na	na	na	na	na	na	na	na	na	na	na
Netherlands	24	**23**	21	24	14	19	30	36	18	15	29	21	18	43	22	15
New Zealand	na	**na**	na	na	na	na	na	na	na	na	na	na	na	na	na	na
Nigeria	75	**na**	na	na	na	na	na	na	na	na	na	na	na	na	na	na
Northern Ireland	40	**34**	38	31	26	33	39	40	26	37	42	33	26	34	35	30
Norway	21	**na**	na	na	na	na	na	na	na	na	na	na	na	na	na	na
Pakistan	na	**na**	na	na	na	na	na	na	na	na	na	na	na	na	na	na
Peru	na	**na**	na	na	na	na	na	na	na	na	na	na	na	na	na	na
Philippines	na	**na**	na	na	na	na	na	na	na	na	na	na	na	na	na	na
Poland	na	**45**	45	45	37	43	52	51	40	33	54	41	37	47	46	34
Portugal	49	**36**	34	38	38	35	34	39	34	15	39	35	37	32	37	34
Puerto Rico	na	**na**	na	na	na	na	na	na	na	na	na	na	na	na	na	na
Romania	45	**54**	56	53	52	54	56	54	55	54	52	58	54	52	57	57
Russian Fed.	54	**54**	55	53	53	57	51	55	56	46	54	55	51	55	53	52
Serbia	na	**na**	na	na	na	na	na	na	na	na	na	na	na	na	na	na
Singapore	na	**na**	na	na	na	na	na	na	na	na	na	na	na	na	na	na
Slovakia	na	**47**	49	45	45	50	45	50	47	37	48	51	43	52	46	31
Slovenia	40	**30**	30	30	18	32	37	41	29	13	39	30	19	37	29	28
South Africa	na	**na**	na	na	na	na	na	na	na	na	na	na	na	na	na	na
Spain	46	**34**	36	32	27	33	38	39	32	25	37	35	33	48	31	26
Sweden	23	**19**	21	17	12	18	24	28	17	14	18	20	18	44	20	9
Switzerland	35	**na**	na	na	na	na	na	na	na	na	na	na	na	na	na	na
Taiwan	na	**na**	na	na	na	na	na	na	na	na	na	na	na	na	na	na
Tanzania	na	**na**	na	na	na	na	na	na	na	na	na	na	na	na	na	na
Turkey	58	**84**	86	82	81	86	90	85	84	75	84	85	83	82	85	87
Uganda	na	**na**	na	na	na	na	na	na	na	na	na	na	na	na	na	na
Ukraine	na	**66**	69	64	61	70	65	70	67	60	71	63	64	69	66	42
United States	46	**na**	na	na	na	na	na	na	na	na	na	na	na	na	na	na
Uruguay	na	**na**	na	na	na	na	na	na	na	na	na	na	na	na	na	na
Venezuela	na	**na**	na	na	na	na	na	na	na	na	na	na	na	na	na	na
Vietnam	na	**na**	na	na	na	na	na	na	na	na	na	na	na	na	na	na
Zimbabwe	na	**na**	na	na	na	na	na	na	na	na	na	na	na	na	na	na
Total	42	**37**	38	36	34	36	39	40	37	31	41	37	34	45	35	26

RANKING

Country	2000
Turkey	84
Ukraine	66
Hungary	58
Romania	54
Greece	54
Russian Fed.	54
Bulgaria	51
Slovakia	47
Ireland	45
Poland	45
Lithuania	42
Belgium	40
Malta	40
Belarus	38
Latvia	36
Czech Republic	36
France	36
Portugal	36
Great Britain	35
Northern Ireland	34
Spain	34
Iceland	31
Slovenia	30
Italy	29
Estonia	29
Austria	28
Germany	26
Luxembourg	26
Croatia	23
Netherlands	23
Sweden	19
Finland	17
Denmark	5
Total	37

D029_1) MARRIAGE SUCCESS: SAME SOCIAL BACKGROUND

Here is a list of things which some people think make for a successful marriage. Please tell me, for each one, whether you think it is...

Very important (%)

(EVS: V135)

Country	Wave		Gender		Age			Education			Income			Values		
	1990	2000	Male	Female	16-29	30-49	50+	Lower	Middle	Upper	Lower	Middle	Upper	Mat	Mixed	Postm.
Albania	na	**na**	na	na	na	na	na	na	na	na	na	na	na	na	na	na
Algeria	na	**na**	na	na	na	na	na	na	na	na	na	na	na	na	na	na
Argentina	26	**na**	na	na	na	na	na	na	na	na	na	na	na	na	na	na
Armenia	na	**na**	na	na	na	na	na	na	na	na	na	na	na	na	na	na
Australia	na	**na**	na	na	na	na	na	na	na	na	na	na	na	na	na	na
Austria	15	**13**	13	13	10	10	18	16	11	7	19	12	9	27	13	9
Azerbaijan	na	**na**	na	na	na	na	na	na	na	na	na	na	na	na	na	na
Bangladesh	na	**na**	na	na	na	na	na	na	na	na	na	na	na	na	na	na
Belarus	16	**11**	11	11	10	11	12	10	11	13	14	10	11	10	10	22
Belgium	22	**21**	18	23	9	14	32	25	20	18	26	21	15	18	23	14
Bosnia and Herz.	na	**na**	na	na	na	na	na	na	na	na	na	na	na	na	na	na
Brazil	28	**na**	na	na	na	na	na	na	na	na	na	na	na	na	na	na
Bulgaria	18	**30**	32	28	32	34	26	27	32	29	30	27	30	29	31	29
Canada	20	**na**	na	na	na	na	na	na	na	na	na	na	na	na	na	na
Chile	34	**na**	na	na	na	na	na	na	na	na	na	na	na	na	na	na
China	13	**na**	na	na	na	na	na	na	na	na	na	na	na	na	na	na
Colombia	na	**na**	na	na	na	na	na	na	na	na	na	na	na	na	na	na
Croatia	na	**7**	10	4	5	5	10	6	8	6	4	7	8	5	8	4
Czech Republic	na	**7**	5	9	4	5	11	9	5	4	11	5	5	10	6	7
Denmark	12	**6**	7	6	3	3	11	8	2	6	9	6	4	8	7	3
Dominican Rep.	na	**na**	na	na	na	na	na	na	na	na	na	na	na	na	na	na
Egypt	na	**na**	na	na	na	na	na	na	na	na	na	na	na	na	na	na
El Salvador	na	**na**	na	na	na	na	na	na	na	na	na	na	na	na	na	na
Estonia	8	**8**	8	9	5	10	9	9	8	10	8	10	7	7	9	13
Finland	8	**9**	6	12	6	7	13	11	4	12	11	9	8	11	8	9
France	21	**16**	17	16	11	12	23	17	18	12	18	15	14	19	17	9
Georgia	na	**na**	na	na	na	na	na	na	na	na	na	na	na	na	na	na
Germany	7	**14**	13	15	11	14	16	17	13	9	18	14	16	19	14	9
Great Britain	21	**18**	19	17	12	15	24	20	17	13	19	16	17	na	na	na
Greece	na	**21**	17	24	14	21	37	34	22	18	20	20	22	25	22	13
Hungary	16	**15**	13	16	11	11	21	17	11	12	16	18	12	17	13	25
Iceland	14	**7**	6	8	5	6	9	6	7	8	8	6	8	9	6	6
India	47	**na**	na	na	na	na	na	na	na	na	na	na	na	na	na	na
Indonesia	na	**na**	na	na	na	na	na	na	na	na	na	na	na	na	na	na
Iran	na	**na**	na	na	na	na	na	na	na	na	na	na	na	na	na	na
Ireland	25	**27**	25	29	11	25	41	37	24	16	37	24	21	32	26	21
Israel	na	**na**	na	na	na	na	na	na	na	na	na	na	na	na	na	na
Italy	17	**13**	11	14	7	10	18	17	9	9	17	12	8	19	13	7
Japan	23	**na**	na	na	na	na	na	na	na	na	na	na	na	na	na	na
Jordan	na	**na**	na	na	na	na	na	na	na	na	na	na	na	na	na	na
Korea, South	22	**na**	na	na	na	na	na	na	na	na	na	na	na	na	na	na
Latvia	12	**15**	15	15	15	12	18	18	15	11	17	16	12	17	14	9
Lithuania	8	**12**	12	12	13	12	11	11	12	13	11	9	13	8	12	18
Luxembourg	na	**15**	15	15	12	14	18	17	14	12	20	13	14	16	16	13
Macedonia	na	**na**	na	na	na	na	na	na	na	na	na	na	na	na	na	na
Malta	na	**51**	49	53	43	52	56	59	50	38	55	52	44	51	52	43
Mexico	30	**na**	na	na	na	na	na	na	na	na	na	na	na	na	na	na
Moldova	na	**na**	na	na	na	na	na	na	na	na	na	na	na	na	na	na
Montenegro	na	**na**	na	na	na	na	na	na	na	na	na	na	na	na	na	na
Morocco	na	**na**	na	na	na	na	na	na	na	na	na	na	na	na	na	na
Netherlands	21	**15**	13	16	7	10	23	18	12	14	16	13	15	21	15	10
New Zealand	na	**na**	na	na	na	na	na	na	na	na	na	na	na	na	na	na
Nigeria	49	**na**	na	na	na	na	na	na	na	na	na	na	na	na	na	na
Northern Ireland	21	**23**	22	24	14	21	28	26	19	20	23	18	13	27	23	18
Norway	14	**na**	na	na	na	na	na	na	na	na	na	na	na	na	na	na
Pakistan	na	**na**	na	na	na	na	na	na	na	na	na	na	na	na	na	na
Peru	na	**na**	na	na	na	na	na	na	na	na	na	na	na	na	na	na
Philippines	na	**na**	na	na	na	na	na	na	na	na	na	na	na	na	na	na
Poland	na	**17**	18	17	10	13	28	22	12	9	19	18	12	19	17	16
Portugal	26	**14**	15	13	13	18	11	14	16	7	16	16	13	8	18	7
Puerto Rico	na	**na**	na	na	na	na	na	na	na	na	na	na	na	na	na	na
Romania	25	**28**	28	29	19	26	36	33	27	24	29	31	26	32	28	12
Russian Fed.	9	**10**	9	10	8	9	11	14	10	7	12	10	7	10	9	11
Serbia	na	**na**	na	na	na	na	na	na	na	na	na	na	na	na	na	na
Singapore	na	**na**	na	na	na	na	na	na	na	na	na	na	na	na	na	na
Slovakia	na	**16**	15	16	12	15	20	20	14	15	22	13	14	17	15	10
Slovenia	24	**15**	13	17	7	14	20	25	11	11	20	15	9	14	15	16
South Africa	na	**na**	na	na	na	na	na	na	na	na	na	na	na	na	na	na
Spain	25	**17**	17	18	10	15	24	23	12	15	18	20	18	26	16	12
Sweden	12	**8**	6	9	2	5	13	6	7	9	8	7	8	12	7	8
Switzerland	16	**na**	na	na	na	na	na	na	na	na	na	na	na	na	na	na
Taiwan	na	**na**	na	na	na	na	na	na	na	na	na	na	na	na	na	na
Tanzania	na	**na**	na	na	na	na	na	na	na	na	na	na	na	na	na	na
Turkey	47	**65**	63	67	62	67	68	69	60	60	68	64	61	64	67	63
Uganda	na	**na**	na	na	na	na	na	na	na	na	na	na	na	na	na	na
Ukraine	na	**16**	14	16	8	16	19	23	13	18	16	14	17	15	15	23
United States	29	**na**	na	na	na	na	na	na	na	na	na	na	na	na	na	na
Uruguay	na	**na**	na	na	na	na	na	na	na	na	na	na	na	na	na	na
Venezuela	na	**na**	na	na	na	na	na	na	na	na	na	na	na	na	na	na
Vietnam	na	**na**	na	na	na	na	na	na	na	na	na	na	na	na	na	na
Zimbabwe	na	**na**	na	na	na	na	na	na	na	na	na	na	na	na	na	na
Total	21	**16**	16	17	12	15	21	18	16	15	19	15	14	18	16	12

RANKING

Country	2000
Turkey	65
Malta	51
Bulgaria	30
Romania	28
Ireland	27
Northern Ireland	23
Greece	21
Belgium	21
Great Britain	18
Poland	17
Spain	17
France	16
Slovakia	16
Ukraine	16
Luxembourg	15
Latvia	15
Hungary	15
Slovenia	15
Netherlands	15
Germany	14
Portugal	14
Austria	13
Italy	13
Lithuania	12
Belarus	11
Russian Fed.	10
Finland	9
Estonia	8
Sweden	8
Croatia	7
Czech Republic	7
Iceland	7
Denmark	6
Total	16

D030_1) MARRIAGE SUCCESS: RESPECT + APPRECIATION

Here is a list of things which some people think make for a successful marriage. Please teil me, for each one, whether you think it is...

Very important (%)

(EVS: V136)

Country	Wave		Gender		Age			Education			Income			Values		
	1990	2000	Male	Female	16-29	30-49	50+	Lower	Middle	Upper	Lower	Middle	Upper	Mat	Mixed	Postm.
Albania	na	**na**	na	na	na	na	na	na	na	na	na	na	na	na	na	na
Algeria	na	**na**	na	na	na	na	na	na	na	na	na	na	na	na	na	na
Argentina	90	**na**	na	na	na	na	na	na	na	na	na	na	na	na	na	na
Armenia	na	**na**	na	na	na	na	na	na	na	na	na	na	na	na	na	na
Australia	na	**na**	na	na	na	na	na	na	na	na	na	na	na	na	na	na
Austria	82	**89**	87	91	88	91	88	89	88	94	84	90	92	86	91	87
Azerbaijan	na	**na**	na	na	na	na	na	na	na	na	na	na	na	na	na	na
Bangladesh	na	**na**	na	na	na	na	na	na	na	na	na	na	na	na	na	na
Belarus	85	**76**	68	83	81	75	73	69	78	82	78	73	80	75	77	80
Belgium	87	**91**	90	92	93	90	90	86	91	93	90	88	93	88	91	94
Bosnia and Herz.	na	**na**	na	na	na	na	na	na	na	na	na	na	na	na	na	na
Brazil	73	**na**	na	na	na	na	na	na	na	na	na	na	na	na	na	na
Bulgaria	68	**81**	79	82	76	80	84	83	79	80	83	78	79	81	80	87
Canada	92	**na**	na	na	na	na	na	na	na	na	na	na	na	na	na	na
Chile	96	**na**	na	na	na	na	na	na	na	na	na	na	na	na	na	na
China	82	**na**	na	na	na	na	na	na	na	na	na	na	na	na	na	na
Colombia	na	**na**	na	na	na	na	na	na	na	na	na	na	na	na	na	na
Croatia	na	**74**	69	79	77	76	71	75	74	75	76	71	80	69	74	80
Czech Republic	na	**87**	84	91	85	87	89	84	90	94	84	88	90	85	88	93
Denmark	83	**85**	80	89	91	87	79	81	89	90	81	84	92	75	85	91
Dominican Rep.	na	**na**	na	na	na	na	na	na	na	na	na	na	na	na	na	na
Egypt	na	**na**	na	na	na	na	na	na	na	na	na	na	na	na	na	na
El Salvador	na	**na**	na	na	na	na	na	na	na	na	na	na	na	na	na	na
Estonia	74	**71**	64	77	67	73	72	65	72	77	68	73	71	72	72	61
Finland	83	**86**	83	88	86	88	82	82	89	94	85	88	85	83	87	88
France	84	**89**	88	91	90	89	90	88	91	91	91	89	86	89	89	90
Georgia	na	**na**	na	na	na	na	na	na	na	na	na	na	na	na	na	na
Germany	78	**81**	78	83	76	84	79	75	84	90	75	80	87	81	80	82
Great Britain	84	**81**	83	79	81	79	83	79	83	82	80	79	81	na	na	na
Greece	na	**94**	92	96	95	92	95	93	93	95	95	92	96	94	95	92
Hungary	90	**87**	83	90	85	87	88	83	93	93	79	90	89	86	89	76
Iceland	96	**97**	95	98	97	97	95	97	96	97	96	97	97	98	96	94
India	80	**na**	na	na	na	na	na	na	na	na	na	na	na	na	na	na
Indonesia	na	**na**	na	na	na	na	na	na	na	na	na	na	na	na	na	na
Iran	na	**na**	na	na	na	na	na	na	na	na	na	na	na	na	na	na
Ireland	83	**87**	84	90	80	90	89	85	86	94	88	84	89	87	87	88
Israel	na	**na**	na	na	na	na	na	na	na	na	na	na	na	na	na	na
Italy	90	**90**	88	92	94	90	89	88	93	92	87	89	93	87	91	92
Japan	74	**na**	na	na	na	na	na	na	na	na	na	na	na	na	na	na
Jordan	na	**na**	na	na	na	na	na	na	na	na	na	na	na	na	na	na
Korea, South	68	**na**	na	na	na	na	na	na	na	na	na	na	na	na	na	na
Latvia	74	**75**	74	77	79	75	74	71	77	76	73	77	77	73	77	67
Lithuania	65	**53**	48	56	52	51	54	47	52	67	50	52	59	47	54	57
Luxembourg	na	**84**	83	85	81	83	87	81	83	91	75	88	89	79	84	88
Macedonia	na	**na**	na	na	na	na	na	na	na	na	na	na	na	na	na	na
Malta	na	**97**	97	97	97	97	97	95	97	100	95	99	99	94	98	99
Mexico	88	**na**	na	na	na	na	na	na	na	na	na	na	na	na	na	na
Moldova	na	**na**	na	na	na	na	na	na	na	na	na	na	na	na	na	na
Montenegro	na	**na**	na	na	na	na	na	na	na	na	na	na	na	na	na	na
Morocco	na	**na**	na	na	na	na	na	na	na	na	na	na	na	na	na	na
Netherlands	93	**95**	94	95	96	97	92	93	95	96	95	93	97	96	95	93
New Zealand	na	**na**	na	na	na	na	na	na	na	na	na	na	na	na	na	na
Nigeria	97	**na**	na	na	na	na	na	na	na	na	na	na	na	na	na	na
Northern Ireland	83	**84**	84	84	79	83	88	85	84	80	87	80	84	88	84	82
Norway	93	**na**	na	na	na	na	na	na	na	na	na	na	na	na	na	na
Pakistan	na	**na**	na	na	na	na	na	na	na	na	na	na	na	na	na	na
Peru	na	**na**	na	na	na	na	na	na	na	na	na	na	na	na	na	na
Philippines	na	**na**	na	na	na	na	na	na	na	na	na	na	na	na	na	na
Poland	na	**88**	84	90	89	86	88	85	91	89	87	88	88	88	88	89
Portugal	83	**66**	66	67	80	60	62	63	70	80	61	64	75	61	71	64
Puerto Rico	na	**na**	na	na	na	na	na	na	na	na	na	na	na	na	na	na
Romania	82	**76**	78	75	81	75	75	69	80	82	65	80	82	75	79	83
Russian Fed.	78	**68**	65	71	67	71	66	65	68	72	66	68	70	67	70	64
Serbia	na	**na**	na	na	na	na	na	na	na	na	na	na	na	na	na	na
Singapore	na	**na**	na	na	na	na	na	na	na	na	na	na	na	na	na	na
Slovakia	na	**81**	76	86	81	79	84	80	81	89	81	80	84	82	81	79
Slovenia	87	**89**	87	91	89	90	89	88	89	91	89	90	91	88	89	91
South Africa	na	**na**	na	na	na	na	na	na	na	na	na	na	na	na	na	na
Spain	78	**79**	77	81	83	79	77	76	80	85	77	85	80	79	78	85
Sweden	91	**94**	92	96	96	94	93	89	94	97	93	93	95	94	93	97
Switzerland	90	**na**	na	na	na	na	na	na	na	na	na	na	na	na	na	na
Taiwan	na	**na**	na	na	na	na	na	na	na	na	na	na	na	na	na	na
Tanzania	na	**na**	na	na	na	na	na	na	na	na	na	na	na	na	na	na
Turkey	89	**95**	96	95	96	95	96	93	99	96	93	97	97	96	96	98
Uganda	na	**na**	na	na	na	na	na	na	na	na	na	na	na	na	na	na
Ukraine	na	**84**	82	86	83	82	87	83	84	85	89	81	81	82	87	84
United States	92	**na**	na	na	na	na	na	na	na	na	na	na	na	na	na	na
Uruguay	na	**na**	na	na	na	na	na	na	na	na	na	na	na	na	na	na
Venezuela	na	**na**	na	na	na	na	na	na	na	na	na	na	na	na	na	na
Vietnam	na	**na**	na	na	na	na	na	na	na	na	na	na	na	na	na	na
Zimbabwe	na	**na**	na	na	na	na	na	na	na	na	na	na	na	na	na	na
Total	84	**83**	81	85	84	83	83	81	83	88	82	83	85	80	85	88

RANKING	
Country	2000
Malta	97
Iceland	97
Turkey	95
Netherlands	95
Greece	94
Sweden	94
Belgium	91
Italy	90
France	89
Slovenia	89
Austria	89
Poland	88
Czech Republic	87
Ireland	87
Hungary	87
Finland	86
Denmark	85
Ukraine	84
Luxembourg	84
Northern Ireland	84
Slovakia	81
Bulgaria	81
Germany	81
Great Britain	81
Spain	79
Romania	76
Belarus	76
Latvia	75
Croatia	74
Estonia	71
Russian Fed.	68
Portugal	66
Lithuania	53
Total	83

D031_1) MARRIAGE SUCCESS: SHARE RELIGIOUS BELIEFS

Here is a list of things which some people think make for a successful marriage. Please tell me, for each one, whether you think it is...

Very important (%)

(EVS: V137)

Country	Wave		Gender		Age			Education			Income			Values		
	1990	2000	Male	Female	16-29	30-49	50+	Lower	Middle	Upper	Lower	Middle	Upper	Mat	Mixed	Postm.
Albania	na	**na**	na	na	na	na	na	na	na	na	na	na	na	na	na	na
Algeria	na	**na**	na	na	na	na	na	na	na	na	na	na	na	na	na	na
Argentina	28	**na**	na	na	na	na	na	na	na	na	na	na	na	na	na	na
Armenia	na	**na**	na	na	na	na	na	na	na	na	na	na	na	na	na	na
Australia	na	**na**	na	na	na	na	na	na	na	na	na	na	na	na	na	na
Austria	23	**19**	16	22	12	16	26	24	15	12	27	19	13	33	20	13
Azerbaijan	na	**na**	na	na	na	na	na	na	na	na	na	na	na	na	na	na
Bangladesh	na	**na**	na	na	na	na	na	na	na	na	na	na	na	na	na	na
Belarus	14	**14**	8	19	8	11	22	22	12	8	18	13	9	16	12	4
Belgium	22	**18**	17	20	14	13	26	28	16	14	27	19	12	21	18	15
Bosnia and Herz.	na	**na**	na	na	na	na	na	na	na	na	na	na	na	na	na	na
Brazil	35	**na**	na	na	na	na	na	na	na	na	na	na	na	na	na	na
Bulgaria	14	**27**	25	28	21	24	32	37	22	17	36	21	21	29	24	22
Canada	28	**na**	na	na	na	na	na	na	na	na	na	na	na	na	na	na
Chile	52	**na**	na	na	na	na	na	na	na	na	na	na	na	na	na	na
China	6	**na**	na	na	na	na	na	na	na	na	na	na	na	na	na	na
Colombia	na	**na**	na	na	na	na	na	na	na	na	na	na	na	na	na	na
Croatia	na	**28**	28	28	19	26	36	32	26	24	36	30	22	39	29	13
Czech Republic	na	**9**	6	10	4	7	12	11	6	8	12	6	7	10	8	9
Denmark	16	**13**	14	12	10	10	18	16	10	8	13	12	12	19	13	11
Dominican Rep.	na	**na**	na	na	na	na	na	na	na	na	na	na	na	na	na	na
Egypt	na	**na**	na	na	na	na	na	na	na	na	na	na	na	na	na	na
El Salvador	na	**na**	na	na	na	na	na	na	na	na	na	na	na	na	na	na
Estonia	8	**11**	10	12	13	9	13	14	10	9	12	12	10	10	11	8
Finland	13	**15**	12	18	9	13	20	18	11	14	18	18	10	16	15	15
France	17	**13**	11	14	9	11	17	15	8	12	14	14	11	14	15	8
Georgia	na	**na**	na	na	na	na	na	na	na	na	na	na	na	na	na	na
Germany	16	**15**	13	17	10	12	20	19	11	10	18	15	17	17	15	11
Great Britain	19	**14**	14	13	10	13	16	13	15	14	16	13	13	na	na	na
Greece	na	**33**	26	38	24	31	55	57	39	23	36	29	32	36	33	25
Hungary	22	**15**	10	20	4	11	25	18	9	13	22	16	10	18	13	na
Iceland	18	**10**	9	11	4	7	19	14	8	8	13	10	8	11	10	6
India	40	**na**	na	na	na	na	na	na	na	na	na	na	na	na	na	na
Indonesia	na	**na**	na	na	na	na	na	na	na	na	na	na	na	na	na	na
Iran	na	**na**	na	na	na	na	na	na	na	na	na	na	na	na	na	na
Ireland	33	**26**	24	28	8	22	44	43	20	11	44	25	15	33	25	24
Israel	na	**na**	na	na	na	na	na	na	na	na	na	na	na	na	na	na
Italy	26	**23**	20	26	16	18	33	34	17	12	32	20	16	38	24	14
Japan	18	**na**	na	na	na	na	na	na	na	na	na	na	na	na	na	na
Jordan	na	**na**	na	na	na	na	na	na	na	na	na	na	na	na	na	na
Korea, South	21	**na**	na	na	na	na	na	na	na	na	na	na	na	na	na	na
Latvia	9	**11**	9	13	8	7	15	18	9	10	15	9	7	10	11	7
Lithuania	14	**16**	15	16	11	11	24	25	12	14	27	13	11	20	14	9
Luxembourg	na	**15**	16	14	11	12	21	22	12	11	20	11	13	19	16	7
Macedonia	na	**na**	na	na	na	na	na	na	na	na	na	na	na	na	na	na
Malta	na	**56**	50	62	39	54	70	73	53	31	66	56	49	58	57	37
Mexico	50	**na**	na	na	na	na	na	na	na	na	na	na	na	na	na	na
Moldova	na	**na**	na	na	na	na	na	na	na	na	na	na	na	na	na	na
Montenegro	na	**na**	na	na	na	na	na	na	na	na	na	na	na	na	na	na
Morocco	na	**na**	na	na	na	na	na	na	na	na	na	na	na	na	na	na
Netherlands	16	**11**	10	12	7	5	20	18	10	7	17	7	10	19	11	6
New Zealand	na	**na**	na	na	na	na	na	na	na	na	na	na	na	na	na	na
Nigeria	83	**na**	na	na	na	na	na	na	na	na	na	na	na	na	na	na
Northern Ireland	37	**33**	33	32	24	25	44	41	24	31	37	28	20	42	32	26
Norway	24	**na**	na	na	na	na	na	na	na	na	na	na	na	na	na	na
Pakistan	na	**na**	na	na	na	na	na	na	na	na	na	na	na	na	na	na
Peru	na	**na**	na	na	na	na	na	na	na	na	na	na	na	na	na	na
Philippines	na	**na**	na	na	na	na	na	na	na	na	na	na	na	na	na	na
Poland	na	**40**	38	41	31	33	52	47	33	25	45	39	29	44	38	33
Portugal	34	**20**	20	19	11	21	24	23	15	7	29	23	16	14	25	7
Puerto Rico	na	**na**	na	na	na	na	na	na	na	na	na	na	na	na	na	na
Romania	31	**41**	38	43	29	36	52	51	37	30	46	43	37	45	40	19
Russian Fed.	11	**12**	9	14	7	12	14	18	11	10	15	11	9	12	11	5
Serbia	na	**na**	na	na	na	na	na	na	na	na	na	na	na	na	na	na
Singapore	na	**na**	na	na	na	na	na	na	na	na	na	na	na	na	na	na
Slovakia	na	**26**	19	32	17	21	39	36	21	20	36	23	21	30	22	14
Slovenia	34	**20**	18	22	9	20	29	37	16	7	31	17	11	27	19	20
South Africa	na	**na**	na	na	na	na	na	na	na	na	na	na	na	na	na	na
Spain	29	**21**	17	24	8	17	31	31	13	13	25	18	12	35	18	9
Sweden	18	**13**	9	17	8	11	18	17	10	14	15	13	11	19	14	7
Switzerland	21	**na**	na	na	na	na	na	na	na	na	na	na	na	na	na	na
Taiwan	na	**na**	na	na	na	na	na	na	na	na	na	na	na	na	na	na
Tanzania	na	**na**	na	na	na	na	na	na	na	na	na	na	na	na	na	na
Turkey	68	**74**	70	77	70	74	84	84	63	44	83	74	54	79	76	63
Uganda	na	**na**	na	na	na	na	na	na	na	na	na	na	na	na	na	na
Ukraine	na	**24**	20	28	18	22	30	37	23	20	29	21	21	23	23	42
United States	44	**na**	na	na	na	na	na	na	na	na	na	na	na	na	na	na
Uruguay	na	**na**	na	na	na	na	na	na	na	na	na	na	na	na	na	na
Venezuela	na	**na**	na	na	na	na	na	na	na	na	na	na	na	na	na	na
Vietnam	na	**na**	na	na	na	na	na	na	na	na	na	na	na	na	na	na
Zimbabwe	na	**na**	na	na	na	na	na	na	na	na	na	na	na	na	na	na
Total	26	**21**	19	23	15	18	28	27	19	17	27	20	16	25	21	15

RANKING	
Country	**2000**
Turkey	74
Malta	56
Romania	41
Poland	40
Northern Ireland	33
Greece	33
Croatia	28
Bulgaria	27
Ireland	26
Slovakia	26
Ukraine	24
Italy	23
Spain	21
Slovenia	20
Portugal	20
Austria	19
Belgium	18
Lithuania	16
Finland	15
Hungary	15
Luxembourg	15
Germany	15
Belarus	14
Great Britain	14
France	13
Sweden	13
Denmark	13
Russian Fed.	12
Netherlands	11
Estonia	11
Latvia	11
Iceland	10
Czech Republic	9
Total	21

D032_1) MARRIAGE SUCCESS: GOOD HOUSING

Here is a list of things which some people think make for a successful marriage. Please tell me, for each one, whether you think it is...

Very important (%)

(EVS: V138)

Country	Wave		Gender		Age			Education			Income			Values		
	1990	2000	Male	Female	16-29	30-49	50+	Lower	Middle	Upper	Lower	Middle	Upper	Mat	Mixed	Postm.
Albania	na	**na**	na	na	na	na	na	na	na	na	na	na	na	na	na	na
Algeria	na	**na**	na	na	na	na	na	na	na	na	na	na	na	na	na	na
Argentina	40	**na**	na	na	na	na	na	na	na	na	na	na	na	na	na	na
Armenia	na	**na**	na	na	na	na	na	na	na	na	na	na	na	na	na	na
Australia	na	**na**	na	na	na	na	na	na	na	na	na	na	na	na	na	na
Austria	40	**33**	31	35	31	28	40	39	30	19	35	35	30	54	34	27
Azerbaijan	na	**na**	na	na	na	na	na	na	na	na	na	na	na	na	na	na
Bangladesh	na	**na**	na	na	na	na	na	na	na	na	na	na	na	na	na	na
Belarus	61	**48**	45	50	46	56	39	37	51	54	48	46	50	47	48	53
Belgium	39	**41**	41	41	41	32	49	58	39	32	51	45	30	51	41	29
Bosnia and Herz.	na	**na**	na	na	na	na	na	na	na	na	na	na	na	na	na	na
Brazil	47	**na**	na	na	na	na	na	na	na	na	na	na	na	na	na	na
Bulgaria	43	**45**	43	46	44	45	45	42	50	38	47	43	45	46	45	60
Canada	33	**na**	na	na	na	na	na	na	na	na	na	na	na	na	na	na
Chile	61	**na**	na	na	na	na	na	na	na	na	na	na	na	na	na	na
China	25	**na**	na	na	na	na	na	na	na	na	na	na	na	na	na	na
Colombia	na	**na**	na	na	na	na	na	na	na	na	na	na	na	na	na	na
Croatia	na	**18**	20	17	15	17	21	18	20	13	23	19	14	22	17	16
Czech Republic	na	**41**	41	40	35	39	44	49	32	26	45	40	37	50	39	26
Denmark	30	**18**	18	19	12	11	29	24	8	12	24	16	12	25	20	11
Dominican Rep.	na	**na**	na	na	na	na	na	na	na	na	na	na	na	na	na	na
Egypt	na	**na**	na	na	na	na	na	na	na	na	na	na	na	na	na	na
El Salvador	na	**na**	na	na	na	na	na	na	na	na	na	na	na	na	na	na
Estonia	35	**26**	25	26	29	23	26	29	27	18	26	25	24	26	27	23
Finland	22	**18**	16	20	12	13	26	23	10	13	26	17	10	26	16	15
France	37	**36**	37	36	34	36	37	41	34	25	37	38	32	43	36	27
Georgia	na	**na**	na	na	na	na	na	na	na	na	na	na	na	na	na	na
Germany	41	**26**	25	27	17	26	30	30	23	19	31	28	23	32	27	16
Great Britain	37	**39**	41	36	38	36	41	45	37	24	44	45	36	na	na	na
Greece	na	**60**	53	64	57	59	70	72	63	54	63	54	60	63	60	54
Hungary	51	**60**	61	59	57	57	64	62	60	48	65	58	59	59	63	62
Iceland	33	**26**	27	24	18	21	38	34	21	15	30	24	22	28	25	19
India	41	**na**	na	na	na	na	na	na	na	na	na	na	na	na	na	na
Indonesia	na	**na**	na	na	na	na	na	na	na	na	na	na	na	na	na	na
Iran	na	**na**	na	na	na	na	na	na	na	na	na	na	na	na	na	na
Ireland	46	**47**	47	47	31	44	62	64	43	26	58	49	36	50	47	39
Israel	na	**na**	na	na	na	na	na	na	na	na	na	na	na	na	na	na
Italy	25	**20**	18	22	17	15	27	28	16	11	28	16	13	29	22	12
Japan	35	**na**	na	na	na	na	na	na	na	na	na	na	na	na	na	na
Jordan	na	**na**	na	na	na	na	na	na	na	na	na	na	na	na	na	na
Korea, South	7	**na**	na	na	na	na	na	na	na	na	na	na	na	na	na	na
Latvia	45	**30**	29	30	33	26	31	33	30	24	34	31	23	31	29	31
Lithuania	33	**27**	28	26	31	22	29	27	28	21	30	26	27	29	26	26
Luxembourg	na	**28**	30	27	26	25	34	35	26	24	34	32	20	29	30	20
Macedonia	na	**na**	na	na	na	na	na	na	na	na	na	na	na	na	na	na
Malta	na	**38**	39	38	34	38	41	43	38	27	44	41	37	39	39	32
Mexico	44	**na**	na	na	na	na	na	na	na	na	na	na	na	na	na	na
Moldova	na	**na**	na	na	na	na	na	na	na	na	na	na	na	na	na	na
Montenegro	na	**na**	na	na	na	na	na	na	na	na	na	na	na	na	na	na
Morocco	na	**na**	na	na	na	na	na	na	na	na	na	na	na	na	na	na
Netherlands	33	**26**	26	26	17	19	37	44	19	16	36	24	14	44	25	21
New Zealand	na	**na**	na	na	na	na	na	na	na	na	na	na	na	na	na	na
Nigeria	74	**na**	na	na	na	na	na	na	na	na	na	na	na	na	na	na
Northern Ireland	36	**36**	38	34	28	31	44	44	28	31	44	34	24	41	34	36
Norway	23	**na**	na	na	na	na	na	na	na	na	na	na	na	na	na	na
Pakistan	na	**na**	na	na	na	na	na	na	na	na	na	na	na	na	na	na
Peru	na	**na**	na	na	na	na	na	na	na	na	na	na	na	na	na	na
Philippines	na	**na**	na	na	na	na	na	na	na	na	na	na	na	na	na	na
Poland	na	**52**	52	53	42	50	61	57	47	45	57	50	46	53	53	46
Portugal	52	**35**	35	34	39	31	35	36	35	23	41	36	32	28	39	31
Puerto Rico	na	**na**	na	na	na	na	na	na	na	na	na	na	na	na	na	na
Romania	51	**51**	54	48	50	49	53	50	52	50	47	53	53	52	52	40
Russian Fed.	51	**45**	44	45	44	46	44	46	48	35	46	44	42	45	45	33
Serbia	na	**na**	na	na	na	na	na	na	na	na	na	na	na	na	na	na
Singapore	na	**na**	na	na	na	na	na	na	na	na	na	na	na	na	na	na
Slovakia	na	**49**	49	48	49	49	48	50	49	38	47	49	48	52	47	39
Slovenia	39	**30**	29	31	20	29	39	42	28	19	40	29	18	38	29	28
South Africa	na	**na**	na	na	na	na	na	na	na	na	na	na	na	na	na	na
Spain	40	**31**	32	30	28	28	35	36	28	22	34	30	33	37	31	22
Sweden	39	**29**	31	27	18	25	39	42	25	24	30	31	24	49	30	20
Switzerland	34	**na**	na	na	na	na	na	na	na	na	na	na	na	na	na	na
Taiwan	na	**na**	na	na	na	na	na	na	na	na	na	na	na	na	na	na
Tanzania	na	**na**	na	na	na	na	na	na	na	na	na	na	na	na	na	na
Turkey	50	**62**	62	61	56	67	68	69	56	40	69	62	50	61	63	61
Uganda	na	**na**	na	na	na	na	na	na	na	na	na	na	na	na	na	na
Ukraine	na	**62**	62	62	57	63	63	68	64	55	68	57	62	65	63	48
United States	40	**na**	na	na	na	na	na	na	na	na	na	na	na	na	na	na
Uruguay	na	**na**	na	na	na	na	na	na	na	na	na	na	na	na	na	na
Venezuela	na	**na**	na	na	na	na	na	na	na	na	na	na	na	na	na	na
Vietnam	na	**na**	na	na	na	na	na	na	na	na	na	na	na	na	na	na
Zimbabwe	na	**na**	na	na	na	na	na	na	na	na	na	na	na	na	na	na
Total	40	**37**	37	37	34	34	41	40	36	32	42	37	33	43	36	27

RANKING	
Country	**2000**
Ukraine	62
Turkey	62
Hungary	60
Greece	60
Poland	52
Romania	51
Slovakia	49
Belarus	48
Ireland	47
Bulgaria	45
Russian Fed.	45
Belgium	41
Czech Republic	41
Great Britain	39
Malta	38
France	36
Northern Ireland	36
Portugal	35
Austria	33
Spain	31
Slovenia	30
Latvia	30
Sweden	29
Luxembourg	28
Lithuania	27
Germany	26
Estonia	26
Netherlands	26
Iceland	26
Italy	20
Denmark	18
Croatia	18
Finland	18
Total	37

D033_1) MARRIAGE SUCCESS: AGREEMENT IN POLITICS

Here is a list of things which some people think make for a successful marriage. Please tell me, for each one, whether you think it is...

(EVS: V139)

Very important (%)

Country	Wave		Gender		Age			Education			Income			Values		
	1990	2000	Male	Female	16-29	30-49	50+	Lower	Middle	Upper	Lower	Middle	Upper	Mat	Mixed	Postm.
Albania	na	na	na	na	na	na	na	na	na	na	na	na	na	na	na	na
Algeria	na	na	na	na	na	na	na	na	na	na	na	na	na	na	na	na
Argentina	8	na	na	na	na	na	na	na	na	na	na	na	na	na	na	na
Armenia	na	na	na	na	na	na	na	na	na	na	na	na	na	na	na	na
Australia	na	na	na	na	na	na	na	na	na	na	na	na	na	na	na	na
Austria	8	6	5	6	4	4	8	5	6	8	8	6	4	9	6	5
Azerbaijan	na	na	na	na	na	na	na	na	na	na	na	na	na	na	na	na
Bangladesh	na	na	na	na	na	na	na	na	na	na	na	na	na	na	na	na
Belarus	9	5	4	6	3	5	7	8	4	7	6	4	6	6	5	6
Belgium	9	7	6	7	4	4	10	11	6	4	10	6	4	7	7	5
Bosnia and Herz.	na	na	na	na	na	na	na	na	na	na	na	na	na	na	na	na
Brazil	13	na	na	na	na	na	na	na	na	na	na	na	na	na	na	na
Bulgaria	15	15	13	17	9	16	18	19	13	14	19	13	12	14	16	5
Canada	6	na	na	na	na	na	na	na	na	na	na	na	na	na	na	na
Chile	18	na	na	na	na	na	na	na	na	na	na	na	na	na	na	na
China	24	na	na	na	na	na	na	na	na	na	na	na	na	na	na	na
Colombia	na	na	na	na	na	na	na	na	na	na	na	na	na	na	na	na
Croatia	na	4	6	2	2	2	7	4	4	3	4	3	5	4	3	5
Czech Republic	na	6	5	7	3	2	10	7	4	4	7	6	4	5	6	7
Denmark	4	2	2	1	1	1	3	3	na	1	1	2	1	na	2	1
Dominican Rep.	na	na	na	na	na	na	na	na	na	na	na	na	na	na	na	na
Egypt	na	na	na	na	na	na	na	na	na	na	na	na	na	na	na	na
El Salvador	na	na	na	na	na	na	na	na	na	na	na	na	na	na	na	na
Estonia	6	5	5	5	3	4	7	5	4	7	5	6	3	5	4	8
Finland	5	4	3	5	2	2	7	6	1	4	6	4	4	5	4	2
France	8	8	7	8	8	6	9	7	9	8	7	7	9	8	7	9
Georgia	na	na	na	na	na	na	na	na	na	na	na	na	na	na	na	na
Germany	12	10	10	10	8	8	13	11	9	11	12	9	12	12	11	7
Great Britain	7	7	8	6	4	6	8	8	5	4	11	5	4	na	na	na
Greece	na	14	13	15	9	11	30	29	13	12	13	14	16	15	13	13
Hungary	11	7	6	9	5	6	10	8	6	10	8	8	7	7	8	5
Iceland	5	2	2	2	2	1	4	3	1	1	3	1	1	3	2	1
India	12	na	na	na	na	na	na	na	na	na	na	na	na	na	na	na
Indonesia	na	na	na	na	na	na	na	na	na	na	na	na	na	na	na	na
Iran	na	na	na	na	na	na	na	na	na	na	na	na	na	na	na	na
Ireland	4	7	5	8	4	6	11	11	5	3	10	8	3	9	7	3
Israel	na	na	na	na	na	na	na	na	na	na	na	na	na	na	na	na
Italy	10	7	7	7	6	5	10	10	6	5	9	8	5	9	7	5
Japan	8	na	na	na	na	na	na	na	na	na	na	na	na	na	na	na
Jordan	na	na	na	na	na	na	na	na	na	na	na	na	na	na	na	na
Korea, South	10	na	na	na	na	na	na	na	na	na	na	na	na	na	na	na
Latvia	13	7	8	6	2	6	9	8	5	8	9	5	5	6	6	9
Lithuania	8	8	8	7	7	6	9	10	7	6	13	6	6	7	7	6
Luxembourg	na	8	8	7	8	6	9	9	7	7	9	7	5	8	8	6
Macedonia	na	na	na	na	na	na	na	na	na	na	na	na	na	na	na	na
Malta	na	24	21	27	16	21	32	33	21	15	30	23	15	26	24	11
Mexico	18	na	na	na	na	na	na	na	na	na	na	na	na	na	na	na
Moldova	na	na	na	na	na	na	na	na	na	na	na	na	na	na	na	na
Montenegro	na	na	na	na	na	na	na	na	na	na	na	na	na	na	na	na
Morocco	na	na	na	na	na	na	na	na	na	na	na	na	na	na	na	na
Netherlands	7	4	3	5	1	2	7	5	4	3	5	3	3	4	4	3
New Zealand	na	na	na	na	na	na	na	na	na	na	na	na	na	na	na	na
Nigeria	20	na	na	na	na	na	na	na	na	na	na	na	na	na	na	na
Northern Ireland	10	13	14	11	13	10	14	15	9	12	13	9	7	14	12	7
Norway	7	na	na	na	na	na	na	na	na	na	na	na	na	na	na	na
Pakistan	na	na	na	na	na	na	na	na	na	na	na	na	na	na	na	na
Peru	na	na	na	na	na	na	na	na	na	na	na	na	na	na	na	na
Philippines	na	na	na	na	na	na	na	na	na	na	na	na	na	na	na	na
Poland	na	13	14	12	10	9	20	15	12	7	16	13	8	15	13	9
Portugal	15	9	9	10	10	8	9	9	11	6	10	9	13	7	12	4
Puerto Rico	na	na	na	na	na	na	na	na	na	na	na	na	na	na	na	na
Romania	7	15	16	15	11	14	20	18	15	11	14	21	13	17	14	10
Russian Fed.	8	3	3	3	1	4	3	2	3	3	3	2	3	2	4	6
Serbia	na	na	na	na	na	na	na	na	na	na	na	na	na	na	na	na
Singapore	na	na	na	na	na	na	na	na	na	na	na	na	na	na	na	na
Slovakia	na	8	7	9	6	8	11	8	9	8	9	8	9	8	9	8
Slovenia	14	6	5	7	2	7	9	12	4	3	8	5	3	5	6	8
South Africa	na	na	na	na	na	na	na	na	na	na	na	na	na	na	na	na
Spain	15	10	10	10	6	9	14	15	7	6	12	10	11	15	9	8
Sweden	10	6	4	8	2	6	8	9	5	4	7	6	5	9	6	6
Switzerland	9	na	na	na	na	na	na	na	na	na	na	na	na	na	na	na
Taiwan	na	na	na	na	na	na	na	na	na	na	na	na	na	na	na	na
Tanzania	na	na	na	na	na	na	na	na	na	na	na	na	na	na	na	na
Turkey	35	49	49	48	45	51	54	53	42	42	54	48	42	38	51	53
Uganda	na	na	na	na	na	na	na	na	na	na	na	na	na	na	na	na
Ukraine	na	10	10	9	4	9	13	13	10	7	11	9	9	9	9	17
United States	12	na	na	na	na	na	na	na	na	na	na	na	na	na	na	na
Uruguay	na	na	na	na	na	na	na	na	na	na	na	na	na	na	na	na
Venezuela	na	na	na	na	na	na	na	na	na	na	na	na	na	na	na	na
Vietnam	na	na	na	na	na	na	na	na	na	na	na	na	na	na	na	na
Zimbabwe	na	na	na	na	na	na	na	na	na	na	na	na	na	na	na	na
Total	11	8	8	9	6	7	11	10	8	7	10	8	7	9	8	7

RANKING	
Country	2000
Turkey	49
Malta	24
Romania	15
Bulgaria	15
Greece	14
Poland	13
Northern Ireland	13
Spain	10
Germany	10
Ukraine	10
Portugal	9
Slovakia	8
France	8
Lithuania	8
Luxembourg	8
Hungary	7
Italy	7
Ireland	7
Belgium	7
Great Britain	7
Latvia	7
Slovenia	6
Sweden	6
Czech Republic	6
Austria	6
Belarus	5
Estonia	5
Finland	4
Netherlands	4
Croatia	4
Russian Fed.	3
Iceland	2
Denmark	2
Total	8

D034_1) MARRIAGE SUCCESS: E10698UNDERSTAND AND TOLERANCE

Here is a list of things which some people think make for a successful marriage. Please tell me, for each one, whether you think it is...

Very important (%) (EVS: V140)

Country	Wave		Gender		Age			Education			Income			Values		
	1990	2000	Male	Female	16-29	30-49	50+	Lower	Middle	Upper	Lower	Middle	Upper	Mat	Mixed	Postm.
Albania	na	**na**	na	na	na	na	na	na	na	na	na	na	na	na	na	na
Algeria	na	**na**	na	na	na	na	na	na	na	na	na	na	na	na	na	na
Argentina	89	**na**	na	na	na	na	na	na	na	na	na	na	na	na	na	na
Armenia	na	**na**	na	na	na	na	na	na	na	na	na	na	na	na	na	na
Australia	na	**na**	na	na	na	na	na	na	na	na	na	na	na	na	na	na
Austria	83	**84**	83	85	86	86	81	81	85	93	77	84	87	83	84	87
Azerbaijan	na	**na**	na	na	na	na	na	na	na	na	na	na	na	na	na	na
Bangladesh	na	**na**	na	na	na	na	na	na	na	na	na	na	na	na	na	na
Belarus	69	**74**	70	77	77	75	70	65	77	76	74	72	76	73	74	82
Belgium	78	**83**	80	85	80	84	83	81	81	86	85	81	83	81	81	85
Bosnia and Herz.	na	**na**	na	na	na	na	na	na	na	na	na	na	na	na	na	na
Brazil	70	**na**	na	na	na	na	na	na	na	na	na	na	na	na	na	na
Bulgaria	63	**75**	73	76	74	73	76	73	75	77	75	72	74	75	74	80
Canada	84	**na**	na	na	na	na	na	na	na	na	na	na	na	na	na	na
Chile	90	**na**	na	na	na	na	na	na	na	na	na	na	na	na	na	na
China	70	**na**	na	na	na	na	na	na	na	na	na	na	na	na	na	na
Colombia	na	**na**	na	na	na	na	na	na	na	na	na	na	na	na	na	na
Croatia	na	**68**	65	71	69	70	65	65	70	68	64	68	71	61	68	74
Czech Republic	na	**86**	84	87	89	83	86	84	87	90	85	86	86	83	86	89
Denmark	80	**79**	72	86	83	80	76	77	80	85	79	77	83	75	80	82
Dominican Rep.	na	**na**	na	na	na	na	na	na	na	na	na	na	na	na	na	na
Egypt	na	**na**	na	na	na	na	na	na	na	na	na	na	na	na	na	na
El Salvador	na	**na**	na	na	na	na	na	na	na	na	na	na	na	na	na	na
Estonia	57	**61**	56	65	60	61	61	56	62	65	58	64	59	61	60	71
Finland	70	**69**	65	73	72	71	66	67	68	77	75	67	65	70	68	77
France	74	**79**	75	83	78	80	79	77	79	84	82	77	78	76	79	85
Georgia	na	**na**	na	na	na	na	na	na	na	na	na	na	na	na	na	na
Germany	74	**81**	79	83	79	85	79	74	87	89	77	82	89	80	81	86
Great Britain	86	**81**	78	84	78	79	86	80	83	80	81	79	81	na	na	na
Greece	na	**90**	86	92	93	88	87	91	87	91	92	87	90	88	91	87
Hungary	76	**80**	75	85	79	81	81	75	90	89	75	81	83	80	81	80
Iceland	86	**88**	87	88	90	87	87	84	90	90	86	88	90	85	89	89
India	81	**na**	na	na	na	na	na	na	na	na	na	na	na	na	na	na
Indonesia	na	**na**	na	na	na	na	na	na	na	na	na	na	na	na	na	na
Iran	na	**na**	na	na	na	na	na	na	na	na	na	na	na	na	na	na
Ireland	81	**86**	85	86	86	87	84	84	86	89	87	83	85	86	85	89
Israel	na	**na**	na	na	na	na	na	na	na	na	na	na	na	na	na	na
Italy	80	**81**	78	85	81	82	81	79	84	83	79	82	84	78	81	85
Japan	77	**na**	na	na	na	na	na	na	na	na	na	na	na	na	na	na
Jordan	na	**na**	na	na	na	na	na	na	na	na	na	na	na	na	na	na
Korea, South	73	**na**	na	na	na	na	na	na	na	na	na	na	na	na	na	na
Latvia	62	**66**	63	69	68	65	67	60	66	75	65	66	69	64	67	63
Lithuania	33	**42**	37	47	46	43	39	34	42	57	39	42	47	42	42	43
Luxembourg	na	**80**	78	83	83	79	80	77	80	89	72	79	85	71	82	86
Macedonia	na	**na**	na	na	na	na	na	na	na	na	na	na	na	na	na	na
Malta	na	**94**	93	95	95	92	95	93	94	98	91	94	96	92	95	96
Mexico	82	**na**	na	na	na	na	na	na	na	na	na	na	na	na	na	na
Moldova	na	**na**	na	na	na	na	na	na	na	na	na	na	na	na	na	na
Montenegro	na	**na**	na	na	na	na	na	na	na	na	na	na	na	na	na	na
Morocco	na	**na**	na	na	na	na	na	na	na	na	na	na	na	na	na	na
Netherlands	87	**87**	85	89	89	87	86	84	90	87	84	86	90	83	87	88
New Zealand	na	**na**	na	na	na	na	na	na	na	na	na	na	na	na	na	na
Nigeria	99	**na**	na	na	na	na	na	na	na	na	na	na	na	na	na	na
Northern Ireland	81	**82**	83	82	78	81	88	82	84	81	84	82	82	88	83	78
Norway	84	**na**	na	na	na	na	na	na	na	na	na	na	na	na	na	na
Pakistan	na	**na**	na	na	na	na	na	na	na	na	na	na	na	na	na	na
Peru	na	**na**	na	na	na	na	na	na	na	na	na	na	na	na	na	na
Philippines	na	**na**	na	na	na	na	na	na	na	na	na	na	na	na	na	na
Poland	na	**78**	75	80	77	76	80	76	81	74	78	76	81	79	77	77
Portugal	76	**59**	58	60	69	53	58	55	66	72	48	60	68	53	63	59
Puerto Rico	na	**na**	na	na	na	na	na	na	na	na	na	na	na	na	na	na
Romania	72	**73**	72	73	72	74	71	68	75	77	64	75	78	71	75	75
Russian Fed.	67	**62**	57	66	58	64	62	61	61	64	60	64	63	61	63	48
Serbia	na	**na**	na	na	na	na	na	na	na	na	na	na	na	na	na	na
Singapore	na	**na**	na	na	na	na	na	na	na	na	na	na	na	na	na	na
Slovakia	na	**79**	74	83	75	80	81	77	79	82	75	82	81	79	80	84
Slovenia	78	**83**	80	86	84	84	81	82	82	88	83	82	84	84	83	86
South Africa	na	**na**	na	na	na	na	na	na	na	na	na	na	na	na	na	na
Spain	73	**76**	74	78	80	78	73	73	79	79	76	78	80	77	75	85
Sweden	89	**87**	82	92	92	88	84	82	87	91	87	85	89	88	86	91
Switzerland	86	**na**	na	na	na	na	na	na	na	na	na	na	na	na	na	na
Taiwan	na	**na**	na	na	na	na	na	na	na	na	na	na	na	na	na	na
Tanzania	na	**na**	na	na	na	na	na	na	na	na	na	na	na	na	na	na
Turkey	80	**92**	93	91	92	92	92	90	96	97	91	92	96	93	92	95
Uganda	na	**na**	na	na	na	na	na	na	na	na	na	na	na	na	na	na
Ukraine	na	**81**	78	84	82	82	81	81	82	80	86	78	79	80	82	76
United States	83	**na**	na	na	na	na	na	na	na	na	na	na	na	na	na	na
Uruguay	na	**na**	na	na	na	na	na	na	na	na	na	na	na	na	na	na
Venezuela	na	**na**	na	na	na	na	na	na	na	na	na	na	na	na	na	na
Vietnam	na	**na**	na	na	na	na	na	na	na	na	na	na	na	na	na	na
Zimbabwe	na	**na**	na	na	na	na	na	na	na	na	na	na	na	na	na	na
Total	77	**77**	75	80	79	78	77	75	78	82	77	77	79	74	78	83

RANKING	
Country	2000
Malta	94
Turkey	92
Greece	90
Iceland	88
Sweden	87
Netherlands	87
Ireland	86
Czech Republic	86
Austria	84
Slovenia	83
Belgium	83
Northern Ireland	82
Italy	81
Germany	81
Ukraine	81
Great Britain	81
Hungary	80
Luxembourg	80
Denmark	79
France	79
Slovakia	79
Poland	78
Spain	76
Bulgaria	75
Belarus	74
Romania	73
Finland	69
Croatia	68
Latvia	66
Russian Fed.	62
Estonia	61
Portugal	59
Lithuania	42
Total	77

D035_1) MARRIAGE SUCCESS: LIVING APART FROM YOUR IN-LAWS

Here is a list of things which some people think make for a successful marriage. Please tell me, for each one, whether you think it is...

Very important (%)

(EVS: V141)

Country	Wave		Gender		Age			Education			Income			Values		
	1990	2000	Male	Female	16-29	30-49	50+	Lower	Middle	Upper	Lower	Middle	Upper	Mat	Mixed	Postm.
Albania	na	**na**	na	na	na	na	na	na	na	na	na	na	na	na	na	na
Algeria	na	**na**	na	na	na	na	na	na	na	na	na	na	na	na	na	na
Argentina	41	**na**	na	na	na	na	na	na	na	na	na	na	na	na	na	na
Armenia	na	**na**	na	na	na	na	na	na	na	na	na	na	na	na	na	na
Australia	na	**na**	na	na	na	na	na	na	na	na	na	na	na	na	na	na
Austria	36	**44**	40	47	40	43	47	43	43	46	46	44	41	36	44	46
Azerbaijan	na	**na**	na	na	na	na	na	na	na	na	na	na	na	na	na	na
Bangladesh	na	**na**	na	na	na	na	na	na	na	na	na	na	na	na	na	na
Belarus	50	**46**	43	48	51	50	36	36	48	53	43	46	48	47	43	53
Belgium	57	**60**	58	62	50	61	65	64	60	58	68	62	54	60	61	63
Bosnia and Herz.	na	**na**	na	na	na	na	na	na	na	na	na	na	na	na	na	na
Brazil	48	**na**	na	na	na	na	na	na	na	na	na	na	na	na	na	na
Bulgaria	43	**58**	58	57	60	62	53	47	63	64	53	58	63	56	62	62
Canada	51	**na**	na	na	na	na	na	na	na	na	na	na	na	na	na	na
Chile	53	**na**	na	na	na	na	na	na	na	na	na	na	na	na	na	na
China	8	**na**	na	na	na	na	na	na	na	na	na	na	na	na	na	na
Colombia	na	**na**	na	na	na	na	na	na	na	na	na	na	na	na	na	na
Croatia	na	**26**	23	29	34	23	24	19	31	29	29	24	28	17	29	24
Czech Republic	na	**40**	38	42	42	41	38	40	39	41	41	38	44	42	40	35
Denmark	54	**55**	54	56	58	55	53	56	57	51	61	55	53	53	57	51
Dominican Rep.	na	**na**	na	na	na	na	na	na	na	na	na	na	na	na	na	na
Egypt	na	**na**	na	na	na	na	na	na	na	na	na	na	na	na	na	na
El Salvador	na	**na**	na	na	na	na	na	na	na	na	na	na	na	na	na	na
Estonia	42	**39**	34	43	47	44	30	38	42	33	32	39	40	40	39	45
Finland	24	**24**	22	26	27	28	20	21	29	24	26	27	23	29	23	20
France	64	**69**	67	71	62	69	73	70	70	68	70	69	67	72	68	70
Georgia	na	**na**	na	na	na	na	na	na	na	na	na	na	na	na	na	na
Germany	44	**31**	33	30	27	37	27	32	30	32	31	38	29	27	34	30
Great Britain	54	**51**	50	51	47	54	49	51	51	44	54	51	54	na	na	na
Greece	na	**51**	47	54	53	50	50	53	55	47	52	53	48	52	51	52
Hungary	48	**49**	46	52	53	53	43	46	57	49	52	50	48	47	53	56
Iceland	43	**40**	37	42	32	48	35	45	36	38	37	40	43	44	38	39
India	20	**na**	na	na	na	na	na	na	na	na	na	na	na	na	na	na
Indonesia	na	**na**	na	na	na	na	na	na	na	na	na	na	na	na	na	na
Iran	na	**na**	na	na	na	na	na	na	na	na	na	na	na	na	na	na
Ireland	46	**45**	44	45	40	47	46	50	44	38	48	45	42	39	47	40
Israel	na	**na**	na	na	na	na	na	na	na	na	na	na	na	na	na	na
Italy	46	**47**	45	49	51	52	40	42	51	51	43	46	48	40	47	50
Japan	7	**na**	na	na	na	na	na	na	na	na	na	na	na	na	na	na
Jordan	na	**na**	na	na	na	na	na	na	na	na	na	na	na	na	na	na
Korea, South	5	**na**	na	na	na	na	na	na	na	na	na	na	na	na	na	na
Latvia	42	**32**	32	33	37	38	26	23	35	35	29	35	37	33	31	31
Lithuania	35	**34**	31	37	44	36	26	20	39	41	28	33	40	33	34	43
Luxembourg	na	**54**	52	57	54	58	51	55	53	57	50	59	52	54	54	58
Macedonia	na	**na**	na	na	na	na	na	na	na	na	na	na	na	na	na	na
Malta	na	**57**	55	58	58	59	54	55	59	50	54	57	60	55	56	72
Mexico	40	**na**	na	na	na	na	na	na	na	na	na	na	na	na	na	na
Moldova	na	**na**	na	na	na	na	na	na	na	na	na	na	na	na	na	na
Montenegro	na	**na**	na	na	na	na	na	na	na	na	na	na	na	na	na	na
Morocco	na	**na**	na	na	na	na	na	na	na	na	na	na	na	na	na	na
Netherlands	59	**56**	53	60	51	54	61	53	57	59	58	54	58	48	57	60
New Zealand	na	**na**	na	na	na	na	na	na	na	na	na	na	na	na	na	na
Nigeria	57	**na**	na	na	na	na	na	na	na	na	na	na	na	na	na	na
Northern Ireland	54	**47**	48	46	47	50	44	44	47	52	51	47	39	52	47	37
Norway	42	**na**	na	na	na	na	na	na	na	na	na	na	na	na	na	na
Pakistan	na	**na**	na	na	na	na	na	na	na	na	na	na	na	na	na	na
Peru	na	**na**	na	na	na	na	na	na	na	na	na	na	na	na	na	na
Philippines	na	**na**	na	na	na	na	na	na	na	na	na	na	na	na	na	na
Poland	na	**61**	56	65	55	65	61	61	61	62	65	59	61	58	64	54
Portugal	54	**31**	32	31	43	32	24	30	36	29	22	34	48	26	35	26
Puerto Rico	na	**na**	na	na	na	na	na	na	na	na	na	na	na	na	na	na
Romania	40	**38**	37	39	47	43	30	28	43	47	27	39	47	37	39	47
Russian Fed.	36	**37**	37	37	45	40	27	26	38	37	31	35	42	35	39	37
Serbia	na	**na**	na	na	na	na	na	na	na	na	na	na	na	na	na	na
Singapore	na	**na**	na	na	na	na	na	na	na	na	na	na	na	na	na	na
Slovakia	na	**18**	20	17	22	21	13	17	19	20	15	21	19	18	20	16
Slovenia	31	**30**	26	34	25	33	30	26	31	33	32	34	28	31	30	31
South Africa	na	**na**	na	na	na	na	na	na	na	na	na	na	na	na	na	na
Spain	36	**33**	34	31	33	36	30	29	36	34	32	35	43	34	32	36
Sweden	54	**42**	37	46	38	41	44	42	42	42	41	41	46	46	43	40
Switzerland	59	**na**	na	na	na	na	na	na	na	na	na	na	na	na	na	na
Taiwan	na	**na**	na	na	na	na	na	na	na	na	na	na	na	na	na	na
Tanzania	na	**na**	na	na	na	na	na	na	na	na	na	na	na	na	na	na
Turkey	42	**60**	61	59	58	61	63	58	63	62	57	57	71	57	58	70
Uganda	na	**na**	na	na	na	na	na	na	na	na	na	na	na	na	na	na
Ukraine	na	**52**	51	53	65	53	44	38	54	55	49	51	59	52	54	63
United States	47	**na**	na	na	na	na	na	na	na	na	na	na	na	na	na	na
Uruguay	na	**na**	na	na	na	na	na	na	na	na	na	na	na	na	na	na
Venezuela	na	**na**	na	na	na	na	na	na	na	na	na	na	na	na	na	na
Vietnam	na	**na**	na	na	na	na	na	na	na	na	na	na	na	na	na	na
Zimbabwe	na	**na**	na	na	na	na	na	na	na	na	na	na	na	na	na	na
Total	42	44	42	46	45	46	41	42	45	47	43	45	45	42	44	46

RANKING	
Country	**2000**
France	69
Poland	61
Belgium	60
Turkey	60
Bulgaria	58
Malta	57
Netherlands	56
Denmark	55
Luxembourg	54
Ukraine	52
Greece	51
Great Britain	51
Hungary	49
Italy	47
Northern Ireland	47
Belarus	46
Ireland	45
Austria	44
Sweden	42
Czech Republic	40
Iceland	40
Estonia	39
Romania	38
Russian Fed.	37
Lithuania	34
Spain	33
Latvia	32
Germany	31
Portugal	31
Slovenia	30
Croatia	26
Finland	24
Slovakia	18
Total	44

D036_1) MARRIAGE SUCCESS: HAPPY SEXUAL RELATIONSHIP

Here is a list of things which some people think make for a successful marriage. Please tell me, for each one, whether you think it is...

Very important (%)

(EVS: V142)

Country	Wave		Gender		Age			Education			Income			Values		
	1990	2000	Male	Female	16-29	30-49	50+	Lower	Middle	Upper	Lower	Middle	Upper	Mat	Mixed	Postm.
Albania	na	**na**	na	na	na	na	na	na	na	na	na	na	na	na	na	na
Algeria	na	**na**	na	na	na	na	na	na	na	na	na	na	na	na	na	na
Argentina	81	**na**	na	na	na	na	na	na	na	na	na	na	na	na	na	na
Armenia	na	**na**	na	na	na	na	na	na	na	na	na	na	na	na	na	na
Australia	na	**na**	na	na	na	na	na	na	na	na	na	na	na	na	na	na
Austria	57	**64**	65	62	71	65	59	63	65	62	57	64	66	59	64	64
Azerbaijan	na	**na**	na	na	na	na	na	na	na	na	na	na	na	na	na	na
Bangladesh	na	**na**	na	na	na	na	na	na	na	na	na	na	na	na	na	na
Belarus	58	**54**	57	52	66	56	41	39	59	60	51	53	63	51	57	64
Belgium	65	**67**	69	64	67	67	66	65	68	66	72	67	64	65	67	67
Bosnia and Herz.	na	**na**	na	na	na	na	na	na	na	na	na	na	na	na	na	na
Brazil	72	**na**	na	na	na	na	na	na	na	na	na	na	na	na	na	na
Bulgaria	48	**61**	65	58	76	62	53	48	70	63	53	61	68	59	66	68
Canada	72	**na**	na	na	na	na	na	na	na	na	na	na	na	na	na	na
Chile	74	**na**	na	na	na	na	na	na	na	na	na	na	na	na	na	na
China	37	**na**	na	na	na	na	na	na	na	na	na	na	na	na	na	na
Colombia	na	**na**	na	na	na	na	na	na	na	na	na	na	na	na	na	na
Croatia	na	**37**	41	34	45	37	31	30	39	50	40	30	44	27	37	45
Czech Republic	na	**56**	59	53	63	56	52	59	54	43	53	56	59	58	54	55
Denmark	65	**56**	55	57	64	53	55	56	58	56	60	52	57	61	56	60
Dominican Rep.	na	**na**	na	na	na	na	na	na	na	na	na	na	na	na	na	na
Egypt	na	**na**	na	na	na	na	na	na	na	na	na	na	na	na	na	na
El Salvador	na	**na**	na	na	na	na	na	na	na	na	na	na	na	na	na	na
Estonia	53	**52**	53	51	63	57	41	49	53	53	48	52	51	53	51	55
Finland	61	**52**	55	49	64	57	40	48	58	49	56	49	51	53	51	55
France	68	**73**	73	72	73	74	71	73	74	71	71	73	69	73	72	72
Georgia	na	**na**	na	na	na	na	na	na	na	na	na	na	na	na	na	na
Germany	54	**48**	49	46	62	58	30	37	59	49	43	51	51	45	50	46
Great Britain	66	**65**	70	59	76	67	57	62	69	64	63	69	67	na	na	na
Greece	na	**82**	81	84	87	83	70	76	84	82	80	82	83	83	84	78
Hungary	69	**70**	75	65	82	73	60	65	79	81	65	66	77	66	74	80
Iceland	73	**71**	72	71	73	72	68	74	71	66	67	69	78	76	71	62
India	78	**na**	na	na	na	na	na	na	na	na	na	na	na	na	na	na
Indonesia	na	**na**	na	na	na	na	na	na	na	na	na	na	na	na	na	na
Iran	na	**na**	na	na	na	na	na	na	na	na	na	na	na	na	na	na
Ireland	68	**72**	72	72	76	72	70	71	73	72	74	74	70	68	73	72
Israel	na	**na**	na	na	na	na	na	na	na	na	na	na	na	na	na	na
Italy	67	**67**	72	63	79	71	57	62	73	69	65	65	65	59	69	68
Japan	28	**na**	na	na	na	na	na	na	na	na	na	na	na	na	na	na
Jordan	na	**na**	na	na	na	na	na	na	na	na	na	na	na	na	na	na
Korea, South	na	**na**	na	na	na	na	na	na	na	na	na	na	na	na	na	na
Latvia	59	**53**	56	51	64	57	46	48	56	52	49	53	57	55	52	50
Lithuania	37	**37**	40	34	51	40	21	17	43	43	29	34	46	35	36	44
Luxembourg	na	**61**	63	59	66	61	57	61	59	66	51	61	68	58	62	65
Macedonia	na	**na**	na	na	na	na	na	na	na	na	na	na	na	na	na	na
Malta	na	**82**	83	81	89	81	79	76	84	85	78	83	88	77	86	82
Mexico	77	**na**	na	na	na	na	na	na	na	na	na	na	na	na	na	na
Moldova	na	**na**	na	na	na	na	na	na	na	na	na	na	na	na	na	na
Montenegro	na	**na**	na	na	na	na	na	na	na	na	na	na	na	na	na	na
Morocco	na	**na**	na	na	na	na	na	na	na	na	na	na	na	na	na	na
Netherlands	62	**51**	55	48	56	48	52	52	54	47	56	49	50	47	52	51
New Zealand	na	**na**	na	na	na	na	na	na	na	na	na	na	na	na	na	na
Nigeria	91	**na**	na	na	na	na	na	na	na	na	na	na	na	na	na	na
Northern Ireland	69	**67**	68	66	67	71	64	63	70	68	70	72	68	69	68	63
Norway	62	**na**	na	na	na	na	na	na	na	na	na	na	na	na	na	na
Pakistan	na	**na**	na	na	na	na	na	na	na	na	na	na	na	na	na	na
Peru	na	**na**	na	na	na	na	na	na	na	na	na	na	na	na	na	na
Philippines	na	**na**	na	na	na	na	na	na	na	na	na	na	na	na	na	na
Poland	na	**66**	69	64	67	67	64	64	71	66	65	65	75	58	71	71
Portugal	69	**41**	47	35	58	37	33	36	52	48	29	39	60	33	47	41
Puerto Rico	na	**na**	na	na	na	na	na	na	na	na	na	na	na	na	na	na
Romania	59	**49**	54	45	62	55	37	37	54	60	37	51	59	46	53	55
Russian Fed.	46	**50**	55	46	58	58	35	35	51	55	46	46	56	47	53	61
Serbia	na	**na**	na	na	na	na	na	na	na	na	na	na	na	na	na	na
Singapore	na	**na**	na	na	na	na	na	na	na	na	na	na	na	na	na	na
Slovakia	na	**59**	59	58	64	65	47	53	60	69	51	60	63	56	61	63
Slovenia	61	**64**	65	63	70	67	57	62	66	58	68	62	65	65	64	69
South Africa	na	**na**	na	na	na	na	na	na	na	na	na	na	na	na	na	na
Spain	63	**60**	62	57	72	61	51	51	66	63	55	67	69	59	60	64
Sweden	67	**60**	59	61	60	62	58	57	60	61	58	63	61	64	61	57
Switzerland	68	**na**	na	na	na	na	na	na	na	na	na	na	na	na	na	na
Taiwan	na	**na**	na	na	na	na	na	na	na	na	na	na	na	na	na	na
Tanzania	na	**na**	na	na	na	na	na	na	na	na	na	na	na	na	na	na
Turkey	73	**84**	85	84	87	83	79	81	89	90	79	86	91	85	84	90
Uganda	na	**na**	na	na	na	na	na	na	na	na	na	na	na	na	na	na
Ukraine	na	**67**	71	63	76	67	62	56	67	72	67	63	73	65	67	84
United States	71	**na**	na	na	na	na	na	na	na	na	na	na	na	na	na	na
Uruguay	na	**na**	na	na	na	na	na	na	na	na	na	na	na	na	na	na
Venezuela	na	**na**	na	na	na	na	na	na	na	na	na	na	na	na	na	na
Vietnam	na	**na**	na	na	na	na	na	na	na	na	na	na	na	na	na	na
Zimbabwe	na	**na**	na	na	na	na	na	na	na	na	na	na	na	na	na	na
Total	63	**60**	62	58	69	62	53	55	63	63	58	59	63	57	61	62

RANKING

Country	2000
Turkey	84
Greece	82
Malta	82
France	73
Ireland	72
Iceland	71
Hungary	70
Italy	67
Ukraine	67
Northern Ireland	67
Belgium	67
Poland	66
Great Britain	65
Slovenia	64
Austria	64
Bulgaria	61
Luxembourg	61
Sweden	60
Spain	60
Slovakia	59
Denmark	56
Czech Republic	56
Belarus	54
Latvia	53
Estonia	52
Finland	52
Netherlands	51
Russian Fed.	50
Romania	49
Germany	48
Portugal	41
Croatia	37
Lithuania	37
Total	60

D037_1) MARRIAGE SUCCESS: SHARING HOUSEHOLD CHORES

Here is a list of things which some people think make for a successful marriage. Please tell me, for each one, whether you think it is...

Very important (%) (EVS: V143)

Country	Wave		Gender		Age			Education			Income			Values		
	1990	2000	Male	Female	16-29	30-49	50+	Lower	Middle	Upper	Lower	Middle	Upper	Mat	Mixed	Postm.
Albania	na	na	na	na	na	na	na	na	na	na	na	na	na	na	na	na
Algeria	na	na	na	na	na	na	na	na	na	na	na	na	na	na	na	na
Argentina	53	na	na	na	na	na	na	na	na	na	na	na	na	na	na	na
Armenia	na	na	na	na	na	na	na	na	na	na	na	na	na	na	na	na
Australia	na	na	na	na	na	na	na	na	na	na	na	na	na	na	na	na
Austria	29	30	30	29	39	28	26	30	29	30	34	26	27	32	29	31
Azerbaijan	na	na	na	na	na	na	na	na	na	na	na	na	na	na	na	na
Bangladesh	na	na	na	na	na	na	na	na	na	na	na	na	na	na	na	na
Belarus	29	45	38	50	44	43	47	49	43	43	48	42	44	44	45	46
Belgium	38	42	45	40	40	43	43	43	42	42	46	44	40	46	39	46
Bosnia and Herz.	na	na	na	na	na	na	na	na	na	na	na	na	na	na	na	na
Brazil	37	na	na	na	na	na	na	na	na	na	na	na	na	na	na	na
Bulgaria	42	34	30	38	38	37	31	29	40	30	35	35	34	30	37	39
Canada	53	na	na	na	na	na	na	na	na	na	na	na	na	na	na	na
Chile	62	na	na	na	na	na	na	na	na	na	na	na	na	na	na	na
China	35	na	na	na	na	na	na	na	na	na	na	na	na	na	na	na
Colombia	na	na	na	na	na	na	na	na	na	na	na	na	na	na	na	na
Croatia	na	23	24	21	25	20	24	20	25	23	24	23	22	21	22	24
Czech Republic	na	24	21	27	23	21	27	26	23	19	26	23	23	25	24	21
Denmark	48	41	40	42	47	41	37	42	39	39	42	41	43	48	40	42
Dominican Rep.	na	na	na	na	na	na	na	na	na	na	na	na	na	na	na	na
Egypt	na	na	na	na	na	na	na	na	na	na	na	na	na	na	na	na
El Salvador	na	na	na	na	na	na	na	na	na	na	na	na	na	na	na	na
Estonia	19	18	16	19	18	18	17	16	18	19	14	21	17	17	19	16
Finland	25	29	27	30	36	30	23	28	33	24	33	30	26	30	27	34
France	35	40	36	43	45	43	35	41	37	38	43	41	37	41	40	40
Georgia	na	na	na	na	na	na	na	na	na	na	na	na	na	na	na	na
Germany	30	20	18	22	22	24	16	17	24	19	23	20	19	18	21	23
Great Britain	44	50	51	49	49	48	53	51	50	46	62	44	49	na	na	na
Greece	na	44	34	51	51	39	35	42	41	46	45	39	42	41	43	49
Hungary	40	41	42	41	36	41	45	42	38	44	38	41	44	40	42	41
Iceland	42	45	44	45	52	44	38	48	42	42	52	41	44	45	45	41
India	58	na	na	na	na	na	na	na	na	na	na	na	na	na	na	na
Indonesia	na	na	na	na	na	na	na	na	na	na	na	na	na	na	na	na
Iran	na	na	na	na	na	na	na	na	na	na	na	na	na	na	na	na
Ireland	38	54	54	53	55	54	53	56	54	48	53	58	50	58	53	55
Israel	na	na	na	na	na	na	na	na	na	na	na	na	na	na	na	na
Italy	30	29	28	30	35	29	26	28	31	27	27	28	27	24	30	28
Japan	10	na	na	na	na	na	na	na	na	na	na	na	na	na	na	na
Jordan	na	na	na	na	na	na	na	na	na	na	na	na	na	na	na	na
Korea, South	na	na	na	na	na	na	na	na	na	na	na	na	na	na	na	na
Latvia	31	26	24	28	23	24	29	29	25	27	29	25	25	27	26	22
Lithuania	25	26	21	30	27	26	25	24	25	33	28	26	28	27	26	20
Luxembourg	na	37	33	40	43	37	32	39	33	41	36	38	35	32	38	44
Macedonia	na	na	na	na	na	na	na	na	na	na	na	na	na	na	na	na
Malta	na	55	55	55	58	52	56	55	53	66	60	58	57	48	57	68
Mexico	47	na	na	na	na	na	na	na	na	na	na	na	na	na	na	na
Moldova	na	na	na	na	na	na	na	na	na	na	na	na	na	na	na	na
Montenegro	na	na	na	na	na	na	na	na	na	na	na	na	na	na	na	na
Morocco	na	na	na	na	na	na	na	na	na	na	na	na	na	na	na	na
Netherlands	34	33	34	31	44	31	28	30	35	32	37	31	30	36	31	36
New Zealand	na	na	na	na	na	na	na	na	na	na	na	na	na	na	na	na
Nigeria	67	na	na	na	na	na	na	na	na	na	na	na	na	na	na	na
Northern Ireland	45	47	46	47	52	47	45	43	49	53	49	45	49	53	44	47
Norway	34	na	na	na	na	na	na	na	na	na	na	na	na	na	na	na
Pakistan	na	na	na	na	na	na	na	na	na	na	na	na	na	na	na	na
Peru	na	na	na	na	na	na	na	na	na	na	na	na	na	na	na	na
Philippines	na	na	na	na	na	na	na	na	na	na	na	na	na	na	na	na
Poland	na	55	51	58	55	54	55	55	55	54	56	53	55	53	56	51
Portugal	50	23	20	26	29	23	20	21	27	33	23	22	31	19	26	27
Puerto Rico	na	na	na	na	na	na	na	na	na	na	na	na	na	na	na	na
Romania	42	43	40	46	46	39	45	44	44	41	42	44	45	43	42	49
Russian Fed.	38	28	24	31	22	31	28	28	30	23	32	28	24	29	28	11
Serbia	na	na	na	na	na	na	na	na	na	na	na	na	na	na	na	na
Singapore	na	na	na	na	na	na	na	na	na	na	na	na	na	na	na	na
Slovakia	na	31	25	36	32	28	32	30	31	30	28	32	30	31	31	23
Slovenia	35	36	30	41	37	36	35	41	35	27	44	34	26	38	33	45
South Africa	na	na	na	na	na	na	na	na	na	na	na	na	na	na	na	na
Spain	40	36	33	39	43	40	29	30	40	42	34	41	38	31	35	44
Sweden	48	52	48	56	61	53	46	42	55	57	52	50	54	48	51	57
Switzerland	33	na	na	na	na	na	na	na	na	na	na	na	na	na	na	na
Taiwan	na	na	na	na	na	na	na	na	na	na	na	na	na	na	na	na
Tanzania	na	na	na	na	na	na	na	na	na	na	na	na	na	na	na	na
Turkey	31	60	58	62	58	60	63	61	57	62	60	58	62	53	61	66
Uganda	na	na	na	na	na	na	na	na	na	na	na	na	na	na	na	na
Ukraine	na	45	40	50	38	43	51	52	45	40	54	37	43	46	46	44
United States	47	na	na	na	na	na	na	na	na	na	na	na	na	na	na	na
Uruguay	na	na	na	na	na	na	na	na	na	na	na	na	na	na	na	na
Venezuela	na	na	na	na	na	na	na	na	na	na	na	na	na	na	na	na
Vietnam	na	na	na	na	na	na	na	na	na	na	na	na	na	na	na	na
Zimbabwe	na	na	na	na	na	na	na	na	na	na	na	na	na	na	na	na
Total	38	37	35	39	40	37	35	36	37	39	40	36	36	36	37	39

RANKING	
Country	2000
Turkey	60
Malta	55
Poland	55
Ireland	54
Sweden	52
Great Britain	50
Northern Ireland	47
Ukraine	45
Belarus	45
Iceland	45
Greece	44
Romania	43
Belgium	42
Hungary	41
Denmark	41
France	40
Luxembourg	37
Spain	36
Slovenia	36
Bulgaria	34
Netherlands	33
Slovakia	31
Austria	30
Italy	29
Finland	29
Russian Fed.	28
Latvia	26
Lithuania	26
Czech Republic	24
Portugal	23
Croatia	23
Germany	20
Estonia	18
Total	37

D038_1) MARRIAGE SUCCESS: CHILDREN

Here is a list of things which some people think make for a successful marriage. Please tell me, for each one, whether you think it is...

Very important (%)

(EVS: V144)

Country	Wave		Gender		Age			Education			Income			Values		
	1990	2000	Male	Female	16-29	30-49	50+	Lower	Middle	Upper	Lower	Middle	Upper	Mat	Mixed	Postm.
Albania	na	**na**	na	na	na	na	na	na	na	na	na	na	na	na	na	na
Algeria	na	**na**	na	na	na	na	na	na	na	na	na	na	na	na	na	na
Argentina	88	**na**	na	na	na	na	na	na	na	na	na	na	na	na	na	na
Armenia	na	**na**	na	na	na	na	na	na	na	na	na	na	na	na	na	na
Australia	na	**na**	na	na	na	na	na	na	na	na	na	na	na	na	na	na
Austria	63	**60**	56	64	51	61	64	65	58	51	62	66	55	65	63	56
Azerbaijan	na	**na**	na	na	na	na	na	na	na	na	na	na	na	na	na	na
Bangladesh	na	**na**	na	na	na	na	na	na	na	na	na	na	na	na	na	na
Belarus	81	**76**	72	80	75	74	80	79	76	74	81	74	74	81	73	70
Belgium	55	**59**	58	59	55	57	61	61	62	50	55	63	56	60	59	55
Bosnia and Herz.	na	**na**	na	na	na	na	na	na	na	na	na	na	na	na	na	na
Brazil	60	**na**	na	na	na	na	na	na	na	na	na	na	na	na	na	na
Bulgaria	84	**79**	77	80	69	80	82	81	78	75	84	74	76	82	75	70
Canada	66	**na**	na	na	na	na	na	na	na	na	na	na	na	na	na	na
Chile	92	**na**	na	na	na	na	na	na	na	na	na	na	na	na	na	na
China	55	**na**	na	na	na	na	na	na	na	na	na	na	na	na	na	na
Colombia	na	**na**	na	na	na	na	na	na	na	na	na	na	na	na	na	na
Croatia	na	**63**	59	66	55	67	64	65	62	59	68	63	61	59	64	63
Czech Republic	na	**78**	73	81	71	77	81	79	76	76	77	80	76	79	78	73
Denmark	42	**36**	36	36	24	32	47	42	23	33	45	33	31	41	37	32
Dominican Rep.	na	**na**	na	na	na	na	na	na	na	na	na	na	na	na	na	na
Egypt	na	**na**	na	na	na	na	na	na	na	na	na	na	na	na	na	na
El Salvador	na	**na**	na	na	na	na	na	na	na	na	na	na	na	na	na	na
Estonia	74	**64**	55	71	51	68	68	58	67	65	65	69	61	64	65	64
Finland	60	**55**	52	58	38	57	62	58	52	49	56	58	54	56	55	55
France	65	**63**	59	66	59	60	66	68	55	55	64	64	59	70	63	53
Georgia	na	**na**	na	na	na	na	na	na	na	na	na	na	na	na	na	na
Germany	65	**48**	43	52	39	50	50	49	48	47	48	54	44	53	46	51
Great Britain	58	**48**	45	51	39	48	53	52	49	38	48	53	46	na	na	na
Greece	na	**72**	72	71	66	72	84	85	72	69	74	70	72	74	73	67
Hungary	85	**83**	79	86	77	84	85	81	86	86	81	82	85	84	82	77
Iceland	66	**51**	52	50	31	51	66	54	49	47	51	50	50	57	49	46
India	79	**na**	na	na	na	na	na	na	na	na	na	na	na	na	na	na
Indonesia	na	**na**	na	na	na	na	na	na	na	na	na	na	na	na	na	na
Iran	na	**na**	na	na	na	na	na	na	na	na	na	na	na	na	na	na
Ireland	62	**59**	58	60	46	61	67	72	56	45	66	63	51	57	60	58
Israel	na	**na**	na	na	na	na	na	na	na	na	na	na	na	na	na	na
Italy	65	**58**	57	59	51	54	66	66	54	46	64	57	53	67	60	51
Japan	52	**na**	na	na	na	na	na	na	na	na	na	na	na	na	na	na
Jordan	na	**na**	na	na	na	na	na	na	na	na	na	na	na	na	na	na
Korea, South	na	**na**	na	na	na	na	na	na	na	na	na	na	na	na	na	na
Latvia	78	**73**	66	79	70	74	74	74	73	74	74	74	72	74	74	70
Lithuania	66	**51**	46	55	49	49	54	54	50	51	57	52	53	54	49	57
Luxembourg	na	**43**	44	43	37	41	49	53	38	39	47	44	36	46	44	34
Macedonia	na	**na**	na	na	na	na	na	na	na	na	na	na	na	na	na	na
Malta	na	**70**	73	68	66	72	72	73	72	57	76	73	70	72	71	60
Mexico	75	**na**	na	na	na	na	na	na	na	na	na	na	na	na	na	na
Moldova	na	**na**	na	na	na	na	na	na	na	na	na	na	na	na	na	na
Montenegro	na	**na**	na	na	na	na	na	na	na	na	na	na	na	na	na	na
Morocco	na	**na**	na	na	na	na	na	na	na	na	na	na	na	na	na	na
Netherlands	56	**47**	40	53	31	45	57	61	48	32	50	47	38	58	47	41
New Zealand	na	**na**	na	na	na	na	na	na	na	na	na	na	na	na	na	na
Nigeria	94	**na**	na	na	na	na	na	na	na	na	na	na	na	na	na	na
Northern Ireland	69	**55**	55	55	50	56	58	61	53	45	59	60	50	55	58	48
Norway	61	**na**	na	na	na	na	na	na	na	na	na	na	na	na	na	na
Pakistan	na	**na**	na	na	na	na	na	na	na	na	na	na	na	na	na	na
Peru	na	**na**	na	na	na	na	na	na	na	na	na	na	na	na	na	na
Philippines	na	**na**	na	na	na	na	na	na	na	na	na	na	na	na	na	na
Poland	na	**73**	73	74	64	77	74	76	73	64	77	72	71	71	74	78
Portugal	65	**43**	41	46	48	39	44	45	43	32	43	50	45	39	46	37
Puerto Rico	na	**na**	na	na	na	na	na	na	na	na	na	na	na	na	na	na
Romania	68	**70**	71	70	59	73	74	73	69	69	67	75	71	73	69	67
Russian Fed.	80	**74**	70	78	64	76	78	75	74	73	76	75	73	76	72	68
Serbia	na	**na**	na	na	na	na	na	na	na	na	na	na	na	na	na	na
Singapore	na	**na**	na	na	na	na	na	na	na	na	na	na	na	na	na	na
Slovakia	na	**70**	66	73	61	72	74	71	69	74	70	70	72	71	71	62
Slovenia	73	**71**	69	73	69	73	71	75	70	67	72	72	67	74	72	70
South Africa	na	**na**	na	na	na	na	na	na	na	na	na	na	na	na	na	na
Spain	68	**66**	63	68	63	63	69	68	64	63	67	69	65	69	64	67
Sweden	61	**59**	57	61	46	61	65	65	57	57	55	60	64	60	60	56
Switzerland	54	**na**	na	na	na	na	na	na	na	na	na	na	na	na	na	na
Taiwan	na	**na**	na	na	na	na	na	na	na	na	na	na	na	na	na	na
Tanzania	na	**na**	na	na	na	na	na	na	na	na	na	na	na	na	na	na
Turkey	69	**78**	78	78	74	80	88	83	72	69	82	79	69	81	79	76
Uganda	na	**na**	na	na	na	na	na	na	na	na	na	na	na	na	na	na
Ukraine	na	**84**	80	88	75	86	88	89	84	83	87	84	82	84	85	78
United States	65	**na**	na	na	na	na	na	na	na	na	na	na	na	na	na	na
Uruguay	na	**na**	na	na	na	na	na	na	na	na	na	na	na	na	na	na
Venezuela	na	**na**	na	na	na	na	na	na	na	na	na	na	na	na	na	na
Vietnam	na	**na**	na	na	na	na	na	na	na	na	na	na	na	na	na	na
Zimbabwe	na	**na**	na	na	na	na	na	na	na	na	na	na	na	na	na	na
Total	68	**63**	60	65	56	63	67	64	63	59	66	64	61	68	63	55

RANKING	
Country	**2000**
Ukraine	84
Hungary	83
Bulgaria	79
Turkey	78
Czech Republic	78
Belarus	76
Russian Fed.	74
Poland	73
Latvia	73
Greece	72
Slovenia	71
Romania	70
Malta	70
Slovakia	70
Spain	66
Estonia	64
Croatia	63
France	63
Austria	60
Ireland	59
Sweden	59
Belgium	59
Italy	58
Northern Ireland	55
Finland	55
Lithuania	51
Iceland	51
Germany	48
Great Britain	48
Netherlands	47
Portugal	43
Luxembourg	43
Denmark	36
Total	63

D039_1) MARRIAGE SUCCESS: WILLING TO DISCUSS PROBLEMS

Here is a list of things which some people think make for a successful marriage. Please tell me, for each one, whether you think it is...

Very important (%)

(EVS: V145)

Country	Wave		Gender		Age			Education			Income			Values		
	1990	2000	Male	Female	16-29	30-49	50+	Lower	Middle	Upper	Lower	Middle	Upper	Mat	Mixed	Postm.
Albania	na	**na**	na	na	na	na	na	na	na	na	na	na	na	na	na	na
Algeria	na	**na**	na	na	na	na	na	na	na	na	na	na	na	na	na	na
Argentina	na	**na**	na	na	na	na	na	na	na	na	na	na	na	na	na	na
Armenia	na	**na**	na	na	na	na	na	na	na	na	na	na	na	na	na	na
Australia	na	**na**	na	na	na	na	na	na	na	na	na	na	na	na	na	na
Austria	na	**75**	74	76	77	80	69	71	77	83	72	76	76	66	76	78
Azerbaijan	na	**na**	na	na	na	na	na	na	na	na	na	na	na	na	na	na
Bangladesh	na	**na**	na	na	na	na	na	na	na	na	na	na	na	na	na	na
Belarus	na	**53**	47	58	64	50	48	44	54	63	53	51	58	54	52	62
Belgium	na	**83**	81	85	86	84	80	79	84	84	83	78	85	81	82	87
Bosnia and Herz.	na	**na**	na	na	na	na	na	na	na	na	na	na	na	na	na	na
Brazil	na	**na**	na	na	na	na	na	na	na	na	na	na	na	na	na	na
Bulgaria	na	**58**	54	62	65	57	55	48	62	65	56	55	60	54	63	62
Canada	na	**na**	na	na	na	na	na	na	na	na	na	na	na	na	na	na
Chile	na	**na**	na	na	na	na	na	na	na	na	na	na	na	na	na	na
China	na	**na**	na	na	na	na	na	na	na	na	na	na	na	na	na	na
Colombia	na	**na**	na	na	na	na	na	na	na	na	na	na	na	na	na	na
Croatia	na	**56**	52	58	63	56	50	51	57	65	52	56	57	47	54	64
Czech Republic	na	**73**	70	76	82	74	67	70	76	77	67	74	77	68	73	83
Denmark	na	**76**	72	81	84	77	72	74	79	82	75	74	82	72	78	79
Dominican Rep.	na	**na**	na	na	na	na	na	na	na	na	na	na	na	na	na	na
Egypt	na	**na**	na	na	na	na	na	na	na	na	na	na	na	na	na	na
El Salvador	na	**na**	na	na	na	na	na	na	na	na	na	na	na	na	na	na
Estonia	na	**51**	43	57	55	54	45	47	53	49	45	52	53	47	53	65
Finland	na	**64**	59	69	78	68	54	58	72	74	69	62	63	59	66	65
France	na	**77**	71	82	79	78	74	77	74	78	79	76	72	79	76	75
Georgia	na	**na**	na	na	na	na	na	na	na	na	na	na	na	na	na	na
Germany	na	**60**	57	63	60	65	56	49	71	68	53	61	69	59	61	63
Great Britain	na	**84**	82	87	83	87	83	82	84	91	85	83	88	na	na	na
Greece	na	**91**	86	95	94	89	88	93	91	91	93	92	89	89	92	91
Hungary	na	**78**	75	82	82	79	77	74	86	87	69	79	85	76	83	67
Iceland	na	**89**	85	93	92	91	84	88	89	92	87	89	92	90	89	89
India	na	**na**	na	na	na	na	na	na	na	na	na	na	na	na	na	na
Indonesia	na	**na**	na	na	na	na	na	na	na	na	na	na	na	na	na	na
Iran	na	**na**	na	na	na	na	na	na	na	na	na	na	na	na	na	na
Ireland	na	**90**	89	90	93	90	87	87	90	92	87	90	90	83	91	94
Israel	na	**na**	na	na	na	na	na	na	na	na	na	na	na	na	na	na
Italy	na	**81**	79	82	87	84	74	75	85	86	76	81	83	76	81	84
Japan	na	**na**	na	na	na	na	na	na	na	na	na	na	na	na	na	na
Jordan	na	**na**	na	na	na	na	na	na	na	na	na	na	na	na	na	na
Korea, South	na	**na**	na	na	na	na	na	na	na	na	na	na	na	na	na	na
Latvia	na	**42**	37	47	53	41	39	42	43	42	41	38	46	41	42	42
Lithuania	na	**33**	28	38	37	35	30	30	33	40	34	28	39	33	33	39
Luxembourg	na	**73**	70	76	73	74	72	76	70	78	66	77	72	69	74	76
Macedonia	na	**na**	na	na	na	na	na	na	na	na	na	na	na	na	na	na
Malta	na	**96**	94	97	96	95	96	95	95	99	95	96	97	92	98	96
Mexico	na	**na**	na	na	na	na	na	na	na	na	na	na	na	na	na	na
Moldova	na	**na**	na	na	na	na	na	na	na	na	na	na	na	na	na	na
Montenegro	na	**na**	na	na	na	na	na	na	na	na	na	na	na	na	na	na
Morocco	na	**na**	na	na	na	na	na	na	na	na	na	na	na	na	na	na
Netherlands	na	**87**	83	91	93	88	83	85	88	88	84	88	89	86	88	87
New Zealand	na	**na**	na	na	na	na	na	na	na	na	na	na	na	na	na	na
Nigeria	na	**na**	na	na	na	na	na	na	na	na	na	na	na	na	na	na
Northern Ireland	na	**82**	81	84	83	84	82	81	83	85	80	81	84	83	84	78
Norway	na	**na**	na	na	na	na	na	na	na	na	na	na	na	na	na	na
Pakistan	na	**na**	na	na	na	na	na	na	na	na	na	na	na	na	na	na
Peru	na	**na**	na	na	na	na	na	na	na	na	na	na	na	na	na	na
Philippines	na	**na**	na	na	na	na	na	na	na	na	na	na	na	na	na	na
Poland	na	**74**	72	76	84	74	69	69	83	73	72	76	76	72	76	78
Portugal	na	**56**	56	56	69	50	53	53	60	64	49	53	69	46	62	54
Puerto Rico	na	**na**	na	na	na	na	na	na	na	na	na	na	na	na	na	na
Romania	na	**66**	69	64	76	68	60	55	70	80	54	66	76	62	70	79
Russian Fed.	na	**43**	41	45	45	45	39	40	43	45	41	45	43	42	43	34
Serbia	na	**na**	na	na	na	na	na	na	na	na	na	na	na	na	na	na
Singapore	na	**na**	na	na	na	na	na	na	na	na	na	na	na	na	na	na
Slovakia	na	**66**	61	70	71	65	63	61	67	76	61	64	72	64	68	74
Slovenia	na	**80**	75	85	84	81	76	77	80	84	77	79	82	81	81	82
South Africa	na	**na**	na	na	na	na	na	na	na	na	na	na	na	na	na	na
Spain	na	**63**	62	65	74	63	57	57	67	70	61	68	67	62	62	74
Sweden	na	**82**	75	88	86	84	77	73	83	87	82	79	85	85	80	87
Switzerland	na	**na**	na	na	na	na	na	na	na	na	na	na	na	na	na	na
Taiwan	na	**na**	na	na	na	na	na	na	na	na	na	na	na	na	na	na
Tanzania	na	**na**	na	na	na	na	na	na	na	na	na	na	na	na	na	na
Turkey	na	**89**	88	89	90	88	88	86	92	96	86	88	95	88	89	95
Uganda	na	**na**	na	na	na	na	na	na	na	na	na	na	na	na	na	na
Ukraine	na	**64**	61	66	68	63	63	60	62	69	68	56	67	58	70	79
United States	na	**na**	na	na	na	na	na	na	na	na	na	na	na	na	na	na
Uruguay	na	**na**	na	na	na	na	na	na	na	na	na	na	na	na	na	na
Venezuela	na	**na**	na	na	na	na	na	na	na	na	na	na	na	na	na	na
Vietnam	na	**na**	na	na	na	na	na	na	na	na	na	na	na	na	na	na
Zimbabwe	na	**na**	na	na	na	na	na	na	na	na	na	na	na	na	na	na
Total	na	**71**	67	73	76	71	66	67	70	77	68	70	73	64	72	78

RANKING	
Country	**2000**
Malta	96
Greece	91
Ireland	90
Iceland	89
Turkey	89
Netherlands	87
Great Britain	84
Belgium	83
Northern Ireland	82
Sweden	82
Italy	81
Slovenia	80
Hungary	78
France	77
Denmark	76
Austria	75
Poland	74
Luxembourg	73
Czech Republic	73
Romania	66
Slovakia	66
Finland	64
Ukraine	64
Spain	63
Germany	60
Bulgaria	58
Portugal	56
Croatia	56
Belarus	53
Estonia	51
Russian Fed.	43
Latvia	42
Lithuania	33
Total	71

D040_1) MARRIAGE SUCCESS: SPENDING TIME TOGETHER

Here is a list of things which some people think make for a successful marriage. Please tell me, for each one, whether you think it is...

Very important (%)

(EVS: V146)

Country	Wave		Gender		Age			Education			Income			Values		
	1990	2000	Male	Female	16-29	30-49	50+	Lower	Middle	Upper	Lower	Middle	Upper	Mat	Mixed	Postm.
Albania	na	**na**	na	na	na	na	na	na	na	na	na	na	na	na	na	na
Algeria	na	**na**	na	na	na	na	na	na	na	na	na	na	na	na	na	na
Argentina	na	**na**	na	na	na	na	na	na	na	na	na	na	na	na	na	na
Armenia	na	**na**	na	na	na	na	na	na	na	na	na	na	na	na	na	na
Australia	na	**na**	na	na	na	na	na	na	na	na	na	na	na	na	na	na
Austria	na	**49**	48	50	45	49	52	58	44	31	50	54	46	50	53	43
Azerbaijan	na	**na**	na	na	na	na	na	na	na	na	na	na	na	na	na	na
Bangladesh	na	**na**	na	na	na	na	na	na	na	na	na	na	na	na	na	na
Belarus	na	**36**	33	38	41	34	33	31	39	33	40	34	34	38	36	35
Belgium	na	**50**	50	50	48	48	53	60	51	40	58	51	44	56	50	41
Bosnia and Herz.	na	**na**	na	na	na	na	na	na	na	na	na	na	na	na	na	na
Brazil	na	**na**	na	na	na	na	na	na	na	na	na	na	na	na	na	na
Bulgaria	na	**41**	38	43	49	40	37	36	46	38	40	41	40	41	42	24
Canada	na	**na**	na	na	na	na	na	na	na	na	na	na	na	na	na	na
Chile	na	**na**	na	na	na	na	na	na	na	na	na	na	na	na	na	na
China	na	**na**	na	na	na	na	na	na	na	na	na	na	na	na	na	na
Colombia	na	**na**	na	na	na	na	na	na	na	na	na	na	na	na	na	na
Croatia	na	**43**	44	43	50	42	40	43	44	44	41	42	48	39	44	46
Czech Republic	na	**33**	31	34	40	28	33	37	30	21	38	35	27	33	33	30
Denmark	na	**39**	37	41	41	33	45	46	29	32	45	38	31	49	41	32
Dominican Rep.	na	**na**	na	na	na	na	na	na	na	na	na	na	na	na	na	na
Egypt	na	**na**	na	na	na	na	na	na	na	na	na	na	na	na	na	na
El Salvador	na	**na**	na	na	na	na	na	na	na	na	na	na	na	na	na	na
Estonia	na	**27**	25	29	34	25	25	29	28	20	26	30	25	26	26	47
Finland	na	**38**	39	38	49	38	32	39	36	43	45	37	35	41	36	45
France	na	**54**	51	57	53	52	56	61	49	42	57	56	48	63	55	40
Georgia	na	**na**	na	na	na	na	na	na	na	na	na	na	na	na	na	na
Germany	na	**39**	38	40	37	41	39	37	42	37	38	39	44	41	41	32
Great Britain	na	**53**	50	55	46	51	58	59	50	46	62	53	50	na	na	na
Greece	na	**61**	58	64	62	58	66	71	65	57	61	63	58	63	59	62
Hungary	na	**58**	55	62	63	55	59	58	62	51	55	60	61	56	61	64
Iceland	na	**48**	45	50	43	47	54	51	45	46	47	49	45	53	48	34
India	na	**na**	na	na	na	na	na	na	na	na	na	na	na	na	na	na
Indonesia	na	**na**	na	na	na	na	na	na	na	na	na	na	na	na	na	na
Iran	na	**na**	na	na	na	na	na	na	na	na	na	na	na	na	na	na
Ireland	na	**58**	56	59	47	61	61	62	58	50	65	65	49	55	58	57
Israel	na	**na**	na	na	na	na	na	na	na	na	na	na	na	na	na	na
Italy	na	**51**	49	52	49	50	51	54	50	42	51	51	45	55	53	47
Japan	na	**na**	na	na	na	na	na	na	na	na	na	na	na	na	na	na
Jordan	na	**na**	na	na	na	na	na	na	na	na	na	na	na	na	na	na
Korea, South	na	**na**	na	na	na	na	na	na	na	na	na	na	na	na	na	na
Latvia	na	**36**	33	39	46	32	35	42	36	28	38	34	35	38	34	33
Lithuania	na	**22**	19	24	25	25	16	12	24	27	22	17	25	18	22	27
Luxembourg	na	**48**	47	49	44	42	56	55	47	37	49	48	41	46	48	41
Macedonia	na	**na**	na	na	na	na	na	na	na	na	na	na	na	na	na	na
Malta	na	**87**	86	88	84	85	91	90	86	86	92	86	83	81	90	94
Mexico	na	**na**	na	na	na	na	na	na	na	na	na	na	na	na	na	na
Moldova	na	**na**	na	na	na	na	na	na	na	na	na	na	na	na	na	na
Montenegro	na	**na**	na	na	na	na	na	na	na	na	na	na	na	na	na	na
Morocco	na	**na**	na	na	na	na	na	na	na	na	na	na	na	na	na	na
Netherlands	na	**31**	29	32	31	23	39	49	28	16	34	33	21	43	31	23
New Zealand	na	**na**	na	na	na	na	na	na	na	na	na	na	na	na	na	na
Nigeria	na	**na**	na	na	na	na	na	na	na	na	na	na	na	na	na	na
Northern Ireland	na	**56**	57	55	55	54	59	57	54	55	59	52	49	53	58	56
Norway	na	**na**	na	na	na	na	na	na	na	na	na	na	na	na	na	na
Pakistan	na	**na**	na	na	na	na	na	na	na	na	na	na	na	na	na	na
Peru	na	**na**	na	na	na	na	na	na	na	na	na	na	na	na	na	na
Philippines	na	**na**	na	na	na	na	na	na	na	na	na	na	na	na	na	na
Poland	na	**61**	59	62	71	56	60	60	63	59	65	58	58	59	62	64
Portugal	na	**34**	36	32	32	31	37	35	33	26	32	36	41	27	38	32
Puerto Rico	na	**na**	na	na	na	na	na	na	na	na	na	na	na	na	na	na
Romania	na	**58**	57	58	65	58	53	53	60	59	50	58	62	57	58	64
Russian Fed.	na	**30**	27	32	28	30	30	34	30	26	31	33	25	29	30	20
Serbia	na	**na**	na	na	na	na	na	na	na	na	na	na	na	na	na	na
Singapore	na	**na**	na	na	na	na	na	na	na	na	na	na	na	na	na	na
Slovakia	na	**43**	39	47	47	41	43	42	45	38	46	41	45	43	42	52
Slovenia	na	**52**	51	53	48	51	57	57	53	40	59	51	42	54	52	52
South Africa	na	**na**	na	na	na	na	na	na	na	na	na	na	na	na	na	na
Spain	na	**46**	45	48	46	46	47	49	45	43	49	50	44	54	46	41
Sweden	na	**37**	39	36	35	36	40	42	36	36	33	39	42	44	39	31
Switzerland	na	**na**	na	na	na	na	na	na	na	na	na	na	na	na	na	na
Taiwan	na	**na**	na	na	na	na	na	na	na	na	na	na	na	na	na	na
Tanzania	na	**na**	na	na	na	na	na	na	na	na	na	na	na	na	na	na
Turkey	na	**78**	79	77	76	79	80	78	77	78	78	77	80	75	79	83
Uganda	na	**na**	na	na	na	na	na	na	na	na	na	na	na	na	na	na
Ukraine	na	**47**	43	50	42	46	50	51	47	44	50	39	51	44	51	53
United States	na	**na**	na	na	na	na	na	na	na	na	na	na	na	na	na	na
Uruguay	na	**na**	na	na	na	na	na	na	na	na	na	na	na	na	na	na
Venezuela	na	**na**	na	na	na	na	na	na	na	na	na	na	na	na	na	na
Vietnam	na	**na**	na	na	na	na	na	na	na	na	na	na	na	na	na	na
Zimbabwe	na	**na**	na	na	na	na	na	na	na	na	na	na	na	na	na	na
Total	na	**46**	45	47	48	44	47	49	46	41	48	46	44	46	47	44

RANKING	
Country	2000
Malta	87
Turkey	78
Greece	61
Poland	61
Hungary	58
Ireland	58
Romania	58
Northern Ireland	56
France	54
Great Britain	53
Slovenia	52
Italy	51
Belgium	50
Austria	49
Luxembourg	48
Iceland	48
Ukraine	47
Spain	46
Croatia	43
Slovakia	43
Bulgaria	41
Germany	39
Denmark	39
Finland	38
Sweden	37
Belarus	36
Latvia	36
Portugal	34
Czech Republic	33
Netherlands	31
Russian Fed.	30
Estonia	27
Lithuania	22
Total	46

D041_1) MARRIAGE SUCCESS: TALKING A LOT

Here is a list of things which some people think make for a successful marriage. Please tell me, for each one, whether you think it is...

Very important (%) (EVS: V147)

Country	Wave		Gender		Age			Education			Income			Values		
	1990	2000	Male	Female	16-29	30-49	50+	Lower	Middle	Upper	Lower	Middle	Upper	Mat	Mixed	Postm.
Albania	na	**na**	na	na	na	na	na	na	na	na	na	na	na	na	na	na
Algeria	na	**na**	na	na	na	na	na	na	na	na	na	na	na	na	na	na
Argentina	na	**na**	na	na	na	na	na	na	na	na	na	na	na	na	na	na
Armenia	na	**na**	na	na	na	na	na	na	na	na	na	na	na	na	na	na
Australia	na	**na**	na	na	na	na	na	na	na	na	na	na	na	na	na	na
Austria	na	**53**	50	56	56	51	54	55	53	46	52	53	53	47	55	52
Azerbaijan	na	**na**	na	na	na	na	na	na	na	na	na	na	na	na	na	na
Bangladesh	na	**na**	na	na	na	na	na	na	na	na	na	na	na	na	na	na
Belarus	na	**34**	31	37	34	32	37	33	34	37	34	35	33	33	34	46
Belgium	na	**50**	49	51	46	50	52	52	50	48	55	51	47	53	48	51
Bosnia and Herz.	na	**na**	na	na	na	na	na	na	na	na	na	na	na	na	na	na
Brazil	na	**na**	na	na	na	na	na	na	na	na	na	na	na	na	na	na
Bulgaria	na	**45**	42	48	53	46	40	36	52	42	44	44	45	43	47	46
Canada	na	**na**	na	na	na	na	na	na	na	na	na	na	na	na	na	na
Chile	na	**na**	na	na	na	na	na	na	na	na	na	na	na	na	na	na
China	na	**na**	na	na	na	na	na	na	na	na	na	na	na	na	na	na
Colombia	na	**na**	na	na	na	na	na	na	na	na	na	na	na	na	na	na
Croatia	na	**46**	44	47	51	47	40	41	48	49	40	46	51	39	45	53
Czech Republic	na	**28**	26	29	29	24	31	29	26	26	31	26	26	26	28	32
Denmark	na	**38**	36	40	35	33	45	39	36	38	42	34	39	31	40	34
Dominican Rep.	na	**na**	na	na	na	na	na	na	na	na	na	na	na	na	na	na
Egypt	na	**na**	na	na	na	na	na	na	na	na	na	na	na	na	na	na
El Salvador	na	**na**	na	na	na	na	na	na	na	na	na	na	na	na	na	na
Estonia	na	**21**	19	22	22	20	21	22	22	16	21	22	20	21	21	29
Finland	na	**41**	36	45	47	39	39	40	41	45	48	39	37	42	39	49
France	na	**49**	46	53	43	51	51	52	47	46	50	48	49	51	51	44
Georgia	na	**na**	na	na	na	na	na	na	na	na	na	na	na	na	na	na
Germany	na	**49**	47	50	46	51	48	44	54	43	48	50	51	57	49	39
Great Britain	na	**48**	45	50	41	45	54	50	48	37	55	45	51	na	na	na
Greece	na	**62**	55	67	58	63	68	74	61	60	63	60	64	63	62	61
Hungary	na	**54**	50	57	52	52	56	52	56	56	51	55	55	52	55	64
Iceland	na	**33**	30	35	27	30	41	37	28	32	35	30	31	37	30	37
India	na	**na**	na	na	na	na	na	na	na	na	na	na	na	na	na	na
Indonesia	na	**na**	na	na	na	na	na	na	na	na	na	na	na	na	na	na
Iran	na	**na**	na	na	na	na	na	na	na	na	na	na	na	na	na	na
Ireland	na	**50**	51	49	44	47	57	55	49	45	56	52	41	53	51	42
Israel	na	**na**	na	na	na	na	na	na	na	na	na	na	na	na	na	na
Italy	na	**64**	60	67	67	64	61	63	66	60	63	64	62	61	64	65
Japan	na	**na**	na	na	na	na	na	na	na	na	na	na	na	na	na	na
Jordan	na	**na**	na	na	na	na	na	na	na	na	na	na	na	na	na	na
Korea, South	na	**na**	na	na	na	na	na	na	na	na	na	na	na	na	na	na
Latvia	na	**31**	26	35	30	29	34	32	32	27	33	31	28	34	29	26
Lithuania	na	**20**	19	21	24	22	15	14	22	22	20	15	25	19	19	24
Luxembourg	na	**54**	52	55	50	50	60	59	52	47	53	53	45	52	55	54
Macedonia	na	**na**	na	na	na	na	na	na	na	na	na	na	na	na	na	na
Malta	na	**83**	82	83	76	84	86	85	82	79	86	82	81	76	86	85
Mexico	na	**na**	na	na	na	na	na	na	na	na	na	na	na	na	na	na
Moldova	na	**na**	na	na	na	na	na	na	na	na	na	na	na	na	na	na
Montenegro	na	**na**	na	na	na	na	na	na	na	na	na	na	na	na	na	na
Morocco	na	**na**	na	na	na	na	na	na	na	na	na	na	na	na	na	na
Netherlands	na	**34**	29	39	35	26	41	43	33	27	42	31	26	41	33	34
New Zealand	na	**na**	na	na	na	na	na	na	na	na	na	na	na	na	na	na
Nigeria	na	**na**	na	na	na	na	na	na	na	na	na	na	na	na	na	na
Northern Ireland	na	**54**	53	55	53	49	60	56	52	53	57	50	46	51	53	59
Norway	na	**na**	na	na	na	na	na	na	na	na	na	na	na	na	na	na
Pakistan	na	**na**	na	na	na	na	na	na	na	na	na	na	na	na	na	na
Peru	na	**na**	na	na	na	na	na	na	na	na	na	na	na	na	na	na
Philippines	na	**na**	na	na	na	na	na	na	na	na	na	na	na	na	na	na
Poland	na	**54**	54	54	58	48	58	53	56	49	54	52	56	50	57	54
Portugal	na	**47**	47	47	52	44	45	45	48	54	45	45	58	35	55	42
Puerto Rico	na	**na**	na	na	na	na	na	na	na	na	na	na	na	na	na	na
Romania	na	**56**	57	56	61	59	52	49	59	63	45	58	64	53	59	68
Russian Fed.	na	**29**	25	32	29	30	27	29	30	26	30	32	26	27	31	25
Serbia	na	**na**	na	na	na	na	na	na	na	na	na	na	na	na	na	na
Singapore	na	**na**	na	na	na	na	na	na	na	na	na	na	na	na	na	na
Slovakia	na	**44**	40	48	46	43	45	46	43	45	45	44	45	44	44	53
Slovenia	na	**60**	56	63	59	58	61	66	59	51	63	59	49	61	61	57
South Africa	na	**na**	na	na	na	na	na	na	na	na	na	na	na	na	na	na
Spain	na	**50**	47	52	56	48	48	47	51	56	49	57	51	52	49	54
Sweden	na	**43**	42	44	37	42	47	44	41	45	42	40	48	46	42	44
Switzerland	na	**na**	na	na	na	na	na	na	na	na	na	na	na	na	na	na
Taiwan	na	**na**	na	na	na	na	na	na	na	na	na	na	na	na	na	na
Tanzania	na	**na**	na	na	na	na	na	na	na	na	na	na	na	na	na	na
Turkey	na	**71**	71	71	69	72	75	73	69	62	72	70	69	78	70	73
Uganda	na	**na**	na	na	na	na	na	na	na	na	na	na	na	na	na	na
Ukraine	na	**50**	48	50	47	48	52	53	49	50	55	42	50	44	56	60
United States	na	**na**	na	na	na	na	na	na	na	na	na	na	na	na	na	na
Uruguay	na	**na**	na	na	na	na	na	na	na	na	na	na	na	na	na	na
Venezuela	na	**na**	na	na	na	na	na	na	na	na	na	na	na	na	na	na
Vietnam	na	**na**	na	na	na	na	na	na	na	na	na	na	na	na	na	na
Zimbabwe	na	**na**	na	na	na	na	na	na	na	na	na	na	na	na	na	na
Total	na	**46**	44	48	46	45	48	47	46	45	47	44	45	44	47	49

RANKING	
Country	**2000**
Malta	83
Turkey	71
Italy	64
Greece	62
Slovenia	60
Romania	56
Northern Ireland	54
Poland	54
Luxembourg	54
Hungary	54
Austria	53
Ireland	50
Belgium	50
Spain	50
Ukraine	50
France	49
Germany	49
Great Britain	48
Portugal	47
Croatia	46
Bulgaria	45
Slovakia	44
Sweden	43
Finland	41
Denmark	38
Belarus	34
Netherlands	34
Iceland	33
Latvia	31
Russian Fed.	29
Czech Republic	28
Estonia	21
Lithuania	20
Total	46

D054) MAKE MY PARENTS PROUD

For each of the following statements I read out, can you tell me how much you agree with each. Do you agree strongly, agree, disagree, or disagree strongly? "One of my main goals in life has been to make my parents proud"

Agree strongly / Agree (%)

(WVS: V113)

Country	Wave		Gender		Age			Education			Income			Values		
	1990	2000	Male	Female	16-29	30-49	50+	Lower	Middle	Upper	Lower	Middle	Upper	Mat	Mixed	Postm.
Albania	na	**94**	93	94	95	94	92	92	94	96	94	92	95	93	94	97
Algeria	na	**92**	90	94	94	90	93	93	92	92	95	94	92	90	93	94
Argentina	na	**85**	87	84	85	84	87	89	82	70	90	88	77	92	87	76
Armenia	na	**84**	84	85	84	87	81	79	85	83	84	84	84	85	85	78
Australia	na	**69**	67	70	72	63	72	76	70	61	72	68	64	79	71	63
Austria	na	**na**	na	na	na	na	na	na	na	na	na	na	na	na	na	na
Azerbaijan	na	**86**	86	87	91	86	76	87	87	85	93	86	82	87	86	87
Bangladesh	na	**96**	96	96	97	95	96	95	98	95	94	94	100	96	96	92
Belarus	na	**na**	na	na	na	na	na	na	na	na	na	na	na	na	na	na
Belgium	na	**na**	na	na	na	na	na	na	na	na	na	na	na	na	na	na
Bosnia and Herz.	na	**88**	88	89	92	88	86	90	87	89	91	88	86	87	89	83
Brazil	na	**88**	89	86	89	87	88	91	88	77	90	88	85	93	86	85
Bulgaria	na	**na**	na	na	na	na	na	na	na	na	na	na	na	na	na	na
Canada	na	**81**	79	82	84	78	82	83	83	76	84	83	77	83	83	76
Chile	na	**84**	85	84	91	84	78	78	88	86	81	86	87	85	84	82
China	na	**61**	59	64	52	64	64	66	60	43	65	61	56	62	57	63
Colombia	na	**93**	93	94	95	92	95	96	96	89	95	95	90	93	95	92
Croatia	na	**na**	na	na	na	na	na	na	na	na	na	na	na	na	na	na
Czech Republic	na	**na**	na	na	na	na	na	na	na	na	na	na	na	na	na	na
Denmark	na	**na**	na	na	na	na	na	na	na	na	na	na	na	na	na	na
Dominican Rep.	na	**89**	87	91	90	88	80	90	89	89	90	86	93	90	90	84
Egypt	na	**99**	98	99	98	98	99	99	99	98	99	98	99	99	99	97
El Salvador	na	**96**	97	96	96	96	98	96	98	94	96	97	94	na	na	na
Estonia	na	**na**	na	na	na	na	na	na	na	na	na	na	na	na	na	na
Finland	na	**na**	na	na	na	na	na	na	na	na	na	na	na	na	na	na
France	na	**na**	na	na	na	na	na	na	na	na	na	na	na	na	na	na
Georgia	na	**85**	85	85	86	87	80	85	85	84	85	86	84	85	85	85
Germany	na	**na**	na	na	na	na	na	na	na	na	na	na	na	na	na	na
Great Britain	na	**na**	na	na	na	na	na	na	na	na	na	na	na	na	na	na
Greece	na	**na**	na	na	na	na	na	na	na	na	na	na	na	na	na	na
Hungary	na	**na**	na	na	na	na	na	na	na	na	na	na	na	na	na	na
Iceland	na	**na**	na	na	na	na	na	na	na	na	na	na	na	na	na	na
India	na	**89**	89	88	90	90	86	89	91	86	88	89	90	88	90	89
Indonesia	na	**92**	92	92	92	93	91	93	93	90	90	93	93	95	90	93
Iran	na	**92**	92	92	93	91	93	92	92	91	92	88	93	93	91	93
Ireland	na	**na**	na	na	na	na	na	na	na	na	na	na	na	na	na	na
Israel	na	**na**	na	na	na	na	na	na	na	na	na	na	na	na	na	na
Italy	na	**na**	na	na	na	na	na	na	na	na	na	na	na	na	na	na
Japan	na	**73**	75	70	70	67	79	80	72	71	76	71	71	80	72	63
Jordan	na	**99**	99	99	99	100	99	99	100	98	99	99	99	100	99	96
Korea, South	na	**75**	80	70	73	72	84	87	75	74	72	74	79	76	73	83
Latvia	na	**na**	na	na	na	na	na	na	na	na	na	na	na	na	na	na
Lithuania	na	**na**	na	na	na	na	na	na	na	na	na	na	na	na	na	na
Luxembourg	na	**na**	na	na	na	na	na	na	na	na	na	na	na	na	na	na
Macedonia	na	**84**	85	83	86	81	87	93	81	77	88	82	81	80	86	92
Malta	na	**na**	na	na	na	na	na	na	na	na	na	na	na	na	na	na
Mexico	na	**93**	93	94	94	93	93	93	94	94	94	92	95	94	93	95
Moldova	na	**93**	90	95	91	93	93	94	92	92	96	91	95	93	92	85
Montenegro	na	**74**	73	75	74	72	75	73	74	72	82	74	74	76	69	72
Morocco	na	**97**	98	97	98	97	97	98	98	96	99	99	93	97	98	98
Netherlands	na	**na**	na	na	na	na	na	na	na	na	na	na	na	na	na	na
New Zealand	na	**55**	55	54	66	45	59	59	55	50	59	53	53	64	53	46
Nigeria	na	**98**	98	98	98	99	96	99	98	98	98	99	98	98	99	99
Northern Ireland	na	**na**	na	na	na	na	na	na	na	na	na	na	na	na	na	na
Norway	na	**54**	55	54	63	46	59	65	56	42	na	na	na	59	55	45
Pakistan	na	**97**	97	97	96	97	98	97	97	97	97	97	98	97	97	92
Peru	na	**96**	96	96	96	96	96	95	96	96	96	96	95	96	96	97
Philippines	na	**96**	97	96	96	95	98	97	97	95	96	95	97	94	98	95
Poland	na	**na**	na	na	na	na	na	na	na	na	na	na	na	na	na	na
Portugal	na	**na**	na	na	na	na	na	na	na	na	na	na	na	na	na	na
Puerto Rico	na	**95**	97	95	93	95	98	97	97	94	97	93	96	95	95	96
Romania	na	**na**	na	na	na	na	na	na	na	na	na	na	na	na	na	na
Russian Fed.	na	**na**	na	na	na	na	na	na	na	na	na	na	na	na	na	na
Serbia	na	**75**	69	81	68	71	83	82	72	71	80	71	75	79	74	57
Singapore	na	**91**	91	91	94	86	92	93	92	83	90	93	90	92	91	85
Slovakia	na	**na**	na	na	na	na	na	na	na	na	na	na	na	na	na	na
Slovenia	na	**na**	na	na	na	na	na	na	na	na	na	na	na	na	na	na
South Africa	na	**95**	94	96	97	94	91	95	95	83	95	99	91	94	95	93
Spain	na	**85**	82	87	79	79	93	89	80	75	92	85	77	87	86	74
Sweden	na	**38**	42	34	43	29	43	50	37	30	43	38	31	55	40	28
Switzerland	na	**45**	45	44	45	39	51	56	42	45	50	51	38	58	46	29
Taiwan	na	**65**	62	67	57	64	71	72	68	56	66	65	63	66	66	53
Tanzania	na	**88**	89	86	91	85	88	88	88	85	90	84	89	87	88	88
Turkey	na	**97**	96	98	97	97	97	98	97	90	98	97	93	98	97	94
Uganda	na	**94**	93	94	97	92	86	93	96	75	96	90	95	94	94	91
Ukraine	na	**na**	na	na	na	na	na	na	na	na	na	na	na	na	na	na
United States	na	**83**	87	78	87	80	83	83	84	82	82	83	82	87	83	80
Uruguay	na	**68**	69	68	67	63	73	73	63	58	68	69	67	68	71	61
Venezuela	na	**97**	97	98	98	97	97	98	97	98	94	99	98	95	98	98
Vietnam	na	**97**	98	97	98	97	97	97	98	96	95	98	98	93	98	100
Zimbabwe	na	**97**	95	98	96	98	98	98	95	100	96	97	97	96	97	97
Total	na	**85**	85	85	88	83	83	88	84	81	86	86	84	88	84	77

RANKING	
Country	2000
Jordan	99
Egypt	99
Nigeria	98
Morocco	97
Venezuela	97
Vietnam	97
Zimbabwe	97
Pakistan	97
Turkey	97
El Salvador	96
Philippines	96
Peru	96
Bangladesh	96
Puerto Rico	95
South Africa	95
Uganda	94
Albania	94
Colombia	93
Mexico	93
Moldova	93
Algeria	92
Iran	92
Indonesia	92
Singapore	91
Dominican Rep.	89
India	89
Bosnia and Herz.	88
Brazil	88
Tanzania	88
Azerbaijan	86
Argentina	85
Georgia	85
Spain	85
Macedonia	84
Armenia	84
Chile	84
United States	83
Canada	81
Serbia	75
Korea, South	75
Montenegro	74
Japan	73
Australia	69
Uruguay	68
Taiwan	65
China	61
New Zealand	55
Norway	54
Switzerland	45
Sweden	38
Total	85

D055) LIVE UP TO WHAT MY FRIENDS EXPECT

For each of the following statements I read out, can you tell me how much you agree with each. Do you agree strongly, agree, disagree, or disagree strongly? "I make a lot of effort to live up to what my friends expect"

(WVS: V114)

Agree strongly / Agree (%)

Country	Wave		Gender		Age			Education			Income			Values		
	1990	2000	Male	Female	16-29	30-49	50+	Lower	Middle	Upper	Lower	Middle	Upper	Mat	Mixed	Postm.
Albania	na	**52**	53	50	42	53	58	56	49	47	58	46	50	52	51	54
Algeria	na	**71**	73	69	71	72	72	70	72	71	73	77	68	67	74	77
Argentina	na	**25**	32	20	25	23	29	28	23	18	28	27	21	30	28	17
Armenia	na	**73**	79	69	72	75	74	71	73	74	72	73	76	71	76	73
Australia	na	**34**	36	32	30	29	43	42	33	29	41	29	30	42	35	31
Austria	na	**na**	na	na	na	na	na	na	na	na	na	na	na	na	na	na
Azerbaijan	na	**74**	76	72	83	72	60	73	73	77	76	76	74	72	77	82
Bangladesh	na	**59**	64	53	60	59	59	55	62	65	45	59	73	54	64	54
Belarus	na	**na**	na	na	na	na	na	na	na	na	na	na	na	na	na	na
Belgium	na	**na**	na	na	na	na	na	na	na	na	na	na	na	na	na	na
Bosnia and Herz.	na	**31**	33	30	30	32	33	38	32	25	32	34	27	26	32	38
Brazil	na	**75**	75	76	70	75	87	85	70	60	81	78	67	81	75	62
Bulgaria	na	**na**	na	na	na	na	na	na	na	na	na	na	na	na	na	na
Canada	na	**44**	48	40	47	38	51	53	45	36	52	46	37	48	46	39
Chile	na	**35**	35	35	38	32	37	36	36	31	39	33	32	33	36	33
China	na	**77**	75	78	74	77	77	77	77	66	80	75	71	72	80	77
Colombia	na	**41**	41	41	40	41	47	52	48	26	54	44	30	55	53	39
Croatia	na	**na**	na	na	na	na	na	na	na	na	na	na	na	na	na	na
Czech Republic	na	**na**	na	na	na	na	na	na	na	na	na	na	na	na	na	na
Denmark	na	**na**	na	na	na	na	na	na	na	na	na	na	na	na	na	na
Dominican Rep.	na	**70**	72	68	70	67	91	83	79	66	75	61	65	83	68	63
Egypt	na	**72**	74	70	76	71	69	67	77	77	73	72	74	71	74	74
El Salvador	na	**na**	na	na	na	na	na	na	na	na	na	na	na	na	na	na
Estonia	na	**na**	na	na	na	na	na	na	na	na	na	na	na	na	na	na
Finland	na	**na**	na	na	na	na	na	na	na	na	na	na	na	na	na	na
France	na	**na**	na	na	na	na	na	na	na	na	na	na	na	na	na	na
Georgia	na	**89**	89	89	91	90	85	89	89	90	88	89	91	89	89	91
Germany	na	**na**	na	na	na	na	na	na	na	na	na	na	na	na	na	na
Great Britain	na	**na**	na	na	na	na	na	na	na	na	na	na	na	na	na	na
Greece	na	**na**	na	na	na	na	na	na	na	na	na	na	na	na	na	na
Hungary	na	**na**	na	na	na	na	na	na	na	na	na	na	na	na	na	na
Iceland	na	**na**	na	na	na	na	na	na	na	na	na	na	na	na	na	na
India	na	**55**	58	51	58	55	53	55	53	57	59	54	54	56	58	44
Indonesia	na	**58**	62	55	48	65	56	61	60	54	62	60	56	56	60	64
Iran	na	**53**	55	51	52	51	57	55	54	48	54	48	53	50	53	53
Ireland	na	**na**	na	na	na	na	na	na	na	na	na	na	na	na	na	na
Israel	na	**na**	na	na	na	na	na	na	na	na	na	na	na	na	na	na
Italy	na	**na**	na	na	na	na	na	na	na	na	na	na	na	na	na	na
Japan	na	**65**	70	60	69	61	67	65	63	68	64	67	63	72	62	65
Jordan	na	**87**	88	87	87	88	87	85	90	88	89	86	89	88	87	84
Korea, South	na	**72**	77	67	74	71	72	64	72	74	67	75	75	69	74	79
Latvia	na	**na**	na	na	na	na	na	na	na	na	na	na	na	na	na	na
Lithuania	na	**na**	na	na	na	na	na	na	na	na	na	na	na	na	na	na
Luxembourg	na	**na**	na	na	na	na	na	na	na	na	na	na	na	na	na	na
Macedonia	na	**35**	37	33	46	33	29	47	30	29	38	36	27	28	37	55
Malta	na	**na**	na	na	na	na	na	na	na	na	na	na	na	na	na	na
Mexico	na	**54**	54	54	57	51	56	56	52	52	56	54	53	58	53	53
Moldova	na	**70**	67	72	71	68	70	74	70	65	77	69	69	72	65	63
Montenegro	na	**69**	69	69	71	69	67	70	70	62	81	65	68	72	63	68
Morocco	na	**73**	77	70	76	73	67	73	73	76	76	70	71	74	76	77
Netherlands	na	**na**	na	na	na	na	na	na	na	na	na	na	na	na	na	na
New Zealand	na	**28**	32	25	27	20	36	33	30	21	36	23	23	38	26	23
Nigeria	na	**77**	80	73	78	76	67	75	79	76	76	76	79	77	76	81
Northern Ireland	na	**na**	na	na	na	na	na	na	na	na	na	na	na	na	na	na
Norway	na	**19**	19	19	22	14	23	23	19	16	na	na	na	29	17	21
Pakistan	na	**48**	48	48	42	51	52	57	32	51	56	45	42	49	47	18
Peru	na	**57**	60	54	58	57	54	58	58	54	59	58	52	55	57	62
Philippines	na	**55**	53	56	56	53	56	55	56	52	56	52	56	55	54	56
Poland	na	**na**	na	na	na	na	na	na	na	na	na	na	na	na	na	na
Portugal	na	**na**	na	na	na	na	na	na	na	na	na	na	na	na	na	na
Puerto Rico	na	**52**	54	51	51	48	56	62	55	50	63	51	46	49	56	45
Romania	na	**na**	na	na	na	na	na	na	na	na	na	na	na	na	na	na
Russian Fed.	na	**na**	na	na	na	na	na	na	na	na	na	na	na	na	na	na
Serbia	na	**63**	61	64	61	60	66	64	63	62	62	62	64	62	64	56
Singapore	na	**43**	48	38	51	36	34	44	44	35	41	47	43	36	46	42
Slovakia	na	**na**	na	na	na	na	na	na	na	na	na	na	na	na	na	na
Slovenia	na	**na**	na	na	na	na	na	na	na	na	na	na	na	na	na	na
South Africa	na	**38**	41	33	38	40	28	39	37	31	40	38	35	32	40	49
Spain	na	**58**	58	59	54	55	64	59	57	56	60	56	58	54	63	46
Sweden	na	**na**	na	na	na	na	na	na	na	na	na	na	na	na	na	na
Switzerland	na	**47**	49	45	47	43	53	53	47	37	50	52	42	55	50	35
Taiwan	na	**59**	57	61	58	59	57	60	66	53	64	62	53	59	60	51
Tanzania	na	**40**	43	36	36	43	38	39	40	42	40	40	47	39	39	46
Turkey	na	**na**	na	na	na	na	na	na	na	na	na	na	na	na	na	na
Uganda	na	**80**	87	73	83	77	77	78	80	87	85	87	81	75	83	79
Ukraine	na	**na**	na	na	na	na	na	na	na	na	na	na	na	na	na	na
United States	na	**33**	35	32	30	28	43	35	32	33	29	35	37	32	35	29
Uruguay	na	**29**	33	26	27	24	34	35	22	17	29	35	23	30	32	20
Venezuela	na	**37**	39	35	38	35	38	45	40	21	46	40	29	36	40	28
Vietnam	na	**77**	78	76	77	78	75	78	75	77	72	76	80	72	80	76
Zimbabwe	na	**50**	50	49	52	47	48	52	47	32	54	49	42	51	49	44
Total	na	**55**	57	53	58	54	54	57	56	52	59	55	54	59	55	46

RANKING	
Country	**2000**
Georgia	89
Jordan	87
Uganda	80
Vietnam	77
Nigeria	77
China	77
Brazil	75
Azerbaijan	74
Armenia	73
Morocco	73
Egypt	72
Korea, South	72
Algeria	71
Dominican Rep.	70
Moldova	70
Montenegro	69
Japan	65
Serbia	63
Bangladesh	59
Taiwan	59
Indonesia	58
Spain	58
Peru	57
India	55
Philippines	55
Mexico	54
Iran	53
Puerto Rico	52
Albania	52
Zimbabwe	50
Pakistan	48
Switzerland	47
Canada	44
Singapore	43
Colombia	41
Tanzania	40
South Africa	38
Venezuela	37
Macedonia	35
Chile	35
Australia	34
United States	33
Bosnia and Herz.	31
Uruguay	29
New Zealand	28
Argentina	25
Norway	19
Total	55

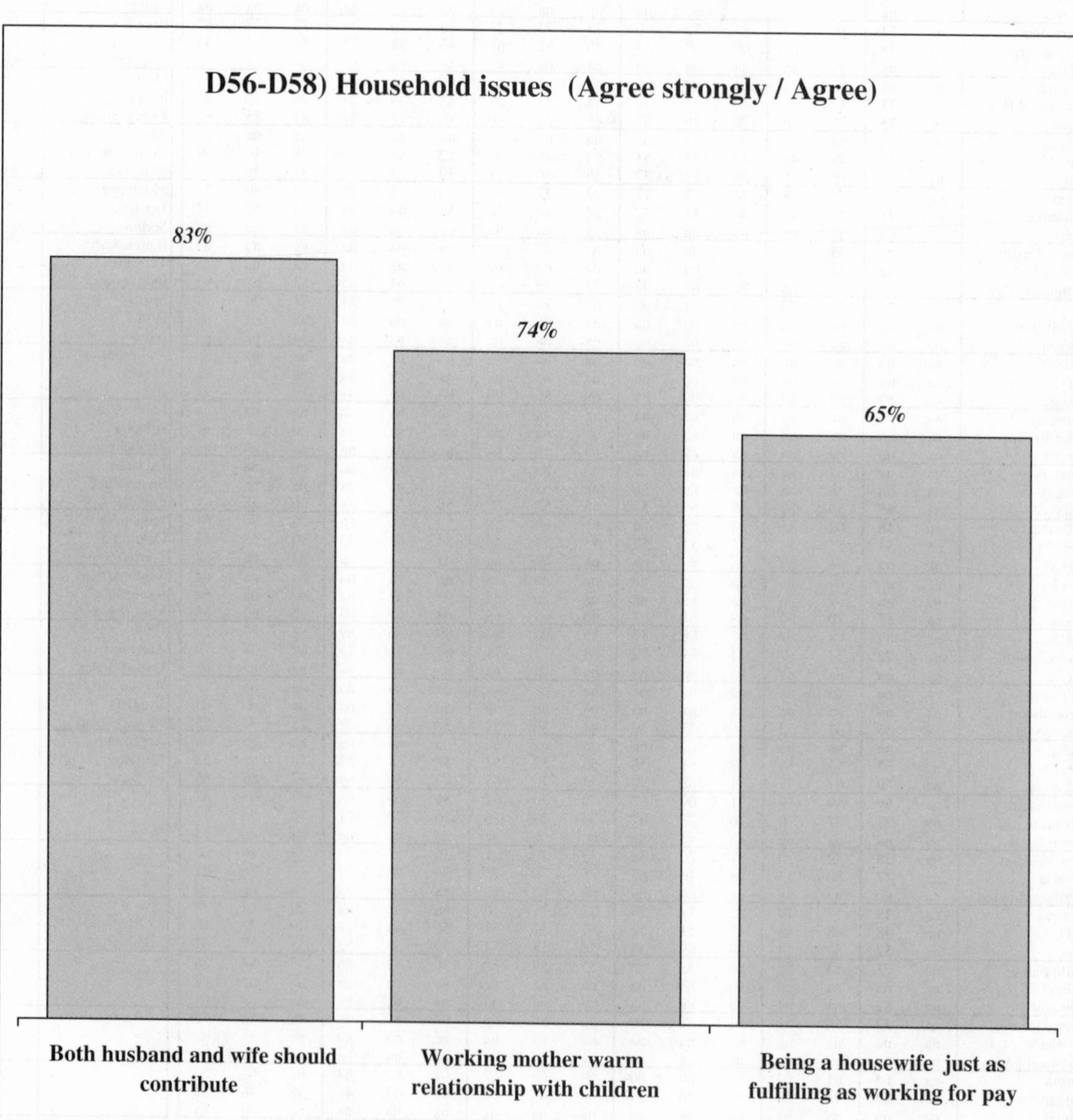
D56-D58) Household issues (Agree strongly / Agree)
83%
74%
65%
Both husband and wife should contribute
Working mother warm relationship with children
Being a housewife just as fulfilling as working for pay

D056) A WORKING MOTHER RELATIONSHIP

Do you agree strongly, agree, disagree, or disagree strongly? "A working mother can establish just as warm and secure a relationship with her children as a mother who does not work"

(WVS: V115; EVS: V154)

Agree strongly / Agree (%)

Country	Wave		Gender		Age			Education			Income			Values		
	1990	2000	Male	Female	16-29	30-49	50+	Lower	Middle	Upper	Lower	Middle	Upper	Mat	Mixed	Postm.
Albania	na	**76**	75	77	78	75	76	73	76	82	70	78	80	75	76	74
Algeria	na	**65**	56	74	63	69	62	58	61	75	62	65	72	61	65	74
Argentina	74	**76**	70	81	77	76	74	72	80	84	75	75	77	76	75	78
Armenia	na	**82**	77	87	82	82	83	82	81	85	83	78	84	80	84	81
Australia	na	**69**	62	75	76	71	59	65	68	72	64	68	75	62	68	73
Austria	53	**na**	na	na	na	na	na	na	na	na	na	na	na	na	na	na
Azerbaijan	na	**80**	77	83	81	80	78	77	79	82	82	79	80	80	79	82
Bangladesh	na	**60**	61	58	62	59	51	53	68	63	38	67	69	51	65	67
Belarus	65	**82**	80	83	87	81	79	79	83	81	83	81	82	85	82	78
Belgium	74	**79**	75	82	80	80	77	68	79	85	72	79	84	70	80	83
Bosnia and Herz.	na	**82**	78	86	83	82	82	79	82	86	74	85	83	83	81	90
Brazil	64	**68**	64	73	75	64	65	61	71	84	62	69	74	61	70	79
Bulgaria	61	**79**	80	78	86	79	77	81	79	77	77	83	77	81	78	67
Canada	70	**78**	75	80	80	80	73	71	80	79	77	76	80	73	77	81
Chile	72	**78**	76	80	81	79	74	71	81	85	74	80	82	77	77	83
China	91	**94**	94	94	88	95	96	94	95	88	94	95	94	95	92	97
Colombia	na	**61**	60	63	61	62	58	53	57	72	54	58	70	55	61	67
Croatia	na	**66**	65	67	77	70	54	54	71	85	49	69	71	67	65	70
Czech Republic	59	**81**	78	84	79	81	82	79	82	86	83	78	83	81	81	79
Denmark	83	**86**	85	88	87	88	85	83	91	91	84	90	89	81	86	93
Dominican Rep.	na	**62**	54	67	63	60	27	34	48	69	54	64	72	57	61	63
Egypt	na	**46**	37	55	50	43	45	42	50	48	45	43	48	45	46	45
El Salvador	na	**47**	46	48	50	46	44	41	47	63	40	45	58	na	na	na
Estonia	82	**71**	63	77	72	73	68	67	71	77	70	74	69	67	74	72
Finland	94	**95**	93	97	94	95	95	93	97	96	93	96	95	94	95	96
France	73	**77**	74	81	78	82	73	72	83	86	72	79	81	74	76	88
Georgia	na	**79**	72	84	82	79	75	74	79	83	77	80	82	80	79	73
Germany	57	**67**	62	71	78	68	62	61	71	79	65	64	69	60	67	77
Great Britain	70	**73**	69	77	83	72	67	71	75	67	69	74	75	na	na	na
Greece	na	**76**	70	80	77	79	66	65	71	81	73	78	78	77	76	72
Hungary	70	**78**	77	79	80	72	81	79	73	82	69	79	81	82	74	69
Iceland	82	**86**	80	92	80	92	82	85	85	92	83	85	91	85	86	92
India	58	**62**	59	67	65	61	59	61	58	66	63	59	64	55	68	51
Indonesia	na	**64**	64	65	60	66	65	67	64	63	59	70	66	63	66	61
Iran	na	**77**	80	74	74	79	84	85	81	68	81	78	72	83	74	74
Ireland	63	**na**	na	na	na	na	na	na	na	na	na	na	na	na	na	na
Israel	na	**na**	na	na	na	na	na	na	na	na	na	na	na	na	na	na
Italy	63	**64**	60	68	69	68	58	55	68	81	56	64	75	52	63	72
Japan	89	**95**	94	97	95	95	96	93	96	94	96	96	93	96	95	96
Jordan	na	**47**	37	57	50	44	49	47	45	50	49	44	46	48	46	53
Korea, South	43	**83**	81	86	89	82	80	59	84	85	82	85	84	79	87	88
Latvia	47	**76**	71	79	71	81	74	73	74	82	74	80	74	78	74	69
Lithuania	42	**77**	75	78	83	75	73	68	79	83	74	74	77	67	80	89
Luxembourg	na	**76**	73	79	82	76	71	72	76	83	65	77	82	71	78	84
Macedonia	na	**74**	75	74	76	75	73	71	74	81	71	73	81	76	75	70
Malta	na	**61**	57	64	73	62	51	52	62	77	47	57	72	56	64	57
Mexico	64	**69**	67	72	71	71	64	66	72	77	66	71	74	69	69	69
Moldova	na	**86**	86	85	81	88	87	86	85	86	89	81	87	84	90	87
Montenegro	na	**77**	73	80	82	80	69	69	79	87	62	78	80	72	81	76
Morocco	na	**60**	50	69	61	60	57	59	63	71	57	66	60	62	58	65
Netherlands	75	**81**	77	86	82	82	80	72	85	86	73	85	88	68	82	88
New Zealand	na	**68**	63	72	74	68	66	68	64	71	65	69	72	70	68	71
Nigeria	65	**74**	71	77	74	75	70	73	75	73	71	75	76	73	75	71
Northern Ireland	71	**na**	na	na	na	na	na	na	na	na	na	na	na	na	na	na
Norway	69	**71**	64	76	66	73	71	62	68	81	na	na	na	66	69	83
Pakistan	na	**18**	14	24	25	19	4	14	19	32	15	14	26	19	17	33
Peru	na	**70**	70	70	67	73	68	61	66	82	62	74	80	70	68	78
Philippines	na	**73**	69	77	73	72	75	74	72	73	73	74	72	72	74	71
Poland	na	**54**	49	59	64	56	46	52	58	55	53	55	56	50	55	58
Portugal	76	**67**	66	68	78	66	62	64	73	80	67	60	71	62	68	78
Puerto Rico	na	**78**	74	80	80	82	74	66	72	84	73	76	84	70	79	81
Romania	84	**83**	83	83	81	87	81	78	84	90	79	84	87	83	83	90
Russian Fed.	64	**83**	82	84	83	83	84	86	83	82	83	84	84	85	83	68
Serbia	na	**79**	74	85	90	82	72	71	81	88	73	81	86	76	83	81
Singapore	na	**74**	72	75	72	73	80	73	75	67	71	71	77	69	76	66
Slovakia	na	**81**	77	85	83	81	79	76	83	82	78	83	83	83	80	86
Slovenia	74	**83**	82	83	89	84	77	76	84	87	79	80	89	77	83	86
South Africa	na	**80**	77	84	80	82	73	79	83	64	79	82	78	78	82	81
Spain	67	**79**	78	80	85	83	71	74	83	85	72	82	81	72	81	86
Sweden	73	**84**	78	90	85	84	83	79	86	86	82	84	87	80	83	87
Switzerland	na	**na**	na	na	na	na	na	na	na	na	na	na	na	na	na	na
Taiwan	na	**92**	92	91	97	90	92	90	92	93	89	92	93	89	94	89
Tanzania	na	**74**	73	76	74	75	74	76	73	70	79	75	76	74	74	83
Turkey	57	**70**	68	72	70	71	68	67	73	81	67	71	78	64	72	73
Uganda	na	**58**	60	56	60	56	57	53	60	60	55	67	65	56	58	61
Ukraine	na	**83**	83	83	80	81	87	83	84	81	85	82	82	82	84	73
United States	72	**79**	75	83	81	80	75	77	79	79	77	77	82	78	77	83
Uruguay	na	**70**	67	72	74	75	64	65	78	69	70	69	70	61	73	68
Venezuela	na	**72**	67	76	74	71	68	68	71	79	70	66	75	64	74	77
Vietnam	na	**84**	81	86	83	87	81	84	84	83	81	85	83	84	83	85
Zimbabwe	na	**73**	73	73	72	72	78	73	74	100	71	70	77	76	71	74
Total	68	74	70	77	74	74	72	68	75	78	71	74	77	71	75	78

RANKING

Country	2000
Japan	95
Finland	95
China	94
Taiwan	92
Denmark	86
Iceland	86
Moldova	86
Sweden	84
Vietnam	84
Korea, South	83
Ukraine	83
Russian Fed.	83
Romania	83
Slovenia	83
Bosnia and Herz.	82
Armenia	82
Belarus	82
Netherlands	81
Slovakia	81
Czech Republic	81
South Africa	80
Azerbaijan	80
Bulgaria	79
Serbia	79
Georgia	79
Spain	79
United States	79
Belgium	79
Chile	78
Puerto Rico	78
Hungary	78
Canada	78
France	77
Iran	77
Lithuania	77
Montenegro	77
Albania	76
Luxembourg	76
Argentina	76
Greece	76
Latvia	76
Macedonia	74
Tanzania	74
Nigeria	74
Singapore	74
Zimbabwe	73
Great Britain	73
Philippines	73
Venezuela	72
Estonia	71
Norway	71
Peru	70
Turkey	70
Uruguay	70
Mexico	69
Australia	69
Brazil	68
New Zealand	68
Germany	67
Portugal	67
Croatia	66
Algeria	65
Indonesia	64
Italy	64
India	62
Dominican Rep.	62
Colombia	61
Malta	61
Morocco	60
Bangladesh	60
Uganda	58
Poland	54
Jordan	47
El Salvador	47
Egypt	46
Pakistan	18
Total	74

D057) BEING A HOUSEWIFE FULFILLING

For each of the following statements I read out, can you tell me how much you agree with each. Do you agree strongly, agree, disagree, or disagree strongly? "Being a housewife is just as fulfilling as working for pay"

Agree strongly / Agree (%)

(WVS: V116; EVS: V157)

Country	Wave		Gender		Age			Education			Income			Values		
	1990	2000	Male	Female	16-29	30-49	50+	Lower	Middle	Upper	Lower	Middle	Upper	Mat	Mixed	Postm.
Albania	na	**46**	46	45	41	46	48	50	44	38	46	49	42	45	45	40
Algeria	na	**66**	63	70	62	69	72	67	67	66	68	69	64	65	65	74
Argentina	62	**75**	79	72	72	75	78	80	71	59	78	79	66	81	77	67
Armenia	na	**75**	81	70	72	78	78	77	78	68	72	77	79	76	75	77
Australia	na	**70**	71	68	68	67	75	76	70	64	73	69	65	72	71	67
Austria	63	**na**	na	na	na	na	na	na	na	na	na	na	na	na	na	na
Azerbaijan	na	**73**	76	70	74	72	74	81	75	67	83	74	62	74	70	82
Bangladesh	na	**29**	29	29	30	28	30	31	25	29	20	31	35	27	30	23
Belarus	81	**64**	61	66	56	60	75	75	61	58	69	63	57	66	63	48
Belgium	67	**64**	68	60	60	58	71	76	64	55	71	67	58	70	64	57
Bosnia and Herz.	na	**71**	75	68	64	71	77	76	73	61	74	74	67	77	67	79
Brazil	61	**61**	66	56	56	59	74	68	59	45	63	62	58	65	61	52
Bulgaria	87	**49**	54	46	49	45	53	58	49	36	59	43	42	49	47	73
Canada	71	**82**	84	81	81	78	88	86	81	81	85	83	80	87	81	83
Chile	74	**69**	71	67	66	65	77	71	68	67	67	73	66	73	69	62
China	88	**90**	90	90	86	91	92	90	90	91	89	91	90	91	89	88
Colombia	na	**66**	67	64	64	65	70	71	68	59	69	67	62	70	70	61
Croatia	na	**56**	55	56	45	59	60	62	57	34	63	58	51	63	55	52
Czech Republic	39	**76**	83	71	74	76	78	77	75	80	82	76	73	78	76	79
Denmark	55	**54**	56	53	51	51	60	54	52	54	58	52	49	51	56	47
Dominican Rep.	na	**49**	50	48	46	51	50	38	53	48	47	54	41	53	49	45
Egypt	na	**74**	77	72	71	75	78	79	71	69	77	75	74	77	73	74
El Salvador	na	**70**	68	72	66	71	75	76	66	60	75	70	59	na	na	na
Estonia	71	**59**	67	53	54	56	64	69	56	51	64	62	54	57	61	50
Finland	54	**81**	81	81	77	76	88	83	80	76	81	80	81	83	80	82
France	60	**62**	66	59	56	60	68	66	59	56	67	64	55	66	64	53
Georgia	na	**79**	80	78	78	79	81	86	80	72	81	80	76	80	78	78
Germany	34	**43**	45	41	29	38	53	55	33	28	52	44	41	56	41	23
Great Britain	60	**61**	59	63	61	54	69	68	59	46	73	57	57	na	na	na
Greece	na	**42**	53	34	31	44	62	74	48	30	55	38	37	50	40	40
Hungary	76	**61**	64	59	58	56	69	69	47	45	61	63	59	64	59	49
Iceland	71	**65**	65	64	58	62	74	65	64	64	66	63	64	66	65	56
India	46	**64**	64	65	63	63	66	64	59	70	59	63	67	61	65	69
Indonesia	na	**23**	20	25	23	24	21	20	24	24	22	22	29	19	24	32
Iran	na	**75**	77	72	74	75	80	80	72	74	74	75	76	75	75	72
Ireland	72	**na**	na	na	na	na	na	na	na	na	na	na	na	na	na	na
Israel	na	**na**	na	na	na	na	na	na	na	na	na	na	na	na	na	na
Italy	57	**55**	59	51	45	49	65	65	50	39	62	57	50	63	56	49
Japan	83	**89**	91	87	82	88	92	91	90	86	91	87	88	88	89	89
Jordan	na	**76**	78	74	74	75	83	77	73	77	73	77	75	74	76	82
Korea, South	67	**89**	84	93	91	89	83	82	89	89	88	90	89	88	89	88
Latvia	66	**40**	44	37	37	35	46	49	38	34	42	41	35	43	39	33
Lithuania	85	**79**	79	78	76	75	84	85	79	67	81	79	76	77	78	85
Luxembourg	na	**65**	70	59	57	62	72	71	63	58	74	64	59	73	65	57
Macedonia	na	**52**	52	51	53	50	52	61	48	45	52	52	48	53	51	58
Malta	na	**87**	89	84	79	87	91	92	86	76	91	90	83	90	87	73
Mexico	68	**73**	74	73	67	76	75	76	71	68	71	71	73	80	71	67
Moldova	na	**72**	76	69	70	73	74	77	75	64	75	71	69	70	78	66
Montenegro	na	**65**	71	60	58	62	72	71	63	59	53	64	66	65	65	58
Morocco	na	**65**	63	67	63	65	74	67	59	57	57	65	70	69	63	65
Netherlands	53	**52**	55	48	46	46	59	65	47	43	60	49	43	60	51	49
New Zealand	na	**66**	63	68	68	61	70	68	71	59	71	67	60	61	64	68
Nigeria	49	**44**	44	44	43	47	44	50	40	42	45	42	45	44	45	42
Northern Ireland	70	**na**	na	na	na	na	na	na	na	na	na	na	na	na	na	na
Norway	53	**61**	62	59	53	60	67	66	61	54	na	na	na	70	58	62
Pakistan	na	**76**	80	72	67	76	94	84	67	68	83	78	70	80	71	73
Peru	na	**73**	72	74	68	76	78	74	72	73	72	76	70	75	72	75
Philippines	na	**86**	84	87	84	86	88	89	85	82	88	85	84	84	88	78
Poland	na	**61**	66	56	58	55	69	68	53	48	65	57	58	61	61	58
Portugal	49	**51**	54	48	41	45	61	55	45	37	61	54	47	56	46	47
Puerto Rico	na	**81**	82	81	72	79	87	77	85	80	82	82	81	81	81	85
Romania	48	**48**	49	48	46	49	49	53	47	40	50	52	44	52	44	54
Russian Fed.	86	**64**	69	59	60	62	67	77	64	55	68	65	59	64	63	55
Serbia	na	**69**	75	64	72	68	69	72	72	61	70	74	65	71	69	61
Singapore	na	**72**	74	71	68	74	82	72	70	81	74	67	77	73	72	71
Slovakia	na	**71**	75	67	67	69	75	75	70	63	74	72	68	70	73	69
Slovenia	63	**54**	60	49	49	48	65	69	54	28	69	53	36	63	53	51
South Africa	na	**56**	59	54	48	59	66	61	50	59	55	50	60	49	61	60
Spain	61	**60**	61	59	50	52	72	68	51	49	69	61	56	72	58	47
Sweden	62	**51**	52	49	44	49	56	61	49	44	52	50	47	53	53	42
Switzerland	na	**na**	na	na	na	na	na	na	na	na	na	na	na	na	na	na
Taiwan	na	**86**	86	86	88	86	87	85	86	88	87	87	86	86	87	89
Tanzania	na	**43**	49	35	33	45	52	47	34	46	47	39	49	42	41	58
Turkey	79	**78**	81	75	76	79	82	83	76	62	83	77	65	78	80	72
Uganda	na	**37**	42	32	35	36	48	40	35	45	49	35	32	39	36	35
Ukraine	na	**58**	63	54	54	56	62	68	60	47	64	53	53	60	57	45
United States	76	**80**	81	79	75	78	87	79	77	82	77	81	82	83	80	79
Uruguay	na	**69**	74	65	62	62	76	74	64	49	72	71	64	70	72	58
Venezuela	na	**65**	66	63	60	65	73	68	64	63	62	64	67	56	67	70
Vietnam	na	**86**	84	88	88	87	84	87	86	78	85	86	87	85	86	88
Zimbabwe	na	**66**	62	70	62	67	75	73	56	52	74	62	56	72	63	57
Total	65	**65**	67	63	60	64	70	69	64	60	67	65	63	67	64	62

RANKING	
Country	**2000**
China	90
Japan	89
Korea, South	89
Malta	87
Taiwan	86
Vietnam	86
Philippines	86
Canada	82
Puerto Rico	81
Finland	81
United States	80
Georgia	79
Lithuania	79
Turkey	78
Czech Republic	76
Pakistan	76
Jordan	76
Armenia	75
Argentina	75
Iran	75
Egypt	74
Mexico	73
Peru	73
Azerbaijan	73
Moldova	72
Singapore	72
Bosnia and Herz.	71
Slovakia	71
El Salvador	70
Australia	70
Serbia	69
Chile	69
Uruguay	69
Algeria	66
Zimbabwe	66
Colombia	66
New Zealand	66
Morocco	65
Montenegro	65
Venezuela	65
Iceland	65
Luxembourg	65
India	64
Belgium	64
Belarus	64
Russian Fed.	64
France	62
Hungary	61
Great Britain	61
Brazil	61
Norway	61
Poland	61
Spain	60
Estonia	59
Ukraine	58
South Africa	56
Croatia	56
Italy	55
Denmark	54
Slovenia	54
Macedonia	52
Netherlands	52
Portugal	51
Sweden	51
Bulgaria	49
Dominican Rep.	49
Romania	48
Albania	46
Nigeria	44
Tanzania	43
Germany	43
Greece	42
Latvia	40
Uganda	37
Bangladesh	29
Indonesia	23
Total	65

D058) HUSBAND AND WIFE SHOULD CONTRIBUTE

For each of the following statements I read out, can you tell me how much you agree with each. Do you agree strongly, agree, disagree, or disagree strongly? "Both the husband and wife should contribute to household income"

(WVS: V117; EVS: V159)

Agree strongly / Agree (%)

Country	Wave		Gender		Age			Education			Income			Values		
	1990	2000	Male	Female	16-29	30-49	50+	Lower	Middle	Upper	Lower	Middle	Upper	Mat	Mixed	Postm.
Albania	na	**96**	96	97	98	96	95	95	96	99	97	96	96	96	96	97
Algeria	na	**71**	62	80	69	73	71	65	72	74	71	79	72	68	75	65
Argentina	77	**91**	86	94	92	91	88	90	92	91	90	91	90	86	91	93
Armenia	na	**80**	69	90	81	78	82	85	79	81	75	81	88	83	77	83
Australia	na	**67**	67	67	73	64	64	70	67	65	70	64	64	65	68	67
Austria	73	**na**	na	na	na	na	na	na	na	na	na	na	na	na	na	na
Azerbaijan	na	**82**	78	87	85	81	80	81	82	83	85	80	84	82	84	85
Bangladesh	na	**87**	82	93	91	85	78	85	89	90	88	86	87	88	86	87
Belarus	83	**85**	84	87	85	81	91	90	84	82	88	85	83	89	83	77
Belgium	67	**70**	64	76	75	67	72	74	67	73	75	71	68	68	71	69
Bosnia and Herz.	na	**94**	93	95	95	94	92	92	94	95	91	94	94	93	94	89
Brazil	93	**96**	94	98	95	97	96	95	97	97	95	98	97	96	96	98
Bulgaria	83	**92**	92	91	91	90	94	93	91	91	93	90	92	93	90	95
Canada	69	**75**	75	76	77	73	77	78	77	70	83	77	70	74	75	78
Chile	88	**87**	85	90	90	89	82	85	88	91	87	90	86	88	86	93
China	95	**98**	98	99	96	98	99	99	98	95	99	97	98	99	97	97
Colombia	na	**95**	93	96	95	95	94	93	94	97	94	94	96	95	96	93
Croatia	na	**94**	93	96	96	96	91	93	95	97	97	94	93	93	94	97
Czech Republic	88	**93**	91	95	87	92	96	95	91	86	96	93	91	96	93	85
Denmark	71	**68**	67	69	75	63	70	70	72	62	70	68	59	75	67	71
Dominican Rep.	na	**92**	88	95	94	88	90	90	94	92	94	91	92	88	92	99
Egypt	na	**76**	67	85	75	74	79	76	75	77	75	77	75	78	75	70
El Salvador	na	**94**	93	96	95	94	94	94	96	93	94	95	93	na	na	na
Estonia	81	**82**	80	84	75	84	85	83	83	81	87	83	80	83	83	79
Finland	78	**71**	71	72	75	69	72	74	72	58	75	74	65	75	71	71
France	80	**81**	81	82	86	76	85	82	81	79	84	80	77	82	82	79
Georgia	na	**88**	83	92	88	87	89	88	88	88	87	91	87	88	88	86
Germany	88	**74**	74	74	89	72	69	65	81	78	74	73	73	67	75	81
Great Britain	70	**70**	71	70	69	63	77	74	66	65	77	72	57	na	na	na
Greece	na	**88**	84	90	90	89	79	78	86	91	84	92	85	87	88	87
Hungary	83	**89**	87	92	90	87	91	92	86	83	93	89	88	91	88	75
Iceland	68	**64**	60	68	67	54	73	68	60	63	69	65	57	64	62	71
India	82	**84**	82	86	85	84	81	86	81	81	89	84	81	83	84	84
Indonesia	na	**85**	85	86	80	84	88	90	86	82	85	86	85	87	84	79
Iran	na	**70**	66	75	74	68	63	67	70	72	68	67	70	72	68	76
Ireland	70	**na**	na	na	na	na	na	na	na	na	na	na	na	na	na	na
Israel	na	**na**	na	na	na	na	na	na	na	na	na	na	na	na	na	na
Italy	80	**81**	78	84	82	80	81	79	83	80	79	78	82	75	82	82
Japan	46	**57**	54	59	63	53	57	62	55	55	65	55	47	56	56	57
Jordan	na	**77**	69	84	72	81	77	78	74	78	79	75	79	77	76	79
Korea, South	59	**75**	73	76	78	72	78	79	77	71	76	75	73	73	75	85
Latvia	77	**89**	89	88	83	88	91	92	87	89	89	94	87	90	88	93
Lithuania	75	**90**	90	89	89	89	90	87	91	87	92	88	89	92	89	95
Luxembourg	na	**54**	54	55	64	52	50	60	52	49	55	57	46	56	55	50
Macedonia	na	**93**	92	95	92	92	95	91	94	95	92	93	95	92	94	96
Malta	na	**74**	75	72	80	73	70	71	74	76	75	73	79	69	76	77
Mexico	82	**89**	87	90	90	90	85	87	91	91	88	87	89	86	90	90
Moldova	na	**92**	92	91	90	91	93	91	93	90	97	93	86	88	94	85
Montenegro	na	**94**	93	94	97	94	91	92	95	96	93	95	96	94	95	83
Morocco	na	**74**	68	81	75	74	74	73	80	84	59	79	81	78	72	79
Netherlands	32	**38**	34	42	42	35	38	41	38	35	42	35	36	36	37	44
New Zealand	na	**60**	61	59	73	53	62	64	55	59	65	57	57	61	60	57
Nigeria	94	**90**	91	88	90	89	90	87	91	93	87	92	91	91	90	85
Northern Ireland	83	**na**	na	na	na	na	na	na	na	na	na	na	na	na	na	na
Norway	74	**80**	79	81	84	76	83	81	80	78	na	na	na	80	80	81
Pakistan	na	**70**	65	76	76	70	61	73	66	67	78	70	58	70	70	58
Peru	na	**94**	93	95	93	96	92	94	94	94	93	95	95	92	95	96
Philippines	na	**92**	91	94	90	93	94	94	92	91	92	92	93	94	91	96
Poland	na	**87**	87	88	83	87	91	88	88	82	89	87	83	86	88	91
Portugal	98	**88**	85	91	95	88	85	87	90	95	90	82	91	88	86	91
Puerto Rico	na	**94**	94	95	97	95	93	92	96	94	95	94	95	95	95	96
Romania	91	**85**	84	87	81	85	88	89	83	83	88	84	82	86	86	76
Russian Fed.	80	**83**	80	85	76	83	86	86	83	81	86	85	80	86	81	72
Serbia	na	**89**	86	92	94	89	87	87	90	92	88	90	89	89	90	86
Singapore	na	**81**	79	83	84	79	77	77	84	76	81	83	79	85	79	83
Slovakia	na	**89**	87	90	90	90	87	87	90	85	87	90	89	89	88	92
Slovenia	93	**91**	89	93	92	89	92	94	91	84	91	92	87	93	91	91
South Africa	na	**88**	87	90	92	86	85	89	88	84	88	96	82	90	88	83
Spain	85	**87**	86	88	91	88	84	85	89	90	81	90	89	85	87	92
Sweden	87	**89**	88	91	90	85	92	91	89	87	90	89	88	92	90	87
Switzerland	na	**na**	na	na	na	na	na	na	na	na	na	na	na	na	na	na
Taiwan	na	**89**	87	91	88	90	87	87	90	90	88	89	89	90	87	97
Tanzania	na	**89**	90	89	89	89	93	88	90	93	86	92	91	89	90	96
Turkey	85	**88**	82	93	87	88	89	87	88	92	85	89	91	86	88	89
Uganda	na	**92**	96	88	93	93	84	90	92	98	92	93	92	88	94	96
Ukraine	na	**86**	83	88	83	84	89	90	86	83	87	86	84	87	85	82
United States	67	**69**	73	65	79	66	63	77	69	65	75	68	60	67	68	72
Uruguay	na	**94**	90	97	96	96	91	93	96	94	93	93	96	92	94	96
Venezuela	na	**95**	95	95	95	96	95	93	96	97	94	94	96	95	96	95
Vietnam	na	**97**	97	98	97	97	97	98	97	96	96	97	98	96	98	98
Zimbabwe	na	**92**	91	93	89	95	95	93	91	100	93	90	92	93	91	92
Total	78	**83**	81	85	85	83	83	84	84	82	84	84	82	85	83	82

RANKING	
Country	2000
China	98
Vietnam	97
Albania	96
Brazil	96
Venezuela	95
Colombia	95
El Salvador	94
Puerto Rico	94
Croatia	94
Peru	94
Uruguay	94
Bosnia and Herz.	94
Montenegro	94
Macedonia	93
Czech Republic	93
Philippines	92
Dominican Rep.	92
Uganda	92
Bulgaria	92
Zimbabwe	92
Moldova	92
Slovenia	91
Argentina	91
Nigeria	90
Lithuania	90
Hungary	89
Tanzania	89
Sweden	89
Serbia	89
Mexico	89
Taiwan	89
Latvia	89
Slovakia	89
Portugal	88
South Africa	88
Georgia	88
Greece	88
Turkey	88
Chile	87
Poland	87
Spain	87
Bangladesh	87
Ukraine	86
Belarus	85
Romania	85
Indonesia	85
India	84
Russian Fed.	83
Estonia	82
Azerbaijan	82
France	81
Italy	81
Singapore	81
Armenia	80
Norway	80
Jordan	77
Egypt	76
Canada	75
Korea, South	75
Morocco	74
Germany	74
Malta	74
Finland	71
Algeria	71
Belgium	70
Great Britain	70
Pakistan	70
Iran	70
United States	69
Denmark	68
Australia	67
Iceland	64
New Zealand	60
Japan	57
Luxembourg	54
Netherlands	38
Total	83

D059) MEN MAKE BETTER POLITICAL LEADERS

For each of the following statements I read out, can you tell me how much you agree with each. Do you agree strongly, agree, disagree, or disagree strongly? "On the whole, men make better political leaders than women do"

Agree strongly / Agree (%)

(WVS: V118)

Country	Wave		Gender		Age			Education			Income			Values		
	1990	2000	Male	Female	16-29	30-49	50+	Lower	Middle	Upper	Lower	Middle	Upper	Mat	Mixed	Postm.
Albania	na	**52**	65	39	43	52	59	60	47	42	53	50	51	52	50	46
Algeria	na	**70**	83	55	72	65	73	79	69	64	71	66	64	74	67	66
Argentina	na	**32**	39	26	35	28	35	35	32	21	42	32	24	40	32	27
Armenia	na	**83**	90	77	80	85	85	87	83	81	82	85	84	88	80	74
Australia	na	**24**	31	18	19	20	34	28	25	21	28	24	19	32	27	17
Austria	na	**na**	na	na	na	na	na	na	na	na	na	na	na	na	na	na
Azerbaijan	na	**72**	77	66	72	71	72	75	71	73	69	73	73	71	72	77
Bangladesh	na	**67**	70	65	66	69	66	69	66	64	83	63	59	69	65	72
Belarus	na	**na**	na	na	na	na	na	na	na	na	na	na	na	na	na	na
Belgium	na	**na**	na	na	na	na	na	na	na	na	na	na	na	na	na	na
Bosnia and Herz.	na	**33**	44	23	31	34	34	37	33	29	33	34	33	34	34	27
Brazil	na	**47**	56	39	43	48	54	55	44	32	55	40	44	54	47	34
Bulgaria	na	**na**	na	na	na	na	na	na	na	na	na	na	na	na	na	na
Canada	na	**21**	25	17	19	20	23	30	19	17	24	22	18	32	22	15
Chile	na	**39**	49	31	33	37	48	46	37	32	48	34	33	42	42	29
China	na	**50**	50	51	41	53	52	61	43	42	53	49	48	53	46	48
Colombia	na	**33**	39	27	32	32	37	46	32	24	42	34	26	44	39	25
Croatia	na	**na**	na	na	na	na	na	na	na	na	na	na	na	na	na	na
Czech Republic	na	**na**	na	na	na	na	na	na	na	na	na	na	na	na	na	na
Denmark	na	**na**	na	na	na	na	na	na	na	na	na	na	na	na	na	na
Dominican Rep.	na	**41**	53	33	42	40	36	63	54	33	39	46	37	51	41	23
Egypt	na	**85**	90	79	80	86	88	87	83	80	88	84	83	85	84	83
El Salvador	na	**37**	38	36	37	38	35	42	37	25	46	33	32	na	na	na
Estonia	na	**na**	na	na	na	na	na	na	na	na	na	na	na	na	na	na
Finland	na	**na**	na	na	na	na	na	na	na	na	na	na	na	na	na	na
France	na	**na**	na	na	na	na	na	na	na	na	na	na	na	na	na	na
Georgia	na	**80**	86	75	77	80	82	81	80	78	82	81	77	82	78	75
Germany	na	**na**	na	na	na	na	na	na	na	na	na	na	na	na	na	na
Great Britain	na	**na**	na	na	na	na	na	na	na	na	na	na	na	na	na	na
Greece	na	**na**	na	na	na	na	na	na	na	na	na	na	na	na	na	na
Hungary	na	**na**	na	na	na	na	na	na	na	na	na	na	na	na	na	na
Iceland	na	**na**	na	na	na	na	na	na	na	na	na	na	na	na	na	na
India	na	**58**	62	53	53	60	61	66	59	43	73	60	50	63	55	31
Indonesia	na	**60**	69	52	58	59	63	67	59	60	56	65	63	64	57	79
Iran	na	**66**	73	58	61	68	76	76	60	66	72	64	62	72	65	54
Ireland	na	**na**	na	na	na	na	na	na	na	na	na	na	na	na	na	na
Israel	na	**na**	na	na	na	na	na	na	na	na	na	na	na	na	na	na
Italy	na	**na**	na	na	na	na	na	na	na	na	na	na	na	na	na	na
Japan	na	**43**	48	40	25	34	58	59	43	34	45	42	45	50	41	33
Jordan	na	**87**	94	80	88	85	91	90	88	81	91	90	82	91	85	76
Korea, South	na	**48**	59	38	27	51	66	61	51	42	51	48	45	54	45	27
Latvia	na	**na**	na	na	na	na	na	na	na	na	na	na	na	na	na	na
Lithuania	na	**na**	na	na	na	na	na	na	na	na	na	na	na	na	na	na
Luxembourg	na	**na**	na	na	na	na	na	na	na	na	na	na	na	na	na	na
Macedonia	na	**41**	50	31	40	38	47	59	35	25	50	42	27	37	43	47
Malta	na	**na**	na	na	na	na	na	na	na	na	na	na	na	na	na	na
Mexico	na	**42**	45	39	37	41	47	51	32	27	49	37	36	48	38	34
Moldova	na	**61**	73	50	56	59	69	72	59	55	71	63	57	66	59	45
Montenegro	na	**55**	72	38	39	52	69	70	49	37	56	57	54	62	51	38
Morocco	na	**73**	81	65	69	76	80	78	59	49	82	70	73	75	73	68
Netherlands	na	**na**	na	na	na	na	na	na	na	na	na	na	na	na	na	na
New Zealand	na	**17**	23	13	13	12	23	22	19	11	23	16	11	25	17	14
Nigeria	na	**80**	87	72	80	80	77	81	81	77	82	78	80	76	82	78
Northern Ireland	na	**na**	na	na	na	na	na	na	na	na	na	na	na	na	na	na
Norway	na	**16**	16	16	14	12	22	21	16	11	na	na	na	28	15	7
Pakistan	na	**49**	53	46	44	48	63	49	50	46	50	47	53	47	52	25
Peru	na	**24**	31	17	21	24	29	30	24	19	27	23	20	33	22	15
Philippines	na	**63**	67	59	59	64	66	70	61	58	64	62	63	61	65	60
Poland	na	**na**	na	na	na	na	na	na	na	na	na	na	na	na	na	na
Portugal	na	**na**	na	na	na	na	na	na	na	na	na	na	na	na	na	na
Puerto Rico	na	**19**	23	17	15	14	25	37	28	11	31	19	8	20	21	10
Romania	na	**na**	na	na	na	na	na	na	na	na	na	na	na	na	na	na
Russian Fed.	na	**na**	na	na	na	na	na	na	na	na	na	na	na	na	na	na
Serbia	na	**47**	58	37	48	43	51	59	46	33	49	48	42	56	40	27
Singapore	na	**50**	51	50	43	56	62	54	48	49	50	53	51	58	50	30
Slovakia	na	**na**	na	na	na	na	na	na	na	na	na	na	na	na	na	na
Slovenia	na	**na**	na	na	na	na	na	na	na	na	na	na	na	na	na	na
South Africa	na	**44**	53	34	40	49	42	53	33	29	54	43	36	48	42	36
Spain	na	**19**	23	15	14	15	25	21	14	17	27	17	18	22	19	11
Sweden	na	**19**	20	18	17	13	26	27	19	13	25	17	13	26	21	11
Switzerland	na	**na**	na	na	na	na	na	na	na	na	na	na	na	na	na	na
Taiwan	na	**49**	46	52	41	48	54	53	45	46	52	46	49	50	45	62
Tanzania	na	**44**	51	34	48	39	49	46	43	37	48	38	43	41	44	63
Turkey	na	**62**	66	58	60	62	67	70	54	43	71	56	50	67	62	49
Uganda	na	**68**	76	61	69	66	75	75	64	79	69	77	59	70	67	69
Ukraine	na	**na**	na	na	na	na	na	na	na	na	na	na	na	na	na	na
United States	na	**23**	28	19	23	19	30	31	24	20	24	22	21	28	23	20
Uruguay	na	**38**	43	33	34	31	45	45	26	36	42	36	33	49	36	31
Venezuela	na	**40**	48	32	38	42	42	46	43	27	43	43	38	53	37	32
Vietnam	na	**56**	58	54	53	54	61	59	53	52	67	57	50	71	55	38
Zimbabwe	na	**52**	60	46	54	48	56	56	48	77	58	53	38	55	50	55
Total	na	49	56	43	49	48	51	56	48	40	54	48	46	59	47	33

RANKING	
Country	**2000**
Jordan	87
Egypt	85
Armenia	83
Georgia	80
Nigeria	80
Morocco	73
Azerbaijan	72
Algeria	70
Uganda	68
Bangladesh	67
Iran	66
Philippines	63
Turkey	62
Moldova	61
Indonesia	60
India	58
Vietnam	56
Montenegro	55
Zimbabwe	52
Albania	52
Singapore	50
China	50
Pakistan	49
Taiwan	49
Korea, South	48
Brazil	47
Serbia	47
South Africa	44
Tanzania	44
Japan	43
Mexico	42
Dominican Rep.	41
Macedonia	41
Venezuela	40
Chile	39
Uruguay	38
El Salvador	37
Bosnia and Herz.	33
Colombia	33
Argentina	32
Australia	24
Peru	24
United States	23
Canada	21
Sweden	19
Puerto Rico	19
Spain	19
New Zealand	17
Norway	16
Total	49

D060) UNIVERSITY IS MORE IMPORTANT FOR A BOY

For each of the following statements I read out, can you tell me how much you agree with each. Do you agree strongly, agree, disagree, or disagree strongly? "A university education is more important for a boy than for a girl"

(WVS: V119)

Agree strongly / Agree (%)

Country	Wave		Gender		Age			Education			Income			Values		
	1990	2000	Male	Female	16-29	30-49	50+	Lower	Middle	Upper	Lower	Middle	Upper	Mat	Mixed	Postm.
Albania	na	**15**	21	10	12	14	20	21	13	9	14	16	15	15	14	11
Algeria	na	**29**	42	15	28	28	30	37	28	23	34	26	20	30	28	22
Argentina	na	**15**	19	12	12	12	22	19	10	9	20	16	10	22	16	10
Armenia	na	**42**	51	35	43	42	43	38	43	40	43	41	41	45	42	25
Australia	na	**11**	15	7	5	8	19	19	7	8	18	6	8	17	12	8
Austria	na	**na**	na	na	na	na	na	na	na	na	na	na	na	na	na	na
Azerbaijan	na	**37**	42	33	37	39	35	37	36	39	37	37	42	37	40	35
Bangladesh	na	**63**	65	59	58	66	64	71	58	48	72	60	58	66	60	54
Belarus	na	**na**	na	na	na	na	na	na	na	na	na	na	na	na	na	na
Belgium	na	**na**	na	na	na	na	na	na	na	na	na	na	na	na	na	na
Bosnia and Herz.	na	**18**	22	14	15	17	21	26	17	12	19	18	17	19	18	12
Brazil	na	**24**	32	16	22	23	31	33	20	9	29	25	18	33	23	10
Bulgaria	na	**na**	na	na	na	na	na	na	na	na	na	na	na	na	na	na
Canada	na	**5**	6	4	2	2	9	10	3	3	7	4	2	7	5	3
Chile	na	**30**	37	24	22	32	35	35	28	26	38	27	25	36	31	18
China	na	**9**	10	9	8	9	13	11	8	10	11	8	8	8	11	6
Colombia	na	**11**	13	9	11	11	14	19	12	6	16	12	8	16	16	11
Croatia	na	**na**	na	na	na	na	na	na	na	na	na	na	na	na	na	na
Czech Republic	na	**na**	na	na	na	na	na	na	na	na	na	na	na	na	na	na
Denmark	na	**na**	na	na	na	na	na	na	na	na	na	na	na	na	na	na
Dominican Rep.	na	**20**	24	17	20	22	10	26	26	17	23	18	13	23	21	8
Egypt	na	**31**	39	22	26	34	33	36	28	22	36	33	25	31	31	26
El Salvador	na	**14**	12	16	15	13	15	16	12	11	20	11	14	na	na	na
Estonia	na	**na**	na	na	na	na	na	na	na	na	na	na	na	na	na	na
Finland	na	**na**	na	na	na	na	na	na	na	na	na	na	na	na	na	na
France	na	**na**	na	na	na	na	na	na	na	na	na	na	na	na	na	na
Georgia	na	**34**	40	29	35	33	34	34	35	29	38	31	29	32	35	32
Germany	na	**na**	na	na	na	na	na	na	na	na	na	na	na	na	na	na
Great Britain	na	**na**	na	na	na	na	na	na	na	na	na	na	na	na	na	na
Greece	na	**na**	na	na	na	na	na	na	na	na	na	na	na	na	na	na
Hungary	na	**na**	na	na	na	na	na	na	na	na	na	na	na	na	na	na
Iceland	na	**na**	na	na	na	na	na	na	na	na	na	na	na	na	na	na
India	na	**42**	42	41	35	43	47	55	38	22	57	48	30	47	38	19
Indonesia	na	**17**	20	14	10	17	20	29	14	12	19	13	17	21	14	11
Iran	na	**38**	43	33	33	39	50	51	33	30	42	36	34	42	37	28
Ireland	na	**na**	na	na	na	na	na	na	na	na	na	na	na	na	na	na
Israel	na	**na**	na	na	na	na	na	na	na	na	na	na	na	na	na	na
Italy	na	**na**	na	na	na	na	na	na	na	na	na	na	na	na	na	na
Japan	na	**23**	26	20	13	17	32	45	22	14	29	23	18	33	21	7
Jordan	na	**39**	51	27	41	33	47	46	32	32	40	43	35	40	38	35
Korea, South	na	**24**	29	19	12	25	36	40	26	18	29	19	23	29	20	18
Latvia	na	**na**	na	na	na	na	na	na	na	na	na	na	na	na	na	na
Lithuania	na	**na**	na	na	na	na	na	na	na	na	na	na	na	na	na	na
Luxembourg	na	**na**	na	na	na	na	na	na	na	na	na	na	na	na	na	na
Macedonia	na	**12**	15	10	9	12	15	21	10	3	18	11	7	10	13	15
Malta	na	**na**	na	na	na	na	na	na	na	na	na	na	na	na	na	na
Mexico	na	**33**	33	33	30	33	38	41	26	19	42	31	28	42	30	27
Moldova	na	**24**	28	20	19	25	27	26	26	17	29	22	24	21	23	29
Montenegro	na	**24**	30	18	14	18	36	36	18	11	25	22	23	27	22	13
Morocco	na	**42**	50	34	37	43	54	47	27	19	67	37	35	41	43	35
Netherlands	na	**na**	na	na	na	na	na	na	na	na	na	na	na	na	na	na
New Zealand	na	**8**	11	6	3	4	14	12	9	4	11	7	4	11	9	4
Nigeria	na	**44**	51	36	45	42	45	53	41	33	48	40	42	42	46	38
Northern Ireland	na	**na**	na	na	na	na	na	na	na	na	na	na	na	na	na	na
Norway	na	**11**	11	11	10	8	16	14	11	8	na	na	na	16	11	3
Pakistan	na	**23**	29	16	15	22	38	30	16	8	31	21	16	24	20	na
Peru	na	**21**	25	17	20	20	23	25	22	15	24	20	16	28	19	15
Philippines	na	**37**	39	36	39	36	39	45	37	30	38	37	37	34	41	33
Poland	na	**na**	na	na	na	na	na	na	na	na	na	na	na	na	na	na
Portugal	na	**na**	na	na	na	na	na	na	na	na	na	na	na	na	na	na
Puerto Rico	na	**11**	16	9	7	9	15	17	15	8	11	13	8	11	11	11
Romania	na	**na**	na	na	na	na	na	na	na	na	na	na	na	na	na	na
Russian Fed.	na	**na**	na	na	na	na	na	na	na	na	na	na	na	na	na	na
Serbia	na	**21**	27	15	21	15	27	31	19	9	25	20	14	26	16	9
Singapore	na	**15**	17	14	15	15	17	17	15	11	18	15	15	16	15	11
Slovakia	na	**na**	na	na	na	na	na	na	na	na	na	na	na	na	na	na
Slovenia	na	**na**	na	na	na	na	na	na	na	na	na	na	na	na	na	na
South Africa	na	**19**	22	16	17	20	25	26	12	4	24	22	13	17	20	25
Spain	na	**12**	14	10	9	9	16	14	8	9	22	13	10	15	11	8
Sweden	na	**7**	8	6	7	6	7	11	6	5	10	6	3	8	6	7
Switzerland	na	**na**	na	na	na	na	na	na	na	na	na	na	na	na	na	na
Taiwan	na	**24**	23	25	20	23	30	31	20	20	26	22	25	23	25	22
Tanzania	na	**16**	16	14	15	14	21	20	12	8	23	12	11	12	17	21
Turkey	na	**29**	35	24	27	28	36	37	22	11	40	21	18	36	27	21
Uganda	na	**23**	35	13	21	25	27	32	17	45	35	31	20	21	21	40
Ukraine	na	**na**	na	na	na	na	na	na	na	na	na	na	na	na	na	na
United States	na	**7**	7	8	6	6	11	13	6	6	8	7	7	15	8	5
Uruguay	na	**13**	15	12	12	8	17	17	7	9	19	11	7	17	12	6
Venezuela	na	**15**	17	14	16	15	15	22	14	10	23	14	11	20	15	8
Vietnam	na	**24**	22	26	19	22	30	28	20	15	27	26	21	42	19	24
Zimbabwe	na	**18**	22	15	17	15	26	24	11	na	25	19	5	21	16	16
Total	na	23	27	19	22	22	25	30	21	16	28	22	20	28	22	14

RANKING	
Country	2000
Bangladesh	63
Nigeria	44
Armenia	42
Morocco	42
India	42
Jordan	39
Iran	38
Azerbaijan	37
Philippines	37
Georgia	34
Mexico	33
Egypt	31
Chile	30
Turkey	29
Algeria	29
Brazil	24
Taiwan	24
Vietnam	24
Montenegro	24
Korea, South	24
Moldova	24
Uganda	23
Japan	23
Pakistan	23
Serbia	21
Peru	21
Dominican Rep.	20
South Africa	19
Zimbabwe	18
Bosnia and Herz.	18
Indonesia	17
Tanzania	16
Albania	15
Argentina	15
Singapore	15
Venezuela	15
El Salvador	14
Uruguay	13
Macedonia	12
Spain	12
Colombia	11
Puerto Rico	11
Norway	11
Australia	11
China	9
New Zealand	8
United States	7
Sweden	7
Canada	5
Total	23

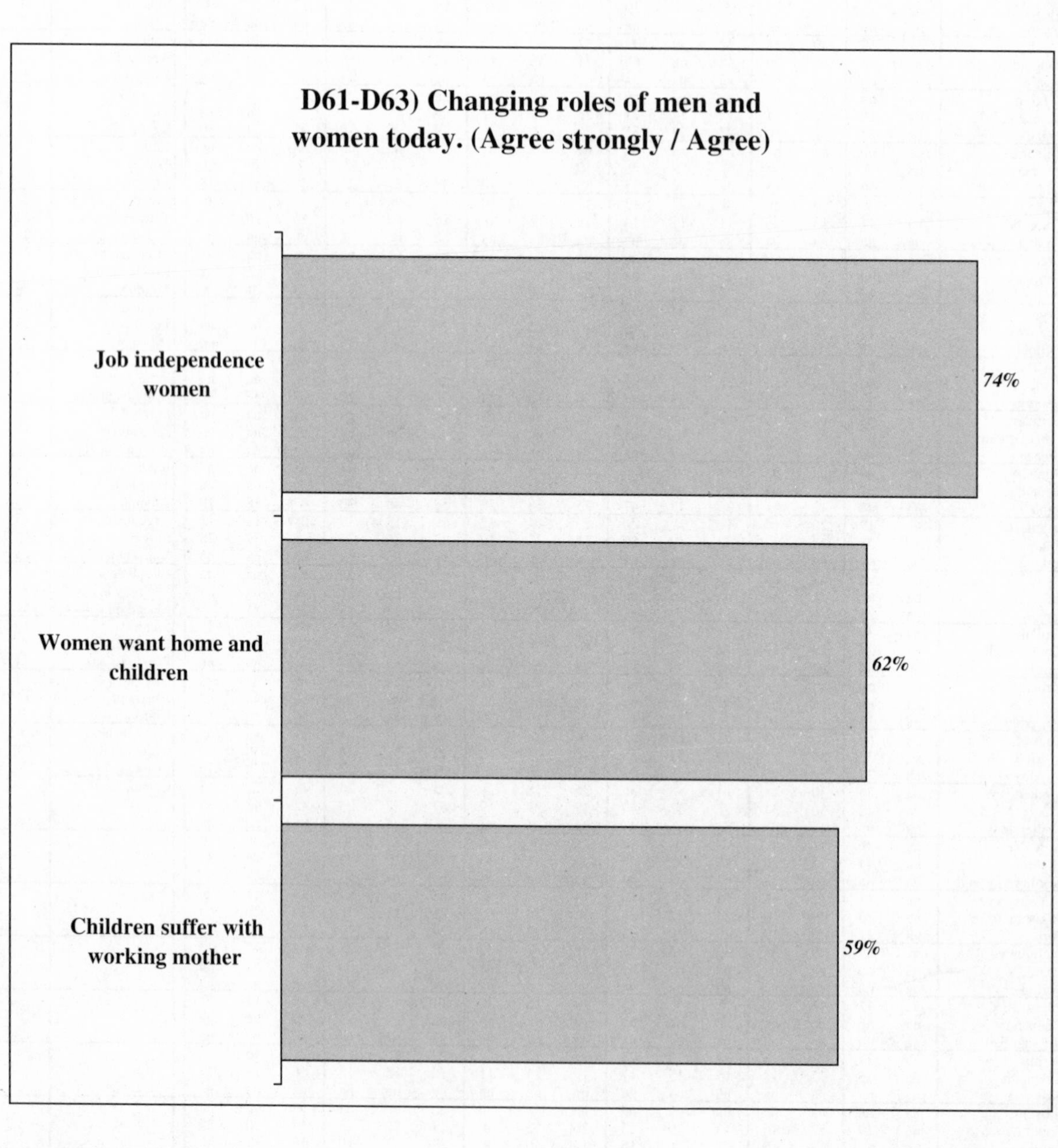
D61-D63) Changing roles of men and women today. (Agree strongly / Agree)
Job independence women
74%
Women want home and children
62%
Children suffer with working mother
59%

D061_1) CHILDREN SUFFER WITH WORKING MOTHER

For each of the following statements I read out, can you tell me how much you agree with each. "A pre-school child is likely to suffer if his or her mother works"

Agree strongly / Agree (%)

(EVS: V155)

Country	Wave		Gender		Age			Education			Income			Values		
	1990	2000	Male	Female	16-29	30-49	50+	Lower	Middle	Upper	Lower	Middle	Upper	Mat	Mixed	Postm.
Albania	na	**na**	na	na	na	na	na	na	na	na	na	na	na	na	na	na
Algeria	na	**na**	na	na	na	na	na	na	na	na	na	na	na	na	na	na
Argentina	78	**na**	na	na	na	na	na	na	na	na	na	na	na	na	na	na
Armenia	na	**na**	na	na	na	na	na	na	na	na	na	na	na	na	na	na
Australia	na	**na**	na	na	na	na	na	na	na	na	na	na	na	na	na	na
Austria	83	**na**	na	na	na	na	na	na	na	na	na	na	na	na	na	na
Azerbaijan	na	**na**	na	na	na	na	na	na	na	na	na	na	na	na	na	na
Bangladesh	na	**na**	na	na	na	na	na	na	na	na	na	na	na	na	na	na
Belarus	81	**60**	58	63	51	63	65	61	58	67	66	59	55	60	59	57
Belgium	61	**51**	56	47	45	46	59	64	53	40	66	53	40	58	53	38
Bosnia and Herz.	na	**na**	na	na	na	na	na	na	na	na	na	na	na	na	na	na
Brazil	75	**na**	na	na	na	na	na	na	na	na	na	na	na	na	na	na
Bulgaria	76	**61**	60	62	49	62	65	67	58	57	60	56	63	59	63	65
Canada	53	**na**	na	na	na	na	na	na	na	na	na	na	na	na	na	na
Chile	82	**na**	na	na	na	na	na	na	na	na	na	na	na	na	na	na
China	61	**na**	na	na	na	na	na	na	na	na	na	na	na	na	na	na
Colombia	na	**na**	na	na	na	na	na	na	na	na	na	na	na	na	na	na
Croatia	na	**64**	66	63	56	64	70	70	64	49	73	68	55	67	63	67
Czech Republic	78	**47**	53	42	36	43	57	51	43	46	54	46	41	51	47	42
Denmark	32	**18**	24	13	9	10	31	24	8	9	23	17	7	18	20	6
Dominican Rep.	na	**na**	na	na	na	na	na	na	na	na	na	na	na	na	na	na
Egypt	na	**na**	na	na	na	na	na	na	na	na	na	na	na	na	na	na
El Salvador	na	**na**	na	na	na	na	na	na	na	na	na	na	na	na	na	na
Estonia	91	**65**	66	65	58	67	67	66	66	61	66	64	63	67	65	48
Finland	52	**41**	47	36	30	31	55	48	33	27	43	40	38	41	41	40
France	65	**56**	60	53	53	48	66	63	51	44	61	55	49	68	56	37
Georgia	na	**na**	na	na	na	na	na	na	na	na	na	na	na	na	na	na
Germany	79	**66**	74	61	53	62	76	76	58	64	69	69	67	73	65	62
Great Britain	55	**46**	54	39	40	41	55	46	46	51	49	42	46	na	na	na
Greece	na	**78**	81	76	76	76	89	84	82	73	81	77	78	79	78	73
Hungary	70	**63**	61	65	50	63	71	67	56	54	65	64	62	66	61	58
Iceland	52	**33**	41	25	25	26	50	40	33	16	40	32	25	35	34	21
India	92	**na**	na	na	na	na	na	na	na	na	na	na	na	na	na	na
Indonesia	na	**na**	na	na	na	na	na	na	na	na	na	na	na	na	na	na
Iran	na	**na**	na	na	na	na	na	na	na	na	na	na	na	na	na	na
Ireland	53	**na**	na	na	na	na	na	na	na	na	na	na	na	na	na	na
Israel	na	**na**	na	na	na	na	na	na	na	na	na	na	na	na	na	na
Italy	78	**81**	83	80	79	77	86	87	80	71	88	85	72	86	83	76
Japan	70	**na**	na	na	na	na	na	na	na	na	na	na	na	na	na	na
Jordan	na	**na**	na	na	na	na	na	na	na	na	na	na	na	na	na	na
Korea, South	72	**na**	na	na	na	na	na	na	na	na	na	na	na	na	na	na
Latvia	92	**75**	76	75	69	77	76	78	73	79	74	77	76	79	74	65
Lithuania	90	**71**	69	74	62	72	77	77	70	69	79	67	72	76	70	61
Luxembourg	na	**68**	73	63	65	62	77	74	66	58	78	72	59	66	69	63
Macedonia	na	**na**	na	na	na	na	na	na	na	na	na	na	na	na	na	na
Malta	na	**87**	89	86	82	87	92	93	86	83	94	91	82	90	87	78
Mexico	78	**na**	na	na	na	na	na	na	na	na	na	na	na	na	na	na
Moldova	na	**na**	na	na	na	na	na	na	na	na	na	na	na	na	na	na
Montenegro	na	**na**	na	na	na	na	na	na	na	na	na	na	na	na	na	na
Morocco	na	**na**	na	na	na	na	na	na	na	na	na	na	na	na	na	na
Netherlands	56	**46**	56	36	47	40	52	59	42	37	53	43	37	58	47	34
New Zealand	na	**na**	na	na	na	na	na	na	na	na	na	na	na	na	na	na
Nigeria	54	**na**	na	na	na	na	na	na	na	na	na	na	na	na	na	na
Northern Ireland	44	**na**	na	na	na	na	na	na	na	na	na	na	na	na	na	na
Norway	46	**na**	na	na	na	na	na	na	na	na	na	na	na	na	na	na
Pakistan	na	**na**	na	na	na	na	na	na	na	na	na	na	na	na	na	na
Peru	na	**na**	na	na	na	na	na	na	na	na	na	na	na	na	na	na
Philippines	na	**na**	na	na	na	na	na	na	na	na	na	na	na	na	na	na
Poland	na	**77**	79	74	68	75	84	81	74	67	79	78	68	80	75	73
Portugal	84	**72**	75	69	71	71	74	74	71	58	81	73	77	71	72	77
Puerto Rico	na	**na**	na	na	na	na	na	na	na	na	na	na	na	na	na	na
Romania	58	**47**	48	46	42	44	53	58	42	42	56	44	43	50	45	39
Russian Fed.	70	**73**	75	72	65	74	78	74	74	71	75	73	71	73	74	67
Serbia	na	**na**	na	na	na	na	na	na	na	na	na	na	na	na	na	na
Singapore	na	**na**	na	na	na	na	na	na	na	na	na	na	na	na	na	na
Slovakia	na	**63**	64	62	55	62	71	70	61	56	69	61	60	63	65	52
Slovenia	67	**47**	51	43	34	40	62	64	43	30	58	48	29	55	45	44
South Africa	na	**na**	na	na	na	na	na	na	na	na	na	na	na	na	na	na
Spain	56	**46**	46	46	30	37	62	58	40	27	55	45	34	59	44	30
Sweden	74	**38**	46	30	26	35	48	59	35	26	40	40	31	50	40	26
Switzerland	na	**na**	na	na	na	na	na	na	na	na	na	na	na	na	na	na
Taiwan	na	**na**	na	na	na	na	na	na	na	na	na	na	na	na	na	na
Tanzania	na	**na**	na	na	na	na	na	na	na	na	na	na	na	na	na	na
Turkey	85	**na**	na	na	na	na	na	na	na	na	na	na	na	na	na	na
Uganda	na	**na**	na	na	na	na	na	na	na	na	na	na	na	na	na	na
Ukraine	na	**73**	75	72	62	74	78	74	75	68	79	72	67	75	70	76
United States	52	**na**	na	na	na	na	na	na	na	na	na	na	na	na	na	na
Uruguay	na	**na**	na	na	na	na	na	na	na	na	na	na	na	na	na	na
Venezuela	na	**na**	na	na	na	na	na	na	na	na	na	na	na	na	na	na
Vietnam	na	**na**	na	na	na	na	na	na	na	na	na	na	na	na	na	na
Zimbabwe	na	**na**	na	na	na	na	na	na	na	na	na	na	na	na	na	na
Total	69	**59**	62	57	52	56	67	64	59	51	64	59	55	66	59	50

RANKING	
Country	**2000**
Malta	87
Italy	81
Greece	78
Poland	77
Latvia	75
Russian Fed.	73
Ukraine	73
Portugal	72
Lithuania	71
Luxembourg	68
Germany	66
Estonia	65
Croatia	64
Slovakia	63
Hungary	63
Bulgaria	61
Belarus	60
France	56
Belgium	51
Czech Republic	47
Romania	47
Slovenia	47
Great Britain	46
Spain	46
Netherlands	46
Finland	41
Sweden	38
Iceland	33
Denmark	18
Total	59

D062_1) WOMEN WANT HOME AND CHILDREN

For each of the following statements I read out, can you tell me how much you agree with each. "A job is alright but what most women really want is a home and children"

Agree strongly / Agree (%) (EVS: V156)

Country	Wave 1990	Wave 2000	Gender Male	Gender Female	Age 16-29	Age 30-49	Age 50+	Education Lower	Education Middle	Education Upper	Income Lower	Income Middle	Income Upper	Values Mat	Values Mixed	Values Postm.
Albania	na	na	na	na	na	na	na	na	na	na	na	na	na	na	na	na
Algeria	na	na	na	na	na	na	na	na	na	na	na	na	na	na	na	na
Argentina	73	na	na	na	na	na	na	na	na	na	na	na	na	na	na	na
Armenia	na	na	na	na	na	na	na	na	na	na	na	na	na	na	na	na
Australia	na	na	na	na	na	na	na	na	na	na	na	na	na	na	na	na
Austria	62	na	na	na	na	na	na	na	na	na	na	na	na	na	na	na
Azerbaijan	na	na	na	na	na	na	na	na	na	na	na	na	na	na	na	na
Bangladesh	na	na	na	na	na	na	na	na	na	na	na	na	na	na	na	na
Belarus	81	68	70	67	59	69	74	74	68	59	75	68	57	73	66	54
Belgium	61	54	55	53	45	46	66	71	54	41	66	59	45	65	53	42
Bosnia and Herz.	na	na	na	na	na	na	na	na	na	na	na	na	na	na	na	na
Brazil	72	na	na	na	na	na	na	na	na	na	na	na	na	na	na	na
Bulgaria	90	76	75	76	75	74	78	80	78	64	80	70	75	77	73	95
Canada	43	na	na	na	na	na	na	na	na	na	na	na	na	na	na	na
Chile	77	na	na	na	na	na	na	na	na	na	na	na	na	na	na	na
China	78	na	na	na	na	na	na	na	na	na	na	na	na	na	na	na
Colombia	na	na	na	na	na	na	na	na	na	na	na	na	na	na	na	na
Croatia	na	66	66	67	52	71	70	77	63	47	77	66	61	77	66	58
Czech Republic	93	72	73	71	64	70	78	79	64	67	76	75	65	77	72	60
Denmark	25	18	19	18	17	16	22	23	12	12	22	18	13	24	19	10
Dominican Rep.	na	na	na	na	na	na	na	na	na	na	na	na	na	na	na	na
Egypt	na	na	na	na	na	na	na	na	na	na	na	na	na	na	na	na
El Salvador	na	na	na	na	na	na	na	na	na	na	na	na	na	na	na	na
Estonia	85	68	69	66	64	64	73	73	66	64	71	70	61	73	64	55
Finland	42	50	54	46	43	38	64	59	40	29	54	53	39	58	48	41
France	68	65	66	64	61	57	75	72	60	51	69	65	60	75	67	46
Georgia	na	na	na	na	na	na	na	na	na	na	na	na	na	na	na	na
Germany	50	44	47	42	32	39	55	55	36	28	51	44	46	62	41	24
Great Britain	45	44	52	38	37	35	58	53	40	37	52	44	33	na	na	na
Greece	na	65	72	60	55	69	79	88	72	55	70	62	64	69	66	59
Hungary	76	70	68	72	63	67	78	76	64	47	73	72	66	74	67	68
Iceland	71	62	65	59	53	55	79	73	61	40	62	66	56	73	61	41
India	91	na	na	na	na	na	na	na	na	na	na	na	na	na	na	na
Indonesia	na	na	na	na	na	na	na	na	na	na	na	na	na	na	na	na
Iran	na	na	na	na	na	na	na	na	na	na	na	na	na	na	na	na
Ireland	59	na	na	na	na	na	na	na	na	na	na	na	na	na	na	na
Israel	na	na	na	na	na	na	na	na	na	na	na	na	na	na	na	na
Italy	72	68	69	66	59	58	81	77	63	52	73	69	62	85	69	56
Japan	81	na	na	na	na	na	na	na	na	na	na	na	na	na	na	na
Jordan	na	na	na	na	na	na	na	na	na	na	na	na	na	na	na	na
Korea, South	70	na	na	na	na	na	na	na	na	na	na	na	na	na	na	na
Latvia	90	67	72	63	66	65	69	72	66	63	68	69	66	69	66	58
Lithuania	97	94	94	94	92	93	96	95	94	91	98	91	93	93	93	96
Luxembourg	na	56	60	52	46	50	69	71	52	34	64	59	41	66	58	32
Macedonia	na	na	na	na	na	na	na	na	na	na	na	na	na	na	na	na
Malta	na	70	71	69	58	70	77	78	69	53	75	71	61	74	69	54
Mexico	61	na	na	na	na	na	na	na	na	na	na	na	na	na	na	na
Moldova	na	na	na	na	na	na	na	na	na	na	na	na	na	na	na	na
Montenegro	na	na	na	na	na	na	na	na	na	na	na	na	na	na	na	na
Morocco	na	na	na	na	na	na	na	na	na	na	na	na	na	na	na	na
Netherlands	37	34	36	33	25	23	52	55	30	20	42	29	28	53	36	22
New Zealand	na	na	na	na	na	na	na	na	na	na	na	na	na	na	na	na
Nigeria	87	na	na	na	na	na	na	na	na	na	na	na	na	na	na	na
Northern Ireland	53	na	na	na	na	na	na	na	na	na	na	na	na	na	na	na
Norway	51	na	na	na	na	na	na	na	na	na	na	na	na	na	na	na
Pakistan	na	na	na	na	na	na	na	na	na	na	na	na	na	na	na	na
Peru	na	na	na	na	na	na	na	na	na	na	na	na	na	na	na	na
Philippines	na	na	na	na	na	na	na	na	na	na	na	na	na	na	na	na
Poland	na	74	79	70	64	74	81	82	68	54	79	71	72	76	74	71
Portugal	62	53	56	50	42	50	61	57	47	36	59	57	48	57	49	47
Puerto Rico	na	na	na	na	na	na	na	na	na	na	na	na	na	na	na	na
Romania	82	85	87	83	76	81	93	93	82	79	88	85	83	90	81	78
Russian Fed.	91	86	88	84	83	85	88	90	87	81	87	87	83	87	85	77
Serbia	na	na	na	na	na	na	na	na	na	na	na	na	na	na	na	na
Singapore	na	na	na	na	na	na	na	na	na	na	na	na	na	na	na	na
Slovakia	na	61	63	60	58	56	69	68	60	45	69	58	57	62	60	61
Slovenia	77	65	69	62	55	59	78	85	62	37	79	66	42	77	64	55
South Africa	na	na	na	na	na	na	na	na	na	na	na	na	na	na	na	na
Spain	57	47	46	47	30	37	65	64	38	26	59	47	30	62	47	23
Sweden	na	40	44	37	36	36	48	61	39	27	43	46	29	43	45	24
Switzerland	na	na	na	na	na	na	na	na	na	na	na	na	na	na	na	na
Taiwan	na	na	na	na	na	na	na	na	na	na	na	na	na	na	na	na
Tanzania	na	na	na	na	na	na	na	na	na	na	na	na	na	na	na	na
Turkey	88	na	na	na	na	na	na	na	na	na	na	na	na	na	na	na
Uganda	na	na	na	na	na	na	na	na	na	na	na	na	na	na	na	na
Ukraine	na	80	84	78	77	80	82	84	81	75	82	79	80	82	79	76
United States	56	na	na	na	na	na	na	na	na	na	na	na	na	na	na	na
Uruguay	na	na	na	na	na	na	na	na	na	na	na	na	na	na	na	na
Venezuela	na	na	na	na	na	na	na	na	na	na	na	na	na	na	na	na
Vietnam	na	na	na	na	na	na	na	na	na	na	na	na	na	na	na	na
Zimbabwe	na	na	na	na	na	na	na	na	na	na	na	na	na	na	na	na
Total	69	62	65	61	56	58	71	70	63	48	68	63	58	73	61	45

RANKING

Country	2000
Lithuania	94
Russian Fed.	86
Romania	85
Ukraine	80
Bulgaria	76
Poland	74
Czech Republic	72
Hungary	70
Malta	70
Belarus	68
Estonia	68
Italy	68
Latvia	67
Croatia	66
France	65
Greece	65
Slovenia	65
Iceland	62
Slovakia	61
Luxembourg	56
Belgium	54
Portugal	53
Finland	50
Spain	47
Great Britain	44
Germany	44
Sweden	40
Netherlands	34
Denmark	18
Total	62

D063_1) JOB INDEPENDENCE WOMEN

For each of the following statements I read out, can you tell me how much you agree with each. "Having a job is the best way for a woman to be an independent person"

Agree strongly / Agree (%)

(EVS: V158)

Country	Wave		Gender		Age			Education			Income			Values		
	1990	2000	Male	Female	16-29	30-49	50+	Lower	Middle	Upper	Lower	Middle	Upper	Mat	Mixed	Postm.
Albania	na	**na**	na	na	na	na	na	na	na	na	na	na	na	na	na	na
Algeria	na	**na**	na	na	na	na	na	na	na	na	na	na	na	na	na	na
Argentina	63	**na**	na	na	na	na	na	na	na	na	na	na	na	na	na	na
Armenia	na	**na**	na	na	na	na	na	na	na	na	na	na	na	na	na	na
Australia	na	**na**	na	na	na	na	na	na	na	na	na	na	na	na	na	na
Austria	74	**na**	na	na	na	na	na	na	na	na	na	na	na	na	na	na
Azerbaijan	na	**na**	na	na	na	na	na	na	na	na	na	na	na	na	na	na
Bangladesh	na	**na**	na	na	na	na	na	na	na	na	na	na	na	na	na	na
Belarus	62	**58**	50	65	57	59	57	52	59	62	60	56	58	56	60	51
Belgium	70	**77**	74	80	72	75	81	80	75	78	77	74	78	78	76	79
Bosnia and Herz.	na	**na**	na	na	na	na	na	na	na	na	na	na	na	na	na	na
Brazil	74	**na**	na	na	na	na	na	na	na	na	na	na	na	na	na	na
Bulgaria	63	**79**	73	85	78	76	83	81	77	81	83	79	78	82	76	81
Canada	55	**na**	na	na	na	na	na	na	na	na	na	na	na	na	na	na
Chile	72	**na**	na	na	na	na	na	na	na	na	na	na	na	na	na	na
China	75	**na**	na	na	na	na	na	na	na	na	na	na	na	na	na	na
Colombia	na	**na**	na	na	na	na	na	na	na	na	na	na	na	na	na	na
Croatia	na	**79**	72	86	77	80	80	87	74	80	90	77	76	77	79	83
Czech Republic	55	**76**	72	79	74	76	77	77	76	69	75	78	75	78	75	76
Denmark	81	**85**	84	85	75	84	90	85	83	85	83	86	88	78	85	86
Dominican Rep.	na	**na**	na	na	na	na	na	na	na	na	na	na	na	na	na	na
Egypt	na	**na**	na	na	na	na	na	na	na	na	na	na	na	na	na	na
El Salvador	na	**na**	na	na	na	na	na	na	na	na	na	na	na	na	na	na
Estonia	56	**79**	74	82	78	79	79	77	79	80	74	81	80	79	78	77
Finland	77	**63**	60	66	58	59	70	66	56	65	67	60	62	66	63	64
France	79	**84**	81	86	85	82	85	83	83	86	86	81	85	84	83	88
Georgia	na	**na**	na	na	na	na	na	na	na	na	na	na	na	na	na	na
Germany	75	**81**	79	83	86	82	78	77	84	89	78	81	84	77	81	89
Great Britain	68	**65**	64	66	63	59	70	65	63	63	72	66	59	na	na	na
Greece	na	**82**	75	88	83	84	81	75	83	83	80	82	83	85	82	82
Hungary	48	**72**	71	74	69	70	77	70	76	74	73	71	74	71	74	62
Iceland	43	**46**	43	49	42	42	54	46	40	56	51	39	50	41	46	53
India	58	**na**	na	na	na	na	na	na	na	na	na	na	na	na	na	na
Indonesia	na	**na**	na	na	na	na	na	na	na	na	na	na	na	na	na	na
Iran	na	**na**	na	na	na	na	na	na	na	na	na	na	na	na	na	na
Ireland	61	**na**	na	na	na	na	na	na	na	na	na	na	na	na	na	na
Israel	na	**na**	na	na	na	na	na	na	na	na	na	na	na	na	na	na
Italy	74	**77**	73	81	75	80	75	73	79	82	73	74	82	70	79	78
Japan	78	**na**	na	na	na	na	na	na	na	na	na	na	na	na	na	na
Jordan	na	**na**	na	na	na	na	na	na	na	na	na	na	na	na	na	na
Korea, South	34	**na**	na	na	na	na	na	na	na	na	na	na	na	na	na	na
Latvia	62	**85**	82	88	83	86	85	84	86	84	85	81	89	85	86	77
Lithuania	41	**77**	73	80	77	74	80	75	76	80	81	79	75	74	80	63
Luxembourg	na	**84**	82	85	86	84	82	83	84	86	84	84	86	81	83	90
Macedonia	na	**na**	na	na	na	na	na	na	na	na	na	na	na	na	na	na
Malta	na	**45**	45	44	52	41	42	42	43	57	48	39	47	36	48	55
Mexico	62	**na**	na	na	na	na	na	na	na	na	na	na	na	na	na	na
Moldova	na	**na**	na	na	na	na	na	na	na	na	na	na	na	na	na	na
Montenegro	na	**na**	na	na	na	na	na	na	na	na	na	na	na	na	na	na
Morocco	na	**na**	na	na	na	na	na	na	na	na	na	na	na	na	na	na
Netherlands	56	**61**	60	61	53	60	65	59	56	67	60	59	64	54	62	61
New Zealand	na	**na**	na	na	na	na	na	na	na	na	na	na	na	na	na	na
Nigeria	62	**na**	na	na	na	na	na	na	na	na	na	na	na	na	na	na
Northern Ireland	70	**na**	na	na	na	na	na	na	na	na	na	na	na	na	na	na
Norway	75	**na**	na	na	na	na	na	na	na	na	na	na	na	na	na	na
Pakistan	na	**na**	na	na	na	na	na	na	na	na	na	na	na	na	na	na
Peru	na	**na**	na	na	na	na	na	na	na	na	na	na	na	na	na	na
Philippines	na	**na**	na	na	na	na	na	na	na	na	na	na	na	na	na	na
Poland	na	**76**	74	78	79	73	78	73	77	84	75	77	75	74	78	74
Portugal	80	**79**	73	84	84	74	80	78	80	79	80	71	80	76	81	77
Puerto Rico	na	**na**	na	na	na	na	na	na	na	na	na	na	na	na	na	na
Romania	68	**82**	78	85	77	80	85	83	80	84	80	84	81	80	81	87
Russian Fed.	58	**70**	62	77	68	71	71	66	71	71	71	69	71	70	71	68
Serbia	na	**na**	na	na	na	na	na	na	na	na	na	na	na	na	na	na
Singapore	na	**na**	na	na	na	na	na	na	na	na	na	na	na	na	na	na
Slovakia	na	**75**	73	76	75	76	73	71	77	72	71	78	74	74	76	74
Slovenia	73	**79**	77	81	74	77	86	83	78	82	80	77	79	84	79	79
South Africa	na	**na**	na	na	na	na	na	na	na	na	na	na	na	na	na	na
Spain	79	**81**	82	80	85	83	77	75	86	85	77	84	84	78	81	86
Sweden	74	**84**	84	83	76	80	91	87	80	86	84	83	84	77	85	82
Switzerland	na	**na**	na	na	na	na	na	na	na	na	na	na	na	na	na	na
Taiwan	na	**na**	na	na	na	na	na	na	na	na	na	na	na	na	na	na
Tanzania	na	**na**	na	na	na	na	na	na	na	na	na	na	na	na	na	na
Turkey	45	**na**	na	na	na	na	na	na	na	na	na	na	na	na	na	na
Uganda	na	**na**	na	na	na	na	na	na	na	na	na	na	na	na	na	na
Ukraine	na	**73**	68	78	73	75	72	67	73	76	72	70	77	75	71	88
United States	60	**na**	na	na	na	na	na	na	na	na	na	na	na	na	na	na
Uruguay	na	**na**	na	na	na	na	na	na	na	na	na	na	na	na	na	na
Venezuela	na	**na**	na	na	na	na	na	na	na	na	na	na	na	na	na	na
Vietnam	na	**na**	na	na	na	na	na	na	na	na	na	na	na	na	na	na
Zimbabwe	na	**na**	na	na	na	na	na	na	na	na	na	na	na	na	na	na
Total	65	**74**	71	77	72	73	76	74	73	77	75	73	75	73	75	77

RANKING	
Country	**2000**
Latvia	85
Denmark	85
Luxembourg	84
France	84
Sweden	84
Greece	82
Romania	82
Germany	81
Spain	81
Croatia	79
Slovenia	79
Bulgaria	79
Portugal	79
Estonia	79
Italy	77
Belgium	77
Lithuania	77
Poland	76
Czech Republic	76
Slovakia	75
Ukraine	73
Hungary	72
Russian Fed.	70
Great Britain	65
Finland	63
Netherlands	61
Belarus	58
Iceland	46
Malta	45
Total	74

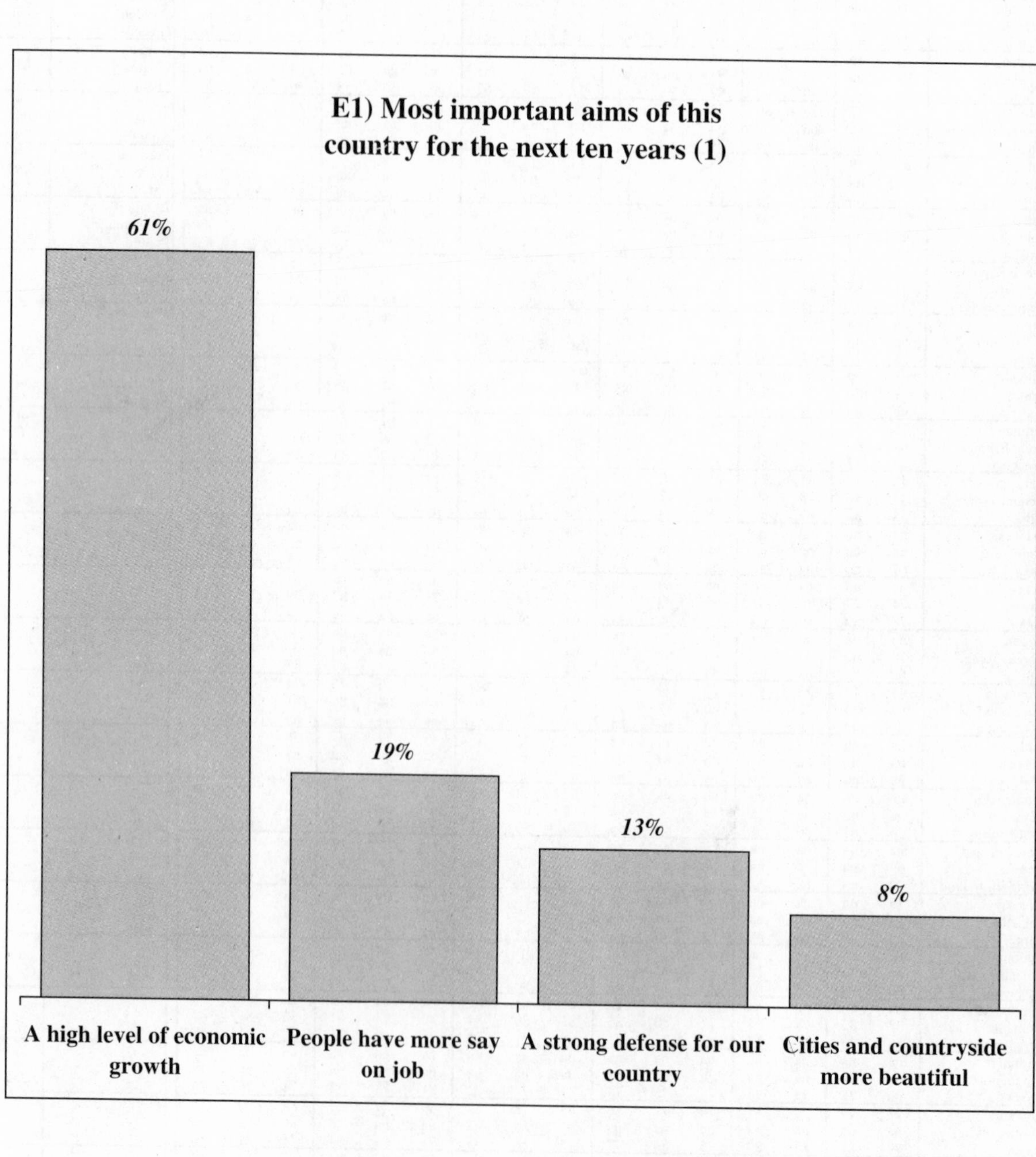
E1) Most important aims of this country for the next ten years (1)
61%
19%
13%
8%
A high level of economic growth
People have more say on job
A strong defense for our country
Cities and countryside more beautiful

E001A) AIMS OF COUNTRY / 1 - MORE SAY ON THE JOB

People sometimes talk about what the aims of this country should be for the next ten years. Would you please say which one of these you, yourself, consider the most important?

Seeing that people have more say about how things are done at their jobs and in their communities (%) (WVS: V120)

Country	Wave		Gender		Age			Education			Income			Values		
	1990	2000	Male	Female	16-29	30-49	50+	Lower	Middle	Upper	Lower	Middle	Upper	Mat	Mixed	Postm.
Albania	na	**3**	4	2	4	3	2	1	4	5	1	3	5	1	5	10
Algeria	na	**13**	14	11	13	14	9	8	13	16	14	9	17	5	14	37
Argentina	25	**31**	29	33	31	35	28	26	38	44	30	27	38	18	27	52
Armenia	na	**11**	7	14	13	9	10	11	11	9	10	11	11	6	13	25
Australia	na	**41**	39	43	47	42	34	34	39	50	39	44	43	16	37	53
Austria	29	**na**	na	na	na	na	na	na	na	na	na	na	na	na	na	na
Azerbaijan	na	**8**	6	9	10	6	5	4	7	9	8	9	7	6	10	13
Bangladesh	na	**11**	10	12	10	11	10	12	10	9	11	8	14	11	10	15
Belarus	17	**na**	na	na	na	na	na	na	na	na	na	na	na	na	na	na
Belgium	38	**na**	na	na	na	na	na	na	na	na	na	na	na	na	na	na
Bosnia and Herz.	na	**6**	6	7	9	6	5	5	7	6	4	6	9	3	7	17
Brazil	26	**29**	30	28	29	30	27	24	31	40	26	30	32	18	30	52
Bulgaria	16	**na**	na	na	na	na	na	na	na	na	na	na	na	na	na	na
Canada	34	**40**	35	45	42	39	40	39	39	42	42	44	36	22	37	51
Chile	25	**26**	24	28	30	23	27	25	24	33	27	23	31	16	28	39
China	2	**5**	4	7	9	4	4	3	7	5	5	7	4	2	7	19
Colombia	na	**na**	na	na	na	na	na	na	na	na	na	na	na	na	na	na
Croatia	na	**na**	na	na	na	na	na	na	na	na	na	na	na	na	na	na
Czech Republic	25	**na**	na	na	na	na	na	na	na	na	na	na	na	na	na	na
Denmark	40	**na**	na	na	na	na	na	na	na	na	na	na	na	na	na	na
Dominican Rep.	na	**29**	28	30	31	27	27	24	28	30	35	30	26	23	25	44
Egypt	na	**10**	10	11	10	11	9	10	11	9	10	12	11	9	11	18
El Salvador	na	**23**	20	25	29	21	14	16	29	30	16	23	28	na	na	na
Estonia	12	**na**	na	na	na	na	na	na	na	na	na	na	na	na	na	na
Finland	54	**na**	na	na	na	na	na	na	na	na	na	na	na	na	na	na
France	36	**na**	na	na	na	na	na	na	na	na	na	na	na	na	na	na
Georgia	na	**9**	9	10	9	9	10	9	9	9	11	9	8	6	12	20
Germany	19	**na**	na	na	na	na	na	na	na	na	na	na	na	na	na	na
Great Britain	40	**na**	na	na	na	na	na	na	na	na	na	na	na	na	na	na
Greece	na	**na**	na	na	na	na	na	na	na	na	na	na	na	na	na	na
Hungary	22	**na**	na	na	na	na	na	na	na	na	na	na	na	na	na	na
Iceland	39	**na**	na	na	na	na	na	na	na	na	na	na	na	na	na	na
India	9	**10**	9	11	10	10	10	10	9	10	12	8	10	8	11	28
Indonesia	na	**3**	2	3	6	2	2	1	2	6	3	3	3	2	4	7
Iran	na	**20**	21	19	20	22	18	18	20	23	21	24	17	10	26	32
Ireland	35	**na**	na	na	na	na	na	na	na	na	na	na	na	na	na	na
Israel	na	**10**	11	10	12	11	8	15	10	7	12	14	6	22	8	9
Italy	38	**na**	na	na	na	na	na	na	na	na	na	na	na	na	na	na
Japan	31	**36**	33	39	46	37	32	33	37	39	38	34	36	22	38	60
Jordan	na	**8**	6	10	9	7	7	7	9	9	7	9	7	5	9	18
Korea, South	25	**23**	22	24	34	20	15	9	20	28	21	19	27	17	27	41
Latvia	8	**na**	na	na	na	na	na	na	na	na	na	na	na	na	na	na
Lithuania	13	**na**	na	na	na	na	na	na	na	na	na	na	na	na	na	na
Luxembourg	na	**na**	na	na	na	na	na	na	na	na	na	na	na	na	na	na
Macedonia	na	**7**	6	7	10	6	5	9	6	5	7	4	8	4	7	26
Malta	na	**na**	na	na	na	na	na	na	na	na	na	na	na	na	na	na
Mexico	25	**27**	27	27	28	30	23	25	29	35	25	29	32	27	25	38
Moldova	na	**11**	12	10	13	10	10	9	11	12	7	11	12	10	12	15
Montenegro	na	**8**	7	8	12	5	8	6	9	9	10	8	5	3	9	26
Morocco	na	**11**	12	10	12	12	7	10	15	21	8	19	10	5	15	18
Netherlands	52	**na**	na	na	na	na	na	na	na	na	na	na	na	na	na	na
New Zealand	na	**22**	20	23	30	23	19	16	23	29	20	25	23	11	21	42
Nigeria	17	**14**	13	15	14	15	14	14	15	13	12	16	13	11	15	21
Northern Ireland	31	**na**	na	na	na	na	na	na	na	na	na	na	na	na	na	na
Norway	43	**49**	46	52	49	50	48	46	49	52	na	na	na	41	48	70
Pakistan	na	**5**	5	4	5	4	5	2	6	13	na	3	13	3	7	33
Peru	na	**28**	27	30	27	29	30	23	28	32	27	27	35	16	30	38
Philippines	na	**22**	20	24	23	25	16	22	26	18	27	22	17	17	26	26
Poland	17	**na**	na	na	na	na	na	na	na	na	na	na	na	na	na	na
Portugal	15	**na**	na	na	na	na	na	na	na	na	na	na	na	na	na	na
Puerto Rico	na	**32**	27	35	38	30	31	17	28	37	24	35	35	20	30	44
Romania	na	**na**	na	na	na	na	na	na	na	na	na	na	na	na	na	na
Russian Fed.	15	**na**	na	na	na	na	na	na	na	na	na	na	na	na	na	na
Serbia	na	**9**	9	10	12	8	9	10	9	10	7	9	11	6	11	28
Singapore	na	**17**	16	19	22	14	7	11	20	21	14	16	21	8	17	58
Slovakia	na	**na**	na	na	na	na	na	na	na	na	na	na	na	na	na	na
Slovenia	29	**na**	na	na	na	na	na	na	na	na	na	na	na	na	na	na
South Africa	26	**22**	22	22	22	22	20	22	22	19	22	28	14	15	25	29
Spain	39	**35**	37	34	40	39	29	32	39	38	30	34	35	21	35	60
Sweden	33	**34**	30	39	40	32	33	35	36	32	38	34	30	18	30	54
Switzerland	42	**42**	39	44	49	39	40	44	42	37	45	48	36	28	37	64
Taiwan	na	**6**	6	6	11	6	3	5	6	7	5	9	5	4	8	11
Tanzania	na	**5**	5	4	4	5	4	5	5	2	6	3	4	4	5	4
Turkey	12	**12**	10	13	15	10	7	9	13	18	12	10	14	5	11	21
Uganda	na	**9**	8	9	7	9	14	12	7	12	6	8	11	5	9	18
Ukraine	na	**na**	na	na	na	na	na	na	na	na	na	na	na	na	na	na
United States	26	**31**	30	33	42	31	23	30	32	31	36	30	28	18	28	44
Uruguay	na	**23**	22	23	29	26	18	19	27	35	21	23	25	16	21	31
Venezuela	na	**22**	19	24	22	22	20	21	23	21	22	22	21	17	23	28
Vietnam	na	**11**	12	11	13	11	11	11	12	16	14	8	14	3	13	29
Zimbabwe	na	**17**	16	17	16	14	22	18	15	na	15	17	17	14	18	23
Total	27	19	17	20	20	18	18	16	19	22	18	18	19	10	20	39

RANKING

Country	2000
Norway	49
Switzerland	42
Australia	41
Canada	40
Japan	36
Spain	35
Sweden	34
Puerto Rico	32
Argentina	31
United States	31
Dominican Rep.	29
Brazil	29
Peru	28
Mexico	27
Chile	26
Uruguay	23
Korea, South	23
El Salvador	23
Philippines	22
New Zealand	22
South Africa	22
Venezuela	22
Iran	20
Singapore	17
Zimbabwe	17
Nigeria	14
Algeria	13
Turkey	12
Vietnam	11
Morocco	11
Moldova	11
Armenia	11
Bangladesh	11
Israel	10
Egypt	10
India	10
Serbia	9
Georgia	9
Uganda	9
Jordan	8
Azerbaijan	8
Montenegro	8
Macedonia	7
Bosnia and Herz.	6
Taiwan	6
China	5
Pakistan	5
Tanzania	5
Albania	3
Indonesia	3
Total	19

E001B) AIMS OF COUNTRY / 1 - HIGHER ECONOMIC GROWTH

People sometimes talk about what the aims of this country should be for the next ten years. Would you please say which one of these you, yourself, consider the most important?

A high level of economic growth (%)

(WVS: V120)

Country	Wave		Gender		Age			Education			Income			Values		
	1990	2000	Male	Female	16-29	30-49	50+	Lower	Middle	Upper	Lower	Middle	Upper	Mat	Mixed	Postm.
Albania	na	**88**	87	89	87	90	87	90	86	89	86	91	88	91	86	80
Algeria	na	**68**	66	71	69	67	70	64	68	71	65	72	67	70	69	54
Argentina	66	**53**	57	50	52	52	55	54	52	51	51	56	51	64	56	38
Armenia	na	**46**	49	43	44	49	45	44	44	54	47	45	44	44	48	41
Australia	na	**44**	45	43	38	47	48	42	49	41	41	44	47	65	48	33
Austria	52	**na**	na	na	na	na	na	na	na	na	na	na	na	na	na	na
Azerbaijan	na	**59**	60	59	61	59	58	53	57	65	52	56	68	59	58	68
Bangladesh	na	**76**	79	72	76	76	76	73	78	79	71	81	73	74	78	65
Belarus	73	**na**	na	na	na	na	na	na	na	na	na	na	na	na	na	na
Belgium	42	**na**	na	na	na	na	na	na	na	na	na	na	na	na	na	na
Bosnia and Herz.	na	**84**	86	82	82	85	83	82	82	90	83	84	82	82	85	70
Brazil	51	**46**	47	45	48	44	47	41	50	49	43	46	49	47	47	35
Bulgaria	76	**na**	na	na	na	na	na	na	na	na	na	na	na	na	na	na
Canada	56	**51**	55	47	45	54	50	45	53	53	47	49	55	63	54	40
Chile	66	**66**	69	63	62	70	65	65	70	60	64	71	62	76	65	53
China	66	**40**	39	41	41	40	40	38	40	50	41	37	41	44	37	29
Colombia	na	**na**	na	na	na	na	na	na	na	na	na	na	na	na	na	na
Croatia	na	**na**	na	na	na	na	na	na	na	na	na	na	na	na	na	na
Czech Republic	66	**na**	na	na	na	na	na	na	na	na	na	na	na	na	na	na
Denmark	47	**na**	na	na	na	na	na	na	na	na	na	na	na	na	na	na
Dominican Rep.	na	**65**	63	65	62	69	55	55	64	66	58	63	73	69	68	53
Egypt	na	**55**	56	54	52	56	57	54	54	58	52	55	58	58	54	44
El Salvador	na	**51**	56	47	46	51	60	48	51	61	45	54	59	na	na	na
Estonia	80	**na**	na	na	na	na	na	na	na	na	na	na	na	na	na	na
Finland	34	**na**	na	na	na	na	na	na	na	na	na	na	na	na	na	na
France	52	**na**	na	na	na	na	na	na	na	na	na	na	na	na	na	na
Georgia	na	**63**	60	65	61	64	62	61	63	63	60	64	65	66	60	53
Germany	73	**na**	na	na	na	na	na	na	na	na	na	na	na	na	na	na
Great Britain	43	**na**	na	na	na	na	na	na	na	na	na	na	na	na	na	na
Greece	na	**na**	na	na	na	na	na	na	na	na	na	na	na	na	na	na
Hungary	63	**na**	na	na	na	na	na	na	na	na	na	na	na	na	na	na
Iceland	53	**na**	na	na	na	na	na	na	na	na	na	na	na	na	na	na
India	54	**54**	57	51	58	55	47	44	56	70	42	53	62	56	57	58
Indonesia	na	**84**	84	85	84	86	84	83	86	84	83	86	84	86	84	75
Iran	na	**56**	55	57	56	55	56	59	56	52	55	55	57	67	51	39
Ireland	55	**na**	na	na	na	na	na	na	na	na	na	na	na	na	na	na
Israel	na	**51**	50	52	51	49	53	45	51	54	50	50	49	36	55	49
Italy	43	**na**	na	na	na	na	na	na	na	na	na	na	na	na	na	na
Japan	43	**42**	41	43	29	41	49	46	44	37	43	44	41	58	40	26
Jordan	na	**66**	67	64	62	67	71	63	65	73	63	65	70	66	66	63
Korea, South	52	**51**	49	52	49	50	54	54	53	46	49	54	49	57	46	32
Latvia	83	**na**	na	na	na	na	na	na	na	na	na	na	na	na	na	na
Lithuania	76	**na**	na	na	na	na	na	na	na	na	na	na	na	na	na	na
Luxembourg	na	**na**	na	na	na	na	na	na	na	na	na	na	na	na	na	na
Macedonia	na	**77**	77	77	76	78	78	70	80	83	76	80	79	81	77	55
Malta	na	**na**	na	na	na	na	na	na	na	na	na	na	na	na	na	na
Mexico	62	**53**	57	49	53	53	54	50	57	55	52	50	54	52	56	45
Moldova	na	**77**	76	79	74	78	79	81	74	80	79	77	79	80	74	73
Montenegro	na	**78**	81	74	78	83	74	73	81	81	74	79	83	79	80	58
Morocco	na	**58**	61	54	60	56	58	56	64	68	58	59	66	60	56	65
Netherlands	41	**na**	na	na	na	na	na	na	na	na	na	na	na	na	na	na
New Zealand	na	**61**	62	61	54	64	62	61	61	64	56	62	68	80	73	53
Nigeria	67	**71**	72	69	71	70	69	70	70	74	71	67	75	74	70	62
Northern Ireland	53	**na**	na	na	na	na	na	na	na	na	na	na	na	na	na	na
Norway	48	**40**	42	37	40	43	35	39	40	40	na	na	na	43	41	25
Pakistan	na	**76**	77	76	79	76	73	81	74	66	83	79	62	79	73	33
Peru	na	**63**	64	61	64	63	61	62	63	62	61	66	61	70	63	55
Philippines	na	**57**	62	52	58	53	62	51	55	67	53	54	64	63	53	57
Poland	74	**na**	na	na	na	na	na	na	na	na	na	na	na	na	na	na
Portugal	71	**na**	na	na	na	na	na	na	na	na	na	na	na	na	na	na
Puerto Rico	na	**56**	63	53	53	61	54	63	60	53	63	53	56	67	58	46
Romania	na	**na**	na	na	na	na	na	na	na	na	na	na	na	na	na	na
Russian Fed.	72	**na**	na	na	na	na	na	na	na	na	na	na	na	na	na	na
Serbia	na	**80**	81	80	80	83	78	76	81	84	78	84	84	80	82	69
Singapore	na	**59**	61	57	49	66	71	64	55	62	60	58	57	71	57	30
Slovakia	na	**na**	na	na	na	na	na	na	na	na	na	na	na	na	na	na
Slovenia	64	**na**	na	na	na	na	na	na	na	na	na	na	na	na	na	na
South Africa	54	**61**	63	58	60	60	63	56	65	77	57	55	71	64	61	40
Spain	46	**50**	50	50	47	48	53	51	46	50	55	55	44	60	52	27
Sweden	51	**57**	61	53	51	59	59	57	57	58	53	59	63	75	61	40
Switzerland	28	**44**	48	39	37	48	42	38	44	51	39	39	50	54	48	26
Taiwan	na	**41**	41	41	33	42	41	43	40	39	40	37	44	44	38	31
Tanzania	na	**82**	83	80	78	85	82	75	89	92	72	88	90	81	82	67
Turkey	59	**65**	69	61	61	68	68	61	71	74	62	68	68	68	66	61
Uganda	na	**65**	69	62	66	65	59	62	67	53	64	69	57	68	65	57
Ukraine	na	**na**	na	na	na	na	na	na	na	na	na	na	na	na	na	na
United States	54	**49**	48	49	44	51	49	46	48	51	41	50	58	70	50	36
Uruguay	na	**66**	68	64	64	62	69	67	65	60	64	64	68	76	66	59
Venezuela	na	**64**	67	60	63	65	62	58	63	73	58	64	70	66	63	61
Vietnam	na	**64**	67	61	60	64	67	65	62	69	55	68	64	85	58	57
Zimbabwe	na	**67**	71	63	67	68	64	64	71	100	64	65	73	73	64	52
Total	58	**61**	63	59	60	62	61	60	61	62	59	62	63	67	61	47

RANKING

Country	2000
Albania	88
Indonesia	84
Bosnia and Herz.	84
Tanzania	82
Serbia	80
Montenegro	78
Moldova	77
Macedonia	77
Pakistan	76
Bangladesh	76
Nigeria	71
Algeria	68
Zimbabwe	67
Chile	66
Jordan	66
Uruguay	66
Turkey	65
Uganda	65
Dominican Rep.	65
Vietnam	64
Venezuela	64
Georgia	63
Peru	63
New Zealand	61
South Africa	61
Azerbaijan	59
Singapore	59
Morocco	58
Sweden	57
Philippines	57
Puerto Rico	56
Iran	56
Egypt	55
India	54
Mexico	53
Argentina	53
El Salvador	51
Israel	51
Canada	51
Korea, South	51
Spain	50
United States	49
Brazil	46
Armenia	46
Australia	44
Switzerland	44
Japan	42
Taiwan	41
China	40
Norway	40
Total	61

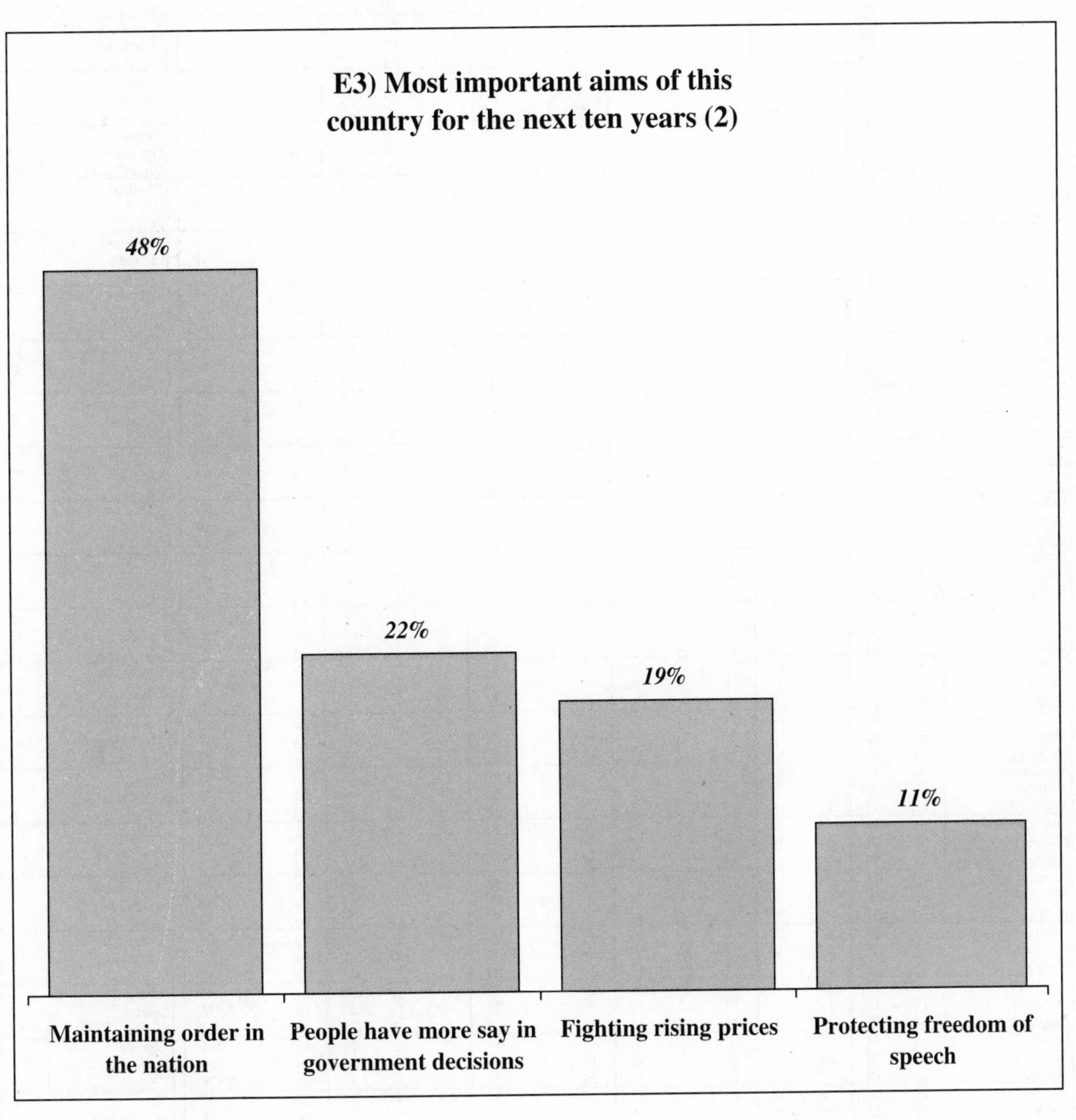
E3) Most important aims of this country for the next ten years (2)
48%
22%
19%
11%
Maintaining order in the nation
People have more say in government decisions
Fighting rising prices
Protecting freedom of speech

E003A) AIMS OF COUNTRY / 2 - MORE SAY IN GOVERNMENT DECISIONS

If you had to choose, which one of the things on this card would you say is most important?

Give people more say in government decisions (%) (WVS: V122; EVS: V190)

Country	Wave		Gender		Age			Education			Income			Values		
	1990	2000	Male	Female	16-29	30-49	50+	Lower	Middle	Upper	Lower	Middle	Upper	Mat	Mixed	Postm.
Albania	na	**11**	14	9	11	12	11	7	13	19	9	11	13	na	15	90
Algeria	na	**12**	14	11	14	12	10	8	11	18	13	10	13	na	14	56
Argentina	32	**30**	31	30	29	34	27	23	38	47	22	28	42	na	22	70
Armenia	na	**13**	14	12	15	14	10	15	11	20	15	12	11	na	21	52
Australia	na	**40**	38	42	44	43	33	39	41	40	39	39	44	na	34	60
Austria	26	**33**	32	34	32	38	29	30	36	35	30	39	31	na	24	60
Azerbaijan	na	**9**	10	9	9	11	6	3	9	11	10	11	9	na	19	82
Bangladesh	na	**19**	20	18	22	18	13	19	19	18	15	25	14	na	26	86
Belarus	35	**13**	16	11	17	16	7	7	14	21	9	14	21	na	22	61
Belgium	18	**25**	27	23	22	28	23	13	24	34	19	28	30	na	23	58
Bosnia and Herz.	na	**15**	16	14	16	15	14	12	17	13	14	14	18	na	19	79
Brazil	22	**32**	35	28	36	33	21	22	37	47	24	31	42	na	40	75
Bulgaria	29	**5**	5	5	8	6	4	4	5	8	6	5	5	na	9	32
Canada	43	**40**	37	42	40	39	41	40	39	42	40	41	38	na	36	60
Chile	31	**28**	30	26	31	31	20	19	30	40	23	29	34	na	31	63
China	14	**12**	13	10	16	12	6	6	15	7	8	16	10	na	20	59
Colombia	na	**23**	24	22	25	23	19	17	25	35	19	23	29	na	25	69
Croatia	na	**45**	48	42	52	47	39	42	49	41	45	44	47	na	47	78
Czech Republic	27	**26**	26	27	29	29	23	26	26	30	27	26	25	na	32	61
Denmark	16	**17**	16	18	17	21	12	13	20	21	12	18	22	na	12	52
Dominican Rep.	na	**26**	29	25	26	27	18	16	23	29	22	31	23	na	23	68
Egypt	na	**8**	10	6	12	6	6	6	9	12	6	8	9	na	9	59
El Salvador	na	**22**	25	20	25	22	19	14	27	37	12	23	39	na	na	na
Estonia	21	**21**	22	19	25	22	17	20	21	22	18	22	22	na	34	77
Finland	59	**24**	23	26	27	26	22	23	25	33	26	24	25	na	27	65
France	21	**24**	25	23	24	26	21	17	27	37	20	23	30	na	22	66
Georgia	na	**11**	14	9	11	12	11	9	11	14	12	10	11	na	18	60
Germany	35	**32**	34	32	40	35	26	27	35	46	27	32	36	na	37	73
Great Britain	29	**na**	na	na	na	na	na	na	na	na	na	na	na	na	na	na
Greece	na	**36**	38	35	39	36	31	40	32	38	39	36	34	na	38	68
Hungary	18	**17**	17	17	22	16	14	14	22	21	19	16	18	na	32	80
Iceland	26	**25**	24	26	28	28	20	20	29	30	23	25	28	na	28	64
India	18	**12**	13	11	12	13	10	7	14	18	6	10	16	na	22	51
Indonesia	na	**6**	8	5	4	7	7	5	5	8	3	6	10	na	8	57
Iran	na	**20**	20	19	22	19	16	13	24	20	17	19	23	na	23	59
Ireland	32	**36**	35	37	40	37	32	31	40	34	33	33	39	na	38	78
Israel	na	**43**	38	48	41	42	46	53	43	37	47	43	43	na	50	84
Italy	29	**39**	39	39	48	42	32	32	44	48	33	42	45	na	35	69
Japan	29	**45**	43	48	55	48	39	39	48	44	44	43	47	na	53	77
Jordan	na	**10**	9	10	12	9	6	8	12	11	9	10	9	na	12	56
Korea, South	15	**18**	21	16	26	17	12	9	15	24	17	19	19	na	31	65
Latvia	26	**24**	31	19	31	28	19	18	25	30	18	31	30	na	35	72
Lithuania	32	**33**	36	31	36	39	26	17	37	47	27	33	38	na	46	66
Luxembourg	na	**30**	27	33	28	34	26	23	32	35	25	31	37	na	30	69
Macedonia	na	**11**	12	10	14	10	9	14	9	10	11	12	9	na	13	71
Malta	na	**20**	23	17	25	21	16	10	21	37	14	22	22	na	25	73
Mexico	23	**22**	25	19	25	23	16	15	27	38	17	26	27	na	24	62
Moldova	na	**14**	14	14	15	15	11	14	13	17	14	11	16	na	23	77
Montenegro	na	**12**	13	10	17	13	6	8	13	17	11	13	12	na	16	69
Morocco	na	**8**	10	7	10	8	3	6	11	25	9	11	9	na	9	55
Netherlands	16	**17**	18	16	16	16	19	13	18	20	15	20	17	na	11	44
New Zealand	na	**38**	35	40	41	40	35	39	37	38	38	42	34	na	42	72
Nigeria	20	**21**	21	21	21	20	26	20	21	22	22	20	21	na	26	78
Northern Ireland	27	**28**	29	28	33	30	25	29	26	32	24	33	28	na	29	69
Norway	14	**14**	15	14	16	15	11	11	14	18	na	na	na	na	12	46
Pakistan	na	**4**	4	3	3	4	3	1	5	10	na	2	11	na	8	83
Peru	na	**31**	34	29	32	30	33	23	28	41	29	29	38	na	32	74
Philippines	na	**18**	20	17	19	17	18	18	17	20	14	21	18	na	26	66
Poland	27	**28**	33	23	23	34	23	23	32	34	24	30	31	na	39	82
Portugal	22	**26**	26	25	34	31	17	20	35	47	12	25	33	na	36	59
Puerto Rico	na	**27**	27	27	30	26	27	23	19	32	17	31	33	na	20	64
Romania	12	**15**	19	12	19	17	12	8	17	25	10	14	20	na	25	56
Russian Fed.	24	**19**	22	16	23	21	14	9	18	27	13	18	24	na	38	82
Serbia	na	**11**	13	8	12	12	9	7	10	19	8	11	13	na	15	68
Singapore	na	**20**	20	20	23	19	12	15	23	20	19	19	21	na	23	63
Slovakia	na	**18**	20	17	21	20	15	12	20	29	13	17	24	na	31	76
Slovenia	28	**36**	36	37	40	38	32	33	39	34	38	40	36	na	36	77
South Africa	27	**21**	21	21	22	22	15	23	17	31	24	21	17	na	30	59
Spain	29	**25**	25	24	29	27	20	21	28	30	24	27	26	na	26	59
Sweden	28	**32**	29	35	34	34	29	20	35	36	31	31	34	na	26	61
Switzerland	18	**16**	17	16	15	18	14	14	17	16	13	16	19	na	14	39
Taiwan	na	**12**	14	10	8	13	11	10	14	12	13	14	9	na	18	65
Tanzania	na	**11**	13	9	9	12	11	9	13	14	10	12	12	na	15	92
Turkey	23	**27**	27	27	30	26	22	27	28	26	27	27	29	na	30	50
Uganda	na	**15**	20	11	15	16	16	15	14	24	14	20	18	na	14	64
Ukraine	na	**22**	24	20	22	26	17	11	22	28	15	25	28	na	38	79
United States	31	**32**	34	30	32	35	29	27	36	32	31	29	37	na	28	55
Uruguay	na	**37**	38	36	46	41	29	30	46	48	30	38	45	na	34	72
Venezuela	na	**20**	23	17	18	23	20	17	19	27	19	18	23	na	19	61
Vietnam	na	**29**	29	28	32	29	26	27	32	24	29	25	32	na	33	79
Zimbabwe	na	**13**	16	10	15	10	12	9	16	48	13	12	20	na	18	55
Total	26	**22**	23	22	24	23	20	18	23	27	20	23	25	na	26	64

RANKING	
Country	**2000**
Japan	45
Croatia	45
Israel	43
Australia	40
Canada	40
Italy	39
New Zealand	38
Uruguay	37
Slovenia	36
Ireland	36
Greece	36
Lithuania	33
Austria	33
Germany	32
United States	32
Sweden	32
Brazil	32
Peru	31
Argentina	30
Luxembourg	30
Vietnam	29
Northern Ireland	28
Poland	28
Chile	28
Puerto Rico	27
Turkey	27
Czech Republic	26
Dominican Rep.	26
Portugal	26
Iceland	25
Belgium	25
Spain	25
Latvia	24
Finland	24
France	24
Colombia	23
El Salvador	22
Mexico	22
Ukraine	22
Nigeria	21
Estonia	21
South Africa	21
Venezuela	20
Malta	20
Singapore	20
Iran	20
Bangladesh	19
Russian Fed.	19
Slovakia	18
Korea, South	18
Philippines	18
Hungary	17
Netherlands	17
Denmark	17
Switzerland	16
Romania	15
Uganda	15
Bosnia and Herz.	15
Norway	14
Moldova	14
Armenia	13
Belarus	13
Zimbabwe	13
Algeria	12
India	12
Taiwan	12
China	12
Montenegro	12
Albania	11
Georgia	11
Tanzania	11
Macedonia	11
Serbia	11
Jordan	10
Azerbaijan	9
Morocco	8
Egypt	8
Indonesia	6
Bulgaria	5
Pakistan	4
Total	22

E003B) AIMS OF COUNTRY / 2 - MAINTAINING ORDER

If you had to choose, which one of the things on this card would you say is most important?

Maintaining order in the nation (%) (WVS: V122; EVS: V190)

Country	Wave		Gender		Age			Education			Income			Values		
	1990	2000	Male	Female	16-29	30-49	50+	Lower	Middle	Upper	Lower	Middle	Upper	Mat	Mixed	Postm.
Albania	na	**70**	70	71	67	73	69	73	69	67	74	68	68	82	66	
Algeria	na	**55**	54	56	53	55	59	55	58	51	52	59	54	72	54	
Argentina	35	**33**	35	32	32	31	38	38	29	23	39	33	30	65	39	
Armenia	na	**61**	63	60	57	64	63	56	62	60	59	64	63	75	55	
Australia	na	**23**	25	21	19	21	28	23	24	20	22	24	22	63	32	
Austria	41	**36**	36	36	29	31	44	41	32	29	40	33	37	76	48	
Azerbaijan	na	**74**	75	73	74	73	78	81	74	73	75	74	72	83	66	
Bangladesh	na	**64**	64	63	60	65	67	64	64	62	61	60	70	80	58	
Belarus	44	**56**	55	57	52	54	62	59	57	48	57	56	54	66	53	
Belgium	21	**38**	36	41	34	36	43	48	39	31	42	38	36	61	43	
Bosnia and Herz.	na	**71**	69	73	72	71	70	72	71	71	71	73	65	85	68	
Brazil	31	**29**	28	30	25	27	39	31	26	30	30	27	28	44	26	
Bulgaria	51	**76**	76	76	76	78	74	75	76	79	71	78	79	82	75	
Canada	21	**22**	21	23	21	22	23	22	24	21	21	23	22	58	28	
Chile	39	**35**	36	33	31	33	41	37	37	24	35	37	32	61	32	
China	67	**57**	57	56	54	59	55	56	56	73	56	55	60	67	51	
Colombia	na	**41**	43	39	38	43	43	41	41	41	41	40	42	70	48	
Croatia	na	**28**	27	29	22	26	34	26	29	28	36	26	24	57	28	
Czech Republic	44	**56**	55	57	48	54	62	55	57	52	56	55	57	77	56	
Denmark	59	**59**	60	58	59	52	65	69	50	41	67	57	47	81	67	
Dominican Rep.	na	**45**	44	45	44	45	46	56	50	42	47	44	44	74	48	
Egypt	na	**63**	65	61	58	66	62	59	67	64	63	63	61	71	63	
El Salvador	na	**26**	25	26	21	27	31	29	22	23	27	24	23	na	na	
Estonia	59	**57**	59	56	52	57	60	54	57	64	55	56	60	70	51	
Finland	11	**52**	56	49	47	49	57	52	55	43	49	52	56	71	53	
France	28	**43**	42	45	39	39	49	50	38	28	49	42	36	69	44	
Georgia	na	**65**	65	66	68	64	64	69	65	65	64	69	65	77	59	
Germany	37	**42**	41	43	29	40	50	48	39	33	46	41	38	67	42	
Great Britain	25	**na**	na	na	na	na	na	na	na	na	na	na	na	na	na	na
Greece	na	**40**	37	41	35	41	46	37	43	37	37	40	41	67	42	
Hungary	37	**53**	55	51	50	52	55	50	55	65	44	57	52	62	45	
Iceland	49	**57**	54	59	54	54	62	64	55	45	56	61	52	75	59	
India	43	**42**	45	38	44	41	43	37	47	47	40	43	43	54	39	
Indonesia	na	**77**	76	78	75	77	78	73	79	76	78	79	74	79	79	
Iran	na	**39**	41	36	38	39	41	40	37	40	38	39	38	63	35	
Ireland	24	**37**	36	38	36	37	39	31	38	46	39	37	38	66	37	
Israel	na	**41**	46	37	39	43	41	35	43	43	35	42	45	65	39	
Italy	29	**32**	33	32	26	30	38	38	30	21	33	32	26	73	37	
Japan	35	**34**	39	29	23	30	42	37	32	34	35	34	34	68	30	
Jordan	na	**63**	67	59	61	62	69	65	59	63	60	65	65	74	61	
Korea, South	43	**43**	48	37	38	41	52	29	43	44	41	43	44	49	41	
Latvia	54	**54**	52	55	51	51	57	55	54	54	56	49	53	73	47	
Lithuania	29	**24**	25	24	21	24	27	31	21	25	22	19	25	45	17	
Luxembourg	na	**45**	49	42	44	40	51	51	45	36	47	41	38	78	47	
Macedonia	na	**77**	76	78	72	76	81	75	78	77	79	74	77	87	76	
Malta	na	**33**	35	30	33	30	35	31	34	33	32	35	35	41	32	
Mexico	28	**32**	33	31	29	32	38	36	29	23	34	35	30	53	31	
Moldova	na	**63**	62	63	59	61	68	69	64	55	69	65	55	71	58	
Montenegro	na	**54**	56	52	41	50	66	62	52	41	69	54	47	75	38	
Morocco	na	**51**	50	53	51	50	55	52	48	45	52	50	47	72	42	
Netherlands	27	**41**	40	41	36	39	45	48	38	37	41	42	37	67	49	
New Zealand	na	**29**	30	28	30	28	30	26	30	33	25	28	35	74	38	
Nigeria	43	**48**	48	48	49	48	43	49	45	52	44	52	50	69	42	
Northern Ireland	36	**41**	40	41	35	37	46	38	43	42	40	36	49	62	44	
Norway	64	**66**	67	65	58	64	75	73	70	56	na	na	na	86	73	
Pakistan	na	**57**	60	55	55	54	70	57	57	60	52	58	63	56	60	
Peru	na	**43**	43	44	42	46	41	47	44	39	43	47	39	70	45	
Philippines	na	**51**	49	52	51	53	45	47	50	56	48	45	60	64	47	
Poland	26	**40**	40	41	37	38	46	39	42	42	37	41	47	57	35	
Portugal	34	**33**	34	32	31	30	37	36	30	20	48	30	39	54	26	
Puerto Rico	na	**46**	49	44	37	48	48	52	53	41	53	43	44	79	57	
Romania	60	**49**	48	50	46	51	49	51	50	46	48	47	50	64	44	
Russian Fed.	59	**56**	57	56	49	58	59	56	56	58	57	57	56	68	45	
Serbia	na	**49**	50	49	47	46	53	46	52	49	49	51	52	57	48	
Singapore	na	**68**	70	66	65	70	73	71	66	71	65	69	70	84	69	
Slovakia	na	**48**	50	46	48	48	47	48	48	47	48	48	48	54	47	
Slovenia	27	**42**	40	43	35	39	50	46	39	45	41	38	39	66	45	
South Africa	38	**41**	39	43	34	43	49	35	48	42	36	40	48	56	36	
Spain	33	**36**	37	35	26	30	47	42	31	30	43	34	32	63	35	
Sweden	38	**45**	47	42	38	42	52	64	42	35	45	49	40	74	56	
Switzerland	32	**32**	32	32	21	28	43	44	30	19	38	36	24	57	36	
Taiwan	na	**69**	71	67	77	69	62	60	68	76	59	70	77	78	65	
Tanzania	na	**83**	81	84	86	82	78	84	83	78	82	83	80	90	81	
Turkey	20	**26**	27	25	21	26	35	28	24	18	28	25	21	48	25	
Uganda	na	**51**	55	46	50	50	54	45	54	37	47	48	46	73	48	
Ukraine	na	**55**	55	54	55	50	58	59	54	54	56	53	53	68	46	
United States	28	**33**	29	36	28	32	38	33	33	32	30	34	33	70	40	
Uruguay	na	**26**	27	25	19	21	34	31	20	17	33	22	22	68	24	
Venezuela	na	**45**	47	44	45	44	50	48	46	42	49	43	45	66	48	
Vietnam	na	**57**	58	55	50	58	59	58	55	60	53	62	53	69	58	
Zimbabwe	na	**37**	40	35	40	36	33	34	42	30	36	36	39	51	31	
Total	38	**48**	48	47	45	47	51	49	48	46	48	48	47	68	47	

RANKING	
Country	**2000**
Tanzania	83
Macedonia	77
Indonesia	77
Bulgaria	76
Azerbaijan	74
Bosnia and Herz.	71
Albania	70
Taiwan	69
Singapore	68
Norway	66
Georgia	65
Bangladesh	64
Jordan	63
Moldova	63
Egypt	63
Armenia	61
Denmark	59
Pakistan	57
Estonia	57
China	57
Iceland	57
Vietnam	57
Russian Fed.	56
Belarus	56
Czech Republic	56
Algeria	55
Ukraine	55
Montenegro	54
Latvia	54
Hungary	53
Finland	52
Morocco	51
Philippines	51
Uganda	51
Serbia	49
Romania	49
Nigeria	48
Slovakia	48
Puerto Rico	46
Venezuela	45
Luxembourg	45
Sweden	45
Dominican Rep.	45
Peru	43
France	43
Korea, South	43
India	42
Germany	42
Slovenia	42
Israel	41
Colombia	41
Netherlands	41
South Africa	41
Northern Ireland	41
Poland	40
Greece	40
Iran	39
Belgium	38
Zimbabwe	37
Ireland	37
Spain	36
Austria	36
Chile	35
Japan	34
Argentina	33
Portugal	33
Malta	33
United States	33
Mexico	32
Italy	32
Switzerland	32
New Zealand	29
Brazil	29
Croatia	28
Uruguay	26
Turkey	26
El Salvador	26
Lithuania	24
Australia	23
Canada	22
Total	48

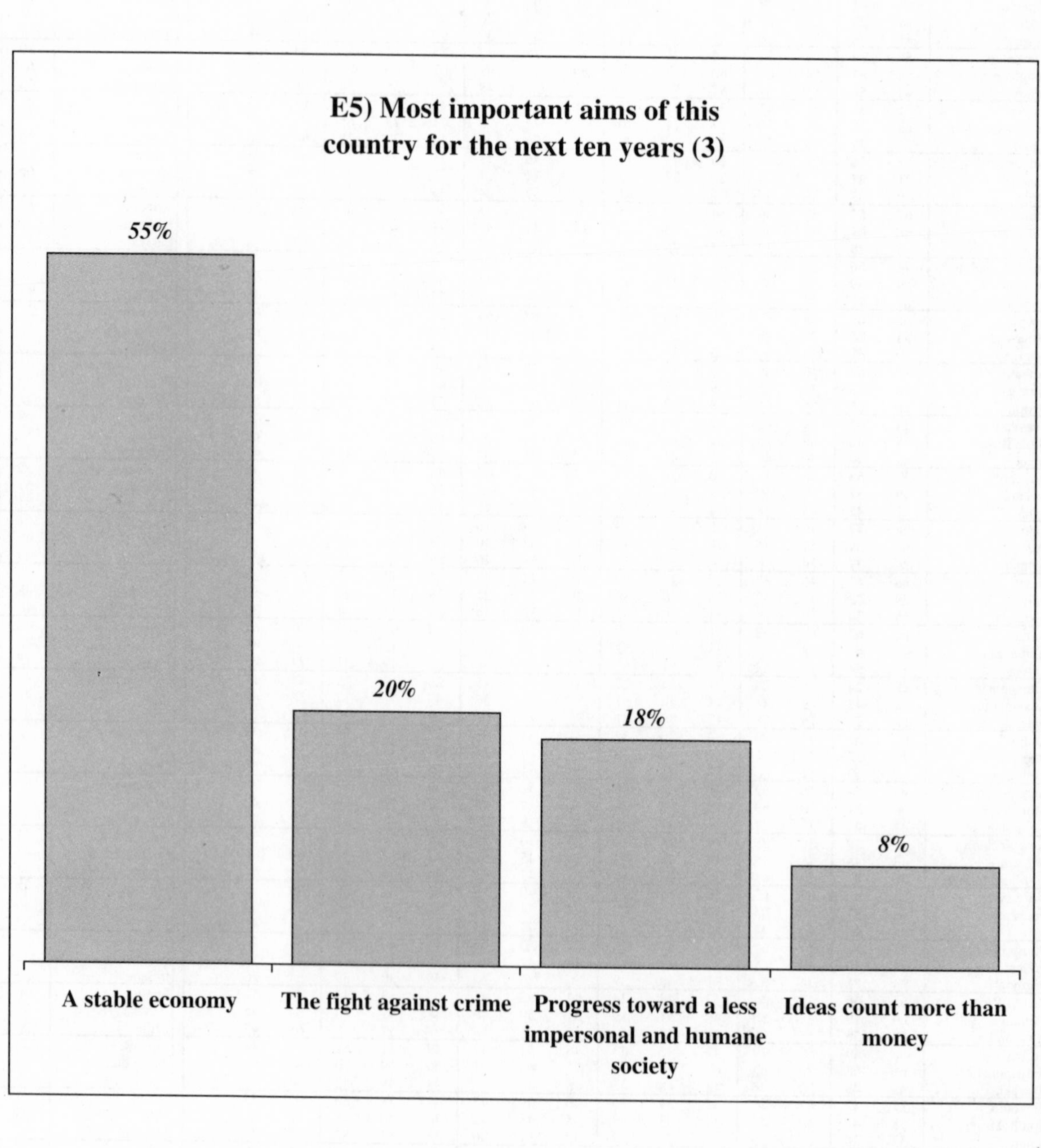
E5) Most important aims of this country for the next ten years (3)
55%
20%
18%
8%
A stable economy
The fight against crime
Progress toward a less impersonal and humane society
Ideas count more than money

E005A) AIMS OF COUNTRY / 3 - LESS IMPERSONAL SOCIETY

Here is another list. In your opinion, which one of these is most important?

(WVS: V124)

Progress toward a less impersonal society (%)

Country	Wave		Gender		Age			Education			Income			Values		
	1990	2000	Male	Female	16-29	30-49	50+	Lower	Middle	Upper	Lower	Middle	Upper	Mat	Mixed	Postm.
Albania	na	**4**	4	4	5	4	3	3	5	6	5	4	3	2	5	10
Algeria	na	**16**	15	18	20	14	12	11	16	20	20	15	17	12	18	24
Argentina	18	**19**	17	21	22	18	18	13	26	37	18	16	24	10	17	32
Armenia	na	**15**	15	15	19	12	13	11	15	18	20	10	13	7	21	25
Australia	na	**23**	21	25	25	26	18	15	20	34	18	25	28	10	20	30
Austria	20	**na**	na	na	na	na	na	na	na	na	na	na	na	na	na	na
Azerbaijan	na	**21**	19	23	22	21	18	15	20	24	21	23	21	18	27	24
Bangladesh	na	**13**	13	14	14	13	12	12	15	13	10	14	15	10	14	27
Belarus	11	**na**	na	na	na	na	na	na	na	na	na	na	na	na	na	na
Belgium	26	**na**	na	na	na	na	na	na	na	na	na	na	na	na	na	na
Bosnia and Herz.	na	**6**	7	6	7	6	6	7	5	10	5	6	8	4	7	8
Brazil	27	**22**	19	24	22	24	18	19	21	35	20	21	25	18	21	37
Bulgaria	9	**na**	na	na	na	na	na	na	na	na	na	na	na	na	na	na
Canada	22	**20**	17	22	24	21	16	13	19	27	17	19	22	8	18	27
Chile	22	**20**	18	22	20	22	18	18	20	26	19	17	27	9	21	36
China	6	**7**	6	9	10	8	4	5	9	7	6	8	9	5	9	22
Colombia	na	**26**	27	24	22	30	21	18	21	39	22	21	35	17	28	37
Croatia	na	**na**	na	na	na	na	na	na	na	na	na	na	na	na	na	na
Czech Republic	9	**na**	na	na	na	na	na	na	na	na	na	na	na	na	na	na
Denmark	21	**na**	na	na	na	na	na	na	na	na	na	na	na	na	na	na
Dominican Rep.	na	**27**	23	30	29	25	27	13	17	33	30	25	25	17	24	50
Egypt	na	**22**	22	23	25	21	21	23	22	23	24	24	19	19	24	32
El Salvador	na	**11**	13	10	11	11	14	8	12	21	6	11	18	na	na	na
Estonia	24	**na**	na	na	na	na	na	na	na	na	na	na	na	na	na	na
Finland	48	**na**	na	na	na	na	na	na	na	na	na	na	na	na	na	na
France	33	**na**	na	na	na	na	na	na	na	na	na	na	na	na	na	na
Georgia	na	**17**	17	17	17	18	16	15	16	23	18	16	16	12	21	31
Germany	17	**na**	na	na	na	na	na	na	na	na	na	na	na	na	na	na
Great Britain	21	**na**	na	na	na	na	na	na	na	na	na	na	na	na	na	na
Greece	na	**na**	na	na	na	na	na	na	na	na	na	na	na	na	na	na
Hungary	8	**na**	na	na	na	na	na	na	na	na	na	na	na	na	na	na
Iceland	25	**na**	na	na	na	na	na	na	na	na	na	na	na	na	na	na
India	20	**16**	16	16	14	16	17	14	20	16	17	17	15	12	20	23
Indonesia	na	**8**	9	8	10	9	7	7	9	9	6	9	12	6	10	18
Iran	na	**16**	15	18	17	15	15	13	17	19	14	17	20	12	18	26
Ireland	19	**na**	na	na	na	na	na	na	na	na	na	na	na	na	na	na
Israel	na	**35**	32	38	41	37	26	19	38	41	30	37	42	40	33	45
Italy	28	**na**	na	na	na	na	na	na	na	na	na	na	na	na	na	na
Japan	44	**36**	39	34	37	38	34	29	35	44	32	35	41	28	36	52
Jordan	na	**14**	13	16	16	12	17	14	17	11	16	16	11	13	14	22
Korea, South	36	**29**	29	28	37	29	17	18	23	39	26	29	31	21	34	47
Latvia	13	**na**	na	na	na	na	na	na	na	na	na	na	na	na	na	na
Lithuania	13	**na**	na	na	na	na	na	na	na	na	na	na	na	na	na	na
Luxembourg	na	**na**	na	na	na	na	na	na	na	na	na	na	na	na	na	na
Macedonia	na	**6**	6	7	8	6	4	7	6	6	4	8	7	5	7	11
Malta	na	**na**	na	na	na	na	na	na	na	na	na	na	na	na	na	na
Mexico	28	**15**	15	15	18	14	12	13	15	24	15	15	17	9	15	26
Moldova	na	**15**	15	16	18	12	16	13	17	15	10	16	14	11	18	31
Montenegro	na	**7**	6	8	12	6	5	6	8	9	6	5	8	3	8	29
Morocco	na	**32**	33	32	30	33	34	33	31	28	43	38	25	26	36	37
Netherlands	30	**na**	na	na	na	na	na	na	na	na	na	na	na	na	na	na
New Zealand	na	**16**	15	16	20	14	15	10	17	22	15	15	18	6	14	34
Nigeria	7	**10**	10	11	10	11	12	12	10	9	11	10	9	7	11	20
Northern Ireland	19	**na**	na	na	na	na	na	na	na	na	na	na	na	na	na	na
Norway	27	**29**	26	33	31	33	23	21	27	40	na	na	na	16	28	54
Pakistan	na	**7**	9	5	7	8	7	5	9	12	3	6	15	7	7	42
Peru	na	**14**	15	14	14	14	16	9	12	22	10	14	23	7	15	22
Philippines	na	**14**	13	14	14	13	15	17	13	12	14	15	13	8	17	24
Poland	9	**na**	na	na	na	na	na	na	na	na	na	na	na	na	na	na
Portugal	24	**na**	na	na	na	na	na	na	na	na	na	na	na	na	na	na
Puerto Rico	na	**23**	23	22	31	21	21	16	15	28	16	23	30	19	18	38
Romania	10	**na**	na	na	na	na	na	na	na	na	na	na	na	na	na	na
Russian Fed.	9	**na**	na	na	na	na	na	na	na	na	na	na	na	na	na	na
Serbia	na	**9**	8	10	10	9	9	7	9	13	8	8	10	7	9	23
Singapore	na	**16**	13	18	17	15	14	14	16	16	14	14	18	11	17	21
Slovakia	na	**na**	na	na	na	na	na	na	na	na	na	na	na	na	na	na
Slovenia	9	**na**	na	na	na	na	na	na	na	na	na	na	na	na	na	na
South Africa	17	**6**	7	6	6	7	5	7	5	8	7	5	7	4	8	10
Spain	27	**27**	27	27	33	28	23	23	30	36	25	30	25	16	30	37
Sweden	31	**24**	23	26	25	24	24	15	23	34	25	21	28	18	20	38
Switzerland	37	**33**	28	38	42	32	29	34	32	37	34	31	33	19	30	48
Taiwan	na	**19**	16	22	24	18	19	20	19	18	19	21	17	15	22	24
Tanzania	na	**17**	13	23	15	19	16	18	15	17	18	17	17	16	18	25
Turkey	27	**24**	21	28	25	24	22	25	20	29	25	23	25	20	24	32
Uganda	na	**12**	12	12	12	13	5	13	11	9	15	11	12	9	12	20
Ukraine	na	**na**	na	na	na	na	na	na	na	na	na	na	na	na	na	na
United States	16	**19**	16	22	19	22	16	12	20	22	20	19	19	20	16	28
Uruguay	na	**26**	26	26	30	30	21	20	33	42	19	25	34	10	24	42
Venezuela	na	**12**	13	11	11	12	12	12	10	16	13	9	12	5	12	20
Vietnam	na	**21**	18	25	20	22	22	19	25	18	26	20	20	13	25	25
Zimbabwe	na	**7**	6	8	9	5	5	8	6	na	7	8	7	4	9	17
Total	21	**18**	16	19	19	18	16	15	17	23	16	17	19	11	19	31

RANKING

Country	2000
Japan	36
Israel	35
Switzerland	33
Morocco	32
Norway	29
Korea, South	29
Dominican Rep.	27
Spain	27
Uruguay	26
Colombia	26
Sweden	24
Turkey	24
Australia	23
Puerto Rico	23
Egypt	22
Brazil	22
Vietnam	21
Azerbaijan	21
Chile	20
Canada	20
Argentina	19
Taiwan	19
United States	19
Georgia	17
Tanzania	17
Algeria	16
Iran	16
India	16
Singapore	16
New Zealand	16
Moldova	15
Armenia	15
Mexico	15
Jordan	14
Peru	14
Philippines	14
Bangladesh	13
Venezuela	12
Uganda	12
El Salvador	11
Nigeria	10
Serbia	9
Indonesia	8
China	7
Pakistan	7
Montenegro	7
Zimbabwe	7
South Africa	6
Macedonia	6
Bosnia and Herz.	6
Albania	4
Total	18

E005B) AIMS OF COUNTRY / 3 - STABLE ECONOMY

Here is another list. In your opinion, which one of these is most important?

A stable economy (%) (WVS: V124)

Country	Wave		Gender		Age			Education			Income			Values		
	1990	2000	Male	Female	16-29	30-49	50+	Lower	Middle	Upper	Lower	Middle	Upper	Mat	Mixed	Postm.
Albania	na	**69**	70	68	69	68	70	71	67	67	68	69	69	73	64	74
Algeria	na	**54**	56	52	53	53	60	62	52	53	51	53	54	65	53	32
Argentina	64	**52**	54	51	46	58	52	54	51	45	50	56	50	64	55	38
Armenia	na	**58**	59	57	53	62	60	61	57	63	55	64	56	64	57	27
Australia	na	**37**	38	35	30	33	47	36	39	35	40	35	34	43	41	29
Austria	51	**na**	na	na	na	na	na	na	na	na	na	na	na	na	na	na
Azerbaijan	na	**55**	59	51	53	55	57	51	52	60	48	51	62	57	52	47
Bangladesh	na	**67**	71	61	64	68	73	65	66	75	69	66	66	68	68	45
Belarus	70	**na**	na	na	na	na	na	na	na	na	na	na	na	na	na	na
Belgium	32	**na**	na	na	na	na	na	na	na	na	na	na	na	na	na	na
Bosnia and Herz.	na	**79**	78	80	78	81	78	77	80	80	75	82	79	82	77	76
Brazil	30	**17**	18	15	16	15	20	15	16	24	15	11	21	13	18	17
Bulgaria	83	**na**	na	na	na	na	na	na	na	na	na	na	na	na	na	na
Canada	54	**49**	54	45	38	48	57	48	51	48	48	51	49	66	52	39
Chile	56	**58**	62	55	58	57	60	56	62	54	57	62	55	69	58	40
China	83	**54**	56	52	59	54	50	43	59	69	47	53	64	60	53	25
Colombia	na	**33**	34	32	34	32	34	31	36	31	30	36	31	46	36	18
Croatia	na	**na**	na	na	na	na	na	na	na	na	na	na	na	na	na	na
Czech Republic	63	**na**	na	na	na	na	na	na	na	na	na	na	na	na	na	na
Denmark	50	**na**	na	na	na	na	na	na	na	na	na	na	na	na	na	na
Dominican Rep.	na	**44**	52	38	42	48	36	47	49	41	38	43	52	57	44	32
Egypt	na	**47**	49	45	40	50	52	48	43	51	46	47	50	53	44	31
El Salvador	na	**24**	28	21	21	24	29	22	25	31	17	26	33	na	na	na
Estonia	60	**na**	na	na	na	na	na	na	na	na	na	na	na	na	na	na
Finland	40	**na**	na	na	na	na	na	na	na	na	na	na	na	na	na	na
France	26	**na**	na	na	na	na	na	na	na	na	na	na	na	na	na	na
Georgia	na	**58**	58	57	57	58	58	63	57	56	57	59	58	64	52	45
Germany	73	**na**	na	na	na	na	na	na	na	na	na	na	na	na	na	na
Great Britain	40	**na**	na	na	na	na	na	na	na	na	na	na	na	na	na	na
Greece	na	**na**	na	na	na	na	na	na	na	na	na	na	na	na	na	na
Hungary	67	**na**	na	na	na	na	na	na	na	na	na	na	na	na	na	na
Iceland	58	**na**	na	na	na	na	na	na	na	na	na	na	na	na	na	na
India	44	**36**	39	32	38	36	34	27	38	50	24	36	42	41	35	23
Indonesia	na	**84**	84	85	82	85	85	82	85	85	88	82	80	87	83	61
Iran	na	**52**	54	50	50	54	55	55	53	51	54	50	51	61	47	44
Ireland	49	**na**	na	na	na	na	na	na	na	na	na	na	na	na	na	na
Israel	na	**39**	43	35	33	39	44	42	38	38	36	37	38	36	41	29
Italy	30	**na**	na	na	na	na	na	na	na	na	na	na	na	na	na	na
Japan	44	**44**	43	45	36	41	50	47	44	40	49	41	42	53	44	33
Jordan	na	**52**	55	49	46	55	58	54	47	54	50	54	51	60	49	26
Korea, South	53	**64**	63	66	55	64	76	75	71	53	67	63	62	74	58	44
Latvia	77	**na**	na	na	na	na	na	na	na	na	na	na	na	na	na	na
Lithuania	61	**na**	na	na	na	na	na	na	na	na	na	na	na	na	na	na
Luxembourg	na	**na**	na	na	na	na	na	na	na	na	na	na	na	na	na	na
Macedonia	na	**76**	77	76	71	77	80	71	78	82	74	78	80	82	76	50
Malta	na	**na**	na	na	na	na	na	na	na	na	na	na	na	na	na	na
Mexico	53	**55**	60	50	52	57	54	53	58	52	53	56	56	58	57	46
Moldova	na	**69**	73	67	64	72	71	76	66	69	75	69	69	73	68	50
Montenegro	na	**68**	70	66	68	72	64	61	72	72	72	72	67	66	73	53
Morocco	na	**38**	39	37	42	35	32	37	38	45	30	33	48	48	33	25
Netherlands	32	**na**	na	na	na	na	na	na	na	na	na	na	na	na	na	na
New Zealand	na	**57**	57	57	45	59	59	59	57	57	54	61	60	80	65	50
Nigeria	61	**65**	66	64	68	63	59	64	66	66	63	66	68	69	64	56
Northern Ireland	51	**na**	na	na	na	na	na	na	na	na	na	na	na	na	na	na
Norway	46	**39**	45	33	30	40	43	41	40	35	na	na	na	43	39	27
Pakistan	na	**69**	70	68	68	68	72	73	67	60	77	70	55	69	70	33
Peru	na	**65**	66	64	62	67	65	65	66	63	67	67	58	72	65	57
Philippines	na	**65**	65	64	61	65	67	62	63	70	60	63	71	68	63	54
Poland	73	**na**	na	na	na	na	na	na	na	na	na	na	na	na	na	na
Portugal	47	**na**	na	na	na	na	na	na	na	na	na	na	na	na	na	na
Puerto Rico	na	**39**	44	37	30	38	45	38	45	37	46	39	36	51	43	25
Romania	67	**na**	na	na	na	na	na	na	na	na	na	na	na	na	na	na
Russian Fed.	65	**na**	na	na	na	na	na	na	na	na	na	na	na	na	na	na
Serbia	na	**69**	74	65	65	72	69	64	74	69	69	75	70	69	71	61
Singapore	na	**73**	77	70	68	79	78	74	72	76	74	75	72	80	73	54
Slovakia	na	**na**	na	na	na	na	na	na	na	na	na	na	na	na	na	na
Slovenia	81	**na**	na	na	na	na	na	na	na	na	na	na	na	na	na	na
South Africa	46	**49**	52	45	49	51	44	44	56	56	49	50	51	51	50	38
Spain	36	**40**	41	38	36	38	43	42	40	31	38	40	38	51	39	24
Sweden	39	**44**	46	41	35	45	48	49	45	37	41	46	45	56	47	31
Switzerland	26	**43**	49	38	33	47	44	37	46	36	40	43	48	54	48	25
Taiwan	na	**50**	52	47	45	52	48	49	53	49	53	50	50	53	49	46
Tanzania	na	**72**	76	67	68	74	73	69	75	79	69	74	77	75	70	58
Turkey	36	**42**	47	37	34	45	51	42	44	43	43	42	40	54	42	29
Uganda	na	**63**	69	58	66	60	61	59	67	53	52	58	65	73	61	45
Ukraine	na	**na**	na	na	na	na	na	na	na	na	na	na	na	na	na	na
United States	50	**46**	50	41	41	43	54	51	45	44	42	46	48	49	50	33
Uruguay	na	**58**	59	57	50	57	63	63	52	48	64	62	48	78	59	42
Venezuela	na	**51**	52	49	49	54	46	48	51	53	51	53	52	63	49	40
Vietnam	na	**68**	71	65	70	69	65	69	66	73	63	69	69	80	64	61
Zimbabwe	na	**64**	71	58	60	65	69	62	66	100	58	65	70	69	62	46
Total	53	55	57	52	51	56	57	54	57	53	54	56	55	63	55	38

RANKING

Country	2000
Indonesia	84
Bosnia and Herz.	79
Macedonia	76
Singapore	73
Tanzania	72
Serbia	69
Moldova	69
Pakistan	69
Albania	69
Vietnam	68
Montenegro	68
Bangladesh	67
Nigeria	65
Peru	65
Philippines	65
Korea, South	64
Zimbabwe	64
Uganda	63
Armenia	58
Chile	58
Uruguay	58
Georgia	58
New Zealand	57
Azerbaijan	55
Mexico	55
Algeria	54
China	54
Iran	52
Argentina	52
Jordan	52
Venezuela	51
Taiwan	50
Canada	49
South Africa	49
Egypt	47
United States	46
Dominican Rep.	44
Japan	44
Sweden	44
Switzerland	43
Turkey	42
Spain	40
Puerto Rico	39
Norway	39
Israel	39
Morocco	38
Australia	37
India	36
Colombia	33
El Salvador	24
Brazil	17
Total	55

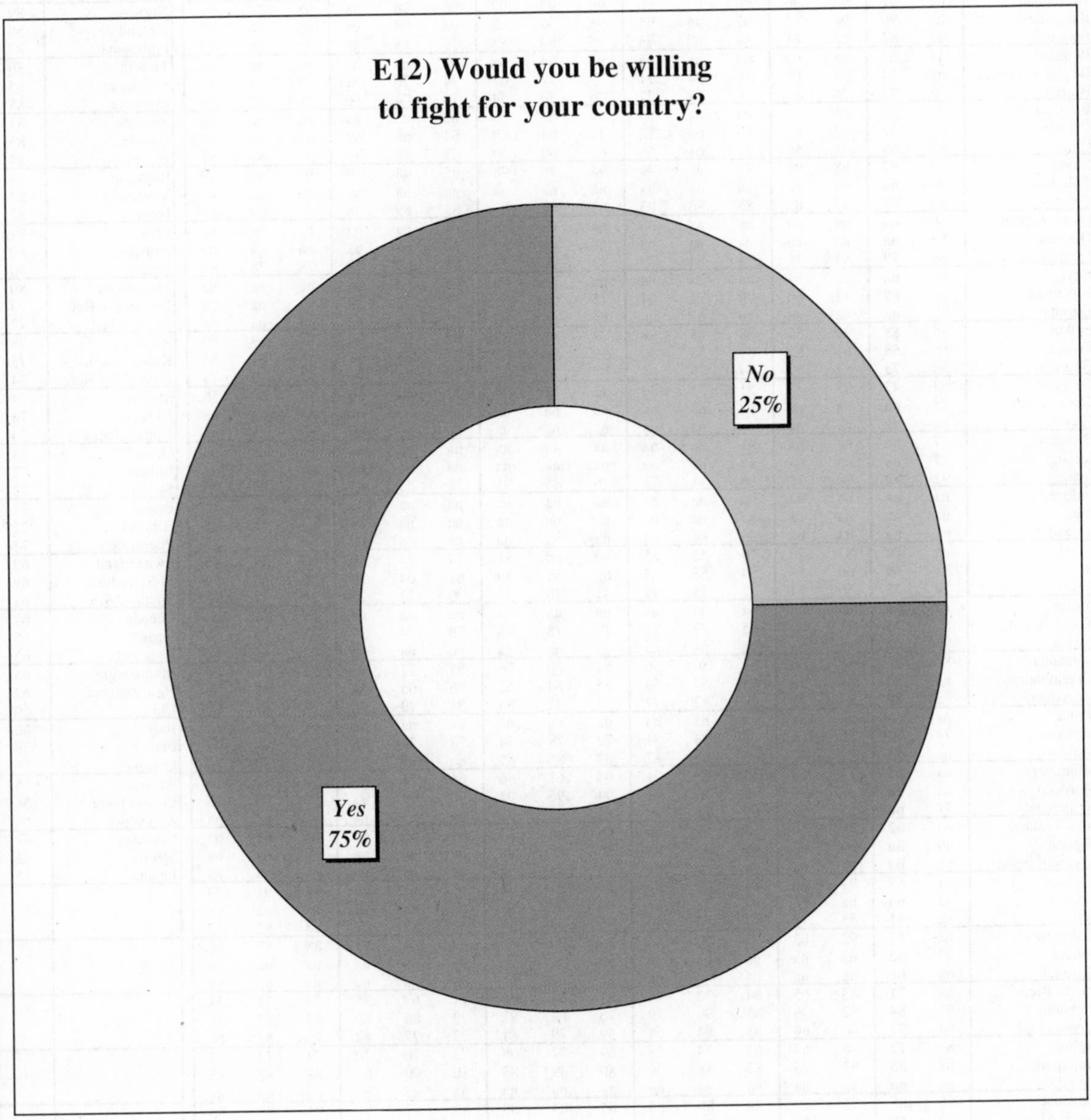

E12) Would you be willing to fight for your country?

No 25%

Yes 75%

E012) BE WILLING TO FIGHT IN WAR FOR YOUR COUNTRY

Of course, we all hope that there will not be another war, but if it were to come to that, would you be willing to fight for your country?

Yes (%)

(WVS: V126; EVS: o24)

Country	Wave		Gender		Age			Education			Income			Values		
	1990	2000	Male	Female	16-29	30-49	50+	Lower	Middle	Upper	Lower	Middle	Upper	Mat	Mixed	Postm.
Albania	na	**72**	83	60	68	73	73	70	72	76	74	68	73	73	72	70
Algeria	na	**na**	na	na	na	na	na	na	na	na	na	na	na	na	na	na
Argentina	63	**65**	71	60	64	66	66	70	59	53	69	67	59	65	69	56
Armenia	na	**80**	88	73	80	83	77	78	80	82	80	81	78	75	85	84
Australia	na	**75**	80	70	63	78	82	79	74	74	76	77	75	72	77	72
Austria	66	**55**	63	47	57	60	49	57	54	53	48	53	63	58	56	54
Azerbaijan	na	**97**	98	96	98	97	96	96	97	97	98	96	98	98	97	94
Bangladesh	na	**96**	98	93	97	95	95	95	97	98	94	98	95	95	96	99
Belarus	92	**84**	88	81	88	90	75	75	89	83	79	88	85	82	89	84
Belgium	41	**na**	na	na	na	na	na	na	na	na	na	na	na	na	na	na
Bosnia and Herz.	na	**74**	81	68	79	74	71	73	77	67	74	76	71	75	74	76
Brazil	36	**72**	76	67	70	71	77	79	70	54	76	74	66	79	72	56
Bulgaria	91	**na**	na	na	na	na	na	na	na	na	na	na	na	na	na	na
Canada	68	**67**	72	61	63	64	72	71	64	68	64	68	69	64	66	68
Chile	83	**60**	71	50	62	61	58	65	60	50	67	58	55	58	64	51
China	97	**97**	98	95	97	98	94	94	98	98	95	98	99	97	97	97
Colombia	na	**na**	na	na	na	na	na	na	na	na	na	na	na	na	na	na
Croatia	na	**85**	87	82	85	86	83	83	87	81	83	89	78	87	84	85
Czech Republic	66	**na**	na	na	na	na	na	na	na	na	na	na	na	na	na	na
Denmark	89	**na**	na	na	na	na	na	na	na	na	na	na	na	na	na	na
Dominican Rep.	na	**79**	84	75	76	84	73	83	79	77	85	69	78	78	78	84
Egypt	na	**na**	na	na	na	na	na	na	na	na	na	na	na	na	na	na
El Salvador	na	**69**	72	66	70	71	64	75	66	56	77	72	55	na	na	na
Estonia	92	**na**	na	na	na	na	na	na	na	na	na	na	na	na	na	na
Finland	88	**88**	90	85	88	88	88	88	87	88	82	90	94	88	89	80
France	66	**58**	61	55	61	58	56	59	56	57	51	63	61	56	61	55
Georgia	na	**73**	87	60	74	76	66	67	73	76	70	74	76	72	74	74
Germany	53	**47**	63	33	51	53	39	42	51	50	37	49	54	40	50	50
Great Britain	75	**na**	na	na	na	na	na	na	na	na	na	na	na	na	na	na
Greece	na	**na**	na	na	na	na	na	na	na	na	na	na	na	na	na	na
Hungary	77	**na**	na	na	na	na	na	na	na	na	na	na	na	na	na	na
Iceland	77	**na**	na	na	na	na	na	na	na	na	na	na	na	na	na	na
India	92	**82**	90	71	88	84	71	76	85	91	78	83	84	84	87	96
Indonesia	na	**na**	na	na	na	na	na	na	na	na	na	na	na	na	na	na
Iran	na	**na**	na	na	na	na	na	na	na	na	na	na	na	na	na	na
Ireland	61	**na**	na	na	na	na	na	na	na	na	na	na	na	na	na	na
Israel	na	**80**	83	78	75	81	85	80	80	81	79	74	88	62	84	85
Italy	31	**60**	66	55	54	58	65	62	59	59	61	64	56	62	60	59
Japan	20	**25**	36	14	12	15	41	41	20	32	30	22	26	28	23	25
Jordan	na	**na**	na	na	na	na	na	na	na	na	na	na	na	na	na	na
Korea, South	87	**75**	82	67	65	77	82	73	78	70	78	74	71	75	75	66
Latvia	97	**na**	na	na	na	na	na	na	na	na	na	na	na	na	na	na
Lithuania	84	**72**	80	64	83	80	56	51	80	76	57	77	78	71	74	75
Luxembourg	na	**54**	59	48	55	54	53	55	54	52	56	65	54	58	59	39
Macedonia	na	**80**	87	72	79	82	77	73	82	84	81	79	78	78	82	68
Malta	na	**na**	na	na	na	na	na	na	na	na	na	na	na	na	na	na
Mexico	74	**74**	80	69	76	74	71	72	78	74	73	76	75	73	78	79
Moldova	na	**85**	87	82	85	88	82	83	86	85	86	83	83	85	89	80
Montenegro	na	**65**	71	59	53	67	71	64	67	66	66	71	66	68	62	75
Morocco	na	**94**	97	92	95	96	91	94	96	94	98	94	93	93	95	96
Netherlands	71	**na**	na	na	na	na	na	na	na	na	na	na	na	na	na	na
New Zealand	na	**62**	76	50	54	62	66	65	68	57	61	63	66	68	61	63
Nigeria	80	**na**	na	na	na	na	na	na	na	na	na	na	na	na	na	na
Northern Ireland	61	**na**	na	na	na	na	na	na	na	na	na	na	na	na	na	na
Norway	91	**89**	91	86	86	89	91	88	91	86	na	na	na	85	91	79
Pakistan	na	**na**	na	na	na	na	na	na	na	na	na	na	na	na	na	na
Peru	na	**81**	85	78	80	83	80	80	83	80	83	82	77	78	82	83
Philippines	na	**87**	92	82	85	90	84	85	90	85	89	84	91	88	87	86
Poland	92	**na**	na	na	na	na	na	na	na	na	na	na	na	na	na	na
Portugal	68	**na**	na	na	na	na	na	na	na	na	na	na	na	na	na	na
Puerto Rico	na	**71**	83	65	64	72	76	81	68	72	71	69	75	77	71	74
Romania	92	**84**	92	76	85	90	79	76	87	92	79	85	89	83	87	88
Russian Fed.	84	**77**	86	69	85	84	64	59	79	81	72	77	82	73	82	86
Serbia	na	**72**	78	67	63	74	75	69	77	68	73	76	70	72	73	67
Singapore	na	**85**	92	79	87	88	70	80	89	83	80	90	87	81	87	85
Slovakia	na	**na**	na	na	na	na	na	na	na	na	na	na	na	na	na	na
Slovenia	95	**85**	91	79	80	89	83	85	84	88	86	87	91	91	83	86
South Africa	70	**68**	74	60	70	72	52	66	71	68	68	71	63	63	73	62
Spain	62	**43**	48	38	38	43	47	45	42	36	46	44	43	44	43	42
Sweden	89	**na**	na	na	na	na	na	na	na	na	na	na	na	na	na	na
Switzerland	78	**69**	74	64	60	70	74	69	70	65	63	74	72	75	73	55
Taiwan	na	**86**	91	81	86	90	76	80	91	89	83	89	87	85	89	90
Tanzania	na	**93**	94	93	92	95	92	93	94	93	91	95	95	93	93	100
Turkey	93	**na**	na	na	na	na	na	na	na	na	na	na	na	na	na	na
Uganda	na	**65**	82	49	69	65	52	61	66	72	78	68	68	62	68	62
Ukraine	na	**74**	82	66	74	79	68	56	77	74	68	75	79	70	77	72
United States	80	**73**	82	63	60	74	82	72	70	75	71	74	74	72	72	76
Uruguay	na	**57**	60	55	53	56	60	64	49	42	62	60	50	58	60	49
Venezuela	na	**82**	87	77	83	85	75	79	85	80	82	81	84	76	83	90
Vietnam	na	**98**	99	96	99	99	95	97	99	100	97	98	98	97	99	99
Zimbabwe	na	**54**	64	45	61	49	42	53	55	32	56	56	48	50	56	56
Total	74	**75**	81	69	75	77	72	74	76	75	74	77	76	76	77	69

RANKING	
Country	**2000**
Vietnam	98
Azerbaijan	97
China	97
Bangladesh	96
Morocco	94
Tanzania	93
Norway	89
Finland	88
Philippines	87
Taiwan	86
Singapore	85
Moldova	85
Slovenia	85
Croatia	85
Belarus	84
Romania	84
Venezuela	82
India	82
Peru	81
Armenia	80
Israel	80
Macedonia	80
Dominican Rep.	79
Russian Fed.	77
Australia	75
Korea, South	75
Bosnia and Herz.	74
Mexico	74
Ukraine	74
United States	73
Georgia	73
Lithuania	72
Serbia	72
Brazil	72
Albania	72
Puerto Rico	71
Switzerland	69
El Salvador	69
South Africa	68
Canada	67
Uganda	65
Argentina	65
Montenegro	65
New Zealand	62
Chile	60
Italy	60
France	58
Uruguay	57
Austria	55
Luxembourg	54
Zimbabwe	54
Germany	47
Spain	43
Japan	25
Total	75

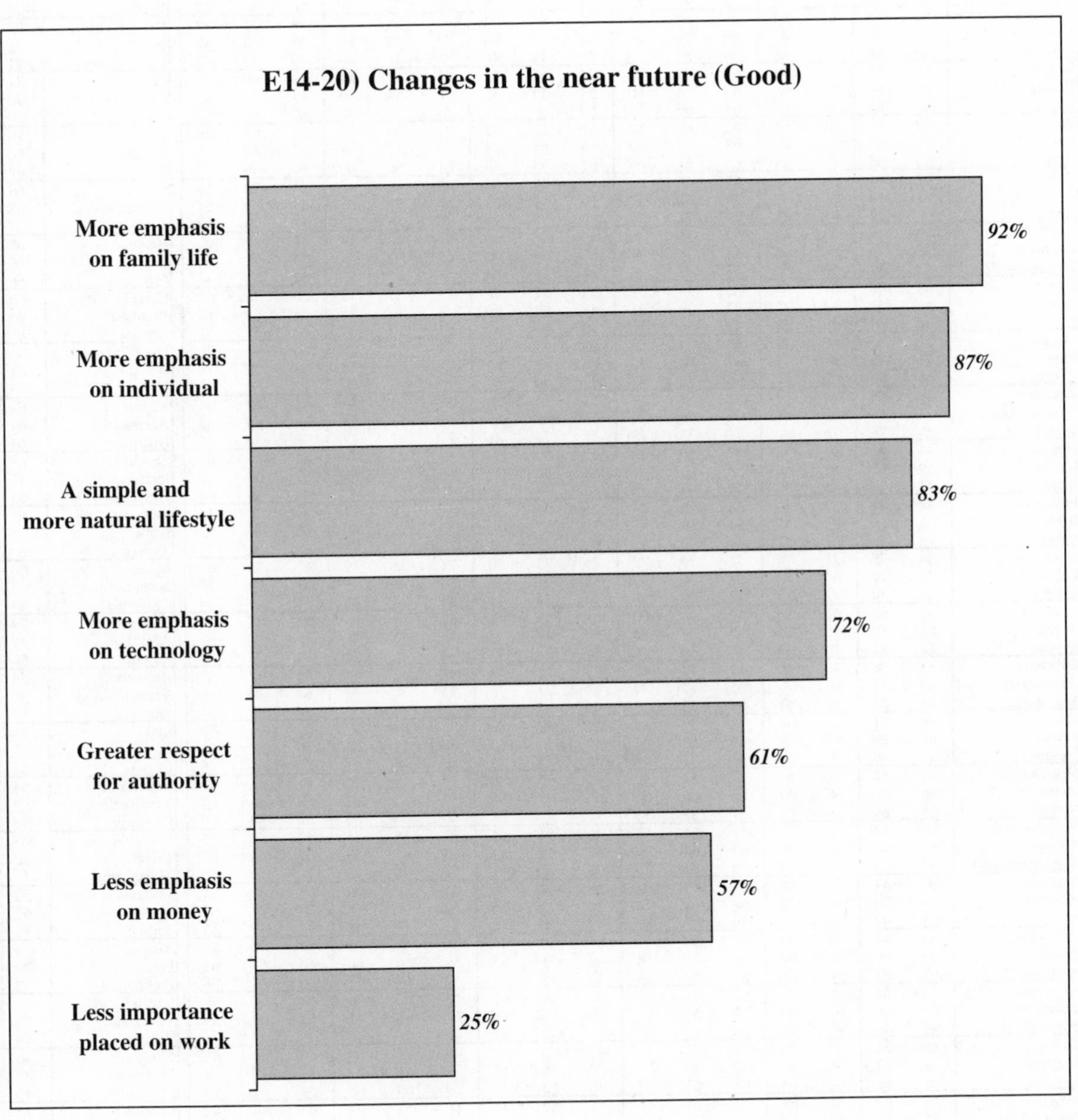
E14-20) Changes in the near future (Good)
More emphasis on family life
92%
More emphasis on individual
87%
A simple and more natural lifestyle
83%
More emphasis on technology
72%
Greater respect for authority
61%
Less emphasis on money
57%
Less importance placed on work
25%

E014) LESS EMPHASIS ON MONEY

I'm going to read out a list of various changes in our way of life that might take place in the near future. If it were to happen, do you think it would be a good thing, a bad thing, or don't you mind?. Less emphasis on money

Good (%)

(WVS: V127; EVS: V192)

Country	Wave		Gender		Age			Education			Income			Values		
	1990	2000	Male	Female	16-29	30-49	50+	Lower	Middle	Upper	Lower	Middle	Upper	Mat	Mixed	Postm.
Albania	na	37	36	37	38	34	40	37	38	35	38	38	34	40	35	21
Algeria	na	40	40	40	36	43	42	37	41	40	39	37	40	44	37	48
Argentina	71	64	61	67	65	64	64	58	74	68	60	63	70	56	63	73
Armenia	na	59	56	61	55	61	62	59	57	63	57	56	62	54	61	76
Australia	na	69	64	73	63	72	71	60	67	78	66	71	72	61	67	74
Austria	55	50	47	53	43	49	55	47	51	58	50	54	46	56	48	52
Azerbaijan	na	64	64	64	68	62	61	57	66	62	61	68	62	58	74	77
Bangladesh	na	36	40	32	39	36	29	30	44	43	31	42	35	27	42	42
Belarus	60	48	47	48	50	44	50	48	48	46	48	47	49	49	47	44
Belgium	65	67	63	71	61	67	70	64	65	72	65	67	67	63	66	74
Bosnia and Herz.	na	54	52	56	49	53	60	54	54	55	60	52	50	47	57	55
Brazil	62	65	62	67	67	66	56	59	68	71	59	66	70	62	66	68
Bulgaria	61	58	55	61	52	62	57	61	55	59	58	56	56	60	58	56
Canada	62	65	62	69	65	69	62	58	65	73	63	66	68	57	64	71
Chile	60	65	65	64	65	63	66	62	65	68	61	66	69	60	66	70
China	67	47	48	45	48	46	48	43	48	64	48	49	45	44	50	56
Colombia	na	59	59	60	57	62	57	59	57	63	56	57	65	64	61	61
Croatia	na	77	73	81	79	75	79	80	75	78	76	75	82	77	76	82
Czech Republic	52	49	48	49	55	46	48	46	50	56	49	48	48	49	48	60
Denmark	78	70	65	75	65	71	71	63	76	79	67	69	76	56	70	80
Dominican Rep.	na	52	55	50	53	51	46	34	55	54	46	61	56	52	52	54
Egypt	na	56	57	54	58	54	57	53	57	59	55	55	57	56	56	54
El Salvador	na	43	44	42	47	39	41	41	43	46	43	40	45	na	na	na
Estonia	na	54	50	58	57	56	51	49	54	62	54	52	57	52	55	51
Finland	71	66	60	72	66	74	59	60	71	82	64	65	71	60	67	75
France	71	71	69	73	67	74	70	67	73	80	73	69	78	63	73	78
Georgia	na	70	69	71	66	73	72	73	70	69	70	73	69	72	69	63
Germany	49	53	49	57	51	51	57	52	54	56	56	56	53	54	49	65
Great Britain	64	66	63	68	68	66	66	66	68	59	59	68	68	na	na	na
Greece	na	78	76	80	79	77	78	71	77	81	77	77	77	78	77	85
Hungary	44	45	46	45	47	50	39	41	50	59	39	47	47	45	44	65
Iceland	59	62	55	68	58	63	62	53	62	77	63	59	65	52	63	72
India	43	43	45	39	44	44	40	36	46	56	37	41	47	41	48	64
Indonesia	na	27	30	24	36	26	24	25	24	33	31	29	21	24	31	20
Iran	na	56	55	56	54	59	55	55	57	56	53	52	60	55	54	63
Ireland	73	69	67	71	64	70	71	67	70	71	70	64	71	68	68	76
Israel	na	75	71	78	72	79	72	73	72	80	72	75	79	77	75	67
Italy	72	71	69	72	67	74	69	68	71	77	70	75	71	63	69	78
Japan	41	39	42	37	33	45	37	26	39	43	34	44	42	36	41	49
Jordan	na	59	62	56	59	58	60	61	55	61	61	58	58	58	58	66
Korea, South	63	53	50	55	57	54	46	50	49	58	51	53	55	51	54	62
Latvia	na	32	30	33	33	38	26	31	31	38	30	30	37	27	34	35
Lithuania	33	46	46	45	49	42	47	53	42	50	42	43	44	56	42	32
Luxembourg	na	71	66	76	65	72	74	67	71	78	73	74	73	67	70	86
Macedonia	na	52	52	51	46	52	55	44	55	58	47	51	61	57	52	40
Malta	na	81	79	84	78	82	83	82	80	88	82	84	82	79	83	83
Mexico	68	58	59	58	60	55	63	59	56	65	58	58	63	56	57	66
Moldova	na	46	46	46	44	47	46	48	43	50	46	46	47	51	43	45
Montenegro	na	52	51	54	57	53	48	45	57	56	57	58	47	47	55	63
Morocco	na	66	65	67	66	66	66	66	68	63	59	69	62	68	66	65
Netherlands	64	60	56	64	67	58	58	51	61	68	60	60	60	51	59	69
New Zealand	na	54	48	59	51	54	54	46	54	64	52	55	55	50	56	62
Nigeria	64	63	62	64	63	64	60	62	63	64	63	61	66	62	63	67
Northern Ireland	60	72	71	73	70	71	73	72	67	81	71	78	73	71	70	78
Norway	60	61	54	68	59	62	61	56	61	66	na	na	na	55	60	74
Pakistan	na	70	70	70	68	69	78	70	72	65	67	69	75	69	71	67
Peru	na	49	46	52	49	47	54	49	50	48	51	48	48	47	49	53
Philippines	na	49	49	50	47	50	50	51	50	46	46	47	53	51	47	53
Poland	59	60	58	62	62	61	58	62	55	65	59	60	60	60	61	61
Portugal	63	57	54	60	58	60	55	57	55	67	52	54	58	56	57	56
Puerto Rico	na	62	65	60	63	62	61	54	56	66	55	62	66	61	60	66
Romania	na	66	64	67	67	69	61	60	68	68	61	64	71	65	69	59
Russian Fed.	42	45	43	48	46	44	46	51	45	44	43	48	45	49	42	41
Serbia	na	51	47	56	58	52	47	42	53	60	46	47	60	46	54	68
Singapore	na	38	36	40	39	38	37	32	39	51	31	41	41	39	38	39
Slovakia	na	61	60	63	63	63	58	56	63	72	59	60	65	59	62	73
Slovenia	50	63	61	65	61	65	61	58	62	74	60	58	71	63	64	62
South Africa	45	35	37	34	33	37	38	33	38	29	28	38	47	36	34	41
Spain	81	76	75	78	74	81	74	75	76	82	77	76	77	72	77	80
Sweden	66	67	61	74	66	68	68	61	65	77	70	66	66	60	65	79
Switzerland	82	68	62	74	72	64	72	67	69	65	78	70	66	59	68	77
Taiwan	na	52	51	54	59	54	44	42	53	62	49	53	56	53	53	70
Tanzania	na	60	61	60	63	59	61	64	57	57	66	64	52	61	60	71
Turkey	56	70	70	70	73	69	66	67	72	80	69	70	73	71	68	75
Uganda	na	25	29	21	19	31	29	26	22	49	35	29	28	19	27	32
Ukraine	na	44	47	42	44	41	48	51	43	44	45	43	44	50	41	35
United States	71	65	59	71	58	70	65	57	63	70	64	66	66	66	64	69
Uruguay	na	75	74	76	75	77	74	74	77	79	74	76	77	75	74	76
Venezuela	na	48	48	49	46	48	55	50	49	45	50	44	49	46	49	48
Vietnam	na	58	58	57	58	59	56	57	61	57	59	55	61	69	62	50
Zimbabwe	na	28	29	27	28	27	30	26	31	14	17	31	36	29	29	13
Total	60	57	55	58	56	57	58	54	57	62	55	57	59	54	58	66

RANKING	
Country	2000
Malta	81
Greece	78
Croatia	77
Spain	76
Uruguay	75
Israel	75
Northern Ireland	72
France	71
Luxembourg	71
Italy	71
Georgia	70
Denmark	70
Pakistan	70
Turkey	70
Ireland	69
Australia	69
Switzerland	68
Sweden	67
Belgium	67
Finland	66
Morocco	66
Great Britain	66
Romania	66
Canada	65
United States	65
Brazil	65
Chile	65
Argentina	64
Azerbaijan	64
Nigeria	63
Slovenia	63
Iceland	62
Puerto Rico	62
Slovakia	61
Norway	61
Tanzania	60
Poland	60
Netherlands	60
Colombia	59
Jordan	59
Armenia	59
Mexico	58
Bulgaria	58
Vietnam	58
Portugal	57
Iran	56
Egypt	56
Estonia	54
Bosnia and Herz.	54
New Zealand	54
Germany	53
Korea, South	53
Taiwan	52
Montenegro	52
Dominican Rep.	52
Macedonia	52
Serbia	51
Austria	50
Peru	49
Philippines	49
Czech Republic	49
Venezuela	48
Belarus	48
China	47
Moldova	46
Lithuania	46
Russian Fed.	45
Hungary	45
Ukraine	44
India	43
El Salvador	43
Algeria	40
Japan	39
Singapore	38
Albania	37
Bangladesh	36
South Africa	35
Latvia	32
Zimbabwe	28
Indonesia	27
Uganda	25
Total	57

E015) LESS IMPORTANCE PLACED ON WORK

I'm going to read out a list of various changes in our way of life that might take place in the near future. If it were to happen, do you think it would be a good thing, a bad thing, or don't you mind? Less importance placed on work in our lives

Good (%) (WVS: V128; EVS: V193)

	Wave		Gender		Age			Education			Income			Values		
Country	1990	2000	Male	Female	16-29	30-49	50+	Lower	Middle	Upper	Lower	Middle	Upper	Mat	Mixed	Postm.
Albania	na	**10**	11	10	11	9	11	10	11	9	10	11	9	9	11	21
Algeria	na	**9**	9	9	10	9	9	10	9	9	9	11	8	8	9	8
Argentina	20	**20**	21	20	21	22	18	18	24	21	16	21	24	17	20	23
Armenia	na	**22**	22	22	25	19	21	26	22	19	18	20	25	24	21	10
Australia	na	**32**	32	32	36	36	24	28	31	36	28	33	37	25	30	37
Austria	23	**30**	29	32	33	29	30	28	32	37	30	29	31	32	29	32
Azerbaijan	na	**30**	31	29	34	28	27	29	30	30	24	34	29	27	37	27
Bangladesh	na	**7**	8	6	7	7	9	7	8	5	5	8	9	5	9	9
Belarus	28	**20**	21	19	22	22	15	18	22	14	21	21	16	18	20	25
Belgium	42	**46**	48	45	48	51	41	44	45	49	45	44	49	40	44	60
Bosnia and Herz.	na	**14**	13	14	11	13	18	15	13	15	14	14	16	12	15	13
Brazil	19	**22**	22	21	23	19	23	25	19	20	25	18	21	24	21	19
Bulgaria	41	**36**	35	37	42	40	30	34	37	39	35	34	39	35	37	44
Canada	31	**33**	34	32	35	38	26	25	32	40	25	30	44	34	31	35
Chile	18	**35**	34	35	38	36	28	29	37	40	31	37	35	30	38	30
China	8	**17**	22	13	17	18	17	16	18	19	19	19	16	20	16	16
Colombia	na	**12**	11	14	12	12	13	16	14	8	14	15	8	20	19	14
Croatia	na	**33**	30	35	33	36	29	31	34	33	31	32	36	32	32	34
Czech Republic	8	**10**	12	9	13	11	9	12	10	7	8	11	11	11	10	13
Denmark	27	**34**	32	35	37	42	23	27	41	46	27	36	41	22	30	48
Dominican Rep.	na	**10**	10	9	9	10	11	15	17	6	13	7	5	6	10	14
Egypt	na	**2**	3	2	2	2	3	3	1	3	3	1	2	3	2	1
El Salvador	na	**18**	18	17	17	19	18	21	15	15	24	13	14	na	na	na
Estonia	na	**13**	15	12	16	17	9	10	13	21	10	10	18	12	13	11
Finland	24	**25**	26	23	34	32	13	20	30	35	24	25	27	23	24	34
France	35	**65**	66	65	70	72	57	62	70	71	61	64	71	58	66	76
Georgia	na	**38**	37	38	36	38	38	44	39	30	37	42	35	40	35	38
Germany	15	**40**	39	41	41	46	34	37	44	35	37	37	40	44	35	48
Great Britain	33	**53**	54	53	63	57	47	52	56	56	48	59	59	na	na	na
Greece	na	**30**	32	28	32	30	25	31	30	28	34	28	26	28	28	37
Hungary	25	**20**	23	17	28	25	10	19	23	19	17	22	20	18	22	25
Iceland	33	**43**	42	44	46	52	30	31	49	57	34	47	49	33	45	54
India	7	**15**	14	15	16	13	16	16	14	11	9	13	18	14	16	11
Indonesia	na	**5**	6	4	3	5	5	6	4	4	6	4	5	4	6	na
Iran	na	**16**	17	16	18	14	16	16	15	16	17	15	15	14	17	17
Ireland	22	**38**	35	41	43	39	31	36	36	46	39	32	40	36	37	46
Israel	na	**34**	36	33	34	35	33	35	32	36	38	37	34	40	33	28
Italy	25	**25**	26	24	28	31	18	19	29	31	19	27	30	16	25	28
Japan	6	**5**	5	5	12	4	4	2	5	7	6	4	5	5	6	5
Jordan	na	**27**	26	28	26	28	30	31	25	23	26	28	28	29	25	27
Korea, South	16	**12**	11	12	8	15	8	13	13	9	14	11	10	11	12	13
Latvia	na	**9**	12	8	13	11	6	8	10	11	8	10	12	5	12	12
Lithuania	12	**13**	15	11	16	14	10	9	15	13	12	10	11	15	13	na
Luxembourg	na	**47**	49	46	54	49	41	45	47	51	44	43	54	51	44	61
Macedonia	na	**24**	22	26	22	21	31	23	27	21	26	23	25	25	25	23
Malta	na	**31**	30	32	30	35	27	26	33	30	30	31	37	31	30	39
Mexico	28	**29**	26	32	32	28	24	31	29	18	36	26	26	25	31	28
Moldova	na	**24**	25	24	26	26	21	25	25	24	26	22	27	23	27	24
Montenegro	na	**20**	20	21	32	20	13	17	24	21	21	21	17	17	22	22
Morocco	na	**44**	40	47	42	44	46	44	44	34	51	46	39	42	47	36
Netherlands	36	**38**	37	38	36	40	36	32	34	47	37	39	39	31	35	51
New Zealand	na	**26**	26	27	37	32	17	19	26	36	19	28	32	30	27	29
Nigeria	15	**34**	32	35	35	34	25	35	34	32	30	34	41	36	31	41
Northern Ireland	22	**42**	44	40	49	41	39	41	44	39	49	43	44	47	41	43
Norway	17	**26**	25	28	29	31	18	22	23	33	na	na	na	22	27	30
Pakistan	na	**10**	9	12	15	9	5	11	8	12	10	8	12	10	11	8
Peru	na	**13**	13	14	14	14	12	13	15	11	14	11	15	15	14	10
Philippines	na	**33**	33	33	30	36	32	34	34	30	32	34	32	33	34	25
Poland	30	**16**	16	16	21	17	13	18	14	13	14	15	22	16	17	16
Portugal	38	**20**	17	23	23	20	19	19	23	23	14	23	19	23	17	23
Puerto Rico	na	**32**	36	30	35	37	28	34	31	33	30	29	40	29	34	30
Romania	na	**19**	22	16	27	19	15	17	21	18	19	16	22	16	19	35
Russian Fed.	26	**16**	15	16	22	15	11	12	16	16	17	14	15	15	16	9
Serbia	na	**14**	13	14	19	13	12	16	13	12	13	15	12	13	14	15
Singapore	na	**29**	28	30	30	28	28	28	27	36	27	25	31	28	29	35
Slovakia	na	**8**	9	7	10	9	6	5	9	11	8	7	8	9	8	14
Slovenia	12	**20**	22	17	24	21	15	22	19	18	21	20	18	18	19	26
South Africa	14	**21**	22	21	21	22	21	26	16	9	27	19	18	19	22	28
Spain	50	**45**	47	43	53	49	37	40	49	55	42	51	46	39	46	54
Sweden	27	**51**	48	54	54	58	42	40	54	54	48	50	55	41	48	61
Switzerland	46	**39**	38	41	47	41	33	38	41	34	48	40	36	42	37	48
Taiwan	na	**12**	10	13	16	11	11	10	9	14	6	15	13	10	13	11
Tanzania	na	**6**	6	7	7	5	8	7	6	6	7	7	6	6	7	13
Turkey	16	**26**	27	26	26	28	22	28	23	25	30	23	24	27	26	26
Uganda	na	**9**	13	6	7	12	14	15	6	17	18	13	7	10	8	14
Ukraine	na	**21**	23	20	26	23	17	18	22	21	18	25	24	25	19	13
United States	23	**32**	31	34	31	35	30	35	29	34	32	31	37	28	32	36
Uruguay	na	**15**	16	14	20	13	14	16	12	15	13	15	16	11	16	13
Venezuela	na	**21**	22	20	22	19	24	20	21	22	21	24	21	23	20	18
Vietnam	na	**28**	28	29	29	28	28	30	26	31	29	30	26	41	28	29
Zimbabwe	na	**11**	14	8	11	11	11	8	15	10	5	14	14	11	11	5
Total	25	25	25	25	26	26	22	24	25	26	23	24	25	21	25	32

RANKING	
Country	2000
France	65
Great Britain	53
Sweden	51
Luxembourg	47
Belgium	46
Spain	45
Morocco	44
Iceland	43
Northern Ireland	42
Germany	40
Switzerland	39
Ireland	38
Netherlands	38
Georgia	38
Bulgaria	36
Chile	35
Israel	34
Nigeria	34
Denmark	34
Philippines	33
Canada	33
Croatia	33
United States	32
Puerto Rico	32
Australia	32
Malta	31
Austria	30
Azerbaijan	30
Greece	30
Mexico	29
Singapore	29
Vietnam	28
Jordan	27
Turkey	26
New Zealand	26
Norway	26
Finland	25
Italy	25
Moldova	24
Macedonia	24
Armenia	22
Brazil	22
Ukraine	21
South Africa	21
Venezuela	21
Argentina	20
Montenegro	20
Portugal	20
Hungary	20
Belarus	20
Slovenia	20
Romania	19
El Salvador	18
China	17
Iran	16
Poland	16
Russian Fed.	16
Uruguay	15
India	15
Bosnia and Herz.	14
Serbia	14
Peru	13
Estonia	13
Lithuania	13
Colombia	12
Taiwan	12
Korea, South	12
Zimbabwe	11
Czech Republic	10
Albania	10
Pakistan	10
Dominican Rep.	10
Latvia	9
Uganda	9
Algeria	9
Slovakia	8
Bangladesh	7
Tanzania	6
Japan	5
Indonesia	5
Egypt	2
Total	25

E016) MORE EMPHASIS ON TECHNOLOGY

I'm going to read out a list of various changes in our way of life that might take place in the near future. If it were to happen, do you think it would be a good thing, a bad thing, or don't you mind?. More emphasis on the development of technology

Good (%) (WVS: V129; EVS: V194)

Country	Wave		Gender		Age			Education			Income			Values		
	1990	2000	Male	Female	16-29	30-49	50+	Lower	Middle	Upper	Lower	Middle	Upper	Mat	Mixed	Postm.
Albania	na	**61**	62	60	65	61	58	56	64	67	55	65	65	61	60	64
Algeria	na	**87**	89	86	87	89	85	84	86	90	86	90	89	87	88	88
Argentina	78	**68**	74	62	64	71	67	65	73	66	65	67	72	65	68	71
Armenia	na	**83**	85	81	81	85	85	84	82	86	85	86	75	80	87	77
Australia	na	**58**	66	51	55	56	63	56	58	60	56	55	65	57	59	59
Austria	42	**57**	65	50	64	59	51	56	57	61	50	59	63	49	60	57
Azerbaijan	na	**77**	79	76	82	74	77	78	74	84	75	80	85	76	79	90
Bangladesh	na	**89**	90	88	87	90	93	87	92	92	92	86	91	92	88	84
Belarus	84	**82**	85	79	89	83	74	61	87	92	76	84	85	79	85	89
Belgium	55	**56**	60	52	52	55	59	57	57	54	50	60	59	56	58	56
Bosnia and Herz.	na	**70**	71	68	71	69	69	62	71	71	71	69	71	71	69	74
Brazil	78	**70**	76	65	67	70	77	68	73	68	71	71	68	71	69	73
Bulgaria	81	**84**	85	83	84	85	82	81	84	86	81	86	85	85	84	78
Canada	63	**58**	65	50	55	59	59	57	57	60	58	58	59	59	59	55
Chile	73	**56**	59	53	56	56	57	54	55	63	57	52	61	53	56	61
China	95	**97**	98	96	96	97	96	96	97	100	97	96	97	98	96	97
Colombia	na	**83**	86	81	85	83	82	76	84	88	75	84	87	80	83	90
Croatia	na	**79**	82	76	78	80	78	80	77	82	82	81	75	82	79	77
Czech Republic	85	**76**	80	72	71	76	78	74	77	80	75	77	75	75	77	78
Denmark	59	**62**	71	52	60	63	62	61	74	58	57	64	68	68	64	49
Dominican Rep.	na	**51**	60	45	52	51	60	38	50	54	50	55	60	53	52	49
Egypt	na	**89**	92	87	92	89	86	86	92	94	87	88	91	86	91	96
El Salvador	na	**72**	74	70	75	72	68	69	73	78	72	72	76	na	na	na
Estonia	84	**75**	78	73	75	79	72	70	76	81	73	75	76	69	78	92
Finland	68	**55**	66	44	61	54	52	54	59	53	55	52	57	53	56	55
France	76	**58**	65	52	58	57	60	57	58	63	57	56	62	57	58	61
Georgia	na	**82**	84	81	83	83	82	86	82	81	84	82	81	84	81	77
Germany	83	**63**	73	55	65	65	60	56	67	74	57	65	70	65	64	60
Great Britain	64	**70**	74	66	70	69	74	71	66	77	64	79	68	na	na	na
Greece	na	**52**	56	49	46	53	63	68	56	45	52	55	52	53	52	52
Hungary	75	**59**	63	55	70	59	52	57	63	60	53	58	64	58	62	40
Iceland	69	**85**	89	80	82	84	88	84	85	84	81	84	89	86	85	80
India	85	**57**	61	51	65	57	49	44	62	80	44	53	67	59	68	75
Indonesia	na	**63**	59	67	66	67	58	62	61	68	65	65	59	65	63	63
Iran	na	**80**	81	79	81	83	71	72	82	87	79	80	80	80	82	84
Ireland	61	**69**	69	69	72	67	70	70	70	67	72	71	67	76	67	70
Israel	na	**78**	81	75	73	79	81	78	79	76	76	78	79	82	79	72
Italy	60	**65**	66	63	67	63	64	63	66	67	60	64	70	65	64	66
Japan	65	**61**	66	56	54	56	68	64	59	62	62	59	62	62	61	61
Jordan	na	**95**	95	94	95	95	92	93	95	97	95	94	94	95	94	93
Korea, South	90	**69**	73	65	63	70	76	73	67	71	70	73	65	70	68	69
Latvia	81	**87**	91	84	87	86	88	83	88	89	83	86	94	87	87	91
Lithuania	88	**79**	84	75	84	81	73	72	81	82	69	81	84	79	79	91
Luxembourg	na	**65**	69	61	63	66	66	59	67	74	62	58	77	63	67	74
Macedonia	na	**65**	66	65	68	64	64	53	72	71	62	63	72	64	70	56
Malta	na	**88**	92	84	91	87	87	83	89	93	85	90	91	85	89	90
Mexico	78	**76**	75	76	75	77	72	73	78	80	72	76	78	68	79	79
Moldova	na	**77**	80	75	79	76	76	73	78	80	74	81	78	79	77	70
Montenegro	na	**76**	77	75	83	78	68	69	77	85	74	79	82	78	75	57
Morocco	na	**93**	93	93	93	94	92	93	94	91	90	92	90	92	94	90
Netherlands	47	**48**	59	38	45	47	52	52	57	35	44	50	49	43	51	45
New Zealand	na	**35**	44	29	38	35	35	29	37	42	28	35	44	39	35	37
Nigeria	96	**86**	88	85	88	85	84	82	88	90	87	86	87	86	87	85
Northern Ireland	60	**62**	68	56	72	58	62	58	63	71	65	58	73	63	59	66
Norway	47	**46**	56	37	46	47	45	44	47	48	na	na	na	48	46	44
Pakistan	na	**77**	76	79	74	77	84	75	80	79	75	77	79	77	77	75
Peru	na	**78**	80	76	77	80	76	77	79	78	75	83	77	70	80	83
Philippines	na	**68**	68	68	69	67	67	64	65	76	66	68	69	68	68	64
Poland	89	**79**	82	77	79	79	80	81	79	76	78	82	75	75	81	84
Portugal	74	**71**	68	74	77	68	70	71	70	78	60	65	75	70	70	74
Puerto Rico	na	**79**	84	77	73	80	82	83	80	79	87	77	78	93	81	70
Romania	na	**85**	87	84	88	88	81	76	88	94	79	87	87	83	88	89
Russian Fed.	84	**88**	90	86	88	88	88	88	88	90	86	89	90	88	89	83
Serbia	na	**81**	83	79	84	81	81	77	83	86	76	80	86	80	83	86
Singapore	na	**67**	71	64	66	67	70	69	66	68	71	70	65	64	69	62
Slovakia	na	**79**	83	75	80	79	78	73	81	77	75	80	79	75	83	90
Slovenia	87	**79**	85	74	77	80	80	72	81	83	78	81	81	79	80	76
South Africa	82	**62**	61	63	65	61	58	58	67	59	57	62	66	60	64	59
Spain	66	**60**	63	57	63	60	58	58	61	63	56	62	61	54	62	63
Sweden	35	**35**	41	30	31	34	40	40	38	28	37	35	33	46	37	26
Switzerland	57	**34**	41	27	35	35	31	26	34	50	27	33	41	34	36	25
Taiwan	na	**93**	93	93	99	94	86	88	96	96	94	95	94	94	94	95
Tanzania	na	**90**	93	87	88	91	92	87	93	97	87	91	95	92	91	88
Turkey	90	**90**	91	88	89	90	90	89	90	91	88	91	90	90	90	90
Uganda	na	**69**	72	67	75	68	49	67	70	70	68	60	70	72	72	52
Ukraine	na	**90**	91	88	89	89	90	89	91	87	90	90	90	90	90	84
United States	70	**57**	63	50	54	55	61	59	56	56	55	60	56	50	57	57
Uruguay	na	**63**	66	61	57	64	66	62	64	69	57	62	71	58	65	62
Venezuela	na	**87**	87	87	87	87	88	85	87	90	83	86	91	78	90	89
Vietnam	na	**79**	84	74	78	78	81	74	85	93	73	80	82	79	86	88
Zimbabwe	na	**77**	79	75	77	77	74	75	78	83	78	77	81	77	76	85
Total	72	72	75	68	73	72	70	69	73	72	70	72	74	74	72	66

RANKING	
Country	**2000**
China	97
Jordan	95
Taiwan	93
Morocco	93
Tanzania	90
Turkey	90
Ukraine	90
Egypt	89
Bangladesh	89
Russian Fed.	88
Malta	88
Algeria	87
Venezuela	87
Latvia	87
Nigeria	86
Romania	85
Iceland	85
Bulgaria	84
Colombia	83
Armenia	83
Georgia	82
Belarus	82
Serbia	81
Iran	80
Poland	79
Puerto Rico	79
Slovenia	79
Lithuania	79
Croatia	79
Slovakia	79
Vietnam	79
Peru	78
Israel	78
Azerbaijan	77
Pakistan	77
Moldova	77
Zimbabwe	77
Czech Republic	76
Montenegro	76
Mexico	76
Estonia	75
El Salvador	72
Portugal	71
Brazil	70
Great Britain	70
Bosnia and Herz.	70
Uganda	69
Ireland	69
Korea, South	69
Argentina	68
Philippines	68
Singapore	67
Luxembourg	65
Macedonia	65
Italy	65
Uruguay	63
Germany	63
Indonesia	63
Denmark	62
South Africa	62
Northern Ireland	62
Albania	61
Japan	61
Spain	60
Hungary	59
France	58
Australia	58
Canada	58
Austria	57
India	57
United States	57
Belgium	56
Chile	56
Finland	55
Greece	52
Dominican Rep.	51
Netherlands	48
Norway	46
New Zealand	35
Sweden	35
Switzerland	34
Total	72

E017_1) MORE EMPHASIS ON INDIVIDUAL

Here is a list of various changes in our way of life that might take place in the near future. If it were to happen do you think it would be a good thing, a bad thing, or don't you mind?. Greater emphasis on the development of the individual

Good (%) (EVS: V195)

Country	Wave		Gender		Age			Education			Income			Values		
	1990	2000	Male	Female	16-29	30-49	50+	Lower	Middle	Upper	Lower	Middle	Upper	Mat	Mixed	Postm.
Albania	na	**na**	na	na	na	na	na	na	na	na	na	na	na	na	na	na
Algeria	na	**na**	na	na	na	na	na	na	na	na	na	na	na	na	na	na
Argentina	95	**na**	na	na	na	na	na	na	na	na	na	na	na	na	na	na
Armenia	na	**na**	na	na	na	na	na	na	na	na	na	na	na	na	na	na
Australia	na	**na**	na	na	na	na	na	na	na	na	na	na	na	na	na	na
Austria	76	**89**	89	89	87	88	91	87	89	96	83	90	90	73	88	96
Azerbaijan	na	**na**	na	na	na	na	na	na	na	na	na	na	na	na	na	na
Bangladesh	na	**na**	na	na	na	na	na	na	na	na	na	na	na	na	na	na
Belarus	96	**87**	89	86	93	90	79	73	91	97	84	89	89	84	91	93
Belgium	81	**86**	86	86	87	86	85	80	84	94	82	86	90	77	87	95
Bosnia and Herz.	na	**na**	na	na	na	na	na	na	na	na	na	na	na	na	na	na
Brazil	92	**na**	na	na	na	na	na	na	na	na	na	na	na	na	na	na
Bulgaria	87	**92**	92	92	91	95	89	91	91	95	89	93	94	93	92	91
Canada	85	**na**	na	na	na	na	na	na	na	na	na	na	na	na	na	na
Chile	90	**na**	na	na	na	na	na	na	na	na	na	na	na	na	na	na
China	40	**na**	na	na	na	na	na	na	na	na	na	na	na	na	na	na
Colombia	na	**na**	na	na	na	na	na	na	na	na	na	na	na	na	na	na
Croatia	na	**75**	77	72	75	73	77	67	78	82	74	73	78	63	75	82
Czech Republic	94	**88**	87	88	88	88	87	85	89	94	86	87	89	83	89	89
Denmark	93	**93**	93	94	91	95	93	91	95	96	92	95	94	93	94	97
Dominican Rep.	na	**na**	na	na	na	na	na	na	na	na	na	na	na	na	na	na
Egypt	na	**na**	na	na	na	na	na	na	na	na	na	na	na	na	na	na
El Salvador	na	**na**	na	na	na	na	na	na	na	na	na	na	na	na	na	na
Estonia	85	**83**	81	86	81	85	83	77	86	87	82	83	85	82	85	85
Finland	93	**90**	88	91	93	90	87	87	93	91	89	89	91	86	91	93
France	88	**87**	86	88	87	87	87	85	87	91	87	87	89	82	87	93
Georgia	na	**na**	na	na	na	na	na	na	na	na	na	na	na	na	na	na
Germany	88	**89**	89	89	92	91	87	84	93	96	85	89	88	85	90	94
Great Britain	78	**75**	74	76	72	74	80	71	77	80	70	80	75	na	na	na
Greece	na	**93**	92	93	94	92	90	92	92	93	92	95	90	94	92	96
Hungary	72	**71**	69	73	79	70	65	65	79	82	68	67	76	68	75	67
Iceland	94	**96**	94	98	91	97	98	94	97	97	95	96	97	92	97	97
India	71	**na**	na	na	na	na	na	na	na	na	na	na	na	na	na	na
Indonesia	na	**na**	na	na	na	na	na	na	na	na	na	na	na	na	na	na
Iran	na	**na**	na	na	na	na	na	na	na	na	na	na	na	na	na	na
Ireland	90	**92**	92	91	91	93	91	90	92	94	90	91	94	88	92	95
Israel	na	**na**	na	na	na	na	na	na	na	na	na	na	na	na	na	na
Italy	93	**92**	91	94	90	93	94	91	93	96	89	93	95	90	92	96
Japan	70	**na**	na	na	na	na	na	na	na	na	na	na	na	na	na	na
Jordan	na	**na**	na	na	na	na	na	na	na	na	na	na	na	na	na	na
Korea, South	84	**na**	na	na	na	na	na	na	na	na	na	na	na	na	na	na
Latvia	86	**90**	90	90	87	89	92	89	90	92	89	87	94	92	90	86
Lithuania	91	**87**	85	88	93	88	82	85	86	94	78	89	91	86	87	94
Luxembourg	na	**78**	78	78	75	79	79	77	77	84	75	84	84	71	81	85
Macedonia	na	**na**	na	na	na	na	na	na	na	na	na	na	na	na	na	na
Malta	na	**96**	97	96	96	96	97	96	96	100	96	98	96	97	97	95
Mexico	88	**na**	na	na	na	na	na	na	na	na	na	na	na	na	na	na
Moldova	na	**na**	na	na	na	na	na	na	na	na	na	na	na	na	na	na
Montenegro	na	**na**	na	na	na	na	na	na	na	na	na	na	na	na	na	na
Morocco	na	**na**	na	na	na	na	na	na	na	na	na	na	na	na	na	na
Netherlands	84	**86**	86	86	88	87	85	80	90	88	84	87	89	77	85	93
New Zealand	na	**na**	na	na	na	na	na	na	na	na	na	na	na	na	na	na
Nigeria	93	**na**	na	na	na	na	na	na	na	na	na	na	na	na	na	na
Northern Ireland	81	**84**	84	83	87	84	83	83	83	86	84	86	84	81	83	85
Norway	88	**na**	na	na	na	na	na	na	na	na	na	na	na	na	na	na
Pakistan	na	**na**	na	na	na	na	na	na	na	na	na	na	na	na	na	na
Peru	na	**na**	na	na	na	na	na	na	na	na	na	na	na	na	na	na
Philippines	na	**na**	na	na	na	na	na	na	na	na	na	na	na	na	na	na
Poland	94	**87**	87	88	87	86	90	86	87	94	87	88	84	83	89	94
Portugal	76	**79**	76	81	88	75	76	78	78	83	74	72	83	77	80	74
Puerto Rico	na	**na**	na	na	na	na	na	na	na	na	na	na	na	na	na	na
Romania	na	**90**	91	90	89	91	90	85	91	96	87	90	92	88	92	96
Russian Fed.	89	**92**	91	93	93	93	91	90	92	95	90	93	94	92	93	79
Serbia	na	**na**	na	na	na	na	na	na	na	na	na	na	na	na	na	na
Singapore	na	**na**	na	na	na	na	na	na	na	na	na	na	na	na	na	na
Slovakia	na	**86**	86	87	85	89	85	80	89	89	83	86	89	85	87	92
Slovenia	81	**na**	na	na	na	na	na	na	na	na	na	na	na	na	na	na
South Africa	90	**na**	na	na	na	na	na	na	na	na	na	na	na	na	na	na
Spain	91	**86**	84	88	85	88	85	86	84	90	85	86	90	79	85	93
Sweden	88	**90**	89	90	92	89	89	85	92	91	87	90	93	86	89	93
Switzerland	91	**na**	na	na	na	na	na	na	na	na	na	na	na	na	na	na
Taiwan	na	**na**	na	na	na	na	na	na	na	na	na	na	na	na	na	na
Tanzania	na	**na**	na	na	na	na	na	na	na	na	na	na	na	na	na	na
Turkey	93	**95**	94	96	95	95	96	93	97	99	94	95	97	90	96	98
Uganda	na	**na**	na	na	na	na	na	na	na	na	na	na	na	na	na	na
Ukraine	na	**94**	93	95	97	92	95	97	93	96	94	94	95	94	95	98
United States	87	**na**	na	na	na	na	na	na	na	na	na	na	na	na	na	na
Uruguay	na	**na**	na	na	na	na	na	na	na	na	na	na	na	na	na	na
Venezuela	na	**na**	na	na	na	na	na	na	na	na	na	na	na	na	na	na
Vietnam	na	**na**	na	na	na	na	na	na	na	na	na	na	na	na	na	na
Zimbabwe	na	**na**	na	na	na	na	na	na	na	na	na	na	na	na	na	na
Total	86	**87**	87	88	88	88	87	83	89	92	86	87	89	85	89	92

RANKING	
Country	2000
Malta	96
Iceland	96
Turkey	95
Ukraine	94
Denmark	93
Greece	93
Italy	92
Russian Fed.	92
Bulgaria	92
Ireland	92
Latvia	90
Romania	90
Finland	90
Sweden	90
Germany	89
Austria	89
Czech Republic	88
Belarus	87
Poland	87
Lithuania	87
France	87
Slovakia	86
Netherlands	86
Spain	86
Belgium	86
Northern Ireland	84
Estonia	83
Portugal	79
Luxembourg	78
Great Britain	75
Croatia	75
Hungary	71
Total	87

E018) GREATER RESPECT FOR AUTHORITY

I'm going to read out a list of various changes in our way of life that might take place in the near future. If it were to happen, do you think it would be a good thing, a bad thing, or don't you mind?. Greater respect for authority

Good (%)

(WVS: V130; EVS: V196)

Country	Wave		Gender		Age			Education			Income			Values		
	1990	2000	Male	Female	16-29	30-49	50+	Lower	Middle	Upper	Lower	Middle	Upper	Mat	Mixed	Postm.
Albania	na	**34**	35	34	30	33	41	34	33	38	35	33	35	37	35	23
Algeria	na	**63**	62	63	59	63	68	67	63	59	66	59	63	66	65	47
Argentina	69	**72**	72	73	66	73	77	80	62	58	81	74	60	82	76	58
Armenia	na	**63**	63	63	60	61	70	67	62	64	56	70	63	61	64	58
Australia	na	**73**	71	75	68	69	82	80	78	61	79	72	67	92	78	61
Austria	47	**39**	35	42	30	34	50	49	32	23	52	37	33	59	43	25
Azerbaijan	na	**61**	62	59	62	59	65	72	58	65	53	68	68	59	61	83
Bangladesh	na	**92**	92	91	91	92	91	89	95	92	92	90	94	93	91	93
Belarus	71	**72**	73	72	71	70	76	68	73	79	72	73	73	73	73	63
Belgium	50	**63**	60	67	55	56	73	76	65	52	70	67	56	79	65	41
Bosnia and Herz.	na	**26**	27	26	21	26	33	34	24	26	29	29	21	28	27	21
Brazil	81	**83**	84	82	78	85	89	88	82	72	87	85	77	90	82	70
Bulgaria	78	**69**	73	65	51	72	75	76	65	68	74	71	62	69	70	66
Canada	64	**66**	64	69	59	63	75	76	69	55	67	72	60	72	70	59
Chile	80	**56**	56	56	53	55	61	61	57	44	61	55	49	60	57	48
China	24	**64**	59	69	68	61	68	74	59	54	67	62	61	61	65	74
Colombia	na	**89**	89	88	86	90	88	90	87	90	88	87	91	89	87	89
Croatia	na	**56**	59	53	50	55	61	66	52	43	66	56	51	56	59	47
Czech Republic	65	**52**	54	51	45	46	62	55	50	46	58	57	44	57	53	44
Denmark	35	**38**	40	36	45	34	39	49	29	23	45	38	23	54	40	17
Dominican Rep.	na	**56**	58	54	56	54	90	57	56	57	53	61	65	57	59	51
Egypt	na	**86**	87	85	86	86	88	86	85	88	88	85	85	85	88	81
El Salvador	na	**86**	86	85	85	85	87	88	87	79	91	85	80	na	na	na
Estonia	na	**44**	45	43	35	40	53	45	43	46	46	48	41	44	44	38
Finland	26	**39**	39	40	40	35	44	42	37	35	43	40	38	38	41	31
France	59	**69**	66	71	61	64	77	76	61	57	72	67	66	82	70	46
Georgia	na	**75**	76	75	68	77	81	77	75	74	77	77	73	78	73	71
Germany	57	**46**	46	45	26	42	58	52	40	42	49	47	43	57	47	25
Great Britain	72	**71**	67	75	59	69	82	75	70	63	71	74	68	na	na	na
Greece	na	**17**	18	16	11	16	32	30	18	14	18	17	16	22	16	13
Hungary	61	**69**	68	69	72	61	74	73	65	52	66	70	68	72	68	57
Iceland	42	**47**	49	44	40	46	54	55	43	36	47	47	46	54	47	27
India	54	**43**	48	38	45	44	41	41	43	49	37	45	45	49	47	36
Indonesia	na	**37**	36	39	31	43	34	34	38	39	33	44	38	35	40	36
Iran	na	**71**	72	70	73	72	66	66	75	74	70	71	71	77	71	72
Ireland	83	**76**	75	77	66	73	86	87	73	65	84	75	69	84	75	69
Israel	na	**58**	57	60	55	57	64	68	59	52	67	58	55	44	61	65
Italy	49	**51**	53	50	42	47	61	57	47	46	55	51	49	65	53	40
Japan	6	**4**	3	5	4	3	5	7	4	2	6	5	3	4	4	2
Jordan	na	**90**	91	90	89	93	87	92	90	88	89	91	90	94	89	78
Korea, South	14	**19**	18	21	14	20	24	34	21	16	22	16	19	20	19	21
Latvia	na	**49**	50	48	42	44	56	52	46	55	50	46	52	50	49	41
Lithuania	53	**44**	46	43	46	41	46	51	40	47	40	40	45	48	42	55
Luxembourg	na	**53**	55	51	50	46	62	62	51	42	63	53	44	63	57	30
Macedonia	na	**49**	48	49	44	47	54	44	54	43	55	44	48	49	50	32
Malta	na	**92**	93	92	91	90	95	93	93	88	91	93	93	93	93	86
Mexico	65	**76**	74	77	71	78	80	79	72	74	77	75	76	77	77	68
Moldova	na	**48**	48	48	39	46	59	52	49	43	57	50	43	51	44	41
Montenegro	na	**45**	44	47	33	46	53	55	40	35	42	42	51	53	39	29
Morocco	na	**89**	87	91	85	91	95	92	80	74	89	82	86	93	87	72
Netherlands	51	**67**	66	68	58	64	74	82	66	53	71	68	59	89	72	41
New Zealand	na	**50**	48	52	37	44	60	55	53	41	51	47	51	57	55	35
Nigeria	91	**83**	83	83	82	83	84	82	82	85	83	82	84	85	82	77
Northern Ireland	82	**77**	75	78	70	71	86	80	73	76	85	77	76	85	78	59
Norway	32	**32**	30	33	30	29	36	34	30	30	na	na	na	50	30	22
Pakistan	na	**62**	63	61	51	64	77	71	52	52	71	64	49	66	57	67
Peru	na	**80**	79	82	78	83	79	83	81	78	80	80	82	78	82	82
Philippines	na	**70**	71	68	69	72	67	69	71	68	72	70	68	71	70	65
Poland	73	**55**	60	49	44	50	68	56	53	51	53	58	49	54	55	58
Portugal	74	**78**	75	80	70	74	85	83	72	51	88	75	74	83	76	66
Puerto Rico	na	**93**	92	95	90	92	97	94	94	93	97	93	92	99	94	94
Romania	na	**85**	83	86	78	83	89	87	82	88	85	85	84	84	87	74
Russian Fed.	68	**56**	54	58	49	55	62	59	54	62	55	55	59	58	55	55
Serbia	na	**55**	56	54	46	49	65	61	53	51	60	59	49	59	52	52
Singapore	na	**52**	53	51	52	52	52	55	52	47	57	51	48	51	54	45
Slovakia	na	**68**	65	71	63	67	74	68	69	64	72	67	68	72	67	56
Slovenia	66	**43**	40	46	28	38	60	56	41	30	54	43	39	51	44	33
South Africa	88	**73**	70	76	75	71	73	71	74	78	69	73	77	77	72	62
Spain	69	**59**	56	63	46	55	72	68	51	50	64	59	56	69	60	41
Sweden	22	**22**	24	21	26	21	21	29	25	12	23	25	17	27	24	15
Switzerland	46	**31**	32	29	20	28	41	37	30	20	36	34	26	44	32	17
Taiwan	na	**45**	42	47	43	46	44	48	46	42	51	45	40	43	49	38
Tanzania	na	**82**	82	83	82	81	87	86	80	75	86	83	76	84	83	79
Turkey	65	**68**	67	69	65	68	75	76	62	43	77	64	53	72	70	54
Uganda	na	**73**	77	70	72	73	82	77	72	69	76	70	69	76	74	66
Ukraine	na	**64**	62	66	56	62	70	70	64	62	66	62	63	67	63	62
United States	78	**70**	65	76	61	71	77	69	75	68	75	70	64	73	73	61
Uruguay	na	**58**	61	56	44	48	72	69	45	37	65	60	49	76	59	42
Venezuela	na	**91**	93	90	90	91	93	92	92	90	90	90	93	87	92	95
Vietnam	na	**80**	82	79	75	82	82	77	86	84	78	80	83	82	87	86
Zimbabwe	na	**90**	87	92	90	89	90	90	89	92	94	88	91	89	90	94
Total	58	**61**	61	61	59	59	65	68	58	55	64	62	59	65	61	50

RANKING	
Country	2000
Puerto Rico	93
Malta	92
Bangladesh	92
Venezuela	91
Jordan	90
Zimbabwe	90
Morocco	89
Colombia	89
Egypt	86
El Salvador	86
Romania	85
Brazil	83
Nigeria	83
Tanzania	82
Peru	80
Vietnam	80
Portugal	78
Northern Ireland	77
Ireland	76
Mexico	76
Georgia	75
Uganda	73
Australia	73
South Africa	73
Belarus	72
Argentina	72
Iran	71
Great Britain	71
United States	70
Philippines	70
Bulgaria	69
France	69
Hungary	69
Slovakia	68
Turkey	68
Netherlands	67
Canada	66
Ukraine	64
China	64
Belgium	63
Armenia	63
Algeria	63
Pakistan	62
Azerbaijan	61
Spain	59
Israel	58
Uruguay	58
Russian Fed.	56
Chile	56
Dominican Rep.	56
Croatia	56
Serbia	55
Poland	55
Luxembourg	53
Czech Republic	52
Singapore	52
Italy	51
New Zealand	50
Latvia	49
Macedonia	49
Moldova	48
Iceland	47
Germany	46
Montenegro	45
Taiwan	45
Lithuania	44
Estonia	44
India	43
Slovenia	43
Finland	39
Austria	39
Denmark	38
Indonesia	37
Albania	34
Norway	32
Switzerland	31
Bosnia and Herz.	26
Sweden	22
Korea, South	19
Greece	17
Japan	4
Total	61

E019) MORE EMPHASIS ON FAMILY LIFE

I'm going to read out a list of various changes in our way of life that might take place in the near future. If it were to happen, do you think it would be a good thing, a bad thing, or don't you mind?. More emphasis on family life

(WVS: V131; EVS: V197)

Good (%)

Country	Wave		Gender		Age			Education			Income			Values		
	1990	2000	Male	Female	16-29	30-49	50+	Lower	Middle	Upper	Lower	Middle	Upper	Mat	Mixed	Postm.
Albania	na	**96**	94	98	93	97	98	95	96	97	97	92	98	97	95	97
Algeria	na	**96**	96	97	96	96	97	98	95	96	96	97	94	96	96	98
Argentina	96	**97**	96	98	96	97	98	97	96	95	97	98	96	97	97	96
Armenia	na	**92**	91	93	92	92	92	94	91	93	94	93	90	93	91	89
Australia	na	**95**	94	96	92	94	98	96	95	93	96	94	94	94	97	92
Austria	92	**92**	90	95	86	92	96	95	91	86	89	96	91	95	93	89
Azerbaijan	na	**95**	95	94	94	95	96	97	96	92	95	96	94	95	94	99
Bangladesh	na	**92**	92	92	92	92	95	93	93	89	95	91	93	95	90	97
Belarus	95	**92**	88	94	90	94	90	89	92	94	89	93	93	93	91	91
Belgium	85	**90**	88	91	85	89	93	94	90	85	91	91	89	94	90	84
Bosnia and Herz.	na	**82**	79	84	82	82	81	83	81	84	82	79	86	85	81	81
Brazil	98	**98**	97	99	98	98	97	98	98	98	98	98	97	99	98	95
Bulgaria	90	**95**	93	97	91	97	96	97	94	95	97	95	92	96	94	94
Canada	94	**94**	91	97	91	95	95	95	95	91	94	96	93	94	95	92
Chile	98	**92**	90	93	92	92	91	91	93	92	92	93	90	93	91	92
China	74	**92**	90	95	89	94	91	94	92	88	94	92	91	95	90	88
Colombia	na	**99**	99	99	99	99	99	99	99	99	99	99	99	98	98	99
Croatia	na	**93**	93	93	91	92	95	96	92	87	95	93	92	96	94	91
Czech Republic	94	**93**	91	95	90	92	95	94	92	92	93	95	91	95	93	89
Denmark	95	**95**	94	97	91	97	96	96	94	94	95	97	96	90	96	95
Dominican Rep.	na	**75**	76	74	74	73	100	75	79	74	71	77	82	75	75	76
Egypt	na	**99**	99	99	100	99	100	99	100	99	100	99	99	99	99	100
El Salvador	na	**95**	95	94	94	95	96	93	97	96	94	95	96	na	na	na
Estonia	86	**89**	86	91	86	88	91	88	90	89	90	90	90	90	89	92
Finland	96	**95**	94	96	93	96	95	95	95	95	94	96	95	96	94	95
France	90	**91**	89	93	88	90	94	95	87	86	92	93	90	95	92	82
Georgia	na	**94**	94	94	92	95	94	94	94	93	93	94	95	94	94	96
Germany	92	**90**	87	92	79	92	93	89	90	93	86	93	92	92	91	86
Great Britain	88	**90**	87	93	81	92	95	95	88	84	89	96	91	na	na	na
Greece	na	**91**	88	93	88	92	97	97	93	89	92	91	91	96	92	87
Hungary	94	**92**	92	92	94	90	93	91	94	91	87	93	94	94	90	84
Iceland	96	**96**	94	99	92	97	99	96	96	97	97	97	96	97	96	95
India	75	**75**	78	72	77	76	71	69	77	87	66	75	81	82	80	89
Indonesia	na	**83**	82	85	93	83	80	77	83	90	78	87	86	86	82	81
Iran	na	**91**	90	92	91	93	89	89	92	92	89	94	90	93	92	90
Ireland	94	**95**	92	97	90	96	96	96	95	92	95	97	92	94	95	93
Israel	na	**93**	92	93	91	93	95	95	93	91	90	94	95	91	93	95
Italy	93	**92**	91	94	90	91	95	95	91	88	92	94	90	95	93	90
Japan	85	**89**	88	90	88	91	87	82	91	88	88	93	87	89	90	93
Jordan	na	**98**	100	97	99	99	96	98	98	99	98	99	98	99	98	98
Korea, South	89	**93**	93	94	92	93	94	89	92	95	91	95	94	94	93	91
Latvia	85	**92**	88	95	89	90	95	93	91	94	95	90	92	94	91	93
Lithuania	96	**97**	96	97	98	97	95	96	97	97	96	98	96	96	98	97
Luxembourg	na	**88**	86	90	85	88	90	90	88	88	89	90	88	93	89	83
Macedonia	na	**82**	82	81	75	84	84	80	84	80	82	83	83	80	85	77
Malta	na	**99**	99	100	98	100	100	100	99	99	100	100	99	99	100	97
Mexico	91	**91**	92	91	92	92	90	91	92	93	91	91	93	90	93	88
Moldova	na	**87**	86	88	86	86	88	89	85	88	90	85	84	90	85	84
Montenegro	na	**95**	93	97	93	96	97	96	94	98	92	97	96	97	96	84
Morocco	na	**99**	99	99	99	99	100	99	99	100	99	99	99	99	99	98
Netherlands	66	**68**	66	71	70	62	74	80	70	55	67	71	64	83	72	51
New Zealand	na	**88**	84	92	81	88	91	88	92	86	91	88	88	90	90	89
Nigeria	92	**94**	94	94	94	95	94	92	95	96	93	95	95	96	93	92
Northern Ireland	92	**91**	89	92	84	89	96	92	89	93	93	94	91	91	93	87
Norway	95	**95**	93	97	95	94	97	96	96	94	na	na	na	97	95	93
Pakistan	na	**89**	87	90	84	91	92	93	84	83	94	89	84	92	84	92
Peru	na	**95**	94	96	94	96	94	95	95	95	95	94	96	93	95	97
Philippines	na	**92**	91	93	94	92	89	88	92	97	89	94	91	94	91	90
Poland	97	**95**	94	96	90	95	98	95	96	91	97	95	91	96	95	89
Portugal	95	**91**	90	93	94	86	93	91	90	93	94	81	94	92	90	92
Puerto Rico	na	**95**	95	95	95	94	95	94	95	95	97	94	94	97	94	98
Romania	na	**96**	95	96	91	97	97	95	96	96	95	96	96	96	96	93
Russian Fed.	95	**94**	91	96	89	94	95	94	94	93	94	94	93	95	92	94
Serbia	na	**95**	94	96	89	96	97	94	95	95	95	96	96	95	95	93
Singapore	na	**93**	92	94	93	92	97	94	94	89	91	94	94	96	93	93
Slovakia	na	**95**	94	96	92	96	95	94	96	93	95	96	96	95	95	94
Slovenia	91	**96**	95	96	96	95	96	96	97	90	98	96	93	98	95	97
South Africa	94	**79**	78	81	81	79	77	77	81	95	72	82	87	78	82	72
Spain	89	**88**	87	89	83	87	92	91	85	83	90	86	85	91	88	82
Sweden	85	**78**	77	79	75	77	81	85	78	73	73	81	79	84	80	70
Switzerland	91	**89**	86	92	84	87	94	93	88	88	91	95	87	92	89	88
Taiwan	na	**96**	96	96	97	97	93	93	98	97	95	98	97	97	98	97
Tanzania	na	**96**	95	96	95	95	98	96	95	95	96	97	92	97	95	100
Turkey	95	**97**	96	97	95	98	98	98	96	91	98	97	93	98	97	94
Uganda	na	**80**	86	75	80	80	81	83	78	80	76	73	77	84	79	72
Ukraine	na	**91**	88	93	86	89	95	95	92	86	92	92	86	92	90	88
United States	95	**94**	92	96	90	96	95	91	97	94	94	95	94	89	95	94
Uruguay	na	**95**	95	94	93	92	97	94	96	90	96	94	94	96	96	92
Venezuela	na	**98**	97	98	98	97	98	97	98	98	94	98	99	98	97	98
Vietnam	na	**88**	88	89	90	90	85	87	92	88	86	91	88	93	91	92
Zimbabwe	na	**96**	96	96	95	97	95	97	94	100	95	97	96	96	96	99
Total	91	**92**	91	93	90	92	93	93	92	90	91	92	92	93	92	89

RANKING

Country	2000
Malta	99
Egypt	99
Morocco	99
Colombia	99
Jordan	98
Brazil	98
Venezuela	98
Argentina	97
Turkey	97
Lithuania	97
Iceland	96
Algeria	96
Albania	96
Taiwan	96
Zimbabwe	96
Slovenia	96
Romania	96
Tanzania	96
Denmark	95
Montenegro	95
Norway	95
Bulgaria	95
Finland	95
Serbia	95
El Salvador	95
Peru	95
Poland	95
Slovakia	95
Azerbaijan	95
Australia	95
Ireland	95
Puerto Rico	95
Uruguay	95
Nigeria	94
Georgia	94
United States	94
Canada	94
Russian Fed.	94
Croatia	93
Korea, South	93
Singapore	93
Czech Republic	93
Israel	93
China	92
Austria	92
Italy	92
Bangladesh	92
Latvia	92
Armenia	92
Hungary	92
Philippines	92
Chile	92
Belarus	92
Mexico	91
France	91
Greece	91
Portugal	91
Iran	91
Northern Ireland	91
Ukraine	91
Germany	90
Great Britain	90
Belgium	90
Estonia	89
Switzerland	89
Pakistan	89
Japan	89
New Zealand	88
Vietnam	88
Luxembourg	88
Spain	88
Moldova	87
Indonesia	83
Bosnia and Herz.	82
Macedonia	82
Uganda	80
South Africa	79
Sweden	78
India	75
Dominican Rep.	75
Netherlands	68
Total	92

E020_1) A SIMPLE AND MORE NATURAL LIFESTYLE

Here is a list of various changes in our way of life that might take place in the near future. If it were to happen do you think it would be a good thing, a bad thing, or don't you mind?. A simple and more natural lifestyle

Good (%)

(EVS: V198)

Country	Wave		Gender		Age			Education			Income			Values		
	1990	2000	Male	Female	16-29	30-49	50+	Lower	Middle	Upper	Lower	Middle	Upper	Mat	Mixed	Postm.
Albania	na	**na**	na	na	na	na	na	na	na	na	na	na	na	na	na	na
Algeria	na	**na**	na	na	na	na	na	na	na	na	na	na	na	na	na	na
Argentina	92	**na**	na	na	na	na	na	na	na	na	na	na	na	na	na	na
Armenia	na	**na**	na	na	na	na	na	na	na	na	na	na	na	na	na	na
Australia	na	**na**	na	na	na	na	na	na	na	na	na	na	na	na	na	na
Austria	85	**82**	76	87	67	83	88	86	79	75	87	83	75	83	81	83
Azerbaijan	na	**na**	na	na	na	na	na	na	na	na	na	na	na	na	na	na
Bangladesh	na	**na**	na	na	na	na	na	na	na	na	na	na	na	na	na	na
Belarus	90	**80**	76	83	75	82	82	78	80	80	77	83	79	80	82	68
Belgium	84	**85**	81	89	76	85	90	89	85	83	91	90	80	85	86	84
Bosnia and Herz.	na	**na**	na	na	na	na	na	na	na	na	na	na	na	na	na	na
Brazil	93	**na**	na	na	na	na	na	na	na	na	na	na	na	na	na	na
Bulgaria	82	**79**	76	83	71	80	83	82	77	82	81	82	76	80	79	94
Canada	84	**na**	na	na	na	na	na	na	na	na	na	na	na	na	na	na
Chile	93	**na**	na	na	na	na	na	na	na	na	na	na	na	na	na	na
China	51	**na**	na	na	na	na	na	na	na	na	na	na	na	na	na	na
Colombia	na	**na**	na	na	na	na	na	na	na	na	na	na	na	na	na	na
Croatia	na	**97**	97	98	93	98	99	98	98	95	100	98	96	99	98	96
Czech Republic	86	**82**	81	83	79	84	82	82	82	84	82	85	79	84	82	81
Denmark	85	**81**	75	87	72	82	86	83	75	81	81	82	83	74	82	85
Dominican Rep.	na	**na**	na	na	na	na	na	na	na	na	na	na	na	na	na	na
Egypt	na	**na**	na	na	na	na	na	na	na	na	na	na	na	na	na	na
El Salvador	na	**na**	na	na	na	na	na	na	na	na	na	na	na	na	na	na
Estonia	84	**86**	85	87	80	87	89	84	86	90	86	89	85	84	88	86
Finland	91	**80**	71	88	72	82	81	81	78	78	85	78	76	80	79	84
France	92	**94**	93	94	90	93	96	95	93	91	96	95	92	94	93	94
Georgia	na	**na**	na	na	na	na	na	na	na	na	na	na	na	na	na	na
Germany	66	**71**	66	75	59	72	75	70	72	72	72	72	75	74	68	75
Great Britain	80	**75**	72	78	74	72	80	79	77	60	78	78	73	na	na	na
Greece	na	**94**	93	94	94	94	95	94	95	93	95	95	93	94	94	96
Hungary	85	**84**	84	84	87	84	82	82	88	83	78	83	87	82	85	94
Iceland	79	**78**	76	80	67	79	86	79	76	78	77	81	74	73	79	82
India	80	**na**	na	na	na	na	na	na	na	na	na	na	na	na	na	na
Indonesia	na	**na**	na	na	na	na	na	na	na	na	na	na	na	na	na	na
Iran	na	**na**	na	na	na	na	na	na	na	na	na	na	na	na	na	na
Ireland	87	**82**	79	86	69	86	89	88	80	79	87	82	77	86	81	83
Israel	na	**na**	na	na	na	na	na	na	na	na	na	na	na	na	na	na
Italy	93	**89**	86	92	85	89	91	90	89	87	90	90	88	88	89	90
Japan	76	**na**	na	na	na	na	na	na	na	na	na	na	na	na	na	na
Jordan	na	**na**	na	na	na	na	na	na	na	na	na	na	na	na	na	na
Korea, South	66	**na**	na	na	na	na	na	na	na	na	na	na	na	na	na	na
Latvia	80	**82**	80	83	76	79	86	86	81	78	82	83	80	86	80	82
Lithuania	89	**90**	92	89	95	93	84	88	91	90	89	88	92	90	90	95
Luxembourg	na	**85**	83	87	83	84	88	85	86	85	81	89	87	83	85	91
Macedonia	na	**na**	na	na	na	na	na	na	na	na	na	na	na	na	na	na
Malta	na	**96**	95	96	91	96	99	98	96	88	97	98	94	96	96	94
Mexico	83	**na**	na	na	na	na	na	na	na	na	na	na	na	na	na	na
Moldova	na	**na**	na	na	na	na	na	na	na	na	na	na	na	na	na	na
Montenegro	na	**na**	na	na	na	na	na	na	na	na	na	na	na	na	na	na
Morocco	na	**na**	na	na	na	na	na	na	na	na	na	na	na	na	na	na
Netherlands	78	**67**	58	75	57	63	76	75	60	67	75	63	62	67	66	70
New Zealand	na	**na**	na	na	na	na	na	na	na	na	na	na	na	na	na	na
Nigeria	90	**na**	na	na	na	na	na	na	na	na	na	na	na	na	na	na
Northern Ireland	86	**75**	70	79	68	75	78	76	75	75	78	73	71	78	74	76
Norway	80	**na**	na	na	na	na	na	na	na	na	na	na	na	na	na	na
Pakistan	na	**na**	na	na	na	na	na	na	na	na	na	na	na	na	na	na
Peru	na	**na**	na	na	na	na	na	na	na	na	na	na	na	na	na	na
Philippines	na	**na**	na	na	na	na	na	na	na	na	na	na	na	na	na	na
Poland	89	**86**	87	85	77	87	90	90	83	77	88	86	81	87	86	84
Portugal	92	**81**	79	83	78	81	83	83	78	73	86	74	78	82	80	76
Puerto Rico	na	**na**	na	na	na	na	na	na	na	na	na	na	na	na	na	na
Romania	na	**84**	80	88	79	84	87	86	83	82	84	85	84	85	84	71
Russian Fed.	89	**59**	58	59	59	58	59	62	60	53	62	61	53	61	57	57
Serbia	na	**na**	na	na	na	na	na	na	na	na	na	na	na	na	na	na
Singapore	na	**na**	na	na	na	na	na	na	na	na	na	na	na	na	na	na
Slovakia	na	**88**	87	90	86	88	90	89	87	88	89	89	88	88	88	88
Slovenia	90	**92**	90	93	90	91	93	92	92	89	94	93	91	93	91	95
South Africa	86	**na**	na	na	na	na	na	na	na	na	na	na	na	na	na	na
Spain	93	**90**	89	91	87	90	92	93	87	90	91	92	86	88	90	90
Sweden	90	**84**	79	89	74	85	89	89	81	84	82	85	84	87	82	88
Switzerland	91	**na**	na	na	na	na	na	na	na	na	na	na	na	na	na	na
Taiwan	na	**na**	na	na	na	na	na	na	na	na	na	na	na	na	na	na
Tanzania	na	**na**	na	na	na	na	na	na	na	na	na	na	na	na	na	na
Turkey	53	**67**	64	70	63	70	75	74	58	58	77	62	58	71	66	65
Uganda	na	**na**	na	na	na	na	na	na	na	na	na	na	na	na	na	na
Ukraine	na	**64**	61	67	55	66	69	73	68	52	70	62	62	67	62	65
United States	85	**na**	na	na	na	na	na	na	na	na	na	na	na	na	na	na
Uruguay	na	**na**	na	na	na	na	na	na	na	na	na	na	na	na	na	na
Venezuela	na	**na**	na	na	na	na	na	na	na	na	na	na	na	na	na	na
Vietnam	na	**na**	na	na	na	na	na	na	na	na	na	na	na	na	na	na
Zimbabwe	na	**na**	na	na	na	na	na	na	na	na	na	na	na	na	na	na
Total	83	**83**	80	85	78	83	85	84	82	81	84	83	81	83	83	85

RANKING

Country	2000
Croatia	97
Malta	96
Greece	94
France	94
Slovenia	92
Lithuania	90
Spain	90
Italy	89
Slovakia	88
Estonia	86
Poland	86
Belgium	85
Luxembourg	85
Romania	84
Hungary	84
Sweden	84
Ireland	82
Czech Republic	82
Austria	82
Latvia	82
Denmark	81
Portugal	81
Finland	80
Belarus	80
Bulgaria	79
Iceland	78
Northern Ireland	75
Great Britain	75
Germany	71
Turkey	67
Netherlands	67
Ukraine	64
Russian Fed.	59
Total	83

E021_1) MORE POWER TO LOCAL AUTHORITIES

Here is a list of various changes in our way of life that might take place in the near future. If it were to happen do you think it would be a good thing, a bad thing, or don't you mind?. More power to local authorities.

Good (%)

(EVS: V199)

Country	Wave 1990	Wave 2000	Gender Male	Gender Female	Age 16-29	Age 30-49	Age 50+	Education Lower	Education Middle	Education Upper	Income Lower	Income Middle	Income Upper	Values Mat	Values Mixed	Values Postm.
Albania	na	**na**	na	na	na	na	na	na	na	na	na	na	na	na	na	na
Algeria	na	**na**	na	na	na	na	na	na	na	na	na	na	na	na	na	na
Argentina	na	**na**	na	na	na	na	na	na	na	na	na	na	na	na	na	na
Armenia	na	**na**	na	na	na	na	na	na	na	na	na	na	na	na	na	na
Australia	na	**na**	na	na	na	na	na	na	na	na	na	na	na	na	na	na
Austria	na	**38**	39	37	34	40	39	40	37	36	37	44	36	46	41	34
Azerbaijan	na	**na**	na	na	na	na	na	na	na	na	na	na	na	na	na	na
Bangladesh	na	**na**	na	na	na	na	na	na	na	na	na	na	na	na	na	na
Belarus	na	**32**	34	31	29	29	39	32	32	35	33	33	31	32	34	33
Belgium	na	**32**	33	32	26	29	38	33	31	33	37	34	28	32	32	35
Bosnia and Herz.	na	**na**	na	na	na	na	na	na	na	na	na	na	na	na	na	na
Brazil	na	**na**	na	na	na	na	na	na	na	na	na	na	na	na	na	na
Bulgaria	na	**51**	57	46	38	52	58	50	50	56	56	54	46	46	55	61
Canada	na	**na**	na	na	na	na	na	na	na	na	na	na	na	na	na	na
Chile	na	**na**	na	na	na	na	na	na	na	na	na	na	na	na	na	na
China	na	**na**	na	na	na	na	na	na	na	na	na	na	na	na	na	na
Colombia	na	**na**	na	na	na	na	na	na	na	na	na	na	na	na	na	na
Croatia	na	**46**	50	43	41	46	49	52	42	48	55	46	42	45	45	50
Czech Republic	na	**70**	71	69	57	71	76	68	70	79	71	72	68	69	70	79
Denmark	na	**44**	43	45	42	49	39	40	47	50	39	47	53	33	42	58
Dominican Rep.	na	**na**	na	na	na	na	na	na	na	na	na	na	na	na	na	na
Egypt	na	**na**	na	na	na	na	na	na	na	na	na	na	na	na	na	na
El Salvador	na	**na**	na	na	na	na	na	na	na	na	na	na	na	na	na	na
Estonia	na	**52**	57	48	42	52	57	50	51	56	54	58	45	45	56	51
Finland	na	**46**	42	50	39	50	48	44	50	51	42	50	44	38	49	49
France	na	**52**	51	54	42	54	56	55	46	50	56	54	47	52	53	51
Georgia	na	**na**	na	na	na	na	na	na	na	na	na	na	na	na	na	na
Germany	na	**46**	48	44	39	45	50	45	47	48	43	46	52	49	43	53
Great Britain	na	**38**	37	38	46	38	34	39	38	37	41	33	40	na	na	na
Greece	na	**51**	52	50	44	53	62	55	47	54	51	52	48	47	51	54
Hungary	na	**25**	25	24	31	25	20	28	17	20	20	26	27	23	26	11
Iceland	na	**49**	49	50	37	55	53	52	46	50	47	51	51	54	46	58
India	na	**na**	na	na	na	na	na	na	na	na	na	na	na	na	na	na
Indonesia	na	**na**	na	na	na	na	na	na	na	na	na	na	na	na	na	na
Iran	na	**na**	na	na	na	na	na	na	na	na	na	na	na	na	na	na
Ireland	na	**47**	48	46	34	46	59	53	45	42	58	44	41	49	48	40
Israel	na	**na**	na	na	na	na	na	na	na	na	na	na	na	na	na	na
Italy	na	**42**	43	41	38	41	45	41	42	46	42	42	46	43	42	44
Japan	na	**na**	na	na	na	na	na	na	na	na	na	na	na	na	na	na
Jordan	na	**na**	na	na	na	na	na	na	na	na	na	na	na	na	na	na
Korea, South	na	**na**	na	na	na	na	na	na	na	na	na	na	na	na	na	na
Latvia	na	**42**	41	43	23	38	53	46	38	49	43	43	41	40	44	34
Lithuania	na	**50**	50	50	50	48	53	56	48	48	50	47	51	50	51	46
Luxembourg	na	**38**	40	36	32	35	46	44	35	38	40	39	40	39	38	38
Macedonia	na	**na**	na	na	na	na	na	na	na	na	na	na	na	na	na	na
Malta	na	**68**	68	67	62	65	74	68	66	74	65	76	73	68	67	74
Mexico	na	**na**	na	na	na	na	na	na	na	na	na	na	na	na	na	na
Moldova	na	**na**	na	na	na	na	na	na	na	na	na	na	na	na	na	na
Montenegro	na	**na**	na	na	na	na	na	na	na	na	na	na	na	na	na	na
Morocco	na	**na**	na	na	na	na	na	na	na	na	na	na	na	na	na	na
Netherlands	na	**26**	23	29	26	28	25	19	28	31	27	28	26	22	26	29
New Zealand	na	**na**	na	na	na	na	na	na	na	na	na	na	na	na	na	na
Nigeria	na	**na**	na	na	na	na	na	na	na	na	na	na	na	na	na	na
Northern Ireland	na	**48**	47	49	49	47	51	52	45	48	60	46	46	50	48	46
Norway	na	**na**	na	na	na	na	na	na	na	na	na	na	na	na	na	na
Pakistan	na	**na**	na	na	na	na	na	na	na	na	na	na	na	na	na	na
Peru	na	**na**	na	na	na	na	na	na	na	na	na	na	na	na	na	na
Philippines	na	**na**	na	na	na	na	na	na	na	na	na	na	na	na	na	na
Poland	na	**55**	58	51	44	55	61	51	56	66	53	55	56	47	59	56
Portugal	na	**57**	58	57	46	56	66	61	54	36	62	56	52	59	55	62
Puerto Rico	na	**na**	na	na	na	na	na	na	na	na	na	na	na	na	na	na
Romania	na	**71**	67	75	60	71	76	74	68	72	70	73	69	72	71	58
Russian Fed.	na	**54**	52	56	43	54	62	58	53	54	52	55	57	57	50	46
Serbia	na	**na**	na	na	na	na	na	na	na	na	na	na	na	na	na	na
Singapore	na	**na**	na	na	na	na	na	na	na	na	na	na	na	na	na	na
Slovakia	na	**74**	75	73	69	74	77	68	75	83	74	71	76	71	77	77
Slovenia	na	**42**	43	41	27	38	56	44	40	45	49	43	46	44	41	41
South Africa	na	**na**	na	na	na	na	na	na	na	na	na	na	na	na	na	na
Spain	na	**40**	41	39	29	34	52	51	34	30	44	40	38	49	38	35
Sweden	na	**35**	33	37	37	34	35	27	37	39	39	35	32	36	34	42
Switzerland	na	**na**	na	na	na	na	na	na	na	na	na	na	na	na	na	na
Taiwan	na	**na**	na	na	na	na	na	na	na	na	na	na	na	na	na	na
Tanzania	na	**na**	na	na	na	na	na	na	na	na	na	na	na	na	na	na
Turkey	na	**59**	60	58	54	62	67	63	53	57	60	60	56	66	59	53
Uganda	na	**na**	na	na	na	na	na	na	na	na	na	na	na	na	na	na
Ukraine	na	**57**	57	57	49	54	66	69	53	61	58	55	60	59	55	67
United States	na	**na**	na	na	na	na	na	na	na	na	na	na	na	na	na	na
Uruguay	na	**na**	na	na	na	na	na	na	na	na	na	na	na	na	na	na
Venezuela	na	**na**	na	na	na	na	na	na	na	na	na	na	na	na	na	na
Vietnam	na	**na**	na	na	na	na	na	na	na	na	na	na	na	na	na	na
Zimbabwe	na	**na**	na	na	na	na	na	na	na	na	na	na	na	na	na	na
Total	na	**47**	48	47	41	47	52	48	47	49	49	48	47	49	48	47

RANKING

Country	2000
Slovakia	74
Romania	71
Czech Republic	70
Malta	68
Turkey	59
Portugal	57
Ukraine	57
Poland	55
Russian Fed.	54
France	52
Estonia	52
Bulgaria	51
Greece	51
Lithuania	50
Iceland	49
Northern Ireland	48
Ireland	47
Finland	46
Croatia	46
Germany	46
Denmark	44
Italy	42
Latvia	42
Slovenia	42
Spain	40
Austria	38
Luxembourg	38
Great Britain	38
Sweden	35
Belarus	32
Belgium	32
Netherlands	26
Hungary	25
Total	47

E22) In the long run, do you think the scientific advances we are making will help or harm mankind?

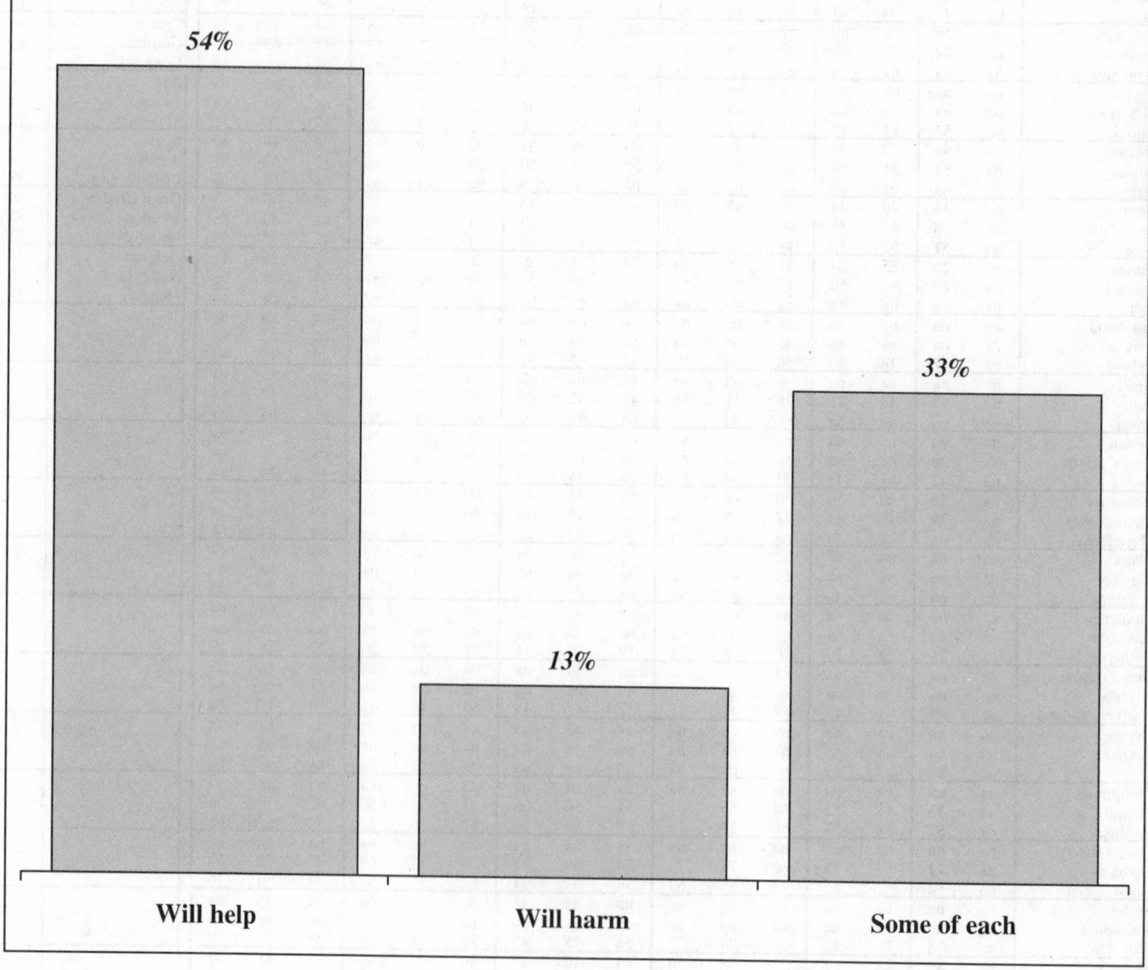

E022) OPINION ABOUT SCIENTIFIC ADVANCE

In the long run, do you think the scientific advances we are making will help or harm mankind?

Will help (%) (WVS: V132; EVS: o25)

Country	Wave		Gender		Age			Education			Income			Values		
	1990	2000	Male	Female	16-29	30-49	50+	Lower	Middle	Upper	Lower	Middle	Upper	Mat	Mixed	Postm.
Albania	na	**55**	56	54	52	56	57	55	55	55	54	55	55	55	56	50
Algeria	na	**55**	55	55	53	53	63	67	59	42	61	57	51	59	55	44
Argentina	47	**51**	52	50	53	52	48	50	50	61	49	50	55	52	49	53
Armenia	na	**74**	76	73	78	71	72	69	76	68	75	72	75	76	72	77
Australia	na	**57**	62	52	52	60	57	50	54	66	51	59	65	55	57	58
Austria	31	**35**	39	32	41	37	31	29	41	42	33	32	39	26	37	37
Azerbaijan	na	**61**	61	61	61	63	57	55	62	62	62	64	59	61	63	65
Bangladesh	na	**70**	67	73	67	71	74	74	68	63	72	68	72	69	71	67
Belarus	38	**56**	58	54	51	60	55	51	58	55	54	55	60	56	58	54
Belgium	34	**na**	na	na	na	na	na	na	na	na	na	na	na	na	na	na
Bosnia and Herz.	na	**54**	54	54	54	52	56	58	55	46	58	57	50	60	51	74
Brazil	64	**66**	68	64	65	66	67	63	67	74	64	66	67	65	66	71
Bulgaria	62	**na**	na	na	na	na	na	na	na	na	na	na	na	na	na	na
Canada	55	**52**	60	44	52	52	52	49	50	58	49	52	56	55	52	51
Chile	43	**42**	44	40	47	41	38	43	43	37	45	38	43	38	44	43
China	58	**80**	79	81	64	81	89	91	74	51	82	81	75	78	77	75
Colombia	na	**67**	67	67	70	66	65	67	67	68	68	65	70	68	67	69
Croatia	na	**38**	41	35	35	38	41	44	35	35	42	39	36	47	38	33
Czech Republic	30	**na**	na	na	na	na	na	na	na	na	na	na	na	na	na	na
Denmark	43	**na**	na	na	na	na	na	na	na	na	na	na	na	na	na	na
Dominican Rep.	na	**44**	54	37	40	50	64	53	50	40	47	48	46	51	44	32
Egypt	na	**80**	77	83	78	80	82	88	78	63	85	82	74	84	77	71
El Salvador	na	**49**	48	50	52	50	42	50	47	51	55	46	48	na	na	na
Estonia	52	**na**	na	na	na	na	na	na	na	na	na	na	na	na	na	na
Finland	42	**na**	na	na	na	na	na	na	na	na	na	na	na	na	na	na
France	42	**na**	na	na	na	na	na	na	na	na	na	na	na	na	na	na
Georgia	na	**70**	70	70	72	69	70	78	71	63	75	71	64	70	70	73
Germany	52	**51**	61	44	56	54	47	49	53	53	51	54	58	53	53	45
Great Britain	48	**40**	44	36	42	43	35	39	38	46	34	47	42	na	na	na
Greece	na	**na**	na	na	na	na	na	na	na	na	na	na	na	na	na	na
Hungary	55	**na**	na	na	na	na	na	na	na	na	na	na	na	na	na	na
Iceland	54	**66**	75	58	66	69	64	62	68	73	60	69	70	67	66	70
India	51	**60**	62	56	65	60	52	57	64	59	58	62	59	59	59	50
Indonesia	na	**49**	53	47	39	54	50	59	47	46	51	51	48	57	45	46
Iran	na	**73**	73	74	70	74	82	81	74	62	74	73	72	75	71	73
Ireland	40	**41**	41	41	43	38	42	38	42	44	41	35	47	42	40	45
Israel	na	**na**	na	na	na	na	na	na	na	na	na	na	na	na	na	na
Italy	37	**31**	36	26	27	31	33	29	31	35	27	32	35	30	32	29
Japan	26	**24**	32	17	17	22	29	30	20	29	25	21	26	24	23	25
Jordan	na	**68**	71	66	63	70	76	75	64	60	70	71	69	72	67	58
Korea, South	40	**49**	54	44	49	46	55	61	47	51	49	50	48	49	50	40
Latvia	34	**na**	na	na	na	na	na	na	na	na	na	na	na	na	na	na
Lithuania	61	**62**	68	57	63	67	56	56	63	67	64	63	63	53	64	73
Luxembourg	na	**na**	na	na	na	na	na	na	na	na	na	na	na	na	na	na
Macedonia	na	**65**	67	63	69	61	67	69	63	62	67	62	65	63	66	76
Malta	na	**na**	na	na	na	na	na	na	na	na	na	na	na	na	na	na
Mexico	44	**50**	52	49	55	48	46	47	53	55	49	48	57	47	49	60
Moldova	na	**56**	54	57	47	58	60	58	60	46	59	56	52	55	58	37
Montenegro	na	**44**	47	41	46	46	41	45	42	45	29	43	54	50	41	19
Morocco	na	**78**	76	80	73	80	87	84	61	47	78	74	80	82	76	58
Netherlands	37	**na**	na	na	na	na	na	na	na	na	na	na	na	na	na	na
New Zealand	na	**26**	34	20	19	25	30	24	21	32	20	23	34	28	26	29
Nigeria	79	**87**	88	87	89	87	84	87	88	87	86	90	88	90	86	91
Northern Ireland	46	**38**	40	36	41	37	37	35	39	42	38	33	37	37	37	43
Norway	36	**39**	53	25	37	43	34	30	39	47	na	na	na	36	38	46
Pakistan	na	**41**	41	42	41	43	39	44	39	38	36	45	39	46	35	58
Peru	na	**54**	54	53	52	56	52	58	55	50	55	58	46	56	54	52
Philippines	na	**68**	69	68	70	69	65	70	65	71	63	72	69	65	71	70
Poland	70	**na**	na	na	na	na	na	na	na	na	na	na	na	na	na	na
Portugal	47	**na**	na	na	na	na	na	na	na	na	na	na	na	na	na	na
Puerto Rico	na	**46**	46	47	41	49	47	45	41	50	48	47	45	49	49	40
Romania	na	**na**	na	na	na	na	na	na	na	na	na	na	na	na	na	na
Russian Fed.	60	**na**	na	na	na	na	na	na	na	na	na	na	na	na	na	na
Serbia	na	**45**	43	46	40	43	48	46	45	41	45	46	48	45	46	43
Singapore	na	**39**	42	37	38	39	44	43	37	37	38	39	39	36	40	46
Slovakia	na	**na**	na	na	na	na	na	na	na	na	na	na	na	na	na	na
Slovenia	41	**35**	40	30	25	34	42	39	32	36	35	38	36	36	35	32
South Africa	57	**57**	57	57	54	60	56	60	53	57	57	61	54	53	60	51
Spain	46	**66**	68	64	65	68	65	66	65	70	67	75	62	65	68	60
Sweden	47	**44**	48	41	42	45	45	39	40	56	43	41	52	39	45	45
Switzerland	na	**39**	43	34	39	38	39	42	38	44	37	40	43	33	41	39
Taiwan	na	**36**	36	36	21	32	56	48	37	24	46	34	27	35	32	51
Tanzania	na	**49**	48	49	47	49	53	56	41	41	55	45	51	50	49	41
Turkey	72	**86**	88	85	84	88	87	88	85	84	87	87	83	89	86	84
Uganda	na	**58**	62	55	70	50	33	54	60	54	56	58	55	57	60	56
Ukraine	na	**na**	na	na	na	na	na	na	na	na	na	na	na	na	na	na
United States	63	**56**	61	50	44	56	65	47	58	59	52	55	65	56	56	55
Uruguay	na	**40**	42	38	33	41	42	37	42	48	42	36	43	50	39	36
Venezuela	na	**63**	63	62	62	64	62	59	64	63	61	56	68	64	63	61
Vietnam	na	**78**	74	83	69	79	85	82	77	60	79	82	74	82	77	76
Zimbabwe	na	**72**	70	74	76	68	65	74	70	23	76	74	64	72	71	80
Total	48	**54**	57	52	55	55	52	57	53	51	55	55	55	58	54	50

RANKING	
Country	2000
Nigeria	87
Turkey	86
Egypt	80
China	80
Vietnam	78
Morocco	78
Armenia	74
Iran	73
Zimbabwe	72
Georgia	70
Bangladesh	70
Jordan	68
Philippines	68
Colombia	67
Iceland	66
Brazil	66
Spain	66
Macedonia	65
Venezuela	63
Lithuania	62
Azerbaijan	61
India	60
Uganda	58
South Africa	57
Australia	57
United States	56
Belarus	56
Moldova	56
Albania	55
Algeria	55
Bosnia and Herz.	54
Peru	54
Canada	52
Germany	51
Argentina	51
Mexico	50
Indonesia	49
El Salvador	49
Korea, South	49
Tanzania	49
Puerto Rico	46
Serbia	45
Sweden	44
Dominican Rep.	44
Montenegro	44
Chile	42
Pakistan	41
Ireland	41
Great Britain	40
Uruguay	40
Singapore	39
Switzerland	39
Norway	39
Croatia	38
Northern Ireland	38
Taiwan	36
Austria	35
Slovenia	35
Italy	31
New Zealand	26
Japan	24
Total	54

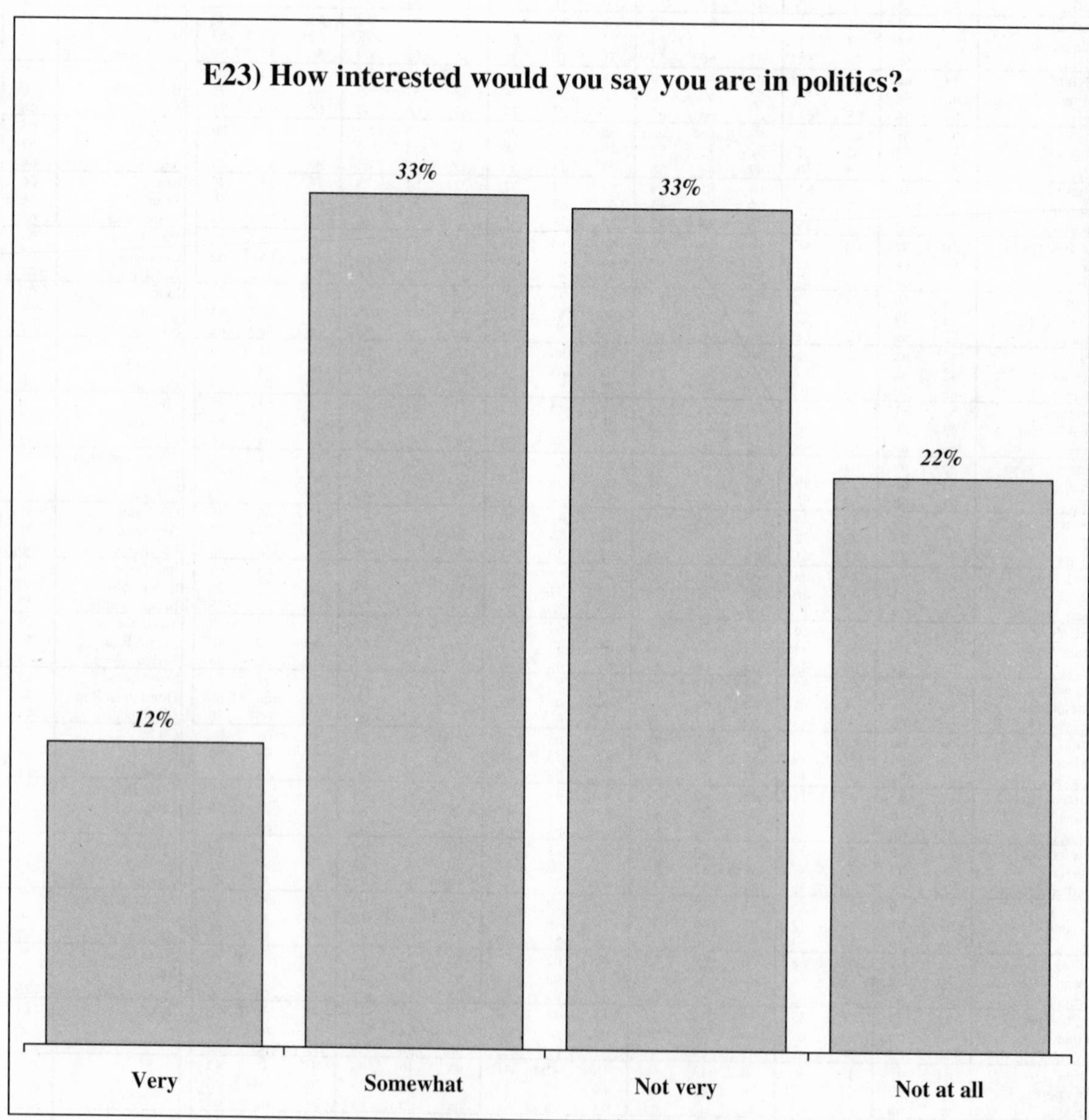
E23) How interested would you say you are in politics?
12%
33%
33%
22%
Very
Somewhat
Not very
Not at all

E023) INTERESTED IN POLITICS

How interested would you say you are in politics?

(WVS: V133; EVS: o17)

Very / Somewhat interested (%)

Country	Wave		Gender		Age			Education			Income			Values		
	1990	2000	Male	Female	16-29	30-49	50+	Lower	Middle	Upper	Lower	Middle	Upper	Mat	Mixed	Postm.
Albania	na	**41**	54	28	26	44	47	35	43	49	38	41	43	37	43	49
Algeria	na	**24**	29	20	21	29	23	17	21	33	21	22	27	19	26	36
Argentina	30	**18**	19	18	13	18	23	13	23	36	13	18	24	12	19	23
Armenia	na	**52**	61	44	43	57	57	45	49	64	51	53	53	48	57	37
Australia	na	**56**	59	53	40	60	65	44	51	71	51	57	66	45	55	60
Austria	54	**67**	75	60	61	67	71	58	71	89	59	68	73	47	67	75
Azerbaijan	na	**43**	49	36	42	43	45	33	37	55	39	46	46	36	54	66
Bangladesh	na	**41**	55	23	40	40	46	30	48	60	30	39	53	37	44	41
Belarus	na	**47**	58	37	46	51	42	27	51	65	38	49	55	39	54	68
Belgium	30	**39**	48	30	32	41	40	19	38	56	31	34	50	24	38	62
Bosnia and Herz.	na	**39**	50	29	29	39	49	34	37	48	37	39	41	32	41	51
Brazil	46	**31**	32	30	32	30	31	20	34	61	22	30	41	18	33	55
Bulgaria	73	**49**	54	45	35	57	49	40	50	64	46	54	53	42	60	53
Canada	58	**49**	55	43	35	48	57	42	43	64	39	50	58	42	45	57
Chile	37	**25**	30	21	26	25	25	19	25	39	21	23	35	20	24	39
China	67	**71**	79	62	75	66	79	65	73	83	68	72	73	71	75	81
Colombia	na	**29**	31	27	25	33	28	22	23	42	22	26	39	27	27	36
Croatia	na	**na**	na	na	na	na	na	na	na	na	na	na	na	na	na	na
Czech Republic	na	**70**	72	67	57	70	77	63	75	86	68	70	72	62	72	82
Denmark	54	**61**	67	55	55	59	65	49	66	80	55	60	74	34	61	76
Dominican Rep.	na	**46**	45	47	43	50	64	34	43	48	47	47	45	38	47	50
Egypt	na	**43**	54	30	40	42	48	36	46	55	42	43	47	37	48	51
El Salvador	na	**15**	17	14	19	12	15	9	16	33	9	14	31	na	na	na
Estonia	60	**na**	na	na	na	na	na	na	na	na	na	na	na	na	na	na
Finland	48	**28**	32	24	22	25	34	24	30	44	23	27	34	17	31	40
France	38	**37**	45	28	27	36	42	29	38	56	28	36	50	25	37	53
Georgia	na	**50**	53	47	34	57	58	45	48	57	53	50	46	50	49	60
Germany	85	**61**	71	52	57	61	62	50	66	87	51	60	64	50	63	75
Great Britain	49	**37**	47	28	31	36	43	27	37	67	25	33	51	na	na	na
Greece	na	**42**	52	35	35	44	53	39	36	47	39	44	49	40	41	49
Hungary	52	**na**	na	na	na	na	na	na	na	na	na	na	na	na	na	na
Iceland	47	**50**	57	44	37	53	57	39	51	72	41	48	62	41	49	74
India	47	**45**	56	28	46	45	43	36	51	56	40	42	50	46	52	54
Indonesia	na	**37**	45	30	54	38	28	19	36	52	32	41	45	36	38	44
Iran	na	**56**	60	51	62	56	40	40	57	70	54	57	58	47	61	72
Ireland	37	**43**	50	37	40	42	47	35	42	63	29	43	56	38	42	61
Israel	na	**70**	77	65	65	72	74	57	69	80	61	75	77	74	72	58
Italy	29	**32**	42	24	29	34	33	22	35	53	25	34	41	19	32	42
Japan	62	**64**	72	57	44	53	81	67	61	69	65	63	65	58	66	77
Jordan	na	**51**	50	51	54	52	42	37	56	70	42	48	66	41	58	72
Korea, South	73	**50**	60	39	39	50	63	46	51	49	50	49	51	45	55	50
Latvia	79	**na**	na	na	na	na	na	na	na	na	na	na	na	na	na	na
Lithuania	74	**46**	52	40	34	49	51	38	44	69	42	44	53	36	51	50
Luxembourg	na	**47**	50	45	30	50	55	32	52	63	34	52	64	39	47	62
Macedonia	na	**46**	54	39	36	47	53	40	48	55	41	49	53	45	49	44
Malta	na	**na**	na	na	na	na	na	na	na	na	na	na	na	na	na	na
Mexico	38	**34**	38	31	36	32	33	28	38	53	31	35	42	25	39	40
Moldova	na	**48**	53	43	36	54	50	33	51	57	45	49	49	42	54	60
Montenegro	na	**45**	55	35	40	44	50	36	49	57	48	44	49	43	49	55
Morocco	na	**20**	26	13	25	18	12	14	36	56	18	23	22	11	25	41
Netherlands	58	**67**	72	61	57	67	71	51	67	81	60	68	74	48	65	79
New Zealand	na	**60**	63	57	41	58	69	56	56	65	63	54	62	51	58	66
Nigeria	35	**53**	61	44	55	50	47	51	52	57	50	51	57	49	54	60
Northern Ireland	34	**40**	50	31	32	40	44	39	36	51	31	42	44	32	42	56
Norway	72	**69**	72	65	61	73	69	58	70	78	na	na	na	51	69	87
Pakistan	na	**30**	38	21	30	30	30	24	36	39	22	33	37	26	36	25
Peru	na	**48**	52	43	50	46	45	36	46	58	40	50	58	39	50	53
Philippines	na	**50**	51	48	50	52	45	48	49	53	50	45	57	50	50	50
Poland	49	**42**	49	35	31	42	48	35	45	65	41	46	35	38	43	58
Portugal	31	**29**	37	23	31	33	26	26	30	53	13	31	40	24	31	40
Puerto Rico	na	**42**	48	39	37	43	44	27	33	49	33	42	51	41	41	47
Romania	18	**na**	na	na	na	na	na	na	na	na	na	na	na	na	na	na
Russian Fed.	53	**39**	49	31	29	40	45	31	36	54	34	41	43	37	42	56
Serbia	na	**38**	46	31	36	39	38	28	40	50	33	39	48	31	46	48
Singapore	na	**36**	39	33	38	35	33	30	39	41	31	35	41	32	36	54
Slovakia	na	**na**	na	na	na	na	na	na	na	na	na	na	na	na	na	na
Slovenia	58	**42**	50	35	33	38	53	32	43	58	38	43	52	44	42	43
South Africa	57	**52**	58	43	47	58	43	50	53	63	54	53	49	40	59	61
Spain	25	**28**	35	22	27	33	25	20	31	49	21	29	41	22	28	43
Sweden	47	**na**	na	na	na	na	na	na	na	na	na	na	na	na	na	na
Switzerland	66	**44**	51	36	35	42	49	31	43	74	41	36	52	28	47	47
Taiwan	na	**41**	44	38	32	46	33	30	50	46	38	41	46	35	48	54
Tanzania	na	**72**	71	72	69	71	81	76	66	67	74	73	69	71	74	79
Turkey	48	**40**	49	32	40	41	38	32	47	74	32	44	58	31	42	55
Uganda	na	**50**	60	41	46	57	48	48	50	65	59	62	56	51	50	54
Ukraine	na	**42**	51	35	37	41	46	34	39	56	41	43	45	38	45	75
United States	61	**66**	69	62	59	61	78	57	62	71	63	66	68	59	65	70
Uruguay	na	**37**	42	34	36	42	34	25	51	64	24	36	53	31	37	45
Venezuela	na	**24**	28	21	22	25	29	20	24	31	24	23	28	26	24	21
Vietnam	na	**80**	88	72	77	81	80	76	86	82	72	80	84	76	86	82
Zimbabwe	na	**31**	38	26	32	32	30	33	29	22	34	32	31	28	33	37
Total	52	**45**	52	39	40	46	49	36	46	58	41	45	51	39	48	56

RANKING

Country	2000
Vietnam	80
Tanzania	72
China	71
Israel	70
Czech Republic	70
Norway	69
Austria	67
Netherlands	67
United States	66
Japan	64
Germany	61
Denmark	61
New Zealand	60
Iran	56
Australia	56
Nigeria	53
Armenia	52
South Africa	52
Jordan	51
Uganda	50
Iceland	50
Philippines	50
Korea, South	50
Georgia	50
Bulgaria	49
Canada	49
Moldova	48
Peru	48
Luxembourg	47
Belarus	47
Macedonia	46
Dominican Rep.	46
Lithuania	46
Montenegro	45
India	45
Switzerland	44
Ireland	43
Azerbaijan	43
Egypt	43
Ukraine	42
Slovenia	42
Puerto Rico	42
Poland	42
Greece	42
Bangladesh	41
Taiwan	41
Albania	41
Turkey	40
Northern Ireland	40
Bosnia and Herz.	39
Russian Fed.	39
Belgium	39
Serbia	38
Great Britain	37
Uruguay	37
Indonesia	37
France	37
Singapore	36
Mexico	34
Italy	32
Zimbabwe	31
Brazil	31
Pakistan	30
Colombia	29
Portugal	29
Spain	28
Finland	28
Chile	25
Venezuela	24
Algeria	24
Morocco	20
Argentina	18
El Salvador	15
Total	45

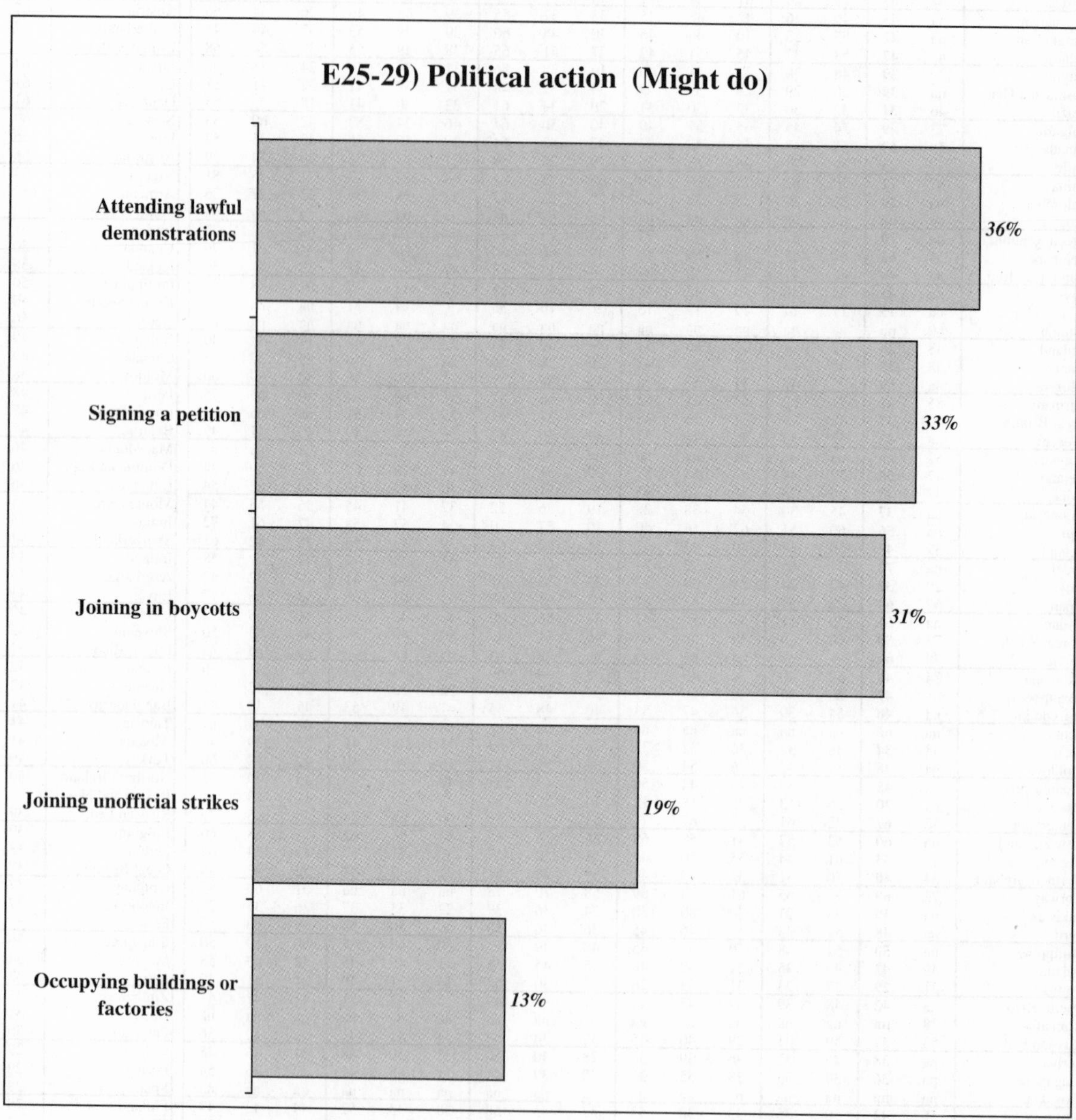

E25-29) Political action (Might do)
Attending lawful demonstrations
36%
Signing a petition
33%
Joining in boycotts
31%
Joining unofficial strikes
19%
Occupying buildings or factories
13%

E025) POLITICAL ACTION: SIGNING A PETITION

I'd like you to tell me, for each one, whether you have actually done any of these things, whether you might do it or would never, under any circumstances, do it.

(WVS: V134; EVS: V179)

Might do (%)

Country	Wave		Gender		Age			Education			Income			Values		
	1990	2000	Male	Female	16-29	30-49	50+	Lower	Middle	Upper	Lower	Middle	Upper	Mat	Mixed	Postm.
Albania	na	**43**	47	37	42	46	39	44	40	47	44	41	43	34	49	44
Algeria	na	**29**	33	25	33	27	22	17	28	38	27	35	26	27	31	29
Argentina	33	**31**	31	32	35	34	26	31	35	23	30	33	31	30	33	31
Armenia	na	**39**	42	36	44	37	36	42	39	38	45	37	36	40	37	55
Australia	na	**16**	18	15	23	14	12	18	20	10	16	17	13	21	17	14
Austria	30	**24**	24	24	29	23	22	29	22	12	28	24	21	31	23	23
Azerbaijan	na	**16**	19	13	15	18	11	8	16	17	14	16	18	10	26	25
Bangladesh	na	**42**	48	35	45	42	34	41	47	38	44	37	48	38	46	44
Belarus	52	**28**	34	23	34	32	18	10	32	45	19	31	35	21	33	52
Belgium	27	**20**	20	20	19	17	24	26	20	15	27	20	15	27	21	8
Bosnia and Herz.	na	**50**	51	48	52	50	47	46	49	53	47	50	50	47	50	53
Brazil	30	**35**	35	35	37	35	30	40	35	15	39	40	26	41	33	25
Bulgaria	39	**37**	42	33	42	45	28	21	43	49	25	42	45	35	43	43
Canada	15	**19**	19	18	24	17	18	26	20	11	21	20	15	22	20	16
Chile	34	**27**	29	25	32	27	23	23	27	38	25	26	33	22	29	32
China	na	**na**	na	na	na	na	na	na	na	na	na	na	na	na	na	na
Colombia	na	**49**	51	46	52	48	42	45	51	51	47	49	51	47	47	53
Croatia	na	**59**	61	58	56	59	62	61	60	54	54	64	55	65	61	50
Czech Republic	na	**27**	27	27	33	28	22	28	28	20	27	28	27	32	26	26
Denmark	25	**27**	29	26	38	26	22	30	27	21	26	26	29	34	28	24
Dominican Rep.	na	**59**	59	58	62	53	40	38	61	61	50	56	70	56	57	68
Egypt	na	**37**	38	37	37	35	42	39	37	34	39	37	36	36	38	40
El Salvador	na	**41**	41	41	48	39	34	39	43	44	37	47	36	na	na	na
Estonia	39	**33**	36	30	37	34	29	31	33	35	27	33	37	26	38	22
Finland	46	**37**	40	34	38	38	34	37	38	29	38	37	34	42	36	31
France	29	**22**	24	21	32	20	20	24	23	17	23	21	21	26	23	18
Georgia	na	**15**	15	15	15	16	13	11	16	14	15	15	15	13	16	19
Germany	25	**35**	38	33	42	31	36	39	34	23	38	35	27	38	37	25
Great Britain	17	**15**	14	16	19	11	18	20	14	8	16	12	11	na	na	na
Greece	na	**38**	36	40	39	38	34	47	45	31	42	39	36	42	40	32
Hungary	30	**32**	35	30	40	35	25	28	42	34	25	34	35	31	33	54
Iceland	37	**37**	36	38	40	32	42	43	37	25	38	38	33	45	36	25
India	45	**29**	29	27	32	30	22	26	30	32	24	32	27	27	33	39
Indonesia	na	**21**	26	16	38	19	16	9	20	31	16	23	25	17	24	43
Iran	na	**na**	na	na	na	na	na	na	na	na	na	na	na	na	na	na
Ireland	40	**26**	25	26	32	21	25	29	27	16	30	27	20	28	27	17
Israel	na	**30**	31	29	32	30	27	29	32	28	31	32	29	32	30	32
Italy	35	**30**	29	32	38	27	30	35	29	21	34	34	26	35	31	28
Japan	25	**30**	33	26	46	28	25	29	28	32	31	26	28	28	32	23
Jordan	na	**9**	10	8	9	10	6	6	10	14	7	12	10	6	11	10
Korea, South	42	**37**	37	37	33	38	41	46	39	34	40	34	37	39	36	32
Latvia	23	**33**	36	31	41	34	28	28	35	33	31	29	37	31	34	41
Lithuania	29	**39**	41	37	46	37	36	36	40	38	32	37	39	41	37	45
Luxembourg	na	**32**	34	31	34	33	30	36	33	25	33	32	31	31	36	22
Macedonia	na	**40**	41	39	40	44	35	35	41	45	35	42	43	38	42	29
Malta	na	**36**	37	35	40	36	32	33	38	30	31	38	40	37	35	37
Mexico	44	**38**	42	35	48	34	31	32	45	45	33	44	42	32	41	48
Moldova	na	**22**	25	19	28	23	15	14	24	26	21	22	27	21	24	22
Montenegro	na	**51**	53	49	59	53	44	43	58	52	55	49	56	52	51	59
Morocco	na	**34**	36	31	39	30	27	32	42	39	42	36	31	24	40	42
Netherlands	33	**30**	28	31	40	25	29	34	33	22	25	29	31	26	32	25
New Zealand	na	**8**	9	7	11	7	7	9	7	6	11	7	5	14	7	3
Nigeria	32	**27**	32	22	32	23	19	22	27	37	25	27	32	26	28	29
Northern Ireland	27	**21**	17	24	26	20	18	20	26	14	17	22	21	23	20	18
Norway	28	**26**	27	25	25	23	30	30	26	22	na	na	na	30	26	18
Pakistan	na	**24**	35	13	26	22	30	23	26	26	24	29	20	24	25	25
Peru	na	**59**	59	58	64	58	46	57	61	55	60	59	57	56	59	63
Philippines	na	**23**	24	22	25	24	18	18	24	28	20	23	27	19	23	43
Poland	52	**29**	32	26	39	32	19	29	28	25	27	32	23	28	29	26
Portugal	46	**39**	43	36	46	47	28	35	52	29	24	39	52	37	43	33
Puerto Rico	na	**44**	45	43	50	47	39	40	48	43	47	43	43	33	46	46
Romania	na	**36**	44	28	49	35	29	24	41	43	29	37	42	30	42	36
Russian Fed.	44	**32**	38	26	33	33	29	27	32	35	30	31	35	28	37	32
Serbia	na	**36**	37	35	42	38	32	33	40	35	33	38	39	36	39	26
Singapore	na	**40**	40	40	53	31	17	26	46	51	32	40	50	27	42	68
Slovakia	na	**23**	24	21	31	21	18	22	24	18	20	27	21	21	25	17
Slovenia	34	**44**	47	41	46	44	41	43	45	38	42	43	43	45	45	40
South Africa	47	**43**	44	43	54	40	26	43	46	19	48	43	41	37	45	64
Spain	36	**37**	42	33	44	37	33	34	42	38	33	40	39	35	39	36
Sweden	24	**10**	12	9	10	8	13	14	9	9	12	10	8	11	11	7
Switzerland	17	**18**	19	17	25	16	16	26	17	5	22	15	11	14	19	15
Taiwan	na	**36**	39	33	45	39	22	23	36	47	31	37	42	31	41	41
Tanzania	na	**47**	50	42	52	45	44	39	55	59	36	48	63	45	49	42
Turkey	41	**42**	46	38	46	41	37	36	51	48	37	45	49	37	43	50
Uganda	na	**43**	52	34	51	37	28	39	44	44	40	47	54	45	42	39
Ukraine	na	**35**	40	31	40	37	32	26	36	37	29	44	34	30	38	44
United States	20	**16**	18	14	31	11	10	27	15	12	20	14	13	15	16	14
Uruguay	na	**30**	30	29	39	28	27	31	31	18	29	35	26	20	32	28
Venezuela	na	**68**	68	68	74	68	56	63	70	69	64	68	71	64	68	78
Vietnam	na	**47**	49	44	54	46	41	41	55	42	56	41	48	40	51	52
Zimbabwe	na	**34**	37	32	38	36	21	30	39	88	28	39	39	30	37	44
Total	34	**33**	35	31	39	32	28	31	35	32	31	34	33	31	34	31

RANKING

Country	2000
Venezuela	68
Croatia	59
Peru	59
Dominican Rep.	59
Montenegro	51
Bosnia and Herz.	50
Colombia	49
Tanzania	47
Vietnam	47
Puerto Rico	44
Slovenia	44
South Africa	43
Uganda	43
Albania	43
Bangladesh	42
Turkey	42
El Salvador	41
Macedonia	40
Singapore	40
Armenia	39
Portugal	39
Lithuania	39
Greece	38
Mexico	38
Egypt	37
Bulgaria	37
Iceland	37
Korea, South	37
Spain	37
Finland	37
Serbia	36
Romania	36
Taiwan	36
Malta	36
Germany	35
Ukraine	35
Brazil	35
Zimbabwe	34
Morocco	34
Latvia	33
Estonia	33
Luxembourg	32
Hungary	32
Russian Fed.	32
Argentina	31
Italy	30
Israel	30
Netherlands	30
Japan	30
Uruguay	30
Algeria	29
India	29
Poland	29
Belarus	28
Chile	27
Nigeria	27
Denmark	27
Czech Republic	27
Norway	26
Ireland	26
Pakistan	24
Austria	24
Philippines	23
Slovakia	23
France	22
Moldova	22
Northern Ireland	21
Indonesia	21
Belgium	20
Canada	19
Switzerland	18
Australia	16
Azerbaijan	16
United States	16
Great Britain	15
Georgia	15
Sweden	10
Jordan	9
New Zealand	8
Total	33

E026) POLITICAL ACTION: JOINING IN BOYCOTTS

I'd like you to tell me, for each one, whether you have actually done any of these things, whether you might do it or would never, under any circumstances, do it.

Might do (%)

(WVS: V135; EVS: V180)

Country	Wave		Gender		Age			Education			Income			Values		
	1990	2000	Male	Female	16-29	30-49	50+	Lower	Middle	Upper	Lower	Middle	Upper	Mat	Mixed	Postm.
Albania	na	**23**	31	15	29	21	21	19	25	27	22	21	27	16	27	41
Algeria	na	**30**	37	22	32	31	22	20	30	36	26	37	31	25	32	38
Argentina	9	**7**	9	6	11	8	3	7	8	10	3	7	11	4	8	8
Armenia	na	**22**	26	18	27	20	16	18	21	25	28	17	17	19	22	40
Australia	na	**43**	44	42	53	43	34	39	44	45	39	45	43	37	42	46
Austria	25	**34**	40	29	41	42	23	26	39	49	28	34	37	14	34	39
Azerbaijan	na	**12**	16	9	12	14	8	11	13	12	15	13	9	7	21	29
Bangladesh	na	**40**	48	29	44	37	38	36	44	44	39	38	43	35	44	48
Belarus	38	**21**	27	16	31	23	10	9	23	33	16	23	25	15	23	47
Belgium	28	**30**	36	23	42	36	19	18	28	40	20	29	37	16	32	39
Bosnia and Herz.	na	**45**	49	42	49	49	37	39	46	49	34	50	45	41	47	49
Brazil	36	**29**	31	27	29	32	23	23	32	40	23	31	35	19	30	48
Bulgaria	33	**27**	35	20	38	35	16	14	30	41	17	30	33	20	36	38
Canada	43	**42**	43	41	52	45	33	34	46	42	37	50	43	45	41	45
Chile	11	**13**	15	11	14	15	10	11	14	17	13	13	14	12	14	14
China	na	**na**	na	na	na	na	na	na	na	na	na	na	na	na	na	na
Colombia	na	**29**	31	27	31	30	21	19	32	39	20	33	34	19	20	31
Croatia	na	**57**	65	49	64	57	52	52	59	66	49	59	60	49	55	71
Czech Republic	na	**30**	36	25	36	35	23	28	30	41	21	32	38	27	31	36
Denmark	32	**37**	38	36	48	42	26	32	45	44	30	39	43	34	37	37
Dominican Rep.	na	**26**	29	24	25	28	27	21	25	27	17	35	23	17	26	37
Egypt	na	**30**	31	29	29	30	32	29	30	32	30	28	32	28	32	27
El Salvador	na	**na**	na	na	na	na	na	na	na	na	na	na	na	na	na	na
Estonia	40	**27**	34	21	31	32	20	19	28	40	13	24	38	20	31	37
Finland	69	**54**	58	49	65	59	42	48	62	57	49	55	60	55	53	52
France	40	**43**	48	38	54	47	33	38	47	53	37	40	51	34	44	54
Georgia	na	**10**	11	8	10	10	9	8	9	12	10	10	9	9	10	16
Germany	32	**42**	46	39	53	46	33	34	48	53	36	46	44	33	43	54
Great Britain	34	**44**	51	38	50	50	36	40	50	53	36	53	50	na	na	na
Greece	na	**22**	21	22	28	19	13	16	20	25	15	22	27	19	23	19
Hungary	14	**19**	22	15	22	26	10	12	26	38	16	18	20	13	23	27
Iceland	53	**59**	61	58	61	61	56	55	65	57	61	60	58	59	62	49
India	45	**27**	33	18	30	27	22	25	28	31	26	28	27	27	29	36
Indonesia	na	**20**	25	16	37	18	15	8	20	29	20	20	24	19	21	54
Iran	na	**na**	na	na	na	na	na	na	na	na	na	na	na	na	na	na
Ireland	33	**36**	38	34	52	35	24	22	43	45	25	45	39	32	38	34
Israel	na	**32**	35	28	33	36	25	25	30	38	23	34	44	33	32	45
Italy	46	**44**	45	42	53	49	33	34	49	56	31	47	54	29	44	52
Japan	53	**64**	66	63	54	68	65	54	63	73	61	64	68	62	66	71
Jordan	na	**6**	8	5	6	6	6	5	7	8	4	8	7	4	8	5
Korea, South	50	**62**	64	59	71	62	50	33	58	69	58	61	66	57	65	71
Latvia	37	**27**	32	22	34	33	19	16	29	33	20	25	38	23	28	42
Lithuania	60	**37**	43	33	38	47	29	22	42	48	20	33	45	30	40	47
Luxembourg	na	**40**	40	39	43	43	33	28	41	57	31	38	46	33	40	49
Macedonia	na	**40**	42	38	42	44	32	40	39	44	37	42	40	36	43	42
Malta	na	**28**	32	25	37	30	21	20	30	41	22	30	41	25	29	41
Mexico	35	**18**	20	16	22	17	13	13	21	26	20	19	19	9	22	19
Moldova	na	**13**	15	11	17	15	8	7	14	17	10	13	17	11	14	26
Montenegro	na	**57**	58	55	68	59	47	45	67	56	57	56	61	56	58	62
Morocco	na	**28**	32	23	32	25	23	26	34	33	28	34	27	20	34	34
Netherlands	36	**39**	43	34	49	44	27	32	42	41	35	41	40	27	41	37
New Zealand	na	**54**	58	51	62	59	48	49	56	60	51	59	58	55	56	60
Nigeria	25	**23**	28	18	26	20	15	19	25	27	24	25	22	21	25	16
Northern Ireland	30	**26**	26	26	36	29	20	19	31	36	21	26	35	19	31	24
Norway	52	**56**	56	57	62	61	46	52	59	57	na	na	na	49	57	62
Pakistan	na	**5**	9	1	6	5	6	5	6	4	4	7	4	5	6	8
Peru	na	**42**	43	40	43	44	32	35	42	45	42	42	40	41	43	36
Philippines	na	**12**	15	10	15	12	10	7	13	18	9	12	16	11	13	18
Poland	35	**24**	30	19	30	28	15	22	28	24	23	23	27	19	28	22
Portugal	31	**33**	39	27	45	40	20	24	49	53	20	31	40	29	37	41
Puerto Rico	na	**27**	32	24	35	27	23	15	26	30	20	30	31	18	25	37
Romania	na	**17**	22	12	22	17	13	9	18	23	11	15	22	11	21	25
Russian Fed.	36	**22**	29	16	25	24	18	16	22	27	21	21	25	18	28	43
Serbia	na	**33**	37	28	41	39	23	22	38	38	28	32	37	27	38	36
Singapore	na	**18**	20	16	24	13	8	11	19	33	10	19	24	12	18	37
Slovakia	na	**29**	36	23	34	37	16	19	32	43	20	28	36	24	33	52
Slovenia	46	**54**	63	46	65	58	42	37	59	67	47	57	65	43	54	65
South Africa	36	**29**	28	31	34	27	21	30	27	45	34	25	31	30	30	19
Spain	26	**23**	28	19	37	27	12	16	29	35	18	25	31	17	24	33
Sweden	62	**55**	57	53	59	53	54	59	59	45	54	56	54	64	58	43
Switzerland	na	**34**	37	32	41	41	22	22	37	36	30	33	37	27	33	44
Taiwan	na	**33**	34	31	43	34	21	19	32	45	26	32	39	29	37	32
Tanzania	na	**23**	26	18	27	21	18	12	32	39	15	18	36	19	23	44
Turkey	23	**29**	34	23	33	27	21	21	38	44	23	30	37	20	29	42
Uganda	na	**37**	47	28	38	40	25	37	37	49	40	46	43	41	35	39
Ukraine	na	**25**	34	17	31	28	18	16	27	24	19	32	25	19	30	18
United States	45	**51**	52	50	60	52	43	48	50	53	49	53	54	53	54	44
Uruguay	na	**18**	21	16	25	22	12	13	23	34	11	17	24	9	19	22
Venezuela	na	**6**	7	5	7	6	6	6	6	6	8	4	6	7	5	8
Vietnam	na	**16**	19	14	18	16	15	15	18	11	22	17	12	13	17	20
Zimbabwe	na	**29**	30	28	33	30	18	28	29	46	28	30	30	25	32	33
Total	37	**31**	35	28	35	33	25	25	33	37	27	32	35	24	34	39

RANKING	
Country	**2000**
Japan	64
Korea, South	62
Iceland	59
Croatia	57
Montenegro	57
Norway	56
Sweden	55
New Zealand	54
Slovenia	54
Finland	54
United States	51
Bosnia and Herz.	45
Great Britain	44
Italy	44
France	43
Australia	43
Canada	42
Germany	42
Peru	42
Bangladesh	40
Macedonia	40
Luxembourg	40
Netherlands	39
Lithuania	37
Uganda	37
Denmark	37
Ireland	36
Switzerland	34
Austria	34
Portugal	33
Taiwan	33
Serbia	33
Israel	32
Czech Republic	30
Egypt	30
Algeria	30
Belgium	30
South Africa	29
Brazil	29
Slovakia	29
Colombia	29
Zimbabwe	29
Turkey	29
Malta	28
Morocco	28
India	27
Bulgaria	27
Estonia	27
Puerto Rico	27
Latvia	27
Northern Ireland	26
Dominican Rep.	26
Ukraine	25
Poland	24
Spain	23
Albania	23
Nigeria	23
Tanzania	23
Russian Fed.	22
Armenia	22
Greece	22
Belarus	21
Indonesia	20
Hungary	19
Singapore	18
Uruguay	18
Mexico	18
Romania	17
Vietnam	16
Chile	13
Moldova	13
Azerbaijan	12
Philippines	12
Georgia	10
Argentina	7
Jordan	6
Venezuela	6
Pakistan	5
Total	31

E027) POLITICAL ACTION: ATTENDING LAWFUL DEMONSTRATIONS

I'd like you to tell me, for each one, whether you have actually done any of these things, whether you might do it or would never, under any circumstances, do it.

(WVS: V136; EVS: V181)

Might do (%)

Country	Wave		Gender		Age			Education			Income			Values		
	1990	2000	Male	Female	16-29	30-49	50+	Lower	Middle	Upper	Lower	Middle	Upper	Mat	Mixed	Postm.
Albania	na	**52**	50	54	54	52	51	54	53	46	57	53	46	57	50	40
Algeria	na	**30**	34	27	36	31	17	22	31	36	32	33	29	28	32	34
Argentina	21	**23**	24	22	32	23	14	19	30	24	22	23	24	16	24	27
Armenia	na	**28**	31	26	36	25	21	26	29	27	33	24	28	30	26	35
Australia	na	**42**	46	39	56	43	28	35	43	47	33	46	47	35	43	44
Austria	33	**36**	38	34	48	40	26	33	40	35	24	43	37	23	36	41
Azerbaijan	na	**22**	25	19	23	22	18	18	21	24	26	20	22	19	29	20
Bangladesh	na	**40**	51	26	43	39	34	33	48	45	35	40	45	32	47	48
Belarus	55	**30**	36	24	39	33	18	18	32	41	26	29	36	21	35	59
Belgium	29	**31**	32	30	43	32	23	25	34	29	22	31	33	29	32	26
Bosnia and Herz.	na	**49**	52	45	53	52	40	43	50	49	42	51	50	47	49	51
Brazil	40	**38**	36	40	50	36	18	35	44	30	37	40	36	39	38	34
Bulgaria	48	**38**	45	32	46	50	24	23	43	52	21	44	48	34	47	28
Canada	43	**41**	41	40	53	45	30	32	45	42	37	43	45	38	40	45
Chile	24	**23**	25	21	30	22	18	17	26	26	20	26	24	19	23	30
China	na	**na**	na	na	na	na	na	na	na	na	na	na	na	na	na	na
Colombia	na	**42**	45	40	47	41	36	36	46	47	39	44	45	38	42	45
Croatia	na	**65**	71	59	75	66	56	61	65	73	53	67	68	53	63	78
Czech Republic	56	**42**	42	42	54	44	33	39	44	45	39	41	45	38	44	41
Denmark	32	**39**	39	40	50	43	30	39	45	38	33	44	38	37	41	35
Dominican Rep.	na	**53**	47	57	60	40	40	26	54	56	52	50	56	46	56	57
Egypt	na	**15**	15	16	15	15	16	16	15	14	18	15	13	15	15	15
El Salvador	na	**14**	17	12	18	13	11	11	19	18	14	15	13	na	na	na
Estonia	42	**31**	35	28	36	34	26	25	31	39	22	32	37	22	35	49
Finland	53	**44**	49	40	60	52	28	39	52	48	41	44	49	41	45	45
France	32	**34**	33	35	44	37	26	34	38	29	32	35	30	33	37	28
Georgia	na	**15**	15	15	14	17	13	14	14	17	15	15	15	14	15	19
Germany	34	**42**	43	41	48	46	34	37	46	41	36	42	39	29	46	49
Great Britain	35	**39**	46	32	49	45	28	32	45	47	30	44	46	na	na	na
Greece	na	**38**	32	43	44	34	33	38	43	35	40	42	35	46	39	33
Hungary	27	**29**	34	25	36	39	16	23	38	45	23	31	32	25	33	35
Iceland	53	**59**	63	56	65	60	54	58	65	51	58	63	56	59	62	44
India	43	**29**	35	21	36	30	20	25	32	35	27	30	30	33	27	43
Indonesia	na	**25**	30	21	37	27	19	13	28	31	23	28	27	25	25	48
Iran	na	**na**	na	na	na	na	na	na	na	na	na	na	na	na	na	na
Ireland	42	**45**	45	46	62	43	35	34	52	52	36	47	51	41	49	41
Israel	na	**31**	33	29	37	31	25	24	34	32	28	30	37	30	32	48
Italy	37	**39**	40	39	43	43	34	39	41	35	37	42	39	39	39	40
Japan	25	**37**	40	34	39	38	35	29	35	45	30	41	41	27	40	44
Jordan	na	**6**	7	6	8	6	3	4	8	9	5	8	6	4	8	9
Korea, South	33	**45**	44	45	51	44	38	24	44	47	43	43	47	43	46	46
Latvia	42	**37**	39	35	47	41	30	28	40	38	30	39	44	32	40	52
Lithuania	51	**48**	51	46	46	57	43	35	53	53	37	50	53	40	52	50
Luxembourg	na	**43**	43	42	51	44	36	39	43	48	40	47	38	46	43	40
Macedonia	na	**43**	46	40	47	46	35	36	45	48	36	44	48	42	44	34
Malta	na	**22**	24	21	32	24	14	11	27	27	13	24	31	24	21	25
Mexico	43	**10**	14	7	14	9	7	8	11	19	9	11	12	8	12	11
Moldova	na	**27**	29	25	29	30	20	26	27	26	31	23	28	26	28	25
Montenegro	na	**47**	52	41	56	49	38	38	53	51	42	48	49	47	49	47
Morocco	na	**29**	33	24	34	26	20	26	41	38	25	34	30	22	34	38
Netherlands	41	**37**	43	31	56	37	27	32	45	33	36	33	40	28	40	33
New Zealand	na	**50**	52	49	60	52	47	46	53	54	47	55	51	54	51	55
Nigeria	30	**35**	39	32	39	32	27	32	36	40	35	35	37	32	38	31
Northern Ireland	31	**30**	31	30	39	34	24	25	35	36	22	33	42	28	31	31
Norway	56	**52**	52	52	58	53	49	53	58	45	na	na	na	52	54	42
Pakistan	na	**7**	11	2	6	6	8	7	7	7	6	9	5	7	6	8
Peru	na	**51**	53	50	57	49	43	52	53	49	51	53	50	50	52	54
Philippines	na	**14**	16	11	19	13	9	9	15	18	13	13	17	11	15	19
Poland	51	**31**	35	28	36	37	21	28	36	34	32	32	29	25	36	30
Portugal	49	**39**	45	34	52	43	28	31	56	47	23	36	51	34	43	38
Puerto Rico	na	**38**	45	34	46	41	33	24	37	42	37	37	43	31	38	45
Romania	na	**41**	48	34	53	43	33	29	48	44	36	39	48	36	46	45
Russian Fed.	42	**33**	37	29	37	35	27	24	34	32	32	33	34	30	36	36
Serbia	na	**32**	38	27	33	40	24	24	37	36	26	35	37	30	36	30
Singapore	na	**23**	24	22	33	16	8	14	25	39	17	24	27	14	23	53
Slovakia	na	**43**	49	38	51	49	31	33	48	46	34	45	49	41	45	60
Slovenia	50	**58**	63	54	72	59	47	49	61	63	55	61	60	54	58	63
South Africa	41	**32**	33	32	41	29	21	30	35	35	35	27	36	30	32	46
Spain	34	**37**	42	33	47	38	30	36	39	38	31	43	38	31	41	34
Sweden	59	**53**	54	52	55	55	49	53	57	45	49	58	53	52	57	40
Switzerland	21	**33**	34	32	48	39	17	25	34	44	28	30	37	29	34	35
Taiwan	na	**36**	35	37	51	37	22	24	35	47	33	34	41	30	43	38
Tanzania	na	**56**	58	53	60	52	59	50	65	59	51	54	67	53	58	67
Turkey	32	**35**	41	28	39	34	27	25	46	52	29	36	47	26	36	45
Uganda	na	**36**	45	28	37	38	24	40	34	45	40	41	43	33	36	41
Ukraine	na	**34**	37	31	38	40	27	24	36	35	28	39	37	29	40	20
United States	44	**54**	54	55	60	58	44	50	57	54	56	55	52	59	55	51
Uruguay	na	**16**	17	16	22	20	11	13	19	29	13	18	18	10	19	15
Venezuela	na	**34**	39	30	39	34	26	25	36	41	30	36	40	38	31	45
Vietnam	na	**38**	38	38	46	38	33	33	44	38	43	34	40	23	44	49
Zimbabwe	na	**37**	40	34	41	38	25	36	38	92	34	42	40	33	41	33
Total	40	36	38	33	42	37	28	30	39	39	32	37	38	30	39	40

RANKING

Country	2000
Croatia	65
Iceland	59
Slovenia	58
Tanzania	56
United States	54
Dominican Rep.	53
Sweden	53
Norway	52
Albania	52
Peru	51
New Zealand	50
Bosnia and Herz.	49
Lithuania	48
Montenegro	47
Ireland	45
Korea, South	45
Finland	44
Slovakia	43
Macedonia	43
Luxembourg	43
Colombia	42
Australia	42
Czech Republic	42
Germany	42
Romania	41
Canada	41
Bangladesh	40
Italy	39
Denmark	39
Portugal	39
Great Britain	39
Greece	38
Bulgaria	38
Puerto Rico	38
Brazil	38
Vietnam	38
Spain	37
Latvia	37
Japan	37
Netherlands	37
Zimbabwe	37
Uganda	36
Austria	36
Taiwan	36
Nigeria	35
Turkey	35
Venezuela	34
Ukraine	34
France	34
Switzerland	33
Russian Fed.	33
South Africa	32
Serbia	32
Poland	31
Estonia	31
Israel	31
Belgium	31
Algeria	30
Northern Ireland	30
Belarus	30
Hungary	29
India	29
Morocco	29
Armenia	28
Moldova	27
Indonesia	25
Chile	23
Argentina	23
Singapore	23
Malta	22
Azerbaijan	22
Uruguay	16
Egypt	15
Georgia	15
El Salvador	14
Philippines	14
Mexico	10
Pakistan	7
Jordan	6
Total	36

E028) POLITICAL ACTION: JOINING UNOFFICIAL STRIKES

I'd like you to tell me, for each one, whether you have actually done any of these things, whether you might do it or would never, under any circumstances, do it.

Might do (%) (WVS: V137; EVS: V182)

Country	Wave		Gender		Age			Education			Income			Values		
	1990	2000	Male	Female	16-29	30-49	50+	Lower	Middle	Upper	Lower	Middle	Upper	Mat	Mixed	Postm.
Albania	na	**5**	7	3	4	6	3	5	4	5	5	4	5	5	4	11
Algeria	na	**8**	10	6	10	8	4	5	6	12	7	7	9	6	8	12
Argentina	11	**10**	10	10	15	10	5	8	14	12	7	11	12	5	11	14
Armenia	na	**19**	23	14	24	16	13	13	19	19	21	17	14	16	21	23
Australia	na	**33**	33	32	52	31	16	28	31	38	26	34	36	27	32	35
Austria	8	**18**	23	13	29	23	7	10	21	37	15	18	21	5	14	29
Azerbaijan	na	**11**	13	9	12	12	7	6	12	11	14	9	12	8	17	12
Bangladesh	na	**24**	30	15	26	23	17	20	27	27	15	30	22	19	27	28
Belarus	29	**16**	24	9	21	19	8	9	17	24	12	16	22	10	19	42
Belgium	18	**19**	23	15	28	25	9	12	18	26	14	16	24	12	16	33
Bosnia and Herz.	na	**31**	34	28	36	35	20	20	33	33	25	31	34	28	31	33
Brazil	19	**15**	16	14	21	14	5	13	16	18	17	10	17	13	16	17
Bulgaria	25	**21**	27	15	24	30	11	16	20	29	12	26	25	20	23	50
Canada	28	**26**	26	26	41	30	14	18	28	31	21	27	32	24	26	29
Chile	16	**16**	16	15	20	16	10	11	16	22	12	17	19	12	16	21
China	na	**na**	na	na	na	na	na	na	na	na	na	na	na	na	na	na
Colombia	na	**18**	21	16	22	18	12	12	19	28	14	20	22	15	17	19
Croatia	na	**37**	41	33	54	35	26	29	39	52	33	35	38	21	35	53
Czech Republic	na	**29**	34	24	45	31	18	26	31	34	22	30	35	27	30	31
Denmark	23	**31**	27	35	54	34	16	24	44	37	25	33	36	29	29	42
Dominican Rep.	na	**12**	14	10	12	13	na	7	12	12	9	13	9	7	14	14
Egypt	na	**3**	2	3	3	3	2	2	3	2	3	3	2	3	2	1
El Salvador	na	**6**	6	6	9	6	2	5	7	8	8	5	6	na	na	na
Estonia	19	**12**	15	9	18	15	6	9	11	18	4	12	18	8	13	23
Finland	35	**25**	29	21	41	31	11	21	31	28	27	26	24	19	25	37
France	25	**32**	36	29	47	38	19	25	38	45	27	31	39	19	34	45
Georgia	na	**6**	8	4	6	7	4	5	5	9	5	7	6	5	6	14
Germany	15	**16**	20	14	32	18	8	12	22	15	15	18	18	7	17	29
Great Britain	19	**28**	33	24	47	30	19	23	33	34	25	32	28	na	na	na
Greece	na	**33**	36	30	42	29	17	16	26	41	28	34	39	22	32	44
Hungary	27	**10**	12	8	13	14	3	8	14	13	9	11	9	7	10	28
Iceland	20	**30**	36	24	43	34	13	21	31	45	28	25	37	18	30	52
India	16	**18**	21	12	20	18	15	16	20	20	17	15	20	17	21	13
Indonesia	na	**6**	9	4	13	6	4	4	6	9	4	8	8	7	6	20
Iran	na	**na**	na	na	na	na	na	na	na	na	na	na	na	na	na	na
Ireland	23	**31**	34	28	46	33	17	15	37	47	20	38	34	27	32	37
Israel	na	**24**	25	23	37	22	13	12	25	32	20	24	31	25	24	42
Italy	18	**16**	19	13	24	21	7	7	20	27	10	20	19	10	14	22
Japan	13	**19**	22	17	24	24	14	15	20	22	14	21	23	11	20	35
Jordan	na	**3**	4	2	4	2	1	1	5	4	2	3	4	2	4	3
Korea, South	na	**55**	53	56	68	55	39	31	52	61	53	58	54	52	56	66
Latvia	30	**15**	19	10	23	16	10	8	16	17	12	11	21	9	17	30
Lithuania	50	**24**	31	18	32	28	16	11	28	31	11	20	32	16	26	36
Luxembourg	na	**23**	26	19	34	26	13	17	25	29	22	19	26	20	22	28
Macedonia	na	**28**	29	27	34	30	20	24	31	30	22	31	30	28	30	21
Malta	na	**16**	20	13	26	17	10	9	17	30	14	13	25	15	17	23
Mexico	36	**12**	15	9	18	10	7	8	14	22	11	15	12	8	13	16
Moldova	na	**23**	25	21	24	26	18	19	22	28	25	24	23	22	25	30
Montenegro	na	**31**	38	24	36	34	25	19	39	38	29	33	27	25	37	39
Morocco	na	**2**	4	1	4	1	1	2	5	2	2	3	4	1	3	7
Netherlands	22	**28**	32	24	35	36	16	19	28	38	29	27	31	11	27	39
New Zealand	na	**33**	33	33	55	41	19	22	34	47	30	39	34	26	31	52
Nigeria	14	**19**	19	18	21	16	18	17	19	20	20	17	19	16	20	22
Northern Ireland	17	**20**	25	16	27	23	15	17	25	20	19	21	24	14	20	31
Norway	58	**28**	29	27	43	32	12	18	32	33	na	na	na	13	29	42
Pakistan	na	**1**	2	na	2	1	2	2	1	1	1	2	1	1	2	na
Peru	na	**15**	16	14	17	14	12	17	13	16	18	15	10	14	14	17
Philippines	na	**6**	8	5	7	7	5	4	8	7	6	6	7	4	8	5
Poland	24	**16**	19	13	23	19	9	16	18	13	16	14	21	13	19	13
Portugal	19	**21**	26	15	34	23	11	13	34	38	11	22	24	17	24	20
Puerto Rico	na	**11**	14	9	21	11	6	3	6	14	4	12	15	7	10	15
Romania	na	**8**	11	5	16	7	5	6	10	8	7	9	9	7	10	12
Russian Fed.	30	**16**	22	12	20	18	11	9	17	18	15	16	17	11	22	33
Serbia	na	**29**	35	24	51	37	14	17	31	44	22	27	37	22	36	46
Singapore	na	**na**	na	na	na	na	na	na	na	na	na	na	na	na	na	na
Slovakia	na	**21**	27	15	29	25	11	13	24	31	13	22	25	17	24	35
Slovenia	8	**33**	37	29	47	35	19	23	34	47	27	33	38	25	33	42
South Africa	24	**14**	16	11	16	14	7	12	17	10	16	11	12	10	17	19
Spain	21	**21**	26	16	31	26	10	12	28	32	16	20	29	9	23	34
Sweden	41	**48**	50	45	62	57	31	33	54	49	48	46	49	34	46	56
Switzerland	22	**16**	20	13	25	20	7	9	17	26	15	17	19	7	14	29
Taiwan	na	**12**	14	10	25	11	5	7	12	16	9	13	13	8	15	15
Tanzania	na	**7**	9	5	6	9	7	3	8	18	5	4	19	6	8	9
Turkey	6	**13**	15	10	16	12	6	8	15	31	11	12	21	8	12	22
Uganda	na	**22**	29	17	21	24	21	24	20	36	33	28	14	26	19	27
Ukraine	na	**16**	25	9	22	20	10	9	17	18	13	17	19	12	20	20
United States	30	**38**	40	37	49	44	22	31	38	41	37	40	42	33	38	44
Uruguay	na	**20**	23	17	34	23	11	16	24	34	13	23	22	6	21	27
Venezuela	na	**6**	7	6	7	6	5	7	6	6	8	5	7	5	6	9
Vietnam	na	**11**	11	10	14	9	9	11	9	12	11	8	14	7	11	10
Zimbabwe	na	**11**	14	7	12	11	7	10	12	na	10	13	11	11	11	6
Total	23	**19**	22	16	25	21	12	13	21	25	16	19	22	13	20	29

RANKING	
Country	2000
Korea, South	55
Sweden	48
United States	38
Croatia	37
New Zealand	33
Slovenia	33
Australia	33
Greece	33
France	32
Ireland	31
Montenegro	31
Bosnia and Herz.	31
Denmark	31
Iceland	30
Serbia	29
Czech Republic	29
Great Britain	28
Macedonia	28
Netherlands	28
Norway	28
Canada	26
Finland	25
Lithuania	24
Israel	24
Bangladesh	24
Luxembourg	23
Moldova	23
Uganda	22
Slovakia	21
Bulgaria	21
Spain	21
Portugal	21
Northern Ireland	20
Uruguay	20
Japan	19
Belgium	19
Nigeria	19
Armenia	19
Colombia	18
India	18
Austria	18
Germany	16
Malta	16
Russian Fed.	16
Switzerland	16
Ukraine	16
Poland	16
Belarus	16
Italy	16
Chile	16
Brazil	15
Peru	15
Latvia	15
South Africa	14
Turkey	13
Dominican Rep.	12
Estonia	12
Taiwan	12
Mexico	12
Azerbaijan	11
Puerto Rico	11
Vietnam	11
Zimbabwe	11
Argentina	10
Hungary	10
Romania	8
Algeria	8
Tanzania	7
Indonesia	6
Philippines	6
Venezuela	6
El Salvador	6
Georgia	6
Albania	5
Jordan	3
Egypt	3
Morocco	2
Pakistan	1
Total	19

E029) POLITICAL ACTION: OCCUPYING BUILDINGS OR FACTORIES

I'd like you to tell me, for each one, whether you have actually done any of these things, whether you might do it or would never, under any circumstances, do it.

Might do (%)

(WVS: V138; EVS: V183)

Country	Wave		Gender		Age			Education			Income			Values		
	1990	2000	Male	Female	16-29	30-49	50+	Lower	Middle	Upper	Lower	Middle	Upper	Mat	Mixed	Postm.
Albania	na	**2**	3	1	4	2	na	2	2	1	2	1	2	2	2	na
Algeria	na	**4**	6	2	5	3	4	4	3	4	5	3	3	2	5	4
Argentina	8	**9**	11	8	13	10	5	8	11	14	8	9	11	5	10	11
Armenia	na	**12**	18	8	18	10	8	9	13	12	18	10	7	9	15	26
Australia	na	**17**	19	16	28	18	8	14	16	22	15	18	19	13	16	21
Austria	6	**10**	12	7	15	12	5	5	13	18	9	7	14	4	7	16
Azerbaijan	na	**3**	5	2	4	3	1	5	3	3	4	3	2	2	5	7
Bangladesh	na	**6**	8	4	5	6	11	6	6	6	3	6	8	4	7	4
Belarus	12	**4**	8	1	7	4	2	2	5	8	2	5	7	2	5	16
Belgium	21	**26**	31	21	44	32	12	15	26	33	19	23	31	16	24	43
Bosnia and Herz.	na	**12**	15	9	14	15	7	8	15	8	10	13	12	15	10	19
Brazil	12	**16**	15	17	19	19	6	15	17	16	20	14	15	15	16	22
Bulgaria	14	**14**	18	10	17	19	8	10	16	17	9	13	20	11	18	27
Canada	21	**18**	21	15	33	19	9	13	20	19	16	22	19	17	16	23
Chile	11	**10**	10	9	12	11	7	7	8	19	8	10	12	6	10	14
China	na	**na**	na	na	na	na	na	na	na	na	na	na	na	na	na	na
Colombia	na	**11**	11	11	15	10	6	8	12	14	9	12	11	10	10	15
Croatia	na	**18**	25	13	23	20	14	15	21	18	17	17	20	11	17	29
Czech Republic	na	**10**	15	6	16	11	7	10	10	13	8	11	12	9	10	15
Denmark	7	**12**	15	10	18	14	8	11	15	12	10	14	9	13	11	18
Dominican Rep.	na	**28**	27	28	29	27	18	25	31	26	27	28	22	34	26	27
Egypt	na	**2**	2	3	3	2	2	3	3	2	3	2	2	2	3	1
El Salvador	na	**5**	6	5	7	5	2	4	5	6	6	4	5	na	na	na
Estonia	7	**5**	8	3	9	6	2	3	5	10	3	5	6	3	5	27
Finland	20	**15**	18	13	25	18	7	13	17	16	17	14	16	13	14	22
France	25	**35**	38	33	56	41	20	28	45	46	31	35	40	22	37	50
Georgia	na	**2**	3	1	3	2	1	2	2	3	2	2	3	1	3	7
Germany	14	**14**	16	13	27	14	7	11	17	14	15	15	16	7	15	24
Great Britain	10	**16**	20	12	26	19	9	13	20	18	14	22	18	na	na	na
Greece	na	**27**	25	27	27	31	17	15	27	28	21	33	29	20	29	27
Hungary	4	**4**	6	3	6	7	1	4	6	6	3	5	5	4	4	16
Iceland	9	**12**	17	8	18	14	5	9	12	20	11	12	14	7	11	31
India	6	**13**	15	8	13	11	15	13	13	11	13	13	13	11	16	13
Indonesia	na	**10**	12	7	16	8	8	5	10	13	9	9	12	10	8	40
Iran	na	**na**	na	na	na	na	na	na	na	na	na	na	na	na	na	na
Ireland	19	**16**	19	13	21	17	10	7	20	22	10	25	16	13	15	26
Israel	na	**7**	8	6	10	7	2	3	7	8	5	7	9	10	5	18
Italy	20	**18**	19	16	26	21	10	12	21	26	14	21	19	10	16	26
Japan	7	**8**	10	6	9	8	7	8	6	11	7	8	9	5	6	19
Jordan	na	**1**	1	1	na	1	1	1	na	na	1	na	1	1	1	na
Korea, South	37	**na**	na	na	na	na	na	na	na	na	na	na	na	na	na	na
Latvia	5	**4**	7	2	6	4	3	3	5	2	3	2	6	2	5	12
Lithuania	21	**12**	19	7	20	12	7	5	15	10	5	12	14	11	12	23
Luxembourg	na	**19**	20	17	28	20	11	15	19	22	18	18	18	14	18	29
Macedonia	na	**16**	17	14	17	15	15	13	17	15	17	19	10	14	17	18
Malta	na	**13**	16	11	19	15	8	7	15	23	13	15	20	12	12	25
Mexico	29	**7**	9	5	11	5	6	5	9	14	7	8	7	4	9	7
Moldova	na	**11**	14	8	12	12	10	8	12	12	10	11	15	12	11	15
Montenegro	na	**16**	23	10	20	16	15	12	20	18	12	14	17	12	19	30
Morocco	na	**5**	6	3	7	3	2	3	8	12	4	7	7	3	5	14
Netherlands	22	**23**	26	21	31	27	16	17	22	31	25	23	25	7	22	36
New Zealand	na	**19**	21	16	35	24	8	11	20	27	17	21	20	8	19	30
Nigeria	11	**33**	36	29	35	32	18	28	35	37	27	36	37	33	34	29
Northern Ireland	8	**10**	14	7	16	13	5	8	14	8	9	9	13	6	9	20
Norway	10	**10**	12	9	14	12	6	8	10	13	na	na	na	5	9	25
Pakistan	na	**0**	na	na	na	na	1	na	na	1	na	1	na	na	na	na
Peru	na	**12**	14	10	14	13	7	14	11	14	13	13	10	10	13	11
Philippines	na	**7**	8	5	7	7	5	5	7	8	5	6	8	5	7	4
Poland	19	**16**	19	13	27	17	7	14	21	11	15	16	20	14	18	13
Portugal	11	**22**	27	17	36	25	12	15	34	43	11	23	25	18	25	24
Puerto Rico	na	**7**	10	6	17	6	4	6	3	9	5	7	9	11	6	9
Romania	na	**6**	7	4	9	5	4	6	6	5	5	7	6	5	7	5
Russian Fed.	12	**8**	13	4	11	10	5	5	9	9	9	7	8	6	11	23
Serbia	na	**17**	22	12	31	20	7	8	18	26	13	17	19	12	21	28
Singapore	na	**na**	na	na	na	na	na	na	na	na	na	na	na	na	na	na
Slovakia	na	**15**	21	9	16	19	9	11	15	26	10	14	16	11	17	27
Slovenia	12	**24**	28	20	29	27	17	20	25	26	23	25	24	18	25	25
South Africa	24	**20**	24	16	24	20	11	22	18	8	28	14	16	18	21	25
Spain	23	**16**	20	12	26	19	7	8	22	25	14	14	20	8	17	26
Sweden	19	**19**	19	19	24	23	12	12	22	21	21	19	18	14	16	30
Switzerland	na	**13**	16	10	19	16	6	10	13	20	12	15	14	6	12	19
Taiwan	na	**5**	4	6	10	5	2	3	8	5	5	4	6	4	5	14
Tanzania	na	**4**	5	3	4	5	3	2	7	8	3	3	10	3	4	8
Turkey	3	**5**	6	3	6	5	2	3	6	9	5	4	6	3	4	9
Uganda	na	**45**	66	34	53	41	32	42	45	66	51	48	51	47	42	55
Ukraine	na	**5**	8	3	8	6	3	4	5	5	5	6	5	4	7	7
United States	17	**25**	29	21	38	27	13	24	26	25	29	25	21	18	24	29
Uruguay	na	**17**	19	15	28	18	10	12	22	26	10	19	20	5	18	22
Venezuela	na	**8**	9	7	10	7	7	9	8	8	11	6	8	10	7	12
Vietnam	na	**22**	21	24	25	19	25	23	21	19	26	18	25	23	23	16
Zimbabwe	na	**4**	5	4	6	2	2	3	6	9	3	6	5	4	5	2
Total	14	13	15	10	17	13	8	10	14	15	11	13	14	9	13	22

RANKING

Country	2000
Uganda	45
France	35
Nigeria	33
Dominican Rep.	28
Greece	27
Belgium	26
United States	25
Slovenia	24
Netherlands	23
Vietnam	22
Portugal	22
South Africa	20
Sweden	19
New Zealand	19
Luxembourg	19
Croatia	18
Canada	18
Italy	18
Australia	17
Uruguay	17
Serbia	17
Montenegro	16
Brazil	16
Great Britain	16
Ireland	16
Poland	16
Spain	16
Macedonia	16
Finland	15
Slovakia	15
Bulgaria	14
Germany	14
Malta	13
Switzerland	13
India	13
Armenia	12
Peru	12
Iceland	12
Denmark	12
Lithuania	12
Bosnia and Herz.	12
Moldova	11
Colombia	11
Norway	10
Northern Ireland	10
Czech Republic	10
Chile	10
Austria	10
Indonesia	10
Argentina	9
Russian Fed.	8
Venezuela	8
Japan	8
Mexico	7
Puerto Rico	7
Israel	7
Philippines	7
Bangladesh	6
Romania	6
Taiwan	5
Ukraine	5
El Salvador	5
Estonia	5
Morocco	5
Turkey	5
Hungary	4
Tanzania	4
Belarus	4
Zimbabwe	4
Latvia	4
Algeria	4
Azerbaijan	3
Egypt	2
Georgia	2
Albania	2
Jordan	1
Pakistan	0
Total	13

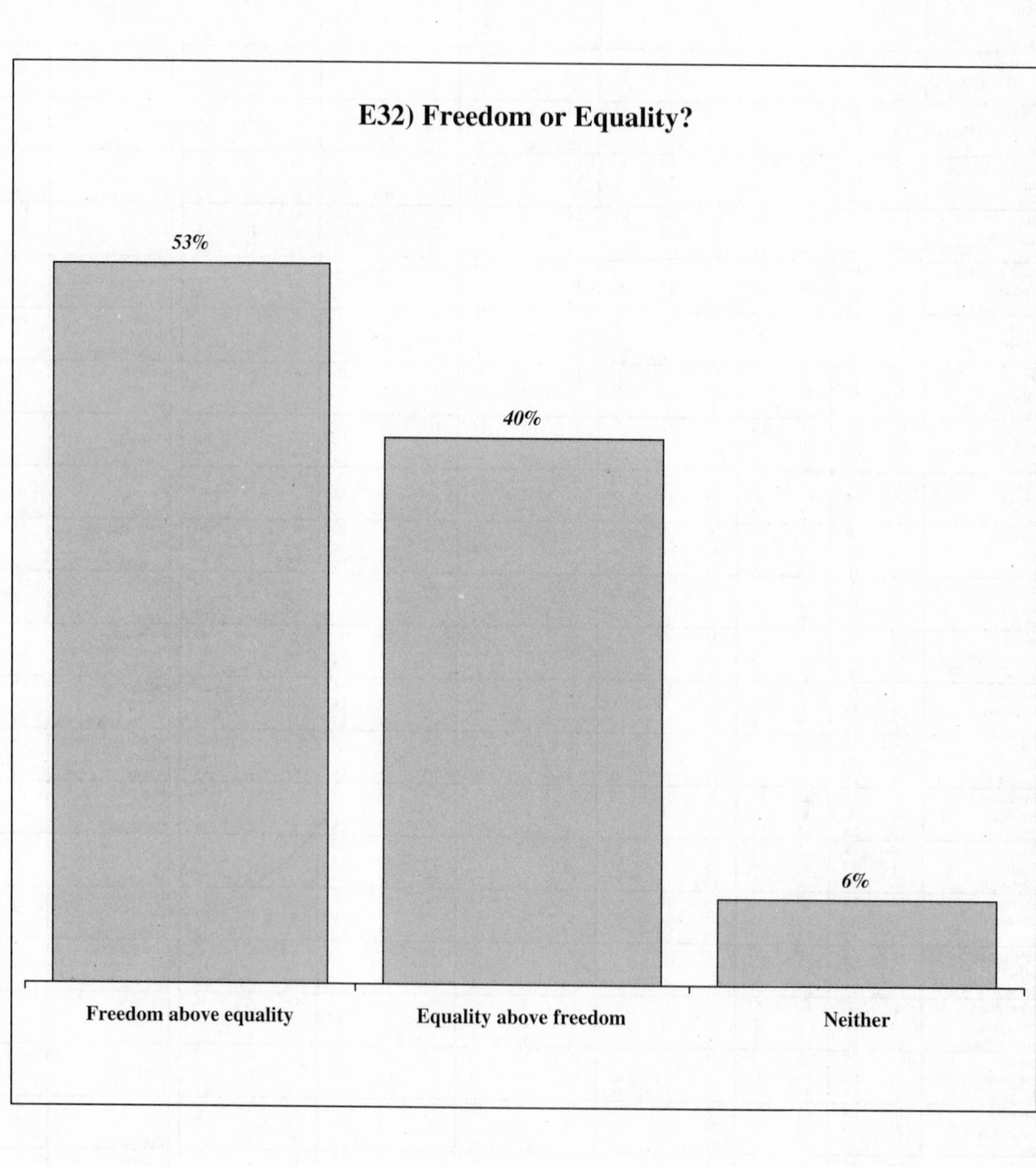
E32) Freedom or Equality?
53%
40%
6%
Freedom above equality
Equality above freedom
Neither

E032_1) FREEDOM OR EQUALITY?

Both freedom and equality are important, but if you were to choose one or the other, which of these two statements comes closest to your own opinion? A. personal freedom more important, or B equality more important

Freedom above equality (%)

(EVS: V184)

Country	Wave		Gender		Age			Education			Income			Values		
	1990	2000	Male	Female	16-29	30-49	50+	Lower	Middle	Upper	Lower	Middle	Upper	Mat	Mixed	Postm.
Albania	na	**na**	na	na	na	na	na	na	na	na	na	na	na	na	na	na
Algeria	na	**na**	na	na	na	na	na	na	na	na	na	na	na	na	na	na
Argentina	58	**na**	na	na	na	na	na	na	na	na	na	na	na	na	na	na
Armenia	na	**na**	na	na	na	na	na	na	na	na	na	na	na	na	na	na
Australia	na	**na**	na	na	na	na	na	na	na	na	na	na	na	na	na	na
Austria	64	**56**	61	51	62	56	54	52	59	65	50	52	61	55	55	58
Azerbaijan	na	**na**	na	na	na	na	na	na	na	na	na	na	na	na	na	na
Bangladesh	na	**na**	na	na	na	na	na	na	na	na	na	na	na	na	na	na
Belarus	41	**62**	65	59	75	63	47	44	66	71	54	65	67	58	63	83
Belgium	52	**46**	49	44	53	45	45	36	46	55	39	43	55	43	48	47
Bosnia and Herz.	na	**na**	na	na	na	na	na	na	na	na	na	na	na	na	na	na
Brazil	41	**na**	na	na	na	na	na	na	na	na	na	na	na	na	na	na
Bulgaria	48	**60**	60	60	70	65	50	43	64	77	47	59	72	54	64	78
Canada	61	**na**	na	na	na	na	na	na	na	na	na	na	na	na	na	na
Chile	53	**na**	na	na	na	na	na	na	na	na	na	na	na	na	na	na
China	21	**na**	na	na	na	na	na	na	na	na	na	na	na	na	na	na
Colombia	na	**na**	na	na	na	na	na	na	na	na	na	na	na	na	na	na
Croatia	na	**42**	47	38	49	42	38	37	44	52	36	34	55	38	42	45
Czech Republic	42	**59**	61	56	66	63	51	51	65	71	52	58	66	47	62	69
Denmark	62	**69**	74	65	76	72	63	69	72	69	65	72	70	65	74	57
Dominican Rep.	na	**na**	na	na	na	na	na	na	na	na	na	na	na	na	na	na
Egypt	na	**na**	na	na	na	na	na	na	na	na	na	na	na	na	na	na
El Salvador	na	**na**	na	na	na	na	na	na	na	na	na	na	na	na	na	na
Estonia	71	**55**	59	51	65	54	49	50	55	62	50	50	61	52	57	66
Finland	74	**53**	56	50	63	51	50	47	63	57	49	50	56	49	55	52
France	53	**50**	52	48	49	51	50	50	50	51	50	50	52	51	50	51
Georgia	na	**na**	na	na	na	na	na	na	na	na	na	na	na	na	na	na
Germany	50	**62**	66	58	60	61	63	63	61	61	59	65	65	62	61	67
Great Britain	65	**60**	62	57	57	57	63	58	62	57	62	58	58	na	na	na
Greece	na	**na**	na	na	na	na	na	na	na	na	na	na	na	na	na	na
Hungary	51	**45**	48	42	47	49	38	39	53	59	36	42	53	41	50	24
Iceland	45	**46**	48	44	52	48	37	39	51	49	38	46	52	44	46	47
India	45	**na**	na	na	na	na	na	na	na	na	na	na	na	na	na	na
Indonesia	na	**na**	na	na	na	na	na	na	na	na	na	na	na	na	na	na
Iran	na	**na**	na	na	na	na	na	na	na	na	na	na	na	na	na	na
Ireland	45	**48**	49	48	44	47	54	54	45	46	56	40	47	54	48	40
Israel	na	**na**	na	na	na	na	na	na	na	na	na	na	na	na	na	na
Italy	46	**40**	42	37	41	38	41	41	40	36	39	40	38	41	42	36
Japan	46	**na**	na	na	na	na	na	na	na	na	na	na	na	na	na	na
Jordan	na	**na**	na	na	na	na	na	na	na	na	na	na	na	na	na	na
Korea, South	51	**na**	na	na	na	na	na	na	na	na	na	na	na	na	na	na
Latvia	58	**52**	52	52	68	52	46	53	52	53	50	49	57	50	54	55
Lithuania	73	**58**	61	55	69	62	45	47	58	73	46	54	67	60	55	78
Luxembourg	na	**49**	52	47	51	46	52	51	48	53	49	52	51	52	50	47
Macedonia	na	**na**	na	na	na	na	na	na	na	na	na	na	na	na	na	na
Malta	na	**58**	61	55	65	54	56	54	58	68	59	57	63	62	54	66
Mexico	61	**na**	na	na	na	na	na	na	na	na	na	na	na	na	na	na
Moldova	na	**na**	na	na	na	na	na	na	na	na	na	na	na	na	na	na
Montenegro	na	**na**	na	na	na	na	na	na	na	na	na	na	na	na	na	na
Morocco	na	**na**	na	na	na	na	na	na	na	na	na	na	na	na	na	na
Netherlands	56	**56**	60	53	64	62	46	49	59	61	55	54	64	45	60	52
New Zealand	na	**na**	na	na	na	na	na	na	na	na	na	na	na	na	na	na
Nigeria	62	**na**	na	na	na	na	na	na	na	na	na	na	na	na	na	na
Northern Ireland	64	**47**	51	44	50	43	50	45	50	47	48	49	47	56	46	43
Norway	67	**na**	na	na	na	na	na	na	na	na	na	na	na	na	na	na
Pakistan	na	**na**	na	na	na	na	na	na	na	na	na	na	na	na	na	na
Peru	na	**na**	na	na	na	na	na	na	na	na	na	na	na	na	na	na
Philippines	na	**na**	na	na	na	na	na	na	na	na	na	na	na	na	na	na
Poland	55	**55**	58	52	57	57	50	51	55	68	49	60	57	48	56	69
Portugal	42	**49**	53	46	46	55	46	49	48	56	52	53	51	47	52	46
Puerto Rico	na	**na**	na	na	na	na	na	na	na	na	na	na	na	na	na	na
Romania	54	**na**	na	na	na	na	na	na	na	na	na	na	na	na	na	na
Russian Fed.	45	**47**	51	44	65	46	36	32	46	56	41	42	55	42	51	60
Serbia	na	**na**	na	na	na	na	na	na	na	na	na	na	na	na	na	na
Singapore	na	**na**	na	na	na	na	na	na	na	na	na	na	na	na	na	na
Slovakia	na	**64**	63	64	67	64	60	57	66	69	60	62	67	61	64	81
Slovenia	42	**46**	46	47	54	54	33	33	47	69	40	42	56	37	49	46
South Africa	48	**na**	na	na	na	na	na	na	na	na	na	na	na	na	na	na
Spain	43	**49**	52	46	54	46	49	48	51	47	49	51	51	49	50	46
Sweden	67	**62**	62	61	68	63	57	49	65	67	56	64	66	67	61	64
Switzerland	58	**na**	na	na	na	na	na	na	na	na	na	na	na	na	na	na
Taiwan	na	**na**	na	na	na	na	na	na	na	na	na	na	na	na	na	na
Tanzania	na	**na**	na	na	na	na	na	na	na	na	na	na	na	na	na	na
Turkey	58	**42**	47	36	41	39	53	45	37	39	50	37	36	44	41	41
Uganda	na	**na**	na	na	na	na	na	na	na	na	na	na	na	na	na	na
Ukraine	na	**53**	56	50	64	57	42	34	54	60	44	53	65	49	56	78
United States	71	**na**	na	na	na	na	na	na	na	na	na	na	na	na	na	na
Uruguay	na	**na**	na	na	na	na	na	na	na	na	na	na	na	na	na	na
Venezuela	na	**na**	na	na	na	na	na	na	na	na	na	na	na	na	na	na
Vietnam	na	**na**	na	na	na	na	na	na	na	na	na	na	na	na	na	na
Zimbabwe	na	**na**	na	na	na	na	na	na	na	na	na	na	na	na	na	na
Total	54	**53**	56	51	59	54	49	48	55	59	50	52	58	51	54	53

RANKING	
Country	**2000**
Denmark	69
Slovakia	64
Belarus	62
Germany	62
Sweden	62
Bulgaria	60
Great Britain	60
Czech Republic	59
Lithuania	58
Malta	58
Austria	56
Netherlands	56
Poland	55
Estonia	55
Finland	53
Ukraine	53
Latvia	52
France	50
Luxembourg	49
Portugal	49
Spain	49
Ireland	48
Northern Ireland	47
Russian Fed.	47
Belgium	46
Slovenia	46
Iceland	46
Hungary	45
Croatia	42
Turkey	42
Italy	40
Total	53

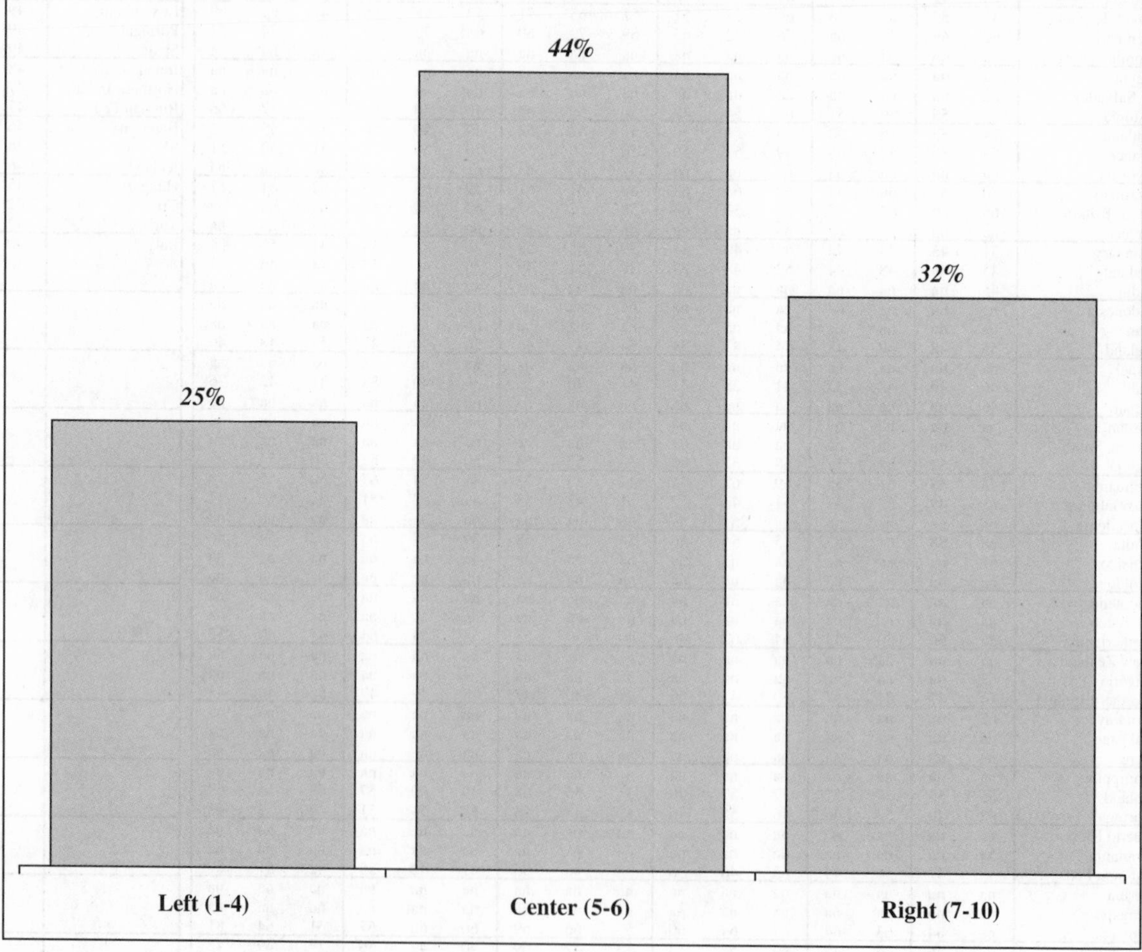
E33) In political matters, people talk of "the left" and "the right." How would you place your views on this scale, generally speaking?
25%
44%
32%
Left (1-4)
Center (5-6)
Right (7-10)

E033) SELF POSITIONING IN POLITICAL SCALE: RIGHT

In political matters, people talk of "the left" and "the right."

How would you place your views on this scale, generally speaking?

% Right (codes 7 to 10 on a 10-point scale)

(WVS: V139; EVS: V185)

Country	Wave		Gender		Age			Education			Income			Values		
	1990	2000	Male	Female	16-29	30-49	50+	Lower	Middle	Upper	Lower	Middle	Upper	Mat	Mixed	Postm.
Albania	na	**36**	40	33	37	37	35	32	39	41	32	36	41	35	38	33
Algeria	na	**43**	45	41	45	42	44	34	42	49	42	39	51	36	49	34
Argentina	21	**33**	34	31	32	31	35	35	28	33	38	33	28	37	34	27
Armenia	na	**27**	27	27	34	24	22	25	28	27	33	21	24	27	26	32
Australia	na	**22**	24	21	15	21	30	24	20	25	23	21	25	24	25	18
Austria	41	**19**	19	20	14	18	23	21	17	20	22	18	21	23	18	20
Azerbaijan	na	**29**	30	27	32	28	25	32	27	32	27	32	32	24	35	49
Bangladesh	na	**66**	70	60	64	67	77	72	62	61	74	62	68	77	62	51
Belarus	10	**28**	31	25	33	29	20	24	26	37	19	29	36	18	29	64
Belgium	31	**21**	22	20	17	18	26	20	22	21	23	16	23	21	24	13
Bosnia and Herz.	na	**18**	21	15	19	18	17	22	17	18	13	17	24	16	19	18
Brazil	31	**41**	43	38	36	39	54	49	36	29	45	39	36	46	40	31
Bulgaria	22	**36**	39	33	46	34	33	25	40	41	29	35	42	32	38	50
Canada	26	**25**	30	20	20	26	27	25	23	29	22	23	30	19	24	28
Chile	18	**21**	20	22	19	22	21	19	22	22	17	20	28	29	20	12
China	na	**na**	na	na	na	na	na	na	na	na	na	na	na	na	na	na
Colombia	na	**45**	45	45	42	45	51	57	46	36	53	44	41	55	50	45
Croatia	na	**16**	16	16	18	17	14	19	16	13	13	16	15	18	18	10
Czech Republic	30	**39**	39	39	44	40	35	34	43	48	29	38	48	27	41	56
Denmark	35	**32**	38	26	36	29	33	32	46	26	27	31	36	34	35	16
Dominican Rep.	na	**52**	47	57	57	46	46	65	53	51	54	46	57	54	53	48
Egypt	na	**na**	na	na	na	na	na	na	na	na	na	na	na	na	na	na
El Salvador	na	**41**	37	46	39	42	44	48	35	34	46	40	35	na	na	na
Estonia	na	**31**	34	28	37	27	32	32	29	35	26	24	39	24	34	30
Finland	43	**36**	38	33	33	35	39	30	42	49	29	37	43	33	39	23
France	20	**21**	22	21	14	17	28	22	20	21	18	20	22	26	22	12
Georgia	na	**37**	36	38	35	38	39	38	38	33	40	36	35	36	38	43
Germany	18	**23**	26	21	12	23	28	26	20	19	25	24	26	28	23	15
Great Britain	27	**16**	14	18	8	12	24	15	16	17	16	14	17	na	na	na
Greece	na	**22**	23	22	17	25	28	37	23	19	26	18	24	34	21	15
Hungary	18	**14**	15	12	10	13	16	13	14	16	16	11	15	15	13	na
Iceland	36	**39**	42	35	39	39	37	36	41	39	27	39	47	44	39	23
India	29	**32**	31	32	33	30	34	32	31	31	29	35	30	36	29	26
Indonesia	na	**43**	40	46	49	41	42	34	45	47	33	51	55	41	44	68
Iran	na	**22**	18	27	20	24	24	24	23	16	18	21	25	25	21	12
Ireland	33	**22**	21	23	12	22	28	26	21	17	26	21	20	24	23	10
Israel	na	**30**	32	28	33	29	28	22	28	39	18	34	36	56	26	23
Italy	18	**28**	31	25	30	25	29	27	31	23	28	24	30	33	30	23
Japan	31	**28**	30	25	12	21	38	34	27	25	30	27	29	39	25	21
Jordan	na	**36**	32	41	40	37	22	34	37	36	37	29	40	40	33	35
Korea, South	50	**30**	31	29	20	29	45	48	33	25	32	26	32	37	25	18
Latvia	na	**31**	29	34	28	25	38	33	31	31	34	31	28	30	32	28
Lithuania	na	**25**	25	25	17	19	39	40	20	26	35	25	23	21	26	21
Luxembourg	na	**22**	23	22	14	22	27	22	24	20	25	28	19	27	23	15
Macedonia	na	**22**	23	20	21	24	20	24	21	22	21	23	23	22	20	39
Malta	na	**24**	26	23	25	21	27	20	25	29	21	32	26	20	27	27
Mexico	32	**51**	49	53	49	49	58	60	42	45	58	45	48	51	51	48
Moldova	na	**36**	37	36	41	38	31	31	32	47	36	38	37	32	39	49
Montenegro	na	**25**	28	20	31	27	17	20	27	26	22	23	24	21	27	30
Morocco	na	**38**	35	42	37	37	43	41	34	24	52	36	34	39	38	32
Netherlands	30	**23**	28	18	21	23	25	22	25	23	20	20	32	29	25	15
New Zealand	na	**31**	31	32	20	34	32	27	33	37	24	23	44	40	34	24
Nigeria	34	**39**	43	36	42	37	32	37	40	41	37	38	44	39	41	34
Northern Ireland	33	**28**	32	23	33	24	28	27	32	22	24	31	35	34	27	25
Norway	34	**30**	32	28	28	26	38	28	28	37	na	na	na	27	33	17
Pakistan	na	**35**	28	44	42	30	29	51	44	18	47	47	23	38	32	50
Peru	na	**31**	29	32	29	31	35	32	31	29	30	29	33	34	30	24
Philippines	na	**41**	41	41	40	38	50	45	39	40	40	36	50	40	44	33
Poland	30	**27**	25	29	21	23	35	26	27	29	24	25	37	29	26	27
Portugal	31	**26**	27	25	28	31	20	25	26	31	25	26	24	22	29	25
Puerto Rico	na	**42**	44	42	27	36	54	51	51	37	53	36	41	42	44	40
Romania	29	**32**	35	29	40	31	29	39	31	30	40	29	30	32	30	42
Russian Fed.	11	**19**	20	17	24	17	17	18	18	21	14	19	23	16	20	17
Serbia	na	**30**	32	27	42	32	21	21	32	34	29	29	29	27	33	29
Singapore	na	**na**	na	na	na	na	na	na	na	na	na	na	na	na	na	na
Slovakia	na	**22**	22	21	23	20	23	19	21	29	19	19	25	18	24	39
Slovenia	14	**14**	17	12	13	12	17	19	14	11	14	12	13	16	13	17
South Africa	29	**33**	35	31	37	32	29	37	31	31	38	40	22	30	35	32
Spain	17	**17**	16	18	11	15	23	19	14	17	19	15	18	23	16	10
Sweden	35	**32**	34	31	33	31	34	18	35	40	25	33	40	32	35	24
Switzerland	30	**23**	27	19	21	20	28	29	22	24	22	23	25	30	26	13
Taiwan	na	**43**	38	48	25	44	52	52	41	36	42	45	43	47	37	44
Tanzania	na	**57**	58	56	52	58	67	62	51	49	56	56	60	57	58	67
Turkey	25	**33**	34	32	30	33	40	37	29	23	34	35	26	42	34	23
Uganda	na	**43**	42	43	43	38	61	48	39	51	41	56	33	46	41	43
Ukraine	na	**29**	33	25	32	36	22	17	28	37	21	30	38	24	29	48
United States	29	**32**	33	30	32	28	36	31	30	33	29	34	35	32	32	31
Uruguay	na	**33**	32	35	18	25	46	43	21	19	40	31	28	48	32	18
Venezuela	na	**40**	39	40	40	38	44	42	40	36	43	42	35	44	37	44
Vietnam	na	**92**	92	92	90	93	92	93	90	89	87	92	95	94	93	88
Zimbabwe	na	**11**	12	10	10	12	13	12	11	na	9	12	13	13	10	18
Total	27	**32**	33	31	32	31	33	33	30	32	31	31	34	33	32	26

RANKING

Country	2000
Vietnam	92
Bangladesh	66
Tanzania	57
Dominican Rep.	52
Mexico	51
Colombia	45
Algeria	43
Taiwan	43
Indonesia	43
Uganda	43
Puerto Rico	42
El Salvador	41
Philippines	41
Brazil	41
Venezuela	40
Nigeria	39
Czech Republic	39
Iceland	39
Morocco	38
Georgia	37
Moldova	36
Albania	36
Bulgaria	36
Jordan	36
Finland	36
Pakistan	35
Uruguay	33
South Africa	33
Turkey	33
Argentina	33
Romania	32
Sweden	32
Denmark	32
United States	32
India	32
Latvia	31
New Zealand	31
Estonia	31
Peru	31
Norway	30
Israel	30
Korea, South	30
Serbia	30
Ukraine	29
Azerbaijan	29
Belarus	28
Italy	28
Northern Ireland	28
Japan	28
Armenia	27
Poland	27
Portugal	26
Canada	25
Lithuania	25
Montenegro	25
Malta	24
Switzerland	23
Netherlands	23
Germany	23
Luxembourg	22
Australia	22
Greece	22
Ireland	22
Macedonia	22
Iran	22
Slovakia	22
France	21
Belgium	21
Chile	21
Austria	19
Russian Fed.	19
Bosnia and Herz.	18
Spain	17
Croatia	16
Great Britain	16
Slovenia	14
Hungary	14
Zimbabwe	11
Total	32

E033B) SELF POSITIONING IN POLITICAL SCALE: LEFT

In political matters, people talk of "the left" and "the right."
How would you place your views on this scale, generally speaking?
% Left (codes 1 to 4 on a 10-point scale)

(WVS: V139; EVS: V185)

Country	Wave		Gender		Age			Education			Income			Values		
	1990	2000	Male	Female	16-29	30-49	50+	Lower	Middle	Upper	Lower	Middle	Upper	Mat	Mixed	Postm.
Albania	na	**40**	38	41	37	37	46	43	36	38	44	37	38	40	40	31
Algeria	na	**20**	18	22	16	22	26	29	20	14	17	19	14	20	19	20
Argentina	18	**14**	15	12	16	13	12	12	14	17	12	14	14	8	11	21
Armenia	na	**29**	29	28	21	29	40	35	28	29	22	30	40	32	28	19
Australia	na	**23**	23	24	24	26	20	18	20	31	22	23	26	21	18	32
Austria	11	**20**	21	19	19	21	20	16	21	28	21	20	21	11	17	28
Azerbaijan	na	**25**	24	26	21	27	26	24	27	21	23	23	26	27	21	21
Bangladesh	na	**8**	8	9	9	6	11	4	10	14	5	7	10	5	9	12
Belarus	60	**15**	16	14	8	16	23	19	14	17	17	16	12	20	13	4
Belgium	27	**25**	28	23	28	29	21	22	21	33	23	26	26	20	22	41
Bosnia and Herz.	na	**24**	24	25	21	24	27	23	24	27	28	23	24	22	25	25
Brazil	30	**27**	27	27	31	27	17	27	25	30	28	28	26	26	26	34
Bulgaria	31	**25**	27	23	16	21	34	40	19	21	38	23	18	32	20	3
Canada	16	**21**	21	21	28	21	18	17	17	30	22	17	25	22	19	26
Chile	30	**31**	37	25	34	29	31	30	29	36	31	31	31	22	31	44
China	na	**na**	na	na	na	na	na	na	na	na	na	na	na	na	na	na
Colombia	na	**10**	10	10	11	10	8	8	9	12	9	10	10	13	8	14
Croatia	na	**19**	17	20	23	17	18	16	17	32	20	16	22	13	16	32
Czech Republic	22	**21**	24	19	11	18	29	25	17	20	30	22	14	32	19	14
Denmark	24	**26**	24	29	27	33	20	20	20	41	23	26	32	16	22	54
Dominican Rep.	na	**19**	17	19	16	21	18	26	22	16	19	22	13	20	18	24
Egypt	na	**na**	na	na	na	na	na	na	na	na	na	na	na	na	na	na
El Salvador	na	**17**	18	16	19	16	15	14	21	20	15	17	20	na	na	na
Estonia	na	**11**	11	12	11	9	14	10	14	7	12	14	8	14	11	10
Finland	21	**24**	27	21	22	28	21	27	20	19	28	24	21	24	21	43
France	42	**39**	41	37	39	43	35	34	43	48	39	43	41	30	37	56
Georgia	na	**20**	22	18	18	20	21	20	20	20	21	20	18	19	21	25
Germany	36	**29**	28	29	39	30	23	21	33	40	27	32	28	25	29	34
Great Britain	24	**26**	27	25	31	29	21	24	24	36	27	30	24	na	na	na
Greece	na	**35**	37	33	32	38	33	24	31	39	32	35	33	19	32	54
Hungary	18	**23**	23	22	11	26	28	19	26	34	17	31	17	19	25	43
Iceland	30	**28**	26	29	27	27	30	26	25	37	38	26	23	18	26	57
India	30	**22**	23	21	20	23	23	23	22	21	30	21	20	21	22	19
Indonesia	na	**9**	13	5	9	8	11	14	9	7	13	6	4	11	9	na
Iran	na	**39**	42	35	43	38	27	32	41	46	39	36	39	38	42	49
Ireland	12	**15**	16	13	19	16	9	12	16	16	11	14	17	8	15	23
Israel	na	**42**	41	43	42	44	39	45	46	33	53	40	36	21	46	53
Italy	41	**32**	34	30	32	36	29	27	33	42	29	34	35	25	29	40
Japan	16	**19**	20	18	29	19	16	24	18	18	19	19	21	8	20	32
Jordan	na	**17**	18	17	20	15	17	17	18	17	18	17	17	18	15	26
Korea, South	14	**32**	34	31	44	32	18	25	25	43	31	32	34	22	39	56
Latvia	na	**13**	15	12	8	15	14	15	13	12	17	14	8	15	11	21
Lithuania	na	**25**	24	26	18	23	32	33	25	18	29	26	19	34	22	14
Luxembourg	na	**26**	27	25	24	28	26	26	26	28	29	30	27	22	23	41
Macedonia	na	**27**	26	29	22	28	31	29	27	26	31	25	25	25	29	31
Malta	na	**13**	14	12	12	15	11	14	13	9	19	10	16	15	12	10
Mexico	21	**16**	17	15	19	14	14	14	19	16	13	17	18	14	16	18
Moldova	na	**31**	32	29	19	28	44	44	31	20	36	36	23	39	24	27
Montenegro	na	**46**	44	49	41	42	55	50	44	45	64	45	43	48	45	47
Morocco	na	**26**	30	20	27	27	22	25	27	32	24	29	25	25	28	25
Netherlands	33	**36**	34	38	32	43	31	23	35	49	37	36	35	25	31	53
New Zealand	na	**21**	22	20	38	19	19	17	20	27	24	23	19	12	19	34
Nigeria	22	**33**	32	35	33	33	38	36	31	34	37	32	34	32	33	41
Northern Ireland	10	**19**	21	17	12	28	16	19	18	23	22	17	17	13	18	30
Norway	27	**24**	23	25	26	30	16	23	22	29	na	na	na	21	21	51
Pakistan	na	**5**	4	5	4	5	3	2	9	1	5	9	2	6	4	na
Peru	na	**21**	22	20	22	22	16	20	21	21	23	20	17	20	21	21
Philippines	na	**10**	11	10	12	10	9	9	10	13	14	9	9	9	10	16
Poland	20	**27**	26	27	23	26	30	24	28	29	31	27	20	28	27	22
Portugal	23	**35**	31	38	35	29	40	35	32	35	45	30	34	33	33	45
Puerto Rico	na	**13**	16	11	15	16	9	9	11	14	13	10	15	13	11	16
Romania	19	**18**	20	15	12	16	25	14	19	20	16	24	17	22	18	8
Russian Fed.	33	**30**	31	29	17	26	43	44	29	27	37	33	21	31	29	34
Serbia	na	**25**	25	24	11	22	33	31	23	21	28	21	26	29	21	19
Singapore	na	**na**	na	na	na	na	na	na	na	na	na	na	na	na	na	na
Slovakia	na	**33**	34	32	24	35	36	35	32	32	33	35	30	38	31	11
Slovenia	23	**25**	25	24	16	28	27	16	25	35	15	30	35	23	26	23
South Africa	39	**26**	25	27	24	26	32	23	29	38	24	27	27	29	24	25
Spain	50	**40**	44	36	48	44	31	36	42	49	40	40	44	31	38	61
Sweden	28	**34**	34	34	36	36	31	39	34	30	40	32	29	31	30	46
Switzerland	23	**28**	27	29	33	31	22	20	27	44	29	26	31	13	23	48
Taiwan	na	**4**	6	3	8	4	3	4	5	5	3	6	4	3	6	9
Tanzania	na	**24**	23	26	31	21	20	23	29	19	30	21	17	22	25	24
Turkey	25	**20**	21	19	23	20	15	15	24	36	17	19	33	13	19	34
Uganda	na	**34**	35	33	34	37	23	30	37	23	37	25	37	32	35	36
Ukraine	na	**27**	28	26	18	21	38	43	28	19	37	26	19	34	25	8
United States	17	**18**	20	15	24	17	15	16	15	20	19	17	19	10	16	25
Uruguay	na	**28**	27	28	39	34	18	18	37	50	23	26	37	17	26	45
Venezuela	na	**17**	18	16	16	18	17	19	17	16	21	15	18	20	18	11
Vietnam	na	**2**	3	2	3	2	3	2	2	2	7	2	na	1	2	5
Zimbabwe	na	**59**	57	61	62	57	56	59	61	40	63	53	62	56	61	66
Total	27	**25**	25	24	25	25	24	24	25	26	26	24	23	24	23	33

RANKING	
Country	2000
Zimbabwe	59
Montenegro	46
Israel	42
Spain	40
Albania	40
Iran	39
France	39
Netherlands	36
Portugal	35
Greece	35
Uganda	34
Sweden	34
Nigeria	33
Slovakia	33
Korea, South	32
Italy	32
Chile	31
Moldova	31
Russian Fed.	30
Armenia	29
Germany	29
Switzerland	28
Uruguay	28
Iceland	28
Macedonia	27
Ukraine	27
Brazil	27
Poland	27
Denmark	26
Luxembourg	26
Morocco	26
South Africa	26
Great Britain	26
Belgium	25
Bulgaria	25
Lithuania	25
Azerbaijan	25
Slovenia	25
Serbia	25
Norway	24
Finland	24
Tanzania	24
Bosnia and Herz.	24
Australia	23
Hungary	23
India	22
Czech Republic	21
New Zealand	21
Canada	21
Peru	21
Turkey	20
Austria	20
Georgia	20
Algeria	20
Northern Ireland	19
Japan	19
Croatia	19
Dominican Rep.	19
Romania	18
United States	18
Jordan	17
Venezuela	17
El Salvador	17
Mexico	16
Belarus	15
Ireland	15
Argentina	14
Latvia	13
Malta	13
Puerto Rico	13
Estonia	11
Philippines	10
Colombia	10
Indonesia	9
Bangladesh	8
Pakistan	5
Taiwan	4
Vietnam	2
Total	25

E033C) SELF POSITIONING IN POLITICAL SCALE: CENTER

In political matters, people talk of "the left" and "the right."

How would you place your views on this scale, generally speaking?

% Center (codes 5 & 6 on a 10-point scale) (WVS: V139; EVS: V185)

Country	Wave 1990	Wave 2000	Gender Male	Gender Female	Age 16-29	Age 30-49	Age 50+	Education Lower	Education Middle	Education Upper	Income Lower	Income Middle	Income Upper	Values Mat	Values Mixed	Values Postm.
Albania	na	**24**	23	26	27	26	19	25	25	21	24	28	22	25	22	36
Algeria	na	**37**	37	37	40	37	31	37	37	37	41	42	35	43	32	46
Argentina	61	**54**	51	57	53	56	53	53	57	50	50	54	58	55	55	52
Armenia	na	**44**	44	45	45	47	38	40	44	45	45	50	36	41	46	50
Australia	na	**54**	53	56	61	53	50	59	60	45	55	57	48	55	57	51
Austria	48	**61**	61	61	67	62	57	63	62	52	57	62	58	66	65	53
Azerbaijan	na	**47**	46	47	47	45	50	44	46	47	50	45	42	49	44	30
Bangladesh	na	**26**	22	32	27	27	13	24	28	25	21	31	22	18	29	37
Belarus	30	**57**	53	61	59	55	57	58	60	47	63	55	52	62	58	31
Belgium	42	**54**	50	58	55	53	54	58	57	47	53	58	52	59	54	47
Bosnia and Herz.	na	**58**	56	60	60	58	56	55	60	55	60	60	52	61	56	57
Brazil	39	**33**	31	35	33	34	30	24	39	41	27	34	38	29	35	34
Bulgaria	47	**39**	35	44	38	45	32	36	41	38	33	42	40	36	42	47
Canada	58	**54**	50	59	52	54	55	59	60	41	55	61	45	59	57	46
Chile	52	**48**	43	54	48	50	48	51	49	42	52	49	41	50	49	44
China	na	**na**	na	na	na	na	na	na	na	na	na	na	na	na	na	na
Colombia	na	**46**	46	45	47	46	41	35	46	52	38	46	49	31	42	41
Croatia	na	**65**	67	63	59	66	68	65	68	55	67	68	62	69	66	59
Czech Republic	49	**40**	38	42	45	42	35	41	40	33	41	40	38	42	40	30
Denmark	41	**42**	39	45	37	38	47	49	35	33	51	43	32	50	43	31
Dominican Rep.	na	**29**	36	24	27	33	36	10	25	33	27	32	30	26	29	29
Egypt	na	**na**	na	na	na	na	na	na	na	na	na	na	na	na	na	na
El Salvador	na	**42**	45	39	42	42	41	38	44	46	39	43	45	na	na	na
Estonia	na	**58**	56	60	52	64	54	58	57	58	62	62	52	62	56	61
Finland	36	**40**	35	45	45	36	40	44	38	32	44	39	36	43	40	34
France	38	**40**	38	42	47	40	37	45	37	31	43	38	37	44	41	32
Georgia	na	**43**	42	44	47	42	40	42	42	46	39	45	48	45	42	32
Germany	46	**48**	46	51	49	47	49	52	46	41	48	44	47	47	48	51
Great Britain	50	**58**	59	58	61	60	55	61	61	48	58	55	59	na	na	na
Greece	na	**43**	41	45	52	37	39	39	46	42	42	47	43	48	47	31
Hungary	65	**64**	62	65	78	62	56	68	59	49	67	58	68	65	62	57
Iceland	34	**34**	32	36	34	34	34	38	34	24	35	36	30	38	35	20
India	41	**47**	47	46	47	47	44	45	47	48	41	43	51	43	49	55
Indonesia	na	**47**	47	49	42	51	47	52	46	47	54	44	41	49	48	32
Iran	na	**39**	40	39	37	38	49	44	36	39	43	43	36	37	37	39
Ireland	55	**64**	63	64	70	62	62	62	63	67	63	65	63	69	62	67
Israel	na	**28**	27	28	24	27	33	32	26	28	29	26	27	24	29	25
Italy	42	**40**	36	45	38	39	42	47	36	35	43	42	36	42	42	37
Japan	54	**54**	50	58	59	61	46	42	55	57	52	54	51	54	54	47
Jordan	na	**47**	50	43	40	48	61	49	46	47	46	54	43	42	52	39
Korea, South	36	**38**	35	40	37	39	37	27	42	33	37	43	35	41	36	27
Latvia	na	**56**	57	54	64	61	48	53	56	56	50	55	64	55	57	51
Lithuania	na	**50**	51	49	65	58	29	27	56	56	36	49	58	44	52	64
Luxembourg	na	**51**	50	53	62	50	47	53	50	52	46	43	54	51	53	45
Macedonia	na	**51**	51	50	56	49	50	47	52	52	49	52	52	54	50	30
Malta	na	**63**	60	66	63	64	62	66	62	63	60	58	58	65	62	63
Mexico	48	**33**	34	33	32	36	28	27	39	38	29	38	34	35	33	34
Moldova	na	**33**	31	35	40	34	26	25	37	33	29	26	40	30	37	24
Montenegro	na	**29**	28	31	28	31	28	29	28	30	15	32	33	31	28	23
Morocco	na	**36**	35	38	37	36	35	34	39	44	25	35	41	36	35	43
Netherlands	37	**41**	38	44	47	35	45	56	41	29	43	44	34	46	44	32
New Zealand	na	**42**	43	41	39	43	42	48	42	33	46	49	33	43	42	41
Nigeria	44	**27**	26	29	25	30	30	27	29	26	26	30	22	29	26	26
Northern Ireland	57	**53**	46	60	55	48	56	54	51	55	54	52	48	53	55	45
Norway	39	**45**	44	46	46	45	46	50	51	35	na	na	na	52	46	32
Pakistan	na	**61**	68	51	54	65	68	47	47	81	47	44	75	56	64	50
Peru	na	**49**	50	48	50	48	50	49	48	50	46	51	51	46	49	55
Philippines	na	**49**	48	49	49	52	42	47	51	47	47	55	41	51	46	51
Poland	50	**47**	49	44	57	51	35	50	45	42	45	48	43	43	47	51
Portugal	46	**40**	42	38	37	40	41	39	42	34	30	43	42	45	38	29
Puerto Rico	na	**45**	40	48	58	48	37	40	38	50	34	54	43	45	45	45
Romania	53	**49**	45	56	47	53	46	47	50	51	45	47	53	46	52	50
Russian Fed.	56	**52**	49	54	59	56	40	38	53	52	49	49	56	52	51	49
Serbia	na	**46**	43	49	47	45	46	48	45	46	44	51	45	44	46	53
Singapore	na	**na**	na	na	na	na	na	na	na	na	na	na	na	na	na	na
Slovakia	na	**46**	44	48	53	46	41	46	47	39	48	46	45	44	46	50
Slovenia	63	**61**	59	64	71	60	56	65	62	54	71	58	52	61	61	60
South Africa	32	**41**	40	42	39	43	39	40	41	51	38	33	51	41	41	42
Spain	33	**43**	41	45	41	41	46	45	44	34	41	45	38	46	46	30
Sweden	37	**34**	33	35	31	34	35	43	31	30	35	35	31	37	35	30
Switzerland	47	**49**	46	52	46	49	51	51	51	32	49	51	44	57	51	39
Taiwan	na	**53**	57	49	67	52	44	44	55	60	54	49	53	50	58	47
Tanzania	na	**19**	19	18	17	22	13	15	20	32	14	24	23	21	17	10
Turkey	51	**43**	42	44	44	44	39	43	44	40	43	43	40	42	44	40
Uganda	na	**23**	23	24	23	25	17	22	24	27	22	20	30	22	25	21
Ukraine	na	**44**	39	49	50	44	40	40	44	45	43	44	44	43	46	44
United States	54	**51**	47	55	45	55	49	54	55	47	53	49	47	58	51	45
Uruguay	na	**39**	41	37	44	41	36	39	41	32	37	43	35	35	42	37
Venezuela	na	**43**	43	44	44	44	39	39	43	48	37	43	46	36	46	44
Vietnam	na	**6**	6	6	7	6	6	4	7	9	7	6	5	5	6	7
Zimbabwe	na	**29**	30	29	28	30	32	30	29	60	28	35	25	31	30	16
Total	46	**44**	43	45	44	44	43	43	45	42	43	45	43	44	44	41

RANKING Country	2000
Croatia	65
Hungary	64
Ireland	64
Malta	63
Slovenia	61
Austria	61
Pakistan	61
Bosnia and Herz.	58
Great Britain	58
Estonia	58
Belarus	57
Latvia	56
Australia	54
Argentina	54
Canada	54
Belgium	54
Japan	54
Northern Ireland	53
Taiwan	53
Russian Fed.	52
Luxembourg	51
Macedonia	51
United States	51
Lithuania	50
Romania	49
Peru	49
Switzerland	49
Philippines	49
Chile	48
Germany	48
Indonesia	47
Jordan	47
Poland	47
Azerbaijan	47
India	47
Slovakia	46
Serbia	46
Colombia	46
Norway	45
Puerto Rico	45
Armenia	44
Ukraine	44
Greece	43
Venezuela	43
Georgia	43
Spain	43
Turkey	43
New Zealand	42
Denmark	42
El Salvador	42
Netherlands	41
South Africa	41
Finland	40
Italy	40
France	40
Czech Republic	40
Portugal	40
Iran	39
Uruguay	39
Bulgaria	39
Korea, South	38
Algeria	37
Morocco	36
Sweden	34
Iceland	34
Mexico	33
Moldova	33
Brazil	33
Zimbabwe	29
Montenegro	29
Dominican Rep.	29
Israel	28
Nigeria	27
Bangladesh	26
Albania	24
Uganda	23
Tanzania	19
Vietnam	6
Total	44

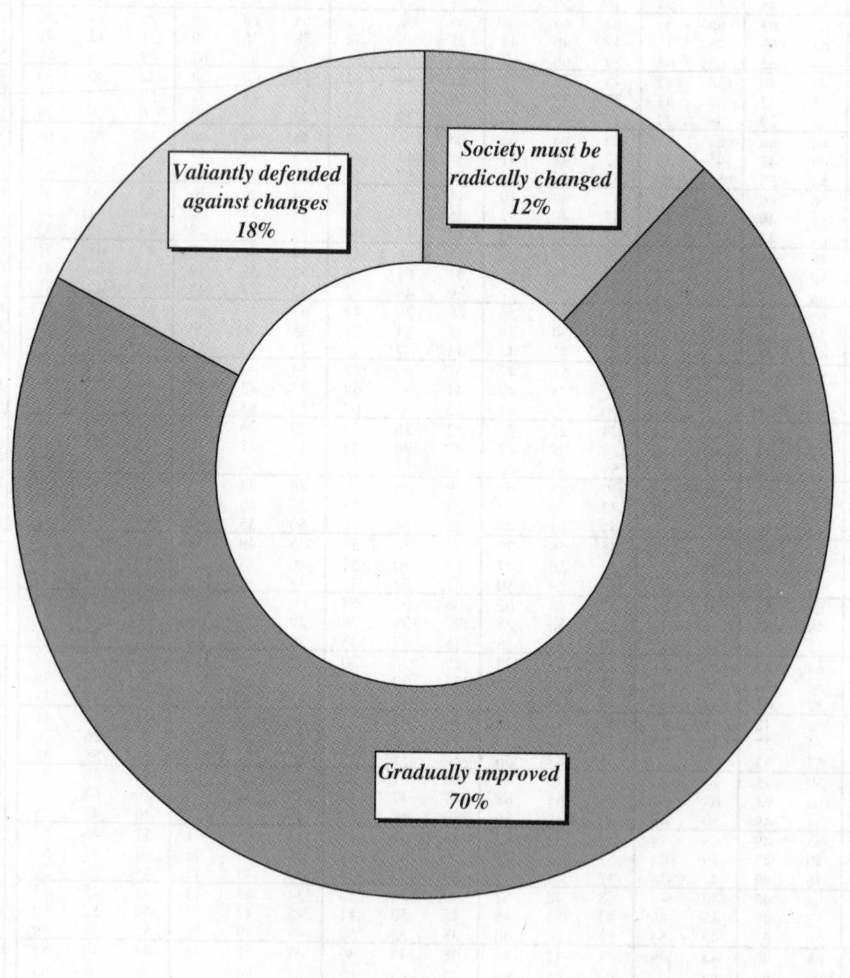
E34) Society Changes
Society must be radically changed 12%
Gradually improved 70%
Valiantly defended against changes 18%

E034A) SOCIAL CHANGE: CONSERVATIVE

On this card are three basic kinds of attitudes concerning the society we live in.
Please choose the one which best describes your own opinion.
Our present society must be valiantly defended against all subversive forces (%) (WVS: V140; EVS: o23)

	Wave		Gender		Age			Education			Income			Values		
Country	1990	2000	Male	Female	16-29	30-49	50+	Lower	Middle	Upper	Lower	Middle	Upper	Mat	Mixed	Postm.
Albania	na	**20**	18	22	21	19	21	26	19	9	22	17	20	18	22	22
Algeria	na	**20**	18	23	21	20	21	25	20	17	19	23	21	25	19	15
Argentina	11	**15**	14	15	14	14	16	18	11	5	18	14	11	20	14	10
Armenia	na	**7**	8	7	8	5	10	15	8	4	8	6	8	8	7	3
Australia	na	**17**	15	18	11	14	24	26	16	10	21	13	14	18	17	15
Austria	20	**17**	15	19	14	14	21	21	14	9	23	14	14	26	19	11
Azerbaijan	na	**4**	4	5	4	4	6	12	5	3	5	5	5	5	4	na
Bangladesh	na	**44**	43	47	42	47	44	51	38	35	41	40	54	48	43	41
Belarus	28	**8**	6	9	5	7	10	12	8	1	8	8	5	8	7	2
Belgium	21	**na**	na	na	na	na	na	na	na	na	na	na	na	na	na	na
Bosnia and Herz.	na	**13**	12	13	11	12	15	11	14	9	12	14	11	16	11	15
Brazil	10	**21**	22	21	19	22	24	24	20	15	22	26	17	22	23	14
Bulgaria	19	**na**	na	na	na	na	na	na	na	na	na	na	na	na	na	na
Canada	13	**15**	13	17	13	12	21	23	14	11	20	17	10	27	16	12
Chile	23	**13**	15	11	13	11	15	15	12	10	16	10	13	16	13	8
China	25	**na**	na	na	na	na	na	na	na	na	na	na	na	na	na	na
Colombia	na	**19**	16	22	26	15	17	22	24	10	25	22	12	18	20	23
Croatia	na	**na**	na	na	na	na	na	na	na	na	na	na	na	na	na	na
Czech Republic	15	**19**	19	19	28	16	16	21	17	18	22	18	18	22	17	18
Denmark	22	**na**	na	na	na	na	na	na	na	na	na	na	na	na	na	na
Dominican Rep.	na	**16**	19	15	16	16	18	28	24	12	16	17	11	30	14	9
Egypt	na	**17**	18	15	15	18	17	19	17	12	17	18	15	15	18	20
El Salvador	na	**15**	12	18	16	15	13	18	14	9	20	15	7	na	na	na
Estonia	17	**na**	na	na	na	na	na	na	na	na	na	na	na	na	na	na
Finland	9	**na**	na	na	na	na	na	na	na	na	na	na	na	na	na	na
France	21	**na**	na	na	na	na	na	na	na	na	na	na	na	na	na	na
Georgia	na	**3**	3	3	4	2	3	4	3	2	3	3	3	3	3	6
Germany	4	**na**	na	na	na	na	na	na	na	na	na	na	na	na	na	na
Great Britain	14	**na**	na	na	na	na	na	na	na	na	na	na	na	na	na	na
Greece	na	**na**	na	na	na	na	na	na	na	na	na	na	na	na	na	na
Hungary	17	**na**	na	na	na	na	na	na	na	na	na	na	na	na	na	na
Iceland	15	**na**	na	na	na	na	na	na	na	na	na	na	na	na	na	na
India	17	**19**	19	18	17	19	20	17	20	21	17	17	21	19	19	22
Indonesia	na	**16**	17	17	17	17	16	19	19	12	16	17	17	19	15	33
Iran	na	**na**	na	na	na	na	na	na	na	na	na	na	na	na	na	na
Ireland	20	**na**	na	na	na	na	na	na	na	na	na	na	na	na	na	na
Israel	na	**na**	na	na	na	na	na	na	na	na	na	na	na	na	na	na
Italy	10	**9**	8	10	8	7	12	13	8	3	12	11	6	14	9	6
Japan	21	**14**	17	12	5	14	18	22	15	11	17	10	17	27	12	11
Jordan	na	**49**	48	49	47	50	47	52	45	46	51	49	50	50	48	41
Korea, South	11	**32**	29	35	21	34	40	70	37	19	35	32	28	37	28	12
Latvia	11	**na**	na	na	na	na	na	na	na	na	na	na	na	na	na	na
Lithuania	10	**10**	8	12	11	11	8	8	11	9	8	11	8	13	8	22
Luxembourg	na	**na**	na	na	na	na	na	na	na	na	na	na	na	na	na	na
Macedonia	na	**24**	24	24	27	23	22	23	26	19	27	23	21	23	23	37
Malta	na	**na**	na	na	na	na	na	na	na	na	na	na	na	na	na	na
Mexico	13	**26**	22	30	25	26	27	29	25	15	27	27	25	29	24	25
Moldova	na	**14**	15	14	13	13	17	15	17	10	15	15	14	18	12	9
Montenegro	na	**12**	11	13	13	8	16	14	10	9	5	9	16	14	9	16
Morocco	na	**9**	9	9	8	10	6	8	7	16	2	10	11	7	9	13
Netherlands	23	**na**	na	na	na	na	na	na	na	na	na	na	na	na	na	na
New Zealand	na	**10**	10	10	7	7	15	16	7	6	13	10	8	8	11	7
Nigeria	13	**13**	14	12	15	12	9	12	14	14	12	14	14	13	13	15
Northern Ireland	21	**na**	na	na	na	na	na	na	na	na	na	na	na	na	na	na
Norway	31	**30**	29	32	23	24	44	43	31	18	na	na	na	46	30	15
Pakistan	na	**17**	16	18	14	20	13	17	16	18	19	16	18	14	21	20
Peru	na	**20**	17	22	21	19	18	25	20	17	22	19	17	23	20	16
Philippines	na	**16**	13	19	21	15	12	14	16	19	15	15	18	14	17	24
Poland	12	**na**	na	na	na	na	na	na	na	na	na	na	na	na	na	na
Portugal	11	**na**	na	na	na	na	na	na	na	na	na	na	na	na	na	na
Puerto Rico	na	**17**	17	17	22	10	20	19	19	15	19	17	13	15	17	16
Romania	na	**na**	na	na	na	na	na	na	na	na	na	na	na	na	na	na
Russian Fed.	34	**6**	5	6	5	5	7	11	6	2	7	6	4	6	6	na
Serbia	na	**12**	10	14	12	10	14	17	12	5	16	11	9	15	10	5
Singapore	na	**na**	na	na	na	na	na	na	na	na	na	na	na	na	na	na
Slovakia	na	**na**	na	na	na	na	na	na	na	na	na	na	na	na	na	na
Slovenia	12	**11**	10	12	12	10	13	17	11	2	14	5	8	16	10	9
South Africa	21	**15**	17	14	15	16	17	17	14	5	20	14	11	18	13	16
Spain	6	**9**	10	8	8	8	11	9	9	10	13	8	10	7	11	6
Sweden	8	**na**	na	na	na	na	na	na	na	na	na	na	na	na	na	na
Switzerland	na	**17**	16	19	12	15	23	31	16	5	20	20	10	26	19	8
Taiwan	na	**24**	23	25	21	27	19	27	22	23	27	24	19	27	23	14
Tanzania	na	**41**	37	48	43	38	49	49	36	28	46	44	30	42	42	38
Turkey	26	**20**	18	23	20	20	22	25	16	9	21	20	16	23	21	12
Uganda	na	**15**	22	9	17	14	14	15	15	25	17	16	19	11	17	21
Ukraine	na	**4**	4	4	6	2	4	5	4	3	4	3	4	5	2	3
United States	18	**16**	19	14	12	12	26	27	17	12	19	15	13	16	18	15
Uruguay	na	**19**	19	20	22	16	21	25	12	10	22	23	13	24	20	16
Venezuela	na	**30**	26	33	32	26	33	33	30	26	28	37	27	27	31	29
Vietnam	na	**16**	17	15	16	16	16	16	15	16	18	14	16	11	17	20
Zimbabwe	na	**20**	18	21	21	17	22	21	19	8	21	18	17	20	20	14
Total	17	**18**	17	18	18	17	18	22	16	13	19	17	16	19	18	14

RANKING	
Country	**2000**
Jordan	49
Bangladesh	44
Tanzania	41
Korea, South	32
Norway	30
Venezuela	30
Mexico	26
Taiwan	24
Macedonia	24
Brazil	21
Algeria	20
Turkey	20
Albania	20
Peru	20
Zimbabwe	20
Uruguay	19
Colombia	19
Czech Republic	19
India	19
Switzerland	17
Egypt	17
Pakistan	17
Austria	17
Australia	17
Puerto Rico	17
Indonesia	16
United States	16
Dominican Rep.	16
Philippines	16
Vietnam	16
Uganda	15
Canada	15
South Africa	15
El Salvador	15
Argentina	15
Moldova	14
Japan	14
Nigeria	13
Chile	13
Bosnia and Herz.	13
Serbia	12
Montenegro	12
Slovenia	11
New Zealand	10
Lithuania	10
Spain	9
Italy	9
Morocco	9
Belarus	8
Armenia	7
Russian Fed.	6
Azerbaijan	4
Ukraine	4
Georgia	3
Total	18

E034B) SOCIAL CHANGE: RADICAL

On this card are three basic kinds of attitudes concerning the society we live in.
Please choose the one which best describes your own opinion.
Our society must be radically changed by revolutionary action (%)

(WVS: V140; EVS: o23)

Country	Wave		Gender		Age			Education			Income			Values		
	1990	2000	Male	Female	16-29	30-49	50+	Lower	Middle	Upper	Lower	Middle	Upper	Mat	Mixed	Postm.
Albania	na	**11**	14	7	8	12	11	12	11	5	14	11	6	9	11	8
Algeria	na	**7**	9	5	9	6	7	9	7	7	8	7	6	6	8	7
Argentina	8	**4**	5	3	6	3	3	3	5	4	5	4	3	3	4	5
Armenia	na	**16**	19	13	17	15	16	17	16	14	13	15	22	15	18	12
Australia	na	**6**	6	7	11	5	3	8	7	3	8	5	4	9	5	7
Austria	2	**2**	2	2	4	2	1	2	3	2	3	2	2	4	2	2
Azerbaijan	na	**24**	22	25	23	26	20	23	25	22	29	25	19	22	26	31
Bangladesh	na	**13**	14	12	13	13	13	12	14	15	7	17	14	10	15	8
Belarus	26	**5**	7	4	7	5	4	4	5	8	6	4	7	5	5	8
Belgium	3	**na**	na	na	na	na	na	na	na	na	na	na	na	na	na	na
Bosnia and Herz.	na	**12**	12	12	11	13	12	11	12	14	13	12	13	13	12	15
Brazil	16	**18**	18	18	20	19	13	18	19	16	19	18	17	17	19	18
Bulgaria	22	**na**	na	na	na	na	na	na	na	na	na	na	na	na	na	na
Canada	5	**7**	6	8	17	5	3	8	9	4	10	9	4	9	7	8
Chile	5	**8**	9	7	9	9	6	9	8	7	9	7	7	4	8	14
China	5	**na**	na	na	na	na	na	na	na	na	na	na	na	na	na	na
Colombia	na	**7**	8	7	8	7	6	8	6	8	7	7	8	na	na	na
Croatia	na	**na**	na	na	na	na	na	na	na	na	na	na	na	11	6	11
Czech Republic	42	**6**	7	6	6	7	5	8	5	2	9	7	3	10	6	3
Denmark	2	**na**	na	na	na	na	na	na	na	na	na	na	na	na	na	na
Dominican Rep.	na	**13**	11	14	12	14	18	21	13	12	17	8	14	16	12	14
Egypt	na	**5**	5	5	5	5	5	5	5	6	5	6	6	7	4	5
El Salvador	na	**6**	6	6	7	6	5	7	6	6	6	6	6	na	na	na
Estonia	22	**na**	na	na	na	na	na	na	na	na	na	na	na	na	na	na
Finland	3	**na**	na	na	na	na	na	na	na	na	na	na	na	na	na	na
France	4	**na**	na	na	na	na	na	na	na	na	na	na	na	na	na	na
Georgia	na	**10**	11	9	10	9	11	9	10	10	11	9	8	9	10	16
Germany	13	**na**	na	na	na	na	na	na	na	na	na	na	na	na	na	na
Great Britain	5	**na**	na	na	na	na	na	na	na	na	na	na	na	na	na	na
Greece	na	**na**	na	na	na	na	na	na	na	na	na	na	na	na	na	na
Hungary	6	**na**	na	na	na	na	na	na	na	na	na	na	na	na	na	na
Iceland	3	**na**	na	na	na	na	na	na	na	na	na	na	na	na	na	na
India	14	**14**	17	10	19	12	12	13	15	16	14	16	12	15	14	10
Indonesia	na	**5**	6	4	4	3	8	8	5	4	9	3	4	8	3	4
Iran	na	**na**	na	na	na	na	na	na	na	na	na	na	na	na	na	na
Ireland	4	**na**	na	na	na	na	na	na	na	na	na	na	na	na	na	na
Israel	na	**na**	na	na	na	na	na	na	na	na	na	na	na	na	na	na
Italy	7	**4**	5	3	8	4	3	4	5	4	5	3	4	2	4	5
Japan	2	**5**	4	6	10	6	2	9	5	3	5	5	4	2	5	5
Jordan	na	**10**	10	9	12	8	7	6	11	13	8	6	10	10	9	15
Korea, South	7	**10**	11	8	10	11	6	4	10	10	13	8	8	7	10	25
Latvia	31	**na**	na	na	na	na	na	na	na	na	na	na	na	na	na	na
Lithuania	32	**23**	25	21	17	27	23	17	27	14	30	22	21	20	25	23
Luxembourg	na	**na**	na	na	na	na	na	na	na	na	na	na	na	na	na	na
Macedonia	na	**15**	16	15	16	14	16	20	14	12	19	14	14	14	17	5
Malta	na	**na**	na	na	na	na	na	na	na	na	na	na	na	na	na	na
Mexico	17	**16**	15	17	16	15	16	18	15	10	18	15	13	na	na	na
Moldova	na	**28**	28	27	32	26	27	28	26	30	28	26	28	23	29	28
Montenegro	na	**11**	12	9	11	9	11	10	11	11	12	9	7	8	13	11
Morocco	na	**6**	8	4	9	4	4	5	9	9	5	7	9	4	7	14
Netherlands	2	**na**	na	na	na	na	na	na	na	na	na	na	na	na	na	na
New Zealand	na	**5**	5	5	14	5	2	5	5	5	6	5	4	6	4	6
Nigeria	28	**31**	32	30	32	32	28	29	34	31	29	31	36	33	29	37
Northern Ireland	5	**na**	na	na	na	na	na	na	na	na	na	na	na	na	na	na
Norway	2	**3**	2	4	4	4	1	4	3	1	na	na	na	1	3	2
Pakistan	na	**20**	20	19	28	17	12	18	23	18	18	22	19	20	19	20
Peru	na	**6**	7	5	6	7	6	4	6	7	7	5	5	6	6	4
Philippines	na	**21**	21	20	23	19	22	25	21	16	19	19	25	19	22	22
Poland	23	**na**	na	na	na	na	na	na	na	na	na	na	na	na	na	na
Portugal	4	**na**	na	na	na	na	na	na	na	na	na	na	na	na	na	na
Puerto Rico	na	**4**	7	3	7	5	2	3	3	5	4	4	5	6	4	5
Romania	na	**na**	na	na	na	na	na	na	na	na	na	na	na	na	na	na
Russian Fed.	17	**15**	16	13	14	15	15	16	15	13	18	14	12	13	16	24
Serbia	na	**9**	11	7	8	8	9	10	9	5	10	7	7	8	9	12
Singapore	na	**na**	na	na	na	na	na	na	na	na	na	na	na	na	na	na
Slovakia	na	**na**	na	na	na	na	na	na	na	na	na	na	na	na	na	na
Slovenia	14	**7**	8	7	8	9	4	12	7	2	10	9	2	5	8	7
South Africa	19	**20**	20	20	19	20	18	23	15	25	20	26	12	16	21	25
Spain	4	**6**	6	5	7	7	4	6	6	6	2	5	9	4	6	7
Sweden	6	**na**	na	na	na	na	na	na	na	na	na	na	na	na	na	na
Switzerland	na	**7**	8	5	10	7	5	7	7	6	8	6	6	7	7	6
Taiwan	na	**3**	4	2	5	3	3	2	4	3	4	3	3	2	5	na
Tanzania	na	**27**	29	24	27	28	21	26	28	31	26	28	24	28	26	42
Turkey	14	**22**	22	23	25	22	17	20	26	25	23	21	27	15	22	33
Uganda	na	**9**	11	8	8	13	2	8	10	16	11	9	11	8	10	9
Ukraine	na	**10**	13	7	7	10	10	13	11	5	14	10	5	9	11	2
United States	7	**9**	9	9	16	8	4	16	9	5	12	7	5	9	7	12
Uruguay	na	**9**	10	8	8	13	6	6	12	13	8	9	9	6	10	7
Venezuela	na	**13**	14	11	11	15	12	11	13	14	13	9	14	15	12	9
Vietnam	na	**54**	55	54	58	54	51	59	50	43	57	54	53	55	53	48
Zimbabwe	na	**13**	14	12	12	16	10	13	12	30	15	11	14	13	13	10
Total	12	**12**	13	11	14	12	9	13	13	10	13	12	12	13	12	11

RANKING	
Country	2000
Vietnam	54
Nigeria	31
Moldova	28
Tanzania	27
Azerbaijan	24
Lithuania	23
Turkey	22
Philippines	21
South Africa	20
Pakistan	20
Brazil	18
Armenia	16
Mexico	16
Macedonia	15
Russian Fed.	15
India	14
Bangladesh	13
Dominican Rep.	13
Zimbabwe	13
Venezuela	13
Bosnia and Herz.	12
Albania	11
Montenegro	11
Georgia	10
Ukraine	10
Jordan	10
Korea, South	10
Uganda	9
United States	9
Serbia	9
Uruguay	9
Chile	8
Algeria	7
Slovenia	7
Colombia	7
Canada	7
Switzerland	7
Czech Republic	6
El Salvador	6
Australia	6
Morocco	6
Peru	6
Spain	6
Belarus	5
Indonesia	5
Egypt	5
New Zealand	5
Japan	5
Puerto Rico	4
Italy	4
Argentina	4
Taiwan	3
Norway	3
Austria	2
Total	12

E034C) SOCIAL CHANGE: REFORMS

On this card are three basic kinds of attitudes concerning the society we live in.

Please choose the one which best describes your own opinion.

Our society must be gradually improved by reforms (%)

(WVS: V140; EVS: o23)

Country	Wave		Gender		Age			Education			Income			Values		
	1990	2000	Male	Female	16-29	30-49	50+	Lower	Middle	Upper	Lower	Middle	Upper	Mat	Mixed	Postm.
Albania	na	**69**	68	71	72	69	68	61	70	86	64	72	74	73	68	69
Algeria	na	**72**	73	71	70	75	72	66	73	75	73	70	73	70	73	78
Argentina	81	**82**	81	82	80	84	81	79	84	91	77	82	86	76	82	84
Armenia	na	**77**	74	80	76	80	74	68	76	82	79	79	70	77	75	85
Australia	na	**77**	79	76	78	81	73	67	77	87	72	82	82	73	78	78
Austria	78	**81**	83	79	82	85	78	77	83	90	74	84	85	70	80	87
Azerbaijan	na	**72**	75	70	73	70	74	65	71	76	66	70	77	73	70	69
Bangladesh	na	**42**	43	41	44	41	43	37	48	50	52	44	32	42	42	51
Belarus	46	**87**	87	87	88	88	85	85	87	91	86	88	87	86	89	90
Belgium	75	**na**	na	na	na	na	na	na	na	na	na	na	na	na	na	na
Bosnia and Herz.	na	**75**	76	75	77	75	73	78	74	77	74	74	76	71	78	71
Brazil	74	**61**	60	61	61	59	63	59	61	70	59	56	66	61	59	68
Bulgaria	59	**na**	na	na	na	na	na	na	na	na	na	na	na	na	na	na
Canada	82	**78**	81	75	70	83	76	69	78	85	71	75	86	64	78	81
Chile	72	**79**	76	82	78	80	78	76	80	83	74	84	80	80	79	78
China	70	**na**	na	na	na	na	na	na	na	na	na	na	na	na	na	na
Colombia	na	**74**	76	71	66	78	77	70	70	82	68	71	81	71	74	66
Croatia	na	**na**	na	na	na	na	na	na	na	na	na	na	na	na	na	na
Czech Republic	42	**75**	75	75	66	76	78	71	78	81	70	76	79	69	77	79
Denmark	77	**na**	na	na	na	na	na	na	na	na	na	na	na	na	na	na
Dominican Rep.	na	**71**	71	71	72	71	64	52	63	76	67	75	75	54	74	77
Egypt	na	**78**	77	80	80	77	78	76	78	81	78	76	80	78	78	76
El Salvador	na	**79**	82	76	77	79	82	76	80	85	74	80	87	na	na	na
Estonia	61	**na**	na	na	na	na	na	na	na	na	na	na	na	na	na	na
Finland	88	**na**	na	na	na	na	na	na	na	na	na	na	na	na	na	na
France	75	**na**	na	na	na	na	na	na	na	na	na	na	na	na	na	na
Georgia	na	**87**	86	88	86	88	87	87	87	89	86	88	89	88	87	78
Germany	84	**na**	na	na	na	na	na	na	na	na	na	na	na	na	na	na
Great Britain	81	**na**	na	na	na	na	na	na	na	na	na	na	na	na	na	na
Greece	na	**na**	na	na	na	na	na	na	na	na	na	na	na	na	na	na
Hungary	77	**na**	na	na	na	na	na	na	na	na	na	na	na	na	na	na
Iceland	82	**na**	na	na	na	na	na	na	na	na	na	na	na	na	na	na
India	69	**67**	64	72	64	69	68	70	65	64	69	67	67	66	67	68
Indonesia	na	**78**	77	79	80	80	75	73	76	84	75	79	79	72	82	63
Iran	na	**na**	na	na	na	na	na	na	na	na	na	na	na	na	na	na
Ireland	76	**na**	na	na	na	na	na	na	na	na	na	na	na	na	na	na
Israel	na	**na**	na	na	na	na	na	na	na	na	na	na	na	na	na	na
Italy	83	**87**	87	87	84	90	86	84	88	93	84	86	90	84	87	89
Japan	77	**81**	80	82	85	80	80	68	80	87	78	84	79	72	83	84
Jordan	na	**42**	42	42	41	41	46	41	44	41	41	44	40	40	43	44
Korea, South	81	**59**	60	58	70	55	54	27	53	72	52	61	64	56	62	63
Latvia	59	**na**	na	na	na	na	na	na	na	na	na	na	na	na	na	na
Lithuania	59	**67**	67	68	72	62	69	74	63	77	61	68	71	67	67	55
Luxembourg	na	**na**	na	na	na	na	na	na	na	na	na	na	na	na	na	na
Macedonia	na	**61**	61	62	57	63	63	57	60	69	55	64	65	63	60	59
Malta	na	**na**	na	na	na	na	na	na	na	na	na	na	na	na	na	na
Mexico	71	**59**	64	54	59	59	57	53	61	75	55	59	62	52	60	64
Moldova	na	**58**	57	59	55	61	57	57	57	60	57	59	58	59	59	63
Montenegro	na	**78**	78	78	76	83	73	76	79	80	83	82	76	78	78	73
Morocco	na	**85**	84	87	83	86	90	87	84	75	93	84	80	89	85	74
Netherlands	75	**na**	na	na	na	na	na	na	na	na	na	na	na	na	na	na
New Zealand	na	**82**	82	81	78	84	81	76	85	87	79	83	86	84	83	85
Nigeria	59	**56**	54	58	54	57	64	59	53	55	60	55	50	54	58	49
Northern Ireland	75	**na**	na	na	na	na	na	na	na	na	na	na	na	na	na	na
Norway	66	**67**	69	65	73	72	56	54	66	81	na	na	na	53	67	82
Pakistan	na	**64**	64	64	59	63	75	65	61	64	63	63	63	66	60	60
Peru	na	**74**	76	72	73	74	77	72	74	76	71	76	78	71	74	80
Philippines	na	**63**	66	60	56	67	66	61	63	65	66	66	58	67	61	54
Poland	65	**na**	na	na	na	na	na	na	na	na	na	na	na	na	na	na
Portugal	85	**na**	na	na	na	na	na	na	na	na	na	na	na	na	na	na
Puerto Rico	na	**79**	77	80	71	84	78	79	78	79	77	79	82	80	79	79
Romania	na	**na**	na	na	na	na	na	na	na	na	na	na	na	na	na	na
Russian Fed.	49	**80**	78	81	81	80	78	74	79	84	75	80	84	81	78	76
Serbia	na	**80**	80	80	81	82	77	73	79	90	74	82	84	77	81	84
Singapore	na	**na**	na	na	na	na	na	na	na	na	na	na	na	na	na	na
Slovakia	na	**na**	na	na	na	na	na	na	na	na	na	na	na	na	na	na
Slovenia	73	**82**	82	81	81	81	83	71	83	96	76	86	90	79	82	84
South Africa	60	**65**	64	67	66	64	66	60	71	70	60	61	78	66	66	59
Spain	91	**85**	84	86	85	86	85	85	85	85	84	87	82	89	83	87
Sweden	86	**na**	na	na	na	na	na	na	na	na	na	na	na	na	na	na
Switzerland	na	**76**	76	76	78	78	73	62	78	89	72	74	84	67	75	87
Taiwan	na	**73**	73	72	74	71	78	71	74	74	69	73	78	72	72	86
Tanzania	na	**32**	34	29	30	34	30	26	36	42	28	28	46	30	32	21
Turkey	61	**53**	56	50	52	53	56	50	54	64	50	55	54	56	53	51
Uganda	na	**75**	67	83	75	73	84	77	76	60	73	76	70	80	73	70
Ukraine	na	**87**	83	90	87	88	85	82	86	92	82	87	92	86	86	95
United States	75	**75**	73	78	73	81	70	57	74	83	69	77	82	75	76	74
Uruguay	na	**72**	71	73	70	71	74	69	75	78	71	68	78	71	70	77
Venezuela	na	**58**	60	56	57	59	56	56	57	61	59	54	59	58	57	63
Vietnam	na	**30**	29	32	26	31	33	25	34	41	25	32	31	34	30	33
Zimbabwe	na	**68**	68	68	68	67	68	67	69	62	64	71	69	68	67	76
Total	71	**70**	70	71	69	71	72	65	71	77	68	71	73	69	70	75

RANKING	
Country	2000
Georgia	87
Belarus	87
Italy	87
Ukraine	87
Morocco	85
Spain	85
Argentina	82
New Zealand	82
Slovenia	82
Austria	81
Japan	81
Russian Fed.	80
Serbia	80
Chile	79
El Salvador	79
Puerto Rico	79
Egypt	78
Indonesia	78
Montenegro	78
Canada	78
Australia	77
Armenia	77
Switzerland	76
Uganda	75
Bosnia and Herz.	75
United States	75
Czech Republic	75
Peru	74
Colombia	74
Taiwan	73
Algeria	72
Azerbaijan	72
Uruguay	72
Dominican Rep.	71
Albania	69
Zimbabwe	68
Lithuania	67
India	67
Norway	67
South Africa	65
Pakistan	64
Philippines	63
Macedonia	61
Brazil	61
Korea, South	59
Mexico	59
Moldova	58
Venezuela	58
Nigeria	56
Turkey	53
Bangladesh	42
Jordan	42
Tanzania	32
Vietnam	30
Total	70

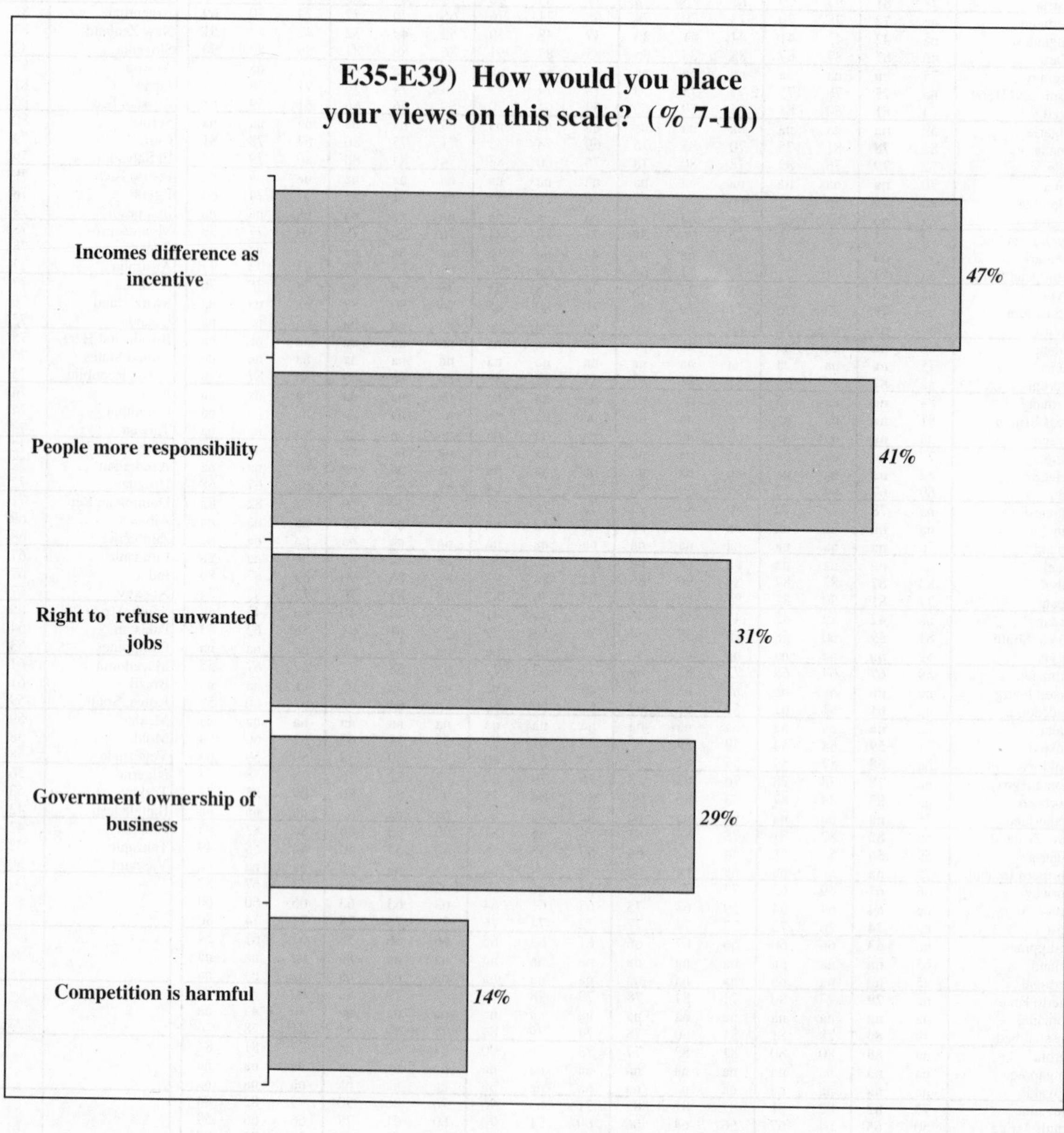
E35-E39) How would you place your views on this scale? (% 7-10)
Incomes difference as incentive
47%
People more responsibility
41%
Right to refuse unwanted jobs
31%
Government ownership of business
29%
Competition is harmful
14%

E035) INCOME: MORE EQUAL OR MORE UNEQUAL?

Now I'd like you to tell me your views on various issues. How would you place your views on this scale?

% "We need larger income differences as incentives for individual effort" (codes 7to 10) (WVS: V141; EVS: o18)

Country	Wave 1990	Wave 2000	Gender Male	Gender Female	Age 16-29	Age 30-49	Age 50+	Education Lower	Education Middle	Education Upper	Income Lower	Income Middle	Income Upper	Values Mat	Values Mixed	Values Postm.
Albania	na	**49**	54	43	53	50	43	40	52	62	43	43	61	48	51	44
Algeria	na	**77**	76	78	78	80	69	66	78	84	76	82	77	68	81	85
Argentina	65	**35**	38	32	35	37	33	29	45	39	28	38	39	28	35	41
Armenia	na	**53**	57	49	54	58	45	47	52	61	62	46	47	51	56	52
Australia	na	**41**	43	39	38	43	41	38	42	43	35	44	45	51	43	36
Austria	42	**26**	32	20	31	26	23	18	29	44	16	23	38	20	27	26
Azerbaijan	na	**43**	44	43	39	47	44	38	39	52	36	36	60	38	52	50
Bangladesh	na	**67**	67	66	64	68	70	62	70	74	65	59	79	73	63	58
Belarus	71	**36**	42	31	49	35	26	21	37	57	30	35	49	27	40	80
Belgium	50	**42**	46	39	43	43	41	36	43	47	41	41	47	39	44	39
Bosnia and Herz.	na	**46**	49	43	49	44	44	34	44	60	40	44	54	50	43	51
Brazil	48	**47**	48	46	42	50	51	44	47	57	42	45	53	42	49	51
Bulgaria	61	**48**	52	44	61	56	33	23	56	72	28	49	64	37	59	70
Canada	63	**40**	43	37	36	43	39	38	39	44	36	38	46	43	42	36
Chile	47	**22**	22	22	23	24	18	21	22	25	21	23	23	21	21	24
China	80	**56**	59	53	55	56	58	58	54	60	62	53	55	54	58	61
Colombia	na	**52**	53	51	52	53	48	45	52	55	47	50	57	51	47	54
Croatia	na	**22**	23	22	27	21	21	19	22	35	20	21	27	12	23	27
Czech Republic	78	**42**	48	37	43	47	37	34	49	60	33	41	51	28	46	52
Denmark	57	**na**	na	na	na	na	na	na	na	na	na	na	na	na	na	na
Dominican Rep.	na	**75**	76	74	74	76	82	75	69	77	80	70	79	75	73	79
Egypt	na	**87**	87	87	87	87	86	85	88	91	87	88	89	88	87	88
El Salvador	na	**63**	64	61	62	62	66	58	65	70	55	64	71	na	na	na
Estonia	77	**62**	63	61	60	68	58	59	62	68	55	61	65	56	66	72
Finland	61	**28**	31	25	29	28	27	20	38	42	25	23	34	19	32	25
France	40	**34**	36	31	31	31	37	32	35	37	29	32	41	31	35	33
Georgia	na	**72**	73	72	73	75	68	75	70	75	70	74	74	72	72	75
Germany	74	**na**	na	na	na	na	na	na	na	na	na	na	na	na	na	na
Great Britain	58	**39**	43	35	33	43	39	34	43	47	29	37	56	na	na	na
Greece	na	**na**	na	na	na	na	na	na	na	na	na	na	na	na	na	na
Hungary	49	**na**	na	na	na	na	na	na	na	na	na	na	na	na	na	na
Iceland	47	**44**	46	43	52	44	39	41	51	40	42	39	53	48	46	29
India	47	**31**	33	27	32	32	25	24	35	36	23	31	34	32	31	48
Indonesia	na	**65**	65	66	68	69	61	55	68	71	58	72	79	66	68	64
Iran	na	**33**	32	34	33	34	32	39	32	28	37	29	32	35	32	34
Ireland	58	**50**	53	47	56	50	46	42	50	63	42	47	62	44	52	48
Israel	na	**12**	13	12	13	13	10	10	11	16	11	13	13	8	14	5
Italy	47	**49**	53	45	51	54	43	40	54	59	40	48	59	43	50	50
Japan	34	**35**	42	30	35	33	38	35	32	46	34	32	44	33	36	42
Jordan	na	**72**	76	69	71	72	77	65	80	77	67	74	78	72	72	77
Korea, South	39	**60**	60	60	60	60	61	59	59	62	55	61	65	57	62	63
Latvia	68	**na**	na	na	na	na	na	na	na	na	na	na	na	na	na	na
Lithuania	73	**34**	34	33	41	39	23	18	36	51	27	24	46	24	35	54
Luxembourg	na	**62**	62	62	64	63	61	55	64	68	60	61	68	58	65	61
Macedonia	na	**35**	35	36	35	36	34	29	35	47	31	34	42	36	36	27
Malta	na	**na**	na	na	na	na	na	na	na	na	na	na	na	na	na	na
Mexico	50	**39**	42	36	42	38	38	35	41	51	30	38	50	34	41	40
Moldova	na	**58**	57	59	60	59	54	53	55	67	64	57	54	51	61	75
Montenegro	na	**40**	44	36	55	42	29	26	45	61	42	29	53	38	44	42
Morocco	na	**73**	72	74	74	72	72	73	73	74	61	73	72	75	70	74
Netherlands	48	**51**	55	47	44	53	52	53	52	47	43	49	61	54	54	40
New Zealand	na	**35**	42	29	32	39	32	32	35	39	25	34	47	41	36	32
Nigeria	74	**55**	56	54	56	54	54	55	53	56	54	54	59	53	56	58
Northern Ireland	67	**44**	46	42	47	41	45	36	48	55	39	43	50	47	44	40
Norway	47	**34**	37	30	32	34	34	25	34	40	na	na	na	33	35	26
Pakistan	na	**11**	12	11	13	10	13	4	19	16	3	10	23	7	17	50
Peru	na	**70**	69	71	68	72	72	70	71	70	71	73	66	68	71	74
Philippines	na	**51**	52	49	51	50	51	46	49	57	48	50	54	50	51	49
Poland	79	**51**	53	49	52	55	46	42	59	73	41	58	60	44	54	68
Portugal	25	**na**	na	na	na	na	na	na	na	na	na	na	na	na	na	na
Puerto Rico	na	**70**	71	70	68	70	72	66	69	72	66	70	74	74	72	65
Romania	55	**20**	18	22	19	21	19	20	17	27	23	19	18	18	20	28
Russian Fed.	63	**65**	68	63	72	67	58	57	65	68	60	65	70	62	69	61
Serbia	na	**47**	50	44	52	51	42	35	48	62	35	46	59	40	53	63
Singapore	na	**63**	62	63	61	66	59	61	62	68	58	64	65	63	64	53
Slovakia	na	**na**	na	na	na	na	na	na	na	na	na	na	na	na	na	na
Slovenia	48	**20**	21	20	21	21	19	10	22	35	15	20	30	19	21	17
South Africa	37	**39**	43	34	45	36	33	33	45	59	31	38	50	37	40	48
Spain	32	**35**	36	35	39	33	35	34	34	42	34	37	35	36	37	29
Sweden	58	**na**	na	na	na	na	na	na	na	na	na	na	na	na	na	na
Switzerland	na	**35**	38	31	36	36	31	28	35	45	26	31	41	42	34	29
Taiwan	na	**46**	46	47	38	48	49	50	39	47	44	44	51	52	42	44
Tanzania	na	**38**	41	35	41	36	37	36	40	39	39	33	43	39	38	46
Turkey	31	**25**	25	25	25	26	25	25	25	28	23	26	27	25	26	25
Uganda	na	**67**	60	74	65	69	72	65	69	63	63	76	63	66	67	75
Ukraine	na	**66**	67	65	66	68	63	63	64	71	64	65	68	62	69	80
United States	62	**44**	45	42	39	43	48	43	42	45	42	40	55	39	46	38
Uruguay	na	**36**	36	36	36	34	38	34	38	38	31	31	46	28	37	39
Venezuela	na	**44**	44	43	45	44	39	34	44	55	34	41	53	41	44	47
Vietnam	na	**50**	55	46	54	54	41	45	55	61	46	45	58	32	57	52
Zimbabwe	na	**63**	63	62	59	64	70	63	62	70	66	59	67	57	68	52
Total	56	**47**	49	46	50	48	43	41	48	55	44	46	53	46	48	45

RANKING

Country	2000
Egypt	87
Algeria	77
Dominican Rep.	75
Morocco	73
Jordan	72
Georgia	72
Peru	70
Puerto Rico	70
Uganda	67
Bangladesh	67
Ukraine	66
Indonesia	65
Russian Fed.	65
El Salvador	63
Singapore	63
Zimbabwe	63
Luxembourg	62
Estonia	62
Korea, South	60
Moldova	58
China	56
Nigeria	55
Armenia	53
Colombia	52
Poland	51
Netherlands	51
Philippines	51
Vietnam	50
Ireland	50
Italy	49
Albania	49
Bulgaria	48
Serbia	47
Brazil	47
Taiwan	46
Bosnia and Herz.	46
Iceland	44
Northern Ireland	44
United States	44
Venezuela	44
Azerbaijan	43
Belgium	42
Czech Republic	42
Australia	41
Canada	40
Montenegro	40
Mexico	39
South Africa	39
Great Britain	39
Tanzania	38
Uruguay	36
Belarus	36
Japan	35
Macedonia	35
Spain	35
New Zealand	35
Argentina	35
Switzerland	35
Lithuania	34
France	34
Norway	34
Iran	33
India	31
Finland	28
Austria	26
Turkey	25
Croatia	22
Chile	22
Slovenia	20
Romania	20
Israel	12
Pakistan	11
Total	47

E036) OWNERSHIP OF BUSINESS: PRIVATE OR GOVERNMENT?

Now I'd like you to tell me your views on various issues. How would you place your views on this scale?

% Government ownership of business and industry should be increased (codes 7-10) (WVS: V142; EVS: o19)

Country	Wave		Gender		Age			Education			Income			Values		
	1990	2000	Male	Female	16-29	30-49	50+	Lower	Middle	Upper	Lower	Middle	Upper	Mat	Mixed	Postm.
Albania	na	**16**	16	16	12	15	21	17	16	13	20	16	12	16	14	36
Algeria	na	**32**	30	34	28	33	40	35	31	31	33	32	34	27	34	36
Argentina	18	**40**	38	42	44	38	38	44	36	30	45	44	30	41	42	35
Armenia	na	**47**	41	53	38	48	62	56	49	36	36	50	62	54	41	52
Australia	na	**12**	14	11	12	14	11	13	13	11	13	13	12	12	12	12
Austria	8	**7**	7	8	6	6	8	10	5	2	10	6	6	16	8	4
Azerbaijan	na	**38**	34	41	38	34	46	51	36	38	44	38	31	38	37	31
Bangladesh	na	**34**	32	37	34	34	33	39	31	24	39	28	37	45	26	26
Belarus	42	**30**	27	33	21	28	43	41	28	25	34	32	19	38	26	11
Belgium	14	**na**	na	na	na	na	na	na	na	na	na	na	na	na	na	na
Bosnia and Herz.	na	**21**	18	25	21	20	23	23	22	19	29	22	15	22	21	21
Brazil	37	**35**	30	40	39	32	34	41	34	20	42	35	28	42	34	25
Bulgaria	20	**na**	na	na	na	na	na	na	na	na	na	na	na	na	na	na
Canada	10	**11**	10	12	12	13	9	13	12	10	16	12	8	16	12	10
Chile	41	**39**	41	38	40	39	38	40	39	39	42	39	36	36	38	48
China	61	**61**	62	60	51	62	69	69	58	40	66	63	54	64	56	63
Colombia	na	**58**	54	62	58	56	61	71	61	44	69	62	44	67	56	58
Croatia	na	**28**	21	34	22	28	31	35	26	13	47	30	15	33	30	18
Czech Republic	19	**24**	22	25	21	21	27	28	21	11	30	24	18	35	21	16
Denmark	11	**na**	na	na	na	na	na	na	na	na	na	na	na	na	na	na
Dominican Rep.	na	**50**	46	53	48	56	46	58	58	47	65	42	43	56	47	57
Egypt	na	**57**	56	59	54	59	58	63	58	41	61	64	50	62	53	50
El Salvador	na	**52**	47	57	53	53	49	54	53	48	56	52	51	na	na	na
Estonia	19	**40**	35	44	32	33	50	45	41	28	52	46	30	46	36	20
Finland	6	**15**	13	16	11	14	17	19	9	9	17	16	12	12	15	19
France	18	**12**	11	13	12	13	11	14	10	9	12	15	9	10	11	17
Georgia	na	**39**	35	43	33	36	52	43	42	29	48	36	30	42	37	33
Germany	9	**12**	13	12	13	14	11	11	14	9	14	12	11	10	14	13
Great Britain	22	**21**	22	19	20	21	21	23	22	13	22	26	22	na	na	na
Greece	na	**na**	na	na	na	na	na	na	na	na	na	na	na	na	na	na
Hungary	17	**na**	na	na	na	na	na	na	na	na	na	na	na	na	na	na
Iceland	11	**9**	9	10	8	7	13	12	6	9	14	9	7	11	9	9
India	31	**51**	48	55	50	51	49	59	52	38	57	59	42	58	46	37
Indonesia	na	**37**	39	35	40	40	33	42	35	36	36	38	41	41	34	54
Iran	na	**35**	33	38	34	34	44	42	35	29	35	33	35	37	35	27
Ireland	15	**14**	13	15	10	13	18	20	13	6	16	19	9	14	12	21
Israel	na	**na**	na	na	na	na	na	na	na	na	na	na	na	na	na	na
Italy	18	**13**	11	15	10	13	15	17	10	9	17	11	10	19	13	9
Japan	17	**9**	7	12	11	8	10	16	9	7	10	9	9	9	9	8
Jordan	na	**43**	39	46	40	45	43	45	40	41	46	43	39	42	42	54
Korea, South	29	**23**	20	25	16	24	26	36	25	17	26	19	22	23	22	22
Latvia	22	**na**	na	na	na	na	na	na	na	na	na	na	na	na	na	na
Lithuania	28	**27**	22	31	17	29	33	35	27	17	33	36	20	33	26	11
Luxembourg	na	**na**	na	na	na	na	na	na	na	na	na	na	na	na	na	na
Macedonia	na	**18**	19	17	13	20	20	25	16	12	22	17	14	21	15	15
Malta	na	**na**	na	na	na	na	na	na	na	na	na	na	na	na	na	na
Mexico	24	**41**	40	42	41	39	44	42	42	30	45	40	37	39	43	38
Moldova	na	**52**	49	55	46	49	63	57	53	47	58	54	44	55	50	40
Montenegro	na	**25**	24	27	15	22	36	37	20	15	25	27	22	30	22	19
Morocco	na	**32**	31	32	30	32	39	35	26	16	33	30	33	36	30	29
Netherlands	10	**13**	11	14	11	9	17	18	10	12	17	12	10	20	11	16
New Zealand	na	**15**	16	15	12	15	17	17	13	14	20	15	11	18	12	17
Nigeria	50	**na**	na	na	na	na	na	na	na	na	na	na	na	na	na	na
Northern Ireland	21	**17**	17	17	18	17	16	20	17	11	22	17	17	13	18	21
Norway	14	**14**	10	17	17	12	13	15	13	14	na	na	na	11	14	16
Pakistan	na	**17**	17	16	17	16	18	22	13	13	21	19	9	19	14	10
Peru	na	**49**	44	53	50	50	42	59	54	34	60	49	30	54	48	45
Philippines	na	**48**	48	49	45	50	51	46	50	49	49	44	55	48	48	55
Poland	24	**38**	35	41	29	36	46	47	28	25	45	37	28	42	37	24
Portugal	18	**20**	19	22	23	21	17	21	18	18	18	21	17	19	21	19
Puerto Rico	na	**22**	19	23	18	19	26	35	29	16	34	18	17	29	23	15
Romania	31	**27**	21	34	23	22	34	45	22	9	39	30	16	35	22	8
Russian Fed.	40	**44**	41	46	26	42	59	62	44	35	52	47	36	49	39	40
Serbia	na	**28**	22	34	16	23	38	41	25	16	40	27	20	35	22	15
Singapore	na	**19**	17	21	19	17	24	25	18	10	26	20	14	19	20	17
Slovakia	na	**na**	na	na	na	na	na	na	na	na	na	na	na	na	na	na
Slovenia	17	**na**	na	na	na	na	na	na	na	na	na	na	na	na	na	na
South Africa	25	**36**	37	36	38	37	30	42	31	15	46	40	20	32	39	34
Spain	36	**34**	36	32	33	33	36	37	31	28	47	36	30	34	32	43
Sweden	14	**na**	na	na	na	na	na	na	na	na	na	na	na	na	na	na
Switzerland	na	**8**	8	9	11	8	8	17	7	5	13	7	6	13	9	6
Taiwan	na	**21**	17	26	18	20	27	30	24	12	27	21	16	23	20	24
Tanzania	na	**38**	33	44	44	35	33	44	31	30	47	37	22	38	38	21
Turkey	42	**33**	31	36	34	33	33	38	29	19	38	32	25	33	33	34
Uganda	na	**21**	10	30	19	21	27	31	17	7	15	29	15	18	21	26
Ukraine	na	**37**	35	39	23	31	53	64	36	27	48	34	28	44	34	24
United States	7	**10**	10	11	12	9	10	17	11	7	14	9	6	12	11	7
Uruguay	na	**36**	40	33	42	36	34	36	36	40	40	36	33	37	38	33
Venezuela	na	**41**	39	43	43	40	40	44	42	35	40	45	43	41	41	42
Vietnam	na	**30**	30	29	24	29	36	27	32	38	32	31	28	22	32	31
Zimbabwe	na	**27**	23	31	29	25	27	30	25	na	32	25	27	24	30	30
Total	23	**29**	27	31	29	29	30	34	29	24	35	30	25	34	27	23

RANKING	
Country	2000
China	61
Colombia	58
Egypt	57
Moldova	52
El Salvador	52
India	51
Dominican Rep.	50
Peru	49
Philippines	48
Armenia	47
Russian Fed.	44
Jordan	43
Venezuela	41
Mexico	41
Argentina	40
Estonia	40
Georgia	39
Chile	39
Poland	38
Tanzania	38
Azerbaijan	38
Ukraine	37
Indonesia	37
South Africa	36
Uruguay	36
Brazil	35
Iran	35
Spain	34
Bangladesh	34
Turkey	33
Algeria	32
Morocco	32
Belarus	30
Vietnam	30
Croatia	28
Serbia	28
Zimbabwe	27
Romania	27
Lithuania	27
Montenegro	25
Czech Republic	24
Korea, South	23
Puerto Rico	22
Bosnia and Herz.	21
Taiwan	21
Uganda	21
Great Britain	21
Portugal	20
Singapore	19
Macedonia	18
Northern Ireland	17
Pakistan	17
Albania	16
New Zealand	15
Finland	15
Ireland	14
Norway	14
Italy	13
Netherlands	13
Australia	12
Germany	12
France	12
Canada	11
United States	10
Japan	9
Iceland	9
Switzerland	8
Austria	7
Total	29

E037) RESPONSIBILITY TO PROVIDE FOR PEOPLE

Now I'd like you to tell me your views on various issues. How would you place your views on this scale?

% "People should take more responsibility to provide for themselves" (codes 7 to 10) (WVS: V143; EVS: V186)

Country	Wave 1990	Wave 2000	Gender Male	Gender Female	Age 16-29	Age 30-49	Age 50+	Education Lower	Education Middle	Education Upper	Income Lower	Income Middle	Income Upper	Values Mat	Values Mixed	Values Postm.
Albania	na	**50**	47	54	48	49	54	56	49	40	53	54	44	52	47	54
Algeria	na	**43**	45	41	45	40	45	51	42	39	47	41	35	45	42	42
Argentina	33	**53**	52	54	52	52	54	53	54	50	56	55	46	60	52	50
Armenia	na	**66**	63	68	63	63	73	70	66	63	61	67	72	69	64	55
Australia	na	**27**	30	25	37	22	25	34	27	22	32	25	20	24	27	28
Austria	14	**18**	17	19	17	18	19	20	17	15	20	19	16	28	16	20
Azerbaijan	na	**64**	66	63	63	63	70	72	64	62	61	65	70	63	68	53
Bangladesh	na	**36**	32	41	36	36	36	42	31	29	45	33	31	50	28	19
Belarus	43	**39**	38	41	36	39	43	45	39	31	44	39	32	45	34	24
Belgium	29	**33**	31	34	30	34	33	43	32	26	40	37	27	39	31	29
Bosnia and Herz.	na	**47**	45	49	45	48	50	47	49	43	50	48	44	48	48	43
Brazil	41	**39**	34	43	40	38	38	42	36	40	43	38	35	42	40	28
Bulgaria	35	**32**	29	35	23	29	39	43	29	19	43	30	24	40	25	16
Canada	19	**24**	23	25	27	24	22	25	24	24	29	24	19	23	22	29
Chile	55	**60**	59	60	58	61	59	63	60	51	64	58	56	61	58	61
China	33	**35**	32	38	28	36	40	37	34	33	38	36	32	36	33	39
Colombia	na	**45**	45	45	44	46	42	49	42	46	50	45	43	46	44	42
Croatia	na	**36**	36	35	36	34	37	39	34	33	33	42	30	40	37	29
Czech Republic	40	**28**	29	28	28	25	31	34	24	15	35	32	19	42	25	22
Denmark	16	**17**	16	18	18	19	14	17	16	18	16	18	17	17	14	30
Dominican Rep.	na	**41**	36	44	41	41	27	38	38	42	41	43	38	44	37	52
Egypt	na	**54**	54	55	52	57	53	62	52	39	60	62	48	62	50	43
El Salvador	na	**37**	36	38	35	36	41	36	36	38	35	35	41	na	na	na
Estonia	35	**43**	42	43	39	41	47	49	44	29	58	46	32	51	37	40
Finland	20	**26**	24	27	21	27	28	31	20	13	33	24	20	31	23	30
France	19	**16**	14	18	18	16	15	18	12	14	22	17	10	20	15	14
Georgia	na	**65**	63	67	56	66	74	69	63	69	69	65	60	66	65	59
Germany	23	**21**	21	22	18	23	21	24	20	14	25	21	12	23	22	17
Great Britain	33	**20**	21	18	23	20	18	24	16	16	23	23	20	na	na	na
Greece	na	**39**	40	38	36	39	47	46	41	35	38	38	38	37	37	42
Hungary	50	**48**	48	48	45	48	50	52	45	28	57	49	41	49	47	56
Iceland	26	**24**	22	27	23	25	24	30	17	27	29	26	18	25	23	36
India	20	**52**	48	57	50	52	52	59	50	40	63	54	44	52	47	41
Indonesia	na	**36**	36	36	42	35	35	38	33	39	29	41	40	40	32	59
Iran	na	**38**	35	42	38	38	41	43	39	33	41	39	37	42	37	40
Ireland	30	**24**	22	25	18	24	29	34	19	17	38	19	20	19	25	24
Israel	na	**79**	78	80	78	79	79	84	78	76	82	81	73	80	78	83
Italy	39	**37**	34	41	34	36	41	44	35	25	44	40	27	42	38	34
Japan	55	**51**	44	57	54	54	47	50	53	47	52	55	45	45	51	53
Jordan	na	**56**	58	54	55	57	55	57	57	53	58	57	51	54	58	52
Korea, South	25	**76**	74	79	82	77	69	73	74	80	76	74	78	75	76	91
Latvia	55	**54**	54	54	53	51	57	63	53	46	60	53	47	53	56	43
Lithuania	44	**34**	28	39	29	27	45	40	34	23	48	39	26	32	37	26
Luxembourg	na	**18**	20	17	19	18	18	24	16	15	19	21	12	20	19	12
Macedonia	na	**70**	68	72	67	67	77	76	73	52	74	70	65	72	69	71
Malta	na	**33**	33	33	32	31	36	38	33	25	37	26	28	28	37	28
Mexico	35	**45**	46	44	43	45	47	52	38	35	47	41	42	52	41	44
Moldova	na	**56**	58	55	55	54	60	56	60	51	57	55	55	60	52	54
Montenegro	na	**78**	75	80	67	75	87	89	75	60	89	82	63	83	71	75
Morocco	na	**50**	52	49	49	51	54	53	42	34	51	41	56	52	51	44
Netherlands	23	**23**	21	25	17	21	28	29	23	17	27	24	18	31	20	26
New Zealand	na	**26**	26	26	36	27	23	25	26	28	31	29	21	30	25	28
Nigeria	54	**68**	66	69	67	69	64	68	69	66	69	66	70	70	68	62
Northern Ireland	36	**25**	27	23	21	26	25	28	22	19	28	24	21	20	26	24
Norway	21	**30**	29	31	40	30	23	28	31	30	na	na	na	29	30	34
Pakistan	na	**57**	55	58	55	59	53	68	46	42	73	58	36	63	48	33
Peru	na	**34**	35	33	37	33	30	38	34	32	34	38	28	28	35	36
Philippines	na	**34**	33	35	35	33	34	38	31	34	37	33	32	34	34	33
Poland	37	**35**	35	36	37	33	38	41	33	16	46	30	26	38	34	32
Portugal	28	**26**	25	27	26	27	26	27	27	18	27	24	24	25	28	14
Puerto Rico	na	**20**	22	19	15	21	22	27	22	18	25	15	21	20	21	17
Romania	37	**33**	29	38	28	31	38	43	32	18	46	31	24	37	31	22
Russian Fed.	32	**40**	37	42	30	39	47	48	41	31	49	42	29	44	35	40
Serbia	na	**62**	57	66	58	58	67	71	58	55	72	61	52	69	56	46
Singapore	na	**40**	38	43	42	37	44	45	39	30	41	42	35	44	38	46
Slovakia	na	**50**	49	51	46	49	54	59	47	39	57	52	45	57	48	34
Slovenia	44	**50**	47	53	47	51	52	65	47	33	57	48	42	58	49	48
South Africa	39	**50**	51	50	44	54	57	57	43	31	57	49	42	54	47	57
Spain	44	**48**	47	50	52	49	45	48	47	51	43	52	50	49	48	49
Sweden	11	**17**	17	17	20	16	17	21	16	16	20	16	14	20	16	22
Switzerland	na	**13**	12	15	18	14	10	20	13	5	18	13	8	22	12	15
Taiwan	na	**32**	33	31	33	30	36	34	29	32	37	30	30	30	33	43
Tanzania	na	**65**	66	64	63	62	74	74	58	50	75	70	50	66	65	63
Turkey	50	**51**	48	54	51	50	50	51	48	50	54	49	45	50	51	51
Uganda	na	**45**	45	46	43	47	50	64	37	45	58	49	40	45	46	40
Ukraine	na	**47**	43	50	37	44	55	66	45	41	58	43	39	52	45	33
United States	14	**20**	19	21	25	20	16	23	19	20	21	18	20	20	18	25
Uruguay	na	**62**	66	60	62	64	61	64	62	56	66	65	59	58	68	57
Venezuela	na	**41**	39	44	41	42	42	45	45	29	51	45	33	50	41	30
Vietnam	na	**21**	16	25	16	21	24	21	21	13	30	21	15	15	21	21
Zimbabwe	na	**60**	58	62	60	59	63	66	52	40	63	59	57	64	58	50
Total	33	**41**	40	42	42	41	41	45	41	36	47	41	36	48	39	35

RANKING

Country	2000
Israel	79
Montenegro	78
Korea, South	76
Macedonia	70
Nigeria	68
Armenia	66
Georgia	65
Tanzania	65
Azerbaijan	64
Uruguay	62
Serbia	62
Zimbabwe	60
Chile	60
Pakistan	57
Moldova	56
Jordan	56
Egypt	54
Latvia	54
Argentina	53
India	52
Japan	51
Turkey	51
Albania	50
South Africa	50
Morocco	50
Slovenia	50
Slovakia	50
Spain	48
Hungary	48
Bosnia and Herz.	47
Ukraine	47
Uganda	45
Colombia	45
Mexico	45
Algeria	43
Estonia	43
Venezuela	41
Dominican Rep.	41
Singapore	40
Russian Fed.	40
Belarus	39
Brazil	39
Greece	39
Iran	38
Italy	37
El Salvador	37
Bangladesh	36
Indonesia	36
Croatia	36
Poland	35
China	35
Lithuania	34
Peru	34
Philippines	34
Malta	33
Romania	33
Belgium	33
Taiwan	32
Bulgaria	32
Norway	30
Czech Republic	28
Australia	27
New Zealand	26
Portugal	26
Finland	26
Northern Ireland	25
Iceland	24
Canada	24
Ireland	24
Netherlands	23
Germany	21
Vietnam	21
Puerto Rico	20
United States	20
Great Britain	20
Luxembourg	18
Austria	18
Sweden	17
Denmark	17
France	16
Switzerland	13
Total	41

E038_7) RIGHT TO REFUSE UNWANTED JOBS

Now I'd like you to tell me your views on various issues. How would you place your views on this scale?

(%) Unemployed should have the right to refuse a job they do not want (codes 7 to 10) (EVS: V187)

Country	Wave		Gender		Age			Education			Income			Values		
	1990	2000	Male	Female	16-29	30-49	50+	Lower	Middle	Upper	Lower	Middle	Upper	Mat	Mixed	Postm.
Albania	na	**na**	na	na	na	na	na	na	na	na	na	na	na	na	na	na
Algeria	na	**na**	na	na	na	na	na	na	na	na	na	na	na	na	na	na
Argentina	23	**na**	na	na	na	na	na	na	na	na	na	na	na	na	na	na
Armenia	na	**na**	na	na	na	na	na	na	na	na	na	na	na	na	na	na
Australia	na	**na**	na	na	na	na	na	na	na	na	na	na	na	na	na	na
Austria	16	**18**	21	16	21	23	12	14	20	29	16	22	19	14	14	28
Azerbaijan	na	**na**	na	na	na	na	na	na	na	na	na	na	na	na	na	na
Bangladesh	na	**na**	na	na	na	na	na	na	na	na	na	na	na	na	na	na
Belarus	39	**44**	45	44	51	46	36	31	49	49	45	46	41	41	45	43
Belgium	29	**32**	32	31	34	36	27	27	32	36	32	34	30	25	31	39
Bosnia and Herz.	na	**na**	na	na	na	na	na	na	na	na	na	na	na	na	na	na
Brazil	38	**na**	na	na	na	na	na	na	na	na	na	na	na	na	na	na
Bulgaria	59	**35**	39	32	48	40	24	20	41	48	26	40	43	35	37	31
Canada	30	**na**	na	na	na	na	na	na	na	na	na	na	na	na	na	na
Chile	26	**na**	na	na	na	na	na	na	na	na	na	na	na	na	na	na
China	36	**na**	na	na	na	na	na	na	na	na	na	na	na	na	na	na
Colombia	na	**na**	na	na	na	na	na	na	na	na	na	na	na	na	na	na
Croatia	na	**33**	31	34	43	32	26	27	35	36	28	36	32	31	31	37
Czech Republic	41	**28**	28	27	36	30	21	29	26	27	27	28	28	25	28	34
Denmark	26	**32**	33	31	32	35	29	30	33	35	31	34	33	28	29	46
Dominican Rep.	na	**na**	na	na	na	na	na	na	na	na	na	na	na	na	na	na
Egypt	na	**na**	na	na	na	na	na	na	na	na	na	na	na	na	na	na
El Salvador	na	**na**	na	na	na	na	na	na	na	na	na	na	na	na	na	na
Estonia	57	**52**	51	52	55	55	47	50	52	52	52	52	49	57	47	65
Finland	12	**33**	32	33	39	38	25	37	24	32	37	36	27	39	29	41
France	25	**28**	27	29	32	34	20	24	29	36	31	27	26	22	25	45
Georgia	na	**na**	na	na	na	na	na	na	na	na	na	na	na	na	na	na
Germany	40	**22**	20	23	27	25	15	19	25	18	19	17	14	13	23	32
Great Britain	37	**27**	30	24	35	29	21	29	27	27	31	31	27	na	na	na
Greece	na	**39**	38	40	40	43	32	35	36	43	36	38	43	32	39	46
Hungary	39	**25**	27	22	24	33	18	22	29	29	31	26	20	20	29	38
Iceland	22	**31**	29	32	31	29	32	31	30	30	38	30	25	28	31	35
India	20	**na**	na	na	na	na	na	na	na	na	na	na	na	na	na	na
Indonesia	na	**na**	na	na	na	na	na	na	na	na	na	na	na	na	na	na
Iran	na	**na**	na	na	na	na	na	na	na	na	na	na	na	na	na	na
Ireland	37	**39**	38	40	39	39	38	43	38	33	49	41	32	34	37	53
Israel	na	**na**	na	na	na	na	na	na	na	na	na	na	na	na	na	na
Italy	16	**13**	12	14	17	16	8	10	16	14	11	16	14	8	13	16
Japan	24	**na**	na	na	na	na	na	na	na	na	na	na	na	na	na	na
Jordan	na	**na**	na	na	na	na	na	na	na	na	na	na	na	na	na	na
Korea, South	33	**na**	na	na	na	na	na	na	na	na	na	na	na	na	na	na
Latvia	68	**45**	47	43	55	54	32	36	45	54	40	45	53	37	47	64
Lithuania	45	**40**	41	40	47	50	26	27	45	43	40	38	42	38	44	34
Luxembourg	na	**17**	17	17	18	21	12	16	18	17	12	21	20	14	17	24
Macedonia	na	**na**	na	na	na	na	na	na	na	na	na	na	na	na	na	na
Malta	na	**36**	35	38	35	39	34	37	35	39	33	38	34	34	38	31
Mexico	31	**na**	na	na	na	na	na	na	na	na	na	na	na	na	na	na
Moldova	na	**na**	na	na	na	na	na	na	na	na	na	na	na	na	na	na
Montenegro	na	**na**	na	na	na	na	na	na	na	na	na	na	na	na	na	na
Morocco	na	**na**	na	na	na	na	na	na	na	na	na	na	na	na	na	na
Netherlands	28	**32**	33	31	28	35	30	25	32	39	33	33	29	18	27	51
New Zealand	na	**na**	na	na	na	na	na	na	na	na	na	na	na	na	na	na
Nigeria	29	**na**	na	na	na	na	na	na	na	na	na	na	na	na	na	na
Northern Ireland	39	**31**	32	30	34	33	28	33	31	23	36	30	23	25	31	40
Norway	12	**na**	na	na	na	na	na	na	na	na	na	na	na	na	na	na
Pakistan	na	**na**	na	na	na	na	na	na	na	na	na	na	na	na	na	na
Peru	na	**na**	na	na	na	na	na	na	na	na	na	na	na	na	na	na
Philippines	na	**na**	na	na	na	na	na	na	na	na	na	na	na	na	na	na
Poland	39	**26**	28	25	36	29	18	27	26	26	22	29	31	23	30	28
Portugal	27	**25**	26	24	33	26	19	22	32	26	11	22	31	22	26	33
Puerto Rico	na	**na**	na	na	na	na	na	na	na	na	na	na	na	na	na	na
Romania	42	**39**	38	40	50	43	28	27	45	45	31	33	48	32	43	53
Russian Fed.	41	**50**	52	48	56	52	43	38	52	50	48	52	50	46	54	57
Serbia	na	**na**	na	na	na	na	na	na	na	na	na	na	na	na	na	na
Singapore	na	**na**	na	na	na	na	na	na	na	na	na	na	na	na	na	na
Slovakia	na	**27**	29	26	35	30	19	23	30	26	27	28	25	24	31	32
Slovenia	11	**16**	17	15	23	15	11	14	16	16	13	16	17	13	16	20
South Africa	28	**na**	na	na	na	na	na	na	na	na	na	na	na	na	na	na
Spain	30	**19**	20	18	27	24	10	11	23	31	15	22	26	10	21	28
Sweden	19	**15**	16	15	15	18	13	17	17	11	18	16	12	10	15	18
Switzerland	na	**na**	na	na	na	na	na	na	na	na	na	na	na	na	na	na
Taiwan	na	**na**	na	na	na	na	na	na	na	na	na	na	na	na	na	na
Tanzania	na	**na**	na	na	na	na	na	na	na	na	na	na	na	na	na	na
Turkey	na	**na**	na	na	na	na	na	na	na	na	na	na	na	na	na	na
Uganda	na	**na**	na	na	na	na	na	na	na	na	na	na	na	na	na	na
Ukraine	na	**53**	52	54	55	56	49	45	53	57	51	52	57	56	51	69
United States	26	**na**	na	na	na	na	na	na	na	na	na	na	na	na	na	na
Uruguay	na	**na**	na	na	na	na	na	na	na	na	na	na	na	na	na	na
Venezuela	na	**na**	na	na	na	na	na	na	na	na	na	na	na	na	na	na
Vietnam	na	**na**	na	na	na	na	na	na	na	na	na	na	na	na	na	na
Zimbabwe	na	**na**	na	na	na	na	na	na	na	na	na	na	na	na	na	na
Total	32	31	32	31	36	35	25	26	34	36	31	33	32	31	31	35

RANKING	
Country	**2000**
Ukraine	53
Estonia	52
Russian Fed.	50
Latvia	45
Belarus	44
Lithuania	40
Greece	39
Romania	39
Ireland	39
Malta	36
Bulgaria	35
Finland	33
Croatia	33
Denmark	32
Netherlands	32
Belgium	32
Iceland	31
Northern Ireland	31
Czech Republic	28
France	28
Slovakia	27
Great Britain	27
Poland	26
Portugal	25
Hungary	25
Germany	22
Spain	19
Austria	18
Luxembourg	17
Slovenia	16
Sweden	15
Italy	13
Total	31

E039A) COMPETITION IS GOOD

Now I'd like you to tell me your views on various issues. How would you place your views on this scale?

% Competition is good. It stimulates people to work hard and develop new ideas (codes 1 to 4) (WVS: V144; EVS: V188)

Country	Wave		Gender		Age			Education			Income			Values		
	1990	2000	Male	Female	16-29	30-49	50+	Lower	Middle	Upper	Lower	Middle	Upper	Mat	Mixed	Postm.
Albania	na	80	83	78	84	81	76	76	82	86	79	79	82	79	80	84
Algeria	na	na	na	na	na	na	na	na	na	na	na	na	na	na	na	na
Argentina	na	59	64	54	50	63	63	54	65	68	52	59	64	57	59	59
Armenia	na	56	58	54	50	63	54	52	53	64	55	56	55	52	59	57
Australia	na	76	76	75	71	77	78	74	74	80	72	79	79	75	76	75
Austria	na	74	78	71	74	75	74	73	74	79	73	72	79	65	76	74
Azerbaijan	na	64	67	60	63	65	62	59	64	64	64	62	71	59	73	60
Bangladesh	na	71	72	70	70	70	78	69	72	74	74	69	70	78	67	60
Belarus	na	65	69	61	75	64	56	51	68	72	60	63	76	62	65	93
Belgium	na	48	52	44	50	45	49	41	50	50	44	44	49	46	51	41
Bosnia and Herz.	na	74	75	73	75	74	71	65	74	79	70	73	80	77	73	79
Brazil	na	69	72	66	63	72	77	65	70	81	62	66	77	65	69	81
Bulgaria	na	66	70	61	72	70	59	52	69	77	58	65	72	62	70	84
Canada	na	70	75	66	68	70	71	68	69	73	63	72	75	72	70	70
Chile	na	46	48	45	49	44	48	42	48	50	42	50	48	43	49	46
China	na	80	82	78	79	78	88	83	79	83	81	79	84	76	85	77
Colombia	na	na	na	na	na	na	na	na	na	na	na	na	na	na	na	na
Croatia	na	75	79	71	69	79	74	76	73	78	68	75	76	71	77	71
Czech Republic	na	77	77	76	79	78	75	73	80	84	74	75	82	69	79	87
Denmark	na	61	68	55	71	62	55	60	76	55	54	61	70	54	65	52
Dominican Rep.	na	72	75	70	70	74	82	68	67	74	65	76	75	65	71	77
Egypt	na	na	na	na	na	na	na	na	na	na	na	na	na	na	na	na
El Salvador	na	66	68	64	66	64	68	63	68	72	62	65	76	na	na	na
Estonia	na	52	56	49	56	55	47	47	50	64	44	47	59	48	55	54
Finland	na	59	63	55	66	56	57	53	67	65	53	57	63	61	59	54
France	na	46	45	46	45	43	49	44	44	51	44	42	53	45	48	39
Georgia	na	73	76	71	75	75	68	71	73	76	70	72	78	71	75	78
Germany	na	66	69	64	65	64	69	65	66	73	69	74	66	71	66	59
Great Britain	na	59	61	57	53	58	63	57	56	68	55	58	64	na	na	na
Greece	na	55	56	55	49	58	62	58	60	51	57	56	55	61	57	45
Hungary	na	61	65	59	66	61	58	56	69	70	57	59	66	57	65	74
Iceland	na	84	87	81	88	87	75	80	88	83	75	86	88	87	85	71
India	na	64	65	63	62	65	64	64	64	63	64	64	64	64	64	61
Indonesia	na	na	na	na	na	na	na	na	na	na	na	na	na	na	na	na
Iran	na	na	na	na	na	na	na	na	na	na	na	na	na	na	na	na
Ireland	na	65	67	62	67	65	62	59	64	77	59	61	74	62	68	61
Israel	na	na	na	na	na	na	na	na	na	na	na	na	na	na	na	na
Italy	na	57	62	53	58	55	58	54	60	61	55	57	61	59	57	58
Japan	na	56	62	51	54	55	58	54	53	64	56	52	64	57	56	62
Jordan	na	na	na	na	na	na	na	na	na	na	na	na	na	na	na	na
Korea, South	na	58	61	54	58	57	58	38	57	60	58	57	57	54	60	63
Latvia	na	68	71	65	69	67	69	57	71	71	69	64	68	63	71	63
Lithuania	na	60	62	57	68	59	54	41	63	69	43	58	68	53	62	69
Luxembourg	na	52	57	47	48	49	57	49	55	50	51	53	56	50	51	56
Macedonia	na	77	78	76	78	75	80	71	78	84	73	77	82	73	80	74
Malta	na	76	79	74	78	76	75	68	78	83	73	76	79	69	80	81
Mexico	na	60	66	54	59	62	55	55	61	75	54	62	68	56	61	67
Moldova	na	61	65	59	65	63	57	59	61	64	61	57	63	58	65	59
Montenegro	na	73	72	74	80	74	67	71	72	81	80	73	71	74	73	64
Morocco	na	83	86	81	82	85	81	83	84	90	74	82	86	82	84	92
Netherlands	na	50	58	43	50	51	49	53	45	53	44	50	57	51	52	44
New Zealand	na	69	72	66	70	69	69	67	67	73	62	68	78	70	72	65
Nigeria	na	na	na	na	na	na	na	na	na	na	na	na	na	na	na	na
Northern Ireland	na	64	64	64	63	63	68	62	66	67	64	64	66	67	66	55
Norway	na	70	78	63	69	73	68	65	71	75	na	na	na	67	72	61
Pakistan	na	na	na	na	na	na	na	na	na	na	na	na	na	na	na	na
Peru	na	67	67	67	65	69	69	64	65	72	64	69	69	59	68	73
Philippines	na	55	56	55	55	56	55	54	51	63	60	56	50	54	57	49
Poland	na	59	62	56	63	60	55	57	60	65	55	60	69	53	61	62
Portugal	na	49	49	50	47	49	51	48	49	60	44	44	47	55	47	41
Puerto Rico	na	73	78	70	61	74	78	71	70	75	72	73	74	63	76	71
Romania	na	79	82	76	83	77	78	72	79	89	75	76	84	78	81	80
Russian Fed.	na	58	63	53	65	58	52	46	55	72	51	53	69	54	62	57
Serbia	na	70	72	69	73	68	71	63	73	75	69	69	75	65	76	68
Singapore	na	75	79	71	78	75	66	72	75	87	67	75	82	70	77	75
Slovakia	na	68	70	66	71	69	65	62	69	82	64	68	72	64	70	80
Slovenia	na	73	74	72	75	73	70	72	70	83	71	73	79	70	74	71
South Africa	na	65	62	68	66	63	67	60	70	83	62	66	65	71	60	64
Spain	na	52	55	48	50	50	54	51	52	53	52	49	55	56	51	47
Sweden	na	74	79	68	75	72	75	69	75	74	69	73	82	80	75	66
Switzerland	na	75	79	72	71	75	79	70	76	79	67	74	80	76	77	67
Taiwan	na	60	66	54	56	63	56	55	60	64	55	60	66	58	62	62
Tanzania	na	75	80	69	67	78	84	75	75	78	75	80	81	76	76	57
Turkey	na	65	69	59	61	68	64	59	71	72	59	65	73	55	67	69
Uganda	na	78	85	72	81	77	67	73	79	90	83	71	78	78	76	85
Ukraine	na	62	72	54	73	68	50	36	63	72	53	65	69	56	66	66
United States	na	71	75	67	67	69	77	60	73	74	64	72	81	72	71	73
Uruguay	na	50	53	47	51	46	52	48	51	53	45	48	57	47	50	51
Venezuela	na	65	68	62	63	67	65	63	63	72	67	65	69	63	66	64
Vietnam	na	59	63	54	57	59	60	57	61	58	53	57	63	56	61	55
Zimbabwe	na	82	86	79	80	82	87	81	83	70	79	86	86	82	83	87
Total	na	66	69	62	66	66	64	62	67	69	62	65	70	64	67	64

RANKING	
Country	2000
Iceland	84
Morocco	83
Zimbabwe	82
China	80
Albania	80
Romania	79
Uganda	78
Macedonia	77
Czech Republic	77
Malta	76
Australia	76
Switzerland	75
Singapore	75
Tanzania	75
Croatia	75
Austria	74
Bosnia and Herz.	74
Sweden	74
Georgia	73
Montenegro	73
Puerto Rico	73
Slovenia	73
Dominican Rep.	72
United States	71
Bangladesh	71
Serbia	70
Norway	70
Canada	70
Brazil	69
New Zealand	69
Slovakia	68
Latvia	68
Peru	67
Germany	66
El Salvador	66
Bulgaria	66
Venezuela	65
Belarus	65
Ireland	65
South Africa	65
Turkey	65
Northern Ireland	64
India	64
Azerbaijan	64
Ukraine	62
Hungary	61
Moldova	61
Denmark	61
Taiwan	60
Lithuania	60
Mexico	60
Great Britain	59
Poland	59
Finland	59
Argentina	59
Vietnam	59
Russian Fed.	58
Korea, South	58
Italy	57
Japan	56
Armenia	56
Philippines	55
Greece	55
Estonia	52
Luxembourg	52
Spain	52
Netherlands	50
Uruguay	50
Portugal	49
Belgium	48
Chile	46
France	46
Total	66

E039B) COMPETITION IS HARMFUL

Now I'd like you to tell me your views on various issues. How would you place your views on this scale?

% Competition is harmful. It brings out the worst in people (codes 7 to 10) (WVS: V144; EVS: V188)

Country	Wave		Gender		Age			Education			Income			Values		
	1990	2000	Male	Female	16-29	30-49	50+	Lower	Middle	Upper	Lower	Middle	Upper	Mat	Mixed	Postm.
Albania	na	**7**	7	6	5	6	9	8	6	5	7	6	7	8	6	8
Algeria	na	**na**	na	na	na	na	na	na	na	na	na	na	na	na	na	na
Argentina	11	**23**	19	27	31	22	17	27	19	12	25	26	18	25	23	22
Armenia	na	**15**	13	16	15	11	20	24	15	10	14	15	17	15	15	11
Australia	na	**8**	8	8	9	8	6	10	8	7	11	6	6	8	7	9
Austria	7	**6**	5	7	4	7	7	7	6	3	10	5	5	6	6	7
Azerbaijan	na	**13**	13	13	13	12	14	16	12	13	10	16	11	14	11	16
Bangladesh	na	**10**	11	9	11	10	10	11	10	7	5	10	14	10	10	19
Belarus	13	**13**	13	12	8	13	17	22	11	6	18	11	7	15	11	4
Belgium	16	**25**	23	26	23	26	25	30	24	22	30	28	22	24	22	32
Bosnia and Herz.	na	**6**	6	7	7	5	9	7	6	7	8	7	5	8	5	8
Brazil	18	**16**	14	19	20	15	13	21	14	8	23	16	10	19	17	6
Bulgaria	7	**14**	13	16	13	10	19	24	11	10	18	17	10	18	10	na
Canada	10	**11**	11	12	12	12	10	14	12	7	17	8	10	14	11	11
Chile	21	**25**	24	26	23	29	20	30	22	21	31	20	21	25	23	30
China	5	**8**	7	9	9	8	6	8	8	7	8	9	5	9	7	10
Colombia	na	**na**	na	na	na	na	na	na	na	na	na	na	na	na	na	na
Croatia	na	**10**	8	11	15	10	7	8	11	10	13	11	7	11	9	13
Czech Republic	5	**10**	10	9	10	9	10	11	9	7	11	10	9	14	9	7
Denmark	13	**15**	10	19	10	15	17	16	6	17	17	15	12	26	13	15
Dominican Rep.	na	**18**	15	19	19	15	18	26	21	16	25	15	14	27	17	9
Egypt	na	**na**	na	na	na	na	na	na	na	na	na	na	na	na	na	na
El Salvador	na	**23**	22	23	23	23	23	25	22	16	23	26	13	na	na	na
Estonia	8	**20**	21	20	19	18	24	24	20	15	27	21	16	25	17	23
Finland	8	**17**	14	19	11	17	20	19	13	18	19	20	14	15	16	21
France	16	**25**	25	25	27	27	22	26	26	21	28	26	24	27	22	31
Georgia	na	**10**	9	11	9	9	13	10	11	9	12	12	7	11	10	12
Germany	8	**11**	8	13	10	11	12	13	10	7	11	9	8	8	12	13
Great Britain	15	**13**	13	13	15	15	11	12	16	10	14	11	18	na	na	na
Greece	na	**20**	22	18	22	19	18	25	19	20	20	20	19	14	19	27
Hungary	13	**14**	12	15	11	15	15	17	9	9	15	15	11	13	15	na
Iceland	5	**4**	4	5	2	4	6	5	3	4	8	4	2	4	5	3
India	7	**14**	14	16	15	14	14	17	15	11	17	15	13	15	14	11
Indonesia	na	**na**	na	na	na	na	na	na	na	na	na	na	na	na	na	na
Iran	na	**na**	na	na	na	na	na	na	na	na	na	na	na	na	na	na
Ireland	13	**13**	15	11	11	13	14	15	12	11	17	13	8	12	13	12
Israel	na	**na**	na	na	na	na	na	na	na	na	na	na	na	na	na	na
Italy	18	**17**	14	20	15	19	16	18	17	15	18	17	16	15	17	18
Japan	13	**9**	8	11	8	7	12	13	10	5	11	10	7	9	9	11
Jordan	na	**na**	na	na	na	na	na	na	na	na	na	na	na	na	na	na
Korea, South	9	**13**	13	14	12	14	12	14	13	13	13	10	15	15	12	15
Latvia	8	**10**	10	10	8	10	10	16	8	6	11	11	8	12	9	7
Lithuania	10	**17**	15	19	12	18	20	22	16	13	25	18	11	18	17	12
Luxembourg	na	**21**	19	23	23	21	20	24	19	20	21	19	17	22	22	19
Macedonia	na	**10**	10	9	10	10	9	13	9	6	13	8	7	12	7	12
Malta	na	**8**	7	8	8	7	9	10	8	3	8	7	7	8	8	8
Mexico	16	**23**	18	27	23	21	26	28	20	10	25	21	17	28	21	17
Moldova	na	**17**	15	18	17	15	19	17	18	14	19	17	16	17	17	15
Montenegro	na	**13**	14	12	9	11	17	17	12	7	13	13	11	11	14	20
Morocco	na	**5**	3	6	6	5	2	5	5	2	6	4	3	5	4	1
Netherlands	14	**20**	17	23	14	20	24	24	20	18	25	20	15	28	18	22
New Zealand	na	**10**	9	10	7	9	12	11	10	8	14	8	7	14	7	10
Nigeria	7	**na**	na	na	na	na	na	na	na	na	na	na	na	na	na	na
Northern Ireland	16	**9**	9	10	9	10	8	11	8	8	10	10	9	6	9	14
Norway	7	**7**	6	9	8	6	8	9	8	5	na	na	na	9	7	10
Pakistan	na	**na**	na	na	na	na	na	na	na	na	na	na	na	na	na	na
Peru	na	**14**	14	15	15	14	15	17	15	12	17	14	11	17	14	12
Philippines	na	**14**	13	15	12	15	15	14	15	12	12	11	19	16	12	18
Poland	12	**18**	18	18	18	18	17	21	15	13	20	18	12	20	17	18
Portugal	19	**20**	18	21	24	19	18	19	25	10	21	19	22	15	22	26
Puerto Rico	na	**12**	9	13	16	11	10	15	17	8	14	11	9	15	10	17
Romania	6	**8**	5	12	9	9	7	11	8	5	11	7	6	10	7	8
Russian Fed.	12	**19**	16	21	15	19	20	24	20	12	23	20	14	21	17	21
Serbia	na	**13**	11	15	11	15	11	16	13	9	16	12	10	14	11	15
Singapore	na	**6**	5	7	5	6	11	9	6	3	8	7	4	7	6	7
Slovakia	na	**11**	11	10	9	10	13	14	9	9	11	13	8	13	9	4
Slovenia	9	**10**	9	10	10	8	11	11	11	1	14	8	6	13	8	11
South Africa	14	**13**	14	12	12	14	13	16	11	3	15	11	15	11	14	16
Spain	22	**16**	16	17	18	17	14	16	17	17	18	18	13	14	16	21
Sweden	7	**8**	7	9	6	9	9	9	9	6	9	8	6	2	8	11
Switzerland	na	**9**	8	9	12	9	6	13	8	3	15	9	4	13	8	8
Taiwan	na	**11**	8	13	8	9	17	15	10	7	14	11	6	12	8	16
Tanzania	na	**15**	12	20	21	12	11	19	12	10	20	12	10	16	14	22
Turkey	23	**21**	18	25	24	19	17	26	16	12	28	18	15	23	20	20
Uganda	na	**8**	3	12	5	9	15	14	6	1	6	14	8	6	8	12
Ukraine	na	**21**	15	26	12	17	31	42	20	13	27	18	17	24	19	18
United States	10	**12**	11	13	14	11	11	21	12	8	17	10	6	13	12	9
Uruguay	na	**27**	26	27	26	27	27	32	21	18	32	28	21	33	27	24
Venezuela	na	**19**	16	22	21	16	21	21	21	13	17	21	16	19	19	19
Vietnam	na	**14**	12	15	12	14	14	15	12	13	18	14	11	12	13	14
Zimbabwe	na	**10**	8	13	12	9	8	14	6	na	14	7	3	11	10	10
Total	12	14	12	15	14	13	14	17	13	11	16	14	11	15	13	15

RANKING	
Country	2000
Uruguay	27
France	25
Belgium	25
Chile	25
Argentina	23
Mexico	23
El Salvador	23
Turkey	21
Luxembourg	21
Ukraine	21
Estonia	20
Netherlands	20
Greece	20
Portugal	20
Venezuela	19
Russian Fed.	19
Poland	18
Dominican Rep.	18
Lithuania	17
Italy	17
Finland	17
Moldova	17
Spain	16
Brazil	16
Tanzania	15
Armenia	15
Denmark	15
India	14
Peru	14
Bulgaria	14
Philippines	14
Hungary	14
Vietnam	14
Korea, South	13
South Africa	13
Great Britain	13
Azerbaijan	13
Serbia	13
Montenegro	13
Belarus	13
Ireland	13
United States	12
Puerto Rico	12
Canada	11
Germany	11
Taiwan	11
Slovakia	11
Georgia	10
Zimbabwe	10
Bangladesh	10
Croatia	10
New Zealand	10
Czech Republic	10
Latvia	10
Slovenia	10
Macedonia	10
Japan	9
Northern Ireland	9
Switzerland	9
Romania	8
Australia	8
Sweden	8
Malta	8
China	8
Uganda	8
Norway	7
Albania	7
Bosnia and Herz.	6
Singapore	6
Austria	6
Morocco	5
Iceland	4
Total	14

E042) FIRMS: CONTROL OR FREEDOM?

Now I'd like you to tell me your views on various issues. How would you place your views on this scale?.
The state should give more freedom to firms or the state should control firms more effectively.

% More control (codes 7 to 10)

(EVS: V189)

Country	Wave		Gender		Age			Education			Income			Values		
	1990	2000	Male	Female	16-29	30-49	50+	Lower	Middle	Upper	Lower	Middle	Upper	Mat	Mixed	Postm.
Albania	na	**na**	na	na	na	na	na	na	na	na	na	na	na	na	na	na
Algeria	na	**na**	na	na	na	na	na	na	na	na	na	na	na	na	na	na
Argentina	na	**na**	na	na	na	na	na	na	na	na	na	na	na	na	na	na
Armenia	na	**na**	na	na	na	na	na	na	na	na	na	na	na	na	na	na
Australia	na	**na**	na	na	na	na	na	na	na	na	na	na	na	na	na	na
Austria	na	**19**	17	21	15	17	22	24	15	11	24	17	18	34	18	16
Azerbaijan	na	**na**	na	na	na	na	na	na	na	na	na	na	na	na	na	na
Bangladesh	na	**na**	na	na	na	na	na	na	na	na	na	na	na	na	na	na
Belarus	na	**30**	27	33	19	27	43	49	25	19	35	28	24	38	26	2
Belgium	na	**42**	42	42	35	40	46	55	41	32	49	49	33	46	37	46
Bosnia and Herz.	na	**na**	na	na	na	na	na	na	na	na	na	na	na	na	na	na
Brazil	na	**na**	na	na	na	na	na	na	na	na	na	na	na	na	na	na
Bulgaria	na	**41**	37	45	31	40	48	53	39	30	50	48	32	48	38	13
Canada	na	**na**	na	na	na	na	na	na	na	na	na	na	na	na	na	na
Chile	na	**na**	na	na	na	na	na	na	na	na	na	na	na	na	na	na
China	na	**na**	na	na	na	na	na	na	na	na	na	na	na	na	na	na
Colombia	na	**na**	na	na	na	na	na	na	na	na	na	na	na	na	na	na
Croatia	na	**40**	39	41	35	39	46	50	37	28	59	41	30	41	43	28
Czech Republic	na	**46**	42	50	46	43	49	52	41	34	54	48	35	57	44	34
Denmark	na	**21**	18	24	23	22	18	23	11	23	25	19	18	23	19	31
Dominican Rep.	na	**na**	na	na	na	na	na	na	na	na	na	na	na	na	na	na
Egypt	na	**na**	na	na	na	na	na	na	na	na	na	na	na	na	na	na
El Salvador	na	**na**	na	na	na	na	na	na	na	na	na	na	na	na	na	na
Estonia	na	**48**	45	50	38	46	55	52	50	36	56	54	41	53	45	46
Finland	na	**23**	22	24	17	24	26	26	19	16	26	24	22	25	22	27
France	na	**29**	29	30	27	29	31	34	25	22	35	35	20	32	26	37
Georgia	na	**na**	na	na	na	na	na	na	na	na	na	na	na	na	na	na
Germany	na	**25**	26	24	25	24	25	25	23	27	27	25	16	16	28	30
Great Britain	na	**20**	22	19	18	20	24	22	19	15	21	21	24	na	na	na
Greece	na	**40**	40	40	37	39	48	54	41	36	45	40	34	33	41	39
Hungary	na	**53**	53	54	47	51	59	58	48	38	55	58	48	57	52	39
Iceland	na	**8**	9	8	8	6	11	13	4	7	12	7	6	10	8	7
India	na	**na**	na	na	na	na	na	na	na	na	na	na	na	na	na	na
Indonesia	na	**na**	na	na	na	na	na	na	na	na	na	na	na	na	na	na
Iran	na	**na**	na	na	na	na	na	na	na	na	na	na	na	na	na	na
Ireland	na	**26**	30	22	21	28	27	32	23	23	30	28	25	25	25	31
Israel	na	**na**	na	na	na	na	na	na	na	na	na	na	na	na	na	na
Italy	na	**29**	28	31	25	28	33	35	27	23	32	31	23	42	29	26
Japan	na	**na**	na	na	na	na	na	na	na	na	na	na	na	na	na	na
Jordan	na	**na**	na	na	na	na	na	na	na	na	na	na	na	na	na	na
Korea, South	na	**na**	na	na	na	na	na	na	na	na	na	na	na	na	na	na
Latvia	na	**67**	66	68	53	66	74	74	66	63	74	69	55	71	65	57
Lithuania	na	**26**	25	27	18	26	33	30	27	17	30	31	23	27	27	14
Luxembourg	na	**50**	50	51	44	52	52	53	53	41	56	56	43	52	52	38
Macedonia	na	**na**	na	na	na	na	na	na	na	na	na	na	na	na	na	na
Malta	na	**31**	29	33	23	34	34	38	31	14	38	31	23	36	30	14
Mexico	na	**na**	na	na	na	na	na	na	na	na	na	na	na	na	na	na
Moldova	na	**na**	na	na	na	na	na	na	na	na	na	na	na	na	na	na
Montenegro	na	**na**	na	na	na	na	na	na	na	na	na	na	na	na	na	na
Morocco	na	**na**	na	na	na	na	na	na	na	na	na	na	na	na	na	na
Netherlands	na	**35**	31	38	32	33	38	42	33	29	40	36	27	46	32	34
New Zealand	na	**na**	na	na	na	na	na	na	na	na	na	na	na	na	na	na
Nigeria	na	**na**	na	na	na	na	na	na	na	na	na	na	na	na	na	na
Northern Ireland	na	**19**	21	18	25	19	16	19	22	16	19	25	19	14	21	26
Norway	na	**na**	na	na	na	na	na	na	na	na	na	na	na	na	na	na
Pakistan	na	**na**	na	na	na	na	na	na	na	na	na	na	na	na	na	na
Peru	na	**na**	na	na	na	na	na	na	na	na	na	na	na	na	na	na
Philippines	na	**na**	na	na	na	na	na	na	na	na	na	na	na	na	na	na
Poland	na	**56**	56	56	46	57	60	59	55	45	64	52	46	62	52	52
Portugal	na	**35**	35	35	39	33	34	36	33	28	22	34	38	31	36	40
Puerto Rico	na	**na**	na	na	na	na	na	na	na	na	na	na	na	na	na	na
Romania	na	**53**	46	61	47	48	63	69	51	33	66	59	39	61	48	29
Russian Fed.	na	**48**	44	51	35	45	59	60	49	38	54	52	40	53	43	35
Serbia	na	**na**	na	na	na	na	na	na	na	na	na	na	na	na	na	na
Singapore	na	**na**	na	na	na	na	na	na	na	na	na	na	na	na	na	na
Slovakia	na	**64**	58	69	59	65	66	72	62	50	70	66	61	69	63	34
Slovenia	na	**40**	38	42	28	41	48	56	38	21	47	46	31	48	39	40
South Africa	na	**na**	na	na	na	na	na	na	na	na	na	na	na	na	na	na
Spain	na	**31**	33	28	29	32	31	32	29	33	35	35	24	33	28	41
Sweden	na	**11**	11	11	8	11	13	18	10	7	16	9	7	18	10	15
Switzerland	na	**na**	na	na	na	na	na	na	na	na	na	na	na	na	na	na
Taiwan	na	**na**	na	na	na	na	na	na	na	na	na	na	na	na	na	na
Tanzania	na	**na**	na	na	na	na	na	na	na	na	na	na	na	na	na	na
Turkey	na	**61**	61	60	61	57	72	63	61	50	61	64	55	64	59	62
Uganda	na	**na**	na	na	na	na	na	na	na	na	na	na	na	na	na	na
Ukraine	na	**39**	36	42	25	32	55	66	39	28	52	35	30	47	38	12
United States	na	**na**	na	na	na	na	na	na	na	na	na	na	na	na	na	na
Uruguay	na	**na**	na	na	na	na	na	na	na	na	na	na	na	na	na	na
Venezuela	na	**na**	na	na	na	na	na	na	na	na	na	na	na	na	na	na
Vietnam	na	**na**	na	na	na	na	na	na	na	na	na	na	na	na	na	na
Zimbabwe	na	**na**	na	na	na	na	na	na	na	na	na	na	na	na	na	na
Total	na	**36**	35	38	31	35	40	41	36	28	42	38	31	44	34	30

RANKING	
Country	2000
Latvia	67
Slovakia	64
Turkey	61
Poland	56
Hungary	53
Romania	53
Luxembourg	50
Estonia	48
Russian Fed.	48
Czech Republic	46
Belgium	42
Bulgaria	41
Croatia	40
Slovenia	40
Greece	40
Ukraine	39
Portugal	35
Netherlands	35
Malta	31
Spain	31
Belarus	30
Italy	29
France	29
Lithuania	26
Ireland	26
Germany	25
Finland	23
Denmark	21
Great Britain	20
Northern Ireland	19
Austria	19
Sweden	11
Iceland	8
Total	36

E042) FIRMS: CONTROL OR FREEDOM?

Now I'd like you to tell me your views on various issues. How would you place your views on this scale?.
The state should give more freedom to firms or the state should control firms more effectively.

% More freedom (codes 1 to 4) (EVS: V189)

Country	Wave		Gender		Age			Education			Income			Values		
	1990	2000	Male	Female	16-29	30-49	50+	Lower	Middle	Upper	Lower	Middle	Upper	Mat	Mixed	Postm.
Albania	na	**na**	na	na	na	na	na	na	na	na	na	na	na	na	na	na
Algeria	na	**na**	na	na	na	na	na	na	na	na	na	na	na	na	na	na
Argentina	na	**na**	na	na	na	na	na	na	na	na	na	na	na	na	na	na
Armenia	na	**na**	na	na	na	na	na	na	na	na	na	na	na	na	na	na
Australia	na	**na**	na	na	na	na	na	na	na	na	na	na	na	na	na	na
Austria	na	**59**	64	54	62	62	55	53	63	69	49	60	63	49	59	62
Azerbaijan	na	**na**	na	na	na	na	na	na	na	na	na	na	na	na	na	na
Bangladesh	na	**na**	na	na	na	na	na	na	na	na	na	na	na	na	na	na
Belarus	na	**49**	53	46	57	53	36	32	53	58	41	49	62	42	50	82
Belgium	na	**32**	36	28	33	34	29	25	31	38	27	28	38	26	36	30
Bosnia and Herz.	na	**na**	na	na	na	na	na	na	na	na	na	na	na	na	na	na
Brazil	na	**na**	na	na	na	na	na	na	na	na	na	na	na	na	na	na
Bulgaria	na	**40**	45	35	51	43	31	27	44	50	30	36	49	31	44	71
Canada	na	**na**	na	na	na	na	na	na	na	na	na	na	na	na	na	na
Chile	na	**na**	na	na	na	na	na	na	na	na	na	na	na	na	na	na
China	na	**na**	na	na	na	na	na	na	na	na	na	na	na	na	na	na
Colombia	na	**na**	na	na	na	na	na	na	na	na	na	na	na	na	na	na
Croatia	na	**40**	47	34	42	40	38	28	45	54	24	40	48	35	39	48
Czech Republic	na	**30**	34	26	30	33	27	25	33	42	23	28	40	21	31	47
Denmark	na	**49**	54	43	43	50	51	48	56	46	37	53	57	44	51	41
Dominican Rep.	na	**na**	na	na	na	na	na	na	na	na	na	na	na	na	na	na
Egypt	na	**na**	na	na	na	na	na	na	na	na	na	na	na	na	na	na
El Salvador	na	**na**	na	na	na	na	na	na	na	na	na	na	na	na	na	na
Estonia	na	**27**	32	24	32	30	23	25	25	38	19	23	33	22	30	27
Finland	na	**50**	54	46	51	51	49	45	56	59	42	50	55	48	52	44
France	na	**44**	46	42	44	44	44	42	45	48	38	40	54	40	50	33
Georgia	na	**na**	na	na	na	na	na	na	na	na	na	na	na	na	na	na
Germany	na	**52**	54	51	46	53	55	51	54	51	52	55	57	63	50	45
Great Britain	na	**40**	40	39	36	41	41	37	40	46	37	39	43	na	na	na
Greece	na	**31**	33	29	29	34	29	23	33	30	30	28	34	37	29	32
Hungary	na	**21**	21	21	23	22	19	16	28	34	15	20	26	18	23	18
Iceland	na	**71**	75	66	70	76	64	65	76	71	63	71	77	71	71	65
India	na	**na**	na	na	na	na	na	na	na	na	na	na	na	na	na	na
Indonesia	na	**na**	na	na	na	na	na	na	na	na	na	na	na	na	na	na
Iran	na	**na**	na	na	na	na	na	na	na	na	na	na	na	na	na	na
Ireland	na	**40**	42	38	41	40	40	38	42	38	36	37	43	29	44	41
Israel	na	**na**	na	na	na	na	na	na	na	na	na	na	na	na	na	na
Italy	na	**46**	51	41	48	46	44	42	47	52	40	43	56	37	46	48
Japan	na	**na**	na	na	na	na	na	na	na	na	na	na	na	na	na	na
Jordan	na	**na**	na	na	na	na	na	na	na	na	na	na	na	na	na	na
Korea, South	na	**na**	na	na	na	na	na	na	na	na	na	na	na	na	na	na
Latvia	na	**15**	16	14	21	16	13	12	16	17	12	14	22	11	17	17
Lithuania	na	**50**	51	50	58	50	44	43	50	60	46	47	54	52	49	62
Luxembourg	na	**21**	23	18	23	19	21	20	20	23	17	24	23	18	21	26
Macedonia	na	**na**	na	na	na	na	na	na	na	na	na	na	na	na	na	na
Malta	na	**44**	48	40	50	43	41	35	45	59	34	40	53	36	46	64
Mexico	na	**na**	na	na	na	na	na	na	na	na	na	na	na	na	na	na
Moldova	na	**na**	na	na	na	na	na	na	na	na	na	na	na	na	na	na
Montenegro	na	**na**	na	na	na	na	na	na	na	na	na	na	na	na	na	na
Morocco	na	**na**	na	na	na	na	na	na	na	na	na	na	na	na	na	na
Netherlands	na	**30**	37	24	27	33	30	26	30	35	25	31	37	24	32	29
New Zealand	na	**na**	na	na	na	na	na	na	na	na	na	na	na	na	na	na
Nigeria	na	**na**	na	na	na	na	na	na	na	na	na	na	na	na	na	na
Northern Ireland	na	**49**	52	47	51	40	57	49	47	53	51	42	45	51	50	50
Norway	na	**na**	na	na	na	na	na	na	na	na	na	na	na	na	na	na
Pakistan	na	**na**	na	na	na	na	na	na	na	na	na	na	na	na	na	na
Peru	na	**na**	na	na	na	na	na	na	na	na	na	na	na	na	na	na
Philippines	na	**na**	na	na	na	na	na	na	na	na	na	na	na	na	na	na
Poland	na	**22**	24	21	32	21	18	20	24	28	18	23	31	20	23	34
Portugal	na	**31**	32	30	30	33	30	30	35	30	29	31	36	30	31	34
Puerto Rico	na	**na**	na	na	na	na	na	na	na	na	na	na	na	na	na	na
Romania	na	**36**	42	30	42	41	27	23	38	53	26	31	49	29	40	62
Russian Fed.	na	**30**	33	27	39	32	22	19	29	37	26	26	35	26	34	44
Serbia	na	**na**	na	na	na	na	na	na	na	na	na	na	na	na	na	na
Singapore	na	**na**	na	na	na	na	na	na	na	na	na	na	na	na	na	na
Slovakia	na	**15**	19	10	18	15	11	11	14	28	11	14	17	10	17	30
Slovenia	na	**39**	44	34	46	40	32	30	41	45	32	34	45	31	39	40
South Africa	na	**na**	na	na	na	na	na	na	na	na	na	na	na	na	na	na
Spain	na	**29**	31	28	29	30	29	29	29	32	27	32	40	31	29	25
Sweden	na	**61**	65	58	64	61	60	52	64	65	54	62	69	62	63	56
Switzerland	na	**na**	na	na	na	na	na	na	na	na	na	na	na	na	na	na
Taiwan	na	**na**	na	na	na	na	na	na	na	na	na	na	na	na	na	na
Tanzania	na	**na**	na	na	na	na	na	na	na	na	na	na	na	na	na	na
Turkey	na	**25**	25	25	24	29	16	26	22	37	27	21	30	24	26	25
Uganda	na	**na**	na	na	na	na	na	na	na	na	na	na	na	na	na	na
Ukraine	na	**40**	46	36	49	48	27	13	42	50	28	42	52	33	43	58
United States	na	**na**	na	na	na	na	na	na	na	na	na	na	na	na	na	na
Uruguay	na	**na**	na	na	na	na	na	na	na	na	na	na	na	na	na	na
Venezuela	na	**na**	na	na	na	na	na	na	na	na	na	na	na	na	na	na
Vietnam	na	**na**	na	na	na	na	na	na	na	na	na	na	na	na	na	na
Zimbabwe	na	**na**	na	na	na	na	na	na	na	na	na	na	na	na	na	na
Total	na	39	42	35	41	40	36	34	40	44	32	37	45	32	41	44

RANKING

Country	2000
Iceland	71
Sweden	61
Austria	59
Germany	52
Lithuania	50
Finland	50
Northern Ireland	49
Belarus	49
Denmark	49
Italy	46
France	44
Malta	44
Ukraine	40
Bulgaria	40
Ireland	40
Croatia	40
Great Britain	40
Slovenia	39
Romania	36
Belgium	32
Portugal	31
Greece	31
Netherlands	30
Russian Fed.	30
Czech Republic	30
Spain	29
Estonia	27
Turkey	25
Poland	22
Hungary	21
Luxembourg	21
Latvia	15
Slovakia	15
Total	39

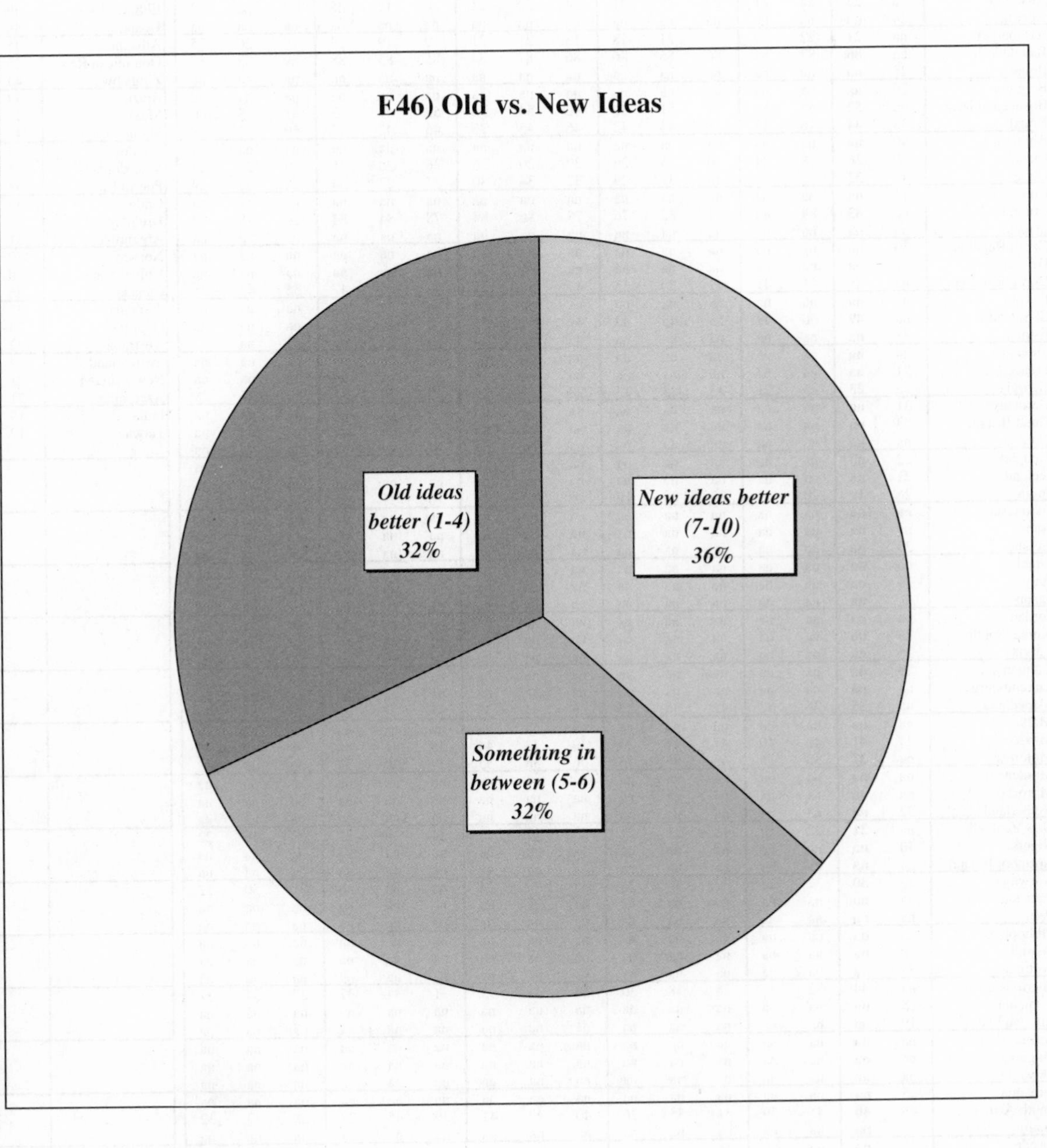
E46) Old vs. New Ideas
Old ideas better (1-4) 32%
New ideas better (7-10) 36%
Something in between (5-6) 32%

E046A) NEW IDEAS ARE BETTER THAN OLD ONES

Now I'd like you to tell me your views on various issues. How would you place your views on this scale?

% New ideas are better than old ones (codes 7 to 10)

(WVS: V145)

Country	Wave		Gender		Age			Education			Income			Values		
	1990	2000	Male	Female	16-29	30-49	50+	Lower	Middle	Upper	Lower	Middle	Upper	Mat	Mixed	Postm.
Albania	na	**45**	45	45	51	47	37	42	46	52	42	48	46	41	48	47
Algeria	na	**na**	na	na	na	na	na	na	na	na	na	na	na	na	na	na
Argentina	32	**31**	33	29	39	29	25	33	29	24	31	32	29	31	35	23
Armenia	na	**25**	27	23	29	26	16	21	24	28	33	16	22	22	26	36
Australia	na	**22**	24	21	22	24	21	24	22	21	24	19	25	27	22	22
Austria	24	**na**	na	na	na	na	na	na	na	na	na	na	na	na	na	na
Azerbaijan	na	**21**	22	19	22	21	18	13	21	21	19	19	24	18	26	25
Bangladesh	na	**86**	87	84	86	85	86	86	87	84	85	85	88	89	83	87
Belarus	28	**na**	na	na	na	na	na	na	na	na	na	na	na	na	na	na
Belgium	26	**na**	na	na	na	na	na	na	na	na	na	na	na	na	na	na
Bosnia and Herz.	na	**52**	55	50	57	51	49	42	54	56	52	47	63	51	53	60
Brazil	38	**44**	46	42	45	44	42	46	45	33	46	42	43	50	42	38
Bulgaria	40	**na**	na	na	na	na	na	na	na	na	na	na	na	na	na	na
Canada	30	**26**	28	24	30	25	26	29	26	25	26	28	25	29	27	25
Chile	42	**33**	32	33	40	31	29	32	34	30	37	27	34	28	35	29
China	14	**na**	na	na	na	na	na	na	na	na	na	na	na	na	na	na
Colombia	na	**83**	84	82	87	82	76	77	86	84	78	84	84	80	78	83
Croatia	na	**na**	na	na	na	na	na	na	na	na	na	na	na	na	na	na
Czech Republic	30	**na**	na	na	na	na	na	na	na	na	na	na	na	na	na	na
Denmark	31	**na**	na	na	na	na	na	na	na	na	na	na	na	na	na	na
Dominican Rep.	na	**45**	51	41	42	50	55	47	56	41	47	45	47	55	43	35
Egypt	na	**na**	na	na	na	na	na	na	na	na	na	na	na	na	na	na
El Salvador	na	**49**	50	48	55	48	42	47	52	51	52	49	51	na	na	na
Estonia	33	**na**	na	na	na	na	na	na	na	na	na	na	na	na	na	na
Finland	24	**na**	na	na	na	na	na	na	na	na	na	na	na	na	na	na
France	21	**na**	na	na	na	na	na	na	na	na	na	na	na	na	na	na
Georgia	na	**23**	25	21	33	23	13	20	24	23	19	20	32	20	25	28
Germany	31	**na**	na	na	na	na	na	na	na	na	na	na	na	na	na	na
Great Britain	23	**na**	na	na	na	na	na	na	na	na	na	na	na	na	na	na
Greece	na	**na**	na	na	na	na	na	na	na	na	na	na	na	na	na	na
Hungary	22	**na**	na	na	na	na	na	na	na	na	na	na	na	na	na	na
Iceland	21	**na**	na	na	na	na	na	na	na	na	na	na	na	na	na	na
India	26	**19**	20	19	20	20	18	20	20	18	16	21	20	14	23	28
Indonesia	na	**na**	na	na	na	na	na	na	na	na	na	na	na	na	na	na
Iran	na	**na**	na	na	na	na	na	na	na	na	na	na	na	na	na	na
Ireland	29	**na**	na	na	na	na	na	na	na	na	na	na	na	na	na	na
Israel	na	**na**	na	na	na	na	na	na	na	na	na	na	na	na	na	na
Italy	29	**na**	na	na	na	na	na	na	na	na	na	na	na	na	na	na
Japan	5	**na**	na	na	na	na	na	na	na	na	na	na	na	na	na	na
Jordan	na	**na**	na	na	na	na	na	na	na	na	na	na	na	na	na	na
Korea, South	23	**na**	na	na	na	na	na	na	na	na	na	na	na	na	na	na
Latvia	26	**na**	na	na	na	na	na	na	na	na	na	na	na	na	na	na
Lithuania	29	**na**	na	na	na	na	na	na	na	na	na	na	na	na	na	na
Luxembourg	na	**na**	na	na	na	na	na	na	na	na	na	na	na	na	na	na
Macedonia	na	**35**	36	33	42	36	27	36	34	35	33	37	35	40	33	35
Malta	na	**na**	na	na	na	na	na	na	na	na	na	na	na	na	na	na
Mexico	34	**41**	42	40	47	41	29	39	43	44	36	41	46	39	42	42
Moldova	na	**37**	38	36	43	36	33	36	38	35	39	30	37	36	38	52
Montenegro	na	**na**	na	na	na	na	na	na	na	na	na	na	na	na	na	na
Morocco	na	**na**	na	na	na	na	na	na	na	na	na	na	na	na	na	na
Netherlands	32	**na**	na	na	na	na	na	na	na	na	na	na	na	na	na	na
New Zealand	na	**21**	22	19	18	21	21	23	17	20	24	16	21	22	16	22
Nigeria	40	**na**	na	na	na	na	na	na	na	na	na	na	na	na	na	na
Northern Ireland	24	**na**	na	na	na	na	na	na	na	na	na	na	na	na	na	na
Norway	33	**30**	32	28	32	30	28	35	30	24	na	na	na	36	30	22
Pakistan	na	**na**	na	na	na	na	na	na	na	na	na	na	na	na	na	na
Peru	na	**na**	na	na	na	na	na	na	na	na	na	na	na	na	na	na
Philippines	na	**na**	na	na	na	na	na	na	na	na	na	na	na	na	na	na
Poland	40	**na**	na	na	na	na	na	na	na	na	na	na	na	na	na	na
Portugal	37	**na**	na	na	na	na	na	na	na	na	na	na	na	na	na	na
Puerto Rico	na	**34**	32	35	36	38	30	29	34	35	31	34	37	27	34	37
Romania	25	**na**	na	na	na	na	na	na	na	na	na	na	na	na	na	na
Russian Fed.	19	**na**	na	na	na	na	na	na	na	na	na	na	na	na	na	na
Serbia	na	**na**	na	na	na	na	na	na	na	na	na	na	na	na	na	na
Singapore	na	**na**	na	na	na	na	na	na	na	na	na	na	na	na	na	na
Slovakia	na	**na**	na	na	na	na	na	na	na	na	na	na	na	na	na	na
Slovenia	25	**na**	na	na	na	na	na	na	na	na	na	na	na	na	na	na
South Africa	46	**40**	41	39	51	35	26	40	40	41	39	45	39	38	43	32
Spain	37	**na**	na	na	na	na	na	na	na	na	na	na	na	na	na	na
Sweden	36	**na**	na	na	na	na	na	na	na	na	na	na	na	na	na	na
Switzerland	na	**22**	25	20	31	23	16	22	23	20	22	21	21	17	21	30
Taiwan	na	**12**	12	11	13	10	14	12	14	9	15	11	9	9	13	24
Tanzania	na	**na**	na	na	na	na	na	na	na	na	na	na	na	na	na	na
Turkey	44	**na**	na	na	na	na	na	na	na	na	na	na	na	na	na	na
Uganda	na	**48**	47	48	55	42	31	42	51	37	42	49	46	50	46	49
Ukraine	na	**na**	na	na	na	na	na	na	na	na	na	na	na	na	na	na
United States	20	**30**	28	31	35	29	27	37	33	25	36	27	27	31	31	27
Uruguay	na	**32**	34	30	45	30	27	33	31	25	33	37	25	31	32	32
Venezuela	na	**50**	52	49	55	48	47	47	53	49	51	49	54	51	50	51
Vietnam	na	**na**	na	na	na	na	na	na	na	na	na	na	na	na	na	na
Zimbabwe	na	**44**	49	40	51	41	33	40	50	44	45	47	44	44	44	53
Total	29	**36**	38	35	43	36	29	38	37	33	36	37	37	35	36	33

RANKING	
Country	**2000**
Bangladesh	86
Colombia	83
Bosnia and Herz.	52
Venezuela	50
El Salvador	49
Uganda	48
Albania	45
Dominican Rep.	45
Zimbabwe	44
Brazil	44
Mexico	41
South Africa	40
Moldova	37
Macedonia	35
Puerto Rico	34
Chile	33
Uruguay	32
Argentina	31
Norway	30
United States	30
Canada	26
Armenia	25
Georgia	23
Australia	22
Switzerland	22
New Zealand	21
Azerbaijan	21
India	19
Taiwan	12
Total	36

046B) OLD IDEAS ARE BETTER THAN NEW ONES

ow I'd like you to tell me your views on various issues. How would you place your views on this scale?

Ideas that have stood the test of time are generally best (code 1 to 4) (WVS: V145)

Country	Wave		Gender		Age			Education			Income			Values		
	1990	2000	Male	Female	16-29	30-49	50+	Lower	Middle	Upper	Lower	Middle	Upper	Mat	Mixed	Postm.
bania	na	**33**	35	31	31	30	39	35	32	29	34	32	33	35	30	45
geria	na	**na**	na	na	na	na	na	na	na	na	na	na	na	na	na	na
gentina	32	**32**	34	31	27	30	41	37	28	25	39	34	25	42	31	27
rmenia	na	**38**	36	39	25	38	58	59	36	34	28	43	45	39	38	25
ustralia	na	**31**	34	27	25	29	37	36	29	29	35	28	28	35	32	27
ustria	24	**na**	na	na	na	na	na	na	na	na	na	na	na	na	na	na
zerbaijan	na	**62**	60	64	61	61	68	74	64	57	71	66	53	68	54	50
angladesh	na	**3**	3	3	3	3	5	3	3	5	4	2	4	2	4	1
elarus	28	**na**	na	na	na	na	na	na	na	na	na	na	na	na	na	na
elgium	26	**na**	na	na	na	na	na	na	na	na	na	na	na	na	na	na
osnia and Herz.	na	**14**	12	15	13	12	16	19	13	12	15	15	12	14	14	9
razil	38	**36**	32	39	35	34	42	37	34	37	38	34	35	35	37	34
ulgaria	40	**na**	na	na	na	na	na	na	na	na	na	na	na	na	na	na
anada	30	**24**	24	24	16	24	28	32	22	21	32	22	19	22	26	20
hile	42	**33**	32	34	27	33	38	37	32	27	33	36	28	38	31	32
hina	14	**na**	na	na	na	na	na	na	na	na	na	na	na	na	na	na
olombia	na	**8**	8	8	5	9	12	14	6	6	13	7	6	10	13	10
roatia	na	**na**	na	na	na	na	na	na	na	na	na	na	na	na	na	na
zech Republic	30	**na**	na	na	na	na	na	na	na	na	na	na	na	na	na	na
enmark	31	**na**	na	na	na	na	na	na	na	na	na	na	na	na	na	na
ominican Rep.	na	**24**	21	25	24	23	9	31	22	23	22	23	20	27	22	23
gypt	na	**na**	na	na	na	na	na	na	na	na	na	na	na	na	na	na
Salvador	na	**34**	31	37	29	38	37	38	32	28	34	36	29	na	na	na
stonia	33	**na**	na	na	na	na	na	na	na	na	na	na	na	na	na	na
nland	24	**na**	na	na	na	na	na	na	na	na	na	na	na	na	na	na
ance	21	**na**	na	na	na	na	na	na	na	na	na	na	na	na	na	na
eorgia	na	**51**	49	53	40	51	64	55	52	47	58	54	39	55	49	47
ermany	31	**na**	na	na	na	na	na	na	na	na	na	na	na	na	na	na
reat Britain	23	**na**	na	na	na	na	na	na	na	na	na	na	na	na	na	na
reece	na	**na**	na	na	na	na	na	na	na	na	na	na	na	na	na	na
ungary	22	**na**	na	na	na	na	na	na	na	na	na	na	na	na	na	na
eland	21	**na**	na	na	na	na	na	na	na	na	na	na	na	na	na	na
dia	26	**61**	59	64	61	59	64	65	60	56	70	60	58	67	56	54
donesia	na	**na**	na	na	na	na	na	na	na	na	na	na	na	na	na	na
an	na	**na**	na	na	na	na	na	na	na	na	na	na	na	na	na	na
eland	29	**na**	na	na	na	na	na	na	na	na	na	na	na	na	na	na
rael	na	**na**	na	na	na	na	na	na	na	na	na	na	na	na	na	na
aly	29	**na**	na	na	na	na	na	na	na	na	na	na	na	na	na	na
pan	5	**na**	na	na	na	na	na	na	na	na	na	na	na	na	na	na
rdan	na	**na**	na	na	na	na	na	na	na	na	na	na	na	na	na	na
orea, South	23	**na**	na	na	na	na	na	na	na	na	na	na	na	na	na	na
atvia	26	**na**	na	na	na	na	na	na	na	na	na	na	na	na	na	na
ithuania	29	**na**	na	na	na	na	na	na	na	na	na	na	na	na	na	na
uxembourg	na	**na**	na	na	na	na	na	na	na	na	na	na	na	na	na	na
acedonia	na	**34**	35	33	26	32	43	39	34	27	40	34	26	31	35	46
alta	na	**na**	na	na	na	na	na	na	na	na	na	na	na	na	na	na
exico	34	**35**	34	35	27	35	46	42	28	21	39	35	28	39	34	27
oldova	na	**31**	31	31	27	30	35	33	31	30	31	32	31	30	29	32
ontenegro	na	**na**	na	na	na	na	na	na	na	na	na	na	na	na	na	na
orocco	na	**na**	na	na	na	na	na	na	na	na	na	na	na	na	na	na
etherlands	32	**na**	na	na	na	na	na	na	na	na	na	na	na	na	na	na
ew Zealand	na	**27**	29	25	16	25	33	29	28	24	32	26	24	35	25	22
igeria	40	**na**	na	na	na	na	na	na	na	na	na	na	na	na	na	na
orthern Ireland	24	**na**	na	na	na	na	na	na	na	na	na	na	na	na	na	na
orway	33	**22**	26	18	21	20	25	22	21	23	na	na	na	20	22	21
akistan	na	**na**	na	na	na	na	na	na	na	na	na	na	na	na	na	na
eru	na	**na**	na	na	na	na	na	na	na	na	na	na	na	na	na	na
hilippines	na	**na**	na	na	na	na	na	na	na	na	na	na	na	na	na	na
oland	40	**na**	na	na	na	na	na	na	na	na	na	na	na	na	na	na
ortugal	37	**na**	na	na	na	na	na	na	na	na	na	na	na	na	na	na
uerto Rico	na	**17**	16	18	15	11	23	43	21	11	25	14	13	27	15	16
omania	25	**na**	na	na	na	na	na	na	na	na	na	na	na	na	na	na
ussian Fed.	19	**na**	na	na	na	na	na	na	na	na	na	na	na	na	na	na
erbia	na	**na**	na	na	na	na	na	na	na	na	na	na	na	na	na	na
ingapore	na	**na**	na	na	na	na	na	na	na	na	na	na	na	na	na	na
lovakia	na	**na**	na	na	na	na	na	na	na	na	na	na	na	na	na	na
lovenia	25	**na**	na	na	na	na	na	na	na	na	na	na	na	na	na	na
outh Africa	46	**30**	29	30	22	33	38	31	28	26	29	34	28	32	27	35
pain	37	**na**	na	na	na	na	na	na	na	na	na	na	na	na	na	na
weden	36	**na**	na	na	na	na	na	na	na	na	na	na	na	na	na	na
witzerland	na	**38**	38	38	27	36	48	48	36	31	41	44	36	47	39	27
aiwan	na	**55**	60	51	46	57	57	57	49	58	53	54	59	56	53	62
anzania	na	**na**	na	na	na	na	na	na	na	na	na	na	na	na	na	na
urkey	44	**na**	na	na	na	na	na	na	na	na	na	na	na	na	na	na
ganda	na	**27**	23	30	22	30	39	36	23	33	32	33	24	26	28	26
kraine	na	**na**	na	na	na	na	na	na	na	na	na	na	na	na	na	na
nited States	20	**23**	25	21	21	24	23	23	24	22	22	25	22	19	23	25
ruguay	na	**30**	27	33	19	24	40	34	25	27	29	34	27	40	28	25
enezuela	na	**25**	25	26	21	26	33	34	23	21	31	28	18	29	24	21
ietnam	na	**na**	na	na	na	na	na	na	na	na	na	na	na	na	na	na
imbabwe	na	**36**	33	38	31	40	40	40	30	18	32	36	36	33	37	35
otal	29	**32**	31	32	27	32	38	36	31	28	35	32	29	38	30	26

RANKING	
Country	**2000**
Azerbaijan	62
India	61
Taiwan	55
Georgia	51
Switzerland	38
Armenia	38
Zimbabwe	36
Brazil	36
Mexico	35
El Salvador	34
Macedonia	34
Chile	33
Albania	33
Argentina	32
Moldova	31
Australia	31
Uruguay	30
South Africa	30
Uganda	27
New Zealand	27
Venezuela	25
Canada	24
Dominican Rep.	24
United States	23
Norway	22
Puerto Rico	17
Bosnia and Herz.	14
Colombia	8
Bangladesh	3
Total	32

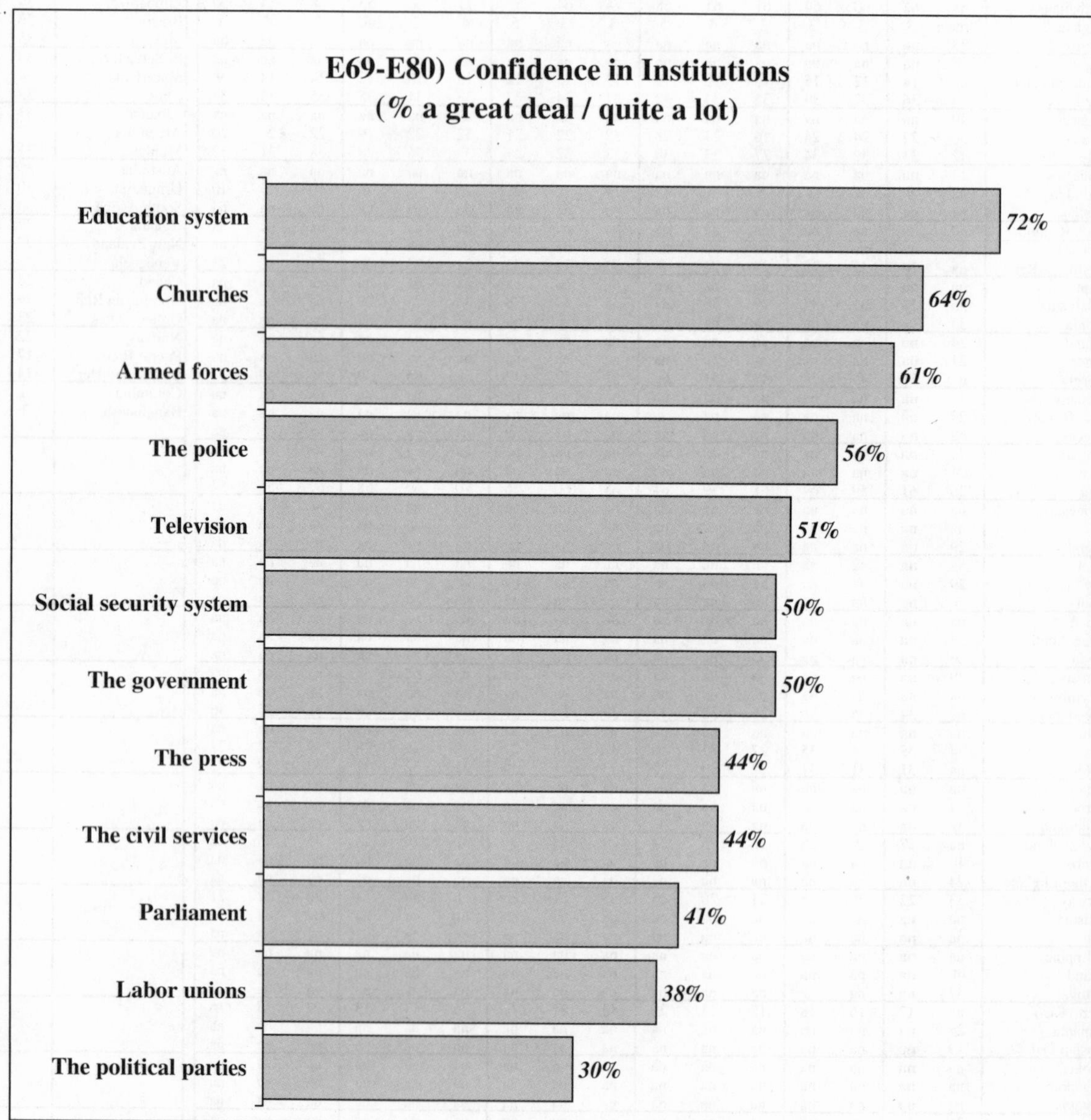
E69-E80) Confidence in Institutions
(% a great deal / quite a lot)
Education system
72%
Churches
64%
Armed forces
61%
The police
56%
Television
51%
Social security system
50%
The government
50%
The press
44%
The civil services
44%
Parliament
41%
Labor unions
38%
The political parties
30%

E069) CONFIDENCE: CHURCHES

I am going to name a number of organizations. For each one, could you tell me how much confidence you have in them: is it a great deal of confidence, quite a lot of confidence, not very much confidence or none at all? The churches.

A great deal / Quite a lot (%) (WVS: V147; EVS: V200)

Country	Wave		Gender		Age			Education			Income			Values		
	1990	2000	Male	Female	16-29	30-49	50+	Lower	Middle	Upper	Lower	Middle	Upper	Mat	Mixed	Postm.
Albania	na	**67**	61	72	64	63	74	67	68	63	66	68	66	65	66	76
Algeria	na	**89**	90	89	90	86	91	91	89	87	92	91	81	92	87	86
Argentina	45	**60**	56	63	54	58	67	63	54	57	69	60	51	68	62	47
Armenia	na	**68**	60	75	67	68	69	70	69	65	68	68	70	68	69	61
Australia	na	**43**	38	47	39	41	48	48	39	42	45	42	39	45	46	36
Austria	50	**39**	36	42	27	35	49	44	33	37	48	41	34	46	40	34
Azerbaijan	na	**72**	74	71	70	71	79	91	73	68	71	75	70	73	70	72
Bangladesh	na	**99**	98	100	98	99	99	100	98	97	99	98	99	99	98	99
Belarus	53	**71**	56	81	65	67	79	81	69	56	77	68	64	73	69	54
Belgium	50	**40**	34	46	32	32	51	50	36	38	52	38	35	45	40	35
Bosnia and Herz.	na	**50**	45	54	54	46	50	63	47	48	49	47	56	57	46	42
Brazil	75	**74**	72	77	74	73	77	75	75	72	76	75	71	77	75	67
Bulgaria	30	**36**	28	42	31	27	45	50	28	27	47	29	31	38	32	33
Canada	64	**59**	54	63	49	57	66	65	59	54	62	58	57	58	63	51
Chile	76	**78**	73	83	73	77	84	82	75	77	79	75	81	80	78	74
China	5	**na**	na	na	na	na	na	na	na	na	na	na	na	na	na	na
Colombia	na	**82**	79	85	80	83	85	84	82	79	83	82	79	84	82	80
Croatia	na	**64**	59	70	60	65	67	71	62	57	72	62	63	71	67	52
Czech Republic	43	**20**	17	22	15	13	28	22	17	16	27	18	13	21	19	22
Denmark	47	**59**	56	62	50	58	65	57	56	65	60	58	62	56	60	57
Dominican Rep.	na	**72**	72	72	71	73	82	72	72	72	74	73	69	72	72	72
Egypt	na	**84**	82	86	85	84	83	87	84	76	87	86	79	87	82	77
El Salvador	na	**63**	64	62	63	59	68	58	64	72	62	61	67	na	na	na
Estonia	54	**44**	38	49	37	39	53	49	42	41	53	48	38	47	42	40
Finland	32	**58**	52	64	53	54	65	56	57	70	60	49	63	59	59	52
France	50	**46**	41	50	37	41	55	49	40	43	46	43	45	53	47	32
Georgia	na	**80**	77	83	84	81	76	78	80	83	79	81	82	79	82	84
Germany	43	**39**	35	43	32	29	54	46	33	41	44	40	41	46	40	32
Great Britain	43	**34**	30	39	31	31	40	33	34	36	33	33	37	na	na	na
Greece	na	**55**	50	58	49	58	63	71	59	48	61	54	50	69	56	35
Hungary	56	**48**	39	55	35	41	61	53	37	37	57	47	43	53	42	44
Iceland	68	**65**	59	70	54	63	76	69	62	61	66	66	61	72	65	42
India	85	**82**	79	86	81	81	86	88	81	70	86	87	76	86	75	76
Indonesia	na	**96**	96	98	95	97	98	97	97	96	97	96	98	97	97	93
Iran	na	**86**	86	87	85	87	90	92	86	80	84	88	85	92	84	71
Ireland	72	**52**	48	56	30	48	72	66	44	46	64	50	44	54	53	43
Israel	na	**na**	na	na	na	na	na	na	na	na	na	na	na	na	na	na
Italy	63	**67**	61	73	55	65	75	72	65	61	74	65	63	79	68	59
Japan	11	**10**	9	10	5	10	12	9	11	7	11	9	9	11	9	10
Jordan	na	**91**	87	95	92	90	90	94	90	87	93	92	86	92	91	81
Korea, South	58	**49**	46	52	46	49	52	45	51	47	47	46	53	51	48	42
Latvia	64	**67**	59	73	60	64	72	73	64	68	70	62	67	67	67	60
Lithuania	73	**71**	60	79	58	61	88	88	65	66	83	65	67	77	71	55
Luxembourg	na	**48**	46	50	38	43	59	56	44	43	46	46	38	51	48	42
Macedonia	na	**46**	43	50	46	44	50	55	44	36	55	43	40	48	46	30
Malta	na	**82**	78	87	69	80	94	90	81	74	86	84	79	84	83	71
Mexico	76	**82**	78	85	80	81	85	84	80	73	86	79	77	84	81	76
Moldova	na	**82**	74	89	75	81	89	86	82	78	87	77	79	83	81	72
Montenegro	na	**48**	43	53	41	47	53	56	46	36	48	48	45	48	47	42
Morocco	na	**97**	96	98	97	98	98	98	97	93	100	96	96	97	97	94
Netherlands	31	**29**	26	32	20	23	39	35	28	24	30	29	24	46	28	21
New Zealand	na	**39**	37	41	38	32	45	36	40	40	41	38	35	46	40	35
Nigeria	88	**95**	93	96	95	95	97	95	95	93	94	96	95	95	95	95
Northern Ireland	80	**64**	59	68	58	52	76	73	54	59	65	63	60	64	64	62
Norway	45	**54**	48	59	44	51	64	57	55	49	na	na	na	59	54	41
Pakistan	na	**88**	90	86	89	86	92	88	89	86	88	88	87	90	87	83
Peru	na	**71**	64	78	67	74	71	73	73	66	74	71	67	74	70	70
Philippines	na	**92**	89	94	92	92	90	94	91	90	89	93	92	93	90	91
Poland	84	**69**	64	74	69	63	77	75	65	56	73	69	62	77	66	59
Portugal	56	**80**	72	87	68	85	83	84	72	68	83	81	76	83	80	71
Puerto Rico	na	**83**	82	84	78	82	87	89	82	84	86	85	83	80	84	83
Romania	72	**83**	76	89	72	81	90	92	81	69	91	85	76	87	81	61
Russian Fed.	65	**61**	50	70	58	58	66	73	60	58	68	60	55	64	58	44
Serbia	na	**53**	50	56	53	50	56	64	47	48	58	51	51	54	51	44
Singapore	na	**na**	na	na	na	na	na	na	na	na	na	na	na	na	na	na
Slovakia	na	**69**	61	76	59	64	81	76	66	59	78	68	65	73	67	59
Slovenia	39	**35**	35	36	29	30	46	51	32	21	46	37	24	42	35	31
South Africa	83	**83**	78	90	87	79	86	85	82	73	82	91	78	84	82	84
Spain	46	**42**	33	50	24	35	59	52	32	31	54	42	34	52	42	23
Sweden	38	**45**	44	47	43	44	48	51	43	45	43	47	47	55	46	41
Switzerland	na	**39**	34	44	24	36	51	47	36	41	45	46	31	48	39	33
Taiwan	na	**62**	59	66	67	60	65	67	59	61	59	67	60	66	58	53
Tanzania	na	**93**	92	94	91	93	94	92	92	95	93	94	94	92	94	92
Turkey	66	**71**	70	73	67	71	82	77	67	57	75	71	63	82	72	55
Uganda	na	**89**	85	93	87	92	90	84	92	89	88	95	89	90	90	85
Ukraine	na	**66**	54	75	61	64	70	79	64	61	67	64	66	69	61	60
United States	68	**75**	69	81	70	75	78	76	75	74	75	75	73	84	76	68
Uruguay	na	**56**	52	59	50	47	65	62	48	47	60	52	54	64	58	42
Venezuela	na	**77**	73	81	75	75	81	76	77	76	76	76	76	82	75	72
Vietnam	na	**23**	19	26	19	23	25	29	14	12	18	22	25	19	24	21
Zimbabwe	na	**85**	76	92	86	83	84	88	80	31	86	87	76	84	83	92
Total	56	64	60	68	64	62	67	69	61	61	68	64	61	71	63	53

RANKING	
Country	2000
Bangladesh	99
Morocco	97
Indonesia	96
Nigeria	95
Tanzania	93
Philippines	92
Jordan	91
Uganda	89
Algeria	89
Pakistan	88
Iran	86
Zimbabwe	85
Egypt	84
Puerto Rico	83
South Africa	83
Romania	83
Malta	82
India	82
Colombia	82
Moldova	82
Mexico	82
Georgia	80
Portugal	80
Chile	78
Venezuela	77
United States	75
Brazil	74
Azerbaijan	72
Dominican Rep.	72
Turkey	71
Lithuania	71
Peru	71
Belarus	71
Poland	69
Slovakia	69
Armenia	68
Italy	67
Latvia	67
Albania	67
Ukraine	66
Iceland	65
Croatia	64
Northern Ireland	64
El Salvador	63
Taiwan	62
Russian Fed.	61
Argentina	60
Denmark	59
Canada	59
Finland	58
Uruguay	56
Greece	55
Norway	54
Serbia	53
Ireland	52
Bosnia and Herz.	50
Korea, South	49
Montenegro	48
Luxembourg	48
Hungary	48
Macedonia	46
France	46
Sweden	45
Estonia	44
Australia	43
Spain	42
Belgium	40
Germany	39
New Zealand	39
Switzerland	39
Austria	39
Bulgaria	36
Slovenia	35
Great Britain	34
Netherlands	29
Vietnam	23
Czech Republic	20
Japan	10
Total	64

E070) CONFIDENCE: ARMED FORCES

I am going to name a number of organizations. For each one, could you tell me how much confidence you have in them: is it a great deal of confidence, quite a lot of confidence, not very much confidence or none at all? The armed forces.

A great deal / Quite a lot (%)

(WVS: V148; EVS: V201

Country	Wave 1990	Wave 2000	Gender Male	Gender Female	Age 16-29	Age 30-49	Age 50+	Education Lower	Education Middle	Education Upper	Income Lower	Income Middle	Income Upper	Values Mat	Values Mixed	Values Postm.
Albania	na	**57**	54	59	54	54	64	61	54	54	60	57	51	60	54	50
Algeria	na	**67**	69	65	64	66	76	79	67	58	69	67	58	76	65	45
Argentina	28	**27**	34	21	24	28	28	29	25	17	32	26	23	32	28	19
Armenia	na	**72**	71	73	71	71	76	73	72	71	72	71	70	73	71	81
Australia	na	**68**	66	70	67	65	72	74	69	62	69	65	66	70	70	63
Austria	29	**39**	35	43	37	36	44	46	35	29	44	39	37	46	42	34
Azerbaijan	na	**56**	60	52	57	53	61	60	55	57	53	57	57	55	57	57
Bangladesh	na	**74**	74	76	74	73	85	81	67	68	82	69	76	75	75	60
Belarus	61	**70**	67	72	59	65	84	82	68	55	80	66	60	77	66	40
Belgium	33	**37**	36	39	41	32	41	38	41	31	38	38	37	45	36	32
Bosnia and Herz.	na	**61**	59	62	59	58	67	77	59	52	61	65	58	65	59	55
Brazil	67	**71**	79	64	69	70	81	71	71	75	70	70	73	72	72	69
Bulgaria	69	**58**	58	58	49	53	66	67	52	56	65	53	55	59	58	36
Canada	57	**63**	60	66	61	60	67	68	65	55	65	66	59	68	65	57
Chile	41	**48**	45	50	43	47	54	51	48	40	50	45	49	58	46	36
China	90	**97**	98	97	94	98	100	98	97	98	97	98	97	97	98	97
Colombia	na	**61**	65	57	59	62	64	57	62	65	56	62	67	61	60	60
Croatia	na	**66**	61	70	65	64	69	77	62	49	76	65	60	79	66	58
Czech Republic	39	**25**	23	27	26	23	27	29	24	14	29	28	19	26	25	23
Denmark	46	**61**	61	62	68	56	63	61	62	61	59	59	65	63	63	53
Dominican Rep.	na	**30**	35	26	29	30	36	41	32	27	33	27	31	33	30	25
Egypt	na	**57**	57	57	57	56	60	58	57	54	59	56	56	56	59	55
El Salvador	na	**45**	47	44	40	45	55	52	39	37	56	42	40	na	na	na
Estonia	23	**35**	36	34	29	26	46	39	32	34	35	40	33	33	37	30
Finland	57	**84**	84	85	83	82	88	84	86	85	83	82	90	86	86	77
France	56	**63**	62	64	60	58	69	67	57	58	61	64	63	73	64	46
Georgia	na	**52**	58	48	50	53	53	52	53	51	52	52	52	50	54	50
Germany	14	**55**	63	49	46	52	62	62	50	48	54	60	51	61	56	45
Great Britain	81	**84**	83	84	74	84	88	89	82	74	84	84	82	na	na	na
Greece	na	**68**	70	67	62	68	82	82	68	66	68	70	67	73	70	61
Hungary	52	**46**	46	47	42	45	49	47	44	45	50	44	48	46	48	40
Iceland	24	**40**	40	40	54	37	32	43	41	34	38	39	43	43	41	29
India	93	**92**	92	92	95	91	90	90	94	93	89	93	92	96	90	88
Indonesia	na	**74**	72	76	62	73	80	80	77	67	77	70	76	75	74	61
Iran	na	**na**	na	na	na	na	na	na	na	na	na	na	na	na	na	na
Ireland	61	**59**	56	62	45	56	72	65	59	47	64	65	51	69	56	57
Israel	na	**na**	na	na	na	na	na	na	na	na	na	na	na	na	na	na
Italy	48	**52**	50	53	47	46	59	59	49	39	55	52	45	66	53	41
Japan	24	**67**	68	67	61	63	74	71	68	62	72	66	63	81	67	50
Jordan	na	**92**	92	93	89	94	96	95	92	87	96	91	88	96	92	75
Korea, South	80	**64**	67	62	48	65	81	72	70	55	64	63	66	67	65	41
Latvia	25	**48**	43	52	40	40	59	58	45	43	53	45	45	51	47	38
Lithuania	22	**50**	48	52	46	38	64	66	46	39	63	47	45	53	50	37
Luxembourg	na	**54**	55	54	57	50	57	60	54	43	53	55	41	58	56	45
Macedonia	na	**55**	56	53	47	53	64	48	59	57	54	55	58	58	56	17
Malta	na	**72**	71	73	63	69	81	78	71	64	77	75	64	76	71	66
Mexico	47	**54**	57	51	53	54	54	54	52	57	48	55	55	56	53	50
Moldova	na	**57**	54	60	50	55	66	65	60	44	64	55	51	57	59	41
Montenegro	na	**51**	50	51	37	46	65	59	45	45	57	58	42	55	47	51
Morocco	na	**71**	72	70	61	76	85	75	55	61	77	63	67	75	68	57
Netherlands	32	**40**	44	36	54	35	38	39	46	35	42	41	35	41	42	35
New Zealand	na	**60**	60	60	59	56	64	64	60	56	65	62	53	67	62	54
Nigeria	61	**47**	50	43	48	47	38	52	43	44	47	45	49	46	47	46
Northern Ireland	79	**56**	53	59	43	52	66	56	55	61	54	58	61	66	60	34
Norway	65	**73**	68	78	70	71	77	74	73	71	na	na	na	74	75	57
Pakistan	na	**86**	87	85	85	84	93	87	85	83	87	84	86	88	84	82
Peru	na	**22**	24	20	23	21	23	26	23	17	26	20	18	26	21	20
Philippines	na	**74**	76	72	71	74	79	77	75	70	75	71	78	78	72	70
Poland	65	**68**	67	68	46	67	82	74	60	57	72	68	58	71	68	56
Portugal	47	**71**	75	67	70	69	73	72	67	77	70	74	64	71	69	74
Puerto Rico	na	**53**	56	51	37	51	62	67	52	51	55	52	56	63	53	51
Romania	82	**83**	81	84	71	82	89	89	80	76	86	85	78	86	82	65
Russian Fed.	69	**67**	65	69	61	63	75	80	68	55	70	69	62	71	64	56
Serbia	na	**74**	72	76	63	68	85	84	71	65	80	77	71	81	70	51
Singapore	na	**na**	na	na	na	na	na	na	na	na	na	na	na	na	na	na
Slovakia	na	**77**	74	80	70	77	82	79	77	71	82	74	78	78	76	70
Slovenia	45	**42**	44	39	35	39	50	52	41	25	46	46	37	48	41	41
South Africa	61	**55**	56	54	56	53	60	62	49	22	64	58	39	58	54	52
Spain	37	**42**	42	43	32	36	55	48	37	36	54	41	38	52	43	25
Sweden	49	**44**	46	43	47	40	47	39	45	48	41	46	46	59	45	39
Switzerland	na	**50**	49	51	42	43	62	55	49	46	47	53	49	63	54	29
Taiwan	na	**76**	76	77	62	77	84	87	73	69	79	79	71	82	71	69
Tanzania	na	**91**	90	93	90	91	96	94	89	87	94	91	88	91	93	79
Turkey	91	**86**	85	87	83	87	91	87	85	81	84	87	85	91	87	77
Uganda	na	**76**	78	73	72	81	69	70	77	84	78	83	80	79	75	70
Ukraine	na	**69**	68	70	58	67	76	74	71	62	72	67	67	68	69	61
United States	48	**82**	80	83	76	83	85	80	79	84	79	82	86	86	84	74
Uruguay	na	**38**	37	39	27	27	52	46	29	23	46	36	31	56	40	20
Venezuela	na	**64**	68	60	58	65	74	66	64	61	61	61	66	65	63	64
Vietnam	na	**96**	97	96	94	97	98	96	97	94	95	97	96	96	97	91
Zimbabwe	na	**62**	60	64	61	62	66	71	51	17	72	63	46	64	61	60
Total	52	**61**	62	61	57	60	66	66	60	56	64	61	59	67	61	49

RANKING

Country	2000
China	97
Vietnam	96
Jordan	92
India	92
Tanzania	91
Pakistan	86
Turkey	86
Finland	84
Great Britain	84
Romania	83
United States	82
Slovakia	77
Taiwan	76
Uganda	76
Bangladesh	74
Philippines	74
Serbia	74
Indonesia	74
Norway	73
Armenia	72
Malta	72
Brazil	71
Portugal	71
Morocco	71
Belarus	70
Ukraine	69
Greece	68
Australia	68
Poland	68
Japan	67
Algeria	67
Russian Fed.	67
Croatia	66
Korea, South	64
Venezuela	64
Canada	63
France	63
Zimbabwe	62
Denmark	61
Colombia	61
Bosnia and Herz.	61
New Zealand	60
Ireland	59
Bulgaria	58
Moldova	57
Egypt	57
Albania	57
Northern Ireland	56
Azerbaijan	56
Germany	55
South Africa	55
Macedonia	55
Luxembourg	54
Mexico	54
Puerto Rico	53
Georgia	52
Italy	52
Montenegro	51
Lithuania	50
Switzerland	50
Chile	48
Latvia	48
Nigeria	47
Hungary	46
El Salvador	45
Sweden	44
Spain	42
Slovenia	42
Netherlands	40
Iceland	40
Austria	39
Uruguay	38
Belgium	37
Estonia	35
Dominican Rep.	30
Argentina	27
Czech Republic	25
Peru	22
Total	61

E071_1) CONFIDENCE: EDUCATION SYSTEM

Please look at this card and tell me, for each item listed, how much confidence you have in them, is it a great deal, quite a lot, not very much or none at all? The education system.

(EVS: V202)

A great deal / Quite a lot (%)

Country	Wave		Gender		Age			Education			Income			Values		
	1990	2000	Male	Female	16-29	30-49	50+	Lower	Middle	Upper	Lower	Middle	Upper	Mat	Mixed	Postm.
Albania	na	**na**	na	na	na	na	na	na	na	na	na	na	na	na	na	na
Algeria	na	**na**	na	na	na	na	na	na	na	na	na	na	na	na	na	na
Argentina	38	**na**	na	na	na	na	na	na	na	na	na	na	na	na	na	na
Armenia	na	**na**	na	na	na	na	na	na	na	na	na	na	na	na	na	na
Australia	na	**na**	na	na	na	na	na	na	na	na	na	na	na	na	na	na
Austria	65	**86**	85	88	84	87	87	87	86	84	80	89	87	86	88	84
Azerbaijan	na	**na**	na	na	na	na	na	na	na	na	na	na	na	na	na	na
Bangladesh	na	**na**	na	na	na	na	na	na	na	na	na	na	na	na	na	na
Belarus	43	**84**	84	84	78	82	92	93	83	74	89	81	81	89	82	70
Belgium	73	**80**	79	82	80	80	81	81	81	78	76	81	80	82	81	78
Bosnia and Herz.	na	**na**	na	na	na	na	na	na	na	na	na	na	na	na	na	na
Brazil	67	**na**	na	na	na	na	na	na	na	na	na	na	na	na	na	na
Bulgaria	53	**58**	55	60	51	57	62	62	54	58	60	54	58	52	61	66
Canada	73	**na**	na	na	na	na	na	na	na	na	na	na	na	na	na	na
Chile	73	**na**	na	na	na	na	na	na	na	na	na	na	na	na	na	na
China	93	**na**	na	na	na	na	na	na	na	na	na	na	na	na	na	na
Colombia	na	**na**	na	na	na	na	na	na	na	na	na	na	na	na	na	na
Croatia	na	**64**	62	67	56	65	70	75	61	46	67	65	63	79	65	52
Czech Republic	61	**55**	52	57	52	50	60	57	53	47	58	55	50	56	54	54
Denmark	81	**75**	75	75	73	72	79	74	77	77	74	76	75	73	75	78
Dominican Rep.	na	**na**	na	na	na	na	na	na	na	na	na	na	na	na	na	na
Egypt	na	**na**	na	na	na	na	na	na	na	na	na	na	na	na	na	na
El Salvador	na	**na**	na	na	na	na	na	na	na	na	na	na	na	na	na	na
Estonia	48	**74**	72	76	70	69	81	78	73	71	72	81	72	75	75	63
Finland	78	**89**	88	90	90	88	89	88	92	84	86	90	91	92	89	83
France	66	**68**	67	70	68	69	68	69	62	73	68	69	70	71	67	71
Georgia	na	**na**	na	na	na	na	na	na	na	na	na	na	na	na	na	na
Germany	40	**73**	74	72	71	71	75	76	70	72	73	74	73	76	73	69
Great Britain	47	**66**	68	65	67	68	64	67	67	64	67	70	65	na	na	na
Greece	na	**29**	29	29	22	30	41	44	26	29	33	28	27	33	29	22
Hungary	61	**64**	64	65	66	64	64	66	60	61	61	65	67	66	63	72
Iceland	80	**82**	81	83	77	84	85	85	80	81	83	84	81	87	83	68
India	73	**na**	na	na	na	na	na	na	na	na	na	na	na	na	na	na
Indonesia	na	**na**	na	na	na	na	na	na	na	na	na	na	na	na	na	na
Iran	na	**na**	na	na	na	na	na	na	na	na	na	na	na	na	na	na
Ireland	73	**86**	84	89	84	86	88	84	87	89	86	84	88	89	86	84
Israel	na	**na**	na	na	na	na	na	na	na	na	na	na	na	na	na	na
Italy	48	**53**	51	55	42	52	60	65	45	44	62	53	47	71	52	47
Japan	46	**na**	na	na	na	na	na	na	na	na	na	na	na	na	na	na
Jordan	na	**na**	na	na	na	na	na	na	na	na	na	na	na	na	na	na
Korea, South	64	**na**	na	na	na	na	na	na	na	na	na	na	na	na	na	na
Latvia	53	**74**	71	76	77	70	76	80	74	68	77	71	73	78	72	75
Lithuania	57	**67**	64	69	61	56	81	86	61	58	72	69	63	73	66	46
Luxembourg	na	**68**	69	67	62	67	72	74	60	74	70	64	68	71	69	61
Macedonia	na	**na**	na	na	na	na	na	na	na	na	na	na	na	na	na	na
Malta	na	**84**	83	86	80	81	91	90	83	80	88	83	84	85	84	86
Mexico	76	**na**	na	na	na	na	na	na	na	na	na	na	na	na	na	na
Moldova	na	**na**	na	na	na	na	na	na	na	na	na	na	na	na	na	na
Montenegro	na	**na**	na	na	na	na	na	na	na	na	na	na	na	na	na	na
Morocco	na	**na**	na	na	na	na	na	na	na	na	na	na	na	na	na	na
Netherlands	67	**73**	76	69	84	71	68	71	74	73	72	76	71	77	72	73
New Zealand	na	**na**	na	na	na	na	na	na	na	na	na	na	na	na	na	na
Nigeria	84	**na**	na	na	na	na	na	na	na	na	na	na	na	na	na	na
Northern Ireland	66	**83**	82	83	79	81	85	83	82	82	85	85	85	84	84	78
Norway	79	**na**	na	na	na	na	na	na	na	na	na	na	na	na	na	na
Pakistan	na	**na**	na	na	na	na	na	na	na	na	na	na	na	na	na	na
Peru	na	**na**	na	na	na	na	na	na	na	na	na	na	na	na	na	na
Philippines	na	**na**	na	na	na	na	na	na	na	na	na	na	na	na	na	na
Poland	75	**81**	81	82	76	79	87	87	79	63	85	82	70	82	80	89
Portugal	51	**60**	56	63	59	56	64	61	54	65	72	58	54	59	60	64
Puerto Rico	na	**na**	na	na	na	na	na	na	na	na	na	na	na	na	na	na
Romania	79	**79**	77	82	73	77	85	85	77	74	84	81	76	83	77	69
Russian Fed.	55	**71**	70	72	67	69	77	82	70	70	74	71	68	74	69	62
Serbia	na	**na**	na	na	na	na	na	na	na	na	na	na	na	na	na	na
Singapore	na	**na**	na	na	na	na	na	na	na	na	na	na	na	na	na	na
Slovakia	na	**76**	73	80	73	75	81	79	76	70	80	78	75	79	75	72
Slovenia	67	**80**	80	80	79	77	85	84	80	77	82	80	82	81	80	81
South Africa	77	**na**	na	na	na	na	na	na	na	na	na	na	na	na	na	na
Spain	67	**68**	63	72	66	61	74	76	64	56	75	68	58	70	70	56
Sweden	70	**68**	67	69	71	72	63	64	68	71	66	72	65	59	67	71
Switzerland	na	**na**	na	na	na	na	na	na	na	na	na	na	na	na	na	na
Taiwan	na	**na**	na	na	na	na	na	na	na	na	na	na	na	na	na	na
Tanzania	na	**na**	na	na	na	na	na	na	na	na	na	na	na	na	na	na
Turkey	65	**57**	50	65	54	58	71	69	45	29	66	58	41	69	57	45
Uganda	na	**na**	na	na	na	na	na	na	na	na	na	na	na	na	na	na
Ukraine	na	**72**	69	74	61	69	80	83	71	69	72	71	72	70	72	67
United States	55	**na**	na	na	na	na	na	na	na	na	na	na	na	na	na	na
Uruguay	na	**na**	na	na	na	na	na	na	na	na	na	na	na	na	na	na
Venezuela	na	**na**	na	na	na	na	na	na	na	na	na	na	na	na	na	na
Vietnam	na	**na**	na	na	na	na	na	na	na	na	na	na	na	na	na	na
Zimbabwe	na	**na**	na	na	na	na	na	na	na	na	na	na	na	na	na	na
Total	64	72	70	73	67	70	76	76	70	67	74	72	70	74	72	68

RANKING	
Country	2000
Finland	89
Ireland	86
Austria	86
Malta	84
Belarus	84
Northern Ireland	83
Iceland	82
Poland	81
Slovenia	80
Belgium	80
Romania	79
Slovakia	76
Denmark	75
Estonia	74
Latvia	74
Netherlands	73
Germany	73
Ukraine	72
Russian Fed.	71
France	68
Sweden	68
Luxembourg	68
Spain	68
Lithuania	67
Great Britain	66
Croatia	64
Hungary	64
Portugal	60
Bulgaria	58
Turkey	57
Czech Republic	55
Italy	53
Greece	29
Total	72

E072) CONFIDENCE: THE PRESS

I am going to name a number of organizations. For each one, could you tell me how much confidence you have in them: is it a great deal of confidence, quite a lot of confidence, not very much confidence or none at all? The press.

A great deal / Quite a lot (%)

(WVS: V149; EVS: V203)

Country	Wave		Gender		Age			Education			Income			Values		
	1990	2000	Male	Female	16-29	30-49	50+	Lower	Middle	Upper	Lower	Middle	Upper	Mat	Mixed	Postm.
Albania	na	**35**	39	31	32	34	40	33	37	37	33	41	32	37	33	50
Algeria	na	**48**	45	51	49	45	50	47	50	46	49	46	48	53	45	46
Argentina	27	**38**	37	39	32	42	41	37	42	35	45	35	37	40	36	42
Armenia	na	**34**	34	34	34	35	33	33	34	34	34	35	30	37	34	15
Australia	na	**17**	18	16	20	16	15	16	16	19	17	14	18	19	17	16
Austria	18	**32**	32	32	34	31	31	31	33	32	35	30	32	35	31	33
Azerbaijan	na	**32**	36	27	37	29	27	33	29	36	28	32	34	30	34	50
Bangladesh	na	**93**	92	95	93	92	98	94	92	92	93	92	95	93	94	93
Belarus	25	**41**	38	43	40	38	45	48	40	31	44	37	41	43	39	28
Belgium	44	**37**	39	36	38	41	33	30	36	45	32	36	41	31	37	46
Bosnia and Herz.	na	**25**	26	24	26	19	32	30	25	21	25	26	23	23	24	40
Brazil	55	**61**	65	58	61	62	63	64	59	58	60	66	61	56	63	67
Bulgaria	35	**26**	26	26	31	24	26	25	24	33	24	26	29	20	31	34
Canada	46	**35**	36	34	33	34	37	34	36	34	36	34	37	37	35	35
Chile	43	**48**	45	51	43	48	53	48	48	46	43	51	56	48	48	46
China	55	**69**	70	69	65	67	78	76	65	65	73	69	62	67	68	71
Colombia	na	**45**	47	44	47	45	43	43	47	47	43	44	50	46	47	47
Croatia	na	**18**	23	14	13	18	22	20	18	14	21	15	19	23	18	15
Czech Republic	43	**38**	38	38	43	36	36	38	37	38	37	37	40	36	37	46
Denmark	31	**33**	35	31	38	29	34	31	33	39	34	30	35	29	34	30
Dominican Rep.	na	**33**	35	31	35	27	50	19	33	35	30	37	34	32	32	35
Egypt	na	**69**	66	73	68	68	74	72	68	67	70	71	69	73	68	59
El Salvador	na	**46**	47	46	48	44	48	47	41	50	50	48	47	na	na	na
Estonia	64	**42**	44	40	47	39	42	43	43	39	39	44	43	38	45	40
Finland	38	**36**	37	36	38	36	37	31	43	47	34	32	44	33	39	35
France	38	**36**	35	36	39	36	34	32	36	44	33	36	38	34	34	44
Georgia	na	**60**	63	58	62	60	58	60	60	60	56	62	63	61	60	61
Germany	21	**36**	36	36	40	33	38	36	36	32	38	38	38	43	36	27
Great Britain	14	**16**	17	15	14	14	19	15	17	17	17	22	12	na	na	na
Greece	na	**31**	25	35	33	29	30	31	29	32	31	31	32	35	31	29
Hungary	40	**31**	32	30	24	35	31	32	27	33	28	32	32	29	32	53
Iceland	20	**39**	40	39	48	37	35	33	43	44	39	37	42	33	41	42
India	66	**70**	71	70	76	66	72	66	72	75	64	69	74	76	71	52
Indonesia	na	**55**	56	54	48	58	56	50	56	57	51	58	52	52	57	50
Iran	na	**36**	36	37	34	38	40	40	37	31	34	33	39	39	33	39
Ireland	36	**35**	34	36	26	38	37	36	29	45	35	32	31	33	35	35
Israel	na	**na**	na	na	na	na	na	na	na	na	na	na	na	na	na	na
Italy	39	**35**	33	38	40	32	35	34	37	34	36	35	34	37	33	38
Japan	56	**73**	69	76	78	71	73	71	75	69	74	74	70	73	76	61
Jordan	na	**59**	53	65	60	60	55	66	60	46	70	53	53	65	57	43
Korea, South	66	**66**	62	70	62	66	69	72	71	58	64	68	66	67	66	56
Latvia	60	**45**	44	46	45	41	48	57	42	40	46	44	43	46	44	45
Lithuania	68	**77**	76	78	74	71	84	86	74	74	80	75	76	80	77	72
Luxembourg	na	**46**	46	46	43	45	49	46	46	47	43	43	46	47	49	40
Macedonia	na	**20**	18	21	20	18	21	23	17	21	19	20	20	18	20	20
Malta	na	**36**	38	35	37	31	41	36	37	37	39	38	37	37	37	33
Mexico	49	**42**	44	39	43	41	40	42	38	53	33	45	49	42	42	41
Moldova	na	**44**	42	45	39	42	50	49	45	35	45	45	44	44	45	39
Montenegro	na	**24**	27	20	25	22	25	19	25	31	14	23	29	20	27	32
Morocco	na	**37**	34	40	32	39	50	41	24	29	41	27	36	40	36	29
Netherlands	34	**56**	57	55	60	59	51	42	59	67	50	56	67	41	57	62
New Zealand	na	**33**	35	31	33	31	35	35	31	33	32	30	36	37	34	30
Nigeria	71	**64**	67	62	64	66	57	63	63	69	63	64	68	61	65	70
Northern Ireland	16	**18**	18	19	14	14	24	20	14	23	18	15	19	17	18	21
Norway	43	**33**	30	35	32	32	33	35	32	32	na	na	na	33	33	34
Pakistan	na	**53**	52	54	52	55	47	50	54	59	49	52	58	48	60	83
Peru	na	**23**	25	21	22	25	21	23	24	22	26	21	21	29	22	21
Philippines	na	**67**	68	66	72	67	61	68	68	64	62	67	72	67	68	61
Poland	47	**47**	46	47	40	46	52	50	43	44	48	46	45	44	48	54
Portugal	36	**66**	63	68	71	62	65	66	68	59	68	62	67	69	64	73
Puerto Rico	na	**41**	44	39	30	40	46	57	37	39	44	41	38	37	42	40
Romania	28	**39**	40	37	33	37	44	42	34	43	43	36	38	38	37	49
Russian Fed.	44	**30**	28	31	30	27	33	37	29	29	33	31	28	30	30	33
Serbia	na	**29**	31	27	32	26	31	34	26	27	27	29	32	29	28	36
Singapore	na	**na**	na	na	na	na	na	na	na	na	na	na	na	na	na	na
Slovakia	na	**49**	48	50	52	49	47	47	50	50	46	47	53	45	52	53
Slovenia	50	**61**	61	62	59	56	68	68	60	53	63	64	66	66	61	59
South Africa	58	**65**	67	63	71	62	60	64	67	61	67	75	55	62	67	66
Spain	45	**41**	40	42	40	42	41	40	43	39	40	43	40	37	42	41
Sweden	33	**46**	47	45	54	42	45	43	46	49	53	45	39	51	45	48
Switzerland	na	**22**	23	21	23	22	21	21	22	27	18	25	25	27	22	20
Taiwan	na	**41**	38	44	36	41	44	44	40	39	45	39	41	42	40	32
Tanzania	na	**76**	73	81	78	74	76	80	72	72	79	73	73	73	78	83
Turkey	42	**35**	32	37	33	34	39	37	31	28	38	32	31	35	34	32
Uganda	na	**67**	70	64	70	69	49	56	71	73	67	72	67	61	69	74
Ukraine	na	**47**	46	47	38	44	53	51	48	42	50	43	45	44	50	39
United States	56	**27**	28	25	28	27	26	26	30	25	27	29	21	37	26	26
Uruguay	na	**61**	61	61	55	58	66	63	56	63	63	61	59	68	60	58
Venezuela	na	**65**	64	65	66	62	68	62	66	65	63	66	64	70	64	63
Vietnam	na	**84**	87	82	81	86	84	83	85	90	77	87	86	80	87	77
Zimbabwe	na	**54**	51	58	57	48	58	59	48	52	64	54	43	47	59	66
Total	42	44	45	44	46	44	44	46	44	43	45	44	45	46	45	41

RANKING

Country	2000
Bangladesh	93
Vietnam	84
Lithuania	77
Tanzania	76
Japan	73
India	70
Egypt	69
China	69
Philippines	67
Uganda	67
Korea, South	66
Portugal	66
South Africa	65
Venezuela	65
Nigeria	64
Brazil	61
Slovenia	61
Uruguay	61
Georgia	60
Jordan	59
Netherlands	56
Indonesia	55
Zimbabwe	54
Pakistan	53
Slovakia	49
Algeria	48
Chile	48
Poland	47
Ukraine	47
El Salvador	46
Luxembourg	46
Sweden	46
Colombia	45
Latvia	45
Moldova	44
Estonia	42
Mexico	42
Spain	41
Taiwan	41
Belarus	41
Puerto Rico	41
Iceland	39
Romania	39
Argentina	38
Czech Republic	38
Belgium	37
Morocco	37
Malta	36
Finland	36
Iran	36
Germany	36
France	36
Albania	35
Italy	35
Canada	35
Ireland	35
Turkey	35
Armenia	34
Denmark	33
Dominican Rep.	33
New Zealand	33
Norway	33
Austria	32
Azerbaijan	32
Greece	31
Hungary	31
Russian Fed.	30
Serbia	29
United States	27
Bulgaria	26
Bosnia and Herz.	25
Montenegro	24
Peru	23
Switzerland	22
Macedonia	20
Northern Ireland	18
Croatia	18
Australia	17
Great Britain	16
Total	44

E073) CONFIDENCE: LABOR UNIONS

I am going to name a number of organizations. For each one, could you tell me how much confidence you have in them: is it a great deal of confidence, quite a lot of confidence, not very much confidence or none at all? Labor unions.

A great deal / Quite a lot (%) (WVS: V151; EVS: V204)

Country	Wave		Gender		Age			Education			Income			Values		
	1990	2000	Male	Female	16-29	30-49	50+	Lower	Middle	Upper	Lower	Middle	Upper	Mat	Mixed	Postm.
Albania	na	**33**	36	29	30	34	32	32	32	35	26	38	34	27	38	29
Algeria	na	**29**	26	33	25	31	34	33	28	28	29	29	23	30	28	34
Argentina	8	**12**	13	11	13	14	9	13	10	9	14	13	9	22	9	11
Armenia	na	**19**	17	21	18	17	25	22	19	18	18	20	18	20	20	9
Australia	na	**26**	28	23	30	25	22	24	25	28	26	27	25	25	25	27
Austria	35	**31**	32	31	39	27	32	36	27	25	37	32	27	36	32	30
Azerbaijan	na	**30**	32	28	26	32	31	27	27	36	25	33	34	29	32	40
Bangladesh	na	**72**	71	73	71	72	78	76	71	63	76	70	71	70	73	74
Belarus	25	**28**	32	24	38	29	18	15	31	38	23	27	39	21	31	54
Belgium	37	**37**	36	37	46	37	32	36	38	35	36	39	35	37	37	36
Bosnia and Herz.	na	**23**	22	23	18	22	29	26	21	27	26	25	18	27	21	22
Brazil	48	**55**	56	55	57	52	59	55	54	60	57	55	52	51	57	58
Bulgaria	32	**15**	12	19	14	17	14	18	13	19	13	16	18	11	18	16
Canada	35	**36**	36	36	47	34	32	33	38	34	42	35	33	38	35	38
Chile	47	**46**	44	47	47	43	48	43	47	47	44	48	45	38	49	49
China	42	**73**	69	79	63	75	79	80	72	62	78	76	68	73	74	52
Colombia	na	**35**	33	36	38	33	33	31	35	39	32	35	37	34	36	42
Croatia	na	**29**	33	26	20	29	35	31	30	21	35	28	28	36	29	25
Czech Republic	27	**22**	23	21	23	20	24	25	20	15	24	25	19	26	22	14
Denmark	46	**48**	44	52	54	48	45	48	44	52	52	47	43	53	48	47
Dominican Rep.	na	**19**	22	18	19	20	10	23	16	21	25	21	16	21	17	20
Egypt	na	**68**	66	70	70	67	65	70	70	60	71	70	64	66	70	57
El Salvador	na	**18**	18	18	20	16	16	16	19	20	17	18	19	na	na	na
Estonia	27	**33**	30	35	32	26	39	32	34	30	31	38	33	32	33	32
Finland	32	**54**	50	57	62	52	52	57	50	45	57	51	53	57	52	52
France	32	**35**	35	35	38	34	34	32	37	41	31	36	37	28	36	45
Georgia	na	**28**	28	29	23	27	35	30	28	28	31	26	27	30	27	20
Germany	28	**38**	39	37	43	35	39	37	40	32	39	39	39	43	37	33
Great Britain	26	**28**	30	26	33	28	26	26	28	36	29	30	27	na	na	na
Greece	na	**14**	13	15	14	15	14	13	14	15	14	14	15	14	13	17
Hungary	30	**24**	26	21	24	22	26	25	21	20	15	24	28	20	28	31
Iceland	51	**49**	44	54	53	44	52	55	47	40	54	50	42	47	51	44
India	52	**48**	51	43	51	45	53	51	49	43	52	52	44	51	46	33
Indonesia	na	**38**	38	38	29	42	39	45	39	34	37	40	31	36	40	35
Iran	na	**37**	37	38	36	38	41	44	37	31	34	34	38	37	36	45
Ireland	43	**46**	46	47	46	44	49	45	46	50	43	52	46	49	45	49
Israel	na	**na**	na	na	na	na	na	na	na	na	na	na	na	na	na	na
Italy	34	**29**	28	30	31	26	30	31	28	26	33	29	25	34	28	29
Japan	26	**43**	39	47	48	44	40	41	45	39	39	49	41	48	44	28
Jordan	na	**51**	41	62	55	48	53	60	45	43	63	43	44	57	49	39
Korea, South	67	**52**	49	56	52	54	49	66	55	47	52	50	54	48	56	61
Latvia	24	**32**	27	37	34	32	32	47	29	29	34	34	29	35	32	23
Lithuania	27	**40**	37	43	35	32	52	55	36	37	50	37	38	38	42	43
Luxembourg	na	**52**	54	51	50	52	54	57	52	44	50	48	45	46	56	46
Macedonia	na	**13**	13	13	10	12	16	13	12	15	13	13	14	11	15	9
Malta	na	**49**	50	48	48	39	59	53	47	47	53	52	42	51	50	34
Mexico	38	**29**	28	29	30	28	28	30	24	38	26	29	31	30	29	28
Moldova	na	**33**	31	35	26	32	41	36	32	32	41	32	30	31	35	37
Montenegro	na	**20**	22	18	20	20	20	18	23	17	17	17	25	21	20	19
Morocco	na	**22**	20	24	20	19	37	24	14	23	22	15	23	24	20	19
Netherlands	54	**58**	59	56	68	56	54	53	59	61	60	64	50	51	57	64
New Zealand	na	**22**	20	23	35	22	18	19	20	27	26	23	20	21	22	23
Nigeria	66	**65**	68	62	63	68	62	65	63	69	64	64	70	63	67	62
Northern Ireland	24	**38**	39	37	37	34	41	39	36	39	39	35	36	28	39	47
Norway	59	**66**	61	71	74	66	61	62	65	72	na	na	na	63	66	70
Pakistan	na	**26**	25	27	26	22	35	28	22	25	29	26	20	26	26	14
Peru	na	**22**	24	20	23	21	24	23	24	20	24	23	17	25	22	18
Philippines	na	**54**	54	55	53	58	50	54	55	54	55	51	58	50	57	60
Poland	23	**34**	35	33	28	33	39	39	31	21	36	36	29	30	36	35
Portugal	29	**47**	42	52	50	45	47	47	48	46	49	48	43	50	44	51
Puerto Rico	na	**42**	43	41	50	40	39	46	42	41	48	38	41	40	43	40
Romania	30	**27**	28	26	25	26	30	31	27	21	29	25	27	30	25	24
Russian Fed.	47	**31**	27	34	29	28	35	45	31	23	36	31	27	32	30	22
Serbia	na	**23**	25	22	20	20	28	27	23	20	25	29	20	23	24	22
Singapore	na	**na**	na	na	na	na	na	na	na	na	na	na	na	na	na	na
Slovakia	na	**43**	42	44	42	44	43	42	45	35	43	41	46	42	44	45
Slovenia	27	**31**	30	32	27	29	37	41	30	22	41	34	29	41	29	30
South Africa	61	**52**	54	48	48	55	52	59	46	20	58	56	36	48	55	48
Spain	40	**30**	31	30	33	30	28	30	30	31	31	35	29	29	30	36
Sweden	40	**43**	43	42	50	39	42	47	43	38	46	46	33	45	41	49
Switzerland	na	**37**	38	37	46	36	34	41	37	33	43	35	36	43	34	43
Taiwan	na	**58**	56	60	53	58	61	64	60	52	56	58	57	58	56	64
Tanzania	na	**70**	67	73	67	71	72	74	65	67	69	73	69	67	72	63
Turkey	40	**52**	50	55	53	51	55	56	50	43	56	52	44	50	53	54
Uganda	na	**58**	64	51	60	56	52	48	60	69	56	65	65	46	62	69
Ukraine	na	**38**	35	40	28	34	47	50	36	35	39	37	38	37	40	31
United States	33	**38**	37	40	49	35	35	50	42	32	42	43	31	45	39	35
Uruguay	na	**39**	40	38	38	38	40	37	39	52	39	37	41	36	38	42
Venezuela	na	**23**	24	22	24	22	23	23	25	18	24	27	21	25	21	29
Vietnam	na	**80**	80	80	74	80	83	78	82	79	80	82	77	80	81	81
Zimbabwe	na	**63**	60	66	60	64	70	70	54	92	68	67	50	61	63	69
Total	37	38	38	38	39	38	38	41	37	36	40	39	37	38	40	38

RANKING	
Country	2000
Vietnam	80
China	73
Bangladesh	72
Tanzania	70
Egypt	68
Norway	66
Nigeria	65
Zimbabwe	63
Taiwan	58
Netherlands	58
Uganda	58
Brazil	55
Philippines	54
Finland	54
Korea, South	52
Turkey	52
Luxembourg	52
South Africa	52
Jordan	51
Iceland	49
Malta	49
India	48
Denmark	48
Portugal	47
Ireland	46
Chile	46
Slovakia	43
Japan	43
Sweden	43
Puerto Rico	42
Lithuania	40
Uruguay	39
United States	38
Germany	38
Indonesia	38
Ukraine	38
Northern Ireland	38
Iran	37
Switzerland	37
Belgium	37
Canada	36
France	35
Colombia	35
Poland	34
Moldova	33
Albania	33
Estonia	33
Latvia	32
Austria	31
Slovenia	31
Russian Fed.	31
Spain	30
Azerbaijan	30
Algeria	29
Croatia	29
Italy	29
Mexico	29
Georgia	28
Great Britain	28
Belarus	28
Romania	27
Pakistan	26
Australia	26
Hungary	24
Serbia	23
Venezuela	23
Bosnia and Herz.	23
Peru	22
Morocco	22
Czech Republic	22
New Zealand	22
Montenegro	20
Armenia	19
Dominican Rep.	19
El Salvador	18
Bulgaria	15
Greece	14
Macedonia	13
Argentina	12
Total	38

E074) CONFIDENCE: THE POLICE

I am going to name a number of organizations. For each one, could you tell me how much confidence you have in them: is it a great deal of confidence, quite a lot of confidence, not very much confidence or none at all? The police.

A great deal / Quite a lot (%)

(WVS: V152; EVS: V205)

Country	Wave		Gender		Age			Education			Income			Values		
	1990	2000	Male	Female	16-29	30-49	50+	Lower	Middle	Upper	Lower	Middle	Upper	Mat	Mixed	Postm.
Albania	na	65	63	67	62	64	70	69	62	62	70	66	58	69	62	67
Algeria	na	67	64	69	64	65	75	73	65	64	69	68	59	74	65	53
Argentina	26	24	29	20	19	25	29	28	20	17	31	25	17	32	25	17
Armenia	na	32	32	32	32	32	32	30	33	28	34	28	31	34	30	41
Australia	na	76	73	78	72	78	77	75	77	76	76	78	76	76	78	73
Austria	68	76	74	77	72	73	80	79	74	66	74	78	75	81	79	67
Azerbaijan	na	41	44	38	44	40	38	44	41	42	37	42	43	41	40	59
Bangladesh	na	53	53	54	49	57	49	56	52	47	50	57	52	49	57	49
Belarus	22	40	35	44	30	34	56	53	36	34	45	38	37	44	39	19
Belgium	51	56	52	59	56	54	57	54	58	54	55	58	57	56	58	48
Bosnia and Herz.	na	64	65	63	62	60	70	73	63	57	69	63	63	69	60	76
Brazil	38	45	48	43	43	42	56	49	43	42	46	51	41	45	47	40
Bulgaria	46	47	44	50	42	44	51	52	45	44	49	47	47	47	47	31
Canada	84	79	75	82	70	81	81	78	80	77	76	78	82	78	82	72
Chile	59	55	55	55	56	51	61	56	54	58	57	53	57	55	57	51
China	68	73	68	77	64	73	80	80	69	56	75	77	64	72	70	66
Colombia	na	50	51	48	48	51	50	47	50	53	48	49	53	48	49	44
Croatia	na	53	48	58	45	52	60	62	52	33	65	54	46	66	53	45
Czech Republic	32	33	32	34	36	28	36	33	34	32	34	34	34	34	33	28
Denmark	89	91	89	92	92	88	93	90	95	90	88	91	93	91	93	81
Dominican Rep.	na	13	15	11	11	16	30	17	7	14	15	12	11	21	12	6
Egypt	na	87	88	87	87	88	88	88	87	85	89	85	87	89	86	90
El Salvador	na	49	50	48	50	44	56	55	43	43	60	45	47	na	na	na
Estonia	19	34	32	36	34	28	40	38	33	32	37	37	32	34	34	42
Finland	76	90	87	93	89	90	91	88	95	91	87	91	93	91	90	88
France	67	66	64	69	63	60	74	68	64	64	63	67	65	71	67	59
Georgia	na	38	38	38	34	38	42	41	39	32	38	39	37	40	37	37
Germany	39	74	72	75	60	73	80	74	73	70	75	74	72	81	73	64
Great Britain	77	70	68	71	61	72	74	70	69	71	70	73	71	na	na	na
Greece	na	28	27	29	21	30	38	53	26	26	29	27	32	37	28	19
Hungary	51	45	44	47	45	40	50	47	39	51	45	45	49	47	44	34
Iceland	85	83	78	88	78	86	83	84	81	85	81	85	84	85	84	72
India	39	38	37	40	35	35	47	39	40	34	45	37	36	35	41	28
Indonesia	na	52	52	52	40	51	59	59	53	46	50	50	57	52	52	61
Iran	na	61	61	60	59	62	61	65	61	55	57	61	61	67	56	62
Ireland	86	84	82	85	77	83	89	81	85	86	82	86	84	90	82	79
Israel	na	na	na	na	na	na	na	na	na	na	na	na	na	na	na	na
Italy	67	67	66	69	62	65	72	72	64	62	70	68	65	73	67	64
Japan	59	50	52	49	40	49	57	54	49	52	53	49	49	61	50	34
Jordan	na	91	89	92	91	90	93	94	92	83	94	91	86	94	90	78
Korea, South	53	50	49	52	42	49	64	67	55	42	48	50	53	53	50	37
Latvia	20	40	37	42	42	33	45	48	37	39	42	35	41	40	41	28
Lithuania	29	26	24	29	23	18	37	38	22	24	41	26	20	24	26	34
Luxembourg	na	72	70	75	68	70	79	74	73	67	72	71	71	75	74	65
Macedonia	na	51	53	49	42	49	61	41	56	56	49	54	54	53	53	16
Malta	na	67	65	69	64	62	73	65	67	71	66	69	64	68	67	59
Mexico	32	30	29	30	28	30	31	35	23	25	31	29	29	32	28	28
Moldova	na	35	34	35	27	33	43	42	33	31	38	36	32	41	29	29
Montenegro	na	40	41	39	39	39	41	41	41	35	47	37	44	42	38	38
Morocco	na	53	48	58	44	55	71	57	34	42	55	49	49	57	48	51
Netherlands	73	64	67	62	62	65	64	62	68	62	61	68	65	60	65	63
New Zealand	na	79	78	80	72	76	84	80	80	78	79	80	77	81	81	74
Nigeria	44	35	36	34	34	36	31	40	32	31	36	35	35	32	36	39
Northern Ireland	80	63	56	69	50	62	71	62	64	64	57	62	71	70	67	44
Norway	88	86	82	89	84	85	87	81	86	90	na	na	na	86	86	81
Pakistan	na	29	28	30	31	26	34	30	28	27	32	27	29	26	32	33
Peru	na	16	18	15	16	16	18	17	17	15	16	16	17	18	17	14
Philippines	na	61	61	61	61	62	59	67	64	50	62	61	60	60	63	49
Poland	30	55	56	55	54	52	59	58	55	43	56	54	58	54	57	56
Portugal	44	66	62	69	61	66	68	67	62	69	71	64	62	69	62	70
Puerto Rico	na	56	57	56	47	56	62	79	58	52	63	53	57	62	55	60
Romania	45	45	43	48	44	39	52	58	39	36	57	41	38	49	44	25
Russian Fed.	35	29	24	33	26	25	35	44	28	24	32	30	25	30	28	24
Serbia	na	47	46	49	44	40	56	57	45	38	54	44	43	56	40	25
Singapore	na	na	na	na	na	na	na	na	na	na	na	na	na	na	na	na
Slovakia	na	45	44	45	41	45	46	48	43	41	45	45	47	47	43	37
Slovenia	52	50	47	53	46	47	57	57	47	48	55	54	47	50	52	42
South Africa	64	57	59	54	56	57	57	65	48	31	66	55	45	56	56	63
Spain	58	59	55	63	47	54	70	65	53	51	65	61	55	68	60	44
Sweden	75	76	73	78	73	80	74	73	73	82	73	76	82	72	76	77
Switzerland	na	69	66	72	67	70	68	69	69	66	66	70	70	81	71	57
Taiwan	na	59	56	62	49	58	70	71	54	53	67	57	54	63	56	46
Tanzania	na	67	61	75	66	64	78	74	62	58	71	68	65	66	69	67
Turkey	63	71	68	74	68	71	77	78	65	50	76	71	55	81	71	56
Uganda	na	55	56	55	56	59	40	53	56	58	65	61	55	48	60	53
Ukraine	na	33	30	34	26	26	42	44	31	30	33	31	33	33	33	15
United States	75	71	69	74	66	71	77	67	69	75	67	74	75	77	74	65
Uruguay	na	53	53	53	42	46	64	60	47	36	61	53	46	69	52	48
Venezuela	na	41	45	38	40	40	47	42	43	36	45	39	43	44	40	43
Vietnam	na	93	93	94	90	93	95	94	93	91	89	93	95	94	93	86
Zimbabwe	na	64	60	68	64	63	67	71	55	17	71	73	44	60	65	78
Total	55	56	55	57	51	55	62	61	53	52	57	55	54	55	57	54

RANKING	
Country	2000
Vietnam	93
Denmark	91
Jordan	91
Finland	90
Egypt	87
Norway	86
Ireland	84
Iceland	83
New Zealand	79
Canada	79
Australia	76
Austria	76
Sweden	76
Germany	74
China	73
Luxembourg	72
United States	71
Turkey	71
Great Britain	70
Switzerland	69
Italy	67
Tanzania	67
Malta	67
Algeria	67
France	66
Portugal	66
Albania	65
Netherlands	64
Zimbabwe	64
Bosnia and Herz.	64
Northern Ireland	63
Philippines	61
Iran	61
Taiwan	59
Spain	59
South Africa	57
Puerto Rico	56
Belgium	56
Uganda	55
Chile	55
Poland	55
Bangladesh	53
Uruguay	53
Croatia	53
Morocco	53
Indonesia	52
Macedonia	51
Japan	50
Korea, South	50
Slovenia	50
Colombia	50
El Salvador	49
Serbia	47
Bulgaria	47
Romania	45
Brazil	45
Hungary	45
Slovakia	45
Venezuela	41
Azerbaijan	41
Belarus	40
Latvia	40
Montenegro	40
Georgia	38
India	38
Nigeria	35
Moldova	35
Estonia	34
Czech Republic	33
Ukraine	33
Armenia	32
Mexico	30
Russian Fed.	29
Pakistan	29
Greece	28
Lithuania	26
Argentina	24
Peru	16
Dominican Rep.	13
Total	56

E075) CONFIDENCE: PARLIAMENT

I am going to name a number of organizations. For each one, could you tell me how much confidence you have in them: is it a great deal of confidence, quite a lot of confidence, not very much confidence or none at all? Parliament.

A great deal / Quite a lot (%)

(WVS: V155; EVS: V206)

Country	Wave		Gender		Age			Education			Income			Values		
	1990	2000	Male	Female	16-29	30-49	50+	Lower	Middle	Upper	Lower	Middle	Upper	Mat	Mixed	Postm.
Albania	na	**45**	47	44	36	45	54	47	42	47	51	45	40	48	42	49
Algeria	na	**33**	32	34	28	35	41	40	31	32	35	37	27	35	35	23
Argentina	17	**11**	14	9	8	14	12	11	12	14	10	12	12	13	12	10
Armenia	na	**30**	29	32	33	28	30	25	33	24	32	28	29	36	25	29
Australia	na	**31**	36	25	28	31	33	25	26	41	28	32	34	27	31	31
Austria	41	**41**	46	36	41	37	45	38	44	41	42	38	42	40	42	38
Azerbaijan	na	**74**	77	71	74	73	75	81	72	77	68	75	80	72	75	74
Bangladesh	na	**89**	87	91	89	87	94	91	88	84	89	87	91	91	88	84
Belarus	29	**38**	37	38	26	30	56	53	33	26	42	36	31	41	37	9
Belgium	43	**36**	39	33	36	38	34	22	35	47	29	32	44	23	37	45
Bosnia and Herz.	na	**20**	19	21	17	20	24	31	18	19	21	21	19	19	21	23
Brazil	24	**34**	35	32	30	35	38	35	33	34	34	35	32	33	33	37
Bulgaria	49	**27**	27	27	30	25	28	25	27	33	28	23	30	22	32	17
Canada	38	**41**	45	37	39	41	43	38	37	51	38	38	47	47	41	41
Chile	63	**35**	33	37	34	35	36	35	37	30	33	35	38	33	37	32
China	81	**95**	94	96	91	96	96	96	95	88	95	97	92	95	93	93
Colombia	na	**25**	25	25	25	24	26	25	24	24	26	23	25	25	29	25
Croatia	na	**23**	23	22	19	22	25	26	20	22	30	19	22	23	24	15
Czech Republic	44	**12**	11	13	15	10	12	11	14	13	14	11	14	14	12	12
Denmark	42	**49**	53	45	53	44	51	42	55	56	47	47	57	41	49	50
Dominican Rep.	na	**12**	15	11	13	12	20	10	15	11	13	11	12	18	12	6
Egypt	na	**68**	67	69	67	68	67	70	68	61	71	70	63	68	69	58
El Salvador	na	**31**	32	30	32	28	35	32	29	31	35	31	29	na	na	na
Estonia	69	**27**	27	27	24	23	32	31	24	29	25	27	30	23	30	22
Finland	34	**44**	40	47	42	39	48	38	47	64	47	39	45	41	44	44
France	48	**41**	42	39	38	41	42	37	41	50	35	38	47	40	40	47
Georgia	na	**41**	39	42	38	40	44	46	41	37	40	40	42	42	40	34
Germany	41	**36**	36	36	30	33	41	36	34	42	39	34	37	47	35	23
Great Britain	46	**36**	38	33	36	36	35	27	39	50	33	39	36	na	na	na
Greece	na	**24**	24	25	20	24	35	27	19	28	19	21	32	28	26	16
Hungary	40	**34**	33	35	31	35	35	34	31	40	30	34	36	34	35	20
Iceland	54	**72**	71	73	65	73	76	70	71	77	72	70	73	73	72	64
India	67	**55**	58	50	56	53	58	53	57	57	58	53	56	62	52	45
Indonesia	na	**43**	44	42	31	45	47	46	47	38	41	44	43	43	43	32
Iran	na	**70**	70	69	68	69	76	75	68	67	68	68	70	75	64	75
Ireland	50	**31**	32	30	25	31	37	30	27	42	31	30	30	37	30	27
Israel	na	**na**	na	na	na	na	na	na	na	na	na	na	na	na	na	na
Italy	32	**34**	36	32	28	34	38	33	34	36	35	36	36	41	32	36
Japan	29	**22**	24	20	14	15	31	34	20	21	24	23	20	32	21	12
Jordan	na	**65**	58	72	67	63	67	70	67	55	74	60	58	72	61	62
Korea, South	34	**11**	10	12	6	10	19	25	13	6	10	11	11	11	11	6
Latvia	73	**28**	25	30	32	20	31	33	25	30	28	24	30	28	28	23
Lithuania	66	**11**	10	11	11	7	14	15	9	13	16	7	9	13	9	10
Luxembourg	na	**63**	63	62	58	62	67	60	61	69	56	62	64	62	63	61
Macedonia	na	**7**	8	6	3	6	12	7	7	7	7	7	6	7	7	8
Malta	na	**52**	52	52	44	46	63	52	51	57	51	54	53	52	52	51
Mexico	35	**23**	26	20	20	23	28	27	16	28	22	23	25	25	22	25
Moldova	na	**35**	33	36	26	31	46	44	36	24	39	32	29	38	34	26
Montenegro	na	**33**	32	34	21	31	43	38	29	32	31	41	26	35	30	38
Morocco	na	**22**	18	28	19	22	33	25	10	21	28	16	22	26	19	21
Netherlands	52	**55**	58	53	64	56	50	42	60	63	52	55	61	46	55	60
New Zealand	na	**15**	17	13	12	15	15	11	10	21	13	11	20	18	15	15
Nigeria	54	**45**	49	40	44	48	40	48	42	45	47	43	47	44	45	52
Northern Ireland	46	**40**	34	46	30	37	46	40	37	48	35	34	47	41	41	37
Norway	59	**70**	73	66	69	73	65	59	71	77	na	na	na	58	70	77
Pakistan	na	**76**	77	74	74	76	80	76	75	77	77	76	77	76	77	82
Peru	na	**10**	10	9	9	10	9	10	9	11	11	8	9	11	10	6
Philippines	na	**62**	62	61	61	64	57	69	60	55	60	60	65	59	63	60
Poland	79	**33**	35	31	27	30	40	34	32	28	32	33	33	29	36	37
Portugal	34	**49**	45	54	44	48	54	51	44	53	50	48	40	59	42	50
Puerto Rico	na	**28**	28	28	24	25	32	39	31	24	33	28	23	35	28	25
Romania	21	**19**	19	20	20	16	22	26	15	17	25	16	17	19	18	23
Russian Fed.	47	**19**	17	21	18	17	24	25	19	18	24	19	17	19	20	26
Serbia	na	**23**	24	23	21	20	27	26	23	21	23	25	23	25	21	18
Singapore	na	**na**	na	na	na	na	na	na	na	na	na	na	na	na	na	na
Slovakia	na	**43**	39	47	41	42	45	42	42	51	40	39	49	40	44	49
Slovenia	36	**25**	25	25	17	24	32	34	23	17	34	23	24	31	26	18
South Africa	66	**60**	60	59	65	57	55	68	52	26	74	67	37	62	58	62
Spain	32	**48**	47	49	38	46	56	51	43	47	56	50	45	51	49	42
Sweden	47	**51**	54	49	52	48	54	49	47	60	49	53	54	59	49	57
Switzerland	na	**44**	41	47	49	42	43	44	43	48	41	42	49	56	45	34
Taiwan	na	**46**	41	51	43	45	53	57	45	38	52	45	42	47	45	49
Tanzania	na	**79**	77	81	78	77	86	85	73	75	84	75	77	80	80	75
Turkey	58	**43**	39	48	40	44	47	47	38	32	46	43	36	46	43	36
Uganda	na	**77**	85	69	79	78	60	69	78	88	86	80	85	74	78	76
Ukraine	na	**27**	25	29	23	24	32	36	26	25	28	24	28	24	28	42
United States	46	**38**	40	37	41	35	40	37	37	39	36	40	40	48	39	32
Uruguay	na	**42**	42	42	34	37	49	41	41	47	41	43	41	56	39	39
Venezuela	na	**34**	39	30	34	32	39	35	36	30	34	37	35	32	35	35
Vietnam	na	**97**	97	96	94	98	97	96	98	96	94	98	97	98	97	94
Zimbabwe	na	**50**	46	54	48	49	57	57	41	16	59	51	37	47	51	60
Total	46	**41**	41	40	39	40	42	44	38	39	41	40	40	43	40	36

RANKING	
Country	2000
Vietnam	97
China	95
Bangladesh	89
Tanzania	79
Uganda	77
Pakistan	76
Azerbaijan	74
Iceland	72
Iran	70
Norway	70
Egypt	68
Jordan	65
Luxembourg	63
Philippines	62
South Africa	60
Netherlands	55
India	55
Malta	52
Sweden	51
Zimbabwe	50
Portugal	49
Denmark	49
Spain	48
Taiwan	46
Albania	45
Nigeria	45
Switzerland	44
Finland	44
Turkey	43
Indonesia	43
Slovakia	43
Uruguay	42
Canada	41
Austria	41
France	41
Georgia	41
Northern Ireland	40
United States	38
Belarus	38
Belgium	36
Germany	36
Great Britain	36
Chile	35
Moldova	35
Venezuela	34
Italy	34
Hungary	34
Brazil	34
Algeria	33
Poland	33
Montenegro	33
Ireland	31
El Salvador	31
Australia	31
Armenia	30
Puerto Rico	28
Latvia	28
Bulgaria	27
Estonia	27
Ukraine	27
Slovenia	25
Colombia	25
Greece	24
Serbia	23
Mexico	23
Croatia	23
Morocco	22
Japan	22
Bosnia and Herz.	20
Russian Fed.	19
Romania	19
New Zealand	15
Dominican Rep.	12
Czech Republic	12
Argentina	11
Korea, South	11
Lithuania	11
Peru	10
Macedonia	7
Total	41

E076) CONFIDENCE: THE CIVIL SERVICES

I am going to name a number of organizations. For each one, could you tell me how much confidence you have in them: is it a great deal of confidence, quite a lot of confidence, not very much confidence or none at all? The Civil Service.

A great deal / Quite a lot (%) (WVS: V156; EVS: V207)

Country	Wave		Gender		Age			Education			Income			Values		
	1990	2000	Male	Female	16-29	30-49	50+	Lower	Middle	Upper	Lower	Middle	Upper	Mat	Mixed	Postm.
Albania	na	**40**	41	38	36	40	43	44	37	39	43	38	38	41	38	47
Algeria	na	**58**	55	62	55	62	57	61	59	54	56	57	55	69	51	59
Argentina	7	**7**	8	6	5	6	10	8	5	6	7	7	6	11	7	5
Armenia	na	**37**	35	38	36	39	34	28	39	33	36	33	41	39	35	33
Australia	na	**38**	38	38	44	35	36	38	35	42	36	37	43	34	39	38
Austria	42	**42**	45	40	39	41	45	43	41	46	46	42	45	41	44	38
Azerbaijan	na	**44**	45	42	45	42	45	47	43	44	43	44	44	41	47	56
Bangladesh	na	**96**	95	97	96	96	96	97	96	92	97	96	96	96	96	95
Belarus	20	**23**	22	24	15	18	35	37	18	17	26	22	20	25	22	2
Belgium	43	**45**	48	43	41	47	45	42	47	45	45	47	46	40	45	49
Bosnia and Herz.	na	**30**	31	29	29	29	33	34	30	27	27	33	31	33	29	32
Brazil	49	**59**	61	58	62	56	59	59	59	58	58	64	57	60	60	57
Bulgaria	30	**24**	20	28	20	19	31	33	19	22	30	18	22	25	23	16
Canada	50	**50**	51	49	51	50	50	54	46	54	49	48	53	55	51	48
Chile	49	**40**	39	42	38	39	44	41	40	41	39	43	41	35	43	41
China	59	**66**	65	67	57	68	72	70	64	67	67	70	61	64	68	56
Colombia	na	**32**	34	31	33	32	31	31	33	33	33	30	34	33	35	35
Croatia	na	**35**	34	36	37	30	40	44	32	23	46	30	36	40	37	26
Czech Republic	32	**22**	20	24	23	19	24	23	21	21	24	20	21	22	22	18
Denmark	51	**55**	53	57	63	50	56	50	60	63	55	55	57	57	56	55
Dominican Rep.	na	**10**	11	9	9	11	30	7	14	9	12	7	12	15	9	5
Egypt	na	**63**	66	61	64	63	64	66	64	55	66	66	58	60	66	63
El Salvador	na	**na**	na	na	na	na	na	na	na	na	na	na	na	na	na	na
Estonia	39	**40**	40	41	41	37	43	39	41	41	38	40	44	40	42	29
Finland	33	**41**	39	43	41	35	45	35	47	55	43	38	42	35	43	40
France	49	**46**	47	45	40	44	50	44	47	49	39	49	48	46	48	43
Georgia	na	**56**	55	58	50	58	60	59	56	55	54	58	59	60	55	45
Germany	18	**39**	39	39	35	35	45	42	35	37	42	35	37	44	38	34
Great Britain	44	**46**	48	44	52	42	47	45	46	53	46	46	42	na	na	na
Greece	na	**14**	11	17	11	16	20	17	15	14	13	13	18	16	14	11
Hungary	50	**50**	48	51	51	47	51	49	47	57	42	51	53	47	53	49
Iceland	46	**56**	52	60	52	53	63	56	54	59	58	55	55	57	56	52
India	74	**49**	49	48	47	48	52	46	52	48	49	48	49	50	49	45
Indonesia	na	**59**	60	59	44	61	65	65	64	52	56	63	67	61	59	52
Iran	na	**44**	43	46	43	44	48	49	44	40	38	49	47	51	41	40
Ireland	59	**59**	60	59	58	55	65	59	60	58	61	60	60	64	58	58
Israel	na	**na**	na	na	na	na	na	na	na	na	na	na	na	na	na	na
Italy	27	**33**	33	33	28	33	36	38	32	21	39	32	29	43	33	28
Japan	34	**32**	33	31	19	25	44	46	30	32	33	33	31	44	31	23
Jordan	na	**66**	60	72	68	61	71	73	69	50	78	61	56	74	62	52
Korea, South	61	**67**	64	69	67	70	59	77	67	65	65	67	69	64	69	72
Latvia	34	**49**	45	53	52	46	51	53	47	50	50	44	54	51	49	39
Lithuania	52	**21**	20	21	22	16	24	23	19	23	32	12	20	25	19	12
Luxembourg	na	**60**	62	57	53	57	67	60	59	60	59	57	63	63	60	54
Macedonia	na	**17**	17	17	13	18	19	14	18	19	18	16	18	18	18	10
Malta	na	**49**	46	51	42	46	56	54	48	42	52	52	41	49	50	38
Mexico	28	**22**	24	20	23	20	27	23	20	27	21	22	23	22	23	24
Moldova	na	**47**	46	49	42	46	54	50	50	41	48	48	43	51	45	35
Montenegro	na	**29**	29	29	29	28	29	22	31	36	19	27	36	26	33	28
Morocco	na	**41**	36	48	36	46	46	44	28	46	37	35	43	45	39	36
Netherlands	46	**37**	38	37	45	34	37	33	36	43	33	41	38	40	37	39
New Zealand	na	**28**	28	28	36	26	28	27	24	32	34	24	27	37	25	31
Nigeria	76	**71**	72	70	69	73	68	72	68	72	70	69	75	69	72	71
Northern Ireland	58	**52**	45	59	46	48	59	53	50	54	50	48	55	50	55	47
Norway	44	**51**	49	53	56	49	50	42	52	58	na	na	na	48	51	52
Pakistan	na	**50**	51	49	43	52	58	50	52	47	51	49	49	51	48	73
Peru	na	**9**	10	8	9	9	11	11	10	6	12	8	6	12	8	8
Philippines	na	**71**	70	72	72	73	65	73	70	70	72	69	73	70	71	74
Poland	79	**33**	34	31	41	28	33	35	31	25	33	33	33	30	34	39
Portugal	32	**54**	49	58	60	48	54	52	56	57	49	51	52	57	50	61
Puerto Rico	na	**27**	28	26	21	23	32	42	29	23	33	29	20	40	26	22
Romania	31	**27**	25	29	32	23	29	31	25	25	35	27	24	32	25	20
Russian Fed.	48	**38**	34	42	38	37	39	40	37	38	34	38	42	40	36	35
Serbia	na	**29**	30	28	27	25	34	34	25	29	32	31	25	32	26	22
Singapore	na	**na**	na	na	na	na	na	na	na	na	na	na	na	na	na	na
Slovakia	na	**39**	35	42	38	35	44	39	38	40	37	40	40	39	38	40
Slovenia	40	**25**	24	26	18	24	32	34	24	16	34	25	24	31	25	20
South Africa	60	**58**	58	58	59	58	53	61	56	38	59	73	49	62	54	68
Spain	34	**41**	38	45	32	37	50	46	35	39	51	40	43	47	42	31
Sweden	44	**49**	51	46	50	48	49	48	45	55	47	51	49	52	47	53
Switzerland	na	**46**	43	49	45	43	49	47	46	45	44	46	47	57	47	38
Taiwan	na	**60**	60	60	54	58	69	69	55	54	61	60	58	60	59	56
Tanzania	na	**71**	70	73	67	72	79	76	66	70	70	72	75	72	72	58
Turkey	50	**60**	57	64	58	61	65	63	56	54	62	63	52	62	61	56
Uganda	na	**69**	73	65	67	73	60	64	71	70	71	70	77	69	70	68
Ukraine	na	**39**	36	41	36	40	40	38	40	38	35	40	43	39	38	38
United States	59	**55**	55	55	60	52	55	52	56	56	53	56	56	61	54	57
Uruguay	na	**45**	46	44	35	39	54	46	42	50	47	45	42	46	44	46
Venezuela	na	**38**	41	34	40	33	42	39	40	30	36	43	36	40	36	42
Vietnam	na	**79**	82	77	79	79	79	79	81	73	77	84	75	83	80	75
Zimbabwe	na	**59**	56	62	58	59	63	66	50	40	69	58	46	58	58	75
Total	44	44	44	44	44	44	46	47	43	42	45	44	44	47	44	40

RANKING

Country	2000
Bangladesh	96
Vietnam	79
Tanzania	71
Philippines	71
Nigeria	71
Uganda	69
Korea, South	67
China	66
Jordan	66
Egypt	63
Turkey	60
Taiwan	60
Luxembourg	60
Ireland	59
Indonesia	59
Brazil	59
Zimbabwe	59
Algeria	58
South Africa	58
Georgia	56
Iceland	56
Denmark	55
United States	55
Portugal	54
Northern Ireland	52
Norway	51
Canada	50
Pakistan	50
Hungary	50
Latvia	49
Sweden	49
Malta	49
India	49
Moldova	47
France	46
Great Britain	46
Switzerland	46
Belgium	45
Uruguay	45
Iran	44
Azerbaijan	44
Austria	42
Morocco	41
Spain	41
Finland	41
Chile	40
Estonia	40
Albania	40
Ukraine	39
Germany	39
Slovakia	39
Australia	38
Russian Fed.	38
Venezuela	38
Netherlands	37
Armenia	37
Croatia	35
Italy	33
Poland	33
Colombia	32
Japan	32
Bosnia and Herz.	30
Serbia	29
Montenegro	29
New Zealand	28
Romania	27
Puerto Rico	27
Slovenia	25
Bulgaria	24
Belarus	23
Mexico	22
Czech Republic	22
Lithuania	21
Macedonia	17
Greece	14
Dominican Rep.	10
Peru	9
Argentina	7
Total	44

E077_1) CONFIDENCE: SOCIAL SECURITY SYSTEM

Please look at this card and tell me, for each item listed, how much confidence you have in them, is it a great deal, quite a lot, not very much or none at all? The social security.

(EVS: V208)

A great deal / Quite a lot (%)

Country	Wave		Gender		Age			Education			Income			Values		
	1990	2000	Male	Female	16-29	30-49	50+	Lower	Middle	Upper	Lower	Middle	Upper	Mat	Mixed	Postm.
Albania	na	**na**	na	na	na	na	na	na	na	na	na	na	na	na	na	na
Algeria	na	**na**	na	na	na	na	na	na	na	na	na	na	na	na	na	na
Argentina	20	**na**	na	na	na	na	na	na	na	na	na	na	na	na	na	na
Armenia	na	**na**	na	na	na	na	na	na	na	na	na	na	na	na	na	na
Australia	na	**na**	na	na	na	na	na	na	na	na	na	na	na	na	na	na
Austria	68	**67**	66	67	65	60	74	72	63	57	70	70	64	74	66	67
Azerbaijan	na	**na**	na	na	na	na	na	na	na	na	na	na	na	na	na	na
Bangladesh	na	**na**	na	na	na	na	na	na	na	na	na	na	na	na	na	na
Belarus	32	**56**	55	57	46	52	69	66	54	45	58	55	54	60	54	31
Belgium	67	**69**	70	68	66	64	75	70	69	68	68	71	70	66	69	69
Bosnia and Herz.	na	**na**	na	na	na	na	na	na	na	na	na	na	na	na	na	na
Brazil	32	**na**	na	na	na	na	na	na	na	na	na	na	na	na	na	na
Bulgaria	36	**26**	21	30	27	25	25	28	22	29	24	27	28	23	28	21
Canada	61	**na**	na	na	na	na	na	na	na	na	na	na	na	na	na	na
Chile	54	**na**	na	na	na	na	na	na	na	na	na	na	na	na	na	na
China	81	**na**	na	na	na	na	na	na	na	na	na	na	na	na	na	na
Colombia	na	**na**	na	na	na	na	na	na	na	na	na	na	na	na	na	na
Croatia	na	**32**	31	33	32	30	34	40	29	23	42	29	28	45	33	16
Czech Republic	42	**34**	31	35	33	30	37	37	30	31	35	34	34	36	32	35
Denmark	69	**67**	67	67	76	63	67	61	73	74	68	66	69	66	70	59
Dominican Rep.	na	**na**	na	na	na	na	na	na	na	na	na	na	na	na	na	na
Egypt	na	**na**	na	na	na	na	na	na	na	na	na	na	na	na	na	na
El Salvador	na	**na**	na	na	na	na	na	na	na	na	na	na	na	na	na	na
Estonia	46	**51**	45	56	38	44	64	54	50	46	56	52	49	50	53	39
Finland	75	**71**	69	72	72	68	72	72	69	71	70	70	73	74	71	61
France	70	**67**	69	65	61	64	72	65	66	72	66	67	69	67	66	72
Georgia	na	**na**	na	na	na	na	na	na	na	na	na	na	na	na	na	na
Germany	58	**44**	42	46	41	39	51	51	39	38	46	41	38	48	47	32
Great Britain	34	**36**	37	36	34	36	39	37	38	35	43	38	28	na	na	na
Greece	na	**19**	16	21	14	18	32	24	19	17	17	18	22	21	19	15
Hungary	50	**42**	39	45	45	38	44	44	39	42	35	45	43	40	46	51
Iceland	69	**50**	49	51	44	41	66	55	43	49	55	50	43	48	49	53
India	67	**na**	na	na	na	na	na	na	na	na	na	na	na	na	na	na
Indonesia	na	**na**	na	na	na	na	na	na	na	na	na	na	na	na	na	na
Iran	na	**na**	na	na	na	na	na	na	na	na	na	na	na	na	na	na
Ireland	59	**56**	53	58	48	51	67	62	53	51	62	56	51	52	58	50
Israel	na	**na**	na	na	na	na	na	na	na	na	na	na	na	na	na	na
Italy	38	**34**	35	33	30	29	41	40	32	23	42	31	30	46	34	27
Japan	44	**na**	na	na	na	na	na	na	na	na	na	na	na	na	na	na
Jordan	na	**na**	na	na	na	na	na	na	na	na	na	na	na	na	na	na
Korea, South	98	**na**	na	na	na	na	na	na	na	na	na	na	na	na	na	na
Latvia	37	**57**	54	60	60	52	61	65	57	49	62	49	58	58	59	43
Lithuania	53	**32**	28	36	28	23	45	50	27	22	47	33	22	39	30	23
Luxembourg	na	**79**	77	80	70	81	82	79	79	79	74	83	84	79	78	83
Macedonia	na	**na**	na	na	na	na	na	na	na	na	na	na	na	na	na	na
Malta	na	**76**	74	78	67	75	84	81	75	71	81	83	70	79	76	66
Mexico	48	**na**	na	na	na	na	na	na	na	na	na	na	na	na	na	na
Moldova	na	**na**	na	na	na	na	na	na	na	na	na	na	na	na	na	na
Montenegro	na	**na**	na	na	na	na	na	na	na	na	na	na	na	na	na	na
Morocco	na	**na**	na	na	na	na	na	na	na	na	na	na	na	na	na	na
Netherlands	68	**65**	68	62	66	63	66	59	65	71	68	63	63	58	65	69
New Zealand	na	**na**	na	na	na	na	na	na	na	na	na	na	na	na	na	na
Nigeria	65	**na**	na	na	na	na	na	na	na	na	na	na	na	na	na	na
Northern Ireland	48	**54**	50	58	49	47	62	56	52	50	50	49	54	56	55	46
Norway	48	**na**	na	na	na	na	na	na	na	na	na	na	na	na	na	na
Pakistan	na	**na**	na	na	na	na	na	na	na	na	na	na	na	na	na	na
Peru	na	**na**	na	na	na	na	na	na	na	na	na	na	na	na	na	na
Philippines	na	**na**	na	na	na	na	na	na	na	na	na	na	na	na	na	na
Poland	43	**39**	40	38	43	35	41	43	37	26	39	39	39	39	38	48
Portugal	47	**51**	48	53	54	46	53	53	49	40	48	55	48	50	48	60
Puerto Rico	na	**na**	na	na	na	na	na	na	na	na	na	na	na	na	na	na
Romania	36	**31**	31	30	35	25	33	37	28	24	39	33	24	36	27	21
Russian Fed.	67	**45**	41	49	40	41	53	55	46	40	45	46	45	46	45	39
Serbia	na	**na**	na	na	na	na	na	na	na	na	na	na	na	na	na	na
Singapore	na	**na**	na	na	na	na	na	na	na	na	na	na	na	na	na	na
Slovakia	na	**37**	33	40	39	32	41	40	34	42	40	36	35	35	39	37
Slovenia	40	**47**	44	49	45	44	51	56	43	46	53	46	47	50	48	43
South Africa	60	**na**	na	na	na	na	na	na	na	na	na	na	na	na	na	na
Spain	50	**63**	60	65	58	56	71	68	58	61	69	65	57	68	64	54
Sweden	46	**51**	50	51	51	48	54	54	46	56	49	53	50	54	51	52
Switzerland	na	**na**	na	na	na	na	na	na	na	na	na	na	na	na	na	na
Taiwan	na	**na**	na	na	na	na	na	na	na	na	na	na	na	na	na	na
Tanzania	na	**na**	na	na	na	na	na	na	na	na	na	na	na	na	na	na
Turkey	75	**66**	61	70	62	67	72	69	62	55	66	69	58	72	66	57
Uganda	na	**na**	na	na	na	na	na	na	na	na	na	na	na	na	na	na
Ukraine	na	**44**	38	49	40	42	48	51	43	43	44	42	49	43	46	42
United States	53	**na**	na	na	na	na	na	na	na	na	na	na	na	na	na	na
Uruguay	na	**na**	na	na	na	na	na	na	na	na	na	na	na	na	na	na
Venezuela	na	**na**	na	na	na	na	na	na	na	na	na	na	na	na	na	na
Vietnam	na	**na**	na	na	na	na	na	na	na	na	na	na	na	na	na	na
Zimbabwe	na	**na**	na	na	na	na	na	na	na	na	na	na	na	na	na	na
Total	54	**50**	48	51	46	46	56	54	47	48	52	49	47	50	51	49

RANKING	
Country	2000
Luxembourg	79
Malta	76
Finland	71
Belgium	69
Denmark	67
France	67
Austria	67
Turkey	66
Netherlands	65
Spain	63
Latvia	57
Belarus	56
Ireland	56
Northern Ireland	54
Sweden	51
Estonia	51
Portugal	51
Iceland	50
Slovenia	47
Russian Fed.	45
Germany	44
Ukraine	44
Hungary	42
Poland	39
Slovakia	37
Great Britain	36
Italy	34
Czech Republic	34
Lithuania	32
Croatia	32
Romania	31
Bulgaria	26
Greece	19
Total	50

E078) CONFIDENCE: TELEVISION

I am going to name a number of organizations. For each one, could you tell me how much confidence you have in them: is it a great deal of confidence, quite a lot of confidence, not very much confidence or none at all? Television

A great deal / Quite a lot (%)

(WVS: V150)

Country	Wave		Gender		Age			Education			Income			Values		
	1990	2000	Male	Female	16-29	30-49	50+	Lower	Middle	Upper	Lower	Middle	Upper	Mat	Mixed	Postm.
Albania	na	**54**	53	55	52	51	60	56	53	52	52	60	51	52	54	61
Algeria	na	**45**	42	49	47	41	51	50	48	39	49	41	45	55	40	37
Argentina	na	**33**	33	32	32	34	32	35	32	22	41	32	25	40	32	30
Armenia	na	**45**	43	47	47	42	48	50	46	42	46	45	43	48	44	33
Australia	na	**26**	25	27	31	22	25	34	26	18	32	22	21	26	29	21
Austria	na	**na**	na	na	na	na	na	na	na	na	na	na	na	na	na	na
Azerbaijan	na	**42**	46	38	45	40	39	35	42	42	44	42	40	41	43	48
Bangladesh	na	**84**	80	89	83	84	83	88	82	75	88	83	81	84	84	78
Belarus	na	**na**	na	na	na	na	na	na	na	na	na	na	na	na	na	na
Belgium	66	**na**	na	na	na	na	na	na	na	na	na	na	na	na	na	na
Bosnia and Herz.	na	**35**	33	37	35	31	41	43	36	26	34	35	37	37	33	47
Brazil	38	**57**	60	55	58	54	61	57	58	57	54	62	58	52	59	61
Bulgaria	50	**na**	na	na	na	na	na	na	na	na	na	na	na	na	na	na
Canada	50	**38**	37	39	33	36	43	44	39	30	46	37	32	43	40	32
Chile	32	**53**	48	57	50	51	58	56	51	50	54	51	55	53	54	47
China	30	**75**	74	75	69	74	80	81	70	67	77	76	67	72	75	65
Colombia	na	**50**	50	50	52	49	48	51	51	47	51	48	51	53	52	53
Croatia	na	**na**	na	na	na	na	na	na	na	na	na	na	na	na	na	na
Czech Republic	66	**na**	na	na	na	na	na	na	na	na	na	na	na	na	na	na
Denmark	39	**na**	na	na	na	na	na	na	na	na	na	na	na	na	na	na
Dominican Rep.	na	**38**	44	34	44	29	30	20	39	40	34	43	42	45	35	34
Egypt	na	**68**	61	75	67	69	68	72	66	62	71	70	65	70	67	61
El Salvador	na	**49**	48	50	48	48	50	52	42	51	56	48	46	na	na	na
Estonia	na	**na**	na	na	na	na	na	na	na	na	na	na	na	na	na	na
Finland	47	**na**	na	na	na	na	na	na	na	na	na	na	na	na	na	na
France	73	**na**	na	na	na	na	na	na	na	na	na	na	na	na	na	na
Georgia	na	**61**	62	60	64	60	59	62	61	60	58	63	63	63	60	55
Germany	64	**na**	na	na	na	na	na	na	na	na	na	na	na	na	na	na
Great Britain	47	**na**	na	na	na	na	na	na	na	na	na	na	na	na	na	na
Greece	na	**na**	na	na	na	na	na	na	na	na	na	na	na	na	na	na
Hungary	63	**na**	na	na	na	na	na	na	na	na	na	na	na	na	na	na
Iceland	36	**na**	na	na	na	na	na	na	na	na	na	na	na	na	na	na
India	33	**72**	72	71	78	69	71	68	75	75	66	72	75	75	73	63
Indonesia	na	**61**	59	64	54	64	62	63	61	61	60	61	62	59	63	57
Iran	na	**50**	47	52	48	47	57	61	49	38	48	49	51	60	43	37
Ireland	71	**na**	na	na	na	na	na	na	na	na	na	na	na	na	na	na
Israel	na	**na**	na	na	na	na	na	na	na	na	na	na	na	na	na	na
Italy	74	**na**	na	na	na	na	na	na	na	na	na	na	na	na	na	na
Japan	27	**68**	62	73	71	65	69	70	71	59	68	70	65	72	70	48
Jordan	na	**59**	52	65	58	59	56	68	56	44	69	53	48	64	55	53
Korea, South	na	**63**	61	66	58	65	67	78	70	53	62	63	66	64	64	54
Latvia	na	**na**	na	na	na	na	na	na	na	na	na	na	na	na	na	na
Lithuania	na	**na**	na	na	na	na	na	na	na	na	na	na	na	na	na	na
Luxembourg	na	**na**	na	na	na	na	na	na	na	na	na	na	na	na	na	na
Macedonia	na	**22**	21	23	20	22	24	28	19	21	25	22	19	18	24	23
Malta	na	**na**	na	na	na	na	na	na	na	na	na	na	na	na	na	na
Mexico	27	**47**	47	47	49	45	48	49	44	48	44	50	49	48	48	42
Moldova	na	**49**	47	51	47	46	55	57	51	39	49	51	49	48	51	47
Montenegro	na	**37**	40	35	42	34	37	36	38	39	37	34	41	36	37	41
Morocco	na	**30**	25	35	27	30	38	33	16	25	34	21	33	31	29	24
Netherlands	58	**na**	na	na	na	na	na	na	na	na	na	na	na	na	na	na
New Zealand	na	**36**	37	36	43	36	35	41	35	33	37	33	38	52	38	26
Nigeria	69	**72**	74	71	74	72	60	70	73	75	71	72	76	73	73	67
Northern Ireland	49	**na**	na	na	na	na	na	na	na	na	na	na	na	na	na	na
Norway	40	**49**	46	52	50	52	44	52	50	45	na	na	na	54	49	46
Pakistan	na	**57**	55	59	55	58	58	58	59	49	60	56	57	56	58	83
Peru	na	**25**	27	24	23	28	25	28	28	19	30	22	21	31	25	17
Philippines	na	**71**	73	70	74	70	70	72	71	70	66	71	76	70	73	71
Poland	na	**na**	na	na	na	na	na	na	na	na	na	na	na	na	na	na
Portugal	57	**na**	na	na	na	na	na	na	na	na	na	na	na	na	na	na
Puerto Rico	na	**26**	27	26	30	26	26	33	29	24	33	24	24	29	29	17
Romania	na	**na**	na	na	na	na	na	na	na	na	na	na	na	na	na	na
Russian Fed.	56	**na**	na	na	na	na	na	na	na	na	na	na	na	na	na	na
Serbia	na	**29**	28	30	33	24	32	37	26	24	30	26	29	29	28	33
Singapore	na	**na**	na	na	na	na	na	na	na	na	na	na	na	na	na	na
Slovakia	na	**na**	na	na	na	na	na	na	na	na	na	na	na	na	na	na
Slovenia	46	**na**	na	na	na	na	na	na	na	na	na	na	na	na	na	na
South Africa	na	**77**	79	74	82	75	68	80	74	61	79	87	64	77	76	84
Spain	48	**39**	38	39	36	38	40	43	37	25	44	40	34	40	40	31
Sweden	58	**na**	na	na	na	na	na	na	na	na	na	na	na	na	na	na
Switzerland	na	**31**	30	32	35	29	31	35	31	23	28	37	30	45	32	22
Taiwan	na	**51**	49	52	46	51	54	56	55	44	51	50	50	54	48	38
Tanzania	na	**80**	77	83	83	77	80	83	76	75	85	76	75	83	78	88
Turkey	37	**37**	34	41	37	37	39	39	37	31	38	38	36	36	38	38
Uganda	na	**67**	69	64	72	61	58	55	71	60	66	66	68	63	68	68
Ukraine	na	**na**	na	na	na	na	na	na	na	na	na	na	na	na	na	na
United States	45	**25**	25	25	25	25	25	32	26	21	28	25	20	40	25	18
Uruguay	na	**57**	57	57	51	52	63	64	48	47	65	58	48	73	56	47
Venezuela	na	**64**	63	65	66	60	67	63	65	62	62	65	64	71	62	61
Vietnam	na	**93**	94	92	89	94	94	93	93	90	91	92	94	92	94	91
Zimbabwe	na	**59**	54	63	64	55	50	65	51	53	67	59	49	54	60	76
Total	49	**51**	51	52	53	51	50	56	51	43	53	51	51	55	51	40

RANKING	
Country	**2000**
Vietnam	93
Bangladesh	84
Tanzania	80
South Africa	77
China	75
Nigeria	72
India	72
Philippines	71
Egypt	68
Japan	68
Uganda	67
Venezuela	64
Korea, South	63
Indonesia	61
Georgia	61
Zimbabwe	59
Jordan	59
Brazil	57
Pakistan	57
Uruguay	57
Albania	54
Chile	53
Taiwan	51
Colombia	50
Iran	50
Moldova	49
Norway	49
El Salvador	49
Mexico	47
Algeria	45
Armenia	45
Azerbaijan	42
Spain	39
Canada	38
Dominican Rep.	38
Turkey	37
Montenegro	37
New Zealand	36
Bosnia and Herz.	35
Argentina	33
Switzerland	31
Morocco	30
Serbia	29
Puerto Rico	26
Australia	26
Peru	25
United States	25
Macedonia	22
Total	51

E079) CONFIDENCE: THE GOVERNMENT

I am going to name a number of organizations. For each one, could you tell me how much confidence you have in them: is it a great deal of confidence, quite a lot of confidence, not very much confidence or none at all? The government.

A great deal / Quite a lot (%) (WVS: V153)

Country	Wave		Gender		Age			Education			Income			Values		
	1990	2000	Male	Female	16-29	30-49	50+	Lower	Middle	Upper	Lower	Middle	Upper	Mat	Mixed	Postm.
Albania	na	**58**	57	59	51	59	64	64	53	56	66	58	50	65	53	55
Algeria	na	**54**	53	56	50	53	64	64	55	45	59	56	47	64	52	28
Argentina	7	**19**	23	17	15	20	23	21	17	20	23	19	17	21	22	13
Armenia	na	**42**	42	42	46	40	41	38	45	36	44	42	39	45	39	57
Australia	na	**26**	30	22	26	30	23	22	23	34	21	30	30	23	27	27
Austria	42	**na**	na	na	na	na	na	na	na	na	na	na	na	na	na	na
Azerbaijan	na	**92**	94	91	93	92	91	93	94	90	93	93	89	92	92	92
Bangladesh	na	**87**	85	91	87	87	87	91	86	82	89	87	85	91	85	84
Belarus	20	**na**	na	na	na	na	na	na	na	na	na	na	na	na	na	na
Belgium	43	**na**	na	na	na	na	na	na	na	na	na	na	na	na	na	na
Bosnia and Herz.	na	**30**	29	30	25	28	36	39	28	26	30	32	26	34	28	37
Brazil	49	**49**	51	47	41	48	66	53	45	46	50	50	46	48	50	44
Bulgaria	30	**na**	na	na	na	na	na	na	na	na	na	na	na	na	na	na
Canada	50	**42**	43	41	39	41	45	40	39	50	40	39	45	51	43	40
Chile	49	**58**	56	59	56	55	64	60	55	61	58	59	57	55	58	63
China	59	**97**	97	97	93	97	98	98	96	93	97	97	97	98	95	100
Colombia	na	**37**	37	36	37	36	36	36	37	35	38	33	36	35	38	34
Croatia	na	**na**	na	na	na	na	na	na	na	na	na	na	na	na	na	na
Czech Republic	32	**na**	na	na	na	na	na	na	na	na	na	na	na	na	na	na
Denmark	51	**na**	na	na	na	na	na	na	na	na	na	na	na	na	na	na
Dominican Rep.	na	**13**	18	9	11	14	27	16	13	12	19	8	11	22	12	5
Egypt	na	**61**	58	64	61	62	60	65	61	50	65	63	55	61	61	51
El Salvador	na	**41**	40	41	39	37	49	46	36	34	49	38	32	na	na	na
Estonia	39	**na**	na	na	na	na	na	na	na	na	na	na	na	na	na	na
Finland	33	**na**	na	na	na	na	na	na	na	na	na	na	na	na	na	na
France	49	**na**	na	na	na	na	na	na	na	na	na	na	na	na	na	na
Georgia	na	**51**	52	51	48	51	55	58	51	46	52	51	51	52	50	50
Germany	18	**na**	na	na	na	na	na	na	na	na	na	na	na	na	na	na
Great Britain	44	**na**	na	na	na	na	na	na	na	na	na	na	na	na	na	na
Greece	na	**na**	na	na	na	na	na	na	na	na	na	na	na	na	na	na
Hungary	50	**na**	na	na	na	na	na	na	na	na	na	na	na	na	na	na
Iceland	46	**na**	na	na	na	na	na	na	na	na	na	na	na	na	na	na
India	74	**56**	58	53	56	55	58	56	57	55	59	57	54	61	54	39
Indonesia	na	**52**	52	53	36	54	58	61	55	44	55	51	44	52	51	54
Iran	na	**69**	68	69	67	69	73	73	67	66	64	69	70	74	64	63
Ireland	59	**na**	na	na	na	na	na	na	na	na	na	na	na	na	na	na
Israel	na	**na**	na	na	na	na	na	na	na	na	na	na	na	na	na	na
Italy	27	**na**	na	na	na	na	na	na	na	na	na	na	na	na	na	na
Japan	34	**27**	30	25	14	22	38	40	25	26	31	26	26	36	27	16
Jordan	na	**83**	80	87	83	83	85	87	86	74	91	79	78	90	80	69
Korea, South	61	**30**	28	32	21	29	45	44	34	23	27	31	33	33	29	25
Latvia	34	**na**	na	na	na	na	na	na	na	na	na	na	na	na	na	na
Lithuania	52	**na**	na	na	na	na	na	na	na	na	na	na	na	na	na	na
Luxembourg	na	**na**	na	na	na	na	na	na	na	na	na	na	na	na	na	na
Macedonia	na	**11**	12	10	7	9	18	12	11	8	13	10	10	10	12	7
Malta	na	**na**	na	na	na	na	na	na	na	na	na	na	na	na	na	na
Mexico	28	**37**	39	35	35	36	43	42	29	40	43	36	37	39	36	36
Moldova	na	**38**	37	38	27	34	50	47	39	26	43	32	33	42	35	25
Montenegro	na	**34**	32	36	21	32	45	41	29	32	33	41	27	37	31	40
Morocco	na	**59**	53	64	52	60	75	64	37	45	63	52	57	67	52	47
Netherlands	46	**na**	na	na	na	na	na	na	na	na	na	na	na	na	na	na
New Zealand	na	**16**	17	15	14	17	15	14	11	20	13	13	20	18	15	13
Nigeria	76	**48**	49	47	48	50	43	53	46	43	50	46	50	49	48	47
Northern Ireland	58	**na**	na	na	na	na	na	na	na	na	na	na	na	na	na	na
Norway	44	**66**	68	64	65	72	59	55	69	74	na	na	na	59	66	78
Pakistan	na	**39**	37	42	43	38	36	39	39	38	39	42	33	37	42	36
Peru	na	**19**	21	18	17	20	23	20	19	20	19	19	22	21	18	21
Philippines	na	**51**	51	51	54	52	45	51	53	48	54	46	55	48	52	55
Poland	79	**na**	na	na	na	na	na	na	na	na	na	na	na	na	na	na
Portugal	32	**na**	na	na	na	na	na	na	na	na	na	na	na	na	na	na
Puerto Rico	na	**44**	46	43	33	39	54	67	45	41	55	45	36	51	45	39
Romania	31	**na**	na	na	na	na	na	na	na	na	na	na	na	na	na	na
Russian Fed.	48	**na**	na	na	na	na	na	na	na	na	na	na	na	na	na	na
Serbia	na	**31**	32	31	31	26	36	36	28	32	31	32	30	33	30	23
Singapore	na	**na**	na	na	na	na	na	na	na	na	na	na	na	na	na	na
Slovakia	na	**na**	na	na	na	na	na	na	na	na	na	na	na	na	na	na
Slovenia	40	**na**	na	na	na	na	na	na	na	na	na	na	na	na	na	na
South Africa	60	**61**	61	61	60	61	62	68	53	43	72	68	39	58	64	53
Spain	34	**44**	43	45	31	43	54	47	41	38	50	47	38	52	44	29
Sweden	44	**na**	na	na	na	na	na	na	na	na	na	na	na	na	na	na
Switzerland	na	**52**	50	55	53	49	55	51	51	65	49	50	58	56	55	43
Taiwan	na	**70**	68	72	63	69	77	76	64	67	73	66	69	72	70	51
Tanzania	na	**83**	81	85	80	82	92	87	78	78	85	83	81	84	85	78
Turkey	50	**46**	40	53	44	47	51	52	39	36	48	46	43	50	47	33
Uganda	na	**78**	84	72	78	80	67	76	77	88	88	84	83	76	78	81
Ukraine	na	**na**	na	na	na	na	na	na	na	na	na	na	na	na	na	na
United States	59	**38**	37	39	43	33	41	36	40	38	36	40	38	50	39	30
Uruguay	na	**42**	44	40	28	34	53	45	36	38	46	42	37	52	42	32
Venezuela	na	**56**	60	52	50	57	67	65	55	49	58	58	57	59	55	54
Vietnam	na	**98**	98	98	97	98	98	98	98	97	97	98	98	99	98	94
Zimbabwe	na	**51**	46	55	51	49	52	58	42	na	60	53	36	50	49	65
Total	44	**50**	50	49	48	50	52	56	48	43	51	49	47	55	49	40

RANKING	
Country	2000
Vietnam	98
China	97
Azerbaijan	92
Bangladesh	87
Jordan	83
Tanzania	83
Uganda	78
Taiwan	70
Iran	69
Norway	66
South Africa	61
Egypt	61
Morocco	59
Albania	58
Chile	58
India	56
Venezuela	56
Algeria	54
Switzerland	52
Indonesia	52
Georgia	51
Philippines	51
Zimbabwe	51
Brazil	49
Nigeria	48
Turkey	46
Spain	44
Puerto Rico	44
Armenia	42
Canada	42
Uruguay	42
El Salvador	41
Pakistan	39
United States	38
Moldova	38
Mexico	37
Colombia	37
Montenegro	34
Serbia	31
Korea, South	30
Bosnia and Herz.	30
Japan	27
Australia	26
Argentina	19
Peru	19
New Zealand	16
Dominican Rep.	13
Macedonia	11
Total	50

E080) CONFIDENCE: THE POLITICAL PARTIES

I am going to name a number of organizations. For each one, could you tell me how much confidence you have in them: is it a great deal of confidence, quite a lot of confidence, not very much confidence or none at all? Political parties

A great deal / Quite a lot (%)

(WVS: V154)

Country	Wave		Gender		Age			Education			Income			Values		
	1990	2000	Male	Female	16-29	30-49	50+	Lower	Middle	Upper	Lower	Middle	Upper	Mat	Mixed	Postm.
Albania	na	**29**	36	23	24	29	34	30	30	27	28	30	30	32	28	26
Algeria	na	**19**	19	19	16	21	23	20	17	21	22	18	16	19	19	19
Argentina	na	**7**	7	7	5	8	9	7	6	11	7	7	8	8	7	7
Armenia	na	**16**	16	16	14	17	16	13	17	13	15	13	19	16	16	11
Australia	na	**16**	19	13	17	14	17	16	14	18	16	15	18	18	16	15
Austria	na	**na**	na	na	na	na	na	na	na	na	na	na	na	na	na	na
Azerbaijan	na	**54**	56	52	57	52	51	53	50	61	45	58	54	51	56	75
Bangladesh	na	**79**	78	81	78	80	80	82	80	72	83	75	80	82	77	75
Belarus	23	**na**	na	na	na	na	na	na	na	na	na	na	na	na	na	na
Belgium	na	**na**	na	na	na	na	na	na	na	na	na	na	na	na	na	na
Bosnia and Herz.	na	**15**	16	14	12	14	18	20	14	12	10	16	16	15	15	19
Brazil	na	**33**	35	30	33	29	38	34	30	34	35	35	28	28	34	35
Bulgaria	29	**na**	na	na	na	na	na	na	na	na	na	na	na	na	na	na
Canada	38	**23**	25	21	23	22	25	22	23	24	23	21	26	30	23	22
Chile	50	**28**	28	28	25	27	32	26	29	28	23	27	35	29	29	23
China	80	**93**	93	93	84	95	95	95	93	79	93	92	93	94	91	84
Colombia	na	**17**	18	17	17	17	17	19	16	15	19	15	18	20	21	19
Croatia	na	**na**	na	na	na	na	na	na	na	na	na	na	na	na	na	na
Czech Republic	44	**na**	na	na	na	na	na	na	na	na	na	na	na	na	na	na
Denmark	na	**na**	na	na	na	na	na	na	na	na	na	na	na	na	na	na
Dominican Rep.	na	**9**	12	7	9	8	10	10	11	8	7	9	10	11	8	10
Egypt	na	**51**	50	52	50	50	52	52	50	48	50	54	49	51	51	47
El Salvador	na	**17**	17	16	18	16	17	18	15	17	19	16	18	na	na	na
Estonia	17	**na**	na	na	na	na	na	na	na	na	na	na	na	na	na	na
Finland	na	**na**	na	na	na	na	na	na	na	na	na	na	na	na	na	na
France	na	**na**	na	na	na	na	na	na	na	na	na	na	na	na	na	na
Georgia	na	**34**	35	33	34	33	34	35	35	28	32	35	34	33	34	41
Germany	na	**na**	na	na	na	na	na	na	na	na	na	na	na	na	na	na
Great Britain	na	**na**	na	na	na	na	na	na	na	na	na	na	na	na	na	na
Greece	na	**na**	na	na	na	na	na	na	na	na	na	na	na	na	na	na
Hungary	na	**na**	na	na	na	na	na	na	na	na	na	na	na	na	na	na
Iceland	na	**na**	na	na	na	na	na	na	na	na	na	na	na	na	na	na
India	55	**34**	37	29	35	29	40	36	33	30	40	32	32	38	33	22
Indonesia	na	**33**	34	32	24	36	35	43	33	27	29	35	32	36	30	32
Iran	na	**34**	34	34	33	33	42	35	36	31	30	35	40	31	34	40
Ireland	na	**na**	na	na	na	na	na	na	na	na	na	na	na	na	na	na
Israel	na	**na**	na	na	na	na	na	na	na	na	na	na	na	na	na	na
Italy	na	**na**	na	na	na	na	na	na	na	na	na	na	na	na	na	na
Japan	na	**18**	20	17	10	14	26	35	16	16	20	20	16	24	18	13
Jordan	na	**26**	19	35	28	25	26	30	24	23	32	25	21	26	26	37
Korea, South	na	**11**	9	13	6	11	16	29	13	6	12	12	9	11	12	5
Latvia	18	**na**	na	na	na	na	na	na	na	na	na	na	na	na	na	na
Lithuania	13	**na**	na	na	na	na	na	na	na	na	na	na	na	na	na	na
Luxembourg	na	**na**	na	na	na	na	na	na	na	na	na	na	na	na	na	na
Macedonia	na	**10**	10	9	10	9	10	12	8	9	10	10	9	8	9	27
Malta	na	**na**	na	na	na	na	na	na	na	na	na	na	na	na	na	na
Mexico	30	**25**	27	23	22	25	29	30	15	30	27	27	24	28	22	27
Moldova	na	**24**	24	25	16	22	34	32	24	17	30	23	22	27	22	19
Montenegro	na	**26**	27	24	23	26	28	22	28	30	21	25	32	22	32	26
Morocco	na	**19**	17	20	18	18	24	20	11	21	17	15	17	21	16	21
Netherlands	na	**na**	na	na	na	na	na	na	na	na	na	na	na	na	na	na
New Zealand	na	**6**	6	6	5	6	6	6	5	7	7	4	7	8	5	5
Nigeria	38	**44**	49	39	43	47	38	49	41	41	46	42	46	44	44	47
Northern Ireland	na	**na**	na	na	na	na	na	na	na	na	na	na	na	na	na	na
Norway	na	**33**	32	34	34	33	31	25	35	38	na	na	na	25	33	40
Pakistan	na	**28**	31	25	25	29	32	27	27	34	28	26	32	27	30	42
Peru	na	**8**	10	6	7	9	8	9	7	8	8	8	7	11	8	4
Philippines	na	**46**	44	48	48	49	37	45	50	40	45	41	53	41	48	54
Poland	9	**na**	na	na	na	na	na	na	na	na	na	na	na	na	na	na
Portugal	na	**na**	na	na	na	na	na	na	na	na	na	na	na	na	na	na
Puerto Rico	na	**20**	19	20	14	15	26	32	22	16	25	23	12	36	19	16
Romania	na	**na**	na	na	na	na	na	na	na	na	na	na	na	na	na	na
Russian Fed.	46	**na**	na	na	na	na	na	na	na	na	na	na	na	na	na	na
Serbia	na	**15**	15	14	17	14	14	14	14	17	16	14	14	15	13	17
Singapore	na	**na**	na	na	na	na	na	na	na	na	na	na	na	na	na	na
Slovakia	na	**na**	na	na	na	na	na	na	na	na	na	na	na	na	na	na
Slovenia	na	**na**	na	na	na	na	na	na	na	na	na	na	na	na	na	na
South Africa	58	**44**	47	41	44	45	45	52	36	22	54	47	30	43	46	45
Spain	23	**27**	27	28	22	24	33	29	24	27	37	30	25	32	28	15
Sweden	na	**na**	na	na	na	na	na	na	na	na	na	na	na	na	na	na
Switzerland	na	**27**	27	27	31	25	28	27	26	34	24	26	29	36	27	20
Taiwan	na	**36**	32	39	26	35	44	44	38	27	42	38	28	35	35	40
Tanzania	na	**59**	58	62	56	58	71	66	52	53	66	55	57	55	62	63
Turkey	49	**29**	27	31	28	28	33	33	25	21	32	29	24	30	29	25
Uganda	na	**41**	50	32	39	44	36	36	42	45	45	45	38	32	44	50
Ukraine	na	**na**	na	na	na	na	na	na	na	na	na	na	na	na	na	na
United States	55	**23**	22	23	24	21	24	26	24	21	24	23	22	25	23	22
Uruguay	na	**37**	40	34	27	34	42	35	37	44	34	38	37	46	33	37
Venezuela	na	**20**	23	17	19	20	24	21	23	13	21	22	20	23	20	16
Vietnam	na	**92**	92	91	89	91	94	92	91	94	92	92	91	90	92	92
Zimbabwe	na	**29**	29	30	29	30	31	35	22	na	42	28	14	29	29	32
Total	37	30	32	29	29	31	31	35	30	25	31	31	30	33	30	25

RANKING	
Country	**2000**
China	93
Vietnam	92
Bangladesh	79
Tanzania	59
Azerbaijan	54
Egypt	51
Philippines	46
Nigeria	44
South Africa	44
Uganda	41
Uruguay	37
Taiwan	36
Iran	34
Georgia	34
India	34
Indonesia	33
Norway	33
Brazil	33
Albania	29
Zimbabwe	29
Turkey	29
Pakistan	28
Chile	28
Spain	27
Switzerland	27
Jordan	26
Montenegro	26
Mexico	25
Moldova	24
Canada	23
United States	23
Venezuela	20
Puerto Rico	20
Algeria	19
Morocco	19
Japan	18
Colombia	17
El Salvador	17
Australia	16
Armenia	16
Bosnia and Herz.	15
Serbia	15
Korea, South	11
Macedonia	10
Dominican Rep.	9
Peru	8
Argentina	7
New Zealand	6
Total	30

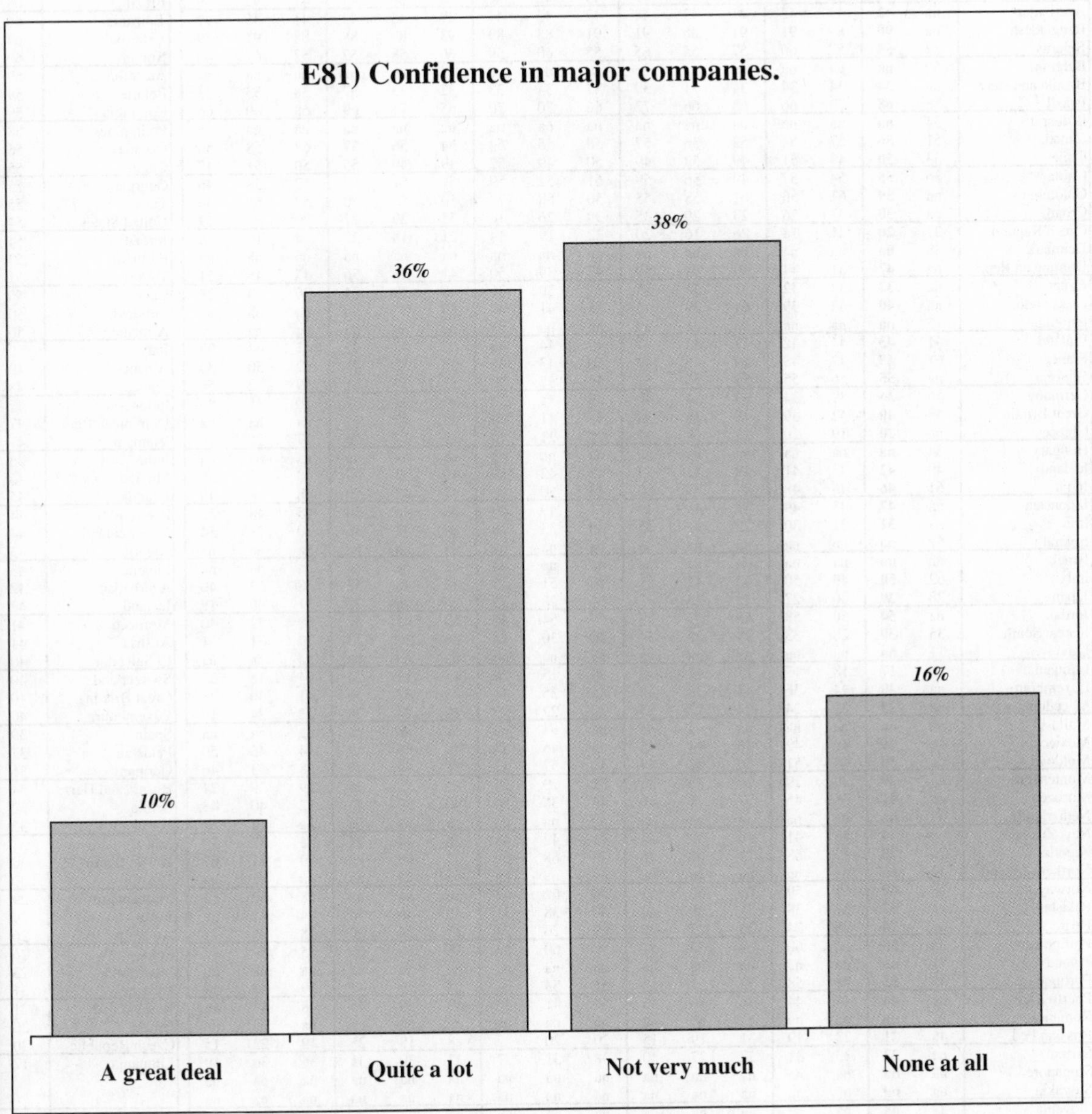
E81) Confidence in major companies.
10%
36%
38%
16%
A great deal
Quite a lot
Not very much
None at all

E081) CONFIDENCE: MAJOR COMPANIES

I am going to name a number of organizations. For each one, could you tell me how much confidence you have in them: is it a great deal of confidence, quite a lot of confidence, not very much confidence or none at all? Major companies.

A great deal / Quite a lot (%)

(WVS: V157; EVS: o27)

Country	Wave		Gender		Age			Education			Income			Values		
	1990	2000	Male	Female	16-29	30-49	50+	Lower	Middle	Upper	Lower	Middle	Upper	Mat	Mixed	Postm.
Albania	na	**49**	52	47	52	49	47	51	48	48	47	51	51	53	49	39
Algeria	na	**43**	42	45	44	44	40	41	43	44	41	44	43	47	41	41
Argentina	25	**26**	33	20	28	25	25	27	26	25	26	27	25	32	26	22
Armenia	na	**50**	50	50	50	48	51	45	51	47	55	45	45	53	47	43
Australia	na	**59**	62	56	66	57	54	56	60	60	51	63	66	62	61	55
Austria	42	**41**	41	42	48	37	42	43	42	32	38	38	44	41	42	39
Azerbaijan	na	**42**	43	42	41	43	44	47	42	41	39	43	43	41	45	49
Bangladesh	na	**90**	89	91	91	88	91	91	88	89	93	89	88	88	91	89
Belarus	37	**59**	57	60	57	55	65	55	60	59	60	58	57	57	62	46
Belgium	50	**na**	na	na	na	na	na	na	na	na	na	na	na	na	na	na
Bosnia and Herz.	na	**34**	34	34	34	31	39	37	34	33	32	35	37	38	33	33
Brazil	58	**68**	70	66	68	66	72	66	70	70	65	71	69	68	69	66
Bulgaria	34	**na**	na	na	na	na	na	na	na	na	na	na	na	na	na	na
Canada	51	**56**	57	54	52	56	57	58	55	54	54	56	57	62	58	50
Chile	53	**50**	49	51	49	52	49	50	49	52	49	49	55	50	51	47
China	36	**55**	54	57	49	56	59	61	52	59	57	57	52	52	58	46
Colombia	na	**59**	61	56	61	58	55	50	58	73	50	58	70	57	55	56
Croatia	na	**30**	33	26	23	29	35	39	26	18	35	29	27	30	33	19
Czech Republic	27	**20**	21	18	26	16	20	22	19	14	21	18	22	24	19	15
Denmark	38	**na**	na	na	na	na	na	na	na	na	na	na	na	na	na	na
Dominican Rep.	na	**47**	51	44	48	44	50	47	39	50	41	48	56	47	46	51
Egypt	na	**32**	32	32	31	31	35	31	30	36	30	29	34	30	34	23
El Salvador	na	**40**	42	39	41	39	42	38	41	47	39	39	50	na	na	na
Estonia	15	**na**	na	na	na	na	na	na	na	na	na	na	na	na	na	na
Finland	41	**43**	44	42	47	42	41	42	44	45	42	42	45	41	44	37
France	67	**48**	47	48	49	46	49	50	43	45	46	52	47	52	50	34
Georgia	na	**55**	56	55	53	56	57	58	57	50	52	54	61	59	52	54
Germany	46	**36**	39	34	33	34	40	39	34	34	40	33	37	50	35	23
Great Britain	48	**40**	42	39	48	38	38	36	41	44	38	42	41	na	na	na
Greece	na	**20**	19	20	22	18	17	20	21	19	19	17	26	27	21	10
Hungary	34	**na**	na	na	na	na	na	na	na	na	na	na	na	na	na	na
Iceland	40	**42**	43	41	49	41	37	42	42	39	40	37	47	48	42	25
India	61	**46**	45	48	47	43	50	43	50	46	41	43	50	48	48	40
Indonesia	na	**47**	45	49	39	48	49	54	49	40	48	45	50	45	48	52
Iran	na	**31**	31	30	29	32	35	30	33	28	24	32	36	30	28	34
Ireland	52	**na**	na	na	na	na	na	na	na	na	na	na	na	na	na	na
Israel	na	**na**	na	na	na	na	na	na	na	na	na	na	na	na	na	na
Italy	62	**50**	49	50	52	47	51	50	51	45	47	48	52	58	53	40
Japan	28	**29**	30	27	32	23	32	24	28	33	25	29	32	31	30	19
Jordan	na	**54**	50	58	55	52	58	59	54	46	63	47	52	59	52	40
Korea, South	35	**30**	28	33	28	29	34	40	30	28	26	32	33	29	31	31
Latvia	11	**na**	na	na	na	na	na	na	na	na	na	na	na	na	na	na
Lithuania	16	**17**	18	17	17	17	18	20	15	20	15	11	24	14	18	22
Luxembourg	na	**40**	44	36	43	38	40	45	35	41	44	37	36	41	40	38
Macedonia	na	**23**	22	24	24	22	23	20	22	29	19	24	28	22	24	19
Malta	na	**na**	na	na	na	na	na	na	na	na	na	na	na	na	na	na
Mexico	46	**46**	49	42	48	44	45	43	46	58	40	43	59	44	46	50
Moldova	na	**50**	48	51	50	52	47	44	52	52	51	49	49	48	53	46
Montenegro	na	**29**	29	29	26	26	35	32	29	25	25	32	30	29	29	24
Morocco	na	**41**	38	45	37	44	48	43	30	50	40	30	46	42	40	43
Netherlands	48	**na**	na	na	na	na	na	na	na	na	na	na	na	na	na	na
New Zealand	na	**44**	48	41	49	49	37	41	42	48	38	44	54	52	47	39
Nigeria	76	**70**	72	68	71	68	76	73	68	69	71	68	73	70	71	67
Northern Ireland	47	**na**	na	na	na	na	na	na	na	na	na	na	na	na	na	na
Norway	53	**60**	61	59	65	60	57	56	62	63	na	na	na	58	62	52
Pakistan	na	**37**	37	38	36	36	44	40	38	31	45	36	36	34	41	55
Peru	na	**26**	28	24	25	27	26	29	26	24	25	24	30	28	26	21
Philippines	na	**58**	56	60	64	57	51	59	60	54	58	56	60	55	59	72
Poland	71	**na**	na	na	na	na	na	na	na	na	na	na	na	na	na	na
Portugal	45	**53**	48	58	52	54	53	51	53	64	44	50	45	59	49	53
Puerto Rico	na	**44**	44	44	38	46	46	58	41	43	49	39	46	48	43	46
Romania	35	**na**	na	na	na	na	na	na	na	na	na	na	na	na	na	na
Russian Fed.	46	**21**	23	19	31	19	15	20	20	22	18	19	25	19	22	15
Serbia	na	**32**	33	31	27	27	40	38	31	27	37	30	31	36	30	19
Singapore	na	**na**	na	na	na	na	na	na	na	na	na	na	na	na	na	na
Slovakia	na	**na**	na	na	na	na	na	na	na	na	na	na	na	na	na	na
Slovenia	33	**na**	na	na	na	na	na	na	na	na	na	na	na	na	na	na
South Africa	76	**74**	76	71	76	73	70	73	74	74	70	79	74	75	74	64
Spain	43	**39**	37	41	34	37	45	43	35	39	41	42	39	45	42	25
Sweden	53	**na**	na	na	na	na	na	na	na	na	na	na	na	na	na	na
Switzerland	na	**40**	43	38	45	40	37	36	40	47	36	36	49	49	43	27
Taiwan	na	**55**	55	55	49	57	54	58	53	53	55	56	56	54	56	44
Tanzania	na	**66**	62	72	72	61	72	69	63	64	65	64	68	62	68	63
Turkey	29	**51**	48	54	53	51	50	53	48	53	50	52	54	51	52	46
Uganda	na	**70**	76	64	71	69	63	72	68	79	73	69	74	64	72	72
Ukraine	na	**21**	22	21	32	20	15	14	21	24	15	23	27	19	23	29
United States	51	**54**	58	50	53	53	56	54	54	54	48	55	61	57	57	47
Uruguay	na	**45**	47	43	39	42	49	45	43	46	44	44	47	52	45	37
Venezuela	na	**64**	66	63	65	65	60	54	66	72	56	67	69	64	63	74
Vietnam	na	**47**	48	46	47	47	47	50	45	41	38	50	48	42	49	43
Zimbabwe	na	**77**	75	79	77	75	81	81	72	58	80	71	74	78	76	77
Total	44	**46**	47	45	48	45	44	49	45	45	45	45	48	48	47	41

RANKING

Country	2000
Bangladesh	90
Zimbabwe	77
South Africa	74
Nigeria	70
Uganda	70
Brazil	68
Tanzania	66
Venezuela	64
Norway	60
Australia	59
Belarus	59
Colombia	59
Philippines	58
Canada	56
China	55
Georgia	55
Taiwan	55
United States	54
Jordan	54
Portugal	53
Turkey	51
Chile	50
Moldova	50
Armenia	50
Italy	50
Albania	49
France	48
Indonesia	47
Dominican Rep.	47
Vietnam	47
India	46
Mexico	46
Uruguay	45
Puerto Rico	44
New Zealand	44
Algeria	43
Finland	43
Azerbaijan	42
Iceland	42
Morocco	41
Austria	41
El Salvador	40
Switzerland	40
Great Britain	40
Luxembourg	40
Spain	39
Pakistan	37
Germany	36
Bosnia and Herz.	34
Serbia	32
Egypt	32
Iran	31
Korea, South	30
Croatia	30
Montenegro	29
Japan	29
Argentina	26
Peru	26
Macedonia	23
Ukraine	21
Russian Fed.	21
Greece	20
Czech Republic	20
Lithuania	17
Total	46

E082) CONFIDENCE: THE ENVIRONMENTAL PROTECTION MOVEMENT

I am going to name a number of organizations. For each one, could you tell me how much confidence you have in them: is it a great deal of confidence, quite a lot of confidence, not very much confidence or none at all? Environmental Protection

(WVS: V158)

A great deal / Quite a lot (%)

Country	Wave		Gender		Age			Education			Income			Values		
	1990	2000	Male	Female	16-29	30-49	50+	Lower	Middle	Upper	Lower	Middle	Upper	Mat	Mixed	Postm.
Albania	na	**38**	38	38	40	39	35	34	37	48	34	40	41	34	43	27
Algeria	na	**na**	na	na	na	na	na	na	na	na	na	na	na	na	na	na
Argentina	na	**67**	69	66	68	66	67	64	72	69	66	66	69	61	65	74
Armenia	na	**47**	42	51	49	44	47	42	48	45	55	36	44	45	47	53
Australia	na	**56**	52	61	66	60	43	46	57	64	47	62	62	50	54	63
Austria	na	**na**	na	na	na	na	na	na	na	na	na	na	na	na	na	na
Azerbaijan	na	**14**	15	13	13	15	16	13	14	14	11	14	19	13	15	26
Bangladesh	na	**83**	82	85	84	82	87	83	86	79	81	81	89	84	84	76
Belarus	na	**na**	na	na	na	na	na	na	na	na	na	na	na	na	na	na
Belgium	na	**na**	na	na	na	na	na	na	na	na	na	na	na	na	na	na
Bosnia and Herz.	na	**52**	52	53	53	47	58	50	51	59	52	51	55	54	52	69
Brazil	na	**80**	82	79	84	78	78	76	84	83	75	84	83	76	82	87
Bulgaria	na	**na**	na	na	na	na	na	na	na	na	na	na	na	na	na	na
Canada	na	**68**	68	68	66	69	67	66	69	67	70	69	66	71	66	71
Chile	na	**65**	65	66	70	66	60	61	66	72	63	67	69	57	66	77
China	na	**88**	87	89	86	88	90	91	87	75	90	91	82	86	88	90
Colombia	na	**70**	71	69	73	70	65	59	71	85	63	68	81	66	70	76
Croatia	na	**na**	na	na	na	na	na	na	na	na	na	na	na	na	na	na
Czech Republic	na	**na**	na	na	na	na	na	na	na	na	na	na	na	na	na	na
Denmark	na	**na**	na	na	na	na	na	na	na	na	na	na	na	na	na	na
Dominican Rep.	na	**64**	66	63	65	63	60	42	58	69	63	68	67	61	65	63
Egypt	na	**77**	76	78	79	75	77	79	76	73	80	76	75	77	77	73
El Salvador	na	**38**	38	38	39	36	40	35	38	44	37	37	44	na	na	na
Estonia	na	**na**	na	na	na	na	na	na	na	na	na	na	na	na	na	na
Finland	na	**na**	na	na	na	na	na	na	na	na	na	na	na	na	na	na
France	na	**na**	na	na	na	na	na	na	na	na	na	na	na	na	na	na
Georgia	na	**42**	39	45	38	44	44	45	42	41	40	42	46	43	42	42
Germany	na	**na**	na	na	na	na	na	na	na	na	na	na	na	na	na	na
Great Britain	na	**na**	na	na	na	na	na	na	na	na	na	na	na	na	na	na
Greece	na	**na**	na	na	na	na	na	na	na	na	na	na	na	na	na	na
Hungary	na	**na**	na	na	na	na	na	na	na	na	na	na	na	na	na	na
Iceland	na	**na**	na	na	na	na	na	na	na	na	na	na	na	na	na	na
India	na	**52**	52	51	55	49	55	43	56	58	42	51	57	51	54	58
Indonesia	na	**55**	56	54	53	56	54	53	56	56	55	57	49	52	57	59
Iran	na	**55**	55	55	54	55	58	59	54	51	50	53	56	54	52	62
Ireland	na	**na**	na	na	na	na	na	na	na	na	na	na	na	na	na	na
Israel	na	**na**	na	na	na	na	na	na	na	na	na	na	na	na	na	na
Italy	na	**na**	na	na	na	na	na	na	na	na	na	na	na	na	na	na
Japan	na	**57**	52	62	59	56	57	56	56	61	57	58	53	54	59	57
Jordan	na	**69**	60	77	71	65	72	71	72	61	79	60	65	72	67	61
Korea, South	na	**75**	73	76	75	76	71	71	76	73	71	74	79	72	76	85
Latvia	na	**na**	na	na	na	na	na	na	na	na	na	na	na	na	na	na
Lithuania	na	**na**	na	na	na	na	na	na	na	na	na	na	na	na	na	na
Luxembourg	na	**na**	na	na	na	na	na	na	na	na	na	na	na	na	na	na
Macedonia	na	**42**	43	41	38	43	44	35	44	47	36	42	48	40	45	31
Malta	na	**na**	na	na	na	na	na	na	na	na	na	na	na	na	na	na
Mexico	na	**54**	56	52	60	52	49	49	58	64	47	55	62	53	54	58
Moldova	na	**52**	52	52	54	51	52	45	53	56	58	51	49	54	53	40
Montenegro	na	**34**	32	37	38	35	31	31	34	42	34	34	34	33	36	40
Morocco	na	**66**	63	69	63	65	74	67	59	64	69	57	64	63	67	65
Netherlands	na	**na**	na	na	na	na	na	na	na	na	na	na	na	na	na	na
New Zealand	na	**46**	40	52	46	53	42	39	45	54	46	48	47	46	43	59
Nigeria	na	**61**	60	62	62	60	58	64	58	60	61	62	62	60	61	67
Northern Ireland	na	**na**	na	na	na	na	na	na	na	na	na	na	na	na	na	na
Norway	na	**63**	57	68	67	68	52	55	63	69	na	na	na	56	62	74
Pakistan	na	**36**	35	37	37	31	46	41	33	29	44	31	33	34	37	22
Peru	na	**48**	49	46	48	47	49	49	44	51	45	45	56	42	49	50
Philippines	na	**74**	74	75	75	77	69	76	75	71	75	75	72	72	76	72
Poland	na	**na**	na	na	na	na	na	na	na	na	na	na	na	na	na	na
Portugal	na	**na**	na	na	na	na	na	na	na	na	na	na	na	na	na	na
Puerto Rico	na	**69**	74	67	68	71	68	55	67	73	67	66	75	61	69	77
Romania	na	**na**	na	na	na	na	na	na	na	na	na	na	na	na	na	na
Russian Fed.	na	**na**	na	na	na	na	na	na	na	na	na	na	na	na	na	na
Serbia	na	**44**	45	42	43	41	47	40	42	51	42	42	50	41	44	50
Singapore	na	**na**	na	na	na	na	na	na	na	na	na	na	na	na	na	na
Slovakia	na	**na**	na	na	na	na	na	na	na	na	na	na	na	na	na	na
Slovenia	na	**na**	na	na	na	na	na	na	na	na	na	na	na	na	na	na
South Africa	na	**61**	61	62	61	60	64	67	54	61	66	60	56	62	60	69
Spain	na	**61**	57	65	68	60	57	59	65	61	56	63	63	55	63	65
Sweden	na	**na**	na	na	na	na	na	na	na	na	na	na	na	na	na	na
Switzerland	na	**44**	39	48	56	45	35	36	44	52	37	39	52	38	40	57
Taiwan	na	**79**	77	81	77	79	81	80	79	79	79	78	80	79	80	70
Tanzania	na	**61**	61	62	66	55	70	66	57	56	65	54	61	56	65	57
Turkey	na	**70**	67	73	70	70	67	69	70	67	67	72	68	67	71	69
Uganda	na	**76**	82	70	75	77	73	74	76	78	83	72	79	70	77	83
Ukraine	na	**na**	na	na	na	na	na	na	na	na	na	na	na	na	na	na
United States	na	**60**	59	61	65	57	60	60	61	60	59	62	56	62	58	65
Uruguay	na	**69**	68	70	68	69	70	66	75	73	69	64	77	68	69	74
Venezuela	na	**68**	69	67	71	67	66	61	69	75	65	68	74	61	70	75
Vietnam	na	**79**	80	79	80	78	81	79	81	82	78	84	76	83	81	80
Zimbabwe	na	**69**	67	72	74	63	71	70	69	52	74	68	63	63	72	83
Total	na	**60**	59	61	62	60	58	60	59	62	59	59	62	57	61	67

RANKING

Country	2000
China	88
Bangladesh	83
Brazil	80
Vietnam	79
Taiwan	79
Egypt	77
Uganda	76
Korea, South	75
Philippines	74
Colombia	70
Turkey	70
Zimbabwe	69
Uruguay	69
Puerto Rico	69
Jordan	69
Venezuela	68
Canada	68
Argentina	67
Morocco	66
Chile	65
Dominican Rep.	64
Norway	63
Tanzania	61
South Africa	61
Spain	61
Nigeria	61
United States	60
Japan	57
Australia	56
Iran	55
Indonesia	55
Mexico	54
Bosnia and Herz.	52
India	52
Moldova	52
Peru	48
Armenia	47
New Zealand	46
Serbia	44
Switzerland	44
Georgia	42
Macedonia	42
Albania	38
El Salvador	38
Pakistan	36
Montenegro	34
Azerbaijan	14
Total	60

E083) CONFIDENCE: THE WOMEN'S MOVEMENT

I am going to name a number of organizations. For each one, could you tell me how much confidence you have in them: is it a great deal of confidence, quite a lot of confidence, not very much confidence or none at all? The women's movement

A great deal / Quite a lot (%)

(WVS: V159)

Country	Wave		Gender		Age			Education			Income			Values		
	1990	2000	Male	Female	16-29	30-49	50+	Lower	Middle	Upper	Lower	Middle	Upper	Mat	Mixed	Postm.
Albania	na	**38**	30	46	42	39	34	34	39	47	36	40	39	37	40	27
Algeria	na	**30**	17	43	31	29	28	30	30	29	30	27	25	34	26	36
Argentina	na	**36**	39	33	37	36	35	38	34	30	40	37	31	35	37	33
Armenia	na	**29**	22	36	31	28	27	22	30	31	30	26	30	29	30	22
Australia	na	**43**	38	49	53	42	36	44	40	47	42	45	40	33	41	51
Austria	na	**na**	na	na	na	na	na	na	na	na	na	na	na	na	na	na
Azerbaijan	na	**20**	13	26	19	20	20	11	19	22	18	19	23	18	22	31
Bangladesh	na	**80**	78	83	81	80	79	82	81	75	83	75	84	82	79	76
Belarus	na	**na**	na	na	na	na	na	na	na	na	na	na	na	na	na	na
Belgium	na	**na**	na	na	na	na	na	na	na	na	na	na	na	na	na	na
Bosnia and Herz.	na	**45**	36	53	47	40	50	43	46	45	45	46	46	49	45	54
Brazil	na	**69**	68	70	73	66	67	70	70	63	67	77	65	68	69	74
Bulgaria	na	**na**	na	na	na	na	na	na	na	na	na	na	na	na	na	na
Canada	na	**63**	60	65	65	64	60	60	65	60	66	63	59	59	61	67
Chile	na	**47**	40	53	53	46	42	43	48	52	41	52	50	45	47	50
China	na	**92**	90	94	88	93	93	92	92	90	90	94	91	92	90	96
Colombia	na	**52**	51	54	56	51	48	48	52	58	51	50	57	52	55	63
Croatia	na	**na**	na	na	na	na	na	na	na	na	na	na	na	na	na	na
Czech Republic	na	**na**	na	na	na	na	na	na	na	na	na	na	na	na	na	na
Denmark	na	**na**	na	na	na	na	na	na	na	na	na	na	na	na	na	na
Dominican Rep.	na	**52**	52	52	51	54	50	54	45	54	54	45	63	54	49	59
Egypt	na	**74**	63	86	76	72	74	75	72	73	73	73	75	76	73	69
El Salvador	na	**na**	na	na	na	na	na	na	na	na	na	na	na	na	na	na
Estonia	na	**na**	na	na	na	na	na	na	na	na	na	na	na	na	na	na
Finland	na	**na**	na	na	na	na	na	na	na	na	na	na	na	na	na	na
France	na	**na**	na	na	na	na	na	na	na	na	na	na	na	na	na	na
Georgia	na	**41**	35	45	37	43	43	45	40	40	38	43	42	41	41	40
Germany	na	**na**	na	na	na	na	na	na	na	na	na	na	na	na	na	na
Great Britain	na	**na**	na	na	na	na	na	na	na	na	na	na	na	na	na	na
Greece	na	**na**	na	na	na	na	na	na	na	na	na	na	na	na	na	na
Hungary	na	**na**	na	na	na	na	na	na	na	na	na	na	na	na	na	na
Iceland	na	**na**	na	na	na	na	na	na	na	na	na	na	na	na	na	na
India	na	**53**	48	60	54	52	53	48	53	57	46	52	55	57	50	49
Indonesia	na	**51**	44	58	47	49	55	54	58	41	52	51	49	50	51	50
Iran	na	**43**	38	49	42	45	41	42	45	41	39	39	46	36	43	56
Ireland	na	**na**	na	na	na	na	na	na	na	na	na	na	na	na	na	na
Israel	na	**na**	na	na	na	na	na	na	na	na	na	na	na	na	na	na
Italy	na	**na**	na	na	na	na	na	na	na	na	na	na	na	na	na	na
Japan	na	**45**	39	50	51	40	46	42	45	45	47	41	43	42	46	46
Jordan	na	**53**	37	68	53	53	52	56	50	50	60	41	53	55	51	52
Korea, South	na	**71**	63	78	74	72	64	69	72	68	65	71	76	68	72	79
Latvia	na	**na**	na	na	na	na	na	na	na	na	na	na	na	na	na	na
Lithuania	na	**na**	na	na	na	na	na	na	na	na	na	na	na	na	na	na
Luxembourg	na	**na**	na	na	na	na	na	na	na	na	na	na	na	na	na	na
Macedonia	na	**45**	38	52	45	46	44	42	43	53	39	47	50	44	47	43
Malta	na	**na**	na	na	na	na	na	na	na	na	na	na	na	na	na	na
Mexico	na	**39**	35	42	42	36	38	37	39	44	39	36	42	36	39	42
Moldova	na	**47**	42	51	44	46	50	44	49	45	54	46	45	48	46	45
Montenegro	na	**29**	18	40	32	31	25	26	29	36	28	29	24	28	30	37
Morocco	na	**41**	25	58	42	39	43	41	38	51	39	36	42	38	41	49
Netherlands	na	**na**	na	na	na	na	na	na	na	na	na	na	na	na	na	na
New Zealand	na	**36**	26	44	35	39	34	36	33	40	39	36	34	39	34	43
Nigeria	na	**54**	44	63	53	56	52	57	53	49	52	55	54	53	55	49
Northern Ireland	na	**na**	na	na	na	na	na	na	na	na	na	na	na	na	na	na
Norway	na	**43**	37	49	46	42	43	40	45	44	na	na	na	40	41	62
Pakistan	na	**29**	21	37	34	26	25	27	31	27	29	27	32	25	33	56
Peru	na	**36**	30	42	32	36	46	42	36	33	41	30	37	33	38	35
Philippines	na	**77**	74	80	76	79	74	79	75	77	78	77	76	75	79	77
Poland	na	**na**	na	na	na	na	na	na	na	na	na	na	na	na	na	na
Portugal	na	**na**	na	na	na	na	na	na	na	na	na	na	na	na	na	na
Puerto Rico	na	**56**	59	54	62	54	54	48	54	58	53	54	61	57	55	60
Romania	na	**na**	na	na	na	na	na	na	na	na	na	na	na	na	na	na
Russian Fed.	na	**na**	na	na	na	na	na	na	na	na	na	na	na	na	na	na
Serbia	na	**39**	36	42	37	35	44	37	39	42	42	39	39	37	41	41
Singapore	na	**na**	na	na	na	na	na	na	na	na	na	na	na	na	na	na
Slovakia	na	**na**	na	na	na	na	na	na	na	na	na	na	na	na	na	na
Slovenia	na	**na**	na	na	na	na	na	na	na	na	na	na	na	na	na	na
South Africa	na	**63**	58	69	66	59	63	61	65	60	59	77	54	60	66	57
Spain	na	**48**	43	53	56	49	42	47	49	53	43	52	52	44	50	51
Sweden	na	**na**	na	na	na	na	na	na	na	na	na	na	na	na	na	na
Switzerland	na	**39**	31	46	47	38	35	33	40	40	38	36	45	34	36	54
Taiwan	na	**76**	72	80	77	77	74	81	77	71	76	75	77	75	78	75
Tanzania	na	**80**	76	85	81	78	84	83	78	75	82	78	77	76	83	68
Turkey	na	**65**	56	75	64	66	68	66	65	59	63	69	64	62	65	70
Uganda	na	**75**	72	78	74	78	71	74	75	81	79	79	74	73	75	79
Ukraine	na	**na**	na	na	na	na	na	na	na	na	na	na	na	na	na	na
United States	na	**59**	57	62	69	54	58	60	63	56	62	62	54	61	58	63
Uruguay	na	**49**	48	50	45	46	53	49	51	45	48	51	51	42	50	53
Venezuela	na	**50**	44	56	53	50	43	44	53	50	46	52	55	47	50	56
Vietnam	na	**85**	83	87	81	84	90	83	89	82	86	89	80	89	85	82
Zimbabwe	na	**61**	45	73	63	59	56	66	54	22	67	62	49	59	61	69
Total	na	**53**	47	58	54	53	50	55	52	51	53	53	54	52	53	55

RANKING

Country	2000
China	92
Vietnam	85
Bangladesh	80
Tanzania	80
Philippines	77
Taiwan	76
Uganda	75
Egypt	74
Korea, South	71
Brazil	69
Turkey	65
South Africa	63
Canada	63
Zimbabwe	61
United States	59
Puerto Rico	56
Nigeria	54
Jordan	53
India	53
Colombia	52
Dominican Rep.	52
Indonesia	51
Venezuela	50
Uruguay	49
Spain	48
Chile	47
Moldova	47
Bosnia and Herz.	45
Macedonia	45
Japan	45
Australia	43
Norway	43
Iran	43
Georgia	41
Morocco	41
Serbia	39
Mexico	39
Switzerland	39
Albania	38
New Zealand	36
Peru	36
Argentina	36
Algeria	30
Armenia	29
Montenegro	29
Pakistan	29
Azerbaijan	20
Total	53

E084_1) CONFIDENCE: HEALTH CARE SYSTEM

Please look at this card and tell me, for each item listed, how much confidence you have in them, is it a great deal, quite a lot, not very much or none at all? Health care system

A great deal / Quite a lot (%) (EVS: V211)

Country	Wave		Gender		Age			Education			Income			Values		
	1990	2000	Male	Female	16-29	30-49	50+	Lower	Middle	Upper	Lower	Middle	Upper	Mat	Mixed	Postm.
Albania	na	**na**	na	na	na	na	na	na	na	na	na	na	na	na	na	na
Algeria	na	**na**	na	na	na	na	na	na	na	na	na	na	na	na	na	na
Argentina	na	**na**	na	na	na	na	na	na	na	na	na	na	na	na	na	na
Armenia	na	**na**	na	na	na	na	na	na	na	na	na	na	na	na	na	na
Australia	na	**na**	na	na	na	na	na	na	na	na	na	na	na	na	na	na
Austria	na	**86**	87	86	86	84	88	89	86	80	84	89	86	90	86	86
Azerbaijan	na	**na**	na	na	na	na	na	na	na	na	na	na	na	na	na	na
Bangladesh	na	**na**	na	na	na	na	na	na	na	na	na	na	na	na	na	na
Belarus	na	**67**	68	67	61	64	76	78	66	51	69	65	71	74	62	61
Belgium	na	**83**	84	83	84	81	85	84	82	85	83	84	86	83	83	83
Bosnia and Herz.	na	**na**	na	na	na	na	na	na	na	na	na	na	na	na	na	na
Brazil	na	**na**	na	na	na	na	na	na	na	na	na	na	na	na	na	na
Bulgaria	na	**34**	30	38	35	35	33	36	32	35	35	36	34	33	34	15
Canada	na	**na**	na	na	na	na	na	na	na	na	na	na	na	na	na	na
Chile	na	**na**	na	na	na	na	na	na	na	na	na	na	na	na	na	na
China	na	**na**	na	na	na	na	na	na	na	na	na	na	na	na	na	na
Colombia	na	**na**	na	na	na	na	na	na	na	na	na	na	na	na	na	na
Croatia	na	**44**	44	44	47	39	47	53	40	30	57	40	39	46	47	32
Czech Republic	na	**43**	44	42	47	39	44	48	38	38	50	41	41	47	40	50
Denmark	na	**70**	75	64	77	67	68	67	76	72	70	70	70	70	70	71
Dominican Rep.	na	**na**	na	na	na	na	na	na	na	na	na	na	na	na	na	na
Egypt	na	**na**	na	na	na	na	na	na	na	na	na	na	na	na	na	na
El Salvador	na	**na**	na	na	na	na	na	na	na	na	na	na	na	na	na	na
Estonia	na	**62**	60	63	70	53	66	65	62	57	59	64	62	62	63	64
Finland	na	**84**	86	83	90	84	82	85	85	82	85	86	85	85	85	82
France	na	**77**	77	78	75	75	81	78	77	77	78	78	77	81	76	78
Georgia	na	**na**	na	na	na	na	na	na	na	na	na	na	na	na	na	na
Germany	na	**53**	52	54	53	49	57	56	49	56	59	48	56	53	53	55
Great Britain	na	**59**	62	56	57	59	60	60	57	60	59	69	50	na	na	na
Greece	na	**26**	25	27	20	25	38	32	26	25	23	24	30	30	27	19
Hungary	na	**44**	43	45	49	40	45	49	32	42	39	43	48	45	44	36
Iceland	na	**85**	86	84	82	84	88	86	84	84	84	88	84	87	86	76
India	na	**na**	na	na	na	na	na	na	na	na	na	na	na	na	na	na
Indonesia	na	**na**	na	na	na	na	na	na	na	na	na	na	na	na	na	na
Iran	na	**na**	na	na	na	na	na	na	na	na	na	na	na	na	na	na
Ireland	na	**58**	58	57	61	52	62	62	55	55	64	56	50	59	56	61
Israel	na	**na**	na	na	na	na	na	na	na	na	na	na	na	na	na	na
Italy	na	**37**	38	36	34	35	40	39	34	36	43	33	37	42	38	32
Japan	na	**na**	na	na	na	na	na	na	na	na	na	na	na	na	na	na
Jordan	na	**na**	na	na	na	na	na	na	na	na	na	na	na	na	na	na
Korea, South	na	**na**	na	na	na	na	na	na	na	na	na	na	na	na	na	na
Latvia	na	**67**	67	67	74	61	70	78	68	52	70	68	63	72	65	57
Lithuania	na	**37**	36	38	37	31	42	46	34	35	48	33	34	39	36	34
Luxembourg	na	**78**	81	75	75	75	83	78	78	79	74	80	78	78	78	80
Macedonia	na	**na**	na	na	na	na	na	na	na	na	na	na	na	na	na	na
Malta	na	**86**	88	85	81	86	91	89	86	83	89	90	86	92	83	85
Mexico	na	**na**	na	na	na	na	na	na	na	na	na	na	na	na	na	na
Moldova	na	**na**	na	na	na	na	na	na	na	na	na	na	na	na	na	na
Montenegro	na	**na**	na	na	na	na	na	na	na	na	na	na	na	na	na	na
Morocco	na	**na**	na	na	na	na	na	na	na	na	na	na	na	na	na	na
Netherlands	na	**76**	80	72	80	75	74	70	79	78	76	72	82	80	76	74
New Zealand	na	**na**	na	na	na	na	na	na	na	na	na	na	na	na	na	na
Nigeria	na	**na**	na	na	na	na	na	na	na	na	na	na	na	na	na	na
Northern Ireland	na	**68**	68	68	66	64	74	70	65	68	74	65	69	72	68	56
Norway	na	**na**	na	na	na	na	na	na	na	na	na	na	na	na	na	na
Pakistan	na	**na**	na	na	na	na	na	na	na	na	na	na	na	na	na	na
Peru	na	**na**	na	na	na	na	na	na	na	na	na	na	na	na	na	na
Philippines	na	**na**	na	na	na	na	na	na	na	na	na	na	na	na	na	na
Poland	na	**57**	54	59	58	53	60	62	53	40	61	54	56	58	56	56
Portugal	na	**44**	43	45	51	41	42	44	44	42	46	49	41	39	45	53
Puerto Rico	na	**na**	na	na	na	na	na	na	na	na	na	na	na	na	na	na
Romania	na	**59**	58	60	57	54	65	71	54	49	70	61	49	65	55	42
Russian Fed.	na	**56**	55	57	58	52	60	69	55	52	58	57	53	58	55	52
Serbia	na	**na**	na	na	na	na	na	na	na	na	na	na	na	na	na	na
Singapore	na	**na**	na	na	na	na	na	na	na	na	na	na	na	na	na	na
Slovakia	na	**51**	48	55	53	51	50	53	51	47	55	50	51	52	51	52
Slovenia	na	**68**	68	69	72	66	69	71	68	68	70	69	66	73	67	74
South Africa	na	**na**	na	na	na	na	na	na	na	na	na	na	na	na	na	na
Spain	na	**66**	61	70	60	61	73	70	63	59	72	68	63	71	67	58
Sweden	na	**76**	81	72	80	79	72	72	75	82	75	78	77	69	77	77
Switzerland	na	**na**	na	na	na	na	na	na	na	na	na	na	na	na	na	na
Taiwan	na	**na**	na	na	na	na	na	na	na	na	na	na	na	na	na	na
Tanzania	na	**na**	na	na	na	na	na	na	na	na	na	na	na	na	na	na
Turkey	na	**56**	51	60	52	58	63	65	46	37	64	56	42	60	56	49
Uganda	na	**na**	na	na	na	na	na	na	na	na	na	na	na	na	na	na
Ukraine	na	**48**	46	49	48	43	52	48	49	44	46	49	49	44	51	54
United States	na	**na**	na	na	na	na	na	na	na	na	na	na	na	na	na	na
Uruguay	na	**na**	na	na	na	na	na	na	na	na	na	na	na	na	na	na
Venezuela	na	**na**	na	na	na	na	na	na	na	na	na	na	na	na	na	na
Vietnam	na	**na**	na	na	na	na	na	na	na	na	na	na	na	na	na	na
Zimbabwe	na	**na**	na	na	na	na	na	na	na	na	na	na	na	na	na	na
Total	na	**61**	61	61	61	58	64	64	59	59	63	60	59	61	62	62

RANKING	
Country	2000
Malta	86
Austria	86
Iceland	85
Finland	84
Belgium	83
Luxembourg	78
France	77
Sweden	76
Netherlands	76
Denmark	70
Slovenia	68
Northern Ireland	68
Belarus	67
Latvia	67
Spain	66
Estonia	62
Romania	59
Great Britain	59
Ireland	58
Poland	57
Russian Fed.	56
Turkey	56
Germany	53
Slovakia	51
Ukraine	48
Portugal	44
Croatia	44
Hungary	44
Czech Republic	43
Lithuania	37
Italy	37
Bulgaria	34
Greece	26
Total	61

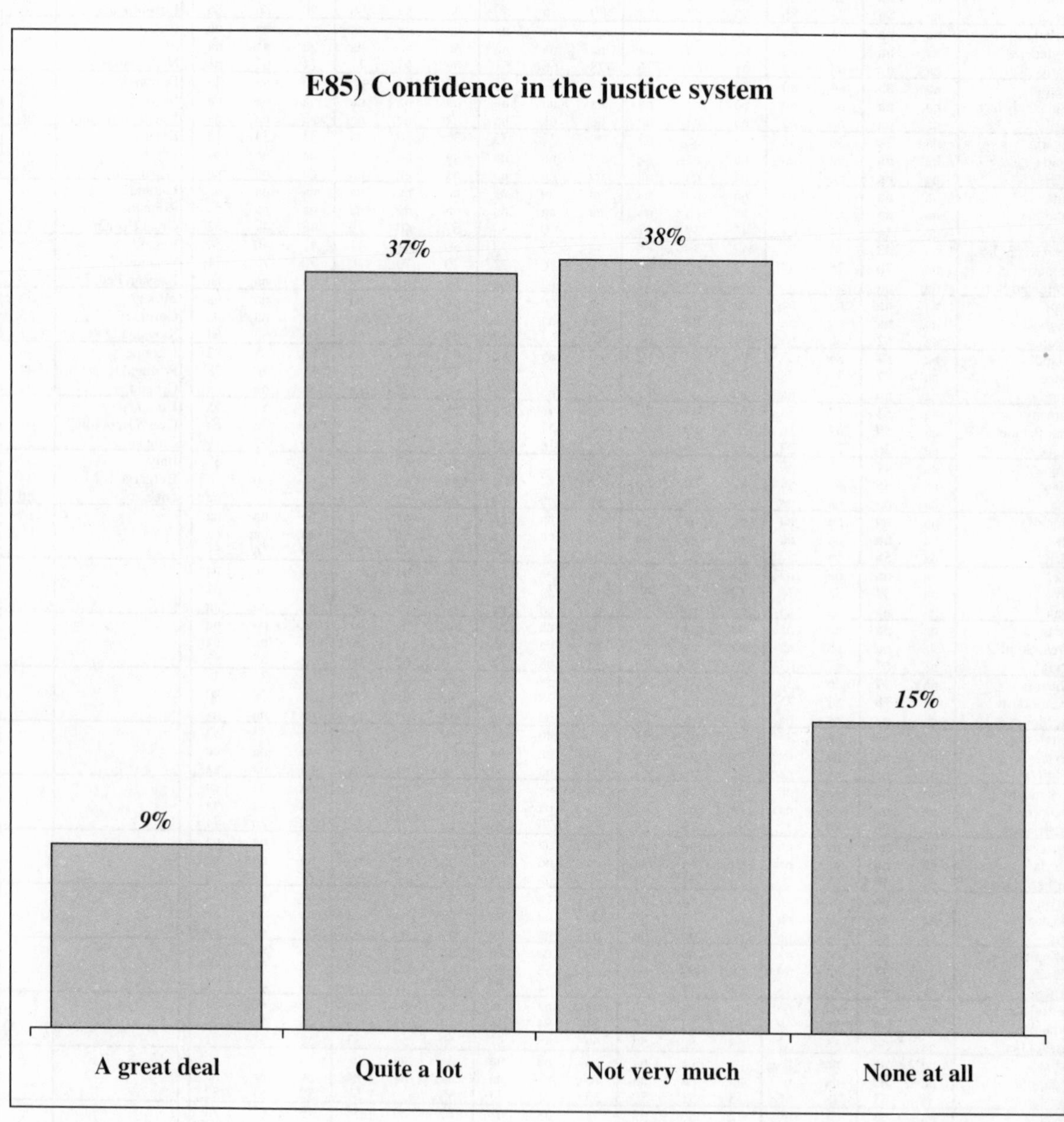

E85) Confidence in the justice system
9%
37%
38%
15%
A great deal
Quite a lot
Not very much
None at all

E085_1) CONFIDENCE: JUSTICE SYSTEM

Please look at this card and tell me, for each item listed, how much confidence you have in them, is it a great deal, quite a lot, not very much or none at all? The justice system

A great deal / Quite a lot (%)

(EVS: V212)

Country	Wave		Gender		Age			Education			Income			Values		
	1990	2000	Male	Female	16-29	30-49	50+	Lower	Middle	Upper	Lower	Middle	Upper	Mat	Mixed	Postm.
Albania	na	**na**	na	na	na	na	na	na	na	na	na	na	na	na	na	na
Algeria	na	**na**	na	na	na	na	na	na	na	na	na	na	na	na	na	na
Argentina	23	**na**	na	na	na	na	na	na	na	na	na	na	na	na	na	na
Armenia	na	**31**	30	33	31	31	32	26	33	28	32	29	31	33	28	45
Australia	na	**35**	35	35	38	34	33	31	32	41	34	34	36	35	35	35
Austria	58	**69**	71	68	73	68	68	66	71	75	65	67	75	70	70	67
Azerbaijan	na	**47**	51	42	50	45	45	48	44	51	40	45	54	45	49	52
Bangladesh	na	**na**	na	na	na	na	na	na	na	na	na	na	na	na	na	na
Belarus	26	**46**	45	48	44	40	55	59	43	37	51	43	48	49	46	24
Belgium	45	**34**	32	36	35	34	35	33	33	38	32	34	36	31	35	34
Bosnia and Herz.	na	**na**	na	na	na	na	na	na	na	na	na	na	na	na	na	na
Brazil	44	**55**	57	53	53	54	61	58	53	51	59	56	49	56	56	49
Bulgaria	46	**28**	25	31	31	28	26	30	26	28	30	28	28	25	29	20
Canada	54	**na**	na	na	na	na	na	na	na	na	na	na	na	na	na	na
Chile	45	**na**	na	na	na	na	na	na	na	na	na	na	na	na	na	na
China	76	**na**	na	na	na	na	na	na	na	na	na	na	na	na	na	na
Colombia	na	**48**	51	45	44	51	48	42	48	57	43	45	58	46	48	48
Croatia	na	**35**	33	38	35	35	36	44	32	21	44	30	35	40	38	23
Czech Republic	43	**23**	21	26	31	21	22	25	22	20	26	23	23	27	21	28
Denmark	79	**79**	79	78	77	79	79	76	85	83	79	76	85	75	78	79
Dominican Rep.	na	**15**	20	12	16	14	9	17	18	14	15	16	18	17	13	22
Egypt	na	**na**	na	na	na	na	na	na	na	na	na	na	na	na	na	na
El Salvador	na	**41**	40	41	39	39	46	46	37	34	53	37	33	na	na	na
Estonia	33	**32**	31	34	38	27	35	35	32	27	29	35	33	30	35	35
Finland	66	**66**	64	68	75	65	61	61	74	68	67	63	70	64	67	61
France	58	**46**	45	46	49	47	43	45	42	51	43	47	47	49	45	45
Georgia	na	**46**	45	46	45	45	48	51	45	44	44	46	47	46	46	40
Germany	41	**62**	62	61	59	59	65	61	62	64	63	54	63	71	58	57
Great Britain	54	**49**	49	49	47	50	51	47	47	58	45	56	50	na	na	na
Greece	na	**44**	41	46	41	42	54	55	40	45	45	42	48	49	46	35
Hungary	60	**45**	43	48	47	45	45	46	39	53	42	45	47	45	46	38
Iceland	67	**74**	74	73	66	78	75	69	74	83	68	76	76	76	73	69
India	64	**na**	na	na	na	na	na	na	na	na	na	na	na	na	na	na
Indonesia	na	**na**	na	na	na	na	na	na	na	na	na	na	na	na	na	na
Iran	na	**na**	na	na	na	na	na	na	na	na	na	na	na	na	na	na
Ireland	47	**55**	50	59	55	50	60	53	53	61	53	50	57	55	54	54
Israel	na	**na**	na	na	na	na	na	na	na	na	na	na	na	na	na	na
Italy	32	**32**	32	32	28	33	32	34	31	27	37	30	28	38	32	27
Japan	62	**na**	na	na	na	na	na	na	na	na	na	na	na	na	na	na
Jordan	na	**na**	na	na	na	na	na	na	na	na	na	na	na	na	na	na
Korea, South	67	**na**	na	na	na	na	na	na	na	na	na	na	na	na	na	na
Latvia	36	**47**	42	52	50	44	49	59	45	39	51	45	45	52	45	38
Lithuania	39	**19**	19	19	21	13	25	29	17	15	34	12	18	20	19	15
Luxembourg	na	**59**	60	58	57	57	62	64	55	59	55	57	55	63	59	53
Macedonia	na	**na**	na	na	na	na	na	na	na	na	na	na	na	na	na	na
Malta	na	**45**	43	47	49	37	50	44	45	47	43	49	44	47	46	33
Mexico	53	**na**	na	na	na	na	na	na	na	na	na	na	na	na	na	na
Moldova	na	**na**	na	na	na	na	na	na	na	na	na	na	na	na	na	na
Montenegro	na	**na**	na	na	na	na	na	na	na	na	na	na	na	na	na	na
Morocco	na	**na**	na	na	na	na	na	na	na	na	na	na	na	na	na	na
Netherlands	64	**49**	48	50	59	45	47	42	49	54	48	47	54	49	45	58
New Zealand	na	**45**	44	47	47	46	45	41	42	55	42	44	50	54	47	41
Nigeria	64	**na**	na	na	na	na	na	na	na	na	na	na	na	na	na	na
Northern Ireland	56	**48**	46	50	44	43	54	47	43	61	47	49	52	51	50	34
Norway	75	**70**	70	70	71	74	63	55	73	80	na	na	na	65	70	74
Pakistan	na	**na**	na	na	na	na	na	na	na	na	na	na	na	na	na	na
Peru	na	**na**	na	na	na	na	na	na	na	na	na	na	na	na	na	na
Philippines	na	**na**	na	na	na	na	na	na	na	na	na	na	na	na	na	na
Poland	48	**42**	38	46	48	40	40	45	41	32	41	42	45	41	43	37
Portugal	41	**41**	38	44	36	41	44	42	37	38	42	41	38	43	37	51
Puerto Rico	na	**na**	na	na	na	na	na	na	na	na	na	na	na	na	na	na
Romania	48	**40**	38	42	46	36	40	50	37	32	50	41	31	45	37	30
Russian Fed.	38	**36**	34	38	37	33	40	45	36	34	38	37	34	38	35	30
Serbia	na	**na**	na	na	na	na	na	na	na	na	na	na	na	na	na	na
Singapore	na	**na**	na	na	na	na	na	na	na	na	na	na	na	na	na	na
Slovakia	na	**36**	32	38	41	33	34	35	36	35	35	34	37	37	34	40
Slovenia	51	**44**	41	46	45	44	43	48	43	38	52	45	42	46	44	44
South Africa	74	**na**	na	na	na	na	na	na	na	na	na	na	na	na	na	na
Spain	49	**42**	38	47	38	39	47	47	39	38	48	39	39	48	46	31
Sweden	56	**61**	62	60	67	62	57	54	61	66	57	59	69	59	59	69
Switzerland	na	**66**	65	67	70	64	66	58	67	76	65	62	72	74	65	67
Taiwan	na	**59**	53	66	57	57	67	67	57	55	58	59	59	61	57	68
Tanzania	na	**na**	na	na	na	na	na	na	na	na	na	na	na	na	na	na
Turkey	64	**57**	53	62	58	56	62	63	52	42	64	58	45	62	59	46
Uganda	na	**na**	na	na	na	na	na	na	na	na	na	na	na	na	na	na
Ukraine	na	**32**	29	35	31	27	38	39	31	33	31	30	35	29	33	51
United States	58	**na**	na	na	na	na	na	na	na	na	na	na	na	na	na	na
Uruguay	na	**60**	62	58	44	52	72	62	55	62	57	58	62	68	60	55
Venezuela	na	**na**	na	na	na	na	na	na	na	na	na	na	na	na	na	na
Vietnam	na	**na**	na	na	na	na	na	na	na	na	na	na	na	na	na	na
Zimbabwe	na	**na**	na	na	na	na	na	na	na	na	na	na	na	na	na	na
Total	52	**46**	46	47	45	45	48	49	44	46	46	45	47	46	47	46

RANKING	
Country	2000
Denmark	79
Iceland	74
Norway	70
Austria	69
Switzerland	66
Finland	66
Germany	62
Sweden	61
Uruguay	60
Taiwan	59
Luxembourg	59
Turkey	57
Brazil	55
Ireland	55
Great Britain	49
Netherlands	49
Northern Ireland	48
Colombia	48
Latvia	47
Azerbaijan	47
Belarus	46
France	46
Georgia	46
New Zealand	45
Hungary	45
Malta	45
Greece	44
Slovenia	44
Spain	42
Poland	42
El Salvador	41
Portugal	41
Romania	40
Russian Fed.	36
Slovakia	36
Croatia	35
Australia	35
Belgium	34
Estonia	32
Ukraine	32
Italy	32
Armenia	31
Bulgaria	28
Czech Republic	23
Lithuania	19
Dominican Rep.	15
Total	46

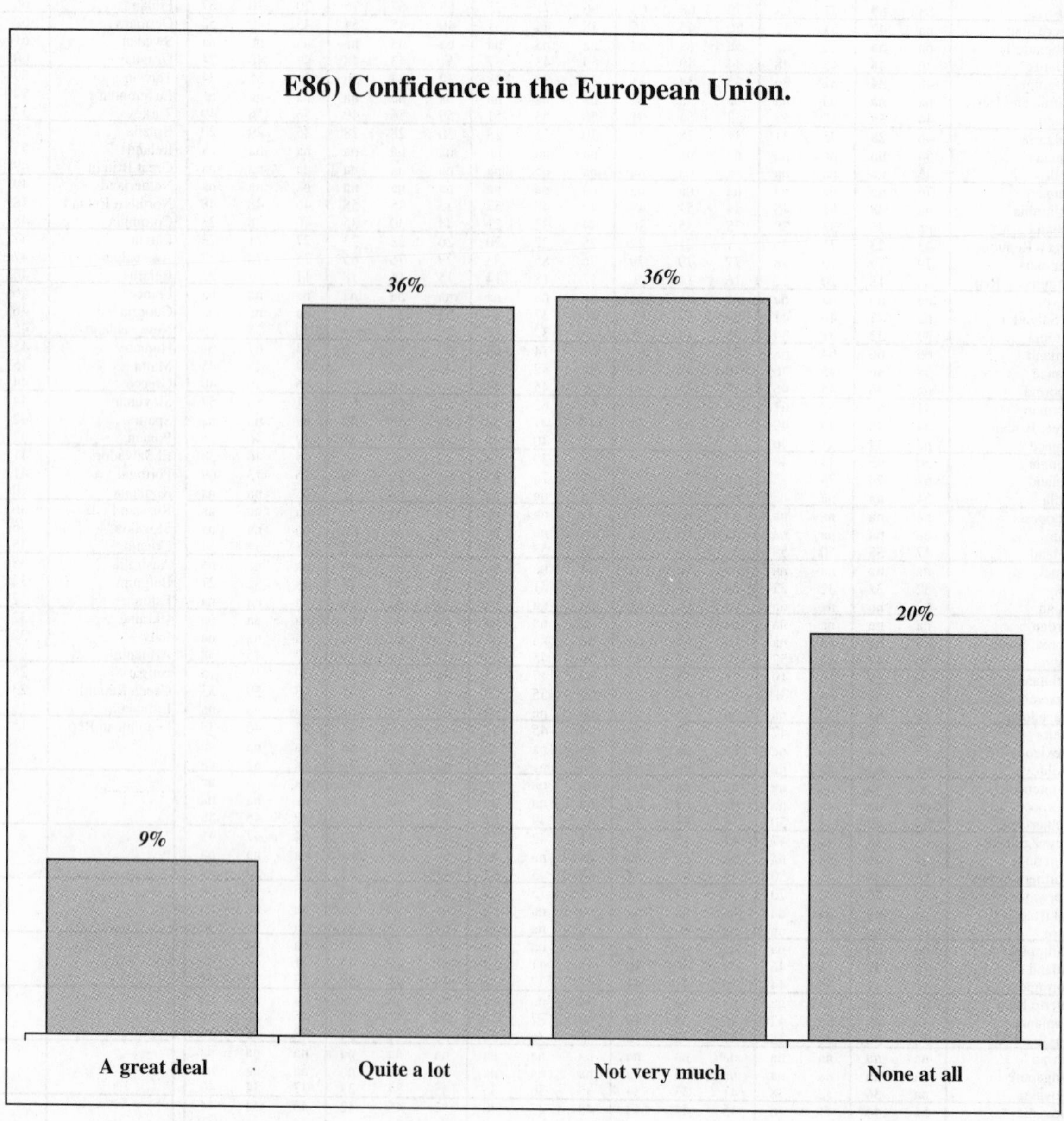
E86) Confidence in the European Union.
9%
36%
36%
20%
A great deal
Quite a lot
Not very much
None at all

E086) CONFIDENCE: THE EUROPEAN UNION

I am going to name a number of organizations. For each one, could you tell me how much confidence you have in them: is it a great deal of confidence, quite a lot of confidence, not very much confidence or none at all? The European Union.

(WVS: V160; EVS: V209)

A great deal / Quite a lot (%)

Country	Wave		Gender		Age			Education			Income			Values		
	1990	2000	Male	Female	16-29	30-49	50+	Lower	Middle	Upper	Lower	Middle	Upper	Mat	Mixed	Postm.
Albania	na	**84**	85	83	79	85	86	85	83	85	83	85	85	84	85	82
Algeria	na	**16**	17	14	18	15	12	14	16	17	16	16	14	18	15	14
Argentina	na	**na**	na	na	na	na	na	na	na	na	na	na	na	na	na	na
Armenia	na	**60**	56	63	63	56	60	55	59	64	64	57	53	60	61	43
Australia	na	**na**	na	na	na	na	na	na	na	na	na	na	na	na	na	na
Austria	na	**38**	42	33	42	36	37	33	41	45	34	37	45	40	36	40
Azerbaijan	na	**28**	30	25	24	31	27	24	24	35	15	29	37	26	28	42
Bangladesh	na	**na**	na	na	na	na	na	na	na	na	na	na	na	na	na	na
Belarus	na	**47**	45	49	52	46	43	48	46	50	48	43	56	51	44	46
Belgium	66	**47**	49	46	59	48	42	35	47	57	41	42	55	41	48	55
Bosnia and Herz.	na	**48**	48	49	47	46	53	54	47	46	46	47	54	49	49	57
Brazil	38	**na**	na	na	na	na	na	na	na	na	na	na	na	na	na	na
Bulgaria	50	**43**	43	44	47	42	43	42	43	47	41	47	46	42	43	40
Canada	50	**na**	na	na	na	na	na	na	na	na	na	na	na	na	na	na
Chile	32	**na**	na	na	na	na	na	na	na	na	na	na	na	na	na	na
China	30	**39**	32	54	33	45	31	43	39	33	46	37	36	34	44	36
Colombia	na	**na**	na	na	na	na	na	na	na	na	na	na	na	na	na	na
Croatia	na	**44**	47	40	48	39	47	49	42	34	46	42	45	51	43	42
Czech Republic	66	**43**	44	42	55	42	36	40	44	54	32	46	48	33	44	54
Denmark	39	**27**	31	23	41	18	29	24	32	28	29	25	26	23	30	14
Dominican Rep.	na	**na**	na	na	na	na	na	na	na	na	na	na	na	na	na	na
Egypt	na	**na**	na	na	na	na	na	na	na	na	na	na	na	na	na	na
El Salvador	na	**na**	na	na	na	na	na	na	na	na	na	na	na	na	na	na
Estonia	na	**31**	33	30	39	26	32	28	31	39	19	32	36	25	35	51
Finland	47	**25**	26	24	32	23	22	21	28	30	26	21	26	20	27	20
France	73	**48**	49	48	54	48	46	42	51	61	43	47	56	47	48	54
Georgia	na	**60**	59	61	59	61	58	62	60	59	56	63	63	61	59	59
Germany	64	**37**	38	37	38	36	38	35	39	44	37	35	36	45	38	24
Great Britain	47	**26**	28	24	35	28	20	20	29	39	24	30	28	na	na	na
Greece	na	**25**	25	26	26	21	33	25	21	29	22	23	33	32	26	12
Hungary	63	**59**	59	58	68	58	52	54	64	70	47	57	66	53	64	75
Iceland	36	**45**	41	50	55	43	39	41	49	44	42	45	47	42	46	46
India	33	**na**	na	na	na	na	na	na	na	na	na	na	na	na	na	na
Indonesia	na	**na**	na	na	na	na	na	na	na	na	na	na	na	na	na	na
Iran	na	**na**	na	na	na	na	na	na	na	na	na	na	na	na	na	na
Ireland	71	**60**	63	57	62	61	59	54	59	73	53	57	68	63	59	62
Israel	na	**na**	na	na	na	na	na	na	na	na	na	na	na	na	na	na
Italy	74	**69**	70	68	73	69	66	66	70	72	65	66	76	66	68	70
Japan	27	**na**	na	na	na	na	na	na	na	na	na	na	na	na	na	na
Jordan	na	**na**	na	na	na	na	na	na	na	na	na	na	na	na	na	na
Korea, South	na	**na**	na	na	na	na	na	na	na	na	na	na	na	na	na	na
Latvia	na	**35**	33	37	46	29	35	38	33	37	33	36	38	32	36	42
Lithuania	na	**31**	29	33	38	26	30	32	30	31	30	27	31	35	27	42
Luxembourg	na	**58**	59	57	61	56	58	64	52	59	59	59	54	60	58	49
Macedonia	na	**33**	33	33	39	34	27	45	25	33	33	33	30	29	33	56
Malta	na	**56**	59	53	60	53	56	42	57	82	47	55	68	43	60	80
Mexico	27	**na**	na	na	na	na	na	na	na	na	na	na	na	na	na	na
Moldova	na	**75**	73	78	76	77	72	69	75	81	72	78	76	72	78	83
Montenegro	na	**51**	53	50	59	51	46	45	51	65	44	49	58	46	58	60
Morocco	na	**24**	22	27	27	23	17	22	25	33	21	20	29	18	24	36
Netherlands	58	**33**	32	35	44	33	27	32	32	37	31	32	37	31	35	29
New Zealand	na	**na**	na	na	na	na	na	na	na	na	na	na	na	na	na	na
Nigeria	69	**na**	na	na	na	na	na	na	na	na	na	na	na	na	na	na
Northern Ireland	49	**40**	36	44	43	41	38	32	42	53	35	35	44	31	40	49
Norway	40	**29**	32	26	28	29	29	22	30	34	na	na	na	25	29	31
Pakistan	na	**na**	na	na	na	na	na	na	na	na	na	na	na	na	na	na
Peru	na	**na**	na	na	na	na	na	na	na	na	na	na	na	na	na	na
Philippines	na	**na**	na	na	na	na	na	na	na	na	na	na	na	na	na	na
Poland	na	**43**	42	44	50	38	45	39	49	48	38	43	54	41	45	48
Portugal	57	**69**	64	74	77	64	67	66	71	81	58	65	71	67	69	68
Puerto Rico	na	**na**	na	na	na	na	na	na	na	na	na	na	na	na	na	na
Romania	na	**39**	41	37	46	36	38	38	40	38	38	37	40	37	39	44
Russian Fed.	56	**26**	24	27	32	25	22	20	24	32	21	25	30	25	27	30
Serbia	na	**27**	30	23	35	27	23	18	30	32	26	21	30	22	30	42
Singapore	na	**na**	na	na	na	na	na	na	na	na	na	na	na	na	na	na
Slovakia	na	**55**	56	53	63	53	49	50	55	67	47	55	59	46	60	72
Slovenia	46	**37**	37	37	39	32	41	39	35	37	37	38	41	37	38	37
South Africa	na	**na**	na	na	na	na	na	na	na	na	na	na	na	na	na	na
Spain	48	**53**	53	53	52	52	54	51	55	54	52	55	58	51	54	53
Sweden	58	**29**	34	24	31	27	30	20	27	39	24	29	35	38	28	30
Switzerland	na	**43**	38	47	54	39	40	35	44	45	41	42	47	42	43	42
Taiwan	na	**64**	63	65	62	62	70	69	62	60	67	59	64	65	62	58
Tanzania	na	**na**	na	na	na	na	na	na	na	na	na	na	na	na	na	na
Turkey	37	**40**	36	45	39	43	37	41	38	41	39	38	47	41	40	39
Uganda	na	**na**	na	na	na	na	na	na	na	na	na	na	na	na	na	na
Ukraine	na	**45**	44	47	55	47	37	22	46	51	36	45	56	42	48	63
United States	45	**na**	na	na	na	na	na	na	na	na	na	na	na	na	na	na
Uruguay	na	**na**	na	na	na	na	na	na	na	na	na	na	na	na	na	na
Venezuela	na	**na**	na	na	na	na	na	na	na	na	na	na	na	na	na	na
Vietnam	na	**na**	na	na	na	na	na	na	na	na	na	na	na	na	na	na
Zimbabwe	na	**na**	na	na	na	na	na	na	na	na	na	na	na	na	na	na
Total	49	**44**	44	44	48	43	43	43	44	47	41	44	49	44	45	45

RANKING

Country	2000
Albania	84
Moldova	75
Italy	69
Portugal	69
Taiwan	64
Ireland	60
Georgia	60
Armenia	60
Hungary	59
Luxembourg	58
Malta	56
Slovakia	55
Spain	53
Montenegro	51
France	48
Bosnia and Herz.	48
Belgium	47
Belarus	47
Ukraine	45
Iceland	45
Croatia	44
Bulgaria	43
Poland	43
Czech Republic	43
Switzerland	43
Turkey	40
Northern Ireland	40
China	39
Romania	39
Austria	38
Germany	37
Slovenia	37
Latvia	35
Netherlands	33
Macedonia	33
Estonia	31
Lithuania	31
Norway	29
Sweden	29
Azerbaijan	28
Serbia	27
Denmark	27
Great Britain	26
Russian Fed.	26
Greece	25
Finland	25
Morocco	24
Algeria	16
Total	44

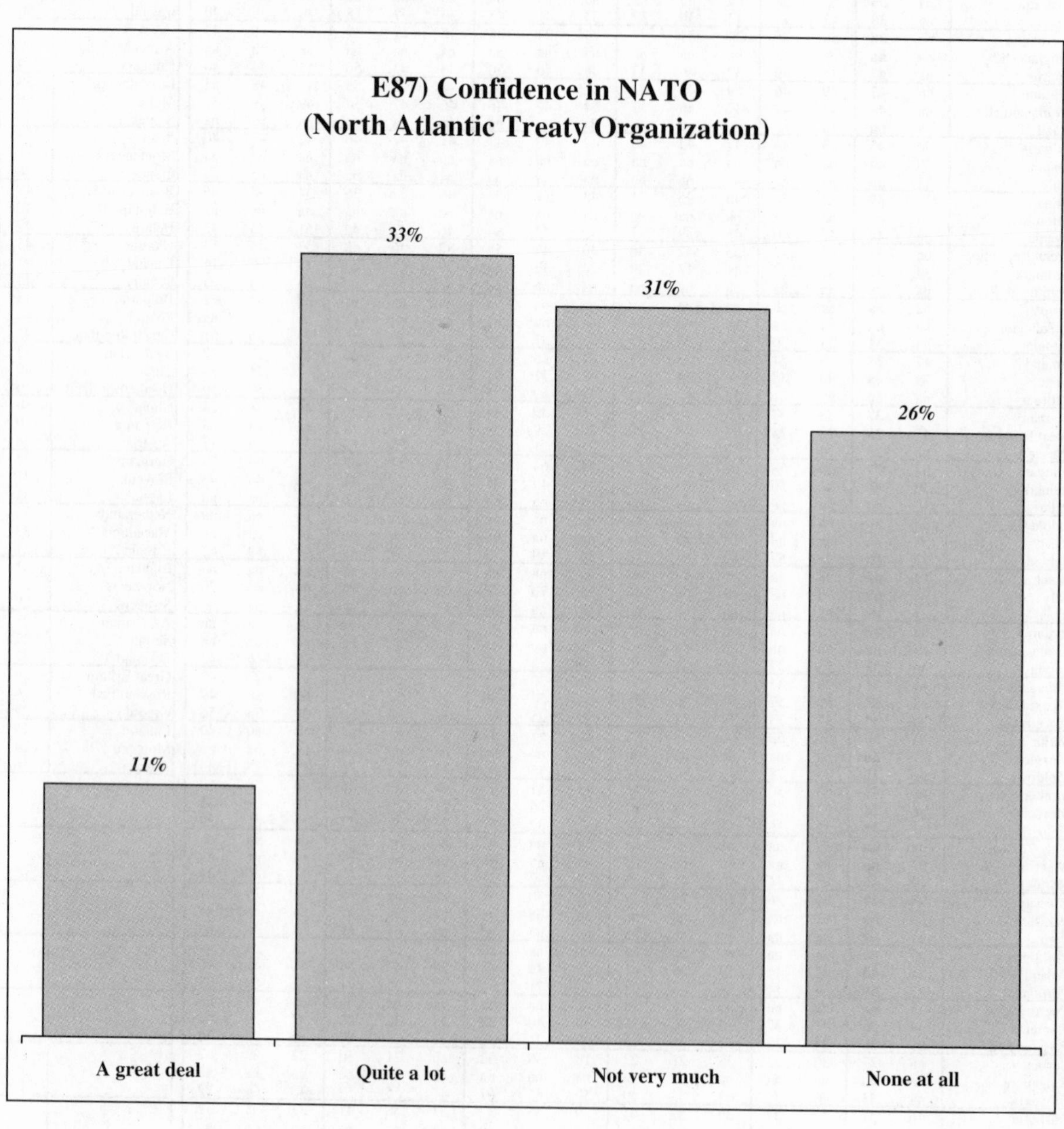
E87) Confidence in NATO
(North Atlantic Treaty Organization)
11%
33%
31%
26%
A great deal
Quite a lot
Not very much
None at all

E087) CONFIDENCE: NATO

I am going to name a number of organizations. For each one, could you tell me how much confidence you have in them: is it a great deal of confidence, quite a lot of confidence, not very much confidence or none at all? NATO (North Atlantic Treaty

(WVS: V161; EVS: o26)

A great deal / Quite a lot (%)

Country	Wave		Gender		Age			Education			Income			Values		
	1990	2000	Male	Female	16-29	30-49	50+	Lower	Middle	Upper	Lower	Middle	Upper	Mat	Mixed	Postm.
Albania	na	**86**	88	85	86	87	86	86	86	87	86	87	87	85	88	82
Algeria	na	**6**	7	5	7	6	5	11	6	5	7	4	6	9	6	1
Argentina	na	**na**	na	na	na	na	na	na	na	na	na	na	na	na	na	na
Armenia	na	**na**	na	na	na	na	na	na	na	na	na	na	na	na	na	na
Australia	na	**na**	na	na	na	na	na	na	na	na	na	na	na	na	na	na
Austria	na	**28**	28	28	31	27	27	24	31	32	21	31	32	21	29	27
Azerbaijan	na	**na**	na	na	na	na	na	na	na	na	na	na	na	na	na	na
Bangladesh	na	**89**	90	87	87	90	92	88	88	91	89	88	90	87	91	80
Belarus	na	**21**	18	24	25	21	19	20	21	24	19	20	28	22	22	18
Belgium	46	**44**	46	42	50	45	41	34	43	53	34	42	51	42	45	47
Bosnia and Herz.	na	**38**	40	37	36	37	42	45	39	30	38	39	42	40	39	44
Brazil	na	**na**	na	na	na	na	na	na	na	na	na	na	na	na	na	na
Bulgaria	28	**na**	na	na	na	na	na	na	na	na	na	na	na	na	na	na
Canada	50	**57**	62	51	57	57	57	47	60	59	49	60	61	61	57	55
Chile	29	**50**	49	52	53	49	49	49	52	51	47	52	54	48	52	50
China	22	**26**	23	32	21	32	18	29	28	12	27	24	25	25	25	39
Colombia	na	**na**	na	na	na	na	na	na	na	na	na	na	na	na	na	na
Croatia	na	**56**	58	53	59	54	55	62	54	42	60	57	52	63	57	47
Czech Republic	35	**44**	45	43	53	42	40	41	45	54	36	46	47	29	47	54
Denmark	52	**59**	64	54	64	56	60	57	73	58	61	59	62	56	62	44
Dominican Rep.	na	**na**	na	na	na	na	na	na	na	na	na	na	na	na	na	na
Egypt	na	**na**	na	na	na	na	na	na	na	na	na	na	na	na	na	na
El Salvador	na	**na**	na	na	na	na	na	na	na	na	na	na	na	na	na	na
Estonia	na	**37**	43	31	41	34	38	34	36	41	24	37	42	26	44	51
Finland	29	**na**	na	na	na	na	na	na	na	na	na	na	na	na	na	na
France	60	**na**	na	na	na	na	na	na	na	na	na	na	na	na	na	na
Georgia	na	**na**	na	na	na	na	na	na	na	na	na	na	na	na	na	na
Germany	18	**51**	57	47	44	53	53	49	53	55	48	51	54	59	50	46
Great Britain	60	**59**	64	53	57	57	62	57	61	62	56	62	62	na	na	na
Greece	na	**7**	6	7	6	6	11	8	7	7	7	4	11	12	7	1
Hungary	42	**na**	na	na	na	na	na	na	na	na	na	na	na	na	na	na
Iceland	35	**47**	50	44	52	45	46	45	51	44	42	45	53	49	49	33
India	35	**na**	na	na	na	na	na	na	na	na	na	na	na	na	na	na
Indonesia	na	**na**	na	na	na	na	na	na	na	na	na	na	na	na	na	na
Iran	na	**na**	na	na	na	na	na	na	na	na	na	na	na	na	na	na
Ireland	59	**na**	na	na	na	na	na	na	na	na	na	na	na	na	na	na
Israel	na	**na**	na	na	na	na	na	na	na	na	na	na	na	na	na	na
Italy	54	**56**	57	54	61	52	56	56	59	49	56	56	55	60	59	49
Japan	27	**na**	na	na	na	na	na	na	na	na	na	na	na	na	na	na
Jordan	na	**na**	na	na	na	na	na	na	na	na	na	na	na	na	na	na
Korea, South	na	**na**	na	na	na	na	na	na	na	na	na	na	na	na	na	na
Latvia	na	**36**	36	35	40	32	38	35	35	38	34	38	37	30	38	49
Lithuania	na	**36**	38	34	46	30	33	31	37	36	32	32	40	39	33	40
Luxembourg	na	**62**	65	59	66	61	61	65	59	64	62	59	55	66	65	51
Macedonia	na	**27**	30	25	34	30	18	41	19	25	27	28	23	23	27	54
Malta	na	**52**	53	51	53	47	56	45	51	74	43	50	65	45	55	66
Mexico	27	**32**	35	29	34	30	34	30	32	40	30	29	39	31	32	36
Moldova	na	**66**	63	68	67	66	63	61	65	71	64	67	65	59	70	84
Montenegro	na	**19**	21	16	25	17	16	17	20	20	8	17	24	12	25	24
Morocco	na	**11**	11	11	10	12	15	11	8	15	15	6	11	13	10	15
Netherlands	50	**52**	55	48	60	52	47	47	59	47	51	50	55	51	55	42
New Zealand	na	**na**	na	na	na	na	na	na	na	na	na	na	na	na	na	na
Nigeria	55	**na**	na	na	na	na	na	na	na	na	na	na	na	na	na	na
Northern Ireland	53	**na**	na	na	na	na	na	na	na	na	na	na	na	na	na	na
Norway	67	**na**	na	na	na	na	na	na	na	na	na	na	na	na	na	na
Pakistan	na	**na**	na	na	na	na	na	na	na	na	na	na	na	na	na	na
Peru	na	**na**	na	na	na	na	na	na	na	na	na	na	na	na	na	na
Philippines	na	**63**	66	61	65	61	65	65	62	64	59	65	65	67	62	58
Poland	na	**57**	61	52	63	52	59	53	61	61	50	60	62	55	60	52
Portugal	35	**68**	70	65	71	66	67	65	71	73	58	69	61	67	68	67
Puerto Rico	na	**na**	na	na	na	na	na	na	na	na	na	na	na	na	na	na
Romania	47	**35**	38	32	42	32	33	30	38	34	35	33	36	33	37	43
Russian Fed.	68	**8**	8	8	10	10	5	6	7	12	8	7	9	8	9	3
Serbia	na	**6**	7	4	8	6	5	5	6	6	5	4	7	4	7	11
Singapore	na	**na**	na	na	na	na	na	na	na	na	na	na	na	na	na	na
Slovakia	na	**36**	36	35	42	37	29	31	36	48	27	34	42	26	42	59
Slovenia	25	**37**	38	36	41	32	40	39	36	34	37	37	38	42	36	39
South Africa	na	**60**	62	56	61	60	53	68	54	26	66	65	51	55	63	66
Spain	19	**33**	33	34	30	32	37	34	32	33	35	34	35	36	36	22
Sweden	36	**41**	43	39	43	40	41	30	44	46	34	44	47	49	44	33
Switzerland	na	**na**	na	na	na	na	na	na	na	na	na	na	na	na	na	na
Taiwan	na	**na**	na	na	na	na	na	na	na	na	na	na	na	na	na	na
Tanzania	na	**na**	na	na	na	na	na	na	na	na	na	na	na	na	na	na
Turkey	47	**39**	35	43	38	38	42	37	43	34	36	40	42	42	39	34
Uganda	na	**53**	60	45	53	51	64	42	56	63	43	55	56	56	48	76
Ukraine	na	**32**	31	33	41	32	26	22	30	39	24	32	41	30	33	52
United States	52	**53**	56	50	52	51	58	46	53	57	45	54	63	62	54	50
Uruguay	na	**na**	na	na	na	na	na	na	na	na	na	na	na	na	na	na
Venezuela	na	**49**	50	47	49	51	44	39	50	56	44	47	55	40	51	55
Vietnam	na	**na**	na	na	na	na	na	na	na	na	na	na	na	na	na	na
Zimbabwe	na	**38**	35	42	37	40	35	43	34	47	49	36	32	29	41	42
Total	41	**44**	46	41	46	43	43	45	42	43	40	45	46	40	45	43

RANKING

Country	2000
Bangladesh	89
Albania	86
Portugal	68
Moldova	66
Philippines	63
Luxembourg	62
South Africa	60
Denmark	59
Great Britain	59
Canada	57
Poland	57
Italy	56
Croatia	56
Uganda	53
United States	53
Malta	52
Netherlands	52
Germany	51
Chile	50
Venezuela	49
Iceland	47
Belgium	44
Czech Republic	44
Sweden	41
Turkey	39
Bosnia and Herz.	38
Zimbabwe	38
Estonia	37
Slovenia	37
Latvia	36
Lithuania	36
Slovakia	36
Romania	35
Spain	33
Mexico	32
Ukraine	32
Austria	28
Macedonia	27
China	26
Belarus	21
Montenegro	19
Morocco	11
Russian Fed.	8
Greece	7
Algeria	6
Serbia	6
Total	44

E088) CONFIDENCE: THE UNITED NATIONS

I am going to name a number of organizations. For each one, could you tell me how much confidence you have in them: is it a great deal of confidence, quite a lot of confidence, not very much confidence or none at all? United Nations.

A great deal / Quite a lot (%)

(WVS: V162; EVS: V210)

Country	Wave		Gender		Age			Education			Income			Values		
	1990	2000	Male	Female	16-29	30-49	50+	Lower	Middle	Upper	Lower	Middle	Upper	Mat	Mixed	Postm.
Albania	na	**86**	87	84	85	87	85	85	86	86	84	87	87	85	87	86
Algeria	na	**15**	12	18	13	20	8	16	16	12	15	14	14	17	13	12
Argentina	na	**42**	45	38	42	42	41	36	47	51	37	40	47	42	42	40
Armenia	na	**70**	66	73	76	63	69	70	70	70	74	65	67	69	70	74
Australia	na	**50**	50	51	56	48	47	47	52	51	50	54	46	47	52	49
Austria	na	**42**	42	41	48	40	40	38	44	50	37	42	46	31	41	46
Azerbaijan	na	**33**	35	31	30	36	29	32	30	38	20	33	44	31	33	48
Bangladesh	na	**93**	93	94	94	93	94	94	90	95	94	92	94	93	93	88
Belarus	na	**53**	51	55	56	53	52	54	54	51	53	51	59	51	54	62
Belgium	na	**45**	47	43	54	46	40	34	44	54	37	42	51	38	47	50
Bosnia and Herz.	na	**39**	38	40	37	37	44	44	39	36	39	40	42	39	40	42
Brazil	na	**70**	74	66	73	68	69	64	73	79	63	72	76	66	70	81
Bulgaria	na	**40**	39	42	44	37	41	37	38	49	37	42	44	39	42	25
Canada	na	**65**	67	63	70	65	63	60	66	68	59	66	67	59	65	68
Chile	na	**58**	57	59	57	57	60	54	60	58	52	62	63	55	58	62
China	na	**69**	67	73	62	70	76	79	67	55	78	73	56	67	70	77
Colombia	na	**na**	na	na	na	na	na	na	na	na	na	na	na	na	na	na
Croatia	na	**47**	47	47	48	44	49	54	45	33	52	45	45	53	47	43
Czech Republic	na	**48**	49	47	57	47	45	44	52	53	39	50	53	37	51	56
Denmark	na	**64**	66	62	67	61	66	62	72	65	65	65	65	53	65	60
Dominican Rep.	na	**44**	46	42	47	34	80	22	39	48	36	44	65	44	43	48
Egypt	na	**32**	27	37	34	32	29	32	34	29	33	31	31	30	34	27
El Salvador	na	**51**	53	50	51	48	57	48	53	57	52	49	59	na	na	na
Estonia	na	**43**	47	40	50	43	40	37	47	44	26	45	51	40	46	59
Finland	na	**44**	42	47	56	46	36	41	51	44	50	41	43	43	45	43
France	na	**54**	52	56	56	54	53	52	52	60	48	55	56	58	54	52
Georgia	na	**61**	59	62	61	62	58	62	61	59	57	63	65	61	60	60
Germany	na	**52**	54	51	50	52	53	50	55	50	48	56	50	59	53	38
Great Britain	na	**60**	61	59	66	56	62	59	64	56	64	64	57	na	na	na
Greece	na	**19**	16	21	20	15	24	16	19	19	18	16	23	25	20	10
Hungary	na	**59**	59	59	65	61	52	54	67	68	50	57	66	55	63	72
Iceland	na	**72**	72	73	77	70	72	70	74	74	70	75	72	65	75	68
India	na	**47**	50	41	52	43	48	37	47	56	37	44	51	54	45	43
Indonesia	na	**48**	47	50	45	49	49	51	51	44	51	43	46	45	50	50
Iran	na	**36**	37	35	35	39	34	36	38	34	33	36	36	30	38	41
Ireland	na	**63**	61	64	65	64	59	56	65	66	56	64	65	62	63	60
Israel	na	**na**	na	na	na	na	na	na	na	na	na	na	na	na	na	na
Italy	na	**68**	66	70	72	67	66	66	71	66	68	66	70	68	68	68
Japan	na	**61**	59	64	64	58	63	54	60	68	58	62	63	70	63	49
Jordan	na	**36**	24	50	38	37	32	39	36	31	46	30	32	41	33	35
Korea, South	na	**62**	61	63	53	64	69	63	65	58	60	63	64	64	62	52
Latvia	na	**48**	50	45	51	44	50	45	46	56	45	46	54	44	49	54
Lithuania	na	**47**	49	45	53	47	42	38	49	52	39	41	52	45	47	60
Luxembourg	na	**65**	65	65	66	65	65	66	64	65	68	62	61	69	64	62
Macedonia	na	**37**	41	33	42	39	30	49	28	38	37	37	34	34	36	58
Malta	na	**63**	62	64	67	58	66	51	64	84	56	64	71	56	66	77
Mexico	na	**46**	48	43	47	44	45	41	46	60	43	45	55	42	47	50
Moldova	na	**74**	71	77	76	74	71	70	73	79	72	73	75	68	78	84
Montenegro	na	**44**	49	40	55	44	39	38	44	61	26	42	57	35	55	50
Morocco	na	**13**	11	16	12	15	12	13	11	18	11	12	12	12	12	18
Netherlands	na	**55**	58	53	61	55	52	50	62	53	53	53	62	50	58	51
New Zealand	na	**54**	53	55	64	57	50	51	52	59	52	55	57	65	56	55
Nigeria	na	**70**	72	68	71	70	67	64	74	74	68	73	69	71	70	70
Northern Ireland	na	**53**	49	57	51	56	51	47	54	63	49	53	55	51	51	59
Norway	na	**73**	73	74	77	73	72	72	76	72	na	na	na	68	74	76
Pakistan	na	**22**	22	22	22	23	19	22	25	18	22	22	25	23	21	50
Peru	na	**44**	47	41	44	44	44	39	42	50	38	43	55	36	46	45
Philippines	na	**77**	80	73	79	75	75	73	77	79	75	77	77	77	77	69
Poland	na	**58**	61	55	60	55	61	54	63	61	56	58	63	58	59	58
Portugal	na	**71**	74	68	74	70	70	69	75	78	59	71	67	70	72	73
Puerto Rico	na	**67**	70	65	61	64	73	70	67	67	69	67	66	68	67	68
Romania	na	**44**	48	40	51	44	41	41	46	46	41	40	49	40	45	61
Russian Fed.	na	**27**	28	25	35	26	22	21	26	33	23	25	30	25	30	22
Serbia	na	**17**	18	16	23	14	17	17	16	19	15	15	16	15	18	23
Singapore	na	**na**	na	na	na	na	na	na	na	na	na	na	na	na	na	na
Slovakia	na	**52**	55	50	59	52	47	46	53	63	43	51	60	46	56	72
Slovenia	na	**49**	47	51	52	42	55	54	49	40	48	53	47	54	50	46
South Africa	na	**67**	71	63	72	65	63	70	65	61	66	75	61	68	67	65
Spain	na	**49**	47	51	51	45	51	49	49	50	48	54	52	50	51	45
Sweden	na	**74**	72	76	77	75	71	73	76	71	70	80	72	76	74	71
Switzerland	na	**43**	42	44	55	43	37	39	43	49	40	36	49	45	42	46
Taiwan	na	**49**	47	52	45	48	56	61	54	37	57	48	45	52	47	42
Tanzania	na	**82**	78	86	83	79	86	84	81	76	83	79	86	81	84	71
Turkey	na	**46**	42	51	46	45	49	47	46	46	46	45	49	44	47	43
Uganda	na	**87**	91	84	89	85	92	86	87	90	85	85	86	88	87	89
Ukraine	na	**55**	56	55	63	56	49	30	56	63	50	50	66	52	58	66
United States	na	**57**	55	60	60	55	59	55	57	59	54	58	62	66	57	54
Uruguay	na	**56**	60	53	53	53	59	54	57	62	52	59	58	60	58	52
Venezuela	na	**52**	52	52	54	52	49	41	54	59	47	52	58	50	52	57
Vietnam	na	**61**	60	62	60	61	62	54	70	57	68	60	59	75	58	68
Zimbabwe	na	**70**	65	76	68	72	72	76	66	52	71	71	70	69	71	74
Total	na	**54**	54	54	56	53	53	53	55	54	52	53	56	52	55	54

RANKING	
Country	**2000**
Bangladesh	93
Uganda	87
Albania	86
Tanzania	82
Philippines	77
Moldova	74
Sweden	74
Norway	73
Iceland	72
Portugal	71
Zimbabwe	70
Brazil	70
Nigeria	70
Armenia	70
China	69
Italy	68
South Africa	67
Puerto Rico	67
Canada	65
Luxembourg	65
Denmark	64
Malta	63
Ireland	63
Korea, South	62
Japan	61
Vietnam	61
Georgia	61
Great Britain	60
Hungary	59
Poland	58
Chile	58
United States	57
Uruguay	56
Ukraine	55
Netherlands	55
New Zealand	54
France	54
Belarus	53
Northern Ireland	53
Slovakia	52
Venezuela	52
Germany	52
El Salvador	51
Australia	50
Taiwan	49
Slovenia	49
Spain	49
Czech Republic	48
Latvia	48
Indonesia	48
Lithuania	47
India	47
Croatia	47
Turkey	46
Mexico	46
Belgium	45
Montenegro	44
Romania	44
Finland	44
Peru	44
Dominican Rep.	44
Estonia	43
Switzerland	43
Austria	42
Argentina	42
Bulgaria	40
Bosnia and Herz.	39
Macedonia	37
Jordan	36
Iran	36
Azerbaijan	33
Egypt	32
Russian Fed.	27
Pakistan	22
Greece	19
Serbia	17
Algeria	15
Morocco	13
Total	54

E110) SATISFACTION WITH DEMOCRACY

On the whole are you very satisfied, rather satisfied, not very satisfied or not at all satisfied with the way democracy is developing in our country?

(WVS: V168; EVS: V213)

Very satisfied / Rather satisfied (%)

Country	Wave 1990	Wave 2000	Gender Male	Gender Female	Age 16-29	Age 30-49	Age 50+	Education Lower	Education Middle	Education Upper	Income Lower	Income Middle	Income Upper	Values Mat	Values Mixed	Values Postm.
Albania	na	**27**	27	27	28	27	25	23	29	32	22	32	28	25	27	39
Algeria	na	**41**	40	43	40	41	44	43	41	39	44	45	37	40	45	25
Argentina	na	**44**	44	44	42	49	41	42	48	45	45	44	44	39	48	40
Armenia	na	**na**	na	na	na	na	na	na	na	na	na	na	na	na	na	na
Australia	na	**na**	na	na	na	na	na	na	na	na	na	na	na	na	na	na
Austria	na	**77**	79	75	77	75	78	77	77	76	77	78	81	67	80	73
Azerbaijan	na	**na**	na	na	na	na	na	na	na	na	na	na	na	na	na	na
Bangladesh	na	**77**	73	83	78	76	80	81	76	70	84	75	74	81	74	76
Belarus	na	**33**	33	33	21	28	53	54	29	22	36	34	26	38	32	8
Belgium	na	**49**	48	50	57	45	50	45	48	53	41	49	55	53	48	46
Bosnia and Herz.	na	**34**	37	32	34	34	34	37	33	33	33	34	40	33	34	37
Brazil	na	**na**	na	na	na	na	na	na	na	na	na	na	na	na	na	na
Bulgaria	na	**28**	28	27	34	28	24	20	30	35	22	25	33	22	33	42
Canada	na	**67**	69	66	68	67	67	62	68	71	60	66	74	73	67	66
Chile	na	**60**	59	60	60	61	57	56	59	69	55	64	63	55	62	60
China	na	**88**	86	91	85	88	90	92	87	76	90	89	85	89	87	77
Colombia	na	**na**	na	na	na	na	na	na	na	na	na	na	na	na	na	na
Croatia	na	**17**	17	17	13	19	18	18	16	19	26	17	12	22	18	8
Czech Republic	na	**37**	39	36	43	39	33	34	39	47	29	36	47	33	38	47
Denmark	na	**67**	68	66	70	69	64	60	77	74	66	68	70	63	68	63
Dominican Rep.	na	**na**	na	na	na	na	na	na	na	na	na	na	na	na	na	na
Egypt	na	**95**	96	94	94	95	95	95	95	94	95	94	94	94	95	97
El Salvador	na	**na**	na	na	na	na	na	na	na	na	na	na	na	na	na	na
Estonia	na	**36**	40	32	47	32	33	33	35	41	27	33	43	30	41	30
Finland	na	**57**	57	56	74	51	53	50	62	72	51	56	62	60	56	52
France	na	**49**	52	47	44	50	51	47	51	55	45	46	59	46	52	49
Georgia	na	**na**	na	na	na	na	na	na	na	na	na	na	na	na	na	na
Germany	na	**75**	75	76	80	74	75	74	77	74	72	77	81	77	74	76
Great Britain	na	**54**	54	53	57	58	49	51	54	66	52	57	59	na	na	na
Greece	na	**55**	57	54	55	55	59	53	51	59	52	58	59	60	59	46
Hungary	na	**33**	33	33	34	29	36	33	29	38	24	30	44	32	35	16
Iceland	na	**65**	68	62	78	64	57	62	70	65	60	66	67	68	67	46
India	na	**63**	64	62	67	62	63	63	65	62	65	64	62	66	63	56
Indonesia	na	**29**	33	25	20	30	32	29	29	29	30	28	34	27	29	30
Iran	na	**67**	66	67	67	67	67	67	66	65	63	71	68	73	63	67
Ireland	na	**64**	61	66	64	63	63	62	61	70	63	62	64	64	65	58
Israel	na	**na**	na	na	na	na	na	na	na	na	na	na	na	na	na	na
Italy	na	**36**	37	35	35	38	35	34	38	36	32	38	40	37	36	35
Japan	na	**41**	43	40	31	39	47	44	41	41	42	41	42	57	40	29
Jordan	na	**72**	70	74	73	71	74	75	75	63	76	66	73	78	70	53
Korea, South	na	**33**	33	33	30	32	36	52	35	27	29	32	37	37	30	27
Latvia	na	**30**	31	30	33	29	30	30	29	36	27	27	37	26	32	21
Lithuania	na	**26**	24	27	29	20	29	26	25	27	20	29	29	24	24	31
Luxembourg	na	**83**	83	84	84	81	86	83	84	80	82	83	84	89	85	77
Macedonia	na	**18**	18	17	18	16	20	15	20	15	17	18	18	18	18	4
Malta	na	**78**	79	77	78	76	80	73	79	85	73	82	83	74	79	85
Mexico	na	**41**	41	42	41	40	45	43	40	37	45	44	42	44	41	41
Moldova	na	**10**	11	10	11	9	12	13	11	8	8	9	13	10	12	9
Montenegro	na	**33**	34	32	41	31	29	27	35	37	20	25	47	27	40	35
Morocco	na	**44**	39	50	40	45	55	50	30	27	53	34	42	51	41	28
Netherlands	na	**74**	75	73	78	73	73	66	80	74	68	74	79	73	74	75
New Zealand	na	**na**	na	na	na	na	na	na	na	na	na	na	na	na	na	na
Nigeria	na	**60**	60	60	59	60	59	63	57	58	59	58	61	58	61	58
Northern Ireland	na	**29**	30	27	29	26	32	27	26	38	25	29	30	34	28	23
Norway	na	**na**	na	na	na	na	na	na	na	na	na	na	na	na	na	na
Pakistan	na	**18**	16	21	23	16	15	11	28	21	10	21	23	14	24	27
Peru	na	**35**	37	33	33	36	38	30	36	37	31	34	42	34	36	34
Philippines	na	**45**	46	44	48	44	44	46	45	44	41	44	50	44	46	51
Poland	na	**45**	47	43	58	44	39	39	49	64	33	50	60	41	47	42
Portugal	na	**77**	78	75	76	77	77	76	74	88	82	73	78	81	74	73
Puerto Rico	na	**54**	62	49	50	53	56	53	51	55	54	56	53	53	56	49
Romania	na	**21**	22	19	24	18	22	22	19	22	24	15	23	19	21	31
Russian Fed.	na	**7**	7	7	11	7	5	7	7	7	6	7	8	6	8	8
Serbia	na	**45**	45	46	53	46	41	43	45	49	41	45	48	46	45	45
Singapore	na	**na**	na	na	na	na	na	na	na	na	na	na	na	na	na	na
Slovakia	na	**23**	23	24	30	22	21	22	23	32	19	22	28	20	26	39
Slovenia	na	**45**	46	44	46	44	46	42	44	53	44	40	60	42	47	46
South Africa	na	**61**	63	59	61	63	54	59	64	52	66	64	56	60	61	71
Spain	na	**66**	66	67	63	65	70	67	64	69	63	73	66	71	67	60
Sweden	na	**60**	61	59	58	60	61	63	60	58	59	57	65	63	63	52
Switzerland	na	**na**	na	na	na	na	na	na	na	na	na	na	na	na	na	na
Taiwan	na	**na**	na	na	na	na	na	na	na	na	na	na	na	na	na	na
Tanzania	na	**76**	75	77	76	74	79	77	76	71	76	74	77	78	77	57
Turkey	na	**24**	21	27	23	22	34	25	22	24	24	24	24	33	23	18
Uganda	na	**68**	64	71	69	67	66	63	70	64	67	68	63	69	66	70
Ukraine	na	**16**	17	14	17	18	12	13	13	23	11	16	20	14	17	19
United States	na	**65**	66	64	66	60	69	61	61	68	60	65	72	72	66	58
Uruguay	na	**na**	na	na	na	na	na	na	na	na	na	na	na	na	na	na
Venezuela	na	**62**	65	60	58	63	70	69	62	56	63	63	61	64	62	62
Vietnam	na	**97**	97	96	96	97	96	97	97	94	98	94	98	90	99	96
Zimbabwe	na	**30**	29	31	32	28	28	32	28	na	35	36	20	30	29	38
Total	na	**49**	50	49	51	49	48	51	48	50	47	49	52	46	51	51

RANKING

Country	2000
Vietnam	97
Egypt	95
China	88
Luxembourg	83
Malta	78
Bangladesh	77
Austria	77
Portugal	77
Tanzania	76
Germany	75
Netherlands	74
Jordan	72
Uganda	68
Canada	67
Denmark	67
Iran	67
Spain	66
Iceland	65
United States	65
Ireland	64
India	63
Venezuela	62
South Africa	61
Sweden	60
Nigeria	60
Chile	60
Finland	57
Greece	55
Great Britain	54
Puerto Rico	54
France	49
Belgium	49
Serbia	45
Poland	45
Philippines	45
Slovenia	45
Argentina	44
Morocco	44
Japan	41
Mexico	41
Algeria	41
Czech Republic	37
Italy	36
Estonia	36
Peru	35
Bosnia and Herz.	34
Belarus	33
Hungary	33
Montenegro	33
Korea, South	33
Latvia	30
Zimbabwe	30
Indonesia	29
Northern Ireland	29
Bulgaria	28
Albania	27
Lithuania	26
Turkey	24
Slovakia	23
Romania	21
Pakistan	18
Macedonia	18
Croatia	17
Ukraine	16
Moldova	10
Russian Fed.	7
Total	49

E111A) RATE POLITICAL SYSTEM TODAY

People have different views about the system for governing this country. Here is a scale for rating how well things are going? (1 = very bad; 10 = very good)

% Very good (codes 7 to 10)

(WVS: V163A; EVS: V214)

Country	Wave 1990	Wave 2000	Gender Male	Gender Female	Age 16-29	Age 30-49	Age 50+	Education Lower	Education Middle	Education Upper	Income Lower	Income Middle	Income Upper	Values Mat	Values Mixed	Values Postm.
Albania	na	**26**	27	26	27	28	24	23	28	30	26	27	27	27	27	15
Algeria	na	**23**	20	26	17	26	28	28	22	19	21	29	25	25	23	11
Argentina	na	**25**	27	24	22	28	25	25	24	31	26	25	25	22	28	21
Armenia	na	**14**	14	13	15	14	11	12	15	11	17	11	12	13	13	27
Australia	na	**18**	22	13	18	20	15	16	16	20	14	20	19	19	17	19
Austria	na	**39**	43	35	41	39	37	36	39	47	37	38	45	33	39	39
Azerbaijan	na	**54**	56	53	59	51	52	60	48	65	42	53	73	52	57	60
Bangladesh	na	**na**	na	na	na	na	na	na	na	na	na	na	na	na	na	na
Belarus	na	**18**	18	18	11	13	30	28	16	9	21	16	18	19	18	10
Belgium	na	**22**	26	18	19	21	24	19	23	23	20	19	29	20	23	20
Bosnia and Herz.	na	**11**	11	11	9	10	14	13	11	9	11	12	10	10	12	4
Brazil	na	**18**	22	14	16	16	25	19	17	17	22	16	15	18	19	13
Bulgaria	na	**21**	23	20	25	21	20	12	25	27	18	18	27	20	22	23
Canada	na	**na**	na	na	na	na	na	na	na	na	na	na	na	na	na	na
Chile	na	**na**	na	na	na	na	na	na	na	na	na	na	na	na	na	na
China	na	**na**	na	na	na	na	na	na	na	na	na	na	na	na	na	na
Colombia	na	**na**	na	na	na	na	na	na	na	na	na	na	na	na	na	na
Croatia	na	**7**	7	7	5	9	6	5	8	7	11	6	5	5	7	4
Czech Republic	na	**12**	13	11	13	12	11	11	11	19	9	12	15	9	12	16
Denmark	na	**28**	29	26	30	29	25	24	34	31	27	28	30	26	27	32
Dominican Rep.	na	**15**	16	14	16	14	9	20	11	16	17	15	13	16	16	11
Egypt	na	**na**	na	na	na	na	na	na	na	na	na	na	na	na	na	na
El Salvador	na	**25**	24	25	29	22	21	23	26	26	26	22	25	na	na	na
Estonia	na	**15**	18	12	21	12	15	14	13	22	10	14	17	11	16	11
Finland	na	**41**	43	38	51	38	37	34	46	56	37	39	44	41	40	40
France	na	**16**	19	13	13	18	15	12	16	26	11	14	25	11	16	25
Georgia	na	**15**	18	12	16	13	15	15	16	12	13	18	15	13	17	12
Germany	na	**46**	47	45	44	44	49	45	48	44	46	52	52	58	45	36
Great Britain	na	**23**	25	20	24	24	22	17	24	37	17	22	28	na	na	na
Greece	na	**20**	24	18	16	23	26	21	18	22	18	22	26	23	22	13
Hungary	na	**9**	9	8	6	5	13	8	8	16	7	6	13	9	9	na
Iceland	na	**45**	51	40	45	49	41	38	48	56	39	47	51	43	47	42
India	na	**28**	28	29	26	28	31	33	26	21	38	30	22	34	24	17
Indonesia	na	**23**	29	17	21	22	25	30	22	19	18	23	35	24	23	7
Iran	na	**38**	37	39	36	40	37	36	40	36	31	32	41	35	38	46
Ireland	na	**36**	40	33	32	35	40	36	33	43	37	34	38	42	36	30
Israel	na	**na**	na	na	na	na	na	na	na	na	na	na	na	na	na	na
Italy	na	**11**	14	8	8	11	12	10	10	13	9	12	14	11	10	12
Japan	na	**na**	na	na	na	na	na	na	na	na	na	na	na	na	na	na
Jordan	na	**39**	34	43	40	38	38	43	41	28	40	37	36	42	36	39
Korea, South	na	**na**	na	na	na	na	na	na	na	na	na	na	na	na	na	na
Latvia	na	**9**	9	9	11	7	10	9	9	11	10	6	11	10	9	6
Lithuania	na	**7**	8	7	7	7	8	6	7	12	8	5	9	10	5	15
Luxembourg	na	**49**	53	46	45	49	51	43	50	60	53	49	58	51	52	48
Macedonia	na	**8**	7	8	9	6	9	7	8	7	6	9	8	5	10	4
Malta	na	**60**	62	58	59	57	64	60	60	59	58	62	65	59	60	65
Mexico	na	**na**	na	na	na	na	na	na	na	na	na	na	na	na	na	na
Moldova	na	**21**	22	19	16	18	28	26	20	16	19	25	20	19	23	12
Montenegro	na	**na**	na	na	na	na	na	na	na	na	na	na	na	na	na	na
Morocco	na	**31**	27	35	27	31	43	34	17	21	36	21	27	37	26	24
Netherlands	na	**52**	58	46	59	53	47	39	53	63	47	53	59	47	53	51
New Zealand	na	**7**	8	6	9	6	7	4	7	10	7	7	6	4	6	12
Nigeria	na	**na**	na	na	na	na	na	na	na	na	na	na	na	na	na	na
Northern Ireland	na	**31**	34	29	18	28	42	31	29	39	27	35	36	35	34	20
Norway	na	**51**	59	42	56	53	44	43	51	57	na	na	na	44	51	56
Pakistan	na	**8**	8	8	9	8	7	6	10	10	8	8	8	6	11	17
Peru	na	**36**	35	37	36	36	36	35	37	36	34	36	39	38	35	37
Philippines	na	**na**	na	na	na	na	na	na	na	na	na	na	na	na	na	na
Poland	na	**11**	12	10	17	10	8	10	11	12	8	10	19	9	12	13
Portugal	na	**36**	35	37	35	30	41	37	35	28	45	34	33	38	34	33
Puerto Rico	na	**31**	29	32	27	29	34	36	31	30	38	32	25	40	30	29
Romania	na	**13**	13	13	16	11	14	15	12	14	19	11	12	13	12	18
Russian Fed.	na	**3**	2	3	4	2	3	3	3	3	2	2	4	3	2	na
Serbia	na	**na**	na	na	na	na	na	na	na	na	na	na	na	na	na	na
Singapore	na	**na**	na	na	na	na	na	na	na	na	na	na	na	na	na	na
Slovakia	na	**8**	7	9	8	8	7	8	7	13	8	7	9	7	9	6
Slovenia	na	**13**	17	9	12	12	14	10	12	20	12	14	17	8	14	8
South Africa	na	**37**	36	38	41	36	30	38	37	19	43	48	22	34	39	37
Spain	na	**33**	32	35	28	33	37	33	33	37	34	36	36	39	33	28
Sweden	na	**27**	33	21	26	26	28	22	24	35	24	26	33	32	25	33
Switzerland	na	**24**	26	23	32	20	25	24	24	27	21	25	28	27	24	23
Taiwan	na	**28**	30	27	19	31	28	30	29	27	30	29	26	24	30	42
Tanzania	na	**54**	59	48	56	53	55	51	60	52	53	52	54	55	55	50
Turkey	na	**6**	5	6	5	6	7	6	5	3	6	4	8	6	6	4
Uganda	na	**na**	na	na	na	na	na	na	na	na	na	na	na	na	na	na
Ukraine	na	**7**	10	6	7	11	4	3	8	8	5	6	12	6	9	6
United States	na	**na**	na	na	na	na	na	na	na	na	na	na	na	na	na	na
Uruguay	na	**14**	15	13	9	7	21	17	7	15	16	11	13	21	13	11
Venezuela	na	**na**	na	na	na	na	na	na	na	na	na	na	na	na	na	na
Vietnam	na	**91**	90	91	88	90	94	91	92	84	82	94	92	94	91	83
Zimbabwe	na	**na**	na	na	na	na	na	na	na	na	na	na	na	na	na	na
Total	na	**26**	27	24	25	25	26	26	24	27	24	25	27	24	26	25

RANKING

Country	2000
Vietnam	91
Malta	60
Azerbaijan	54
Tanzania	54
Netherlands	52
Norway	51
Luxembourg	49
Germany	46
Iceland	45
Finland	41
Austria	39
Jordan	39
Iran	38
South Africa	37
Ireland	36
Peru	36
Portugal	36
Spain	33
Northern Ireland	31
Morocco	31
Puerto Rico	31
Taiwan	28
India	28
Denmark	28
Sweden	27
Albania	26
Argentina	25
El Salvador	25
Switzerland	24
Indonesia	23
Great Britain	23
Algeria	23
Belgium	22
Bulgaria	21
Moldova	21
Greece	20
Brazil	18
Belarus	18
Australia	18
France	16
Estonia	15
Dominican Rep.	15
Georgia	15
Armenia	14
Uruguay	14
Romania	13
Slovenia	13
Czech Republic	12
Italy	11
Bosnia and Herz.	11
Poland	11
Latvia	9
Hungary	9
Pakistan	8
Slovakia	8
Macedonia	8
Lithuania	7
Ukraine	7
New Zealand	7
Croatia	7
Turkey	6
Russian Fed.	3
Total	26

E111B) RATE POLITICAL SYSTEM TODAY

People have different views about the system for governing this country. Here is a scale for rating how well things are going? (1 = very bad; 10 = very good)

% Bad (codes 1 to 4)

(WVS: V163A; EVS: V214)

Country	Wave		Gender		Age			Education			Income			Values		
	1990	2000	Male	Female	16-29	30-49	50+	Lower	Middle	Upper	Lower	Middle	Upper	Mat	Mixed	Postm.
Albania	na	**51**	51	50	51	51	50	51	52	47	52	49	49	49	52	64
Algeria	na	**52**	55	48	56	50	45	45	51	58	50	49	52	49	51	68
Argentina	na	**37**	35	40	35	35	41	38	35	35	40	38	33	40	36	39
Armenia	na	**62**	63	62	55	65	70	62	62	65	52	71	69	64	63	52
Australia	na	**50**	47	53	47	48	56	55	52	44	56	48	46	50	51	49
Austria	na	**21**	21	22	22	23	20	21	21	21	24	20	18	30	19	23
Azerbaijan	na	**2**	2	2	2	2	3	2	2	2	2	2	2	2	2	na
Bangladesh	na	**na**	na	na	na	na	na	na	na	na	na	na	na	na	na	na
Belarus	na	**55**	58	52	61	59	44	43	56	66	50	55	61	50	58	78
Belgium	na	**36**	37	35	39	40	31	42	37	30	46	36	31	38	35	38
Bosnia and Herz.	na	**60**	62	58	61	61	58	52	60	65	63	57	60	57	60	71
Brazil	na	**52**	48	56	55	55	41	50	54	50	48	55	55	49	52	56
Bulgaria	na	**49**	48	50	44	46	53	60	46	38	58	46	42	54	43	50
Canada	na	**na**	na	na	na	na	na	na	na	na	na	na	na	na	na	na
Chile	na	**na**	na	na	na	na	na	na	na	na	na	na	na	na	na	na
China	na	**na**	na	na	na	na	na	na	na	na	na	na	na	na	na	na
Colombia	na	**na**	na	na	na	na	na	na	na	na	na	na	na	na	na	na
Croatia	na	**67**	67	67	76	67	61	63	69	73	62	65	72	64	64	83
Czech Republic	na	**53**	56	50	46	58	52	55	51	50	56	53	50	60	51	45
Denmark	na	**36**	35	37	36	36	35	38	36	33	33	35	40	35	37	32
Dominican Rep.	na	**61**	57	64	65	57	27	53	65	61	57	62	59	66	59	64
Egypt	na	**na**	na	na	na	na	na	na	na	na	na	na	na	na	na	na
El Salvador	na	**44**	45	44	37	49	49	46	43	42	43	46	44	na	na	na
Estonia	na	**43**	40	45	34	46	44	42	45	38	49	39	41	49	38	56
Finland	na	**22**	23	20	15	24	23	24	20	13	25	22	17	21	21	24
France	na	**40**	36	44	42	42	38	44	38	33	48	40	33	41	41	38
Georgia	na	**55**	52	57	53	57	54	58	53	57	58	53	51	57	52	64
Germany	na	**23**	26	22	28	23	22	24	23	23	23	22	19	21	26	22
Great Britain	na	**32**	31	33	30	31	33	35	31	25	38	29	27	na	na	na
Greece	na	**43**	42	43	47	41	33	41	46	40	47	41	40	35	40	57
Hungary	na	**57**	58	55	55	61	53	57	58	53	68	58	47	52	59	87
Iceland	na	**18**	17	20	17	18	21	21	18	15	24	18	16	18	17	27
India	na	**24**	25	23	23	26	24	23	27	25	24	22	27	22	28	37
Indonesia	na	**37**	36	37	46	34	36	32	36	42	42	33	35	36	38	46
Iran	na	**23**	24	21	24	22	19	20	22	28	28	22	20	20	24	28
Ireland	na	**24**	23	24	23	29	19	28	25	16	22	25	22	19	26	23
Israel	na	**na**	na	na	na	na	na	na	na	na	na	na	na	na	na	na
Italy	na	**51**	51	51	57	46	51	52	51	47	51	48	49	49	52	51
Japan	na	**na**	na	na	na	na	na	na	na	na	na	na	na	na	na	na
Jordan	na	**17**	20	14	15	19	19	16	13	23	18	16	17	15	17	29
Korea, South	na	**na**	na	na	na	na	na	na	na	na	na	na	na	na	na	na
Latvia	na	**46**	48	45	48	51	42	44	46	52	47	48	43	47	45	53
Lithuania	na	**73**	75	72	70	76	73	71	76	68	77	76	71	70	75	67
Luxembourg	na	**12**	13	12	11	13	12	12	13	11	14	11	13	12	10	19
Macedonia	na	**76**	75	77	75	77	77	80	75	71	80	74	73	79	74	81
Malta	na	**12**	12	13	12	14	11	16	11	9	16	9	11	14	12	10
Mexico	na	**na**	na	na	na	na	na	na	na	na	na	na	na	na	na	na
Moldova	na	**54**	56	52	64	53	46	46	53	62	50	52	58	53	52	62
Montenegro	na	**na**	na	na	na	na	na	na	na	na	na	na	na	na	na	na
Morocco	na	**30**	37	24	35	27	25	28	42	37	30	39	32	24	34	44
Netherlands	na	**11**	11	12	8	14	10	12	11	11	11	11	10	14	10	12
New Zealand	na	**72**	71	73	61	73	76	80	75	61	75	73	69	79	75	61
Nigeria	na	**na**	na	na	na	na	na	na	na	na	na	na	na	na	na	na
Northern Ireland	na	**33**	34	32	39	40	23	34	35	22	36	29	32	28	29	51
Norway	na	**13**	14	13	11	13	16	19	11	10	na	na	na	16	13	10
Pakistan	na	**63**	63	63	63	64	61	66	60	61	66	59	65	66	59	58
Peru	na	**27**	27	27	27	28	25	27	29	25	33	25	20	26	27	31
Philippines	na	**na**	na	na	na	na	na	na	na	na	na	na	na	na	na	na
Poland	na	**55**	54	55	45	55	60	56	53	52	61	54	43	59	52	56
Portugal	na	**16**	13	19	17	19	14	17	14	20	14	18	16	13	18	21
Puerto Rico	na	**25**	28	24	29	27	23	30	27	24	28	20	28	20	26	24
Romania	na	**65**	65	65	62	67	64	65	67	60	62	69	65	67	65	58
Russian Fed.	na	**83**	83	84	82	83	85	86	84	81	87	85	79	84	84	72
Serbia	na	**na**	na	na	na	na	na	na	na	na	na	na	na	na	na	na
Singapore	na	**na**	na	na	na	na	na	na	na	na	na	na	na	na	na	na
Slovakia	na	**64**	66	62	59	65	66	66	63	58	68	63	60	68	61	33
Slovenia	na	**48**	46	50	51	53	40	49	50	40	47	49	41	51	45	56
South Africa	na	**34**	34	33	29	36	38	32	34	52	26	27	48	37	31	35
Spain	na	**23**	24	22	28	22	21	24	20	25	25	23	25	17	23	35
Sweden	na	**37**	34	41	34	40	37	35	39	36	39	37	35	22	39	35
Switzerland	na	**33**	31	34	28	35	33	40	31	29	37	35	29	31	32	40
Taiwan	na	**25**	23	27	33	26	17	24	18	30	26	20	29	27	25	8
Tanzania	na	**23**	19	28	24	21	24	30	17	12	30	24	10	23	23	25
Turkey	na	**75**	78	73	79	74	70	75	76	78	75	75	76	73	75	81
Uganda	na	**na**	na	na	na	na	na	na	na	na	na	na	na	na	na	na
Ukraine	na	**70**	69	70	66	64	77	76	70	65	77	71	59	71	70	59
United States	na	**na**	na	na	na	na	na	na	na	na	na	na	na	na	na	na
Uruguay	na	**63**	66	61	67	72	56	61	70	58	60	67	63	57	63	66
Venezuela	na	**na**	na	na	na	na	na	na	na	na	na	na	na	na	na	na
Vietnam	na	**1**	1	1	na	1	na	1	1	na	2	1	na	1	1	na
Zimbabwe	na	**na**	na	na	na	na	na	na	na	na	na	na	na	na	na	na
Total	na	**41**	41	42	42	42	40	41	43	40	45	42	41	43	40	43

RANKING	
Country	2000
Russian Fed.	83
Macedonia	76
Turkey	75
Lithuania	73
New Zealand	72
Ukraine	70
Croatia	67
Romania	65
Slovakia	64
Uruguay	63
Pakistan	63
Armenia	62
Dominican Rep.	61
Bosnia and Herz.	60
Hungary	57
Georgia	55
Poland	55
Belarus	55
Moldova	54
Czech Republic	53
Algeria	52
Brazil	52
Italy	51
Albania	51
Australia	50
Bulgaria	49
Slovenia	48
Latvia	46
El Salvador	44
Estonia	43
Greece	43
France	40
Sweden	37
Argentina	37
Indonesia	37
Belgium	36
Denmark	36
South Africa	34
Switzerland	33
Northern Ireland	33
Great Britain	32
Morocco	30
Peru	27
Puerto Rico	25
Taiwan	25
India	24
Ireland	24
Germany	23
Tanzania	23
Spain	23
Iran	23
Finland	22
Austria	21
Iceland	18
Jordan	17
Portugal	16
Norway	13
Malta	12
Luxembourg	12
Netherlands	11
Azerbaijan	2
Vietnam	1
Total	41

E112A) RATE POLITICAL SYSTEM TEN YEARS AGO

Where on this scale would you put the political system as it was ten years ago (1 = very bad; 10 = very good)

% Very good (codes 7 to 10)

(WVS: V163; EVS: V215)

Country	Wave		Gender		Age			Education			Income			Values		
	1990	2000	Male	Female	16-29	30-49	50+	Lower	Middle	Upper	Lower	Middle	Upper	Mat	Mixed	Postm.
Albania	na	**11**	11	10	10	8	15	12	9	11	13	8	11	11	11	5
Algeria	na	**na**	na	na	na	na	na	na	na	na	na	na	na	na	na	na
Argentina	na	**15**	17	15	17	13	17	16	15	10	16	17	13	18	15	16
Armenia	na	**43**	43	44	32	46	56	56	44	37	34	50	49	47	42	25
Australia	na	**31**	34	29	25	32	35	36	30	31	31	32	31	29	34	28
Austria	na	**48**	50	46	47	45	52	52	43	46	50	47	50	46	51	41
Azerbaijan	na	**58**	54	62	55	59	63	53	60	56	58	57	59	59	57	65
Bangladesh	na	**26**	25	27	24	25	32	28	23	23	24	23	30	32	20	26
Belarus	na	**36**	33	38	19	32	54	52	31	29	43	33	30	43	32	14
Belgium	na	**26**	25	26	21	23	30	30	27	20	29	27	23	25	27	24
Bosnia and Herz.	na	**54**	51	57	47	54	61	60	53	52	61	56	42	52	54	52
Brazil	na	**25**	28	22	21	24	35	31	21	19	30	23	21	28	24	23
Bulgaria	na	**31**	28	35	11	28	43	57	20	15	48	31	16	43	20	21
Canada	na	**32**	31	32	30	29	36	37	26	36	35	28	31	34	33	29
Chile	na	**23**	25	21	22	22	25	22	21	28	20	23	26	21	24	22
China	na	**64**	65	64	69	61	68	70	60	61	59	66	69	66	61	58
Colombia	na	**na**	na	na	na	na	na	na	na	na	na	na	na	na	na	na
Croatia	na	**17**	17	17	17	19	14	27	10	11	20	18	13	12	18	15
Czech Republic	na	**14**	15	13	10	12	18	21	8	6	23	14	7	27	11	5
Denmark	na	**35**	38	32	37	31	39	33	43	35	30	34	41	36	40	20
Dominican Rep.	na	**12**	13	12	14	9	na	10	7	14	14	12	15	18	11	8
Egypt	na	**68**	68	68	67	69	68	67	70	67	69	68	67	68	69	67
El Salvador	na	**39**	37	40	38	39	39	45	35	29	40	43	31	na	na	na
Estonia	na	**21**	21	22	17	22	22	24	22	16	19	27	18	21	22	13
Finland	na	**36**	39	34	36	33	39	35	39	40	37	37	34	34	37	32
France	na	**23**	24	22	22	23	24	23	26	22	26	26	20	21	23	26
Georgia	na	**41**	36	44	32	38	53	43	44	29	49	33	34	43	39	34
Germany	na	**47**	47	48	42	46	51	51	43	51	48	48	55	58	45	40
Great Britain	na	**25**	27	24	20	22	31	24	27	22	25	22	30	na	na	na
Greece	na	**23**	22	23	21	23	26	34	24	19	27	20	22	25	24	18
Hungary	na	**33**	33	34	31	30	37	34	36	24	36	34	30	38	27	39
Iceland	na	**25**	25	25	17	25	29	24	24	29	28	25	23	28	24	25
India	na	**na**	na	na	na	na	na	na	na	na	na	na	na	na	na	na
Indonesia	na	**na**	na	na	na	na	na	na	na	na	na	na	na	na	na	na
Iran	na	**na**	na	na	na	na	na	na	na	na	na	na	na	na	na	na
Ireland	na	**27**	29	25	19	25	33	34	25	20	30	25	24	38	25	20
Israel	na	**na**	na	na	na	na	na	na	na	na	na	na	na	na	na	na
Italy	na	**18**	18	19	15	17	21	22	17	13	23	18	15	29	17	16
Japan	na	**11**	13	9	4	7	16	15	10	11	12	10	11	17	10	8
Jordan	na	**na**	na	na	na	na	na	na	na	na	na	na	na	na	na	na
Korea, South	na	**8**	8	8	4	10	10	8	10	6	6	10	10	9	8	5
Latvia	na	**19**	18	20	19	18	19	24	19	11	23	19	14	22	17	17
Lithuania	na	**38**	34	42	22	34	52	56	36	14	48	46	26	36	41	18
Luxembourg	na	**46**	49	42	34	42	54	43	45	55	49	44	58	52	43	47
Macedonia	na	**47**	45	49	34	44	62	48	50	38	52	45	45	55	44	19
Malta	na	**46**	48	44	42	46	48	48	45	47	43	44	55	47	46	45
Mexico	na	**37**	36	38	36	35	42	42	34	26	42	39	30	40	36	34
Moldova	na	**22**	23	20	23	17	27	26	21	18	24	22	21	23	22	16
Montenegro	na	**19**	18	19	9	18	25	24	16	16	19	22	20	23	16	10
Morocco	na	**na**	na	na	na	na	na	na	na	na	na	na	na	na	na	na
Netherlands	na	**44**	47	42	41	44	46	43	44	46	41	44	46	44	48	33
New Zealand	na	**38**	40	37	38	38	39	38	38	40	32	39	44	37	42	28
Nigeria	na	**na**	na	na	na	na	na	na	na	na	na	na	na	na	na	na
Northern Ireland	na	**27**	28	27	19	22	34	28	24	32	26	27	27	26	31	17
Norway	na	**36**	43	29	31	39	34	29	34	46	na	na	na	34	35	42
Pakistan	na	**na**	na	na	na	na	na	na	na	na	na	na	na	na	na	na
Peru	na	**na**	na	na	na	na	na	na	na	na	na	na	na	na	na	na
Philippines	na	**27**	26	28	24	30	26	33	26	21	27	22	34	25	27	41
Poland	na	**24**	21	26	14	23	29	30	18	11	31	19	17	30	19	23
Portugal	na	**19**	20	18	16	22	19	19	18	21	18	18	24	16	22	20
Puerto Rico	na	**na**	na	na	na	na	na	na	na	na	na	na	na	na	na	na
Romania	na	**30**	27	32	18	28	37	43	25	18	46	29	21	38	24	10
Russian Fed.	na	**41**	37	45	26	37	54	63	42	25	53	44	27	46	36	48
Serbia	na	**10**	10	9	1	8	15	13	9	6	11	8	9	13	7	4
Singapore	na	**na**	na	na	na	na	na	na	na	na	na	na	na	na	na	na
Slovakia	na	**33**	32	34	23	36	37	39	32	18	38	35	29	39	30	8
Slovenia	na	**23**	22	23	18	23	25	29	22	14	29	22	17	22	22	23
South Africa	na	**13**	13	14	12	13	18	12	16	12	8	12	23	17	12	7
Spain	na	**25**	24	26	21	27	26	24	26	27	22	26	29	24	25	27
Sweden	na	**39**	41	36	34	35	44	40	36	42	42	33	41	57	36	42
Switzerland	na	**46**	48	44	40	43	52	50	45	45	42	48	50	50	49	36
Taiwan	na	**34**	30	39	35	35	31	34	32	36	33	37	32	39	32	31
Tanzania	na	**51**	46	58	50	48	60	60	39	40	61	49	38	54	49	50
Turkey	na	**51**	50	52	50	50	60	60	40	32	60	51	33	49	53	44
Uganda	na	**31**	37	26	30	28	49	28	31	41	26	37	27	26	32	42
Ukraine	na	**33**	29	36	19	28	44	53	33	19	43	29	24	37	33	19
United States	na	**39**	41	37	36	37	45	43	35	40	38	39	41	53	40	33
Uruguay	na	**22**	23	22	17	15	31	27	14	20	27	21	20	32	24	14
Venezuela	na	**23**	22	23	25	21	22	24	25	17	26	27	16	24	23	21
Vietnam	na	**71**	71	70	68	74	68	73	68	64	63	70	75	77	69	53
Zimbabwe	na	**52**	54	51	48	56	55	54	49	85	58	54	44	53	52	56
Total	na	**32**	32	32	28	31	36	36	31	28	34	33	30	36	32	26

RANKING	
Country	2000
Vietnam	71
Egypt	68
China	64
Azerbaijan	58
Bosnia and Herz.	54
Zimbabwe	52
Turkey	51
Tanzania	51
Austria	48
Germany	47
Macedonia	47
Switzerland	46
Malta	46
Luxembourg	46
Netherlands	44
Armenia	43
Russian Fed.	41
Georgia	41
United States	39
Sweden	39
El Salvador	39
Lithuania	38
New Zealand	38
Mexico	37
Finland	36
Belarus	36
Norway	36
Denmark	35
Taiwan	34
Hungary	33
Slovakia	33
Ukraine	33
Canada	32
Australia	31
Bulgaria	31
Uganda	31
Romania	30
Northern Ireland	27
Philippines	27
Ireland	27
Belgium	26
Bangladesh	26
Spain	25
Great Britain	25
Brazil	25
Iceland	25
Poland	24
France	23
Chile	23
Slovenia	23
Venezuela	23
Greece	23
Uruguay	22
Moldova	22
Estonia	21
Portugal	19
Latvia	19
Montenegro	19
Italy	18
Croatia	17
Argentina	15
Czech Republic	14
South Africa	13
Dominican Rep.	12
Albania	11
Japan	11
Serbia	10
Korea, South	8
Total	32

E112B) RATE POLITICAL SYSTEM TEN YEARS AGO

Where on this scale would you put the political system as it was ten years ago (1 = very bad; 10 = very good)

% Bad (codes 1 to 4) (WVS: V163; EVS: V215)

Country	Wave		Gender		Age			Education			Income			Values		
	1990	2000	Male	Female	16-29	30-49	50+	Lower	Middle	Upper	Lower	Middle	Upper	Mat	Mixed	Postm.
Albania	na	**74**	72	76	76	76	68	69	77	79	70	75	77	71	77	77
Algeria	na	**na**	na	na	na	na	na	na	na	na	na	na	na	na	na	na
Argentina	na	**62**	62	63	61	63	62	60	63	74	58	63	66	58	63	62
Armenia	na	**26**	28	24	28	27	21	17	24	35	32	24	21	22	28	37
Australia	na	**27**	26	27	29	28	24	29	28	24	28	26	24	23	26	30
Austria	na	**17**	17	16	15	18	16	13	20	19	22	18	12	24	15	19
Azerbaijan	na	**25**	28	23	30	24	20	27	26	25	27	23	26	23	30	30
Bangladesh	na	**29**	34	23	31	28	30	27	31	35	20	31	36	27	31	32
Belarus	na	**38**	39	36	57	40	19	23	41	51	31	39	45	33	39	65
Belgium	na	**30**	34	26	29	33	27	27	31	31	28	29	35	25	29	40
Bosnia and Herz.	na	**23**	25	21	28	23	18	23	22	24	16	21	33	25	22	17
Brazil	na	**48**	45	51	50	51	37	44	49	59	44	47	55	45	48	53
Bulgaria	na	**47**	52	43	66	50	36	23	55	70	33	50	59	37	57	63
Canada	na	**29**	34	23	33	32	23	26	29	29	26	33	27	28	27	32
Chile	na	**37**	38	37	41	37	33	41	35	34	43	31	37	37	37	37
China	na	**12**	11	12	7	14	10	10	13	7	15	11	8	10	14	13
Colombia	na	**na**	na	na	na	na	na	na	na	na	na	na	na	na	na	na
Croatia	na	**56**	58	55	59	55	56	46	61	67	55	54	60	68	52	61
Czech Republic	na	**65**	66	65	72	67	60	56	72	83	56	65	74	44	70	83
Denmark	na	**30**	28	32	21	37	26	29	27	36	35	29	31	30	23	57
Dominican Rep.	na	**73**	71	74	70	75	100	67	77	73	66	78	69	65	72	83
Egypt	na	**10**	10	9	10	10	10	10	10	10	10	9	11	10	10	10
El Salvador	na	**34**	35	34	31	35	38	30	34	44	33	30	38	na	na	na
Estonia	na	**53**	54	51	60	50	52	53	51	57	51	47	58	48	54	66
Finland	na	**24**	27	22	23	29	21	24	26	23	24	23	27	25	23	29
France	na	**30**	29	30	32	29	30	29	30	33	28	29	32	25	31	33
Georgia	na	**36**	40	33	46	35	29	33	32	52	29	40	46	34	38	45
Germany	na	**23**	23	22	31	23	19	20	25	21	21	25	17	22	25	18
Great Britain	na	**34**	32	37	37	37	30	31	34	42	38	32	33	na	na	na
Greece	na	**38**	41	36	39	35	39	28	39	39	38	36	37	29	37	46
Hungary	na	**31**	33	28	33	33	26	26	35	50	23	33	32	27	34	42
Iceland	na	**29**	31	26	28	30	27	29	29	26	28	29	29	28	28	35
India	na	**na**	na	na	na	na	na	na	na	na	na	na	na	na	na	na
Indonesia	na	**na**	na	na	na	na	na	na	na	na	na	na	na	na	na	na
Iran	na	**na**	na	na	na	na	na	na	na	na	na	na	na	na	na	na
Ireland	na	**40**	39	42	43	44	35	33	43	49	37	43	43	33	41	48
Israel	na	**na**	na	na	na	na	na	na	na	na	na	na	na	na	na	na
Italy	na	**49**	51	47	53	51	46	44	51	58	46	51	50	35	49	56
Japan	na	**53**	52	54	63	62	40	48	53	55	52	54	50	40	56	58
Jordan	na	**na**	na	na	na	na	na	na	na	na	na	na	na	na	na	na
Korea, South	na	**69**	68	70	73	68	66	73	68	71	72	68	67	67	70	77
Latvia	na	**52**	54	51	54	51	52	46	51	63	48	47	61	49	54	57
Lithuania	na	**38**	41	35	54	39	28	22	40	61	31	30	48	40	33	67
Luxembourg	na	**11**	10	13	11	13	10	13	11	10	11	12	11	9	11	16
Macedonia	na	**30**	32	27	40	32	18	36	26	27	27	31	28	20	33	56
Malta	na	**18**	21	15	20	19	15	15	18	24	18	19	18	13	19	27
Mexico	na	**36**	39	34	39	40	26	30	41	50	33	37	46	35	37	44
Moldova	na	**51**	54	48	54	53	45	43	50	59	43	53	53	49	49	62
Montenegro	na	**68**	69	66	77	69	60	64	70	72	68	64	64	62	72	77
Morocco	na	**na**	na	na	na	na	na	na	na	na	na	na	na	na	na	na
Netherlands	na	**10**	12	9	8	12	10	13	9	10	13	9	10	13	8	15
New Zealand	na	**30**	32	30	29	30	31	30	32	30	37	27	27	26	27	41
Nigeria	na	**na**	na	na	na	na	na	na	na	na	na	na	na	na	na	na
Northern Ireland	na	**43**	44	41	54	46	38	42	46	36	52	42	42	40	40	58
Norway	na	**18**	20	16	19	18	17	20	18	15	na	na	na	19	17	21
Pakistan	na	**na**	na	na	na	na	na	na	na	na	na	na	na	na	na	na
Peru	na	**na**	na	na	na	na	na	na	na	na	na	na	na	na	na	na
Philippines	na	**30**	30	30	33	28	31	26	31	34	33	31	26	30	31	24
Poland	na	**53**	57	50	68	52	47	43	62	74	45	55	70	45	58	62
Portugal	na	**36**	36	36	34	33	39	36	34	35	37	34	28	39	33	36
Puerto Rico	na	**na**	na	na	na	na	na	na	na	na	na	na	na	na	na	na
Romania	na	**51**	54	48	65	55	40	36	54	69	37	48	64	41	55	83
Russian Fed.	na	**30**	34	26	40	33	20	16	27	46	21	25	43	25	34	24
Serbia	na	**72**	74	70	90	77	59	58	75	86	62	74	78	65	77	94
Singapore	na	**na**	na	na	na	na	na	na	na	na	na	na	na	na	na	na
Slovakia	na	**37**	39	36	46	33	36	32	37	57	33	35	42	31	40	69
Slovenia	na	**44**	45	42	50	42	41	40	45	46	37	42	48	43	45	43
South Africa	na	**69**	71	67	72	69	65	72	66	70	76	71	59	68	70	69
Spain	na	**32**	35	29	32	34	30	31	31	34	31	31	36	26	35	31
Sweden	na	**23**	22	23	20	25	22	24	23	21	20	27	21	13	23	25
Switzerland	na	**12**	13	10	14	13	9	10	12	12	15	10	10	7	11	19
Taiwan	na	**25**	31	20	27	25	26	21	30	27	22	25	31	21	30	29
Tanzania	na	**27**	31	21	31	25	24	23	34	25	24	28	24	26	28	29
Turkey	na	**28**	31	25	30	28	21	20	37	49	20	27	45	24	25	39
Uganda	na	**46**	35	56	45	49	36	53	43	45	52	45	44	51	46	30
Ukraine	na	**44**	49	39	61	48	31	25	43	57	33	46	54	37	46	64
United States	na	**25**	25	26	26	27	23	22	27	26	28	24	23	17	24	33
Uruguay	na	**43**	45	42	47	51	37	37	53	50	38	43	48	39	42	49
Venezuela	na	**53**	55	51	52	55	50	51	53	55	51	50	58	56	52	51
Vietnam	na	**6**	6	7	9	6	6	6	7	6	10	6	5	7	6	13
Zimbabwe	na	**33**	32	33	35	31	32	34	32	15	32	30	36	30	34	38
Total	na	**37**	38	37	43	38	33	34	38	42	36	37	41	36	38	42

RANKING	
Country	2000
Albania	74
Dominican Rep.	73
Serbia	72
South Africa	69
Korea, South	69
Montenegro	68
Czech Republic	65
Argentina	62
Croatia	56
Poland	53
Venezuela	53
Japan	53
Estonia	53
Latvia	52
Romania	51
Moldova	51
Italy	49
Brazil	48
Bulgaria	47
Uganda	46
Ukraine	44
Slovenia	44
Uruguay	43
Northern Ireland	43
Ireland	40
Greece	38
Lithuania	38
Belarus	38
Slovakia	37
Chile	37
Georgia	36
Mexico	36
Portugal	36
El Salvador	34
Great Britain	34
Zimbabwe	33
Spain	32
Hungary	31
New Zealand	30
Philippines	30
Belgium	30
Denmark	30
France	30
Russian Fed.	30
Macedonia	30
Bangladesh	29
Iceland	29
Canada	29
Turkey	28
Australia	27
Tanzania	27
Armenia	26
Azerbaijan	25
Taiwan	25
United States	25
Finland	24
Bosnia and Herz.	23
Germany	23
Sweden	23
Malta	18
Norway	18
Austria	17
China	12
Switzerland	12
Luxembourg	11
Netherlands	10
Egypt	10
Vietnam	6
Total	

E114A) HAVING A STRONG LEADER

I'm going to describe various types of political systems and ask what you think about each as a way of governing this country. Having a strong leader who does not have to bother with parliament and elections

Very good / Fairly good (%) (WVS: V164; EVS: V216)

Country	Wave		Gender		Age			Education			Income			Values		
	1990	2000	Male	Female	16-29	30-49	50+	Lower	Middle	Upper	Lower	Middle	Upper	Mat	Mixed	Postm.
Albania	na	**17**	18	16	16	15	22	20	17	13	17	17	18	16	18	19
Algeria	na	**39**	35	43	40	37	41	47	40	32	43	40	39	44	38	27
Argentina	na	**42**	43	41	43	42	40	52	30	22	49	47	29	50	45	29
Armenia	na	**53**	52	55	49	54	61	65	55	44	49	57	60	61	48	36
Australia	na	**25**	25	24	32	22	22	37	26	14	29	21	20	32	28	19
Austria	na	**16**	15	17	18	13	18	21	13	4	24	15	12	34	16	11
Azerbaijan	na	**7**	8	6	5	7	11	6	7	7	6	7	7	6	8	9
Bangladesh	na	**12**	10	13	14	10	10	7	17	15	11	15	7	11	11	21
Belarus	na	**40**	39	41	28	40	52	52	39	27	42	44	27	46	37	15
Belgium	na	**33**	32	35	31	30	37	48	34	23	39	34	28	50	34	18
Bosnia and Herz.	na	**37**	36	37	37	34	40	40	37	32	35	39	37	32	38	48
Brazil	na	**61**	58	63	62	60	57	68	58	42	67	64	52	68	59	51
Bulgaria	na	**48**	49	46	44	50	47	52	51	35	53	49	43	54	45	31
Canada	na	**23**	22	24	26	24	21	30	25	14	34	22	17	31	25	19
Chile	na	**43**	43	43	46	43	40	43	46	35	44	40	45	42	47	31
China	na	**19**	16	21	21	18	18	16	20	18	15	19	21	19	16	31
Colombia	na	**54**	54	53	57	51	53	61	52	44	60	50	49	61	62	63
Croatia	na	**12**	9	15	14	12	11	16	11	5	17	14	8	14	13	7
Czech Republic	na	**17**	17	16	16	14	19	21	14	7	21	17	14	22	15	12
Denmark	na	**14**	15	13	12	13	16	17	10	9	16	13	13	19	16	7
Dominican Rep.	na	**28**	30	27	28	28	20	36	36	25	28	26	26	32	28	21
Egypt	na	**8**	9	7	7	8	8	8	7	8	9	7	7	7	8	6
El Salvador	na	**59**	59	60	64	55	59	59	64	53	61	60	56	na	na	na
Estonia	na	**18**	21	16	26	15	17	20	19	13	17	17	18	22	15	15
Finland	na	**27**	27	26	21	25	30	35	19	11	34	28	20	32	25	26
France	na	**35**	32	38	32	33	39	41	31	24	42	37	31	44	37	20
Georgia	na	**66**	65	67	66	62	72	65	68	62	71	63	61	68	65	59
Germany	na	**16**	17	15	17	15	17	21	12	10	21	18	10	21	17	8
Great Britain	na	**25**	24	26	28	26	23	31	22	19	36	23	20	na	na	na
Greece	na	**9**	11	7	6	10	12	13	11	6	9	8	8	12	8	6
Hungary	na	**22**	21	22	16	23	23	28	10	10	26	21	21	25	19	1
Iceland	na	**11**	8	14	12	9	13	18	8	2	19	8	6	19	10	3
India	na	**59**	61	55	64	57	55	66	56	52	73	57	55	62	56	58
Indonesia	na	**19**	18	21	18	21	19	19	19	20	17	19	21	20	20	18
Iran	na	**39**	38	41	42	38	33	35	38	43	38	39	42	40	38	41
Ireland	na	**27**	22	31	24	24	32	36	25	14	37	28	18	30	26	20
Israel	na	**na**	na	na	na	na	na	na	na	na	na	na	na	na	na	na
Italy	na	**16**	17	15	14	14	18	21	13	8	15	14	12	22	17	9
Japan	na	**28**	30	27	28	25	31	46	28	20	31	27	26	28	28	21
Jordan	na	**42**	42	42	41	42	44	45	39	41	40	43	47	48	37	40
Korea, South	na	**28**	33	24	16	29	43	50	32	21	35	23	25	32	27	16
Latvia	na	**58**	55	60	54	55	62	63	60	46	62	58	51	62	58	38
Lithuania	na	**56**	56	56	58	55	55	65	57	38	64	50	55	61	54	46
Luxembourg	na	**45**	45	45	47	42	47	50	46	35	55	49	34	53	45	31
Macedonia	na	**74**	75	73	77	70	76	79	72	71	74	76	70	75	73	74
Malta	na	**19**	21	17	25	15	19	17	21	16	17	15	19	20	19	15
Mexico	na	**56**	53	59	54	56	60	64	52	38	65	55	49	57	57	49
Moldova	na	**62**	63	62	64	57	67	70	64	53	62	61	63	62	62	63
Montenegro	na	**15**	15	15	11	13	20	21	15	4	18	16	13	17	12	8
Morocco	na	**18**	19	17	16	19	22	17	21	14	24	14	23	20	18	16
Netherlands	na	**27**	25	29	17	24	35	43	26	13	31	27	21	40	28	18
New Zealand	na	**19**	18	19	23	15	21	25	19	11	25	17	13	22	18	10
Nigeria	na	**43**	41	45	41	45	44	49	39	39	40	43	46	43	42	45
Northern Ireland	na	**19**	19	20	27	17	15	22	19	14	19	20	19	17	19	19
Norway	na	**14**	15	13	14	13	15	20	13	9	na	na	na	25	13	6
Pakistan	na	**34**	33	35	33	33	38	35	34	29	36	34	28	36	31	50
Peru	na	**39**	38	39	39	37	41	48	39	32	41	38	36	42	38	37
Philippines	na	**63**	65	60	65	60	63	69	61	57	62	64	61	61	64	53
Poland	na	**22**	27	17	21	23	22	28	17	15	23	24	17	25	21	21
Portugal	na	**36**	36	35	29	39	37	33	39	41	47	37	27	36	37	25
Puerto Rico	na	**33**	31	35	40	32	31	38	40	28	39	33	29	36	33	31
Romania	na	**67**	61	73	61	62	74	82	64	48	78	71	56	74	63	39
Russian Fed.	na	**49**	50	48	47	49	50	60	51	39	53	50	44	51	47	45
Serbia	na	**19**	18	21	17	16	24	31	17	9	25	21	16	25	16	4
Singapore	na	**23**	21	25	25	20	22	21	25	16	24	21	23	15	25	22
Slovakia	na	**20**	19	20	18	18	23	23	19	12	25	22	15	24	16	17
Slovenia	na	**24**	23	25	22	21	29	33	24	8	34	21	16	34	23	14
South Africa	na	**34**	33	36	34	34	35	37	31	35	32	35	35	34	31	56
Spain	na	**21**	21	21	19	16	27	22	21	18	23	19	22	28	22	12
Sweden	na	**22**	24	19	16	20	26	37	20	11	24	26	14	33	24	10
Switzerland	na	**31**	32	30	27	34	31	36	31	25	37	30	29	43	32	26
Taiwan	na	**41**	38	44	44	38	48	52	38	34	43	43	36	42	41	32
Tanzania	na	**3**	2	3	3	2	4	4	1	2	4	2	1	2	3	na
Turkey	na	**71**	68	75	70	71	74	76	68	59	75	70	64	75	73	60
Uganda	na	**30**	39	22	25	36	33	30	26	67	37	44	28	29	29	39
Ukraine	na	**60**	60	59	52	60	64	68	61	52	62	59	57	65	58	43
United States	na	**30**	30	29	37	29	25	43	33	22	35	29	24	37	31	24
Uruguay	na	**27**	29	26	28	25	29	34	19	17	31	30	21	38	28	18
Venezuela	na	**48**	49	46	50	46	47	51	48	45	55	46	45	51	48	42
Vietnam	na	**99**	99	99	99	100	99	99	100	100	100	99	99	99	100	100
Zimbabwe	na	**27**	26	27	32	24	20	26	28	30	28	30	23	27	27	23
Total	na	**33**	33	33	34	32	34	37	34	26	37	34	31	37	32	24

RANKING	
Country	2000
Vietnam	99
Macedonia	74
Turkey	71
Romania	67
Georgia	66
Philippines	63
Moldova	62
Brazil	61
Ukraine	60
El Salvador	59
India	59
Latvia	58
Mexico	56
Lithuania	56
Colombia	54
Armenia	53
Russian Fed.	49
Venezuela	48
Bulgaria	48
Luxembourg	45
Chile	43
Nigeria	43
Jordan	42
Argentina	42
Taiwan	41
Belarus	40
Algeria	39
Iran	39
Peru	39
Bosnia and Herz.	37
Portugal	36
France	35
South Africa	34
Pakistan	34
Belgium	33
Puerto Rico	33
Switzerland	31
Uganda	30
United States	30
Korea, South	28
Japan	28
Dominican Rep.	28
Uruguay	27
Netherlands	27
Zimbabwe	27
Ireland	27
Finland	27
Australia	25
Great Britain	25
Slovenia	24
Canada	23
Singapore	23
Poland	22
Hungary	22
Sweden	22
Spain	21
Slovakia	20
Serbia	19
Indonesia	19
Northern Ireland	19
Malta	19
New Zealand	19
China	19
Estonia	18
Morocco	18
Albania	17
Czech Republic	17
Germany	16
Austria	16
Italy	16
Montenegro	15
Denmark	14
Norway	14
Croatia	12
Bangladesh	12
Iceland	11
Greece	9
Egypt	8
Azerbaijan	7
Tanzania	3
Total	33

E115) HAVING EXPERTS MAKE DECISIONS

I'm going to describe various types of political systems and ask what you think about each as a way of governing this country.

Having experts, not government, make decisions according to what they think is best for the country

Very good / Fairly good (%) (WVS: V165; EVS: V217)

	Wave		Gender		Age			Education			Income			Values		
Country	1990	2000	Male	Female	16-29	30-49	50+	Lower	Middle	Upper	Lower	Middle	Upper	Mat	Mixed	Postm.
Albania	na	**88**	90	86	87	88	89	90	86	89	88	87	87	90	86	77
Algeria	na	**81**	80	81	80	82	80	77	81	81	79	86	80	78	82	81
Argentina	na	**54**	54	55	54	54	55	61	48	42	56	58	48	59	56	47
Armenia	na	**55**	55	55	57	55	52	57	55	55	56	54	50	47	62	54
Australia	na	**42**	42	43	49	38	41	47	44	37	46	38	41	50	43	39
Austria	na	**61**	59	62	59	61	61	62	62	51	63	60	59	62	61	60
Azerbaijan	na	**2**	1	2	3	1	1	1	1	3	1	2	3	1	3	2
Bangladesh	na	**77**	75	79	78	77	68	76	78	76	72	82	73	78	75	89
Belarus	na	**79**	75	83	83	80	74	77	80	80	80	79	78	76	79	88
Belgium	na	**58**	56	61	64	56	58	60	59	56	58	56	58	67	60	48
Bosnia and Herz.	na	**74**	71	76	74	73	75	75	72	79	77	72	76	76	74	75
Brazil	na	**83**	85	81	80	87	82	84	83	82	80	87	83	84	83	82
Bulgaria	na	**82**	78	87	77	84	84	86	82	80	89	78	80	83	81	81
Canada	na	**44**	41	47	53	43	40	48	47	36	49	42	44	51	46	41
Chile	na	**59**	60	57	66	57	54	59	60	53	60	58	58	62	60	48
China	na	**30**	31	30	34	32	19	27	31	46	22	33	33	31	30	36
Colombia	na	**71**	72	70	72	70	72	73	73	65	72	71	69	73	74	71
Croatia	na	**88**	88	88	86	92	85	88	89	86	85	89	90	93	89	84
Czech Republic	na	**63**	63	63	65	68	58	64	63	58	60	64	65	69	62	56
Denmark	na	**30**	27	32	37	29	27	33	25	25	35	29	22	36	32	19
Dominican Rep.	na	**49**	47	51	47	55	46	62	51	47	56	47	35	40	51	55
Egypt	na	**67**	70	64	66	66	72	68	65	69	67	66	71	68	66	70
El Salvador	na	**69**	69	68	71	68	66	70	70	63	70	70	61	na	na	na
Estonia	na	**57**	55	59	60	55	56	55	59	52	59	58	57	58	56	62
Finland	na	**59**	56	61	62	57	57	59	61	51	65	56	56	57	58	61
France	na	**51**	48	55	55	51	49	56	45	44	58	53	44	58	53	38
Georgia	na	**58**	61	56	59	61	54	60	57	60	58	57	59	54	61	62
Germany	na	**56**	57	55	53	56	57	57	56	50	62	61	57	60	53	58
Great Britain	na	**47**	45	49	54	48	43	49	50	37	57	44	41	na	na	na
Greece	na	**13**	18	10	8	15	20	16	16	11	15	15	12	20	12	8
Hungary	na	**85**	85	85	85	86	85	85	86	84	79	87	87	88	83	77
Iceland	na	**42**	35	49	46	41	40	48	39	35	46	41	39	46	43	29
India	na	**68**	67	69	69	67	67	69	69	65	72	73	63	73	65	76
Indonesia	na	**48**	51	44	40	55	44	45	49	50	48	47	50	39	54	58
Iran	na	**27**	30	23	24	29	32	32	23	27	31	27	23	25	29	26
Ireland	na	**38**	35	42	43	40	35	37	39	37	37	38	41	30	40	34
Israel	na	**na**	na	na	na	na	na	na	na	na	na	na	na	na	na	na
Italy	na	**51**	48	54	47	49	55	59	47	39	55	48	45	60	51	46
Japan	na	**58**	52	65	74	64	47	64	60	55	59	58	58	57	60	61
Jordan	na	**88**	88	89	88	88	89	89	89	87	90	87	89	92	86	85
Korea, South	na	**53**	54	51	55	55	46	51	49	59	51	53	55	53	51	66
Latvia	na	**61**	59	62	61	61	60	59	60	65	64	59	58	60	61	65
Lithuania	na	**57**	55	59	57	56	59	61	57	54	55	57	58	62	57	43
Luxembourg	na	**46**	45	47	51	44	46	53	44	40	53	46	38	39	50	33
Macedonia	na	**84**	84	84	86	83	83	88	84	79	86	85	80	81	85	84
Malta	na	**34**	35	33	40	33	31	31	35	40	29	35	37	32	36	28
Mexico	na	**66**	67	66	68	65	66	69	64	65	76	68	64	67	67	60
Moldova	na	**51**	50	52	54	51	48	50	49	53	62	46	48	50	57	29
Montenegro	na	**89**	89	89	87	89	91	90	88	90	92	90	85	91	87	86
Morocco	na	**70**	70	70	68	74	69	71	65	71	80	67	62	70	71	67
Netherlands	na	**40**	38	42	46	38	39	47	42	31	41	44	37	46	43	31
New Zealand	na	**42**	40	43	49	46	35	44	41	39	42	42	40	53	40	37
Nigeria	na	**73**	71	75	74	72	77	74	74	72	73	71	75	72	75	68
Northern Ireland	na	**38**	36	40	47	40	31	39	38	35	35	40	46	38	38	35
Norway	na	**34**	34	34	43	34	28	35	35	32	na	na	na	41	34	27
Pakistan	na	**19**	19	19	24	17	16	17	24	16	16	20	18	20	17	20
Peru	na	**63**	63	63	63	62	65	67	65	58	64	62	62	67	62	63
Philippines	na	**62**	61	63	64	59	67	62	63	62	56	63	68	59	65	61
Poland	na	**88**	88	88	96	86	85	87	87	93	86	89	89	87	89	88
Portugal	na	**47**	47	48	43	50	48	45	50	56	46	52	46	43	50	49
Puerto Rico	na	**42**	41	43	47	40	42	58	47	38	47	43	39	45	42	41
Romania	na	**85**	85	85	81	85	87	89	83	82	89	87	81	88	81	85
Russian Fed.	na	**52**	51	53	60	50	48	51	53	49	53	51	51	49	56	44
Serbia	na	**88**	85	92	88	88	89	88	87	90	87	88	89	90	86	86
Singapore	na	**40**	41	39	46	33	36	35	42	43	37	41	41	38	40	48
Slovakia	na	**86**	86	85	85	86	86	87	86	78	85	84	86	83	88	71
Slovenia	na	**81**	83	80	81	77	87	80	83	77	82	82	79	82	82	81
South Africa	na	**52**	47	58	52	52	50	53	50	58	47	57	55	50	53	55
Spain	na	**44**	44	45	43	40	49	42	46	45	49	41	40	47	43	43
Sweden	na	**41**	40	43	48	37	42	49	45	30	45	45	34	56	45	27
Switzerland	na	**46**	43	50	48	50	42	39	49	41	49	50	44	54	46	48
Taiwan	na	**60**	59	61	48	61	65	63	60	57	60	59	61	61	59	66
Tanzania	na	**30**	31	28	29	31	29	32	28	28	34	31	24	30	27	30
Turkey	na	**74**	72	76	77	73	70	75	73	69	76	74	72	75	74	74
Uganda	na	**36**	54	19	35	35	41	38	32	55	47	36	26	34	35	43
Ukraine	na	**50**	47	54	50	54	47	50	53	45	51	46	55	52	49	41
United States	na	**44**	42	46	50	48	33	53	46	40	46	42	43	52	45	40
Uruguay	na	**40**	41	39	43	37	41	46	34	29	43	39	36	42	41	36
Venezuela	na	**69**	69	68	69	68	69	69	69	68	69	68	70	66	68	74
Vietnam	na	**98**	98	98	99	98	98	99	98	97	97	98	98	100	97	98
Zimbabwe	na	**69**	71	67	69	71	68	69	70	70	69	70	73	72	69	53
Total	na	**58**	57	58	59	58	56	61	58	52	59	59	58	60	58	51

RANKING	
Country	**2000**
Vietnam	98
Montenegro	89
Jordan	88
Croatia	88
Serbia	88
Poland	88
Albania	88
Slovakia	86
Hungary	85
Romania	85
Macedonia	84
Brazil	83
Bulgaria	82
Slovenia	81
Algeria	81
Belarus	79
Bangladesh	77
Turkey	74
Bosnia and Herz.	74
Nigeria	73
Colombia	71
Morocco	70
Zimbabwe	69
El Salvador	69
Venezuela	69
India	68
Egypt	67
Mexico	66
Czech Republic	63
Peru	63
Philippines	62
Austria	61
Latvia	61
Taiwan	60
Chile	59
Finland	59
Japan	58
Georgia	58
Belgium	58
Lithuania	57
Estonia	57
Germany	56
Armenia	55
Argentina	54
Korea, South	53
South Africa	52
Russian Fed.	52
France	51
Italy	51
Moldova	51
Ukraine	50
Dominican Rep.	49
Indonesia	48
Portugal	47
Great Britain	47
Luxembourg	46
Switzerland	46
Canada	44
Spain	44
United States	44
Puerto Rico	42
Australia	42
Iceland	42
New Zealand	42
Sweden	41
Netherlands	40
Singapore	40
Uruguay	40
Ireland	38
Northern Ireland	38
Uganda	36
Malta	34
Norway	34
China	30
Tanzania	30
Denmark	30
Iran	27
Pakistan	19
Greece	13
Azerbaijan	2
Total	58

E116) HAVING THE ARMY RULE

I'm going to describe various types of political systems and ask what you think about each as a way of governing this country. Having the army rule

Very good / Fairly good (%)

(WVS: V166; EVS: V218)

Country	Wave		Gender		Age			Education			Income			Values		
	1990	2000	Male	Female	16-29	30-49	50+	Lower	Middle	Upper	Lower	Middle	Upper	Mat	Mixed	Postm.
Albania	na	**12**	12	11	15	11	9	11	12	13	11	13	11	10	9	40
Algeria	na	**19**	21	18	16	19	29	30	19	13	21	19	18	20	20	12
Argentina	na	**18**	19	16	15	18	20	23	11	7	22	20	10	28	17	10
Armenia	na	**19**	17	20	18	18	21	24	20	13	15	20	26	15	22	22
Australia	na	**7**	6	8	10	6	6	10	8	3	10	5	5	11	8	4
Austria	na	**2**	1	2	3	1	2	3	1	na	4	1	2	14	1	na
Azerbaijan	na	**2**	3	2	2	2	4	2	2	2	2	2	4	2	3	na
Bangladesh	na	**19**	17	21	19	20	15	22	16	16	18	22	15	17	19	26
Belarus	na	**20**	20	20	15	18	26	27	19	12	18	21	17	25	17	14
Belgium	na	**5**	3	6	5	4	5	7	5	2	6	5	3	8	5	1
Bosnia and Herz.	na	**9**	7	11	10	8	10	15	9	5	10	11	7	10	9	10
Brazil	na	**45**	44	47	46	45	45	60	39	20	57	44	35	63	41	26
Bulgaria	na	**12**	13	11	9	11	15	18	12	7	15	11	11	14	10	9
Canada	na	**6**	4	8	6	6	6	8	6	3	9	6	3	6	7	3
Chile	na	**24**	25	24	24	22	28	28	24	17	26	25	20	31	24	15
China	na	**45**	39	52	37	48	43	59	40	18	55	46	31	44	44	32
Colombia	na	**34**	33	35	37	30	36	39	36	23	39	33	28	43	39	34
Croatia	na	**6**	5	6	8	4	6	11	3	3	9	5	5	9	6	1
Czech Republic	na	**2**	2	3	2	1	3	3	2	na	3	3	1	3	2	2
Denmark	na	**1**	1	1	1	1	1	1	na	na	1	1	1	1	1	na
Dominican Rep.	na	**6**	6	7	7	6	na	7	4	7	9	4	8	14	5	2
Egypt	na	**na**	na	na	na	na	na	na	na	na	na	na	na	na	na	na
El Salvador	na	**39**	33	45	38	40	40	51	31	23	51	36	19	na	na	na
Estonia	na	**3**	3	3	4	3	3	4	4	2	4	2	3	3	3	3
Finland	na	**6**	7	5	5	5	7	9	4	na	10	5	4	8	5	6
France	na	**4**	3	5	6	3	4	5	4	1	6	3	2	6	4	1
Georgia	na	**11**	13	10	13	10	12	9	13	7	13	10	10	10	13	7
Germany	na	**2**	2	1	2	1	2	2	2	1	3	2	1	1	2	1
Great Britain	na	**7**	7	7	11	6	6	10	5	6	14	4	4	na	na	na
Greece	na	**10**	11	9	10	9	11	12	14	6	9	10	10	12	9	7
Hungary	na	**3**	3	3	4	1	5	4	2	1	6	2	3	4	3	na
Iceland	na	**1**	1	na	na	1	1	1	1	na	1	na	na	1	1	na
India	na	**20**	20	20	19	21	21	22	22	15	32	22	14	20	21	14
Indonesia	na	**96**	95	98	97	95	97	97	95	98	96	96	96	95	98	89
Iran	na	**84**	84	84	84	83	84	84	84	83	83	85	82	91	80	82
Ireland	na	**5**	4	6	5	4	5	7	4	1	6	6	2	5	3	6
Israel	na	**na**	na	na	na	na	na	na	na	na	na	na	na	na	na	na
Italy	na	**4**	3	5	4	3	6	7	3	1	7	3	3	5	5	2
Japan	na	**2**	2	1	2	2	2	4	2	1	2	1	2	1	2	na
Jordan	na	**58**	48	67	62	57	51	59	62	51	64	53	55	62	55	48
Korea, South	na	**4**	4	4	1	4	6	10	4	3	5	2	4	4	4	na
Latvia	na	**5**	5	6	8	4	6	11	4	4	7	5	4	5	6	2
Lithuania	na	**4**	4	4	3	4	5	5	4	2	4	4	3	4	4	2
Luxembourg	na	**7**	9	5	9	6	6	8	7	3	11	4	5	10	6	3
Macedonia	na	**26**	26	26	29	23	27	31	25	19	28	28	21	22	28	20
Malta	na	**4**	4	4	4	3	5	7	3	2	4	3	3	6	4	1
Mexico	na	**35**	32	39	36	33	39	43	31	17	41	35	29	37	36	29
Moldova	na	**14**	15	13	13	15	13	13	17	9	18	16	11	15	12	12
Montenegro	na	**7**	7	7	2	7	10	11	6	2	12	8	5	10	4	na
Morocco	na	**15**	16	15	14	15	19	18	7	6	17	7	14	18	14	9
Netherlands	na	**1**	1	2	2	1	1	3	1	na	2	1	na	5	na	2
New Zealand	na	**2**	3	2	4	2	2	3	2	1	5	1	1	2	2	1
Nigeria	na	**26**	25	27	26	26	24	32	23	22	28	21	29	24	28	20
Northern Ireland	na	**2**	2	2	2	2	2	3	1	2	2	3	1	3	2	1
Norway	na	**5**	4	6	7	3	4	9	5	1	na	na	na	9	4	2
Pakistan	na	**4**	3	5	6	3	4	5	5	2	5	5	2	5	4	8
Peru	na	**15**	16	14	17	13	12	18	15	12	18	13	11	20	13	14
Philippines	na	**49**	49	50	51	49	48	55	49	42	48	50	50	47	52	46
Poland	na	**17**	16	18	20	16	16	22	13	7	19	18	12	18	17	15
Portugal	na	**9**	9	10	6	10	11	10	8	11	11	13	7	8	11	7
Puerto Rico	na	**11**	12	10	10	9	12	18	15	8	14	10	8	10	10	12
Romania	na	**28**	23	33	24	21	37	44	22	17	40	28	20	30	27	15
Russian Fed.	na	**19**	22	17	20	17	21	27	21	11	21	20	17	17	21	23
Serbia	na	**10**	10	11	11	6	14	17	9	4	16	12	4	15	7	1
Singapore	na	**13**	11	15	19	8	7	17	12	6	20	13	9	8	15	18
Slovakia	na	**7**	6	8	7	8	8	9	7	4	10	8	5	9	7	2
Slovenia	na	**5**	4	5	4	5	5	9	3	1	9	3	2	7	4	5
South Africa	na	**22**	23	20	20	23	20	26	17	19	26	24	14	17	23	32
Spain	na	**7**	7	7	5	7	9	7	8	6	9	6	9	10	8	3
Sweden	na	**7**	7	7	7	4	9	12	6	4	10	6	3	13	8	2
Switzerland	na	**5**	5	5	6	2	8	10	4	1	4	8	3	7	6	2
Taiwan	na	**16**	11	20	11	16	17	23	14	11	21	16	10	17	14	15
Tanzania	na	**14**	12	16	20	11	8	16	13	8	19	11	8	13	14	9
Turkey	na	**29**	25	33	28	29	30	35	25	10	33	27	22	34	29	21
Uganda	na	**34**	32	36	32	37	28	38	32	40	39	39	29	32	32	46
Ukraine	na	**13**	13	13	10	11	16	21	14	9	18	12	10	14	13	10
United States	na	**9**	8	9	11	8	8	18	8	6	11	9	5	17	9	5
Uruguay	na	**8**	6	10	7	8	9	11	4	6	12	7	7	16	5	6
Venezuela	na	**23**	24	21	25	18	27	25	25	14	26	25	19	25	22	21
Vietnam	na	**99**	99	99	100	99	98	99	98	99	99	99	99	99	99	100
Zimbabwe	na	**12**	11	13	17	9	5	12	13	na	13	13	9	10	13	21
Total	na	**16**	16	17	19	16	15	21	15	12	20	17	14	19	16	10

RANKING	
Country	2000
Vietnam	99
Indonesia	96
Iran	84
Jordan	58
Philippines	49
Brazil	45
China	45
El Salvador	39
Mexico	35
Uganda	34
Colombia	34
Turkey	29
Romania	28
Nigeria	26
Macedonia	26
Chile	24
Venezuela	23
South Africa	22
India	20
Belarus	20
Algeria	19
Russian Fed.	19
Bangladesh	19
Armenia	19
Argentina	18
Poland	17
Taiwan	16
Morocco	15
Peru	15
Tanzania	14
Moldova	14
Singapore	13
Ukraine	13
Bulgaria	12
Zimbabwe	12
Albania	12
Georgia	11
Puerto Rico	11
Serbia	10
Greece	10
Portugal	9
Bosnia and Herz.	9
United States	9
Uruguay	8
Slovakia	7
Spain	7
Australia	7
Great Britain	7
Luxembourg	7
Sweden	7
Montenegro	7
Dominican Rep.	6
Finland	6
Canada	6
Croatia	6
Latvia	5
Switzerland	5
Ireland	5
Norway	5
Slovenia	5
Belgium	5
Italy	4
Pakistan	4
Malta	4
France	4
Korea, South	4
Lithuania	4
Estonia	3
Hungary	3
Azerbaijan	2
Czech Republic	2
New Zealand	2
Northern Ireland	2
Austria	2
Japan	2
Germany	2
Netherlands	1
Denmark	1
Iceland	1
Total	16

E117) HAVING A DEMOCRATIC POLITICAL SYSTEM

I'm going to describe various types of political systems and ask what you think about each as a way of governing this country.

Having a democratic political system

Very good / Fairly good (%) (WVS: V167; EVS: V219)

Country	Wave		Gender		Age			Education			Income			Values		
	1990	2000	Male	Female	16-29	30-49	50+	Lower	Middle	Upper	Lower	Middle	Upper	Mat	Mixed	Postm.
Albania	na	**98**	98	97	98	98	96	97	97	100	97	98	98	99	97	97
Algeria	na	**93**	92	93	92	93	93	95	91	93	92	95	91	93	92	96
Argentina	na	**91**	90	91	88	91	93	86	97	97	86	90	96	85	90	95
Armenia	na	**85**	86	84	87	87	78	77	84	91	89	85	76	79	90	90
Australia	na	**87**	90	85	80	90	90	80	85	96	86	88	91	81	86	90
Austria	na	**96**	97	96	97	96	97	95	97	98	95	97	96	89	96	98
Azerbaijan	na	**98**	98	97	98	97	97	99	98	96	98	96	97	98	97	97
Bangladesh	na	**98**	98	99	99	98	98	98	98	100	98	99	98	98	99	97
Belarus	na	**88**	89	88	90	89	86	84	89	93	90	87	88	88	89	92
Belgium	na	**89**	91	88	92	88	89	79	89	97	87	87	93	80	89	97
Bosnia and Herz.	na	**92**	92	92	94	92	90	92	92	94	93	91	93	94	91	98
Brazil	na	**85**	85	85	84	86	85	80	87	96	84	83	87	79	87	87
Bulgaria	na	**86**	89	84	93	86	83	82	85	93	80	89	89	82	89	94
Canada	na	**88**	90	87	86	86	93	81	87	97	83	86	93	89	86	93
Chile	na	**85**	85	84	84	85	85	84	84	89	82	87	87	80	86	90
China	na	**96**	97	95	95	97	96	95	97	95	96	97	96	96	97	93
Colombia	na	**85**	86	85	86	86	84	80	85	95	82	86	90	80	84	88
Croatia	na	**98**	98	98	97	98	98	97	99	98	96	98	98	100	97	99
Czech Republic	na	**93**	92	93	92	93	92	89	96	98	89	93	95	87	94	97
Denmark	na	**98**	98	98	96	99	98	97	100	99	97	98	99	92	98	100
Dominican Rep.	na	**91**	93	90	90	93	91	90	93	91	93	92	93	84	91	99
Egypt	na	**99**	99	98	99	98	99	99	98	99	98	99	99	98	99	98
El Salvador	na	**86**	88	83	82	86	91	83	86	90	82	86	90	na	na	na
Estonia	na	**87**	84	90	84	86	89	82	87	92	84	86	89	85	88	89
Finland	na	**87**	88	87	89	91	83	83	92	96	85	86	92	83	89	85
France	na	**89**	90	89	87	89	91	86	90	97	89	89	93	87	89	93
Georgia	na	**91**	91	91	91	91	90	92	90	93	88	93	93	90	91	93
Germany	na	**95**	95	95	93	96	95	94	95	98	95	96	94	96	94	97
Great Britain	na	**88**	89	87	83	88	90	84	89	94	85	91	86	na	na	na
Greece	na	**98**	98	98	97	98	98	96	98	98	99	97	98	99	98	99
Hungary	na	**87**	90	84	84	88	89	84	93	96	83	87	89	86	88	88
Iceland	na	**98**	98	98	97	98	99	97	98	100	97	99	99	95	99	100
India	na	**93**	93	93	95	92	92	91	93	96	89	93	94	95	93	92
Indonesia	na	**96**	97	95	95	96	97	97	96	95	95	96	97	96	96	96
Iran	na	**86**	87	83	82	88	93	86	85	88	84	88	84	83	86	91
Ireland	na	**91**	92	90	89	90	93	87	91	98	91	87	93	88	90	96
Israel	na	**na**	na	na	na	na	na	na	na	na	na	na	na	na	na	na
Italy	na	**97**	97	97	94	97	98	96	97	98	96	98	98	96	97	96
Japan	na	**92**	92	92	94	92	91	90	92	94	91	91	94	92	92	98
Jordan	na	**94**	95	94	95	94	93	93	96	96	94	95	94	96	94	89
Korea, South	na	**85**	85	84	81	86	87	80	85	84	84	87	84	86	84	86
Latvia	na	**88**	87	89	80	89	91	83	88	95	87	87	91	89	88	87
Lithuania	na	**86**	84	88	90	86	83	82	86	91	82	83	90	81	86	97
Luxembourg	na	**92**	91	93	91	94	90	87	94	98	90	92	94	91	93	92
Macedonia	na	**91**	93	90	92	91	92	88	92	95	90	90	95	90	92	95
Malta	na	**94**	94	93	95	92	94	90	94	100	90	97	94	93	94	98
Mexico	na	**86**	87	86	85	85	89	85	85	92	87	87	88	84	85	89
Moldova	na	**75**	74	75	79	79	66	66	73	83	70	72	79	70	80	78
Montenegro	na	**95**	94	95	96	95	93	93	94	98	93	95	98	93	97	94
Morocco	na	**96**	96	96	96	96	93	95	98	97	96	94	95	96	95	97
Netherlands	na	**97**	97	96	96	96	97	91	99	99	94	97	98	92	97	97
New Zealand	na	**87**	90	85	81	90	89	84	84	95	87	87	91	88	88	94
Nigeria	na	**95**	96	95	95	96	93	93	96	97	94	96	97	95	95	97
Northern Ireland	na	**92**	93	91	88	92	94	91	93	93	92	92	91	95	92	88
Norway	na	**96**	96	96	94	97	98	94	96	99	na	na	na	90	97	99
Pakistan	na	**88**	89	88	89	88	86	89	88	86	88	89	89	88	88	91
Peru	na	**93**	93	94	93	94	93	92	92	95	92	93	95	92	93	94
Philippines	na	**82**	83	82	84	82	80	81	81	86	79	84	84	81	84	81
Poland	na	**84**	84	83	86	82	84	79	87	94	78	88	82	81	85	89
Portugal	na	**91**	89	92	92	87	93	89	93	96	89	86	93	91	90	92
Puerto Rico	na	**91**	91	92	85	92	94	89	90	92	92	92	91	96	90	93
Romania	na	**89**	89	89	92	89	87	83	90	94	86	89	91	86	90	96
Russian Fed.	na	**63**	65	62	75	64	53	43	59	81	53	59	74	56	69	66
Serbia	na	**94**	95	93	95	96	92	88	95	99	90	94	97	92	96	99
Singapore	na	**94**	94	94	94	94	95	95	92	98	90	93	96	95	94	94
Slovakia	na	**84**	84	84	90	84	80	80	85	92	78	85	89	83	85	98
Slovenia	na	**90**	92	88	89	88	92	83	90	97	86	89	95	81	91	92
South Africa	na	**90**	88	92	94	86	91	90	90	93	91	92	88	91	89	93
Spain	na	**95**	95	95	95	95	95	96	94	95	94	94	94	95	94	97
Sweden	na	**97**	97	98	96	98	98	97	96	100	96	98	99	92	98	98
Switzerland	na	**93**	92	94	90	93	95	90	94	94	92	91	95	90	94	94
Taiwan	na	**93**	95	91	92	93	94	90	93	96	89	95	95	92	95	92
Tanzania	na	**93**	95	90	94	93	92	88	98	99	88	94	99	96	92	100
Turkey	na	**92**	92	92	91	92	94	90	92	97	91	92	94	91	91	94
Uganda	na	**93**	98	89	94	94	84	85	96	94	96	97	94	94	93	89
Ukraine	na	**85**	85	84	85	89	79	70	85	89	79	86	90	83	85	87
United States	na	**89**	91	88	85	88	94	80	87	94	86	90	93	85	89	91
Uruguay	na	**96**	96	96	95	96	97	95	99	96	97	94	98	95	97	98
Venezuela	na	**94**	94	93	91	95	95	91	93	97	91	92	96	93	93	97
Vietnam	na	**96**	95	96	96	96	95	97	93	99	97	96	95	94	96	93
Zimbabwe	na	**88**	90	87	86	90	90	88	88	100	86	89	94	91	87	84
Total	na	**91**	92	91	91	91	91	89	91	94	89	91	93	89	92	94

RANKING	
Country	2000
Egypt	99
Bangladesh	98
Denmark	98
Greece	98
Iceland	98
Albania	98
Croatia	98
Azerbaijan	98
Sweden	97
Italy	97
Netherlands	97
China	96
Norway	96
Austria	96
Uruguay	96
Morocco	96
Indonesia	96
Vietnam	96
Nigeria	95
Germany	95
Spain	95
Montenegro	95
Jordan	94
Serbia	94
Singapore	94
Malta	94
Venezuela	94
Switzerland	93
Taiwan	93
Peru	93
Uganda	93
Tanzania	93
India	93
Algeria	93
Czech Republic	93
Bosnia and Herz.	92
Northern Ireland	92
Japan	92
Luxembourg	92
Turkey	92
Macedonia	91
Dominican Rep.	91
Puerto Rico	91
Ireland	91
Argentina	91
Georgia	91
Portugal	91
South Africa	90
Slovenia	90
France	89
Belgium	89
United States	89
Romania	89
Belarus	88
Canada	88
Latvia	88
Pakistan	88
Zimbabwe	88
Great Britain	88
Finland	87
Australia	87
New Zealand	87
Hungary	87
Estonia	87
Bulgaria	86
Lithuania	86
Mexico	86
Iran	86
El Salvador	86
Colombia	85
Armenia	85
Brazil	85
Chile	85
Korea, South	85
Ukraine	85
Slovakia	84
Poland	84
Philippines	82
Moldova	75
Russian Fed.	63
Total	91

E120) IN DEMOCRACY, THE ECONOMIC SYSTEM RUNS BADLY

I'm going to read off some things that people sometimes say about a democratic political system. In democracy, the economic system runs badly

Disagree / Strongly disagree (%) (WVS: V169; EVS: V221)

Country	Wave		Gender		Age			Education			Income			Values		
	1990	2000	Male	Female	16-29	30-49	50+	Lower	Middle	Upper	Lower	Middle	Upper	Mat	Mixed	Postm.
Albania	na	**79**	82	76	87	75	78	77	76	90	76	77	85	82	78	77
Algeria	na	**69**	68	70	64	72	75	81	65	68	61	73	72	70	69	68
Argentina	na	**55**	58	52	53	56	55	47	62	76	47	53	65	45	54	64
Armenia	na	**58**	61	55	64	58	47	52	55	69	67	55	46	50	62	83
Australia	na	**70**	69	71	62	74	73	55	67	85	64	73	78	68	70	71
Austria	na	**87**	88	86	85	89	86	85	88	95	83	85	90	70	87	91
Azerbaijan	na	**84**	84	83	87	83	80	81	83	85	82	84	85	82	86	91
Bangladesh	na	**90**	89	90	91	89	87	91	89	87	91	90	89	91	89	92
Belarus	na	**69**	73	64	80	70	54	55	70	79	65	66	78	63	71	91
Belgium	na	**67**	70	64	67	68	65	51	65	79	57	63	75	61	67	74
Bosnia and Herz.	na	**75**	75	76	77	75	74	75	74	81	72	75	79	76	75	75
Brazil	na	**30**	34	25	27	31	32	29	25	48	32	21	34	25	32	28
Bulgaria	na	**60**	61	59	77	61	49	38	63	79	45	60	70	49	69	81
Canada	na	**73**	76	69	69	74	73	58	69	89	62	69	84	65	70	79
Chile	na	**63**	65	61	58	65	64	62	64	63	60	65	64	66	60	70
China	na	**74**	78	70	76	72	78	73	75	75	76	71	75	75	74	65
Colombia	na	**na**	na	na	na	na	na	na	na	na	na	na	na	na	na	na
Croatia	na	**71**	73	69	73	72	69	67	70	85	69	67	77	66	69	81
Czech Republic	na	**63**	66	60	67	68	57	53	70	85	54	62	72	51	65	76
Denmark	na	**85**	86	84	81	86	86	80	92	89	81	84	91	70	85	92
Dominican Rep.	na	**73**	72	74	72	75	90	71	61	78	69	74	82	63	74	81
Egypt	na	**82**	81	83	80	82	86	85	79	80	83	85	82	84	82	73
El Salvador	na	**na**	na	na	na	na	na	na	na	na	na	na	na	na	na	na
Estonia	na	**69**	72	66	75	70	65	64	70	72	65	63	72	65	71	83
Finland	na	**80**	80	80	83	82	76	75	85	87	76	83	82	76	82	80
France	na	**50**	52	48	43	54	49	41	57	67	44	47	60	41	50	65
Georgia	na	**69**	70	68	71	71	65	70	67	76	63	71	77	69	69	73
Germany	na	**88**	89	88	85	89	89	87	88	94	83	88	89	87	88	91
Great Britain	na	**71**	69	73	66	73	73	74	68	69	71	70	76	na	na	na
Greece	na	**58**	60	57	60	56	55	37	51	68	53	56	62	52	61	60
Hungary	na	**61**	63	58	64	64	55	51	72	84	51	59	66	59	62	72
Iceland	na	**88**	88	87	88	92	82	82	90	94	83	90	91	83	88	94
India	na	**57**	57	56	60	56	55	49	60	64	50	57	59	63	54	40
Indonesia	na	**78**	79	78	76	78	81	76	80	79	73	83	82	78	79	82
Iran	na	**67**	69	65	68	67	64	68	67	67	64	70	68	70	67	70
Ireland	na	**80**	83	78	84	81	77	72	83	89	71	79	88	83	79	86
Israel	na	**na**	na	na	na	na	na	na	na	na	na	na	na	na	na	na
Italy	na	**67**	70	64	68	71	62	55	71	87	58	69	75	59	66	71
Japan	na	**79**	80	79	75	86	75	68	77	89	72	82	83	81	80	86
Jordan	na	**67**	71	64	63	69	74	65	70	67	71	71	59	63	69	76
Korea, South	na	**82**	81	83	86	82	76	75	79	86	77	86	85	80	83	88
Latvia	na	**52**	56	49	58	52	50	42	50	70	46	49	62	47	55	60
Lithuania	na	**60**	62	59	70	63	49	47	60	75	50	52	69	59	58	79
Luxembourg	na	**79**	78	81	77	81	79	76	77	88	74	78	83	71	81	86
Macedonia	na	**55**	55	55	60	57	48	51	55	62	44	61	60	52	56	71
Malta	na	**88**	87	89	86	89	88	84	89	93	84	93	87	87	87	97
Mexico	na	**45**	46	43	46	43	46	42	41	64	42	44	52	44	46	40
Moldova	na	**58**	61	54	58	64	50	48	58	64	51	57	61	52	64	69
Montenegro	na	**80**	81	80	86	83	74	75	79	90	73	79	87	79	81	89
Morocco	na	**65**	67	61	66	65	59	63	66	73	52	69	72	64	64	73
Netherlands	na	**92**	93	90	93	93	89	82	94	97	88	93	95	82	92	95
New Zealand	na	**72**	76	69	61	82	66	61	73	84	63	73	83	74	74	80
Nigeria	na	**63**	64	62	62	65	60	56	68	67	56	69	68	63	64	61
Northern Ireland	na	**79**	78	81	72	80	81	78	77	85	76	79	83	78	80	77
Norway	na	**66**	72	61	64	68	66	58	65	77	na	na	na	54	67	79
Pakistan	na	**61**	66	56	57	62	68	60	58	71	60	63	63	61	61	71
Peru	na	**45**	44	46	43	47	44	44	43	49	44	41	51	43	45	45
Philippines	na	**48**	49	47	47	50	47	45	50	49	48	48	48	46	49	61
Poland	na	**53**	54	52	54	56	50	42	62	75	44	56	66	47	58	52
Portugal	na	**61**	63	58	60	59	63	58	64	67	54	55	64	63	61	52
Puerto Rico	na	**51**	61	45	49	48	55	41	47	55	48	56	50	58	49	53
Romania	na	**44**	48	40	56	45	36	30	46	63	30	36	58	35	49	76
Russian Fed.	na	**45**	48	43	58	49	32	18	43	65	36	42	56	38	51	61
Serbia	na	**70**	71	68	73	73	63	57	70	81	57	70	79	66	71	78
Singapore	na	**na**	na	na	na	na	na	na	na	na	na	na	na	na	na	na
Slovakia	na	**52**	52	51	55	54	46	46	52	66	40	50	61	47	56	59
Slovenia	na	**53**	60	47	62	58	41	33	56	77	36	55	76	44	55	57
South Africa	na	**56**	56	56	57	56	56	46	68	62	53	50	68	62	53	49
Spain	na	**76**	76	77	76	78	75	75	76	82	71	79	80	70	79	76
Sweden	na	**90**	90	90	93	90	88	78	91	97	87	87	98	80	90	95
Switzerland	na	**78**	78	77	79	76	78	69	78	86	72	72	88	73	76	85
Taiwan	na	**74**	75	73	77	76	63	66	76	78	70	77	74	69	78	77
Tanzania	na	**73**	79	65	72	74	72	67	79	81	69	75	78	74	74	65
Turkey	na	**69**	71	66	68	70	66	64	71	87	66	68	78	66	68	74
Uganda	na	**80**	77	84	85	79	67	67	87	69	71	79	81	80	82	75
Ukraine	na	**64**	69	58	73	68	53	38	63	75	56	65	70	56	67	82
United States	na	**78**	80	75	72	78	82	61	76	86	74	79	83	74	78	80
Uruguay	na	**81**	86	77	80	81	81	79	83	86	79	83	81	79	80	84
Venezuela	na	**56**	58	55	57	54	59	54	53	67	51	56	60	56	57	58
Vietnam	na	**82**	85	80	83	82	82	81	84	82	75	86	82	74	84	88
Zimbabwe	na	**70**	72	68	68	73	69	70	70	85	67	70	75	78	65	60
Total	na	**68**	70	66	68	70	66	63	68	76	63	68	73	64	69	74

RANKING	
Country	2000
Netherlands	92
Sweden	90
Bangladesh	90
Germany	88
Malta	88
Iceland	88
Austria	87
Denmark	85
Azerbaijan	84
Vietnam	82
Korea, South	82
Egypt	82
Uruguay	81
Uganda	80
Ireland	80
Finland	80
Montenegro	80
Japan	79
Luxembourg	79
Northern Ireland	79
Albania	79
Indonesia	78
United States	78
Switzerland	78
Spain	76
Bosnia and Herz.	75
China	74
Taiwan	74
Dominican Rep.	73
Tanzania	73
Canada	73
New Zealand	72
Great Britain	71
Croatia	71
Australia	70
Zimbabwe	70
Serbia	70
Georgia	69
Algeria	69
Estonia	69
Turkey	69
Belarus	69
Iran	67
Jordan	67
Belgium	67
Italy	67
Norway	66
Morocco	65
Ukraine	64
Czech Republic	63
Nigeria	63
Chile	63
Pakistan	61
Portugal	61
Hungary	61
Lithuania	60
Bulgaria	60
Greece	58
Armenia	58
Moldova	58
India	57
Venezuela	56
South Africa	56
Macedonia	55
Argentina	55
Poland	53
Slovenia	53
Latvia	52
Slovakia	52
Puerto Rico	51
France	50
Philippines	48
Russian Fed.	45
Peru	45
Mexico	45
Romania	44
Brazil	30
Total	68

E121) DEMOCRACIES ARE INDECISIVE

I'm going to read off some things that people sometimes say about a democratic political system. Democracies are indecisive and have too much quibbling

Disagree / Strongly disagree (%)

(WVS: V170; EVS: V222)

Country	Wave		Gender		Age			Education			Income			Values		
	1990	2000	Male	Female	16-29	30-49	50+	Lower	Middle	Upper	Lower	Middle	Upper	Mat	Mixed	Postm.
Albania	na	**72**	71	72	74	72	69	68	72	78	67	71	79	74	72	62
Algeria	na	**37**	37	37	33	41	38	43	36	34	32	37	41	39	35	46
Argentina	na	**33**	33	34	32	31	37	26	40	55	25	33	42	30	31	41
Armenia	na	**42**	44	41	52	37	34	43	39	52	50	37	34	34	47	69
Australia	na	**50**	51	49	42	54	53	37	46	65	44	49	61	48	48	55
Austria	na	**60**	56	64	63	62	56	56	61	71	56	57	64	41	60	63
Azerbaijan	na	**81**	81	80	83	81	75	76	81	81	80	80	80	79	84	91
Bangladesh	na	**87**	86	88	86	87	87	92	84	82	88	88	87	88	87	83
Belarus	na	**60**	64	57	67	59	54	49	62	65	56	60	68	56	62	77
Belgium	na	**40**	43	36	47	43	33	27	37	52	28	36	48	32	39	50
Bosnia and Herz.	na	**55**	54	55	56	54	56	56	53	59	54	56	56	53	56	51
Brazil	na	**16**	19	14	15	16	19	17	13	23	18	11	18	14	17	18
Bulgaria	na	**58**	58	57	71	60	48	38	62	70	46	57	65	49	64	70
Canada	na	**50**	51	49	47	49	53	37	46	66	41	47	60	45	47	57
Chile	na	**56**	55	56	54	57	56	50	58	63	48	64	58	54	53	68
China	na	**65**	66	64	63	64	71	68	63	73	72	65	58	66	64	71
Colombia	na	**na**	na	na	na	na	na	na	na	na	na	na	na	na	na	na
Croatia	na	**74**	75	73	82	75	68	69	74	86	76	71	75	71	72	83
Czech Republic	na	**49**	49	49	57	54	40	39	57	66	41	47	58	39	49	67
Denmark	na	**57**	59	55	59	62	50	46	69	67	48	58	71	32	55	73
Dominican Rep.	na	**61**	58	63	62	57	78	46	51	66	47	67	71	51	60	71
Egypt	na	**71**	70	72	67	72	75	77	68	64	72	75	69	74	70	61
El Salvador	na	**na**	na	na	na	na	na	na	na	na	na	na	na	na	na	na
Estonia	na	**54**	56	54	61	59	47	49	56	59	53	44	61	48	57	70
Finland	na	**53**	49	56	58	54	47	48	59	57	50	54	53	52	53	48
France	na	**26**	27	26	26	29	24	18	30	43	19	24	35	16	26	41
Georgia	na	**52**	54	51	55	53	49	54	51	55	46	55	60	50	54	54
Germany	na	**66**	65	67	67	68	64	63	68	74	62	64	68	64	67	68
Great Britain	na	**55**	55	56	51	58	55	55	53	59	56	50	60	na	na	na
Greece	na	**49**	46	52	52	52	39	32	46	56	45	44	55	47	50	55
Hungary	na	**38**	39	36	45	41	29	31	44	58	26	33	46	37	38	32
Iceland	na	**82**	81	82	82	86	75	77	83	86	76	82	85	75	84	80
India	na	**34**	34	33	34	34	35	35	29	37	40	35	31	39	32	27
Indonesia	na	**75**	78	73	66	75	80	74	75	76	69	79	81	74	77	79
Iran	na	**72**	72	72	71	75	67	65	74	74	71	74	71	70	75	75
Ireland	na	**60**	62	58	60	59	63	54	60	72	52	62	66	61	60	63
Israel	na	**na**	na	na	na	na	na	na	na	na	na	na	na	na	na	na
Italy	na	**48**	49	46	52	53	41	34	53	71	41	49	56	34	47	56
Japan	na	**57**	58	55	46	62	56	49	54	64	53	61	60	52	55	74
Jordan	na	**56**	58	54	54	58	56	55	60	53	60	58	47	54	57	58
Korea, South	na	**62**	58	66	66	62	56	58	61	64	57	67	64	60	63	75
Latvia	na	**30**	32	28	35	31	27	23	29	40	24	31	35	27	29	41
Lithuania	na	**37**	43	32	43	45	24	24	37	52	23	33	45	37	33	68
Luxembourg	na	**47**	45	49	50	53	39	42	47	54	42	42	49	44	46	56
Macedonia	na	**59**	60	58	65	58	54	57	56	68	51	61	66	58	58	70
Malta	na	**80**	79	81	78	79	83	77	80	86	77	81	80	77	81	87
Mexico	na	**38**	40	37	39	37	40	38	35	50	38	39	42	36	41	36
Moldova	na	**58**	61	55	58	65	48	48	57	67	46	59	65	54	61	69
Montenegro	na	**73**	73	74	76	77	66	68	71	84	63	74	79	71	75	81
Morocco	na	**29**	30	27	32	27	20	29	29	28	18	25	37	28	30	32
Netherlands	na	**58**	57	58	58	65	50	44	59	68	50	61	66	45	56	67
New Zealand	na	**53**	54	53	41	60	52	44	54	64	48	53	64	46	55	67
Nigeria	na	**45**	45	44	44	47	36	38	50	47	40	46	51	48	44	43
Northern Ireland	na	**67**	66	68	58	67	71	65	67	71	61	64	72	73	66	66
Norway	na	**42**	41	42	45	44	36	33	43	49	na	na	na	30	42	55
Pakistan	na	**71**	73	69	71	70	76	68	74	78	64	72	79	71	72	75
Peru	na	**42**	43	41	42	44	40	45	41	42	43	42	41	43	43	39
Philippines	na	**43**	44	41	37	46	45	46	43	40	46	44	38	42	44	40
Poland	na	**20**	20	21	21	24	16	14	25	35	16	23	24	22	19	26
Portugal	na	**40**	41	39	37	47	35	37	46	41	31	38	45	38	42	35
Puerto Rico	na	**44**	51	40	40	43	46	30	35	50	42	48	44	47	43	46
Romania	na	**27**	31	24	34	28	22	18	27	45	18	23	38	19	32	51
Russian Fed.	na	**28**	30	26	37	31	18	10	25	45	20	25	35	21	33	47
Serbia	na	**51**	56	46	57	56	44	34	56	62	41	51	58	46	54	64
Singapore	na	**na**	na	na	na	na	na	na	na	na	na	na	na	na	na	na
Slovakia	na	**45**	46	44	48	47	40	37	45	67	35	42	55	39	48	66
Slovenia	na	**31**	33	29	36	36	22	13	32	59	18	35	46	17	32	39
South Africa	na	**48**	49	48	55	42	52	43	54	58	48	55	46	50	48	46
Spain	na	**64**	62	66	67	68	58	61	65	69	57	68	65	56	67	64
Sweden	na	**52**	51	54	55	58	45	37	50	67	47	51	60	43	48	68
Switzerland	na	**25**	24	25	24	27	23	22	27	17	25	27	24	32	24	22
Taiwan	na	**39**	42	36	33	40	42	43	38	38	43	37	38	35	42	53
Tanzania	na	**51**	55	45	38	55	62	49	48	63	45	55	63	53	51	46
Turkey	na	**43**	44	42	44	44	40	41	41	58	44	42	46	39	42	51
Uganda	na	**55**	41	69	56	53	53	51	58	35	40	44	56	59	53	49
Ukraine	na	**46**	49	43	57	48	37	26	44	59	35	46	57	36	49	77
United States	na	**61**	62	60	53	60	69	46	56	69	54	59	72	61	61	60
Uruguay	na	**58**	58	58	55	60	58	56	59	64	59	60	56	61	59	56
Venezuela	na	**45**	44	45	45	43	48	42	42	54	41	43	46	47	43	46
Vietnam	na	**70**	71	67	77	67	68	69	71	69	66	73	68	54	73	71
Zimbabwe	na	**63**	66	61	62	66	62	64	62	70	65	61	66	75	57	42
Total	na	**52**	52	51	53	54	48	47	52	59	47	52	56	50	52	57

RANKING	
Country	2000
Bangladesh	87
Iceland	82
Azerbaijan	81
Malta	80
Indonesia	75
Croatia	74
Montenegro	73
Iran	72
Albania	72
Pakistan	71
Egypt	71
Vietnam	70
Northern Ireland	67
Germany	66
China	65
Spain	64
Zimbabwe	63
Korea, South	62
Dominican Rep.	61
United States	61
Ireland	60
Belarus	60
Austria	60
Macedonia	59
Uruguay	58
Bulgaria	58
Moldova	58
Netherlands	58
Denmark	57
Japan	57
Jordan	56
Chile	56
Great Britain	55
Bosnia and Herz.	55
Uganda	55
Estonia	54
New Zealand	53
Finland	53
Georgia	52
Sweden	52
Serbia	51
Tanzania	51
Australia	50
Canada	50
Greece	49
Czech Republic	49
South Africa	48
Italy	48
Luxembourg	47
Ukraine	46
Nigeria	45
Slovakia	45
Venezuela	45
Puerto Rico	44
Turkey	43
Philippines	43
Armenia	42
Peru	42
Norway	42
Portugal	40
Belgium	40
Taiwan	39
Mexico	38
Hungary	38
Lithuania	37
Algeria	37
India	34
Argentina	33
Slovenia	31
Latvia	30
Morocco	29
Russian Fed.	28
Romania	27
France	26
Switzerland	25
Poland	20
Brazil	16
Total	52

E122) DEMOCRACIES AREN'T GOOD AT MAINTAINING ORDER

I'm going to read off some things that people sometimes say about a democratic political system. Democracies aren't good a maintaining order

Disagree / Strongly disagree (%) (WVS: V171; EVS: V223

Country	Wave 1990	Wave 2000	Gender Male	Gender Female	Age 16-29	Age 30-49	Age 50+	Education Lower	Education Middle	Education Upper	Income Lower	Income Middle	Income Upper	Values Mat	Values Mixed	Values Postm.
Albania	na	**71**	73	70	79	70	67	65	74	80	70	70	75	77	69	62
Algeria	na	**68**	67	68	64	71	71	72	65	69	62	70	73	65	69	71
Argentina	na	**65**	65	64	65	66	63	55	75	84	51	66	76	48	65	78
Armenia	na	**49**	50	49	57	48	39	49	47	57	57	45	41	40	55	78
Australia	na	**71**	73	69	67	76	69	58	67	86	63	74	79	65	69	76
Austria	na	**87**	86	88	88	90	84	85	87	93	82	92	89	67	87	93
Azerbaijan	na	**79**	79	79	81	78	75	78	78	81	75	78	83	77	82	90
Bangladesh	na	**88**	87	89	89	87	85	91	86	83	88	88	88	89	88	92
Belarus	na	**59**	60	58	68	61	45	52	59	67	59	57	62	52	63	78
Belgium	na	**62**	65	58	66	66	55	44	60	77	48	58	71	54	61	74
Bosnia and Herz.	na	**82**	81	82	82	83	80	74	82	87	82	81	81	83	82	80
Brazil	na	**44**	47	40	43	42	48	36	44	66	41	38	50	34	47	51
Bulgaria	na	**65**	66	64	76	71	53	40	72	80	52	65	74	56	72	90
Canada	na	**71**	74	67	75	71	68	54	68	89	60	68	81	70	67	78
Chile	na	**64**	65	64	62	65	65	61	65	70	58	68	68	62	63	73
China	na	**82**	84	79	83	80	84	81	81	91	86	78	82	83	81	81
Colombia	na	**na**	na	na	na	na	na	na	na	na	na	na	na	na	na	na
Croatia	na	**81**	80	82	84	82	78	76	82	91	80	77	86	78	78	92
Czech Republic	na	**46**	47	45	55	49	37	39	51	61	43	44	51	35	46	68
Denmark	na	**84**	85	82	86	90	75	77	94	91	77	84	93	71	83	91
Dominican Rep.	na	**64**	62	66	63	68	67	43	61	69	57	69	71	54	65	72
Egypt	na	**80**	80	80	78	80	82	83	78	77	81	81	81	81	79	79
El Salvador	na	**85**	87	83	83	85	88	87	82	86	86	85	87	na	na	na
Estonia	na	**70**	68	71	75	72	64	63	70	77	65	66	71	66	71	77
Finland	na	**81**	84	79	87	83	76	75	87	95	77	83	85	75	83	83
France	na	**45**	45	45	44	50	40	34	48	67	36	42	53	34	43	63
Georgia	na	**55**	57	53	57	55	51	58	52	60	49	55	63	54	54	62
Germany	na	**84**	84	85	83	85	84	83	85	92	83	86	84	82	85	85
Great Britain	na	**67**	65	68	64	69	66	65	64	72	68	60	71	na	na	na
Greece	na	**67**	68	67	71	67	59	46	60	77	61	66	72	59	67	76
Hungary	na	**61**	63	59	68	64	52	54	67	81	46	60	67	59	61	65
Iceland	na	**89**	90	89	90	91	85	83	92	96	84	91	93	84	90	93
India	na	**59**	59	58	59	60	56	54	61	62	57	58	60	62	59	57
Indonesia	na	**77**	79	75	66	82	78	75	78	78	77	79	74	77	77	78
Iran	na	**69**	69	68	67	71	69	62	72	69	69	71	67	65	70	75
Ireland	na	**77**	81	74	75	82	74	72	78	86	67	77	85	74	78	80
Israel	na	**na**	na	na	na	na	na	na	na	na	na	na	na	na	na	na
Italy	na	**80**	79	81	83	83	75	70	85	93	75	82	84	70	79	87
Japan	na	**80**	80	81	78	85	77	66	78	90	75	82	84	78	81	92
Jordan	na	**66**	68	64	67	67	61	63	70	66	71	68	56	62	67	74
Korea, South	na	**77**	75	78	85	75	71	70	72	83	73	81	77	73	79	88
Latvia	na	**56**	58	55	67	57	51	41	57	73	49	53	67	54	56	74
Lithuania	na	**50**	51	49	62	51	38	36	51	58	37	51	53	50	46	71
Luxembourg	na	**79**	78	79	76	82	77	76	77	88	78	74	83	79	78	87
Macedonia	na	**59**	59	59	62	59	55	58	56	66	48	62	64	60	58	58
Malta	na	**87**	86	88	85	86	90	85	87	94	85	91	89	86	87	94
Mexico	na	**49**	52	46	53	47	46	44	49	67	47	52	54	46	51	48
Moldova	na	**57**	59	54	60	60	49	46	58	61	44	63	58	53	60	72
Montenegro	na	**81**	80	81	84	84	74	74	80	92	71	81	86	79	82	90
Morocco	na	**59**	60	58	62	56	53	57	60	66	48	58	68	61	57	70
Netherlands	na	**78**	77	80	83	82	72	67	81	85	78	78	84	68	76	90
New Zealand	na	**69**	73	66	66	77	64	57	68	83	62	70	80	67	71	78
Nigeria	na	**55**	53	56	56	55	47	47	59	59	51	56	61	54	55	59
Northern Ireland	na	**75**	75	76	69	76	77	72	74	84	69	75	79	76	74	78
Norway	na	**68**	67	68	72	72	58	55	68	79	na	na	na	51	68	86
Pakistan	na	**47**	51	43	42	50	49	43	49	57	39	46	58	50	44	20
Peru	na	**52**	55	50	50	55	52	48	52	56	48	52	61	49	54	50
Philippines	na	**50**	51	49	49	52	48	47	50	53	52	52	45	50	49	53
Poland	na	**32**	33	31	35	33	29	25	36	53	28	34	38	25	36	34
Portugal	na	**59**	60	58	56	60	61	58	59	71	57	56	62	58	59	57
Puerto Rico	na	**55**	63	51	54	55	57	43	47	61	51	58	59	59	55	58
Romania	na	**49**	53	45	60	52	40	36	51	64	35	47	59	40	54	69
Russian Fed.	na	**35**	35	34	43	37	25	17	32	50	28	32	43	28	39	56
Serbia	na	**69**	73	64	74	76	59	53	72	80	57	69	77	61	73	86
Singapore	na	**na**	na	na	na	na	na	na	na	na	na	na	na	na	na	na
Slovakia	na	**58**	57	58	61	58	55	56	56	73	49	55	67	52	61	73
Slovenia	na	**54**	59	50	57	59	47	39	54	81	41	56	72	42	55	63
South Africa	na	**61**	63	59	65	60	58	54	69	78	61	62	66	66	60	46
Spain	na	**81**	81	82	85	84	77	78	83	88	79	81	81	74	82	88
Sweden	na	**85**	85	86	89	89	80	73	85	93	81	84	92	74	85	91
Switzerland	na	**73**	74	73	79	72	71	62	75	85	67	68	81	69	71	81
Taiwan	na	**66**	71	61	71	68	59	61	69	70	69	60	69	60	71	76
Tanzania	na	**79**	83	73	79	79	78	72	86	89	71	82	86	76	81	83
Turkey	na	**65**	65	64	65	65	62	60	64	83	62	65	71	63	64	70
Uganda	na	**79**	78	81	84	76	68	70	83	75	69	78	83	77	81	76
Ukraine	na	**50**	51	49	55	55	41	36	48	61	42	52	57	43	51	68
United States	na	**78**	79	77	76	77	80	62	76	85	72	79	84	76	77	80
Uruguay	na	**79**	81	77	78	80	78	74	84	87	74	80	81	70	78	88
Venezuela	na	**64**	62	65	62	64	67	63	60	72	60	64	63	66	62	67
Vietnam	na	**75**	79	70	74	76	74	73	77	75	64	78	76	54	81	72
Zimbabwe	na	**68**	72	65	66	72	70	70	66	78	68	64	73	77	64	52
Total	na	**67**	68	66	68	69	64	62	67	75	62	67	72	62	68	76

RANKING

Country	2000
Iceland	89
Bangladesh	88
Malta	87
Austria	87
El Salvador	85
Sweden	85
Germany	84
Denmark	84
Bosnia and Herz.	82
China	82
Spain	81
Finland	81
Croatia	81
Montenegro	81
Japan	80
Italy	80
Egypt	80
Uganda	79
Luxembourg	79
Tanzania	79
Azerbaijan	79
Uruguay	79
Netherlands	78
United States	78
Ireland	77
Indonesia	77
Korea, South	77
Northern Ireland	75
Vietnam	75
Switzerland	73
Albania	71
Australia	71
Canada	71
Estonia	70
New Zealand	69
Serbia	69
Iran	69
Zimbabwe	68
Algeria	68
Norway	68
Greece	67
Great Britain	67
Taiwan	66
Jordan	66
Bulgaria	65
Argentina	65
Turkey	65
Chile	64
Dominican Rep.	64
Venezuela	64
Belgium	62
South Africa	61
Hungary	61
Portugal	59
Belarus	59
Morocco	59
India	59
Macedonia	59
Slovakia	58
Moldova	57
Latvia	56
Puerto Rico	55
Georgia	55
Nigeria	55
Slovenia	54
Peru	52
Philippines	50
Ukraine	50
Lithuania	50
Armenia	49
Mexico	49
Romania	49
Pakistan	47
Czech Republic	46
France	45
Brazil	44
Russian Fed.	35
Poland	32
Total	67

E123) DEMOCRACY MAY HAVE PROBLEMS BUT IS BETTER

I'm going to read off some things that people sometimes say about a democratic political system. Democracy may have problems but it's better than any other form of government

Agree strongly / Agree (%) (WVS: V172; EVS: V220)

Country	Wave 1990	Wave 2000	Gender Male	Gender Female	Age 16-29	Age 30-49	Age 50+	Education Lower	Education Middle	Education Upper	Income Lower	Income Middle	Income Upper	Values Mat	Values Mixed	Values Postm.
Albania	na	**95**	95	95	96	96	92	91	96	98	92	96	97	94	96	97
Algeria	na	**88**	86	91	88	89	87	90	88	88	88	91	89	88	88	88
Argentina	na	**91**	89	93	91	92	91	89	96	93	87	92	95	86	92	94
Armenia	na	**73**	71	75	76	75	66	68	73	77	75	70	71	69	75	86
Australia	na	**87**	89	84	80	89	89	82	83	95	86	87	89	80	86	89
Austria	na	**97**	97	98	98	96	98	97	97	98	97	97	98	91	98	98
Azerbaijan	na	**96**	97	95	97	96	96	98	97	94	97	96	95	96	98	92
Bangladesh	na	**98**	98	99	98	98	99	99	99	97	98	98	99	99	98	100
Belarus	na	**87**	87	87	91	87	83	82	87	89	86	87	87	84	89	98
Belgium	na	**92**	92	92	89	92	93	88	90	97	90	89	95	90	91	96
Bosnia and Herz.	na	**92**	92	92	94	92	90	92	91	93	92	91	93	91	93	92
Brazil	na	**83**	83	83	83	81	89	81	84	89	83	82	86	80	84	87
Bulgaria	na	**84**	85	82	92	89	74	71	86	93	75	82	91	79	87	92
Canada	na	**87**	88	86	81	87	91	82	86	93	83	86	90	85	87	88
Chile	na	**82**	83	80	80	82	82	79	82	86	78	83	87	77	82	89
China	na	**90**	90	90	85	92	90	89	90	90	92	88	91	92	89	88
Colombia	na	**na**	na	na	na	na	na	na	na	na	na	na	na	na	na	na
Croatia	na	**96**	96	96	95	95	97	95	96	96	97	94	97	96	96	96
Czech Republic	na	**93**	92	93	94	94	91	90	94	98	88	93	95	87	94	96
Denmark	na	**99**	99	99	97	100	99	98	99	100	98	99	100	93	99	99
Dominican Rep.	na	**93**	93	93	91	96	100	97	90	93	91	93	95	81	95	100
Egypt	na	**98**	97	98	96	98	99	98	96	99	98	98	98	98	97	97
El Salvador	na	**na**	na	na	na	na	na	na	na	na	na	na	na	na	na	na
Estonia	na	**90**	90	91	87	92	91	91	89	93	91	91	90	88	92	85
Finland	na	**91**	92	89	89	91	91	88	93	97	87	89	94	91	91	91
France	na	**94**	95	92	92	94	94	91	94	99	92	94	97	92	93	98
Georgia	na	**86**	86	86	86	88	82	87	84	91	82	90	89	85	87	83
Germany	na	**97**	97	97	96	97	97	96	97	99	97	96	97	97	96	97
Great Britain	na	**78**	82	74	74	79	79	71	82	88	69	84	85	na	na	na
Greece	na	**97**	96	97	97	96	97	97	97	97	97	97	97	98	97	97
Hungary	na	**81**	81	82	83	82	79	75	89	97	71	81	86	80	83	77
Iceland	na	**97**	97	97	95	98	99	97	97	100	95	98	99	94	99	97
India	na	**92**	92	91	93	91	91	90	91	95	84	93	93	93	90	97
Indonesia	na	**71**	72	71	62	72	76	68	70	74	74	73	66	69	73	75
Iran	na	**69**	70	68	65	74	74	71	68	71	70	73	65	68	72	60
Ireland	na	**92**	93	92	89	93	93	87	93	99	88	90	96	92	92	95
Israel	na	**na**	na	na	na	na	na	na	na	na	na	na	na	na	na	na
Italy	na	**94**	94	95	92	95	95	93	95	98	94	95	96	92	95	95
Japan	na	**92**	91	93	87	91	95	91	92	94	92	91	93	93	91	99
Jordan	na	**89**	92	87	90	90	86	89	90	90	87	89	92	91	90	87
Korea, South	na	**91**	90	92	92	91	89	86	91	92	88	94	92	92	90	92
Latvia	na	**89**	88	89	85	90	90	85	89	93	88	87	92	87	90	93
Lithuania	na	**88**	88	88	89	90	85	78	89	97	84	90	89	87	88	91
Luxembourg	na	**96**	96	95	94	96	97	94	97	96	96	94	98	93	97	97
Macedonia	na	**81**	79	84	86	80	79	83	78	87	77	80	88	81	82	86
Malta	na	**94**	94	94	95	93	95	93	94	98	93	95	94	94	94	94
Mexico	na	**80**	82	78	78	79	84	79	79	86	77	80	81	78	81	78
Moldova	na	**78**	82	74	79	78	77	81	75	81	76	79	80	77	83	82
Montenegro	na	**92**	91	93	96	92	89	90	91	98	88	91	96	90	94	94
Morocco	na	**96**	96	96	96	97	98	97	95	95	96	97	96	97	96	94
Netherlands	na	**96**	97	96	97	95	98	92	97	99	96	96	98	92	97	97
New Zealand	na	**83**	86	82	79	86	83	76	87	91	81	82	89	89	84	88
Nigeria	na	**45**	47	44	44	45	53	53	41	41	50	45	39	46	45	42
Northern Ireland	na	**93**	94	93	92	92	95	91	97	93	94	93	90	96	93	91
Norway	na	**95**	95	95	92	95	97	93	94	98	na	na	na	94	95	96
Pakistan	na	**82**	83	81	82	83	81	80	85	85	78	83	88	81	84	83
Peru	na	**89**	88	90	89	89	91	88	88	91	87	89	93	89	89	92
Philippines	na	**80**	79	80	81	80	79	80	79	80	77	81	80	78	81	86
Poland	na	**90**	92	88	91	91	88	88	90	98	86	92	92	87	92	87
Portugal	na	**93**	94	92	89	93	95	94	91	91	92	91	93	96	90	96
Puerto Rico	na	**90**	89	92	84	90	95	86	93	91	92	93	88	90	92	89
Romania	na	**78**	81	76	82	78	76	66	80	90	70	78	85	72	81	97
Russian Fed.	na	**63**	62	64	71	67	53	42	60	79	52	60	76	59	67	67
Serbia	na	**89**	89	89	91	92	85	80	92	95	84	90	92	86	92	93
Singapore	na	**na**	na	na	na	na	na	na	na	na	na	na	na	na	na	na
Slovakia	na	**84**	84	85	87	84	83	79	85	94	79	85	88	82	86	98
Slovenia	na	**90**	93	88	88	90	92	85	91	98	84	94	96	89	90	92
South Africa	na	**84**	85	83	85	83	84	85	82	92	85	82	83	86	84	78
Spain	na	**93**	93	93	93	93	93	93	93	93	93	93	91	92	93	95
Sweden	na	**94**	94	94	93	95	95	91	93	99	91	95	97	90	94	95
Switzerland	na	**91**	90	92	92	89	94	89	91	96	92	88	93	88	90	96
Taiwan	na	**84**	85	82	86	82	86	78	84	87	83	82	85	83	86	78
Tanzania	na	**88**	91	85	89	88	91	85	91	93	85	90	92	87	89	92
Turkey	na	**88**	88	89	87	89	91	87	89	92	88	88	89	88	88	89
Uganda	na	**92**	97	87	94	93	79	84	95	93	94	93	95	93	91	91
Ukraine	na	**83**	83	82	82	88	77	65	83	88	76	83	89	80	83	90
United States	na	**88**	87	88	80	87	95	78	86	92	84	88	92	85	88	88
Uruguay	na	**96**	98	95	95	97	97	96	98	95	97	96	97	97	96	98
Venezuela	na	**93**	91	94	92	93	93	93	92	95	89	95	94	92	93	93
Vietnam	na	**72**	71	74	68	75	72	71	75	68	74	70	73	68	76	71
Zimbabwe	na	**88**	86	89	85	89	92	88	87	100	86	87	90	88	88	86
Total	na	**88**	88	88	87	89	89	87	88	91	86	88	90	86	89	92

RANKING

Country	2000
Denmark	99
Bangladesh	98
Egypt	98
Iceland	97
Austria	97
Germany	97
Greece	97
Netherlands	96
Morocco	96
Uruguay	96
Azerbaijan	96
Croatia	96
Luxembourg	96
Norway	95
Albania	95
Italy	94
Sweden	94
Malta	94
France	94
Northern Ireland	93
Spain	93
Dominican Rep.	93
Portugal	93
Czech Republic	93
Venezuela	93
Ireland	92
Bosnia and Herz.	92
Japan	92
Uganda	92
Montenegro	92
Belgium	92
India	92
Argentina	91
Switzerland	91
Korea, South	91
Finland	91
Estonia	90
Puerto Rico	90
Slovenia	90
China	90
Poland	90
Jordan	89
Serbia	89
Peru	89
Latvia	89
Algeria	88
Tanzania	88
Turkey	88
Lithuania	88
Zimbabwe	88
United States	88
Canada	87
Belarus	87
Australia	87
Georgia	86
Slovakia	84
South Africa	84
Bulgaria	84
Taiwan	84
Brazil	83
New Zealand	83
Ukraine	83
Pakistan	82
Chile	82
Macedonia	81
Hungary	81
Philippines	80
Mexico	80
Romania	78
Moldova	78
Great Britain	78
Armenia	73
Vietnam	72
Indonesia	71
Iran	69
Russian Fed.	63
Nigeria	45
Total	88

E124) RESPECT FOR INDIVIDUAL HUMAN RIGHTS

How much respect is there for individual human rights nowadays (in our country)? Do you feel there is ...

A lot of respect for / Some respect (%) (WVS: V173; EVS: V224)

	Wave		Gender		Age			Education			Income			Values		
Country	1990	2000	Male	Female	16-29	30-49	50+	Lower	Middle	Upper	Lower	Middle	Upper	Mat	Mixed	Postm.
Albania	na	**37**	38	37	38	38	36	35	38	42	37	41	35	34	41	45
Algeria	na	**36**	35	37	34	37	37	41	34	34	36	38	31	40	35	27
Argentina	na	**22**	27	17	19	22	24	20	23	33	24	20	22	24	23	20
Armenia	na	**23**	24	22	27	19	22	24	24	21	28	14	22	25	21	19
Australia	na	**na**	na	na	na	na	na	na	na	na	na	na	na	na	na	na
Austria	na	**76**	78	74	75	76	77	75	76	79	71	75	81	76	79	70
Azerbaijan	na	**61**	62	61	57	63	67	66	62	59	59	60	66	64	57	50
Bangladesh	na	**73**	72	76	75	72	71	73	75	71	77	73	70	75	71	79
Belarus	na	**36**	33	40	23	30	56	57	31	25	42	36	28	43	34	15
Belgium	na	**63**	67	59	65	61	63	52	61	73	54	60	74	59	62	71
Bosnia and Herz.	na	**35**	36	33	31	34	39	37	34	34	30	35	40	36	34	43
Brazil	na	**na**	na	na	na	na	na	na	na	na	na	na	na	na	na	na
Bulgaria	na	**34**	38	31	37	36	32	30	34	42	33	29	38	26	41	52
Canada	na	**84**	86	81	82	85	83	75	83	92	77	86	88	84	84	85
Chile	na	**57**	57	56	55	56	58	54	57	62	53	58	64	53	59	58
China	na	**88**	88	87	87	88	88	88	88	88	85	89	89	89	87	83
Colombia	na	**na**	na	na	na	na	na	na	na	na	na	na	na	na	na	na
Croatia	na	**58**	59	56	60	57	56	61	56	55	58	57	57	64	58	49
Czech Republic	na	**65**	65	64	68	61	65	61	66	76	57	65	72	57	66	74
Denmark	na	**88**	90	85	94	90	82	82	95	96	83	88	98	82	86	94
Dominican Rep.	na	**na**	na	na	na	na	na	na	na	na	na	na	na	na	na	na
Egypt	na	**72**	68	76	69	71	77	75	70	65	72	74	69	74	72	51
El Salvador	na	**na**	na	na	na	na	na	na	na	na	na	na	na	na	na	na
Estonia	na	**54**	55	54	54	52	57	52	54	61	50	53	60	48	60	57
Finland	na	**88**	89	87	95	87	86	85	92	95	84	90	92	89	89	85
France	na	**60**	65	55	55	60	62	54	63	73	47	63	70	56	61	62
Georgia	na	**25**	26	24	27	24	23	25	25	23	22	27	27	25	24	27
Germany	na	**79**	79	79	77	79	80	75	81	83	75	80	87	82	78	76
Great Britain	na	**66**	68	65	69	68	65	57	69	85	52	75	73	na	na	na
Greece	na	**63**	68	59	57	66	69	55	60	67	59	64	65	66	65	59
Hungary	na	**57**	60	54	56	61	54	52	61	75	52	55	63	55	60	53
Iceland	na	**86**	87	85	85	87	85	80	89	93	81	88	88	81	87	91
India	na	**75**	73	78	79	74	71	74	75	76	81	77	72	76	76	68
Indonesia	na	**62**	64	60	50	67	62	70	63	55	59	65	63	59	63	68
Iran	na	**73**	71	75	72	73	76	75	74	67	72	72	73	78	72	71
Ireland	na	**76**	78	75	75	83	71	70	78	85	70	72	83	72	77	80
Israel	na	**na**	na	na	na	na	na	na	na	na	na	na	na	na	na	na
Italy	na	**62**	68	57	59	66	61	56	64	78	57	64	72	54	61	69
Japan	na	**62**	64	61	56	58	68	58	60	70	61	61	68	72	64	47
Jordan	na	**74**	67	80	73	74	74	76	75	69	80	69	73	78	71	61
Korea, South	na	**47**	49	45	44	45	56	56	51	41	46	48	48	51	46	30
Latvia	na	**52**	51	54	46	49	58	52	52	54	54	47	54	57	51	47
Lithuania	na	**23**	24	22	28	17	26	20	22	34	19	25	24	22	23	19
Luxembourg	na	**91**	92	89	90	88	94	88	91	96	89	93	93	91	92	88
Macedonia	na	**32**	34	30	30	31	36	25	35	37	28	30	41	32	34	24
Malta	na	**75**	76	75	76	74	76	71	75	87	71	80	79	71	78	77
Mexico	na	**48**	46	49	45	47	52	51	44	43	48	48	48	48	47	48
Moldova	na	**21**	22	20	20	19	26	23	22	19	18	19	21	20	25	27
Montenegro	na	**40**	40	41	46	38	39	35	41	50	30	36	50	34	45	41
Morocco	na	**42**	38	47	39	43	50	45	32	35	40	37	42	52	37	28
Netherlands	na	**80**	83	76	85	81	75	67	83	88	74	82	88	70	80	83
New Zealand	na	**na**	na	na	na	na	na	na	na	na	na	na	na	na	na	na
Nigeria	na	**63**	65	61	63	64	63	64	62	63	58	65	67	63	64	60
Northern Ireland	na	**70**	71	70	65	70	73	66	71	80	64	69	70	69	73	64
Norway	na	**na**	na	na	na	na	na	na	na	na	na	na	na	na	na	na
Pakistan	na	**54**	54	54	55	55	53	57	52	52	56	55	52	54	56	50
Peru	na	**45**	47	43	44	47	43	40	47	46	43	44	52	46	45	46
Philippines	na	**79**	79	79	82	78	78	78	80	79	78	79	80	77	82	77
Poland	na	**57**	56	57	64	57	51	50	61	75	46	59	74	54	58	57
Portugal	na	**62**	65	59	66	62	60	59	65	76	56	64	68	65	59	68
Puerto Rico	na	**56**	61	53	54	60	54	41	51	61	52	57	60	56	58	51
Romania	na	**24**	24	23	24	24	23	19	24	30	23	23	26	23	23	27
Russian Fed.	na	**16**	16	16	20	16	15	14	16	18	15	17	17	16	17	17
Serbia	na	**49**	51	46	45	51	49	50	48	48	45	47	52	49	49	44
Singapore	na	**na**	na	na	na	na	na	na	na	na	na	na	na	na	na	na
Slovakia	na	**59**	59	59	68	57	55	52	61	70	51	57	66	54	63	71
Slovenia	na	**41**	47	36	42	42	40	29	42	61	33	44	60	36	43	39
South Africa	na	**56**	57	54	58	54	57	55	56	71	59	56	54	52	58	58
Spain	na	**63**	63	63	63	66	61	59	65	72	60	64	67	65	64	63
Sweden	na	**75**	82	69	77	75	74	66	77	80	71	76	83	66	76	76
Switzerland	na	**na**	na	na	na	na	na	na	na	na	na	na	na	na	na	na
Taiwan	na	**na**	na	na	na	na	na	na	na	na	na	na	na	na	na	na
Tanzania	na	**70**	71	68	58	74	80	73	63	70	70	72	73	68	72	63
Turkey	na	**26**	26	26	24	27	29	28	24	24	28	26	23	31	26	18
Uganda	na	**70**	76	66	73	66	76	65	72	73	67	75	71	73	68	74
Ukraine	na	**23**	21	25	22	23	23	15	22	28	18	23	28	23	22	31
United States	na	**74**	76	72	70	72	81	69	70	78	67	77	80	70	77	71
Uruguay	na	**na**	na	na	na	na	na	na	na	na	na	na	na	na	na	na
Venezuela	na	**49**	51	46	48	50	46	54	46	48	51	45	51	53	48	43
Vietnam	na	**95**	96	94	95	95	95	95	96	94	94	95	95	96	95	93
Zimbabwe	na	**32**	32	33	36	27	33	33	32	9	37	30	33	34	31	30
Total	na	**57**	58	56	55	57	58	57	55	61	53	57	60	53	58	60

RANKING	
Country	2000
Vietnam	95
Luxembourg	91
Finland	88
Denmark	88
China	88
Iceland	86
Canada	84
Netherlands	80
Philippines	79
Germany	79
Ireland	76
Austria	76
Malta	75
Sweden	75
India	75
United States	74
Jordan	74
Bangladesh	73
Iran	73
Egypt	72
Uganda	70
Northern Ireland	70
Tanzania	70
Great Britain	66
Czech Republic	65
Spain	63
Nigeria	63
Greece	63
Belgium	63
Japan	62
Italy	62
Portugal	62
Indonesia	62
Azerbaijan	61
France	60
Slovakia	59
Croatia	58
Hungary	57
Chile	57
Poland	57
Puerto Rico	56
South Africa	56
Estonia	54
Pakistan	54
Latvia	52
Serbia	49
Venezuela	49
Mexico	48
Korea, South	47
Peru	45
Morocco	42
Slovenia	41
Montenegro	40
Albania	37
Belarus	36
Algeria	36
Bosnia and Herz.	35
Bulgaria	34
Zimbabwe	32
Macedonia	32
Turkey	26
Georgia	25
Romania	24
Armenia	23
Lithuania	23
Ukraine	23
Argentina	22
Moldova	21
Russian Fed.	16
Total	57

E125) SATISFACTION WITH GOVERNMENT

How satisfied are you with the way the people now in national office are handling the country's affairs? Would you say you are very satisfied, fairly satisfied, fairly dissatisfied or very dissatisfied?

Very satisfied / Fairly sátisfied (%) (WVS: V174)

	Wave		Gender		Age			Education			Income			Values		
Country	1990	2000	Male	Female	16-29	30-49	50+	Lower	Middle	Upper	Lower	Middle	Upper	Mat	Mixed	Postm.
Albania	na	**19**	20	19	19	20	18	17	20	23	19	22	17	19	18	28
Algeria	na	**28**	26	31	26	30	31	28	30	26	29	31	28	30	28	16
Argentina	na	**27**	32	23	24	31	26	28	26	28	31	25	27	29	30	22
Armenia	na	**15**	14	16	19	12	13	12	16	14	15	9	18	17	14	9
Australia	na	**45**	48	42	54	45	37	44	44	47	40	50	46	44	44	48
Austria	na	**na**	na	na	na	na	na	na	na	na	na	na	na	na	na	na
Azerbaijan	na	**26**	29	23	24	26	29	30	25	26	23	27	28	26	25	20
Bangladesh	na	**76**	72	81	74	77	80	81	70	71	84	77	69	76	75	81
Belarus	na	**na**	na	na	na	na	na	na	na	na	na	na	na	na	na	na
Belgium	na	**na**	na	na	na	na	na	na	na	na	na	na	na	na	na	na
Bosnia and Herz.	na	**24**	27	22	19	26	28	31	23	22	23	26	26	25	24	21
Brazil	na	**57**	65	50	53	55	71	59	56	57	60	55	56	55	58	62
Bulgaria	na	**na**	na	na	na	na	na	na	na	na	na	na	na	na	na	na
Canada	na	**65**	67	63	66	63	68	65	65	67	62	63	68	73	66	62
Chile	na	**66**	66	67	68	65	68	66	66	68	61	72	70	63	69	65
China	na	**73**	72	74	66	75	74	77	71	66	68	78	73	75	71	61
Colombia	na	**28**	27	30	28	28	29	34	30	22	35	28	24	28	30	33
Croatia	na	**na**	na	na	na	na	na	na	na	na	na	na	na	na	na	na
Czech Republic	na	**na**	na	na	na	na	na	na	na	na	na	na	na	na	na	na
Denmark	na	**na**	na	na	na	na	na	na	na	na	na	na	na	na	na	na
Dominican Rep.	na	**6**	8	5	7	6	na	22	4	5	9	5	6	12	6	5
Egypt	na	**92**	93	92	92	93	93	92	92	92	93	91	92	92	93	92
El Salvador	na	**na**	na	na	na	na	na	na	na	na	na	na	na	na	na	na
Estonia	na	**na**	na	na	na	na	na	na	na	na	na	na	na	na	na	na
Finland	na	**na**	na	na	na	na	na	na	na	na	na	na	na	na	na	na
France	na	**na**	na	na	na	na	na	na	na	na	na	na	na	na	na	na
Georgia	na	**23**	24	23	24	23	22	23	23	25	20	25	26	23	23	19
Germany	na	**na**	na	na	na	na	na	na	na	na	na	na	na	na	na	na
Great Britain	na	**na**	na	na	na	na	na	na	na	na	na	na	na	na	na	na
Greece	na	**na**	na	na	na	na	na	na	na	na	na	na	na	na	na	na
Hungary	na	**na**	na	na	na	na	na	na	na	na	na	na	na	na	na	na
Iceland	na	**na**	na	na	na	na	na	na	na	na	na	na	na	na	na	na
India	na	**60**	62	57	61	61	57	62	60	56	67	61	56	64	59	49
Indonesia	na	**23**	26	19	14	22	28	27	24	18	21	23	27	23	21	29
Iran	na	**71**	70	73	70	74	72	73	71	69	67	70	74	76	69	66
Ireland	na	**na**	na	na	na	na	na	na	na	na	na	na	na	na	na	na
Israel	na	**na**	na	na	na	na	na	na	na	na	na	na	na	na	na	na
Italy	na	**na**	na	na	na	na	na	na	na	na	na	na	na	na	na	na
Japan	na	**8**	10	7	7	5	12	11	7	10	9	6	9	13	7	7
Jordan	na	**77**	72	82	78	76	78	77	82	72	82	70	79	79	76	71
Korea, South	na	**31**	30	33	27	31	38	42	35	25	33	29	31	38	27	22
Latvia	na	**na**	na	na	na	na	na	na	na	na	na	na	na	na	na	na
Lithuania	na	**na**	na	na	na	na	na	na	na	na	na	na	na	na	na	na
Luxembourg	na	**na**	na	na	na	na	na	na	na	na	na	na	na	na	na	na
Macedonia	na	**19**	21	16	19	16	22	18	19	18	20	18	18	19	20	na
Malta	na	**na**	na	na	na	na	na	na	na	na	na	na	na	na	na	na
Mexico	na	**48**	46	50	47	48	49	51	45	41	52	50	44	51	47	43
Moldova	na	**21**	21	21	17	21	24	22	26	11	25	20	18	25	19	18
Montenegro	na	**28**	26	30	33	27	25	24	30	31	16	22	41	25	33	22
Morocco	na	**49**	46	52	43	51	58	53	31	31	53	40	45	58	43	36
Netherlands	na	**na**	na	na	na	na	na	na	na	na	na	na	na	na	na	na
New Zealand	na	**26**	28	26	25	30	23	23	25	31	20	26	33	29	27	25
Nigeria	na	**72**	73	72	73	72	65	75	69	73	69	71	77	72	72	76
Northern Ireland	na	**na**	na	na	na	na	na	na	na	na	na	na	na	na	na	na
Norway	na	**86**	85	86	86	89	82	81	88	89	na	na	na	85	86	82
Pakistan	na	**43**	44	42	43	42	46	40	47	47	40	46	44	42	44	42
Peru	na	**35**	36	33	33	36	36	33	33	38	32	35	39	36	34	37
Philippines	na	**51**	55	48	55	50	48	50	52	52	46	51	56	49	55	41
Poland	na	**na**	na	na	na	na	na	na	na	na	na	na	na	na	na	na
Portugal	na	**na**	na	na	na	na	na	na	na	na	na	na	na	na	na	na
Puerto Rico	na	**42**	42	42	39	40	46	49	44	40	48	45	36	49	41	44
Romania	na	**na**	na	na	na	na	na	na	na	na	na	na	na	na	na	na
Russian Fed.	na	**na**	na	na	na	na	na	na	na	na	na	na	na	na	na	na
Serbia	na	**38**	39	37	45	37	35	33	39	42	32	40	41	35	40	45
Singapore	na	**92**	89	94	92	90	92	94	90	90	93	91	91	95	91	81
Slovakia	na	**na**	na	na	na	na	na	na	na	na	na	na	na	na	na	na
Slovenia	na	**na**	na	na	na	na	na	na	na	na	na	na	na	na	na	na
South Africa	na	**57**	58	56	57	57	57	60	53	58	65	64	40	50	61	68
Spain	na	**46**	47	45	37	41	56	48	41	46	44	49	44	51	46	35
Sweden	na	**44**	48	41	48	43	44	46	45	42	43	48	45	44	43	48
Switzerland	na	**65**	63	68	70	62	66	66	64	67	67	63	66	73	66	59
Taiwan	na	**38**	36	40	25	35	56	50	38	28	40	40	35	37	38	44
Tanzania	na	**60**	57	62	60	58	62	60	60	57	59	56	62	59	61	50
Turkey	na	**28**	25	30	27	28	29	29	27	22	27	29	28	31	28	23
Uganda	na	**68**	63	72	69	67	62	63	69	73	65	77	61	67	68	71
Ukraine	na	**na**	na	na	na	na	na	na	na	na	na	na	na	na	na	na
United States	na	**67**	68	67	68	67	66	68	67	67	62	71	72	74	69	60
Uruguay	na	**31**	33	29	22	21	42	34	27	27	34	26	30	44	28	25
Venezuela	na	**62**	67	56	59	64	64	70	61	55	63	61	63	63	61	64
Vietnam	na	**94**	95	94	93	95	94	96	92	94	91	95	95	95	94	93
Zimbabwe	na	**32**	31	32	33	30	30	34	29	17	37	32	26	30	31	46
Total	na	**47**	48	46	48	47	46	52	46	42	45	46	48	47	48	45

RANKING	
Country	2000
Vietnam	94
Egypt	92
Singapore	92
Norway	86
Jordan	77
Bangladesh	76
China	73
Nigeria	72
Iran	71
Uganda	68
United States	67
Chile	66
Canada	65
Switzerland	65
Venezuela	62
India	60
Tanzania	60
Brazil	57
South Africa	57
Philippines	51
Morocco	49
Mexico	48
Spain	46
Australia	45
Sweden	44
Pakistan	43
Puerto Rico	42
Taiwan	38
Serbia	38
Peru	35
Zimbabwe	32
Korea, South	31
Uruguay	31
Algeria	28
Colombia	28
Montenegro	28
Turkey	28
Argentina	27
New Zealand	26
Azerbaijan	26
Bosnia and Herz.	24
Georgia	23
Indonesia	23
Moldova	21
Albania	19
Macedonia	19
Armenia	15
Japan	8
Dominican Rep.	6
Total	47

E128) COUNTRY IS RUN BY BIG INTEREST

Generally speaking, would you say that this country is run by a few big interests looking out for themselves, or that it is run for the benefit of all the people?

Run by few big interests (%)

(WVS: V175)

Country	Wave 1990	Wave 2000	Gender Male	Gender Female	Age 16-29	Age 30-49	Age 50+	Education Lower	Education Middle	Education Upper	Income Lower	Income Middle	Income Upper	Values Mat	Values Mixed	Values Postm.
Albania	na	**65**	70	61	62	66	67	59	68	71	67	56	72	67	64	66
Algeria	na	**87**	89	85	87	87	88	88	86	89	88	87	82	83	88	96
Argentina	na	**90**	90	90	87	92	91	87	95	91	88	89	94	86	90	92
Armenia	na	**96**	97	96	97	97	95	94	96	98	97	98	95	97	97	98
Australia	na	**68**	65	71	65	67	72	72	72	60	72	68	62	66	67	69
Austria	na	**na**	na	na	na	na	na	na	na	na	na	na	na	na	na	na
Azerbaijan	na	**78**	76	80	80	79	72	66	78	81	79	76	79	77	79	91
Bangladesh	na	**56**	60	52	57	56	54	48	65	66	43	58	65	54	59	62
Belarus	na	**na**	na	na	na	na	na	na	na	na	na	na	na	na	na	na
Belgium	na	**na**	na	na	na	na	na	na	na	na	na	na	na	na	na	na
Bosnia and Herz.	na	**81**	80	82	86	80	78	74	82	82	82	80	81	83	79	90
Brazil	na	**75**	71	80	75	77	74	66	81	88	69	76	82	69	77	85
Bulgaria	na	**na**	na	na	na	na	na	na	na	na	na	na	na	na	na	na
Canada	70	**52**	50	54	51	53	51	56	52	48	58	53	48	42	52	56
Chile	45	**65**	68	63	67	64	65	67	66	60	71	62	60	68	65	63
China	8	**17**	17	16	19	17	12	14	19	8	18	17	16	16	18	20
Colombia	na	**79**	82	76	80	79	75	69	76	90	72	77	86	76	73	81
Croatia	na	**na**	na	na	na	na	na	na	na	na	na	na	na	na	na	na
Czech Republic	67	**na**	na	na	na	na	na	na	na	na	na	na	na	na	na	na
Denmark	na	**na**	na	na	na	na	na	na	na	na	na	na	na	na	na	na
Dominican Rep.	na	**92**	90	93	90	94	100	84	91	93	91	89	93	84	92	98
Egypt	na	**69**	69	68	69	70	65	66	69	74	68	69	71	72	66	72
El Salvador	na	**74**	77	72	71	76	78	65	81	89	59	76	90	na	na	na
Estonia	54	**na**	na	na	na	na	na	na	na	na	na	na	na	na	na	na
Finland	na	**na**	na	na	na	na	na	na	na	na	na	na	na	na	na	na
France	na	**na**	na	na	na	na	na	na	na	na	na	na	na	na	na	na
Georgia	na	**94**	93	94	94	94	92	93	93	95	93	94	94	94	93	97
Germany	na	**na**	na	na	na	na	na	na	na	na	na	na	na	na	na	na
Great Britain	na	**na**	na	na	na	na	na	na	na	na	na	na	na	na	na	na
Greece	na	**na**	na	na	na	na	na	na	na	na	na	na	na	na	na	na
Hungary	na	**na**	na	na	na	na	na	na	na	na	na	na	na	na	na	na
Iceland	na	**na**	na	na	na	na	na	na	na	na	na	na	na	na	na	na
India	55	**66**	65	68	64	67	66	71	64	60	70	64	66	66	64	71
Indonesia	na	**70**	71	69	78	70	65	62	69	76	63	74	76	69	69	80
Iran	na	**49**	48	49	49	49	47	45	50	50	53	49	44	47	45	53
Ireland	na	**na**	na	na	na	na	na	na	na	na	na	na	na	na	na	na
Israel	na	**na**	na	na	na	na	na	na	na	na	na	na	na	na	na	na
Italy	na	**na**	na	na	na	na	na	na	na	na	na	na	na	na	na	na
Japan	na	**84**	83	84	91	87	78	74	85	84	83	86	83	80	84	90
Jordan	na	**69**	74	64	68	70	68	66	71	72	63	74	69	63	72	81
Korea, South	na	**88**	88	89	92	90	80	73	86	93	87	88	89	85	90	94
Latvia	35	**na**	na	na	na	na	na	na	na	na	na	na	na	na	na	na
Lithuania	50	**na**	na	na	na	na	na	na	na	na	na	na	na	na	na	na
Luxembourg	na	**na**	na	na	na	na	na	na	na	na	na	na	na	na	na	na
Macedonia	na	**93**	92	93	94	93	91	94	92	93	93	93	93	93	93	93
Malta	na	**na**	na	na	na	na	na	na	na	na	na	na	na	na	na	na
Mexico	81	**72**	73	70	71	70	75	65	76	87	62	74	80	67	74	72
Moldova	na	**91**	89	92	89	92	90	93	87	94	96	90	87	90	91	88
Montenegro	na	**74**	75	73	67	75	78	80	70	69	87	79	62	78	67	82
Morocco	na	**76**	79	73	79	76	71	73	88	88	76	84	77	71	81	81
Netherlands	na	**na**	na	na	na	na	na	na	na	na	na	na	na	na	na	na
New Zealand	na	**76**	74	79	82	74	76	76	81	74	82	80	68	77	75	78
Nigeria	78	**72**	72	73	72	73	72	74	71	71	77	72	67	74	72	71
Northern Ireland	na	**na**	na	na	na	na	na	na	na	na	na	na	na	na	na	na
Norway	na	**28**	26	31	32	23	32	34	27	24	na	na	na	37	27	26
Pakistan	na	**89**	87	92	88	88	94	93	87	79	97	91	77	90	88	58
Peru	na	**57**	58	56	58	56	55	53	56	61	52	59	63	51	58	59
Philippines	na	**60**	61	60	57	63	60	60	61	60	60	59	64	60	61	60
Poland	na	**na**	na	na	na	na	na	na	na	na	na	na	na	na	na	na
Portugal	na	**na**	na	na	na	na	na	na	na	na	na	na	na	na	na	na
Puerto Rico	na	**52**	52	52	63	53	47	42	50	55	43	55	56	43	51	58
Romania	na	**na**	na	na	na	na	na	na	na	na	na	na	na	na	na	na
Russian Fed.	na	**na**	na	na	na	na	na	na	na	na	na	na	na	na	na	na
Serbia	na	**69**	69	70	63	69	72	76	66	66	72	68	70	75	63	75
Singapore	na	**22**	25	19	25	21	16	15	27	21	16	23	25	15	22	47
Slovakia	na	**na**	na	na	na	na	na	na	na	na	na	na	na	na	na	na
Slovenia	na	**na**	na	na	na	na	na	na	na	na	na	na	na	na	na	na
South Africa	na	**60**	62	58	59	62	54	54	66	71	49	54	79	61	61	48
Spain	51	**60**	60	60	61	63	56	60	61	58	64	58	58	55	60	63
Sweden	na	**na**	na	na	na	na	na	na	na	na	na	na	na	na	na	na
Switzerland	na	**61**	66	55	61	66	56	56	62	63	63	67	59	60	60	66
Taiwan	na	**52**	53	51	67	52	41	37	53	64	39	57	57	56	49	48
Tanzania	na	**48**	51	44	53	46	44	43	61	43	48	47	47	51	46	48
Turkey	53	**82**	84	80	83	82	79	79	86	87	82	82	82	82	82	83
Uganda	na	**51**	44	58	52	50	52	53	51	54	51	39	48	46	51	68
Ukraine	na	**na**	na	na	na	na	na	na	na	na	na	na	na	na	na	na
United States	68	**63**	65	62	65	63	62	61	67	62	65	61	62	56	63	69
Uruguay	na	**76**	74	78	83	86	66	71	84	82	72	78	79	68	76	84
Venezuela	na	**37**	34	41	40	38	29	24	37	52	27	37	45	34	37	40
Vietnam	na	**9**	8	10	7	10	9	9	7	7	14	7	8	9	8	11
Zimbabwe	na	**82**	84	81	81	85	82	81	85	91	79	80	86	84	83	67
Total	55	67	67	67	68	67	65	63	68	71	68	68	68	68	65	70

RANKING

Country	2000
Armenia	96
Georgia	94
Macedonia	93
Dominican Rep.	92
Moldova	91
Argentina	90
Pakistan	89
Korea, South	88
Algeria	87
Japan	84
Zimbabwe	82
Turkey	82
Bosnia and Herz.	81
Colombia	79
Azerbaijan	78
Morocco	76
Uruguay	76
New Zealand	76
Brazil	75
El Salvador	74
Montenegro	74
Nigeria	72
Mexico	72
Indonesia	70
Serbia	69
Jordan	69
Egypt	69
Australia	68
India	66
Chile	65
Albania	65
United States	63
Switzerland	61
Philippines	60
South Africa	60
Spain	60
Peru	57
Bangladesh	56
Canada	52
Puerto Rico	52
Taiwan	52
Uganda	51
Iran	49
Tanzania	48
Venezuela	37
Norway	28
Singapore	22
China	17
Vietnam	9
Total	67

E129) ECONOMIC AID

Some people favor, and others are against, having this country provide economic aid to poorer countries. Do you think that this country should provide more or less economic aid to poorer countries? Would you say we should give …

(WVS: V176)

Provide a lot more that we do / Somewhat more than we do (%)

Country	Wave		Gender		Age			Education			Income			Values		
	1990	2000	Male	Female	16-29	30-49	50+	Lower	Middle	Upper	Lower	Middle	Upper	Mat	Mixed	Postm.
Albania	na	**43**	41	46	36	45	46	33	46	65	36	49	47	37	49	25
Algeria	na	**39**	38	40	41	35	42	40	37	41	39	40	36	41	36	42
Argentina	na	**4**	4	3	4	3	4	3	5	1	5	4	2	3	3	5
Armenia	na	**63**	63	63	64	61	64	62	63	64	66	55	64	61	65	67
Australia	na	**75**	75	75	76	77	72	68	72	85	69	75	82	75	74	76
Austria	na	**na**	na	na	na	na	na	na	na	na	na	na	na	na	na	na
Azerbaijan	na	**57**	59	55	61	55	54	55	54	63	52	60	63	53	62	72
Bangladesh	na	**63**	64	62	64	62	65	61	61	70	65	59	68	67	61	59
Belarus	na	**na**	na	na	na	na	na	na	na	na	na	na	na	na	na	na
Belgium	na	**na**	na	na	na	na	na	na	na	na	na	na	na	na	na	na
Bosnia and Herz.	na	**49**	47	50	49	46	52	45	48	54	44	48	57	48	48	65
Brazil	na	**65**	66	64	66	63	67	66	67	56	69	66	59	68	64	62
Bulgaria	na	**na**	na	na	na	na	na	na	na	na	na	na	na	na	na	na
Canada	na	**56**	58	54	66	54	51	44	55	67	50	53	65	50	54	62
Chile	na	**50**	50	51	54	48	49	50	50	51	50	52	46	43	53	54
China	na	**69**	64	74	77	68	65	70	69	64	65	74	66	64	72	79
Colombia	na	**na**	na	na	na	na	na	na	na	na	na	na	na	na	na	na
Croatia	na	**na**	na	na	na	na	na	na	na	na	na	na	na	na	na	na
Czech Republic	na	**na**	na	na	na	na	na	na	na	na	na	na	na	na	na	na
Denmark	na	**na**	na	na	na	na	na	na	na	na	na	na	na	na	na	na
Dominican Rep.	na	**68**	65	69	64	73	82	68	72	66	71	68	59	73	68	63
Egypt	na	**na**	na	na	na	na	na	na	na	na	na	na	na	na	na	na
El Salvador	na	**na**	na	na	na	na	na	na	na	na	na	na	na	na	na	na
Estonia	na	**na**	na	na	na	na	na	na	na	na	na	na	na	na	na	na
Finland	na	**na**	na	na	na	na	na	na	na	na	na	na	na	na	na	na
France	na	**na**	na	na	na	na	na	na	na	na	na	na	na	na	na	na
Georgia	na	**56**	59	55	54	58	56	56	56	58	58	59	54	55	58	71
Germany	na	**na**	na	na	na	na	na	na	na	na	na	na	na	na	na	na
Great Britain	na	**na**	na	na	na	na	na	na	na	na	na	na	na	na	na	na
Greece	na	**na**	na	na	na	na	na	na	na	na	na	na	na	na	na	na
Hungary	na	**na**	na	na	na	na	na	na	na	na	na	na	na	na	na	na
Iceland	na	**na**	na	na	na	na	na	na	na	na	na	na	na	na	na	na
India	na	**55**	55	54	54	56	52	54	57	54	62	52	53	53	58	45
Indonesia	na	**na**	na	na	na	na	na	na	na	na	na	na	na	na	na	na
Iran	na	**na**	na	na	na	na	na	na	na	na	na	na	na	na	na	na
Ireland	na	**na**	na	na	na	na	na	na	na	na	na	na	na	na	na	na
Israel	na	**na**	na	na	na	na	na	na	na	na	na	na	na	na	na	na
Italy	na	**na**	na	na	na	na	na	na	na	na	na	na	na	na	na	na
Japan	na	**45**	47	44	60	48	37	40	43	56	40	45	49	42	46	51
Jordan	na	**na**	na	na	na	na	na	na	na	na	na	na	na	na	na	na
Korea, South	na	**na**	na	na	na	na	na	na	na	na	na	na	na	na	na	na
Latvia	na	**na**	na	na	na	na	na	na	na	na	na	na	na	na	na	na
Lithuania	na	**na**	na	na	na	na	na	na	na	na	na	na	na	na	na	na
Luxembourg	na	**na**	na	na	na	na	na	na	na	na	na	na	na	na	na	na
Macedonia	na	**20**	21	20	23	22	16	26	16	23	22	16	21	19	22	23
Malta	na	**na**	na	na	na	na	na	na	na	na	na	na	na	na	na	na
Mexico	na	**68**	65	71	68	67	70	71	67	59	70	71	65	70	68	69
Moldova	na	**63**	65	62	55	68	65	60	67	59	67	68	57	60	67	60
Montenegro	na	**48**	46	51	53	46	45	46	48	51	65	47	36	43	52	64
Morocco	na	**62**	58	67	64	60	63	66	53	39	54	51	44	69	60	46
Netherlands	na	**na**	na	na	na	na	na	na	na	na	na	na	na	na	na	na
New Zealand	na	**68**	69	68	69	68	68	58	70	79	63	70	72	68	67	73
Nigeria	na	**na**	na	na	na	na	na	na	na	na	na	na	na	na	na	na
Northern Ireland	na	**na**	na	na	na	na	na	na	na	na	na	na	na	na	na	na
Norway	na	**82**	79	84	83	83	80	77	78	91	na	na	na	70	82	92
Pakistan	na	**na**	na	na	na	na	na	na	na	na	na	na	na	na	na	na
Peru	na	**94**	93	94	94	93	94	93	95	92	95	92	94	92	94	93
Philippines	na	**36**	33	39	43	34	30	33	39	35	35	32	41	37	36	35
Poland	na	**na**	na	na	na	na	na	na	na	na	na	na	na	na	na	na
Portugal	na	**na**	na	na	na	na	na	na	na	na	na	na	na	na	na	na
Puerto Rico	na	**84**	84	85	86	81	86	91	84	84	87	85	82	80	86	82
Romania	na	**na**	na	na	na	na	na	na	na	na	na	na	na	na	na	na
Russian Fed.	na	**na**	na	na	na	na	na	na	na	na	na	na	na	na	na	na
Serbia	na	**26**	25	28	27	25	28	25	25	31	29	25	25	25	24	47
Singapore	na	**68**	67	68	75	61	59	67	67	72	70	65	68	63	70	69
Slovakia	na	**na**	na	na	na	na	na	na	na	na	na	na	na	na	na	na
Slovenia	na	**na**	na	na	na	na	na	na	na	na	na	na	na	na	na	na
South Africa	na	**45**	46	43	42	48	42	50	39	37	49	45	40	37	49	56
Spain	na	**83**	81	85	86	82	82	82	83	87	78	86	86	82	83	84
Sweden	na	**40**	37	42	47	43	31	27	37	53	37	34	50	18	35	58
Switzerland	na	**na**	na	na	na	na	na	na	na	na	na	na	na	na	na	na
Taiwan	na	**76**	74	77	78	75	74	72	81	76	74	73	80	72	80	81
Tanzania	na	**40**	37	45	40	40	42	44	34	42	44	43	35	36	42	32
Turkey	na	**na**	na	na	na	na	na	na	na	na	na	na	na	na	na	na
Uganda	na	**37**	38	37	45	32	21	40	35	39	39	43	26	33	39	39
Ukraine	na	**na**	na	na	na	na	na	na	na	na	na	na	na	na	na	na
United States	na	**44**	47	41	52	40	43	45	38	47	41	46	47	41	44	46
Uruguay	na	**62**	66	60	67	59	63	60	65	68	58	59	72	55	67	63
Venezuela	na	**66**	66	66	67	65	65	68	70	53	73	67	60	70	64	67
Vietnam	na	**74**	77	70	75	69	79	75	70	84	75	71	75	61	76	78
Zimbabwe	na	**54**	48	59	58	50	49	58	50	19	59	55	46	52	55	63
Total	na	**57**	56	58	59	57	55	55	55	63	56	56	57	53	58	61

RANKING	
Country	2000
Peru	94
Puerto Rico	84
Spain	83
Norway	82
Taiwan	76
Australia	75
Vietnam	74
China	69
Mexico	68
New Zealand	68
Dominican Rep.	68
Singapore	68
Venezuela	66
Brazil	65
Bangladesh	63
Armenia	63
Moldova	63
Morocco	62
Uruguay	62
Azerbaijan	57
Georgia	56
Canada	56
India	55
Zimbabwe	54
Chile	50
Bosnia and Herz.	49
Montenegro	48
Japan	45
South Africa	45
United States	44
Albania	43
Tanzania	40
Sweden	40
Algeria	39
Uganda	37
Philippines	36
Serbia	26
Macedonia	20
Argentina	4
Total	57

E135) WHO SHOULD DECIDE: INTERNATIONAL PEACEKEEPING

Who could better handle certain kinds of problems: the United Nations, the respective national governments, or the national governments together with the United Nations?

National governments (%)

(WVS: V177)

Country	Wave		Gender		Age			Education			Income			Values		
	1990	2000	Male	Female	16-29	30-49	50+	Lower	Middle	Upper	Lower	Middle	Upper	Mat	Mixed	Postm.
Albania	na	**60**	60	59	61	60	59	54	63	65	56	62	62	58	61	54
Algeria	na	**49**	48	50	51	46	52	49	50	47	54	44	48	52	47	51
Argentina	na	**2**	2	3	1	2	3	2	2	3	2	2	2	2	2	3
Armenia	na	**na**	na	na	na	na	na	na	na	na	na	na	na	na	na	na
Australia	na	**na**	na	na	na	na	na	na	na	na	na	na	na	na	na	na
Austria	na	**na**	na	na	na	na	na	na	na	na	na	na	na	na	na	na
Azerbaijan	na	**na**	na	na	na	na	na	na	na	na	na	na	na	na	na	na
Bangladesh	na	**43**	42	44	46	43	32	41	45	45	40	42	50	43	44	51
Belarus	na	**na**	na	na	na	na	na	na	na	na	na	na	na	na	na	na
Belgium	na	**na**	na	na	na	na	na	na	na	na	na	na	na	na	na	na
Bosnia and Herz.	na	**56**	56	55	56	57	53	49	56	61	53	56	55	53	57	53
Brazil	na	**na**	na	na	na	na	na	na	na	na	na	na	na	na	na	na
Bulgaria	na	**na**	na	na	na	na	na	na	na	na	na	na	na	na	na	na
Canada	na	**62**	55	69	60	62	63	59	65	59	62	61	61	56	63	62
Chile	na	**51**	54	50	55	54	45	43	54	61	40	57	62	48	53	54
China	na	**46**	45	46	48	44	47	43	47	48	49	42	48	46	47	30
Colombia	na	**na**	na	na	na	na	na	na	na	na	na	na	na	na	na	na
Croatia	na	**na**	na	na	na	na	na	na	na	na	na	na	na	na	na	na
Czech Republic	na	**na**	na	na	na	na	na	na	na	na	na	na	na	na	na	na
Denmark	na	**na**	na	na	na	na	na	na	na	na	na	na	na	na	na	na
Dominican Rep.	na	**na**	na	na	na	na	na	na	na	na	na	na	na	na	na	na
Egypt	na	**48**	44	52	52	46	45	47	49	50	52	46	46	47	49	45
El Salvador	na	**na**	na	na	na	na	na	na	na	na	na	na	na	na	na	na
Estonia	na	**na**	na	na	na	na	na	na	na	na	na	na	na	na	na	na
Finland	na	**na**	na	na	na	na	na	na	na	na	na	na	na	na	na	na
France	na	**na**	na	na	na	na	na	na	na	na	na	na	na	na	na	na
Georgia	na	**na**	na	na	na	na	na	na	na	na	na	na	na	na	na	na
Germany	na	**na**	na	na	na	na	na	na	na	na	na	na	na	na	na	na
Great Britain	na	**na**	na	na	na	na	na	na	na	na	na	na	na	na	na	na
Greece	na	**na**	na	na	na	na	na	na	na	na	na	na	na	na	na	na
Hungary	na	**na**	na	na	na	na	na	na	na	na	na	na	na	na	na	na
Iceland	na	**na**	na	na	na	na	na	na	na	na	na	na	na	na	na	na
India	na	**56**	59	50	56	57	52	45	59	67	41	53	63	64	54	58
Indonesia	na	**57**	55	60	57	61	54	52	57	62	58	59	55	61	55	46
Iran	na	**59**	60	58	58	58	62	58	56	63	60	58	60	59	61	52
Ireland	na	**na**	na	na	na	na	na	na	na	na	na	na	na	na	na	na
Israel	na	**na**	na	na	na	na	na	na	na	na	na	na	na	na	na	na
Italy	na	**na**	na	na	na	na	na	na	na	na	na	na	na	na	na	na
Japan	na	**39**	38	39	29	40	42	28	40	42	41	40	36	41	39	40
Jordan	na	**67**	63	71	66	69	64	65	66	71	71	63	70	63	69	65
Korea, South	na	**65**	61	70	76	64	56	52	62	72	63	65	68	64	66	77
Latvia	na	**na**	na	na	na	na	na	na	na	na	na	na	na	na	na	na
Lithuania	na	**na**	na	na	na	na	na	na	na	na	na	na	na	na	na	na
Luxembourg	na	**na**	na	na	na	na	na	na	na	na	na	na	na	na	na	na
Macedonia	na	**29**	29	29	25	30	30	26	30	28	29	29	30	30	28	24
Malta	na	**na**	na	na	na	na	na	na	na	na	na	na	na	na	na	na
Mexico	na	**47**	45	48	49	47	43	42	50	56	33	50	54	43	47	52
Moldova	na	**66**	63	68	70	65	64	61	64	74	73	68	60	66	66	53
Montenegro	na	**42**	39	44	45	43	40	38	44	46	41	41	44	40	44	39
Morocco	na	**45**	44	46	46	45	41	49	37	33	49	45	39	49	45	37
Netherlands	na	**na**	na	na	na	na	na	na	na	na	na	na	na	na	na	na
New Zealand	na	**na**	na	na	na	na	na	na	na	na	na	na	na	na	na	na
Nigeria	na	**37**	37	38	39	37	27	38	35	40	39	36	35	36	38	36
Northern Ireland	na	**na**	na	na	na	na	na	na	na	na	na	na	na	na	na	na
Norway	na	**na**	na	na	na	na	na	na	na	na	na	na	na	na	na	na
Pakistan	na	**na**	na	na	na	na	na	na	na	na	na	na	na	na	na	na
Peru	na	**na**	na	na	na	na	na	na	na	na	na	na	na	na	na	na
Philippines	na	**36**	36	35	33	37	38	35	36	36	40	36	32	36	36	31
Poland	na	**na**	na	na	na	na	na	na	na	na	na	na	na	na	na	na
Portugal	na	**na**	na	na	na	na	na	na	na	na	na	na	na	na	na	na
Puerto Rico	na	**na**	na	na	na	na	na	na	na	na	na	na	na	na	na	na
Romania	na	**na**	na	na	na	na	na	na	na	na	na	na	na	na	na	na
Russian Fed.	na	**na**	na	na	na	na	na	na	na	na	na	na	na	na	na	na
Serbia	na	**52**	51	53	58	53	48	44	52	61	47	52	55	47	55	60
Singapore	na	**na**	na	na	na	na	na	na	na	na	na	na	na	na	na	na
Slovakia	na	**na**	na	na	na	na	na	na	na	na	na	na	na	na	na	na
Slovenia	na	**na**	na	na	na	na	na	na	na	na	na	na	na	na	na	na
South Africa	na	**44**	43	46	41	48	42	46	41	42	49	45	36	42	46	44
Spain	na	**65**	66	65	66	66	64	64	67	67	64	66	63	65	64	72
Sweden	na	**67**	62	71	66	70	65	64	68	67	66	68	66	67	66	67
Switzerland	na	**na**	na	na	na	na	na	na	na	na	na	na	na	na	na	na
Taiwan	na	**na**	na	na	na	na	na	na	na	na	na	na	na	na	na	na
Tanzania	na	**28**	30	26	28	28	29	27	28	33	27	32	28	31	27	17
Turkey	na	**na**	na	na	na	na	na	na	na	na	na	na	na	na	na	na
Uganda	na	**38**	39	37	42	34	34	36	40	25	40	30	45	35	41	33
Ukraine	na	**na**	na	na	na	na	na	na	na	na	na	na	na	na	na	na
United States	na	**59**	55	62	54	59	63	52	60	61	52	63	61	52	59	61
Uruguay	na	**na**	na	na	na	na	na	na	na	na	na	na	na	na	na	na
Venezuela	na	**na**	na	na	na	na	na	na	na	na	na	na	na	na	na	na
Vietnam	na	**40**	40	40	37	41	41	35	48	39	39	38	43	42	42	51
Zimbabwe	na	**27**	27	27	29	25	26	28	27	30	31	28	25	32	25	20
Total	na	**48**	46	49	47	48	47	42	49	55	47	47	49	47	48	48

RANKING

Country	2000
Jordan	67
Sweden	67
Moldova	66
Korea, South	65
Spain	65
Canada	62
Albania	60
Iran	59
United States	59
Indonesia	57
Bosnia and Herz.	56
India	56
Serbia	52
Chile	51
Algeria	49
Egypt	48
Mexico	47
China	46
Morocco	45
South Africa	44
Bangladesh	43
Montenegro	42
Vietnam	40
Japan	39
Uganda	38
Nigeria	37
Philippines	36
Macedonia	29
Tanzania	28
Zimbabwe	27
Argentina	2
Total	48

E136) WHO SHOULD DECIDE: PROTECTION OF THE ENVIRONMENT

Who could better handle certain kinds of problems: the United Nations, the respective national governments, or the national governments together with the United Nations?

(WVS: V178)

National governments (%)

Country	Wave		Gender		Age			Education			Income			Values		
	1990	2000	Male	Female	16-29	30-49	50+	Lower	Middle	Upper	Lower	Middle	Upper	Mat	Mixed	Postm.
Albania	na	**56**	55	56	54	59	52	53	59	54	57	55	54	58	52	64
Algeria	na	**28**	27	29	29	25	30	29	27	29	29	27	25	24	32	19
Argentina	na	**67**	65	69	64	67	71	72	60	66	77	66	60	78	68	56
Armenia	na	**na**	na	na	na	na	na	na	na	na	na	na	na	na	na	na
Australia	na	**na**	na	na	na	na	na	na	na	na	na	na	na	na	na	na
Austria	na	**na**	na	na	na	na	na	na	na	na	na	na	na	na	na	na
Azerbaijan	na	**na**	na	na	na	na	na	na	na	na	na	na	na	na	na	na
Bangladesh	na	**47**	49	45	47	45	60	50	46	42	46	42	57	52	46	25
Belarus	na	**na**	na	na	na	na	na	na	na	na	na	na	na	na	na	na
Belgium	na	**na**	na	na	na	na	na	na	na	na	na	na	na	na	na	na
Bosnia and Herz.	na	**55**	52	57	57	58	49	56	55	54	56	56	54	51	58	55
Brazil	na	**na**	na	na	na	na	na	na	na	na	na	na	na	na	na	na
Bulgaria	na	**na**	na	na	na	na	na	na	na	na	na	na	na	na	na	na
Canada	na	**37**	35	39	38	35	38	41	37	34	38	39	34	48	39	30
Chile	na	**40**	37	43	41	38	44	48	37	34	47	37	36	41	39	43
China	na	**53**	51	56	52	55	50	54	54	38	60	54	44	52	55	48
Colombia	na	**na**	na	na	na	na	na	na	na	na	na	na	na	na	na	na
Croatia	na	**na**	na	na	na	na	na	na	na	na	na	na	na	na	na	na
Czech Republic	na	**na**	na	na	na	na	na	na	na	na	na	na	na	na	na	na
Denmark	na	**na**	na	na	na	na	na	na	na	na	na	na	na	na	na	na
Dominican Rep.	na	**na**	na	na	na	na	na	na	na	na	na	na	na	na	na	na
Egypt	na	**48**	48	48	46	50	47	50	50	38	50	52	43	48	47	49
El Salvador	na	**na**	na	na	na	na	na	na	na	na	na	na	na	na	na	na
Estonia	na	**na**	na	na	na	na	na	na	na	na	na	na	na	na	na	na
Finland	na	**na**	na	na	na	na	na	na	na	na	na	na	na	na	na	na
France	na	**na**	na	na	na	na	na	na	na	na	na	na	na	na	na	na
Georgia	na	**na**	na	na	na	na	na	na	na	na	na	na	na	na	na	na
Germany	na	**na**	na	na	na	na	na	na	na	na	na	na	na	na	na	na
Great Britain	na	**na**	na	na	na	na	na	na	na	na	na	na	na	na	na	na
Greece	na	**na**	na	na	na	na	na	na	na	na	na	na	na	na	na	na
Hungary	na	**na**	na	na	na	na	na	na	na	na	na	na	na	na	na	na
Iceland	na	**na**	na	na	na	na	na	na	na	na	na	na	na	na	na	na
India	na	**51**	49	54	48	52	50	56	52	43	54	54	47	47	50	61
Indonesia	na	**71**	71	70	76	72	68	75	67	74	76	68	69	72	70	75
Iran	na	**26**	25	28	28	25	22	28	26	25	27	25	25	23	29	28
Ireland	na	**na**	na	na	na	na	na	na	na	na	na	na	na	na	na	na
Israel	na	**na**	na	na	na	na	na	na	na	na	na	na	na	na	na	na
Italy	na	**na**	na	na	na	na	na	na	na	na	na	na	na	na	na	na
Japan	na	**28**	25	30	26	26	30	36	27	28	30	28	25	26	27	25
Jordan	na	**53**	54	52	53	52	57	54	56	48	53	54	54	58	53	31
Korea, South	na	**49**	49	50	41	53	52	64	52	44	55	48	44	50	51	32
Latvia	na	**na**	na	na	na	na	na	na	na	na	na	na	na	na	na	na
Lithuania	na	**na**	na	na	na	na	na	na	na	na	na	na	na	na	na	na
Luxembourg	na	**na**	na	na	na	na	na	na	na	na	na	na	na	na	na	na
Macedonia	na	**63**	59	67	59	64	65	54	68	63	63	62	64	63	66	49
Malta	na	**na**	na	na	na	na	na	na	na	na	na	na	na	na	na	na
Mexico	na	**47**	48	47	47	47	48	50	44	46	53	42	47	49	46	45
Moldova	na	**36**	34	38	35	38	35	38	37	32	30	33	38	38	34	37
Montenegro	na	**59**	59	58	55	59	60	60	58	58	70	62	52	62	55	58
Morocco	na	**47**	47	46	44	52	43	49	43	32	43	43	48	54	42	46
Netherlands	na	**na**	na	na	na	na	na	na	na	na	na	na	na	na	na	na
New Zealand	na	**na**	na	na	na	na	na	na	na	na	na	na	na	na	na	na
Nigeria	na	**57**	56	57	57	56	56	58	56	55	54	58	60	58	56	58
Northern Ireland	na	**na**	na	na	na	na	na	na	na	na	na	na	na	na	na	na
Norway	na	**na**	na	na	na	na	na	na	na	na	na	na	na	na	na	na
Pakistan	na	**na**	na	na	na	na	na	na	na	na	na	na	na	na	na	na
Peru	na	**na**	na	na	na	na	na	na	na	na	na	na	na	na	na	na
Philippines	na	**55**	53	56	60	53	51	48	53	66	49	56	58	50	58	59
Poland	na	**na**	na	na	na	na	na	na	na	na	na	na	na	na	na	na
Portugal	na	**na**	na	na	na	na	na	na	na	na	na	na	na	na	na	na
Puerto Rico	na	**na**	na	na	na	na	na	na	na	na	na	na	na	na	na	na
Romania	na	**na**	na	na	na	na	na	na	na	na	na	na	na	na	na	na
Russian Fed.	na	**na**	na	na	na	na	na	na	na	na	na	na	na	na	na	na
Serbia	na	**54**	52	56	53	54	55	55	57	50	56	58	55	58	52	46
Singapore	na	**na**	na	na	na	na	na	na	na	na	na	na	na	na	na	na
Slovakia	na	**na**	na	na	na	na	na	na	na	na	na	na	na	na	na	na
Slovenia	na	**na**	na	na	na	na	na	na	na	na	na	na	na	na	na	na
South Africa	na	**55**	55	56	58	50	64	53	58	65	50	60	57	55	55	57
Spain	na	**24**	24	24	21	25	26	26	21	25	28	20	30	28	25	17
Sweden	na	**28**	27	30	31	24	31	35	29	22	29	29	25	38	30	21
Switzerland	na	**na**	na	na	na	na	na	na	na	na	na	na	na	na	na	na
Taiwan	na	**na**	na	na	na	na	na	na	na	na	na	na	na	na	na	na
Tanzania	na	**63**	63	63	68	60	61	63	68	52	62	64	54	62	64	63
Turkey	na	**na**	na	na	na	na	na	na	na	na	na	na	na	na	na	na
Uganda	na	**72**	68	75	68	75	74	74	70	75	70	65	68	78	68	72
Ukraine	na	**na**	na	na	na	na	na	na	na	na	na	na	na	na	na	na
United States	na	**38**	36	39	36	39	38	41	40	35	39	34	41	42	38	37
Uruguay	na	**na**	na	na	na	na	na	na	na	na	na	na	na	na	na	na
Venezuela	na	**na**	na	na	na	na	na	na	na	na	na	na	na	na	na	na
Vietnam	na	**43**	43	44	46	43	41	46	39	48	38	49	41	55	38	36
Zimbabwe	na	**69**	70	68	68	70	69	68	70	62	66	71	72	69	69	64
Total	na	50	48	51	50	50	49	53	50	44	51	50	47	53	49	42

RANKING

Country	2000
Uganda	72
Indonesia	71
Zimbabwe	69
Argentina	67
Macedonia	63
Tanzania	63
Montenegro	59
Nigeria	57
Albania	56
South Africa	55
Bosnia and Herz.	55
Philippines	55
Serbia	54
China	53
Jordan	53
India	51
Korea, South	49
Egypt	48
Bangladesh	47
Mexico	47
Morocco	47
Vietnam	43
Chile	40
United States	38
Canada	37
Moldova	36
Sweden	28
Algeria	28
Japan	28
Iran	26
Spain	24
Total	50

E137) WHO SHOULD DECIDE: AID TO DEVELOPING COUNTRIES

Who could better handle certain kinds of problems: the United Nations, the respective national governments, or the national governments together with the United Nations?

National governments (%) (WVS: V179)

Country	Wave 1990	Wave 2000	Gender Male	Gender Female	Age 16-29	Age 30-49	Age 50+	Education Lower	Education Middle	Education Upper	Income Lower	Income Middle	Income Upper	Values Mat	Values Mixed	Values Postm.
Albania	na	**48**	48	47	48	46	50	48	47	49	48	47	48	46	50	44
Algeria	na	**46**	47	44	49	43	45	42	46	47	49	46	44	47	46	44
Argentina	na	**3**	3	2	2	3	2	1	4	5	1	3	4	2	2	5
Armenia	na	**na**	na	na	na	na	na	na	na	na	na	na	na	na	na	na
Australia	na	**na**	na	na	na	na	na	na	na	na	na	na	na	na	na	na
Austria	na	**na**	na	na	na	na	na	na	na	na	na	na	na	na	na	na
Azerbaijan	na	**na**	na	na	na	na	na	na	na	na	na	na	na	na	na	na
Bangladesh	na	**43**	43	43	45	41	41	42	42	43	42	43	42	45	42	47
Belarus	na	**na**	na	na	na	na	na	na	na	na	na	na	na	na	na	na
Belgium	na	**na**	na	na	na	na	na	na	na	na	na	na	na	na	na	na
Bosnia and Herz.	na	**56**	57	55	57	55	56	53	56	56	57	55	55	57	55	53
Brazil	na	**na**	na	na	na	na	na	na	na	na	na	na	na	na	na	na
Bulgaria	na	**na**	na	na	na	na	na	na	na	na	na	na	na	na	na	na
Canada	na	**58**	54	62	56	60	58	56	59	60	57	61	58	60	58	61
Chile	na	**54**	54	53	59	52	51	50	56	55	45	59	59	50	54	58
China	na	**33**	29	38	37	31	36	31	32	52	30	30	38	35	30	39
Colombia	na	**na**	na	na	na	na	na	na	na	na	na	na	na	na	na	na
Croatia	na	**na**	na	na	na	na	na	na	na	na	na	na	na	na	na	na
Czech Republic	na	**na**	na	na	na	na	na	na	na	na	na	na	na	na	na	na
Denmark	na	**na**	na	na	na	na	na	na	na	na	na	na	na	na	na	na
Dominican Rep.	na	**na**	na	na	na	na	na	na	na	na	na	na	na	na	na	na
Egypt	na	**32**	29	36	33	32	32	36	30	27	39	32	28	32	33	27
El Salvador	na	**na**	na	na	na	na	na	na	na	na	na	na	na	na	na	na
Estonia	na	**na**	na	na	na	na	na	na	na	na	na	na	na	na	na	na
Finland	na	**na**	na	na	na	na	na	na	na	na	na	na	na	na	na	na
France	na	**na**	na	na	na	na	na	na	na	na	na	na	na	na	na	na
Georgia	na	**na**	na	na	na	na	na	na	na	na	na	na	na	na	na	na
Germany	na	**na**	na	na	na	na	na	na	na	na	na	na	na	na	na	na
Great Britain	na	**na**	na	na	na	na	na	na	na	na	na	na	na	na	na	na
Greece	na	**na**	na	na	na	na	na	na	na	na	na	na	na	na	na	na
Hungary	na	**na**	na	na	na	na	na	na	na	na	na	na	na	na	na	na
Iceland	na	**na**	na	na	na	na	na	na	na	na	na	na	na	na	na	na
India	na	**50**	51	48	53	49	48	39	50	62	33	44	60	56	48	53
Indonesia	na	**52**	50	54	46	51	57	49	56	49	53	54	43	51	55	36
Iran	na	**52**	53	51	53	53	50	51	52	56	49	55	54	57	48	57
Ireland	na	**na**	na	na	na	na	na	na	na	na	na	na	na	na	na	na
Israel	na	**na**	na	na	na	na	na	na	na	na	na	na	na	na	na	na
Italy	na	**na**	na	na	na	na	na	na	na	na	na	na	na	na	na	na
Japan	na	**42**	39	44	39	40	45	44	42	39	43	44	38	39	41	45
Jordan	na	**54**	47	60	54	54	54	53	52	57	57	52	51	49	55	70
Korea, South	na	**62**	59	65	67	63	55	52	61	64	64	60	62	61	62	71
Latvia	na	**na**	na	na	na	na	na	na	na	na	na	na	na	na	na	na
Lithuania	na	**na**	na	na	na	na	na	na	na	na	na	na	na	na	na	na
Luxembourg	na	**na**	na	na	na	na	na	na	na	na	na	na	na	na	na	na
Macedonia	na	**31**	32	31	32	31	31	26	32	37	28	33	33	33	30	34
Malta	na	**na**	na	na	na	na	na	na	na	na	na	na	na	na	na	na
Mexico	na	**49**	47	51	52	48	47	48	48	57	44	51	53	45	51	53
Moldova	na	**62**	59	64	61	61	63	63	59	65	65	64	58	59	63	67
Montenegro	na	**41**	38	43	44	40	40	38	42	43	29	39	44	33	48	45
Morocco	na	**44**	41	48	44	46	39	46	41	38	51	46	36	45	46	34
Netherlands	na	**na**	na	na	na	na	na	na	na	na	na	na	na	na	na	na
New Zealand	na	**na**	na	na	na	na	na	na	na	na	na	na	na	na	na	na
Nigeria	na	**33**	35	31	34	32	31	33	33	33	32	33	34	34	32	33
Northern Ireland	na	**na**	na	na	na	na	na	na	na	na	na	na	na	na	na	na
Norway	na	**na**	na	na	na	na	na	na	na	na	na	na	na	na	na	na
Pakistan	na	**na**	na	na	na	na	na	na	na	na	na	na	na	na	na	na
Peru	na	**na**	na	na	na	na	na	na	na	na	na	na	na	na	na	na
Philippines	na	**32**	31	32	30	33	32	30	31	35	34	33	29	31	32	38
Poland	na	**na**	na	na	na	na	na	na	na	na	na	na	na	na	na	na
Portugal	na	**na**	na	na	na	na	na	na	na	na	na	na	na	na	na	na
Puerto Rico	na	**na**	na	na	na	na	na	na	na	na	na	na	na	na	na	na
Romania	na	**na**	na	na	na	na	na	na	na	na	na	na	na	na	na	na
Russian Fed.	na	**na**	na	na	na	na	na	na	na	na	na	na	na	na	na	na
Serbia	na	**41**	38	44	44	42	39	37	41	46	39	40	41	35	45	53
Singapore	na	**na**	na	na	na	na	na	na	na	na	na	na	na	na	na	na
Slovakia	na	**na**	na	na	na	na	na	na	na	na	na	na	na	na	na	na
Slovenia	na	**na**	na	na	na	na	na	na	na	na	na	na	na	na	na	na
South Africa	na	**44**	44	43	42	44	46	43	45	33	46	40	44	41	47	37
Spain	na	**73**	71	74	75	73	70	72	72	77	69	73	70	71	71	81
Sweden	na	**64**	62	66	60	67	64	64	63	66	65	63	66	64	62	71
Switzerland	na	**na**	na	na	na	na	na	na	na	na	na	na	na	na	na	na
Taiwan	na	**na**	na	na	na	na	na	na	na	na	na	na	na	na	na	na
Tanzania	na	**35**	38	30	30	37	34	34	31	43	30	38	44	34	35	39
Turkey	na	**na**	na	na	na	na	na	na	na	na	na	na	na	na	na	na
Uganda	na	**39**	50	30	40	37	45	31	42	53	36	40	43	37	39	48
Ukraine	na	**na**	na	na	na	na	na	na	na	na	na	na	na	na	na	na
United States	na	**53**	50	56	47	54	57	49	56	53	49	57	53	48	54	54
Uruguay	na	**na**	na	na	na	na	na	na	na	na	na	na	na	na	na	na
Venezuela	na	**na**	na	na	na	na	na	na	na	na	na	na	na	na	na	na
Vietnam	na	**34**	37	31	34	34	34	32	35	46	33	29	39	35	36	43
Zimbabwe	na	**34**	32	35	34	33	33	33	33	53	36	30	40	36	33	22
Total	na	**45**	44	45	44	44	46	41	45	50	44	44	45	43	45	48

RANKING

Country	2000
Spain	73
Sweden	64
Korea, South	62
Moldova	62
Canada	58
Bosnia and Herz.	56
Chile	54
Jordan	54
United States	53
Iran	52
Indonesia	52
India	50
Mexico	49
Albania	48
Algeria	46
Morocco	44
South Africa	44
Bangladesh	43
Japan	42
Serbia	41
Montenegro	41
Uganda	39
Tanzania	35
Vietnam	34
Zimbabwe	34
China	33
Nigeria	33
Egypt	32
Philippines	32
Macedonia	31
Argentina	3
Total	45

E138) WHO SHOULD DECIDE: REFUGEES

Who could better handle certain kinds of problems: the United Nations, the respective national governments, or the national governments together with the United Nations?

National governments (%) (WVS: V180)

Country	Wave		Gender		Age			Education			Income			Values		
	1990	2000	Male	Female	16-29	30-49	50+	Lower	Middle	Upper	Lower	Middle	Upper	Mat	Mixed	Postm.
Albania	na	**55**	54	57	55	55	55	55	56	56	54	57	56	58	53	49
Algeria	na	**41**	42	40	45	37	42	38	38	47	43	40	41	42	41	43
Argentina	na	**1**	1	1	1	1	na	na	1	1	na	na	2	1	1	1
Armenia	na	**na**	na	na	na	na	na	na	na	na	na	na	na	na	na	na
Australia	na	**na**	na	na	na	na	na	na	na	na	na	na	na	na	na	na
Austria	na	**na**	na	na	na	na	na	na	na	na	na	na	na	na	na	na
Azerbaijan	na	**na**	na	na	na	na	na	na	na	na	na	na	na	na	na	na
Bangladesh	na	**42**	43	42	46	42	34	42	42	44	40	42	46	40	46	41
Belarus	na	**na**	na	na	na	na	na	na	na	na	na	na	na	na	na	na
Belgium	na	**na**	na	na	na	na	na	na	na	na	na	na	na	na	na	na
Bosnia and Herz.	na	**64**	65	63	63	63	66	64	64	63	66	64	61	67	63	64
Brazil	na	**na**	na	na	na	na	na	na	na	na	na	na	na	na	na	na
Bulgaria	na	**na**	na	na	na	na	na	na	na	na	na	na	na	na	na	na
Canada	na	**53**	48	59	52	55	53	53	51	57	52	54	54	49	53	56
Chile	na	**49**	48	50	52	50	44	45	50	53	40	57	51	44	50	54
China	na	**31**	29	33	32	28	37	27	30	51	32	29	32	34	29	9
Colombia	na	**na**	na	na	na	na	na	na	na	na	na	na	na	na	na	na
Croatia	na	**na**	na	na	na	na	na	na	na	na	na	na	na	na	na	na
Czech Republic	na	**na**	na	na	na	na	na	na	na	na	na	na	na	na	na	na
Denmark	na	**na**	na	na	na	na	na	na	na	na	na	na	na	na	na	na
Dominican Rep.	na	**na**	na	na	na	na	na	na	na	na	na	na	na	na	na	na
Egypt	na	**33**	29	37	32	33	34	37	30	28	38	32	31	34	33	27
El Salvador	na	**na**	na	na	na	na	na	na	na	na	na	na	na	na	na	na
Estonia	na	**na**	na	na	na	na	na	na	na	na	na	na	na	na	na	na
Finland	na	**na**	na	na	na	na	na	na	na	na	na	na	na	na	na	na
France	na	**na**	na	na	na	na	na	na	na	na	na	na	na	na	na	na
Georgia	na	**na**	na	na	na	na	na	na	na	na	na	na	na	na	na	na
Germany	na	**na**	na	na	na	na	na	na	na	na	na	na	na	na	na	na
Great Britain	na	**na**	na	na	na	na	na	na	na	na	na	na	na	na	na	na
Greece	na	**na**	na	na	na	na	na	na	na	na	na	na	na	na	na	na
Hungary	na	**na**	na	na	na	na	na	na	na	na	na	na	na	na	na	na
Iceland	na	**na**	na	na	na	na	na	na	na	na	na	na	na	na	na	na
India	na	**46**	49	40	47	45	46	37	46	55	30	43	53	52	44	53
Indonesia	na	**50**	57	44	45	54	49	39	57	49	51	54	43	54	50	39
Iran	na	**50**	49	51	50	50	49	49	48	56	48	50	54	54	50	42
Ireland	na	**na**	na	na	na	na	na	na	na	na	na	na	na	na	na	na
Israel	na	**na**	na	na	na	na	na	na	na	na	na	na	na	na	na	na
Italy	na	**na**	na	na	na	na	na	na	na	na	na	na	na	na	na	na
Japan	na	**46**	46	46	43	48	46	48	46	47	45	48	44	38	49	46
Jordan	na	**53**	47	59	52	53	54	52	50	57	57	49	51	54	50	57
Korea, South	na	**62**	58	65	65	60	60	56	59	66	59	61	64	59	64	62
Latvia	na	**na**	na	na	na	na	na	na	na	na	na	na	na	na	na	na
Lithuania	na	**na**	na	na	na	na	na	na	na	na	na	na	na	na	na	na
Luxembourg	na	**na**	na	na	na	na	na	na	na	na	na	na	na	na	na	na
Macedonia	na	**29**	30	28	27	31	28	29	28	32	28	28	33	32	27	25
Malta	na	**na**	na	na	na	na	na	na	na	na	na	na	na	na	na	na
Mexico	na	**46**	43	48	45	46	45	48	43	46	38	51	47	44	46	46
Moldova	na	**57**	54	60	60	56	56	54	55	64	59	62	53	55	60	60
Montenegro	na	**51**	51	52	57	49	50	47	50	62	61	48	48	48	55	53
Morocco	na	**41**	38	44	41	42	35	42	38	36	48	41	31	40	42	38
Netherlands	na	**na**	na	na	na	na	na	na	na	na	na	na	na	na	na	na
New Zealand	na	**na**	na	na	na	na	na	na	na	na	na	na	na	na	na	na
Nigeria	na	**37**	37	37	39	34	29	32	38	41	37	36	36	35	37	41
Northern Ireland	na	**na**	na	na	na	na	na	na	na	na	na	na	na	na	na	na
Norway	na	**na**	na	na	na	na	na	na	na	na	na	na	na	na	na	na
Pakistan	na	**na**	na	na	na	na	na	na	na	na	na	na	na	na	na	na
Peru	na	**na**	na	na	na	na	na	na	na	na	na	na	na	na	na	na
Philippines	na	**25**	26	25	24	28	22	25	24	27	26	28	21	22	27	27
Poland	na	**na**	na	na	na	na	na	na	na	na	na	na	na	na	na	na
Portugal	na	**na**	na	na	na	na	na	na	na	na	na	na	na	na	na	na
Puerto Rico	na	**na**	na	na	na	na	na	na	na	na	na	na	na	na	na	na
Romania	na	**na**	na	na	na	na	na	na	na	na	na	na	na	na	na	na
Russian Fed.	na	**na**	na	na	na	na	na	na	na	na	na	na	na	na	na	na
Serbia	na	**48**	47	49	54	50	44	43	47	54	44	49	48	44	51	58
Singapore	na	**na**	na	na	na	na	na	na	na	na	na	na	na	na	na	na
Slovakia	na	**na**	na	na	na	na	na	na	na	na	na	na	na	na	na	na
Slovenia	na	**na**	na	na	na	na	na	na	na	na	na	na	na	na	na	na
South Africa	na	**39**	40	39	42	37	41	36	46	32	37	41	38	37	41	39
Spain	na	**67**	66	69	70	67	64	65	66	74	66	66	65	68	65	73
Sweden	na	**62**	61	63	53	66	63	58	58	71	60	62	68	62	59	72
Switzerland	na	**na**	na	na	na	na	na	na	na	na	na	na	na	na	na	na
Taiwan	na	**na**	na	na	na	na	na	na	na	na	na	na	na	na	na	na
Tanzania	na	**35**	35	34	36	34	32	37	34	29	34	43	30	38	34	48
Turkey	na	**na**	na	na	na	na	na	na	na	na	na	na	na	na	na	na
Uganda	na	**33**	42	25	35	33	23	20	39	36	26	38	42	27	38	27
Ukraine	na	**na**	na	na	na	na	na	na	na	na	na	na	na	na	na	na
United States	na	**54**	52	56	49	55	57	49	59	53	52	58	53	51	54	56
Uruguay	na	**na**	na	na	na	na	na	na	na	na	na	na	na	na	na	na
Venezuela	na	**na**	na	na	na	na	na	na	na	na	na	na	na	na	na	na
Vietnam	na	**34**	37	32	32	34	37	30	40	40	35	31	39	28	39	41
Zimbabwe	na	**30**	31	29	31	31	28	28	33	22	31	27	32	32	30	25
Total	na	**44**	43	44	43	44	45	39	45	50	43	44	44	43	44	45

RANKING	
Country	2000
Spain	67
Bosnia and Herz.	64
Sweden	62
Korea, South	62
Moldova	57
Albania	55
United States	54
Canada	53
Jordan	53
Montenegro	51
Indonesia	50
Iran	50
Chile	49
Serbia	48
Japan	46
India	46
Mexico	46
Bangladesh	42
Algeria	41
Morocco	41
South Africa	39
Nigeria	37
Tanzania	35
Vietnam	34
Uganda	33
Egypt	33
China	31
Zimbabwe	30
Macedonia	29
Philippines	25
Argentina	1
Total	44

E139) WHO SHOULD DECIDE: HUMAN RIGHTS

Who could better handle certain kinds of problems: the United Nations, the respective national governments, or the national governments together with the United Nations?

National governments (%)

(WVS: V181)

Country	Wave		Gender		Age			Education			Income			Values		
	1990	2000	Male	Female	16-29	30-49	50+	Lower	Middle	Upper	Lower	Middle	Upper	Mat	Mixed	Postm.
Albania	na	**57**	54	60	50	60	58	61	52	59	58	56	57	58	56	59
Algeria	na	**51**	53	50	53	47	57	54	48	55	53	53	49	50	53	49
Argentina	na	**1**	1	1	1	2	1	1	2	3	na	1	3	2	1	2
Armenia	na	**na**	na	na	na	na	na	na	na	na	na	na	na	na	na	na
Australia	na	**na**	na	na	na	na	na	na	na	na	na	na	na	na	na	na
Austria	na	**na**	na	na	na	na	na	na	na	na	na	na	na	na	na	na
Azerbaijan	na	**na**	na	na	na	na	na	na	na	na	na	na	na	na	na	na
Bangladesh	na	**38**	37	39	36	41	30	39	34	44	46	35	36	36	41	25
Belarus	na	**na**	na	na	na	na	na	na	na	na	na	na	na	na	na	na
Belgium	na	**na**	na	na	na	na	na	na	na	na	na	na	na	na	na	na
Bosnia and Herz.	na	**66**	67	64	66	65	66	66	66	65	68	65	62	67	66	62
Brazil	na	**na**	na	na	na	na	na	na	na	na	na	na	na	na	na	na
Bulgaria	na	**na**	na	na	na	na	na	na	na	na	na	na	na	na	na	na
Canada	na	**55**	50	60	56	54	54	50	54	59	49	56	58	50	54	59
Chile	na	**43**	44	43	45	46	38	36	48	46	33	50	50	45	43	43
China	na	**20**	18	22	24	18	19	20	19	33	18	19	22	21	17	15
Colombia	na	**na**	na	na	na	na	na	na	na	na	na	na	na	na	na	na
Croatia	na	**na**	na	na	na	na	na	na	na	na	na	na	na	na	na	na
Czech Republic	na	**na**	na	na	na	na	na	na	na	na	na	na	na	na	na	na
Denmark	na	**na**	na	na	na	na	na	na	na	na	na	na	na	na	na	na
Dominican Rep.	na	**na**	na	na	na	na	na	na	na	na	na	na	na	na	na	na
Egypt	na	**37**	33	41	39	35	38	39	36	34	39	37	36	38	37	32
El Salvador	na	**na**	na	na	na	na	na	na	na	na	na	na	na	na	na	na
Estonia	na	**na**	na	na	na	na	na	na	na	na	na	na	na	na	na	na
Finland	na	**na**	na	na	na	na	na	na	na	na	na	na	na	na	na	na
France	na	**na**	na	na	na	na	na	na	na	na	na	na	na	na	na	na
Georgia	na	**na**	na	na	na	na	na	na	na	na	na	na	na	na	na	na
Germany	na	**na**	na	na	na	na	na	na	na	na	na	na	na	na	na	na
Great Britain	na	**na**	na	na	na	na	na	na	na	na	na	na	na	na	na	na
Greece	na	**na**	na	na	na	na	na	na	na	na	na	na	na	na	na	na
Hungary	na	**na**	na	na	na	na	na	na	na	na	na	na	na	na	na	na
Iceland	na	**na**	na	na	na	na	na	na	na	na	na	na	na	na	na	na
India	na	**42**	45	37	44	41	40	33	44	51	28	39	48	45	43	33
Indonesia	na	**40**	43	37	35	40	42	34	41	40	40	41	41	39	42	36
Iran	na	**56**	57	55	58	54	54	56	56	57	58	54	56	57	55	61
Ireland	na	**na**	na	na	na	na	na	na	na	na	na	na	na	na	na	na
Israel	na	**na**	na	na	na	na	na	na	na	na	na	na	na	na	na	na
Italy	na	**na**	na	na	na	na	na	na	na	na	na	na	na	na	na	na
Japan	na	**34**	34	34	28	34	36	38	34	31	36	33	31	36	33	35
Jordan	na	**52**	44	59	53	52	48	49	51	55	53	52	52	51	51	59
Korea, South	na	**42**	43	42	52	39	40	35	39	48	38	44	46	41	43	52
Latvia	na	**na**	na	na	na	na	na	na	na	na	na	na	na	na	na	na
Lithuania	na	**na**	na	na	na	na	na	na	na	na	na	na	na	na	na	na
Luxembourg	na	**na**	na	na	na	na	na	na	na	na	na	na	na	na	na	na
Macedonia	na	**28**	29	28	29	30	26	26	28	33	24	32	31	27	29	29
Malta	na	**na**	na	na	na	na	na	na	na	na	na	na	na	na	na	na
Mexico	na	**42**	40	44	43	39	45	40	41	51	30	47	47	39	42	47
Moldova	na	**58**	56	59	63	57	54	54	55	66	61	61	54	56	59	57
Montenegro	na	**50**	52	48	60	48	46	42	52	60	50	49	55	51	50	45
Morocco	na	**37**	37	38	40	37	31	36	38	51	40	40	31	31	41	38
Netherlands	na	**na**	na	na	na	na	na	na	na	na	na	na	na	na	na	na
New Zealand	na	**na**	na	na	na	na	na	na	na	na	na	na	na	na	na	na
Nigeria	na	**27**	27	26	28	26	23	22	29	31	25	28	27	27	28	21
Northern Ireland	na	**na**	na	na	na	na	na	na	na	na	na	na	na	na	na	na
Norway	na	**na**	na	na	na	na	na	na	na	na	na	na	na	na	na	na
Pakistan	na	**na**	na	na	na	na	na	na	na	na	na	na	na	na	na	na
Peru	na	**na**	na	na	na	na	na	na	na	na	na	na	na	na	na	na
Philippines	na	**20**	20	20	21	21	18	19	20	22	18	22	19	21	20	21
Poland	na	**na**	na	na	na	na	na	na	na	na	na	na	na	na	na	na
Portugal	na	**na**	na	na	na	na	na	na	na	na	na	na	na	na	na	na
Puerto Rico	na	**na**	na	na	na	na	na	na	na	na	na	na	na	na	na	na
Romania	na	**na**	na	na	na	na	na	na	na	na	na	na	na	na	na	na
Russian Fed.	na	**na**	na	na	na	na	na	na	na	na	na	na	na	na	na	na
Serbia	na	**47**	49	46	53	48	44	43	47	54	43	45	49	45	50	45
Singapore	na	**na**	na	na	na	na	na	na	na	na	na	na	na	na	na	na
Slovakia	na	**na**	na	na	na	na	na	na	na	na	na	na	na	na	na	na
Slovenia	na	**na**	na	na	na	na	na	na	na	na	na	na	na	na	na	na
South Africa	na	**34**	31	38	33	36	33	34	35	38	36	30	37	35	33	36
Spain	na	**72**	71	73	75	72	68	69	73	77	70	71	71	71	72	74
Sweden	na	**50**	45	56	44	53	52	48	50	53	51	50	50	51	48	55
Switzerland	na	**na**	na	na	na	na	na	na	na	na	na	na	na	na	na	na
Taiwan	na	**na**	na	na	na	na	na	na	na	na	na	na	na	na	na	na
Tanzania	na	**35**	36	35	33	37	34	35	34	35	32	42	34	36	35	39
Turkey	na	**na**	na	na	na	na	na	na	na	na	na	na	na	na	na	na
Uganda	na	**29**	39	19	33	26	23	16	35	23	23	32	38	25	32	23
Ukraine	na	**na**	na	na	na	na	na	na	na	na	na	na	na	na	na	na
United States	na	**53**	55	52	50	53	57	44	52	58	50	55	58	52	52	57
Uruguay	na	**na**	na	na	na	na	na	na	na	na	na	na	na	na	na	na
Venezuela	na	**na**	na	na	na	na	na	na	na	na	na	na	na	na	na	na
Vietnam	na	**27**	26	28	26	27	28	26	27	31	28	28	26	23	31	29
Zimbabwe	na	**29**	31	27	29	30	27	27	32	32	25	28	36	31	29	14
Total	na	**41**	40	41	41	40	41	36	41	48	39	41	42	40	41	42

RANKING

Country	2000
Spain	72
Bosnia and Herz.	66
Moldova	58
Albania	57
Iran	56
Canada	55
United States	53
Jordan	52
Algeria	51
Sweden	50
Montenegro	50
Serbia	47
Chile	43
Korea, South	42
India	42
Mexico	42
Indonesia	40
Bangladesh	38
Morocco	37
Egypt	37
Tanzania	35
South Africa	34
Japan	34
Zimbabwe	29
Uganda	29
Macedonia	28
Vietnam	27
Nigeria	27
Philippines	20
China	20
Argentina	1
Total	41

E143) IMMIGRANT POLICY

How about people from other countries coming here to work.

Which one of the following do you think the government should do?

Let people come as long as there are jobs available (%)

(WVS: V146; EVS: V258)

Country	Wave		Gender		Age			Education			Income			Values		
	1990	2000	Male	Female	16-29	30-49	50+	Lower	Middle	Upper	Lower	Middle	Upper	Mat	Mixed	Postm.
Albania	na	**45**	44	45	40	46	48	47	41	48	44	44	47	49	42	23
Algeria	na	**45**	45	46	43	48	45	36	49	47	42	53	51	48	42	51
Argentina	na	**45**	41	48	51	43	41	41	51	47	44	42	49	34	45	52
Armenia	na	**51**	47	54	57	46	47	43	50	54	55	48	47	49	51	58
Australia	na	**52**	52	53	48	55	53	49	48	59	49	52	56	52	51	55
Austria	na	**52**	52	51	52	53	50	43	58	67	46	53	54	41	50	56
Azerbaijan	na	**60**	61	58	56	62	62	54	61	58	63	60	59	64	53	51
Bangladesh	na	**50**	49	51	49	51	48	47	53	53	58	46	50	56	46	47
Belarus	na	**35**	35	34	38	37	29	27	38	36	30	38	35	30	39	41
Belgium	na	**31**	31	31	34	29	32	26	31	35	29	33	31	27	30	41
Bosnia and Herz.	na	**55**	57	53	56	58	51	51	55	60	49	58	54	55	56	53
Brazil	na	**37**	38	35	39	36	34	29	41	47	33	40	41	31	39	41
Bulgaria	na	**31**	31	31	29	33	30	28	29	39	28	32	32	29	33	49
Canada	na	**49**	52	47	55	46	50	42	46	62	39	48	60	40	48	57
Chile	na	**48**	46	49	50	47	47	43	49	55	48	45	50	41	50	53
China	na	**48**	47	49	58	48	37	37	54	56	38	50	57	47	50	55
Colombia	na	**na**	na	na	na	na	na	na	na	na	na	na	na	na	na	na
Croatia	na	**28**	27	28	26	32	25	22	28	43	24	23	36	27	26	31
Czech Republic	na	**30**	30	31	31	29	32	27	30	45	27	30	35	24	32	39
Denmark	na	**24**	26	22	25	25	22	21	23	30	25	24	27	12	25	27
Dominican Rep.	na	**37**	37	37	37	39	36	32	30	40	27	41	43	30	41	33
Egypt	na	**43**	42	43	41	43	46	44	42	43	42	44	46	46	42	35
El Salvador	na	**na**	na	na	na	na	na	na	na	na	na	na	na	na	na	na
Estonia	na	**37**	34	39	48	36	31	38	37	35	42	32	35	35	38	38
Finland	na	**35**	34	35	30	34	39	32	38	36	31	38	35	27	38	35
France	na	**34**	35	32	34	36	32	28	38	45	29	32	42	23	34	50
Georgia	na	**53**	55	51	53	55	49	50	52	59	50	55	58	53	53	59
Germany	na	**33**	32	33	35	34	29	27	36	43	27	38	36	24	33	45
Great Britain	na	**34**	32	36	37	34	31	24	40	44	30	35	38	na	na	na
Greece	na	**45**	43	46	43	50	40	42	44	47	40	48	46	41	45	49
Hungary	na	**12**	12	13	11	11	14	10	18	15	11	12	13	11	13	4
Iceland	na	**59**	58	61	67	57	56	55	64	61	58	62	57	56	60	64
India	na	**19**	20	19	16	23	18	17	20	24	14	16	25	16	24	21
Indonesia	na	**23**	27	19	17	25	23	24	23	23	20	22	30	24	22	35
Iran	na	**28**	29	27	28	25	33	30	29	26	30	31	26	29	27	33
Ireland	na	**47**	45	49	49	45	46	39	46	62	37	44	56	43	47	49
Israel	na	**na**	na	na	na	na	na	na	na	na	na	na	na	na	na	na
Italy	na	**47**	47	48	42	51	47	44	47	57	47	49	51	36	46	56
Japan	na	**52**	53	51	63	58	42	39	50	64	48	50	57	49	52	68
Jordan	na	**31**	29	34	30	30	38	29	32	35	32	29	30	31	32	33
Korea, South	na	**58**	58	58	71	54	53	36	53	68	53	62	61	57	57	81
Latvia	na	**27**	29	25	38	28	22	21	28	31	25	29	28	24	30	18
Lithuania	na	**37**	33	39	44	35	33	29	38	43	32	37	39	37	37	34
Luxembourg	na	**52**	51	53	49	54	52	51	52	54	47	58	57	54	51	58
Macedonia	na	**20**	20	19	23	22	14	19	19	22	15	21	23	18	20	25
Malta	na	**30**	31	29	33	27	31	23	31	43	25	31	31	22	33	46
Mexico	na	**42**	43	41	43	41	41	37	45	55	33	46	50	37	43	50
Moldova	na	**54**	54	55	51	57	54	54	56	52	56	52	53	55	54	40
Montenegro	na	**27**	30	24	34	28	22	18	30	43	15	25	35	18	37	35
Morocco	na	**38**	40	36	37	38	41	37	41	44	42	42	37	36	40	44
Netherlands	na	**35**	37	35	32	38	35	26	38	41	32	35	41	28	34	45
New Zealand	na	**56**	58	54	47	54	61	48	54	65	53	59	58	51	56	63
Nigeria	na	**41**	42	41	42	42	36	41	41	42	43	42	38	36	45	45
Northern Ireland	na	**35**	34	37	36	37	36	30	39	41	32	38	42	32	37	37
Norway	na	**43**	40	45	46	42	41	34	38	57	na	na	na	31	43	56
Pakistan	na	**43**	40	46	40	46	41	37	48	53	35	38	61	41	45	58
Peru	na	**42**	42	42	41	41	46	43	39	44	39	43	45	39	43	43
Philippines	na	**18**	18	19	18	17	21	20	20	14	21	19	15	19	19	9
Poland	na	**19**	19	18	19	21	15	14	22	28	15	20	22	16	19	23
Portugal	na	**61**	61	61	56	56	69	64	57	49	64	59	58	66	59	56
Puerto Rico	na	**30**	29	31	41	28	27	34	28	31	28	29	34	29	29	35
Romania	na	**39**	38	39	44	42	33	31	43	41	32	40	42	41	37	45
Russian Fed.	na	**46**	44	48	52	48	39	35	44	58	41	45	53	44	48	42
Serbia	na	**36**	38	34	37	39	33	26	37	49	32	38	40	32	41	41
Singapore	na	**24**	28	20	29	19	22	23	22	33	23	19	29	21	24	34
Slovakia	na	**27**	26	28	30	25	28	28	26	37	27	28	28	23	31	32
Slovenia	na	**48**	45	51	43	50	50	42	48	61	42	52	58	42	48	55
South Africa	na	**27**	28	25	23	29	27	22	31	50	21	24	37	20	32	22
Spain	na	**58**	58	58	54	59	59	59	55	61	57	58	59	55	61	52
Sweden	na	**55**	58	51	62	50	55	55	55	54	55	54	55	55	54	57
Switzerland	na	**55**	54	55	60	53	53	41	56	76	50	53	58	48	52	72
Taiwan	na	**32**	34	29	46	31	24	28	26	39	27	34	35	27	36	31
Tanzania	na	**19**	20	18	17	23	17	18	21	23	17	23	16	22	18	26
Turkey	na	**37**	37	38	40	36	33	34	38	45	36	37	40	33	38	41
Uganda	na	**45**	44	46	46	47	31	50	41	54	52	45	50	39	45	60
Ukraine	na	**44**	44	45	48	47	40	28	44	54	43	44	47	41	50	47
United States	na	**45**	45	45	46	40	50	34	45	49	42	43	53	43	44	49
Uruguay	na	**55**	54	56	55	55	55	51	62	54	52	51	64	51	53	64
Venezuela	na	**50**	51	48	50	47	54	48	51	48	49	48	52	52	49	49
Vietnam	na	**55**	56	54	51	53	61	59	49	62	57	53	56	57	54	58
Zimbabwe	na	**53**	52	55	50	54	63	57	50	23	58	54	47	57	52	45
Total	na	**40**	40	40	41	41	39	36	42	45	38	40	43	37	41	48

RANKING	
Country	**2000**
Portugal	61
Azerbaijan	60
Iceland	59
Korea, South	58
Spain	58
New Zealand	56
Bosnia and Herz.	55
Uruguay	55
Vietnam	55
Switzerland	55
Sweden	55
Moldova	54
Zimbabwe	53
Georgia	53
Australia	52
Japan	52
Luxembourg	52
Austria	52
Armenia	51
Bangladesh	50
Venezuela	50
Canada	49
Slovenia	48
Chile	48
China	48
Italy	47
Ireland	47
Russian Fed.	46
Algeria	45
Greece	45
Argentina	45
United States	45
Albania	45
Uganda	45
Ukraine	44
Pakistan	43
Egypt	43
Norway	43
Peru	42
Mexico	42
Nigeria	41
Romania	39
Morocco	38
Dominican Rep.	37
Turkey	37
Brazil	37
Estonia	37
Lithuania	37
Serbia	36
Netherlands	35
Northern Ireland	35
Finland	35
Belarus	35
Great Britain	34
France	34
Germany	33
Taiwan	32
Jordan	31
Belgium	31
Bulgaria	31
Czech Republic	30
Puerto Rico	30
Malta	30
Iran	28
Croatia	28
Slovakia	27
Montenegro	27
Latvia	27
South Africa	27
Singapore	24
Denmark	24
Indonesia	23
Macedonia	20
India	19
Tanzania	19
Poland	19
Philippines	18
Hungary	12
Total	40

E145_2) IMMIGRANTS

Which of these statements is the nearest to your opinion? For the greater good of society it is better if immigrants: A) maintain their distinct customs and traditions; or B) take over the customs of the country

Take over the custom (%)

(EVS: V259)

Country	Wave		Gender		Age			Education			Income			Values		
	1990	2000	Male	Female	16-29	30-49	50+	Lower	Middle	Upper	Lower	Middle	Upper	Mat	Mixed	Postm.
Albania	na	**na**	na	na	na	na	na	na	na	na	na	na	na	na	na	na
Algeria	na	**na**	na	na	na	na	na	na	na	na	na	na	na	na	na	na
Argentina	na	**na**	na	na	na	na	na	na	na	na	na	na	na	na	na	na
Armenia	na	**na**	na	na	na	na	na	na	na	na	na	na	na	na	na	na
Australia	na	**na**	na	na	na	na	na	na	na	na	na	na	na	na	na	na
Austria	na	**82**	82	81	75	80	86	86	78	72	83	83	80	92	85	72
Azerbaijan	na	**na**	na	na	na	na	na	na	na	na	na	na	na	na	na	na
Bangladesh	na	**na**	na	na	na	na	na	na	na	na	na	na	na	na	na	na
Belarus	na	**52**	53	51	42	58	54	53	54	41	54	48	56	55	49	46
Belgium	na	**75**	74	76	68	72	81	81	78	66	75	75	74	86	75	62
Bosnia and Herz.	na	**na**	na	na	na	na	na	na	na	na	na	na	na	na	na	na
Brazil	na	**na**	na	na	na	na	na	na	na	na	na	na	na	na	na	na
Bulgaria	na	**40**	41	38	30	40	44	52	37	32	43	35	38	44	34	42
Canada	na	**na**	na	na	na	na	na	na	na	na	na	na	na	na	na	na
Chile	na	**na**	na	na	na	na	na	na	na	na	na	na	na	na	na	na
China	na	**na**	na	na	na	na	na	na	na	na	na	na	na	na	na	na
Colombia	na	**na**	na	na	na	na	na	na	na	na	na	na	na	na	na	na
Croatia	na	**44**	44	44	34	47	47	53	39	36	52	40	45	45	47	33
Czech Republic	na	**69**	69	70	67	69	71	71	68	66	69	70	70	79	68	51
Denmark	na	**77**	76	77	77	70	83	83	74	63	80	78	65	88	80	54
Dominican Rep.	na	**na**	na	na	na	na	na	na	na	na	na	na	na	na	na	na
Egypt	na	**na**	na	na	na	na	na	na	na	na	na	na	na	na	na	na
El Salvador	na	**na**	na	na	na	na	na	na	na	na	na	na	na	na	na	na
Estonia	na	**48**	50	46	53	41	50	59	46	33	48	46	50	48	48	39
Finland	na	**68**	72	64	64	66	73	73	64	57	70	69	66	73	68	50
France	na	**73**	71	75	67	71	78	79	70	61	75	76	66	83	73	55
Georgia	na	**na**	na	na	na	na	na	na	na	na	na	na	na	na	na	na
Germany	na	**76**	79	74	68	75	81	78	75	75	74	74	80	77	77	72
Great Britain	na	**55**	58	53	42	55	62	61	55	40	49	55	52	na	na	na
Greece	na	**23**	23	22	21	21	29	35	26	18	24	22	25	29	23	17
Hungary	na	**67**	64	68	64	66	68	73	58	49	68	71	61	69	65	50
Iceland	na	**73**	71	75	69	75	74	69	76	72	71	70	76	73	75	57
India	na	**na**	na	na	na	na	na	na	na	na	na	na	na	na	na	na
Indonesia	na	**na**	na	na	na	na	na	na	na	na	na	na	na	na	na	na
Iran	na	**na**	na	na	na	na	na	na	na	na	na	na	na	na	na	na
Ireland	na	**43**	46	41	38	44	47	45	46	34	41	47	39	45	44	36
Israel	na	**na**	na	na	na	na	na	na	na	na	na	na	na	na	na	na
Italy	na	**40**	41	40	30	37	49	49	34	33	43	39	37	56	43	30
Japan	na	**na**	na	na	na	na	na	na	na	na	na	na	na	na	na	na
Jordan	na	**na**	na	na	na	na	na	na	na	na	na	na	na	na	na	na
Korea, South	na	**na**	na	na	na	na	na	na	na	na	na	na	na	na	na	na
Latvia	na	**53**	50	55	47	50	58	59	54	42	57	50	53	57	52	47
Lithuania	na	**64**	66	61	62	62	67	73	64	50	68	70	58	63	65	40
Luxembourg	na	**43**	43	43	40	39	48	42	43	42	40	48	45	40	44	36
Macedonia	na	**na**	na	na	na	na	na	na	na	na	na	na	na	na	na	na
Malta	na	**44**	45	44	41	43	48	48	45	31	52	47	37	43	46	39
Mexico	na	**na**	na	na	na	na	na	na	na	na	na	na	na	na	na	na
Moldova	na	**na**	na	na	na	na	na	na	na	na	na	na	na	na	na	na
Montenegro	na	**na**	na	na	na	na	na	na	na	na	na	na	na	na	na	na
Morocco	na	**na**	na	na	na	na	na	na	na	na	na	na	na	na	na	na
Netherlands	na	**70**	69	71	68	67	74	75	74	61	68	69	71	85	70	61
New Zealand	na	**na**	na	na	na	na	na	na	na	na	na	na	na	na	na	na
Nigeria	na	**na**	na	na	na	na	na	na	na	na	na	na	na	na	na	na
Northern Ireland	na	**46**	48	44	33	40	56	52	42	40	47	39	40	50	47	37
Norway	na	**na**	na	na	na	na	na	na	na	na	na	na	na	na	na	na
Pakistan	na	**na**	na	na	na	na	na	na	na	na	na	na	na	na	na	na
Peru	na	**na**	na	na	na	na	na	na	na	na	na	na	na	na	na	na
Philippines	na	**na**	na	na	na	na	na	na	na	na	na	na	na	na	na	na
Poland	na	**53**	52	53	52	49	57	56	49	49	53	55	44	56	50	57
Portugal	na	**51**	50	52	48	52	52	51	54	39	41	53	58	52	53	49
Puerto Rico	na	**na**	na	na	na	na	na	na	na	na	na	na	na	na	na	na
Romania	na	**38**	37	39	29	34	48	53	32	28	47	41	31	41	39	15
Russian Fed.	na	**57**	58	56	51	57	60	67	58	49	62	56	53	59	54	74
Serbia	na	**na**	na	na	na	na	na	na	na	na	na	na	na	na	na	na
Singapore	na	**na**	na	na	na	na	na	na	na	na	na	na	na	na	na	na
Slovakia	na	**60**	58	62	61	59	61	65	60	49	64	59	58	66	56	46
Slovenia	na	**69**	70	69	66	68	72	71	69	68	71	68	68	73	69	65
South Africa	na	**na**	na	na	na	na	na	na	na	na	na	na	na	na	na	na
Spain	na	**48**	50	47	35	46	58	52	49	33	46	49	47	56	49	35
Sweden	na	**64**	64	64	57	63	68	70	65	58	60	69	65	60	70	49
Switzerland	na	**na**	na	na	na	na	na	na	na	na	na	na	na	na	na	na
Taiwan	na	**na**	na	na	na	na	na	na	na	na	na	na	na	na	na	na
Tanzania	na	**na**	na	na	na	na	na	na	na	na	na	na	na	na	na	na
Turkey	na	**na**	na	na	na	na	na	na	na	na	na	na	na	na	na	na
Uganda	na	**na**	na	na	na	na	na	na	na	na	na	na	na	na	na	na
Ukraine	na	**54**	54	54	46	51	61	62	56	45	57	56	47	55	53	49
United States	na	**na**	na	na	na	na	na	na	na	na	na	na	na	na	na	na
Uruguay	na	**na**	na	na	na	na	na	na	na	na	na	na	na	na	na	na
Venezuela	na	**na**	na	na	na	na	na	na	na	na	na	na	na	na	na	na
Vietnam	na	**na**	na	na	na	na	na	na	na	na	na	na	na	na	na	na
Zimbabwe	na	**na**	na	na	na	na	na	na	na	na	na	na	na	na	na	na
Total	na	**57**	58	57	51	56	63	64	55	47	59	58	55	60	58	48

RANKING

Country	2000
Austria	82
Denmark	77
Germany	76
Belgium	75
France	73
Iceland	73
Netherlands	70
Slovenia	69
Czech Republic	69
Finland	68
Hungary	67
Sweden	64
Lithuania	64
Slovakia	60
Russian Fed.	57
Great Britain	55
Ukraine	54
Latvia	53
Poland	53
Belarus	52
Portugal	51
Spain	48
Estonia	48
Northern Ireland	46
Malta	44
Croatia	44
Ireland	43
Luxembourg	43
Italy	40
Bulgaria	40
Romania	38
Greece	23
Total	57

E146_1) ELIMINATING INEQUALITIES

In order to be considered "just", what should a society provide? Please tell me for each statement if it is important or unimportant to you. 1 means very important; 5 means not important at all.

% Important / very important (codes 1 to 2) (EVS: V260)

	Wave		Gender		Age			Education			Income			Values		
Country	1990	2000	Male	Female	16-29	30-49	50+	Lower	Middle	Upper	Lower	Middle	Upper	Mat	Mixed	Postm.
Albania	na	**na**	na	na	na	na	na	na	na	na	na	na	na	na	na	na
Algeria	na	**na**	na	na	na	na	na	na	na	na	na	na	na	na	na	na
Argentina	na	**na**	na	na	na	na	na	na	na	na	na	na	na	na	na	na
Armenia	na	**na**	na	na	na	na	na	na	na	na	na	na	na	na	na	na
Australia	na	**na**	na	na	na	na	na	na	na	na	na	na	na	na	na	na
Austria	na	**58**	58	58	49	58	62	62	57	43	70	59	49	64	60	55
Azerbaijan	na	**na**	na	na	na	na	na	na	na	na	na	na	na	na	na	na
Bangladesh	na	**na**	na	na	na	na	na	na	na	na	na	na	na	na	na	na
Belarus	na	**59**	52	65	45	57	74	74	56	47	68	56	49	68	54	31
Belgium	na	**63**	61	65	53	62	69	72	63	56	73	66	53	63	61	66
Bosnia and Herz.	na	**na**	na	na	na	na	na	na	na	na	na	na	na	na	na	na
Brazil	na	**na**	na	na	na	na	na	na	na	na	na	na	na	na	na	na
Bulgaria	na	**65**	62	67	56	61	72	77	61	51	80	67	50	74	58	27
Canada	na	**na**	na	na	na	na	na	na	na	na	na	na	na	na	na	na
Chile	na	**na**	na	na	na	na	na	na	na	na	na	na	na	na	na	na
China	na	**na**	na	na	na	na	na	na	na	na	na	na	na	na	na	na
Colombia	na	**na**	na	na	na	na	na	na	na	na	na	na	na	na	na	na
Croatia	na	**84**	80	87	77	83	89	93	79	73	88	86	79	86	85	79
Czech Republic	na	**56**	55	57	54	49	64	67	49	31	69	60	40	70	53	44
Denmark	na	**28**	30	26	28	27	30	29	22	30	33	27	26	25	28	35
Dominican Rep.	na	**na**	na	na	na	na	na	na	na	na	na	na	na	na	na	na
Egypt	na	**na**	na	na	na	na	na	na	na	na	na	na	na	na	na	na
El Salvador	na	**na**	na	na	na	na	na	na	na	na	na	na	na	na	na	na
Estonia	na	**61**	56	64	49	56	72	65	61	53	72	62	56	64	59	52
Finland	na	**67**	64	70	62	70	68	73	62	50	74	69	59	73	64	70
France	na	**70**	68	73	69	71	71	72	69	68	73	71	68	73	69	72
Georgia	na	**na**	na	na	na	na	na	na	na	na	na	na	na	na	na	na
Germany	na	**60**	58	61	55	60	61	63	60	47	66	61	56	66	59	53
Great Britain	na	**56**	54	58	59	53	57	57	56	51	61	58	43	na	na	na
Greece	na	**81**	81	81	79	82	84	82	82	81	84	81	80	72	83	86
Hungary	na	**86**	84	88	84	84	90	91	84	62	92	87	81	88	85	83
Iceland	na	**71**	65	77	62	71	80	80	68	60	78	77	58	73	70	74
India	na	**na**	na	na	na	na	na	na	na	na	na	na	na	na	na	na
Indonesia	na	**na**	na	na	na	na	na	na	na	na	na	na	na	na	na	na
Iran	na	**na**	na	na	na	na	na	na	na	na	na	na	na	na	na	na
Ireland	na	**69**	71	66	59	70	73	73	68	64	77	69	62	66	70	63
Israel	na	**na**	na	na	na	na	na	na	na	na	na	na	na	na	na	na
Italy	na	**61**	59	63	58	58	66	67	59	51	67	68	54	63	61	61
Japan	na	**na**	na	na	na	na	na	na	na	na	na	na	na	na	na	na
Jordan	na	**na**	na	na	na	na	na	na	na	na	na	na	na	na	na	na
Korea, South	na	**na**	na	na	na	na	na	na	na	na	na	na	na	na	na	na
Latvia	na	**82**	78	85	71	80	87	85	83	73	86	85	74	80	84	65
Lithuania	na	**68**	67	68	56	62	82	84	65	49	80	77	58	75	67	52
Luxembourg	na	**64**	62	67	61	65	66	71	66	49	70	66	55	67	63	68
Macedonia	na	**na**	na	na	na	na	na	na	na	na	na	na	na	na	na	na
Malta	na	**36**	36	35	33	32	41	39	35	29	40	34	29	34	39	18
Mexico	na	**na**	na	na	na	na	na	na	na	na	na	na	na	na	na	na
Moldova	na	**na**	na	na	na	na	na	na	na	na	na	na	na	na	na	na
Montenegro	na	**na**	na	na	na	na	na	na	na	na	na	na	na	na	na	na
Morocco	na	**na**	na	na	na	na	na	na	na	na	na	na	na	na	na	na
Netherlands	na	**41**	39	44	39	38	46	44	39	40	49	41	32	46	37	51
New Zealand	na	**na**	na	na	na	na	na	na	na	na	na	na	na	na	na	na
Nigeria	na	**na**	na	na	na	na	na	na	na	na	na	na	na	na	na	na
Northern Ireland	na	**62**	62	63	58	64	63	68	59	55	67	55	60	62	61	70
Norway	na	**na**	na	na	na	na	na	na	na	na	na	na	na	na	na	na
Pakistan	na	**na**	na	na	na	na	na	na	na	na	na	na	na	na	na	na
Peru	na	**na**	na	na	na	na	na	na	na	na	na	na	na	na	na	na
Philippines	na	**na**	na	na	na	na	na	na	na	na	na	na	na	na	na	na
Poland	na	**75**	71	79	69	70	86	81	71	62	85	69	66	76	75	70
Portugal	na	**87**	86	88	82	85	91	89	82	80	89	82	87	86	88	78
Puerto Rico	na	**na**	na	na	na	na	na	na	na	na	na	na	na	na	na	na
Romania	na	**85**	84	86	80	83	90	88	88	73	90	91	80	89	84	62
Russian Fed.	na	**59**	55	63	46	56	71	70	60	52	67	62	51	64	55	54
Serbia	na	**na**	na	na	na	na	na	na	na	na	na	na	na	na	na	na
Singapore	na	**na**	na	na	na	na	na	na	na	na	na	na	na	na	na	na
Slovakia	na	**86**	84	89	82	85	92	92	87	66	92	89	81	92	84	58
Slovenia	na	**67**	65	69	58	63	79	83	66	41	77	76	48	78	66	64
South Africa	na	**na**	na	na	na	na	na	na	na	na	na	na	na	na	na	na
Spain	na	**83**	82	84	84	83	83	83	82	85	84	82	80	82	82	88
Sweden	na	**45**	42	47	37	47	48	58	42	38	53	46	32	57	42	49
Switzerland	na	**na**	na	na	na	na	na	na	na	na	na	na	na	na	na	na
Taiwan	na	**na**	na	na	na	na	na	na	na	na	na	na	na	na	na	na
Tanzania	na	**na**	na	na	na	na	na	na	na	na	na	na	na	na	na	na
Turkey	na	**86**	85	87	86	86	86	86	86	87	84	87	87	83	85	92
Uganda	na	**na**	na	na	na	na	na	na	na	na	na	na	na	na	na	na
Ukraine	na	**na**	na	na	na	na	na	na	na	na	na	na	na	na	na	na
United States	na	**na**	na	na	na	na	na	na	na	na	na	na	na	na	na	na
Uruguay	na	**na**	na	na	na	na	na	na	na	na	na	na	na	na	na	na
Venezuela	na	**na**	na	na	na	na	na	na	na	na	na	na	na	na	na	na
Vietnam	na	**na**	na	na	na	na	na	na	na	na	na	na	na	na	na	na
Zimbabwe	na	**na**	na	na	na	na	na	na	na	na	na	na	na	na	na	na
Total	na	**66**	63	68	61	64	71	72	64	56	72	67	59	72	64	62

RANKING	
Country	**2000**
Portugal	87
Slovakia	86
Hungary	86
Turkey	86
Romania	85
Croatia	84
Spain	83
Latvia	82
Greece	81
Poland	75
Iceland	71
France	70
Ireland	69
Lithuania	68
Slovenia	67
Finland	67
Bulgaria	65
Luxembourg	64
Belgium	63
Northern Ireland	62
Italy	61
Estonia	61
Germany	60
Russian Fed.	59
Belarus	59
Austria	58
Czech Republic	56
Great Britain	56
Sweden	45
Netherlands	41
Malta	36
Denmark	28
Total	66

E147_1) BASIC NEEDS FOR ALL

In order to be considered "just", what should a society provide? Please tell me for each statement if it is important or unimportant to you. 1 means very important; 5 means not important at all.

% Important / very important (codes 1 to 2) (EVS: V261)

Country	Wave 1990	Wave 2000	Gender Male	Gender Female	Age 16-29	Age 30-49	Age 50+	Education Lower	Education Middle	Education Upper	Income Lower	Income Middle	Income Upper	Values Mat	Values Mixed	Values Postm.
Albania	na	**na**	na	na	na	na	na	na	na	na	na	na	na	na	na	na
Algeria	na	**na**	na	na	na	na	na	na	na	na	na	na	na	na	na	na
Argentina	na	**na**	na	na	na	na	na	na	na	na	na	na	na	na	na	na
Armenia	na	**na**	na	na	na	na	na	na	na	na	na	na	na	na	na	na
Australia	na	**na**	na	na	na	na	na	na	na	na	na	na	na	na	na	na
Austria	na	**63**	62	64	62	65	61	62	63	66	63	63	62	64	64	62
Azerbaijan	na	**na**	na	na	na	na	na	na	na	na	na	na	na	na	na	na
Bangladesh	na	**na**	na	na	na	na	na	na	na	na	na	na	na	na	na	na
Belarus	na	**83**	81	85	83	82	84	79	84	83	85	83	79	86	81	66
Belgium	na	**74**	72	76	70	74	76	74	73	76	76	75	71	73	74	78
Bosnia and Herz.	na	**na**	na	na	na	na	na	na	na	na	na	na	na	na	na	na
Brazil	na	**na**	na	na	na	na	na	na	na	na	na	na	na	na	na	na
Bulgaria	na	**72**	70	73	71	68	75	79	67	71	80	66	68	76	69	59
Canada	na	**na**	na	na	na	na	na	na	na	na	na	na	na	na	na	na
Chile	na	**na**	na	na	na	na	na	na	na	na	na	na	na	na	na	na
China	na	**na**	na	na	na	na	na	na	na	na	na	na	na	na	na	na
Colombia	na	**na**	na	na	na	na	na	na	na	na	na	na	na	na	na	na
Croatia	na	**66**	65	66	62	69	65	65	67	65	69	70	62	63	67	67
Czech Republic	na	**53**	50	56	58	47	55	58	49	41	56	54	49	63	51	45
Denmark	na	**48**	48	48	55	50	43	41	54	60	48	45	56	35	49	59
Dominican Rep.	na	**na**	na	na	na	na	na	na	na	na	na	na	na	na	na	na
Egypt	na	**na**	na	na	na	na	na	na	na	na	na	na	na	na	na	na
El Salvador	na	**na**	na	na	na	na	na	na	na	na	na	na	na	na	na	na
Estonia	na	**63**	56	68	53	62	69	64	64	56	70	62	60	70	59	55
Finland	na	**69**	65	72	74	71	65	72	65	64	72	71	65	73	66	72
France	na	**77**	73	79	75	79	74	77	73	78	79	79	71	76	76	79
Georgia	na	**na**	na	na	na	na	na	na	na	na	na	na	na	na	na	na
Germany	na	**61**	58	64	64	63	58	58	64	66	61	59	57	57	61	67
Great Britain	na	**71**	70	72	70	74	70	74	68	75	70	77	69	na	na	na
Greece	na	**84**	81	86	84	85	83	85	83	85	85	83	81	79	85	86
Hungary	na	**75**	75	75	77	76	73	76	75	66	74	78	72	78	71	77
Iceland	na	**78**	72	84	71	81	80	77	75	85	80	80	75	75	79	78
India	na	**na**	na	na	na	na	na	na	na	na	na	na	na	na	na	na
Indonesia	na	**na**	na	na	na	na	na	na	na	na	na	na	na	na	na	na
Iran	na	**na**	na	na	na	na	na	na	na	na	na	na	na	na	na	na
Ireland	na	**76**	77	76	74	78	78	80	72	82	80	72	74	77	75	81
Israel	na	**na**	na	na	na	na	na	na	na	na	na	na	na	na	na	na
Italy	na	**70**	68	73	72	71	69	71	70	70	72	75	67	68	69	74
Japan	na	**na**	na	na	na	na	na	na	na	na	na	na	na	na	na	na
Jordan	na	**na**	na	na	na	na	na	na	na	na	na	na	na	na	na	na
Korea, South	na	**na**	na	na	na	na	na	na	na	na	na	na	na	na	na	na
Latvia	na	**84**	82	85	78	85	85	82	85	83	85	82	81	86	83	75
Lithuania	na	**79**	79	80	78	81	78	81	80	76	78	79	81	79	80	77
Luxembourg	na	**60**	57	63	56	63	61	56	62	66	56	59	66	56	61	71
Macedonia	na	**na**	na	na	na	na	na	na	na	na	na	na	na	na	na	na
Malta	na	**74**	74	74	69	78	74	77	73	74	74	71	77	73	75	72
Mexico	na	**na**	na	na	na	na	na	na	na	na	na	na	na	na	na	na
Moldova	na	**na**	na	na	na	na	na	na	na	na	na	na	na	na	na	na
Montenegro	na	**na**	na	na	na	na	na	na	na	na	na	na	na	na	na	na
Morocco	na	**na**	na	na	na	na	na	na	na	na	na	na	na	na	na	na
Netherlands	na	**70**	68	72	70	71	68	64	71	74	70	74	65	68	67	77
New Zealand	na	**na**	na	na	na	na	na	na	na	na	na	na	na	na	na	na
Nigeria	na	**na**	na	na	na	na	na	na	na	na	na	na	na	na	na	na
Northern Ireland	na	**77**	78	76	77	75	79	79	76	71	75	78	75	79	73	88
Norway	na	**na**	na	na	na	na	na	na	na	na	na	na	na	na	na	na
Pakistan	na	**na**	na	na	na	na	na	na	na	na	na	na	na	na	na	na
Peru	na	**na**	na	na	na	na	na	na	na	na	na	na	na	na	na	na
Philippines	na	**na**	na	na	na	na	na	na	na	na	na	na	na	na	na	na
Poland	na	**79**	76	81	79	77	80	84	75	64	85	74	73	82	78	64
Portugal	na	**81**	80	81	80	75	85	82	78	76	82	76	76	80	80	86
Puerto Rico	na	**na**	na	na	na	na	na	na	na	na	na	na	na	na	na	na
Romania	na	**61**	59	63	56	63	63	59	64	60	62	66	61	64	61	58
Russian Fed.	na	**77**	75	80	72	78	80	80	78	75	78	80	76	79	76	65
Serbia	na	**na**	na	na	na	na	na	na	na	na	na	na	na	na	na	na
Singapore	na	**na**	na	na	na	na	na	na	na	na	na	na	na	na	na	na
Slovakia	na	**78**	77	78	75	78	79	79	79	65	78	80	76	83	75	68
Slovenia	na	**72**	67	77	68	74	73	75	74	58	79	72	70	75	71	76
South Africa	na	**na**	na	na	na	na	na	na	na	na	na	na	na	na	na	na
Spain	na	**71**	70	71	72	71	70	68	70	79	70	72	71	67	68	83
Sweden	na	**71**	68	74	72	73	69	68	72	74	73	69	71	62	70	80
Switzerland	na	**na**	na	na	na	na	na	na	na	na	na	na	na	na	na	na
Taiwan	na	**na**	na	na	na	na	na	na	na	na	na	na	na	na	na	na
Tanzania	na	**na**	na	na	na	na	na	na	na	na	na	na	na	na	na	na
Turkey	na	**79**	78	80	79	79	81	80	77	82	78	80	81	83	77	86
Uganda	na	**na**	na	na	na	na	na	na	na	na	na	na	na	na	na	na
Ukraine	na	**na**	na	na	na	na	na	na	na	na	na	na	na	na	na	na
United States	na	**na**	na	na	na	na	na	na	na	na	na	na	na	na	na	na
Uruguay	na	**na**	na	na	na	na	na	na	na	na	na	na	na	na	na	na
Venezuela	na	**na**	na	na	na	na	na	na	na	na	na	na	na	na	na	na
Vietnam	na	**na**	na	na	na	na	na	na	na	na	na	na	na	na	na	na
Zimbabwe	na	**na**	na	na	na	na	na	na	na	na	na	na	na	na	na	na
Total	na	**72**	69	74	71	72	71	71	72	72	74	72	70	74	70	73

RANKING Country	2000
Greece	84
Latvia	84
Belarus	83
Portugal	81
Lithuania	79
Turkey	79
Poland	79
Iceland	78
Slovakia	78
Russian Fed.	77
Northern Ireland	77
France	77
Ireland	76
Hungary	75
Belgium	74
Malta	74
Slovenia	72
Bulgaria	72
Sweden	71
Great Britain	71
Spain	71
Italy	70
Netherlands	70
Finland	69
Croatia	66
Austria	63
Estonia	63
Germany	61
Romania	61
Luxembourg	60
Czech Republic	53
Denmark	48
Total	72

E148_1) RECOGNIZING MERITS

In order to be considered "just", what should a society provide? Please tell me for each statement if it is important or unimportant to you. 1 means very important; 5 means not important at all.

% Important / very important (codes 1 to 2) (EVS: V262)

	Wave		Gender		Age			Education			Income			Values		
Country	1990	2000	Male	Female	16-29	30-49	50+	Lower	Middle	Upper	Lower	Middle	Upper	Mat	Mixed	Postm.
Albania	na	**na**	na	na	na	na	na	na	na	na	na	na	na	na	na	na
Algeria	na	**na**	na	na	na	na	na	na	na	na	na	na	na	na	na	na
Argentina	na	**na**	na	na	na	na	na	na	na	na	na	na	na	na	na	na
Armenia	na	**na**	na	na	na	na	na	na	na	na	na	na	na	na	na	na
Australia	na	**na**	na	na	na	na	na	na	na	na	na	na	na	na	na	na
Austria	na	**44**	41	47	39	39	51	46	41	41	46	42	43	50	45	41
Azerbaijan	na	**na**	na	na	na	na	na	na	na	na	na	na	na	na	na	na
Bangladesh	na	**na**	na	na	na	na	na	na	na	na	na	na	na	na	na	na
Belarus	na	**78**	73	82	75	79	79	75	78	81	75	80	79	81	75	84
Belgium	na	**51**	52	51	44	47	58	50	53	49	58	52	45	51	49	58
Bosnia and Herz.	na	**na**	na	na	na	na	na	na	na	na	na	na	na	na	na	na
Brazil	na	**na**	na	na	na	na	na	na	na	na	na	na	na	na	na	na
Bulgaria	na	**67**	67	66	67	65	68	66	66	70	69	65	66	67	68	63
Canada	na	**na**	na	na	na	na	na	na	na	na	na	na	na	na	na	na
Chile	na	**na**	na	na	na	na	na	na	na	na	na	na	na	na	na	na
China	na	**na**	na	na	na	na	na	na	na	na	na	na	na	na	na	na
Colombia	na	**na**	na	na	na	na	na	na	na	na	na	na	na	na	na	na
Croatia	na	**47**	42	52	45	47	48	53	44	41	56	47	44	57	46	45
Czech Republic	na	**65**	64	66	58	65	69	64	67	65	66	66	65	61	66	68
Denmark	na	**39**	43	34	32	37	44	40	36	39	37	38	45	27	39	39
Dominican Rep.	na	**na**	na	na	na	na	na	na	na	na	na	na	na	na	na	na
Egypt	na	**na**	na	na	na	na	na	na	na	na	na	na	na	na	na	na
El Salvador	na	**na**	na	na	na	na	na	na	na	na	na	na	na	na	na	na
Estonia	na	**41**	43	40	33	42	45	42	39	46	39	42	43	42	43	46
Finland	na	**39**	35	43	30	36	47	44	33	34	43	44	34	46	36	45
France	na	**54**	53	55	46	50	62	61	46	43	58	55	47	60	55	40
Georgia	na	**na**	na	na	na	na	na	na	na	na	na	na	na	na	na	na
Germany	na	**44**	41	47	41	43	48	44	45	45	46	46	44	48	41	48
Great Britain	na	**50**	54	47	41	50	56	48	49	52	47	50	51	na	na	na
Greece	na	**57**	52	61	53	58	63	68	58	54	63	53	57	51	58	58
Hungary	na	**64**	64	63	62	65	63	66	59	59	65	64	61	63	65	68
Iceland	na	**68**	65	71	48	74	78	70	65	71	71	68	67	65	69	74
India	na	**na**	na	na	na	na	na	na	na	na	na	na	na	na	na	na
Indonesia	na	**na**	na	na	na	na	na	na	na	na	na	na	na	na	na	na
Iran	na	**na**	na	na	na	na	na	na	na	na	na	na	na	na	na	na
Ireland	na	**54**	55	53	45	58	57	58	52	53	59	49	50	56	54	48
Israel	na	**na**	na	na	na	na	na	na	na	na	na	na	na	na	na	na
Italy	na	**43**	44	41	36	43	46	44	40	46	44	40	41	45	43	41
Japan	na	**na**	na	na	na	na	na	na	na	na	na	na	na	na	na	na
Jordan	na	**na**	na	na	na	na	na	na	na	na	na	na	na	na	na	na
Korea, South	na	**na**	na	na	na	na	na	na	na	na	na	na	na	na	na	na
Latvia	na	**52**	52	53	49	51	55	52	51	58	55	53	49	53	52	46
Lithuania	na	**36**	35	38	32	39	37	38	36	36	32	38	36	35	37	42
Luxembourg	na	**56**	59	54	50	52	65	57	58	53	63	60	54	61	59	44
Macedonia	na	**na**	na	na	na	na	na	na	na	na	na	na	na	na	na	na
Malta	na	**64**	63	64	55	69	65	63	63	68	67	67	65	62	65	63
Mexico	na	**na**	na	na	na	na	na	na	na	na	na	na	na	na	na	na
Moldova	na	**na**	na	na	na	na	na	na	na	na	na	na	na	na	na	na
Montenegro	na	**na**	na	na	na	na	na	na	na	na	na	na	na	na	na	na
Morocco	na	**na**	na	na	na	na	na	na	na	na	na	na	na	na	na	na
Netherlands	na	**44**	41	46	34	39	54	41	44	46	49	43	37	38	40	58
New Zealand	na	**na**	na	na	na	na	na	na	na	na	na	na	na	na	na	na
Nigeria	na	**na**	na	na	na	na	na	na	na	na	na	na	na	na	na	na
Northern Ireland	na	**49**	51	47	42	48	54	52	45	51	52	46	41	55	45	56
Norway	na	**na**	na	na	na	na	na	na	na	na	na	na	na	na	na	na
Pakistan	na	**na**	na	na	na	na	na	na	na	na	na	na	na	na	na	na
Peru	na	**na**	na	na	na	na	na	na	na	na	na	na	na	na	na	na
Philippines	na	**na**	na	na	na	na	na	na	na	na	na	na	na	na	na	na
Poland	na	**74**	73	75	73	72	76	77	71	63	78	72	68	73	74	78
Portugal	na	**65**	65	64	61	64	67	68	59	57	62	59	66	63	66	62
Puerto Rico	na	**na**	na	na	na	na	na	na	na	na	na	na	na	na	na	na
Romania	na	**65**	67	63	62	68	65	53	69	77	55	66	76	63	67	71
Russian Fed.	na	**57**	56	58	48	58	62	58	56	60	59	56	57	58	57	48
Serbia	na	**na**	na	na	na	na	na	na	na	na	na	na	na	na	na	na
Singapore	na	**na**	na	na	na	na	na	na	na	na	na	na	na	na	na	na
Slovakia	na	**55**	54	56	56	54	56	54	55	60	59	53	56	54	55	58
Slovenia	na	**51**	50	51	42	53	54	49	52	45	55	48	49	48	51	51
South Africa	na	**na**	na	na	na	na	na	na	na	na	na	na	na	na	na	na
Spain	na	**47**	48	46	44	46	49	49	46	44	44	51	44	44	47	49
Sweden	na	**42**	41	44	34	39	50	46	41	42	46	38	41	43	40	48
Switzerland	na	**na**	na	na	na	na	na	na	na	na	na	na	na	na	na	na
Taiwan	na	**na**	na	na	na	na	na	na	na	na	na	na	na	na	na	na
Tanzania	na	**na**	na	na	na	na	na	na	na	na	na	na	na	na	na	na
Turkey	na	**69**	69	68	70	68	67	64	74	77	65	69	76	67	68	78
Uganda	na	**na**	na	na	na	na	na	na	na	na	na	na	na	na	na	na
Ukraine	na	**na**	na	na	na	na	na	na	na	na	na	na	na	na	na	na
United States	na	**na**	na	na	na	na	na	na	na	na	na	na	na	na	na	na
Uruguay	na	**na**	na	na	na	na	na	na	na	na	na	na	na	na	na	na
Venezuela	na	**na**	na	na	na	na	na	na	na	na	na	na	na	na	na	na
Vietnam	na	**na**	na	na	na	na	na	na	na	na	na	na	na	na	na	na
Zimbabwe	na	**na**	na	na	na	na	na	na	na	na	na	na	na	na	na	na
Total	na	**54**	53	54	49	53	58	55	53	53	56	54	53	57	53	52

RANKING	
Country	**2000**
Belarus	78
Poland	74
Turkey	69
Iceland	68
Bulgaria	67
Czech Republic	65
Romania	65
Portugal	65
Malta	64
Hungary	64
Russian Fed.	57
Greece	57
Luxembourg	56
Slovakia	55
France	54
Ireland	54
Latvia	52
Belgium	51
Slovenia	51
Great Britain	50
Northern Ireland	49
Croatia	47
Spain	47
Germany	44
Austria	44
Netherlands	44
Italy	43
Sweden	42
Estonia	41
Finland	39
Denmark	39
Lithuania	36
Total	54

E150) HOW OFTEN FOLLOWS POLITICS IN THE NEWS

How often do you follow politics in the news on television or on the radio or in the daily papers?

Every day (%) (WVS: V217; EVS: V263)

Country	Wave		Gender		Age			Education			Income			Values		
	1990	2000	Male	Female	16-29	30-49	50+	Lower	Middle	Upper	Lower	Middle	Upper	Mat	Mixed	Postm.
Albania	na	**31**	41	22	16	31	45	26	34	38	30	33	32	30	32	43
Algeria	na	**na**	na	na	na	na	na	na	na	na	na	na	na	na	na	na
Argentina	na	**48**	50	46	34	48	61	46	48	57	49	46	48	42	48	50
Armenia	na	**na**	na	na	na	na	na	na	na	na	na	na	na	na	na	na
Australia	na	**na**	na	na	na	na	na	na	na	na	na	na	na	na	na	na
Austria	na	**57**	60	55	34	55	72	54	57	71	57	58	66	49	58	60
Azerbaijan	na	**na**	na	na	na	na	na	na	na	na	na	na	na	na	na	na
Bangladesh	na	**35**	39	29	38	33	34	19	51	57	19	36	49	34	37	32
Belarus	na	**34**	40	30	27	36	39	22	36	49	28	36	42	31	37	44
Belgium	na	**47**	52	41	27	42	59	36	42	60	43	47	51	42	44	58
Bosnia and Herz.	na	**30**	37	24	20	29	43	26	29	38	32	28	35	27	31	32
Brazil	na	**na**	na	na	na	na	na	na	na	na	na	na	na	na	na	na
Bulgaria	na	**41**	44	39	22	40	52	34	41	56	40	49	40	36	50	39
Canada	na	**34**	39	29	13	29	52	37	27	44	30	38	34	21	33	39
Chile	na	**27**	30	24	20	27	33	26	24	38	25	24	35	25	27	32
China	na	**46**	54	37	43	44	52	36	51	71	37	48	55	49	45	66
Colombia	na	**na**	na	na	na	na	na	na	na	na	na	na	na	na	na	na
Croatia	na	**53**	62	44	33	52	66	49	55	51	55	47	56	47	53	53
Czech Republic	na	**60**	60	60	34	58	75	55	62	74	65	59	57	55	61	65
Denmark	na	**64**	69	59	44	61	77	59	65	73	65	63	70	44	65	73
Dominican Rep.	na	**na**	na	na	na	na	na	na	na	na	na	na	na	na	na	na
Egypt	na	**na**	na	na	na	na	na	na	na	na	na	na	na	na	na	na
El Salvador	na	**na**	na	na	na	na	na	na	na	na	na	na	na	na	na	na
Estonia	na	**48**	52	45	24	44	65	48	43	62	47	52	49	45	51	52
Finland	na	**39**	42	37	21	36	51	37	40	53	33	39	47	35	41	40
France	na	**58**	61	54	36	52	73	57	55	60	55	60	64	56	59	53
Georgia	na	**na**	na	na	na	na	na	na	na	na	na	na	na	na	na	na
Germany	na	**61**	68	56	42	62	68	54	64	86	55	62	66	62	60	66
Great Britain	na	**24**	26	21	8	21	35	22	22	34	20	24	26	na	na	na
Greece	na	**53**	58	49	38	60	76	67	47	56	55	54	53	50	53	56
Hungary	na	**48**	54	44	29	52	56	45	51	66	44	52	48	46	52	53
Iceland	na	**45**	47	44	21	46	65	41	45	57	42	46	49	39	46	55
India	na	**34**	40	26	38	34	31	18	37	64	24	25	48	32	43	52
Indonesia	na	**na**	na	na	na	na	na	na	na	na	na	na	na	na	na	na
Iran	na	**na**	na	na	na	na	na	na	na	na	na	na	na	na	na	na
Ireland	na	**30**	34	26	15	30	40	26	28	39	25	32	37	23	31	37
Israel	na	**80**	82	78	69	81	93	81	78	84	83	82	81	76	82	79
Italy	na	**50**	56	44	37	49	58	46	49	64	48	52	55	46	51	52
Japan	na	**37**	44	32	17	26	56	44	34	43	40	36	42	40	36	51
Jordan	na	**na**	na	na	na	na	na	na	na	na	na	na	na	na	na	na
Korea, South	na	**52**	63	41	35	54	69	46	55	50	50	55	53	52	53	45
Latvia	na	**64**	66	62	44	64	73	57	65	72	64	65	65	61	66	70
Lithuania	na	**68**	69	68	49	74	76	66	69	70	74	67	71	67	70	70
Luxembourg	na	**46**	47	44	23	46	60	39	47	58	36	54	59	46	45	52
Macedonia	na	**56**	65	48	38	59	68	51	57	65	55	54	62	58	57	43
Malta	na	**34**	37	32	17	34	46	47	29	32	43	32	32	33	35	37
Mexico	na	**30**	30	31	25	32	34	27	31	42	27	32	35	31	33	34
Moldova	na	**45**	53	38	37	49	47	31	49	51	44	46	43	37	51	55
Montenegro	na	**28**	37	20	14	27	38	26	27	38	33	26	32	30	29	22
Morocco	na	**19**	25	13	21	19	16	14	31	62	15	21	33	11	25	35
Netherlands	na	**51**	54	48	28	49	65	45	49	59	46	53	56	41	50	58
New Zealand	na	**na**	na	na	na	na	na	na	na	na	na	na	na	na	na	na
Nigeria	na	**na**	na	na	na	na	na	na	na	na	na	na	na	na	na	na
Northern Ireland	na	**32**	38	27	24	32	36	33	30	38	28	26	37	30	33	43
Norway	na	**na**	na	na	na	na	na	na	na	na	na	na	na	na	na	na
Pakistan	na	**na**	na	na	na	na	na	na	na	na	na	na	na	na	na	na
Peru	na	**58**	61	55	51	61	68	49	58	64	54	61	61	51	59	64
Philippines	na	**28**	30	25	27	28	28	22	28	34	26	26	32	26	29	31
Poland	na	**53**	56	50	28	54	66	49	53	70	55	52	52	51	54	55
Portugal	na	**36**	41	32	35	41	34	33	40	58	20	38	47	33	37	50
Puerto Rico	na	**46**	49	45	24	47	56	54	45	45	49	48	44	39	48	46
Romania	na	**43**	49	37	28	46	48	31	43	69	31	46	52	39	50	48
Russian Fed.	na	**67**	72	63	51	70	74	64	66	74	65	68	70	68	68	67
Serbia	na	**45**	54	38	27	41	58	40	45	55	44	45	53	43	48	50
Singapore	na	**29**	33	25	22	36	33	28	27	41	27	28	29	27	30	26
Slovakia	na	**41**	46	36	27	40	53	35	42	53	40	41	42	39	42	57
Slovenia	na	**44**	46	42	17	40	68	41	41	59	46	47	53	48	42	43
South Africa	na	**24**	29	17	17	30	21	21	25	43	18	31	25	23	25	17
Spain	na	**44**	50	38	35	46	47	41	43	53	35	48	49	41	44	50
Sweden	na	**72**	75	69	52	71	86	82	63	79	69	74	76	69	71	76
Switzerland	na	**na**	na	na	na	na	na	na	na	na	na	na	na	na	na	na
Taiwan	na	**na**	na	na	na	na	na	na	na	na	na	na	na	na	na	na
Tanzania	na	**39**	41	35	33	39	45	39	35	43	38	41	40	36	40	50
Turkey	na	**49**	61	37	44	54	53	42	55	71	42	49	63	46	48	58
Uganda	na	**29**	33	25	30	26	34	28	28	33	35	30	29	24	28	49
Ukraine	na	**62**	65	59	49	63	68	50	63	66	59	61	67	59	66	80
United States	na	**34**	37	31	17	31	54	28	33	38	32	34	38	24	34	40
Uruguay	na	**na**	na	na	na	na	na	na	na	na	na	na	na	na	na	na
Venezuela	na	**32**	36	29	27	33	40	32	31	37	29	31	36	28	33	35
Vietnam	na	**59**	69	49	49	58	68	48	72	78	53	57	65	59	64	67
Zimbabwe	na	**15**	21	11	14	18	15	11	21	52	7	14	32	10	18	30
Total	na	**44**	49	40	30	44	56	39	44	54	42	45	49	40	46	50

RANKING	
Country	2000
Israel	80
Sweden	72
Lithuania	68
Russian Fed.	67
Latvia	64
Denmark	64
Ukraine	62
Germany	61
Czech Republic	60
Vietnam	59
Peru	58
France	58
Austria	57
Macedonia	56
Greece	53
Poland	53
Croatia	53
Korea, South	52
Netherlands	51
Italy	50
Turkey	49
Hungary	48
Estonia	48
Argentina	48
Belgium	47
Puerto Rico	46
China	46
Luxembourg	46
Iceland	45
Serbia	45
Moldova	45
Slovenia	44
Spain	44
Romania	43
Bulgaria	41
Slovakia	41
Finland	39
Tanzania	39
Japan	37
Portugal	36
Bangladesh	35
Belarus	34
Malta	34
United States	34
India	34
Canada	34
Venezuela	32
Northern Ireland	32
Albania	31
Bosnia and Herz.	30
Mexico	30
Ireland	30
Singapore	29
Uganda	29
Montenegro	28
Philippines	28
Chile	27
Great Britain	24
South Africa	24
Morocco	19
Zimbabwe	15
Total	44

E151_1) INFORMATION TO HELP JUSTICE

Can you tell me your opinion on each of the following statements? If someone has information that may help justice be done, generally he or she should give it to authorities

Strongly agree (%)

(EVS: V264)

Country	Wave		Gender		Age			Education			Income			Values		
	1990	2000	Male	Female	16-29	30-49	50+	Lower	Middle	Upper	Lower	Middle	Upper	Mat	Mixed	Postm.
Albania	na	**na**	na	na	na	na	na	na	na	na	na	na	na	na	na	na
Algeria	na	**na**	na	na	na	na	na	na	na	na	na	na	na	na	na	na
Argentina	na	**na**	na	na	na	na	na	na	na	na	na	na	na	na	na	na
Armenia	na	**na**	na	na	na	na	na	na	na	na	na	na	na	na	na	na
Australia	na	**na**	na	na	na	na	na	na	na	na	na	na	na	na	na	na
Austria	na	**33**	37	30	27	33	38	33	35	30	30	32	37	39	36	28
Azerbaijan	na	**na**	na	na	na	na	na	na	na	na	na	na	na	na	na	na
Bangladesh	na	**na**	na	na	na	na	na	na	na	na	na	na	na	na	na	na
Belarus	na	**43**	41	44	35	44	48	49	39	46	45	42	39	44	42	44
Belgium	na	**55**	55	54	43	53	61	53	55	54	59	54	54	55	56	54
Bosnia and Herz.	na	**na**	na	na	na	na	na	na	na	na	na	na	na	na	na	na
Brazil	na	**na**	na	na	na	na	na	na	na	na	na	na	na	na	na	na
Bulgaria	na	**50**	47	53	36	49	59	55	46	53	56	52	45	52	51	45
Canada	na	**na**	na	na	na	na	na	na	na	na	na	na	na	na	na	na
Chile	na	**na**	na	na	na	na	na	na	na	na	na	na	na	na	na	na
China	na	**na**	na	na	na	na	na	na	na	na	na	na	na	na	na	na
Colombia	na	**na**	na	na	na	na	na	na	na	na	na	na	na	na	na	na
Croatia	na	**45**	43	46	34	47	50	46	46	38	49	42	47	45	45	43
Czech Republic	na	**42**	41	43	38	38	47	40	44	42	45	39	42	42	41	44
Denmark	na	**46**	45	47	50	43	47	48	45	43	44	49	46	48	47	35
Dominican Rep.	na	**na**	na	na	na	na	na	na	na	na	na	na	na	na	na	na
Egypt	na	**na**	na	na	na	na	na	na	na	na	na	na	na	na	na	na
El Salvador	na	**na**	na	na	na	na	na	na	na	na	na	na	na	na	na	na
Estonia	na	**33**	29	37	25	30	40	32	34	32	34	39	31	31	36	29
Finland	na	**49**	44	53	43	44	57	49	45	56	51	47	50	46	51	48
France	na	**60**	59	60	54	57	65	64	54	54	58	60	59	66	59	51
Georgia	na	**na**	na	na	na	na	na	na	na	na	na	na	na	na	na	na
Germany	na	**25**	27	23	23	21	30	28	21	30	24	26	18	27	23	26
Great Britain	na	**45**	44	46	35	46	49	40	48	51	38	44	53	na	na	na
Greece	na	**35**	35	35	30	34	48	52	34	32	38	33	33	36	36	32
Hungary	na	**36**	34	37	36	27	43	38	30	31	37	35	35	35	37	12
Iceland	na	**49**	50	49	41	52	53	50	49	48	50	50	48	51	50	41
India	na	**na**	na	na	na	na	na	na	na	na	na	na	na	na	na	na
Indonesia	na	**na**	na	na	na	na	na	na	na	na	na	na	na	na	na	na
Iran	na	**na**	na	na	na	na	na	na	na	na	na	na	na	na	na	na
Ireland	na	**49**	47	51	39	51	53	51	46	50	51	52	44	43	49	54
Israel	na	**na**	na	na	na	na	na	na	na	na	na	na	na	na	na	na
Italy	na	**41**	44	38	38	42	41	36	42	51	37	43	43	35	41	44
Japan	na	**na**	na	na	na	na	na	na	na	na	na	na	na	na	na	na
Jordan	na	**na**	na	na	na	na	na	na	na	na	na	na	na	na	na	na
Korea, South	na	**na**	na	na	na	na	na	na	na	na	na	na	na	na	na	na
Latvia	na	**37**	33	40	25	34	43	34	37	40	38	37	35	38	36	28
Lithuania	na	**25**	23	28	20	23	32	24	25	29	23	30	26	25	26	26
Luxembourg	na	**47**	50	44	41	47	51	47	45	52	43	51	54	48	47	54
Macedonia	na	**na**	na	na	na	na	na	na	na	na	na	na	na	na	na	na
Malta	na	**43**	44	43	43	41	46	46	42	48	39	45	44	45	45	30
Mexico	na	**na**	na	na	na	na	na	na	na	na	na	na	na	na	na	na
Moldova	na	**na**	na	na	na	na	na	na	na	na	na	na	na	na	na	na
Montenegro	na	**na**	na	na	na	na	na	na	na	na	na	na	na	na	na	na
Morocco	na	**na**	na	na	na	na	na	na	na	na	na	na	na	na	na	na
Netherlands	na	**31**	35	27	24	27	38	34	32	26	27	32	30	37	30	30
New Zealand	na	**na**	na	na	na	na	na	na	na	na	na	na	na	na	na	na
Nigeria	na	**na**	na	na	na	na	na	na	na	na	na	na	na	na	na	na
Northern Ireland	na	**38**	35	40	34	36	41	36	38	42	31	38	52	43	37	29
Norway	na	**na**	na	na	na	na	na	na	na	na	na	na	na	na	na	na
Pakistan	na	**na**	na	na	na	na	na	na	na	na	na	na	na	na	na	na
Peru	na	**na**	na	na	na	na	na	na	na	na	na	na	na	na	na	na
Philippines	na	**na**	na	na	na	na	na	na	na	na	na	na	na	na	na	na
Poland	na	**45**	46	45	40	46	49	46	49	34	45	47	43	46	46	39
Portugal	na	**47**	51	44	48	44	50	49	46	43	46	44	52	46	51	44
Puerto Rico	na	**na**	na	na	na	na	na	na	na	na	na	na	na	na	na	na
Romania	na	**48**	49	46	41	50	49	46	50	48	45	51	50	48	47	55
Russian Fed.	na	**29**	26	31	21	27	36	34	27	29	32	31	24	29	28	29
Serbia	na	**na**	na	na	na	na	na	na	na	na	na	na	na	na	na	na
Singapore	na	**na**	na	na	na	na	na	na	na	na	na	na	na	na	na	na
Slovakia	na	**53**	52	55	52	50	58	56	52	50	55	52	55	53	53	58
Slovenia	na	**46**	46	47	44	45	49	50	44	47	45	48	47	51	45	46
South Africa	na	**na**	na	na	na	na	na	na	na	na	na	na	na	na	na	na
Spain	na	**38**	36	40	31	39	41	40	34	44	36	43	43	41	36	40
Sweden	na	**27**	29	24	22	26	30	27	26	27	25	27	28	40	25	27
Switzerland	na	**na**	na	na	na	na	na	na	na	na	na	na	na	na	na	na
Taiwan	na	**na**	na	na	na	na	na	na	na	na	na	na	na	na	na	na
Tanzania	na	**na**	na	na	na	na	na	na	na	na	na	na	na	na	na	na
Turkey	na	**na**	na	na	na	na	na	na	na	na	na	na	na	na	na	na
Uganda	na	**na**	na	na	na	na	na	na	na	na	na	na	na	na	na	na
Ukraine	na	**37**	37	38	31	38	40	39	37	38	38	37	39	34	42	32
United States	na	**na**	na	na	na	na	na	na	na	na	na	na	na	na	na	na
Uruguay	na	**na**	na	na	na	na	na	na	na	na	na	na	na	na	na	na
Venezuela	na	**na**	na	na	na	na	na	na	na	na	na	na	na	na	na	na
Vietnam	na	**na**	na	na	na	na	na	na	na	na	na	na	na	na	na	na
Zimbabwe	na	**na**	na	na	na	na	na	na	na	na	na	na	na	na	na	na
Total	na	**42**	41	42	36	40	46	43	40	41	41	42	42	42	42	39

RANKING	
Country	2000
France	60
Belgium	55
Slovakia	53
Bulgaria	50
Iceland	49
Finland	49
Ireland	49
Romania	48
Portugal	47
Luxembourg	47
Slovenia	46
Denmark	46
Poland	45
Croatia	45
Great Britain	45
Malta	43
Belarus	43
Czech Republic	42
Italy	41
Spain	38
Northern Ireland	38
Ukraine	37
Latvia	37
Hungary	36
Greece	35
Austria	33
Estonia	33
Netherlands	31
Russian Fed.	29
Sweden	27
Lithuania	25
Germany	25
Total	42

E152_1) STICK TO OWN AFFAIRS

Can you tell me your opinion on each of the following statements? People should stick to their own affairs and not show too much interest in what others say or do

Strongly agree / Agree (%)

(EVS: V265)

Country	Wave		Gender		Age			Education			Income			Values		
	1990	2000	Male	Female	16-29	30-49	50+	Lower	Middle	Upper	Lower	Middle	Upper	Mat	Mixed	Postm.
Albania	na	**na**	na	na	na	na	na	na	na	na	na	na	na	na	na	na
Algeria	na	**na**	na	na	na	na	na	na	na	na	na	na	na	na	na	na
Argentina	na	**na**	na	na	na	na	na	na	na	na	na	na	na	na	na	na
Armenia	na	**na**	na	na	na	na	na	na	na	na	na	na	na	na	na	na
Australia	na	**na**	na	na	na	na	na	na	na	na	na	na	na	na	na	na
Austria	na	**60**	57	62	54	54	69	68	51	53	69	61	51	72	60	58
Azerbaijan	na	**na**	na	na	na	na	na	na	na	na	na	na	na	na	na	na
Bangladesh	na	**na**	na	na	na	na	na	na	na	na	na	na	na	na	na	na
Belarus	na	**47**	47	48	44	48	49	49	46	49	48	47	47	51	44	37
Belgium	na	**50**	48	53	43	46	58	65	53	37	61	54	43	63	50	37
Bosnia and Herz.	na	**na**	na	na	na	na	na	na	na	na	na	na	na	na	na	na
Brazil	na	**na**	na	na	na	na	na	na	na	na	na	na	na	na	na	na
Bulgaria	na	**46**	48	45	51	43	47	48	47	42	49	46	44	45	46	41
Canada	na	**na**	na	na	na	na	na	na	na	na	na	na	na	na	na	na
Chile	na	**na**	na	na	na	na	na	na	na	na	na	na	na	na	na	na
China	na	**na**	na	na	na	na	na	na	na	na	na	na	na	na	na	na
Colombia	na	**na**	na	na	na	na	na	na	na	na	na	na	na	na	na	na
Croatia	na	**64**	62	67	60	62	70	71	63	48	74	63	61	73	64	60
Czech Republic	na	**31**	33	30	29	31	33	40	23	19	38	33	22	37	30	22
Denmark	na	**35**	37	33	32	28	43	46	23	18	40	33	27	61	34	20
Dominican Rep.	na	**na**	na	na	na	na	na	na	na	na	na	na	na	na	na	na
Egypt	na	**na**	na	na	na	na	na	na	na	na	na	na	na	na	na	na
El Salvador	na	**na**	na	na	na	na	na	na	na	na	na	na	na	na	na	na
Estonia	na	**65**	61	68	60	65	69	67	65	63	68	65	65	66	67	67
Finland	na	**62**	62	62	62	57	66	67	59	49	70	60	57	66	63	55
France	na	**62**	61	63	61	57	67	72	55	43	71	61	50	73	62	46
Georgia	na	**na**	na	na	na	na	na	na	na	na	na	na	na	na	na	na
Germany	na	**41**	41	41	42	41	40	45	39	27	48	47	34	40	41	38
Great Britain	na	**38**	34	41	33	32	43	49	28	29	47	35	31	na	na	na
Greece	na	**47**	48	47	40	49	61	64	53	39	56	47	39	49	48	45
Hungary	na	**54**	53	54	51	56	53	56	50	48	54	51	57	53	54	37
Iceland	na	**55**	55	55	51	51	64	62	54	43	61	57	47	60	55	44
India	na	**na**	na	na	na	na	na	na	na	na	na	na	na	na	na	na
Indonesia	na	**na**	na	na	na	na	na	na	na	na	na	na	na	na	na	na
Iran	na	**na**	na	na	na	na	na	na	na	na	na	na	na	na	na	na
Ireland	na	**43**	43	43	42	40	47	54	42	27	54	45	34	51	40	45
Israel	na	**na**	na	na	na	na	na	na	na	na	na	na	na	na	na	na
Italy	na	**29**	27	31	25	24	35	38	23	18	30	28	23	45	29	21
Japan	na	**na**	na	na	na	na	na	na	na	na	na	na	na	na	na	na
Jordan	na	**na**	na	na	na	na	na	na	na	na	na	na	na	na	na	na
Korea, South	na	**na**	na	na	na	na	na	na	na	na	na	na	na	na	na	na
Latvia	na	**66**	66	66	60	66	68	66	64	69	67	61	67	67	66	66
Lithuania	na	**57**	56	57	60	55	56	54	59	49	60	56	50	59	56	44
Luxembourg	na	**64**	64	65	63	63	67	67	67	52	67	64	54	69	64	57
Macedonia	na	**na**	na	na	na	na	na	na	na	na	na	na	na	na	na	na
Malta	na	**63**	62	64	58	64	65	71	61	53	62	66	66	68	61	51
Mexico	na	**na**	na	na	na	na	na	na	na	na	na	na	na	na	na	na
Moldova	na	**na**	na	na	na	na	na	na	na	na	na	na	na	na	na	na
Montenegro	na	**na**	na	na	na	na	na	na	na	na	na	na	na	na	na	na
Morocco	na	**na**	na	na	na	na	na	na	na	na	na	na	na	na	na	na
Netherlands	na	**29**	25	33	21	25	39	42	27	19	34	30	23	48	29	22
New Zealand	na	**na**	na	na	na	na	na	na	na	na	na	na	na	na	na	na
Nigeria	na	**na**	na	na	na	na	na	na	na	na	na	na	na	na	na	na
Northern Ireland	na	**39**	40	39	38	41	40	44	38	31	46	33	30	44	37	40
Norway	na	**na**	na	na	na	na	na	na	na	na	na	na	na	na	na	na
Pakistan	na	**na**	na	na	na	na	na	na	na	na	na	na	na	na	na	na
Peru	na	**na**	na	na	na	na	na	na	na	na	na	na	na	na	na	na
Philippines	na	**na**	na	na	na	na	na	na	na	na	na	na	na	na	na	na
Poland	na	**63**	66	60	68	64	58	64	62	58	66	59	64	64	63	65
Portugal	na	**69**	68	70	68	66	73	71	68	59	72	69	64	71	69	71
Puerto Rico	na	**na**	na	na	na	na	na	na	na	na	na	na	na	na	na	na
Romania	na	**59**	58	61	60	54	64	68	56	52	66	60	54	66	53	55
Russian Fed.	na	**63**	65	61	60	63	64	62	63	61	60	67	61	63	62	60
Serbia	na	**na**	na	na	na	na	na	na	na	na	na	na	na	na	na	na
Singapore	na	**na**	na	na	na	na	na	na	na	na	na	na	na	na	na	na
Slovakia	na	**27**	27	27	29	27	26	29	28	16	31	28	23	27	27	23
Slovenia	na	**71**	66	75	70	71	72	77	70	65	76	72	61	70	73	61
South Africa	na	**na**	na	na	na	na	na	na	na	na	na	na	na	na	na	na
Spain	na	**53**	51	54	50	50	57	60	52	36	61	50	41	54	56	41
Sweden	na	**28**	31	25	22	22	37	44	28	15	31	33	18	40	30	19
Switzerland	na	**na**	na	na	na	na	na	na	na	na	na	na	na	na	na	na
Taiwan	na	**na**	na	na	na	na	na	na	na	na	na	na	na	na	na	na
Tanzania	na	**na**	na	na	na	na	na	na	na	na	na	na	na	na	na	na
Turkey	na	**na**	na	na	na	na	na	na	na	na	na	na	na	na	na	na
Uganda	na	**na**	na	na	na	na	na	na	na	na	na	na	na	na	na	na
Ukraine	na	**58**	55	59	56	57	59	58	59	55	60	57	54	56	57	59
United States	na	**na**	na	na	na	na	na	na	na	na	na	na	na	na	na	na
Uruguay	na	**na**	na	na	na	na	na	na	na	na	na	na	na	na	na	na
Venezuela	na	**na**	na	na	na	na	na	na	na	na	na	na	na	na	na	na
Vietnam	na	**na**	na	na	na	na	na	na	na	na	na	na	na	na	na	na
Zimbabwe	na	**na**	na	na	na	na	na	na	na	na	na	na	na	na	na	na
Total	na	**51**	50	52	49	49	55	57	50	42	55	51	46	57	51	42

RANKING

Country	2000
Slovenia	71
Portugal	69
Latvia	66
Estonia	65
Luxembourg	64
Croatia	64
Malta	63
Poland	63
Russian Fed.	63
Finland	62
France	62
Austria	60
Romania	59
Ukraine	58
Lithuania	57
Iceland	55
Hungary	54
Spain	53
Belgium	50
Belarus	47
Greece	47
Bulgaria	46
Ireland	43
Germany	41
Northern Ireland	39
Great Britain	38
Denmark	35
Czech Republic	31
Netherlands	29
Italy	29
Sweden	28
Slovakia	27
Total	51

E153_1) CONCERNED WITH IMMEDIATE FAMILY

To what extent do you feel concerned about the living conditions of: Your immediate family

Very much / Much (%)

(EVS: V266)

Country	Wave		Gender		Age			Education			Income			Values		
	1990	2000	Male	Female	16-29	30-49	50+	Lower	Middle	Upper	Lower	Middle	Upper	Mat	Mixed	Postm.
Albania	na	**na**	na	na	na	na	na	na	na	na	na	na	na	na	na	na
Algeria	na	**na**	na	na	na	na	na	na	na	na	na	na	na	na	na	na
Argentina	na	**na**	na	na	na	na	na	na	na	na	na	na	na	na	na	na
Armenia	na	**na**	na	na	na	na	na	na	na	na	na	na	na	na	na	na
Australia	na	**na**	na	na	na	na	na	na	na	na	na	na	na	na	na	na
Austria	na	**76**	74	78	72	76	78	79	76	64	76	80	73	70	78	74
Azerbaijan	na	**na**	na	na	na	na	na	na	na	na	na	na	na	na	na	na
Bangladesh	na	**na**	na	na	na	na	na	na	na	na	na	na	na	na	na	na
Belarus	na	**96**	96	97	94	98	96	97	96	94	97	96	95	97	95	98
Belgium	na	**93**	91	94	94	92	92	90	93	94	87	93	96	94	92	92
Bosnia and Herz.	na	**na**	na	na	na	na	na	na	na	na	na	na	na	na	na	na
Brazil	na	**na**	na	na	na	na	na	na	na	na	na	na	na	na	na	na
Bulgaria	na	**97**	96	97	97	98	96	97	95	99	95	97	98	97	98	100
Canada	na	**na**	na	na	na	na	na	na	na	na	na	na	na	na	na	na
Chile	na	**na**	na	na	na	na	na	na	na	na	na	na	na	na	na	na
China	na	**na**	na	na	na	na	na	na	na	na	na	na	na	na	na	na
Colombia	na	**na**	na	na	na	na	na	na	na	na	na	na	na	na	na	na
Croatia	na	**73**	68	77	67	75	74	75	74	61	84	75	62	84	72	68
Czech Republic	na	**30**	28	32	29	28	33	34	27	23	33	33	26	40	27	23
Denmark	na	**34**	34	35	48	35	27	36	36	30	34	35	31	43	34	35
Dominican Rep.	na	**na**	na	na	na	na	na	na	na	na	na	na	na	na	na	na
Egypt	na	**na**	na	na	na	na	na	na	na	na	na	na	na	na	na	na
El Salvador	na	**na**	na	na	na	na	na	na	na	na	na	na	na	na	na	na
Estonia	na	**88**	85	91	86	91	87	84	89	92	84	90	90	88	88	89
Finland	na	**34**	36	33	25	38	36	37	27	35	35	36	31	36	34	30
France	na	**89**	87	90	91	87	89	86	89	96	85	89	89	89	89	87
Georgia	na	**na**	na	na	na	na	na	na	na	na	na	na	na	na	na	na
Germany	na	**98**	98	98	97	98	98	98	98	98	96	99	97	99	97	98
Great Britain	na	**72**	72	71	75	73	68	69	71	74	68	75	72	na	na	na
Greece	na	**96**	96	96	98	95	96	97	96	97	97	97	95	98	96	96
Hungary	na	**97**	96	97	99	98	94	96	98	98	95	97	97	97	97	100
Iceland	na	**93**	90	96	92	92	95	92	92	97	93	92	93	93	94	88
India	na	**na**	na	na	na	na	na	na	na	na	na	na	na	na	na	na
Indonesia	na	**na**	na	na	na	na	na	na	na	na	na	na	na	na	na	na
Iran	na	**na**	na	na	na	na	na	na	na	na	na	na	na	na	na	na
Ireland	na	**81**	81	81	80	81	81	79	81	84	83	81	83	81	81	82
Israel	na	**na**	na	na	na	na	na	na	na	na	na	na	na	na	na	na
Italy	na	**83**	79	87	79	86	83	82	81	93	82	85	86	84	83	84
Japan	na	**na**	na	na	na	na	na	na	na	na	na	na	na	na	na	na
Jordan	na	**na**	na	na	na	na	na	na	na	na	na	na	na	na	na	na
Korea, South	na	**na**	na	na	na	na	na	na	na	na	na	na	na	na	na	na
Latvia	na	**86**	88	86	83	91	84	80	87	93	86	86	88	87	86	77
Lithuania	na	**99**	98	100	98	100	99	98	99	99	97	100	98	98	99	100
Luxembourg	na	**88**	87	89	88	88	88	86	89	90	86	87	91	83	89	90
Macedonia	na	**na**	na	na	na	na	na	na	na	na	na	na	na	na	na	na
Malta	na	**96**	97	96	96	95	98	98	96	93	95	99	95	98	96	94
Mexico	na	**na**	na	na	na	na	na	na	na	na	na	na	na	na	na	na
Moldova	na	**na**	na	na	na	na	na	na	na	na	na	na	na	na	na	na
Montenegro	na	**na**	na	na	na	na	na	na	na	na	na	na	na	na	na	na
Morocco	na	**na**	na	na	na	na	na	na	na	na	na	na	na	na	na	na
Netherlands	na	**94**	92	96	93	95	94	93	95	95	88	96	99	94	94	96
New Zealand	na	**na**	na	na	na	na	na	na	na	na	na	na	na	na	na	na
Nigeria	na	**na**	na	na	na	na	na	na	na	na	na	na	na	na	na	na
Northern Ireland	na	**74**	75	73	73	72	75	73	75	73	76	74	79	78	73	73
Norway	na	**na**	na	na	na	na	na	na	na	na	na	na	na	na	na	na
Pakistan	na	**na**	na	na	na	na	na	na	na	na	na	na	na	na	na	na
Peru	na	**na**	na	na	na	na	na	na	na	na	na	na	na	na	na	na
Philippines	na	**na**	na	na	na	na	na	na	na	na	na	na	na	na	na	na
Poland	na	**95**	93	96	96	95	93	94	96	96	94	95	95	95	95	96
Portugal	na	**95**	94	95	94	92	97	95	92	97	95	94	96	96	95	92
Puerto Rico	na	**na**	na	na	na	na	na	na	na	na	na	na	na	na	na	na
Romania	na	**89**	88	90	85	92	88	88	90	86	89	91	88	93	88	83
Russian Fed.	na	**87**	86	88	83	92	85	81	89	87	88	88	86	89	87	87
Serbia	na	**na**	na	na	na	na	na	na	na	na	na	na	na	na	na	na
Singapore	na	**na**	na	na	na	na	na	na	na	na	na	na	na	na	na	na
Slovakia	na	**89**	86	91	89	88	89	86	90	91	88	91	90	89	87	98
Slovenia	na	**86**	83	87	83	87	86	88	85	85	88	87	82	87	85	85
South Africa	na	**na**	na	na	na	na	na	na	na	na	na	na	na	na	na	na
Spain	na	**92**	92	92	91	93	92	93	91	93	90	94	91	94	91	90
Sweden	na	**98**	97	99	95	99	98	98	97	98	95	98	99	92	99	96
Switzerland	na	**na**	na	na	na	na	na	na	na	na	na	na	na	na	na	na
Taiwan	na	**na**	na	na	na	na	na	na	na	na	na	na	na	na	na	na
Tanzania	na	**na**	na	na	na	na	na	na	na	na	na	na	na	na	na	na
Turkey	na	**na**	na	na	na	na	na	na	na	na	na	na	na	na	na	na
Uganda	na	**na**	na	na	na	na	na	na	na	na	na	na	na	na	na	na
Ukraine	na	**96**	95	96	95	98	95	95	96	97	96	95	96	97	95	92
United States	na	**na**	na	na	na	na	na	na	na	na	na	na	na	na	na	na
Uruguay	na	**na**	na	na	na	na	na	na	na	na	na	na	na	na	na	na
Venezuela	na	**na**	na	na	na	na	na	na	na	na	na	na	na	na	na	na
Vietnam	na	**na**	na	na	na	na	na	na	na	na	na	na	na	na	na	na
Zimbabwe	na	**na**	na	na	na	na	na	na	na	na	na	na	na	na	na	na
Total	na	**83**	82	85	83	84	83	80	86	85	83	84	83	88	83	81

RANKING	
Country	**2000**
Lithuania	99
Germany	98
Sweden	98
Bulgaria	97
Hungary	97
Greece	96
Belarus	96
Malta	96
Ukraine	96
Poland	95
Portugal	95
Netherlands	94
Iceland	93
Belgium	93
Spain	92
Romania	89
Slovakia	89
France	89
Estonia	88
Luxembourg	88
Russian Fed.	87
Latvia	86
Slovenia	86
Italy	83
Ireland	81
Austria	76
Northern Ireland	74
Croatia	73
Great Britain	72
Denmark	34
Finland	34
Czech Republic	30
Total	83

E154_1) CONCERNED WITH PEOPLE NEIGHBORHOOD

To what extent do you feel concerned about the living conditions of: People in your neighborhood

Very much / Much (%)

(EVS: V267)

Country	Wave		Gender		Age			Education			Income			Values		
	1990	2000	Male	Female	16-29	30-49	50+	Lower	Middle	Upper	Lower	Middle	Upper	Mat	Mixed	Postm.
Albania	na	**na**	na	na	na	na	na	na	na	na	na	na	na	na	na	na
Algeria	na	**na**	na	na	na	na	na	na	na	na	na	na	na	na	na	na
Argentina	na	**na**	na	na	na	na	na	na	na	na	na	na	na	na	na	na
Armenia	na	**na**	na	na	na	na	na	na	na	na	na	na	na	na	na	na
Australia	na	**na**	na	na	na	na	na	na	na	na	na	na	na	na	na	na
Austria	na	**27**	26	27	22	27	29	29	26	19	28	26	29	21	27	27
Azerbaijan	na	**na**	na	na	na	na	na	na	na	na	na	na	na	na	na	na
Bangladesh	na	**na**	na	na	na	na	na	na	na	na	na	na	na	na	na	na
Belarus	na	**38**	35	41	27	35	50	53	34	26	44	35	33	41	38	24
Belgium	na	**36**	35	37	32	34	39	36	36	35	32	43	33	42	35	31
Bosnia and Herz.	na	**na**	na	na	na	na	na	na	na	na	na	na	na	na	na	na
Brazil	na	**na**	na	na	na	na	na	na	na	na	na	na	na	na	na	na
Bulgaria	na	**31**	33	29	20	31	36	41	25	26	37	28	25	32	30	31
Canada	na	**na**	na	na	na	na	na	na	na	na	na	na	na	na	na	na
Chile	na	**na**	na	na	na	na	na	na	na	na	na	na	na	na	na	na
China	na	**na**	na	na	na	na	na	na	na	na	na	na	na	na	na	na
Colombia	na	**na**	na	na	na	na	na	na	na	na	na	na	na	na	na	na
Croatia	na	**37**	38	36	21	39	44	42	34	32	47	36	32	44	37	29
Czech Republic	na	**12**	10	13	11	11	13	13	11	7	12	11	11	14	11	14
Denmark	na	**11**	11	10	11	11	10	11	10	9	9	12	10	14	10	15
Dominican Rep.	na	**na**	na	na	na	na	na	na	na	na	na	na	na	na	na	na
Egypt	na	**na**	na	na	na	na	na	na	na	na	na	na	na	na	na	na
El Salvador	na	**na**	na	na	na	na	na	na	na	na	na	na	na	na	na	na
Estonia	na	**22**	18	26	19	19	27	23	21	25	21	26	21	21	24	15
Finland	na	**8**	8	7	4	6	12	9	5	9	7	9	6	6	8	11
France	na	**32**	29	34	26	29	36	28	32	40	27	36	33	27	31	39
Georgia	na	**na**	na	na	na	na	na	na	na	na	na	na	na	na	na	na
Germany	na	**55**	52	57	48	52	60	55	56	50	52	59	62	54	55	58
Great Britain	na	**32**	31	33	34	35	26	28	33	36	29	31	34	na	na	na
Greece	na	**26**	26	26	21	27	38	38	25	25	28	24	25	27	25	25
Hungary	na	**24**	23	26	18	23	29	24	22	29	25	26	22	25	24	27
Iceland	na	**25**	24	26	20	23	31	25	23	26	23	26	23	21	25	28
India	na	**na**	na	na	na	na	na	na	na	na	na	na	na	na	na	na
Indonesia	na	**na**	na	na	na	na	na	na	na	na	na	na	na	na	na	na
Iran	na	**na**	na	na	na	na	na	na	na	na	na	na	na	na	na	na
Ireland	na	**52**	55	50	45	52	57	53	51	53	57	53	57	48	52	59
Israel	na	**na**	na	na	na	na	na	na	na	na	na	na	na	na	na	na
Italy	na	**25**	22	28	19	23	31	28	23	23	28	27	24	25	24	28
Japan	na	**na**	na	na	na	na	na	na	na	na	na	na	na	na	na	na
Jordan	na	**na**	na	na	na	na	na	na	na	na	na	na	na	na	na	na
Korea, South	na	**na**	na	na	na	na	na	na	na	na	na	na	na	na	na	na
Latvia	na	**10**	9	11	6	9	12	12	9	11	13	8	7	10	11	2
Lithuania	na	**24**	20	26	12	25	30	34	20	22	30	21	21	26	24	18
Luxembourg	na	**32**	31	34	25	31	39	34	31	35	31	37	32	35	31	33
Macedonia	na	**na**	na	na	na	na	na	na	na	na	na	na	na	na	na	na
Malta	na	**44**	42	46	28	42	55	54	41	33	52	45	40	49	41	38
Mexico	na	**na**	na	na	na	na	na	na	na	na	na	na	na	na	na	na
Moldova	na	**na**	na	na	na	na	na	na	na	na	na	na	na	na	na	na
Montenegro	na	**na**	na	na	na	na	na	na	na	na	na	na	na	na	na	na
Morocco	na	**na**	na	na	na	na	na	na	na	na	na	na	na	na	na	na
Netherlands	na	**34**	31	36	21	35	40	35	32	35	30	34	37	32	35	33
New Zealand	na	**na**	na	na	na	na	na	na	na	na	na	na	na	na	na	na
Nigeria	na	**na**	na	na	na	na	na	na	na	na	na	na	na	na	na	na
Northern Ireland	na	**40**	40	40	38	37	43	41	39	39	43	46	46	38	38	47
Norway	na	**na**	na	na	na	na	na	na	na	na	na	na	na	na	na	na
Pakistan	na	**na**	na	na	na	na	na	na	na	na	na	na	na	na	na	na
Peru	na	**na**	na	na	na	na	na	na	na	na	na	na	na	na	na	na
Philippines	na	**na**	na	na	na	na	na	na	na	na	na	na	na	na	na	na
Poland	na	**37**	36	37	30	36	42	38	36	34	38	37	35	35	36	45
Portugal	na	**31**	31	31	24	27	39	34	29	19	38	34	34	39	26	28
Puerto Rico	na	**na**	na	na	na	na	na	na	na	na	na	na	na	na	na	na
Romania	na	**27**	29	26	19	26	33	31	25	24	31	29	25	29	27	23
Russian Fed.	na	**15**	13	16	9	14	20	17	16	11	21	16	8	14	15	24
Serbia	na	**na**	na	na	na	na	na	na	na	na	na	na	na	na	na	na
Singapore	na	**na**	na	na	na	na	na	na	na	na	na	na	na	na	na	na
Slovakia	na	**47**	43	51	43	46	51	48	46	49	46	49	49	46	49	48
Slovenia	na	**23**	26	21	17	22	29	26	23	18	29	26	18	25	22	29
South Africa	na	**na**	na	na	na	na	na	na	na	na	na	na	na	na	na	na
Spain	na	**42**	42	41	35	41	47	42	42	40	43	45	38	45	39	41
Sweden	na	**28**	27	29	12	30	36	39	24	26	25	31	29	33	28	28
Switzerland	na	**na**	na	na	na	na	na	na	na	na	na	na	na	na	na	na
Taiwan	na	**na**	na	na	na	na	na	na	na	na	na	na	na	na	na	na
Tanzania	na	**na**	na	na	na	na	na	na	na	na	na	na	na	na	na	na
Turkey	na	**7**	8	6	9	4	4	4	11	7	4	6	11	6	6	9
Uganda	na	**na**	na	na	na	na	na	na	na	na	na	na	na	na	na	na
Ukraine	na	**21**	20	22	16	20	24	25	20	22	24	19	19	20	24	16
United States	na	**na**	na	na	na	na	na	na	na	na	na	na	na	na	na	na
Uruguay	na	**na**	na	na	na	na	na	na	na	na	na	na	na	na	na	na
Venezuela	na	**na**	na	na	na	na	na	na	na	na	na	na	na	na	na	na
Vietnam	na	**na**	na	na	na	na	na	na	na	na	na	na	na	na	na	na
Zimbabwe	na	**na**	na	na	na	na	na	na	na	na	na	na	na	na	na	na
Total	na	**29**	28	30	23	28	34	31	28	28	30	30	28	30	28	31

RANKING

Country	2000
Germany	55
Ireland	52
Slovakia	47
Malta	44
Spain	42
Northern Ireland	40
Belarus	38
Croatia	37
Poland	37
Belgium	36
Netherlands	34
Luxembourg	32
Great Britain	32
France	32
Portugal	31
Bulgaria	31
Sweden	28
Romania	27
Austria	27
Greece	26
Italy	25
Iceland	25
Hungary	24
Lithuania	24
Slovenia	23
Estonia	22
Ukraine	21
Russian Fed.	15
Czech Republic	12
Denmark	11
Latvia	10
Finland	8
Turkey	7
Total	29

E155_1) CONCERNED WITH PEOPLE OWN REGION

To what extent do you feel concerned about the living conditions of: The people of the region you live in

Very much / Much (%) (EVS: V268)

Country	Wave		Gender		Age			Education			Income			Values		
	1990	2000	Male	Female	16-29	30-49	50+	Lower	Middle	Upper	Lower	Middle	Upper	Mat	Mixed	Postm.
Albania	na	**na**	na	na	na	na	na	na	na	na	na	na	na	na	na	na
Algeria	na	**na**	na	na	na	na	na	na	na	na	na	na	na	na	na	na
Argentina	na	**na**	na	na	na	na	na	na	na	na	na	na	na	na	na	na
Armenia	na	**na**	na	na	na	na	na	na	na	na	na	na	na	na	na	na
Australia	na	**na**	na	na	na	na	na	na	na	na	na	na	na	na	na	na
Austria	na	**15**	16	14	11	15	17	17	13	12	18	14	14	18	15	15
Azerbaijan	na	**na**	na	na	na	na	na	na	na	na	na	na	na	na	na	na
Bangladesh	na	**na**	na	na	na	na	na	na	na	na	na	na	na	na	na	na
Belarus	na	**36**	36	36	30	35	42	41	35	29	39	36	31	38	36	35
Belgium	na	**17**	17	16	12	12	23	19	17	14	20	17	14	18	16	18
Bosnia and Herz.	na	**na**	na	na	na	na	na	na	na	na	na	na	na	na	na	na
Brazil	na	**na**	na	na	na	na	na	na	na	na	na	na	na	na	na	na
Bulgaria	na	**21**	21	20	14	18	26	26	18	17	28	16	15	19	23	18
Canada	na	**na**	na	na	na	na	na	na	na	na	na	na	na	na	na	na
Chile	na	**na**	na	na	na	na	na	na	na	na	na	na	na	na	na	na
China	na	**na**	na	na	na	na	na	na	na	na	na	na	na	na	na	na
Colombia	na	**na**	na	na	na	na	na	na	na	na	na	na	na	na	na	na
Croatia	na	**33**	36	30	21	34	39	40	27	35	42	32	27	32	35	29
Czech Republic	na	**12**	10	13	11	12	12	11	13	12	9	13	12	11	11	14
Denmark	na	**8**	9	8	7	8	9	9	8	8	8	8	10	13	8	13
Dominican Rep.	na	**na**	na	na	na	na	na	na	na	na	na	na	na	na	na	na
Egypt	na	**na**	na	na	na	na	na	na	na	na	na	na	na	na	na	na
El Salvador	na	**na**	na	na	na	na	na	na	na	na	na	na	na	na	na	na
Estonia	na	**12**	9	14	11	8	16	14	11	11	13	15	10	12	12	8
Finland	na	**9**	9	8	5	8	11	10	5	11	9	9	7	5	10	12
France	na	**17**	18	17	13	16	21	16	17	22	16	19	18	15	17	22
Georgia	na	**na**	na	na	na	na	na	na	na	na	na	na	na	na	na	na
Germany	na	**33**	31	35	22	32	39	32	34	36	32	37	39	34	34	33
Great Britain	na	**23**	21	24	23	24	20	23	20	27	21	20	23	na	na	na
Greece	na	**20**	21	19	16	18	33	26	20	19	19	21	18	17	19	23
Hungary	na	**13**	12	14	8	12	18	15	9	12	15	14	11	16	11	14
Iceland	na	**18**	16	19	11	18	23	19	14	22	18	17	18	13	18	25
India	na	**na**	na	na	na	na	na	na	na	na	na	na	na	na	na	na
Indonesia	na	**na**	na	na	na	na	na	na	na	na	na	na	na	na	na	na
Iran	na	**na**	na	na	na	na	na	na	na	na	na	na	na	na	na	na
Ireland	na	**37**	41	34	31	38	42	41	35	36	40	37	41	37	36	47
Israel	na	**na**	na	na	na	na	na	na	na	na	na	na	na	na	na	na
Italy	na	**20**	19	20	17	19	21	20	18	24	18	24	19	16	18	26
Japan	na	**na**	na	na	na	na	na	na	na	na	na	na	na	na	na	na
Jordan	na	**na**	na	na	na	na	na	na	na	na	na	na	na	na	na	na
Korea, South	na	**na**	na	na	na	na	na	na	na	na	na	na	na	na	na	na
Latvia	na	**8**	9	7	7	6	10	11	7	10	10	8	7	9	9	5
Lithuania	na	**19**	14	24	11	17	27	22	17	23	23	23	16	21	20	16
Luxembourg	na	**19**	19	19	15	18	23	20	17	22	18	22	17	18	18	25
Macedonia	na	**na**	na	na	na	na	na	na	na	na	na	na	na	na	na	na
Malta	na	**33**	33	33	18	33	44	45	29	24	43	30	31	39	30	33
Mexico	na	**na**	na	na	na	na	na	na	na	na	na	na	na	na	na	na
Moldova	na	**na**	na	na	na	na	na	na	na	na	na	na	na	na	na	na
Montenegro	na	**na**	na	na	na	na	na	na	na	na	na	na	na	na	na	na
Morocco	na	**na**	na	na	na	na	na	na	na	na	na	na	na	na	na	na
Netherlands	na	**8**	7	9	5	7	12	13	6	6	12	8	5	10	9	7
New Zealand	na	**na**	na	na	na	na	na	na	na	na	na	na	na	na	na	na
Nigeria	na	**na**	na	na	na	na	na	na	na	na	na	na	na	na	na	na
Northern Ireland	na	**26**	27	25	27	25	27	25	24	33	30	27	31	21	25	37
Norway	na	**na**	na	na	na	na	na	na	na	na	na	na	na	na	na	na
Pakistan	na	**na**	na	na	na	na	na	na	na	na	na	na	na	na	na	na
Peru	na	**na**	na	na	na	na	na	na	na	na	na	na	na	na	na	na
Philippines	na	**na**	na	na	na	na	na	na	na	na	na	na	na	na	na	na
Poland	na	**20**	23	17	16	21	20	20	20	19	23	21	11	17	20	31
Portugal	na	**24**	23	25	15	24	29	25	21	22	26	26	21	29	20	22
Puerto Rico	na	**na**	na	na	na	na	na	na	na	na	na	na	na	na	na	na
Romania	na	**34**	36	32	23	36	38	37	30	40	35	37	34	35	33	33
Russian Fed.	na	**16**	15	17	11	17	19	14	17	16	18	18	14	15	18	19
Serbia	na	**na**	na	na	na	na	na	na	na	na	na	na	na	na	na	na
Singapore	na	**na**	na	na	na	na	na	na	na	na	na	na	na	na	na	na
Slovakia	na	**34**	31	36	32	33	35	32	34	36	32	36	35	33	33	37
Slovenia	na	**15**	18	12	10	14	19	15	15	13	19	18	12	14	15	20
South Africa	na	**na**	na	na	na	na	na	na	na	na	na	na	na	na	na	na
Spain	na	**30**	30	31	22	32	34	29	31	35	32	30	30	33	29	32
Sweden	na	**19**	18	19	8	23	22	23	17	19	20	20	16	22	18	21
Switzerland	na	**na**	na	na	na	na	na	na	na	na	na	na	na	na	na	na
Taiwan	na	**na**	na	na	na	na	na	na	na	na	na	na	na	na	na	na
Tanzania	na	**na**	na	na	na	na	na	na	na	na	na	na	na	na	na	na
Turkey	na	**10**	11	10	14	8	5	7	16	13	7	10	17	11	10	10
Uganda	na	**na**	na	na	na	na	na	na	na	na	na	na	na	na	na	na
Ukraine	na	**21**	23	19	18	22	22	19	21	22	24	20	19	21	23	22
United States	na	**na**	na	na	na	na	na	na	na	na	na	na	na	na	na	na
Uruguay	na	**na**	na	na	na	na	na	na	na	na	na	na	na	na	na	na
Venezuela	na	**na**	na	na	na	na	na	na	na	na	na	na	na	na	na	na
Vietnam	na	**na**	na	na	na	na	na	na	na	na	na	na	na	na	na	na
Zimbabwe	na	**na**	na	na	na	na	na	na	na	na	na	na	na	na	na	na
Total	na	**21**	21	21	16	20	24	21	20	21	22	21	19	22	20	23

RANKING	
Country	**2000**
Ireland	37
Belarus	36
Romania	34
Slovakia	34
Germany	33
Malta	33
Croatia	33
Spain	30
Northern Ireland	26
Portugal	24
Great Britain	23
Ukraine	21
Bulgaria	21
Poland	20
Greece	20
Italy	20
Lithuania	19
Luxembourg	19
Sweden	19
Iceland	18
France	17
Belgium	17
Russian Fed.	16
Austria	15
Slovenia	15
Hungary	13
Estonia	12
Czech Republic	12
Turkey	10
Finland	9
Netherlands	8
Denmark	8
Latvia	8
Total	21

E156_1) CONCERNED WITH FELLOW COUNTRYMEN

To what extent do you feel concerned about the living conditions of: Your fellow countrymen

Very much / Much (%) (EVS: V269)

Country	Wave		Gender		Age			Education			Income			Values		
	1990	2000	Male	Female	16-29	30-49	50+	Lower	Middle	Upper	Lower	Middle	Upper	Mat	Mixed	Postm.
Albania	na	**na**	na	na	na	na	na	na	na	na	na	na	na	na	na	na
Algeria	na	**na**	na	na	na	na	na	na	na	na	na	na	na	na	na	na
Argentina	na	**na**	na	na	na	na	na	na	na	na	na	na	na	na	na	na
Armenia	na	**na**	na	na	na	na	na	na	na	na	na	na	na	na	na	na
Australia	na	**na**	na	na	na	na	na	na	na	na	na	na	na	na	na	na
Austria	na	**16**	17	15	10	14	21	17	15	15	20	17	15	11	17	15
Azerbaijan	na	**na**	na	na	na	na	na	na	na	na	na	na	na	na	na	na
Bangladesh	na	**na**	na	na	na	na	na	na	na	na	na	na	na	na	na	na
Belarus	na	**51**	52	50	49	53	50	45	53	53	49	52	51	47	55	59
Belgium	na	**14**	16	11	15	12	15	17	12	13	16	15	10	12	14	16
Bosnia and Herz.	na	**na**	na	na	na	na	na	na	na	na	na	na	na	na	na	na
Brazil	na	**na**	na	na	na	na	na	na	na	na	na	na	na	na	na	na
Bulgaria	na	**30**	30	31	22	30	35	29	30	34	30	28	33	27	34	40
Canada	na	**na**	na	na	na	na	na	na	na	na	na	na	na	na	na	na
Chile	na	**na**	na	na	na	na	na	na	na	na	na	na	na	na	na	na
China	na	**na**	na	na	na	na	na	na	na	na	na	na	na	na	na	na
Colombia	na	**na**	na	na	na	na	na	na	na	na	na	na	na	na	na	na
Croatia	na	**35**	36	34	20	37	42	41	29	38	46	30	34	39	36	28
Czech Republic	na	**17**	16	19	17	17	18	17	18	21	18	18	16	17	18	17
Denmark	na	**12**	12	12	14	11	12	12	11	11	13	11	11	17	11	13
Dominican Rep.	na	**na**	na	na	na	na	na	na	na	na	na	na	na	na	na	na
Egypt	na	**na**	na	na	na	na	na	na	na	na	na	na	na	na	na	na
El Salvador	na	**na**	na	na	na	na	na	na	na	na	na	na	na	na	na	na
Estonia	na	**13**	12	14	13	8	17	12	12	18	11	14	14	12	13	12
Finland	na	**15**	15	15	11	14	20	17	12	15	18	15	13	12	16	17
France	na	**19**	20	17	17	18	20	15	16	28	18	18	20	14	18	27
Georgia	na	**na**	na	na	na	na	na	na	na	na	na	na	na	na	na	na
Germany	na	**30**	30	31	27	29	34	30	30	35	29	37	30	26	32	34
Great Britain	na	**21**	23	19	22	20	21	20	19	27	16	20	20	na	na	na
Greece	na	**31**	32	30	31	30	36	37	31	30	33	29	32	31	30	37
Hungary	na	**20**	18	22	16	19	23	18	19	35	16	18	23	20	22	29
Iceland	na	**27**	25	29	19	28	31	26	24	34	28	25	29	19	27	39
India	na	**na**	na	na	na	na	na	na	na	na	na	na	na	na	na	na
Indonesia	na	**na**	na	na	na	na	na	na	na	na	na	na	na	na	na	na
Iran	na	**na**	na	na	na	na	na	na	na	na	na	na	na	na	na	na
Ireland	na	**35**	40	31	29	35	41	39	31	38	38	34	38	34	34	42
Israel	na	**na**	na	na	na	na	na	na	na	na	na	na	na	na	na	na
Italy	na	**25**	24	25	22	26	25	23	24	33	22	30	24	18	23	33
Japan	na	**na**	na	na	na	na	na	na	na	na	na	na	na	na	na	na
Jordan	na	**na**	na	na	na	na	na	na	na	na	na	na	na	na	na	na
Korea, South	na	**na**	na	na	na	na	na	na	na	na	na	na	na	na	na	na
Latvia	na	**10**	10	10	11	7	11	10	9	12	10	9	10	8	11	11
Lithuania	na	**32**	30	34	23	36	35	28	31	46	30	36	30	28	33	52
Luxembourg	na	**21**	23	19	15	19	26	18	21	26	17	27	22	22	20	25
Macedonia	na	**na**	na	na	na	na	na	na	na	na	na	na	na	na	na	na
Malta	na	**40**	40	39	29	40	46	43	37	47	38	40	45	41	39	38
Mexico	na	**na**	na	na	na	na	na	na	na	na	na	na	na	na	na	na
Moldova	na	**na**	na	na	na	na	na	na	na	na	na	na	na	na	na	na
Montenegro	na	**na**	na	na	na	na	na	na	na	na	na	na	na	na	na	na
Morocco	na	**na**	na	na	na	na	na	na	na	na	na	na	na	na	na	na
Netherlands	na	**11**	11	11	7	9	15	15	9	9	16	9	7	9	12	10
New Zealand	na	**na**	na	na	na	na	na	na	na	na	na	na	na	na	na	na
Nigeria	na	**na**	na	na	na	na	na	na	na	na	na	na	na	na	na	na
Northern Ireland	na	**23**	25	22	26	22	23	21	23	31	29	22	27	14	24	32
Norway	na	**na**	na	na	na	na	na	na	na	na	na	na	na	na	na	na
Pakistan	na	**na**	na	na	na	na	na	na	na	na	na	na	na	na	na	na
Peru	na	**na**	na	na	na	na	na	na	na	na	na	na	na	na	na	na
Philippines	na	**na**	na	na	na	na	na	na	na	na	na	na	na	na	na	na
Poland	na	**30**	33	26	23	31	32	29	29	34	31	30	25	24	33	36
Portugal	na	**32**	33	31	28	33	33	32	32	31	28	34	27	31	32	30
Puerto Rico	na	**na**	na	na	na	na	na	na	na	na	na	na	na	na	na	na
Romania	na	**44**	46	42	40	42	48	43	42	52	44	45	46	42	47	44
Russian Fed.	na	**21**	20	21	17	21	23	15	21	22	21	23	19	17	25	26
Serbia	na	**na**	na	na	na	na	na	na	na	na	na	na	na	na	na	na
Singapore	na	**na**	na	na	na	na	na	na	na	na	na	na	na	na	na	na
Slovakia	na	**29**	28	31	24	32	31	30	29	31	29	33	29	28	31	30
Slovenia	na	**33**	34	32	28	34	36	29	35	31	36	37	32	38	32	38
South Africa	na	**na**	na	na	na	na	na	na	na	na	na	na	na	na	na	na
Spain	na	**28**	28	28	23	28	31	26	27	36	29	26	33	28	26	34
Sweden	na	**28**	30	26	25	27	32	31	23	35	30	31	23	29	27	32
Switzerland	na	**na**	na	na	na	na	na	na	na	na	na	na	na	na	na	na
Taiwan	na	**na**	na	na	na	na	na	na	na	na	na	na	na	na	na	na
Tanzania	na	**na**	na	na	na	na	na	na	na	na	na	na	na	na	na	na
Turkey	na	**8**	8	7	10	7	4	6	11	10	7	9	8	6	8	10
Uganda	na	**na**	na	na	na	na	na	na	na	na	na	na	na	na	na	na
Ukraine	na	**24**	26	22	17	26	25	23	23	26	27	22	23	22	26	32
United States	na	**na**	na	na	na	na	na	na	na	na	na	na	na	na	na	na
Uruguay	na	**na**	na	na	na	na	na	na	na	na	na	na	na	na	na	na
Venezuela	na	**na**	na	na	na	na	na	na	na	na	na	na	na	na	na	na
Vietnam	na	**na**	na	na	na	na	na	na	na	na	na	na	na	na	na	na
Zimbabwe	na	**na**	na	na	na	na	na	na	na	na	na	na	na	na	na	na
Total	na	**25**	26	25	22	25	28	24	25	28	26	26	25	25	26	28

RANKING	
Country	**2000**
Belarus	51
Romania	44
Malta	40
Ireland	35
Croatia	35
Slovenia	33
Lithuania	32
Portugal	32
Greece	31
Bulgaria	30
Germany	30
Poland	30
Slovakia	29
Sweden	28
Spain	28
Iceland	27
Italy	25
Ukraine	24
Northern Ireland	23
Luxembourg	21
Great Britain	21
Russian Fed.	21
Hungary	20
France	19
Czech Republic	17
Austria	16
Finland	15
Belgium	14
Estonia	13
Denmark	12
Netherlands	11
Latvia	10
Turkey	8
Total	25

E157_1) CONCERNED WITH EUROPEANS

To what extent do you feel concerned about the living conditions of: European

Very much / Much (%) (EVS: V270)

Country	Wave 1990	Wave 2000	Gender Male	Gender Female	Age 16-29	Age 30-49	Age 50+	Education Lower	Education Middle	Education Upper	Income Lower	Income Middle	Income Upper	Values Mat	Values Mixed	Values Postm.
Albania	na	**na**	na	na	na	na	na	na	na	na	na	na	na	na	na	na
Algeria	na	**na**	na	na	na	na	na	na	na	na	na	na	na	na	na	na
Argentina	na	**na**	na	na	na	na	na	na	na	na	na	na	na	na	na	na
Armenia	na	**na**	na	na	na	na	na	na	na	na	na	na	na	na	na	na
Australia	na	**na**	na	na	na	na	na	na	na	na	na	na	na	na	na	na
Austria	na	**8**	8	8	7	6	11	7	9	9	9	10	8	7	7	10
Azerbaijan	na	**na**	na	na	na	na	na	na	na	na	na	na	na	na	na	na
Bangladesh	na	**na**	na	na	na	na	na	na	na	na	na	na	na	na	na	na
Belarus	na	**31**	32	31	33	34	26	22	33	41	28	32	35	26	36	45
Belgium	na	**9**	11	7	7	8	11	6	9	11	10	9	8	5	9	15
Bosnia and Herz.	na	**na**	na	na	na	na	na	na	na	na	na	na	na	na	na	na
Brazil	na	**na**	na	na	na	na	na	na	na	na	na	na	na	na	na	na
Bulgaria	na	**13**	11	14	12	12	13	11	13	15	12	10	15	9	15	27
Canada	na	**na**	na	na	na	na	na	na	na	na	na	na	na	na	na	na
Chile	na	**na**	na	na	na	na	na	na	na	na	na	na	na	na	na	na
China	na	**na**	na	na	na	na	na	na	na	na	na	na	na	na	na	na
Colombia	na	**na**	na	na	na	na	na	na	na	na	na	na	na	na	na	na
Croatia	na	**16**	19	14	7	17	22	20	14	15	20	14	17	27	15	12
Czech Republic	na	**11**	10	12	10	12	11	11	11	9	11	12	10	10	11	12
Denmark	na	**10**	10	10	10	8	11	10	11	8	10	8	12	7	10	12
Dominican Rep.	na	**na**	na	na	na	na	na	na	na	na	na	na	na	na	na	na
Egypt	na	**na**	na	na	na	na	na	na	na	na	na	na	na	na	na	na
El Salvador	na	**na**	na	na	na	na	na	na	na	na	na	na	na	na	na	na
Estonia	na	**5**	4	5	5	3	7	6	4	7	3	6	5	5	5	12
Finland	na	**7**	7	7	6	6	9	9	5	6	9	8	5	6	8	10
France	na	**14**	15	13	13	14	13	11	13	21	14	13	15	9	13	21
Georgia	na	**na**	na	na	na	na	na	na	na	na	na	na	na	na	na	na
Germany	na	**18**	17	20	17	18	20	16	20	23	16	22	25	15	19	23
Great Britain	na	**10**	10	10	14	9	8	8	11	14	8	11	11	na	na	na
Greece	na	**12**	12	12	11	12	19	13	10	14	12	14	10	12	11	17
Hungary	na	**9**	9	10	6	9	12	9	8	13	8	8	11	10	8	19
Iceland	na	**13**	12	14	6	14	17	12	10	21	14	12	13	7	13	23
India	na	**na**	na	na	na	na	na	na	na	na	na	na	na	na	na	na
Indonesia	na	**na**	na	na	na	na	na	na	na	na	na	na	na	na	na	na
Iran	na	**na**	na	na	na	na	na	na	na	na	na	na	na	na	na	na
Ireland	na	**20**	22	18	12	21	25	24	17	21	22	18	22	21	19	23
Israel	na	**na**	na	na	na	na	na	na	na	na	na	na	na	na	na	na
Italy	na	**18**	18	18	16	19	17	15	19	23	15	20	19	12	16	25
Japan	na	**na**	na	na	na	na	na	na	na	na	na	na	na	na	na	na
Jordan	na	**na**	na	na	na	na	na	na	na	na	na	na	na	na	na	na
Korea, South	na	**na**	na	na	na	na	na	na	na	na	na	na	na	na	na	na
Latvia	na	**3**	4	3	3	3	4	5	3	2	4	3	3	4	4	2
Lithuania	na	**11**	10	13	8	12	13	7	12	15	9	12	10	12	11	9
Luxembourg	na	**17**	18	16	15	15	20	15	16	22	16	20	19	17	14	27
Macedonia	na	**na**	na	na	na	na	na	na	na	na	na	na	na	na	na	na
Malta	na	**27**	28	25	25	25	29	21	27	41	23	29	32	24	28	38
Mexico	na	**na**	na	na	na	na	na	na	na	na	na	na	na	na	na	na
Moldova	na	**na**	na	na	na	na	na	na	na	na	na	na	na	na	na	na
Montenegro	na	**na**	na	na	na	na	na	na	na	na	na	na	na	na	na	na
Morocco	na	**na**	na	na	na	na	na	na	na	na	na	na	na	na	na	na
Netherlands	na	**6**	6	6	4	5	7	6	4	8	7	7	5	5	5	8
New Zealand	na	**na**	na	na	na	na	na	na	na	na	na	na	na	na	na	na
Nigeria	na	**na**	na	na	na	na	na	na	na	na	na	na	na	na	na	na
Northern Ireland	na	**13**	12	14	12	13	13	12	13	16	17	12	13	9	12	19
Norway	na	**na**	na	na	na	na	na	na	na	na	na	na	na	na	na	na
Pakistan	na	**na**	na	na	na	na	na	na	na	na	na	na	na	na	na	na
Peru	na	**na**	na	na	na	na	na	na	na	na	na	na	na	na	na	na
Philippines	na	**na**	na	na	na	na	na	na	na	na	na	na	na	na	na	na
Poland	na	**12**	14	10	11	13	12	13	11	11	13	11	12	10	14	12
Portugal	na	**18**	19	17	14	20	18	18	17	14	13	20	17	17	17	18
Puerto Rico	na	**na**	na	na	na	na	na	na	na	na	na	na	na	na	na	na
Romania	na	**17**	18	17	16	18	17	17	16	20	15	19	18	16	18	18
Russian Fed.	na	**6**	6	6	4	6	8	6	6	6	8	7	5	5	6	9
Serbia	na	**na**	na	na	na	na	na	na	na	na	na	na	na	na	na	na
Singapore	na	**na**	na	na	na	na	na	na	na	na	na	na	na	na	na	na
Slovakia	na	**16**	15	16	15	16	16	14	16	20	15	15	18	14	16	24
Slovenia	na	**11**	12	10	8	11	13	9	13	9	12	13	9	9	12	12
South Africa	na	**na**	na	na	na	na	na	na	na	na	na	na	na	na	na	na
Spain	na	**18**	17	18	14	20	18	16	18	23	18	17	22	19	15	23
Sweden	na	**16**	15	18	13	17	17	16	13	22	17	17	14	22	15	20
Switzerland	na	**na**	na	na	na	na	na	na	na	na	na	na	na	na	na	na
Taiwan	na	**na**	na	na	na	na	na	na	na	na	na	na	na	na	na	na
Tanzania	na	**na**	na	na	na	na	na	na	na	na	na	na	na	na	na	na
Turkey	na	**60**	59	61	62	58	63	60	61	59	58	62	61	65	61	56
Uganda	na	**na**	na	na	na	na	na	na	na	na	na	na	na	na	na	na
Ukraine	na	**6**	6	7	7	7	5	4	6	8	7	4	8	6	7	9
United States	na	**na**	na	na	na	na	na	na	na	na	na	na	na	na	na	na
Uruguay	na	**na**	na	na	na	na	na	na	na	na	na	na	na	na	na	na
Venezuela	na	**na**	na	na	na	na	na	na	na	na	na	na	na	na	na	na
Vietnam	na	**na**	na	na	na	na	na	na	na	na	na	na	na	na	na	na
Zimbabwe	na	**na**	na	na	na	na	na	na	na	na	na	na	na	na	na	na
Total	na	**14**	14	13	12	14	14	13	13	16	13	14	14	12	13	18

RANKING

Country	2000
Turkey	60
Belarus	31
Malta	27
Ireland	20
Germany	18
Italy	18
Portugal	18
Spain	18
Romania	17
Luxembourg	17
Croatia	16
Sweden	16
Slovakia	16
France	14
Iceland	13
Northern Ireland	13
Bulgaria	13
Greece	12
Poland	12
Lithuania	11
Slovenia	11
Czech Republic	11
Denmark	10
Great Britain	10
Hungary	9
Belgium	9
Austria	8
Finland	7
Ukraine	6
Russian Fed.	6
Netherlands	6
Estonia	5
Latvia	3
Total	14

E158_1) CONCERNED WITH HUMAN KIND

To what extent do you feel concerned about the living conditions of: Human kind

Very much / Much (%) (EVS: V271)

Country	Wave		Gender		Age			Education			Income			Values		
	1990	2000	Male	Female	16-29	30-49	50+	Lower	Middle	Upper	Lower	Middle	Upper	Mat	Mixed	Postm.
Albania	na	**na**	na	na	na	na	na	na	na	na	na	na	na	na	na	na
Algeria	na	**na**	na	na	na	na	na	na	na	na	na	na	na	na	na	na
Argentina	na	**na**	na	na	na	na	na	na	na	na	na	na	na	na	na	na
Armenia	na	**na**	na	na	na	na	na	na	na	na	na	na	na	na	na	na
Australia	na	**na**	na	na	na	na	na	na	na	na	na	na	na	na	na	na
Austria	na	**17**	16	18	17	18	17	13	20	24	17	19	19	14	15	23
Azerbaijan	na	**na**	na	na	na	na	na	na	na	na	na	na	na	na	na	na
Bangladesh	na	**na**	na	na	na	na	na	na	na	na	na	na	na	na	na	na
Belarus	na	**34**	34	35	39	37	29	23	36	48	29	35	41	31	38	43
Belgium	na	**22**	25	20	19	26	21	15	23	27	25	19	22	15	22	34
Bosnia and Herz.	na	**na**	na	na	na	na	na	na	na	na	na	na	na	na	na	na
Brazil	na	**na**	na	na	na	na	na	na	na	na	na	na	na	na	na	na
Bulgaria	na	**24**	22	26	26	25	23	19	26	29	23	24	28	19	30	40
Canada	na	**na**	na	na	na	na	na	na	na	na	na	na	na	na	na	na
Chile	na	**na**	na	na	na	na	na	na	na	na	na	na	na	na	na	na
China	na	**na**	na	na	na	na	na	na	na	na	na	na	na	na	na	na
Colombia	na	**na**	na	na	na	na	na	na	na	na	na	na	na	na	na	na
Croatia	na	**34**	33	35	33	33	36	32	33	43	33	33	34	38	31	43
Czech Republic	na	**29**	26	32	29	29	28	24	31	41	29	27	30	23	31	37
Denmark	na	**36**	37	36	34	37	36	30	40	44	34	35	42	23	35	54
Dominican Rep.	na	**na**	na	na	na	na	na	na	na	na	na	na	na	na	na	na
Egypt	na	**na**	na	na	na	na	na	na	na	na	na	na	na	na	na	na
El Salvador	na	**na**	na	na	na	na	na	na	na	na	na	na	na	na	na	na
Estonia	na	**13**	12	13	17	9	13	13	12	13	11	14	13	13	13	12
Finland	na	**36**	32	40	35	34	39	34	38	43	38	31	38	25	39	51
France	na	**24**	25	22	25	25	22	19	24	36	26	23	24	15	24	35
Georgia	na	**na**	na	na	na	na	na	na	na	na	na	na	na	na	na	na
Germany	na	**23**	21	24	20	23	23	19	25	29	19	28	26	17	24	28
Great Britain	na	**29**	29	29	36	28	28	24	35	31	27	29	28	na	na	na
Greece	na	**46**	42	48	47	44	49	52	46	45	46	43	46	40	45	53
Hungary	na	**23**	22	23	25	25	19	21	26	26	20	22	24	22	23	40
Iceland	na	**20**	20	21	18	20	23	22	15	26	24	18	19	13	21	32
India	na	**na**	na	na	na	na	na	na	na	na	na	na	na	na	na	na
Indonesia	na	**na**	na	na	na	na	na	na	na	na	na	na	na	na	na	na
Iran	na	**na**	na	na	na	na	na	na	na	na	na	na	na	na	na	na
Ireland	na	**35**	36	34	28	37	38	36	32	40	30	38	38	33	35	38
Israel	na	**na**	na	na	na	na	na	na	na	na	na	na	na	na	na	na
Italy	na	**29**	29	29	28	31	27	25	29	37	27	31	29	21	27	36
Japan	na	**na**	na	na	na	na	na	na	na	na	na	na	na	na	na	na
Jordan	na	**na**	na	na	na	na	na	na	na	na	na	na	na	na	na	na
Korea, South	na	**na**	na	na	na	na	na	na	na	na	na	na	na	na	na	na
Latvia	na	**9**	10	9	13	10	7	10	10	8	9	9	10	7	10	18
Lithuania	na	**16**	13	19	15	16	17	10	17	24	14	18	19	11	18	17
Luxembourg	na	**29**	29	29	28	29	30	26	28	38	25	34	30	22	27	46
Macedonia	na	**na**	na	na	na	na	na	na	na	na	na	na	na	na	na	na
Malta	na	**36**	37	34	32	36	38	34	34	50	33	39	42	35	37	37
Mexico	na	**na**	na	na	na	na	na	na	na	na	na	na	na	na	na	na
Moldova	na	**na**	na	na	na	na	na	na	na	na	na	na	na	na	na	na
Montenegro	na	**na**	na	na	na	na	na	na	na	na	na	na	na	na	na	na
Morocco	na	**na**	na	na	na	na	na	na	na	na	na	na	na	na	na	na
Netherlands	na	**33**	32	33	27	34	34	30	31	37	36	33	32	25	32	39
New Zealand	na	**na**	na	na	na	na	na	na	na	na	na	na	na	na	na	na
Nigeria	na	**na**	na	na	na	na	na	na	na	na	na	na	na	na	na	na
Northern Ireland	na	**25**	25	25	24	27	24	21	27	31	32	25	26	18	23	37
Norway	na	**na**	na	na	na	na	na	na	na	na	na	na	na	na	na	na
Pakistan	na	**na**	na	na	na	na	na	na	na	na	na	na	na	na	na	na
Peru	na	**na**	na	na	na	na	na	na	na	na	na	na	na	na	na	na
Philippines	na	**na**	na	na	na	na	na	na	na	na	na	na	na	na	na	na
Poland	na	**14**	16	12	15	12	15	13	15	15	15	13	13	12	16	14
Portugal	na	**40**	41	38	50	38	35	37	43	49	29	42	40	36	40	48
Puerto Rico	na	**na**	na	na	na	na	na	na	na	na	na	na	na	na	na	na
Romania	na	**20**	20	20	20	20	20	19	19	25	18	22	21	20	21	18
Russian Fed.	na	**19**	17	20	18	18	20	14	20	18	20	22	16	16	22	19
Serbia	na	**na**	na	na	na	na	na	na	na	na	na	na	na	na	na	na
Singapore	na	**na**	na	na	na	na	na	na	na	na	na	na	na	na	na	na
Slovakia	na	**20**	18	22	19	20	21	20	19	25	22	17	22	19	20	29
Slovenia	na	**25**	22	27	24	24	26	23	26	22	27	26	23	25	25	27
South Africa	na	**na**	na	na	na	na	na	na	na	na	na	na	na	na	na	na
Spain	na	**35**	35	35	31	38	35	32	34	47	37	34	39	30	34	43
Sweden	na	**34**	30	38	36	34	33	32	32	39	39	35	25	41	31	43
Switzerland	na	**na**	na	na	na	na	na	na	na	na	na	na	na	na	na	na
Taiwan	na	**na**	na	na	na	na	na	na	na	na	na	na	na	na	na	na
Tanzania	na	**na**	na	na	na	na	na	na	na	na	na	na	na	na	na	na
Turkey	na	**16**	16	17	20	13	14	15	18	17	17	16	13	16	17	15
Uganda	na	**na**	na	na	na	na	na	na	na	na	na	na	na	na	na	na
Ukraine	na	**18**	17	20	21	18	16	15	18	20	17	17	21	18	19	32
United States	na	**na**	na	na	na	na	na	na	na	na	na	na	na	na	na	na
Uruguay	na	**na**	na	na	na	na	na	na	na	na	na	na	na	na	na	na
Venezuela	na	**na**	na	na	na	na	na	na	na	na	na	na	na	na	na	na
Vietnam	na	**na**	na	na	na	na	na	na	na	na	na	na	na	na	na	na
Zimbabwe	na	**na**	na	na	na	na	na	na	na	na	na	na	na	na	na	na
Total	na	**26**	26	27	27	26	26	24	26	32	26	27	27	21	27	36

RANKING	
Country	2000
Greece	46
Portugal	40
Finland	36
Denmark	36
Malta	36
Spain	35
Ireland	35
Belarus	34
Croatia	34
Sweden	34
Netherlands	33
Great Britain	29
Luxembourg	29
Czech Republic	29
Italy	29
Northern Ireland	25
Slovenia	25
Bulgaria	24
France	24
Germany	23
Hungary	23
Belgium	22
Iceland	20
Romania	20
Slovakia	20
Russian Fed.	19
Ukraine	18
Austria	17
Lithuania	16
Turkey	16
Poland	14
Estonia	13
Latvia	9
Total	26

E159_1) CONCERNED WITH ELDERLY

To what extent do you feel concerned about the living conditions of: Elderly people in your country

Very much / Much (%) (EVS: V272)

Country	Wave		Gender		Age			Education			Income			Values		
	1990	2000	Male	Female	16-29	30-49	50+	Lower	Middle	Upper	Lower	Middle	Upper	Mat	Mixed	Postm.
Albania	na	**na**	na	na	na	na	na	na	na	na	na	na	na	na	na	na
Algeria	na	**na**	na	na	na	na	na	na	na	na	na	na	na	na	na	na
Argentina	na	**na**	na	na	na	na	na	na	na	na	na	na	na	na	na	na
Armenia	na	**na**	na	na	na	na	na	na	na	na	na	na	na	na	na	na
Australia	na	**na**	na	na	na	na	na	na	na	na	na	na	na	na	na	na
Austria	na	**49**	47	51	40	46	57	52	47	43	50	51	48	41	53	43
Azerbaijan	na	**na**	na	na	na	na	na	na	na	na	na	na	na	na	na	na
Bangladesh	na	**na**	na	na	na	na	na	na	na	na	na	na	na	na	na	na
Belarus	na	**51**	46	55	37	50	64	56	49	51	56	51	43	54	51	45
Belgium	na	**58**	54	62	38	50	75	66	56	56	69	61	53	61	58	56
Bosnia and Herz.	na	**na**	na	na	na	na	na	na	na	na	na	na	na	na	na	na
Brazil	na	**na**	na	na	na	na	na	na	na	na	na	na	na	na	na	na
Bulgaria	na	**70**	66	74	50	66	84	78	65	67	74	68	70	72	70	84
Canada	na	**na**	na	na	na	na	na	na	na	na	na	na	na	na	na	na
Chile	na	**na**	na	na	na	na	na	na	na	na	na	na	na	na	na	na
China	na	**na**	na	na	na	na	na	na	na	na	na	na	na	na	na	na
Colombia	na	**na**	na	na	na	na	na	na	na	na	na	na	na	na	na	na
Croatia	na	**68**	63	72	56	68	76	67	66	75	77	67	66	74	67	65
Czech Republic	na	**47**	44	50	44	42	55	48	47	46	58	44	44	51	48	41
Denmark	na	**53**	48	58	57	56	49	56	54	51	52	51	56	61	53	56
Dominican Rep.	na	**na**	na	na	na	na	na	na	na	na	na	na	na	na	na	na
Egypt	na	**na**	na	na	na	na	na	na	na	na	na	na	na	na	na	na
El Salvador	na	**na**	na	na	na	na	na	na	na	na	na	na	na	na	na	na
Estonia	na	**48**	39	55	28	44	61	46	46	54	54	51	45	51	46	42
Finland	na	**62**	57	67	45	61	73	66	54	61	64	61	62	57	65	59
France	na	**67**	63	70	56	61	77	70	58	66	66	69	65	65	71	58
Georgia	na	**na**	na	na	na	na	na	na	na	na	na	na	na	na	na	na
Germany	na	**64**	63	65	55	61	72	67	60	74	63	67	67	66	64	65
Great Britain	na	**70**	67	73	60	68	77	69	71	65	68	76	70	na	na	na
Greece	na	**68**	64	71	60	69	83	80	70	65	73	68	64	67	68	69
Hungary	na	**57**	53	61	37	52	73	56	58	61	57	57	57	60	55	51
Iceland	na	**62**	54	70	48	64	72	68	57	60	65	61	60	62	62	65
India	na	**na**	na	na	na	na	na	na	na	na	na	na	na	na	na	na
Indonesia	na	**na**	na	na	na	na	na	na	na	na	na	na	na	na	na	na
Iran	na	**na**	na	na	na	na	na	na	na	na	na	na	na	na	na	na
Ireland	na	**81**	78	83	76	80	84	82	79	80	80	83	84	81	79	84
Israel	na	**na**	na	na	na	na	na	na	na	na	na	na	na	na	na	na
Italy	na	**76**	72	79	62	74	84	80	72	76	81	77	71	74	76	76
Japan	na	**na**	na	na	na	na	na	na	na	na	na	na	na	na	na	na
Jordan	na	**na**	na	na	na	na	na	na	na	na	na	na	na	na	na	na
Korea, South	na	**na**	na	na	na	na	na	na	na	na	na	na	na	na	na	na
Latvia	na	**38**	36	40	35	37	41	36	39	40	38	44	36	34	40	47
Lithuania	na	**76**	70	82	58	73	91	86	72	77	85	78	69	78	77	79
Luxembourg	na	**44**	41	47	26	39	60	42	45	44	43	50	44	39	44	51
Macedonia	na	**na**	na	na	na	na	na	na	na	na	na	na	na	na	na	na
Malta	na	**79**	76	83	63	83	88	89	76	74	84	79	76	82	79	70
Mexico	na	**na**	na	na	na	na	na	na	na	na	na	na	na	na	na	na
Moldova	na	**na**	na	na	na	na	na	na	na	na	na	na	na	na	na	na
Montenegro	na	**na**	na	na	na	na	na	na	na	na	na	na	na	na	na	na
Morocco	na	**na**	na	na	na	na	na	na	na	na	na	na	na	na	na	na
Netherlands	na	**53**	47	58	39	46	67	60	51	48	53	56	45	57	54	47
New Zealand	na	**na**	na	na	na	na	na	na	na	na	na	na	na	na	na	na
Nigeria	na	**na**	na	na	na	na	na	na	na	na	na	na	na	na	na	na
Northern Ireland	na	**69**	69	69	62	68	72	68	67	74	70	71	80	67	69	76
Norway	na	**na**	na	na	na	na	na	na	na	na	na	na	na	na	na	na
Pakistan	na	**na**	na	na	na	na	na	na	na	na	na	na	na	na	na	na
Peru	na	**na**	na	na	na	na	na	na	na	na	na	na	na	na	na	na
Philippines	na	**na**	na	na	na	na	na	na	na	na	na	na	na	na	na	na
Poland	na	**72**	71	73	59	74	78	73	72	73	74	72	70	70	75	68
Portugal	na	**83**	81	85	74	82	89	86	75	82	85	86	79	88	80	82
Puerto Rico	na	**na**	na	na	na	na	na	na	na	na	na	na	na	na	na	na
Romania	na	**67**	62	71	56	65	74	68	64	72	66	68	66	71	65	61
Russian Fed.	na	**70**	66	74	51	69	84	72	70	70	74	74	66	70	71	63
Serbia	na	**na**	na	na	na	na	na	na	na	na	na	na	na	na	na	na
Singapore	na	**na**	na	na	na	na	na	na	na	na	na	na	na	na	na	na
Slovakia	na	**69**	65	72	59	64	82	73	66	71	74	70	68	71	68	69
Slovenia	na	**46**	43	48	29	40	64	51	44	41	54	50	40	51	45	43
South Africa	na	**na**	na	na	na	na	na	na	na	na	na	na	na	na	na	na
Spain	na	**63**	61	65	50	64	71	68	59	62	68	68	62	69	61	67
Sweden	na	**68**	61	74	53	66	77	74	62	71	68	67	67	62	66	73
Switzerland	na	**na**	na	na	na	na	na	na	na	na	na	na	na	na	na	na
Taiwan	na	**na**	na	na	na	na	na	na	na	na	na	na	na	na	na	na
Tanzania	na	**na**	na	na	na	na	na	na	na	na	na	na	na	na	na	na
Turkey	na	**6**	7	4	8	3	4	5	8	4	5	6	5	7	5	8
Uganda	na	**na**	na	na	na	na	na	na	na	na	na	na	na	na	na	na
Ukraine	na	**72**	67	77	54	70	84	88	69	71	80	69	67	71	75	77
United States	na	**na**	na	na	na	na	na	na	na	na	na	na	na	na	na	na
Uruguay	na	**na**	na	na	na	na	na	na	na	na	na	na	na	na	na	na
Venezuela	na	**na**	na	na	na	na	na	na	na	na	na	na	na	na	na	na
Vietnam	na	**na**	na	na	na	na	na	na	na	na	na	na	na	na	na	na
Zimbabwe	na	**na**	na	na	na	na	na	na	na	na	na	na	na	na	na	na
Total	na	**63**	59	66	50	60	73	65	61	63	65	63	61	65	62	61

RANKING	
Country	**2000**
Portugal	83
Ireland	81
Malta	79
Lithuania	76
Italy	76
Poland	72
Ukraine	72
Russian Fed.	70
Bulgaria	70
Great Britain	70
Northern Ireland	69
Slovakia	69
Greece	68
Croatia	68
Sweden	68
Romania	67
France	67
Germany	64
Spain	63
Iceland	62
Finland	62
Belgium	58
Hungary	57
Denmark	53
Netherlands	53
Belarus	51
Austria	49
Estonia	48
Czech Republic	47
Slovenia	46
Luxembourg	44
Latvia	38
Turkey	6
Total	63

E160_1) CONCERNED WITH UNEMPLOYED

To what extent do you feel concerned about the living conditions of: Unemployed people in your country

Very much / Much (%) (EVS: V273)

Country	Wave 1990	Wave 2000	Gender Male	Gender Female	Age 16-29	Age 30-49	Age 50+	Education Lower	Education Middle	Education Upper	Income Lower	Income Middle	Income Upper	Values Mat	Values Mixed	Values Postm.
Albania	na	**na**	na	na	na	na	na	na	na	na	na	na	na	na	na	na
Algeria	na	**na**	na	na	na	na	na	na	na	na	na	na	na	na	na	na
Argentina	na	**na**	na	na	na	na	na	na	na	na	na	na	na	na	na	na
Armenia	na	**na**	na	na	na	na	na	na	na	na	na	na	na	na	na	na
Australia	na	**na**	na	na	na	na	na	na	na	na	na	na	na	na	na	na
Austria	na	**32**	32	32	22	30	40	30	31	43	33	33	32	21	33	35
Azerbaijan	na	**na**	na	na	na	na	na	na	na	na	na	na	na	na	na	na
Bangladesh	na	**na**	na	na	na	na	na	na	na	na	na	na	na	na	na	na
Belarus	na	**27**	25	29	25	27	30	28	27	28	29	29	20	29	28	20
Belgium	na	**32**	33	31	26	28	39	35	31	31	41	38	25	30	31	36
Bosnia and Herz.	na	**na**	na	na	na	na	na	na	na	na	na	na	na	na	na	na
Brazil	na	**na**	na	na	na	na	na	na	na	na	na	na	na	na	na	na
Bulgaria	na	**57**	51	63	40	58	65	65	53	55	62	56	59	58	59	63
Canada	na	**na**	na	na	na	na	na	na	na	na	na	na	na	na	na	na
Chile	na	**na**	na	na	na	na	na	na	na	na	na	na	na	na	na	na
China	na	**na**	na	na	na	na	na	na	na	na	na	na	na	na	na	na
Colombia	na	**na**	na	na	na	na	na	na	na	na	na	na	na	na	na	na
Croatia	na	**69**	67	70	59	71	72	66	70	71	77	69	64	71	68	71
Czech Republic	na	**44**	39	48	37	39	51	45	44	35	54	43	36	46	45	39
Denmark	na	**24**	24	24	18	24	28	25	30	23	27	23	25	29	23	32
Dominican Rep.	na	**na**	na	na	na	na	na	na	na	na	na	na	na	na	na	na
Egypt	na	**na**	na	na	na	na	na	na	na	na	na	na	na	na	na	na
El Salvador	na	**na**	na	na	na	na	na	na	na	na	na	na	na	na	na	na
Estonia	na	**38**	32	43	27	37	46	38	38	37	46	40	33	39	38	34
Finland	na	**47**	44	51	37	47	54	53	40	40	55	48	43	47	48	51
France	na	**54**	52	56	49	53	59	52	52	62	55	56	54	48	56	58
Georgia	na	**na**	na	na	na	na	na	na	na	na	na	na	na	na	na	na
Germany	na	**34**	33	35	29	34	37	31	35	44	32	37	38	27	36	39
Great Britain	na	**34**	32	35	31	31	38	32	34	36	35	36	32	na	na	na
Greece	na	**53**	51	53	47	51	71	68	54	48	57	50	49	45	53	58
Hungary	na	**30**	28	31	21	29	34	32	25	26	34	32	25	30	29	50
Iceland	na	**36**	34	37	21	36	48	39	32	36	42	36	30	36	34	42
India	na	**na**	na	na	na	na	na	na	na	na	na	na	na	na	na	na
Indonesia	na	**na**	na	na	na	na	na	na	na	na	na	na	na	na	na	na
Iran	na	**na**	na	na	na	na	na	na	na	na	na	na	na	na	na	na
Ireland	na	**50**	49	50	38	54	54	52	46	54	52	44	58	47	52	45
Israel	na	**na**	na	na	na	na	na	na	na	na	na	na	na	na	na	na
Italy	na	**60**	58	63	54	61	64	61	58	65	64	63	56	59	59	67
Japan	na	**na**	na	na	na	na	na	na	na	na	na	na	na	na	na	na
Jordan	na	**na**	na	na	na	na	na	na	na	na	na	na	na	na	na	na
Korea, South	na	**na**	na	na	na	na	na	na	na	na	na	na	na	na	na	na
Latvia	na	**23**	24	22	20	18	27	21	23	25	26	21	20	22	22	30
Lithuania	na	**63**	59	67	51	60	74	66	62	61	70	67	56	66	63	67
Luxembourg	na	**24**	23	24	18	22	29	20	25	26	19	29	22	16	25	30
Macedonia	na	**na**	na	na	na	na	na	na	na	na	na	na	na	na	na	na
Malta	na	**46**	47	46	36	49	51	51	44	50	51	51	47	50	45	36
Mexico	na	**na**	na	na	na	na	na	na	na	na	na	na	na	na	na	na
Moldova	na	**na**	na	na	na	na	na	na	na	na	na	na	na	na	na	na
Montenegro	na	**na**	na	na	na	na	na	na	na	na	na	na	na	na	na	na
Morocco	na	**na**	na	na	na	na	na	na	na	na	na	na	na	na	na	na
Netherlands	na	**21**	20	21	9	18	30	27	17	19	22	22	17	23	19	26
New Zealand	na	**na**	na	na	na	na	na	na	na	na	na	na	na	na	na	na
Nigeria	na	**na**	na	na	na	na	na	na	na	na	na	na	na	na	na	na
Northern Ireland	na	**33**	35	31	28	32	35	33	29	39	40	31	36	27	32	46
Norway	na	**na**	na	na	na	na	na	na	na	na	na	na	na	na	na	na
Pakistan	na	**na**	na	na	na	na	na	na	na	na	na	na	na	na	na	na
Peru	na	**na**	na	na	na	na	na	na	na	na	na	na	na	na	na	na
Philippines	na	**na**	na	na	na	na	na	na	na	na	na	na	na	na	na	na
Poland	na	**51**	48	53	39	55	53	53	51	41	59	46	41	47	53	49
Portugal	na	**49**	48	49	48	43	54	51	44	39	53	46	55	50	48	52
Puerto Rico	na	**na**	na	na	na	na	na	na	na	na	na	na	na	na	na	na
Romania	na	**58**	55	60	53	56	62	59	57	57	56	62	56	63	56	53
Russian Fed.	na	**53**	46	58	34	52	65	55	53	51	57	56	48	54	53	49
Serbia	na	**na**	na	na	na	na	na	na	na	na	na	na	na	na	na	na
Singapore	na	**na**	na	na	na	na	na	na	na	na	na	na	na	na	na	na
Slovakia	na	**49**	46	53	43	49	54	50	49	49	54	53	46	51	50	39
Slovenia	na	**48**	45	51	38	46	58	53	47	42	56	50	42	54	47	50
South Africa	na	**na**	na	na	na	na	na	na	na	na	na	na	na	na	na	na
Spain	na	**53**	50	55	46	55	56	52	52	58	52	59	54	57	50	57
Sweden	na	**36**	31	40	26	32	46	45	31	37	40	35	32	35	33	46
Switzerland	na	**na**	na	na	na	na	na	na	na	na	na	na	na	na	na	na
Taiwan	na	**na**	na	na	na	na	na	na	na	na	na	na	na	na	na	na
Tanzania	na	**na**	na	na	na	na	na	na	na	na	na	na	na	na	na	na
Turkey	na	**5**	5	5	6	4	5	5	6	5	4	6	4	8	4	5
Uganda	na	**na**	na	na	na	na	na	na	na	na	na	na	na	na	na	na
Ukraine	na	**59**	52	66	45	57	69	69	58	56	69	55	55	59	63	57
United States	na	**na**	na	na	na	na	na	na	na	na	na	na	na	na	na	na
Uruguay	na	**na**	na	na	na	na	na	na	na	na	na	na	na	na	na	na
Venezuela	na	**na**	na	na	na	na	na	na	na	na	na	na	na	na	na	na
Vietnam	na	**na**	na	na	na	na	na	na	na	na	na	na	na	na	na	na
Zimbabwe	na	**na**	na	na	na	na	na	na	na	na	na	na	na	na	na	na
Total	na	**43**	41	45	35	42	49	44	43	42	47	43	41	44	43	45

RANKING Country	2000
Croatia	69
Lithuania	63
Italy	60
Ukraine	59
Romania	58
Bulgaria	57
France	54
Spain	53
Russian Fed.	53
Greece	53
Poland	51
Ireland	50
Slovakia	49
Portugal	49
Slovenia	48
Finland	47
Malta	46
Czech Republic	44
Estonia	38
Sweden	36
Iceland	36
Germany	34
Great Britain	34
Northern Ireland	33
Austria	32
Belgium	32
Hungary	30
Belarus	27
Denmark	24
Luxembourg	24
Latvia	23
Netherlands	21
Turkey	5
Total	43

E161_1) CONCERNED WITH IMMIGRANTS

To what extent do you feel concerned about the living conditions of: Immigrants in your country

Very much / Much (%) (EVS: V274)

Country	Wave		Gender		Age			Education			Income			Values		
	1990	2000	Male	Female	16-29	30-49	50+	Lower	Middle	Upper	Lower	Middle	Upper	Mat	Mixed	Postm.
Albania	na	**na**	na	na	na	na	na	na	na	na	na	na	na	na	na	na
Algeria	na	**na**	na	na	na	na	na	na	na	na	na	na	na	na	na	na
Argentina	na	**na**	na	na	na	na	na	na	na	na	na	na	na	na	na	na
Armenia	na	**na**	na	na	na	na	na	na	na	na	na	na	na	na	na	na
Australia	na	**na**	na	na	na	na	na	na	na	na	na	na	na	na	na	na
Austria	na	**16**	15	17	14	15	18	11	19	24	18	15	14	10	13	23
Azerbaijan	na	**na**	na	na	na	na	na	na	na	na	na	na	na	na	na	na
Bangladesh	na	**na**	na	na	na	na	na	na	na	na	na	na	na	na	na	na
Belarus	na	**9**	9	10	8	9	11	7	10	10	8	11	9	10	10	5
Belgium	na	**16**	16	15	17	16	15	9	13	24	15	16	16	7	15	27
Bosnia and Herz.	na	**na**	na	na	na	na	na	na	na	na	na	na	na	na	na	na
Brazil	na	**na**	na	na	na	na	na	na	na	na	na	na	na	na	na	na
Bulgaria	na	**9**	8	10	5	9	11	8	8	13	9	8	11	8	11	9
Canada	na	**na**	na	na	na	na	na	na	na	na	na	na	na	na	na	na
Chile	na	**na**	na	na	na	na	na	na	na	na	na	na	na	na	na	na
China	na	**na**	na	na	na	na	na	na	na	na	na	na	na	na	na	na
Colombia	na	**na**	na	na	na	na	na	na	na	na	na	na	na	na	na	na
Croatia	na	**20**	20	21	12	28	18	21	20	21	25	18	22	18	21	21
Czech Republic	na	**13**	10	16	14	12	14	13	14	10	13	13	14	14	13	17
Denmark	na	**15**	15	15	16	16	14	10	21	21	13	15	21	5	14	27
Dominican Rep.	na	**na**	na	na	na	na	na	na	na	na	na	na	na	na	na	na
Egypt	na	**na**	na	na	na	na	na	na	na	na	na	na	na	na	na	na
El Salvador	na	**na**	na	na	na	na	na	na	na	na	na	na	na	na	na	na
Estonia	na	**11**	9	13	8	12	12	9	11	15	10	13	10	14	10	16
Finland	na	**15**	15	16	13	18	14	14	15	20	18	15	13	10	17	20
France	na	**27**	26	27	29	28	25	21	29	41	24	25	32	16	27	43
Georgia	na	**na**	na	na	na	na	na	na	na	na	na	na	na	na	na	na
Germany	na	**22**	21	23	24	22	21	18	24	30	17	25	23	13	23	34
Great Britain	na	**15**	15	14	16	16	13	8	17	27	10	19	17	na	na	na
Greece	na	**27**	24	29	28	24	31	22	25	29	28	24	25	18	26	40
Hungary	na	**5**	6	5	3	5	7	6	3	5	5	7	3	6	5	8
Iceland	na	**21**	18	23	17	20	25	21	16	29	23	20	20	13	21	34
India	na	**na**	na	na	na	na	na	na	na	na	na	na	na	na	na	na
Indonesia	na	**na**	na	na	na	na	na	na	na	na	na	na	na	na	na	na
Iran	na	**na**	na	na	na	na	na	na	na	na	na	na	na	na	na	na
Ireland	na	**28**	30	27	21	32	30	25	26	40	22	28	37	28	29	30
Israel	na	**na**	na	na	na	na	na	na	na	na	na	na	na	na	na	na
Italy	na	**35**	32	37	30	40	32	30	35	46	34	37	37	24	33	44
Japan	na	**na**	na	na	na	na	na	na	na	na	na	na	na	na	na	na
Jordan	na	**na**	na	na	na	na	na	na	na	na	na	na	na	na	na	na
Korea, South	na	**na**	na	na	na	na	na	na	na	na	na	na	na	na	na	na
Latvia	na	**5**	6	5	4	6	5	6	5	7	5	6	4	4	5	9
Lithuania	na	**7**	6	9	9	8	6	5	7	13	8	7	8	6	8	8
Luxembourg	na	**23**	22	24	22	24	22	20	24	27	21	27	27	19	22	32
Macedonia	na	**na**	na	na	na	na	na	na	na	na	na	na	na	na	na	na
Malta	na	**21**	20	22	22	22	20	15	23	28	18	21	26	21	22	22
Mexico	na	**na**	na	na	na	na	na	na	na	na	na	na	na	na	na	na
Moldova	na	**na**	na	na	na	na	na	na	na	na	na	na	na	na	na	na
Montenegro	na	**na**	na	na	na	na	na	na	na	na	na	na	na	na	na	na
Morocco	na	**na**	na	na	na	na	na	na	na	na	na	na	na	na	na	na
Netherlands	na	**16**	15	16	13	16	16	11	14	22	16	16	15	7	14	23
New Zealand	na	**na**	na	na	na	na	na	na	na	na	na	na	na	na	na	na
Nigeria	na	**na**	na	na	na	na	na	na	na	na	na	na	na	na	na	na
Northern Ireland	na	**18**	17	19	15	20	17	14	17	29	19	15	22	13	18	27
Norway	na	**na**	na	na	na	na	na	na	na	na	na	na	na	na	na	na
Pakistan	na	**na**	na	na	na	na	na	na	na	na	na	na	na	na	na	na
Peru	na	**na**	na	na	na	na	na	na	na	na	na	na	na	na	na	na
Philippines	na	**na**	na	na	na	na	na	na	na	na	na	na	na	na	na	na
Poland	na	**9**	10	8	7	8	11	9	7	10	9	8	10	7	10	9
Portugal	na	**24**	25	23	21	25	25	26	23	17	27	24	26	28	20	29
Puerto Rico	na	**na**	na	na	na	na	na	na	na	na	na	na	na	na	na	na
Romania	na	**20**	19	20	18	18	22	20	19	18	21	21	18	19	20	19
Russian Fed.	na	**11**	10	12	7	11	14	11	10	13	13	11	9	11	12	15
Serbia	na	**na**	na	na	na	na	na	na	na	na	na	na	na	na	na	na
Singapore	na	**na**	na	na	na	na	na	na	na	na	na	na	na	na	na	na
Slovakia	na	**12**	10	13	11	11	13	12	11	13	12	11	14	11	12	12
Slovenia	na	**13**	12	14	11	13	15	18	12	7	15	15	9	11	13	17
South Africa	na	**na**	na	na	na	na	na	na	na	na	na	na	na	na	na	na
Spain	na	**31**	28	33	24	35	31	29	31	36	29	36	33	28	27	41
Sweden	na	**30**	25	34	35	27	29	25	28	37	30	27	30	26	25	44
Switzerland	na	**na**	na	na	na	na	na	na	na	na	na	na	na	na	na	na
Taiwan	na	**na**	na	na	na	na	na	na	na	na	na	na	na	na	na	na
Tanzania	na	**na**	na	na	na	na	na	na	na	na	na	na	na	na	na	na
Turkey	na	**33**	33	33	38	29	28	31	36	34	30	35	34	38	32	31
Uganda	na	**na**	na	na	na	na	na	na	na	na	na	na	na	na	na	na
Ukraine	na	**9**	8	9	8	10	8	8	8	10	11	4	10	6	10	12
United States	na	**na**	na	na	na	na	na	na	na	na	na	na	na	na	na	na
Uruguay	na	**na**	na	na	na	na	na	na	na	na	na	na	na	na	na	na
Venezuela	na	**na**	na	na	na	na	na	na	na	na	na	na	na	na	na	na
Vietnam	na	**na**	na	na	na	na	na	na	na	na	na	na	na	na	na	na
Zimbabwe	na	**na**	na	na	na	na	na	na	na	na	na	na	na	na	na	na
Total	na	**17**	16	18	16	18	17	16	16	22	17	17	18	13	17	28

RANKING	
Country	2000
Italy	35
Turkey	33
Spain	31
Sweden	30
Ireland	28
France	27
Greece	27
Portugal	24
Luxembourg	23
Germany	22
Malta	21
Iceland	21
Croatia	20
Romania	20
Northern Ireland	18
Austria	16
Belgium	16
Netherlands	16
Denmark	15
Finland	15
Great Britain	15
Czech Republic	13
Slovenia	13
Slovakia	12
Estonia	11
Russian Fed.	11
Belarus	9
Bulgaria	9
Poland	9
Ukraine	9
Lithuania	7
Latvia	5
Hungary	5
Total	17

E162_1) CONCERNED WITH SICK AND DISABLED

To what extent do you feel concerned about the living conditions of: Sick and disabled people in your country

Very much / Much (%)

(EVS: V275)

Country	Wave		Gender		Age			Education			Income			Values		
	1990	2000	Male	Female	16-29	30-49	50+	Lower	Middle	Upper	Lower	Middle	Upper	Mat	Mixed	Postm.
Albania	na	**na**	na	na	na	na	na	na	na	na	na	na	na	na	na	na
Algeria	na	**na**	na	na	na	na	na	na	na	na	na	na	na	na	na	na
Argentina	na	**na**	na	na	na	na	na	na	na	na	na	na	na	na	na	na
Armenia	na	**na**	na	na	na	na	na	na	na	na	na	na	na	na	na	na
Australia	na	**na**	na	na	na	na	na	na	na	na	na	na	na	na	na	na
Austria	na	**49**	48	51	40	49	55	50	50	46	49	50	49	41	51	48
Azerbaijan	na	**na**	na	na	na	na	na	na	na	na	na	na	na	na	na	na
Bangladesh	na	**na**	na	na	na	na	na	na	na	na	na	na	na	na	na	na
Belarus	na	**35**	33	37	32	33	41	36	35	35	37	37	28	36	37	29
Belgium	na	**51**	49	54	43	46	60	56	51	50	60	56	47	53	51	53
Bosnia and Herz.	na	**na**	na	na	na	na	na	na	na	na	na	na	na	na	na	na
Brazil	na	**na**	na	na	na	na	na	na	na	na	na	na	na	na	na	na
Bulgaria	na	**60**	55	65	49	55	69	65	57	59	59	63	63	59	65	55
Canada	na	**na**	na	na	na	na	na	na	na	na	na	na	na	na	na	na
Chile	na	**na**	na	na	na	na	na	na	na	na	na	na	na	na	na	na
China	na	**na**	na	na	na	na	na	na	na	na	na	na	na	na	na	na
Colombia	na	**na**	na	na	na	na	na	na	na	na	na	na	na	na	na	na
Croatia	na	**69**	66	71	61	71	71	66	69	73	79	69	66	71	69	65
Czech Republic	na	**65**	60	69	64	62	67	64	64	69	68	64	64	66	64	70
Denmark	na	**54**	49	58	55	56	50	55	57	53	53	52	55	58	55	57
Dominican Rep.	na	**na**	na	na	na	na	na	na	na	na	na	na	na	na	na	na
Egypt	na	**na**	na	na	na	na	na	na	na	na	na	na	na	na	na	na
El Salvador	na	**na**	na	na	na	na	na	na	na	na	na	na	na	na	na	na
Estonia	na	**42**	36	47	37	37	49	42	42	40	47	43	40	42	42	53
Finland	na	**56**	53	60	41	55	66	60	49	55	61	56	56	55	58	55
France	na	**61**	60	61	53	58	66	62	52	63	62	62	61	58	61	61
Georgia	na	**na**	na	na	na	na	na	na	na	na	na	na	na	na	na	na
Germany	na	**53**	49	55	41	54	56	49	53	68	49	56	57	50	53	55
Great Britain	na	**64**	59	70	51	62	76	67	65	60	66	69	61	na	na	na
Greece	na	**69**	64	72	66	67	78	81	70	65	73	70	64	66	68	74
Hungary	na	**46**	40	52	35	46	53	47	45	40	48	47	44	47	48	32
Iceland	na	**65**	58	71	56	64	73	72	57	65	73	65	58	62	65	67
India	na	**na**	na	na	na	na	na	na	na	na	na	na	na	na	na	na
Indonesia	na	**na**	na	na	na	na	na	na	na	na	na	na	na	na	na	na
Iran	na	**na**	na	na	na	na	na	na	na	na	na	na	na	na	na	na
Ireland	na	**79**	76	82	70	80	85	83	75	82	79	82	82	74	79	85
Israel	na	**na**	na	na	na	na	na	na	na	na	na	na	na	na	na	na
Italy	na	**74**	69	77	64	75	78	76	71	73	75	73	73	71	73	78
Japan	na	**na**	na	na	na	na	na	na	na	na	na	na	na	na	na	na
Jordan	na	**na**	na	na	na	na	na	na	na	na	na	na	na	na	na	na
Korea, South	na	**na**	na	na	na	na	na	na	na	na	na	na	na	na	na	na
Latvia	na	**34**	29	37	33	30	37	31	34	36	36	32	33	31	35	41
Lithuania	na	**64**	56	70	55	62	71	66	62	67	69	64	62	58	67	64
Luxembourg	na	**39**	36	42	28	35	50	37	41	40	39	43	36	34	37	50
Macedonia	na	**na**	na	na	na	na	na	na	na	na	na	na	na	na	na	na
Malta	na	**79**	78	80	71	83	82	82	78	79	82	84	76	82	79	70
Mexico	na	**na**	na	na	na	na	na	na	na	na	na	na	na	na	na	na
Moldova	na	**na**	na	na	na	na	na	na	na	na	na	na	na	na	na	na
Montenegro	na	**na**	na	na	na	na	na	na	na	na	na	na	na	na	na	na
Morocco	na	**na**	na	na	na	na	na	na	na	na	na	na	na	na	na	na
Netherlands	na	**50**	45	54	42	44	59	55	47	47	48	50	47	48	50	49
New Zealand	na	**na**	na	na	na	na	na	na	na	na	na	na	na	na	na	na
Nigeria	na	**na**	na	na	na	na	na	na	na	na	na	na	na	na	na	na
Northern Ireland	na	**61**	63	60	53	60	66	61	58	65	66	65	70	57	61	72
Norway	na	**na**	na	na	na	na	na	na	na	na	na	na	na	na	na	na
Pakistan	na	**na**	na	na	na	na	na	na	na	na	na	na	na	na	na	na
Peru	na	**na**	na	na	na	na	na	na	na	na	na	na	na	na	na	na
Philippines	na	**na**	na	na	na	na	na	na	na	na	na	na	na	na	na	na
Poland	na	**65**	63	66	61	66	65	64	68	61	65	65	60	63	66	61
Portugal	na	**73**	71	76	72	75	73	75	69	77	73	75	70	74	73	71
Puerto Rico	na	**na**	na	na	na	na	na	na	na	na	na	na	na	na	na	na
Romania	na	**65**	62	68	60	63	70	66	63	67	63	68	63	67	66	63
Russian Fed.	na	**62**	56	68	44	63	73	60	63	62	65	64	60	63	62	60
Serbia	na	**na**	na	na	na	na	na	na	na	na	na	na	na	na	na	na
Singapore	na	**na**	na	na	na	na	na	na	na	na	na	na	na	na	na	na
Slovakia	na	**61**	57	65	55	57	70	64	61	55	62	63	62	62	61	61
Slovenia	na	**53**	47	57	43	47	65	58	50	50	61	54	46	59	52	53
South Africa	na	**na**	na	na	na	na	na	na	na	na	na	na	na	na	na	na
Spain	na	**52**	49	55	44	52	56	53	51	51	53	56	52	55	50	58
Sweden	na	**60**	53	67	57	57	66	65	57	63	66	58	56	56	58	69
Switzerland	na	**na**	na	na	na	na	na	na	na	na	na	na	na	na	na	na
Taiwan	na	**na**	na	na	na	na	na	na	na	na	na	na	na	na	na	na
Tanzania	na	**na**	na	na	na	na	na	na	na	na	na	na	na	na	na	na
Turkey	na	**3**	3	2	3	2	3	2	4	na	2	3	4	3	2	4
Uganda	na	**na**	na	na	na	na	na	na	na	na	na	na	na	na	na	na
Ukraine	na	**65**	59	69	51	60	77	82	62	62	74	60	61	65	66	71
United States	na	**na**	na	na	na	na	na	na	na	na	na	na	na	na	na	na
Uruguay	na	**na**	na	na	na	na	na	na	na	na	na	na	na	na	na	na
Venezuela	na	**na**	na	na	na	na	na	na	na	na	na	na	na	na	na	na
Vietnam	na	**na**	na	na	na	na	na	na	na	na	na	na	na	na	na	na
Zimbabwe	na	**na**	na	na	na	na	na	na	na	na	na	na	na	na	na	na
Total	na	**58**	54	62	51	57	64	60	57	59	60	59	57	57	59	60

RANKING	
Country	2000
Malta	79
Ireland	79
Italy	74
Portugal	73
Croatia	69
Greece	69
Romania	65
Iceland	65
Czech Republic	65
Poland	65
Ukraine	65
Great Britain	64
Lithuania	64
Russian Fed.	62
Slovakia	61
Northern Ireland	61
France	61
Sweden	60
Bulgaria	60
Finland	56
Denmark	54
Germany	53
Slovenia	53
Spain	52
Belgium	51
Netherlands	50
Austria	49
Hungary	46
Estonia	42
Luxembourg	39
Belarus	35
Latvia	34
Turkey	3
Total	58

E163_1) PREPARED TO HELP IMMEDIATE FAMILY

Would you be prepared to actually do something to improve the conditions of: Your immediate family

Absolutely yes / Yes (%) (EVS: V276)

	Wave		Gender		Age			Education			Income			Values		
Country	1990	2000	Male	Female	16-29	30-49	50+	Lower	Middle	Upper	Lower	Middle	Upper	Mat	Mixed	Postm.
Albania	na	**na**	na	na	na	na	na	na	na	na	na	na	na	na	na	na
Algeria	na	**na**	na	na	na	na	na	na	na	na	na	na	na	na	na	na
Argentina	na	**na**	na	na	na	na	na	na	na	na	na	na	na	na	na	na
Armenia	na	**na**	na	na	na	na	na	na	na	na	na	na	na	na	na	na
Australia	na	**na**	na	na	na	na	na	na	na	na	na	na	na	na	na	na
Austria	na	**97**	97	97	98	98	96	96	98	98	94	97	99	91	97	98
Azerbaijan	na	**na**	na	na	na	na	na	na	na	na	na	na	na	na	na	na
Bangladesh	na	**na**	na	na	na	na	na	na	na	na	na	na	na	na	na	na
Belarus	na	**66**	73	60	69	73	55	52	69	76	56	67	81	67	65	75
Belgium	na	**96**	95	97	96	96	96	93	96	98	92	97	98	97	96	97
Bosnia and Herz.	na	**na**	na	na	na	na	na	na	na	na	na	na	na	na	na	na
Brazil	na	**na**	na	na	na	na	na	na	na	na	na	na	na	na	na	na
Bulgaria	na	**98**	98	98	98	99	97	97	98	99	96	99	98	98	98	100
Canada	na	**na**	na	na	na	na	na	na	na	na	na	na	na	na	na	na
Chile	na	**na**	na	na	na	na	na	na	na	na	na	na	na	na	na	na
China	na	**na**	na	na	na	na	na	na	na	na	na	na	na	na	na	na
Colombia	na	**na**	na	na	na	na	na	na	na	na	na	na	na	na	na	na
Croatia	na	**99**	98	99	99	98	99	97	100	99	99	98	99	100	98	100
Czech Republic	na	**91**	88	94	89	92	92	89	93	96	88	93	92	92	91	92
Denmark	na	**89**	90	88	88	90	88	86	94	93	85	89	94	81	89	95
Dominican Rep.	na	**na**	na	na	na	na	na	na	na	na	na	na	na	na	na	na
Egypt	na	**na**	na	na	na	na	na	na	na	na	na	na	na	na	na	na
El Salvador	na	**na**	na	na	na	na	na	na	na	na	na	na	na	na	na	na
Estonia	na	**89**	87	90	88	92	86	82	92	92	85	86	94	89	90	89
Finland	na	**91**	90	92	96	94	86	89	94	91	92	91	91	89	92	92
France	na	**95**	94	96	95	93	97	95	94	96	94	94	97	96	95	93
Georgia	na	**na**	na	na	na	na	na	na	na	na	na	na	na	na	na	na
Germany	na	**98**	99	98	96	99	98	98	98	99	97	99	97	98	98	98
Great Britain	na	**91**	93	90	88	93	91	92	89	95	87	94	94	na	na	na
Greece	na	**98**	97	98	98	97	98	98	97	98	97	98	97	96	98	99
Hungary	na	**98**	97	99	98	99	97	97	98	99	96	99	98	98	99	97
Iceland	na	**99**	98	99	98	99	99	98	100	100	98	99	99	100	98	99
India	na	**na**	na	na	na	na	na	na	na	na	na	na	na	na	na	na
Indonesia	na	**na**	na	na	na	na	na	na	na	na	na	na	na	na	na	na
Iran	na	**na**	na	na	na	na	na	na	na	na	na	na	na	na	na	na
Ireland	na	**96**	96	96	95	97	94	93	96	99	93	96	97	95	96	95
Israel	na	**na**	na	na	na	na	na	na	na	na	na	na	na	na	na	na
Italy	na	**92**	91	93	89	93	92	91	91	98	90	94	94	91	92	93
Japan	na	**na**	na	na	na	na	na	na	na	na	na	na	na	na	na	na
Jordan	na	**na**	na	na	na	na	na	na	na	na	na	na	na	na	na	na
Korea, South	na	**na**	na	na	na	na	na	na	na	na	na	na	na	na	na	na
Latvia	na	**95**	95	95	98	98	92	91	96	98	92	95	99	93	96	98
Lithuania	na	**88**	86	91	87	92	86	86	89	90	80	90	93	85	90	97
Luxembourg	na	**95**	94	95	95	95	94	93	95	97	90	95	97	91	95	95
Macedonia	na	**na**	na	na	na	na	na	na	na	na	na	na	na	na	na	na
Malta	na	**99**	99	100	99	100	99	99	100	97	99	100	99	100	99	99
Mexico	na	**na**	na	na	na	na	na	na	na	na	na	na	na	na	na	na
Moldova	na	**na**	na	na	na	na	na	na	na	na	na	na	na	na	na	na
Montenegro	na	**na**	na	na	na	na	na	na	na	na	na	na	na	na	na	na
Morocco	na	**na**	na	na	na	na	na	na	na	na	na	na	na	na	na	na
Netherlands	na	**95**	95	95	96	97	93	92	97	97	91	96	98	94	95	96
New Zealand	na	**na**	na	na	na	na	na	na	na	na	na	na	na	na	na	na
Nigeria	na	**na**	na	na	na	na	na	na	na	na	na	na	na	na	na	na
Northern Ireland	na	**95**	96	95	93	95	96	95	95	96	92	98	97	96	95	95
Norway	na	**na**	na	na	na	na	na	na	na	na	na	na	na	na	na	na
Pakistan	na	**na**	na	na	na	na	na	na	na	na	na	na	na	na	na	na
Peru	na	**na**	na	na	na	na	na	na	na	na	na	na	na	na	na	na
Philippines	na	**na**	na	na	na	na	na	na	na	na	na	na	na	na	na	na
Poland	na	**96**	97	95	95	97	96	95	98	97	95	97	97	95	97	99
Portugal	na	**96**	97	96	96	97	96	96	96	99	91	97	97	97	97	99
Puerto Rico	na	**na**	na	na	na	na	na	na	na	na	na	na	na	na	na	na
Romania	na	**95**	96	94	94	98	93	90	97	99	92	95	97	94	97	96
Russian Fed.	na	**85**	87	83	88	92	75	74	85	91	78	88	90	83	88	80
Serbia	na	**na**	na	na	na	na	na	na	na	na	na	na	na	na	na	na
Singapore	na	**na**	na	na	na	na	na	na	na	na	na	na	na	na	na	na
Slovakia	na	**94**	91	96	95	92	94	91	95	94	92	95	94	93	94	96
Slovenia	na	**98**	97	99	99	97	98	97	98	99	98	98	98	97	99	97
South Africa	na	**na**	na	na	na	na	na	na	na	na	na	na	na	na	na	na
Spain	na	**95**	95	95	96	95	95	96	94	97	95	95	93	96	95	96
Sweden	na	**98**	97	99	98	99	97	98	99	97	98	98	98	98	98	99
Switzerland	na	**na**	na	na	na	na	na	na	na	na	na	na	na	na	na	na
Taiwan	na	**na**	na	na	na	na	na	na	na	na	na	na	na	na	na	na
Tanzania	na	**na**	na	na	na	na	na	na	na	na	na	na	na	na	na	na
Turkey	na	**na**	na	na	na	na	na	na	na	na	na	na	na	na	na	na
Uganda	na	**na**	na	na	na	na	na	na	na	na	na	na	na	na	na	na
Ukraine	na	**88**	92	85	93	94	80	76	90	90	82	90	94	85	93	90
United States	na	**na**	na	na	na	na	na	na	na	na	na	na	na	na	na	na
Uruguay	na	**na**	na	na	na	na	na	na	na	na	na	na	na	na	na	na
Venezuela	na	**na**	na	na	na	na	na	na	na	na	na	na	na	na	na	na
Vietnam	na	**na**	na	na	na	na	na	na	na	na	na	na	na	na	na	na
Zimbabwe	na	**na**	na	na	na	na	na	na	na	na	na	na	na	na	na	na
Total	na	**94**	94	94	94	95	92	92	94	96	90	94	96	92	94	96

RANKING	
Country	**2000**
Malta	99
Iceland	99
Croatia	99
Germany	98
Sweden	98
Slovenia	98
Bulgaria	98
Hungary	98
Greece	98
Austria	97
Portugal	96
Belgium	96
Poland	96
Ireland	96
France	95
Netherlands	95
Northern Ireland	95
Latvia	95
Spain	95
Romania	95
Luxembourg	95
Slovakia	94
Italy	92
Czech Republic	91
Finland	91
Great Britain	91
Estonia	89
Denmark	89
Lithuania	88
Ukraine	88
Russian Fed.	85
Belarus	66
Total	94

E164_1) PREPARED TO HELP PEOPLE NEIGHBORHOOD

Would you be prepared to actually do something to improve the conditions of: People in your neighborhood / community

Absolutely yes / Yes (%) (EVS: V277)

Country	Wave		Gender		Age			Education			Income			Values		
	1990	2000	Male	Female	16-29	30-49	50+	Lower	Middle	Upper	Lower	Middle	Upper	Mat	Mixed	Postm.
Albania	na	**na**	na	na	na	na	na	na	na	na	na	na	na	na	na	na
Algeria	na	**na**	na	na	na	na	na	na	na	na	na	na	na	na	na	na
Argentina	na	**na**	na	na	na	na	na	na	na	na	na	na	na	na	na	na
Armenia	na	**na**	na	na	na	na	na	na	na	na	na	na	na	na	na	na
Australia	na	**na**	na	na	na	na	na	na	na	na	na	na	na	na	na	na
Austria	na	**69**	69	69	58	74	70	69	70	68	63	73	72	59	72	68
Azerbaijan	na	**na**	na	na	na	na	na	na	na	na	na	na	na	na	na	na
Bangladesh	na	**na**	na	na	na	na	na	na	na	na	na	na	na	na	na	na
Belarus	na	**10**	11	10	9	9	13	13	10	9	12	10	8	11	11	5
Belgium	na	**66**	64	68	56	66	70	60	67	69	64	65	69	65	66	67
Bosnia and Herz.	na	**na**	na	na	na	na	na	na	na	na	na	na	na	na	na	na
Brazil	na	**na**	na	na	na	na	na	na	na	na	na	na	na	na	na	na
Bulgaria	na	**43**	45	41	33	47	44	47	39	44	42	47	38	42	44	56
Canada	na	**na**	na	na	na	na	na	na	na	na	na	na	na	na	na	na
Chile	na	**na**	na	na	na	na	na	na	na	na	na	na	na	na	na	na
China	na	**na**	na	na	na	na	na	na	na	na	na	na	na	na	na	na
Colombia	na	**na**	na	na	na	na	na	na	na	na	na	na	na	na	na	na
Croatia	na	**68**	68	69	58	76	67	67	68	75	80	63	71	65	68	70
Czech Republic	na	**51**	45	55	43	47	57	49	52	54	51	52	48	49	51	59
Denmark	na	**47**	48	46	37	48	51	44	51	50	42	51	51	49	45	58
Dominican Rep.	na	**na**	na	na	na	na	na	na	na	na	na	na	na	na	na	na
Egypt	na	**na**	na	na	na	na	na	na	na	na	na	na	na	na	na	na
El Salvador	na	**na**	na	na	na	na	na	na	na	na	na	na	na	na	na	na
Estonia	na	**34**	31	37	26	31	42	34	34	36	34	35	38	32	39	28
Finland	na	**46**	43	49	38	49	47	46	44	49	46	46	46	45	45	50
France	na	**49**	45	52	41	45	56	46	49	55	47	49	49	48	48	51
Georgia	na	**na**	na	na	na	na	na	na	na	na	na	na	na	na	na	na
Germany	na	**60**	58	61	53	58	65	58	61	62	56	62	64	54	61	68
Great Britain	na	**40**	37	43	33	42	41	38	38	47	39	34	43	na	na	na
Greece	na	**42**	40	43	35	41	58	50	41	40	42	38	41	37	42	45
Hungary	na	**53**	50	56	49	52	56	51	56	60	44	59	52	51	56	71
Iceland	na	**51**	47	55	49	54	50	50	52	52	49	53	51	51	51	56
India	na	**na**	na	na	na	na	na	na	na	na	na	na	na	na	na	na
Indonesia	na	**na**	na	na	na	na	na	na	na	na	na	na	na	na	na	na
Iran	na	**na**	na	na	na	na	na	na	na	na	na	na	na	na	na	na
Ireland	na	**72**	74	71	63	75	75	71	71	77	69	73	80	72	72	73
Israel	na	**na**	na	na	na	na	na	na	na	na	na	na	na	na	na	na
Italy	na	**49**	45	52	39	50	54	49	48	53	50	52	51	47	48	53
Japan	na	**na**	na	na	na	na	na	na	na	na	na	na	na	na	na	na
Jordan	na	**na**	na	na	na	na	na	na	na	na	na	na	na	na	na	na
Korea, South	na	**na**	na	na	na	na	na	na	na	na	na	na	na	na	na	na
Latvia	na	**30**	29	31	25	26	35	29	31	29	33	28	29	29	32	17
Lithuania	na	**21**	17	25	14	21	26	28	18	20	24	24	16	25	20	12
Luxembourg	na	**62**	61	64	63	58	67	57	66	65	62	64	68	61	62	68
Macedonia	na	**na**	na	na	na	na	na	na	na	na	na	na	na	na	na	na
Malta	na	**55**	54	56	39	58	63	58	54	53	56	57	57	56	56	50
Mexico	na	**na**	na	na	na	na	na	na	na	na	na	na	na	na	na	na
Moldova	na	**na**	na	na	na	na	na	na	na	na	na	na	na	na	na	na
Montenegro	na	**na**	na	na	na	na	na	na	na	na	na	na	na	na	na	na
Morocco	na	**na**	na	na	na	na	na	na	na	na	na	na	na	na	na	na
Netherlands	na	**68**	65	71	55	70	72	69	70	64	62	70	68	73	67	66
New Zealand	na	**na**	na	na	na	na	na	na	na	na	na	na	na	na	na	na
Nigeria	na	**na**	na	na	na	na	na	na	na	na	na	na	na	na	na	na
Northern Ireland	na	**57**	58	56	57	58	57	54	56	68	54	59	68	53	57	69
Norway	na	**na**	na	na	na	na	na	na	na	na	na	na	na	na	na	na
Pakistan	na	**na**	na	na	na	na	na	na	na	na	na	na	na	na	na	na
Peru	na	**na**	na	na	na	na	na	na	na	na	na	na	na	na	na	na
Philippines	na	**na**	na	na	na	na	na	na	na	na	na	na	na	na	na	na
Poland	na	**55**	56	54	38	59	62	58	51	54	61	53	49	51	57	62
Portugal	na	**44**	40	48	36	44	49	45	42	44	42	47	49	47	42	51
Puerto Rico	na	**na**	na	na	na	na	na	na	na	na	na	na	na	na	na	na
Romania	na	**48**	50	46	41	52	48	46	46	54	45	51	49	49	50	45
Russian Fed.	na	**26**	24	28	20	29	28	29	26	26	29	28	24	25	28	26
Serbia	na	**na**	na	na	na	na	na	na	na	na	na	na	na	na	na	na
Singapore	na	**na**	na	na	na	na	na	na	na	na	na	na	na	na	na	na
Slovakia	na	**72**	68	75	69	68	78	74	70	76	72	72	74	70	74	75
Slovenia	na	**66**	66	66	52	68	74	66	65	69	65	71	72	68	66	68
South Africa	na	**na**	na	na	na	na	na	na	na	na	na	na	na	na	na	na
Spain	na	**52**	48	56	51	50	55	51	50	63	53	54	53	58	48	61
Sweden	na	**67**	65	69	57	73	67	67	66	68	61	68	75	69	65	70
Switzerland	na	**na**	na	na	na	na	na	na	na	na	na	na	na	na	na	na
Taiwan	na	**na**	na	na	na	na	na	na	na	na	na	na	na	na	na	na
Tanzania	na	**na**	na	na	na	na	na	na	na	na	na	na	na	na	na	na
Turkey	na	**na**	na	na	na	na	na	na	na	na	na	na	na	na	na	na
Uganda	na	**na**	na	na	na	na	na	na	na	na	na	na	na	na	na	na
Ukraine	na	**29**	29	29	22	32	31	29	28	32	30	26	33	27	32	24
United States	na	**na**	na	na	na	na	na	na	na	na	na	na	na	na	na	na
Uruguay	na	**na**	na	na	na	na	na	na	na	na	na	na	na	na	na	na
Venezuela	na	**na**	na	na	na	na	na	na	na	na	na	na	na	na	na	na
Vietnam	na	**na**	na	na	na	na	na	na	na	na	na	na	na	na	na	na
Zimbabwe	na	**na**	na	na	na	na	na	na	na	na	na	na	na	na	na	na
Total	na	**50**	49	51	42	51	54	51	49	52	48	51	52	46	52	59

RANKING

Country	2000
Ireland	72
Slovakia	72
Austria	69
Croatia	68
Netherlands	68
Sweden	67
Slovenia	66
Belgium	66
Luxembourg	62
Germany	60
Northern Ireland	57
Poland	55
Malta	55
Hungary	53
Spain	52
Iceland	51
Czech Republic	51
Italy	49
France	49
Romania	48
Denmark	47
Finland	46
Portugal	44
Bulgaria	43
Greece	42
Great Britain	40
Estonia	34
Latvia	30
Ukraine	29
Russian Fed.	26
Lithuania	21
Belarus	10
Total	50

E165_1) PREPARED TO HELP ELDERLY

Would you be prepared to actually do something to improve the conditions of: Elderly people in your country

Absolutely yes / Yes (%) (EVS: V278)

Country	Wave 1990	Wave 2000	Gender Male	Gender Female	Age 16-29	Age 30-49	Age 50+	Education Lower	Education Middle	Education Upper	Income Lower	Income Middle	Income Upper	Values Mat	Values Mixed	Values Postm.
Albania	na	**na**	na	na	na	na	na	na	na	na	na	na	na	na	na	na
Algeria	na	**na**	na	na	na	na	na	na	na	na	na	na	na	na	na	na
Argentina	na	**na**	na	na	na	na	na	na	na	na	na	na	na	na	na	na
Armenia	na	**na**	na	na	na	na	na	na	na	na	na	na	na	na	na	na
Australia	na	**na**	na	na	na	na	na	na	na	na	na	na	na	na	na	na
Austria	na	**58**	58	58	52	59	60	60	56	56	51	63	60	50	58	61
Azerbaijan	na	**na**	na	na	na	na	na	na	na	na	na	na	na	na	na	na
Bangladesh	na	**na**	na	na	na	na	na	na	na	na	na	na	na	na	na	na
Belarus	na	**7**	8	7	7	8	8	5	9	7	6	9	6	5	10	11
Belgium	na	**67**	65	69	55	64	76	69	68	66	69	68	68	68	66	69
Bosnia and Herz.	na	**na**	na	na	na	na	na	na	na	na	na	na	na	na	na	na
Brazil	na	**na**	na	na	na	na	na	na	na	na	na	na	na	na	na	na
Bulgaria	na	**58**	55	61	44	64	61	62	55	60	53	60	63	53	63	83
Canada	na	**na**	na	na	na	na	na	na	na	na	na	na	na	na	na	na
Chile	na	**na**	na	na	na	na	na	na	na	na	na	na	na	na	na	na
China	na	**na**	na	na	na	na	na	na	na	na	na	na	na	na	na	na
Colombia	na	**na**	na	na	na	na	na	na	na	na	na	na	na	na	na	na
Croatia	na	**76**	73	80	72	81	74	77	75	80	87	74	74	76	76	74
Czech Republic	na	**63**	58	67	53	60	70	62	64	62	66	61	61	59	64	65
Denmark	na	**67**	64	69	62	68	68	65	71	70	65	68	67	63	67	74
Dominican Rep.	na	**na**	na	na	na	na	na	na	na	na	na	na	na	na	na	na
Egypt	na	**na**	na	na	na	na	na	na	na	na	na	na	na	na	na	na
El Salvador	na	**na**	na	na	na	na	na	na	na	na	na	na	na	na	na	na
Estonia	na	**33**	29	36	24	35	37	31	34	35	36	28	37	30	37	27
Finland	na	**72**	66	78	61	73	78	73	73	67	75	70	73	65	75	79
France	na	**59**	56	61	49	58	64	62	52	57	63	59	56	59	59	57
Georgia	na	**na**	na	na	na	na	na	na	na	na	na	na	na	na	na	na
Germany	na	**50**	48	52	41	48	56	48	49	63	48	49	57	44	53	54
Great Britain	na	**54**	50	58	37	54	63	57	50	55	54	52	57	na	na	na
Greece	na	**66**	63	68	58	69	78	76	67	63	69	66	60	67	64	71
Hungary	na	**57**	51	63	46	59	62	54	62	67	46	61	59	54	62	58
Iceland	na	**73**	67	79	63	77	76	76	69	73	77	73	70	66	75	78
India	na	**na**	na	na	na	na	na	na	na	na	na	na	na	na	na	na
Indonesia	na	**na**	na	na	na	na	na	na	na	na	na	na	na	na	na	na
Iran	na	**na**	na	na	na	na	na	na	na	na	na	na	na	na	na	na
Ireland	na	**81**	80	81	76	81	83	82	80	80	79	80	86	77	81	82
Israel	na	**na**	na	na	na	na	na	na	na	na	na	na	na	na	na	na
Italy	na	**80**	77	83	74	81	83	81	80	81	81	81	78	75	81	84
Japan	na	**na**	na	na	na	na	na	na	na	na	na	na	na	na	na	na
Jordan	na	**na**	na	na	na	na	na	na	na	na	na	na	na	na	na	na
Korea, South	na	**na**	na	na	na	na	na	na	na	na	na	na	na	na	na	na
Latvia	na	**56**	56	55	59	56	54	46	57	64	54	54	63	51	58	68
Lithuania	na	**35**	29	40	23	39	40	37	33	38	29	40	35	35	36	28
Luxembourg	na	**61**	59	62	47	60	71	56	62	65	55	69	63	64	57	72
Macedonia	na	**na**	na	na	na	na	na	na	na	na	na	na	na	na	na	na
Malta	na	**76**	77	76	65	79	81	81	74	78	77	79	77	75	79	66
Mexico	na	**na**	na	na	na	na	na	na	na	na	na	na	na	na	na	na
Moldova	na	**na**	na	na	na	na	na	na	na	na	na	na	na	na	na	na
Montenegro	na	**na**	na	na	na	na	na	na	na	na	na	na	na	na	na	na
Morocco	na	**na**	na	na	na	na	na	na	na	na	na	na	na	na	na	na
Netherlands	na	**62**	59	66	54	62	67	69	65	53	62	66	57	67	62	60
New Zealand	na	**na**	na	na	na	na	na	na	na	na	na	na	na	na	na	na
Nigeria	na	**na**	na	na	na	na	na	na	na	na	na	na	na	na	na	na
Northern Ireland	na	**62**	64	61	61	64	62	59	63	71	66	66	69	52	65	72
Norway	na	**na**	na	na	na	na	na	na	na	na	na	na	na	na	na	na
Pakistan	na	**na**	na	na	na	na	na	na	na	na	na	na	na	na	na	na
Peru	na	**na**	na	na	na	na	na	na	na	na	na	na	na	na	na	na
Philippines	na	**na**	na	na	na	na	na	na	na	na	na	na	na	na	na	na
Poland	na	**67**	67	68	55	71	70	66	70	67	70	66	65	63	69	77
Portugal	na	**59**	55	61	56	59	60	58	58	68	52	57	59	62	55	62
Puerto Rico	na	**na**	na	na	na	na	na	na	na	na	na	na	na	na	na	na
Romania	na	**67**	65	68	59	71	66	62	65	80	61	67	71	66	70	55
Russian Fed.	na	**50**	50	50	48	54	45	39	50	54	47	51	53	46	55	47
Serbia	na	**na**	na	na	na	na	na	na	na	na	na	na	na	na	na	na
Singapore	na	**na**	na	na	na	na	na	na	na	na	na	na	na	na	na	na
Slovakia	na	**69**	67	71	65	66	77	70	67	80	67	71	73	68	71	75
Slovenia	na	**65**	62	67	49	65	76	68	64	63	73	69	66	66	64	68
South Africa	na	**na**	na	na	na	na	na	na	na	na	na	na	na	na	na	na
Spain	na	**57**	55	59	52	59	58	55	55	69	60	57	55	58	55	65
Sweden	na	**85**	83	87	82	85	87	88	85	85	86	86	87	84	85	88
Switzerland	na	**na**	na	na	na	na	na	na	na	na	na	na	na	na	na	na
Taiwan	na	**na**	na	na	na	na	na	na	na	na	na	na	na	na	na	na
Tanzania	na	**na**	na	na	na	na	na	na	na	na	na	na	na	na	na	na
Turkey	na	**na**	na	na	na	na	na	na	na	na	na	na	na	na	na	na
Uganda	na	**na**	na	na	na	na	na	na	na	na	na	na	na	na	na	na
Ukraine	na	**40**	36	43	31	42	43	46	38	42	44	37	38	38	44	36
United States	na	**na**	na	na	na	na	na	na	na	na	na	na	na	na	na	na
Uruguay	na	**na**	na	na	na	na	na	na	na	na	na	na	na	na	na	na
Venezuela	na	**na**	na	na	na	na	na	na	na	na	na	na	na	na	na	na
Vietnam	na	**na**	na	na	na	na	na	na	na	na	na	na	na	na	na	na
Zimbabwe	na	**na**	na	na	na	na	na	na	na	na	na	na	na	na	na	na
Total	na	**61**	58	63	53	62	64	61	59	63	60	61	62	55	63	68

RANKING

Country	2000
Sweden	85
Ireland	81
Italy	80
Croatia	76
Malta	76
Iceland	73
Finland	72
Slovakia	69
Belgium	67
Poland	67
Denmark	67
Romania	67
Greece	66
Slovenia	65
Czech Republic	63
Northern Ireland	62
Netherlands	62
Luxembourg	61
France	59
Portugal	59
Bulgaria	58
Austria	58
Hungary	57
Spain	57
Latvia	56
Great Britain	54
Germany	50
Russian Fed.	50
Ukraine	40
Lithuania	35
Estonia	33
Belarus	7
Total	61

E166_1) PREPARED TO HELP IMMIGRANTS

Would you be prepared to actually do something to improve the conditions of: Immigrants in your country

Absolutely yes / Yes (%)

(EVS: V279)

Country	Wave		Gender		Age			Education			Income			Values		
	1990	2000	Male	Female	16-29	30-49	50+	Lower	Middle	Upper	Lower	Middle	Upper	Mat	Mixed	Postm.
Albania	na	**na**	na	na	na	na	na	na	na	na	na	na	na	na	na	na
Algeria	na	**na**	na	na	na	na	na	na	na	na	na	na	na	na	na	na
Argentina	na	**na**	na	na	na	na	na	na	na	na	na	na	na	na	na	na
Armenia	na	**na**	na	na	na	na	na	na	na	na	na	na	na	na	na	na
Australia	na	**na**	na	na	na	na	na	na	na	na	na	na	na	na	na	na
Austria	na	**20**	20	20	21	22	17	15	21	32	17	19	23	12	17	28
Azerbaijan	na	**na**	na	na	na	na	na	na	na	na	na	na	na	na	na	na
Bangladesh	na	**na**	na	na	na	na	na	na	na	na	na	na	na	na	na	na
Belarus	na	**1**	2	1	1	2	1	na	2	1	1	2	1	1	2	2
Belgium	na	**29**	31	27	31	30	28	18	27	40	25	29	31	19	27	45
Bosnia and Herz.	na	**na**	na	na	na	na	na	na	na	na	na	na	na	na	na	na
Brazil	na	**na**	na	na	na	na	na	na	na	na	na	na	na	na	na	na
Bulgaria	na	**16**	14	18	10	21	15	11	16	22	12	16	19	12	20	18
Canada	na	**na**	na	na	na	na	na	na	na	na	na	na	na	na	na	na
Chile	na	**na**	na	na	na	na	na	na	na	na	na	na	na	na	na	na
China	na	**na**	na	na	na	na	na	na	na	na	na	na	na	na	na	na
Colombia	na	**na**	na	na	na	na	na	na	na	na	na	na	na	na	na	na
Croatia	na	**32**	30	34	26	35	33	32	30	41	39	26	37	26	34	31
Czech Republic	na	**15**	13	17	16	12	17	13	17	19	15	13	17	11	15	24
Denmark	na	**30**	31	30	28	33	28	21	36	46	28	29	40	13	28	53
Dominican Rep.	na	**na**	na	na	na	na	na	na	na	na	na	na	na	na	na	na
Egypt	na	**na**	na	na	na	na	na	na	na	na	na	na	na	na	na	na
El Salvador	na	**na**	na	na	na	na	na	na	na	na	na	na	na	na	na	na
Estonia	na	**9**	8	10	7	13	7	7	10	10	8	8	10	9	9	9
Finland	na	**23**	20	26	26	23	22	19	27	29	25	22	23	17	23	36
France	na	**25**	25	26	24	27	24	20	24	39	23	24	31	15	25	42
Georgia	na	**na**	na	na	na	na	na	na	na	na	na	na	na	na	na	na
Germany	na	**24**	23	25	26	23	23	19	26	33	20	25	26	15	24	37
Great Britain	na	**14**	13	14	13	16	11	9	15	23	11	15	17	na	na	na
Greece	na	**29**	27	30	27	30	30	23	27	32	30	24	31	19	27	43
Hungary	na	**8**	6	9	5	7	9	6	12	8	6	8	8	6	9	18
Iceland	na	**35**	28	41	32	37	34	31	31	50	35	34	37	22	36	47
India	na	**na**	na	na	na	na	na	na	na	na	na	na	na	na	na	na
Indonesia	na	**na**	na	na	na	na	na	na	na	na	na	na	na	na	na	na
Iran	na	**na**	na	na	na	na	na	na	na	na	na	na	na	na	na	na
Ireland	na	**35**	36	33	29	38	35	29	35	44	29	32	46	30	34	43
Israel	na	**na**	na	na	na	na	na	na	na	na	na	na	na	na	na	na
Italy	na	**46**	45	47	42	51	44	41	48	58	45	51	47	34	45	57
Japan	na	**na**	na	na	na	na	na	na	na	na	na	na	na	na	na	na
Jordan	na	**na**	na	na	na	na	na	na	na	na	na	na	na	na	na	na
Korea, South	na	**na**	na	na	na	na	na	na	na	na	na	na	na	na	na	na
Latvia	na	**12**	14	11	15	11	12	13	11	14	12	10	14	10	13	17
Lithuania	na	**4**	3	5	6	4	4	3	4	6	1	7	4	5	4	3
Luxembourg	na	**41**	40	43	36	44	42	38	38	54	35	45	48	40	38	60
Macedonia	na	**na**	na	na	na	na	na	na	na	na	na	na	na	na	na	na
Malta	na	**26**	27	26	22	26	30	24	27	28	25	27	29	28	25	28
Mexico	na	**na**	na	na	na	na	na	na	na	na	na	na	na	na	na	na
Moldova	na	**na**	na	na	na	na	na	na	na	na	na	na	na	na	na	na
Montenegro	na	**na**	na	na	na	na	na	na	na	na	na	na	na	na	na	na
Morocco	na	**na**	na	na	na	na	na	na	na	na	na	na	na	na	na	na
Netherlands	na	**34**	32	35	29	39	31	26	37	38	33	35	32	24	33	41
New Zealand	na	**na**	na	na	na	na	na	na	na	na	na	na	na	na	na	na
Nigeria	na	**na**	na	na	na	na	na	na	na	na	na	na	na	na	na	na
Northern Ireland	na	**24**	25	23	24	26	23	20	24	36	21	23	31	18	26	31
Norway	na	**na**	na	na	na	na	na	na	na	na	na	na	na	na	na	na
Pakistan	na	**na**	na	na	na	na	na	na	na	na	na	na	na	na	na	na
Peru	na	**na**	na	na	na	na	na	na	na	na	na	na	na	na	na	na
Philippines	na	**na**	na	na	na	na	na	na	na	na	na	na	na	na	na	na
Poland	na	**16**	17	15	10	17	19	16	14	22	15	18	12	13	17	24
Portugal	na	**20**	18	23	22	21	19	18	23	30	18	21	23	20	17	27
Puerto Rico	na	**na**	na	na	na	na	na	na	na	na	na	na	na	na	na	na
Romania	na	**22**	24	20	28	21	19	17	22	29	19	20	26	19	26	23
Russian Fed.	na	**11**	11	12	10	11	12	10	10	15	13	11	10	10	13	9
Serbia	na	**na**	na	na	na	na	na	na	na	na	na	na	na	na	na	na
Singapore	na	**na**	na	na	na	na	na	na	na	na	na	na	na	na	na	na
Slovakia	na	**21**	18	23	20	21	21	19	21	24	20	19	25	18	21	35
Slovenia	na	**28**	24	32	21	32	30	30	26	31	30	29	37	28	26	36
South Africa	na	**na**	na	na	na	na	na	na	na	na	na	na	na	na	na	na
Spain	na	**35**	33	37	37	40	30	26	38	50	33	35	42	26	33	51
Sweden	na	**68**	65	70	68	71	65	63	66	74	66	64	74	63	63	84
Switzerland	na	**na**	na	na	na	na	na	na	na	na	na	na	na	na	na	na
Taiwan	na	**na**	na	na	na	na	na	na	na	na	na	na	na	na	na	na
Tanzania	na	**na**	na	na	na	na	na	na	na	na	na	na	na	na	na	na
Turkey	na	**na**	na	na	na	na	na	na	na	na	na	na	na	na	na	na
Uganda	na	**na**	na	na	na	na	na	na	na	na	na	na	na	na	na	na
Ukraine	na	**9**	8	9	8	9	8	9	7	11	11	5	9	7	10	10
United States	na	**na**	na	na	na	na	na	na	na	na	na	na	na	na	na	na
Uruguay	na	**na**	na	na	na	na	na	na	na	na	na	na	na	na	na	na
Venezuela	na	**na**	na	na	na	na	na	na	na	na	na	na	na	na	na	na
Vietnam	na	**na**	na	na	na	na	na	na	na	na	na	na	na	na	na	na
Zimbabwe	na	**na**	na	na	na	na	na	na	na	na	na	na	na	na	na	na
Total	na	**24**	23	25	22	25	23	20	23	32	23	23	26	16	25	40

RANKING

Country	2000
Sweden	68
Italy	46
Luxembourg	41
Spain	35
Iceland	35
Ireland	35
Netherlands	34
Croatia	32
Denmark	30
Belgium	29
Greece	29
Slovenia	28
Malta	26
France	25
Northern Ireland	24
Germany	24
Finland	23
Romania	22
Slovakia	21
Portugal	20
Austria	20
Poland	16
Bulgaria	16
Czech Republic	15
Great Britain	14
Latvia	12
Russian Fed.	11
Estonia	9
Ukraine	9
Hungary	8
Lithuania	4
Belarus	1
Total	24

E167_1) PREPARED TO HELP SICK AND DISABLED

Would you be prepared to actually do something to improve the conditions of: Sick and disabled people in your country

Absolutely yes / Yes (%) (EVS: V280)

Country	Wave		Gender		Age			Education			Income			Values		
	1990	2000	Male	Female	16-29	30-49	50+	Lower	Middle	Upper	Lower	Middle	Upper	Mat	Mixed	Postm.
Albania	na	**na**	na	na	na	na	na	na	na	na	na	na	na	na	na	na
Algeria	na	**na**	na	na	na	na	na	na	na	na	na	na	na	na	na	na
Argentina	na	**na**	na	na	na	na	na	na	na	na	na	na	na	na	na	na
Armenia	na	**na**	na	na	na	na	na	na	na	na	na	na	na	na	na	na
Australia	na	**na**	na	na	na	na	na	na	na	na	na	na	na	na	na	na
Austria	na	**57**	56	58	52	59	59	57	58	57	53	60	60	55	56	62
Azerbaijan	na	**na**	na	na	na	na	na	na	na	na	na	na	na	na	na	na
Bangladesh	na	**na**	na	na	na	na	na	na	na	na	na	na	na	na	na	na
Belarus	na	**10**	9	10	10	10	9	5	11	10	8	11	10	7	12	13
Belgium	na	**68**	67	69	58	67	74	71	68	67	70	69	68	72	66	70
Bosnia and Herz.	na	**na**	na	na	na	na	na	na	na	na	na	na	na	na	na	na
Brazil	na	**na**	na	na	na	na	na	na	na	na	na	na	na	na	na	na
Bulgaria	na	**65**	61	69	55	69	67	68	62	68	58	69	71	58	72	74
Canada	na	**na**	na	na	na	na	na	na	na	na	na	na	na	na	na	na
Chile	na	**na**	na	na	na	na	na	na	na	na	na	na	na	na	na	na
China	na	**na**	na	na	na	na	na	na	na	na	na	na	na	na	na	na
Colombia	na	**na**	na	na	na	na	na	na	na	na	na	na	na	na	na	na
Croatia	na	**79**	76	83	78	82	78	80	78	84	92	76	76	75	79	80
Czech Republic	na	**76**	74	79	75	76	77	76	77	79	75	78	75	73	78	79
Denmark	na	**70**	69	71	63	69	75	69	69	73	68	72	72	63	72	76
Dominican Rep.	na	**na**	na	na	na	na	na	na	na	na	na	na	na	na	na	na
Egypt	na	**na**	na	na	na	na	na	na	na	na	na	na	na	na	na	na
El Salvador	na	**na**	na	na	na	na	na	na	na	na	na	na	na	na	na	na
Estonia	na	**40**	37	42	33	40	43	36	41	41	39	36	43	36	44	36
Finland	na	**73**	69	78	68	71	79	74	76	66	77	73	74	68	75	78
France	na	**62**	61	63	59	59	66	63	57	62	66	62	60	63	60	63
Georgia	na	**na**	na	na	na	na	na	na	na	na	na	na	na	na	na	na
Germany	na	**49**	44	52	42	49	51	43	50	61	44	48	55	43	50	54
Great Britain	na	**58**	56	61	46	58	65	58	57	56	62	57	59	na	na	na
Greece	na	**71**	69	72	66	71	82	76	72	69	72	71	68	68	70	75
Hungary	na	**60**	54	64	59	60	59	58	63	63	48	62	63	55	65	65
Iceland	na	**83**	80	86	77	84	87	83	82	83	87	81	82	80	84	84
India	na	**na**	na	na	na	na	na	na	na	na	na	na	na	na	na	na
Indonesia	na	**na**	na	na	na	na	na	na	na	na	na	na	na	na	na	na
Iran	na	**na**	na	na	na	na	na	na	na	na	na	na	na	na	na	na
Ireland	na	**81**	80	82	78	82	83	82	82	79	83	80	85	74	83	82
Israel	na	**na**	na	na	na	na	na	na	na	na	na	na	na	na	na	na
Italy	na	**82**	79	85	78	83	83	82	83	83	81	83	83	79	82	85
Japan	na	**na**	na	na	na	na	na	na	na	na	na	na	na	na	na	na
Jordan	na	**na**	na	na	na	na	na	na	na	na	na	na	na	na	na	na
Korea, South	na	**na**	na	na	na	na	na	na	na	na	na	na	na	na	na	na
Latvia	na	**59**	58	59	65	58	57	53	59	64	56	58	66	53	62	70
Lithuania	na	**35**	30	39	29	35	40	36	34	40	28	37	34	38	34	29
Luxembourg	na	**66**	63	68	56	65	72	61	67	70	60	69	69	65	62	79
Macedonia	na	**na**	na	na	na	na	na	na	na	na	na	na	na	na	na	na
Malta	na	**82**	83	81	78	84	84	82	82	85	83	88	81	80	84	78
Mexico	na	**na**	na	na	na	na	na	na	na	na	na	na	na	na	na	na
Moldova	na	**na**	na	na	na	na	na	na	na	na	na	na	na	na	na	na
Montenegro	na	**na**	na	na	na	na	na	na	na	na	na	na	na	na	na	na
Morocco	na	**na**	na	na	na	na	na	na	na	na	na	na	na	na	na	na
Netherlands	na	**66**	61	70	68	61	69	71	69	58	64	70	60	71	67	60
New Zealand	na	**na**	na	na	na	na	na	na	na	na	na	na	na	na	na	na
Nigeria	na	**na**	na	na	na	na	na	na	na	na	na	na	na	na	na	na
Northern Ireland	na	**66**	69	64	64	67	67	63	66	74	68	68	75	62	67	74
Norway	na	**na**	na	na	na	na	na	na	na	na	na	na	na	na	na	na
Pakistan	na	**na**	na	na	na	na	na	na	na	na	na	na	na	na	na	na
Peru	na	**na**	na	na	na	na	na	na	na	na	na	na	na	na	na	na
Philippines	na	**na**	na	na	na	na	na	na	na	na	na	na	na	na	na	na
Poland	na	**72**	73	70	69	73	71	70	75	72	70	73	71	68	72	78
Portugal	na	**65**	61	70	67	65	64	63	68	81	58	62	67	60	66	77
Puerto Rico	na	**na**	na	na	na	na	na	na	na	na	na	na	na	na	na	na
Romania	na	**64**	62	66	65	64	63	59	62	78	58	64	69	64	66	62
Russian Fed.	na	**49**	48	49	47	53	45	36	49	54	44	51	52	46	52	57
Serbia	na	**na**	na	na	na	na	na	na	na	na	na	na	na	na	na	na
Singapore	na	**na**	na	na	na	na	na	na	na	na	na	na	na	na	na	na
Slovakia	na	**72**	70	74	71	68	77	73	70	78	70	73	75	69	75	77
Slovenia	na	**71**	69	72	61	71	77	73	69	72	76	73	74	69	71	78
South Africa	na	**na**	na	na	na	na	na	na	na	na	na	na	na	na	na	na
Spain	na	**55**	52	57	55	56	53	51	55	65	58	54	55	53	54	62
Sweden	na	**88**	87	89	85	88	89	89	88	86	87	88	90	86	87	91
Switzerland	na	**na**	na	na	na	na	na	na	na	na	na	na	na	na	na	na
Taiwan	na	**na**	na	na	na	na	na	na	na	na	na	na	na	na	na	na
Tanzania	na	**na**	na	na	na	na	na	na	na	na	na	na	na	na	na	na
Turkey	na	**na**	na	na	na	na	na	na	na	na	na	na	na	na	na	na
Uganda	na	**na**	na	na	na	na	na	na	na	na	na	na	na	na	na	na
Ukraine	na	**41**	39	42	33	43	43	50	39	41	44	39	40	40	44	48
United States	na	**na**	na	na	na	na	na	na	na	na	na	na	na	na	na	na
Uruguay	na	**na**	na	na	na	na	na	na	na	na	na	na	na	na	na	na
Venezuela	na	**na**	na	na	na	na	na	na	na	na	na	na	na	na	na	na
Vietnam	na	**na**	na	na	na	na	na	na	na	na	na	na	na	na	na	na
Zimbabwe	na	**na**	na	na	na	na	na	na	na	na	na	na	na	na	na	na
Total	na	**64**	62	65	60	64	66	64	63	67	63	64	65	57	66	71

RANKING	
Country	2000
Sweden	88
Iceland	83
Italy	82
Malta	82
Ireland	81
Croatia	79
Czech Republic	76
Finland	73
Slovakia	72
Poland	72
Greece	71
Slovenia	71
Denmark	70
Belgium	68
Northern Ireland	66
Netherlands	66
Luxembourg	66
Portugal	65
Bulgaria	65
Romania	64
France	62
Hungary	60
Latvia	59
Great Britain	58
Austria	57
Spain	55
Russian Fed.	49
Germany	49
Ukraine	41
Estonia	40
Lithuania	35
Belarus	10
Total	64

E188_1) WATCH TV

Do you ever watch television? If yes: How much time do you usually spend watching television on an average weekday (NOT WEEKENDS)?

Less than 3 hours per day (%) (WVS: V237B)

	Wave		Gender		Age			Education			Income			Values		
Country	1990	2000	Male	Female	16-29	30-49	50+	Lower	Middle	Upper	Lower	Middle	Upper	Mat	Mixed	Postm.
Albania	na	**na**	na	na	na	na	na	na	na	na	na	na	na	na	na	na
Algeria	na	**70**	76	64	64	72	80	73	68	70	70	71	75	72	70	69
Argentina	na	**77**	79	75	66	83	81	77	74	83	77	74	80	76	74	82
Armenia	na	**42**	46	38	41	43	42	48	40	45	41	46	35	46	39	28
Australia	na	**70**	72	68	70	77	62	60	66	84	56	75	83	59	69	73
Austria	na	**na**	na	na	na	na	na	na	na	na	na	na	na	na	na	na
Azerbaijan	na	**48**	48	48	42	48	61	62	47	48	44	55	49	49	47	47
Bangladesh	na	**94**	94	94	94	94	95	96	92	91	92	94	96	95	94	88
Belarus	na	**na**	na	na	na	na	na	na	na	na	na	na	na	na	na	na
Belgium	na	**na**	na	na	na	na	na	na	na	na	na	na	na	na	na	na
Bosnia and Herz.	na	**na**	na	na	na	na	na	na	na	na	na	na	na	na	na	na
Brazil	na	**70**	72	69	65	75	71	73	66	76	71	69	70	68	73	65
Bulgaria	na	**na**	na	na	na	na	na	na	na	na	na	na	na	na	na	na
Canada	na	**na**	na	na	na	na	na	na	na	na	na	na	na	na	na	na
Chile	na	**na**	na	na	na	na	na	na	na	na	na	na	na	na	na	na
China	na	**na**	na	na	na	na	na	na	na	na	na	na	na	na	na	na
Colombia	na	**85**	86	83	79	87	88	86	80	89	87	82	87	84	83	78
Croatia	na	**na**	na	na	na	na	na	na	na	na	na	na	na	na	na	na
Czech Republic	na	**na**	na	na	na	na	na	na	na	na	na	na	na	na	na	na
Denmark	na	**na**	na	na	na	na	na	na	na	na	na	na	na	na	na	na
Dominican Rep.	na	**85**	87	84	82	91	91	78	76	89	86	85	89	87	85	85
Egypt	na	**78**	87	69	68	83	84	82	75	76	82	78	76	82	77	68
El Salvador	na	**81**	80	82	77	83	83	84	77	76	87	78	75	na	na	na
Estonia	na	**na**	na	na	na	na	na	na	na	na	na	na	na	na	na	na
Finland	na	**na**	na	na	na	na	na	na	na	na	na	na	na	na	na	na
France	na	**na**	na	na	na	na	na	na	na	na	na	na	na	na	na	na
Georgia	na	**100**	100	100	100	100	100	100	100	100	100	100	100	100	100	100
Germany	na	**na**	na	na	na	na	na	na	na	na	na	na	na	na	na	na
Great Britain	na	**na**	na	na	na	na	na	na	na	na	na	na	na	na	na	na
Greece	na	**na**	na	na	na	na	na	na	na	na	na	na	na	na	na	na
Hungary	na	**na**	na	na	na	na	na	na	na	na	na	na	na	na	na	na
Iceland	na	**na**	na	na	na	na	na	na	na	na	na	na	na	na	na	na
India	na	**na**	na	na	na	na	na	na	na	na	na	na	na	na	na	na
Indonesia	na	**76**	84	68	67	79	77	73	73	81	75	76	75	75	75	89
Iran	na	**na**	na	na	na	na	na	na	na	na	na	na	na	na	na	na
Ireland	na	**na**	na	na	na	na	na	na	na	na	na	na	na	na	na	na
Israel	na	**na**	na	na	na	na	na	na	na	na	na	na	na	na	na	na
Italy	na	**na**	na	na	na	na	na	na	na	na	na	na	na	na	na	na
Japan	na	**na**	na	na	na	na	na	na	na	na	na	na	na	na	na	na
Jordan	na	**73**	76	71	63	78	84	79	66	70	78	74	66	74	74	60
Korea, South	na	**na**	na	na	na	na	na	na	na	na	na	na	na	na	na	na
Latvia	na	**na**	na	na	na	na	na	na	na	na	na	na	na	na	na	na
Lithuania	na	**na**	na	na	na	na	na	na	na	na	na	na	na	na	na	na
Luxembourg	na	**na**	na	na	na	na	na	na	na	na	na	na	na	na	na	na
Macedonia	na	**na**	na	na	na	na	na	na	na	na	na	na	na	na	na	na
Malta	na	**na**	na	na	na	na	na	na	na	na	na	na	na	na	na	na
Mexico	na	**na**	na	na	na	na	na	na	na	na	na	na	na	na	na	na
Moldova	na	**na**	na	na	na	na	na	na	na	na	na	na	na	na	na	na
Montenegro	na	**na**	na	na	na	na	na	na	na	na	na	na	na	na	na	na
Morocco	na	**78**	85	71	75	81	79	76	86	86	93	84	74	80	77	78
Netherlands	na	**na**	na	na	na	na	na	na	na	na	na	na	na	na	na	na
New Zealand	na	**78**	80	77	79	83	73	71	81	85	69	80	89	77	80	79
Nigeria	na	**75**	75	75	70	81	86	86	72	63	84	74	65	79	74	71
Northern Ireland	na	**na**	na	na	na	na	na	na	na	na	na	na	na	na	na	na
Norway	na	**87**	86	87	85	89	85	81	87	92	na	na	na	80	87	93
Pakistan	na	**93**	92	93	88	94	99	95	88	94	95	92	91	94	91	91
Peru	na	**80**	80	79	73	83	86	83	78	80	83	76	79	80	79	79
Philippines	na	**na**	na	na	na	na	na	na	na	na	na	na	na	na	na	na
Poland	na	**na**	na	na	na	na	na	na	na	na	na	na	na	na	na	na
Portugal	na	**na**	na	na	na	na	na	na	na	na	na	na	na	na	na	na
Puerto Rico	na	**78**	80	77	77	80	77	72	72	82	70	80	83	74	78	80
Romania	na	**na**	na	na	na	na	na	na	na	na	na	na	na	na	na	na
Russian Fed.	na	**na**	na	na	na	na	na	na	na	na	na	na	na	na	na	na
Serbia	na	**na**	na	na	na	na	na	na	na	na	na	na	na	na	na	na
Singapore	na	**na**	na	na	na	na	na	na	na	na	na	na	na	na	na	na
Slovakia	na	**na**	na	na	na	na	na	na	na	na	na	na	na	na	na	na
Slovenia	na	**na**	na	na	na	na	na	na	na	na	na	na	na	na	na	na
South Africa	na	**68**	69	67	57	77	72	72	62	79	74	61	72	67	69	66
Spain	na	**79**	78	80	85	84	71	72	87	94	62	81	86	78	79	83
Sweden	na	**na**	na	na	na	na	na	na	na	na	na	na	na	na	na	na
Switzerland	na	**93**	93	93	94	94	92	89	94	98	87	94	96	92	93	94
Taiwan	na	**76**	80	73	64	78	79	75	68	82	75	74	78	76	76	83
Tanzania	na	**na**	na	na	na	na	na	na	na	na	na	na	na	na	na	na
Turkey	na	**na**	na	na	na	na	na	na	na	na	na	na	na	na	na	na
Uganda	na	**88**	95	81	82	93	99	91	86	96	93	96	89	87	88	90
Ukraine	na	**na**	na	na	na	na	na	na	na	na	na	na	na	na	na	na
United States	na	**na**	na	na	na	na	na	na	na	na	na	na	na	na	na	na
Uruguay	na	**70**	72	69	73	76	65	67	71	88	72	70	72	68	70	76
Venezuela	na	**na**	na	na	na	na	na	na	na	na	na	na	na	na	na	na
Vietnam	na	**na**	na	na	na	na	na	na	na	na	na	na	na	na	na	na
Zimbabwe	na	**88**	88	87	83	90	93	94	79	62	95	91	73	86	89	92
Total	na	78	80	76	73	81	78	80	74	80	77	78	78	77	78	78

RANKING

Country	2000
Georgia	100
Bangladesh	94
Switzerland	93
Pakistan	93
Uganda	88
Zimbabwe	88
Norway	87
Dominican Rep.	85
Colombia	85
El Salvador	81
Peru	80
Spain	79
Egypt	78
Morocco	78
New Zealand	78
Puerto Rico	78
Argentina	77
Taiwan	76
Indonesia	76
Nigeria	75
Jordan	73
Algeria	70
Brazil	70
Uruguay	70
Australia	70
South Africa	68
Azerbaijan	48
Armenia	42
Total	78

E189) TV MOST IMPORTANT ENTERTAINMENT

Do you agree strongly, agree, disagree or disagree strongly with the following statement: "Television is my most important form of entertainment."

(WVS: V237)

Strongly agree / Agree (%)

Country	Wave		Gender		Age			Education			Income			Values		
	1990	2000	Male	Female	16-29	30-49	50+	Lower	Middle	Upper	Lower	Middle	Upper	Mat	Mixed	Postm.
Albania	na	**57**	54	61	50	55	67	67	54	42	65	55	51	57	55	51
Algeria	na	**42**	37	47	41	41	47	56	43	31	47	44	30	47	40	29
Argentina	na	**na**	na	na	na	na	na	na	na	na	na	na	na	na	na	na
Armenia	na	**na**	na	na	na	na	na	na	na	na	na	na	na	na	na	na
Australia	na	**na**	na	na	na	na	na	na	na	na	na	na	na	na	na	na
Austria	na	**na**	na	na	na	na	na	na	na	na	na	na	na	na	na	na
Azerbaijan	na	**na**	na	na	na	na	na	na	na	na	na	na	na	na	na	na
Bangladesh	na	**89**	91	86	85	90	96	92	86	84	98	90	79	87	89	88
Belarus	na	**na**	na	na	na	na	na	na	na	na	na	na	na	na	na	na
Belgium	na	**na**	na	na	na	na	na	na	na	na	na	na	na	na	na	na
Bosnia and Herz.	na	**39**	37	41	31	35	53	56	40	22	46	39	32	40	39	43
Brazil	na	**na**	na	na	na	na	na	na	na	na	na	na	na	na	na	na
Bulgaria	na	**na**	na	na	na	na	na	na	na	na	na	na	na	na	na	na
Canada	na	**33**	35	31	27	29	41	45	34	21	42	36	22	43	36	26
Chile	na	**52**	54	50	48	51	58	63	49	38	61	45	50	52	53	46
China	na	**62**	60	64	54	63	67	63	62	48	60	65	62	63	62	42
Colombia	na	**na**	na	na	na	na	na	na	na	na	na	na	na	na	na	na
Croatia	na	**na**	na	na	na	na	na	na	na	na	na	na	na	na	na	na
Czech Republic	na	**na**	na	na	na	na	na	na	na	na	na	na	na	na	na	na
Denmark	na	**na**	na	na	na	na	na	na	na	na	na	na	na	na	na	na
Dominican Rep.	na	**na**	na	na	na	na	na	na	na	na	na	na	na	na	na	na
Egypt	na	**61**	52	70	62	62	58	65	59	52	61	66	58	63	61	54
El Salvador	na	**na**	na	na	na	na	na	na	na	na	na	na	na	na	na	na
Estonia	na	**na**	na	na	na	na	na	na	na	na	na	na	na	na	na	na
Finland	na	**na**	na	na	na	na	na	na	na	na	na	na	na	na	na	na
France	na	**na**	na	na	na	na	na	na	na	na	na	na	na	na	na	na
Georgia	na	**na**	na	na	na	na	na	na	na	na	na	na	na	na	na	na
Germany	na	**na**	na	na	na	na	na	na	na	na	na	na	na	na	na	na
Great Britain	na	**na**	na	na	na	na	na	na	na	na	na	na	na	na	na	na
Greece	na	**na**	na	na	na	na	na	na	na	na	na	na	na	na	na	na
Hungary	na	**na**	na	na	na	na	na	na	na	na	na	na	na	na	na	na
Iceland	na	**na**	na	na	na	na	na	na	na	na	na	na	na	na	na	na
India	na	**63**	63	64	70	64	54	54	75	69	52	61	70	66	63	67
Indonesia	na	**69**	67	71	65	69	71	82	71	57	73	69	60	77	64	57
Iran	na	**na**	na	na	na	na	na	na	na	na	na	na	na	na	na	na
Ireland	na	**na**	na	na	na	na	na	na	na	na	na	na	na	na	na	na
Israel	na	**na**	na	na	na	na	na	na	na	na	na	na	na	na	na	na
Italy	na	**na**	na	na	na	na	na	na	na	na	na	na	na	na	na	na
Japan	na	**69**	67	71	72	63	73	82	70	57	76	67	62	73	68	58
Jordan	na	**41**	34	47	44	37	41	44	40	36	35	44	47	40	41	38
Korea, South	na	**na**	na	na	na	na	na	na	na	na	na	na	na	na	na	na
Latvia	na	**na**	na	na	na	na	na	na	na	na	na	na	na	na	na	na
Lithuania	na	**na**	na	na	na	na	na	na	na	na	na	na	na	na	na	na
Luxembourg	na	**na**	na	na	na	na	na	na	na	na	na	na	na	na	na	na
Macedonia	na	**52**	51	54	46	45	68	71	46	39	63	50	40	54	51	52
Malta	na	**na**	na	na	na	na	na	na	na	na	na	na	na	na	na	na
Mexico	na	**52**	51	53	47	55	54	61	44	33	54	48	48	59	50	41
Moldova	na	**55**	58	53	46	54	64	59	63	38	62	55	52	57	55	48
Montenegro	na	**44**	44	45	32	40	56	59	38	30	59	45	36	48	39	40
Morocco	na	**48**	41	55	46	50	52	54	30	20	47	40	52	49	48	45
Netherlands	na	**na**	na	na	na	na	na	na	na	na	na	na	na	na	na	na
New Zealand	na	**na**	na	na	na	na	na	na	na	na	na	na	na	na	na	na
Nigeria	na	**76**	77	75	80	72	65	71	79	78	73	76	79	73	77	82
Northern Ireland	na	**na**	na	na	na	na	na	na	na	na	na	na	na	na	na	na
Norway	na	**na**	na	na	na	na	na	na	na	na	na	na	na	na	na	na
Pakistan	na	**na**	na	na	na	na	na	na	na	na	na	na	na	na	na	na
Peru	na	**na**	na	na	na	na	na	na	na	na	na	na	na	na	na	na
Philippines	na	**64**	63	65	66	64	62	61	66	64	61	61	71	66	63	60
Poland	na	**na**	na	na	na	na	na	na	na	na	na	na	na	na	na	na
Portugal	na	**na**	na	na	na	na	na	na	na	na	na	na	na	na	na	na
Puerto Rico	na	**na**	na	na	na	na	na	na	na	na	na	na	na	na	na	na
Romania	na	**na**	na	na	na	na	na	na	na	na	na	na	na	na	na	na
Russian Fed.	na	**na**	na	na	na	na	na	na	na	na	na	na	na	na	na	na
Serbia	na	**44**	41	47	32	38	55	66	38	25	53	39	38	55	35	23
Singapore	na	**54**	50	59	52	53	69	64	53	35	66	56	45	56	54	44
Slovakia	na	**na**	na	na	na	na	na	na	na	na	na	na	na	na	na	na
Slovenia	na	**na**	na	na	na	na	na	na	na	na	na	na	na	na	na	na
South Africa	na	**na**	na	na	na	na	na	na	na	na	na	na	na	na	na	na
Spain	na	**na**	na	na	na	na	na	na	na	na	na	na	na	na	na	na
Sweden	na	**29**	31	26	23	24	36	43	25	22	33	28	23	37	30	19
Switzerland	na	**na**	na	na	na	na	na	na	na	na	na	na	na	na	na	na
Taiwan	na	**na**	na	na	na	na	na	na	na	na	na	na	na	na	na	na
Tanzania	na	**55**	54	57	59	52	57	62	54	39	61	54	51	58	53	70
Turkey	na	**na**	na	na	na	na	na	na	na	na	na	na	na	na	na	na
Uganda	na	**45**	44	45	53	39	23	30	52	36	36	48	56	46	45	39
Ukraine	na	**na**	na	na	na	na	na	na	na	na	na	na	na	na	na	na
United States	na	**28**	30	25	23	26	33	35	29	24	33	25	24	35	28	23
Uruguay	na	**na**	na	na	na	na	na	na	na	na	na	na	na	na	na	na
Venezuela	na	**52**	52	52	51	51	56	59	54	38	61	50	47	57	51	46
Vietnam	na	**93**	94	91	91	94	91	92	95	85	90	93	94	95	93	93
Zimbabwe	na	**50**	49	51	59	43	38	43	59	31	41	51	63	45	53	60
Total	na	**54**	53	55	53	53	57	61	54	42	57	55	52	58	53	42

RANKING	
Country	2000
Vietnam	93
Bangladesh	89
Nigeria	76
Japan	69
Indonesia	69
Philippines	64
India	63
China	62
Egypt	61
Albania	57
Tanzania	55
Moldova	55
Singapore	54
Macedonia	52
Chile	52
Mexico	52
Venezuela	52
Zimbabwe	50
Morocco	48
Uganda	45
Serbia	44
Montenegro	44
Algeria	42
Jordan	41
Bosnia and Herz.	39
Canada	33
Sweden	29
United States	28
Total	54

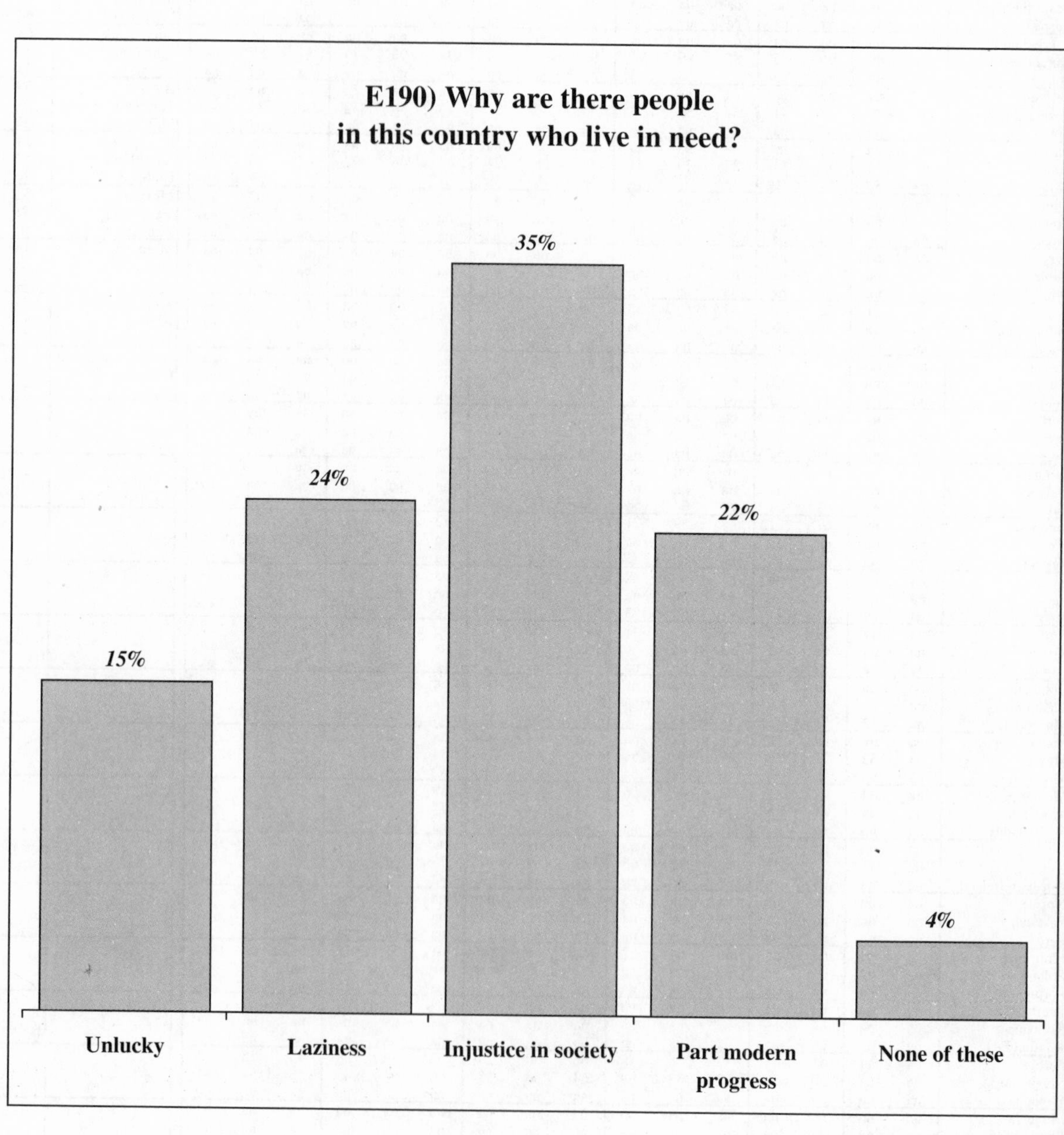
E190) Why are there people
in this country who live in need?
15%
24%
35%
22%
4%
Unlucky
Laziness
Injustice in society
Part modern
progress
None of these

E190_3) WHY ARE THERE PEOPLE LIVING IN NEED: FIRST

Why are there people in this country who live in need? Here are four possible reasons. Which one reason do you consider to be most important?

Injustice in society (%) (EVS: V69)

Country	Wave 1990	Wave 2000	Gender Male	Gender Female	Age 16-29	Age 30-49	Age 50+	Education Lower	Education Middle	Education Upper	Income Lower	Income Middle	Income Upper	Values Mat	Values Mixed	Values Postm.
Albania	na	**na**	na	na	na	na	na	na	na	na	na	na	na	na	na	na
Algeria	na	**na**	na	na	na	na	na	na	na	na	na	na	na	na	na	na
Argentina	49	**na**	na	na	na	na	na	na	na	na	na	na	na	na	na	na
Armenia	na	**na**	na	na	na	na	na	na	na	na	na	na	na	na	na	na
Australia	na	**na**	na	na	na	na	na	na	na	na	na	na	na	na	na	na
Austria	25	**22**	20	23	20	25	20	19	22	32	22	24	23	14	21	25
Azerbaijan	na	**na**	na	na	na	na	na	na	na	na	na	na	na	na	na	na
Bangladesh	na	**na**	na	na	na	na	na	na	na	na	na	na	na	na	na	na
Belarus	60	**46**	43	48	42	49	46	48	47	39	51	44	40	49	46	40
Belgium	33	**34**	33	35	41	37	27	30	36	34	32	35	34	31	30	48
Bosnia and Herz.	na	**na**	na	na	na	na	na	na	na	na	na	na	na	na	na	na
Brazil	40	**na**	na	na	na	na	na	na	na	na	na	na	na	na	na	na
Bulgaria	52	**50**	47	53	46	45	56	59	46	44	58	49	46	60	41	31
Canada	32	**na**	na	na	na	na	na	na	na	na	na	na	na	na	na	na
Chile	41	**na**	na	na	na	na	na	na	na	na	na	na	na	na	na	na
China	36	**na**	na	na	na	na	na	na	na	na	na	na	na	na	na	na
Colombia	na	**na**	na	na	na	na	na	na	na	na	na	na	na	na	na	na
Croatia	na	**70**	69	71	68	68	72	74	67	64	79	72	63	60	70	78
Czech Republic	27	**19**	19	18	16	17	22	20	18	16	23	20	13	23	18	14
Denmark	29	**17**	15	19	15	19	16	16	17	18	18	16	16	17	15	28
Dominican Rep.	na	**na**	na	na	na	na	na	na	na	na	na	na	na	na	na	na
Egypt	na	**na**	na	na	na	na	na	na	na	na	na	na	na	na	na	na
El Salvador	na	**na**	na	na	na	na	na	na	na	na	na	na	na	na	na	na
Estonia	57	**42**	39	44	30	41	49	46	41	37	51	47	34	48	39	39
Finland	20	**24**	20	27	25	25	22	26	22	19	26	25	24	23	24	35
France	42	**44**	41	47	46	47	41	43	42	50	45	46	44	40	44	52
Georgia	na	**na**	na	na	na	na	na	na	na	na	na	na	na	na	na	na
Germany	47	**37**	38	36	35	40	34	34	39	44	43	34	34	38	34	47
Great Britain	34	**31**	29	32	37	33	24	25	35	35	29	33	32	na	na	na
Greece	na	**24**	24	24	26	24	20	16	29	22	28	21	21	21	25	25
Hungary	39	**38**	38	37	34	42	36	39	40	24	42	41	32	38	38	34
Iceland	27	**30**	27	32	28	30	31	31	25	34	35	30	25	29	27	47
India	33	**na**	na	na	na	na	na	na	na	na	na	na	na	na	na	na
Indonesia	na	**na**	na	na	na	na	na	na	na	na	na	na	na	na	na	na
Iran	na	**na**	na	na	na	na	na	na	na	na	na	na	na	na	na	na
Ireland	36	**33**	30	36	35	31	32	26	35	41	31	37	35	28	33	39
Israel	na	**na**	na	na	na	na	na	na	na	na	na	na	na	na	na	na
Italy	43	**38**	36	39	40	39	35	35	40	40	35	40	39	30	37	45
Japan	29	**na**	na	na	na	na	na	na	na	na	na	na	na	na	na	na
Jordan	na	**na**	na	na	na	na	na	na	na	na	na	na	na	na	na	na
Korea, South	35	**na**	na	na	na	na	na	na	na	na	na	na	na	na	na	na
Latvia	65	**32**	34	31	27	33	34	35	33	29	36	34	26	34	32	33
Lithuania	51	**50**	50	50	43	53	52	48	53	38	64	48	47	49	54	35
Luxembourg	na	**23**	21	26	25	24	21	21	23	28	20	25	26	16	22	35
Macedonia	na	**na**	na	na	na	na	na	na	na	na	na	na	na	na	na	na
Malta	na	**24**	25	23	28	22	23	24	24	24	26	23	19	22	24	29
Mexico	32	**na**	na	na	na	na	na	na	na	na	na	na	na	na	na	na
Moldova	na	**na**	na	na	na	na	na	na	na	na	na	na	na	na	na	na
Montenegro	na	**na**	na	na	na	na	na	na	na	na	na	na	na	na	na	na
Morocco	na	**na**	na	na	na	na	na	na	na	na	na	na	na	na	na	na
Netherlands	39	**25**	22	28	22	26	26	28	23	25	27	30	15	23	23	35
New Zealand	na	**na**	na	na	na	na	na	na	na	na	na	na	na	na	na	na
Nigeria	48	**na**	na	na	na	na	na	na	na	na	na	na	na	na	na	na
Northern Ireland	25	**28**	25	31	32	32	21	27	28	29	21	25	29	21	28	40
Norway	49	**na**	na	na	na	na	na	na	na	na	na	na	na	na	na	na
Pakistan	na	**na**	na	na	na	na	na	na	na	na	na	na	na	na	na	na
Peru	na	**na**	na	na	na	na	na	na	na	na	na	na	na	na	na	na
Philippines	na	**na**	na	na	na	na	na	na	na	na	na	na	na	na	na	na
Poland	59	**50**	52	49	50	52	50	53	49	43	58	46	46	49	52	48
Portugal	39	**22**	21	22	26	23	18	17	33	24	14	23	22	18	22	32
Puerto Rico	na	**na**	na	na	na	na	na	na	na	na	na	na	na	na	na	na
Romania	36	**43**	44	43	40	46	42	40	47	41	40	46	46	44	44	37
Russian Fed.	50	**22**	22	22	16	19	30	30	23	17	25	25	17	26	19	9
Serbia	na	**na**	na	na	na	na	na	na	na	na	na	na	na	na	na	na
Singapore	na	**na**	na	na	na	na	na	na	na	na	na	na	na	na	na	na
Slovakia	na	**37**	40	35	35	39	36	35	40	29	40	37	34	41	36	34
Slovenia	44	**35**	37	34	37	35	35	36	39	20	42	37	25	37	35	37
South Africa	58	**na**	na	na	na	na	na	na	na	na	na	na	na	na	na	na
Spain	44	**48**	47	50	56	50	43	44	50	57	47	44	48	40	50	58
Sweden	35	**50**	46	53	51	46	51	55	47	50	51	49	48	40	47	61
Switzerland	na	**na**	na	na	na	na	na	na	na	na	na	na	na	na	na	na
Taiwan	na	**na**	na	na	na	na	na	na	na	na	na	na	na	na	na	na
Tanzania	na	**na**	na	na	na	na	na	na	na	na	na	na	na	na	na	na
Turkey	37	**67**	68	66	70	66	57	64	70	69	67	66	69	64	66	74
Uganda	na	**na**	na	na	na	na	na	na	na	na	na	na	na	na	na	na
Ukraine	na	**26**	24	27	24	24	29	34	26	22	30	27	21	28	25	29
United States	33	**na**	na	na	na	na	na	na	na	na	na	na	na	na	na	na
Uruguay	na	**na**	na	na	na	na	na	na	na	na	na	na	na	na	na	na
Venezuela	na	**na**	na	na	na	na	na	na	na	na	na	na	na	na	na	na
Vietnam	na	**na**	na	na	na	na	na	na	na	na	na	na	na	na	na	na
Zimbabwe	na	**na**	na	na	na	na	na	na	na	na	na	na	na	na	na	na
Total	40	35	34	36	34	36	34	35	36	32	38	36	32	36	34	41

RANKING

Country	2000
Croatia	70
Turkey	67
Poland	50
Lithuania	50
Bulgaria	50
Sweden	50
Spain	48
Belarus	46
France	44
Romania	43
Estonia	42
Italy	38
Hungary	38
Slovakia	37
Germany	37
Slovenia	35
Belgium	34
Ireland	33
Latvia	32
Great Britain	31
Iceland	30
Northern Ireland	28
Ukraine	26
Netherlands	25
Greece	24
Finland	24
Malta	24
Luxembourg	23
Russian Fed.	22
Austria	22
Portugal	22
Czech Republic	19
Denmark	17
Total	35

E190_2) WHY ARE THERE PEOPLE LIVING IN NEED: FIRST

Why are there people in this country who live in need? Here are four possible reasons. Which one reason do you consider to be most important?

Laziness or lack of willpower (%)

(EVS: V69

Country	Wave 1990	Wave 2000	Gender Male	Gender Female	Age 16-29	Age 30-49	Age 50+	Education Lower	Education Middle	Education Upper	Income Lower	Income Middle	Income Upper	Values Mat	Values Mixed	Values Postm.
Albania	na	**na**	na	na	na	na	na	na	na	na	na	na	na	na	na	na
Algeria	na	**na**	na	na	na	na	na	na	na	na	na	na	na	na	na	na
Argentina	34	**na**	na	na	na	na	na	na	na	na	na	na	na	na	na	na
Armenia	na	**na**	na	na	na	na	na	na	na	na	na	na	na	na	na	na
Australia	na	**na**	na	na	na	na	na	na	na	na	na	na	na	na	na	na
Austria	37	**32**	34	31	33	27	37	40	29	14	35	33	31	42	35	25
Azerbaijan	na	**na**	na	na	na	na	na	na	na	na	na	na	na	na	na	na
Bangladesh	na	**na**	na	na	na	na	na	na	na	na	na	na	na	na	na	na
Belarus	27	**21**	26	18	24	20	21	19	22	22	14	21	34	19	22	40
Belgium	22	**18**	18	17	17	15	21	24	18	13	25	16	13	21	19	7
Bosnia and Herz.	na	**na**	na	na	na	na	na	na	na	na	na	na	na	na	na	na
Brazil	27	**na**	na	na	na	na	na	na	na	na	na	na	na	na	na	na
Bulgaria	27	**15**	17	14	13	15	16	14	16	15	14	13	17	13	18	17
Canada	32	**na**	na	na	na	na	na	na	na	na	na	na	na	na	na	na
Chile	35	**na**	na	na	na	na	na	na	na	na	na	na	na	na	na	na
China	12	**na**	na	na	na	na	na	na	na	na	na	na	na	na	na	na
Colombia	na	**na**	na	na	na	na	na	na	na	na	na	na	na	na	na	na
Croatia	na	**12**	11	12	10	12	14	11	13	10	10	9	15	18	12	7
Czech Republic	43	**43**	45	42	42	43	43	44	41	45	41	43	44	47	44	34
Denmark	14	**17**	21	13	25	16	15	21	15	12	16	18	18	28	19	5
Dominican Rep.	na	**na**	na	na	na	na	na	na	na	na	na	na	na	na	na	na
Egypt	na	**na**	na	na	na	na	na	na	na	na	na	na	na	na	na	na
El Salvador	na	**na**	na	na	na	na	na	na	na	na	na	na	na	na	na	na
Estonia	24	**15**	15	15	15	16	15	16	15	14	10	16	17	16	14	19
Finland	26	**23**	25	21	27	17	27	25	23	14	21	26	20	29	21	18
France	15	**11**	14	9	11	8	15	13	11	7	13	11	12	13	13	5
Georgia	na	**na**	na	na	na	na	na	na	na	na	na	na	na	na	na	na
Germany	29	**28**	30	27	19	28	33	33	25	22	28	30	25	33	31	15
Great Britain	27	**25**	28	22	17	20	34	29	21	21	24	24	17	na	na	na
Greece	na	**23**	24	22	15	25	34	36	26	18	24	24	21	29	22	19
Hungary	34	**28**	25	30	26	21	34	30	23	26	28	29	25	32	25	5
Iceland	23	**22**	29	16	30	20	19	22	26	16	24	20	24	28	22	14
India	40	**na**	na	na	na	na	na	na	na	na	na	na	na	na	na	na
Indonesia	na	**na**	na	na	na	na	na	na	na	na	na	na	na	na	na	na
Iran	na	**na**	na	na	na	na	na	na	na	na	na	na	na	na	na	na
Ireland	21	**21**	22	20	17	20	25	26	18	16	22	23	19	22	21	19
Israel	na	**na**	na	na	na	na	na	na	na	na	na	na	na	na	na	na
Italy	30	**23**	24	22	19	21	27	27	22	16	24	24	20	32	24	16
Japan	33	**na**	na	na	na	na	na	na	na	na	na	na	na	na	na	na
Jordan	na	**na**	na	na	na	na	na	na	na	na	na	na	na	na	na	na
Korea, South	36	**na**	na	na	na	na	na	na	na	na	na	na	na	na	na	na
Latvia	17	**29**	30	29	33	27	29	30	30	25	28	32	29	26	30	31
Lithuania	25	**10**	11	9	10	8	12	13	9	11	8	12	9	11	9	12
Luxembourg	na	**23**	23	22	23	20	25	26	24	12	25	22	17	29	23	14
Macedonia	na	**na**	na	na	na	na	na	na	na	na	na	na	na	na	na	na
Malta	na	**50**	50	51	49	53	49	48	52	46	51	52	58	54	48	52
Mexico	39	**na**	na	na	na	na	na	na	na	na	na	na	na	na	na	na
Moldova	na	**na**	na	na	na	na	na	na	na	na	na	na	na	na	na	na
Montenegro	na	**na**	na	na	na	na	na	na	na	na	na	na	na	na	na	na
Morocco	na	**na**	na	na	na	na	na	na	na	na	na	na	na	na	na	na
Netherlands	14	**15**	18	12	25	12	12	19	16	9	19	13	10	24	16	7
New Zealand	na	**na**	na	na	na	na	na	na	na	na	na	na	na	na	na	na
Nigeria	24	**na**	na	na	na	na	na	na	na	na	na	na	na	na	na	na
Northern Ireland	32	**29**	29	29	31	25	32	30	29	27	29	31	25	37	29	16
Norway	11	**na**	na	na	na	na	na	na	na	na	na	na	na	na	na	na
Pakistan	na	**na**	na	na	na	na	na	na	na	na	na	na	na	na	na	na
Peru	na	**na**	na	na	na	na	na	na	na	na	na	na	na	na	na	na
Philippines	na	**na**	na	na	na	na	na	na	na	na	na	na	na	na	na	na
Poland	20	**23**	23	22	24	19	27	24	20	22	19	24	27	26	20	26
Portugal	24	**42**	45	40	37	44	44	45	37	28	48	37	42	45	42	35
Puerto Rico	na	**na**	na	na	na	na	na	na	na	na	na	na	na	na	na	na
Romania	34	**30**	31	29	22	26	38	38	27	24	35	33	25	33	28	20
Russian Fed.	34	**23**	25	22	27	23	20	23	23	24	17	23	27	22	24	29
Serbia	na	**na**	na	na	na	na	na	na	na	na	na	na	na	na	na	na
Singapore	na	**na**	na	na	na	na	na	na	na	na	na	na	na	na	na	na
Slovakia	na	**31**	30	33	28	30	35	33	30	31	31	30	34	33	31	29
Slovenia	24	**33**	33	33	31	33	35	35	33	30	29	34	35	35	35	25
South Africa	22	**na**	na	na	na	na	na	na	na	na	na	na	na	na	na	na
Spain	24	**20**	20	19	20	16	23	23	17	17	22	22	18	23	20	14
Sweden	16	**7**	10	4	8	9	5	5	8	7	7	9	6	15	8	2
Switzerland	na	**na**	na	na	na	na	na	na	na	na	na	na	na	na	na	na
Taiwan	na	**na**	na	na	na	na	na	na	na	na	na	na	na	na	na	na
Tanzania	na	**na**	na	na	na	na	na	na	na	na	na	na	na	na	na	na
Turkey	39	**23**	23	22	21	22	30	23	21	22	21	23	23	24	24	18
Uganda	na	**na**	na	na	na	na	na	na	na	na	na	na	na	na	na	na
Ukraine	na	**17**	16	18	19	17	16	17	17	17	15	14	23	16	19	23
United States	40	**na**	na	na	na	na	na	na	na	na	na	na	na	na	na	na
Uruguay	na	**na**	na	na	na	na	na	na	na	na	na	na	na	na	na	na
Venezuela	na	**na**	na	na	na	na	na	na	na	na	na	na	na	na	na	na
Vietnam	na	**na**	na	na	na	na	na	na	na	na	na	na	na	na	na	na
Zimbabwe	na	**na**	na	na	na	na	na	na	na	na	na	na	na	na	na	na
Total	27	**24**	25	23	23	22	26	27	23	18	23	23	23	27	24	17

RANKING

Country	2000
Malta	50
Czech Republic	43
Portugal	42
Slovenia	33
Austria	32
Slovakia	31
Romania	30
Latvia	29
Northern Ireland	29
Germany	28
Hungary	28
Great Britain	25
Finland	23
Italy	23
Russian Fed.	23
Greece	23
Poland	23
Luxembourg	23
Turkey	23
Iceland	22
Belarus	21
Ireland	21
Spain	20
Belgium	18
Denmark	17
Ukraine	17
Estonia	15
Bulgaria	15
Netherlands	15
Croatia	12
France	11
Lithuania	10
Sweden	7
Total	24

E191_1) WHY ARE THERE PEOPLE LIVING IN NEED: SECOND

And which reason do you consider to be the second most important?

Unlucky (%) (EVS: V70)

Country	Wave		Gender		Age			Education			Income			Values		
	1990	2000	Male	Female	16-29	30-49	50+	Lower	Middle	Upper	Lower	Middle	Upper	Mat	Mixed	Postm.
Albania	na	**na**	na	na	na	na	na	na	na	na	na	na	na	na	na	na
Algeria	na	**na**	na	na	na	na	na	na	na	na	na	na	na	na	na	na
Argentina	na	**na**	na	na	na	na	na	na	na	na	na	na	na	na	na	na
Armenia	na	**na**	na	na	na	na	na	na	na	na	na	na	na	na	na	na
Australia	na	**na**	na	na	na	na	na	na	na	na	na	na	na	na	na	na
Austria	na	**16**	17	16	14	16	18	17	16	17	19	15	16	16	18	14
Azerbaijan	na	**na**	na	na	na	na	na	na	na	na	na	na	na	na	na	na
Bangladesh	na	**na**	na	na	na	na	na	na	na	na	na	na	na	na	na	na
Belarus	na	**18**	18	18	14	19	19	23	17	13	20	18	14	20	17	19
Belgium	na	**30**	31	29	30	28	32	31	29	30	27	29	31	28	32	29
Bosnia and Herz.	na	**na**	na	na	na	na	na	na	na	na	na	na	na	na	na	na
Brazil	na	**na**	na	na	na	na	na	na	na	na	na	na	na	na	na	na
Bulgaria	na	**21**	17	25	20	18	25	32	17	14	29	21	17	27	16	17
Canada	na	**na**	na	na	na	na	na	na	na	na	na	na	na	na	na	na
Chile	na	**na**	na	na	na	na	na	na	na	na	na	na	na	na	na	na
China	na	**na**	na	na	na	na	na	na	na	na	na	na	na	na	na	na
Colombia	na	**na**	na	na	na	na	na	na	na	na	na	na	na	na	na	na
Croatia	na	**13**	11	16	8	13	18	13	13	14	13	14	12	20	12	13
Czech Republic	na	**27**	29	26	27	23	32	28	27	27	26	30	26	27	26	34
Denmark	na	**23**	23	23	24	17	28	24	23	22	24	24	21	31	23	21
Dominican Rep.	na	**na**	na	na	na	na	na	na	na	na	na	na	na	na	na	na
Egypt	na	**na**	na	na	na	na	na	na	na	na	na	na	na	na	na	na
El Salvador	na	**na**	na	na	na	na	na	na	na	na	na	na	na	na	na	na
Estonia	na	**24**	25	23	20	24	26	26	22	25	27	28	19	26	22	28
Finland	na	**23**	22	25	23	20	26	24	23	23	29	20	20	23	23	28
France	na	**21**	19	23	19	20	23	21	21	21	21	23	21	21	21	21
Georgia	na	**na**	na	na	na	na	na	na	na	na	na	na	na	na	na	na
Germany	na	**22**	20	24	24	22	21	23	23	15	25	20	20	24	22	21
Great Britain	na	**20**	22	19	24	19	19	18	19	26	17	19	23	na	na	na
Greece	na	**15**	15	15	15	16	13	18	14	16	14	14	15	19	14	15
Hungary	na	**24**	27	23	24	24	26	25	23	25	26	25	23	28	22	14
Iceland	na	**28**	28	29	20	29	34	28	28	28	30	28	26	35	26	30
India	na	**na**	na	na	na	na	na	na	na	na	na	na	na	na	na	na
Indonesia	na	**na**	na	na	na	na	na	na	na	na	na	na	na	na	na	na
Iran	na	**na**	na	na	na	na	na	na	na	na	na	na	na	na	na	na
Ireland	na	**25**	27	24	23	26	25	27	24	24	27	23	25	24	28	16
Israel	na	**na**	na	na	na	na	na	na	na	na	na	na	na	na	na	na
Italy	na	**22**	20	24	20	21	25	25	20	19	21	26	19	27	24	17
Japan	na	**na**	na	na	na	na	na	na	na	na	na	na	na	na	na	na
Jordan	na	**na**	na	na	na	na	na	na	na	na	na	na	na	na	na	na
Korea, South	na	**na**	na	na	na	na	na	na	na	na	na	na	na	na	na	na
Latvia	na	**19**	20	18	18	19	19	19	19	21	20	18	18	22	17	21
Lithuania	na	**21**	23	19	23	21	20	22	22	16	21	15	24	23	20	25
Luxembourg	na	**26**	26	26	23	26	27	27	24	28	27	29	26	28	24	32
Macedonia	na	**na**	na	na	na	na	na	na	na	na	na	na	na	na	na	na
Malta	na	**18**	18	17	18	17	17	18	19	8	18	12	18	21	16	13
Mexico	na	**na**	na	na	na	na	na	na	na	na	na	na	na	na	na	na
Moldova	na	**na**	na	na	na	na	na	na	na	na	na	na	na	na	na	na
Montenegro	na	**na**	na	na	na	na	na	na	na	na	na	na	na	na	na	na
Morocco	na	**na**	na	na	na	na	na	na	na	na	na	na	na	na	na	na
Netherlands	na	**31**	32	29	30	30	31	30	32	29	31	32	27	33	30	30
New Zealand	na	**na**	na	na	na	na	na	na	na	na	na	na	na	na	na	na
Nigeria	na	**na**	na	na	na	na	na	na	na	na	na	na	na	na	na	na
Northern Ireland	na	**19**	19	20	17	17	22	20	18	20	26	17	20	21	17	26
Norway	na	**na**	na	na	na	na	na	na	na	na	na	na	na	na	na	na
Pakistan	na	**na**	na	na	na	na	na	na	na	na	na	na	na	na	na	na
Peru	na	**na**	na	na	na	na	na	na	na	na	na	na	na	na	na	na
Philippines	na	**na**	na	na	na	na	na	na	na	na	na	na	na	na	na	na
Poland	na	**21**	21	20	23	18	23	24	19	11	23	18	21	22	19	22
Portugal	na	**31**	33	30	23	32	36	36	26	12	34	37	25	32	30	22
Puerto Rico	na	**na**	na	na	na	na	na	na	na	na	na	na	na	na	na	na
Romania	na	**18**	16	20	12	18	21	25	15	13	24	19	14	20	16	14
Russian Fed.	na	**19**	18	20	17	20	19	28	20	12	21	21	14	21	17	10
Serbia	na	**na**	na	na	na	na	na	na	na	na	na	na	na	na	na	na
Singapore	na	**na**	na	na	na	na	na	na	na	na	na	na	na	na	na	na
Slovakia	na	**18**	19	18	16	18	20	22	17	11	22	17	15	21	17	10
Slovenia	na	**14**	14	13	12	12	16	18	13	6	13	14	14	16	13	13
South Africa	na	**na**	na	na	na	na	na	na	na	na	na	na	na	na	na	na
Spain	na	**25**	25	25	26	21	27	26	25	24	24	25	21	32	25	18
Sweden	na	**22**	20	24	22	21	22	20	21	24	22	19	25	18	21	23
Switzerland	na	**na**	na	na	na	na	na	na	na	na	na	na	na	na	na	na
Taiwan	na	**na**	na	na	na	na	na	na	na	na	na	na	na	na	na	na
Tanzania	na	**na**	na	na	na	na	na	na	na	na	na	na	na	na	na	na
Turkey	na	**11**	10	12	10	10	17	13	8	7	13	11	7	15	11	7
Uganda	na	**na**	na	na	na	na	na	na	na	na	na	na	na	na	na	na
Ukraine	na	**19**	20	18	20	21	17	20	20	18	16	21	21	19	19	10
United States	na	**na**	na	na	na	na	na	na	na	na	na	na	na	na	na	na
Uruguay	na	**na**	na	na	na	na	na	na	na	na	na	na	na	na	na	na
Venezuela	na	**na**	na	na	na	na	na	na	na	na	na	na	na	na	na	na
Vietnam	na	**na**	na	na	na	na	na	na	na	na	na	na	na	na	na	na
Zimbabwe	na	**na**	na	na	na	na	na	na	na	na	na	na	na	na	na	na
Total	na	**22**	22	22	20	21	24	24	20	20	23	22	20	24	21	21

RANKING

Country	2000
Portugal	31
Netherlands	31
Belgium	30
Iceland	28
Czech Republic	27
Luxembourg	26
Ireland	25
Spain	25
Hungary	24
Estonia	24
Finland	23
Denmark	23
Germany	22
Italy	22
Sweden	22
Bulgaria	21
France	21
Lithuania	21
Poland	21
Great Britain	20
Northern Ireland	19
Ukraine	19
Latvia	19
Russian Fed.	19
Slovakia	18
Belarus	18
Romania	18
Malta	18
Austria	16
Greece	15
Slovenia	14
Croatia	13
Turkey	11
Total	22

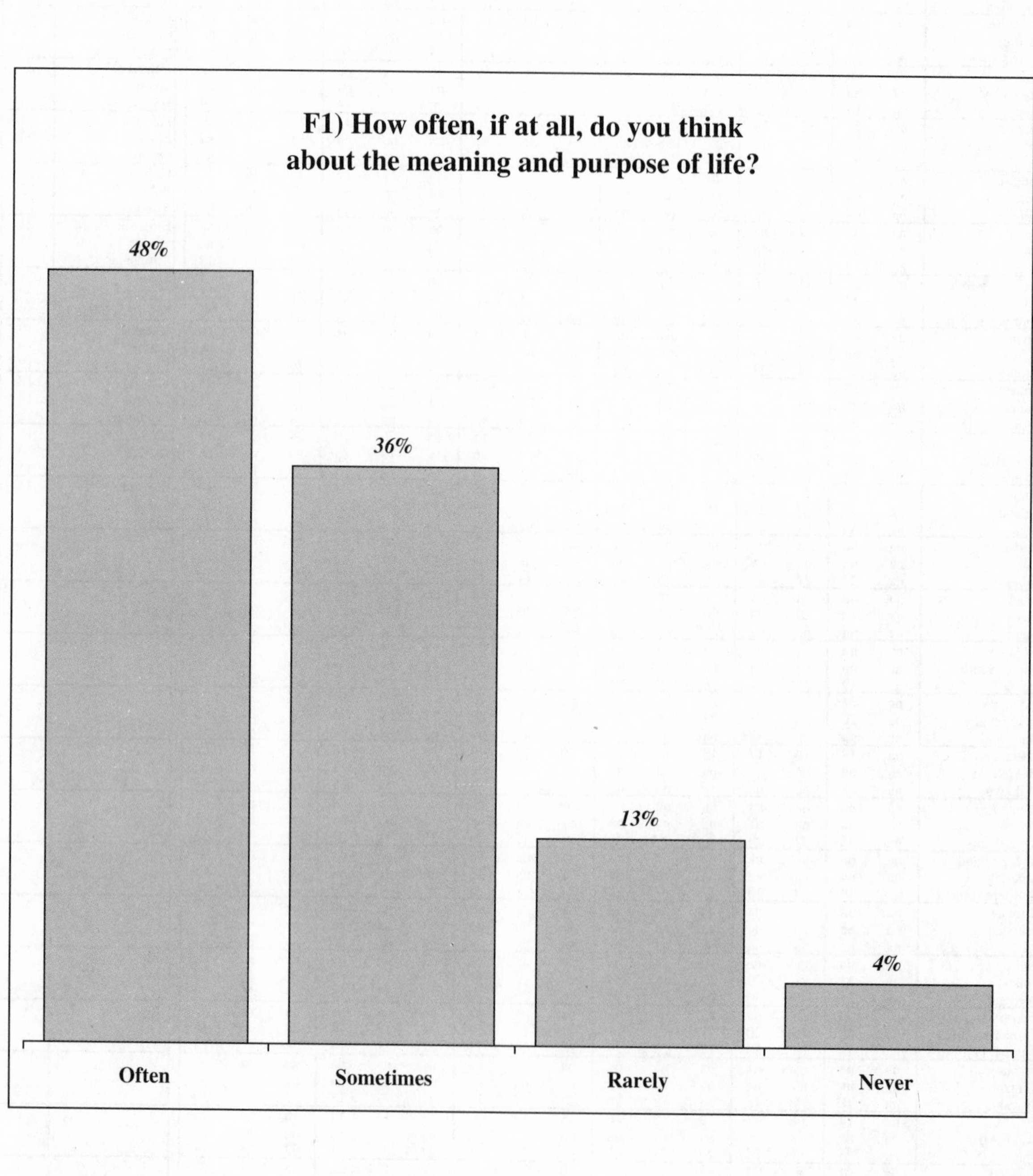
F1) How often, if at all, do you think
about the meaning and purpose of life?
48%
36%
13%
4%
Often
Sometimes
Rarely
Never

F001) THINKING ABOUT MEANING AND PURPOSE OF LIFE

How often, if at all, do you think about the meaning and purpose of life?

Often (%) (WVS: V182; EVS: o6)

Country	Wave		Gender		Age			Education			Income			Values		
	1990	2000	Male	Female	16-29	30-49	50+	Lower	Middle	Upper	Lower	Middle	Upper	Mat	Mixed	Postm.
Albania	na	**53**	53	54	61	54	46	49	53	65	54	55	51	55	50	49
Algeria	na	**50**	47	52	48	49	54	53	48	49	49	50	49	51	49	54
Argentina	57	**51**	46	56	46	56	51	46	57	66	50	48	57	44	52	58
Armenia	na	**60**	55	65	58	58	68	65	60	60	61	54	69	55	64	73
Australia	na	**44**	39	50	41	45	46	42	41	50	48	45	42	33	45	45
Austria	28	**34**	30	38	28	32	38	33	33	38	35	34	30	33	32	37
Azerbaijan	na	**42**	44	41	40	43	44	48	39	48	43	39	47	43	41	42
Bangladesh	na	**47**	53	40	44	45	64	44	47	56	43	43	55	50	43	49
Belarus	35	**36**	32	39	40	33	35	31	37	40	35	35	37	33	39	36
Belgium	29	**na**	na	na	na	na	na	na	na	na	na	na	na	na	na	na
Bosnia and Herz.	na	**41**	42	41	44	40	40	40	42	40	44	39	43	43	40	53
Brazil	44	**37**	36	38	36	37	41	35	36	49	36	33	41	33	37	44
Bulgaria	44	**46**	40	51	44	50	43	38	49	53	46	50	43	38	56	44
Canada	43	**52**	49	54	50	54	49	51	54	48	58	53	48	49	51	55
Chile	53	**50**	49	52	58	49	45	48	50	57	50	50	54	45	48	68
China	32	**32**	37	28	42	32	26	27	36	35	30	36	31	31	38	47
Colombia	na	**70**	70	71	68	72	69	61	66	83	62	68	79	67	66	62
Croatia	na	**41**	38	44	39	46	37	42	40	44	49	39	37	29	43	42
Czech Republic	31	**na**	na	na	na	na	na	na	na	na	na	na	na	na	na	na
Denmark	29	**37**	32	41	36	38	35	33	34	44	43	32	34	25	36	41
Dominican Rep.	na	**56**	52	59	59	49	73	50	50	59	59	50	60	59	55	56
Egypt	na	**52**	55	49	53	52	49	46	56	61	53	52	54	51	53	55
El Salvador	na	**54**	55	52	52	54	55	47	60	62	48	55	63	na	na	na
Estonia	35	**40**	31	47	41	40	39	36	40	44	45	40	41	41	40	50
Finland	38	**42**	31	53	37	38	49	42	42	46	54	40	35	35	43	56
France	39	**na**	na	na	na	na	na	na	na	na	na	na	na	na	na	na
Georgia	na	**73**	69	76	69	77	72	76	72	73	77	74	67	73	73	76
Germany	40	**22**	21	23	17	23	23	19	23	33	17	27	23	16	24	27
Great Britain	36	**24**	23	26	24	19	29	22	24	29	24	23	22	na	na	na
Greece	na	**na**	na	na	na	na	na	na	na	na	na	na	na	na	na	na
Hungary	45	**na**	na	na	na	na	na	na	na	na	na	na	na	na	na	na
Iceland	36	**na**	na	na	na	na	na	na	na	na	na	na	na	na	na	na
India	34	**36**	37	35	37	36	36	32	34	46	28	32	43	38	39	44
Indonesia	na	**58**	58	59	65	59	55	50	58	67	51	60	73	59	60	71
Iran	na	**46**	46	46	44	44	54	48	41	49	48	43	46	44	47	56
Ireland	34	**na**	na	na	na	na	na	na	na	na	na	na	na	na	na	na
Israel	na	**na**	na	na	na	na	na	na	na	na	na	na	na	na	na	na
Italy	47	**50**	43	57	47	53	50	46	53	56	51	50	50	46	50	53
Japan	21	**26**	27	25	30	23	27	25	24	32	28	24	26	25	25	34
Jordan	na	**60**	57	64	60	65	50	56	60	69	61	61	62	60	61	62
Korea, South	39	**41**	40	43	52	40	33	29	37	49	41	43	41	34	48	50
Latvia	36	**na**	na	na	na	na	na	na	na	na	na	na	na	na	na	na
Lithuania	41	**40**	32	46	31	40	45	42	38	44	48	43	31	39	41	42
Luxembourg	na	**36**	32	40	27	36	42	34	35	43	37	42	39	30	35	47
Macedonia	na	**50**	48	53	57	51	44	46	52	55	54	48	50	47	52	64
Malta	na	**na**	na	na	na	na	na	na	na	na	na	na	na	na	na	na
Mexico	40	**44**	46	43	50	44	36	37	50	64	35	45	58	43	43	57
Moldova	na	**57**	55	59	50	60	61	57	55	62	61	56	57	58	58	50
Montenegro	na	**37**	34	40	43	36	34	30	38	50	41	38	37	37	39	27
Morocco	na	**75**	77	73	75	76	73	75	72	77	68	71	77	75	77	64
Netherlands	30	**na**	na	na	na	na	na	na	na	na	na	na	na	na	na	na
New Zealand	na	**43**	38	48	38	45	45	41	44	46	48	43	39	48	42	44
Nigeria	59	**56**	59	53	55	58	52	50	58	61	55	55	58	60	54	54
Northern Ireland	33	**na**	na	na	na	na	na	na	na	na	na	na	na	na	na	na
Norway	31	**32**	27	37	30	32	33	31	30	35	na	na	na	27	31	42
Pakistan	na	**36**	34	37	28	34	52	34	37	37	35	34	40	32	40	27
Peru	na	**54**	55	53	51	54	58	44	54	60	53	52	58	43	55	64
Philippines	na	**64**	62	66	62	65	64	60	66	66	65	62	65	65	62	71
Poland	34	**na**	na	na	na	na	na	na	na	na	na	na	na	na	na	na
Portugal	43	**na**	na	na	na	na	na	na	na	na	na	na	na	na	na	na
Puerto Rico	na	**76**	77	76	77	83	71	57	75	80	68	79	80	74	76	81
Romania	45	**na**	na	na	na	na	na	na	na	na	na	na	na	na	na	na
Russian Fed.	41	**49**	43	53	45	49	50	47	50	47	49	52	45	50	48	47
Serbia	na	**39**	37	40	43	42	33	34	39	45	40	41	38	32	43	49
Singapore	na	**32**	34	30	41	26	18	22	36	44	28	32	36	22	35	41
Slovakia	na	**na**	na	na	na	na	na	na	na	na	na	na	na	na	na	na
Slovenia	37	**na**	na	na	na	na	na	na	na	na	na	na	na	na	na	na
South Africa	57	**56**	56	57	58	56	52	49	66	72	49	58	63	52	62	42
Spain	26	**22**	20	24	22	22	23	21	22	27	24	21	25	19	22	29
Sweden	24	**37**	32	41	27	40	39	36	34	42	39	39	31	32	34	47
Switzerland	44	**43**	38	47	40	43	44	42	43	45	47	47	39	36	42	51
Taiwan	na	**28**	29	28	33	29	23	19	32	35	23	26	36	24	33	38
Tanzania	na	**84**	84	85	84	84	87	84	84	88	83	83	87	81	87	83
Turkey	38	**na**	na	na	na	na	na	na	na	na	na	na	na	na	na	na
Uganda	na	**59**	57	61	63	54	64	62	60	41	53	45	55	61	58	60
Ukraine	na	**51**	46	54	47	47	56	51	51	51	59	47	46	48	51	64
United States	48	**58**	54	62	56	59	60	60	58	58	61	58	54	61	55	65
Uruguay	na	**42**	38	45	48	46	36	36	50	54	36	41	49	32	41	53
Venezuela	na	**66**	64	67	65	69	60	56	68	71	64	64	66	60	68	66
Vietnam	na	**58**	63	54	55	59	59	47	73	72	61	53	63	47	66	69
Zimbabwe	na	**70**	69	70	67	75	67	69	70	92	70	69	77	73	66	76
Total	38	**48**	46	49	49	48	46	44	48	54	49	47	49	46	49	52

RANKING	
Country	2000
Tanzania	84
Puerto Rico	76
Morocco	75
Georgia	73
Colombia	70
Zimbabwe	70
Venezuela	66
Philippines	64
Armenia	60
Jordan	60
Uganda	59
Vietnam	58
Indonesia	58
United States	58
Moldova	57
South Africa	56
Dominican Rep.	56
Nigeria	56
Peru	54
El Salvador	54
Albania	53
Egypt	52
Canada	52
Argentina	51
Ukraine	51
Chile	50
Italy	50
Macedonia	50
Algeria	50
Russian Fed.	49
Bangladesh	47
Iran	46
Bulgaria	46
Australia	44
Mexico	44
New Zealand	43
Switzerland	43
Finland	42
Azerbaijan	42
Uruguay	42
Korea, South	41
Bosnia and Herz.	41
Croatia	41
Estonia	40
Lithuania	40
Serbia	39
Brazil	37
Montenegro	37
Sweden	37
Denmark	37
India	36
Luxembourg	36
Belarus	36
Pakistan	36
Austria	34
China	32
Norway	32
Singapore	32
Taiwan	28
Japan	26
Great Britain	24
Spain	22
Germany	22
Total	48

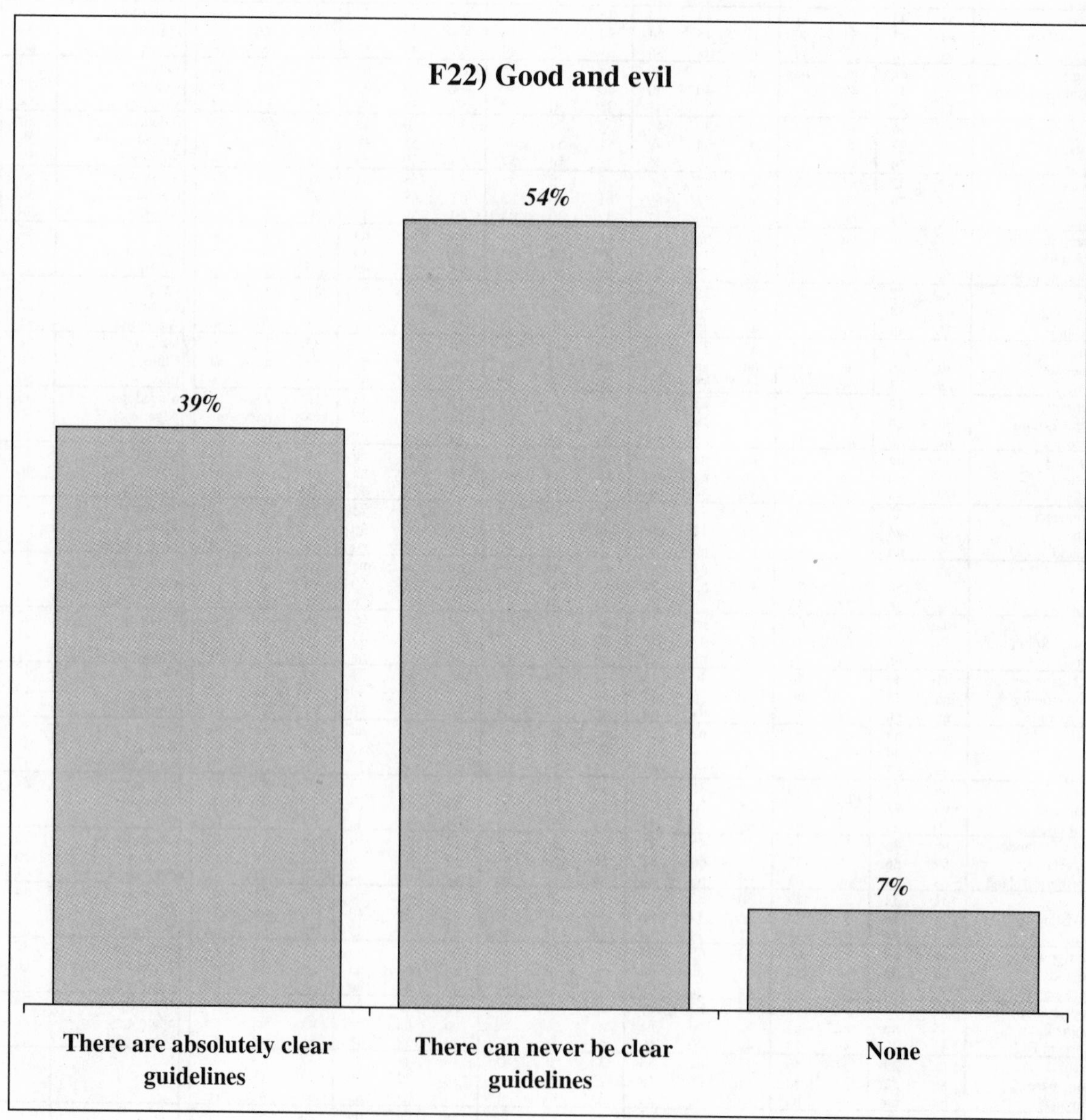
F22) Good and evil
39%
54%
7%
There are absolutely clear guidelines
There can never be clear guidelines
None

F022) GOOD AND EVIL

Here are two statements which people sometimes make when discussing good and evil.
Which one comes closest to your own point of view?
There are absolutely clear guidelines about what is good and evil (%)

(WVS: V183; EVS: V100)

Country	Wave		Gender		Age			Education			Income			Values		
	1990	2000	Male	Female	16-29	30-49	50+	Lower	Middle	Upper	Lower	Middle	Upper	Mat	Mixed	Postm.
Albania	na	**49**	48	50	50	49	49	52	47	49	47	51	50	44	52	58
Algeria	na	**na**	na	na	na	na	na	na	na	na	na	na	na	na	na	na
Argentina	33	**39**	39	39	36	40	40	39	39	38	44	34	40	43	40	32
Armenia	na	**41**	41	41	39	40	45	45	43	32	38	46	38	43	42	24
Australia	na	**42**	42	41	33	43	48	44	44	37	45	44	36	57	43	37
Austria	28	**20**	21	20	15	16	28	23	18	18	25	20	18	28	22	15
Azerbaijan	na	**57**	58	56	57	55	60	53	55	60	57	53	62	59	52	62
Bangladesh	na	**48**	48	48	43	49	61	51	44	44	55	48	42	49	47	40
Belarus	26	**25**	21	28	17	24	32	34	24	15	32	22	20	26	25	15
Belgium	33	**31**	31	30	22	29	37	39	31	25	37	28	26	38	32	21
Bosnia and Herz.	na	**54**	56	52	50	56	55	59	53	52	50	54	57	55	53	56
Brazil	46	**49**	50	48	48	50	50	49	51	47	52	48	47	49	50	44
Bulgaria	47	**33**	32	34	24	32	39	41	31	27	37	35	30	31	36	41
Canada	31	**42**	41	44	35	46	43	46	44	37	40	46	40	46	44	38
Chile	35	**53**	54	52	47	54	57	57	52	47	56	53	47	60	53	41
China	35	**36**	37	36	29	36	45	47	32	20	34	40	34	37	33	35
Colombia	na	**38**	37	39	35	39	41	38	38	37	36	39	38	42	42	32
Croatia	na	**35**	37	34	23	37	41	40	31	36	54	28	33	35	38	23
Czech Republic	na	**24**	24	23	17	21	29	26	20	24	30	21	20	28	22	18
Denmark	10	**10**	13	8	10	9	13	11	6	8	16	8	7	12	10	5
Dominican Rep.	na	**35**	40	31	32	40	55	34	38	34	40	35	32	30	36	36
Egypt	na	**na**	na	na	na	na	na	na	na	na	na	na	na	na	na	na
El Salvador	na	**49**	49	48	48	48	53	49	50	49	50	47	52	na	na	na
Estonia	23	**30**	32	28	24	24	39	34	27	33	37	32	26	30	30	43
Finland	26	**29**	27	32	21	26	37	29	27	34	31	26	33	35	28	28
France	24	**25**	28	23	16	23	33	30	20	19	24	26	24	30	28	13
Georgia	na	**60**	61	60	55	59	66	59	61	59	61	59	59	61	60	52
Germany	23	**35**	35	34	34	31	40	43	27	29	41	36	30	38	34	32
Great Britain	36	**42**	41	42	30	40	49	47	38	39	47	33	41	na	na	na
Greece	na	**16**	18	15	11	20	19	25	17	13	16	17	15	18	15	15
Hungary	17	**15**	16	15	15	13	18	15	14	19	14	18	13	18	14	5
Iceland	11	**9**	9	9	7	9	10	8	10	9	12	8	8	10	9	7
India	45	**30**	30	30	32	29	31	30	27	32	34	31	27	30	31	22
Indonesia	na	**na**	na	na	na	na	na	na	na	na	na	na	na	na	na	na
Iran	na	**na**	na	na	na	na	na	na	na	na	na	na	na	na	na	na
Ireland	42	**39**	37	40	33	36	45	40	39	36	42	38	32	43	40	29
Israel	na	**na**	na	na	na	na	na	na	na	na	na	na	na	na	na	na
Italy	45	**36**	37	36	24	37	43	40	33	36	40	36	36	39	37	32
Japan	15	**19**	21	18	8	17	26	27	19	16	19	18	22	18	19	16
Jordan	na	**na**	na	na	na	na	na	na	na	na	na	na	na	na	na	na
Korea, South	23	**37**	37	37	26	38	48	45	40	32	39	37	35	40	34	32
Latvia	27	**41**	40	42	38	37	46	42	41	41	43	43	38	47	38	40
Lithuania	23	**35**	31	38	23	31	47	55	30	22	49	39	26	48	29	34
Luxembourg	na	**23**	24	22	19	20	30	25	20	28	28	21	20	18	25	23
Macedonia	na	**55**	54	57	57	53	56	62	54	49	60	51	52	57	54	50
Malta	na	**48**	48	48	41	48	54	57	47	37	59	56	45	56	45	39
Mexico	38	**41**	42	40	37	42	45	45	36	35	45	36	38	48	39	29
Moldova	na	**39**	37	41	30	39	48	47	40	32	47	40	38	37	41	40
Montenegro	na	**49**	48	49	33	48	60	61	43	36	62	55	39	59	42	24
Morocco	na	**79**	79	78	74	81	87	81	71	66	91	79	71	78	79	79
Netherlands	23	**27**	28	25	20	27	29	35	24	21	30	27	22	37	28	17
New Zealand	na	**42**	41	43	29	41	47	45	49	35	47	40	39	46	42	35
Nigeria	60	**na**	na	na	na	na	na	na	na	na	na	na	na	na	na	na
Northern Ireland	51	**47**	46	48	42	41	52	52	46	37	50	47	39	52	45	49
Norway	32	**29**	31	27	24	30	32	31	26	31	na	na	na	34	29	21
Pakistan	na	**na**	na	na	na	na	na	na	na	na	na	na	na	na	na	na
Peru	na	**53**	55	51	51	53	58	53	52	54	54	51	53	53	53	52
Philippines	na	**55**	56	55	53	56	57	54	55	57	58	54	54	58	53	53
Poland	33	**51**	52	49	42	50	58	50	50	54	51	50	53	55	50	44
Portugal	31	**39**	38	40	36	40	40	39	43	27	43	40	32	44	36	37
Puerto Rico	na	**45**	46	45	44	47	44	34	50	44	41	49	42	39	47	42
Romania	23	**40**	37	42	35	33	49	49	38	27	45	47	32	42	38	21
Russian Fed.	31	**39**	37	40	27	39	46	44	38	38	43	39	33	39	39	39
Serbia	na	**47**	46	47	38	44	53	55	43	41	48	48	45	50	44	39
Singapore	na	**38**	38	38	36	41	38	40	36	40	44	36	34	39	38	33
Slovakia	na	**36**	36	37	29	36	43	42	34	32	38	39	35	40	35	28
Slovenia	21	**22**	23	21	18	20	27	21	23	18	24	20	17	20	24	15
South Africa	52	**63**	62	64	58	65	66	60	66	78	60	64	70	68	59	63
Spain	34	**39**	38	40	32	34	48	46	34	30	42	42	39	52	39	25
Sweden	19	**16**	19	13	10	15	21	21	13	16	15	19	14	30	16	13
Switzerland	22	**28**	29	27	18	27	36	32	26	31	33	31	25	35	29	15
Taiwan	na	**28**	28	28	23	29	30	25	37	26	26	26	31	28	29	17
Tanzania	na	**69**	68	70	68	68	74	73	65	64	71	64	68	67	69	63
Turkey	34	**35**	38	33	32	39	37	37	32	38	39	34	32	33	37	31
Uganda	na	**59**	58	60	57	61	60	59	59	63	55	59	52	63	57	58
Ukraine	na	**43**	42	43	32	44	48	47	45	36	50	39	40	44	41	41
United States	50	**49**	46	52	41	56	47	51	49	49	50	49	49	54	53	41
Uruguay	na	**32**	33	31	27	29	36	34	29	29	34	34	29	39	35	20
Venezuela	na	**41**	42	40	41	38	46	47	43	30	46	41	37	48	40	32
Vietnam	na	**58**	57	60	57	56	63	60	58	53	64	63	51	64	58	50
Zimbabwe	na	**57**	59	56	56	56	64	58	56	62	58	54	53	60	55	58
Total	31	39	40	39	36	39	43	43	38	35	43	39	36	44	38	31

RANKING

Country	2000
Morocco	79
Tanzania	69
South Africa	63
Georgia	60
Uganda	59
Vietnam	58
Zimbabwe	57
Azerbaijan	57
Philippines	55
Macedonia	55
Bosnia and Herz.	54
Chile	53
Peru	53
Poland	51
Brazil	49
United States	49
Albania	49
Montenegro	49
El Salvador	49
Malta	48
Bangladesh	48
Northern Ireland	47
Serbia	47
Puerto Rico	45
Ukraine	43
Canada	42
Australia	42
New Zealand	42
Great Britain	42
Armenia	41
Latvia	41
Mexico	41
Venezuela	41
Romania	40
Moldova	39
Portugal	39
Spain	39
Ireland	39
Argentina	39
Russian Fed.	39
Colombia	38
Singapore	38
Korea, South	37
Italy	36
Slovakia	36
China	36
Turkey	35
Croatia	35
Lithuania	35
Dominican Rep.	35
Germany	35
Bulgaria	33
Uruguay	32
Belgium	31
India	30
Estonia	30
Finland	29
Norway	29
Taiwan	28
Switzerland	28
Netherlands	27
France	25
Belarus	25
Czech Republic	24
Luxembourg	23
Slovenia	22
Austria	20
Japan	19
Greece	16
Sweden	16
Hungary	15
Denmark	10
Iceland	9
Total	39

F024) BELONG TO RELIGIOUS DENOMINATION

Do you belong to a religious denomination?

Yes (%) (WVS: *V184; EVS: V101

Country	Wave 1990	Wave 2000	Gender Male	Gender Female	Age 16-29	Age 30-49	Age 50+	Education Lower	Education Middle	Education Upper	Income Lower	Income Middle	Income Upper	Values Mat	Values Mixed	Values Postm.
Albania	na	**87**	85	89	85	84	93	89	84	89	89	88	84	91	83	92
Algeria	na	**na**	na	na	na	na	na	na	na	na	na	na	na	na	na	na
Argentina	84	**87**	84	90	83	87	91	87	87	89	90	85	87	87	89	82
Armenia	na	**87**	82	91	86	88	85	88	86	86	85	86	88	87	88	75
Australia	na	**81**	77	85	77	78	89	86	82	76	85	81	76	85	84	76
Austria	86	**88**	86	90	91	88	86	88	88	88	86	88	89	89	89	86
Azerbaijan	na	**94**	94	94	93	95	94	97	96	90	97	97	86	95	91	94
Bangladesh	na	**100**	100	100	100	100	100	100	100	100	100	100	100	100	100	100
Belarus	30	**52**	41	61	51	49	57	61	51	43	61	49	43	54	51	50
Belgium	68	**64**	59	68	53	57	74	72	61	61	66	63	60	72	64	54
Bosnia and Herz.	na	**75**	75	76	79	74	73	83	75	69	74	75	77	79	73	79
Brazil	88	**88**	84	92	83	90	94	88	88	89	89	89	86	91	87	89
Bulgaria	34	**70**	65	75	62	64	79	81	64	65	79	66	65	72	70	71
Canada	74	**69**	64	73	55	67	79	75	68	65	72	71	62	71	74	59
Chile	82	**66**	60	72	65	61	75	72	63	63	69	65	63	73	67	53
China	4	**6**	5	7	6	6	6	5	7	9	5	6	8	5	7	3
Colombia	na	**92**	89	95	88	94	95	93	92	90	92	93	90	91	93	87
Croatia	na	**89**	87	90	88	89	90	97	85	80	88	89	89	94	91	78
Czech Republic	56	**34**	28	39	21	23	50	35	34	25	43	32	25	39	31	36
Denmark	92	**90**	88	92	90	88	92	92	90	87	91	91	88	94	93	78
Dominican Rep.	na	**76**	71	80	75	78	91	74	70	79	77	76	76	77	74	85
Egypt	na	**100**	100	100	100	100	100	100	100	100	100	100	100	100	100	100
El Salvador	na	**84**	82	86	81	83	90	83	85	86	82	83	88	na	na	na
Estonia	13	**25**	18	30	14	23	33	29	22	25	30	30	18	28	23	20
Finland	89	**88**	84	91	92	85	88	88	88	89	90	85	88	92	89	80
France	62	**58**	55	60	46	54	67	60	53	55	54	61	54	65	59	43
Georgia	na	**94**	93	95	94	95	92	92	94	94	93	94	94	94	93	100
Germany	35	**77**	73	79	73	72	83	83	73	67	76	76	83	78	77	75
Great Britain	58	**83**	80	87	76	84	89	83	86	78	82	83	86	na	na	na
Greece	na	**96**	94	97	95	96	97	98	97	95	97	96	95	98	97	92
Hungary	58	**57**	53	61	43	54	68	61	48	54	61	59	53	64	51	46
Iceland	98	**96**	96	95	93	95	99	97	98	90	97	96	95	98	96	89
India	99	**93**	94	92	95	93	92	94	92	93	90	94	94	94	92	93
Indonesia	na	**100**	100	100	100	100	100	100	100	100	100	100	100	100	100	100
Iran	na	**99**	99	99	99	99	99	99	99	99	99	99	99	100	99	100
Ireland	96	**91**	88	93	86	89	96	89	92	92	91	92	90	91	91	87
Israel	na	**100**	100	100	100	100	100	100	100	100	100	100	100	100	100	100
Italy	85	**82**	78	87	80	80	86	88	79	74	83	82	78	90	82	79
Japan	na	**41**	43	39	19	32	59	56	42	34	45	46	37	43	41	36
Jordan	na	**100**	100	100	100	100	100	100	100	100	100	100	100	100	100	100
Korea, South	72	**63**	57	69	60	63	69	64	65	60	60	63	68	63	63	62
Latvia	37	**59**	53	64	44	54	70	67	54	66	63	60	54	63	59	57
Lithuania	63	**81**	72	89	72	75	94	92	77	81	88	79	78	83	82	74
Luxembourg	na	**72**	70	74	59	71	82	78	69	72	69	77	71	76	73	63
Macedonia	na	**86**	88	84	85	86	86	92	85	79	89	83	85	89	85	90
Malta	na	**99**	97	100	97	99	100	99	99	96	100	99	98	98	99	97
Mexico	85	**81**	78	83	76	80	88	85	76	72	83	80	77	84	80	67
Moldova	na	**100**	100	100	100	100	100	100	100	100	100	100	100	100	100	100
Montenegro	na	**97**	97	98	97	97	97	98	96	97	97	99	99	98	97	95
Morocco	na	**100**	100	100	100	100	100	100	100	100	100	100	100	100	100	100
Netherlands	51	**45**	42	48	34	38	58	49	44	43	43	45	43	58	46	34
New Zealand	na	**82**	80	84	64	80	90	86	83	76	84	80	82	78	84	77
Nigeria	95	**99**	99	99	99	99	99	99	99	99	99	99	99	98	100	100
Northern Ireland	91	**86**	83	89	81	78	95	91	81	84	88	86	85	88	86	87
Norway	90	**91**	89	93	90	89	93	92	93	86	na	na	na	95	92	78
Pakistan	na	**71**	69	73	69	71	74	79	70	41	78	70	63	73	68	67
Peru	na	**95**	94	97	93	97	97	95	97	94	96	96	94	96	95	97
Philippines	na	**90**	92	89	89	90	92	89	89	92	92	90	90	88	92	91
Poland	na	**96**	95	97	95	96	97	98	95	87	97	96	94	98	95	92
Portugal	72	**89**	84	94	82	93	91	93	82	79	94	92	85	92	89	75
Puerto Rico	na	**88**	87	90	83	86	93	90	90	88	89	90	88	88	90	85
Romania	94	**98**	97	99	98	97	98	99	97	97	97	98	97	98	98	92
Russian Fed.	37	**51**	39	60	43	46	61	62	49	50	61	50	42	55	46	36
Serbia	na	**94**	93	95	94	95	94	97	93	91	96	93	94	96	93	87
Singapore	na	**80**	78	82	78	79	92	87	79	67	92	80	73	88	78	69
Slovakia	na	**77**	71	82	66	74	88	83	76	65	85	78	73	79	76	69
Slovenia	74	**70**	69	71	65	66	78	82	70	50	76	71	59	78	68	70
South Africa	na	**86**	79	94	85	84	96	85	87	88	85	92	80	86	87	86
Spain	85	**83**	77	89	74	81	91	88	78	77	87	81	81	90	84	68
Sweden	82	**76**	74	78	76	73	78	79	74	76	75	76	78	70	77	74
Switzerland	92	**100**	100	100	100	100	100	100	100	100	100	100	100	100	100	100
Taiwan	na	**79**	72	86	67	81	83	89	79	70	82	82	72	81	79	62
Tanzania	na	**98**	99	99	99	99	99	99	99	98	98	99	99	100	99	100
Turkey	97	**98**	98	98	97	98	100	99	98	90	99	98	94	99	98	94
Uganda	na	**99**	98	100	100	99	97	98	99	100	99	99	99	99	99	99
Ukraine	na	**56**	43	67	53	53	62	77	53	52	59	56	55	57	53	64
United States	77	**79**	73	84	65	80	88	70	75	84	74	78	85	84	80	73
Uruguay	na	**52**	40	61	43	47	60	57	45	48	55	51	50	61	54	42
Venezuela	na	**73**	69	77	65	76	83	76	70	78	71	70	73	76	72	70
Vietnam	na	**54**	50	58	54	51	57	62	43	45	48	57	52	62	49	40
Zimbabwe	na	**100**	100	100	100	100	100	100	100	100	100	100	100	100	100	100
Total	70	80	78	83	79	79	83	84	78	79	81	80	78	82	80	75

RANKING

Country	2000
Jordan	100
Moldova	100
Morocco	100
Zimbabwe	100
Switzerland	100
Egypt	100
Bangladesh	100
Israel	100
Indonesia	100
Nigeria	99
Uganda	99
Iran	99
Malta	99
Tanzania	98
Turkey	98
Romania	98
Montenegro	97
Greece	96
Iceland	96
Poland	96
Peru	95
Azerbaijan	94
Serbia	94
Georgia	94
India	93
Colombia	92
Ireland	91
Norway	91
Philippines	90
Denmark	90
Portugal	89
Croatia	89
Puerto Rico	88
Austria	88
Finland	88
Brazil	88
Albania	87
Argentina	87
Armenia	87
South Africa	86
Northern Ireland	86
Macedonia	86
El Salvador	84
Great Britain	83
Spain	83
Italy	82
New Zealand	82
Lithuania	81
Australia	81
Mexico	81
Singapore	80
Taiwan	79
United States	79
Slovakia	77
Germany	77
Dominican Rep.	76
Sweden	76
Bosnia and Herz.	75
Venezuela	73
Luxembourg	72
Pakistan	71
Bulgaria	70
Slovenia	70
Canada	69
Chile	66
Belgium	64
Korea, South	63
Latvia	59
France	58
Hungary	57
Ukraine	56
Vietnam	54
Belarus	52
Uruguay	52
Russian Fed.	51
Netherlands	45
Japan	41
Czech Republic	34
Estonia	25
China	6
Total	80

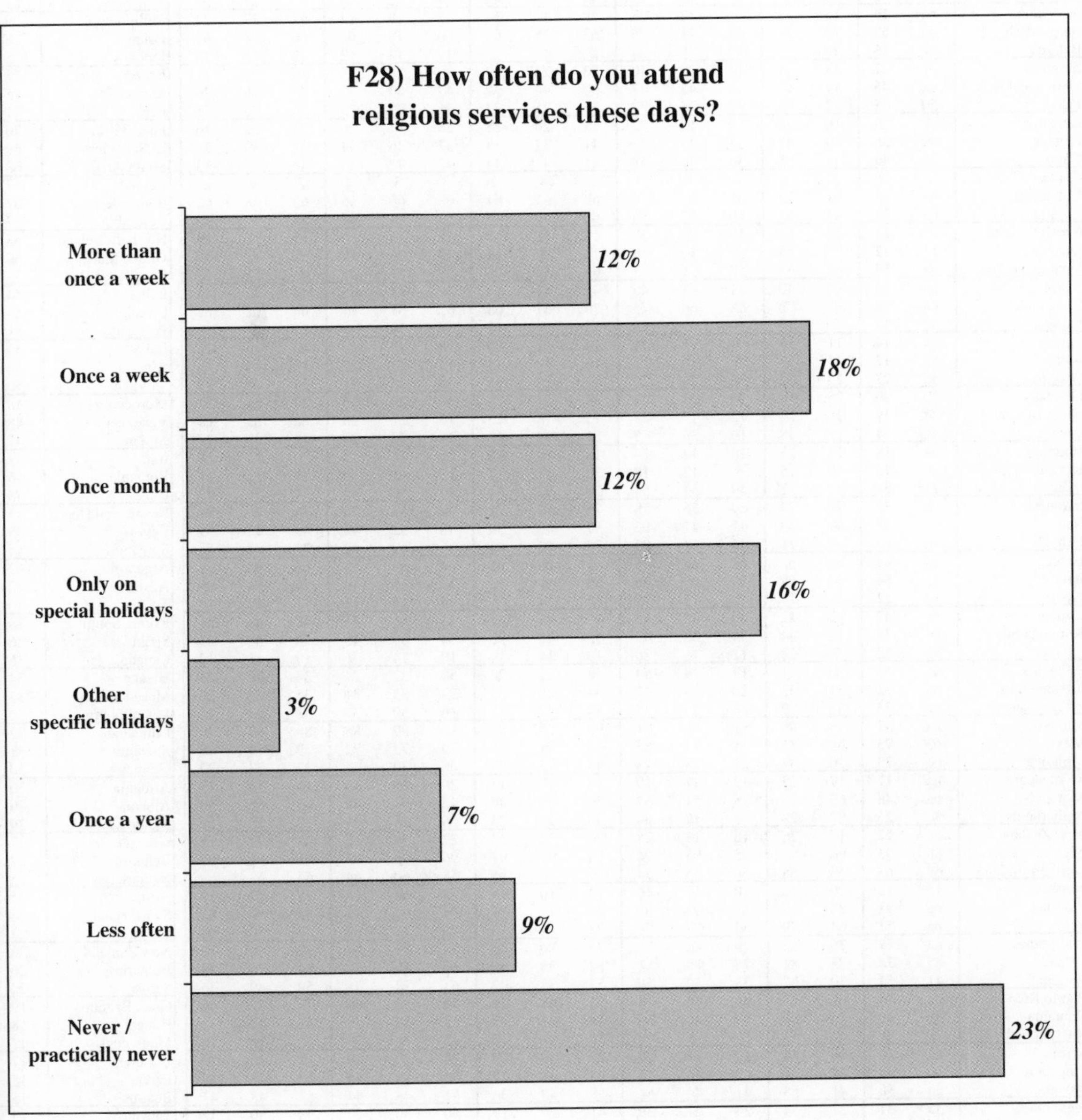
F28) How often do you attend religious services these days?
More than once a week
12%
Once a week
18%
Once month
12%
Only on special holidays
16%
Other specific holidays
3%
Once a year
7%
Less often
9%
Never / practically never
23%

F028) HOW OFTEN DO YOU ATTEND RELIGIOUS SERVICES

Apart from weddings, funerals and christenings, about how often do you attend religious services these days

Once a month or more (%) (WVS: V185; EVS: V105)

Country	Wave		Gender		Age			Education			Income			Values		
	1990	2000	Male	Female	16-29	30-49	50+	Lower	Middle	Upper	Lower	Middle	Upper	Mat	Mixed	Postm.
Albania	na	**29**	25	34	25	27	37	34	27	24	33	30	26	28	29	39
Algeria	na	**50**	73	27	43	50	65	58	49	46	53	50	50	50	52	47
Argentina	55	**43**	33	52	34	44	50	44	40	44	46	44	39	42	45	38
Armenia	na	**30**	21	37	32	29	28	30	30	28	27	32	31	31	28	25
Australia	na	**25**	21	29	23	23	30	28	22	27	26	26	20	29	28	19
Austria	44	**42**	40	45	25	43	51	44	40	44	47	42	40	38	45	39
Azerbaijan	na	**14**	15	13	11	13	25	28	13	14	12	19	14	12	17	24
Bangladesh	na	**67**	75	57	60	71	76	63	75	69	66	73	61	66	68	61
Belarus	6	**15**	6	21	10	9	24	22	13	8	17	13	12	18	11	13
Belgium	31	**27**	23	31	14	20	40	33	23	29	33	28	23	30	28	21
Bosnia and Herz.	na	**45**	44	47	46	43	47	60	44	36	47	44	47	47	46	26
Brazil	50	**75**	72	78	74	75	77	75	75	73	76	79	73	74	76	71
Bulgaria	9	**20**	16	24	23	16	22	18	20	25	23	17	20	21	22	16
Canada	40	**36**	30	41	23	33	47	41	32	38	37	36	34	38	39	28
Chile	47	**45**	35	55	36	43	58	51	41	44	47	42	48	46	49	33
China	1	**3**	2	4	3	3	3	3	4	2	3	3	4	3	4	na
Colombia	na	**67**	61	72	61	69	73	69	65	64	68	66	66	65	68	65
Croatia	na	**53**	44	61	50	52	56	62	47	47	62	54	47	58	55	40
Czech Republic	21	**12**	10	14	10	5	18	13	10	11	17	10	7	15	10	14
Denmark	11	**12**	9	15	5	10	18	11	8	14	17	8	12	6	12	9
Dominican Rep.	na	**55**	44	63	57	51	73	61	53	56	58	59	49	61	53	58
Egypt	na	**45**	45	45	44	45	46	45	44	44	47	45	45	44	45	46
El Salvador	na	**69**	65	72	68	66	75	70	67	68	67	67	71	na	na	na
Estonia	na	**11**	7	15	5	8	18	15	9	11	17	14	6	14	9	4
Finland	11	**14**	11	17	7	11	21	14	12	20	18	12	15	12	15	12
France	17	**12**	11	13	5	10	17	12	10	13	13	11	12	13	13	7
Georgia	na	**27**	22	32	36	26	20	24	26	35	25	28	31	26	28	37
Germany	20	**30**	25	34	20	22	43	34	27	28	31	30	33	29	31	32
Great Britain	24	**19**	16	22	12	17	24	15	18	25	13	22	25	na	na	na
Greece	na	**34**	27	38	19	39	55	51	39	26	41	33	27	43	32	27
Hungary	34	**18**	11	23	10	12	27	18	15	18	21	18	15	20	15	9
Iceland	9	**12**	10	15	5	12	18	10	11	17	13	11	10	11	12	11
India	71	**51**	51	52	49	51	54	50	52	54	46	50	55	54	54	47
Indonesia	na	**75**	77	74	69	76	78	78	77	71	70	82	76	76	76	71
Iran	na	**47**	49	43	41	47	62	57	43	39	48	52	44	49	45	39
Ireland	88	**67**	63	71	44	64	89	75	63	66	76	69	62	73	67	58
Israel	na	**na**	na	na	na	na	na	na	na	na	na	na	na	na	na	na
Italy	53	**54**	44	63	40	50	65	59	49	52	59	53	49	59	54	49
Japan	14	**12**	11	14	2	12	17	13	14	7	14	15	11	13	12	14
Jordan	na	**47**	83	12	40	45	66	49	47	41	43	56	42	48	48	36
Korea, South	64	**38**	32	44	34	38	43	35	40	36	34	38	43	38	38	43
Latvia	9	**15**	7	22	11	11	20	19	14	14	19	14	9	19	13	13
Lithuania	na	**32**	20	41	17	19	54	58	21	28	50	32	24	38	29	23
Luxembourg	na	**32**	31	33	20	24	47	34	29	35	27	35	31	35	32	26
Macedonia	na	**33**	36	29	28	33	37	44	27	28	36	30	31	38	29	40
Malta	na	**87**	83	90	81	86	91	90	85	88	85	89	85	88	87	79
Mexico	63	**75**	68	81	71	74	83	79	71	67	79	73	72	79	74	68
Moldova	na	**29**	20	37	21	23	43	44	23	27	38	30	25	33	23	22
Montenegro	na	**17**	17	17	15	17	19	18	17	17	20	15	15	16	18	19
Morocco	na	**48**	69	28	38	51	67	50	40	46	45	54	48	45	50	50
Netherlands	30	**25**	22	28	13	17	39	30	24	23	25	25	21	38	25	19
New Zealand	na	**22**	17	26	18	17	28	20	22	23	27	21	16	25	22	15
Nigeria	88	**95**	96	94	95	95	94	93	97	97	96	96	93	95	96	97
Northern Ireland	69	**63**	58	68	56	55	74	69	56	65	58	60	64	63	63	69
Norway	13	**12**	10	15	10	11	16	12	10	16	na	na	na	15	12	12
Pakistan	na	**91**	88	95	87	93	95	94	87	89	94	90	91	92	90	83
Peru	na	**71**	64	79	63	77	78	73	74	66	73	71	69	77	70	69
Philippines	na	**79**	76	83	79	80	78	73	80	86	78	79	82	79	80	78
Poland	85	**78**	75	81	74	78	81	82	75	69	80	80	70	84	76	73
Portugal	41	**51**	39	62	38	52	59	57	38	42	61	54	45	59	49	36
Puerto Rico	na	**70**	65	73	61	66	78	73	68	71	70	76	66	72	72	66
Romania	31	**46**	33	60	34	40	59	58	41	37	53	49	39	50	44	33
Russian Fed.	6	**9**	5	13	7	7	13	15	8	10	12	9	7	10	8	16
Serbia	na	**20**	16	24	19	17	23	26	16	19	24	20	19	19	20	23
Singapore	na	**44**	44	44	42	46	47	45	43	47	46	44	44	50	43	34
Slovakia	na	**50**	41	58	41	44	64	58	48	36	61	48	44	53	48	43
Slovenia	35	**31**	27	34	24	27	39	41	29	19	40	30	20	38	30	27
South Africa	na	**68**	59	79	67	67	77	69	67	65	67	66	70	71	65	76
Spain	39	**36**	24	47	16	29	54	44	27	30	48	33	30	47	35	18
Sweden	10	**9**	8	11	7	6	14	12	7	12	11	8	8	11	9	9
Switzerland	43	**25**	22	27	9	19	40	38	21	25	31	28	16	30	25	20
Taiwan	na	**15**	12	17	17	10	24	21	10	11	17	13	12	15	12	3
Tanzania	na	**87**	86	88	85	88	87	86	89	86	87	88	84	87	87	92
Turkey	38	**40**	71	8	37	38	51	40	41	39	45	38	31	40	41	40
Uganda	na	**88**	84	92	86	93	82	84	90	91	89	85	92	86	89	92
Ukraine	na	**17**	11	22	12	17	20	30	16	13	17	18	15	17	15	16
United States	58	**60**	54	67	47	64	66	54	59	63	58	63	59	69	61	56
Uruguay	na	**23**	14	30	18	20	28	27	18	21	28	21	22	32	21	19
Venezuela	na	**48**	39	57	38	52	62	52	45	49	49	51	45	54	46	44
Vietnam	na	**13**	9	17	11	10	18	16	8	10	10	14	13	19	12	12
Zimbabwe	na	**81**	68	93	83	82	76	82	80	47	75	87	84	80	81	93
Total	36	41	39	43	40	39	45	46	38	40	44	42	38	43	41	37

RANKING

Country	2000
Nigeria	95
Pakistan	91
Uganda	88
Malta	87
Tanzania	87
Zimbabwe	81
Philippines	79
Poland	78
Indonesia	75
Brazil	75
Mexico	75
Peru	71
Puerto Rico	70
El Salvador	69
South Africa	68
Ireland	67
Bangladesh	67
Colombia	67
Northern Ireland	63
United States	60
Dominican Rep.	55
Italy	54
Croatia	53
Portugal	51
India	51
Algeria	50
Slovakia	50
Morocco	48
Venezuela	48
Jordan	47
Iran	47
Romania	46
Chile	45
Bosnia and Herz.	45
Egypt	45
Singapore	44
Argentina	43
Austria	42
Turkey	40
Korea, South	38
Spain	36
Canada	36
Greece	34
Macedonia	33
Luxembourg	32
Lithuania	32
Slovenia	31
Germany	30
Armenia	30
Albania	29
Moldova	29
Georgia	27
Belgium	27
Netherlands	25
Australia	25
Switzerland	25
Uruguay	23
New Zealand	22
Bulgaria	20
Serbia	20
Great Britain	19
Hungary	18
Montenegro	17
Ukraine	17
Latvia	15
Belarus	15
Taiwan	15
Finland	14
Azerbaijan	14
Vietnam	13
Japan	12
Norway	12
Iceland	12
Denmark	12
France	12
Czech Republic	12
Estonia	11
Sweden	9
Russian Fed.	9
China	3
Total	41

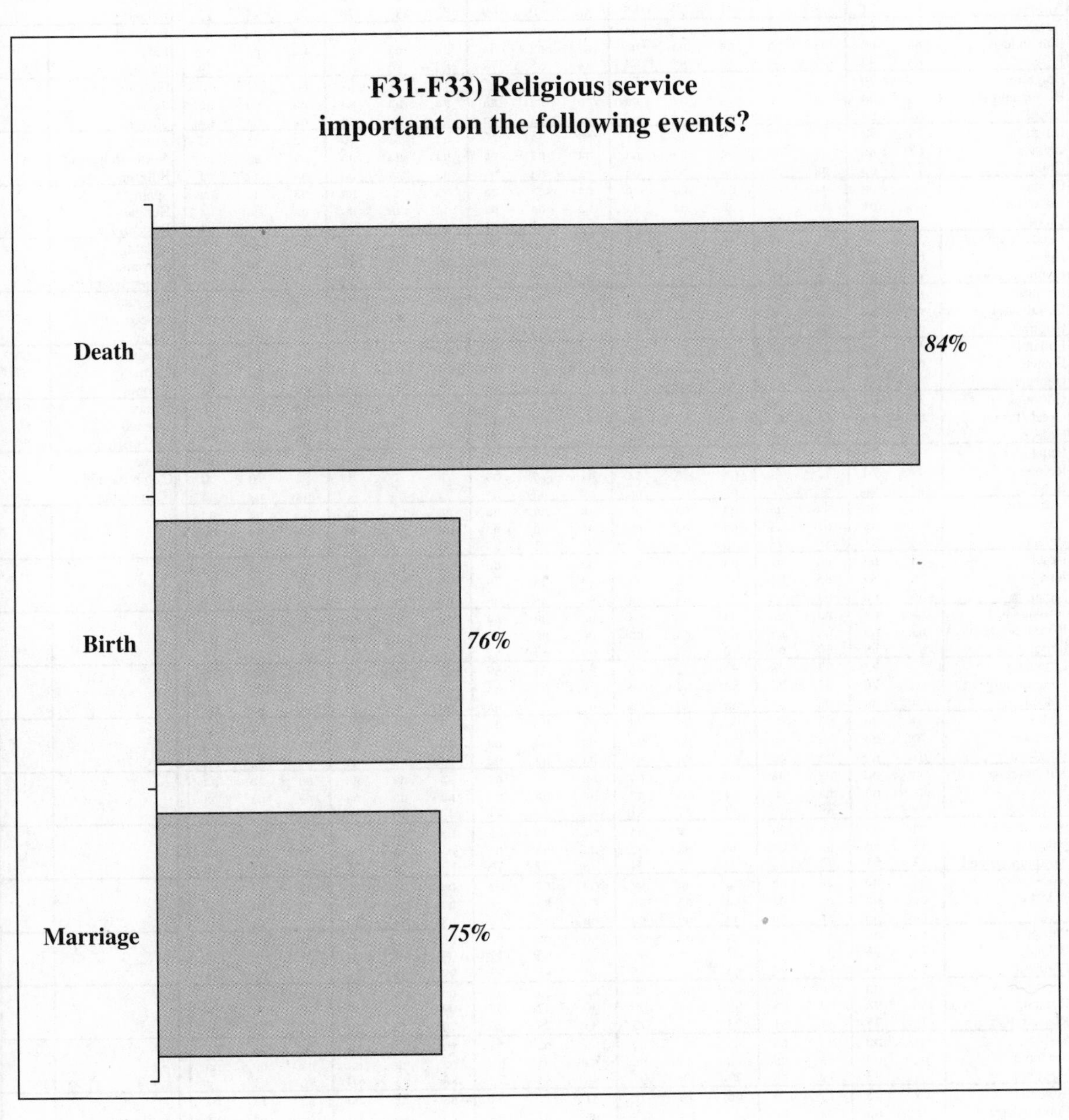
F31-F33) Religious service
important on the following events?
Death
84%
Birth
76%
Marriage
75%

F031_1) RELIGIOUS SERVICE BIRTH

Do you personally think it is important to hold a religious service for any of the following events? Birth

Yes (%)

(EVS: V107)

Country	Wave		Gender		Age			Education			Income			Values		
	1990	2000	Male	Female	16-29	30-49	50+	Lower	Middle	Upper	Lower	Middle	Upper	Mat	Mixed	Postm.
Albania	na	**na**	na	na	na	na	na	na	na	na	na	na	na	na	na	na
Algeria	na	**na**	na	na	na	na	na	na	na	na	na	na	na	na	na	na
Argentina	67	**na**	na	na	na	na	na	na	na	na	na	na	na	na	na	na
Armenia	na	**na**	na	na	na	na	na	na	na	na	na	na	na	na	na	na
Australia	na	**na**	na	na	na	na	na	na	na	na	na	na	na	na	na	na
Austria	87	**81**	78	84	81	78	85	86	80	69	82	82	79	88	83	77
Azerbaijan	na	**na**	na	na	na	na	na	na	na	na	na	na	na	na	na	na
Bangladesh	na	**na**	na	na	na	na	na	na	na	na	na	na	na	na	na	na
Belarus	83	**84**	77	88	81	85	84	84	85	78	82	86	81	85	83	79
Belgium	74	**70**	66	74	65	63	79	78	69	65	71	71	67	80	71	56
Bosnia and Herz.	na	**na**	na	na	na	na	na	na	na	na	na	na	na	na	na	na
Brazil	81	**na**	na	na	na	na	na	na	na	na	na	na	na	na	na	na
Bulgaria	78	**78**	77	79	79	74	81	84	75	76	82	77	76	82	75	72
Canada	68	**na**	na	na	na	na	na	na	na	na	na	na	na	na	na	na
Chile	77	**na**	na	na	na	na	na	na	na	na	na	na	na	na	na	na
China	4	**na**	na	na	na	na	na	na	na	na	na	na	na	na	na	na
Colombia	na	**na**	na	na	na	na	na	na	na	na	na	na	na	na	na	na
Croatia	na	**91**	89	93	89	93	90	95	91	81	91	92	90	92	94	84
Czech Republic	52	**42**	36	47	35	34	52	46	40	30	49	43	31	45	41	39
Denmark	69	**65**	64	66	63	62	70	70	60	59	66	64	67	62	68	55
Dominican Rep.	na	**na**	na	na	na	na	na	na	na	na	na	na	na	na	na	na
Egypt	na	**na**	na	na	na	na	na	na	na	na	na	na	na	na	na	na
El Salvador	na	**na**	na	na	na	na	na	na	na	na	na	na	na	na	na	na
Estonia	66	**64**	56	69	57	61	69	69	63	57	66	68	57	67	62	53
Finland	58	**84**	82	86	81	81	89	86	82	84	84	80	87	88	85	76
France	65	**61**	57	64	60	52	70	66	57	50	64	60	54	72	62	41
Georgia	na	**na**	na	na	na	na	na	na	na	na	na	na	na	na	na	na
Germany	39	**64**	58	68	52	59	74	70	59	57	62	63	66	73	63	56
Great Britain	66	**59**	55	63	50	53	69	67	54	44	63	58	55	na	na	na
Greece	na	**67**	65	68	63	68	71	75	69	64	68	64	66	70	67	61
Hungary	79	**75**	71	79	65	69	88	79	67	70	81	74	74	81	70	64
Iceland	67	**74**	72	77	68	74	81	81	73	65	78	75	70	82	76	50
India	74	**na**	na	na	na	na	na	na	na	na	na	na	na	na	na	na
Indonesia	na	**na**	na	na	na	na	na	na	na	na	na	na	na	na	na	na
Iran	na	**na**	na	na	na	na	na	na	na	na	na	na	na	na	na	na
Ireland	94	**91**	88	93	88	89	94	92	91	88	90	94	88	93	92	82
Israel	na	**na**	na	na	na	na	na	na	na	na	na	na	na	na	na	na
Italy	86	**89**	85	93	88	86	93	94	88	79	92	88	85	94	91	83
Japan	36	**na**	na	na	na	na	na	na	na	na	na	na	na	na	na	na
Jordan	na	**na**	na	na	na	na	na	na	na	na	na	na	na	na	na	na
Korea, South	na	**na**	na	na	na	na	na	na	na	na	na	na	na	na	na	na
Latvia	84	**65**	60	69	62	65	66	69	64	62	66	63	65	68	64	59
Lithuania	87	**93**	87	98	91	92	96	98	92	89	97	89	93	93	96	75
Luxembourg	na	**70**	67	74	68	64	79	79	67	63	75	72	58	77	72	54
Macedonia	na	**na**	na	na	na	na	na	na	na	na	na	na	na	na	na	na
Malta	na	**96**	95	98	96	95	98	97	96	97	98	95	96	96	97	93
Mexico	76	**na**	na	na	na	na	na	na	na	na	na	na	na	na	na	na
Moldova	na	**na**	na	na	na	na	na	na	na	na	na	na	na	na	na	na
Montenegro	na	**na**	na	na	na	na	na	na	na	na	na	na	na	na	na	na
Morocco	na	**na**	na	na	na	na	na	na	na	na	na	na	na	na	na	na
Netherlands	48	**40**	39	42	39	31	51	42	39	41	42	40	36	48	41	35
New Zealand	na	**na**	na	na	na	na	na	na	na	na	na	na	na	na	na	na
Nigeria	92	**na**	na	na	na	na	na	na	na	na	na	na	na	na	na	na
Northern Ireland	83	**81**	77	85	79	79	84	86	77	76	83	78	78	80	83	79
Norway	66	**na**	na	na	na	na	na	na	na	na	na	na	na	na	na	na
Pakistan	na	**na**	na	na	na	na	na	na	na	na	na	na	na	na	na	na
Peru	na	**na**	na	na	na	na	na	na	na	na	na	na	na	na	na	na
Philippines	na	**na**	na	na	na	na	na	na	na	na	na	na	na	na	na	na
Poland	95	**96**	95	97	97	95	97	98	95	91	97	97	94	98	95	95
Portugal	75	**90**	88	93	84	90	95	94	85	75	97	92	83	95	90	81
Puerto Rico	na	**na**	na	na	na	na	na	na	na	na	na	na	na	na	na	na
Romania	86	**98**	97	98	95	98	99	99	97	97	99	97	97	98	98	96
Russian Fed.	78	**75**	67	81	75	73	77	85	75	70	79	77	69	79	72	57
Serbia	na	**na**	na	na	na	na	na	na	na	na	na	na	na	na	na	na
Singapore	na	**na**	na	na	na	na	na	na	na	na	na	na	na	na	na	na
Slovakia	na	**83**	79	86	77	78	91	88	81	72	88	83	80	86	81	74
Slovenia	79	**73**	73	73	66	73	78	87	71	54	86	72	60	82	73	64
South Africa	78	**na**	na	na	na	na	na	na	na	na	na	na	na	na	na	na
Spain	74	**78**	72	83	67	74	87	87	72	68	81	78	68	90	80	53
Sweden	56	**60**	58	62	54	58	65	67	59	56	59	63	55	65	62	52
Switzerland	na	**na**	na	na	na	na	na	na	na	na	na	na	na	na	na	na
Taiwan	na	**na**	na	na	na	na	na	na	na	na	na	na	na	na	na	na
Tanzania	na	**na**	na	na	na	na	na	na	na	na	na	na	na	na	na	na
Turkey	42	**42**	37	47	40	41	51	47	37	29	44	42	35	55	40	32
Uganda	na	**na**	na	na	na	na	na	na	na	na	na	na	na	na	na	na
Ukraine	na	**86**	79	91	83	85	88	90	85	84	86	87	85	87	85	75
United States	57	**na**	na	na	na	na	na	na	na	na	na	na	na	na	na	na
Uruguay	na	**na**	na	na	na	na	na	na	na	na	na	na	na	na	na	na
Venezuela	na	**na**	na	na	na	na	na	na	na	na	na	na	na	na	na	na
Vietnam	na	**na**	na	na	na	na	na	na	na	na	na	na	na	na	na	na
Zimbabwe	na	**na**	na	na	na	na	na	na	na	na	na	na	na	na	na	na
Total	70	**76**	72	79	72	73	81	80	75	68	77	75	73	82	76	65

RANKING	
Country	**2000**
Romania	98
Malta	96
Poland	96
Lithuania	93
Croatia	91
Ireland	91
Portugal	90
Italy	89
Ukraine	86
Finland	84
Belarus	84
Slovakia	83
Austria	81
Northern Ireland	81
Bulgaria	78
Spain	78
Hungary	75
Russian Fed.	75
Iceland	74
Slovenia	73
Luxembourg	70
Belgium	70
Greece	67
Denmark	65
Latvia	65
Germany	64
Estonia	64
France	61
Sweden	60
Great Britain	59
Turkey	42
Czech Republic	42
Netherlands	40
Total	76

F032_1) RELIGIOUS SERVICE MARRIAGE

Do you personally think it is important to hold a religious service for any of the following events? Marriage

Yes (%) (EVS: V108)

Country	Wave 1990	Wave 2000	Gender Male	Gender Female	Age 16-29	Age 30-49	Age 50+	Education Lower	Education Middle	Education Upper	Income Lower	Income Middle	Income Upper	Values Mat	Values Mixed	Values Postm.
Albania	na	**na**	na	na	na	na	na	na	na	na	na	na	na	na	na	na
Algeria	na	**na**	na	na	na	na	na	na	na	na	na	na	na	na	na	na
Argentina	73	**na**	na	na	na	na	na	na	na	na	na	na	na	na	na	na
Armenia	na	**na**	na	na	na	na	na	na	na	na	na	na	na	na	na	na
Australia	na	**na**	na	na	na	na	na	na	na	na	na	na	na	na	na	na
Austria	85	**76**	74	79	71	73	82	82	73	64	77	79	72	89	79	68
Azerbaijan	na	**na**	na	na	na	na	na	na	na	na	na	na	na	na	na	na
Bangladesh	na	**na**	na	na	na	na	na	na	na	na	na	na	na	na	na	na
Belarus	62	**61**	54	67	59	57	68	70	58	59	63	59	63	63	59	49
Belgium	76	**70**	66	73	70	60	79	79	69	65	73	69	66	77	71	55
Bosnia and Herz.	na	**na**	na	na	na	na	na	na	na	na	na	na	na	na	na	na
Brazil	82	**na**	na	na	na	na	na	na	na	na	na	na	na	na	na	na
Bulgaria	81	**83**	82	84	84	81	85	86	82	79	86	82	83	86	80	79
Canada	82	**na**	na	na	na	na	na	na	na	na	na	na	na	na	na	na
Chile	87	**na**	na	na	na	na	na	na	na	na	na	na	na	na	na	na
China	13	**na**	na	na	na	na	na	na	na	na	na	na	na	na	na	na
Colombia	na	**na**	na	na	na	na	na	na	na	na	na	na	na	na	na	na
Croatia	na	**95**	94	96	95	97	94	98	95	88	92	97	96	95	96	94
Czech Republic	50	**40**	35	45	40	30	50	44	38	31	47	40	31	44	39	42
Denmark	64	**63**	62	64	66	57	68	68	54	57	66	63	57	70	65	49
Dominican Rep.	na	**na**	na	na	na	na	na	na	na	na	na	na	na	na	na	na
Egypt	na	**na**	na	na	na	na	na	na	na	na	na	na	na	na	na	na
El Salvador	na	**na**	na	na	na	na	na	na	na	na	na	na	na	na	na	na
Estonia	64	**65**	61	68	67	57	71	77	61	55	67	68	59	65	66	50
Finland	64	**83**	80	86	80	79	88	83	81	84	84	78	84	87	83	71
France	68	**66**	64	67	66	58	73	71	63	54	72	65	57	77	66	44
Georgia	na	**na**	na	na	na	na	na	na	na	na	na	na	na	na	na	na
Germany	46	**68**	63	72	63	61	78	74	63	63	67	67	70	71	68	64
Great Britain	80	**69**	62	76	65	63	75	74	66	57	74	65	66	na	na	na
Greece	na	**83**	80	85	83	82	84	96	88	76	86	84	81	90	85	71
Hungary	76	**75**	71	79	73	66	86	79	72	60	80	73	74	82	69	77
Iceland	66	**67**	64	71	65	65	71	73	68	56	66	68	66	76	68	42
India	79	**na**	na	na	na	na	na	na	na	na	na	na	na	na	na	na
Indonesia	na	**na**	na	na	na	na	na	na	na	na	na	na	na	na	na	na
Iran	na	**na**	na	na	na	na	na	na	na	na	na	na	na	na	na	na
Ireland	94	**92**	90	94	92	88	96	94	92	89	92	93	91	96	93	83
Israel	na	**na**	na	na	na	na	na	na	na	na	na	na	na	na	na	na
Italy	83	**85**	82	88	83	81	90	91	82	76	89	84	81	92	86	77
Japan	56	**na**	na	na	na	na	na	na	na	na	na	na	na	na	na	na
Jordan	na	**na**	na	na	na	na	na	na	na	na	na	na	na	na	na	na
Korea, South	na	**na**	na	na	na	na	na	na	na	na	na	na	na	na	na	na
Latvia	79	**78**	74	81	78	76	79	81	77	76	77	77	82	82	76	76
Lithuania	84	**89**	83	93	83	86	95	97	86	85	96	84	88	90	92	67
Luxembourg	na	**66**	64	67	63	59	75	75	63	57	71	68	52	75	67	47
Macedonia	na	**na**	na	na	na	na	na	na	na	na	na	na	na	na	na	na
Malta	na	**96**	94	98	94	95	98	98	95	94	98	96	95	96	97	89
Mexico	82	**na**	na	na	na	na	na	na	na	na	na	na	na	na	na	na
Moldova	na	**na**	na	na	na	na	na	na	na	na	na	na	na	na	na	na
Montenegro	na	**na**	na	na	na	na	na	na	na	na	na	na	na	na	na	na
Morocco	na	**na**	na	na	na	na	na	na	na	na	na	na	na	na	na	na
Netherlands	52	**46**	44	47	45	33	59	53	42	43	49	45	39	61	45	37
New Zealand	na	**na**	na	na	na	na	na	na	na	na	na	na	na	na	na	na
Nigeria	95	**na**	na	na	na	na	na	na	na	na	na	na	na	na	na	na
Northern Ireland	93	**90**	87	93	88	86	94	94	86	88	90	92	86	88	91	91
Norway	70	**na**	na	na	na	na	na	na	na	na	na	na	na	na	na	na
Pakistan	na	**na**	na	na	na	na	na	na	na	na	na	na	na	na	na	na
Peru	na	**na**	na	na	na	na	na	na	na	na	na	na	na	na	na	na
Philippines	na	**na**	na	na	na	na	na	na	na	na	na	na	na	na	na	na
Poland	97	**95**	94	95	91	95	96	97	94	87	96	95	90	96	94	93
Portugal	79	**89**	86	91	76	91	94	94	79	73	98	91	79	92	90	76
Puerto Rico	na	**na**	na	na	na	na	na	na	na	na	na	na	na	na	na	na
Romania	92	**98**	97	99	96	99	99	99	98	99	99	99	98	99	98	96
Russian Fed.	62	**54**	45	60	52	46	63	71	53	47	59	56	46	56	51	38
Serbia	na	**na**	na	na	na	na	na	na	na	na	na	na	na	na	na	na
Singapore	na	**na**	na	na	na	na	na	na	na	na	na	na	na	na	na	na
Slovakia	na	**80**	76	84	75	76	89	87	78	72	87	80	78	82	80	70
Slovenia	76	**70**	71	70	64	69	76	85	68	51	79	74	54	75	70	66
South Africa	93	**na**	na	na	na	na	na	na	na	na	na	na	na	na	na	na
Spain	74	**75**	71	80	62	69	88	87	68	62	79	77	65	87	78	48
Sweden	59	**62**	64	61	64	58	66	70	62	58	62	64	59	72	65	50
Switzerland	na	**na**	na	na	na	na	na	na	na	na	na	na	na	na	na	na
Taiwan	na	**na**	na	na	na	na	na	na	na	na	na	na	na	na	na	na
Tanzania	na	**na**	na	na	na	na	na	na	na	na	na	na	na	na	na	na
Turkey	76	**82**	79	84	81	81	87	89	76	54	92	79	68	88	82	72
Uganda	na	**na**	na	na	na	na	na	na	na	na	na	na	na	na	na	na
Ukraine	na	**69**	61	74	64	69	71	81	66	67	67	75	65	69	67	68
United States	86	**na**	na	na	na	na	na	na	na	na	na	na	na	na	na	na
Uruguay	na	**na**	na	na	na	na	na	na	na	na	na	na	na	na	na	na
Venezuela	na	**na**	na	na	na	na	na	na	na	na	na	na	na	na	na	na
Vietnam	na	**na**	na	na	na	na	na	na	na	na	na	na	na	na	na	na
Zimbabwe	na	**na**	na	na	na	na	na	na	na	na	na	na	na	na	na	na
Total	73	**75**	72	78	73	71	81	81	73	68	77	75	72	80	76	65

RANKING	
Country	2000
Romania	98
Malta	96
Croatia	95
Poland	95
Ireland	92
Northern Ireland	90
Lithuania	89
Portugal	89
Italy	85
Bulgaria	83
Greece	83
Finland	83
Turkey	82
Slovakia	80
Latvia	78
Austria	76
Hungary	75
Spain	75
Slovenia	70
Belgium	70
Ukraine	69
Great Britain	69
Germany	68
Iceland	67
Luxembourg	66
France	66
Estonia	65
Denmark	63
Sweden	62
Belarus	61
Russian Fed.	54
Netherlands	46
Czech Republic	40
Total	75

F033_1) RELIGIOUS SERVICE DEATH

Do you personally think it is important to hold a religious service for any of the following events? Death

Yes (%)

(EVS: V109)

Country	Wave		Gender		Age			Education			Income			Values		
	1990	2000	Male	Female	16-29	30-49	50+	Lower	Middle	Upper	Lower	Middle	Upper	Mat	Mixed	Postm.
Albania	na	**na**	na	na	na	na	na	na	na	na	na	na	na	na	na	na
Algeria	na	**na**	na	na	na	na	na	na	na	na	na	na	na	na	na	na
Argentina	67	**na**	na	na	na	na	na	na	na	na	na	na	na	na	na	na
Armenia	na	**na**	na	na	na	na	na	na	na	na	na	na	na	na	na	na
Australia	na	**na**	na	na	na	na	na	na	na	na	na	na	na	na	na	na
Austria	88	**85**	83	87	83	84	87	88	83	79	85	85	84	89	86	81
Azerbaijan	na	**na**	na	na	na	na	na	na	na	na	na	na	na	na	na	na
Bangladesh	na	**na**	na	na	na	na	na	na	na	na	na	na	na	na	na	na
Belarus	76	**88**	84	91	85	90	88	89	88	86	90	87	86	90	86	88
Belgium	79	**74**	71	77	76	66	81	80	75	70	75	75	72	83	75	61
Bosnia and Herz.	na	**na**	na	na	na	na	na	na	na	na	na	na	na	na	na	na
Brazil	76	**na**	na	na	na	na	na	na	na	na	na	na	na	na	na	na
Bulgaria	87	**89**	88	89	92	86	90	92	87	87	90	89	89	91	86	85
Canada	84	**na**	na	na	na	na	na	na	na	na	na	na	na	na	na	na
Chile	82	**na**	na	na	na	na	na	na	na	na	na	na	na	na	na	na
China	11	**na**	na	na	na	na	na	na	na	na	na	na	na	na	na	na
Colombia	na	**na**	na	na	na	na	na	na	na	na	na	na	na	na	na	na
Croatia	na	**96**	95	96	94	97	94	98	95	89	94	97	95	98	96	92
Czech Republic	62	**50**	46	54	50	46	54	55	48	39	54	50	43	53	50	49
Denmark	80	**80**	77	83	81	77	83	83	76	77	82	79	79	81	83	68
Dominican Rep.	na	**na**	na	na	na	na	na	na	na	na	na	na	na	na	na	na
Egypt	na	**na**	na	na	na	na	na	na	na	na	na	na	na	na	na	na
El Salvador	na	**na**	na	na	na	na	na	na	na	na	na	na	na	na	na	na
Estonia	72	**76**	72	78	72	73	79	80	75	70	80	77	69	78	75	63
Finland	83	**90**	87	93	88	86	95	90	89	90	90	89	91	92	91	80
France	73	**73**	71	75	77	68	76	78	68	64	77	73	67	81	75	55
Georgia	na	**na**	na	na	na	na	na	na	na	na	na	na	na	na	na	na
Germany	61	**74**	69	77	67	69	81	79	69	68	70	73	77	77	74	68
Great Britain	86	**79**	72	85	77	76	81	83	78	65	84	79	73	na	na	na
Greece	na	**87**	83	90	85	88	91	95	92	82	91	87	84	90	89	78
Hungary	86	**82**	78	86	78	77	89	85	76	75	86	80	81	86	78	77
Iceland	93	**91**	91	92	87	90	96	94	91	84	91	91	91	97	92	77
India	75	**na**	na	na	na	na	na	na	na	na	na	na	na	na	na	na
Indonesia	na	**na**	na	na	na	na	na	na	na	na	na	na	na	na	na	na
Iran	na	**na**	na	na	na	na	na	na	na	na	na	na	na	na	na	na
Ireland	97	**96**	94	97	96	93	98	97	96	93	94	96	96	98	96	88
Israel	na	**na**	na	na	na	na	na	na	na	na	na	na	na	na	na	na
Italy	87	**89**	86	93	89	86	92	92	89	83	91	88	87	92	91	84
Japan	87	**na**	na	na	na	na	na	na	na	na	na	na	na	na	na	na
Jordan	na	**na**	na	na	na	na	na	na	na	na	na	na	na	na	na	na
Korea, South	na	**na**	na	na	na	na	na	na	na	na	na	na	na	na	na	na
Latvia	85	**88**	86	90	88	86	90	90	87	88	87	88	90	88	89	86
Lithuania	89	**95**	93	98	94	94	98	98	95	93	98	94	95	96	97	88
Luxembourg	na	**77**	73	80	78	71	82	84	73	71	81	75	65	83	78	58
Macedonia	na	**na**	na	na	na	na	na	na	na	na	na	na	na	na	na	na
Malta	na	**97**	96	98	95	96	99	99	96	97	99	97	97	96	98	92
Mexico	81	**na**	na	na	na	na	na	na	na	na	na	na	na	na	na	na
Moldova	na	**na**	na	na	na	na	na	na	na	na	na	na	na	na	na	na
Montenegro	na	**na**	na	na	na	na	na	na	na	na	na	na	na	na	na	na
Morocco	na	**na**	na	na	na	na	na	na	na	na	na	na	na	na	na	na
Netherlands	62	**56**	54	57	54	48	64	62	52	53	57	55	52	67	57	47
New Zealand	na	**na**	na	na	na	na	na	na	na	na	na	na	na	na	na	na
Nigeria	90	**na**	na	na	na	na	na	na	na	na	na	na	na	na	na	na
Northern Ireland	96	**93**	91	95	92	90	95	96	90	92	92	93	91	93	94	91
Norway	81	**na**	na	na	na	na	na	na	na	na	na	na	na	na	na	na
Pakistan	na	**na**	na	na	na	na	na	na	na	na	na	na	na	na	na	na
Peru	na	**na**	na	na	na	na	na	na	na	na	na	na	na	na	na	na
Philippines	na	**na**	na	na	na	na	na	na	na	na	na	na	na	na	na	na
Poland	95	**96**	95	97	93	97	97	98	96	89	97	97	92	98	95	94
Portugal	79	**92**	91	94	84	96	95	97	87	73	97	96	85	96	93	81
Puerto Rico	na	**na**	na	na	na	na	na	na	na	na	na	na	na	na	na	na
Romania	89	**98**	97	99	96	98	99	99	97	97	99	98	97	98	98	96
Russian Fed.	74	**79**	71	85	79	78	80	88	79	74	81	80	75	81	76	67
Serbia	na	**na**	na	na	na	na	na	na	na	na	na	na	na	na	na	na
Singapore	na	**na**	na	na	na	na	na	na	na	na	na	na	na	na	na	na
Slovakia	na	**85**	82	87	81	82	90	89	83	78	90	85	83	85	84	87
Slovenia	81	**77**	79	76	77	75	80	89	76	59	88	78	61	82	77	73
South Africa	86	**na**	na	na	na	na	na	na	na	na	na	na	na	na	na	na
Spain	75	**80**	75	85	70	77	88	89	75	71	82	78	75	91	83	57
Sweden	80	**78**	76	79	80	72	81	82	79	72	79	77	76	80	80	70
Switzerland	na	**na**	na	na	na	na	na	na	na	na	na	na	na	na	na	na
Taiwan	na	**na**	na	na	na	na	na	na	na	na	na	na	na	na	na	na
Tanzania	na	**na**	na	na	na	na	na	na	na	na	na	na	na	na	na	na
Turkey	95	**95**	94	96	94	96	97	97	93	89	96	97	90	98	94	93
Uganda	na	**na**	na	na	na	na	na	na	na	na	na	na	na	na	na	na
Ukraine	na	**85**	78	91	84	86	85	94	83	84	84	86	86	86	84	82
United States	87	**na**	na	na	na	na	na	na	na	na	na	na	na	na	na	na
Uruguay	na	**na**	na	na	na	na	na	na	na	na	na	na	na	na	na	na
Venezuela	na	**na**	na	na	na	na	na	na	na	na	na	na	na	na	na	na
Vietnam	na	**na**	na	na	na	na	na	na	na	na	na	na	na	na	na	na
Zimbabwe	na	**na**	na	na	na	na	na	na	na	na	na	na	na	na	na	na
Total	80	84	81	86	83	81	87	88	83	78	85	84	82	88	84	75

RANKING

Country	2000
Romania	98
Malta	97
Poland	96
Croatia	96
Ireland	96
Lithuania	95
Turkey	95
Northern Ireland	93
Portugal	92
Iceland	91
Finland	90
Italy	89
Bulgaria	89
Belarus	88
Latvia	88
Greece	87
Austria	85
Ukraine	85
Slovakia	85
Hungary	82
Spain	80
Denmark	80
Russian Fed.	79
Great Britain	79
Sweden	78
Slovenia	77
Luxembourg	77
Estonia	76
Belgium	74
Germany	74
France	73
Netherlands	56
Czech Republic	50
Total	84

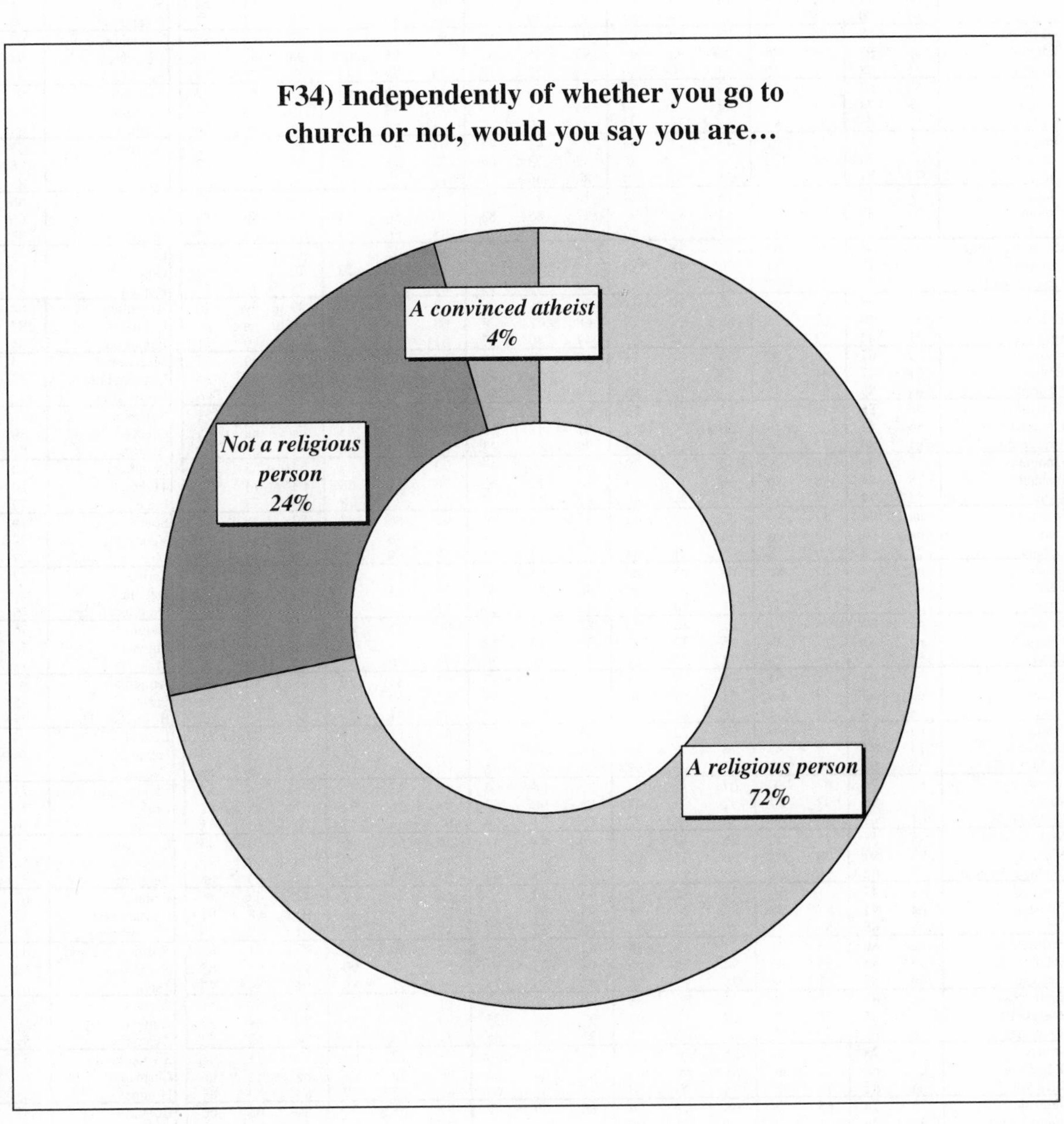
F34) Independently of whether you go to church or not, would you say you are…
A convinced atheist
4%
Not a religious person
24%
A religious person
72%

F034) RELIGIOUS PERSON

Independently of whether you go to church or not, would you say you are...

A religious person (%)

(WVS: V186; EVS: V110)

Country	Wave		Gender		Age			Education			Income			Values		
	1990	2000	Male	Female	16-29	30-49	50+	Lower	Middle	Upper	Lower	Middle	Upper	Mat	Mixed	Postm.
Albania	na	**68**	63	74	67	65	75	72	69	58	69	70	66	70	66	64
Algeria	na	**59**	60	58	53	58	74	68	56	56	62	64	50	57	60	59
Argentina	73	**84**	80	88	79	84	90	86	83	80	89	85	79	89	86	77
Armenia	na	**75**	66	82	78	73	73	74	76	71	75	73	77	73	78	65
Australia	na	**59**	52	66	48	59	70	67	54	58	63	57	54	63	61	54
Austria	81	**80**	75	84	71	79	84	82	79	72	82	80	76	78	81	77
Azerbaijan	na	**88**	86	90	87	89	90	92	89	86	90	87	87	89	86	88
Bangladesh	na	**97**	96	98	94	98	99	99	95	94	99	95	97	98	96	96
Belarus	41	**28**	17	36	23	20	40	43	22	18	35	26	18	30	26	15
Belgium	68	**67**	62	72	55	63	78	74	66	64	71	66	63	81	68	52
Bosnia and Herz.	na	**74**	71	77	84	72	69	83	75	65	75	74	74	75	74	69
Brazil	88	**85**	84	87	81	87	91	84	87	87	83	88	87	85	86	84
Bulgaria	36	**52**	42	61	43	43	63	65	44	45	62	47	45	51	53	52
Canada	71	**74**	67	80	59	71	85	82	73	67	77	75	68	76	77	67
Chile	77	**71**	62	79	64	69	79	80	66	65	71	71	68	70	73	65
China	5	**15**	12	17	16	15	14	14	15	21	9	14	24	14	15	17
Colombia	na	**85**	82	89	82	85	92	87	85	83	86	86	84	88	86	88
Croatia	na	**85**	78	91	77	89	86	91	84	74	88	86	84	94	85	75
Czech Republic	46	**43**	36	50	34	35	55	44	43	41	50	42	36	45	42	47
Denmark	73	**77**	69	84	60	78	84	81	65	73	78	78	73	72	78	72
Dominican Rep.	na	**76**	75	77	77	76	82	74	69	79	81	77	75	75	76	77
Egypt	na	**99**	98	99	98	99	100	99	98	99	99	99	99	99	99	96
El Salvador	na	**70**	67	73	66	67	79	68	71	74	68	68	72	na	na	na
Estonia	21	**42**	32	50	34	34	52	47	40	37	51	45	36	44	40	31
Finland	59	**67**	56	76	50	64	78	69	62	69	68	64	67	64	69	62
France	51	**47**	41	52	35	42	56	51	39	43	50	47	41	56	47	31
Georgia	na	**89**	86	93	93	90	84	90	90	88	88	90	90	90	89	96
Germany	38	**56**	48	62	43	51	66	60	52	50	55	60	59	57	57	51
Great Britain	56	**42**	37	46	26	37	53	41	43	32	39	41	43	na	na	na
Greece	na	**80**	74	84	76	82	84	90	86	73	81	78	80	88	81	67
Hungary	57	**59**	48	69	47	53	72	66	46	43	70	59	53	64	55	47
Iceland	75	**74**	68	80	60	76	83	81	72	65	76	76	68	83	74	51
India	84	**79**	78	82	77	81	80	82	78	75	77	82	78	83	73	73
Indonesia	na	**84**	83	87	80	83	88	85	86	82	83	86	83	82	86	87
Iran	na	**95**	94	96	94	95	97	96	94	94	95	96	94	97	94	94
Ireland	72	**74**	70	78	68	71	84	77	72	74	79	69	74	79	74	69
Israel	na	**na**	na	na	na	na	na	na	na	na	na	na	na	na	na	na
Italy	86	**86**	80	91	82	85	89	90	83	80	89	85	82	94	88	77
Japan	26	**27**	23	30	15	24	33	33	28	19	31	26	23	26	26	27
Jordan	na	**86**	76	95	81	88	93	87	83	87	90	85	84	87	86	76
Korea, South	na	**31**	27	35	25	32	37	36	33	28	27	29	36	31	30	35
Latvia	54	**77**	65	86	71	75	81	81	76	76	79	80	73	80	76	77
Lithuania	55	**84**	72	94	76	79	94	93	80	87	95	83	79	85	86	70
Luxembourg	na	**63**	58	68	51	59	76	71	62	55	62	69	60	62	64	58
Macedonia	na	**84**	84	84	86	84	82	93	80	77	90	81	80	86	82	85
Malta	na	**75**	69	80	64	72	85	85	71	71	81	75	67	77	74	66
Mexico	75	**77**	74	80	74	76	85	80	75	74	85	75	75	78	78	73
Moldova	na	**91**	86	95	87	92	93	94	92	86	94	90	89	93	88	86
Montenegro	na	**73**	67	80	67	72	78	83	68	62	73	76	70	78	70	53
Morocco	na	**95**	93	97	92	96	100	95	96	92	93	95	92	97	93	92
Netherlands	61	**62**	54	69	54	55	72	67	61	59	60	63	57	76	61	55
New Zealand	na	**51**	45	56	38	49	57	49	54	51	56	52	46	50	55	43
Nigeria	93	**97**	96	97	96	97	99	97	97	96	96	97	97	96	97	97
Northern Ireland	72	**62**	56	68	53	57	72	69	55	62	63	58	61	62	63	68
Norway	48	**47**	37	56	35	46	57	48	42	51	na	na	na	47	47	46
Pakistan	na	**91**	87	94	87	94	88	95	87	85	96	89	88	93	88	91
Peru	na	**88**	85	91	85	90	93	89	89	87	87	91	87	91	87	90
Philippines	na	**80**	78	81	72	82	85	82	76	81	82	80	76	77	81	82
Poland	95	**94**	93	96	94	95	95	98	93	83	97	94	90	98	93	85
Portugal	69	**88**	81	94	78	93	90	93	80	74	91	91	85	91	89	77
Puerto Rico	na	**82**	77	86	76	80	88	90	81	82	81	86	80	84	82	84
Romania	75	**85**	78	92	77	81	92	92	83	75	90	87	78	89	84	57
Russian Fed.	56	**66**	52	77	64	62	71	73	65	65	71	64	64	70	60	52
Serbia	na	**75**	67	82	76	76	72	81	72	70	78	77	69	77	73	63
Singapore	na	**na**	na	na	na	na	na	na	na	na	na	na	na	na	na	na
Slovakia	na	**82**	76	87	74	79	90	85	82	69	87	82	79	83	80	83
Slovenia	73	**70**	65	74	66	67	76	86	69	47	82	68	51	80	68	66
South Africa	83	**79**	71	88	77	77	90	76	82	87	74	81	83	80	78	79
Spain	70	**61**	50	72	46	57	74	69	53	54	68	61	59	74	61	43
Sweden	31	**39**	32	46	26	35	51	43	34	44	40	38	37	46	38	37
Switzerland	74	**57**	51	64	41	58	66	65	55	61	61	57	54	54	56	59
Taiwan	na	**75**	70	80	65	77	78	81	73	72	75	80	71	76	75	59
Tanzania	na	**94**	93	96	93	95	96	94	94	97	94	95	93	94	95	91
Turkey	75	**80**	75	84	76	81	84	87	74	59	84	79	68	84	80	69
Uganda	na	**94**	95	94	95	94	89	93	95	95	98	94	94	91	96	97
Ukraine	na	**75**	62	86	77	71	78	83	73	78	76	76	74	74	74	83
United States	84	**83**	77	88	75	84	87	82	83	83	83	80	86	87	83	80
Uruguay	na	**55**	42	64	47	47	64	60	48	46	59	51	55	60	57	47
Venezuela	na	**79**	75	82	73	83	82	78	77	84	72	80	81	81	78	80
Vietnam	na	**38**	31	46	33	36	46	46	29	27	42	38	36	45	37	39
Zimbabwe	na	**89**	82	95	89	90	86	89	89	70	85	93	93	87	90	93
Total	63	**72**	66	77	69	70	75	76	69	69	74	72	69	75	72	66

RANKING	
Country	2000
Egypt	99
Bangladesh	97
Nigeria	97
Iran	95
Morocco	95
Poland	94
Tanzania	94
Uganda	94
Moldova	91
Pakistan	91
Georgia	89
Zimbabwe	89
Azerbaijan	88
Peru	88
Portugal	88
Jordan	86
Italy	86
Brazil	85
Croatia	85
Colombia	85
Romania	85
Argentina	84
Lithuania	84
Indonesia	84
Macedonia	84
United States	83
Puerto Rico	82
Slovakia	82
Greece	80
Austria	80
Philippines	80
Turkey	80
India	79
South Africa	79
Venezuela	79
Mexico	77
Latvia	77
Denmark	77
Dominican Rep.	76
Ukraine	75
Taiwan	75
Malta	75
Armenia	75
Serbia	75
Bosnia and Herz.	74
Ireland	74
Iceland	74
Canada	74
Montenegro	73
Chile	71
Slovenia	70
El Salvador	70
Albania	68
Belgium	67
Finland	67
Russian Fed.	66
Luxembourg	63
Northern Ireland	62
Netherlands	62
Spain	61
Algeria	59
Hungary	59
Australia	59
Switzerland	57
Germany	56
Uruguay	55
Bulgaria	52
New Zealand	51
Norway	47
France	47
Czech Republic	43
Estonia	42
Great Britain	42
Sweden	39
Vietnam	38
Korea, South	31
Belarus	28
Japan	27
China	15
Total	72

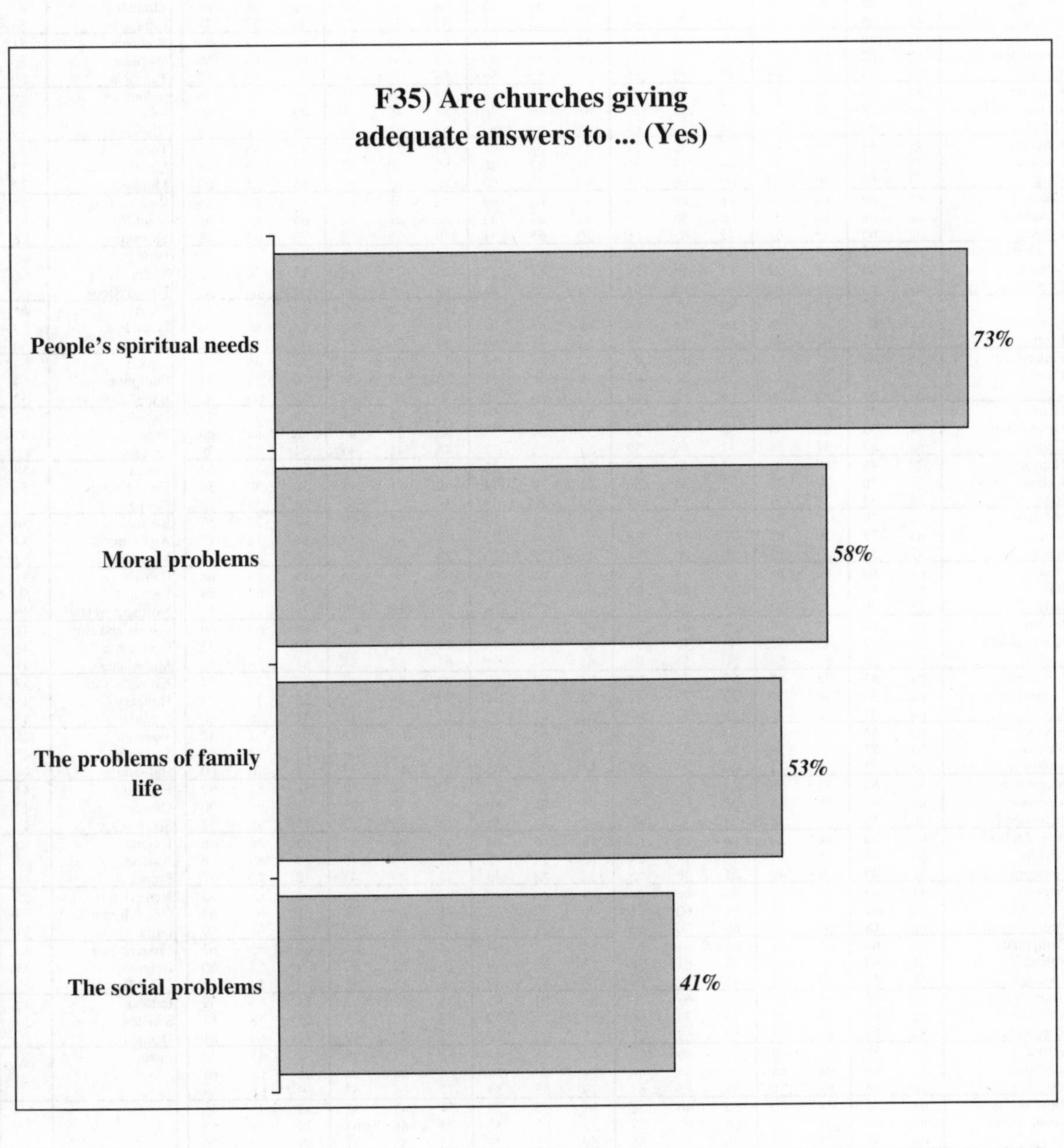
F35) Are churches giving adequate answers to ... (Yes)
People's spiritual needs
73%
Moral problems
58%
The problems of family life
53%
The social problems
41%

F035) CHURCHES GIVE ANSWERS: MORAL PROBLEMS

Generally speaking, do you think that the churches in your country are giving adequate answers to ...

The moral problems and needs of the individual

Yes (%)

(WVS: V187; EVS: V111)

Country	Wave		Gender		Age			Education			Income			Values		
	1990	2000	Male	Female	16-29	30-49	50+	Lower	Middle	Upper	Lower	Middle	Upper	Mat	Mixed	Postm.
Albania	na	**64**	61	67	60	61	71	71	60	59	65	66	62	65	63	54
Algeria	na	**91**	92	89	90	89	96	95	89	89	92	90	86	95	89	90
Argentina	42	**54**	49	58	47	53	61	59	46	48	62	56	44	66	57	38
Armenia	na	**na**	na	na	na	na	na	na	na	na	na	na	na	na	na	na
Australia	na	**na**	na	na	na	na	na	na	na	na	na	na	na	na	na	na
Austria	47	**38**	37	38	29	37	43	38	35	42	43	38	37	30	37	38
Azerbaijan	na	**na**	na	na	na	na	na	na	na	na	na	na	na	na	na	na
Bangladesh	na	**62**	64	57	60	63	64	66	58	60	65	64	57	65	60	66
Belarus	83	**56**	46	63	48	53	66	67	51	56	58	57	49	57	53	52
Belgium	42	**33**	32	34	29	26	41	42	32	28	43	33	27	39	32	26
Bosnia and Herz.	na	**48**	48	49	47	47	51	61	46	46	53	46	49	43	51	49
Brazil	44	**na**	na	na	na	na	na	na	na	na	na	na	na	na	na	na
Bulgaria	49	**44**	36	52	37	38	52	57	37	42	55	38	42	41	45	45
Canada	55	**51**	48	53	44	49	56	59	49	46	55	50	47	55	55	42
Chile	77	**65**	60	69	60	66	68	69	63	60	66	65	62	65	65	63
China	na	**na**	na	na	na	na	na	na	na	na	na	na	na	na	na	na
Colombia	na	**na**	na	na	na	na	na	na	na	na	na	na	na	na	na	na
Croatia	na	**60**	55	65	45	63	66	70	55	51	78	55	58	73	61	48
Czech Republic	na	**35**	32	38	30	28	45	37	32	38	42	34	28	33	35	43
Denmark	20	**20**	17	23	14	19	24	21	17	22	20	23	18	15	20	22
Dominican Rep.	na	**na**	na	na	na	na	na	na	na	na	na	na	na	na	na	na
Egypt	na	**92**	89	95	90	93	95	94	90	90	92	93	92	94	92	86
El Salvador	na	**na**	na	na	na	na	na	na	na	na	na	na	na	na	na	na
Estonia	na	**45**	41	49	33	41	55	52	41	46	54	50	37	51	41	44
Finland	25	**44**	41	46	37	38	51	42	44	52	43	40	44	38	46	44
France	38	**36**	35	36	33	31	41	36	30	41	36	35	38	40	35	31
Georgia	na	**na**	na	na	na	na	na	na	na	na	na	na	na	na	na	na
Germany	58	**48**	43	52	38	42	60	53	43	50	52	47	51	56	47	43
Great Britain	34	**33**	32	34	29	34	33	30	34	33	36	33	36	na	na	na
Greece	na	**43**	41	44	37	45	52	57	50	35	48	41	44	54	42	36
Hungary	79	**46**	39	53	33	40	60	51	39	36	53	47	42	50	42	44
Iceland	37	**40**	39	42	33	38	50	43	36	44	40	41	41	50	38	30
India	38	**33**	31	37	32	33	34	36	29	33	31	31	35	33	33	23
Indonesia	na	**79**	77	83	67	80	84	87	81	72	81	77	79	84	77	67
Iran	na	**79**	76	83	77	78	88	87	79	72	78	81	78	84	78	75
Ireland	42	**30**	27	33	16	26	44	42	25	20	38	30	23	33	30	21
Israel	na	**na**	na	na	na	na	na	na	na	na	na	na	na	na	na	na
Italy	55	**62**	58	65	53	59	69	67	58	57	68	61	56	70	63	54
Japan	28	**20**	16	24	21	22	17	15	23	16	20	18	19	21	21	14
Jordan	na	**64**	54	74	64	61	70	69	63	56	69	61	62	65	63	69
Korea, South	na	**47**	43	52	44	47	51	53	48	45	44	46	52	48	47	35
Latvia	88	**58**	52	64	50	54	65	64	57	55	63	58	55	61	58	49
Lithuania	na	**83**	78	85	75	75	91	94	77	80	90	79	80	88	83	54
Luxembourg	na	**33**	34	32	27	29	41	38	30	34	39	28	25	32	34	31
Macedonia	na	**47**	48	47	48	47	47	62	41	37	52	45	42	44	46	66
Malta	na	**66**	60	71	49	64	78	79	61	59	71	69	55	68	67	42
Mexico	65	**73**	71	76	68	73	82	79	68	63	79	72	66	75	73	65
Moldova	na	**73**	71	75	60	76	81	83	75	63	81	65	73	74	76	60
Montenegro	na	**52**	47	58	44	50	60	62	48	42	50	56	49	52	52	52
Morocco	na	**97**	96	98	95	97	98	97	98	88	97	97	95	98	96	90
Netherlands	36	**36**	33	38	33	32	40	42	34	32	33	39	35	45	38	27
New Zealand	na	**na**	na	na	na	na	na	na	na	na	na	na	na	na	na	na
Nigeria	86	**79**	78	79	78	79	84	83	77	75	79	79	78	77	80	78
Northern Ireland	55	**49**	49	49	51	40	55	52	48	43	45	49	47	48	49	51
Norway	41	**na**	na	na	na	na	na	na	na	na	na	na	na	na	na	na
Pakistan	na	**62**	58	67	61	60	72	70	57	47	71	63	52	61	65	64
Peru	na	**68**	63	72	66	70	66	71	71	61	73	68	57	73	67	59
Philippines	na	**64**	66	62	65	63	65	64	64	64	64	64	64	62	65	62
Poland	na	**64**	63	66	49	61	78	73	56	49	70	62	59	69	63	60
Portugal	57	**57**	53	60	46	49	69	63	43	49	68	55	52	60	54	52
Puerto Rico	na	**65**	59	69	51	63	73	82	64	63	71	65	63	73	65	59
Romania	62	**81**	76	85	73	79	86	89	79	70	88	83	75	85	78	65
Russian Fed.	88	**71**	65	75	62	69	78	75	69	72	72	73	67	72	69	81
Serbia	na	**50**	44	55	52	46	52	63	43	43	53	51	45	52	47	42
Singapore	na	**na**	na	na	na	na	na	na	na	na	na	na	na	na	na	na
Slovakia	na	**68**	62	75	59	63	81	79	65	59	77	65	67	69	68	68
Slovenia	64	**45**	44	46	36	40	58	61	42	29	54	47	38	53	45	36
South Africa	na	**69**	64	75	66	69	77	73	67	38	73	68	64	78	65	55
Spain	40	**41**	33	48	26	33	56	50	32	29	53	42	31	53	40	20
Sweden	19	**26**	25	28	21	25	31	36	21	27	27	28	23	33	28	18
Switzerland	na	**na**	na	na	na	na	na	na	na	na	na	na	na	na	na	na
Taiwan	na	**na**	na	na	na	na	na	na	na	na	na	na	na	na	na	na
Tanzania	na	**80**	76	85	79	82	74	78	80	85	78	81	82	82	79	71
Turkey	50	**76**	76	76	77	74	82	83	69	61	87	74	62	78	76	71
Uganda	na	**89**	90	88	90	90	85	86	90	93	92	96	92	88	90	90
Ukraine	na	**80**	72	86	68	81	85	91	78	77	83	80	74	80	78	83
United States	68	**58**	55	60	54	61	56	64	57	55	60	59	51	63	61	49
Uruguay	na	**na**	na	na	na	na	na	na	na	na	na	na	na	na	na	na
Venezuela	na	**na**	na	na	na	na	na	na	na	na	na	na	na	na	na	na
Vietnam	na	**45**	41	49	40	46	47	50	39	42	41	43	49	45	45	48
Zimbabwe	na	**87**	80	93	86	88	88	92	81	62	88	89	78	90	85	83
Total	53	**58**	54	61	56	56	61	64	55	52	62	57	54	64	57	47

RANKING

Country	2000
Morocco	97
Egypt	92
Algeria	91
Uganda	89
Zimbabwe	87
Lithuania	83
Romania	81
Ukraine	80
Tanzania	80
Indonesia	79
Iran	79
Nigeria	79
Turkey	76
Mexico	73
Moldova	73
Russian Fed.	71
South Africa	69
Slovakia	68
Peru	68
Malta	66
Puerto Rico	65
Chile	65
Poland	64
Albania	64
Jordan	64
Philippines	64
Bangladesh	62
Pakistan	62
Italy	62
Croatia	60
Latvia	58
United States	58
Portugal	57
Belarus	56
Argentina	54
Montenegro	52
Canada	51
Serbia	50
Northern Ireland	49
Bosnia and Herz.	48
Germany	48
Macedonia	47
Korea, South	47
Hungary	46
Estonia	45
Vietnam	45
Slovenia	45
Bulgaria	44
Finland	44
Greece	43
Spain	41
Iceland	40
Austria	38
France	36
Netherlands	36
Czech Republic	35
India	33
Luxembourg	33
Belgium	33
Great Britain	33
Ireland	30
Sweden	26
Denmark	20
Japan	20
Total	58

F036) CHURCHES GIVE ANSWERS: THE PROBLEMS OF FAMILY LIFE

Generally speaking, do you think that the churches in your country are giving adequate answers to ...
The problems of family life.

Yes (%) (WVS: V188; EVS: V112)

Country	Wave		Gender		Age			Education			Income			Values		
	1990	2000	Male	Female	16-29	30-49	50+	Lower	Middle	Upper	Lower	Middle	Upper	Mat	Mixed	Postm.
Albania	na	**53**	53	54	47	51	61	58	48	54	54	55	51	53	53	51
Algeria	na	**90**	90	89	92	88	88	91	88	90	92	85	88	95	86	92
Argentina	49	**59**	55	62	55	58	63	63	52	52	68	59	49	69	61	46
Armenia	na	**na**	na	na	na	na	na	na	na	na	na	na	na	na	na	na
Australia	na	**na**	na	na	na	na	na	na	na	na	na	na	na	na	na	na
Austria	34	**29**	28	30	26	28	31	27	28	38	33	29	29	30	29	29
Azerbaijan	na	**na**	na	na	na	na	na	na	na	na	na	na	na	na	na	na
Bangladesh	na	**54**	54	54	52	54	61	61	44	50	60	57	46	55	53	58
Belarus	83	**36**	29	42	27	32	49	50	33	27	39	35	33	40	33	24
Belgium	37	**30**	29	31	25	25	37	38	28	27	36	28	26	36	30	21
Bosnia and Herz.	na	**34**	33	34	34	31	37	43	31	33	37	29	39	28	35	26
Brazil	51	**na**	na	na	na	na	na	na	na	na	na	na	na	na	na	na
Bulgaria	38	**29**	25	34	22	23	39	45	22	23	40	25	26	28	30	21
Canada	56	**48**	45	50	39	48	52	57	48	40	48	48	44	53	50	42
Chile	83	**68**	66	70	67	68	71	75	66	62	69	70	64	69	65	77
China	na	**na**	na	na	na	na	na	na	na	na	na	na	na	na	na	na
Colombia	na	**na**	na	na	na	na	na	na	na	na	na	na	na	na	na	na
Croatia	na	**59**	51	66	50	58	65	67	55	51	77	57	52	70	59	48
Czech Republic	na	**30**	26	35	25	23	40	32	28	32	36	28	24	28	32	23
Denmark	13	**15**	14	17	13	12	20	18	12	13	15	16	14	12	16	13
Dominican Rep.	na	**na**	na	na	na	na	na	na	na	na	na	na	na	na	na	na
Egypt	na	**87**	84	91	85	88	90	90	84	88	88	89	87	90	87	81
El Salvador	na	**na**	na	na	na	na	na	na	na	na	na	na	na	na	na	na
Estonia	na	**31**	29	32	23	27	38	37	26	32	36	35	25	33	28	20
Finland	27	**42**	35	48	32	38	51	43	42	42	45	36	42	37	44	45
France	28	**28**	26	29	22	23	36	29	25	27	30	26	30	31	28	23
Georgia	na	**na**	na	na	na	na	na	na	na	na	na	na	na	na	na	na
Germany	43	**39**	35	42	34	32	48	44	35	34	39	41	48	46	38	33
Great Britain	36	**30**	28	32	25	29	33	29	31	25	33	36	30	na	na	na
Greece	na	**31**	30	30	24	29	46	53	35	23	38	27	28	39	30	21
Hungary	70	**41**	31	49	29	33	54	46	30	34	47	40	39	44	37	24
Iceland	40	**45**	41	49	35	45	54	50	42	41	44	47	45	52	45	28
India	28	**27**	24	32	25	28	28	30	22	27	26	27	27	26	27	30
Indonesia	na	**77**	73	83	68	81	79	88	76	71	77	79	72	83	74	71
Iran	na	**73**	71	76	74	69	80	79	72	68	75	73	72	77	70	70
Ireland	36	**27**	25	29	20	23	37	34	22	25	31	26	23	33	27	14
Israel	na	**na**	na	na	na	na	na	na	na	na	na	na	na	na	na	na
Italy	47	**48**	43	52	34	46	57	54	43	41	56	44	43	61	48	40
Japan	22	**16**	12	20	10	17	18	16	19	9	20	14	13	15	17	11
Jordan	na	**61**	54	68	61	59	66	65	58	57	64	58	64	63	59	63
Korea, South	na	**39**	34	44	34	41	41	40	42	34	35	42	40	41	38	31
Latvia	63	**48**	43	52	35	44	56	55	44	50	53	45	44	50	47	37
Lithuania	na	**81**	75	85	71	72	93	95	77	70	88	76	78	87	81	57
Luxembourg	na	**24**	26	23	19	18	34	26	23	24	22	22	22	29	24	19
Macedonia	na	**31**	30	32	32	29	33	44	25	24	37	30	25	30	29	45
Malta	na	**74**	72	76	61	69	87	84	72	60	75	75	71	76	75	55
Mexico	64	**74**	71	76	71	74	79	78	71	66	80	74	64	73	74	70
Moldova	na	**67**	61	71	56	69	73	80	66	55	78	60	60	66	67	70
Montenegro	na	**34**	30	39	26	34	40	41	32	26	34	38	28	32	35	36
Morocco	na	**97**	97	97	96	97	99	97	97	94	97	97	96	97	97	92
Netherlands	34	**31**	29	33	29	27	36	41	27	26	35	32	23	46	33	20
New Zealand	na	**na**	na	na	na	na	na	na	na	na	na	na	na	na	na	na
Nigeria	86	**79**	78	80	79	79	81	82	78	74	80	78	78	77	80	77
Northern Ireland	59	**48**	47	49	47	37	56	52	45	42	48	48	42	47	47	51
Norway	29	**na**	na	na	na	na	na	na	na	na	na	na	na	na	na	na
Pakistan	na	**49**	47	51	45	46	63	53	43	43	51	49	44	52	44	55
Peru	na	**76**	71	80	75	76	78	79	80	67	80	76	67	80	76	67
Philippines	na	**63**	60	65	64	63	61	67	60	61	61	61	67	63	62	67
Poland	na	**64**	62	66	53	62	73	71	57	49	67	63	59	70	63	50
Portugal	56	**46**	42	50	43	36	56	51	32	47	52	44	45	52	43	37
Puerto Rico	na	**72**	64	77	65	69	78	88	71	70	78	73	69	79	72	67
Romania	53	**79**	74	82	71	75	86	88	77	63	85	80	72	83	75	60
Russian Fed.	74	**55**	47	61	50	50	64	65	53	55	60	60	46	55	55	54
Serbia	na	**39**	35	42	43	32	43	49	31	37	43	36	36	40	37	32
Singapore	na	**na**	na	na	na	na	na	na	na	na	na	na	na	na	na	na
Slovakia	na	**64**	57	71	55	58	77	75	60	58	74	65	58	65	63	64
Slovenia	54	**43**	42	43	40	35	54	55	42	26	53	45	34	50	43	37
South Africa	na	**73**	66	81	66	77	78	77	70	54	75	72	72	80	71	59
Spain	42	**37**	31	42	20	31	52	46	29	24	49	36	28	48	35	21
Sweden	14	**18**	17	20	11	15	25	31	13	17	19	19	16	32	19	13
Switzerland	na	**na**	na	na	na	na	na	na	na	na	na	na	na	na	na	na
Taiwan	na	**na**	na	na	na	na	na	na	na	na	na	na	na	na	na	na
Tanzania	na	**81**	78	84	86	79	77	80	82	80	81	83	81	83	80	87
Turkey	34	**67**	66	69	66	66	76	77	56	47	77	68	49	72	69	58
Uganda	na	**84**	88	80	84	84	85	80	85	91	86	91	86	82	85	86
Ukraine	na	**63**	54	70	50	63	71	76	61	62	66	64	59	61	61	75
United States	69	**61**	59	63	61	62	59	66	63	58	65	59	58	59	63	57
Uruguay	na	**na**	na	na	na	na	na	na	na	na	na	na	na	na	na	na
Venezuela	na	**na**	na	na	na	na	na	na	na	na	na	na	na	na	na	na
Vietnam	na	**30**	28	33	28	31	32	36	25	21	26	24	38	22	31	38
Zimbabwe	na	**88**	83	93	89	87	89	90	86	60	87	90	86	90	87	87
Total	48	**53**	49	56	52	50	56	59	50	47	57	51	49	58	52	44

RANKING	
Country	**2000**
Morocco	97
Algeria	90
Zimbabwe	88
Egypt	87
Uganda	84
Lithuania	81
Tanzania	81
Nigeria	79
Romania	79
Indonesia	77
Peru	76
Malta	74
Mexico	74
Iran	73
South Africa	73
Puerto Rico	72
Chile	68
Turkey	67
Moldova	67
Poland	64
Slovakia	64
Ukraine	63
Philippines	63
Jordan	61
United States	61
Croatia	59
Argentina	59
Russian Fed.	55
Bangladesh	54
Albania	53
Pakistan	49
Latvia	48
Italy	48
Northern Ireland	48
Canada	48
Portugal	46
Iceland	45
Slovenia	43
Finland	42
Hungary	41
Germany	39
Korea, South	39
Serbia	39
Spain	37
Belarus	36
Montenegro	34
Bosnia and Herz.	34
Netherlands	31
Macedonia	31
Greece	31
Estonia	31
Czech Republic	30
Vietnam	30
Great Britain	30
Belgium	30
Bulgaria	29
Austria	29
France	28
India	27
Ireland	27
Luxembourg	24
Sweden	18
Japan	16
Denmark	15
Total	53

F037) CHURCHES GIVE ANSWERS: PEOPLE'S SPIRITUAL NEEDS

Generally speaking, do you think that the churches in your country are giving adequate answers to ...
People's spiritual needs.
Yes (%)

(WVS: V189; EVS: V113)

Country	Wave		Gender		Age			Education			Income			Values		
	1990	2000	Male	Female	16-29	30-49	50+	Lower	Middle	Upper	Lower	Middle	Upper	Mat	Mixed	Postm.
Albania	na	**79**	75	82	81	76	81	83	76	75	79	80	78	75	81	75
Algeria	na	**98**	99	97	97	98	98	98	97	98	98	98	96	98	97	97
Argentina	59	**68**	64	72	68	65	73	71	67	59	75	67	63	75	71	58
Armenia	na	**na**	na	na	na	na	na	na	na	na	na	na	na	na	na	na
Australia	na	**na**	na	na	na	na	na	na	na	na	na	na	na	na	na	na
Austria	68	**60**	58	62	55	61	62	59	60	68	58	62	60	47	62	59
Azerbaijan	na	**na**	na	na	na	na	na	na	na	na	na	na	na	na	na	na
Bangladesh	na	**78**	80	73	76	78	84	79	76	77	88	76	72	81	76	78
Belarus	83	**70**	63	76	64	67	78	81	66	68	71	70	69	71	68	72
Belgium	58	**49**	47	52	50	43	55	48	49	50	50	45	52	49	50	47
Bosnia and Herz.	na	**67**	65	68	66	68	65	76	66	61	67	64	70	69	66	61
Brazil	57	**na**	na	na	na	na	na	na	na	na	na	na	na	na	na	na
Bulgaria	56	**55**	43	66	50	50	61	65	50	51	63	49	54	52	55	48
Canada	75	**72**	69	75	69	73	73	72	73	70	72	70	73	70	74	69
Chile	86	**83**	80	86	83	80	88	89	80	78	86	82	79	83	83	82
China	na	**na**	na	na	na	na	na	na	na	na	na	na	na	na	na	na
Colombia	na	**na**	na	na	na	na	na	na	na	na	na	na	na	na	na	na
Croatia	na	**87**	84	90	81	89	89	92	85	83	89	85	87	96	87	79
Czech Republic	na	**69**	64	74	71	67	70	71	68	63	68	68	67	67	70	71
Denmark	49	**51**	46	55	47	48	57	57	46	48	51	52	51	56	52	42
Dominican Rep.	na	**na**	na	na	na	na	na	na	na	na	na	na	na	na	na	na
Egypt	na	**93**	92	94	91	93	94	95	90	92	94	95	92	95	92	89
El Salvador	na	**na**	na	na	na	na	na	na	na	na	na	na	na	na	na	na
Estonia	na	**73**	66	79	64	70	80	78	69	74	78	73	70	75	73	73
Finland	51	**68**	60	76	67	65	71	70	66	71	73	61	68	69	68	72
France	59	**55**	54	57	56	53	58	52	53	67	51	55	63	55	55	55
Georgia	na	**na**	na	na	na	na	na	na	na	na	na	na	na	na	na	na
Germany	64	**56**	51	59	51	49	64	60	51	57	53	59	56	58	55	54
Great Britain	63	**58**	57	60	55	61	56	55	57	71	59	59	62	na	na	na
Greece	na	**62**	59	64	59	63	68	81	65	56	63	62	64	71	63	50
Hungary	90	**67**	57	76	60	63	76	71	62	55	74	65	68	69	65	68
Iceland	58	**54**	51	57	47	51	65	60	50	50	54	56	49	63	54	32
India	59	**43**	39	49	40	45	44	47	41	40	35	45	45	46	40	48
Indonesia	na	**84**	82	87	74	84	90	91	84	80	83	85	83	87	82	74
Iran	na	**75**	73	77	71	77	81	83	73	66	75	76	70	81	73	59
Ireland	71	**64**	60	67	60	60	70	69	62	60	68	63	62	74	62	54
Israel	na	**na**	na	na	na	na	na	na	na	na	na	na	na	na	na	na
Italy	72	**72**	69	75	67	70	78	77	68	70	79	70	69	81	72	69
Japan	42	**34**	29	39	48	35	27	24	36	34	36	33	32	40	34	21
Jordan	na	**64**	58	71	63	63	73	69	60	61	66	64	64	68	61	62
Korea, South	na	**59**	53	65	54	58	67	63	61	55	54	63	61	61	58	46
Latvia	87	**81**	75	86	76	78	86	88	79	76	84	80	80	81	81	86
Lithuania	na	**87**	81	91	86	77	95	97	84	78	94	86	83	92	88	65
Luxembourg	na	**46**	45	47	43	45	49	46	44	50	42	41	42	40	46	49
Macedonia	na	**75**	76	75	76	74	76	82	72	72	82	73	68	77	73	82
Malta	na	**85**	83	88	83	81	90	90	83	84	83	86	85	86	86	78
Mexico	80	**83**	82	84	80	85	86	86	81	78	88	81	81	85	83	78
Moldova	na	**82**	78	86	73	83	88	91	82	75	87	80	78	84	80	85
Montenegro	na	**75**	71	79	74	72	78	81	71	72	74	76	70	74	75	81
Morocco	na	**97**	97	97	96	98	99	98	97	92	98	98	96	98	97	97
Netherlands	55	**49**	46	53	55	48	49	50	50	48	49	49	48	62	53	35
New Zealand	na	**na**	na	na	na	na	na	na	na	na	na	na	na	na	na	na
Nigeria	89	**85**	85	85	85	84	92	86	85	86	86	84	86	86	85	81
Northern Ireland	80	**77**	73	80	80	68	82	80	74	73	73	81	77	75	77	76
Norway	55	**na**	na	na	na	na	na	na	na	na	na	na	na	na	na	na
Pakistan	na	**65**	62	69	61	66	72	71	62	51	71	67	57	64	68	91
Peru	na	**80**	78	83	80	79	83	84	84	72	84	82	72	85	81	69
Philippines	na	**81**	80	81	82	80	80	79	79	85	77	82	83	79	82	85
Poland	na	**83**	83	83	79	83	86	87	79	74	84	84	80	87	82	75
Portugal	62	**73**	65	80	68	68	79	77	62	65	77	72	67	76	71	68
Puerto Rico	na	**76**	70	80	67	73	83	90	74	75	82	76	74	78	78	71
Romania	78	**89**	88	90	85	90	91	89	90	85	90	91	86	90	89	80
Russian Fed.	92	**74**	67	81	74	73	77	80	75	71	77	76	69	76	73	66
Serbia	na	**73**	69	77	77	69	74	80	68	72	74	74	71	74	73	56
Singapore	na	**na**	na	na	na	na	na	na	na	na	na	na	na	na	na	na
Slovakia	na	**83**	80	86	79	80	89	88	82	77	90	84	80	86	81	82
Slovenia	77	**70**	69	72	70	69	72	78	70	58	75	71	62	78	70	65
South Africa	na	**83**	78	88	81	82	86	83	82	74	84	81	78	85	81	79
Spain	54	**55**	48	61	44	47	67	62	48	48	66	54	47	63	55	39
Sweden	51	**57**	55	58	55	53	61	66	56	51	53	61	53	64	60	46
Switzerland	na	**na**	na	na	na	na	na	na	na	na	na	na	na	na	na	na
Taiwan	na	**na**	na	na	na	na	na	na	na	na	na	na	na	na	na	na
Tanzania	na	**91**	91	90	88	93	90	89	91	93	88	92	92	94	90	82
Turkey	59	**83**	82	85	83	82	87	87	78	77	87	84	75	83	85	78
Uganda	na	**93**	93	93	94	95	83	93	92	99	92	96	93	92	94	94
Ukraine	na	**82**	74	88	77	82	85	90	79	86	81	83	82	80	82	95
United States	84	**75**	73	76	74	75	74	75	75	74	74	75	75	79	75	73
Uruguay	na	**na**	na	na	na	na	na	na	na	na	na	na	na	na	na	na
Venezuela	na	**na**	na	na	na	na	na	na	na	na	na	na	na	na	na	na
Vietnam	na	**60**	59	62	57	61	63	66	54	56	56	55	68	56	61	63
Zimbabwe	na	**91**	86	95	90	91	95	94	88	70	91	93	89	93	89	91
Total	68	73	69	76	72	71	75	76	71	69	75	72	71	76	72	65

RANKING

Country	2000
Algeria	98
Morocco	97
Uganda	93
Egypt	93
Zimbabwe	91
Tanzania	91
Romania	89
Croatia	87
Lithuania	87
Malta	85
Nigeria	85
Indonesia	84
Mexico	83
Slovakia	83
Turkey	83
Chile	83
Poland	83
South Africa	83
Ukraine	82
Moldova	82
Latvia	81
Philippines	81
Peru	80
Albania	79
Bangladesh	78
Northern Ireland	77
Puerto Rico	76
Macedonia	75
Montenegro	75
Iran	75
United States	75
Russian Fed.	74
Estonia	73
Serbia	73
Portugal	73
Italy	72
Canada	72
Slovenia	70
Belarus	70
Czech Republic	69
Argentina	68
Finland	68
Hungary	67
Bosnia and Herz.	67
Pakistan	65
Jordan	64
Ireland	64
Greece	62
Vietnam	60
Austria	60
Korea, South	59
Great Britain	58
Sweden	57
Germany	56
France	55
Bulgaria	55
Spain	55
Iceland	54
Denmark	51
Netherlands	49
Belgium	49
Luxembourg	46
India	43
Japan	34
Total	73

F038) CHURCHES GIVE ANSWERS: THE SOCIAL PROBLEMS

Generally speaking, do you think that the churches in your country are giving adequate answers to ...

The social problems facing our country today.

Yes (%) (WVS: V190; EVS: V114)

Country	Wave 1990	Wave 2000	Gender Male	Gender Female	Age 16-29	Age 30-49	Age 50+	Education Lower	Education Middle	Education Upper	Income Lower	Income Middle	Income Upper	Values Mat	Values Mixed	Values Postm.
Albania	na	**33**	32	34	28	28	43	40	26	33	36	27	35	39	31	12
Algeria	na	**77**	81	72	79	75	75	83	75	75	81	72	71	84	72	76
Argentina	37	**50**	47	52	43	47	58	53	45	42	57	51	41	59	52	37
Armenia	na	**na**	na	na	na	na	na	na	na	na	na	na	na	na	na	na
Australia	na	**na**	na	na	na	na	na	na	na	na	na	na	na	na	na	na
Austria	39	**30**	27	33	20	30	35	27	31	38	30	30	29	28	29	34
Azerbaijan	na	**na**	na	na	na	na	na	na	na	na	na	na	na	na	na	na
Bangladesh	na	**58**	59	55	57	57	65	62	50	57	58	59	56	62	55	59
Belarus	83	**23**	18	27	18	19	33	36	20	15	26	22	19	26	20	11
Belgium	29	**27**	28	26	22	24	33	32	25	27	33	25	26	31	28	20
Bosnia and Herz.	na	**27**	26	28	27	26	27	32	26	26	28	23	31	23	28	26
Brazil	42	**na**	na	na	na	na	na	na	na	na	na	na	na	na	na	na
Bulgaria	23	**15**	12	18	12	13	18	24	12	10	25	12	9	12	16	12
Canada	44	**35**	32	38	27	35	40	42	34	31	39	37	31	37	38	31
Chile	76	**50**	47	53	44	50	55	59	46	40	54	49	46	55	51	38
China	na	**na**	na	na	na	na	na	na	na	na	na	na	na	na	na	na
Colombia	na	**na**	na	na	na	na	na	na	na	na	na	na	na	na	na	na
Croatia	na	**44**	39	49	38	44	48	49	43	35	56	40	42	59	45	29
Czech Republic	na	**15**	12	19	10	11	23	17	13	17	22	15	9	16	15	19
Denmark	8	**12**	11	12	9	12	13	14	10	10	12	11	12	8	12	13
Dominican Rep.	na	**na**	na	na	na	na	na	na	na	na	na	na	na	na	na	na
Egypt	na	**83**	80	86	81	82	86	84	80	84	83	82	84	86	81	76
El Salvador	na	**na**	na	na	na	na	na	na	na	na	na	na	na	na	na	na
Estonia	na	**14**	11	16	15	10	17	17	13	14	17	16	12	17	12	5
Finland	12	**31**	26	36	23	27	40	34	24	37	33	29	31	31	30	37
France	24	**21**	19	23	15	20	26	23	18	21	22	21	21	24	22	15
Georgia	na	**na**	na	na	na	na	na	na	na	na	na	na	na	na	na	na
Germany	58	**32**	29	34	22	26	42	37	27	30	33	34	35	39	30	25
Great Britain	29	**27**	25	29	23	25	30	27	27	21	33	31	28	na	na	na
Greece	na	**31**	30	31	26	31	42	51	37	22	37	30	27	37	31	23
Hungary	55	**25**	20	30	12	23	35	29	16	19	32	24	24	25	24	23
Iceland	24	**28**	26	30	23	26	35	36	23	21	34	24	26	31	28	17
India	24	**29**	26	33	28	29	29	33	24	26	26	28	29	29	27	32
Indonesia	na	**64**	64	65	56	66	66	76	62	59	61	64	70	70	60	52
Iran	na	**62**	58	66	58	62	72	75	59	49	61	60	61	68	58	51
Ireland	33	**27**	28	25	18	24	36	32	25	22	29	28	24	31	27	19
Israel	na	**na**	na	na	na	na	na	na	na	na	na	na	na	na	na	na
Italy	43	**44**	40	46	30	42	53	50	39	39	50	42	41	52	43	40
Japan	7	**7**	5	9	4	7	9	13	8	4	9	4	7	7	6	3
Jordan	na	**65**	57	72	65	63	68	67	65	60	65	67	60	68	61	64
Korea, South	na	**23**	23	23	15	23	34	23	26	18	22	23	24	24	22	19
Latvia	42	**26**	22	30	23	21	32	32	24	27	31	23	22	26	27	19
Lithuania	na	**61**	57	65	46	50	77	85	52	46	77	57	52	69	62	35
Luxembourg	na	**24**	25	24	14	22	34	27	20	29	20	25	25	25	24	25
Macedonia	na	**22**	23	20	23	19	24	29	19	16	24	23	15	19	22	23
Malta	na	**56**	51	61	40	52	69	67	53	45	63	57	49	61	55	43
Mexico	47	**54**	49	59	49	53	63	64	44	36	65	51	40	60	51	44
Moldova	na	**39**	34	43	27	41	48	54	39	28	46	37	33	40	40	38
Montenegro	na	**22**	21	22	12	24	25	23	21	20	21	24	17	21	21	18
Morocco	na	**91**	91	92	89	92	96	93	87	77	95	88	89	92	91	84
Netherlands	33	**37**	35	39	34	35	40	37	37	36	35	37	36	49	38	29
New Zealand	na	**na**	na	na	na	na	na	na	na	na	na	na	na	na	na	na
Nigeria	83	**73**	72	74	73	72	75	75	72	69	72	75	70	72	74	66
Northern Ireland	52	**36**	34	39	36	26	45	41	33	30	34	33	32	36	36	38
Norway	19	**na**	na	na	na	na	na	na	na	na	na	na	na	na	na	na
Pakistan	na	**45**	44	46	44	45	47	51	40	34	52	44	35	46	44	36
Peru	na	**64**	59	70	64	65	66	70	68	55	70	63	55	70	64	56
Philippines	na	**52**	52	53	52	51	56	55	49	54	51	55	49	49	55	53
Poland	na	**39**	36	43	28	37	50	45	35	28	46	38	29	43	39	36
Portugal	44	**36**	31	41	30	30	47	41	25	31	43	37	36	42	32	30
Puerto Rico	na	**65**	61	69	53	63	74	79	67	63	74	64	64	75	66	59
Romania	32	**52**	46	59	39	46	65	69	48	34	65	52	43	58	49	33
Russian Fed.	60	**25**	19	30	19	22	33	37	24	23	31	27	18	26	25	23
Serbia	na	**28**	24	32	26	25	31	35	26	24	33	30	21	29	27	25
Singapore	na	**na**	na	na	na	na	na	na	na	na	na	na	na	na	na	na
Slovakia	na	**30**	23	37	20	24	45	46	24	20	43	28	24	33	28	24
Slovenia	49	**34**	32	36	28	25	48	45	30	26	45	38	21	39	33	31
South Africa	na	**62**	56	69	60	61	70	62	64	53	60	70	58	72	55	66
Spain	33	**31**	26	35	15	25	46	39	22	25	40	29	27	41	30	15
Sweden	12	**17**	16	18	11	16	22	25	15	16	17	20	14	16	18	15
Switzerland	na	**na**	na	na	na	na	na	na	na	na	na	na	na	na	na	na
Taiwan	na	**na**	na	na	na	na	na	na	na	na	na	na	na	na	na	na
Tanzania	na	**74**	71	77	77	73	69	72	77	73	73	77	72	73	75	70
Turkey	29	**44**	45	42	40	45	54	50	36	34	47	45	34	47	44	39
Uganda	na	**70**	78	63	72	67	72	68	70	83	76	84	67	67	69	84
Ukraine	na	**30**	22	37	25	32	32	41	30	25	31	31	28	25	31	52
United States	57	**46**	42	49	40	48	46	49	47	44	52	42	42	52	48	37
Uruguay	na	**na**	na	na	na	na	na	na	na	na	na	na	na	na	na	na
Venezuela	na	**na**	na	na	na	na	na	na	na	na	na	na	na	na	na	na
Vietnam	na	**18**	16	20	12	18	22	22	14	13	21	15	21	16	19	19
Zimbabwe	na	**72**	63	81	70	71	82	80	63	48	79	70	67	76	70	63
Total	40	**41**	39	44	41	39	44	48	38	37	46	40	37	45	41	35

RANKING

Country	2000
Morocco	91
Egypt	83
Algeria	77
Tanzania	74
Nigeria	73
Zimbabwe	72
Uganda	70
Puerto Rico	65
Jordan	65
Peru	64
Indonesia	64
South Africa	62
Iran	62
Lithuania	61
Bangladesh	58
Malta	56
Mexico	54
Philippines	52
Romania	52
Chile	50
Argentina	50
United States	46
Pakistan	45
Croatia	44
Turkey	44
Italy	44
Poland	39
Moldova	39
Netherlands	37
Portugal	36
Northern Ireland	36
Canada	35
Slovenia	34
Albania	33
Germany	32
Greece	31
Finland	31
Spain	31
Ukraine	30
Austria	30
Slovakia	30
India	29
Iceland	28
Serbia	28
Belgium	27
Great Britain	27
Bosnia and Herz.	27
Ireland	27
Latvia	26
Hungary	25
Russian Fed.	25
Luxembourg	24
Belarus	23
Korea, South	23
Montenegro	22
Macedonia	22
France	21
Vietnam	18
Sweden	17
Czech Republic	15
Bulgaria	15
Estonia	14
Denmark	12
Japan	7
Total	41

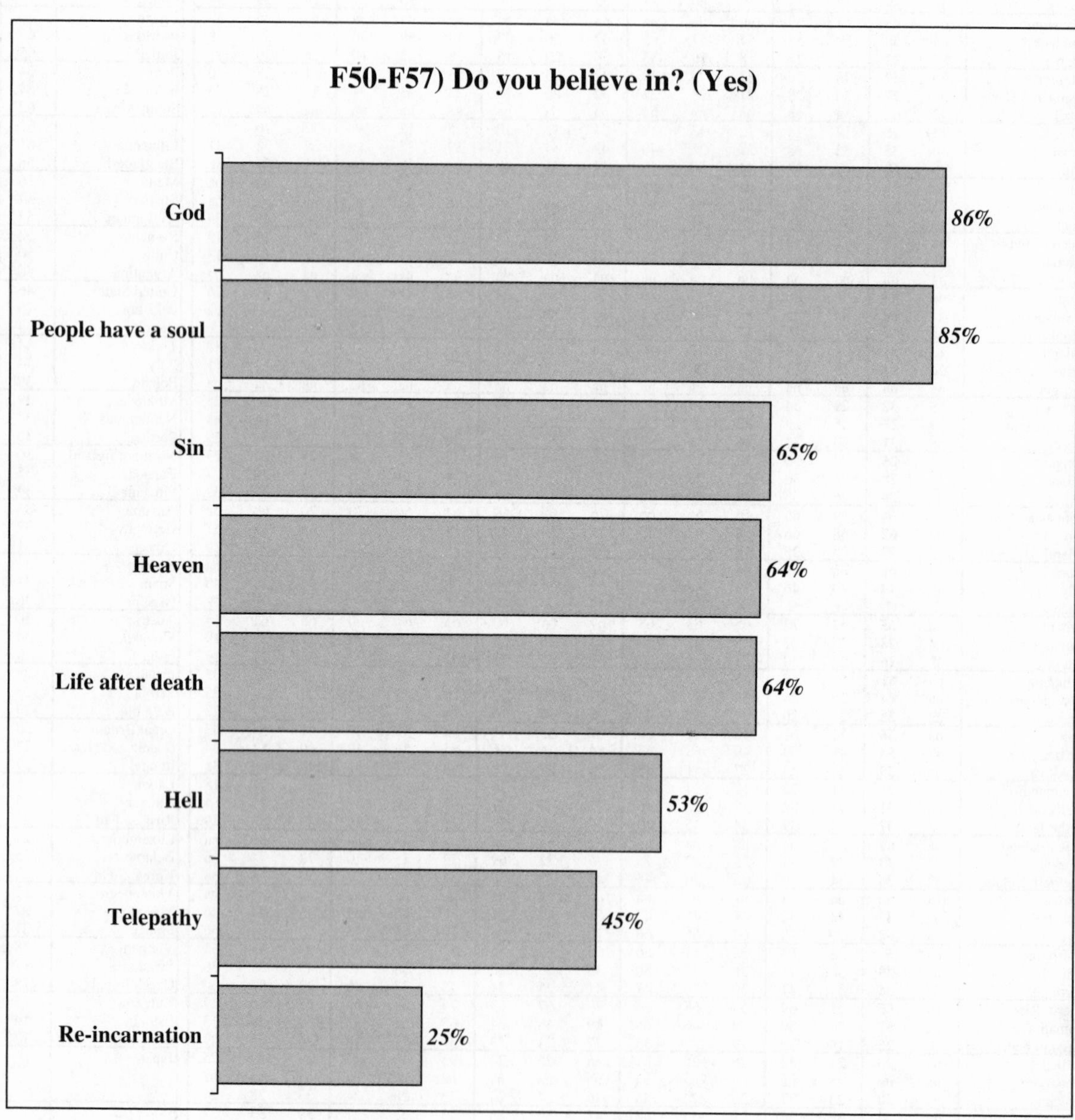
F50-F57) Do you believe in? (Yes)
God
86%
People have a soul
85%
Sin
65%
Heaven
64%
Life after death
64%
Hell
53%
Telepathy
45%
Re-incarnation
25%

F050) BELIEVE IN GOD

Which, if any, of the following do you believe in? Believe in God.

Yes (%) (WVS: V191; EVS: V115)

Country	Wave		Gender		Age			Education			Income			Values		
	1990	2000	Male	Female	16-29	30-49	50+	Lower	Middle	Upper	Lower	Middle	Upper	Mat	Mixed	Postm.
Albania	na	**92**	88	96	90	93	92	94	91	88	92	91	92	91	92	87
Algeria	na	**100**	100	100	100	99	100	100	100	99	100	100	99	100	100	99
Argentina	92	**96**	94	98	95	97	97	98	95	91	98	97	94	99	97	93
Armenia	na	**86**	80	91	89	84	82	83	87	83	84	86	88	85	88	70
Australia	na	**80**	75	86	79	77	85	86	78	78	84	80	73	83	82	76
Austria	87	**87**	83	90	80	87	91	87	88	83	86	88	86	90	88	82
Azerbaijan	na	**98**	97	99	98	98	97	97	99	96	99	99	95	98	98	97
Bangladesh	na	**100**	99	100	99	100	100	100	99	99	100	99	100	100	99	100
Belarus	43	**83**	72	91	79	82	86	90	82	73	86	83	75	85	82	69
Belgium	69	**71**	65	76	56	67	81	79	69	69	76	71	66	79	71	62
Bosnia and Herz.	na	**88**	86	90	93	90	81	94	90	78	88	88	87	90	87	88
Brazil	99	**99**	99	100	99	99	100	100	99	98	99	100	99	99	99	99
Bulgaria	40	**66**	60	72	66	61	71	77	61	59	73	68	60	68	64	67
Canada	89	**89**	86	93	84	88	94	92	91	85	92	90	86	94	92	82
Chile	95	**97**	96	98	97	97	97	98	97	93	99	97	94	98	98	91
China	na	**na**	na	na	na	na	na	na	na	na	na	na	na	na	na	na
Colombia	na	**99**	99	100	99	99	99	100	99	98	100	100	98	100	99	98
Croatia	na	**93**	92	95	89	96	93	96	94	85	93	94	92	98	93	89
Czech Republic	na	**39**	32	46	34	31	49	40	38	40	46	36	32	43	37	40
Denmark	64	**69**	61	77	55	67	79	74	55	64	72	70	63	64	71	59
Dominican Rep.	na	**93**	95	91	95	89	91	87	94	93	90	93	95	92	93	92
Egypt	na	**100**	100	100	100	100	100	100	100	100	100	100	100	100	100	100
El Salvador	na	**99**	99	100	99	100	99	100	99	99	100	99	100	na	na	na
Estonia	na	**51**	40	61	43	46	61	58	49	45	61	58	44	54	51	31
Finland	76	**83**	73	91	73	79	91	83	83	83	83	75	89	81	85	74
France	62	**62**	58	64	53	60	67	63	59	60	61	61	61	67	63	48
Georgia	na	**93**	90	96	96	94	89	92	94	93	92	94	94	94	92	99
Germany	36	**68**	61	73	56	63	78	74	62	66	64	70	71	68	69	65
Great Britain	78	**72**	63	80	64	71	76	74	71	62	68	74	67	na	na	na
Greece	na	**91**	88	93	90	91	95	97	95	87	93	91	89	96	93	80
Hungary	65	**68**	56	79	53	63	82	74	57	52	76	71	62	75	62	54
Iceland	85	**84**	78	90	76	86	89	87	84	80	85	87	82	88	85	73
India	94	**95**	94	96	94	96	94	95	93	94	93	96	95	96	93	93
Indonesia	na	**100**	100	100	99	100	100	100	100	100	100	100	99	100	100	100
Iran	na	**99**	99	100	99	100	99	100	100	99	99	100	99	100	100	99
Ireland	98	**96**	93	98	93	94	98	95	95	97	96	96	95	99	95	90
Israel	na	**na**	na	na	na	na	na	na	na	na	na	na	na	na	na	na
Italy	91	**94**	90	97	94	92	95	96	92	90	94	94	90	97	94	89
Japan	65	**53**	46	59	47	55	53	56	53	49	55	55	49	54	52	51
Jordan	na	**100**	100	100	100	100	100	100	100	99	100	100	100	100	100	100
Korea, South	na	**na**	na	na	na	na	na	na	na	na	na	na	na	na	na	na
Latvia	58	**80**	67	90	75	79	82	83	78	80	82	80	76	80	80	80
Lithuania	na	**87**	75	95	80	83	93	95	83	85	95	82	86	88	87	68
Luxembourg	na	**73**	67	79	63	73	81	73	74	73	70	74	71	75	73	67
Macedonia	na	**91**	89	92	91	92	88	98	87	86	96	89	85	92	90	89
Malta	na	**100**	99	100	100	99	100	100	99	100	99	100	99	100	99	99
Mexico	93	**98**	98	98	98	98	99	99	97	97	99	98	97	98	98	97
Moldova	na	**96**	94	98	94	97	97	98	97	92	97	96	95	97	96	96
Montenegro	na	**83**	80	86	77	84	86	89	80	75	84	87	83	85	83	72
Morocco	na	**100**	100	100	100	100	100	100	100	100	100	100	100	100	100	100
Netherlands	64	**60**	55	64	50	54	70	66	58	56	58	62	52	76	57	58
New Zealand	na	**78**	74	81	76	73	83	77	82	77	79	79	74	84	80	71
Nigeria	100	**100**	100	99	100	100	100	100	100	100	100	100	100	100	100	99
Northern Ireland	97	**93**	90	96	89	94	95	95	92	92	95	94	92	96	92	92
Norway	65	**69**	60	77	55	68	80	74	68	65	na	na	na	75	70	53
Pakistan	na	**100**	100	100	100	100	100	100	100	100	100	100	100	100	100	100
Peru	na	**99**	98	99	98	99	99	98	99	97	99	99	97	99	98	98
Philippines	na	**99**	99	100	100	99	99	99	100	99	100	99	99	99	100	100
Poland	97	**97**	97	98	97	98	97	99	96	93	98	97	95	99	96	95
Portugal	86	**96**	94	98	92	98	98	99	94	82	100	97	94	97	97	90
Puerto Rico	na	**99**	99	99	99	99	99	100	99	99	99	100	99	99	99	99
Romania	94	**96**	94	99	94	98	97	98	96	94	97	97	96	96	97	92
Russian Fed.	44	**70**	57	81	70	66	75	80	69	68	76	68	66	75	66	55
Serbia	na	**83**	76	88	86	82	81	90	78	79	86	83	78	85	81	75
Singapore	na	**87**	84	90	84	89	94	90	86	83	89	89	84	92	86	76
Slovakia	na	**83**	77	88	76	80	91	87	82	72	89	85	78	84	82	85
Slovenia	63	**65**	61	69	59	64	71	81	64	41	76	62	50	81	62	62
South Africa	98	**99**	98	100	99	99	99	99	99	99	99	100	98	99	99	99
Spain	86	**85**	79	90	73	84	93	91	80	75	89	83	81	92	84	72
Sweden	45	**53**	46	61	43	50	63	61	49	54	52	57	50	58	54	47
Switzerland	na	**83**	78	89	66	85	91	86	82	85	84	86	82	89	83	82
Taiwan	na	**76**	70	83	79	74	82	81	76	72	77	78	71	78	75	68
Tanzania	na	**99**	99	99	100	99	100	99	100	99	99	100	99	100	100	100
Turkey	na	**98**	97	99	97	98	99	100	97	91	99	98	94	100	98	94
Uganda	na	**99**	99	100	99	100	97	98	100	100	100	100	100	99	100	99
Ukraine	na	**80**	68	90	80	81	80	85	79	80	82	81	79	81	77	83
United States	96	**96**	94	98	93	97	96	94	97	95	96	95	96	97	96	95
Uruguay	na	**87**	81	91	81	83	92	91	83	71	91	85	86	87	89	80
Venezuela	na	**na**	na	na	na	na	na	na	na	na	na	na	na	na	na	na
Vietnam	na	**19**	14	24	22	19	17	25	10	15	15	19	20	32	15	17
Zimbabwe	na	**99**	100	99	99	100	100	99	99	100	99	99	100	99	100	100
Total	76	86	83	89	86	85	87	89	85	84	88	87	84	89	85	81

RANKING Country	2000
Morocco	100
Pakistan	100
Egypt	100
Algeria	100
Jordan	100
Nigeria	100
Bangladesh	100
Indonesia	100
Malta	100
El Salvador	99
Iran	99
Philippines	99
Zimbabwe	99
Uganda	99
Tanzania	99
Brazil	99
Colombia	99
South Africa	99
Puerto Rico	99
Peru	99
Mexico	98
Turkey	98
Azerbaijan	98
Poland	97
Chile	97
Argentina	96
Portugal	96
Romania	96
Moldova	96
United States	96
Ireland	96
India	95
Italy	94
Croatia	93
Georgia	93
Northern Ireland	93
Dominican Rep.	93
Albania	92
Greece	91
Macedonia	91
Canada	89
Bosnia and Herz.	88
Singapore	87
Austria	87
Uruguay	87
Lithuania	87
Armenia	86
Spain	85
Iceland	84
Switzerland	83
Montenegro	83
Belarus	83
Slovakia	83
Finland	83
Serbia	83
Ukraine	80
Australia	80
Latvia	80
New Zealand	78
Taiwan	76
Luxembourg	73
Great Britain	72
Belgium	71
Russian Fed.	70
Denmark	69
Norway	69
Hungary	68
Germany	68
Bulgaria	66
Slovenia	65
France	62
Netherlands	60
Sweden	53
Japan	53
Estonia	51
Czech Republic	39
Vietnam	19
Total	86

F051) BELIEVE IN LIFE AFTER DEATH

Which, if any, of the following do you believe in? Believe in life after death

Yes (%) (WVS: V192; EVS: V116)

Country	Wave		Gender		Age			Education			Income			Values		
	1990	2000	Male	Female	16-29	30-49	50+	Lower	Middle	Upper	Lower	Middle	Upper	Mat	Mixed	Postm.
Albania	na	**47**	41	54	47	42	56	55	42	40	43	51	49	45	48	39
Algeria	na	**100**	100	100	100	99	100	100	100	99	100	100	99	100	100	99
Argentina	65	**63**	56	70	64	67	59	60	69	67	59	64	67	62	64	63
Armenia	na	**36**	30	42	41	36	29	36	37	35	40	37	29	33	41	32
Australia	na	**64**	55	73	69	63	60	67	64	62	66	64	57	59	66	62
Austria	56	**59**	53	65	62	61	56	55	65	59	59	61	56	44	58	65
Azerbaijan	na	**56**	50	61	58	51	64	69	53	57	55	59	49	52	60	70
Bangladesh	na	**56**	55	57	53	56	68	61	50	49	73	50	46	60	51	51
Belarus	18	**41**	30	50	43	36	45	45	40	40	39	39	48	42	40	39
Belgium	44	**44**	40	48	45	41	45	39	42	50	48	44	40	42	45	42
Bosnia and Herz.	na	**60**	56	64	68	57	57	73	59	54	67	58	61	62	60	57
Brazil	74	**71**	70	71	73	68	71	64	76	76	72	65	74	64	73	77
Bulgaria	18	**36**	30	42	40	30	39	46	31	32	42	29	34	36	35	49
Canada	69	**73**	67	78	74	71	73	68	76	71	71	77	70	70	74	72
Chile	70	**82**	75	87	84	81	81	80	82	85	81	80	85	86	82	75
China	na	**na**	na	na	na	na	na	na	na	na	na	na	na	na	na	na
Colombia	na	**70**	68	71	70	68	76	73	66	72	74	68	70	67	70	62
Croatia	na	**68**	62	73	72	71	62	71	66	64	63	64	75	74	68	64
Czech Republic	na	**36**	30	42	48	30	35	36	36	35	36	36	31	33	36	42
Denmark	34	**38**	28	49	49	39	32	36	35	42	41	37	35	31	38	39
Dominican Rep.	na	**72**	72	72	75	66	82	62	68	75	66	75	77	58	74	81
Egypt	na	**100**	100	100	100	100	100	100	100	100	100	100	100	100	100	100
El Salvador	na	**83**	80	86	84	83	84	84	82	84	87	81	83	na	na	na
Estonia	na	**36**	29	43	43	38	31	36	35	40	36	33	40	32	39	38
Finland	60	**57**	44	68	50	54	62	57	55	62	60	49	59	55	57	63
France	44	**45**	35	54	49	48	39	43	49	45	44	47	41	46	44	44
Georgia	na	**58**	54	60	68	56	48	52	56	66	52	57	67	56	59	62
Germany	21	**39**	34	43	38	38	40	41	37	35	33	40	42	36	40	45
Great Britain	52	**58**	48	68	58	58	58	54	62	57	55	61	60	na	na	na
Greece	na	**61**	57	63	62	61	58	62	65	56	61	60	59	67	61	49
Hungary	26	**33**	24	41	37	31	32	31	36	37	35	32	34	31	36	44
Iceland	81	**78**	72	85	79	77	79	83	79	69	80	79	75	85	78	65
India	41	**66**	63	69	63	67	67	70	62	59	67	65	65	75	52	66
Indonesia	na	**99**	100	99	99	99	100	100	99	100	100	99	99	100	99	100
Iran	na	**98**	97	98	98	97	99	98	97	98	98	99	97	99	98	97
Ireland	83	**79**	75	83	67	80	86	80	77	82	82	78	82	76	81	75
Israel	na	**na**	na	na	na	na	na	na	na	na	na	na	na	na	na	na
Italy	68	**73**	63	81	74	74	71	70	75	76	73	72	72	75	73	71
Japan	54	**51**	41	60	61	61	35	48	54	46	52	56	43	48	53	48
Jordan	na	**98**	98	97	97	97	99	97	99	98	97	99	97	97	98	95
Korea, South	na	**na**	na	na	na	na	na	na	na	na	na	na	na	na	na	na
Latvia	30	**45**	30	59	53	44	43	52	42	48	47	47	43	47	44	50
Lithuania	na	**79**	66	88	77	72	85	95	72	73	91	70	77	85	77	64
Luxembourg	na	**54**	47	61	54	50	59	54	54	54	57	50	57	57	51	57
Macedonia	na	**47**	45	50	61	47	36	63	39	39	47	47	45	43	47	69
Malta	na	**86**	84	89	85	86	87	87	85	93	86	89	87	85	88	81
Mexico	61	**76**	73	78	72	76	80	75	77	76	75	76	77	78	75	77
Moldova	na	**59**	52	65	62	55	63	68	57	55	66	54	58	61	59	48
Montenegro	na	**23**	18	28	16	24	27	34	18	13	29	20	20	22	21	24
Morocco	na	**100**	100	100	100	100	100	100	99	100	100	100	100	100	100	98
Netherlands	47	**51**	46	55	54	51	49	49	53	49	51	49	48	57	51	46
New Zealand	na	**64**	53	73	77	64	60	58	67	69	65	67	61	63	65	62
Nigeria	82	**88**	88	87	87	88	88	89	86	88	88	87	87	86	89	83
Northern Ireland	78	**75**	70	80	66	73	83	78	69	82	77	80	75	78	76	71
Norway	45	**47**	37	58	47	47	48	47	47	49	na	na	na	42	49	44
Pakistan	na	**100**	100	100	100	100	100	100	100	100	100	100	100	100	100	100
Peru	na	**72**	68	76	70	74	72	75	71	72	70	74	74	71	73	69
Philippines	na	**86**	87	86	86	87	86	85	85	90	87	87	86	86	87	84
Poland	78	**80**	74	86	85	80	79	81	81	75	83	79	79	85	77	81
Portugal	39	**47**	41	54	43	47	50	46	50	46	54	42	41	52	44	47
Puerto Rico	na	**78**	76	80	74	82	78	86	71	80	74	79	81	73	80	76
Romania	58	**68**	61	75	79	66	64	70	68	63	68	67	68	71	64	72
Russian Fed.	21	**37**	26	46	47	31	36	42	36	36	40	34	35	36	36	33
Serbia	na	**27**	23	32	38	25	24	32	21	31	30	24	26	22	32	34
Singapore	na	**74**	71	77	72	76	76	76	74	69	79	74	72	79	72	73
Slovakia	na	**68**	62	74	62	64	78	73	68	58	73	68	67	69	67	76
Slovenia	28	**32**	28	36	37	27	34	39	30	29	38	30	24	29	32	37
South Africa	78	**73**	64	83	71	71	83	70	77	64	66	74	78	76	70	77
Spain	52	**53**	43	63	47	50	59	56	48	54	59	52	51	61	51	44
Sweden	38	**46**	32	59	53	46	42	40	48	48	51	47	37	45	46	44
Switzerland	64	**64**	57	70	68	64	60	65	63	64	61	62	63	68	62	70
Taiwan	na	**61**	55	66	71	60	55	61	54	64	55	63	61	64	59	39
Tanzania	na	**87**	88	86	84	89	90	86	87	92	87	86	90	90	86	82
Turkey	80	**90**	89	91	90	89	93	93	88	77	94	90	80	94	90	84
Uganda	na	**85**	83	87	82	90	79	80	87	86	82	92	85	84	85	87
Ukraine	na	**40**	30	49	48	37	38	48	37	43	40	40	38	35	41	50
United States	78	**81**	79	84	77	83	83	77	83	82	81	81	83	83	81	80
Uruguay	na	**45**	37	51	48	44	45	43	47	51	42	45	50	43	45	49
Venezuela	na	**na**	na	na	na	na	na	na	na	na	na	na	na	na	na	na
Vietnam	na	**16**	11	20	18	15	16	20	10	13	14	14	19	15	16	15
Zimbabwe	na	**75**	73	76	72	75	80	73	76	100	67	77	77	77	73	71
Total	53	64	59	69	69	63	60	66	62	65	66	63	63	64	63	63

RANKING	
Country	2000
Pakistan	100
Egypt	100
Algeria	100
Morocco	100
Indonesia	99
Iran	98
Jordan	98
Turkey	90
Nigeria	88
Tanzania	87
Philippines	86
Malta	86
Uganda	85
El Salvador	83
Chile	82
United States	81
Poland	80
Ireland	79
Lithuania	79
Iceland	78
Puerto Rico	78
Mexico	76
Northern Ireland	75
Zimbabwe	75
Singapore	74
Italy	73
South Africa	73
Canada	73
Dominican Rep.	72
Peru	72
Brazil	71
Colombia	70
Slovakia	68
Croatia	68
Romania	68
India	66
Australia	64
New Zealand	64
Switzerland	64
Argentina	63
Taiwan	61
Greece	61
Bosnia and Herz.	60
Moldova	59
Austria	59
Great Britain	58
Georgia	58
Finland	57
Bangladesh	56
Azerbaijan	56
Luxembourg	54
Spain	53
Japan	51
Netherlands	51
Norway	47
Portugal	47
Albania	47
Macedonia	47
Sweden	46
Latvia	45
Uruguay	45
France	45
Belgium	44
Belarus	41
Ukraine	40
Germany	39
Denmark	38
Russian Fed.	37
Armenia	36
Estonia	36
Czech Republic	36
Bulgaria	36
Hungary	33
Slovenia	32
Serbia	27
Montenegro	23
Vietnam	16
Total	64

F052) BELIEVE IN PEOPLE HAVE A SOUL

Which, if any, of the following do you believe in? Do you believe people have a soul?.

Yes (%) (WVS: V193)

Country	Wave 1990	Wave 2000	Gender Male	Gender Female	Age 16-29	Age 30-49	Age 50+	Education Lower	Education Middle	Education Upper	Income Lower	Income Middle	Income Upper	Values Mat	Values Mixed	Values Postm.
Albania	na	**75**	69	81	74	74	78	80	72	68	75	77	73	73	75	72
Algeria	na	**99**	100	99	99	99	99	99	100	99	100	99	98	100	99	99
Argentina	81	**85**	82	88	83	88	86	84	89	85	86	85	86	88	86	83
Armenia	na	**65**	59	70	69	65	58	56	64	71	70	62	59	59	71	65
Australia	na	**85**	77	93	87	85	83	88	83	85	86	85	84	85	86	85
Austria	73	**na**	na	na	na	na	na	na	na	na	na	na	na	na	na	na
Azerbaijan	na	**69**	62	76	70	67	76	79	70	67	75	72	58	67	72	81
Bangladesh	na	**99**	99	99	100	99	100	100	99	99	100	99	99	100	99	100
Belarus	45	**na**	na	na	na	na	na	na	na	na	na	na	na	na	na	na
Belgium	60	**na**	na	na	na	na	na	na	na	na	na	na	na	na	na	na
Bosnia and Herz.	na	**85**	83	87	90	84	81	89	85	82	91	84	82	85	85	90
Brazil	84	**82**	81	84	83	81	83	78	85	86	82	81	83	76	85	88
Bulgaria	38	**na**	na	na	na	na	na	na	na	na	na	na	na	na	na	na
Canada	85	**91**	86	96	92	90	92	92	92	88	93	93	88	92	92	89
Chile	81	**89**	85	93	90	89	89	90	89	89	90	89	89	91	91	82
China	na	**na**	na	na	na	na	na	na	na	na	na	na	na	na	na	na
Colombia	na	**87**	85	89	87	87	88	89	85	89	88	87	88	89	87	76
Croatia	na	**na**	na	na	na	na	na	na	na	na	na	na	na	na	na	na
Czech Republic	na	**na**	na	na	na	na	na	na	na	na	na	na	na	na	na	na
Denmark	47	**na**	na	na	na	na	na	na	na	na	na	na	na	na	na	na
Dominican Rep.	na	**89**	88	90	91	84	91	86	91	88	84	87	95	88	87	95
Egypt	na	**100**	100	100	100	100	100	100	100	100	100	100	100	100	100	100
El Salvador	na	**94**	93	95	95	92	94	94	93	94	95	93	93	na	na	na
Estonia	na	**na**	na	na	na	na	na	na	na	na	na	na	na	na	na	na
Finland	73	**na**	na	na	na	na	na	na	na	na	na	na	na	na	na	na
France	55	**na**	na	na	na	na	na	na	na	na	na	na	na	na	na	na
Georgia	na	**76**	71	81	83	78	66	73	75	83	73	76	82	76	75	79
Germany	37	**na**	na	na	na	na	na	na	na	na	na	na	na	na	na	na
Great Britain	70	**na**	na	na	na	na	na	na	na	na	na	na	na	na	na	na
Greece	na	**na**	na	na	na	na	na	na	na	na	na	na	na	na	na	na
Hungary	14	**na**	na	na	na	na	na	na	na	na	na	na	na	na	na	na
Iceland	88	**na**	na	na	na	na	na	na	na	na	na	na	na	na	na	na
India	75	**81**	79	83	78	83	82	82	81	80	80	81	82	88	74	71
Indonesia	na	**99**	99	99	98	99	100	98	99	100	99	100	99	99	99	100
Iran	na	**99**	99	99	98	99	99	99	99	98	99	99	98	99	99	98
Ireland	88	**na**	na	na	na	na	na	na	na	na	na	na	na	na	na	na
Israel	na	**na**	na	na	na	na	na	na	na	na	na	na	na	na	na	na
Italy	78	**na**	na	na	na	na	na	na	na	na	na	na	na	na	na	na
Japan	75	**71**	63	78	80	78	60	71	73	68	72	75	64	71	73	63
Jordan	na	**100**	99	100	100	100	99	99	100	99	100	100	99	100	99	100
Korea, South	na	**na**	na	na	na	na	na	na	na	na	na	na	na	na	na	na
Latvia	78	**na**	na	na	na	na	na	na	na	na	na	na	na	na	na	na
Lithuania	na	**na**	na	na	na	na	na	na	na	na	na	na	na	na	na	na
Luxembourg	na	**na**	na	na	na	na	na	na	na	na	na	na	na	na	na	na
Macedonia	na	**80**	77	84	86	81	74	87	75	80	82	78	80	78	80	89
Malta	na	**na**	na	na	na	na	na	na	na	na	na	na	na	na	na	na
Mexico	72	**93**	92	94	93	93	94	94	93	89	94	93	91	93	93	95
Moldova	na	**81**	75	86	83	78	82	83	80	81	82	77	81	82	81	69
Montenegro	na	**35**	30	39	28	36	37	41	31	29	40	34	28	35	33	29
Morocco	na	**100**	100	100	100	100	100	100	100	100	100	100	100	100	100	100
Netherlands	75	**na**	na	na	na	na	na	na	na	na	na	na	na	na	na	na
New Zealand	na	**84**	78	90	92	87	80	79	88	88	84	86	84	88	84	87
Nigeria	92	**97**	97	97	97	97	96	95	98	97	96	97	97	98	96	97
Northern Ireland	92	**na**	na	na	na	na	na	na	na	na	na	na	na	na	na	na
Norway	54	**60**	49	70	62	57	61	57	59	63	na	na	na	50	61	62
Pakistan	na	**100**	100	100	100	100	100	100	100	100	100	100	100	100	100	100
Peru	na	**89**	87	91	87	91	90	90	89	89	90	88	89	91	89	89
Philippines	na	**96**	96	96	97	96	96	97	96	96	96	97	95	98	96	90
Poland	86	**na**	na	na	na	na	na	na	na	na	na	na	na	na	na	na
Portugal	66	**na**	na	na	na	na	na	na	na	na	na	na	na	na	na	na
Puerto Rico	na	**96**	94	97	95	96	97	99	94	97	96	95	97	96	96	98
Romania	76	**na**	na	na	na	na	na	na	na	na	na	na	na	na	na	na
Russian Fed.	54	**na**	na	na	na	na	na	na	na	na	na	na	na	na	na	na
Serbia	na	**34**	28	40	46	31	32	37	28	42	32	34	35	30	38	35
Singapore	na	**92**	89	93	91	92	95	91	93	90	95	90	90	96	90	93
Slovakia	na	**na**	na	na	na	na	na	na	na	na	na	na	na	na	na	na
Slovenia	46	**na**	na	na	na	na	na	na	na	na	na	na	na	na	na	na
South Africa	91	**94**	93	95	95	93	94	92	96	96	90	96	96	94	94	92
Spain	65	**72**	61	81	66	69	78	75	66	70	82	70	67	78	71	61
Sweden	58	**na**	na	na	na	na	na	na	na	na	na	na	na	na	na	na
Switzerland	81	**89**	86	93	89	87	93	94	89	87	91	90	87	90	88	93
Taiwan	na	**77**	70	84	83	76	77	78	71	81	78	76	76	80	76	68
Tanzania	na	**98**	98	98	97	98	99	98	98	99	98	99	97	99	98	100
Turkey	87	**91**	92	91	92	91	92	94	90	79	95	90	84	95	92	83
Uganda	na	**92**	94	91	91	94	91	86	94	95	91	94	93	90	94	90
Ukraine	na	**na**	na	na	na	na	na	na	na	na	na	na	na	na	na	na
United States	93	**96**	94	97	95	97	95	96	95	96	96	95	95	97	95	97
Uruguay	na	**61**	53	67	57	60	63	62	61	58	62	61	62	69	58	64
Venezuela	na	**na**	na	na	na	na	na	na	na	na	na	na	na	na	na	na
Vietnam	na	**38**	31	45	43	38	35	40	37	31	44	33	41	38	40	41
Zimbabwe	na	**93**	91	95	92	94	94	93	94	57	91	94	94	94	92	94
Total	70	**85**	82	87	88	84	81	86	83	86	86	85	83	84	84	85

RANKING

Country	2000
Morocco	100
Pakistan	100
Egypt	100
Jordan	100
Bangladesh	99
Algeria	99
Indonesia	99
Iran	99
Tanzania	98
Nigeria	97
Philippines	96
Puerto Rico	96
United States	96
South Africa	94
El Salvador	94
Mexico	93
Zimbabwe	93
Uganda	92
Singapore	92
Turkey	91
Canada	91
Chile	89
Switzerland	89
Peru	89
Dominican Rep.	89
Colombia	87
Argentina	85
Australia	85
Bosnia and Herz.	85
New Zealand	84
Brazil	82
India	81
Moldova	81
Macedonia	80
Taiwan	77
Georgia	76
Albania	75
Spain	72
Japan	71
Azerbaijan	69
Armenia	65
Uruguay	61
Norway	60
Vietnam	38
Montenegro	35
Serbia	34
Total	85

F053) BELIEVE IN HELL

Which, if any, of the following do you believe in? Believe in hell

Yes (%) (WVS: V194; EVS: V117)

Country	Wave		Gender		Age			Education			Income			Values		
	1990	2000	Male	Female	16-29	30-49	50+	Lower	Middle	Upper	Lower	Middle	Upper	Mat	Mixed	Postm.
Albania	na	**41**	34	48	38	36	51	52	35	31	41	40	43	39	45	13
Algeria	na	**99**	99	98	99	98	99	98	99	99	99	99	99	99	99	98
Argentina	41	**44**	40	47	42	46	42	42	46	46	44	44	44	46	45	39
Armenia	na	**36**	31	41	41	34	33	37	37	33	41	35	30	31	43	28
Australia	na	**41**	36	46	46	39	39	46	41	36	43	42	35	45	45	33
Austria	20	**18**	16	20	14	18	21	21	16	16	22	19	15	18	20	15
Azerbaijan	na	**59**	54	63	60	56	66	69	57	60	60	61	55	55	64	76
Bangladesh	na	**95**	96	95	96	95	94	98	93	92	98	95	93	91	99	96
Belarus	9	**35**	24	45	30	30	45	47	33	20	41	30	34	39	32	22
Belgium	17	**16**	15	17	18	14	17	16	17	15	20	16	12	15	19	11
Bosnia and Herz.	na	**60**	56	64	68	58	55	72	59	53	67	60	58	57	62	57
Brazil	39	**49**	49	49	49	50	47	52	48	42	56	50	42	51	50	38
Bulgaria	11	**30**	25	35	34	24	33	42	25	22	38	23	27	31	29	39
Canada	42	**50**	48	53	58	49	47	52	54	42	53	53	44	53	54	43
Chile	45	**65**	59	71	62	65	69	71	64	58	70	65	58	70	68	49
China	na	**na**	na	na	na	na	na	na	na	na	na	na	na	na	na	na
Colombia	na	**40**	38	43	46	37	40	39	42	39	40	42	39	45	42	29
Croatia	na	**57**	49	64	57	59	55	61	57	46	58	53	59	64	58	49
Czech Republic	na	**13**	12	14	17	9	15	16	10	12	16	12	9	14	12	14
Denmark	8	**10**	8	11	10	8	11	9	8	9	13	8	6	8	10	6
Dominican Rep.	na	**68**	67	69	70	64	55	85	71	66	71	63	63	59	66	79
Egypt	na	**100**	100	100	100	100	100	100	100	100	100	100	100	100	100	100
El Salvador	na	**76**	74	79	76	78	75	79	76	70	79	76	72	na	na	na
Estonia	na	**16**	14	18	17	17	15	20	15	15	15	20	15	18	15	11
Finland	27	**31**	25	38	27	28	37	33	26	36	31	33	30	32	31	30
France	17	**20**	17	22	23	20	18	21	17	18	20	21	17	23	20	13
Georgia	na	**59**	55	63	70	57	50	54	58	66	56	57	67	59	59	57
Germany	9	**20**	17	22	17	17	25	23	19	10	20	20	21	19	22	17
Great Britain	28	**35**	32	38	33	39	33	34	38	36	30	43	36	na	na	na
Greece	na	**41**	38	42	40	40	40	57	46	32	44	39	37	45	43	27
Hungary	16	**20**	13	27	21	15	25	20	20	21	24	20	18	20	20	26
Iceland	12	**18**	21	14	21	18	14	18	18	15	19	19	13	20	17	15
India	39	**69**	65	73	65	69	72	74	65	59	72	71	64	78	57	54
Indonesia	na	**100**	100	100	99	100	100	100	100	100	100	100	99	100	100	100
Iran	na	**98**	98	98	98	98	99	99	98	97	98	99	98	100	98	97
Ireland	53	**53**	50	57	43	49	66	63	48	49	65	52	45	54	54	49
Israel	na	**na**	na	na	na	na	na	na	na	na	na	na	na	na	na	na
Italy	42	**49**	44	54	45	45	56	55	47	40	54	50	44	53	50	44
Japan	32	**30**	24	36	32	39	21	36	32	25	29	36	27	27	31	27
Jordan	na	**99**	99	99	99	99	99	99	100	99	100	100	98	99	99	100
Korea, South	na	**na**	na	na	na	na	na	na	na	na	na	na	na	na	na	na
Latvia	7	**28**	19	37	34	26	28	32	29	23	29	29	27	31	27	32
Lithuania	na	**68**	52	81	60	54	82	90	61	43	88	60	58	72	68	48
Luxembourg	na	**22**	21	23	20	19	25	26	20	15	27	21	18	23	22	19
Macedonia	na	**47**	44	49	61	46	36	66	37	35	49	48	38	45	43	76
Malta	na	**81**	76	85	77	72	91	87	78	82	82	82	77	78	82	80
Mexico	48	**75**	72	77	74	74	76	77	74	65	75	77	71	79	73	72
Moldova	na	**65**	55	72	66	59	70	77	63	56	73	59	61	66	63	63
Montenegro	na	**21**	17	24	16	21	23	29	18	9	29	22	13	24	16	17
Morocco	na	**100**	100	100	100	100	100	100	100	98	100	100	100	100	100	100
Netherlands	13	**14**	14	13	16	14	12	15	14	12	16	13	11	22	14	10
New Zealand	na	**33**	33	34	42	35	29	29	40	34	36	38	27	39	36	22
Nigeria	51	**94**	93	94	94	94	91	93	93	96	93	93	95	93	94	95
Northern Ireland	73	**74**	72	76	67	72	79	78	72	68	74	76	67	76	74	71
Norway	19	**20**	18	21	21	19	20	23	18	19	na	na	na	23	20	16
Pakistan	na	**100**	100	100	100	100	100	100	100	100	100	100	100	100	100	100
Peru	na	**65**	62	68	62	69	64	66	64	66	67	64	63	63	66	66
Philippines	na	**93**	91	94	91	93	94	94	92	92	92	93	92	92	94	83
Poland	54	**66**	56	74	72	64	64	66	70	53	68	65	61	71	61	66
Portugal	25	**38**	30	44	25	36	47	42	29	30	46	41	24	45	35	30
Puerto Rico	na	**73**	71	75	75	76	71	68	68	77	70	75	75	76	74	72
Romania	43	**71**	63	79	73	66	76	86	69	49	81	73	63	77	66	57
Russian Fed.	16	**36**	24	46	39	30	40	51	35	30	41	35	31	38	33	19
Serbia	na	**18**	16	20	24	14	19	23	14	20	17	17	19	15	21	22
Singapore	na	**79**	77	81	78	80	83	79	80	77	83	81	75	88	76	72
Slovakia	na	**46**	38	53	34	42	60	57	43	31	55	44	42	50	44	45
Slovenia	17	**20**	16	24	16	19	25	33	17	11	27	20	11	24	20	21
South Africa	52	**61**	53	70	55	63	67	57	67	52	54	56	71	61	62	48
Spain	30	**37**	29	44	25	32	48	45	28	29	44	35	31	45	36	22
Sweden	8	**10**	10	9	9	8	11	12	8	10	12	8	8	13	9	9
Switzerland	24	**21**	19	22	18	20	22	28	18	23	24	25	17	27	21	16
Taiwan	na	**62**	52	72	73	60	58	67	56	60	62	67	56	65	60	41
Tanzania	na	**96**	96	95	93	97	97	96	94	98	96	95	95	97	95	96
Turkey	85	**94**	93	95	93	93	94	97	92	75	97	94	84	97	94	85
Uganda	na	**77**	79	74	74	84	61	75	76	90	83	87	83	69	81	77
Ukraine	na	**38**	26	49	38	36	41	53	36	34	43	34	37	39	35	31
United States	71	**75**	72	77	77	78	68	84	74	71	77	76	72	73	77	69
Uruguay	na	**25**	22	28	22	25	27	27	23	20	27	21	29	29	24	22
Venezuela	na	**na**	na	na	na	na	na	na	na	na	na	na	na	na	na	na
Vietnam	na	**17**	12	22	20	17	15	22	13	5	20	15	17	18	17	19
Zimbabwe	na	**79**	73	85	76	79	89	83	74	100	83	77	79	76	81	85
Total	31	**53**	50	56	58	52	48	57	50	51	57	53	49	58	52	43

RANKING	
Country	**2000**
Pakistan	100
Egypt	100
Morocco	100
Indonesia	100
Jordan	99
Algeria	99
Iran	98
Tanzania	96
Bangladesh	95
Nigeria	94
Turkey	94
Philippines	93
Malta	81
Zimbabwe	79
Singapore	79
Uganda	77
El Salvador	76
Mexico	75
United States	75
Northern Ireland	74
Puerto Rico	73
Romania	71
India	69
Lithuania	68
Dominican Rep.	68
Poland	66
Chile	65
Peru	65
Moldova	65
Taiwan	62
South Africa	61
Bosnia and Herz.	60
Georgia	59
Azerbaijan	59
Croatia	57
Ireland	53
Canada	50
Brazil	49
Italy	49
Macedonia	47
Slovakia	46
Argentina	44
Australia	41
Albania	41
Greece	41
Colombia	40
Ukraine	38
Portugal	38
Spain	37
Armenia	36
Russian Fed.	36
Great Britain	35
Belarus	35
New Zealand	33
Finland	31
Japan	30
Bulgaria	30
Latvia	28
Uruguay	25
Luxembourg	22
Montenegro	21
Switzerland	21
Slovenia	20
Hungary	20
Germany	20
Norway	20
France	20
Austria	18
Serbia	18
Iceland	18
Vietnam	17
Estonia	16
Belgium	16
Netherlands	14
Czech Republic	13
Denmark	10
Sweden	10
Total	53

F054) BELIEVE IN HEAVEN

Which, if any, of the following do you believe in? Believe in heaven

Yes (%) (WVS: V195; EVS: V118)

Country	Wave		Gender		Age			Education			Income			Values		
	1990	2000	Male	Female	16-29	30-49	50+	Lower	Middle	Upper	Lower	Middle	Upper	Mat	Mixed	Postm.
Albania	na	**48**	41	56	49	43	56	57	44	37	48	50	47	43	50	42
Algeria	na	**100**	100	100	100	99	100	100	100	99	100	100	99	100	100	99
Argentina	69	**81**	76	85	82	80	80	84	77	73	84	83	75	85	83	72
Armenia	na	**41**	36	46	48	38	36	42	42	37	46	38	36	34	50	31
Australia	na	**64**	53	73	67	60	64	75	64	53	67	63	54	71	66	57
Austria	47	**41**	35	48	41	39	44	45	38	39	43	43	35	46	42	40
Azerbaijan	na	**61**	57	66	63	58	67	72	60	61	62	62	58	58	65	76
Bangladesh	na	**100**	99	100	99	100	100	100	99	99	100	100	99	100	100	99
Belarus	12	**37**	25	47	30	33	45	45	35	26	38	36	34	38	34	36
Belgium	34	**31**	27	35	34	28	32	35	30	29	37	33	25	33	33	24
Bosnia and Herz.	na	**62**	58	66	71	59	57	75	61	55	68	61	61	58	64	61
Brazil	76	**82**	82	83	86	80	80	87	83	65	88	86	73	90	83	65
Bulgaria	16	**33**	28	37	39	27	34	42	29	25	41	28	29	34	32	41
Canada	72	**74**	67	80	74	72	76	81	77	61	78	75	68	84	78	63
Chile	77	**80**	70	88	80	79	81	87	76	75	85	78	72	86	81	67
China	na	**na**	na	na	na	na	na	na	na	na	na	na	na	na	na	na
Colombia	na	**82**	77	87	86	78	86	93	86	69	93	85	71	89	84	74
Croatia	na	**64**	58	70	65	69	58	69	64	50	65	61	65	68	65	55
Czech Republic	na	**21**	19	23	22	15	25	25	15	17	27	20	13	23	19	22
Denmark	19	**18**	13	24	22	15	20	20	13	17	22	16	15	19	19	11
Dominican Rep.	na	**81**	80	82	83	79	70	89	83	80	84	76	81	80	80	85
Egypt	na	**100**	100	100	100	100	100	100	100	100	100	100	100	100	100	100
El Salvador	na	**86**	82	90	88	84	87	90	84	79	92	84	81	na	na	na
Estonia	na	**19**	16	22	19	20	19	26	16	18	21	22	16	20	18	10
Finland	55	**61**	47	74	54	59	68	62	60	63	63	55	66	65	61	59
France	32	**31**	25	37	34	30	31	34	28	27	34	32	26	40	30	20
Georgia	na	**63**	59	66	73	61	53	57	62	68	59	61	69	61	64	63
Germany	25	**31**	25	36	28	27	36	36	27	21	30	33	33	26	35	28
Great Britain	59	**56**	44	67	50	53	60	64	53	43	60	58	50	na	na	na
Greece	na	**47**	45	48	48	45	47	64	53	38	51	47	43	50	49	34
Hungary	27	**29**	21	37	28	24	34	32	23	29	36	29	26	30	29	42
Iceland	57	**59**	54	63	53	59	63	67	60	41	63	60	51	72	57	36
India	43	**72**	69	76	69	72	75	77	69	64	75	73	69	80	62	56
Indonesia	na	**100**	100	100	99	100	100	100	100	100	100	100	99	100	100	100
Iran	na	**98**	98	99	98	98	100	99	98	98	98	99	98	100	98	99
Ireland	90	**85**	81	89	80	82	93	91	84	79	91	85	82	88	86	78
Israel	na	**na**	na	na	na	na	na	na	na	na	na	na	na	na	na	na
Italy	54	**59**	52	65	55	54	65	65	56	49	64	59	52	67	60	53
Japan	43	**38**	28	46	43	46	27	46	39	33	37	40	35	33	40	35
Jordan	na	**100**	99	100	100	100	99	99	100	100	100	100	99	100	99	100
Korea, South	na	**na**	na	na	na	na	na	na	na	na	na	na	na	na	na	na
Latvia	12	**33**	22	44	41	30	33	41	32	27	34	37	29	35	32	33
Lithuania	na	**71**	53	83	61	57	84	92	63	49	89	64	60	76	70	50
Luxembourg	na	**33**	30	35	34	31	34	40	30	24	39	33	24	39	32	30
Macedonia	na	**50**	47	54	63	50	40	69	42	40	54	51	41	49	48	76
Malta	na	**88**	82	93	83	82	96	93	86	85	90	90	83	88	87	88
Mexico	70	**88**	85	91	87	88	90	92	87	75	93	90	83	91	88	85
Moldova	na	**68**	58	76	71	63	71	76	66	62	75	59	65	69	67	63
Montenegro	na	**19**	17	20	13	20	20	26	16	7	28	20	12	21	14	12
Morocco	na	**100**	100	100	100	100	100	100	99	98	100	100	100	100	100	98
Netherlands	37	**38**	31	45	42	35	38	45	38	31	37	39	32	54	38	28
New Zealand	na	**61**	53	68	66	60	61	61	68	56	66	64	52	74	63	47
Nigeria	96	**99**	99	99	99	99	100	99	100	100	99	99	100	99	99	99
Northern Ireland	90	**87**	83	90	83	84	90	90	83	84	86	88	81	88	87	85
Norway	44	**47**	38	55	42	45	53	54	45	42	na	na	na	49	49	31
Pakistan	na	**100**	100	100	100	100	100	100	100	100	100	100	100	100	100	100
Peru	na	**85**	81	88	82	87	85	89	87	77	88	83	80	88	84	82
Philippines	na	**96**	95	98	96	96	97	98	96	96	97	97	95	97	97	91
Poland	80	**80**	74	85	86	77	79	83	80	63	82	79	74	87	75	76
Portugal	56	**60**	53	67	48	58	69	67	46	38	66	66	43	65	58	48
Puerto Rico	na	**91**	88	93	93	92	90	90	90	92	89	92	90	88	92	92
Romania	58	**75**	67	83	78	70	78	87	75	54	82	78	68	80	71	62
Russian Fed.	18	**36**	24	47	38	30	41	51	35	30	42	35	30	38	33	22
Serbia	na	**17**	16	19	25	13	18	24	13	17	19	17	17	15	19	25
Singapore	na	**81**	77	85	79	82	83	83	80	79	85	81	77	88	79	71
Slovakia	na	**55**	46	63	44	50	70	65	53	37	66	55	49	59	53	53
Slovenia	30	**28**	25	30	25	23	34	45	23	14	38	26	16	34	27	26
South Africa	91	**91**	87	96	90	91	93	90	91	90	88	95	89	90	91	91
Spain	52	**51**	40	61	38	45	64	61	40	43	62	49	43	62	50	33
Sweden	31	**31**	24	38	25	29	37	41	30	26	35	34	21	38	32	26
Switzerland	44	**45**	37	52	37	44	51	62	41	35	51	49	36	56	44	36
Taiwan	na	**62**	52	71	68	60	60	66	56	60	64	64	55	64	60	43
Tanzania	na	**93**	93	92	91	94	93	92	92	96	92	93	94	93	93	91
Turkey	87	**94**	93	95	94	94	95	98	93	76	97	94	84	98	95	85
Uganda	na	**92**	90	94	91	97	84	90	93	98	92	96	95	91	94	90
Ukraine	na	**40**	28	51	41	37	43	58	38	35	45	38	36	40	37	38
United States	87	**88**	84	91	87	90	85	92	89	85	89	88	85	91	89	83
Uruguay	na	**51**	39	60	42	46	58	58	43	34	56	48	49	67	47	43
Venezuela	na	**na**	na	na	na	na	na	na	na	na	na	na	na	na	na	na
Vietnam	na	**17**	12	21	20	17	14	21	11	7	18	15	16	17	16	17
Zimbabwe	na	**93**	91	95	93	92	96	94	91	100	92	94	92	93	93	96
Total	51	**64**	60	69	69	63	61	70	61	61	69	65	60	68	64	56

RANKING	
Country	2000
Pakistan	100
Egypt	100
Algeria	100
Morocco	100
Jordan	100
Bangladesh	100
Indonesia	100
Nigeria	99
Iran	98
Philippines	96
Turkey	94
Zimbabwe	93
Tanzania	93
Uganda	92
Puerto Rico	91
South Africa	91
Mexico	88
Malta	88
United States	88
Northern Ireland	87
El Salvador	86
Ireland	85
Peru	85
Brazil	82
Colombia	82
Dominican Rep.	81
Singapore	81
Argentina	81
Chile	80
Poland	80
Romania	75
Canada	74
India	72
Lithuania	71
Moldova	68
Croatia	64
Australia	64
Georgia	63
Bosnia and Herz.	62
Taiwan	62
Azerbaijan	61
Finland	61
New Zealand	61
Portugal	60
Iceland	59
Italy	59
Great Britain	56
Slovakia	55
Uruguay	51
Spain	51
Macedonia	50
Albania	48
Greece	47
Norway	47
Switzerland	45
Austria	41
Armenia	41
Ukraine	40
Netherlands	38
Japan	38
Belarus	37
Russian Fed.	36
Latvia	33
Luxembourg	33
Bulgaria	33
France	31
Sweden	31
Germany	31
Belgium	31
Hungary	29
Slovenia	28
Czech Republic	21
Estonia	19
Montenegro	19
Denmark	18
Serbia	17
Vietnam	17
Total	64

F055_1) BELIEVE IN SIN

Which, if any, of the following do you believe in? Sin.

Yes (%) (EVS: V119)

Country	Wave		Gender		Age			Education			Income			Values		
	1990	2000	Male	Female	16-29	30-49	50+	Lower	Middle	Upper	Lower	Middle	Upper	Mat	Mixed	Postm.
Albania	na	**na**	na	na	na	na	na	na	na	na	na	na	na	na	na	na
Algeria	na	**na**	na	na	na	na	na	na	na	na	na	na	na	na	na	na
Argentina	72	**na**	na	na	na	na	na	na	na	na	na	na	na	na	na	na
Armenia	na	**65**	60	70	68	64	64	61	64	71	72	58	62	59	72	65
Australia	na	**74**	73	75	74	74	75	73	75	73	72	79	74	73	76	72
Austria	66	**61**	58	64	56	59	67	63	61	57	63	62	56	66	64	54
Azerbaijan	na	**75**	75	76	71	75	84	85	73	78	77	75	75	73	77	85
Bangladesh	na	**na**	na	na	na	na	na	na	na	na	na	na	na	na	na	na
Belarus	48	**59**	46	70	49	58	68	68	56	53	62	58	56	60	59	41
Belgium	45	**43**	43	43	41	39	47	44	42	44	47	42	42	42	47	35
Bosnia and Herz.	na	**na**	na	na	na	na	na	na	na	na	na	na	na	na	na	na
Brazil	82	**89**	89	89	88	90	89	93	90	74	93	94	82	95	90	71
Bulgaria	30	**53**	44	61	49	47	59	58	50	49	58	51	51	58	50	54
Canada	74	**na**	na	na	na	na	na	na	na	na	na	na	na	na	na	na
Chile	88	**na**	na	na	na	na	na	na	na	na	na	na	na	na	na	na
China	na	**na**	na	na	na	na	na	na	na	na	na	na	na	na	na	na
Colombia	na	**85**	84	87	89	84	85	89	89	78	88	89	79	89	88	83
Croatia	na	**76**	70	82	76	79	74	82	74	67	84	76	73	78	77	71
Czech Republic	na	**59**	52	65	54	56	64	56	60	68	61	58	55	52	60	65
Denmark	24	**21**	20	21	20	16	26	23	15	20	30	15	16	19	22	12
Dominican Rep.	na	**84**	82	84	86	81	64	90	86	82	89	74	81	81	83	86
Egypt	na	**na**	na	na	na	na	na	na	na	na	na	na	na	na	na	na
El Salvador	na	**95**	95	95	94	96	96	96	95	93	95	96	95	na	na	na
Estonia	na	**52**	48	56	46	53	56	53	51	56	53	55	50	52	52	38
Finland	66	**67**	62	72	56	65	75	69	63	72	73	62	67	58	72	64
France	43	**40**	36	43	35	36	46	42	37	38	43	40	37	45	40	29
Georgia	na	**84**	81	87	88	85	79	82	83	89	82	84	87	83	85	92
Germany	37	**41**	36	45	35	37	49	46	39	31	39	42	48	41	42	42
Great Britain	72	**67**	66	68	61	67	71	65	67	71	65	63	71	na	na	na
Greece	na	**74**	69	77	69	75	82	90	80	65	75	74	71	81	76	59
Hungary	39	**46**	36	54	44	39	52	45	45	48	52	46	41	47	45	39
Iceland	70	**64**	66	63	55	63	76	69	62	59	68	68	58	67	66	45
India	67	**na**	na	na	na	na	na	na	na	na	na	na	na	na	na	na
Indonesia	na	**na**	na	na	na	na	na	na	na	na	na	na	na	na	na	na
Iran	na	**na**	na	na	na	na	na	na	na	na	na	na	na	na	na	na
Ireland	87	**86**	86	86	85	85	88	85	86	85	85	85	87	89	85	84
Israel	na	**na**	na	na	na	na	na	na	na	na	na	na	na	na	na	na
Italy	73	**73**	66	79	70	70	78	79	71	63	80	69	67	80	75	65
Japan	28	**na**	na	na	na	na	na	na	na	na	na	na	na	na	na	na
Jordan	na	**na**	na	na	na	na	na	na	na	na	na	na	na	na	na	na
Korea, South	na	**na**	na	na	na	na	na	na	na	na	na	na	na	na	na	na
Latvia	51	**74**	63	83	74	75	72	74	72	78	74	71	75	75	72	90
Lithuania	na	**91**	83	96	85	89	95	96	88	88	95	89	90	90	91	96
Luxembourg	na	**47**	43	51	42	45	54	50	45	48	49	46	48	54	47	38
Macedonia	na	**na**	na	na	na	na	na	na	na	na	na	na	na	na	na	na
Malta	na	**93**	90	96	89	91	97	94	92	97	93	95	91	92	93	96
Mexico	74	**na**	na	na	na	na	na	na	na	na	na	na	na	na	na	na
Moldova	na	**na**	na	na	na	na	na	na	na	na	na	na	na	na	na	na
Montenegro	na	**na**	na	na	na	na	na	na	na	na	na	na	na	na	na	na
Morocco	na	**na**	na	na	na	na	na	na	na	na	na	na	na	na	na	na
Netherlands	43	**40**	40	40	33	32	52	46	37	36	44	37	34	56	38	36
New Zealand	na	**66**	65	68	73	70	61	60	71	71	65	68	68	70	68	63
Nigeria	62	**na**	na	na	na	na	na	na	na	na	na	na	na	na	na	na
Northern Ireland	91	**90**	88	93	88	87	93	92	90	87	91	91	87	92	91	89
Norway	44	**45**	42	49	37	42	57	53	42	42	na	na	na	53	46	33
Pakistan	na	**na**	na	na	na	na	na	na	na	na	na	na	na	na	na	na
Peru	na	**na**	na	na	na	na	na	na	na	na	na	na	na	na	na	na
Philippines	na	**na**	na	na	na	na	na	na	na	na	na	na	na	na	na	na
Poland	91	**90**	87	93	92	90	90	92	89	85	90	91	88	95	88	85
Portugal	68	**71**	63	78	59	73	77	77	62	55	79	74	58	76	70	67
Puerto Rico	na	**na**	na	na	na	na	na	na	na	na	na	na	na	na	na	na
Romania	77	**91**	87	95	89	90	93	95	91	81	93	93	87	93	90	77
Russian Fed.	47	**68**	56	77	71	64	72	72	67	70	68	68	68	68	68	62
Serbia	na	**na**	na	na	na	na	na	na	na	na	na	na	na	na	na	na
Singapore	na	**na**	na	na	na	na	na	na	na	na	na	na	na	na	na	na
Slovakia	na	**76**	70	81	66	74	86	80	74	70	84	75	72	77	76	69
Slovenia	47	**43**	39	47	39	40	49	56	41	32	51	47	31	52	42	43
South Africa	69	**na**	na	na	na	na	na	na	na	na	na	na	na	na	na	na
Spain	56	**51**	40	62	33	43	68	65	40	44	61	50	45	69	49	31
Sweden	31	**26**	25	27	21	18	36	36	23	22	31	24	20	36	26	20
Switzerland	64	**57**	54	60	48	54	66	70	55	52	60	60	52	60	58	52
Taiwan	na	**46**	38	53	51	44	45	53	42	42	49	45	42	48	45	33
Tanzania	na	**na**	na	na	na	na	na	na	na	na	na	na	na	na	na	na
Turkey	91	**96**	95	96	94	97	99	99	94	82	98	97	88	98	97	90
Uganda	na	**na**	na	na	na	na	na	na	na	na	na	na	na	na	na	na
Ukraine	na	**74**	65	81	77	74	73	74	73	76	75	73	74	76	72	83
United States	89	**na**	na	na	na	na	na	na	na	na	na	na	na	na	na	na
Uruguay	na	**53**	42	60	46	45	61	60	44	37	58	50	50	64	52	44
Venezuela	na	**na**	na	na	na	na	na	na	na	na	na	na	na	na	na	na
Vietnam	na	**na**	na	na	na	na	na	na	na	na	na	na	na	na	na	na
Zimbabwe	na	**na**	na	na	na	na	na	na	na	na	na	na	na	na	na	na
Total	61	**65**	61	69	65	63	68	68	65	63	69	65	64	69	64	56

RANKING

Country	2000
Turkey	96
El Salvador	95
Malta	93
Romania	91
Lithuania	91
Poland	90
Northern Ireland	90
Brazil	89
Ireland	86
Colombia	85
Georgia	84
Dominican Rep.	84
Croatia	76
Slovakia	76
Azerbaijan	75
Australia	74
Ukraine	74
Greece	74
Latvia	74
Italy	73
Portugal	71
Russian Fed.	68
Finland	67
Great Britain	67
New Zealand	66
Armenia	65
Iceland	64
Austria	61
Belarus	59
Czech Republic	59
Switzerland	57
Bulgaria	53
Uruguay	53
Estonia	52
Spain	51
Luxembourg	47
Taiwan	46
Hungary	46
Norway	45
Slovenia	43
Belgium	43
Germany	41
France	40
Netherlands	40
Sweden	26
Denmark	21
Total	65

F056_1) BELIEVE IN TELEPATHY

Which, if any, of the following do you believe in? Telepathy

Yes (%) (EVS: V120)

Country	Wave		Gender		Age			Education			Income			Values		
	1990	2000	Male	Female	16-29	30-49	50+	Lower	Middle	Upper	Lower	Middle	Upper	Mat	Mixed	Postm.
Albania	na	**na**	na	na	na	na	na	na	na	na	na	na	na	na	na	na
Algeria	na	**na**	na	na	na	na	na	na	na	na	na	na	na	na	na	na
Argentina	na	**na**	na	na	na	na	na	na	na	na	na	na	na	na	na	na
Armenia	na	**na**	na	na	na	na	na	na	na	na	na	na	na	na	na	na
Australia	na	**na**	na	na	na	na	na	na	na	na	na	na	na	na	na	na
Austria	na	**48**	41	55	51	52	43	43	53	53	41	50	50	45	46	55
Azerbaijan	na	**na**	na	na	na	na	na	na	na	na	na	na	na	na	na	na
Bangladesh	na	**na**	na	na	na	na	na	na	na	na	na	na	na	na	na	na
Belarus	na	**32**	29	34	43	32	21	27	33	33	29	30	39	27	37	26
Belgium	na	**38**	33	43	39	41	35	30	41	39	38	35	41	37	40	38
Bosnia and Herz.	na	**na**	na	na	na	na	na	na	na	na	na	na	na	na	na	na
Brazil	na	**na**	na	na	na	na	na	na	na	na	na	na	na	na	na	na
Bulgaria	na	**45**	37	52	46	56	34	29	47	62	30	45	56	43	46	62
Canada	na	**na**	na	na	na	na	na	na	na	na	na	na	na	na	na	na
Chile	na	**na**	na	na	na	na	na	na	na	na	na	na	na	na	na	na
China	na	**na**	na	na	na	na	na	na	na	na	na	na	na	na	na	na
Colombia	na	**na**	na	na	na	na	na	na	na	na	na	na	na	na	na	na
Croatia	na	**39**	41	37	47	42	30	32	42	46	29	37	47	26	40	45
Czech Republic	na	**73**	70	76	80	76	67	68	78	77	64	73	79	69	75	72
Denmark	na	**36**	29	43	34	40	32	35	38	38	39	34	30	31	36	41
Dominican Rep.	na	**na**	na	na	na	na	na	na	na	na	na	na	na	na	na	na
Egypt	na	**na**	na	na	na	na	na	na	na	na	na	na	na	na	na	na
El Salvador	na	**na**	na	na	na	na	na	na	na	na	na	na	na	na	na	na
Estonia	na	**55**	51	58	55	62	48	41	61	60	42	53	64	53	56	71
Finland	na	**46**	34	57	41	48	46	45	50	44	51	41	45	47	45	49
France	na	**40**	35	44	44	43	34	38	43	41	39	41	38	39	39	42
Georgia	na	**na**	na	na	na	na	na	na	na	na	na	na	na	na	na	na
Germany	na	**29**	22	34	37	31	22	24	32	27	26	28	34	25	28	33
Great Britain	na	**45**	40	50	50	45	43	43	46	46	43	46	42	na	na	na
Greece	na	**55**	53	56	62	49	50	43	56	56	52	56	58	50	55	54
Hungary	na	**46**	40	52	51	52	37	39	59	56	44	48	46	43	50	56
Iceland	na	**61**	56	66	43	60	79	65	60	56	64	61	56	61	61	58
India	na	**na**	na	na	na	na	na	na	na	na	na	na	na	na	na	na
Indonesia	na	**na**	na	na	na	na	na	na	na	na	na	na	na	na	na	na
Iran	na	**na**	na	na	na	na	na	na	na	na	na	na	na	na	na	na
Ireland	na	**42**	38	45	47	42	36	37	42	49	35	39	48	39	43	42
Israel	na	**na**	na	na	na	na	na	na	na	na	na	na	na	na	na	na
Italy	na	**37**	32	42	41	41	32	31	42	43	31	39	39	34	36	42
Japan	na	**na**	na	na	na	na	na	na	na	na	na	na	na	na	na	na
Jordan	na	**na**	na	na	na	na	na	na	na	na	na	na	na	na	na	na
Korea, South	na	**na**	na	na	na	na	na	na	na	na	na	na	na	na	na	na
Latvia	na	**52**	49	55	57	58	46	41	52	66	45	49	66	49	53	66
Lithuania	na	**79**	69	87	82	82	74	79	78	86	77	74	83	83	78	90
Luxembourg	na	**38**	34	43	39	45	31	35	43	35	43	39	39	39	37	45
Macedonia	na	**na**	na	na	na	na	na	na	na	na	na	na	na	na	na	na
Malta	na	**34**	31	36	39	33	31	29	34	44	27	28	45	34	35	19
Mexico	na	**na**	na	na	na	na	na	na	na	na	na	na	na	na	na	na
Moldova	na	**na**	na	na	na	na	na	na	na	na	na	na	na	na	na	na
Montenegro	na	**na**	na	na	na	na	na	na	na	na	na	na	na	na	na	na
Morocco	na	**na**	na	na	na	na	na	na	na	na	na	na	na	na	na	na
Netherlands	na	**50**	45	55	56	58	39	42	52	56	44	57	51	47	49	54
New Zealand	na	**na**	na	na	na	na	na	na	na	na	na	na	na	na	na	na
Nigeria	na	**na**	na	na	na	na	na	na	na	na	na	na	na	na	na	na
Northern Ireland	na	**38**	34	41	38	41	37	32	40	49	33	33	45	35	40	37
Norway	na	**na**	na	na	na	na	na	na	na	na	na	na	na	na	na	na
Pakistan	na	**na**	na	na	na	na	na	na	na	na	na	na	na	na	na	na
Peru	na	**na**	na	na	na	na	na	na	na	na	na	na	na	na	na	na
Philippines	na	**na**	na	na	na	na	na	na	na	na	na	na	na	na	na	na
Poland	na	**40**	35	44	46	41	34	30	48	57	30	44	50	36	42	44
Portugal	na	**35**	33	37	45	33	30	31	40	46	17	38	33	36	32	45
Puerto Rico	na	**na**	na	na	na	na	na	na	na	na	na	na	na	na	na	na
Romania	na	**67**	63	70	73	66	62	54	67	78	51	64	75	64	69	75
Russian Fed.	na	**59**	55	63	68	62	47	40	57	70	50	58	67	57	61	46
Serbia	na	**na**	na	na	na	na	na	na	na	na	na	na	na	na	na	na
Singapore	na	**na**	na	na	na	na	na	na	na	na	na	na	na	na	na	na
Slovakia	na	**53**	50	56	56	56	46	42	56	60	46	53	57	51	53	63
Slovenia	na	**27**	27	28	35	31	18	19	28	40	24	29	37	30	27	30
South Africa	na	**na**	na	na	na	na	na	na	na	na	na	na	na	na	na	na
Spain	na	**27**	24	30	30	32	21	21	30	33	27	22	38	26	25	29
Sweden	na	**48**	40	57	52	45	49	44	54	43	53	45	45	51	48	49
Switzerland	na	**na**	na	na	na	na	na	na	na	na	na	na	na	na	na	na
Taiwan	na	**na**	na	na	na	na	na	na	na	na	na	na	na	na	na	na
Tanzania	na	**na**	na	na	na	na	na	na	na	na	na	na	na	na	na	na
Turkey	na	**8**	7	9	8	9	7	8	10	8	8	8	9	7	8	10
Uganda	na	**na**	na	na	na	na	na	na	na	na	na	na	na	na	na	na
Ukraine	na	**57**	58	56	65	61	46	29	57	68	52	56	64	58	57	52
United States	na	**na**	na	na	na	na	na	na	na	na	na	na	na	na	na	na
Uruguay	na	**na**	na	na	na	na	na	na	na	na	na	na	na	na	na	na
Venezuela	na	**na**	na	na	na	na	na	na	na	na	na	na	na	na	na	na
Vietnam	na	**na**	na	na	na	na	na	na	na	na	na	na	na	na	na	na
Zimbabwe	na	**na**	na	na	na	na	na	na	na	na	na	na	na	na	na	na
Total	na	**45**	41	49	49	48	40	38	48	51	41	45	51	44	46	46

RANKING

Country	2000
Lithuania	79
Czech Republic	73
Romania	67
Iceland	61
Russian Fed.	59
Ukraine	57
Estonia	55
Greece	55
Slovakia	53
Latvia	52
Netherlands	50
Austria	48
Sweden	48
Hungary	46
Finland	46
Great Britain	45
Bulgaria	45
Ireland	42
France	40
Poland	40
Croatia	39
Luxembourg	38
Belgium	38
Northern Ireland	38
Italy	37
Denmark	36
Portugal	35
Malta	34
Belarus	32
Germany	29
Slovenia	27
Spain	27
Turkey	8
Total	45

F057_1) BELIEVE IN RE-INCARNATION

Do you believe in re-incarnation, that is, that we are born into this world again?

Yes (%)

(EVS: V121)

Country	Wave		Gender		Age			Education			Income			Values		
	1990	2000	Male	Female	16-29	30-49	50+	Lower	Middle	Upper	Lower	Middle	Upper	Mat	Mixed	Postm.
Albania	na	**na**	na	na	na	na	na	na	na	na	na	na	na	na	na	na
Algeria	na	**na**	na	na	na	na	na	na	na	na	na	na	na	na	na	na
Argentina	39	**na**	na	na	na	na	na	na	na	na	na	na	na	na	na	na
Armenia	na	**na**	na	na	na	na	na	na	na	na	na	na	na	na	na	na
Australia	na	**na**	na	na	na	na	na	na	na	na	na	na	na	na	na	na
Austria	29	**23**	20	26	27	26	18	20	27	22	24	21	24	22	22	24
Azerbaijan	na	**na**	na	na	na	na	na	na	na	na	na	na	na	na	na	na
Bangladesh	na	**na**	na	na	na	na	na	na	na	na	na	na	na	na	na	na
Belarus	24	**33**	27	37	41	31	27	29	34	31	30	29	44	34	30	33
Belgium	16	**17**	13	21	29	18	11	15	19	16	22	20	12	15	18	20
Bosnia and Herz.	na	**na**	na	na	na	na	na	na	na	na	na	na	na	na	na	na
Brazil	57	**na**	na	na	na	na	na	na	na	na	na	na	na	na	na	na
Bulgaria	25	**30**	24	37	43	31	22	19	32	45	22	29	37	26	33	49
Canada	31	**na**	na	na	na	na	na	na	na	na	na	na	na	na	na	na
Chile	49	**na**	na	na	na	na	na	na	na	na	na	na	na	na	na	na
China	na	**na**	na	na	na	na	na	na	na	na	na	na	na	na	na	na
Colombia	na	**na**	na	na	na	na	na	na	na	na	na	na	na	na	na	na
Croatia	na	**23**	22	24	38	23	14	21	25	22	17	21	28	7	25	31
Czech Republic	na	**23**	20	26	36	25	15	24	24	19	16	27	23	22	24	22
Denmark	17	**17**	11	24	24	20	11	17	20	17	19	15	16	17	18	18
Dominican Rep.	na	**na**	na	na	na	na	na	na	na	na	na	na	na	na	na	na
Egypt	na	**na**	na	na	na	na	na	na	na	na	na	na	na	na	na	na
El Salvador	na	**na**	na	na	na	na	na	na	na	na	na	na	na	na	na	na
Estonia	na	**37**	30	43	49	43	25	33	39	37	34	30	44	34	38	57
Finland	34	**18**	12	25	19	19	17	22	16	7	23	13	17	16	20	17
France	28	**29**	23	35	36	34	20	29	30	26	31	31	26	28	28	32
Georgia	na	**na**	na	na	na	na	na	na	na	na	na	na	na	na	na	na
Germany	13	**19**	15	22	23	21	16	19	22	10	16	21	26	22	18	20
Great Britain	29	**na**	na	na	na	na	na	na	na	na	na	na	na	na	na	na
Greece	na	**26**	27	25	32	26	15	25	28	25	26	26	26	27	27	20
Hungary	23	**20**	17	23	28	23	12	19	24	18	17	18	23	17	22	34
Iceland	40	**41**	34	49	47	45	31	49	41	27	47	41	35	51	39	33
India	91	**na**	na	na	na	na	na	na	na	na	na	na	na	na	na	na
Indonesia	na	**na**	na	na	na	na	na	na	na	na	na	na	na	na	na	na
Iran	na	**na**	na	na	na	na	na	na	na	na	na	na	na	na	na	na
Ireland	20	**23**	19	27	25	26	18	26	23	17	26	24	18	17	24	28
Israel	na	**na**	na	na	na	na	na	na	na	na	na	na	na	na	na	na
Italy	27	**18**	15	21	24	19	14	17	21	14	17	20	14	13	19	18
Japan	50	**na**	na	na	na	na	na	na	na	na	na	na	na	na	na	na
Jordan	na	**na**	na	na	na	na	na	na	na	na	na	na	na	na	na	na
Korea, South	na	**na**	na	na	na	na	na	na	na	na	na	na	na	na	na	na
Latvia	45	**33**	26	41	42	38	25	28	34	39	29	36	38	33	34	33
Lithuania	na	**44**	37	50	47	43	43	44	43	46	46	40	43	38	48	31
Luxembourg	na	**24**	21	27	30	25	19	25	25	17	23	25	22	21	25	24
Macedonia	na	**na**	na	na	na	na	na	na	na	na	na	na	na	na	na	na
Malta	na	**12**	11	13	14	12	11	10	13	9	12	11	10	11	13	10
Mexico	43	**na**	na	na	na	na	na	na	na	na	na	na	na	na	na	na
Moldova	na	**na**	na	na	na	na	na	na	na	na	na	na	na	na	na	na
Montenegro	na	**na**	na	na	na	na	na	na	na	na	na	na	na	na	na	na
Morocco	na	**na**	na	na	na	na	na	na	na	na	na	na	na	na	na	na
Netherlands	22	**22**	16	28	27	27	14	20	24	22	22	22	24	25	21	23
New Zealand	na	**na**	na	na	na	na	na	na	na	na	na	na	na	na	na	na
Nigeria	39	**na**	na	na	na	na	na	na	na	na	na	na	na	na	na	na
Northern Ireland	33	**17**	16	18	24	21	11	15	19	17	18	20	20	12	16	25
Norway	15	**na**	na	na	na	na	na	na	na	na	na	na	na	na	na	na
Pakistan	na	**na**	na	na	na	na	na	na	na	na	na	na	na	na	na	na
Peru	na	**na**	na	na	na	na	na	na	na	na	na	na	na	na	na	na
Philippines	na	**na**	na	na	na	na	na	na	na	na	na	na	na	na	na	na
Poland	26	**25**	20	29	32	27	19	26	24	18	26	25	22	22	26	33
Portugal	29	**29**	24	35	34	24	31	29	31	32	19	29	25	31	30	27
Puerto Rico	na	**na**	na	na	na	na	na	na	na	na	na	na	na	na	na	na
Romania	24	**28**	24	33	34	27	25	24	27	34	25	23	31	27	29	31
Russian Fed.	22	**32**	24	39	45	31	25	28	32	35	29	32	35	31	33	39
Serbia	na	**na**	na	na	na	na	na	na	na	na	na	na	na	na	na	na
Singapore	na	**na**	na	na	na	na	na	na	na	na	na	na	na	na	na	na
Slovakia	na	**20**	20	20	25	21	14	16	22	20	15	20	23	16	20	36
Slovenia	17	**17**	16	17	30	17	7	12	18	21	14	11	22	14	17	20
South Africa	43	**na**	na	na	na	na	na	na	na	na	na	na	na	na	na	na
Spain	28	**20**	18	23	21	21	19	18	23	18	21	18	23	23	20	18
Sweden	20	**22**	15	29	27	24	18	19	26	18	27	19	17	36	21	23
Switzerland	36	**na**	na	na	na	na	na	na	na	na	na	na	na	na	na	na
Taiwan	na	**na**	na	na	na	na	na	na	na	na	na	na	na	na	na	na
Tanzania	na	**na**	na	na	na	na	na	na	na	na	na	na	na	na	na	na
Turkey	54	**33**	32	34	31	34	38	33	35	28	28	39	29	35	36	24
Uganda	na	**na**	na	na	na	na	na	na	na	na	na	na	na	na	na	na
Ukraine	na	**28**	25	32	37	28	24	27	26	35	30	27	30	26	31	35
United States	26	**na**	na	na	na	na	na	na	na	na	na	na	na	na	na	na
Uruguay	na	**na**	na	na	na	na	na	na	na	na	na	na	na	na	na	na
Venezuela	na	**na**	na	na	na	na	na	na	na	na	na	na	na	na	na	na
Vietnam	na	**na**	na	na	na	na	na	na	na	na	na	na	na	na	na	na
Zimbabwe	na	**na**	na	na	na	na	na	na	na	na	na	na	na	na	na	na
Total	32	**25**	20	29	32	26	18	23	26	24	24	24	26	24	25	24

RANKING	
Country	**2000**
Lithuania	44
Iceland	41
Estonia	37
Latvia	33
Turkey	33
Belarus	33
Russian Fed.	32
Bulgaria	30
Portugal	29
France	29
Ukraine	28
Romania	28
Greece	26
Poland	25
Luxembourg	24
Croatia	23
Czech Republic	23
Ireland	23
Austria	23
Netherlands	22
Sweden	22
Spain	20
Hungary	20
Slovakia	20
Germany	19
Finland	18
Italy	18
Denmark	17
Belgium	17
Slovenia	17
Northern Ireland	17
Malta	12
Total	25

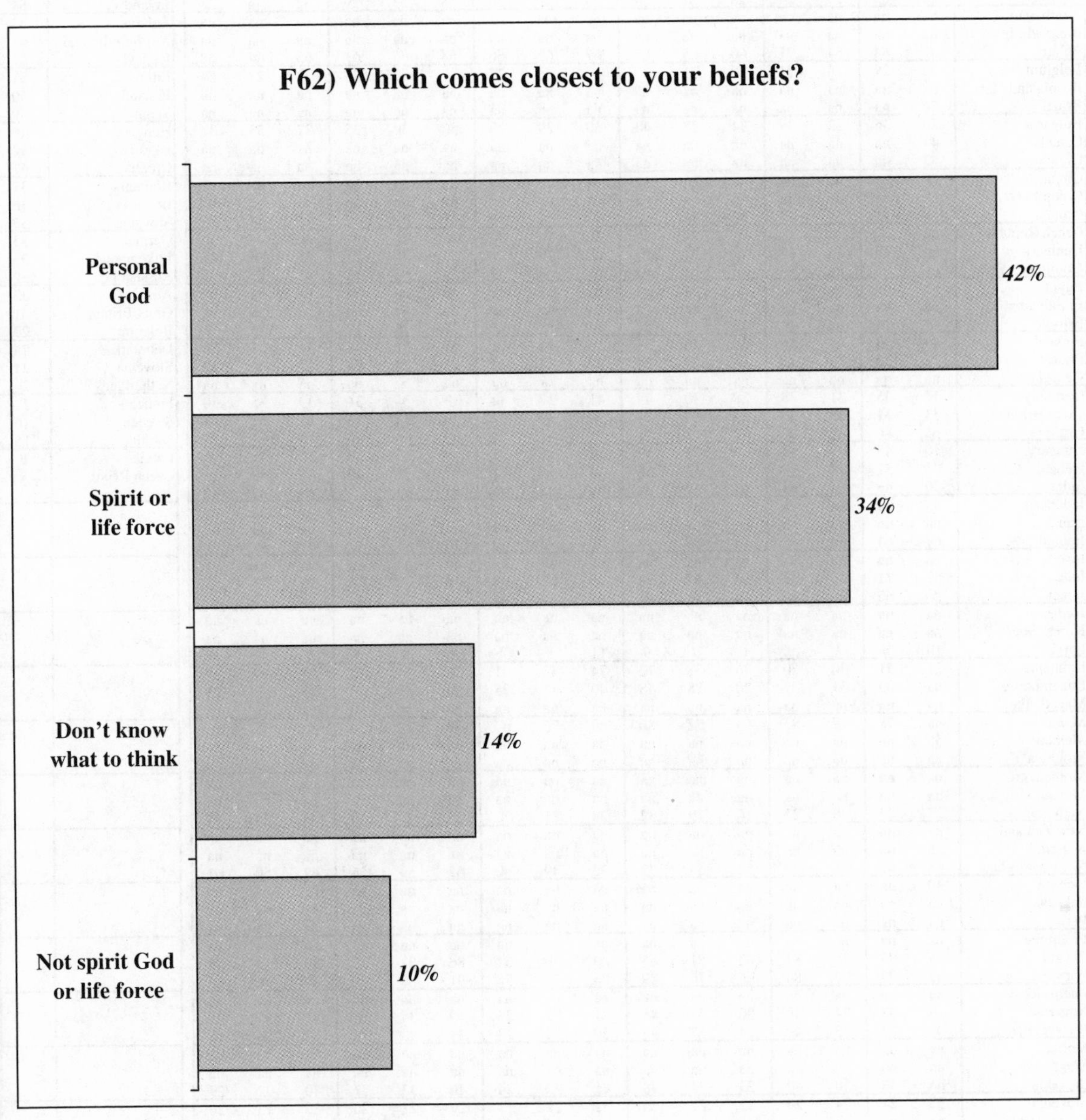
F62) Which comes closest to your beliefs?
Personal God
42%
Spirit or life force
34%
Don't know what to think
14%
Not spirit God or life force
10%

F062_1) STATEMENT OF YOUR BELIEF

Which of these statements comes closest to your beliefs?

Personal God (%)

(EVS: V122)

Country	Wave		Gender		Age			Education			Income			Values		
	1990	2000	Male	Female	16-29	30-49	50+	Lower	Middle	Upper	Lower	Middle	Upper	Mat	Mixed	Postm.
Albania	na	**na**	na	na	na	na	na	na	na	na	na	na	na	na	na	na
Algeria	na	**na**	na	na	na	na	na	na	na	na	na	na	na	na	na	na
Argentina	58	**na**	na	na	na	na	na	na	na	na	na	na	na	na	na	na
Armenia	na	**na**	na	na	na	na	na	na	na	na	na	na	na	na	na	na
Australia	na	**na**	na	na	na	na	na	na	na	na	na	na	na	na	na	na
Austria	29	**32**	29	34	28	31	34	33	29	34	35	33	29	32	32	28
Azerbaijan	na	**na**	na	na	na	na	na	na	na	na	na	na	na	na	na	na
Bangladesh	na	**na**	na	na	na	na	na	na	na	na	na	na	na	na	na	na
Belarus	6	**64**	54	71	60	65	65	67	62	66	63	65	61	65	64	68
Belgium	32	**29**	26	31	20	21	40	40	24	27	37	27	23	37	27	24
Bosnia and Herz.	na	**na**	na	na	na	na	na	na	na	na	na	na	na	na	na	na
Brazil	56	**na**	na	na	na	na	na	na	na	na	na	na	na	na	na	na
Bulgaria	10	**36**	32	39	34	28	43	50	29	25	50	30	25	37	33	32
Canada	44	**na**	na	na	na	na	na	na	na	na	na	na	na	na	na	na
Chile	52	**na**	na	na	na	na	na	na	na	na	na	na	na	na	na	na
China	3	**na**	na	na	na	na	na	na	na	na	na	na	na	na	na	na
Colombia	na	**na**	na	na	na	na	na	na	na	na	na	na	na	na	na	na
Croatia	na	**41**	35	47	30	41	50	42	44	30	45	41	40	45	44	29
Czech Republic	na	**7**	6	7	5	5	9	9	4	6	8	6	4	9	5	8
Denmark	20	**25**	23	27	22	22	29	28	19	21	27	25	23	23	26	18
Dominican Rep.	na	**na**	na	na	na	na	na	na	na	na	na	na	na	na	na	na
Egypt	na	**na**	na	na	na	na	na	na	na	na	na	na	na	na	na	na
El Salvador	na	**na**	na	na	na	na	na	na	na	na	na	na	na	na	na	na
Estonia	7	**16**	12	19	13	12	21	22	15	9	25	16	12	18	15	9
Finland	29	**50**	43	56	38	46	59	53	44	51	51	51	46	51	51	38
France	22	**22**	19	25	16	23	24	22	22	23	21	22	24	27	22	13
Georgia	na	**na**	na	na	na	na	na	na	na	na	na	na	na	na	na	na
Germany	17	**35**	31	38	28	30	44	41	31	32	33	34	34	39	35	30
Great Britain	33	**31**	25	36	27	30	34	30	32	27	29	33	33	na	na	na
Greece	na	**66**	61	69	62	68	71	76	73	58	68	66	66	75	67	55
Hungary	40	**45**	35	53	37	37	57	50	35	35	58	44	38	50	41	26
Iceland	51	**51**	48	55	40	53	58	54	53	42	52	51	49	61	50	35
India	30	**na**	na	na	na	na	na	na	na	na	na	na	na	na	na	na
Indonesia	na	**na**	na	na	na	na	na	na	na	na	na	na	na	na	na	na
Iran	na	**na**	na	na	na	na	na	na	na	na	na	na	na	na	na	na
Ireland	67	**64**	60	68	49	60	79	75	57	60	70	66	57	69	65	48
Israel	na	**na**	na	na	na	na	na	na	na	na	na	na	na	na	na	na
Italy	67	**71**	65	76	64	67	78	76	67	65	78	70	65	78	72	63
Japan	5	**na**	na	na	na	na	na	na	na	na	na	na	na	na	na	na
Jordan	na	**na**	na	na	na	na	na	na	na	na	na	na	na	na	na	na
Korea, South	na	**na**	na	na	na	na	na	na	na	na	na	na	na	na	na	na
Latvia	10	**8**	7	9	6	7	9	11	8	4	9	9	5	7	7	16
Lithuania	21	**51**	40	60	36	38	72	74	43	41	71	46	43	55	49	39
Luxembourg	na	**33**	31	35	20	28	48	40	31	25	30	35	30	35	35	21
Macedonia	na	**na**	na	na	na	na	na	na	na	na	na	na	na	na	na	na
Malta	na	**78**	72	83	68	77	86	89	75	67	78	78	74	83	76	66
Mexico	56	**na**	na	na	na	na	na	na	na	na	na	na	na	na	na	na
Moldova	na	**na**	na	na	na	na	na	na	na	na	na	na	na	na	na	na
Montenegro	na	**na**	na	na	na	na	na	na	na	na	na	na	na	na	na	na
Morocco	na	**na**	na	na	na	na	na	na	na	na	na	na	na	na	na	na
Netherlands	27	**24**	20	27	16	19	32	28	21	22	25	23	19	38	24	14
New Zealand	na	**na**	na	na	na	na	na	na	na	na	na	na	na	na	na	na
Nigeria	68	**na**	na	na	na	na	na	na	na	na	na	na	na	na	na	na
Northern Ireland	66	**61**	58	65	52	53	72	72	49	60	62	59	56	67	60	61
Norway	30	**na**	na	na	na	na	na	na	na	na	na	na	na	na	na	na
Pakistan	na	**na**	na	na	na	na	na	na	na	na	na	na	na	na	na	na
Peru	na	**na**	na	na	na	na	na	na	na	na	na	na	na	na	na	na
Philippines	na	**na**	na	na	na	na	na	na	na	na	na	na	na	na	na	na
Poland	na	**83**	78	87	82	81	85	89	79	64	86	82	75	89	79	78
Portugal	62	**79**	72	84	66	76	89	84	72	55	91	80	70	87	76	66
Puerto Rico	na	**na**	na	na	na	na	na	na	na	na	na	na	na	na	na	na
Romania	36	**37**	34	40	30	33	45	47	35	25	49	34	34	41	35	25
Russian Fed.	8	**32**	23	40	24	27	43	50	32	23	41	30	25	37	26	16
Serbia	na	**na**	na	na	na	na	na	na	na	na	na	na	na	na	na	na
Singapore	na	**na**	na	na	na	na	na	na	na	na	na	na	na	na	na	na
Slovakia	na	**35**	30	40	23	33	48	45	32	24	46	33	31	40	32	29
Slovenia	22	**24**	24	24	22	21	30	32	22	17	29	21	20	30	23	20
South Africa	na	**na**	na	na	na	na	na	na	na	na	na	na	na	na	na	na
Spain	49	**49**	42	56	29	44	64	61	41	38	56	46	44	60	48	34
Sweden	16	**16**	14	19	13	13	21	19	14	17	17	17	14	13	16	13
Switzerland	23	**na**	na	na	na	na	na	na	na	na	na	na	na	na	na	na
Taiwan	na	**na**	na	na	na	na	na	na	na	na	na	na	na	na	na	na
Tanzania	na	**na**	na	na	na	na	na	na	na	na	na	na	na	na	na	na
Turkey	na	**na**	na	na	na	na	na	na	na	na	na	na	na	na	na	na
Uganda	na	**na**	na	na	na	na	na	na	na	na	na	na	na	na	na	na
Ukraine	na	**42**	30	51	39	39	46	64	41	30	45	41	38	43	37	46
United States	69	**na**	na	na	na	na	na	na	na	na	na	na	na	na	na	na
Uruguay	na	**na**	na	na	na	na	na	na	na	na	na	na	na	na	na	na
Venezuela	na	**na**	na	na	na	na	na	na	na	na	na	na	na	na	na	na
Vietnam	na	**na**	na	na	na	na	na	na	na	na	na	na	na	na	na	na
Zimbabwe	na	**na**	na	na	na	na	na	na	na	na	na	na	na	na	na	na
Total	34	**42**	37	46	36	38	49	49	39	36	45	42	37	48	41	34

RANKING	
Country	2000
Poland	83
Portugal	79
Malta	78
Italy	71
Greece	66
Ireland	64
Belarus	64
Northern Ireland	61
Iceland	51
Lithuania	51
Finland	50
Spain	49
Hungary	45
Ukraine	42
Croatia	41
Romania	37
Bulgaria	36
Slovakia	35
Germany	35
Luxembourg	33
Russian Fed.	32
Austria	32
Great Britain	31
Belgium	29
Denmark	25
Slovenia	24
Netherlands	24
France	22
Sweden	16
Estonia	16
Latvia	8
Czech Republic	7
Total	42

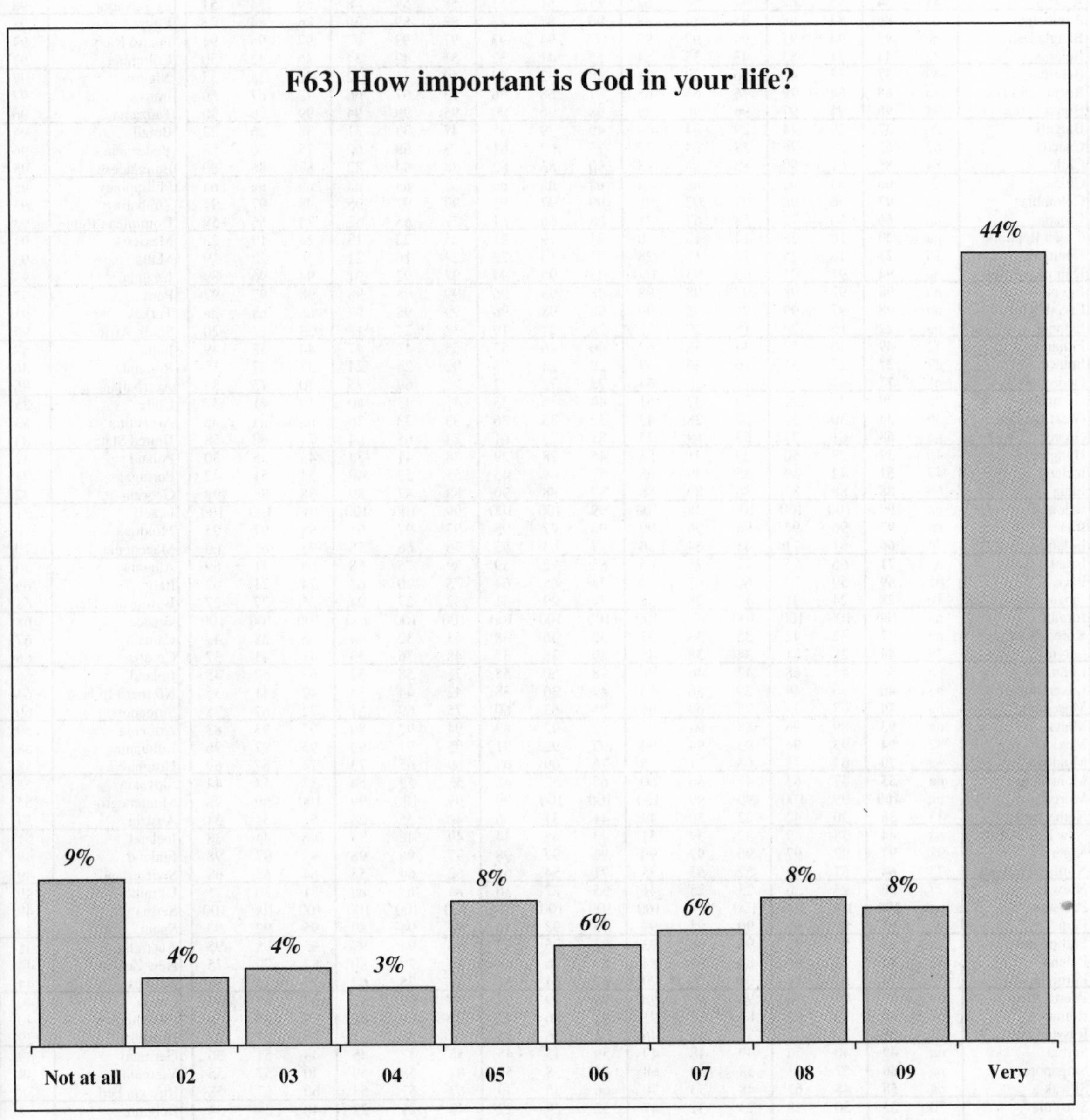

F63) How important is God in your life?
9%
4%
4%
3%
8%
6%
6%
8%
8%
44%
Not at all
02
03
04
05
06
07
08
09
Very

F063) HOW IMPORTANT IS GOD IN YOUR LIFE

How important is God in your life? Please use this scale to indicate.
(10 means very important and 1 means not at all important)
% Important (codes 7 to 10)

(WVS: V196; EVS: V123)

	Wave		Gender		Age			Education			Income			Values		
Country	1990	2000	Male	Female	16-29	30-49	50+	Lower	Middle	Upper	Lower	Middle	Upper	Mat	Mixed	Postm.
Albania	na	**70**	64	75	68	66	76	75	68	61	72	70	67	72	68	63
Algeria	na	**98**	98	99	99	98	98	97	98	99	98	99	98	99	98	98
Argentina	74	**83**	78	87	76	85	87	88	77	73	89	84	76	87	85	75
Armenia	na	**59**	49	67	61	56	59	63	59	57	59	55	63	56	63	48
Australia	na	**45**	39	51	38	42	55	51	42	43	48	46	37	49	46	41
Austria	41	**54**	45	62	47	50	62	57	51	51	58	53	48	59	54	51
Azerbaijan	na	**86**	83	88	85	86	88	90	87	83	88	89	79	86	84	91
Bangladesh	na	**95**	94	97	94	97	97	97	94	93	97	93	97	97	95	91
Belarus	22	**44**	31	53	43	35	54	55	41	32	51	42	34	46	42	30
Belgium	39	**37**	33	42	26	28	51	48	32	37	49	35	32	40	38	33
Bosnia and Herz.	na	**68**	64	72	76	65	65	81	68	56	73	67	66	72	67	60
Brazil	94	**96**	95	97	96	96	96	98	96	90	95	99	94	99	96	90
Bulgaria	20	**37**	29	44	29	34	44	49	29	35	47	33	31	38	36	22
Canada	62	**67**	58	76	58	64	77	75	67	61	73	68	60	75	70	58
Chile	84	**85**	81	89	83	85	88	90	83	82	88	84	82	87	86	80
China	3	**na**	na	na	na	na	na	na	na	na	na	na	na	na	na	na
Colombia	na	**97**	96	98	97	97	98	99	97	95	99	97	95	98	97	97
Croatia	na	**66**	60	72	58	67	71	68	66	61	77	65	62	75	66	58
Czech Republic	na	**20**	16	25	14	13	30	21	19	21	25	22	13	23	19	23
Denmark	18	**21**	16	25	14	17	28	21	13	23	24	16	21	9	22	19
Dominican Rep.	na	**94**	91	97	95	93	100	100	95	94	97	92	91	94	96	89
Egypt	na	**98**	97	98	97	98	98	98	98	96	99	98	98	98	97	97
El Salvador	na	**98**	97	99	97	98	99	98	98	96	99	98	97	na	na	na
Estonia	na	**22**	15	29	15	20	28	28	21	19	32	24	18	23	22	20
Finland	42	**49**	40	58	34	43	62	50	46	52	55	43	47	44	52	49
France	27	**27**	22	31	16	26	33	29	24	23	32	26	24	33	27	15
Georgia	na	**72**	67	76	77	73	64	72	72	72	72	69	75	70	73	84
Germany	26	**39**	35	42	30	32	51	44	35	35	41	43	40	39	41	37
Great Britain	36	**34**	30	38	27	28	43	32	33	36	33	33	36	na	na	na
Greece	na	**68**	61	73	63	69	75	81	73	61	73	65	64	74	68	58
Hungary	40	**39**	28	50	29	31	53	45	28	29	48	41	33	43	35	30
Iceland	47	**51**	42	59	35	49	68	57	49	43	55	53	40	54	51	42
India	68	**88**	88	87	86	89	88	87	88	90	88	87	89	88	88	93
Indonesia	na	**99**	100	100	100	100	100	99	100	100	99	100	100	100	100	100
Iran	na	**97**	96	97	96	96	99	98	97	95	97	97	95	98	97	93
Ireland	74	**66**	61	71	43	64	86	77	63	53	76	66	58	73	65	60
Israel	na	**71**	66	75	72	75	65	85	72	59	79	75	58	68	71	69
Italy	65	**69**	59	77	60	67	74	73	65	64	75	70	63	74	71	62
Japan	20	**28**	24	31	17	28	32	34	29	21	32	27	24	25	27	27
Jordan	na	**100**	100	100	100	100	100	100	100	100	100	100	100	100	100	100
Korea, South	na	**37**	32	42	35	38	37	32	36	38	33	32	44	35	38	43
Latvia	26	**40**	28	51	34	38	45	49	38	37	48	36	33	41	41	37
Lithuania	na	**58**	45	68	47	46	76	78	50	55	75	58	52	63	57	45
Luxembourg	na	**40**	36	44	29	36	53	47	36	38	42	44	34	42	41	35
Macedonia	na	**70**	67	73	75	69	66	85	63	60	75	69	61	72	67	75
Malta	na	**93**	89	96	85	94	97	97	92	89	94	97	89	95	93	83
Mexico	82	**94**	93	94	93	94	94	95	92	91	95	91	93	95	92	96
Moldova	na	**70**	64	75	63	71	75	76	69	67	69	65	73	74	67	69
Montenegro	na	**55**	47	63	47	56	60	63	52	45	53	57	54	57	54	44
Morocco	na	**100**	99	100	99	99	100	100	100	99	99	100	99	100	99	98
Netherlands	33	**36**	30	42	22	30	49	41	31	36	42	35	24	51	34	34
New Zealand	na	**44**	38	49	37	39	51	43	45	44	49	46	35	46	44	38
Nigeria	98	**97**	97	97	96	97	99	96	97	98	97	96	98	97	97	98
Northern Ireland	73	**64**	57	69	52	57	75	71	54	62	62	64	55	64	63	68
Norway	27	**30**	23	36	23	25	41	35	27	30	na	na	na	31	30	25
Pakistan	na	**100**	100	100	100	100	100	100	100	100	100	100	100	100	100	100
Peru	na	**92**	89	96	90	95	93	95	93	89	93	94	89	95	92	90
Philippines	na	**95**	95	95	96	96	93	92	96	97	95	94	97	95	95	95
Poland	87	**82**	77	86	80	80	84	89	76	64	85	79	80	87	79	75
Portugal	57	**74**	63	84	61	78	79	81	64	51	81	75	67	77	73	68
Puerto Rico	na	**97**	97	98	96	98	98	99	99	97	97	99	97	99	98	97
Romania	67	**86**	79	92	83	82	91	92	86	72	92	86	81	89	85	66
Russian Fed.	21	**38**	27	47	31	34	46	51	36	35	44	38	31	40	34	23
Serbia	na	**49**	40	56	49	48	49	59	43	45	55	47	45	48	51	36
Singapore	na	**60**	57	63	58	60	68	64	58	59	67	58	59	70	57	55
Slovakia	na	**58**	48	67	48	53	70	66	55	49	67	57	53	60	57	58
Slovenia	30	**35**	30	38	23	31	47	52	29	22	49	29	27	40	34	34
South Africa	88	**90**	87	93	91	88	90	91	88	89	89	88	94	90	89	85
Spain	48	**46**	34	57	32	43	58	54	38	39	58	43	43	54	45	34
Sweden	19	**23**	18	28	15	20	31	26	20	25	24	24	18	31	21	24
Switzerland	56	**49**	43	55	29	46	64	58	45	55	56	51	45	49	48	49
Taiwan	na	**31**	25	36	19	28	45	43	28	21	37	28	22	33	27	24
Tanzania	na	**96**	96	96	97	96	96	97	96	95	97	96	96	98	96	100
Turkey	86	**91**	89	94	90	91	94	96	90	75	95	90	84	95	92	83
Uganda	na	**93**	90	95	95	92	83	89	95	87	90	89	93	91	94	93
Ukraine	na	**49**	38	58	39	48	55	62	47	46	55	47	44	48	46	62
United States	77	**83**	78	88	76	86	85	84	84	82	85	80	85	85	84	80
Uruguay	na	**58**	48	65	52	53	65	63	55	40	63	57	54	54	60	55
Venezuela	na	**96**	94	98	96	96	94	96	96	93	95	95	96	95	96	96
Vietnam	na	**39**	37	40	38	39	38	43	35	19	39	35	42	27	40	40
Zimbabwe	na	**95**	93	96	95	94	94	94	96	100	95	94	94	92	96	100
Total	50	**66**	61	70	68	64	66	71	63	63	71	66	62	70	65	59

RANKING	
Country	2000
Pakistan	100
Jordan	100
Morocco	100
Indonesia	99
Algeria	98
El Salvador	98
Egypt	98
Puerto Rico	97
Colombia	97
Nigeria	97
Iran	97
Tanzania	96
Brazil	96
Venezuela	96
Bangladesh	95
Philippines	95
Zimbabwe	95
Dominican Rep.	94
Mexico	94
Malta	93
Uganda	93
Peru	92
Turkey	91
South Africa	90
India	88
Romania	86
Azerbaijan	86
Chile	85
Argentina	83
United States	83
Poland	82
Portugal	74
Georgia	72
Israel	71
Moldova	70
Macedonia	70
Albania	70
Italy	69
Bosnia and Herz.	68
Greece	68
Canada	67
Croatia	66
Ireland	66
Northern Ireland	64
Singapore	60
Armenia	59
Lithuania	58
Uruguay	58
Slovakia	58
Montenegro	55
Austria	54
Iceland	51
Finland	49
Switzerland	49
Ukraine	49
Serbia	49
Spain	46
Australia	45
New Zealand	44
Belarus	44
Latvia	40
Luxembourg	40
Hungary	39
Germany	39
Vietnam	39
Russian Fed.	38
Belgium	37
Bulgaria	37
Korea, South	37
Netherlands	36
Slovenia	35
Great Britain	34
Taiwan	31
Norway	30
Japan	28
France	27
Sweden	23
Estonia	22
Denmark	21
Czech Republic	20
Total	66

F064) COMFORT AND STRENGTH FROM RELIGION

Do you find that you get comfort and strength from religion?

Yes (%) (WVS: V197; EVS: V124)

Country	Wave		Gender		Age			Education			Income			Values		
	1990	2000	Male	Female	16-29	30-49	50+	Lower	Middle	Upper	Lower	Middle	Upper	Mat	Mixed	Postm.
Albania	na	**73**	69	77	67	73	78	75	73	68	72	75	72	72	74	73
Algeria	na	**99**	99	99	99	99	99	100	99	98	100	99	98	100	99	98
Argentina	66	**77**	70	84	66	80	86	82	71	72	84	80	68	84	79	68
Armenia	na	**70**	59	79	74	67	68	70	72	63	66	72	73	69	73	61
Australia	na	**49**	41	57	41	48	58	56	46	47	54	49	42	54	51	43
Austria	61	**62**	54	69	53	59	69	65	60	58	67	62	56	65	64	55
Azerbaijan	na	**88**	86	89	86	88	91	92	87	88	88	89	84	88	87	92
Bangladesh	na	**99**	98	100	98	99	99	100	100	95	100	99	98	100	98	99
Belarus	31	**54**	38	67	47	48	67	69	50	44	64	51	46	61	49	31
Belgium	47	**49**	41	56	35	42	62	58	45	47	59	48	43	56	49	40
Bosnia and Herz.	na	**72**	67	77	80	70	68	82	73	62	74	71	73	74	71	65
Brazil	86	**89**	86	92	85	90	94	91	89	84	91	89	87	91	89	86
Bulgaria	33	**45**	34	55	34	36	57	61	34	40	58	37	37	43	44	53
Canada	62	**63**	54	72	47	60	76	76	61	56	69	66	53	69	67	54
Chile	83	**75**	66	83	66	74	85	86	68	69	81	72	69	78	75	69
China	4	**na**	na	na	na	na	na	na	na	na	na	na	na	na	na	na
Colombia	na	**91**	89	93	89	90	95	96	92	85	96	92	86	94	94	92
Croatia	na	**82**	76	87	77	83	85	85	82	78	86	82	81	89	82	74
Czech Republic	na	**26**	20	32	21	18	35	27	25	24	33	24	20	30	24	28
Denmark	27	**33**	24	41	25	31	39	34	24	36	39	27	35	23	36	24
Dominican Rep.	na	**81**	75	85	79	83	91	88	84	79	86	78	77	84	82	76
Egypt	na	**100**	100	100	100	100	100	100	100	100	100	100	100	100	100	99
El Salvador	na	**89**	86	90	86	89	91	89	90	86	91	87	88	na	na	na
Estonia	na	**36**	23	46	22	29	49	43	33	33	45	44	28	40	33	26
Finland	49	**59**	46	71	42	55	71	60	56	64	64	52	57	59	59	59
France	36	**35**	28	41	24	32	43	36	32	33	39	34	34	40	37	21
Georgia	na	**83**	78	88	87	85	78	84	83	85	81	82	87	82	84	96
Germany	31	**50**	41	57	35	43	63	56	45	44	53	51	52	53	50	46
Great Britain	45	**37**	30	44	28	31	48	37	37	35	37	36	40	na	na	na
Greece	na	**76**	70	81	71	78	84	91	82	68	77	77	75	86	77	64
Hungary	49	**49**	35	63	33	43	65	55	39	37	58	50	44	55	45	23
Iceland	75	**75**	68	81	59	76	86	81	72	69	79	76	67	80	76	56
India	81	**85**	83	87	82	84	88	87	85	79	82	87	84	87	81	78
Indonesia	na	**100**	100	100	100	100	100	100	100	100	100	100	100	100	100	100
Iran	na	**96**	96	97	95	96	99	98	97	93	97	97	95	99	95	94
Ireland	83	**75**	67	83	56	73	90	82	71	73	82	76	68	78	75	69
Israel	na	**na**	na	na	na	na	na	na	na	na	na	na	na	na	na	na
Italy	71	**72**	62	80	57	71	81	80	65	64	81	69	63	82	73	61
Japan	42	**35**	31	38	10	31	49	46	37	26	42	35	31	37	33	38
Jordan	na	**100**	100	100	100	100	100	100	99	100	100	100	100	100	100	99
Korea, South	na	**67**	58	75	63	68	69	68	67	68	62	66	73	67	67	65
Latvia	37	**63**	48	76	53	62	69	70	61	62	70	62	57	66	62	61
Lithuania	na	**72**	57	83	61	62	87	91	63	70	86	69	66	77	71	59
Luxembourg	na	**49**	44	54	34	45	63	56	45	47	50	51	45	51	48	45
Macedonia	na	**71**	70	72	76	71	67	84	66	61	75	68	67	72	69	78
Malta	na	**93**	89	95	85	92	98	98	91	87	95	95	88	96	92	82
Mexico	77	**89**	86	93	87	89	94	92	87	80	94	89	85	93	89	82
Moldova	na	**92**	87	96	83	94	96	96	93	85	95	91	89	93	90	89
Montenegro	na	**66**	57	74	57	67	70	74	62	53	60	66	67	70	62	55
Morocco	na	**100**	100	100	100	100	100	100	100	99	100	100	100	100	100	99
Netherlands	45	**43**	37	49	39	38	51	47	41	42	49	40	36	58	42	38
New Zealand	na	**50**	45	54	39	43	61	49	51	49	57	49	42	53	50	43
Nigeria	96	**98**	98	98	98	98	100	99	98	97	98	98	98	98	99	98
Northern Ireland	77	**69**	62	75	56	61	80	75	61	68	71	66	64	71	68	71
Norway	36	**40**	31	48	28	36	53	43	37	41	na	na	na	39	40	33
Pakistan	na	**96**	95	97	95	96	98	96	96	94	96	96	96	97	94	92
Peru	na	**91**	87	95	87	93	94	92	93	86	93	92	86	92	91	88
Philippines	na	**91**	91	92	90	92	91	90	93	90	91	91	91	93	90	91
Poland	90	**82**	75	88	80	81	85	89	77	66	84	81	80	89	78	82
Portugal	67	**80**	69	89	66	82	85	87	66	59	83	84	72	85	77	73
Puerto Rico	na	**86**	79	91	80	83	93	97	89	84	90	90	81	89	88	83
Romania	76	**87**	79	93	79	84	93	94	87	74	92	90	80	91	84	67
Russian Fed.	35	**57**	42	69	49	53	66	69	55	56	63	57	50	59	54	44
Serbia	na	**63**	53	72	63	64	63	76	56	58	71	60	59	66	63	45
Singapore	na	**77**	73	81	71	80	87	83	74	71	82	80	71	83	76	60
Slovakia	na	**64**	54	72	52	59	77	72	61	56	74	60	61	66	62	63
Slovenia	51	**48**	42	54	37	44	60	64	45	32	59	48	35	59	47	45
South Africa	89	**89**	83	96	88	89	92	92	85	83	90	92	86	88	90	88
Spain	56	**54**	41	66	32	50	72	65	43	44	67	53	45	65	55	32
Sweden	27	**33**	26	40	23	30	43	38	30	34	36	33	27	38	32	34
Switzerland	na	**55**	47	63	36	55	66	64	53	52	66	57	49	59	53	56
Taiwan	na	**68**	58	78	70	68	67	72	65	66	69	68	65	67	70	52
Tanzania	na	**96**	95	97	95	97	96	94	97	100	93	97	99	96	97	96
Turkey	88	**92**	90	95	91	93	95	97	89	76	96	91	84	96	93	83
Uganda	na	**95**	93	98	95	95	95	95	95	99	98	94	93	93	96	96
Ukraine	na	**65**	49	77	58	62	71	81	61	63	68	65	62	64	63	66
United States	80	**80**	72	87	68	82	85	82	80	79	82	77	80	85	81	75
Uruguay	na	**55**	42	65	45	49	64	61	49	43	61	48	56	64	56	47
Venezuela	na	**na**	na	na	na	na	na	na	na	na	na	na	na	na	na	na
Vietnam	na	**27**	17	37	24	26	32	34	18	21	23	24	32	34	26	18
Zimbabwe	na	**93**	87	98	93	94	91	93	93	70	91	97	92	93	92	100
Total	57	**71**	65	77	70	70	74	76	68	68	76	71	68	77	70	61

RANKING	
Country	**2000**
Egypt	100
Jordan	100
Morocco	100
Indonesia	100
Algeria	99
Bangladesh	99
Nigeria	98
Iran	96
Tanzania	96
Pakistan	96
Uganda	95
Zimbabwe	93
Malta	93
Turkey	92
Moldova	92
Philippines	91
Peru	91
Colombia	91
Mexico	89
South Africa	89
Brazil	89
El Salvador	89
Azerbaijan	88
Romania	87
Puerto Rico	86
India	85
Georgia	83
Croatia	82
Poland	82
Dominican Rep.	81
Portugal	80
United States	80
Argentina	77
Singapore	77
Greece	76
Chile	75
Ireland	75
Iceland	75
Albania	73
Lithuania	72
Bosnia and Herz.	72
Italy	72
Macedonia	71
Armenia	70
Northern Ireland	69
Taiwan	68
Korea, South	67
Montenegro	66
Ukraine	65
Slovakia	64
Serbia	63
Latvia	63
Canada	63
Austria	62
Finland	59
Russian Fed.	57
Uruguay	55
Switzerland	55
Belarus	54
Spain	54
New Zealand	50
Germany	50
Hungary	49
Australia	49
Luxembourg	49
Belgium	49
Slovenia	48
Bulgaria	45
Netherlands	43
Norway	40
Great Britain	37
Estonia	36
Japan	35
France	35
Sweden	33
Denmark	33
Vietnam	27
Czech Republic	26
Total	71

F65) Do you take some moments of prayer, meditation or contemplation or something like that?

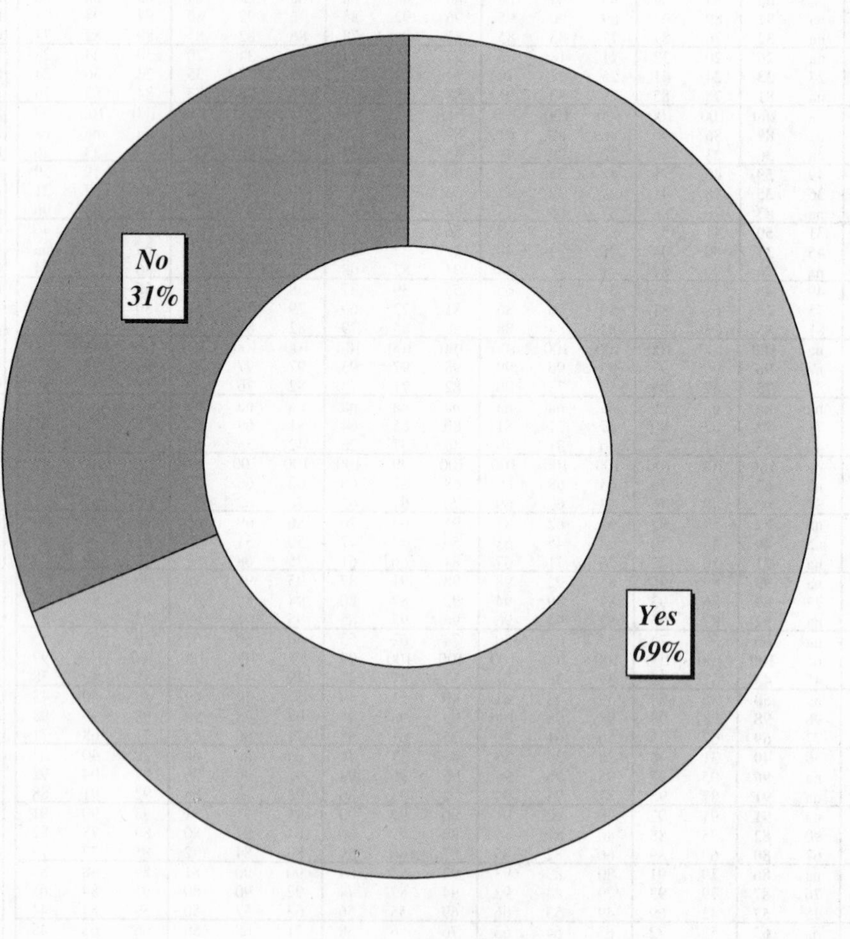

F065) MOMENTS OF PRAYER, MEDITATION...

Do you take some moments of prayer, meditation or contemplation or something like that?

Yes (%) (WVS: V198; EVS: V125)

Country	Wave		Gender		Age			Education			Income			Values		
	1990	2000	Male	Female	16-29	30-49	50+	Lower	Middle	Upper	Lower	Middle	Upper	Mat	Mixed	Postm.
Albania	na	**81**	75	87	78	81	85	81	81	83	79	83	82	79	82	78
Algeria	na	**na**	na	na	na	na	na	na	na	na	na	na	na	na	na	na
Argentina	75	**78**	69	86	70	82	82	79	77	80	81	78	75	81	79	74
Armenia	na	**na**	na	na	na	na	na	na	na	na	na	na	na	na	na	na
Australia	na	**na**	na	na	na	na	na	na	na	na	na	na	na	na	na	na
Austria	72	**69**	60	77	55	68	78	67	68	77	71	71	67	65	70	68
Azerbaijan	na	**na**	na	na	na	na	na	na	na	na	na	na	na	na	na	na
Bangladesh	na	**96**	95	97	94	96	99	98	94	89	95	95	97	98	94	94
Belarus	40	**71**	54	84	68	67	79	79	70	61	73	71	67	72	70	68
Belgium	55	**62**	55	68	51	57	71	65	56	69	71	58	60	65	61	64
Bosnia and Herz.	na	**80**	77	83	86	80	76	87	80	77	82	80	79	80	80	84
Brazil	89	**na**	na	na	na	na	na	na	na	na	na	na	na	na	na	na
Bulgaria	36	**34**	22	45	33	22	44	46	25	30	45	31	23	33	34	30
Canada	74	**80**	73	86	73	79	84	82	79	79	83	81	76	85	79	79
Chile	85	**82**	76	88	79	82	86	86	80	82	84	80	82	85	81	83
China	20	**na**	na	na	na	na	na	na	na	na	na	na	na	na	na	na
Colombia	na	**na**	na	na	na	na	na	na	na	na	na	na	na	na	na	na
Croatia	na	**75**	67	82	68	76	77	80	72	68	81	77	68	84	75	65
Czech Republic	na	**37**	32	43	34	30	46	34	38	51	42	33	37	35	37	47
Denmark	43	**51**	39	63	42	48	59	48	48	56	54	48	54	36	52	55
Dominican Rep.	na	**na**	na	na	na	na	na	na	na	na	na	na	na	na	na	na
Egypt	na	**na**	na	na	na	na	na	na	na	na	na	na	na	na	na	na
El Salvador	na	**na**	na	na	na	na	na	na	na	na	na	na	na	na	na	na
Estonia	na	**51**	39	60	46	46	58	51	51	49	51	53	54	49	53	46
Finland	22	**75**	63	86	65	73	82	73	75	85	79	70	75	73	75	78
France	46	**41**	34	48	35	40	46	39	38	49	43	37	44	41	42	38
Georgia	na	**na**	na	na	na	na	na	na	na	na	na	na	na	na	na	na
Germany	53	**54**	44	62	46	50	63	58	51	53	53	52	57	56	54	54
Great Britain	54	**50**	44	56	45	46	56	43	52	57	49	49	53	na	na	na
Greece	na	**61**	50	69	61	59	65	72	62	58	66	62	55	64	61	55
Hungary	58	**61**	47	73	45	57	74	63	58	55	66	61	58	64	59	40
Iceland	46	**54**	45	63	46	55	60	54	53	54	58	52	51	48	56	53
India	85	**88**	85	91	86	89	88	90	85	85	89	89	86	89	87	73
Indonesia	na	**na**	na	na	na	na	na	na	na	na	na	na	na	na	na	na
Iran	na	**na**	na	na	na	na	na	na	na	na	na	na	na	na	na	na
Ireland	84	**82**	76	88	76	80	89	83	81	85	89	78	79	84	83	76
Israel	na	**na**	na	na	na	na	na	na	na	na	na	na	na	na	na	na
Italy	76	**79**	70	87	71	80	83	80	77	83	83	78	77	80	80	77
Japan	41	**40**	38	41	19	36	52	49	41	32	44	42	36	41	39	38
Jordan	na	**na**	na	na	na	na	na	na	na	na	na	na	na	na	na	na
Korea, South	na	**59**	51	66	54	62	58	66	58	59	57	55	64	59	59	53
Latvia	66	**65**	52	75	63	64	66	64	63	72	67	63	64	63	66	63
Lithuania	na	**62**	45	75	52	48	81	83	52	66	82	56	55	66	60	47
Luxembourg	na	**58**	52	64	41	57	71	63	56	59	57	61	57	55	58	59
Macedonia	na	**62**	59	65	70	61	57	76	54	55	65	59	59	61	60	71
Malta	na	**91**	87	95	85	91	95	96	89	90	93	91	86	92	91	86
Mexico	82	**87**	84	91	85	87	91	89	85	85	88	86	86	89	87	87
Moldova	na	**88**	81	94	78	91	93	94	85	87	93	88	83	88	87	85
Montenegro	na	**58**	50	66	49	57	66	67	53	52	56	56	60	61	56	51
Morocco	na	**na**	na	na	na	na	na	na	na	na	na	na	na	na	na	na
Netherlands	68	**69**	65	73	63	69	72	59	70	77	67	67	74	76	65	76
New Zealand	na	**na**	na	na	na	na	na	na	na	na	na	na	na	na	na	na
Nigeria	99	**na**	na	na	na	na	na	na	na	na	na	na	na	na	na	na
Northern Ireland	76	**73**	65	79	65	69	80	79	65	71	74	70	69	74	72	78
Norway	64	**na**	na	na	na	na	na	na	na	na	na	na	na	na	na	na
Pakistan	na	**na**	na	na	na	na	na	na	na	na	na	na	na	na	na	na
Peru	na	**80**	76	83	75	82	85	79	83	75	85	77	75	80	78	85
Philippines	na	**97**	96	99	96	98	98	97	98	97	97	97	97	97	98	95
Poland	89	**87**	82	92	85	87	89	88	88	84	90	85	88	89	87	87
Portugal	61	**73**	60	84	59	73	80	79	59	63	74	80	68	75	72	70
Puerto Rico	na	**90**	85	94	84	87	97	96	87	92	92	91	90	94	90	90
Romania	86	**94**	89	98	88	92	97	97	93	90	97	94	91	94	92	93
Russian Fed.	37	**33**	18	46	26	27	45	52	31	31	42	31	26	36	29	29
Serbia	na	**59**	49	68	52	60	62	68	52	59	66	55	58	58	61	53
Singapore	na	**70**	65	74	66	70	83	75	68	63	72	72	67	78	67	64
Slovakia	na	**66**	55	77	57	62	79	73	63	65	75	68	61	70	64	69
Slovenia	45	**46**	36	55	39	43	55	62	40	40	59	40	40	53	45	46
South Africa	86	**89**	85	94	88	90	91	90	88	89	89	91	87	90	90	84
Spain	62	**55**	42	67	38	49	70	62	48	48	69	49	48	64	54	40
Sweden	34	**44**	36	52	37	40	52	38	40	56	45	42	43	43	42	49
Switzerland	na	**na**	na	na	na	na	na	na	na	na	na	na	na	na	na	na
Taiwan	na	**na**	na	na	na	na	na	na	na	na	na	na	na	na	na	na
Tanzania	na	**97**	96	99	96	98	97	96	99	99	95	98	98	97	97	100
Turkey	90	**93**	90	96	92	94	95	96	90	82	96	94	87	95	94	88
Uganda	na	**95**	92	98	95	95	96	95	95	97	97	93	91	94	96	96
Ukraine	na	**49**	32	64	43	46	56	73	45	46	54	47	47	51	47	57
United States	84	**89**	85	94	83	92	91	85	91	90	90	90	90	92	89	91
Uruguay	na	**na**	na	na	na	na	na	na	na	na	na	na	na	na	na	na
Venezuela	na	**na**	na	na	na	na	na	na	na	na	na	na	na	na	na	na
Vietnam	na	**30**	20	39	25	30	33	37	20	24	26	27	33	41	27	25
Zimbabwe	na	**92**	85	97	91	93	91	93	89	100	90	95	92	90	92	97
Total	63	69	61	76	66	68	73	73	66	69	72	68	67	71	69	69

RANKING	
Country	2000
Philippines	97
Tanzania	97
Bangladesh	96
Uganda	95
Romania	94
Turkey	93
Zimbabwe	92
Malta	91
Puerto Rico	90
United States	89
South Africa	89
Moldova	88
India	88
Mexico	87
Poland	87
Chile	82
Ireland	82
Albania	81
Bosnia and Herz.	80
Canada	80
Peru	80
Italy	79
Argentina	78
Croatia	75
Finland	75
Portugal	73
Northern Ireland	73
Belarus	71
Singapore	70
Austria	69
Netherlands	69
Slovakia	66
Latvia	65
Macedonia	62
Belgium	62
Lithuania	62
Greece	61
Hungary	61
Serbia	59
Korea, South	59
Montenegro	58
Luxembourg	58
Spain	55
Germany	54
Iceland	54
Denmark	51
Estonia	51
Great Britain	50
Ukraine	49
Slovenia	46
Sweden	44
France	41
Japan	40
Czech Republic	37
Bulgaria	34
Russian Fed.	33
Vietnam	30
Total	69

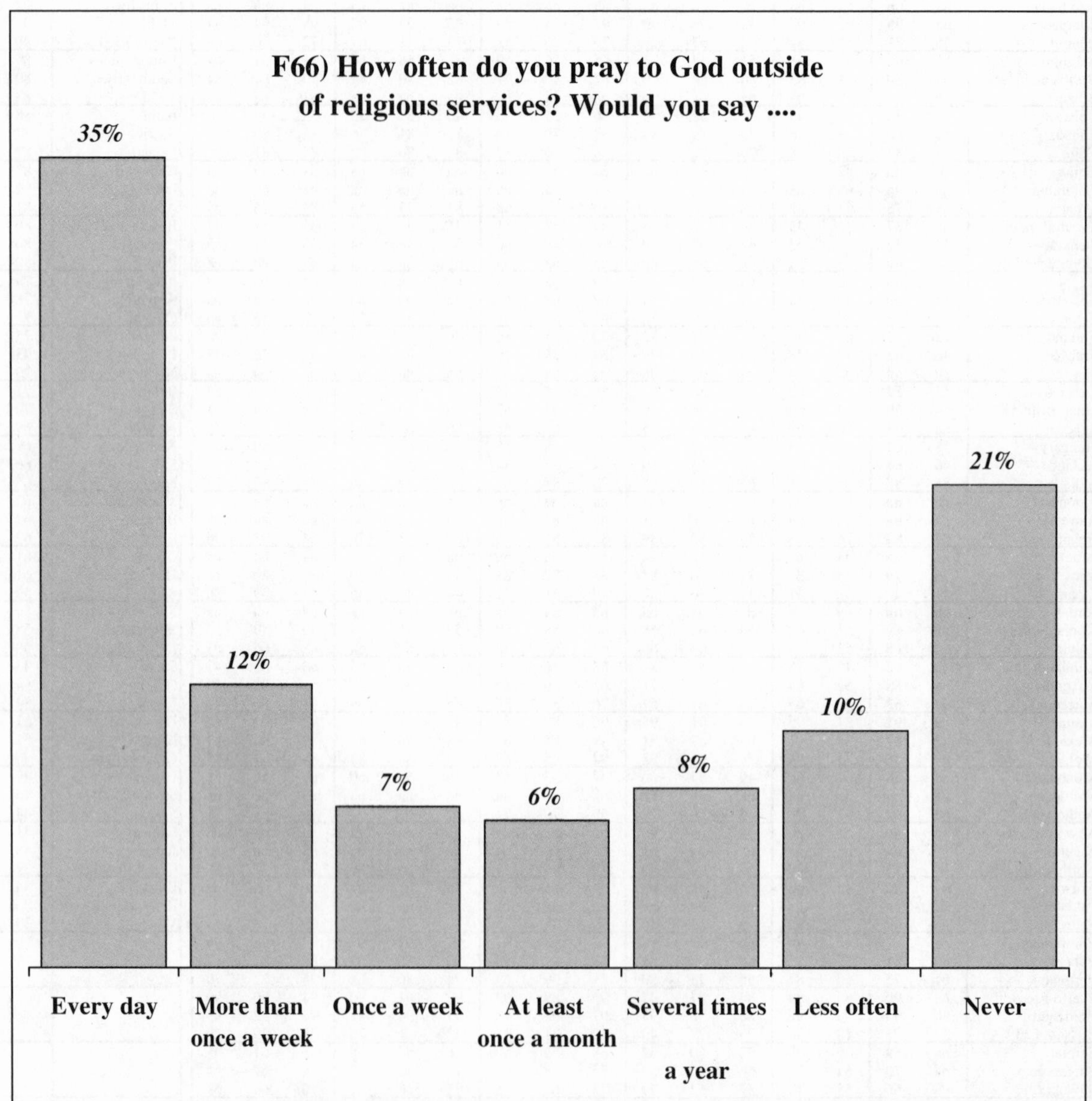
F66) How often do you pray to God outside of religious services? Would you say ....
35%
12%
7%
6%
8%
10%
21%
Every day
More than once a week
Once a week
At least once a month
Several times a year
Less often
Never

F066) PRAY TO GOD OUTSIDE OF RELIGIOUS SERVICES

How often do you pray to God outside of religious services? Would you say...

Every day / More than once a week (%) (WVS: V199; EVS: V126)

Country	Wave		Gender		Age			Education			Income			Values		
	1990	2000	Male	Female	16-29	30-49	50+	Lower	Middle	Upper	Lower	Middle	Upper	Mat	Mixed	Postm.
Albania	na	**48**	38	57	46	43	57	51	47	40	49	52	43	49	45	50
Algeria	na	**na**	na	na	na	na	na	na	na	na	na	na	na	na	na	na
Argentina	66	**51**	36	64	35	56	60	53	48	47	55	52	45	54	51	48
Armenia	na	**na**	na	na	na	na	na	na	na	na	na	na	na	na	na	na
Australia	na	**na**	na	na	na	na	na	na	na	na	na	na	na	na	na	na
Austria	57	**34**	26	42	19	30	46	37	30	33	39	34	28	33	35	31
Azerbaijan	na	**na**	na	na	na	na	na	na	na	na	na	na	na	na	na	na
Bangladesh	na	**81**	79	83	77	82	89	81	83	77	78	84	78	83	78	87
Belarus	6	**27**	11	39	21	17	41	41	22	20	33	27	16	28	24	25
Belgium	41	**27**	20	33	15	18	40	38	22	25	42	26	17	27	27	25
Bosnia and Herz.	na	**40**	34	46	45	35	43	53	38	36	45	38	40	36	42	33
Brazil	87	**na**	na	na	na	na	na	na	na	na	na	na	na	na	na	na
Bulgaria	21	**20**	10	29	13	14	27	29	13	18	30	18	11	20	20	7
Canada	62	**49**	38	60	35	45	62	58	48	43	56	48	40	55	51	43
Chile	76	**55**	44	65	47	55	64	60	53	51	61	48	55	61	53	52
China	6	**na**	na	na	na	na	na	na	na	na	na	na	na	na	na	na
Colombia	na	**na**	na	na	na	na	na	na	na	na	na	na	na	na	na	na
Croatia	na	**53**	39	65	49	52	56	62	47	47	65	51	48	60	54	39
Czech Republic	na	**15**	10	18	10	7	23	15	14	15	23	11	10	17	14	15
Denmark	25	**17**	11	22	7	13	25	18	10	17	24	12	15	9	18	10
Dominican Rep.	na	**na**	na	na	na	na	na	na	na	na	na	na	na	na	na	na
Egypt	na	**na**	na	na	na	na	na	na	na	na	na	na	na	na	na	na
El Salvador	na	**na**	na	na	na	na	na	na	na	na	na	na	na	na	na	na
Estonia	na	**15**	7	21	9	11	22	16	15	12	26	15	10	17	13	9
Finland	53	**35**	24	45	23	29	47	36	33	41	42	30	33	34	35	42
France	34	**15**	11	18	7	13	21	16	14	13	20	14	12	18	15	10
Georgia	na	**na**	na	na	na	na	na	na	na	na	na	na	na	na	na	na
Germany	28	**27**	20	33	17	22	38	32	24	25	25	30	32	28	26	32
Great Britain	43	**24**	17	31	15	19	34	23	24	23	21	26	25	na	na	na
Greece	na	**48**	38	55	43	50	54	68	51	42	52	47	41	54	48	40
Hungary	38	**30**	16	42	17	19	47	33	22	25	41	31	23	32	29	14
Iceland	51	**37**	25	48	21	35	52	41	30	38	46	33	29	34	38	30
India	73	**62**	57	69	61	62	63	63	60	62	54	62	65	61	60	42
Indonesia	na	**na**	na	na	na	na	na	na	na	na	na	na	na	na	na	na
Iran	na	**60**	61	60	62	58	60	61	59	60	63	59	60	61	61	60
Ireland	81	**60**	51	68	35	55	84	73	55	49	77	60	49	62	60	56
Israel	na	**na**	na	na	na	na	na	na	na	na	na	na	na	na	na	na
Italy	67	**55**	38	70	44	51	64	60	51	51	62	53	48	60	55	51
Japan	38	**20**	15	24	5	17	28	20	22	12	24	20	17	21	20	18
Jordan	na	**na**	na	na	na	na	na	na	na	na	na	na	na	na	na	na
Korea, South	na	**40**	35	45	33	43	41	33	42	39	42	34	43	42	38	45
Latvia	28	**27**	12	39	18	20	35	35	25	21	34	21	19	28	26	24
Lithuania	na	**32**	16	44	17	22	52	54	23	31	55	33	21	38	29	27
Luxembourg	na	**25**	21	29	16	20	37	32	19	27	29	24	25	23	25	23
Macedonia	na	**44**	40	48	49	43	40	64	34	33	48	41	39	41	42	68
Malta	na	**80**	73	88	67	77	92	89	78	74	85	80	75	85	79	70
Mexico	71	**66**	58	74	56	68	78	72	57	67	66	65	63	65	68	64
Moldova	na	**60**	46	72	45	60	71	75	57	50	68	58	52	66	52	51
Montenegro	na	**19**	15	23	13	18	23	25	15	15	21	21	18	22	16	8
Morocco	na	**74**	67	81	64	80	87	76	67	70	74	75	72	76	71	68
Netherlands	46	**29**	23	35	20	21	42	33	27	28	34	28	21	42	28	24
New Zealand	na	**na**	na	na	na	na	na	na	na	na	na	na	na	na	na	na
Nigeria	97	**na**	na	na	na	na	na	na	na	na	na	na	na	na	na	na
Northern Ireland	75	**55**	49	61	42	47	69	63	45	55	60	53	46	61	54	57
Norway	36	**na**	na	na	na	na	na	na	na	na	na	na	na	na	na	na
Pakistan	na	**na**	na	na	na	na	na	na	na	na	na	na	na	na	na	na
Peru	na	**75**	66	83	66	78	85	79	75	71	77	73	73	76	74	77
Philippines	na	**86**	82	90	83	86	90	84	86	88	85	86	86	84	87	85
Poland	na	**68**	57	77	61	61	80	71	67	56	73	66	58	75	64	60
Portugal	58	**53**	38	67	38	51	64	61	36	39	70	60	44	59	51	47
Puerto Rico	na	**86**	77	92	76	86	92	92	80	89	88	86	86	89	87	85
Romania	72	**70**	58	81	58	62	82	84	64	56	82	69	60	74	67	41
Russian Fed.	17	**22**	10	33	13	16	35	42	19	19	30	20	15	25	18	14
Serbia	na	**30**	20	38	26	25	36	40	23	27	37	29	26	31	29	19
Singapore	na	**45**	42	48	39	51	49	46	44	47	51	48	43	52	42	44
Slovakia	na	**50**	37	62	39	45	64	63	45	39	64	48	43	54	47	41
Slovenia	38	**na**	na	na	na	na	na	na	na	na	na	na	na	na	na	na
South Africa	na	**76**	68	85	75	74	84	76	76	84	74	73	80	75	76	80
Spain	56	**33**	19	45	17	28	46	40	25	27	41	30	30	42	31	19
Sweden	25	**na**	na	na	na	na	na	na	na	na	na	na	na	na	na	na
Switzerland	na	**na**	na	na	na	na	na	na	na	na	na	na	na	na	na	na
Taiwan	na	**na**	na	na	na	na	na	na	na	na	na	na	na	na	na	na
Tanzania	na	**87**	84	89	85	86	90	84	88	92	85	90	84	88	86	92
Turkey	na	**82**	76	87	77	84	90	90	72	62	87	82	71	82	83	73
Uganda	na	**83**	81	84	82	84	83	81	83	86	87	79	86	78	83	95
Ukraine	na	**35**	20	47	21	31	46	63	30	30	39	34	30	37	32	27
United States	78	**71**	62	80	57	75	78	70	69	73	72	72	69	85	72	66
Uruguay	na	**na**	na	na	na	na	na	na	na	na	na	na	na	na	na	na
Venezuela	na	**72**	63	81	63	75	84	77	70	71	72	73	67	76	72	66
Vietnam	na	**9**	8	10	7	9	10	12	5	5	6	7	12	6	9	11
Zimbabwe	na	**78**	65	90	76	82	77	80	76	60	74	87	80	77	79	93
Total	49	**48**	39	55	44	46	53	53	43	46	53	47	43	50	47	45

RANKING

Country	2000
Tanzania	87
Puerto Rico	86
Philippines	86
Uganda	83
Turkey	82
Bangladesh	81
Malta	80
Zimbabwe	78
South Africa	76
Peru	75
Morocco	74
Venezuela	72
United States	71
Romania	70
Poland	68
Mexico	66
India	62
Iran	60
Ireland	60
Moldova	60
Chile	55
Northern Ireland	55
Italy	55
Portugal	53
Croatia	53
Argentina	51
Slovakia	50
Canada	49
Greece	48
Albania	48
Singapore	45
Macedonia	44
Bosnia and Herz.	40
Korea, South	40
Iceland	37
Finland	35
Ukraine	35
Austria	34
Spain	33
Lithuania	32
Hungary	30
Serbia	30
Netherlands	29
Germany	27
Belarus	27
Belgium	27
Latvia	27
Luxembourg	25
Great Britain	24
Russian Fed.	22
Japan	20
Bulgaria	20
Montenegro	19
Denmark	17
France	15
Estonia	15
Czech Republic	15
Vietnam	9
Total	48

F102) POLITICIANS WHO DON'T BELIEVE IN GOD UNFIT FOR PUBLIC OFFICE

How much do you agree or disagree with each of the following statements:

Politicians who do not believe in God are unfit for public office

Disagree / Strongly disagree (%) (WVS: V200; EVS: V129)

	Wave		Gender		Age			Education			Income			Values		
Country	1990	2000	Male	Female	16-29	30-49	50+	Lower	Middle	Upper	Lower	Middle	Upper	Mat	Mixed	Postm.
Albania	na	**29**	31	26	28	29	29	26	29	35	29	26	31	29	30	27
Algeria	na	**13**	12	14	13	14	11	13	12	14	14	12	16	11	14	14
Argentina	na	**46**	49	43	52	44	42	38	54	68	37	45	56	38	43	60
Armenia	na	**na**	na	na	na	na	na	na	na	na	na	na	na	na	na	na
Australia	na	**na**	na	na	na	na	na	na	na	na	na	na	na	na	na	na
Austria	na	**69**	71	66	73	73	62	64	71	82	62	69	74	55	69	72
Azerbaijan	na	**na**	na	na	na	na	na	na	na	na	na	na	na	na	na	na
Bangladesh	na	**24**	25	22	27	23	10	16	30	33	15	31	22	16	28	38
Belarus	na	**55**	64	48	63	58	45	51	57	56	55	54	60	56	55	60
Belgium	na	**82**	86	79	84	88	77	73	83	89	74	83	89	76	84	89
Bosnia and Herz.	na	**51**	53	49	46	51	57	43	52	57	51	52	52	51	52	48
Brazil	na	**na**	na	na	na	na	na	na	na	na	na	na	na	na	na	na
Bulgaria	na	**52**	56	49	63	53	47	42	58	55	43	58	56	55	51	58
Canada	na	**59**	64	53	63	61	53	50	56	70	52	56	69	55	54	69
Chile	na	**55**	57	53	58	54	54	48	59	59	48	60	63	56	52	63
China	na	**na**	na	na	na	na	na	na	na	na	na	na	na	na	na	na
Colombia	na	**na**	na	na	na	na	na	na	na	na	na	na	na	na	na	na
Croatia	na	**57**	64	51	66	54	55	48	61	69	56	53	61	53	55	68
Czech Republic	na	**80**	82	79	85	84	75	76	85	86	75	80	87	73	82	85
Denmark	na	**92**	93	90	93	94	89	89	95	96	89	94	94	94	91	94
Dominican Rep.	na	**na**	na	na	na	na	na	na	na	na	na	na	na	na	na	na
Egypt	na	**10**	10	9	9	11	9	10	9	11	9	11	10	9	10	9
El Salvador	na	**na**	na	na	na	na	na	na	na	na	na	na	na	na	na	na
Estonia	na	**59**	64	55	70	60	52	49	64	61	57	53	65	55	61	71
Finland	na	**65**	67	63	71	71	56	61	68	74	63	68	68	58	68	72
France	na	**78**	82	75	78	80	77	75	84	80	73	79	82	73	78	87
Georgia	na	**na**	na	na	na	na	na	na	na	na	na	na	na	na	na	na
Germany	na	**67**	72	63	75	73	57	61	71	76	66	66	66	63	66	72
Great Britain	na	**71**	73	70	73	75	69	70	73	75	67	65	78	na	na	na
Greece	na	**37**	42	33	42	34	32	22	30	45	32	36	39	34	35	46
Hungary	na	**66**	70	62	72	72	55	61	73	76	58	64	71	61	70	79
Iceland	na	**79**	81	78	87	84	66	74	81	88	72	78	87	75	79	89
India	na	**44**	49	36	50	44	38	32	43	63	37	35	55	44	48	55
Indonesia	na	**9**	9	10	6	10	10	11	11	7	12	6	7	6	12	4
Iran	na	**na**	na	na	na	na	na	na	na	na	na	na	na	na	na	na
Ireland	na	**70**	74	67	78	75	60	60	74	80	58	74	78	67	71	77
Israel	na	**na**	na	na	na	na	na	na	na	na	na	na	na	na	na	na
Italy	na	**64**	68	61	71	70	55	53	72	75	55	68	73	48	64	74
Japan	na	**41**	43	40	59	44	31	24	38	59	35	40	50	39	45	43
Jordan	na	**17**	16	18	16	16	21	19	14	15	15	17	18	16	18	14
Korea, South	na	**59**	61	57	69	57	52	45	57	63	59	60	59	57	61	61
Latvia	na	**59**	65	54	73	62	51	52	63	58	55	58	65	54	62	64
Lithuania	na	**51**	61	42	65	57	35	32	56	59	34	58	54	49	48	74
Luxembourg	na	**67**	67	68	67	68	66	57	68	81	53	74	81	56	68	78
Macedonia	na	**47**	47	47	40	50	49	33	54	52	44	44	58	50	48	29
Malta	na	**43**	46	40	58	46	29	30	45	63	34	41	49	36	45	51
Mexico	na	**49**	50	48	54	49	41	41	56	62	45	47	60	43	51	60
Moldova	na	**32**	34	30	40	29	29	24	33	38	27	39	34	35	26	35
Montenegro	na	**55**	60	50	63	57	47	45	58	68	45	58	60	54	58	47
Morocco	na	**9**	10	8	11	8	7	8	15	17	5	13	16	6	11	11
Netherlands	na	**94**	96	93	96	95	92	92	94	97	92	95	97	86	95	97
New Zealand	na	**na**	na	na	na	na	na	na	na	na	na	na	na	na	na	na
Nigeria	na	**11**	11	11	10	11	10	10	11	10	8	11	13	12	10	9
Northern Ireland	na	**68**	73	64	71	77	61	61	73	77	58	72	78	59	69	81
Norway	na	**na**	na	na	na	na	na	na	na	na	na	na	na	na	na	na
Pakistan	na	**1**	1	1	1	1	1	2	na	na	1	1	na	1	1	na
Peru	na	**na**	na	na	na	na	na	na	na	na	na	na	na	na	na	na
Philippines	na	**14**	15	13	13	15	12	13	16	11	21	12	10	14	15	11
Poland	na	**64**	66	63	62	71	58	55	73	79	59	68	70	56	69	68
Portugal	na	**66**	71	62	78	64	61	61	77	81	47	61	77	62	66	77
Puerto Rico	na	**23**	26	22	26	23	22	25	21	24	23	21	26	21	21	30
Romania	na	**23**	27	19	32	27	15	13	28	30	16	24	29	19	26	37
Russian Fed.	na	**58**	65	52	60	60	54	48	57	65	52	57	64	56	59	65
Serbia	na	**57**	62	52	56	58	57	45	62	64	53	58	63	53	60	66
Singapore	na	**na**	na	na	na	na	na	na	na	na	na	na	na	na	na	na
Slovakia	na	**53**	58	48	61	54	44	43	55	68	42	52	60	47	57	65
Slovenia	na	**74**	73	75	76	78	68	63	76	86	63	77	82	72	73	81
South Africa	na	**29**	35	22	29	30	23	29	29	32	30	25	33	28	30	27
Spain	na	**69**	73	64	77	73	59	62	75	76	59	70	73	57	71	81
Sweden	na	**85**	84	85	89	88	78	78	82	93	81	85	88	79	84	88
Switzerland	na	**na**	na	na	na	na	na	na	na	na	na	na	na	na	na	na
Taiwan	na	**na**	na	na	na	na	na	na	na	na	na	na	na	na	na	na
Tanzania	na	**23**	22	24	20	23	27	24	19	25	24	21	27	24	21	26
Turkey	na	**28**	27	29	31	27	23	19	33	57	19	29	46	18	28	44
Uganda	na	**22**	22	22	23	20	26	22	22	16	14	20	29	27	21	14
Ukraine	na	**46**	54	38	60	42	41	33	48	47	40	48	51	44	47	50
United States	na	**36**	42	30	39	33	37	32	33	39	35	36	37	25	35	43
Uruguay	na	**na**	na	na	na	na	na	na	na	na	na	na	na	na	na	na
Venezuela	na	**32**	32	32	39	27	28	28	34	34	29	34	35	28	35	28
Vietnam	na	**62**	71	52	65	62	60	57	66	66	59	61	64	42	68	61
Zimbabwe	na	**37**	37	38	41	36	31	38	38	10	38	38	32	37	38	40
Total	na	**49**	51	47	48	50	49	43	51	54	43	49	54	41	50	61

RANKING	
Country	2000
Netherlands	94
Denmark	92
Sweden	85
Belgium	82
Czech Republic	80
Iceland	79
France	78
Slovenia	74
Great Britain	71
Ireland	70
Spain	69
Austria	69
Northern Ireland	68
Luxembourg	67
Germany	67
Portugal	66
Hungary	66
Finland	65
Italy	64
Poland	64
Vietnam	62
Latvia	59
Korea, South	59
Estonia	59
Canada	59
Russian Fed.	58
Serbia	57
Croatia	57
Belarus	55
Chile	55
Montenegro	55
Slovakia	53
Bulgaria	52
Bosnia and Herz.	51
Lithuania	51
Mexico	49
Macedonia	47
Argentina	46
Ukraine	46
India	44
Malta	43
Japan	41
Zimbabwe	37
Greece	37
United States	36
Moldova	32
Venezuela	32
South Africa	29
Albania	29
Turkey	28
Bangladesh	24
Puerto Rico	23
Romania	23
Tanzania	23
Uganda	22
Jordan	17
Philippines	14
Algeria	13
Nigeria	11
Egypt	10
Indonesia	9
Morocco	9
Pakistan	1
Total	49

F103) RELIGIOUS LEADERS SHOULD NOT INFLUENCE PEOPLE VOTE

How much do you agree or disagree with each of the following statements:

Religious leaders should not influence how people vote in elections

Agree strongly / Agree (%)

(WVS: V201; EVS: V130)

Country	Wave		Gender		Age			Education			Income			Values		
	1990	2000	Male	Female	16-29	30-49	50+	Lower	Middle	Upper	Lower	Middle	Upper	Mat	Mixed	Postm.
Albania	na	**77**	77	77	74	78	78	77	75	81	78	75	78	82	73	68
Algeria	na	**38**	34	42	40	37	36	34	38	41	42	39	34	32	43	29
Argentina	na	**75**	76	74	74	75	75	74	77	76	74	74	77	69	73	82
Armenia	na	**na**	na	na	na	na	na	na	na	na	na	na	na	na	na	na
Australia	na	**na**	na	na	na	na	na	na	na	na	na	na	na	na	na	na
Austria	na	**85**	83	86	82	84	86	84	85	85	79	87	86	84	84	88
Azerbaijan	na	**na**	na	na	na	na	na	na	na	na	na	na	na	na	na	na
Bangladesh	na	**75**	73	76	77	74	63	73	75	77	79	71	75	78	72	73
Belarus	na	**82**	86	79	86	84	77	79	83	85	82	83	82	82	82	91
Belgium	na	**79**	80	79	80	79	79	77	79	81	81	79	83	75	81	83
Bosnia and Herz.	na	**76**	76	77	75	75	79	71	76	82	77	74	79	80	76	77
Brazil	na	**na**	na	na	na	na	na	na	na	na	na	na	na	na	na	na
Bulgaria	na	**83**	84	82	79	87	82	78	86	83	80	82	86	83	84	86
Canada	na	**77**	78	77	78	78	77	79	78	76	76	78	79	84	76	78
Chile	na	**69**	70	68	68	71	68	68	70	71	67	71	70	74	68	65
China	na	**na**	na	na	na	na	na	na	na	na	na	na	na	na	na	na
Colombia	na	**na**	na	na	na	na	na	na	na	na	na	na	na	na	na	na
Croatia	na	**84**	82	86	88	85	80	87	81	87	87	81	86	84	84	86
Czech Republic	na	**81**	83	78	81	80	81	80	82	78	81	83	80	81	81	79
Denmark	na	**85**	83	86	84	82	88	87	83	80	85	88	77	89	87	84
Dominican Rep.	na	**na**	na	na	na	na	na	na	na	na	na	na	na	na	na	na
Egypt	na	**57**	60	54	53	58	60	56	56	61	59	58	57	58	56	54
El Salvador	na	**na**	na	na	na	na	na	na	na	na	na	na	na	na	na	na
Estonia	na	**84**	82	86	87	84	84	80	86	87	83	85	84	85	85	74
Finland	na	**68**	70	65	67	69	67	71	64	58	67	71	65	73	68	59
France	na	**86**	87	85	87	87	85	87	88	84	88	87	84	87	85	89
Georgia	na	**na**	na	na	na	na	na	na	na	na	na	na	na	na	na	na
Germany	na	**75**	76	74	81	78	68	69	79	84	74	72	71	69	73	88
Great Britain	na	**70**	69	70	70	68	72	70	71	69	71	67	68	na	na	na
Greece	na	**78**	80	77	81	79	72	74	79	78	80	81	77	77	79	79
Hungary	na	**77**	79	75	78	79	73	74	82	83	69	77	80	74	79	89
Iceland	na	**81**	81	82	81	82	80	83	81	78	83	80	80	83	81	79
India	na	**68**	67	70	69	68	67	66	69	70	63	70	69	61	75	69
Indonesia	na	**86**	87	86	81	90	86	86	89	85	88	87	87	90	86	75
Iran	na	**na**	na	na	na	na	na	na	na	na	na	na	na	na	na	na
Ireland	na	**79**	78	79	82	78	77	78	81	74	77	82	78	76	79	79
Israel	na	**na**	na	na	na	na	na	na	na	na	na	na	na	na	na	na
Italy	na	**79**	80	77	82	80	76	78	81	76	74	83	80	70	79	83
Japan	na	**74**	78	71	73	73	76	62	74	80	68	77	80	75	78	74
Jordan	na	**75**	76	74	76	74	76	73	78	77	76	73	76	78	73	74
Korea, South	na	**69**	73	66	74	66	71	53	69	72	71	67	69	66	73	67
Latvia	na	**84**	87	82	80	85	85	78	87	83	80	88	86	84	84	84
Lithuania	na	**81**	82	79	83	87	73	74	84	80	68	88	79	76	82	91
Luxembourg	na	**82**	82	82	82	83	81	80	83	85	72	85	85	81	82	82
Macedonia	na	**80**	79	82	79	79	83	75	82	85	81	79	82	81	81	78
Malta	na	**90**	88	91	92	90	88	92	90	86	91	88	88	87	91	92
Mexico	na	**64**	66	62	63	66	61	62	65	71	60	63	66	62	63	64
Moldova	na	**69**	68	69	73	68	65	64	68	73	62	68	70	69	64	75
Montenegro	na	**83**	85	82	90	84	78	77	86	91	81	84	89	85	84	76
Morocco	na	**76**	74	77	72	75	87	80	63	53	87	64	72	77	76	64
Netherlands	na	**66**	66	65	58	65	71	68	64	65	63	67	68	60	65	73
New Zealand	na	**na**	na	na	na	na	na	na	na	na	na	na	na	na	na	na
Nigeria	na	**73**	73	72	72	74	68	73	73	72	73	74	72	74	72	75
Northern Ireland	na	**76**	73	78	75	79	75	76	81	65	75	79	77	80	74	75
Norway	na	**na**	na	na	na	na	na	na	na	na	na	na	na	na	na	na
Pakistan	na	**74**	73	76	85	74	55	66	83	87	69	72	86	70	80	100
Peru	na	**na**	na	na	na	na	na	na	na	na	na	na	na	na	na	na
Philippines	na	**75**	77	73	79	73	73	72	74	80	75	75	75	76	75	71
Poland	na	**86**	87	85	89	86	83	84	88	85	87	86	83	84	86	89
Portugal	na	**80**	84	77	86	79	78	78	87	83	72	80	79	79	81	79
Puerto Rico	na	**70**	71	69	68	72	70	68	70	71	73	70	72	59	72	70
Romania	na	**78**	79	77	81	81	74	72	80	83	75	79	80	73	81	87
Russian Fed.	na	**82**	84	81	84	84	79	76	82	87	76	82	88	82	84	74
Serbia	na	**85**	86	85	82	86	86	80	88	88	84	85	88	83	89	81
Singapore	na	**na**	na	na	na	na	na	na	na	na	na	na	na	na	na	na
Slovakia	na	**74**	75	73	79	76	68	72	76	72	70	75	77	73	77	66
Slovenia	na	**78**	77	78	73	81	78	74	78	82	76	79	85	83	78	75
South Africa	na	**65**	63	66	62	68	63	62	69	57	60	71	64	59	69	60
Spain	na	**67**	69	64	72	69	61	61	71	72	62	65	72	57	69	78
Sweden	na	**68**	67	69	63	67	72	79	69	58	69	73	62	64	70	65
Switzerland	na	**na**	na	na	na	na	na	na	na	na	na	na	na	na	na	na
Taiwan	na	**na**	na	na	na	na	na	na	na	na	na	na	na	na	na	na
Tanzania	na	**70**	69	71	69	68	77	71	69	66	72	70	64	69	71	67
Turkey	na	**79**	80	78	79	79	78	76	82	88	76	81	82	77	80	81
Uganda	na	**63**	61	65	62	62	68	62	63	66	69	61	65	61	63	69
Ukraine	na	**83**	84	81	88	84	78	76	82	86	83	85	79	82	83	88
United States	na	**64**	66	61	67	61	65	73	69	57	72	60	59	68	62	65
Uruguay	na	**na**	na	na	na	na	na	na	na	na	na	na	na	na	na	na
Venezuela	na	**56**	55	58	53	59	59	61	52	61	55	59	57	55	58	55
Vietnam	na	**69**	76	61	65	70	69	64	73	75	71	66	71	68	70	65
Zimbabwe	na	**63**	64	62	63	62	65	63	64	78	59	64	69	65	62	65
Total	na	**75**	76	75	74	75	75	74	76	75	74	76	76	75	76	76

RANKING

Country	2000
Malta	90
Indonesia	86
France	86
Poland	86
Serbia	85
Denmark	85
Austria	85
Estonia	84
Croatia	84
Latvia	84
Montenegro	83
Bulgaria	83
Ukraine	83
Belarus	82
Luxembourg	82
Russian Fed.	82
Iceland	81
Lithuania	81
Czech Republic	81
Portugal	80
Macedonia	80
Belgium	79
Turkey	79
Italy	79
Ireland	79
Greece	78
Romania	78
Slovenia	78
Canada	77
Albania	77
Hungary	77
Bosnia and Herz.	76
Northern Ireland	76
Morocco	76
Jordan	75
Philippines	75
Germany	75
Argentina	75
Bangladesh	75
Pakistan	74
Japan	74
Slovakia	74
Nigeria	73
Puerto Rico	70
Tanzania	70
Great Britain	70
Korea, South	69
Chile	69
Moldova	69
Vietnam	69
India	68
Sweden	68
Finland	68
Spain	67
Netherlands	66
South Africa	65
United States	64
Mexico	64
Zimbabwe	63
Uganda	63
Egypt	57
Venezuela	56
Algeria	38
Total	75

F104) PEOPLE WITH STRONG RELIGIOUS BELIEFS SHOULD HELD PUBLIC OFFICE

How much do you agree or disagree with each of the following statements: It would be better for [country] if more people with strong religious beliefs held public office

Disagree / Strongly disagree (%) (WVS: V202; EVS: V131)

	Wave		Gender		Age			Education			Income			Values		
Country	1990	2000	Male	Female	16-29	30-49	50+	Lower	Middle	Upper	Lower	Middle	Upper	Mat	Mixed	Postm.
Albania	na	**32**	35	30	34	33	29	30	33	35	33	30	33	33	32	32
Algeria	na	**30**	28	33	27	34	28	23	33	31	28	27	40	27	31	38
Argentina	na	**44**	45	44	51	40	43	36	55	57	34	44	54	33	43	56
Armenia	na	**na**	na	na	na	na	na	na	na	na	na	na	na	na	na	na
Australia	na	**na**	na	na	na	na	na	na	na	na	na	na	na	na	na	na
Austria	na	**49**	51	47	58	51	43	45	51	57	44	47	55	41	46	58
Azerbaijan	na	**na**	na	na	na	na	na	na	na	na	na	na	na	na	na	na
Bangladesh	na	**54**	57	50	55	54	50	47	59	66	57	51	57	55	53	60
Belarus	na	**36**	44	29	39	38	31	29	38	36	37	34	37	38	33	42
Belgium	na	**66**	67	64	71	71	58	57	67	70	61	65	71	58	65	77
Bosnia and Herz.	na	**41**	45	38	37	41	45	32	42	46	43	41	39	38	43	46
Brazil	na	**na**	na	na	na	na	na	na	na	na	na	na	na	na	na	na
Bulgaria	na	**42**	45	39	46	43	38	30	49	41	30	46	49	42	44	32
Canada	na	**50**	54	45	55	53	43	47	49	54	46	48	55	48	46	58
Chile	na	**49**	51	47	48	50	47	43	52	53	39	53	58	48	47	57
China	na	**na**	na	na	na	na	na	na	na	na	na	na	na	na	na	na
Colombia	na	**na**	na	na	na	na	na	na	na	na	na	na	na	na	na	na
Croatia	na	**29**	32	27	32	31	25	23	32	38	21	30	33	23	28	40
Czech Republic	na	**72**	73	71	73	76	67	70	74	70	69	73	75	69	72	73
Denmark	na	**88**	88	88	89	93	82	87	91	88	86	90	90	92	87	93
Dominican Rep.	na	**na**	na	na	na	na	na	na	na	na	na	na	na	na	na	na
Egypt	na	**4**	4	4	5	4	4	3	5	7	3	3	6	4	4	7
El Salvador	na	**na**	na	na	na	na	na	na	na	na	na	na	na	na	na	na
Estonia	na	**42**	46	39	51	41	39	39	43	44	43	36	48	42	40	70
Finland	na	**58**	61	55	65	67	47	57	60	57	58	61	58	54	59	58
France	na	**68**	70	65	68	71	64	67	69	69	68	68	68	62	67	77
Georgia	na	**na**	na	na	na	na	na	na	na	na	na	na	na	na	na	na
Germany	na	**48**	54	43	60	53	36	39	53	58	49	45	42	42	49	49
Great Britain	na	**54**	56	52	51	56	55	55	53	56	50	55	55	na	na	na
Greece	na	**31**	35	27	31	30	29	21	28	35	27	31	31	20	30	45
Hungary	na	**50**	58	43	57	56	40	45	60	59	48	46	56	45	56	53
Iceland	na	**59**	60	58	65	63	48	53	62	65	53	55	70	60	57	72
India	na	**49**	52	44	51	49	48	42	51	58	43	44	57	50	50	71
Indonesia	na	**na**	na	na	na	na	na	na	na	na	na	na	na	na	na	na
Iran	na	**na**	na	na	na	na	na	na	na	na	na	na	na	na	na	na
Ireland	na	**60**	63	57	72	64	46	50	64	66	49	65	67	49	63	64
Israel	na	**na**	na	na	na	na	na	na	na	na	na	na	na	na	na	na
Italy	na	**49**	53	46	57	53	42	41	57	53	42	51	55	38	48	57
Japan	na	**63**	66	61	71	67	56	59	61	69	55	65	69	63	66	64
Jordan	na	**25**	28	22	27	26	19	17	30	33	24	17	34	23	26	30
Korea, South	na	**40**	44	35	42	40	35	28	37	44	44	42	34	40	38	50
Latvia	na	**33**	39	28	42	37	27	24	37	33	28	36	40	31	32	43
Lithuania	na	**26**	37	18	34	34	15	10	31	37	18	34	28	22	25	46
Luxembourg	na	**53**	50	55	57	58	45	45	55	60	43	58	64	45	53	66
Macedonia	na	**51**	51	51	45	53	55	38	57	58	49	49	59	55	51	38
Malta	na	**21**	24	18	32	24	11	12	24	29	19	19	24	18	21	35
Mexico	na	**40**	44	37	45	39	35	31	50	56	34	40	53	39	41	52
Moldova	na	**11**	13	9	17	8	10	5	12	15	10	11	13	12	11	16
Montenegro	na	**38**	43	32	43	37	34	32	38	48	27	42	41	37	40	30
Morocco	na	**24**	24	24	25	26	18	20	40	38	15	26	47	24	24	30
Netherlands	na	**73**	73	73	74	79	67	67	74	78	66	79	76	61	73	79
New Zealand	na	**na**	na	na	na	na	na	na	na	na	na	na	na	na	na	na
Nigeria	na	**5**	5	5	5	4	4	3	6	5	3	5	7	5	4	8
Northern Ireland	na	**59**	63	56	58	65	55	56	59	70	55	63	66	52	61	66
Norway	na	**na**	na	na	na	na	na	na	na	na	na	na	na	na	na	na
Pakistan	na	**50**	48	52	57	52	32	38	60	71	38	53	61	45	56	67
Peru	na	**na**	na	na	na	na	na	na	na	na	na	na	na	na	na	na
Philippines	na	**7**	9	5	8	7	6	7	7	7	8	9	5	6	8	6
Poland	na	**45**	46	43	39	50	42	37	56	54	42	49	40	40	47	55
Portugal	na	**47**	50	44	56	47	42	45	50	60	35	47	50	43	47	55
Puerto Rico	na	**34**	39	32	35	37	33	24	34	37	32	32	42	20	35	43
Romania	na	**13**	17	9	18	15	8	5	15	21	5	15	16	10	14	22
Russian Fed.	na	**25**	32	20	28	27	22	16	26	27	22	24	30	23	27	46
Serbia	na	**37**	45	29	29	39	39	29	41	39	30	37	43	34	39	46
Singapore	na	**na**	na	na	na	na	na	na	na	na	na	na	na	na	na	na
Slovakia	na	**35**	42	29	40	40	26	28	38	46	25	36	40	33	36	39
Slovenia	na	**71**	70	71	70	76	65	58	73	82	64	72	80	67	72	70
South Africa	na	**16**	23	8	18	14	14	12	19	37	14	14	21	15	16	19
Spain	na	**56**	60	51	64	61	45	50	59	63	46	59	59	42	57	72
Sweden	na	**70**	68	72	66	73	69	68	67	75	67	70	74	62	70	76
Switzerland	na	**na**	na	na	na	na	na	na	na	na	na	na	na	na	na	na
Taiwan	na	**na**	na	na	na	na	na	na	na	na	na	na	na	na	na	na
Tanzania	na	**25**	25	26	26	26	24	26	22	27	24	23	30	25	24	38
Turkey	na	**27**	27	28	28	29	21	17	36	53	18	29	48	19	27	40
Uganda	na	**10**	9	11	10	9	15	10	11	5	10	5	12	11	10	10
Ukraine	na	**22**	29	16	27	20	22	16	23	23	22	21	24	21	23	26
United States	na	**25**	30	20	28	24	24	20	24	28	23	25	27	19	23	33
Uruguay	na	**na**	na	na	na	na	na	na	na	na	na	na	na	na	na	na
Venezuela	na	**27**	28	25	30	26	21	22	27	31	24	24	33	22	29	27
Vietnam	na	**46**	53	38	50	45	43	39	51	65	50	46	44	39	49	49
Zimbabwe	na	**24**	27	22	27	22	22	24	23	70	26	26	23	20	26	37
Total	na	41	44	38	41	43	39	37	42	46	36	42	45	34	42	53

RANKING	
Country	**2000**
Denmark	88
Netherlands	73
Czech Republic	72
Slovenia	71
Sweden	70
France	68
Belgium	66
Japan	63
Ireland	60
Northern Ireland	59
Iceland	59
Finland	58
Spain	56
Bangladesh	54
Great Britain	54
Luxembourg	53
Macedonia	51
Hungary	50
Pakistan	50
Canada	50
Italy	49
India	49
Austria	49
Chile	49
Germany	48
Portugal	47
Vietnam	46
Poland	45
Argentina	44
Estonia	42
Bulgaria	42
Bosnia and Herz.	41
Mexico	40
Korea, South	40
Montenegro	38
Serbia	37
Belarus	36
Slovakia	35
Puerto Rico	34
Latvia	33
Albania	32
Greece	31
Algeria	30
Croatia	29
Turkey	27
Venezuela	27
Lithuania	26
Russian Fed.	25
Tanzania	25
Jordan	25
United States	25
Zimbabwe	24
Morocco	24
Ukraine	22
Malta	21
South Africa	16
Romania	13
Moldova	11
Uganda	10
Philippines	7
Nigeria	5
Egypt	4
Total	41

F105) RELIGIOUS LEADERS SHOULD NOT INFLUENCE GOVERNMENT

How much do you agree or disagree with each of the following statements.

Religious leaders should not influence government

Agree strongly / Agree (%)

(WVS: V203; EVS: V132)

Country	Wave		Gender		Age			Education			Income			Values		
	1990	2000	Male	Female	16-29	30-49	50+	Lower	Middle	Upper	Lower	Middle	Upper	Mat	Mixed	Postm.
Albania	na	**76**	77	74	71	76	79	74	75	83	74	75	79	79	74	73
Algeria	na	**40**	39	40	43	37	37	37	40	41	45	40	38	37	40	43
Argentina	na	**65**	65	64	61	65	68	64	66	63	63	64	68	60	64	70
Armenia	na	**na**	na	na	na	na	na	na	na	na	na	na	na	na	na	na
Australia	na	**na**	na	na	na	na	na	na	na	na	na	na	na	na	na	na
Austria	na	**80**	80	79	80	79	80	80	80	76	78	81	78	82	79	80
Azerbaijan	na	**na**	na	na	na	na	na	na	na	na	na	na	na	na	na	na
Bangladesh	na	**71**	69	73	73	70	61	66	75	75	77	69	66	71	69	75
Belarus	na	**73**	76	71	75	76	67	68	75	74	73	73	73	73	73	74
Belgium	na	**74**	74	73	75	74	72	73	73	75	76	73	77	69	73	79
Bosnia and Herz.	na	**72**	71	72	70	71	75	67	72	76	73	71	74	76	71	71
Brazil	na	**na**	na	na	na	na	na	na	na	na	na	na	na	na	na	na
Bulgaria	na	**80**	80	79	77	81	79	74	82	82	74	80	81	80	79	89
Canada	na	**67**	68	67	67	68	67	69	67	66	67	68	68	75	64	72
Chile	na	**68**	69	66	64	69	69	67	67	72	63	74	70	68	67	69
China	na	**na**	na	na	na	na	na	na	na	na	na	na	na	na	na	na
Colombia	na	**na**	na	na	na	na	na	na	na	na	na	na	na	na	na	na
Croatia	na	**79**	83	76	81	80	77	82	78	77	76	80	80	82	81	75
Czech Republic	na	**74**	77	71	70	74	76	73	75	77	74	72	78	73	75	71
Denmark	na	**85**	82	89	83	85	87	88	84	80	87	89	77	93	86	83
Dominican Rep.	na	**na**	na	na	na	na	na	na	na	na	na	na	na	na	na	na
Egypt	na	**na**	na	na	na	na	na	na	na	na	na	na	na	na	na	na
El Salvador	na	**na**	na	na	na	na	na	na	na	na	na	na	na	na	na	na
Estonia	na	**75**	74	75	73	75	76	74	74	77	79	75	71	76	74	51
Finland	na	**58**	61	55	56	65	52	61	57	47	54	62	61	65	57	50
France	na	**82**	81	82	82	83	80	81	85	81	80	83	83	81	80	88
Georgia	na	**na**	na	na	na	na	na	na	na	na	na	na	na	na	na	na
Germany	na	**71**	74	69	75	75	65	68	74	77	72	68	70	71	68	82
Great Britain	na	**65**	67	64	62	64	70	69	66	60	68	63	63	na	na	na
Greece	na	**59**	65	55	55	62	62	59	59	60	56	60	63	54	60	63
Hungary	na	**70**	73	67	71	70	69	68	76	69	64	70	72	67	72	63
Iceland	na	**70**	71	69	72	70	69	68	75	67	71	72	67	74	68	72
India	na	**71**	73	68	72	71	72	66	72	79	63	69	77	67	75	81
Indonesia	na	**91**	89	93	86	91	93	91	92	90	89	94	92	89	92	86
Iran	na	**na**	na	na	na	na	na	na	na	na	na	na	na	na	na	na
Ireland	na	**73**	74	72	78	71	72	72	76	68	73	70	74	76	73	73
Israel	na	**na**	na	na	na	na	na	na	na	na	na	na	na	na	na	na
Italy	na	**68**	70	66	64	70	68	67	69	67	64	72	70	59	68	73
Japan	na	**72**	78	68	71	73	72	62	71	81	66	74	80	76	75	74
Jordan	na	**na**	na	na	na	na	na	na	na	na	na	na	na	na	na	na
Korea, South	na	**57**	61	53	55	58	59	53	57	58	61	54	56	57	59	47
Latvia	na	**73**	75	71	67	74	75	68	77	69	71	77	73	75	71	81
Lithuania	na	**76**	81	71	81	82	66	65	80	78	67	83	76	70	77	88
Luxembourg	na	**77**	78	75	77	78	76	73	79	78	68	76	79	76	78	77
Macedonia	na	**74**	72	75	69	74	76	66	77	77	69	76	77	73	73	79
Malta	na	**78**	77	80	81	80	74	79	79	73	82	77	72	77	78	80
Mexico	na	**65**	67	63	64	65	65	65	64	68	62	65	66	63	64	64
Moldova	na	**58**	56	60	59	58	59	56	57	62	56	65	56	66	48	55
Montenegro	na	**78**	79	75	83	78	74	72	80	86	76	79	81	78	79	78
Morocco	na	**65**	62	68	66	63	65	63	72	61	71	63	65	67	64	58
Netherlands	na	**60**	61	59	57	60	62	57	63	59	59	60	64	50	60	65
New Zealand	na	**na**	na	na	na	na	na	na	na	na	na	na	na	na	na	na
Nigeria	na	**na**	na	na	na	na	na	na	na	na	na	na	na	na	na	na
Northern Ireland	na	**66**	63	68	65	70	64	67	68	57	65	67	62	68	64	70
Norway	na	**na**	na	na	na	na	na	na	na	na	na	na	na	na	na	na
Pakistan	na	**na**	na	na	na	na	na	na	na	na	na	na	na	na	na	na
Peru	na	**na**	na	na	na	na	na	na	na	na	na	na	na	na	na	na
Philippines	na	**76**	78	74	80	74	74	73	78	77	77	76	74	78	75	68
Poland	na	**81**	82	80	79	83	80	80	83	81	82	84	73	78	82	85
Portugal	na	**80**	82	77	84	78	78	79	79	83	73	78	84	76	81	82
Puerto Rico	na	**59**	63	57	65	56	59	60	61	58	61	60	56	53	59	63
Romania	na	**78**	80	75	78	78	76	73	80	79	76	78	78	75	78	85
Russian Fed.	na	**68**	72	65	68	69	67	67	67	71	63	68	72	68	68	61
Serbia	na	**82**	84	80	78	83	83	78	84	83	79	85	82	82	82	81
Singapore	na	**na**	na	na	na	na	na	na	na	na	na	na	na	na	na	na
Slovakia	na	**71**	72	69	72	73	67	69	72	72	65	71	74	71	71	68
Slovenia	na	**73**	75	72	69	77	72	71	73	77	72	77	78	75	74	74
South Africa	na	**52**	54	51	49	57	48	52	55	32	49	60	51	51	54	51
Spain	na	**69**	72	65	75	71	63	63	74	75	67	67	71	59	70	82
Sweden	na	**52**	53	50	49	53	52	55	55	45	54	53	48	50	53	52
Switzerland	na	**na**	na	na	na	na	na	na	na	na	na	na	na	na	na	na
Taiwan	na	**na**	na	na	na	na	na	na	na	na	na	na	na	na	na	na
Tanzania	na	**69**	68	70	71	66	74	74	69	51	77	66	57	70	69	65
Turkey	na	**72**	71	73	73	72	72	69	73	84	68	73	76	72	74	72
Uganda	na	**55**	52	58	53	57	58	55	54	65	64	53	45	51	55	65
Ukraine	na	**72**	78	67	76	73	69	63	74	72	73	73	71	70	74	82
United States	na	**51**	55	47	55	47	53	56	53	48	52	54	48	52	50	53
Uruguay	na	**na**	na	na	na	na	na	na	na	na	na	na	na	na	na	na
Venezuela	na	**57**	58	56	55	58	58	55	56	60	55	58	60	60	57	53
Vietnam	na	**67**	72	61	63	67	70	60	75	69	74	66	64	67	69	62
Zimbabwe	na	**52**	51	52	53	50	53	53	51	10	51	56	51	53	51	44
Total	na	**69**	71	68	68	70	70	69	70	68	68	71	69	70	69	70

RANKING

Country	2000
Indonesia	91
Denmark	85
Serbia	82
France	82
Poland	81
Austria	80
Bulgaria	80
Portugal	80
Croatia	79
Malta	78
Romania	78
Montenegro	78
Luxembourg	77
Philippines	76
Lithuania	76
Albania	76
Estonia	75
Czech Republic	74
Macedonia	74
Belgium	74
Slovenia	73
Latvia	73
Belarus	73
Ireland	73
Japan	72
Turkey	72
Ukraine	72
Bosnia and Herz.	72
India	71
Germany	71
Slovakia	71
Bangladesh	71
Iceland	70
Hungary	70
Spain	69
Tanzania	69
Russian Fed.	68
Italy	68
Chile	68
Canada	67
Vietnam	67
Northern Ireland	66
Great Britain	65
Argentina	65
Mexico	65
Morocco	65
Netherlands	60
Greece	59
Puerto Rico	59
Moldova	58
Finland	58
Korea, South	57
Venezuela	57
Uganda	55
South Africa	52
Sweden	52
Zimbabwe	52
United States	51
Algeria	40
Total	69

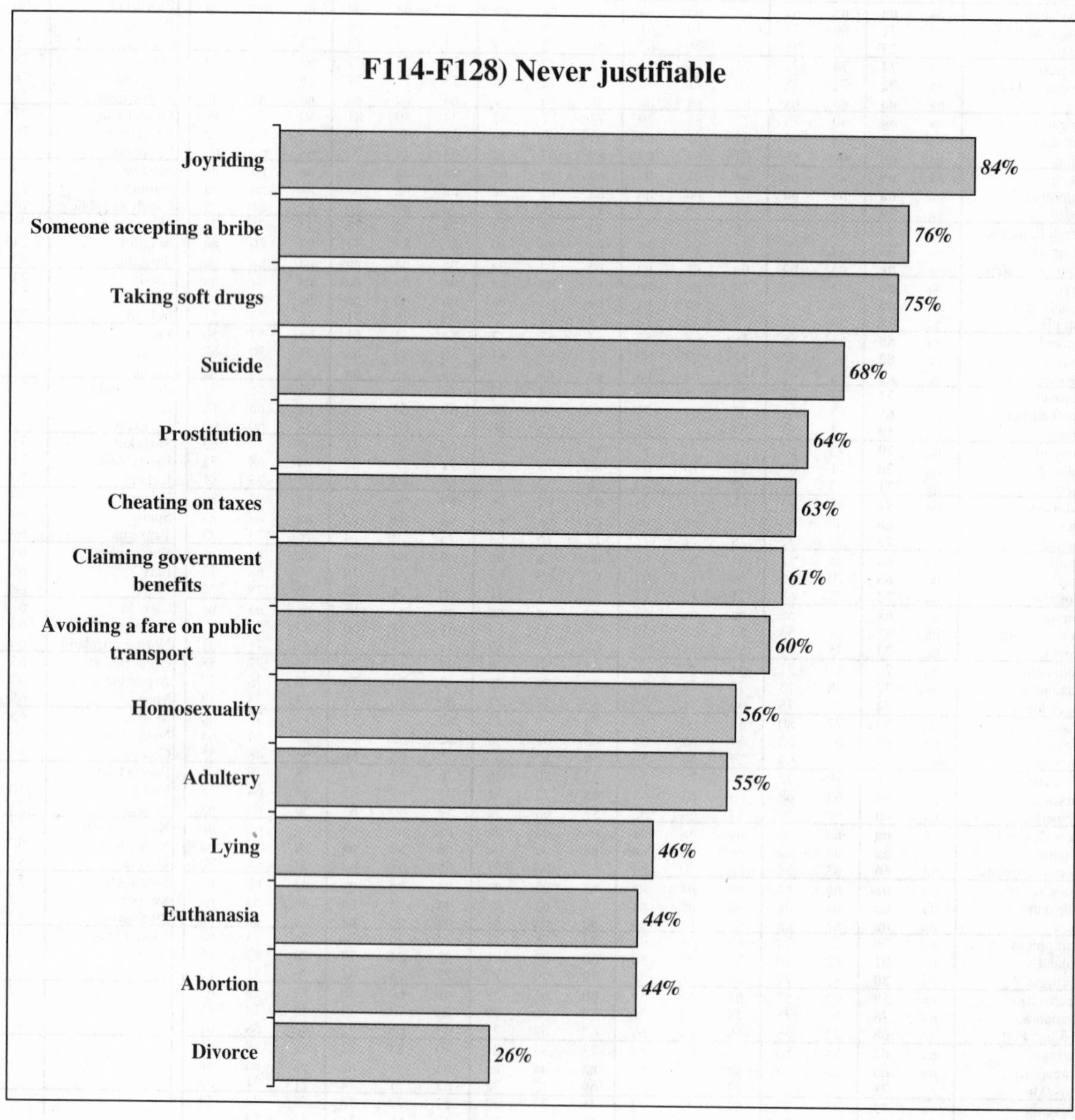

F114-F128) Never justifiable
Joyriding
84%
Someone accepting a bribe
76%
Taking soft drugs
75%
Suicide
68%
Prostitution
64%
Cheating on taxes
63%
Claiming government benefits
61%
Avoiding a fare on public transport
60%
Homosexuality
56%
Adultery
55%
Lying
46%
Euthanasia
44%
Abortion
44%
Divorce
26%

F114) JUSTIFIABLE: CLAIMING GOVERNMENT BENEFITS

Please tell me for each of the following statements whether you think it can always be justified, never be justified, or something in between: Claiming government benefits to which you have no right

(WVS: V204; EVS: V225)

Never justifiable (%)

Country	Wave		Gender		Age			Education			Income			Values		
	1990	2000	Male	Female	16-29	30-49	50+	Lower	Middle	Upper	Lower	Middle	Upper	Mat	Mixed	Postm.
Albania	na	**58**	56	61	52	59	63	54	59	70	54	58	64	60	58	56
Algeria	na	**51**	49	53	51	49	54	53	48	53	55	45	47	51	49	60
Argentina	79	**64**	63	66	55	66	72	65	61	72	62	66	65	62	65	65
Armenia	na	**44**	43	44	40	45	47	43	43	47	43	40	46	39	49	35
Australia	na	**73**	71	75	53	77	87	71	74	74	72	74	76	77	75	69
Austria	69	**58**	56	59	39	58	67	63	52	53	56	58	57	69	62	48
Azerbaijan	na	**62**	61	64	61	62	64	69	65	55	74	60	57	66	57	52
Bangladesh	na	**92**	90	94	92	92	95	94	89	90	95	89	94	95	90	91
Belarus	58	**35**	33	37	24	38	42	38	33	38	38	35	30	35	37	27
Belgium	52	**57**	56	58	37	56	69	57	56	59	58	56	60	55	61	51
Bosnia and Herz.	na	**76**	77	74	73	73	81	80	73	79	79	76	71	77	75	74
Brazil	72	**55**	55	55	48	55	67	54	52	66	52	47	62	49	55	64
Bulgaria	69	**70**	68	71	56	67	78	76	66	66	75	73	62	70	69	81
Canada	70	**71**	69	73	56	69	81	78	68	71	70	69	72	77	72	68
Chile	51	**47**	45	50	46	46	51	48	48	44	48	45	51	58	44	41
China	76	**62**	64	60	56	62	68	66	60	55	61	65	62	61	59	71
Colombia	na	**72**	70	74	67	74	77	75	67	75	74	70	72	76	73	73
Croatia	na	**78**	72	82	72	78	81	81	76	75	79	77	80	84	76	80
Czech Republic	2	**64**	63	65	47	64	73	63	65	66	69	66	59	62	66	61
Denmark	81	**83**	82	85	71	85	88	84	81	84	79	85	86	78	85	85
Dominican Rep.	na	**70**	71	69	68	71	100	78	75	68	69	69	71	71	70	69
Egypt	na	**73**	72	75	72	74	74	73	72	77	76	69	75	75	73	65
El Salvador	na	**74**	75	73	68	79	75	76	72	70	75	75	73	na	na	na
Estonia	63	**36**	35	37	25	34	45	34	38	36	41	37	37	33	39	31
Finland	13	**51**	48	54	31	54	60	50	52	61	45	49	57	50	52	47
France	40	**41**	40	41	26	36	52	42	38	39	43	39	41	47	41	30
Georgia	na	**47**	48	47	41	49	51	49	48	45	54	52	33	46	48	44
Germany	74	**63**	60	65	49	60	71	66	57	77	65	58	58	68	61	62
Great Britain	70	**67**	65	69	45	66	79	69	63	67	69	63	70	na	na	na
Greece	na	**24**	26	23	18	27	33	36	25	21	29	24	20	26	24	21
Hungary	67	**74**	70	77	64	69	85	74	75	73	76	77	71	77	70	74
Iceland	73	**68**	64	72	50	71	79	73	64	68	65	66	72	76	68	52
India	77	**75**	77	73	77	74	76	72	76	81	66	73	81	78	75	72
Indonesia	na	**42**	39	45	28	45	46	53	44	31	47	36	41	44	39	19
Iran	na	**67**	65	70	64	69	74	72	71	56	65	70	64	77	64	58
Ireland	69	**67**	62	71	54	65	78	72	64	63	71	67	66	64	68	60
Israel	na	**na**	na	na	na	na	na	na	na	na	na	na	na	na	na	na
Italy	68	**65**	65	65	46	67	73	67	63	67	67	65	63	60	66	66
Japan	67	**64**	66	63	42	62	76	78	64	59	69	65	60	69	64	55
Jordan	na	**80**	84	76	74	80	92	82	79	76	73	87	79	78	81	78
Korea, South	78	**na**	na	na	na	na	na	na	na	na	na	na	na	na	na	na
Latvia	75	**62**	60	64	48	65	66	64	60	67	63	59	65	65	60	58
Lithuania	61	**54**	51	57	45	49	66	64	50	53	54	62	51	52	54	66
Luxembourg	na	**46**	44	48	31	47	55	46	44	51	43	46	52	41	47	52
Macedonia	na	**47**	49	45	41	45	55	48	45	52	47	44	52	51	46	43
Malta	na	**85**	83	86	75	86	90	88	83	83	85	87	85	86	84	84
Mexico	25	**45**	46	45	37	47	56	48	42	43	44	44	43	46	45	37
Moldova	na	**28**	26	30	23	32	27	24	27	33	35	28	25	27	30	19
Montenegro	na	**42**	43	41	33	39	52	45	40	41	44	43	45	45	39	42
Morocco	na	**86**	84	89	84	88	91	87	84	81	89	86	81	87	85	88
Netherlands	71	**77**	76	78	62	75	87	79	80	72	71	79	81	76	80	70
New Zealand	na	**69**	67	72	48	67	81	76	75	60	68	69	71	71	70	64
Nigeria	69	**62**	60	64	61	62	70	62	64	59	61	63	61	59	64	65
Northern Ireland	77	**66**	63	70	62	60	75	66	66	67	68	66	65	73	67	53
Norway	80	**71**	68	74	43	75	86	76	68	71	na	na	na	70	72	64
Pakistan	na	**77**	79	76	72	76	90	78	75	79	78	79	78	74	81	80
Peru	na	**44**	42	46	39	46	48	38	44	48	40	40	56	34	47	46
Philippines	na	**28**	27	29	23	29	33	31	25	28	34	31	18	30	26	27
Poland	65	**53**	54	52	40	55	59	52	53	61	52	57	44	51	54	55
Portugal	58	**59**	59	59	57	59	60	61	54	61	52	57	58	57	60	60
Puerto Rico	na	**71**	69	73	51	70	81	76	67	72	72	71	70	74	72	71
Romania	71	**70**	70	70	62	67	77	72	67	74	72	71	71	72	67	76
Russian Fed.	66	**58**	55	61	46	57	66	67	56	58	62	59	53	57	59	60
Serbia	na	**61**	59	62	42	61	68	62	59	61	61	66	61	64	55	68
Singapore	na	**48**	49	47	38	58	57	50	46	54	49	47	50	52	49	31
Slovakia	na	**37**	34	40	31	37	43	38	37	37	37	39	37	37	38	28
Slovenia	51	**49**	47	52	29	53	60	49	48	55	48	53	52	50	51	44
South Africa	77	**50**	48	51	51	46	59	42	60	62	39	53	59	56	49	27
Spain	70	**56**	52	60	48	53	64	62	50	49	61	58	53	63	56	49
Sweden	75	**55**	53	58	38	57	64	64	48	60	55	55	55	65	56	49
Switzerland	75	**67**	63	70	53	66	76	67	67	67	66	64	68	68	68	63
Taiwan	na	**55**	57	52	53	56	52	49	56	59	53	54	58	57	53	49
Tanzania	na	**87**	89	85	87	87	92	86	88	92	86	86	90	88	88	87
Turkey	84	**90**	89	91	88	92	90	90	89	94	88	92	90	88	92	92
Uganda	na	**72**	76	68	68	77	72	72	71	86	75	68	76	71	71	78
Ukraine	na	**48**	43	52	32	46	59	58	46	47	57	45	40	50	46	50
United States	69	**64**	60	67	48	66	74	58	66	65	61	65	67	56	63	68
Uruguay	na	**79**	77	80	69	77	84	80	78	72	84	79	75	89	78	73
Venezuela	na	**54**	53	54	53	57	47	50	54	58	45	52	63	48	56	54
Vietnam	na	**73**	76	70	72	72	76	76	72	58	70	76	72	79	70	63
Zimbabwe	na	**80**	77	82	77	83	81	81	79	62	82	76	83	81	79	81
Total	64	**61**	60	62	53	62	68	65	58	61	61	61	61	61	61	59

RANKING

Country	2000
Bangladesh	92
Turkey	90
Tanzania	87
Morocco	86
Malta	85
Denmark	83
Jordan	80
Zimbabwe	80
Uruguay	79
Croatia	78
Pakistan	77
Netherlands	77
Bosnia and Herz.	76
India	75
Hungary	74
El Salvador	74
Egypt	73
Vietnam	73
Australia	73
Uganda	72
Colombia	72
Canada	71
Norway	71
Puerto Rico	71
Dominican Rep.	70
Romania	70
Bulgaria	70
New Zealand	69
Iceland	68
Iran	67
Great Britain	67
Ireland	67
Switzerland	67
Northern Ireland	66
Italy	65
Argentina	64
Japan	64
Czech Republic	64
United States	64
Germany	63
Latvia	62
Nigeria	62
Azerbaijan	62
China	62
Serbia	61
Portugal	59
Albania	58
Russian Fed.	58
Austria	58
Belgium	57
Spain	56
Sweden	55
Brazil	55
Taiwan	55
Lithuania	54
Venezuela	54
Poland	53
Finland	51
Algeria	51
South Africa	50
Slovenia	49
Singapore	48
Ukraine	48
Chile	47
Georgia	47
Macedonia	47
Luxembourg	46
Mexico	45
Peru	44
Armenia	44
Montenegro	42
Indonesia	42
France	41
Slovakia	37
Estonia	36
Belarus	35
Moldova	28
Philippines	28
Greece	24
Total	61

F115) JUSTIFIABLE: AVOIDING A FARE ON PUBLIC TRANSPORT

Please tell me for each of the following statements whether you think it can always be justified, never be justified, or something in between: Avoiding a fare on public transport

Never justifiable (%) (WVS: V205; EVS: o33)

	Wave		Gender		Age			Education			Income			Values		
Country	1990	2000	Male	Female	16-29	30-49	50+	Lower	Middle	Upper	Lower	Middle	Upper	Mat	Mixed	Postm.
Albania	na	**47**	46	49	38	46	58	44	47	55	43	45	54	46	49	51
Algeria	na	**64**	63	65	61	65	70	62	62	68	66	65	62	60	65	72
Argentina	73	**67**	66	67	56	68	76	68	64	71	66	67	67	65	69	63
Armenia	na	**37**	34	40	34	39	39	37	35	44	36	34	38	35	40	26
Australia	na	**63**	60	66	41	64	82	69	65	56	70	59	59	71	65	57
Austria	66	**53**	49	57	39	49	64	64	47	33	57	54	48	71	58	40
Azerbaijan	na	**49**	47	50	49	50	46	56	52	42	54	46	50	50	48	44
Bangladesh	na	**96**	95	98	96	97	97	98	95	96	98	94	99	98	95	97
Belarus	50	**21**	20	22	13	19	30	30	18	19	23	22	15	21	21	20
Belgium	59	**61**	56	64	43	58	71	66	61	56	66	64	59	65	58	60
Bosnia and Herz.	na	**73**	73	72	66	71	82	81	71	71	76	74	66	75	72	70
Brazil	67	**56**	56	55	51	55	66	54	55	64	50	55	62	53	56	58
Bulgaria	65	**na**	na	na	na	na	na	na	na	na	na	na	na	na	na	na
Canada	63	**63**	60	67	45	60	78	75	61	58	67	65	57	63	66	58
Chile	60	**47**	45	48	43	44	53	43	48	50	42	46	54	53	44	49
China	80	**83**	83	84	77	85	84	84	82	88	83	83	86	82	83	78
Colombia	na	**49**	50	49	42	52	56	50	44	55	43	48	55	49	46	45
Croatia	na	**56**	55	58	36	58	68	66	53	42	66	54	55	59	57	53
Czech Republic	na	**41**	36	46	23	35	57	45	39	31	54	40	32	42	42	38
Denmark	75	**71**	68	74	47	68	86	78	61	62	75	71	63	65	74	65
Dominican Rep.	na	**71**	72	70	68	75	82	81	72	70	70	72	72	69	73	66
Egypt	na	**74**	72	76	72	75	75	72	74	80	73	70	79	76	73	74
El Salvador	na	**na**	na	na	na	na	na	na	na	na	na	na	na	na	na	na
Estonia	61	**na**	na	na	na	na	na	na	na	na	na	na	na	na	na	na
Finland	54	**50**	43	57	25	43	71	58	41	42	53	50	47	53	50	47
France	55	**54**	53	54	32	50	68	60	46	44	54	54	54	63	56	35
Georgia	na	**47**	46	48	39	49	53	49	47	47	53	48	38	46	48	47
Germany	73	**54**	54	54	39	50	64	57	49	59	57	51	48	57	53	50
Great Britain	60	**48**	42	53	30	43	59	48	46	42	54	47	46	na	na	na
Greece	na	**36**	37	36	23	43	56	58	40	29	43	33	29	37	38	31
Hungary	59	**na**	na	na	na	na	na	na	na	na	na	na	na	na	na	na
Iceland	56	**na**	na	na	na	na	na	na	na	na	na	na	na	na	na	na
India	84	**80**	80	79	79	81	79	75	82	88	70	77	87	82	82	80
Indonesia	na	**87**	84	90	83	87	89	92	86	84	87	85	89	91	84	68
Iran	na	**84**	83	84	80	89	86	84	83	83	82	84	84	90	79	85
Ireland	58	**na**	na	na	na	na	na	na	na	na	na	na	na	na	na	na
Israel	na	**na**	na	na	na	na	na	na	na	na	na	na	na	na	na	na
Italy	67	**61**	59	62	35	60	75	70	54	51	69	56	55	65	63	55
Japan	79	**77**	77	78	59	75	87	86	79	69	80	79	76	80	77	73
Jordan	na	**89**	91	86	87	88	92	89	90	87	89	91	88	88	89	85
Korea, South	69	**41**	44	38	25	43	56	64	44	34	44	43	37	42	41	38
Latvia	61	**na**	na	na	na	na	na	na	na	na	na	na	na	na	na	na
Lithuania	56	**38**	37	39	24	37	49	45	36	33	47	38	34	35	39	43
Luxembourg	na	**51**	49	53	31	52	63	55	50	46	45	61	52	54	52	43
Macedonia	na	**69**	67	71	62	68	76	73	68	66	74	66	68	72	68	59
Malta	na	**na**	na	na	na	na	na	na	na	na	na	na	na	na	na	na
Mexico	32	**49**	52	46	40	52	55	52	46	44	47	48	47	52	47	44
Moldova	na	**22**	23	20	16	28	20	18	21	25	29	20	19	20	22	22
Montenegro	na	**42**	43	42	32	39	53	45	40	40	47	38	48	43	41	48
Morocco	na	**82**	79	86	77	84	90	84	76	75	87	80	78	81	82	83
Netherlands	56	**44**	40	48	26	36	62	57	45	32	43	47	39	60	44	36
New Zealand	na	**64**	61	67	37	58	80	74	66	52	70	63	59	68	64	60
Nigeria	61	**56**	54	58	54	57	63	56	56	53	55	57	53	53	57	62
Northern Ireland	72	**na**	na	na	na	na	na	na	na	na	na	na	na	na	na	na
Norway	76	**70**	68	72	44	73	86	77	70	64	na	na	na	70	71	64
Pakistan	na	**87**	89	85	83	85	99	86	87	89	86	87	89	85	89	83
Peru	na	**54**	51	57	49	56	60	52	54	56	49	55	61	44	57	58
Philippines	na	**35**	33	36	30	38	34	33	33	39	38	37	28	37	33	37
Poland	na	**na**	na	na	na	na	na	na	na	na	na	na	na	na	na	na
Portugal	57	**na**	na	na	na	na	na	na	na	na	na	na	na	na	na	na
Puerto Rico	na	**80**	79	81	66	78	89	93	78	79	87	75	79	81	82	77
Romania	64	**na**	na	na	na	na	na	na	na	na	na	na	na	na	na	na
Russian Fed.	54	**33**	31	34	22	29	43	47	32	26	39	32	27	33	32	37
Serbia	na	**59**	58	60	38	57	72	60	61	56	61	66	57	61	57	60
Singapore	na	**55**	57	52	45	64	63	54	55	59	56	53	58	57	56	37
Slovakia	na	**na**	na	na	na	na	na	na	na	na	na	na	na	na	na	na
Slovenia	63	**na**	na	na	na	na	na	na	na	na	na	na	na	na	na	na
South Africa	na	**54**	53	56	54	53	60	48	63	63	46	55	63	58	56	31
Spain	68	**57**	53	61	46	54	68	62	51	52	67	53	56	64	56	49
Sweden	68	**na**	na	na	na	na	na	na	na	na	na	na	na	na	na	na
Switzerland	79	**59**	56	62	37	57	76	65	58	59	63	59	59	63	61	52
Taiwan	na	**60**	59	61	58	62	57	59	60	61	58	65	60	64	60	49
Tanzania	na	**90**	91	88	89	89	93	88	91	92	89	88	91	91	90	92
Turkey	76	**na**	na	na	na	na	na	na	na	na	na	na	na	na	na	na
Uganda	na	**66**	75	58	63	70	64	67	64	82	76	60	75	60	68	76
Ukraine	na	**34**	33	34	17	33	43	43	30	37	40	30	30	34	35	37
United States	62	**50**	49	51	32	51	63	43	53	51	49	52	50	48	51	49
Uruguay	na	**72**	71	72	60	69	78	73	71	63	72	75	70	79	71	65
Venezuela	na	**56**	58	54	55	58	55	53	56	59	44	55	64	50	59	57
Vietnam	na	**89**	90	87	88	87	91	89	88	85	90	93	83	91	87	87
Zimbabwe	na	**83**	82	85	78	89	86	85	81	83	86	81	83	86	82	83
Total	63	**60**	59	60	52	60	68	65	56	57	61	60	58	60	61	55

RANKING	
Country	**2000**
Bangladesh	96
Tanzania	90
Vietnam	89
Jordan	89
Pakistan	87
Indonesia	87
Iran	84
China	83
Zimbabwe	83
Morocco	82
Puerto Rico	80
India	80
Japan	77
Egypt	74
Bosnia and Herz.	73
Uruguay	72
Dominican Rep.	71
Denmark	71
Norway	70
Macedonia	69
Argentina	67
Uganda	66
Algeria	64
New Zealand	64
Canada	63
Australia	63
Belgium	61
Italy	61
Taiwan	60
Switzerland	59
Serbia	59
Spain	57
Croatia	56
Venezuela	56
Brazil	56
Nigeria	56
Singapore	55
South Africa	54
Peru	54
Germany	54
France	54
Austria	53
Luxembourg	51
Finland	50
United States	50
Colombia	49
Mexico	49
Azerbaijan	49
Great Britain	48
Albania	47
Georgia	47
Chile	47
Netherlands	44
Montenegro	42
Czech Republic	41
Korea, South	41
Lithuania	38
Armenia	37
Greece	36
Philippines	35
Ukraine	34
Russian Fed.	33
Moldova	22
Belarus	21
Total	60

F116) JUSTIFIABLE: CHEATING ON TAXES

Please tell me for each of the following statements whether you think it can always be justified, never be justified, or something in between: Cheating on taxes if you have a chance

(WVS: V206; EVS: V226)

Never justifiable (%)

Country	Wave 1990	Wave 2000	Gender Male	Gender Female	Age 16-29	Age 30-49	Age 50+	Education Lower	Education Middle	Education Upper	Income Lower	Income Middle	Income Upper	Values Mat	Values Mixed	Values Postm.
Albania	na	**59**	56	61	54	57	65	55	59	67	60	55	60	58	61	51
Algeria	na	**76**	73	80	72	79	81	75	77	76	79	79	73	76	77	75
Argentina	81	**77**	73	81	71	77	83	78	75	79	77	77	78	74	79	75
Armenia	na	**41**	38	44	37	42	46	42	40	44	42	35	46	41	42	32
Australia	na	**62**	57	67	47	62	76	68	63	58	69	60	55	67	63	59
Austria	63	**58**	54	62	47	58	64	65	55	42	59	59	55	65	61	53
Azerbaijan	na	**48**	44	51	49	47	49	40	50	45	53	46	51	50	46	41
Bangladesh	na	**99**	98	99	98	99	98	99	98	97	100	98	99	99	98	97
Belarus	47	**26**	22	30	17	26	35	33	23	27	30	26	22	27	28	14
Belgium	38	**38**	33	43	28	34	46	45	38	32	49	40	30	37	38	33
Bosnia and Herz.	na	**77**	75	79	72	76	83	86	75	75	84	78	68	78	77	74
Brazil	65	**47**	47	47	40	47	61	47	47	49	45	47	48	44	47	54
Bulgaria	60	**67**	63	71	52	59	81	75	65	58	76	68	58	65	70	67
Canada	61	**67**	61	73	58	66	74	76	66	62	73	67	60	66	69	63
Chile	78	**70**	70	70	68	71	70	67	73	68	66	71	74	72	67	78
China	82	**77**	78	77	71	78	80	81	75	70	78	79	72	76	76	78
Colombia	na	**72**	70	74	68	74	77	78	67	71	78	68	70	78	75	76
Croatia	na	**61**	57	65	48	63	68	69	58	50	73	57	61	65	62	56
Czech Republic	na	**59**	55	63	49	53	70	61	58	53	69	61	48	60	60	56
Denmark	59	**66**	57	74	64	61	72	69	59	63	69	64	63	70	66	71
Dominican Rep.	na	**70**	70	71	69	72	80	86	64	71	74	68	64	66	73	65
Egypt	na	**80**	76	84	78	80	82	79	81	80	80	77	82	81	79	74
El Salvador	na	**81**	81	81	78	83	83	82	80	81	81	79	85	na	na	na
Estonia	66	**40**	38	42	24	32	56	41	39	41	49	43	37	40	41	20
Finland	42	**53**	45	60	38	49	64	57	47	54	56	50	51	53	53	52
France	48	**48**	46	51	33	47	57	53	36	46	54	49	47	55	49	37
Georgia	na	**53**	53	52	46	54	58	57	52	53	56	56	45	52	53	53
Germany	68	**57**	53	60	46	55	64	58	53	70	60	51	53	64	53	57
Great Britain	55	**56**	51	61	33	56	67	58	51	56	58	55	58	na	na	na
Greece	na	**37**	38	37	32	39	46	49	40	33	43	36	30	39	36	40
Hungary	62	**66**	63	67	52	57	82	71	60	47	69	70	60	71	62	50
Iceland	59	**58**	52	63	48	55	70	66	54	51	62	59	52	64	57	50
India	82	**80**	80	81	80	81	79	75	85	87	71	78	86	83	82	80
Indonesia	na	**79**	76	83	79	78	82	85	77	78	79	77	82	82	78	68
Iran	na	**89**	89	90	87	91	92	91	89	87	87	91	89	92	87	89
Ireland	50	**58**	53	62	48	56	68	67	50	58	66	53	53	56	58	57
Israel	na	**na**	na	na	na	na	na	na	na	na	na	na	na	na	na	na
Italy	57	**57**	55	58	44	56	64	57	56	55	59	58	52	53	58	57
Japan	82	**84**	80	87	74	83	89	90	85	79	86	85	81	86	84	82
Jordan	na	**84**	85	82	79	84	93	89	83	76	84	85	83	85	83	84
Korea, South	91	**75**	72	77	71	75	79	82	77	71	77	75	72	76	74	71
Latvia	68	**60**	56	63	39	59	69	66	57	59	62	63	54	63	59	47
Lithuania	58	**39**	37	41	27	33	53	48	36	37	42	48	38	39	39	47
Luxembourg	na	**41**	38	44	30	44	44	49	37	37	43	43	45	42	42	38
Macedonia	na	**68**	67	69	57	67	79	70	67	69	74	65	67	72	68	44
Malta	na	**80**	75	84	71	80	86	87	77	77	85	80	76	81	80	80
Mexico	41	**69**	67	71	62	71	78	73	65	67	68	68	71	75	66	66
Moldova	na	**26**	27	25	21	30	26	22	25	31	37	25	20	22	30	21
Montenegro	na	**46**	43	48	37	40	57	50	41	47	50	46	46	48	43	50
Morocco	na	**96**	94	98	94	96	99	96	95	92	96	95	95	97	95	96
Netherlands	44	**46**	42	51	34	41	59	52	48	39	49	49	39	54	46	45
New Zealand	na	**59**	52	66	41	57	69	65	60	53	61	59	57	57	60	55
Nigeria	64	**58**	57	59	59	56	67	56	59	60	59	56	57	57	58	64
Northern Ireland	71	**59**	52	65	54	53	67	61	57	59	61	56	55	69	58	47
Norway	45	**48**	38	57	43	40	60	54	43	47	na	na	na	50	47	44
Pakistan	na	**91**	91	91	91	89	97	91	92	88	92	91	91	90	92	83
Peru	na	**64**	61	67	63	64	68	62	64	65	62	62	71	53	68	65
Philippines	na	**41**	38	44	37	44	41	39	40	45	45	42	35	42	39	49
Poland	51	**60**	61	59	46	61	67	62	56	58	62	60	53	58	62	52
Portugal	45	**55**	55	55	56	50	59	57	48	61	59	48	57	52	58	53
Puerto Rico	na	**77**	76	78	65	75	85	85	77	76	83	76	74	80	79	71
Romania	69	**57**	56	59	44	54	67	61	53	61	61	55	59	57	56	58
Russian Fed.	56	**46**	42	49	29	43	60	60	45	40	52	46	40	49	41	50
Serbia	na	**64**	63	65	51	60	73	61	64	69	67	68	64	64	62	80
Singapore	na	**68**	66	69	60	74	73	71	67	63	69	68	65	67	70	46
Slovakia	na	**59**	55	64	54	58	65	60	60	56	60	61	60	60	60	53
Slovenia	70	**60**	56	63	48	61	67	61	61	53	61	63	55	69	60	53
South Africa	68	**55**	52	59	56	50	68	49	62	73	51	55	57	54	58	42
Spain	65	**57**	53	60	48	53	65	63	49	52	66	56	56	64	56	51
Sweden	58	**51**	47	55	45	47	57	60	45	53	54	48	50	52	51	51
Switzerland	66	**54**	48	59	40	48	69	59	53	48	57	55	49	52	58	43
Taiwan	na	**64**	67	62	62	64	67	65	63	65	63	64	66	67	63	60
Tanzania	na	**85**	86	84	86	83	89	86	84	85	85	84	84	88	86	75
Turkey	90	**92**	91	93	91	94	92	91	93	95	91	93	93	91	93	92
Uganda	na	**58**	62	55	54	64	56	61	55	77	65	58	68	53	59	71
Ukraine	na	**41**	38	43	26	36	54	51	40	38	47	38	36	43	39	45
United States	69	**62**	55	69	53	61	71	64	62	61	63	63	59	60	63	60
Uruguay	na	**80**	79	81	77	77	84	82	78	75	82	80	79	84	79	77
Venezuela	na	**70**	70	70	70	71	69	69	70	72	60	69	79	60	73	75
Vietnam	na	**88**	90	86	90	85	91	88	89	83	89	91	83	87	87	86
Zimbabwe	na	**84**	79	87	82	86	82	85	82	83	84	84	81	85	81	91
Total	61	63	60	65	58	62	69	68	60	61	66	63	61	63	63	59

RANKING

Country	2000
Bangladesh	99
Morocco	96
Turkey	92
Pakistan	91
Iran	89
Vietnam	88
Tanzania	85
Jordan	84
Japan	84
Zimbabwe	84
El Salvador	81
India	80
Uruguay	80
Malta	80
Egypt	80
Indonesia	79
Argentina	77
China	77
Bosnia and Herz.	77
Puerto Rico	77
Algeria	76
Korea, South	75
Colombia	72
Dominican Rep.	70
Venezuela	70
Chile	70
Mexico	69
Macedonia	68
Singapore	68
Canada	67
Bulgaria	67
Denmark	66
Hungary	66
Taiwan	64
Peru	64
Serbia	64
Australia	62
United States	62
Croatia	61
Slovenia	60
Latvia	60
Poland	60
Slovakia	59
New Zealand	59
Czech Republic	59
Northern Ireland	59
Albania	59
Austria	58
Nigeria	58
Uganda	58
Iceland	58
Ireland	58
Germany	57
Romania	57
Spain	57
Italy	57
Great Britain	56
South Africa	55
Portugal	55
Switzerland	54
Finland	53
Georgia	53
Sweden	51
France	48
Azerbaijan	48
Norway	48
Brazil	47
Netherlands	46
Russian Fed.	46
Montenegro	46
Armenia	41
Philippines	41
Luxembourg	41
Ukraine	41
Estonia	40
Lithuania	39
Belgium	38
Greece	37
Belarus	26
Moldova	26
Total	63

F117) JUSTIFIABLE: SOMEONE ACCEPTING A BRIBE

Please tell me for each of the following statements whether you think it can always be justified, never be justified, or something in between: Someone accepting a bribe in the course of his / her duties

Never justifiable (%)

(WVS: V207; EVS: V231)

Country	Wave		Gender		Age			Education			Income			Values		
	1990	2000	Male	Female	16-29	30-49	50+	Lower	Middle	Upper	Lower	Middle	Upper	Mat	Mixed	Postm.
Albania	na	**53**	51	55	50	51	60	50	53	61	52	52	56	54	52	59
Algeria	na	**89**	88	89	87	90	89	84	90	90	91	90	84	88	89	89
Argentina	95	**92**	90	94	87	93	96	92	92	95	93	91	94	89	91	95
Armenia	na	**63**	60	66	56	64	72	69	63	62	59	65	66	63	66	43
Australia	na	**86**	83	88	72	88	95	88	85	85	89	83	84	87	88	82
Austria	72	**72**	69	76	66	72	77	77	70	63	72	75	70	83	72	71
Azerbaijan	na	**53**	55	52	55	50	61	60	53	54	57	59	52	50	58	61
Bangladesh	na	**99**	98	100	98	100	99	99	99	98	100	98	100	99	99	99
Belarus	75	**39**	35	43	24	40	52	49	36	36	50	37	26	43	39	18
Belgium	61	**68**	65	70	52	68	75	69	67	68	74	69	66	65	67	72
Bosnia and Herz.	na	**86**	85	86	80	87	89	90	83	89	89	84	83	84	86	89
Brazil	88	**46**	43	49	39	48	56	41	48	60	39	47	54	47	44	52
Bulgaria	81	**78**	77	78	64	76	86	86	73	74	86	75	71	80	77	93
Canada	77	**80**	77	84	66	81	88	83	80	79	79	81	81	79	81	78
Chile	85	**71**	71	71	71	70	72	67	73	72	66	73	75	76	67	75
China	87	**83**	84	83	79	85	83	85	83	74	83	86	80	83	83	90
Colombia	na	**81**	81	82	76	84	85	83	77	85	81	80	82	84	79	79
Croatia	na	**79**	76	82	66	81	86	84	76	76	87	77	80	83	79	75
Czech Republic	57	**51**	47	56	37	47	63	50	53	52	60	52	43	48	52	52
Denmark	91	**93**	90	96	86	94	95	94	92	92	92	94	92	91	93	94
Dominican Rep.	na	**76**	78	74	72	81	91	87	73	76	82	73	71	71	76	80
Egypt	na	**94**	93	95	93	94	96	95	93	93	94	93	95	95	93	96
El Salvador	na	**89**	88	90	86	90	93	89	88	91	90	88	92	na	na	na
Estonia	70	**67**	62	71	57	63	77	67	67	67	71	68	66	67	68	52
Finland	74	**80**	76	83	71	82	83	81	76	82	81	78	80	81	79	82
France	64	**67**	63	71	53	68	73	69	62	68	69	70	64	70	67	65
Georgia	na	**73**	71	74	63	76	78	77	73	70	77	75	63	73	72	77
Germany	64	**67**	62	70	61	64	72	70	62	73	66	64	67	68	66	67
Great Britain	75	**67**	65	69	50	67	77	67	67	65	66	68	73	na	na	na
Greece	na	**64**	61	67	59	66	78	81	66	60	70	62	58	60	65	70
Hungary	70	**53**	47	59	45	44	67	55	49	56	52	55	54	54	53	54
Iceland	84	**87**	82	92	75	89	95	90	84	88	86	87	88	90	86	85
India	86	**85**	85	85	85	85	84	81	89	91	75	85	90	89	84	84
Indonesia	na	**82**	79	86	81	81	85	87	81	81	84	81	78	84	82	71
Iran	na	**93**	93	94	92	95	96	95	93	91	93	96	92	96	93	90
Ireland	85	**83**	79	87	77	83	88	86	79	88	83	84	80	79	85	81
Israel	na	**86**	83	88	79	88	92	91	83	86	84	80	89	83	86	88
Italy	77	**79**	76	82	67	82	83	81	76	83	84	78	77	77	79	82
Japan	71	**83**	80	86	73	83	87	85	84	81	86	84	79	85	83	83
Jordan	na	**96**	98	95	96	96	98	97	96	96	97	96	97	98	96	95
Korea, South	85	**80**	77	83	79	79	85	91	81	77	84	78	78	81	80	81
Latvia	76	**74**	72	77	62	74	79	81	73	72	79	76	69	76	73	68
Lithuania	60	**67**	60	73	53	61	81	80	62	62	78	69	60	64	68	64
Luxembourg	na	**71**	69	73	57	75	76	67	72	77	62	75	83	71	71	70
Macedonia	na	**87**	86	87	84	85	92	85	87	89	86	86	89	88	87	74
Malta	na	**94**	93	96	91	96	95	96	94	94	95	95	92	95	95	91
Mexico	55	**73**	73	72	65	76	80	75	69	75	68	74	76	74	71	71
Moldova	na	**49**	46	52	39	54	53	55	47	48	67	54	34	51	50	33
Montenegro	na	**84**	81	88	79	82	91	89	78	88	90	87	82	86	84	82
Morocco	na	**98**	97	99	97	98	100	98	97	96	98	97	97	98	97	97
Netherlands	68	**73**	69	76	57	73	80	77	73	68	73	71	76	70	73	73
New Zealand	na	**81**	80	84	56	83	90	85	84	78	82	81	83	79	82	83
Nigeria	66	**63**	63	64	63	62	69	59	66	65	63	64	62	64	63	65
Northern Ireland	85	**78**	75	80	72	74	86	81	77	73	85	78	73	90	76	71
Norway	80	**85**	83	86	73	86	91	87	83	85	na	na	na	82	85	86
Pakistan	na	**92**	91	93	91	90	97	90	94	93	90	93	93	91	93	91
Peru	na	**73**	71	75	70	75	74	72	73	73	74	68	77	63	76	74
Philippines	na	**40**	39	41	36	41	41	36	40	44	39	44	34	40	39	42
Poland	83	**77**	75	79	65	77	84	79	74	73	78	77	69	77	77	73
Portugal	74	**74**	71	77	74	69	78	74	71	76	72	69	74	75	72	75
Puerto Rico	na	**89**	89	90	83	92	91	90	84	93	92	87	90	92	90	90
Romania	68	**80**	79	82	71	80	86	83	79	80	83	80	80	81	78	81
Russian Fed.	85	**70**	66	74	52	69	83	84	70	64	76	70	66	71	69	74
Serbia	na	**86**	84	89	78	86	91	86	85	89	89	87	88	88	84	87
Singapore	na	**77**	77	76	75	80	73	74	78	77	75	79	76	77	78	66
Slovakia	na	**39**	36	43	29	41	46	43	38	34	41	40	39	39	41	34
Slovenia	81	**74**	69	77	59	76	81	76	73	71	77	76	71	80	72	75
South Africa	80	**61**	58	65	65	56	66	55	69	76	54	63	67	62	63	47
Spain	83	**72**	69	75	67	70	77	76	68	68	78	70	73	74	72	69
Sweden	74	**69**	65	72	65	67	72	75	66	68	70	69	67	69	68	68
Switzerland	84	**79**	72	86	66	80	85	80	80	69	82	78	76	80	79	79
Taiwan	na	**75**	75	74	73	74	77	72	77	76	73	74	77	77	74	70
Tanzania	na	**92**	93	91	93	90	96	90	94	95	91	91	94	94	93	88
Turkey	92	**94**	93	95	92	96	95	93	94	98	92	95	95	94	95	95
Uganda	na	**73**	78	68	70	75	76	75	71	86	79	77	79	68	73	85
Ukraine	na	**64**	61	67	44	64	76	76	63	62	76	57	57	68	62	72
United States	80	**80**	77	83	68	81	89	77	80	82	79	79	82	75	81	82
Uruguay	na	**91**	90	92	90	91	91	90	93	90	93	88	91	88	91	90
Venezuela	na	**75**	75	75	73	76	78	74	74	78	64	74	83	72	77	76
Vietnam	na	**94**	93	94	93	93	95	94	94	85	96	96	90	94	93	93
Zimbabwe	na	**92**	92	92	89	94	96	94	89	100	91	92	92	93	91	92
Total	76	76	74	78	70	76	81	79	74	76	77	76	75	75	76	77

RANKING	
Country	2000
Bangladesh	99
Morocco	98
Jordan	96
Malta	94
Egypt	94
Vietnam	94
Turkey	94
Iran	93
Denmark	93
Tanzania	92
Argentina	92
Pakistan	92
Zimbabwe	92
Uruguay	91
Puerto Rico	89
El Salvador	89
Algeria	89
Iceland	87
Macedonia	87
Serbia	86
Israel	86
Australia	86
Bosnia and Herz.	86
India	85
Norway	85
Montenegro	84
China	83
Ireland	83
Japan	83
Indonesia	82
New Zealand	81
Colombia	81
Canada	80
Korea, South	80
Romania	80
United States	80
Finland	80
Italy	79
Croatia	79
Switzerland	79
Northern Ireland	78
Bulgaria	78
Poland	77
Singapore	77
Dominican Rep.	76
Venezuela	75
Taiwan	75
Latvia	74
Portugal	74
Slovenia	74
Peru	73
Georgia	73
Netherlands	73
Uganda	73
Mexico	73
Austria	72
Spain	72
Chile	71
Luxembourg	71
Russian Fed.	70
Sweden	69
Belgium	68
Great Britain	67
France	67
Estonia	67
Lithuania	67
Germany	67
Greece	64
Ukraine	64
Nigeria	63
Armenia	63
South Africa	61
Azerbaijan	53
Hungary	53
Albania	53
Czech Republic	51
Moldova	49
Brazil	46
Philippines	40
Slovakia	39
Belarus	39
Total	76

F118) JUSTIFIABLE: HOMOSEXUALITY

Please tell me for each of the following statements whether you think it can always be justified, never be justified, or something in between: Homosexuality

Never justifiable (%)

(WVS: V208; EVS: V232)

Country	Wave		Gender		Age			Education			Income			Values		
	1990	2000	Male	Female	16-29	30-49	50+	Lower	Middle	Upper	Lower	Middle	Upper	Mat	Mixed	Postm.
Albania	na	**81**	81	81	70	83	88	82	82	74	84	79	80	83	80	74
Algeria	na	**93**	93	94	92	93	96	95	93	92	94	94	91	95	92	95
Argentina	63	**40**	45	35	32	37	52	50	28	23	49	41	30	53	42	27
Armenia	na	**71**	75	68	60	75	83	87	71	67	68	73	75	74	70	58
Australia	na	**31**	38	25	23	25	46	49	30	17	40	33	16	51	32	24
Austria	52	**26**	30	23	13	22	37	37	19	5	36	27	21	54	26	19
Azerbaijan	na	**89**	90	88	86	90	93	94	90	85	93	91	80	91	85	95
Bangladesh	na	**99**	99	99	98	100	99	100	98	98	100	98	100	99	99	99
Belarus	84	**57**	57	58	39	59	72	73	53	50	62	58	48	66	51	40
Belgium	46	**27**	31	23	19	20	36	41	26	16	37	30	16	34	26	17
Bosnia and Herz.	na	**72**	76	69	63	72	82	85	72	63	80	75	64	74	72	60
Brazil	73	**56**	62	50	54	55	61	63	52	46	61	56	51	67	52	45
Bulgaria	81	**60**	64	56	49	55	70	75	57	42	74	61	45	67	53	61
Canada	40	**27**	29	24	21	22	35	42	26	15	32	28	17	31	29	18
Chile	78	**37**	41	34	33	34	46	45	36	24	43	38	25	44	38	22
China	93	**92**	93	91	87	93	96	93	93	86	88	95	94	92	92	88
Colombia	na	**61**	62	60	54	63	72	72	59	48	69	62	51	67	60	51
Croatia	na	**70**	71	69	54	69	81	78	68	53	78	68	67	77	71	61
Czech Republic	39	**27**	31	23	18	21	37	33	21	15	32	28	19	36	25	19
Denmark	44	**21**	27	15	6	12	39	31	9	6	29	17	12	41	22	6
Dominican Rep.	na	**53**	57	50	49	58	70	77	63	46	62	50	38	53	52	49
Egypt	na	**100**	100	100	100	100	100	100	100	100	100	100	100	100	100	100
El Salvador	na	**81**	83	79	75	83	88	86	79	69	87	80	76	na	na	na
Estonia	78	**57**	60	54	42	51	71	61	56	53	62	64	51	59	55	49
Finland	36	**29**	38	20	17	21	44	38	19	15	32	31	22	33	28	25
France	42	**23**	28	18	12	17	35	30	15	12	29	23	20	33	22	11
Georgia	na	**82**	84	80	79	81	87	87	83	76	88	84	71	80	83	80
Germany	50	**19**	21	17	10	12	29	27	11	16	25	17	12	27	17	10
Great Britain	42	**25**	30	19	12	20	33	28	20	21	24	28	17	na	na	na
Greece	na	**24**	29	20	13	24	51	60	27	15	33	24	19	30	24	18
Hungary	85	**88**	89	88	86	87	91	91	86	76	89	87	87	89	88	78
Iceland	30	**12**	17	7	3	11	23	15	13	3	16	12	9	15	11	7
India	94	**71**	71	70	66	74	70	67	75	74	70	67	73	76	72	83
Indonesia	na	**95**	94	96	91	95	97	97	95	93	97	94	94	97	94	89
Iran	na	**94**	94	94	92	96	96	95	95	92	95	95	92	97	93	92
Ireland	52	**37**	39	35	20	26	62	64	26	15	60	34	21	46	38	19
Israel	na	**38**	39	37	32	36	46	61	37	23	51	39	19	51	34	35
Italy	49	**30**	35	26	17	22	44	45	19	16	43	26	19	49	30	18
Japan	61	**30**	33	27	12	18	49	50	30	21	36	26	30	35	27	22
Jordan	na	**98**	99	98	98	98	99	99	99	96	98	100	97	99	97	96
Korea, South	91	**53**	56	50	29	58	69	79	59	41	56	53	49	56	52	34
Latvia	84	**77**	81	74	64	73	86	85	75	70	83	76	70	82	75	64
Lithuania	89	**78**	79	77	61	76	92	92	73	72	89	77	73	81	78	76
Luxembourg	na	**20**	23	18	12	18	29	32	15	14	22	26	15	26	21	12
Macedonia	na	**76**	80	71	66	78	80	89	72	62	87	73	65	72	76	78
Malta	na	**61**	61	61	44	57	76	77	57	39	74	59	51	69	59	37
Mexico	58	**53**	57	49	40	56	66	65	43	29	59	52	44	64	51	33
Moldova	na	**65**	66	63	51	68	73	74	65	57	81	66	49	66	65	43
Montenegro	na	**86**	88	83	81	82	93	93	85	71	93	86	83	92	81	73
Morocco	na	**na**	na	na	na	na	na	na	na	na	na	na	na	na	na	na
Netherlands	20	**7**	9	5	6	5	9	14	5	3	11	5	3	12	7	5
New Zealand	na	**30**	39	22	18	21	42	40	32	17	38	28	21	41	30	18
Nigeria	73	**78**	78	77	78	78	74	75	79	80	79	76	76	76	79	78
Northern Ireland	65	**42**	46	39	31	33	55	52	38	26	49	41	26	56	43	26
Norway	53	**27**	36	19	18	22	41	39	26	18	na	na	na	36	28	9
Pakistan	na	**96**	96	97	94	97	99	98	94	95	99	96	94	97	96	92
Peru	na	**57**	55	58	53	60	59	62	59	50	65	51	49	57	56	59
Philippines	na	**29**	28	30	28	29	32	26	30	32	31	31	24	29	30	24
Poland	81	**60**	65	55	38	59	74	72	50	34	67	55	54	64	57	64
Portugal	67	**43**	43	44	30	41	55	50	35	22	58	42	37	49	42	32
Puerto Rico	na	**50**	55	48	36	46	61	67	56	45	60	52	43	61	51	45
Romania	87	**80**	81	78	70	75	91	92	75	71	88	83	73	86	77	57
Russian Fed.	89	**71**	73	69	56	69	83	80	71	64	77	72	63	73	68	70
Serbia	na	**75**	77	73	60	70	87	86	77	55	84	74	68	81	71	56
Singapore	na	**55**	58	52	48	62	61	58	56	41	59	59	50	58	54	48
Slovakia	na	**24**	23	25	18	21	33	33	22	9	32	26	18	27	21	14
Slovenia	66	**42**	47	37	26	42	53	59	40	18	54	43	25	59	39	33
South Africa	78	**48**	51	43	51	45	46	48	46	60	47	48	47	52	47	30
Spain	46	**17**	18	16	7	10	28	24	10	9	25	12	13	25	16	5
Sweden	45	**9**	12	5	5	5	15	21	5	4	10	12	4	17	10	3
Switzerland	49	**17**	20	15	11	14	25	25	16	13	23	19	11	21	19	8
Taiwan	na	**65**	66	65	52	66	74	70	72	58	68	67	63	66	65	65
Tanzania	na	**94**	95	94	96	93	96	93	97	95	93	96	93	96	95	96
Turkey	85	**85**	84	86	79	89	91	91	80	59	90	88	69	87	86	80
Uganda	na	**91**	92	90	90	92	94	93	90	93	92	94	90	91	92	86
Ukraine	na	**71**	74	68	53	71	82	81	72	65	78	67	65	73	68	69
United States	57	**32**	34	30	28	35	31	45	33	26	36	29	29	38	33	27
Uruguay	na	**46**	49	44	35	38	57	55	33	32	49	47	41	56	46	33
Venezuela	na	**62**	63	60	59	62	66	69	64	47	64	60	62	66	62	52
Vietnam	na	**82**	83	81	83	78	87	82	83	76	80	86	79	90	79	83
Zimbabwe	na	**96**	95	97	95	97	97	98	94	92	98	95	92	98	95	99
Total	63	56	59	53	52	55	61	63	55	46	63	57	50	68	53	36

RANKING	
Country	2000
Egypt	100
Bangladesh	99
Jordan	98
Pakistan	96
Zimbabwe	96
Indonesia	95
Tanzania	94
Iran	94
Algeria	93
China	92
Uganda	91
Azerbaijan	89
Hungary	88
Montenegro	86
Turkey	85
Georgia	82
Vietnam	82
El Salvador	81
Albania	81
Romania	80
Lithuania	78
Nigeria	78
Latvia	77
Macedonia	76
Serbia	75
Bosnia and Herz.	72
Armenia	71
Ukraine	71
India	71
Russian Fed.	71
Croatia	70
Taiwan	65
Moldova	65
Venezuela	62
Colombia	61
Malta	61
Poland	60
Bulgaria	60
Belarus	57
Estonia	57
Peru	57
Brazil	56
Singapore	55
Mexico	53
Dominican Rep.	53
Korea, South	53
Puerto Rico	50
South Africa	48
Uruguay	46
Portugal	43
Northern Ireland	42
Slovenia	42
Argentina	40
Israel	38
Chile	37
Ireland	37
United States	32
Australia	31
Italy	30
Japan	30
New Zealand	30
Philippines	29
Finland	29
Norway	27
Czech Republic	27
Canada	27
Belgium	27
Austria	26
Great Britain	25
Greece	24
Slovakia	24
France	23
Denmark	21
Luxembourg	20
Germany	19
Switzerland	17
Spain	17
Iceland	12
Sweden	9
Netherlands	7
Total	56

F119) JUSTIFIABLE: PROSTITUTION

Please tell me for each of the following statements whether you think it can always be justified, never be justified, or something in between: Prostitution

Never justifiable (%)

(WVS: V209; EVS: o35)

Country	Wave		Gender		Age			Education			Income			Values		
	1990	2000	Male	Female	16-29	30-49	50+	Lower	Middle	Upper	Lower	Middle	Upper	Mat	Mixed	Postm.
Albania	na	**80**	78	82	69	81	88	85	77	75	83	80	77	83	79	71
Algeria	na	**93**	93	93	91	94	96	92	94	93	94	94	92	95	93	93
Argentina	75	**51**	46	57	45	48	62	60	41	32	60	54	40	61	52	41
Armenia	na	**65**	62	68	58	64	78	78	67	53	59	67	74	72	62	41
Australia	na	**29**	26	32	26	22	41	43	29	18	36	29	17	43	31	23
Austria	49	**36**	35	36	28	32	44	47	29	15	44	35	33	56	37	28
Azerbaijan	na	**85**	85	84	80	86	91	90	87	79	90	88	75	87	80	83
Bangladesh	na	**95**	94	96	93	96	99	98	94	88	98	92	97	97	95	87
Belarus	73	**49**	38	57	28	48	66	64	44	39	56	48	35	54	46	25
Belgium	48	**na**	na	na	na	na	na	na	na	na	na	na	na	na	na	na
Bosnia and Herz.	na	**76**	71	80	70	72	85	86	74	73	82	78	66	74	77	70
Brazil	75	**68**	69	67	69	66	70	74	65	59	73	68	63	77	65	63
Bulgaria	72	**na**	na	na	na	na	na	na	na	na	na	na	na	na	na	na
Canada	44	**44**	38	49	40	39	52	60	42	33	50	44	34	45	48	34
Chile	78	**48**	47	50	47	46	54	56	47	37	53	51	36	58	47	34
China	92	**93**	92	93	89	94	92	91	94	93	89	94	96	93	91	97
Colombia	na	**64**	63	66	61	65	71	76	65	56	73	66	57	64	58	57
Croatia	na	**82**	75	88	70	82	90	90	78	73	86	80	84	87	84	72
Czech Republic	43	**45**	34	55	33	34	60	50	42	29	55	46	33	48	44	41
Denmark	45	**na**	na	na	na	na	na	na	na	na	na	na	na	na	na	na
Dominican Rep.	na	**55**	58	52	52	58	73	68	66	49	53	58	45	55	55	48
Egypt	na	**93**	92	94	93	93	92	93	92	93	92	93	94	92	93	94
El Salvador	na	**85**	86	85	81	86	91	91	83	74	92	84	79	na	na	na
Estonia	63	**na**	na	na	na	na	na	na	na	na	na	na	na	na	na	na
Finland	31	**45**	32	56	28	37	60	51	35	41	52	42	37	48	45	43
France	48	**na**	na	na	na	na	na	na	na	na	na	na	na	na	na	na
Georgia	na	**74**	69	77	68	73	81	80	74	68	81	74	62	74	74	68
Germany	53	**35**	30	39	23	31	44	41	30	25	39	32	27	41	34	26
Great Britain	43	**42**	36	48	32	33	54	49	36	27	47	44	34	na	na	na
Greece	na	**41**	34	46	31	44	61	70	46	32	48	40	37	40	43	37
Hungary	78	**na**	na	na	na	na	na	na	na	na	na	na	na	na	na	na
Iceland	54	**50**	35	64	39	45	66	62	44	37	60	47	42	64	48	28
India	84	**74**	73	75	71	75	74	72	76	75	75	75	72	82	71	84
Indonesia	na	**94**	94	94	94	94	95	96	94	93	94	95	93	94	94	89
Iran	na	**95**	95	96	95	95	98	96	96	93	96	97	94	98	94	95
Ireland	61	**58**	51	64	49	51	73	71	52	48	71	57	46	63	59	46
Israel	na	**48**	41	54	43	49	54	64	50	34	57	47	31	52	47	58
Italy	60	**57**	50	64	45	52	69	69	49	45	65	55	47	68	58	49
Japan	71	**64**	53	74	40	64	76	71	68	51	69	63	63	67	64	57
Jordan	na	**98**	99	98	98	98	99	99	99	97	98	99	98	99	98	97
Korea, South	79	**59**	53	65	44	63	67	75	65	48	59	63	55	62	58	44
Latvia	68	**na**	na	na	na	na	na	na	na	na	na	na	na	na	na	na
Lithuania	78	**65**	56	73	44	58	87	90	57	54	84	69	57	71	63	57
Luxembourg	na	**45**	43	48	38	42	55	58	38	40	48	48	31	50	46	35
Macedonia	na	**81**	80	83	77	81	86	92	77	74	88	79	74	80	82	86
Malta	na	**na**	na	na	na	na	na	na	na	na	na	na	na	na	na	na
Mexico	52	**61**	60	62	51	61	74	71	51	39	65	61	53	70	56	52
Moldova	na	**61**	57	64	47	65	68	73	57	56	79	63	45	64	59	48
Montenegro	na	**81**	80	81	73	77	88	89	79	65	85	82	77	87	75	71
Morocco	na	**na**	na	na	na	na	na	na	na	na	na	na	na	na	na	na
Netherlands	21	**na**	na	na	na	na	na	na	na	na	na	na	na	na	na	na
New Zealand	na	**29**	23	33	20	18	43	37	29	19	41	25	18	33	30	15
Nigeria	68	**77**	77	77	76	77	81	75	78	79	76	78	76	78	77	76
Northern Ireland	65	**69**	62	75	63	61	80	79	64	55	79	68	59	81	67	57
Norway	66	**43**	40	46	35	36	58	56	39	37	na	na	na	51	44	30
Pakistan	na	**96**	96	96	95	96	98	99	94	90	100	96	91	97	95	82
Peru	na	**66**	60	72	62	69	69	71	67	62	71	62	63	64	66	68
Philippines	na	**43**	40	47	41	44	45	39	44	47	47	44	38	45	43	34
Poland	76	**na**	na	na	na	na	na	na	na	na	na	na	na	na	na	na
Portugal	68	**na**	na	na	na	na	na	na	na	na	na	na	na	na	na	na
Puerto Rico	na	**na**	na	na	na	na	na	na	na	na	na	na	na	na	na	na
Romania	80	**74**	66	81	62	68	85	89	69	58	85	76	64	81	70	43
Russian Fed.	78	**61**	53	68	39	60	76	76	62	51	71	62	50	66	57	47
Serbia	na	**75**	72	78	60	71	87	82	79	60	81	75	70	81	71	62
Singapore	na	**54**	54	55	51	59	53	57	55	45	59	57	51	56	54	45
Slovakia	na	**na**	na	na	na	na	na	na	na	na	na	na	na	na	na	na
Slovenia	63	**50**	40	57	34	47	63	72	46	23	63	50	29	63	49	38
South Africa	81	**58**	57	59	61	54	61	57	59	55	59	53	57	59	57	49
Spain	50	**30**	27	34	21	26	40	36	25	24	42	25	26	40	29	19
Sweden	66	**na**	na	na	na	na	na	na	na	na	na	na	na	na	na	na
Switzerland	45	**22**	21	22	18	17	30	29	20	21	26	25	14	25	22	14
Taiwan	na	**66**	62	70	60	69	65	67	70	64	65	67	69	67	66	61
Tanzania	na	**93**	93	93	95	90	95	93	93	92	93	94	89	96	93	88
Turkey	83	**na**	na	na	na	na	na	na	na	na	na	na	na	na	na	na
Uganda	na	**78**	79	78	77	78	89	85	75	82	78	80	76	80	77	80
Ukraine	na	**67**	58	75	39	66	84	86	66	60	75	64	61	71	63	70
United States	61	**47**	40	55	47	46	49	55	50	43	52	44	45	45	50	41
Uruguay	na	**44**	43	46	34	33	58	52	34	33	49	42	41	57	44	33
Venezuela	na	**66**	63	68	64	66	69	69	66	60	65	63	68	68	67	57
Vietnam	na	**92**	93	92	92	91	96	92	94	85	96	95	87	96	90	94
Zimbabwe	na	**94**	91	96	91	95	99	97	90	92	95	95	91	95	93	97
Total	62	**64**	61	67	60	63	70	72	62	56	70	65	59	73	62	47

RANKING	
Country	2000
Jordan	98
Pakistan	96
Iran	95
Bangladesh	95
Zimbabwe	94
Indonesia	94
Algeria	93
Tanzania	93
China	93
Egypt	93
Vietnam	92
El Salvador	85
Azerbaijan	85
Croatia	82
Macedonia	81
Montenegro	81
Albania	80
Uganda	78
Nigeria	77
Bosnia and Herz.	76
Serbia	75
India	74
Romania	74
Georgia	74
Northern Ireland	69
Brazil	68
Ukraine	67
Taiwan	66
Peru	66
Venezuela	66
Armenia	65
Lithuania	65
Colombia	64
Japan	64
Russian Fed.	61
Moldova	61
Mexico	61
Korea, South	59
Ireland	58
South Africa	58
Italy	57
Dominican Rep.	55
Singapore	54
Argentina	51
Iceland	50
Slovenia	50
Belarus	49
Chile	48
Israel	48
United States	47
Luxembourg	45
Czech Republic	45
Finland	45
Uruguay	44
Canada	44
Norway	43
Philippines	43
Great Britain	42
Greece	41
Austria	36
Germany	35
Spain	30
Australia	29
New Zealand	29
Switzerland	22
Total	64

F120) JUSTIFIABLE: ABORTION

Please tell me for each of the following statements whether you think it can always be justified, never be justified, or something in between: Abortion.

Never justifiable (%)

(WVS: V210; EVS: V233)

Country	Wave		Gender		Age			Education			Income			Values		
	1990	2000	Male	Female	16-29	30-49	50+	Lower	Middle	Upper	Lower	Middle	Upper	Mat	Mixed	Postm.
Albania	na	**26**	25	27	24	25	30	28	26	23	25	30	24	22	29	23
Algeria	na	**79**	78	80	76	80	84	83	79	76	82	79	74	78	80	78
Argentina	48	**66**	64	67	63	66	68	74	56	47	76	67	54	73	68	55
Armenia	na	**23**	26	20	23	20	28	33	23	18	19	22	28	24	23	18
Australia	na	**24**	22	25	20	20	32	38	22	14	30	22	14	31	25	18
Austria	34	**24**	22	25	17	19	32	28	23	10	28	22	24	32	24	21
Azerbaijan	na	**30**	34	26	39	22	31	44	29	29	27	30	36	29	32	35
Bangladesh	na	**90**	89	90	86	92	96	95	86	82	96	88	86	94	88	76
Belarus	28	**18**	16	19	12	14	26	27	15	13	22	18	8	21	15	7
Belgium	24	**30**	29	31	27	23	39	47	29	19	36	32	21	41	29	21
Bosnia and Herz.	na	**35**	35	35	32	34	40	43	35	27	45	33	30	30	37	32
Brazil	66	**75**	74	76	76	74	76	80	73	64	82	79	67	82	73	67
Bulgaria	29	**20**	21	19	16	16	27	30	16	13	28	20	12	22	20	7
Canada	23	**30**	26	33	25	27	36	46	28	18	36	29	21	40	32	22
Chile	76	**67**	66	68	64	66	72	72	66	60	69	68	60	76	66	54
China	16	**56**	53	59	54	58	53	56	59	29	56	56	55	52	57	58
Colombia	na	**74**	72	77	73	73	81	82	76	59	82	75	63	79	76	75
Croatia	na	**44**	44	44	27	46	52	50	43	28	52	42	42	55	43	34
Czech Republic	9	**14**	13	14	11	10	18	17	10	7	21	12	9	16	13	9
Denmark	na	**13**	10	16	10	11	17	18	4	8	19	11	7	25	13	6
Dominican Rep.	na	**59**	60	59	59	58	90	77	64	55	64	58	47	60	61	55
Egypt	na	**57**	62	51	55	56	59	59	55	54	61	52	55	55	57	59
El Salvador	na	**91**	90	92	89	91	93	94	89	83	96	92	84	na	na	na
Estonia	15	**21**	23	19	20	15	26	27	19	14	26	22	18	24	19	8
Finland	14	**11**	11	12	7	7	17	15	8	6	15	11	8	11	11	15
France	20	**14**	15	14	13	11	19	19	9	8	20	14	9	21	14	5
Georgia	na	**29**	36	24	32	26	32	35	30	23	35	29	21	29	30	36
Germany	21	**27**	26	27	14	20	39	36	19	18	30	27	23	34	26	17
Great Britain	19	**26**	22	29	18	19	34	35	19	11	33	25	15	na	na	na
Greece	na	**18**	18	19	11	18	39	41	21	12	26	18	13	18	19	13
Hungary	27	**33**	32	35	34	24	42	37	27	24	38	33	30	33	34	30
Iceland	12	**12**	11	12	8	9	18	19	9	2	17	8	8	15	12	4
India	39	**65**	66	65	63	66	67	67	67	61	66	67	64	75	61	59
Indonesia	na	**88**	90	86	83	88	91	94	87	85	87	89	88	90	87	86
Iran	na	**77**	77	77	76	75	83	82	75	71	77	76	74	82	72	79
Ireland	53	**51**	49	53	29	44	74	69	44	35	70	49	38	62	49	39
Israel	na	**27**	26	27	26	28	26	41	29	14	34	29	10	38	23	23
Italy	26	**32**	28	36	20	28	42	41	25	25	44	26	24	44	33	22
Japan	29	**15**	16	13	8	13	19	20	15	10	17	15	12	14	15	10
Jordan	na	**85**	86	84	85	83	88	87	82	84	84	85	84	87	84	83
Korea, South	40	**37**	41	32	26	37	48	54	42	28	41	39	31	40	35	31
Latvia	27	**37**	37	36	37	27	45	53	33	28	43	36	31	40	34	33
Lithuania	31	**33**	28	37	19	21	54	65	22	20	53	33	20	39	31	28
Luxembourg	na	**18**	19	17	12	16	24	28	13	10	25	19	10	19	19	11
Macedonia	na	**40**	43	38	44	39	40	56	37	24	48	38	31	38	40	54
Malta	na	**89**	86	92	78	90	95	97	88	77	97	91	82	90	90	76
Mexico	43	**69**	68	71	62	71	77	77	63	52	71	70	64	78	66	59
Moldova	na	**42**	41	42	35	40	50	51	39	37	57	42	30	47	38	23
Montenegro	na	**32**	32	32	21	26	46	45	25	20	33	28	24	41	25	15
Morocco	na	**84**	85	84	80	86	93	89	69	56	87	79	83	89	82	70
Netherlands	13	**15**	15	15	10	13	20	28	12	7	23	12	8	28	16	7
New Zealand	na	**18**	16	20	16	14	23	23	17	12	29	15	11	25	19	8
Nigeria	53	**74**	74	74	73	75	79	75	74	72	73	75	73	77	73	72
Northern Ireland	41	**46**	45	48	40	34	59	58	40	30	54	48	30	52	45	45
Norway	16	**15**	15	15	14	11	20	23	15	6	na	na	na	27	14	4
Pakistan	na	**60**	66	53	61	57	65	57	60	65	58	59	58	60	60	9
Peru	na	**74**	70	77	71	76	75	78	75	68	77	71	71	71	75	72
Philippines	na	**55**	52	59	55	55	57	47	59	60	60	57	48	57	55	50
Poland	43	**44**	42	46	35	39	55	53	36	27	49	42	37	50	40	41
Portugal	28	**36**	32	39	25	32	44	40	27	29	52	32	33	43	34	24
Puerto Rico	na	**74**	71	76	68	67	82	90	77	70	85	73	65	82	74	70
Romania	25	**40**	40	40	34	33	49	54	36	23	52	39	31	45	35	26
Russian Fed.	20	**17**	18	16	14	13	23	30	16	12	24	15	12	18	15	18
Serbia	na	**20**	25	16	19	16	25	28	18	14	27	20	13	21	18	22
Singapore	na	**41**	41	41	37	45	44	47	39	33	47	40	39	40	42	32
Slovakia	na	**25**	22	29	18	20	38	38	21	15	37	25	19	28	23	20
Slovenia	19	**20**	20	19	14	18	26	34	16	6	29	17	10	30	17	17
South Africa	66	**53**	55	50	53	51	57	55	51	49	52	51	55	55	52	45
Spain	33	**28**	24	32	15	19	44	39	17	15	43	22	23	39	26	13
Sweden	15	**5**	6	5	1	5	8	10	4	4	8	5	2	11	6	2
Switzerland	56	**22**	20	25	13	19	31	32	20	20	31	25	14	23	24	14
Taiwan	na	**46**	44	48	39	47	51	53	50	39	52	43	44	48	44	44
Tanzania	na	**90**	90	90	94	88	92	91	92	84	91	91	82	92	91	92
Turkey	40	**64**	68	61	61	65	73	73	57	39	74	65	46	69	64	59
Uganda	na	**76**	78	74	73	75	91	85	71	83	80	75	76	75	77	74
Ukraine	na	**33**	36	31	24	30	41	52	30	30	41	29	28	34	33	29
United States	35	**30**	27	33	26	28	35	41	33	24	36	28	23	31	31	26
Uruguay	na	**48**	43	51	41	37	59	59	33	30	53	48	39	60	48	32
Venezuela	na	**71**	69	73	71	72	72	77	71	66	72	72	70	73	72	69
Vietnam	na	**61**	59	63	67	61	57	69	52	45	56	68	55	58	61	54
Zimbabwe	na	**92**	89	95	90	92	98	96	87	44	96	92	84	94	90	99
Total	31	**44**	44	44	45	42	46	54	40	36	50	44	38	49	42	34

RANKING	
Country	2000
Zimbabwe	92
El Salvador	91
Tanzania	90
Bangladesh	90
Malta	89
Indonesia	88
Jordan	85
Morocco	84
Algeria	79
Iran	77
Uganda	76
Brazil	75
Colombia	74
Nigeria	74
Peru	74
Puerto Rico	74
Venezuela	71
Mexico	69
Chile	67
Argentina	66
India	65
Turkey	64
Vietnam	61
Pakistan	60
Dominican Rep.	59
Egypt	57
China	56
Philippines	55
South Africa	53
Ireland	51
Uruguay	48
Taiwan	46
Northern Ireland	46
Poland	44
Croatia	44
Moldova	42
Singapore	41
Macedonia	40
Romania	40
Korea, South	37
Latvia	37
Portugal	36
Bosnia and Herz.	35
Hungary	33
Lithuania	33
Ukraine	33
Montenegro	32
Italy	32
Belgium	30
Azerbaijan	30
Canada	30
United States	30
Georgia	29
Spain	28
Israel	27
Germany	27
Albania	26
Great Britain	26
Slovakia	25
Austria	24
Australia	24
Armenia	23
Switzerland	22
Estonia	21
Bulgaria	20
Serbia	20
Slovenia	20
Greece	18
New Zealand	18
Luxembourg	18
Belarus	18
Russian Fed.	17
Netherlands	15
Norway	15
Japan	15
France	14
Czech Republic	14
Denmark	13
Iceland	12
Finland	11
Sweden	5
Total	44

F121) JUSTIFIABLE: DIVORCE

Please tell me for each of the following statements whether you think it can always be justified, never be justified, or something in between: Divorce.

Never justifiable (%)

(WVS: V211; EVS: V234)

Country	Wave		Gender		Age			Education			Income			Values		
	1990	2000	Male	Female	16-29	30-49	50+	Lower	Middle	Upper	Lower	Middle	Upper	Mat	Mixed	Postm.
Albania	na	**18**	19	17	17	18	20	19	18	17	16	21	18	16	19	18
Algeria	na	**26**	25	27	22	26	33	35	25	20	32	23	19	27	26	16
Argentina	32	**25**	24	25	19	24	31	32	16	12	30	28	15	37	26	14
Armenia	na	**18**	18	18	16	16	26	31	19	11	12	20	24	21	17	11
Australia	na	**10**	12	8	9	8	13	17	8	6	13	8	6	19	11	6
Austria	19	**11**	12	10	8	8	16	15	8	3	15	9	11	25	10	10
Azerbaijan	na	**27**	29	24	29	24	28	35	27	25	32	29	22	28	24	29
Bangladesh	na	**82**	78	87	80	83	86	88	80	69	88	80	80	86	80	68
Belarus	22	**9**	7	10	5	6	14	12	7	10	11	8	5	8	9	5
Belgium	18	**14**	14	13	10	10	19	24	13	7	18	17	7	21	12	6
Bosnia and Herz.	na	**15**	15	15	9	17	18	26	14	11	21	16	12	13	16	8
Brazil	39	**30**	32	29	29	30	35	38	27	16	37	34	21	39	29	20
Bulgaria	33	**18**	19	18	13	14	25	28	15	9	27	16	11	20	17	21
Canada	15	**11**	11	10	9	8	15	22	8	5	16	8	8	13	12	7
Chile	49	**27**	26	28	23	22	37	36	24	16	34	23	18	38	25	15
China	16	**57**	53	61	48	61	57	64	54	26	57	60	53	54	54	66
Colombia	na	**34**	33	35	30	33	43	53	34	20	47	37	21	41	37	26
Croatia	na	**31**	28	33	16	33	37	36	29	21	36	28	31	32	31	25
Czech Republic	8	**7**	6	8	4	5	10	10	5	2	11	7	3	9	6	5
Denmark	17	**7**	8	7	5	5	10	11	4	2	12	4	4	17	7	1
Dominican Rep.	na	**27**	29	25	27	24	60	47	34	22	37	18	17	22	28	25
Egypt	na	**16**	18	14	15	16	17	16	17	13	18	13	13	16	15	19
El Salvador	na	**57**	58	56	52	58	64	64	53	45	58	60	47	na	na	na
Estonia	12	**11**	11	11	10	8	14	18	10	5	17	11	9	12	10	na
Finland	7	**3**	4	3	2	3	4	4	2	2	5	3	3	3	4	1
France	13	**7**	8	7	5	6	10	10	4	3	9	9	4	12	7	3
Georgia	na	**21**	22	21	21	20	25	27	23	13	27	21	12	20	23	20
Germany	14	**13**	12	14	5	9	21	19	8	8	16	13	7	15	13	11
Great Britain	12	**12**	13	11	6	10	14	13	9	11	16	11	10	na	na	na
Greece	na	**7**	8	6	3	8	14	19	6	5	9	6	5	6	7	5
Hungary	26	**24**	21	28	15	22	32	29	16	15	28	24	22	25	24	34
Iceland	5	**4**	4	4	2	2	8	7	3	na	8	3	2	5	4	1
India	52	**51**	49	54	47	51	55	54	52	45	54	55	46	57	47	47
Indonesia	na	**54**	53	56	41	61	53	61	57	46	55	53	51	56	53	39
Iran	na	**55**	55	55	52	56	62	65	54	42	55	56	50	62	47	46
Ireland	31	**26**	24	26	15	15	46	42	19	13	41	23	16	37	23	19
Israel	na	**12**	14	10	12	11	12	20	12	5	14	13	3	19	10	10
Italy	21	**19**	16	21	8	13	29	28	12	10	30	14	11	31	20	9
Japan	19	**6**	6	5	2	3	9	11	6	2	8	3	5	5	6	3
Jordan	na	**42**	33	51	38	43	50	44	38	44	46	36	47	46	39	39
Korea, South	40	**21**	24	18	10	21	34	46	23	15	26	20	16	22	21	16
Latvia	20	**25**	26	25	20	19	32	45	20	15	29	29	18	30	22	19
Lithuania	25	**20**	17	23	8	13	35	44	11	15	32	25	12	21	20	13
Luxembourg	na	**10**	10	9	6	10	12	18	7	4	11	13	5	11	10	5
Macedonia	na	**36**	37	35	35	36	37	52	32	20	44	35	27	35	35	51
Malta	na	**59**	56	62	41	53	77	76	55	41	69	62	46	65	57	44
Mexico	29	**40**	41	40	29	42	53	51	30	17	50	39	30	49	36	31
Moldova	na	**29**	28	30	18	32	35	42	26	22	45	30	18	34	24	18
Montenegro	na	**9**	9	10	3	6	18	16	6	3	14	9	3	11	8	6
Morocco	na	**44**	40	47	38	46	52	47	37	11	44	39	37	45	43	28
Netherlands	7	**5**	5	4	4	3	6	9	2	3	6	5	2	11	5	1
New Zealand	na	**6**	7	6	1	5	9	8	7	3	11	4	3	10	5	2
Nigeria	44	**55**	51	58	55	53	55	52	57	54	54	58	49	53	55	59
Northern Ireland	28	**24**	22	25	19	17	31	28	23	12	28	28	11	32	22	18
Norway	16	**7**	8	5	5	4	11	10	7	3	na	na	na	13	6	1
Pakistan	na	**67**	68	65	67	65	70	62	70	74	64	67	70	65	69	33
Peru	na	**42**	37	46	37	43	52	49	46	31	49	38	35	42	43	38
Philippines	na	**43**	38	47	43	41	46	39	46	43	46	46	36	47	40	37
Poland	33	**26**	27	25	18	22	37	33	19	15	28	25	22	31	25	18
Portugal	20	**17**	15	19	10	14	24	20	13	7	31	14	16	21	17	6
Puerto Rico	na	**35**	35	35	24	29	45	56	42	28	46	36	25	46	34	30
Romania	25	**33**	31	34	26	25	43	49	26	19	46	30	23	37	28	12
Russian Fed.	18	**11**	12	10	6	9	16	22	10	6	16	10	7	11	10	7
Serbia	na	**13**	15	12	8	10	18	20	12	6	18	15	7	14	13	4
Singapore	na	**31**	31	31	26	35	36	34	31	23	34	26	33	30	32	20
Slovakia	na	**14**	11	16	7	12	20	20	12	4	20	15	9	14	13	10
Slovenia	20	**14**	14	14	10	13	19	26	12	1	23	11	5	20	12	17
South Africa	53	**32**	33	30	30	32	35	31	32	43	30	35	30	36	31	18
Spain	25	**12**	11	13	4	7	21	17	6	6	17	10	10	20	10	3
Sweden	9	**2**	3	1	2	1	3	5	2	1	3	3	na	4	2	na
Switzerland	26	**9**	9	8	5	6	15	16	7	6	14	13	3	11	10	4
Taiwan	na	**33**	31	36	19	33	44	44	37	21	38	32	29	33	33	42
Tanzania	na	**53**	54	53	52	54	57	52	57	53	54	53	47	55	53	57
Turkey	27	**42**	43	41	36	45	55	53	29	20	55	41	23	48	43	34
Uganda	na	**62**	67	58	57	64	77	65	59	81	63	76	62	62	62	63
Ukraine	na	**24**	22	25	15	22	30	40	22	19	31	19	20	26	23	21
United States	20	**8**	9	6	9	7	8	13	10	4	10	7	6	6	8	6
Uruguay	na	**22**	21	23	16	15	30	29	11	17	23	22	19	27	22	13
Venezuela	na	**30**	27	32	25	29	41	39	30	18	31	31	27	32	30	25
Vietnam	na	**50**	48	53	54	49	49	54	49	33	45	62	40	46	51	50
Zimbabwe	na	**74**	69	79	75	72	77	79	68	44	80	77	59	75	72	87
Total	23	26	26	26	25	25	29	34	24	18	31	27	21	31	24	16

RANKING	
Country	2000
Bangladesh	82
Zimbabwe	74
Pakistan	67
Uganda	62
Malta	59
China	57
El Salvador	57
Iran	55
Nigeria	55
Indonesia	54
Tanzania	53
India	51
Vietnam	50
Morocco	44
Philippines	43
Turkey	42
Jordan	42
Peru	42
Mexico	40
Macedonia	36
Puerto Rico	35
Colombia	34
Taiwan	33
Romania	33
South Africa	32
Singapore	31
Croatia	31
Brazil	30
Venezuela	30
Moldova	29
Chile	27
Azerbaijan	27
Dominican Rep.	27
Poland	26
Algeria	26
Ireland	26
Latvia	25
Argentina	25
Hungary	24
Ukraine	24
Northern Ireland	24
Uruguay	22
Georgia	21
Korea, South	21
Lithuania	20
Italy	19
Albania	18
Bulgaria	18
Armenia	18
Portugal	17
Egypt	16
Bosnia and Herz.	15
Slovenia	14
Slovakia	14
Belgium	14
Serbia	13
Germany	13
Great Britain	12
Spain	12
Israel	12
Austria	11
Estonia	11
Russian Fed.	11
Canada	11
Australia	10
Luxembourg	10
Montenegro	9
Switzerland	9
Belarus	9
United States	8
France	7
Denmark	7
Czech Republic	7
Greece	7
Norway	7
New Zealand	6
Japan	6
Netherlands	5
Iceland	4
Finland	3
Sweden	2
Total	26

F122) JUSTIFIABLE: EUTHANASIA

Please tell me for each of the following statements whether you think it can always be justified, never be justified, or something in between: Euthanasia - ending the life of the incurably sick

Never justifiable (%) (WVS: V212; EVS: V235)

Country	Wave		Gender		Age			Education			Income			Values		
	1990	2000	Male	Female	16-29	30-49	50+	Lower	Middle	Upper	Lower	Middle	Upper	Mat	Mixed	Postm.
Albania	na	**47**	46	49	43	47	50	49	44	49	46	48	47	47	47	43
Algeria	na	**86**	85	86	84	86	88	87	88	81	91	84	78	90	83	82
Argentina	61	**49**	45	52	42	50	54	58	37	32	59	47	42	62	47	42
Armenia	na	**39**	39	39	37	37	45	45	39	35	38	34	44	41	38	32
Australia	na	**15**	16	15	11	12	23	24	13	11	22	12	9	17	16	13
Austria	42	**31**	28	33	22	26	40	35	27	27	35	31	31	36	31	29
Azerbaijan	na	**47**	47	47	46	46	49	54	45	49	48	41	52	51	42	29
Bangladesh	na	**97**	96	97	96	97	97	99	96	92	99	96	95	97	96	93
Belarus	40	**20**	17	22	13	19	26	27	18	13	26	18	13	21	18	11
Belgium	23	**12**	12	12	11	8	16	19	10	10	19	11	6	14	12	10
Bosnia and Herz.	na	**43**	43	43	37	42	51	56	42	37	44	45	40	45	43	32
Brazil	71	**61**	59	63	57	65	61	67	58	47	71	61	51	69	58	55
Bulgaria	52	**45**	45	45	40	38	54	60	42	28	58	44	34	52	41	39
Canada	25	**20**	16	23	14	15	28	31	18	12	26	21	11	22	22	14
Chile	68	**45**	42	48	42	40	55	55	41	36	49	44	41	55	44	33
China	24	**53**	51	54	46	53	58	63	49	21	62	54	38	50	50	45
Colombia	na	**45**	43	48	45	43	54	64	48	29	63	49	30	53	49	34
Croatia	na	**45**	40	50	22	47	59	55	40	36	54	45	41	58	43	40
Czech Republic	na	**18**	16	19	11	11	27	21	15	11	25	17	13	21	16	18
Denmark	26	**12**	11	13	8	9	17	14	10	9	16	11	6	21	12	6
Dominican Rep.	na	**53**	52	53	53	51	70	70	60	48	62	53	36	51	49	61
Egypt	na	**78**	77	78	77	78	78	77	78	80	76	78	80	78	78	71
El Salvador	na	**83**	81	85	81	84	83	87	81	73	89	85	74	na	na	na
Estonia	40	**23**	18	27	15	18	32	30	21	18	34	23	17	25	21	8
Finland	14	**18**	16	19	6	12	30	23	11	14	22	16	13	18	18	13
France	24	**12**	11	14	13	10	14	15	10	9	15	13	9	15	12	9
Georgia	na	**57**	55	58	53	55	62	61	58	50	63	57	47	55	58	49
Germany	43	**28**	28	28	21	22	38	36	22	21	32	25	24	29	27	29
Great Britain	23	**21**	20	22	15	16	26	25	16	16	26	21	16	na	na	na
Greece	na	**30**	27	32	23	31	43	49	34	22	35	29	25	30	30	25
Hungary	48	**44**	42	46	39	36	54	50	35	29	47	44	44	48	42	11
Iceland	22	**18**	16	19	12	15	28	26	14	8	22	20	11	22	17	11
India	57	**63**	63	64	62	63	66	64	66	60	67	63	62	69	62	57
Indonesia	na	**84**	83	85	67	85	90	92	86	75	83	84	83	87	82	71
Iran	na	**76**	73	80	73	78	83	83	76	68	78	79	72	83	73	69
Ireland	56	**49**	46	52	32	41	69	62	43	38	63	46	39	58	48	38
Israel	na	**na**	na	na	na	na	na	na	na	na	na	na	na	na	na	na
Italy	47	**40**	38	42	27	35	52	51	32	31	52	39	31	50	41	32
Japan	21	**10**	10	11	3	5	19	20	10	6	13	10	8	10	11	7
Jordan	na	**90**	88	91	87	91	93	91	88	89	93	91	88	92	89	87
Korea, South	na	**24**	26	23	14	24	36	52	27	17	27	27	19	26	23	19
Latvia	48	**30**	27	32	18	25	40	44	27	23	38	30	19	34	28	16
Lithuania	45	**26**	23	28	16	18	40	46	19	18	39	21	17	28	23	22
Luxembourg	na	**19**	22	16	15	17	24	29	14	13	21	21	14	18	21	13
Macedonia	na	**56**	56	56	50	58	58	68	54	43	64	54	47	55	55	63
Malta	na	**69**	64	74	50	67	84	87	64	54	78	67	56	74	69	48
Mexico	38	**59**	59	58	53	58	68	67	54	33	62	55	51	71	54	44
Moldova	na	**50**	47	53	35	53	59	63	48	43	68	50	37	54	49	22
Montenegro	na	**35**	33	38	30	33	41	46	30	26	52	40	25	43	30	16
Morocco	na	**93**	92	94	91	94	96	94	90	83	95	88	92	95	91	92
Netherlands	13	**8**	9	8	6	6	12	15	5	5	15	5	3	16	8	5
New Zealand	na	**12**	11	12	8	9	15	12	14	10	16	9	8	19	11	8
Nigeria	56	**64**	63	65	65	62	65	65	63	64	66	66	57	63	63	72
Northern Ireland	43	**41**	38	43	29	31	55	49	34	30	46	36	26	48	41	33
Norway	32	**18**	15	21	9	14	31	26	14	16	na	na	na	24	18	12
Pakistan	na	**100**	100	100	100	100	100	100	100	100	100	100	100	100	100	100
Peru	na	**na**	na	na	na	na	na	na	na	na	na	na	na	na	na	na
Philippines	na	**50**	47	54	46	51	56	48	50	53	53	52	45	53	49	40
Poland	67	**50**	51	50	38	45	65	61	42	30	55	50	40	53	49	49
Portugal	53	**41**	40	43	34	36	50	46	34	28	55	36	38	49	38	34
Puerto Rico	na	**68**	62	72	55	64	78	83	72	64	74	70	62	69	69	70
Romania	54	**56**	54	58	39	51	71	70	52	45	66	63	47	63	51	41
Russian Fed.	54	**23**	21	25	15	20	32	38	22	17	29	22	18	24	21	20
Serbia	na	**35**	34	37	21	33	45	47	33	26	46	35	29	39	33	27
Singapore	na	**40**	40	41	36	44	46	51	38	22	51	40	35	46	39	30
Slovakia	na	**25**	22	27	18	22	34	34	22	16	31	25	21	26	23	35
Slovenia	51	**28**	28	27	17	26	38	41	25	14	36	27	20	33	28	21
South Africa	61	**40**	40	41	39	40	46	42	38	35	38	44	37	43	39	31
Spain	45	**24**	20	27	12	15	38	33	14	14	35	21	18	36	21	10
Sweden	21	**10**	10	11	6	9	14	17	7	10	12	10	8	7	11	8
Switzerland	32	**15**	13	16	11	10	22	25	11	18	20	15	13	14	16	9
Taiwan	na	**27**	23	30	15	28	31	37	30	16	33	25	22	25	28	28
Tanzania	na	**89**	88	90	91	87	92	90	88	86	92	88	83	90	90	88
Turkey	70	**65**	62	69	58	71	75	77	53	36	75	67	45	65	66	61
Uganda	na	**83**	89	77	78	88	81	85	81	90	89	82	86	82	84	82
Ukraine	na	**30**	26	33	13	30	40	44	30	23	33	29	28	29	27	36
United States	34	**24**	21	27	19	23	30	33	22	22	29	21	19	23	26	20
Uruguay	na	**40**	39	41	29	33	50	51	25	24	47	40	31	50	41	28
Venezuela	na	**55**	53	58	51	58	60	63	56	44	61	54	53	57	57	46
Vietnam	na	**51**	47	55	52	53	47	51	54	28	43	55	50	51	50	55
Zimbabwe	na	**90**	86	93	89	91	92	93	86	82	93	90	82	91	89	93
Total	42	**44**	43	45	43	42	47	54	40	36	50	44	38	52	42	32

RANKING	
Country	2000
Pakistan	100
Bangladesh	97
Morocco	93
Zimbabwe	90
Jordan	90
Tanzania	89
Algeria	86
Indonesia	84
El Salvador	83
Uganda	83
Egypt	78
Iran	76
Malta	69
Puerto Rico	68
Turkey	65
Nigeria	64
India	63
Brazil	61
Mexico	59
Georgia	57
Romania	56
Macedonia	56
Venezuela	55
China	53
Dominican Rep.	53
Vietnam	51
Poland	50
Philippines	50
Moldova	50
Argentina	49
Ireland	49
Albania	47
Azerbaijan	47
Colombia	45
Chile	45
Croatia	45
Bulgaria	45
Hungary	44
Bosnia and Herz.	43
Portugal	41
Northern Ireland	41
Singapore	40
South Africa	40
Italy	40
Uruguay	40
Armenia	39
Serbia	35
Montenegro	35
Austria	31
Ukraine	30
Latvia	30
Greece	30
Germany	28
Slovenia	28
Taiwan	27
Lithuania	26
Slovakia	25
Korea, South	24
United States	24
Spain	24
Estonia	23
Russian Fed.	23
Great Britain	21
Canada	20
Belarus	20
Luxembourg	19
Norway	18
Iceland	18
Czech Republic	18
Finland	18
Australia	15
Switzerland	15
France	12
Denmark	12
Belgium	12
New Zealand	12
Japan	10
Sweden	10
Netherlands	8
Total	44

F123) JUSTIFIABLE: SUICIDE

Please tell me for each of the following statements whether you think it can always be justified, never be justified, or something in between: Suicide

Never justifiable (%)

(WVS: V213; EVS: V236)

Country	Wave		Gender		Age			Education			Income			Values		
	1990	2000	Male	Female	16-29	30-49	50+	Lower	Middle	Upper	Lower	Middle	Upper	Mat	Mixed	Postm.
Albania	na	68	67	69	66	69	69	67	69	70	62	73	70	68	68	72
Algeria	na	94	94	94	93	94	95	93	94	94	95	93	91	95	93	96
Argentina	83	78	76	79	71	79	82	81	76	66	84	77	73	81	78	74
Armenia	na	60	61	59	52	64	66	68	59	62	58	58	63	58	63	51
Australia	na	48	49	46	41	46	55	59	50	36	54	46	40	57	51	40
Austria	50	47	44	49	35	42	57	59	39	25	56	47	41	58	47	42
Azerbaijan	na	73	75	71	65	77	77	76	74	70	75	67	71	76	68	55
Bangladesh	na	99	99	100	99	100	100	100	100	98	100	99	100	99	99	100
Belarus	64	50	42	56	37	53	57	56	47	49	59	46	41	54	47	36
Belgium	51	45	45	44	35	37	57	56	48	32	52	49	36	51	47	29
Bosnia and Herz.	na	80	79	81	78	78	86	88	80	76	83	82	75	80	82	64
Brazil	90	87	88	87	87	88	89	87	87	88	88	90	85	87	87	87
Bulgaria	68	71	70	71	61	67	78	80	67	63	78	66	66	74	68	91
Canada	53	52	49	54	44	50	59	68	52	38	57	55	43	60	52	48
Chile	82	71	71	72	70	70	75	76	72	61	73	72	69	79	69	65
China	55	83	83	83	76	86	82	83	85	63	80	88	82	82	83	81
Colombia	na	82	81	83	79	83	88	89	83	76	87	83	78	82	79	72
Croatia	na	84	81	86	75	83	90	89	83	74	89	84	82	85	84	84
Czech Republic	na	48	46	51	36	44	59	56	42	33	56	53	37	57	46	43
Denmark	60	51	54	48	47	48	57	61	46	34	55	51	42	63	52	42
Dominican Rep.	na	76	77	76	73	80	100	90	81	73	78	76	70	76	76	74
Egypt	na	95	96	94	92	96	96	95	93	97	94	93	96	96	93	93
El Salvador	na	94	94	94	91	96	96	97	91	90	98	92	93	na	na	na
Estonia	59	62	58	64	53	60	68	60	63	60	62	64	61	62	62	51
Finland	33	41	38	44	25	35	56	48	31	34	43	43	36	42	42	38
France	34	26	27	26	24	26	28	30	22	21	28	29	24	34	25	18
Georgia	na	79	77	80	77	78	82	76	80	76	82	78	74	77	80	75
Germany	56	54	51	56	40	51	63	62	44	57	58	52	47	64	52	43
Great Britain	40	39	39	40	31	39	43	47	34	26	39	45	32	na	na	na
Greece	na	53	51	55	47	57	64	70	58	47	62	50	47	55	56	48
Hungary	73	81	81	80	78	79	84	83	78	70	79	82	80	81	81	72
Iceland	57	63	61	65	54	62	74	72	63	46	66	65	55	67	64	52
India	82	72	74	70	69	74	72	70	74	76	70	72	73	77	72	80
Indonesia	na	97	97	98	97	96	99	100	97	97	98	96	99	98	97	93
Iran	na	95	94	95	93	96	97	96	95	91	94	95	94	97	93	92
Ireland	63	69	67	70	57	67	80	80	67	53	78	63	60	74	68	63
Israel	na	na	na	na	na	na	na	na	na	na	na	na	na	na	na	na
Italy	70	62	62	63	52	59	71	72	57	49	71	63	54	73	63	56
Japan	58	48	45	51	37	47	55	59	52	35	54	52	40	54	46	40
Jordan	na	97	99	96	95	98	99	97	97	98	97	98	97	98	97	91
Korea, South	66	51	52	50	35	53	63	70	56	41	56	51	45	51	52	37
Latvia	64	76	72	78	70	76	78	78	76	69	78	77	74	76	76	78
Lithuania	70	76	69	81	67	74	84	89	71	71	86	72	70	79	74	81
Luxembourg	na	38	38	39	30	35	47	50	35	21	47	39	25	42	40	24
Macedonia	na	83	84	83	80	84	84	90	81	79	87	81	81	82	84	82
Malta	na	93	92	95	88	95	96	96	94	82	97	93	89	95	94	79
Mexico	51	82	82	83	76	84	88	87	79	74	82	82	78	86	80	76
Moldova	na	67	63	71	56	71	72	73	65	66	81	69	54	71	66	43
Montenegro	na	53	51	55	45	50	61	60	50	41	70	51	44	60	47	46
Morocco	na	98	98	99	98	99	99	98	98	98	99	98	97	99	98	99
Netherlands	32	28	27	28	26	21	35	43	28	13	36	25	17	40	29	18
New Zealand	na	47	46	48	35	44	54	55	53	34	51	47	42	55	45	41
Nigeria	74	76	75	77	75	78	75	74	77	78	78	77	72	76	76	79
Northern Ireland	58	68	65	71	53	62	81	79	63	50	78	67	54	78	67	57
Norway	58	52	57	48	43	51	61	68	51	38	na	na	na	65	53	34
Pakistan	na	97	96	97	95	97	98	99	94	92	99	96	94	97	96	83
Peru	na	75	72	78	70	78	79	76	76	73	78	72	75	68	78	73
Philippines	na	57	55	60	55	58	59	52	58	63	60	59	52	60	57	45
Poland	75	64	63	65	47	63	74	72	54	48	66	63	57	67	60	65
Portugal	72	63	58	67	63	60	66	66	55	61	71	55	56	66	60	59
Puerto Rico	na	90	89	92	79	93	94	92	91	90	95	88	88	92	92	89
Romania	77	87	85	90	82	86	91	92	86	83	90	87	86	89	87	76
Russian Fed.	68	67	65	69	58	66	73	73	68	61	73	66	63	69	65	63
Serbia	na	73	72	75	65	71	79	75	75	69	78	74	70	74	73	69
Singapore	na	69	69	68	61	77	73	73	69	55	73	70	66	68	70	57
Slovakia	na	37	36	38	28	31	51	46	34	24	45	39	31	39	34	46
Slovenia	59	47	48	46	32	47	57	59	45	31	56	52	31	59	46	39
South Africa	78	65	67	63	70	62	62	61	72	49	54	72	70	64	68	50
Spain	72	52	47	56	42	45	64	61	45	37	61	49	44	64	50	38
Sweden	47	29	31	27	25	32	28	41	29	19	28	33	25	31	30	23
Switzerland	58	38	38	38	33	37	43	48	37	28	45	37	33	40	39	35
Taiwan	na	63	63	63	59	61	71	69	68	56	69	61	59	65	62	50
Tanzania	na	96	97	95	96	95	97	95	96	96	95	96	96	97	96	96
Turkey	81	90	89	90	86	93	93	92	87	82	91	90	85	91	91	87
Uganda	na	93	95	92	92	95	93	94	93	95	96	92	95	92	93	96
Ukraine	na	73	70	76	62	72	81	82	73	70	76	69	76	76	71	75
United States	62	57	55	59	57	57	57	68	62	50	64	55	51	58	60	51
Uruguay	na	71	70	71	61	68	78	77	63	56	74	71	66	78	71	61
Venezuela	na	80	78	81	78	82	80	79	80	80	77	78	84	75	81	82
Vietnam	na	86	86	86	82	87	87	86	86	79	82	90	83	84	88	87
Zimbabwe	na	93	91	95	91	95	94	95	90	100	95	92	87	93	92	98
Total	62	68	68	69	66	68	71	75	67	61	72	69	64	74	68	57

RANKING

Country	2000
Bangladesh	99
Morocco	98
Indonesia	97
Jordan	97
Pakistan	97
Tanzania	96
Egypt	95
Iran	95
El Salvador	94
Algeria	94
Malta	93
Uganda	93
Zimbabwe	93
Puerto Rico	90
Turkey	90
Brazil	87
Romania	87
Vietnam	86
Croatia	84
Macedonia	83
China	83
Mexico	82
Colombia	82
Hungary	81
Bosnia and Herz.	80
Venezuela	80
Georgia	79
Argentina	78
Nigeria	76
Dominican Rep.	76
Lithuania	76
Latvia	76
Peru	75
Ukraine	73
Serbia	73
Azerbaijan	73
India	72
Chile	71
Uruguay	71
Bulgaria	71
Ireland	69
Singapore	69
Albania	68
Northern Ireland	68
Moldova	67
Russian Fed.	67
South Africa	65
Poland	64
Iceland	63
Taiwan	63
Portugal	63
Italy	62
Estonia	62
Armenia	60
Philippines	57
United States	57
Germany	54
Greece	53
Montenegro	53
Norway	52
Canada	52
Spain	52
Denmark	51
Korea, South	51
Belarus	50
Czech Republic	48
Japan	48
Australia	48
Austria	47
New Zealand	47
Slovenia	47
Belgium	45
Finland	41
Great Britain	39
Luxembourg	38
Switzerland	38
Slovakia	37
Sweden	29
Netherlands	28
France	26
Total	68

F125_1) JUSTIFIABLE: JOYRIDING

Please tell me for each of the following statements whether you think it can always be justified, never be justified, or something in between: Taking and driving away a car belonging to someone else (joyriding)

Never justifiable (%) (EVS: V227)

Country	Wave 1990	Wave 2000	Gender Male	Gender Female	Age 16-29	Age 30-49	Age 50+	Education Lower	Education Middle	Education Upper	Income Lower	Income Middle	Income Upper	Values Mat	Values Mixed	Values Postm.
Albania	na	**na**	na	na	na	na	na	na	na	na	na	na	na	na	na	na
Algeria	na	**na**	na	na	na	na	na	na	na	na	na	na	na	na	na	na
Argentina	95	**na**	na	na	na	na	na	na	na	na	na	na	na	na	na	na
Armenia	na	**na**	na	na	na	na	na	na	na	na	na	na	na	na	na	na
Australia	na	**na**	na	na	na	na	na	na	na	na	na	na	na	na	na	na
Austria	94	**92**	90	93	87	92	94	93	91	90	88	93	92	90	93	89
Azerbaijan	na	**na**	na	na	na	na	na	na	na	na	na	na	na	na	na	na
Bangladesh	na	**na**	na	na	na	na	na	na	na	na	na	na	na	na	na	na
Belarus	75	**67**	60	72	55	67	75	72	63	72	70	66	61	70	65	52
Belgium	83	**93**	92	94	84	94	95	93	93	93	93	93	93	94	93	90
Bosnia and Herz.	na	**na**	na	na	na	na	na	na	na	na	na	na	na	na	na	na
Brazil	90	**na**	na	na	na	na	na	na	na	na	na	na	na	na	na	na
Bulgaria	86	**90**	90	91	82	89	95	95	88	87	92	93	86	92	89	96
Canada	83	**na**	na	na	na	na	na	na	na	na	na	na	na	na	na	na
Chile	88	**na**	na	na	na	na	na	na	na	na	na	na	na	na	na	na
China	85	**na**	na	na	na	na	na	na	na	na	na	na	na	na	na	na
Colombia	na	**na**	na	na	na	na	na	na	na	na	na	na	na	na	na	na
Croatia	na	**91**	91	92	89	90	94	95	89	88	93	93	90	91	92	92
Czech Republic	na	**67**	65	69	54	62	78	66	67	66	75	66	59	69	65	63
Denmark	96	**97**	97	96	95	96	97	97	99	95	96	96	97	96	97	95
Dominican Rep.	na	**na**	na	na	na	na	na	na	na	na	na	na	na	na	na	na
Egypt	na	**na**	na	na	na	na	na	na	na	na	na	na	na	na	na	na
El Salvador	na	**na**	na	na	na	na	na	na	na	na	na	na	na	na	na	na
Estonia	93	**83**	80	85	79	82	86	78	85	88	83	84	85	85	82	80
Finland	78	**82**	82	83	66	82	91	86	75	81	80	85	82	85	82	76
France	84	**86**	86	86	76	87	90	87	85	83	84	85	89	88	87	80
Georgia	na	**na**	na	na	na	na	na	na	na	na	na	na	na	na	na	na
Germany	93	**88**	88	88	80	90	89	88	87	91	86	86	84	93	87	83
Great Britain	89	**89**	86	92	75	92	94	89	89	85	86	91	92	na	na	na
Greece	na	**74**	73	75	70	76	83	88	76	70	80	73	70	75	76	67
Hungary	85	**93**	92	94	88	93	95	91	96	96	91	94	93	93	92	87
Iceland	72	**75**	73	77	64	76	84	84	73	61	77	74	73	85	74	61
India	84	**na**	na	na	na	na	na	na	na	na	na	na	na	na	na	na
Indonesia	na	**na**	na	na	na	na	na	na	na	na	na	na	na	na	na	na
Iran	na	**na**	na	na	na	na	na	na	na	na	na	na	na	na	na	na
Ireland	95	**96**	96	96	94	96	97	97	95	96	96	96	95	96	96	93
Israel	na	**na**	na	na	na	na	na	na	na	na	na	na	na	na	na	na
Italy	83	**80**	78	82	69	79	87	83	78	79	85	78	78	78	82	78
Japan	91	**na**	na	na	na	na	na	na	na	na	na	na	na	na	na	na
Jordan	na	**na**	na	na	na	na	na	na	na	na	na	na	na	na	na	na
Korea, South	83	**na**	na	na	na	na	na	na	na	na	na	na	na	na	na	na
Latvia	92	**92**	92	92	84	94	94	90	92	94	92	93	92	92	93	83
Lithuania	94	**93**	92	94	88	94	97	97	92	92	95	96	93	96	93	94
Luxembourg	na	**77**	74	80	64	81	82	79	75	79	70	83	86	76	78	77
Macedonia	na	**na**	na	na	na	na	na	na	na	na	na	na	na	na	na	na
Malta	na	**93**	91	96	89	96	94	95	93	91	95	94	91	94	94	87
Mexico	56	**na**	na	na	na	na	na	na	na	na	na	na	na	na	na	na
Moldova	na	**na**	na	na	na	na	na	na	na	na	na	na	na	na	na	na
Montenegro	na	**na**	na	na	na	na	na	na	na	na	na	na	na	na	na	na
Morocco	na	**na**	na	na	na	na	na	na	na	na	na	na	na	na	na	na
Netherlands	80	**82**	79	85	76	81	87	84	82	81	83	83	79	85	83	78
New Zealand	na	**na**	na	na	na	na	na	na	na	na	na	na	na	na	na	na
Nigeria	63	**na**	na	na	na	na	na	na	na	na	na	na	na	na	na	na
Northern Ireland	98	**93**	93	93	90	92	97	94	92	93	94	97	96	97	93	85
Norway	89	**na**	na	na	na	na	na	na	na	na	na	na	na	na	na	na
Pakistan	na	**na**	na	na	na	na	na	na	na	na	na	na	na	na	na	na
Peru	na	**na**	na	na	na	na	na	na	na	na	na	na	na	na	na	na
Philippines	na	**na**	na	na	na	na	na	na	na	na	na	na	na	na	na	na
Poland	na	**91**	91	90	86	91	93	89	91	94	91	90	90	89	91	94
Portugal	87	**79**	76	81	80	73	83	80	75	81	84	72	78	81	78	75
Puerto Rico	na	**na**	na	na	na	na	na	na	na	na	na	na	na	na	na	na
Romania	87	**93**	92	94	89	93	94	94	91	95	94	91	94	94	94	85
Russian Fed.	93	**85**	84	86	76	86	91	90	85	85	86	86	83	85	86	89
Serbia	na	**na**	na	na	na	na	na	na	na	na	na	na	na	na	na	na
Singapore	na	**na**	na	na	na	na	na	na	na	na	na	na	na	na	na	na
Slovakia	na	**42**	40	44	35	42	49	43	41	47	43	41	46	42	43	39
Slovenia	90	**78**	75	81	67	80	84	80	77	78	80	82	77	80	78	78
South Africa	na	**na**	na	na	na	na	na	na	na	na	na	na	na	na	na	na
Spain	84	**71**	69	74	64	68	78	78	67	64	77	69	67	76	72	65
Sweden	97	**87**	86	89	81	88	90	93	86	85	85	90	88	88	90	79
Switzerland	85	**na**	na	na	na	na	na	na	na	na	na	na	na	na	na	na
Taiwan	na	**na**	na	na	na	na	na	na	na	na	na	na	na	na	na	na
Tanzania	na	**na**	na	na	na	na	na	na	na	na	na	na	na	na	na	na
Turkey	88	**92**	91	93	91	93	92	90	94	96	89	94	93	91	93	94
Uganda	na	**na**	na	na	na	na	na	na	na	na	na	na	na	na	na	na
Ukraine	na	**82**	80	84	72	84	87	87	81	83	85	80	81	84	81	83
United States	88	**na**	na	na	na	na	na	na	na	na	na	na	na	na	na	na
Uruguay	na	**na**	na	na	na	na	na	na	na	na	na	na	na	na	na	na
Venezuela	na	**na**	na	na	na	na	na	na	na	na	na	na	na	na	na	na
Vietnam	na	**na**	na	na	na	na	na	na	na	na	na	na	na	na	na	na
Zimbabwe	na	**na**	na	na	na	na	na	na	na	na	na	na	na	na	na	na
Total	86	**84**	83	85	76	84	89	86	82	84	85	84	84	85	85	81

RANKING

Country	2000
Denmark	97
Ireland	96
Lithuania	93
Malta	93
Romania	93
Northern Ireland	93
Hungary	93
Belgium	93
Latvia	92
Turkey	92
Austria	92
Croatia	91
Poland	91
Bulgaria	90
Great Britain	89
Germany	88
Sweden	87
France	86
Russian Fed.	85
Estonia	83
Finland	82
Ukraine	82
Netherlands	82
Italy	80
Portugal	79
Slovenia	78
Luxembourg	77
Iceland	75
Greece	74
Spain	71
Belarus	67
Czech Republic	67
Slovakia	42
Total	84

F126_1) JUSTIFIABLE: TAKING SOFT DRUGS

Please tell me for each of the following statements whether you think it can always be justified, never be justified, or something in between: Taking the drug marijuana or hashish

Never justifiable (%)

(EVS: V228)

Country	Wave		Gender		Age			Education			Income			Values		
	1990	2000	Male	Female	16-29	30-49	50+	Lower	Middle	Upper	Lower	Middle	Upper	Mat	Mixed	Postm.
Albania	na	**na**	na	na	na	na	na	na	na	na	na	na	na	na	na	na
Algeria	na	**na**	na	na	na	na	na	na	na	na	na	na	na	na	na	na
Argentina	95	**na**	na	na	na	na	na	na	na	na	na	na	na	na	na	na
Armenia	na	**na**	na	na	na	na	na	na	na	na	na	na	na	na	na	na
Australia	na	**na**	na	na	na	na	na	na	na	na	na	na	na	na	na	na
Austria	86	**75**	73	77	57	73	87	85	70	52	77	77	74	85	81	62
Azerbaijan	na	**na**	na	na	na	na	na	na	na	na	na	na	na	na	na	na
Bangladesh	na	**na**	na	na	na	na	na	na	na	na	na	na	na	na	na	na
Belarus	85	**76**	71	80	64	75	87	84	72	77	80	76	68	79	74	71
Belgium	85	**80**	77	84	66	76	91	90	82	71	86	83	75	89	83	63
Bosnia and Herz.	na	**na**	na	na	na	na	na	na	na	na	na	na	na	na	na	na
Brazil	91	**na**	na	na	na	na	na	na	na	na	na	na	na	na	na	na
Bulgaria	88	**84**	84	85	69	84	92	91	81	81	92	86	77	86	83	93
Canada	65	**na**	na	na	na	na	na	na	na	na	na	na	na	na	na	na
Chile	90	**na**	na	na	na	na	na	na	na	na	na	na	na	na	na	na
China	96	**na**	na	na	na	na	na	na	na	na	na	na	na	na	na	na
Colombia	na	**na**	na	na	na	na	na	na	na	na	na	na	na	na	na	na
Croatia	na	**87**	82	92	74	89	95	94	83	82	93	88	83	94	88	82
Czech Republic	77	**77**	75	79	58	75	88	80	75	67	85	79	67	85	75	67
Denmark	73	**62**	57	67	42	55	82	75	46	44	70	59	52	74	66	43
Dominican Rep.	na	**na**	na	na	na	na	na	na	na	na	na	na	na	na	na	na
Egypt	na	**na**	na	na	na	na	na	na	na	na	na	na	na	na	na	na
El Salvador	na	**na**	na	na	na	na	na	na	na	na	na	na	na	na	na	na
Estonia	89	**81**	76	86	69	82	88	80	83	81	83	86	79	85	79	77
Finland	79	**79**	76	82	54	78	94	85	71	72	77	82	78	84	79	63
France	83	**69**	67	72	55	63	82	80	61	50	73	71	66	81	70	53
Georgia	na	**na**	na	na	na	na	na	na	na	na	na	na	na	na	na	na
Germany	95	**68**	68	69	48	65	80	75	61	70	71	69	64	80	67	54
Great Britain	77	**52**	48	56	28	46	69	63	45	32	59	50	44	na	na	na
Greece	na	**51**	45	55	37	56	77	81	59	39	58	50	44	57	53	41
Hungary	90	**91**	89	92	84	88	97	93	89	85	94	89	91	93	89	81
Iceland	80	**72**	67	78	52	72	91	82	66	63	73	76	66	78	72	58
India	91	**na**	na	na	na	na	na	na	na	na	na	na	na	na	na	na
Indonesia	na	**na**	na	na	na	na	na	na	na	na	na	na	na	na	na	na
Iran	na	**na**	na	na	na	na	na	na	na	na	na	na	na	na	na	na
Ireland	88	**72**	68	76	51	70	89	87	69	55	86	70	61	80	72	61
Israel	na	**na**	na	na	na	na	na	na	na	na	na	na	na	na	na	na
Italy	85	**71**	66	76	50	67	87	83	64	54	81	71	59	84	73	62
Japan	92	**na**	na	na	na	na	na	na	na	na	na	na	na	na	na	na
Jordan	na	**na**	na	na	na	na	na	na	na	na	na	na	na	na	na	na
Korea, South	94	**na**	na	na	na	na	na	na	na	na	na	na	na	na	na	na
Latvia	92	**93**	91	94	78	95	96	93	92	93	95	92	91	94	93	83
Lithuania	94	**88**	86	89	78	89	93	94	85	88	92	89	85	91	86	90
Luxembourg	na	**67**	66	68	52	64	80	76	64	59	62	76	63	71	71	47
Macedonia	na	**na**	na	na	na	na	na	na	na	na	na	na	na	na	na	na
Malta	na	**96**	95	96	90	98	98	97	96	91	97	97	93	98	95	90
Mexico	69	**na**	na	na	na	na	na	na	na	na	na	na	na	na	na	na
Moldova	na	**na**	na	na	na	na	na	na	na	na	na	na	na	na	na	na
Montenegro	na	**na**	na	na	na	na	na	na	na	na	na	na	na	na	na	na
Morocco	na	**na**	na	na	na	na	na	na	na	na	na	na	na	na	na	na
Netherlands	66	**47**	42	51	31	39	63	69	45	27	53	48	35	69	49	31
New Zealand	na	**na**	na	na	na	na	na	na	na	na	na	na	na	na	na	na
Nigeria	71	**na**	na	na	na	na	na	na	na	na	na	na	na	na	na	na
Northern Ireland	91	**69**	64	74	54	62	83	81	61	53	79	68	55	80	70	49
Norway	91	**na**	na	na	na	na	na	na	na	na	na	na	na	na	na	na
Pakistan	na	**na**	na	na	na	na	na	na	na	na	na	na	na	na	na	na
Peru	na	**na**	na	na	na	na	na	na	na	na	na	na	na	na	na	na
Philippines	na	**na**	na	na	na	na	na	na	na	na	na	na	na	na	na	na
Poland	91	**84**	81	86	73	84	91	88	80	76	87	84	75	86	83	78
Portugal	82	**70**	64	75	54	67	82	77	55	60	84	67	58	73	71	52
Puerto Rico	na	**na**	na	na	na	na	na	na	na	na	na	na	na	na	na	na
Romania	91	**95**	94	95	90	96	97	96	95	94	96	94	95	96	95	89
Russian Fed.	94	**88**	85	91	74	90	95	93	88	85	90	90	84	90	87	87
Serbia	na	**na**	na	na	na	na	na	na	na	na	na	na	na	na	na	na
Singapore	na	**na**	na	na	na	na	na	na	na	na	na	na	na	na	na	na
Slovakia	na	**51**	47	55	39	52	60	56	50	44	54	53	50	55	50	47
Slovenia	88	**68**	63	72	41	72	83	79	65	57	80	75	53	80	66	60
South Africa	84	**na**	na	na	na	na	na	na	na	na	na	na	na	na	na	na
Spain	82	**66**	61	72	46	60	83	82	54	53	73	66	50	83	66	47
Sweden	93	**72**	70	75	58	70	83	88	72	60	69	79	69	81	76	59
Switzerland	79	**na**	na	na	na	na	na	na	na	na	na	na	na	na	na	na
Taiwan	na	**na**	na	na	na	na	na	na	na	na	na	na	na	na	na	na
Tanzania	na	**na**	na	na	na	na	na	na	na	na	na	na	na	na	na	na
Turkey	93	**93**	92	95	91	96	94	93	95	92	91	95	94	94	95	94
Uganda	na	**na**	na	na	na	na	na	na	na	na	na	na	na	na	na	na
Ukraine	na	**87**	83	90	73	89	93	90	87	86	91	84	87	89	86	86
United States	74	**na**	na	na	na	na	na	na	na	na	na	na	na	na	na	na
Uruguay	na	**na**	na	na	na	na	na	na	na	na	na	na	na	na	na	na
Venezuela	na	**na**	na	na	na	na	na	na	na	na	na	na	na	na	na	na
Vietnam	na	**na**	na	na	na	na	na	na	na	na	na	na	na	na	na	na
Zimbabwe	na	**na**	na	na	na	na	na	na	na	na	na	na	na	na	na	na
Total	85	75	72	78	59	73	86	82	73	65	80	76	71	84	76	60

RANKING

Country	2000
Malta	96
Romania	95
Turkey	93
Latvia	93
Hungary	91
Russian Fed.	88
Lithuania	88
Croatia	87
Ukraine	87
Bulgaria	84
Poland	84
Estonia	81
Belgium	80
Finland	79
Czech Republic	77
Belarus	76
Austria	75
Iceland	72
Sweden	72
Ireland	72
Italy	71
Portugal	70
France	69
Northern Ireland	69
Germany	68
Slovenia	68
Luxembourg	67
Spain	66
Denmark	62
Great Britain	52
Slovakia	51
Greece	51
Netherlands	47
Total	75

F127_1) JUSTIFIABLE: LYING

Please tell me for each of the following statements whether you think it can always be justified, never be justified, or something in between: Lying in your own interest

(EVS: V229)

Never justifiable (%)

Country	Wave		Gender		Age			Education			Income			Values		
	1990	2000	Male	Female	16-29	30-49	50+	Lower	Middle	Upper	Lower	Middle	Upper	Mat	Mixed	Postm.
Albania	na	**na**	na	na	na	na	na	na	na	na	na	na	na	na	na	na
Algeria	na	**na**	na	na	na	na	na	na	na	na	na	na	na	na	na	na
Argentina	65	**na**	na	na	na	na	na	na	na	na	na	na	na	na	na	na
Armenia	na	**na**	na	na	na	na	na	na	na	na	na	na	na	na	na	na
Australia	na	**na**	na	na	na	na	na	na	na	na	na	na	na	na	na	na
Austria	39	**33**	30	36	28	30	39	37	31	25	39	32	29	49	35	26
Azerbaijan	na	**na**	na	na	na	na	na	na	na	na	na	na	na	na	na	na
Bangladesh	na	**na**	na	na	na	na	na	na	na	na	na	na	na	na	na	na
Belarus	47	**20**	16	22	10	17	30	29	16	18	26	16	16	21	19	11
Belgium	30	**31**	30	32	16	30	39	36	30	28	36	36	24	33	30	31
Bosnia and Herz.	na	**na**	na	na	na	na	na	na	na	na	na	na	na	na	na	na
Brazil	63	**na**	na	na	na	na	na	na	na	na	na	na	na	na	na	na
Bulgaria	70	**80**	80	79	64	78	88	88	75	76	88	77	71	80	78	83
Canada	46	**na**	na	na	na	na	na	na	na	na	na	na	na	na	na	na
Chile	64	**na**	na	na	na	na	na	na	na	na	na	na	na	na	na	na
China	34	**na**	na	na	na	na	na	na	na	na	na	na	na	na	na	na
Colombia	na	**na**	na	na	na	na	na	na	na	na	na	na	na	na	na	na
Croatia	na	**56**	50	60	39	56	66	57	55	51	64	54	53	60	55	50
Czech Republic	29	**34**	31	37	22	29	44	38	30	25	45	33	23	38	33	24
Denmark	59	**61**	57	64	45	60	70	68	52	49	65	59	55	67	62	55
Dominican Rep.	na	**na**	na	na	na	na	na	na	na	na	na	na	na	na	na	na
Egypt	na	**na**	na	na	na	na	na	na	na	na	na	na	na	na	na	na
El Salvador	na	**na**	na	na	na	na	na	na	na	na	na	na	na	na	na	na
Estonia	47	**36**	34	38	27	32	45	34	36	41	41	37	34	40	33	17
Finland	31	**40**	35	46	21	36	55	46	32	37	44	39	37	36	42	38
France	34	**34**	32	37	20	31	44	40	24	28	40	33	31	42	33	28
Georgia	na	**na**	na	na	na	na	na	na	na	na	na	na	na	na	na	na
Germany	37	**30**	27	32	17	27	39	34	26	32	35	27	25	32	28	33
Great Britain	40	**40**	36	43	19	37	51	43	34	37	43	39	35	na	na	na
Greece	na	**33**	33	33	22	38	49	57	37	26	43	30	25	33	32	38
Hungary	40	**48**	49	48	35	38	66	52	42	37	47	49	48	52	45	51
Iceland	69	**69**	65	73	51	72	81	77	68	55	73	72	61	73	70	54
India	58	**na**	na	na	na	na	na	na	na	na	na	na	na	na	na	na
Indonesia	na	**na**	na	na	na	na	na	na	na	na	na	na	na	na	na	na
Iran	na	**na**	na	na	na	na	na	na	na	na	na	na	na	na	na	na
Ireland	52	**54**	48	60	37	52	71	67	47	50	67	53	43	54	56	49
Israel	na	**na**	na	na	na	na	na	na	na	na	na	na	na	na	na	na
Italy	50	**51**	46	55	30	49	63	59	45	44	59	46	45	57	51	48
Japan	55	**na**	na	na	na	na	na	na	na	na	na	na	na	na	na	na
Jordan	na	**na**	na	na	na	na	na	na	na	na	na	na	na	na	na	na
Korea, South	70	**na**	na	na	na	na	na	na	na	na	na	na	na	na	na	na
Latvia	61	**60**	53	65	38	56	71	68	57	57	65	61	51	64	58	38
Lithuania	58	**35**	29	40	23	32	46	45	31	33	47	40	28	35	34	36
Luxembourg	na	**40**	40	41	24	42	50	46	39	36	40	47	40	39	43	36
Macedonia	na	**na**	na	na	na	na	na	na	na	na	na	na	na	na	na	na
Malta	na	**76**	73	79	64	79	82	84	74	67	81	79	67	76	76	76
Mexico	31	**na**	na	na	na	na	na	na	na	na	na	na	na	na	na	na
Moldova	na	**na**	na	na	na	na	na	na	na	na	na	na	na	na	na	na
Montenegro	na	**na**	na	na	na	na	na	na	na	na	na	na	na	na	na	na
Morocco	na	**na**	na	na	na	na	na	na	na	na	na	na	na	na	na	na
Netherlands	25	**27**	22	32	13	24	38	34	28	20	25	29	26	30	29	22
New Zealand	na	**na**	na	na	na	na	na	na	na	na	na	na	na	na	na	na
Nigeria	45	**na**	na	na	na	na	na	na	na	na	na	na	na	na	na	na
Northern Ireland	60	**54**	48	59	46	48	65	59	51	49	59	54	51	65	53	44
Norway	56	**na**	na	na	na	na	na	na	na	na	na	na	na	na	na	na
Pakistan	na	**na**	na	na	na	na	na	na	na	na	na	na	na	na	na	na
Peru	na	**na**	na	na	na	na	na	na	na	na	na	na	na	na	na	na
Philippines	na	**na**	na	na	na	na	na	na	na	na	na	na	na	na	na	na
Poland	63	**59**	58	61	43	60	69	62	56	55	60	61	52	58	61	52
Portugal	38	**56**	53	59	48	51	65	60	48	50	68	49	48	57	55	57
Puerto Rico	na	**na**	na	na	na	na	na	na	na	na	na	na	na	na	na	na
Romania	38	**51**	47	55	36	48	62	63	44	47	58	51	46	53	49	45
Russian Fed.	50	**32**	30	34	19	30	43	42	33	25	38	34	26	34	30	32
Serbia	na	**na**	na	na	na	na	na	na	na	na	na	na	na	na	na	na
Singapore	na	**na**	na	na	na	na	na	na	na	na	na	na	na	na	na	na
Slovakia	na	**31**	29	32	24	28	39	33	30	27	39	31	27	29	31	38
Slovenia	67	**56**	53	58	31	60	69	63	54	50	65	58	47	64	55	50
South Africa	62	**na**	na	na	na	na	na	na	na	na	na	na	na	na	na	na
Spain	52	**41**	37	44	30	35	52	51	35	29	52	42	32	49	42	29
Sweden	55	**41**	38	45	27	38	53	60	37	34	42	44	39	42	43	38
Switzerland	51	**na**	na	na	na	na	na	na	na	na	na	na	na	na	na	na
Taiwan	na	**na**	na	na	na	na	na	na	na	na	na	na	na	na	na	na
Tanzania	na	**na**	na	na	na	na	na	na	na	na	na	na	na	na	na	na
Turkey	67	**84**	81	87	78	89	87	87	78	86	83	87	79	81	84	87
Uganda	na	**na**	na	na	na	na	na	na	na	na	na	na	na	na	na	na
Ukraine	na	**44**	41	46	25	42	56	55	40	45	53	37	40	45	44	62
United States	56	**na**	na	na	na	na	na	na	na	na	na	na	na	na	na	na
Uruguay	na	**na**	na	na	na	na	na	na	na	na	na	na	na	na	na	na
Venezuela	na	**na**	na	na	na	na	na	na	na	na	na	na	na	na	na	na
Vietnam	na	**na**	na	na	na	na	na	na	na	na	na	na	na	na	na	na
Zimbabwe	na	**na**	na	na	na	na	na	na	na	na	na	na	na	na	na	na
Total	50	**46**	43	49	32	44	57	53	42	40	52	45	40	48	46	40

RANKING	
Country	2000
Turkey	84
Bulgaria	80
Malta	76
Iceland	69
Denmark	61
Latvia	60
Poland	59
Portugal	56
Croatia	56
Slovenia	56
Ireland	54
Northern Ireland	54
Romania	51
Italy	51
Hungary	48
Ukraine	44
Sweden	41
Spain	41
Finland	40
Luxembourg	40
Great Britain	40
Estonia	36
Lithuania	35
France	34
Czech Republic	34
Austria	33
Greece	33
Russian Fed.	32
Belgium	31
Slovakia	31
Germany	30
Netherlands	27
Belarus	20
Total	46

F128_1) JUSTIFIABLE: ADULTERY

Please tell me for each of the following statements whether you think it can always be justified, never be justified, or something in between: Married men/women having an affair

Never justifiable (%)

(EVS: V230)

Country	Wave		Gender		Age			Education			Income			Values		
	1990	2000	Male	Female	16-29	30-49	50+	Lower	Middle	Upper	Lower	Middle	Upper	Mat	Mixed	Postm.
Albania	na	**na**	na	na	na	na	na	na	na	na	na	na	na	na	na	na
Algeria	na	**na**	na	na	na	na	na	na	na	na	na	na	na	na	na	na
Argentina	72	**na**	na	na	na	na	na	na	na	na	na	na	na	na	na	na
Armenia	na	**na**	na	na	na	na	na	na	na	na	na	na	na	na	na	na
Australia	na	**na**	na	na	na	na	na	na	na	na	na	na	na	na	na	na
Austria	52	**50**	45	55	44	47	57	58	48	29	55	48	46	69	52	41
Azerbaijan	na	**na**	na	na	na	na	na	na	na	na	na	na	na	na	na	na
Bangladesh	na	**na**	na	na	na	na	na	na	na	na	na	na	na	na	na	na
Belarus	45	**37**	27	45	31	34	45	44	33	43	42	36	30	37	37	26
Belgium	52	**54**	48	60	48	49	62	68	54	44	57	56	50	62	55	43
Bosnia and Herz.	na	**na**	na	na	na	na	na	na	na	na	na	na	na	na	na	na
Brazil	68	**na**	na	na	na	na	na	na	na	na	na	na	na	na	na	na
Bulgaria	49	**40**	33	47	28	26	58	57	33	26	58	36	27	44	36	43
Canada	55	**na**	na	na	na	na	na	na	na	na	na	na	na	na	na	na
Chile	63	**na**	na	na	na	na	na	na	na	na	na	na	na	na	na	na
China	72	**na**	na	na	na	na	na	na	na	na	na	na	na	na	na	na
Colombia	na	**na**	na	na	na	na	na	na	na	na	na	na	na	na	na	na
Croatia	na	**59**	52	66	42	61	68	65	55	57	62	57	62	73	59	48
Czech Republic	31	**40**	36	44	35	32	49	45	36	27	48	41	29	44	40	31
Denmark	67	**67**	65	69	68	65	69	75	58	58	70	67	56	80	70	49
Dominican Rep.	na	**na**	na	na	na	na	na	na	na	na	na	na	na	na	na	na
Egypt	na	**na**	na	na	na	na	na	na	na	na	na	na	na	na	na	na
El Salvador	na	**na**	na	na	na	na	na	na	na	na	na	na	na	na	na	na
Estonia	31	**36**	28	41	34	27	44	37	37	29	36	41	34	35	36	13
Finland	42	**53**	50	55	50	47	59	58	46	45	57	51	49	50	54	50
France	35	**38**	33	42	36	34	42	42	37	27	45	37	31	48	37	23
Georgia	na	**na**	na	na	na	na	na	na	na	na	na	na	na	na	na	na
Germany	57	**41**	36	45	27	39	51	47	36	39	44	41	33	42	43	36
Great Britain	53	**55**	50	59	39	55	61	57	56	40	53	56	56	na	na	na
Greece	na	**43**	35	49	36	45	60	79	45	34	48	43	38	48	43	39
Hungary	64	**66**	55	75	51	62	78	69	62	56	62	71	62	68	64	52
Iceland	72	**79**	74	84	74	80	82	85	80	64	79	82	75	87	80	55
India	91	**na**	na	na	na	na	na	na	na	na	na	na	na	na	na	na
Indonesia	na	**na**	na	na	na	na	na	na	na	na	na	na	na	na	na	na
Iran	na	**na**	na	na	na	na	na	na	na	na	na	na	na	na	na	na
Ireland	69	**73**	68	78	61	69	86	82	71	62	84	75	62	80	74	58
Israel	na	**na**	na	na	na	na	na	na	na	na	na	na	na	na	na	na
Italy	52	**51**	43	58	39	46	62	62	44	36	61	47	40	64	52	42
Japan	47	**na**	na	na	na	na	na	na	na	na	na	na	na	na	na	na
Jordan	na	**na**	na	na	na	na	na	na	na	na	na	na	na	na	na	na
Korea, South	72	**na**	na	na	na	na	na	na	na	na	na	na	na	na	na	na
Latvia	48	**46**	41	51	31	42	56	61	43	38	51	48	39	49	44	40
Lithuania	61	**60**	50	68	45	52	77	80	53	50	70	63	54	61	58	60
Luxembourg	na	**56**	52	59	45	54	65	61	53	55	50	66	55	58	59	42
Macedonia	na	**na**	na	na	na	na	na	na	na	na	na	na	na	na	na	na
Malta	na	**94**	91	97	92	95	95	97	94	89	96	94	90	95	94	91
Mexico	43	**na**	na	na	na	na	na	na	na	na	na	na	na	na	na	na
Moldova	na	**na**	na	na	na	na	na	na	na	na	na	na	na	na	na	na
Montenegro	na	**na**	na	na	na	na	na	na	na	na	na	na	na	na	na	na
Morocco	na	**na**	na	na	na	na	na	na	na	na	na	na	na	na	na	na
Netherlands	45	**49**	44	53	51	43	53	65	50	32	50	50	42	62	51	37
New Zealand	na	**na**	na	na	na	na	na	na	na	na	na	na	na	na	na	na
Nigeria	58	**na**	na	na	na	na	na	na	na	na	na	na	na	na	na	na
Northern Ireland	78	**74**	71	76	65	70	84	80	70	66	78	77	63	81	73	69
Norway	62	**na**	na	na	na	na	na	na	na	na	na	na	na	na	na	na
Pakistan	na	**na**	na	na	na	na	na	na	na	na	na	na	na	na	na	na
Peru	na	**na**	na	na	na	na	na	na	na	na	na	na	na	na	na	na
Philippines	na	**na**	na	na	na	na	na	na	na	na	na	na	na	na	na	na
Poland	69	**67**	63	71	56	68	73	73	64	47	67	70	59	69	66	60
Portugal	62	**59**	50	67	50	53	69	64	47	55	66	59	47	60	59	48
Puerto Rico	na	**na**	na	na	na	na	na	na	na	na	na	na	na	na	na	na
Romania	62	**72**	65	78	56	69	83	84	67	61	80	73	64	79	66	49
Russian Fed.	51	**49**	47	51	38	48	58	63	50	38	56	52	41	52	48	39
Serbia	na	**na**	na	na	na	na	na	na	na	na	na	na	na	na	na	na
Singapore	na	**na**	na	na	na	na	na	na	na	na	na	na	na	na	na	na
Slovakia	na	**36**	29	44	28	33	47	47	33	27	44	39	31	41	34	13
Slovenia	43	**44**	39	49	35	39	57	62	41	24	52	45	31	56	43	37
South Africa	73	**na**	na	na	na	na	na	na	na	na	na	na	na	na	na	na
Spain	59	**54**	44	63	37	50	67	69	42	46	63	58	41	68	53	35
Sweden	63	**51**	53	48	49	47	55	68	50	38	50	55	45	58	53	40
Switzerland	56	**na**	na	na	na	na	na	na	na	na	na	na	na	na	na	na
Taiwan	na	**na**	na	na	na	na	na	na	na	na	na	na	na	na	na	na
Tanzania	na	**na**	na	na	na	na	na	na	na	na	na	na	na	na	na	na
Turkey	87	**na**	na	na	na	na	na	na	na	na	na	na	na	na	na	na
Uganda	na	**na**	na	na	na	na	na	na	na	na	na	na	na	na	na	na
Ukraine	na	**57**	48	64	37	56	68	72	55	51	66	50	51	59	54	61
United States	71	**na**	na	na	na	na	na	na	na	na	na	na	na	na	na	na
Uruguay	na	**na**	na	na	na	na	na	na	na	na	na	na	na	na	na	na
Venezuela	na	**na**	na	na	na	na	na	na	na	na	na	na	na	na	na	na
Vietnam	na	**na**	na	na	na	na	na	na	na	na	na	na	na	na	na	na
Zimbabwe	na	**na**	na	na	na	na	na	na	na	na	na	na	na	na	na	na
Total	58	55	49	60	46	51	64	63	51	46	59	56	48	59	55	44

RANKING

Country	2000
Malta	94
Iceland	79
Northern Ireland	74
Ireland	73
Romania	72
Denmark	67
Poland	67
Hungary	66
Lithuania	60
Croatia	59
Portugal	59
Ukraine	57
Luxembourg	56
Great Britain	55
Belgium	54
Spain	54
Finland	53
Italy	51
Sweden	51
Austria	50
Russian Fed.	49
Netherlands	49
Latvia	46
Slovenia	44
Greece	43
Germany	41
Bulgaria	40
Czech Republic	40
France	38
Belarus	37
Slovakia	36
Estonia	36
Total	55

F129_1) JUSTIFIABLE: THROWING AWAY LITTER

Please tell me for each of the following statements whether you think it can always be justified, never be justified, or something in between: Throwing away litter in a public place

(EVS: V237)

Never justifiable (%)

Country	Wave		Gender		Age			Education			Income			Values		
	1990	2000	Male	Female	16-29	30-49	50+	Lower	Middle	Upper	Lower	Middle	Upper	Mat	Mixed	Postm.
Albania	na	**na**	na	na	na	na	na	na	na	na	na	na	na	na	na	na
Algeria	na	**na**	na	na	na	na	na	na	na	na	na	na	na	na	na	na
Argentina	na	**na**	na	na	na	na	na	na	na	na	na	na	na	na	na	na
Armenia	na	**na**	na	na	na	na	na	na	na	na	na	na	na	na	na	na
Australia	na	**na**	na	na	na	na	na	na	na	na	na	na	na	na	na	na
Austria	na	**57**	55	59	49	55	63	63	54	40	55	59	54	67	61	48
Azerbaijan	na	**na**	na	na	na	na	na	na	na	na	na	na	na	na	na	na
Bangladesh	na	**na**	na	na	na	na	na	na	na	na	na	na	na	na	na	na
Belarus	na	**44**	38	50	33	46	51	44	42	52	49	46	33	46	43	38
Belgium	na	**79**	77	82	63	78	87	82	82	74	84	83	74	81	79	77
Bosnia and Herz.	na	**na**	na	na	na	na	na	na	na	na	na	na	na	na	na	na
Brazil	na	**na**	na	na	na	na	na	na	na	na	na	na	na	na	na	na
Bulgaria	na	**76**	76	76	62	79	79	77	75	76	77	78	72	76	77	89
Canada	na	**na**	na	na	na	na	na	na	na	na	na	na	na	na	na	na
Chile	na	**na**	na	na	na	na	na	na	na	na	na	na	na	na	na	na
China	na	**na**	na	na	na	na	na	na	na	na	na	na	na	na	na	na
Colombia	na	**na**	na	na	na	na	na	na	na	na	na	na	na	na	na	na
Croatia	na	**90**	90	89	89	88	93	95	86	87	90	91	88	91	90	89
Czech Republic	na	**68**	65	72	55	67	76	69	68	64	75	69	64	69	69	64
Denmark	na	**80**	77	82	67	80	87	86	77	73	80	79	80	84	80	83
Dominican Rep.	na	**na**	na	na	na	na	na	na	na	na	na	na	na	na	na	na
Egypt	na	**na**	na	na	na	na	na	na	na	na	na	na	na	na	na	na
El Salvador	na	**na**	na	na	na	na	na	na	na	na	na	na	na	na	na	na
Estonia	na	**62**	56	67	53	60	69	59	63	66	64	64	61	62	62	55
Finland	na	**51**	48	55	31	46	67	58	42	48	54	52	48	53	52	41
France	na	**76**	76	76	65	76	82	79	73	72	74	78	78	76	77	75
Georgia	na	**na**	na	na	na	na	na	na	na	na	na	na	na	na	na	na
Germany	na	**52**	51	53	41	50	59	57	46	55	54	52	47	51	53	50
Great Britain	na	**49**	42	56	30	48	58	47	49	45	49	47	51	na	na	na
Greece	na	**60**	57	62	56	62	65	69	61	57	69	60	50	57	61	61
Hungary	na	**68**	66	70	60	62	79	70	67	63	72	70	65	70	67	73
Iceland	na	**63**	58	68	38	65	80	69	57	60	66	63	57	66	63	54
India	na	**na**	na	na	na	na	na	na	na	na	na	na	na	na	na	na
Indonesia	na	**na**	na	na	na	na	na	na	na	na	na	na	na	na	na	na
Iran	na	**na**	na	na	na	na	na	na	na	na	na	na	na	na	na	na
Ireland	na	**71**	69	72	64	73	75	69	69	77	75	64	73	68	71	71
Israel	na	**na**	na	na	na	na	na	na	na	na	na	na	na	na	na	na
Italy	na	**74**	72	76	62	77	78	75	73	73	75	71	71	75	74	74
Japan	na	**na**	na	na	na	na	na	na	na	na	na	na	na	na	na	na
Jordan	na	**na**	na	na	na	na	na	na	na	na	na	na	na	na	na	na
Korea, South	na	**na**	na	na	na	na	na	na	na	na	na	na	na	na	na	na
Latvia	na	**84**	82	86	69	87	88	84	84	84	87	86	82	87	83	77
Lithuania	na	**64**	59	67	55	62	71	68	62	60	67	63	62	57	65	73
Luxembourg	na	**71**	69	73	61	73	75	72	71	70	63	77	76	67	73	68
Macedonia	na	**na**	na	na	na	na	na	na	na	na	na	na	na	na	na	na
Malta	na	**95**	93	97	96	96	94	95	95	94	96	94	96	95	96	94
Mexico	na	**na**	na	na	na	na	na	na	na	na	na	na	na	na	na	na
Moldova	na	**na**	na	na	na	na	na	na	na	na	na	na	na	na	na	na
Montenegro	na	**na**	na	na	na	na	na	na	na	na	na	na	na	na	na	na
Morocco	na	**na**	na	na	na	na	na	na	na	na	na	na	na	na	na	na
Netherlands	na	**66**	60	72	43	66	80	74	63	63	70	66	63	71	66	66
New Zealand	na	**na**	na	na	na	na	na	na	na	na	na	na	na	na	na	na
Nigeria	na	**na**	na	na	na	na	na	na	na	na	na	na	na	na	na	na
Northern Ireland	na	**53**	49	56	48	46	63	57	47	56	60	49	60	56	53	47
Norway	na	**na**	na	na	na	na	na	na	na	na	na	na	na	na	na	na
Pakistan	na	**na**	na	na	na	na	na	na	na	na	na	na	na	na	na	na
Peru	na	**na**	na	na	na	na	na	na	na	na	na	na	na	na	na	na
Philippines	na	**na**	na	na	na	na	na	na	na	na	na	na	na	na	na	na
Poland	na	**69**	69	68	57	70	73	70	68	65	69	69	66	68	68	72
Portugal	na	**68**	67	69	72	63	69	67	67	77	66	58	73	73	65	69
Puerto Rico	na	**na**	na	na	na	na	na	na	na	na	na	na	na	na	na	na
Romania	na	**86**	84	87	79	84	90	88	84	84	89	84	86	84	87	80
Russian Fed.	na	**75**	70	78	68	76	78	75	75	75	74	77	76	75	75	74
Serbia	na	**na**	na	na	na	na	na	na	na	na	na	na	na	na	na	na
Singapore	na	**na**	na	na	na	na	na	na	na	na	na	na	na	na	na	na
Slovakia	na	**39**	36	42	31	39	45	40	38	45	39	42	39	39	39	48
Slovenia	na	**71**	65	75	55	74	78	76	70	63	76	76	63	73	71	69
South Africa	na	**na**	na	na	na	na	na	na	na	na	na	na	na	na	na	na
Spain	na	**65**	64	66	59	64	70	68	61	67	74	69	59	66	65	66
Sweden	na	**44**	45	43	31	43	52	59	37	43	48	45	38	56	45	38
Switzerland	na	**na**	na	na	na	na	na	na	na	na	na	na	na	na	na	na
Taiwan	na	**na**	na	na	na	na	na	na	na	na	na	na	na	na	na	na
Tanzania	na	**na**	na	na	na	na	na	na	na	na	na	na	na	na	na	na
Turkey	na	**89**	87	91	87	91	89	88	89	92	86	89	93	87	90	94
Uganda	na	**na**	na	na	na	na	na	na	na	na	na	na	na	na	na	na
Ukraine	na	**66**	63	69	55	67	73	68	66	66	72	63	64	69	66	76
United States	na	**na**	na	na	na	na	na	na	na	na	na	na	na	na	na	na
Uruguay	na	**na**	na	na	na	na	na	na	na	na	na	na	na	na	na	na
Venezuela	na	**na**	na	na	na	na	na	na	na	na	na	na	na	na	na	na
Vietnam	na	**na**	na	na	na	na	na	na	na	na	na	na	na	na	na	na
Zimbabwe	na	**na**	na	na	na	na	na	na	na	na	na	na	na	na	na	na
Total	na	**67**	64	69	57	67	74	70	65	65	69	67	65	68	68	65

RANKING

Country	2000
Malta	95
Croatia	90
Turkey	89
Romania	86
Latvia	84
Denmark	80
Belgium	79
France	76
Bulgaria	76
Russian Fed.	75
Italy	74
Luxembourg	71
Ireland	71
Slovenia	71
Poland	69
Hungary	68
Czech Republic	68
Portugal	68
Ukraine	66
Netherlands	66
Spain	65
Lithuania	64
Iceland	63
Estonia	62
Greece	60
Austria	57
Northern Ireland	53
Germany	52
Finland	51
Great Britain	49
Belarus	44
Sweden	44
Slovakia	39
Total	67

F130_1) JUSTIFIABLE: DRIVING UNDER INFLUENCE OF ALCOHOL

Please tell me for each of the following statements whether you think it can always be justified, never be justified, or something in between: Driving under the influence of alcohol

Never justifiable (%)

(EVS: V238)

Country	Wave		Gender		Age			Education			Income			Values		
	1990	2000	Male	Female	16-29	30-49	50+	Lower	Middle	Upper	Lower	Middle	Upper	Mat	Mixed	Postm.
Albania	na	**na**	na	na	na	na	na	na	na	na	na	na	na	na	na	na
Algeria	na	**na**	na	na	na	na	na	na	na	na	na	na	na	na	na	na
Argentina	na	**na**	na	na	na	na	na	na	na	na	na	na	na	na	na	na
Armenia	na	**na**	na	na	na	na	na	na	na	na	na	na	na	na	na	na
Australia	na	**na**	na	na	na	na	na	na	na	na	na	na	na	na	na	na
Austria	na	**75**	69	81	69	73	81	78	74	70	73	77	73	85	76	73
Azerbaijan	na	**na**	na	na	na	na	na	na	na	na	na	na	na	na	na	na
Bangladesh	na	**na**	na	na	na	na	na	na	na	na	na	na	na	na	na	na
Belarus	na	**56**	46	63	42	59	63	62	53	53	62	55	44	56	55	48
Belgium	na	**74**	65	82	67	68	82	80	75	67	78	77	67	81	74	67
Bosnia and Herz.	na	**na**	na	na	na	na	na	na	na	na	na	na	na	na	na	na
Brazil	na	**na**	na	na	na	na	na	na	na	na	na	na	na	na	na	na
Bulgaria	na	**81**	79	83	69	81	88	89	77	77	90	77	76	84	79	81
Canada	na	**na**	na	na	na	na	na	na	na	na	na	na	na	na	na	na
Chile	na	**na**	na	na	na	na	na	na	na	na	na	na	na	na	na	na
China	na	**na**	na	na	na	na	na	na	na	na	na	na	na	na	na	na
Colombia	na	**na**	na	na	na	na	na	na	na	na	na	na	na	na	na	na
Croatia	na	**80**	70	89	64	82	88	88	75	76	90	80	76	88	82	68
Czech Republic	na	**73**	67	80	63	71	81	76	73	64	82	73	66	76	74	66
Denmark	na	**93**	89	96	92	93	94	94	91	92	95	93	90	93	93	93
Dominican Rep.	na	**na**	na	na	na	na	na	na	na	na	na	na	na	na	na	na
Egypt	na	**na**	na	na	na	na	na	na	na	na	na	na	na	na	na	na
El Salvador	na	**na**	na	na	na	na	na	na	na	na	na	na	na	na	na	na
Estonia	na	**75**	67	81	69	71	81	75	76	71	80	81	67	79	73	65
Finland	na	**82**	75	89	69	83	88	85	79	78	80	81	84	80	83	77
France	na	**66**	59	73	56	64	74	70	62	62	69	67	61	70	68	57
Georgia	na	**na**	na	na	na	na	na	na	na	na	na	na	na	na	na	na
Germany	na	**78**	75	81	72	79	80	77	79	84	79	76	75	87	76	76
Great Britain	na	**81**	76	85	74	80	84	81	84	71	82	75	82	na	na	na
Greece	na	**69**	66	70	63	73	74	83	70	65	76	70	59	67	69	72
Hungary	na	**90**	87	93	89	86	95	90	92	86	91	92	89	92	90	82
Iceland	na	**78**	72	85	72	77	86	87	77	63	83	81	70	83	80	60
India	na	**na**	na	na	na	na	na	na	na	na	na	na	na	na	na	na
Indonesia	na	**na**	na	na	na	na	na	na	na	na	na	na	na	na	na	na
Iran	na	**na**	na	na	na	na	na	na	na	na	na	na	na	na	na	na
Ireland	na	**82**	78	86	80	81	87	85	80	81	84	82	80	81	82	84
Israel	na	**na**	na	na	na	na	na	na	na	na	na	na	na	na	na	na
Italy	na	**81**	76	85	67	82	87	86	76	77	86	81	74	84	82	78
Japan	na	**na**	na	na	na	na	na	na	na	na	na	na	na	na	na	na
Jordan	na	**na**	na	na	na	na	na	na	na	na	na	na	na	na	na	na
Korea, South	na	**na**	na	na	na	na	na	na	na	na	na	na	na	na	na	na
Latvia	na	**79**	72	85	63	81	84	80	80	75	83	80	76	81	78	72
Lithuania	na	**76**	67	84	70	72	84	85	73	69	87	77	68	79	74	81
Luxembourg	na	**55**	51	60	48	54	62	61	55	46	50	59	58	56	57	44
Macedonia	na	**na**	na	na	na	na	na	na	na	na	na	na	na	na	na	na
Malta	na	**95**	92	98	93	95	96	97	94	93	95	94	94	95	95	92
Mexico	na	**na**	na	na	na	na	na	na	na	na	na	na	na	na	na	na
Moldova	na	**na**	na	na	na	na	na	na	na	na	na	na	na	na	na	na
Montenegro	na	**na**	na	na	na	na	na	na	na	na	na	na	na	na	na	na
Morocco	na	**na**	na	na	na	na	na	na	na	na	na	na	na	na	na	na
Netherlands	na	**76**	67	83	66	77	79	81	76	70	75	79	72	82	76	72
New Zealand	na	**na**	na	na	na	na	na	na	na	na	na	na	na	na	na	na
Nigeria	na	**na**	na	na	na	na	na	na	na	na	na	na	na	na	na	na
Northern Ireland	na	**87**	83	91	89	85	90	87	87	89	92	89	86	89	87	83
Norway	na	**na**	na	na	na	na	na	na	na	na	na	na	na	na	na	na
Pakistan	na	**na**	na	na	na	na	na	na	na	na	na	na	na	na	na	na
Peru	na	**na**	na	na	na	na	na	na	na	na	na	na	na	na	na	na
Philippines	na	**na**	na	na	na	na	na	na	na	na	na	na	na	na	na	na
Poland	na	**90**	86	95	87	91	92	89	91	94	90	92	89	92	91	80
Portugal	na	**70**	65	74	72	64	73	71	65	71	81	65	64	70	69	67
Puerto Rico	na	**na**	na	na	na	na	na	na	na	na	na	na	na	na	na	na
Romania	na	**87**	84	91	78	88	92	93	85	83	91	88	86	88	88	76
Russian Fed.	na	**77**	70	84	63	76	88	86	77	73	80	81	74	78	76	73
Serbia	na	**na**	na	na	na	na	na	na	na	na	na	na	na	na	na	na
Singapore	na	**na**	na	na	na	na	na	na	na	na	na	na	na	na	na	na
Slovakia	na	**54**	45	61	46	53	60	57	52	52	56	58	52	58	50	56
Slovenia	na	**68**	58	76	53	68	77	76	65	60	73	69	59	77	67	60
South Africa	na	**na**	na	na	na	na	na	na	na	na	na	na	na	na	na	na
Spain	na	**75**	70	79	66	72	82	82	69	68	79	80	64	82	74	69
Sweden	na	**83**	78	88	79	81	88	92	81	79	83	88	78	83	84	81
Switzerland	na	**na**	na	na	na	na	na	na	na	na	na	na	na	na	na	na
Taiwan	na	**na**	na	na	na	na	na	na	na	na	na	na	na	na	na	na
Tanzania	na	**na**	na	na	na	na	na	na	na	na	na	na	na	na	na	na
Turkey	na	**93**	91	95	91	95	92	93	92	95	92	93	93	92	93	95
Uganda	na	**na**	na	na	na	na	na	na	na	na	na	na	na	na	na	na
Ukraine	na	**74**	65	80	56	74	83	83	72	72	80	70	71	73	73	86
United States	na	**na**	na	na	na	na	na	na	na	na	na	na	na	na	na	na
Uruguay	na	**na**	na	na	na	na	na	na	na	na	na	na	na	na	na	na
Venezuela	na	**na**	na	na	na	na	na	na	na	na	na	na	na	na	na	na
Vietnam	na	**na**	na	na	na	na	na	na	na	na	na	na	na	na	na	na
Zimbabwe	na	**na**	na	na	na	na	na	na	na	na	na	na	na	na	na	na
Total	na	**77**	71	82	69	76	83	82	75	73	81	78	73	79	77	72

RANKING	
Country	2000
Malta	95
Denmark	93
Turkey	93
Poland	90
Hungary	90
Romania	87
Northern Ireland	87
Sweden	83
Finland	82
Ireland	82
Bulgaria	81
Great Britain	81
Italy	81
Croatia	80
Latvia	79
Germany	78
Iceland	78
Russian Fed.	77
Lithuania	76
Netherlands	76
Austria	75
Estonia	75
Spain	75
Belgium	74
Ukraine	74
Czech Republic	73
Portugal	70
Greece	69
Slovenia	68
France	66
Belarus	56
Luxembourg	55
Slovakia	54
Total	77

F131_1) JUSTIFIABLE: AVOID TAXES

Please tell me for each of the following statements whether you think it can always be justified, never be justified, or something in between: Paying cash for services to avoid taxes

Never justifiable (%) (EVS: V239)

Country	Wave		Gender		Age			Education			Income			Values		
	1990	2000	Male	Female	16-29	30-49	50+	Lower	Middle	Upper	Lower	Middle	Upper	Mat	Mixed	Postm.
Albania	na	**na**	na	na	na	na	na	na	na	na	na	na	na	na	na	na
Algeria	na	**na**	na	na	na	na	na	na	na	na	na	na	na	na	na	na
Argentina	na	**na**	na	na	na	na	na	na	na	na	na	na	na	na	na	na
Armenia	na	**na**	na	na	na	na	na	na	na	na	na	na	na	na	na	na
Australia	na	**na**	na	na	na	na	na	na	na	na	na	na	na	na	na	na
Austria	na	**37**	34	40	36	32	43	43	35	21	42	33	34	56	38	31
Azerbaijan	na	**na**	na	na	na	na	na	na	na	na	na	na	na	na	na	na
Bangladesh	na	**na**	na	na	na	na	na	na	na	na	na	na	na	na	na	na
Belarus	na	**26**	23	29	16	27	36	33	23	31	34	24	18	29	25	11
Belgium	na	**27**	25	29	18	23	35	34	25	24	33	27	23	31	26	27
Bosnia and Herz.	na	**na**	na	na	na	na	na	na	na	na	na	na	na	na	na	na
Brazil	na	**na**	na	na	na	na	na	na	na	na	na	na	na	na	na	na
Bulgaria	na	**77**	75	79	61	73	88	84	73	74	87	76	70	79	76	76
Canada	na	**na**	na	na	na	na	na	na	na	na	na	na	na	na	na	na
Chile	na	**na**	na	na	na	na	na	na	na	na	na	na	na	na	na	na
China	na	**na**	na	na	na	na	na	na	na	na	na	na	na	na	na	na
Colombia	na	**na**	na	na	na	na	na	na	na	na	na	na	na	na	na	na
Croatia	na	**58**	53	63	42	60	67	69	53	46	69	56	55	62	58	55
Czech Republic	na	**46**	39	52	33	41	57	48	45	34	57	45	36	47	46	38
Denmark	na	**24**	22	26	16	20	32	27	23	16	31	21	21	34	22	25
Dominican Rep.	na	**na**	na	na	na	na	na	na	na	na	na	na	na	na	na	na
Egypt	na	**na**	na	na	na	na	na	na	na	na	na	na	na	na	na	na
El Salvador	na	**na**	na	na	na	na	na	na	na	na	na	na	na	na	na	na
Estonia	na	**40**	35	45	27	34	53	40	42	35	52	43	35	40	41	20
Finland	na	**30**	26	33	14	24	43	34	24	24	31	31	24	33	29	26
France	na	**32**	27	36	23	31	36	35	27	28	35	32	32	36	31	27
Georgia	na	**na**	na	na	na	na	na	na	na	na	na	na	na	na	na	na
Germany	na	**42**	41	44	34	39	49	47	36	50	45	38	35	45	40	46
Great Britain	na	**34**	29	39	20	29	44	35	31	30	38	35	31	na	na	na
Greece	na	**34**	31	37	29	35	47	50	36	30	41	32	31	34	34	36
Hungary	na	**53**	51	56	47	43	67	60	41	43	55	59	48	57	50	50
Iceland	na	**44**	43	46	32	47	51	53	41	35	48	44	40	51	44	32
India	na	**na**	na	na	na	na	na	na	na	na	na	na	na	na	na	na
Indonesia	na	**na**	na	na	na	na	na	na	na	na	na	na	na	na	na	na
Iran	na	**na**	na	na	na	na	na	na	na	na	na	na	na	na	na	na
Ireland	na	**48**	44	51	47	39	59	55	45	41	61	41	42	48	48	43
Israel	na	**na**	na	na	na	na	na	na	na	na	na	na	na	na	na	na
Italy	na	**54**	52	55	43	53	60	59	50	52	58	54	44	53	55	51
Japan	na	**na**	na	na	na	na	na	na	na	na	na	na	na	na	na	na
Jordan	na	**na**	na	na	na	na	na	na	na	na	na	na	na	na	na	na
Korea, South	na	**na**	na	na	na	na	na	na	na	na	na	na	na	na	na	na
Latvia	na	**46**	39	51	27	40	58	59	44	35	55	51	32	47	46	35
Lithuania	na	**30**	25	34	15	22	49	46	24	28	37	41	23	27	30	34
Luxembourg	na	**29**	29	30	19	28	37	38	25	26	32	32	26	29	31	22
Macedonia	na	**na**	na	na	na	na	na	na	na	na	na	na	na	na	na	na
Malta	na	**72**	70	74	62	73	77	76	70	70	75	76	68	72	72	70
Mexico	na	**na**	na	na	na	na	na	na	na	na	na	na	na	na	na	na
Moldova	na	**na**	na	na	na	na	na	na	na	na	na	na	na	na	na	na
Montenegro	na	**na**	na	na	na	na	na	na	na	na	na	na	na	na	na	na
Morocco	na	**na**	na	na	na	na	na	na	na	na	na	na	na	na	na	na
Netherlands	na	**16**	13	18	6	15	22	25	14	8	17	14	14	23	16	12
New Zealand	na	**na**	na	na	na	na	na	na	na	na	na	na	na	na	na	na
Nigeria	na	**na**	na	na	na	na	na	na	na	na	na	na	na	na	na	na
Northern Ireland	na	**50**	44	56	42	44	60	56	46	46	59	50	42	64	49	39
Norway	na	**na**	na	na	na	na	na	na	na	na	na	na	na	na	na	na
Pakistan	na	**na**	na	na	na	na	na	na	na	na	na	na	na	na	na	na
Peru	na	**na**	na	na	na	na	na	na	na	na	na	na	na	na	na	na
Philippines	na	**na**	na	na	na	na	na	na	na	na	na	na	na	na	na	na
Poland	na	**44**	42	47	33	45	52	50	40	33	45	46	39	43	45	47
Portugal	na	**57**	59	56	53	49	67	60	48	61	69	51	54	57	57	59
Puerto Rico	na	**na**	na	na	na	na	na	na	na	na	na	na	na	na	na	na
Romania	na	**56**	49	63	47	49	68	67	50	52	64	57	50	56	54	49
Russian Fed.	na	**41**	36	45	27	37	56	52	42	32	52	43	31	44	39	40
Serbia	na	**na**	na	na	na	na	na	na	na	na	na	na	na	na	na	na
Singapore	na	**na**	na	na	na	na	na	na	na	na	na	na	na	na	na	na
Slovakia	na	**24**	21	27	18	25	27	29	22	17	26	29	20	23	25	18
Slovenia	na	**44**	39	48	23	46	57	56	41	33	54	42	34	53	43	36
South Africa	na	**na**	na	na	na	na	na	na	na	na	na	na	na	na	na	na
Spain	na	**41**	38	43	29	36	51	54	31	30	51	40	30	52	39	30
Sweden	na	**26**	23	28	23	22	31	40	21	21	30	26	19	29	26	23
Switzerland	na	**na**	na	na	na	na	na	na	na	na	na	na	na	na	na	na
Taiwan	na	**na**	na	na	na	na	na	na	na	na	na	na	na	na	na	na
Tanzania	na	**na**	na	na	na	na	na	na	na	na	na	na	na	na	na	na
Turkey	na	**87**	85	89	84	90	88	87	87	88	86	88	87	89	87	90
Uganda	na	**na**	na	na	na	na	na	na	na	na	na	na	na	na	na	na
Ukraine	na	**42**	39	45	22	38	57	56	41	37	49	40	35	44	40	50
United States	na	**na**	na	na	na	na	na	na	na	na	na	na	na	na	na	na
Uruguay	na	**na**	na	na	na	na	na	na	na	na	na	na	na	na	na	na
Venezuela	na	**na**	na	na	na	na	na	na	na	na	na	na	na	na	na	na
Vietnam	na	**na**	na	na	na	na	na	na	na	na	na	na	na	na	na	na
Zimbabwe	na	**na**	na	na	na	na	na	na	na	na	na	na	na	na	na	na
Total	na	**42**	38	45	32	38	51	49	39	35	48	41	37	47	41	36

RANKING

Country	2000
Turkey	87
Bulgaria	77
Malta	72
Croatia	58
Portugal	57
Romania	56
Italy	54
Hungary	53
Northern Ireland	50
Ireland	48
Latvia	46
Czech Republic	46
Poland	44
Iceland	44
Slovenia	44
Germany	42
Ukraine	42
Russian Fed.	41
Spain	41
Estonia	40
Austria	37
Greece	34
Great Britain	34
France	32
Finland	30
Lithuania	30
Luxembourg	29
Belgium	27
Belarus	26
Sweden	26
Slovakia	24
Denmark	24
Netherlands	16
Total	42

F132_1) JUSTIFIABLE: HAVING CASUAL SEX

Please tell me for each of the following statements whether you think it can always be justified, never be justified, or something in between: Having casual sex

Never justifiable (%) (EVS: V240)

Country	Wave		Gender		Age			Education			Income			Values		
	1990	2000	Male	Female	16-29	30-49	50+	Lower	Middle	Upper	Lower	Middle	Upper	Mat	Mixed	Postm.
Albania	na	**na**	na	na	na	na	na	na	na	na	na	na	na	na	na	na
Algeria	na	**na**	na	na	na	na	na	na	na	na	na	na	na	na	na	na
Argentina	na	**na**	na	na	na	na	na	na	na	na	na	na	na	na	na	na
Armenia	na	**na**	na	na	na	na	na	na	na	na	na	na	na	na	na	na
Australia	na	**na**	na	na	na	na	na	na	na	na	na	na	na	na	na	na
Austria	na	**46**	41	51	28	42	60	56	40	27	56	47	40	68	49	36
Azerbaijan	na	**na**	na	na	na	na	na	na	na	na	na	na	na	na	na	na
Bangladesh	na	**na**	na	na	na	na	na	na	na	na	na	na	na	na	na	na
Belarus	na	**29**	18	37	18	25	42	42	25	22	36	27	20	31	26	20
Belgium	na	**54**	47	61	33	48	69	68	55	42	61	58	47	65	54	39
Bosnia and Herz.	na	**na**	na	na	na	na	na	na	na	na	na	na	na	na	na	na
Brazil	na	**na**	na	na	na	na	na	na	na	na	na	na	na	na	na	na
Bulgaria	na	**51**	43	59	30	46	66	68	42	43	65	52	40	56	46	51
Canada	na	**na**	na	na	na	na	na	na	na	na	na	na	na	na	na	na
Chile	na	**na**	na	na	na	na	na	na	na	na	na	na	na	na	na	na
China	na	**na**	na	na	na	na	na	na	na	na	na	na	na	na	na	na
Colombia	na	**na**	na	na	na	na	na	na	na	na	na	na	na	na	na	na
Croatia	na	**62**	49	73	44	63	72	71	58	51	69	60	61	75	62	52
Czech Republic	na	**41**	31	51	31	33	53	44	40	29	49	44	30	43	42	32
Denmark	na	**46**	41	52	27	43	61	56	35	34	50	44	41	59	49	30
Dominican Rep.	na	**na**	na	na	na	na	na	na	na	na	na	na	na	na	na	na
Egypt	na	**na**	na	na	na	na	na	na	na	na	na	na	na	na	na	na
El Salvador	na	**na**	na	na	na	na	na	na	na	na	na	na	na	na	na	na
Estonia	na	**42**	29	52	29	33	57	42	43	39	48	48	38	42	42	29
Finland	na	**34**	30	37	18	27	49	40	24	28	37	35	29	32	35	29
France	na	**36**	29	43	26	32	46	43	29	25	40	40	30	47	37	20
Georgia	na	**na**	na	na	na	na	na	na	na	na	na	na	na	na	na	na
Germany	na	**39**	37	41	26	35	49	49	30	33	45	40	35	37	42	36
Great Britain	na	**37**	32	43	19	31	51	44	31	26	37	34	33	na	na	na
Greece	na	**21**	16	25	12	25	38	52	22	15	26	21	16	23	22	14
Hungary	na	**56**	44	67	42	53	69	60	52	42	59	61	50	58	54	56
Iceland	na	**21**	18	23	7	18	36	24	21	12	22	20	18	26	20	11
India	na	**na**	na	na	na	na	na	na	na	na	na	na	na	na	na	na
Indonesia	na	**na**	na	na	na	na	na	na	na	na	na	na	na	na	na	na
Iran	na	**na**	na	na	na	na	na	na	na	na	na	na	na	na	na	na
Ireland	na	**55**	50	60	25	52	81	71	50	39	69	56	43	54	55	53
Israel	na	**na**	na	na	na	na	na	na	na	na	na	na	na	na	na	na
Italy	na	**49**	38	58	28	44	64	64	39	32	58	47	37	63	51	37
Japan	na	**na**	na	na	na	na	na	na	na	na	na	na	na	na	na	na
Jordan	na	**na**	na	na	na	na	na	na	na	na	na	na	na	na	na	na
Korea, South	na	**na**	na	na	na	na	na	na	na	na	na	na	na	na	na	na
Latvia	na	**59**	47	68	36	59	68	68	56	55	63	61	55	63	58	37
Lithuania	na	**58**	44	69	41	49	77	80	50	48	72	61	48	59	57	49
Luxembourg	na	**44**	40	48	24	44	58	53	41	32	43	57	38	45	47	34
Macedonia	na	**na**	na	na	na	na	na	na	na	na	na	na	na	na	na	na
Malta	na	**94**	90	97	88	95	96	97	93	89	97	93	91	93	95	88
Mexico	na	**na**	na	na	na	na	na	na	na	na	na	na	na	na	na	na
Moldova	na	**na**	na	na	na	na	na	na	na	na	na	na	na	na	na	na
Montenegro	na	**na**	na	na	na	na	na	na	na	na	na	na	na	na	na	na
Morocco	na	**na**	na	na	na	na	na	na	na	na	na	na	na	na	na	na
Netherlands	na	**41**	35	46	26	32	58	61	41	21	44	41	33	63	41	29
New Zealand	na	**na**	na	na	na	na	na	na	na	na	na	na	na	na	na	na
Nigeria	na	**na**	na	na	na	na	na	na	na	na	na	na	na	na	na	na
Northern Ireland	na	**51**	47	55	31	39	72	61	44	44	60	50	42	59	53	40
Norway	na	**na**	na	na	na	na	na	na	na	na	na	na	na	na	na	na
Pakistan	na	**na**	na	na	na	na	na	na	na	na	na	na	na	na	na	na
Peru	na	**na**	na	na	na	na	na	na	na	na	na	na	na	na	na	na
Philippines	na	**na**	na	na	na	na	na	na	na	na	na	na	na	na	na	na
Poland	na	**61**	56	66	38	61	75	66	58	49	66	59	54	66	58	54
Portugal	na	**51**	38	62	39	47	61	56	39	49	65	49	41	54	50	40
Puerto Rico	na	**na**	na	na	na	na	na	na	na	na	na	na	na	na	na	na
Romania	na	**73**	61	83	52	71	85	83	67	68	80	72	69	75	72	47
Russian Fed.	na	**45**	38	51	27	42	62	63	46	35	54	46	37	47	44	36
Serbia	na	**na**	na	na	na	na	na	na	na	na	na	na	na	na	na	na
Singapore	na	**na**	na	na	na	na	na	na	na	na	na	na	na	na	na	na
Slovakia	na	**37**	28	45	26	33	49	48	33	26	46	36	33	41	33	28
Slovenia	na	**38**	30	46	20	37	53	55	34	27	49	42	24	50	36	35
South Africa	na	**na**	na	na	na	na	na	na	na	na	na	na	na	na	na	na
Spain	na	**34**	22	45	13	28	52	53	19	23	46	35	20	48	32	17
Sweden	na	**27**	29	24	13	25	37	50	21	17	21	33	26	33	29	17
Switzerland	na	**na**	na	na	na	na	na	na	na	na	na	na	na	na	na	na
Taiwan	na	**na**	na	na	na	na	na	na	na	na	na	na	na	na	na	na
Tanzania	na	**na**	na	na	na	na	na	na	na	na	na	na	na	na	na	na
Turkey	na	**79**	74	84	72	84	87	86	69	65	84	78	70	84	79	73
Uganda	na	**na**	na	na	na	na	na	na	na	na	na	na	na	na	na	na
Ukraine	na	**50**	37	60	27	48	65	65	49	43	61	42	43	53	46	60
United States	na	**na**	na	na	na	na	na	na	na	na	na	na	na	na	na	na
Uruguay	na	**na**	na	na	na	na	na	na	na	na	na	na	na	na	na	na
Venezuela	na	**na**	na	na	na	na	na	na	na	na	na	na	na	na	na	na
Vietnam	na	**na**	na	na	na	na	na	na	na	na	na	na	na	na	na	na
Zimbabwe	na	**na**	na	na	na	na	na	na	na	na	na	na	na	na	na	na
Total	na	**47**	39	53	30	43	61	56	43	36	53	47	41	53	47	35

RANKING

Country	2000
Malta	94
Turkey	79
Romania	73
Croatia	62
Poland	61
Latvia	59
Lithuania	58
Hungary	56
Ireland	55
Belgium	54
Bulgaria	51
Northern Ireland	51
Portugal	51
Ukraine	50
Italy	49
Austria	46
Denmark	46
Russian Fed.	45
Luxembourg	44
Estonia	42
Czech Republic	41
Netherlands	41
Germany	39
Slovenia	38
Great Britain	37
Slovakia	37
France	36
Spain	34
Finland	34
Belarus	29
Sweden	27
Greece	21
Iceland	21
Total	47

F133_1) JUSTIFIABLE: SMOKING IN PUBLIC BUILDINGS

Please tell me for each of the following statements whether you think it can always be justified, never be justified, or something in between: smoking in public buildings

Never justifiable (%) (EVS: V241)

	Wave		Gender		Age			Education			Income			Values		
Country	1990	2000	Male	Female	16-29	30-49	50+	Lower	Middle	Upper	Lower	Middle	Upper	Mat	Mixed	Postm.
Albania	na	**na**	na	na	na	na	na	na	na	na	na	na	na	na	na	na
Algeria	na	**na**	na	na	na	na	na	na	na	na	na	na	na	na	na	na
Argentina	na	**na**	na	na	na	na	na	na	na	na	na	na	na	na	na	na
Armenia	na	**na**	na	na	na	na	na	na	na	na	na	na	na	na	na	na
Australia	na	**na**	na	na	na	na	na	na	na	na	na	na	na	na	na	na
Austria	na	**24**	25	23	17	19	33	27	23	16	28	25	21	43	26	16
Azerbaijan	na	**na**	na	na	na	na	na	na	na	na	na	na	na	na	na	na
Bangladesh	na	**na**	na	na	na	na	na	na	na	na	na	na	na	na	na	na
Belarus	na	**22**	17	25	13	21	29	25	20	20	26	21	14	22	20	13
Belgium	na	**49**	45	52	37	42	60	50	50	45	54	50	44	48	49	46
Bosnia and Herz.	na	**na**	na	na	na	na	na	na	na	na	na	na	na	na	na	na
Brazil	na	**na**	na	na	na	na	na	na	na	na	na	na	na	na	na	na
Bulgaria	na	**38**	34	42	32	30	49	48	35	30	48	35	31	41	36	42
Canada	na	**na**	na	na	na	na	na	na	na	na	na	na	na	na	na	na
Chile	na	**na**	na	na	na	na	na	na	na	na	na	na	na	na	na	na
China	na	**na**	na	na	na	na	na	na	na	na	na	na	na	na	na	na
Colombia	na	**na**	na	na	na	na	na	na	na	na	na	na	na	na	na	na
Croatia	na	**52**	48	57	37	52	63	60	48	49	65	50	48	56	54	42
Czech Republic	na	**34**	33	35	22	29	46	34	36	32	41	35	29	34	36	29
Denmark	na	**26**	25	26	18	23	32	28	26	21	28	28	19	28	27	19
Dominican Rep.	na	**na**	na	na	na	na	na	na	na	na	na	na	na	na	na	na
Egypt	na	**na**	na	na	na	na	na	na	na	na	na	na	na	na	na	na
El Salvador	na	**na**	na	na	na	na	na	na	na	na	na	na	na	na	na	na
Estonia	na	**34**	32	36	28	28	43	33	36	31	38	35	34	35	34	29
Finland	na	**38**	36	40	24	34	50	41	33	38	38	37	37	40	37	37
France	na	**42**	38	45	29	37	53	45	35	38	42	40	42	46	42	35
Georgia	na	**na**	na	na	na	na	na	na	na	na	na	na	na	na	na	na
Germany	na	**25**	24	26	15	22	33	29	22	20	31	24	22	25	25	26
Great Britain	na	**31**	28	34	16	22	44	33	27	27	37	24	32	na	na	na
Greece	na	**22**	22	23	13	25	41	44	27	14	29	20	18	23	23	20
Hungary	na	**51**	48	55	46	43	63	52	55	43	51	52	52	54	51	41
Iceland	na	**44**	44	44	33	41	57	49	43	37	48	43	41	47	44	32
India	na	**na**	na	na	na	na	na	na	na	na	na	na	na	na	na	na
Indonesia	na	**na**	na	na	na	na	na	na	na	na	na	na	na	na	na	na
Iran	na	**na**	na	na	na	na	na	na	na	na	na	na	na	na	na	na
Ireland	na	**43**	41	44	36	40	51	41	45	41	45	42	40	44	44	37
Israel	na	**na**	na	na	na	na	na	na	na	na	na	na	na	na	na	na
Italy	na	**39**	39	39	21	38	49	46	33	37	46	38	34	47	40	34
Japan	na	**na**	na	na	na	na	na	na	na	na	na	na	na	na	na	na
Jordan	na	**na**	na	na	na	na	na	na	na	na	na	na	na	na	na	na
Korea, South	na	**na**	na	na	na	na	na	na	na	na	na	na	na	na	na	na
Latvia	na	**51**	43	58	37	45	63	59	49	49	53	53	50	55	51	35
Lithuania	na	**32**	23	40	19	26	48	46	27	31	44	36	26	25	35	37
Luxembourg	na	**25**	26	25	19	25	30	32	20	27	29	29	25	30	26	20
Macedonia	na	**na**	na	na	na	na	na	na	na	na	na	na	na	na	na	na
Malta	na	**89**	85	92	83	90	91	92	87	88	92	89	87	89	89	84
Mexico	na	**na**	na	na	na	na	na	na	na	na	na	na	na	na	na	na
Moldova	na	**na**	na	na	na	na	na	na	na	na	na	na	na	na	na	na
Montenegro	na	**na**	na	na	na	na	na	na	na	na	na	na	na	na	na	na
Morocco	na	**na**	na	na	na	na	na	na	na	na	na	na	na	na	na	na
Netherlands	na	**31**	27	34	15	25	46	38	30	26	35	32	25	34	30	32
New Zealand	na	**na**	na	na	na	na	na	na	na	na	na	na	na	na	na	na
Nigeria	na	**na**	na	na	na	na	na	na	na	na	na	na	na	na	na	na
Northern Ireland	na	**35**	34	36	28	29	45	38	34	32	37	31	38	44	34	30
Norway	na	**na**	na	na	na	na	na	na	na	na	na	na	na	na	na	na
Pakistan	na	**na**	na	na	na	na	na	na	na	na	na	na	na	na	na	na
Peru	na	**na**	na	na	na	na	na	na	na	na	na	na	na	na	na	na
Philippines	na	**na**	na	na	na	na	na	na	na	na	na	na	na	na	na	na
Poland	na	**39**	36	42	21	36	53	42	35	38	43	37	34	41	38	33
Portugal	na	**36**	33	40	26	33	45	40	27	39	54	36	29	40	35	33
Puerto Rico	na	**na**	na	na	na	na	na	na	na	na	na	na	na	na	na	na
Romania	na	**57**	51	63	41	52	70	71	52	45	65	57	50	63	52	37
Russian Fed.	na	**42**	35	47	29	39	53	50	42	35	50	42	34	42	42	37
Serbia	na	**na**	na	na	na	na	na	na	na	na	na	na	na	na	na	na
Singapore	na	**na**	na	na	na	na	na	na	na	na	na	na	na	na	na	na
Slovakia	na	**32**	28	36	25	33	37	35	30	32	37	34	29	32	31	32
Slovenia	na	**46**	44	47	32	42	61	58	43	34	57	48	32	52	46	36
South Africa	na	**na**	na	na	na	na	na	na	na	na	na	na	na	na	na	na
Spain	na	**33**	28	37	23	29	41	41	24	34	41	38	28	39	34	22
Sweden	na	**40**	42	38	26	40	48	50	39	33	36	47	35	55	40	37
Switzerland	na	**na**	na	na	na	na	na	na	na	na	na	na	na	na	na	na
Taiwan	na	**na**	na	na	na	na	na	na	na	na	na	na	na	na	na	na
Tanzania	na	**na**	na	na	na	na	na	na	na	na	na	na	na	na	na	na
Turkey	na	**74**	73	75	71	77	78	79	69	67	80	73	67	72	77	71
Uganda	na	**na**	na	na	na	na	na	na	na	na	na	na	na	na	na	na
Ukraine	na	**43**	35	49	29	39	54	54	41	40	50	39	39	45	42	59
United States	na	**na**	na	na	na	na	na	na	na	na	na	na	na	na	na	na
Uruguay	na	**na**	na	na	na	na	na	na	na	na	na	na	na	na	na	na
Venezuela	na	**na**	na	na	na	na	na	na	na	na	na	na	na	na	na	na
Vietnam	na	**na**	na	na	na	na	na	na	na	na	na	na	na	na	na	na
Zimbabwe	na	**na**	na	na	na	na	na	na	na	na	na	na	na	na	na	na
Total	na	**39**	37	42	28	36	50	44	38	34	44	39	36	43	40	33

RANKING

Country	2000
Malta	89
Turkey	74
Romania	57
Croatia	52
Hungary	51
Latvia	51
Belgium	49
Slovenia	46
Iceland	44
Ireland	43
Ukraine	43
Russian Fed.	42
France	42
Sweden	40
Italy	39
Poland	39
Bulgaria	38
Finland	38
Portugal	36
Northern Ireland	35
Czech Republic	34
Estonia	34
Spain	33
Lithuania	32
Slovakia	32
Netherlands	31
Great Britain	31
Denmark	26
Luxembourg	25
Germany	25
Austria	24
Greece	22
Belarus	22
Total	39

F134_1) JUSTIFIABLE: SPEEDING OVER LIMIT

Please tell me for each of the following statements whether you think it can always be justified, never be justified, or something in between: Speeding over the limit in built-up areas

Never justifiable (%)

(EVS: V242)

Country	Wave		Gender		Age			Education			Income			Values		
	1990	2000	Male	Female	16-29	30-49	50+	Lower	Middle	Upper	Lower	Middle	Upper	Mat	Mixed	Postm.
Albania	na	**na**	na	na	na	na	na	na	na	na	na	na	na	na	na	na
Algeria	na	**na**	na	na	na	na	na	na	na	na	na	na	na	na	na	na
Argentina	na	**na**	na	na	na	na	na	na	na	na	na	na	na	na	na	na
Armenia	na	**na**	na	na	na	na	na	na	na	na	na	na	na	na	na	na
Australia	na	**na**	na	na	na	na	na	na	na	na	na	na	na	na	na	na
Austria	na	**58**	53	64	46	57	66	64	56	43	57	60	59	72	62	49
Azerbaijan	na	**na**	na	na	na	na	na	na	na	na	na	na	na	na	na	na
Bangladesh	na	**na**	na	na	na	na	na	na	na	na	na	na	na	na	na	na
Belarus	na	**22**	15	27	12	19	33	32	17	21	28	22	9	23	20	9
Belgium	na	**59**	53	65	36	54	74	73	59	49	71	62	49	66	58	52
Bosnia and Herz.	na	**na**	na	na	na	na	na	na	na	na	na	na	na	na	na	na
Brazil	na	**na**	na	na	na	na	na	na	na	na	na	na	na	na	na	na
Bulgaria	na	**68**	65	71	56	63	79	79	65	57	77	69	61	74	63	66
Canada	na	**na**	na	na	na	na	na	na	na	na	na	na	na	na	na	na
Chile	na	**na**	na	na	na	na	na	na	na	na	na	na	na	na	na	na
China	na	**na**	na	na	na	na	na	na	na	na	na	na	na	na	na	na
Colombia	na	**na**	na	na	na	na	na	na	na	na	na	na	na	na	na	na
Croatia	na	**78**	71	84	62	78	88	84	74	75	87	74	78	87	77	74
Czech Republic	na	**50**	44	56	39	44	62	55	48	34	62	51	41	57	49	43
Denmark	na	**56**	49	63	42	50	71	64	43	49	66	51	47	63	58	51
Dominican Rep.	na	**na**	na	na	na	na	na	na	na	na	na	na	na	na	na	na
Egypt	na	**na**	na	na	na	na	na	na	na	na	na	na	na	na	na	na
El Salvador	na	**na**	na	na	na	na	na	na	na	na	na	na	na	na	na	na
Estonia	na	**54**	44	63	37	51	67	54	57	48	61	61	48	61	49	59
Finland	na	**37**	30	44	17	33	52	44	27	30	44	34	29	36	37	38
France	na	**45**	40	50	30	41	56	50	37	38	51	44	40	52	44	36
Georgia	na	**na**	na	na	na	na	na	na	na	na	na	na	na	na	na	na
Germany	na	**56**	51	60	43	55	63	60	52	57	58	55	50	64	55	48
Great Britain	na	**56**	50	63	41	53	67	63	51	43	66	52	45	na	na	na
Greece	na	**50**	45	54	38	58	65	71	55	43	61	48	43	50	52	47
Hungary	na	**67**	59	74	57	60	79	72	63	46	74	68	63	76	60	40
Iceland	na	**39**	31	46	22	37	56	55	31	22	48	37	30	49	39	18
India	na	**na**	na	na	na	na	na	na	na	na	na	na	na	na	na	na
Indonesia	na	**na**	na	na	na	na	na	na	na	na	na	na	na	na	na	na
Iran	na	**na**	na	na	na	na	na	na	na	na	na	na	na	na	na	na
Ireland	na	**69**	65	73	65	67	77	76	69	57	81	68	57	67	69	69
Israel	na	**na**	na	na	na	na	na	na	na	na	na	na	na	na	na	na
Italy	na	**48**	42	54	32	45	59	60	40	35	58	48	33	56	49	43
Japan	na	**na**	na	na	na	na	na	na	na	na	na	na	na	na	na	na
Jordan	na	**na**	na	na	na	na	na	na	na	na	na	na	na	na	na	na
Korea, South	na	**na**	na	na	na	na	na	na	na	na	na	na	na	na	na	na
Latvia	na	**66**	57	74	41	67	76	72	66	57	74	69	55	75	62	52
Lithuania	na	**55**	47	62	35	51	73	77	48	45	69	62	45	55	54	68
Luxembourg	na	**44**	43	46	26	44	57	53	44	32	48	56	45	49	46	36
Macedonia	na	**na**	na	na	na	na	na	na	na	na	na	na	na	na	na	na
Malta	na	**92**	88	96	88	94	94	95	92	85	95	92	90	92	93	89
Mexico	na	**na**	na	na	na	na	na	na	na	na	na	na	na	na	na	na
Moldova	na	**na**	na	na	na	na	na	na	na	na	na	na	na	na	na	na
Montenegro	na	**na**	na	na	na	na	na	na	na	na	na	na	na	na	na	na
Morocco	na	**na**	na	na	na	na	na	na	na	na	na	na	na	na	na	na
Netherlands	na	**60**	51	68	43	56	73	71	59	51	66	63	49	72	58	61
New Zealand	na	**na**	na	na	na	na	na	na	na	na	na	na	na	na	na	na
Nigeria	na	**na**	na	na	na	na	na	na	na	na	na	na	na	na	na	na
Northern Ireland	na	**63**	58	67	55	56	73	72	55	55	71	64	61	67	61	60
Norway	na	**na**	na	na	na	na	na	na	na	na	na	na	na	na	na	na
Pakistan	na	**na**	na	na	na	na	na	na	na	na	na	na	na	na	na	na
Peru	na	**na**	na	na	na	na	na	na	na	na	na	na	na	na	na	na
Philippines	na	**na**	na	na	na	na	na	na	na	na	na	na	na	na	na	na
Poland	na	**59**	55	63	38	60	72	66	55	42	64	59	48	62	58	53
Portugal	na	**50**	45	54	38	45	61	56	38	40	65	48	44	52	50	44
Puerto Rico	na	**na**	na	na	na	na	na	na	na	na	na	na	na	na	na	na
Romania	na	**68**	61	75	50	63	82	81	63	56	78	71	59	74	64	44
Russian Fed.	na	**59**	51	67	41	56	75	72	59	53	68	62	49	61	57	53
Serbia	na	**na**	na	na	na	na	na	na	na	na	na	na	na	na	na	na
Singapore	na	**na**	na	na	na	na	na	na	na	na	na	na	na	na	na	na
Slovakia	na	**29**	25	33	20	30	36	35	27	23	36	33	23	31	27	22
Slovenia	na	**50**	44	55	28	48	68	67	47	33	61	53	31	61	48	47
South Africa	na	**na**	na	na	na	na	na	na	na	na	na	na	na	na	na	na
Spain	na	**60**	57	63	50	59	67	69	53	58	72	61	54	67	59	58
Sweden	na	**39**	35	42	23	38	48	54	35	31	43	43	26	41	40	35
Switzerland	na	**na**	na	na	na	na	na	na	na	na	na	na	na	na	na	na
Taiwan	na	**na**	na	na	na	na	na	na	na	na	na	na	na	na	na	na
Tanzania	na	**na**	na	na	na	na	na	na	na	na	na	na	na	na	na	na
Turkey	na	**90**	89	92	88	93	91	91	89	95	90	91	91	88	91	95
Uganda	na	**na**	na	na	na	na	na	na	na	na	na	na	na	na	na	na
Ukraine	na	**58**	48	65	36	57	70	70	56	53	67	53	52	61	54	67
United States	na	**na**	na	na	na	na	na	na	na	na	na	na	na	na	na	na
Uruguay	na	**na**	na	na	na	na	na	na	na	na	na	na	na	na	na	na
Venezuela	na	**na**	na	na	na	na	na	na	na	na	na	na	na	na	na	na
Vietnam	na	**na**	na	na	na	na	na	na	na	na	na	na	na	na	na	na
Zimbabwe	na	**na**	na	na	na	na	na	na	na	na	na	na	na	na	na	na
Total	na	**55**	49	61	41	53	67	63	53	47	63	55	48	60	54	50

RANKING	
Country	2000
Malta	92
Turkey	90
Croatia	78
Ireland	69
Bulgaria	68
Romania	68
Hungary	67
Latvia	66
Northern Ireland	63
Spain	60
Netherlands	60
Russian Fed.	59
Poland	59
Belgium	59
Austria	58
Ukraine	58
Denmark	56
Great Britain	56
Germany	56
Lithuania	55
Estonia	54
Greece	50
Czech Republic	50
Slovenia	50
Portugal	50
Italy	48
France	45
Luxembourg	44
Iceland	39
Sweden	39
Finland	37
Slovakia	29
Belarus	22
Total	55

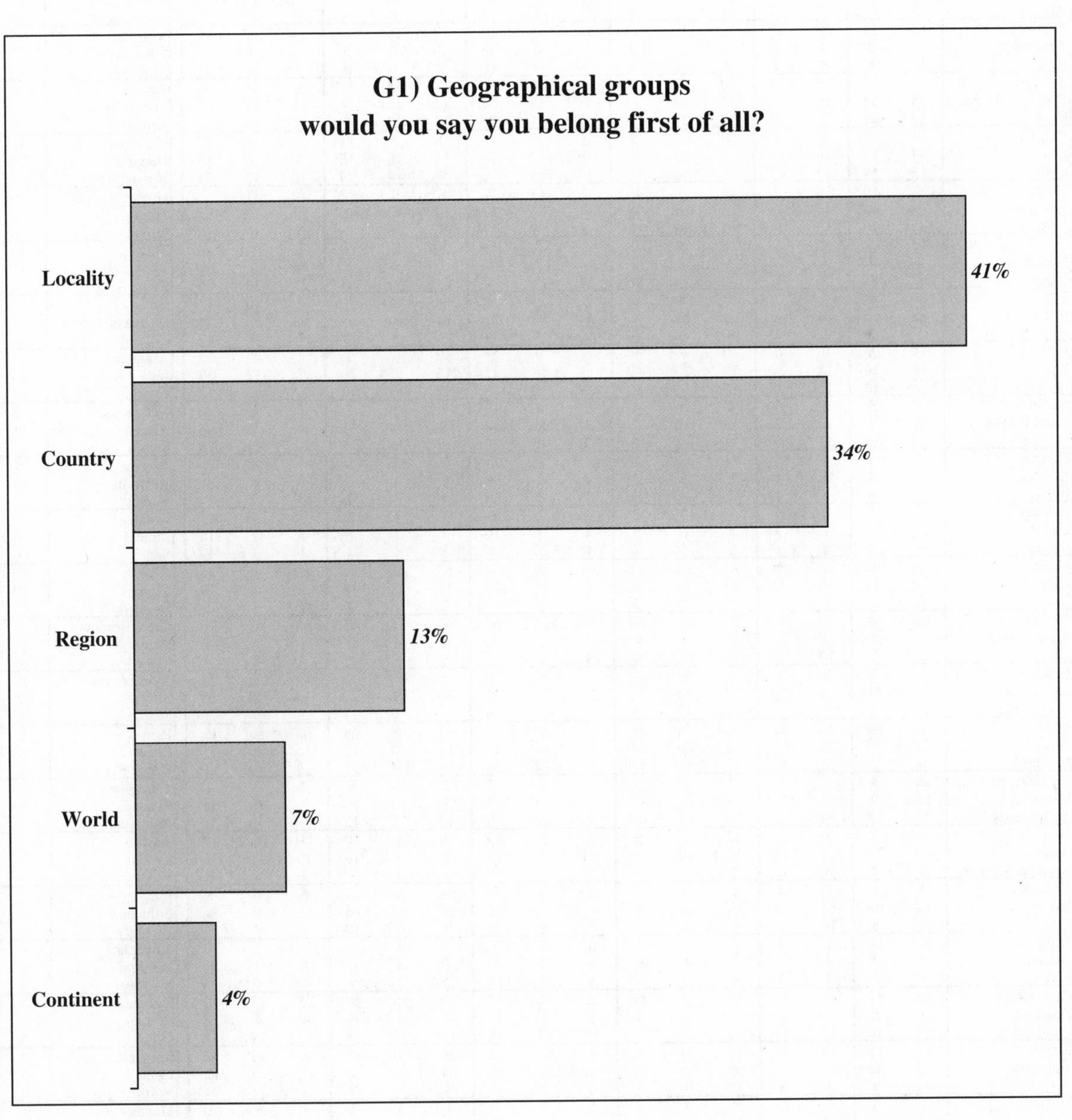
G1) Geographical groups
would you say you belong first of all?
Locality
41%
Country
34%
Region
13%
World
7%
Continent
4%

G001) BELONG FIRST TO CONTINENT OR THE WORLD

To which of these geographical groups would you say you belong first of all?

Continent / The world (%)

(WVS: V214; EVS: V251)

Country	Wave		Gender		Age			Education			Income			Values		
	1990	2000	Male	Female	16-29	30-49	50+	Lower	Middle	Upper	Lower	Middle	Upper	Mat	Mixed	Postm.
Albania	na	**2**	2	2	4	1	1	1	2	4	1	3	3	3	2	na
Algeria	na	**10**	10	10	14	8	6	5	10	13	8	14	11	8	10	14
Argentina	11	**13**	13	13	15	15	9	11	15	22	9	14	15	8	12	19
Armenia	na	**11**	12	11	13	11	9	5	11	15	12	9	15	9	12	18
Australia	na	**11**	12	10	15	11	7	6	10	15	10	10	10	6	10	13
Austria	7	**7**	7	7	6	8	8	7	7	9	6	8	9	6	8	7
Azerbaijan	na	**18**	19	17	19	19	14	14	18	19	19	16	24	19	17	19
Bangladesh	na	**3**	4	2	4	2	5	1	4	8	2	2	5	2	4	8
Belarus	6	**8**	9	7	9	10	5	3	9	13	7	8	10	7	7	21
Belgium	18	**17**	19	14	20	20	12	8	16	24	17	15	17	8	15	30
Bosnia and Herz.	na	**14**	16	12	15	14	12	6	13	24	12	12	16	11	15	23
Brazil	22	**29**	30	28	32	28	26	26	31	31	28	27	30	26	29	34
Bulgaria	11	**7**	8	7	16	8	3	3	7	17	2	8	11	4	10	12
Canada	13	**16**	18	13	19	17	12	9	17	18	12	16	18	6	16	19
Chile	13	**14**	15	13	16	14	11	11	15	18	9	14	18	10	12	24
China	4	**10**	12	7	13	8	10	4	14	7	8	9	12	10	11	7
Colombia	na	**14**	14	13	16	13	11	11	14	17	13	12	16	11	15	17
Croatia	na	**10**	13	8	10	14	7	6	12	17	7	10	13	3	10	16
Czech Republic	13	**8**	9	7	12	9	5	7	8	13	8	7	9	3	9	14
Denmark	4	**3**	4	3	5	4	2	3	3	4	2	3	3	na	3	8
Dominican Rep.	na	**33**	34	32	32	34	36	28	23	37	22	35	44	28	34	35
Egypt	na	**9**	9	9	13	8	6	8	11	9	9	9	8	7	10	14
El Salvador	na	**na**	na	na	na	na	na	na	na	na	na	na	na	na	na	na
Estonia	5	**5**	6	4	8	6	3	2	5	11	3	5	6	5	5	12
Finland	14	**8**	9	6	10	6	8	6	9	9	10	6	7	4	8	16
France	18	**16**	18	14	19	20	10	11	18	25	13	15	20	7	12	39
Georgia	na	**13**	12	13	13	14	10	11	12	15	12	13	13	12	13	17
Germany	10	**5**	6	4	7	6	4	3	6	13	3	5	5	1	6	8
Great Britain	12	**9**	12	7	13	10	7	5	11	14	8	9	11	na	na	na
Greece	na	**16**	17	15	21	14	6	7	16	17	17	16	15	12	14	25
Hungary	9	**6**	8	5	11	8	2	5	8	11	7	5	8	4	8	26
Iceland	5	**5**	6	4	8	5	2	4	4	6	5	4	6	3	4	9
India	9	**5**	5	4	7	4	4	3	4	10	4	3	7	3	7	9
Indonesia	na	**3**	2	4	9	2	2	2	2	6	3	3	3	3	3	21
Iran	na	**7**	7	7	8	6	5	4	7	10	7	7	6	5	7	10
Ireland	5	**4**	4	3	2	5	3	1	5	4	4	4	4	1	3	8
Israel	na	**na**	na	na	na	na	na	na	na	na	na	na	na	na	na	na
Italy	20	**13**	14	12	15	16	9	7	15	24	11	13	16	7	11	19
Japan	3	**2**	2	3	3	2	2	2	2	3	3	1	2	1	2	5
Jordan	na	**68**	66	69	73	67	60	66	72	67	67	71	68	65	69	75
Korea, South	na	**3**	4	3	5	3	1	2	3	4	4	4	2	1	5	4
Latvia	5	**7**	10	5	15	7	4	8	6	9	6	6	8	5	8	9
Lithuania	6	**7**	8	6	8	8	4	6	6	10	5	7	8	6	6	14
Luxembourg	na	**21**	23	20	27	26	13	22	16	33	20	21	27	14	20	35
Macedonia	na	**9**	9	9	12	10	5	6	8	16	5	10	13	7	9	20
Malta	na	**na**	na	na	na	na	na	na	na	na	na	na	na	na	na	na
Mexico	18	**19**	22	17	22	20	14	14	24	32	14	20	26	15	20	31
Moldova	na	**19**	21	16	22	19	16	13	17	26	16	18	23	19	19	23
Montenegro	na	**4**	5	3	7	4	2	1	5	7	2	2	6	2	5	10
Morocco	na	**9**	11	6	11	7	7	7	14	17	7	10	10	7	10	15
Netherlands	13	**13**	14	11	16	15	8	8	12	18	12	13	12	6	13	16
New Zealand	na	**9**	9	9	13	9	8	5	9	13	10	8	10	4	9	13
Nigeria	20	**11**	11	11	13	10	7	10	10	15	9	9	16	10	11	13
Northern Ireland	8	**4**	5	4	7	7	2	3	5	7	3	4	7	5	3	6
Norway	4	**6**	7	4	9	6	3	4	5	9	na	na	na	6	6	8
Pakistan	na	**na**	na	na	na	na	na	na	na	na	na	na	na	na	na	na
Peru	na	**8**	10	7	8	9	7	8	8	9	9	6	10	5	9	8
Philippines	na	**4**	4	4	5	3	4	3	4	5	3	3	6	5	3	4
Poland	7	**3**	4	2	3	4	2	3	3	6	3	3	6	1	4	6
Portugal	14	**6**	7	5	9	8	3	3	11	13	2	7	9	4	6	13
Puerto Rico	na	**17**	16	18	16	19	17	22	18	17	19	15	18	25	17	17
Romania	5	**5**	5	5	7	5	4	3	5	9	4	4	6	4	4	18
Russian Fed.	16	**16**	17	15	21	18	11	12	17	17	14	16	18	13	19	12
Serbia	na	**11**	13	10	17	14	6	4	11	22	9	10	15	5	14	42
Singapore	na	**na**	na	na	na	na	na	na	na	na	na	na	na	na	na	na
Slovakia	na	**9**	10	8	11	10	6	6	9	17	6	8	9	5	11	24
Slovenia	4	**6**	7	5	8	7	4	5	7	7	4	5	7	3	6	10
South Africa	11	**14**	13	16	17	14	10	14	13	35	12	20	12	18	11	23
Spain	10	**10**	12	9	15	13	5	6	14	18	8	9	12	6	10	19
Sweden	7	**10**	10	10	12	10	7	3	11	13	11	8	8	6	9	13
Switzerland	12	**23**	24	22	35	26	11	14	24	35	20	19	26	12	21	34
Taiwan	na	**15**	18	11	12	15	14	11	14	19	13	13	17	12	17	19
Tanzania	na	**8**	8	8	10	6	8	7	8	11	7	8	11	9	8	17
Turkey	9	**11**	12	9	13	11	4	7	13	24	7	11	21	7	10	19
Uganda	na	**19**	14	23	17	20	20	27	16	9	16	12	17	22	19	7
Ukraine	na	**17**	20	14	25	17	11	10	16	23	15	18	18	13	19	43
United States	19	**22**	22	23	28	20	21	24	27	19	25	18	25	14	21	29
Uruguay	na	**17**	16	18	19	19	15	12	23	27	14	11	26	13	13	30
Venezuela	na	**15**	15	14	17	14	10	10	14	20	12	13	15	14	14	18
Vietnam	na	**7**	8	6	8	8	5	7	6	11	6	9	6	5	8	9
Zimbabwe	na	**10**	12	9	13	9	8	8	13	38	9	10	13	9	12	6
Total	11	11	12	11	15	12	8	8	12	16	10	11	13	9	11	18

RANKING	
Country	2000
Jordan	68
Dominican Rep.	33
Brazil	29
Switzerland	23
United States	22
Luxembourg	21
Mexico	19
Uganda	19
Moldova	19
Azerbaijan	18
Puerto Rico	17
Uruguay	17
Ukraine	17
Belgium	17
Russian Fed.	16
Greece	16
France	16
Canada	16
Taiwan	15
Venezuela	15
South Africa	14
Chile	14
Bosnia and Herz.	14
Colombia	14
Argentina	13
Italy	13
Georgia	13
Netherlands	13
Armenia	11
Serbia	11
Nigeria	11
Australia	11
Turkey	11
Croatia	10
Zimbabwe	10
Spain	10
Algeria	10
China	10
Sweden	10
Great Britain	9
Egypt	9
Macedonia	9
New Zealand	9
Slovakia	9
Morocco	9
Peru	8
Belarus	8
Czech Republic	8
Tanzania	8
Finland	8
Bulgaria	7
Austria	7
Latvia	7
Vietnam	7
Iran	7
Lithuania	7
Hungary	6
Slovenia	6
Portugal	6
Norway	6
Estonia	5
Germany	5
India	5
Romania	5
Iceland	5
Northern Ireland	4
Montenegro	4
Philippines	4
Ireland	4
Korea, South	3
Bangladesh	3
Denmark	3
Poland	3
Indonesia	3
Japan	2
Albania	2
Total	11

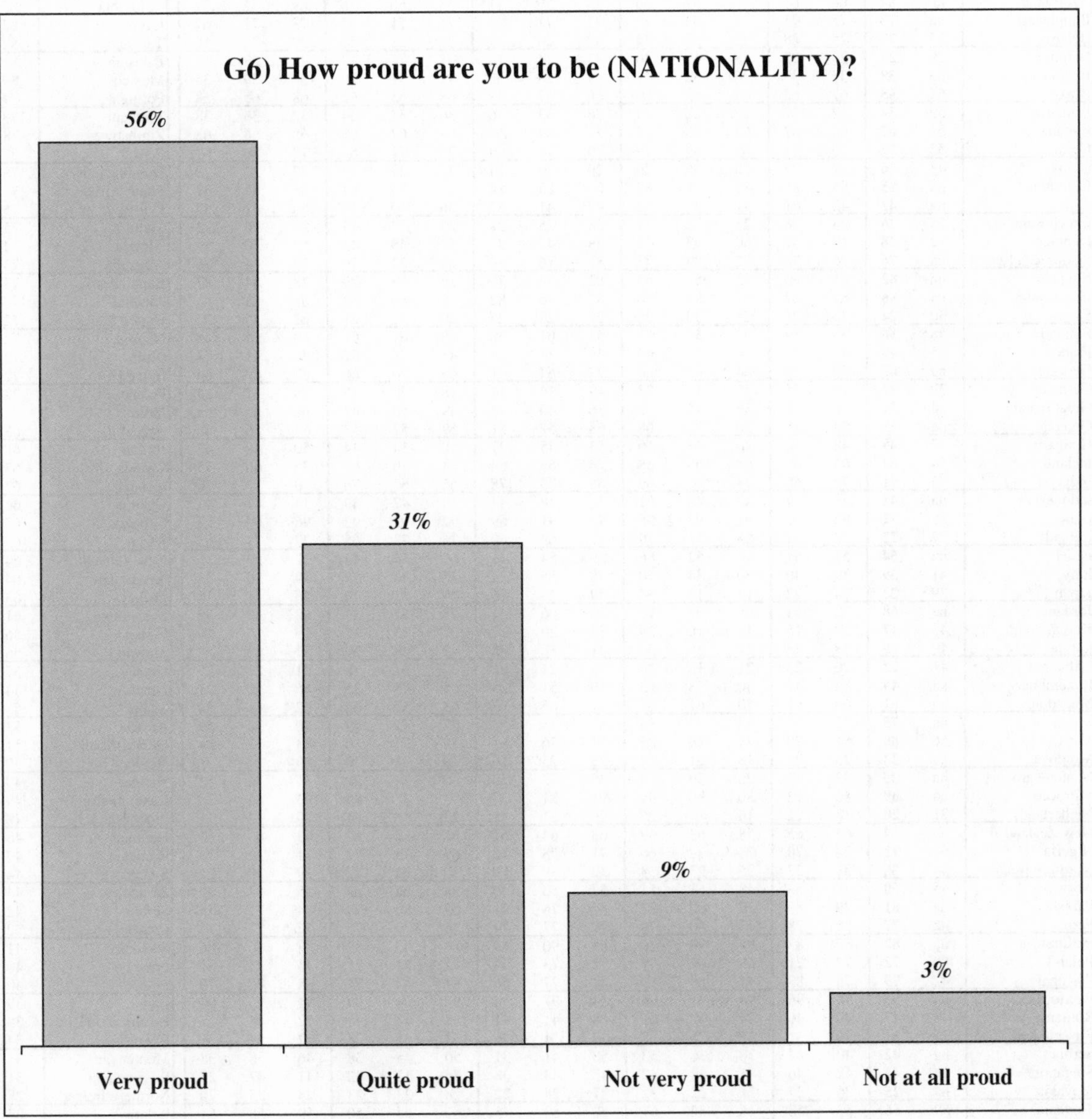
G6) How proud are you to be (NATIONALITY)?
56%
31%
9%
3%
Very proud
Quite proud
Not very proud
Not at all proud

G006) HOW PROUD OF YOUR NATIONALITY

How proud are you to be (NATIONALITY)?

Very proud (%) (WVS: V216; EVS: V255)

Country	Wave		Gender		Age			Education			Income			Values		
	1990	2000	Male	Female	16-29	30-49	50+	Lower	Middle	Upper	Lower	Middle	Upper	Mat	Mixed	Postm.
Albania	na	**73**	74	71	67	71	81	72	73	74	74	65	78	77	71	74
Algeria	na	**74**	73	74	68	75	83	80	73	71	75	71	72	78	71	71
Argentina	55	**68**	69	67	65	66	73	72	65	54	74	68	61	69	70	62
Armenia	na	**44**	46	41	39	48	45	50	44	39	47	36	46	42	44	52
Australia	na	**73**	73	74	68	72	81	83	74	65	75	72	73	73	75	72
Austria	53	**53**	52	53	47	49	59	57	52	35	51	50	57	55	59	39
Azerbaijan	na	**64**	66	61	64	62	66	75	59	71	55	60	76	69	55	57
Bangladesh	na	**73**	75	71	71	73	79	75	71	72	71	71	77	77	71	67
Belarus	35	**27**	25	28	22	23	34	32	26	21	29	28	20	29	27	16
Belgium	29	**23**	23	23	18	17	30	33	24	14	31	26	17	28	22	17
Bosnia and Herz.	na	**38**	37	39	36	32	47	49	36	33	47	41	29	34	39	33
Brazil	64	**65**	67	62	64	63	69	66	67	49	68	65	62	68	65	58
Bulgaria	39	**34**	32	37	28	27	44	36	33	36	36	33	34	32	36	38
Canada	61	**67**	66	67	62	65	72	74	64	64	64	67	68	68	66	68
Chile	53	**72**	70	73	69	69	79	79	71	59	75	71	67	78	70	67
China	43	**26**	27	25	29	25	26	20	30	24	20	29	29	27	27	28
Colombia	na	**85**	85	85	83	85	87	86	85	84	85	85	84	83	85	87
Croatia	na	**42**	42	41	31	39	52	47	41	32	56	40	36	50	41	37
Czech Republic	25	**26**	24	28	23	22	32	28	25	22	29	27	23	28	26	23
Denmark	42	**48**	49	47	50	43	52	59	41	32	52	48	43	55	50	39
Dominican Rep.	na	**76**	76	76	72	83	73	81	76	76	80	72	76	72	74	86
Egypt	na	**82**	84	80	82	82	83	82	84	79	86	79	79	78	84	87
El Salvador	na	**86**	84	87	82	87	90	87	86	82	89	86	84	na	na	na
Estonia	30	**24**	23	25	25	20	26	27	20	27	29	22	21	22	25	22
Finland	38	**56**	53	59	53	58	57	53	61	58	49	61	61	59	56	48
France	35	**40**	40	40	34	32	49	46	34	29	48	37	32	46	41	27
Georgia	na	**65**	70	60	64	64	66	73	64	61	65	70	60	67	63	69
Germany	29	**17**	19	15	9	13	23	19	14	16	18	20	15	18	17	14
Great Britain	54	**51**	54	48	36	44	62	56	46	43	49	50	47	na	na	na
Greece	na	**55**	54	55	50	54	68	68	57	51	59	52	53	63	56	48
Hungary	47	**49**	48	50	40	45	59	53	45	37	50	54	44	50	48	42
Iceland	54	**67**	65	69	68	66	66	74	65	54	64	70	65	75	66	55
India	75	**71**	74	66	73	70	69	66	73	78	66	67	76	70	73	76
Indonesia	na	**48**	53	44	43	48	51	54	48	44	50	47	49	54	47	43
Iran	na	**92**	92	93	91	93	95	96	91	89	92	92	92	96	92	83
Ireland	77	**72**	72	71	65	71	79	77	69	69	76	73	65	77	71	63
Israel	na	**54**	51	57	46	52	66	69	54	45	61	54	48	32	59	56
Italy	41	**39**	39	40	30	34	50	48	35	24	45	44	29	49	40	33
Japan	29	**23**	24	22	14	13	34	39	23	16	29	21	20	26	21	15
Jordan	na	**68**	72	64	65	68	72	73	66	61	73	67	63	68	68	59
Korea, South	45	**17**	20	15	11	16	29	34	20	12	22	13	15	19	16	15
Latvia	49	**40**	38	43	21	35	54	41	38	48	43	40	39	37	43	33
Lithuania	41	**22**	20	23	21	18	26	23	21	21	27	24	18	21	21	27
Luxembourg	na	**49**	52	47	40	38	63	59	51	25	65	48	35	66	50	27
Macedonia	na	**61**	60	61	50	61	69	54	65	59	63	57	62	62	61	34
Malta	na	**75**	72	77	63	72	84	83	74	55	77	75	69	80	74	59
Mexico	56	**80**	81	79	75	80	85	82	76	81	78	77	80	83	77	84
Moldova	na	**23**	25	22	18	21	29	23	25	19	26	23	20	25	17	31
Montenegro	na	**33**	33	32	26	30	39	35	32	30	30	34	29	31	34	52
Morocco	na	**89**	86	92	86	90	94	91	81	77	93	87	85	93	86	78
Netherlands	21	**20**	18	22	16	16	26	29	21	11	23	15	21	29	22	11
New Zealand	na	**64**	64	65	58	63	69	68	64	61	61	62	67	63	65	60
Nigeria	68	**72**	74	70	73	72	66	71	73	71	69	75	72	71	72	76
Northern Ireland	54	**28**	31	27	25	23	33	32	30	19	30	32	22	29	30	22
Norway	45	**50**	48	53	48	51	51	57	53	40	na	na	na	55	53	27
Pakistan	na	**81**	79	83	79	80	91	87	76	71	85	80	79	84	77	100
Peru	na	**77**	75	78	72	80	79	79	77	74	76	79	75	77	77	75
Philippines	na	**87**	87	87	84	90	86	85	90	85	88	87	87	88	86	86
Poland	69	**72**	72	71	69	67	79	75	73	54	72	71	71	71	71	81
Portugal	42	**79**	75	83	71	80	83	84	71	56	84	84	74	88	75	70
Puerto Rico	na	**95**	94	96	94	91	98	94	97	94	97	94	94	94	95	96
Romania	48	**47**	49	46	29	42	61	58	41	41	57	43	44	52	44	27
Russian Fed.	26	**31**	30	31	25	28	38	39	31	26	33	31	28	32	29	31
Serbia	na	**42**	40	44	30	36	53	50	41	31	50	45	38	46	38	38
Singapore	na	**44**	42	46	45	42	42	45	44	38	46	45	42	41	47	27
Slovakia	na	**25**	26	24	21	22	32	27	24	22	28	23	23	28	23	20
Slovenia	59	**56**	53	58	46	52	67	68	53	45	61	54	50	59	56	54
South Africa	64	**75**	75	75	78	75	68	78	72	67	76	82	67	73	77	74
Spain	45	**53**	51	56	43	51	61	61	44	47	54	56	53	58	55	40
Sweden	41	**41**	42	41	38	40	44	52	39	36	43	40	41	42	42	39
Switzerland	38	**25**	25	25	18	20	36	34	24	12	26	26	24	34	27	13
Taiwan	na	**15**	14	16	8	16	17	19	17	10	18	16	12	13	15	22
Tanzania	na	**82**	81	83	78	80	92	85	76	82	87	80	83	83	81	92
Turkey	67	**63**	60	66	57	65	73	67	61	46	62	65	54	70	65	48
Uganda	na	**66**	80	54	71	64	57	65	67	70	79	73	70	54	72	78
Ukraine	na	**24**	25	23	18	23	28	23	25	23	22	17	33	22	25	38
United States	76	**72**	72	72	61	71	83	76	75	69	71	71	76	74	74	68
Uruguay	na	**75**	72	77	61	70	84	77	73	66	78	76	71	76	77	70
Venezuela	na	**92**	92	92	91	92	95	95	91	91	92	93	92	88	93	95
Vietnam	na	**78**	82	75	76	75	86	76	83	77	81	76	80	79	82	79
Zimbabwe	na	**78**	78	78	78	78	79	80	76	52	80	77	78	76	79	87
Total	47	**56**	57	56	56	54	59	63	53	52	59	56	54	56	56	53

RANKING	
Country	2000
Puerto Rico	95
Iran	92
Venezuela	92
Morocco	89
Philippines	87
El Salvador	86
Colombia	85
Egypt	82
Tanzania	82
Pakistan	81
Mexico	80
Portugal	79
Vietnam	78
Zimbabwe	78
Peru	77
Dominican Rep.	76
South Africa	75
Uruguay	75
Malta	75
Algeria	74
Australia	73
Bangladesh	73
Albania	73
United States	72
Nigeria	72
Chile	72
Ireland	72
Poland	72
India	71
Argentina	68
Jordan	68
Canada	67
Iceland	67
Uganda	66
Georgia	65
Brazil	65
New Zealand	64
Azerbaijan	64
Turkey	63
Macedonia	61
Finland	56
Slovenia	56
Greece	55
Israel	54
Spain	53
Austria	53
Great Britain	51
Norway	50
Hungary	49
Luxembourg	49
Indonesia	48
Denmark	48
Romania	47
Singapore	44
Armenia	44
Serbia	42
Croatia	42
Sweden	41
Latvia	40
France	40
Italy	39
Bosnia and Herz.	38
Bulgaria	34
Montenegro	33
Russian Fed.	31
Northern Ireland	28
Belarus	27
Czech Republic	26
China	26
Switzerland	25
Slovakia	25
Ukraine	24
Estonia	24
Belgium	23
Moldova	23
Japan	23
Lithuania	22
Netherlands	20
Korea, South	17
Germany	17
Taiwan	15
Total	56

Y002) MATERIALIST

MATERIALIST-POSTMATERIALIST VALUES

% Materialist values (WVS: V405)

Country	Wave		Gender		Age			Education			Income			Values		
	1990	2000	Male	Female	16-29	30-49	50+	Lower	Middle	Upper	Lower	Middle	Upper	Mat	Mixed	Postm.
Albania	na	**44**	40	47	37	44	48	52	39	34	49	47	36	100	na	na
Algeria	na	**35**	34	37	34	31	47	45	39	23	37	36	30	100	na	na
Argentina	25	**18**	19	18	16	15	24	24	11	9	25	17	13	100	na	na
Armenia	na	**45**	41	48	41	46	49	52	47	32	38	51	49	100	na	na
Australia	na	**8**	9	7	7	7	10	9	9	6	8	9	6	100	na	na
Austria	14	**8**	7	8	8	5	10	10	6	5	11	8	7	100	na	na
Azerbaijan	na	**60**	56	64	59	60	62	72	61	57	64	61	56	100	na	na
Bangladesh	na	**39**	34	45	37	40	40	43	37	30	47	34	37	100	na	na
Belarus	34	**50**	43	55	38	46	63	66	46	36	59	46	40	100	na	na
Belgium	22	**23**	18	28	17	21	28	42	21	12	28	26	15	100	na	na
Bosnia and Herz.	na	**30**	28	33	29	29	34	35	31	23	33	30	27	100	na	na
Brazil	40	**31**	28	33	26	34	33	39	27	16	37	34	21	100	na	na
Bulgaria	28	**49**	46	51	41	40	60	67	43	31	62	45	41	100	na	na
Canada	12	**8**	8	8	6	9	9	12	8	7	7	9	8	100	na	na
Chile	25	**28**	24	32	22	26	36	32	27	20	32	27	22	100	na	na
China	51	**42**	45	40	35	45	42	41	44	30	40	42	51	100	na	na
Colombia	na	**14**	13	15	14	13	16	21	12	6	20	12	9	100	na	na
Croatia	na	**15**	13	18	7	18	19	18	15	10	12	20	12	100	na	na
Czech Republic	26	**25**	22	28	22	24	28	32	21	11	31	25	21	100	na	na
Denmark	16	**9**	9	8	11	5	11	11	6	4	11	9	4	100	na	na
Dominican Rep.	na	**19**	15	21	20	16	18	28	30	13	25	13	17	100	na	na
Egypt	na	**43**	38	48	32	47	51	54	36	25	50	45	39	100	na	na
El Salvador	na	**na**	na	na	na	na	na	na	na	na	na	na	na	na	na	na
Estonia	32	**41**	34	47	35	38	47	46	41	32	43	44	39	100	na	na
Finland	6	**26**	24	28	24	28	26	31	20	17	25	26	27	100	na	na
France	21	**28**	25	30	21	24	35	35	20	15	35	29	17	100	na	na
Georgia	na	**46**	45	48	40	47	51	52	46	44	47	48	43	100	na	na
Germany	12	**28**	26	30	13	25	37	36	24	14	33	30	30	100	na	na
Great Britain	20	**na**	na	na	na	na	na	na	na	na	na	na	na	na	na	na
Greece	na	**19**	18	20	17	20	21	16	21	18	15	20	22	100	na	na
Hungary	45	**51**	48	53	45	44	60	57	41	34	55	52	45	100	na	na
Iceland	25	**22**	19	24	20	23	22	29	20	11	24	20	20	100	na	na
India	40	**39**	41	36	40	40	34	39	42	36	42	44	34	100	na	na
Indonesia	na	**38**	35	42	29	36	45	54	41	24	38	39	43	100	na	na
Iran	na	**25**	25	26	25	26	27	30	26	20	26	27	23	100	na	na
Ireland	24	**20**	19	20	17	20	22	14	17	26	25	17	16	100	na	na
Israel	na	**16**	17	14	19	17	10	13	16	16	10	17	17	100	na	na
Italy	25	**14**	12	16	8	11	20	21	9	9	21	12	8	100	na	na
Japan	29	**17**	17	16	11	17	19	13	17	18	17	16	19	100	na	na
Jordan	na	**40**	39	41	32	43	51	47	31	36	43	39	37	100	na	na
Korea, South	46	**46**	43	50	35	47	57	77	50	37	50	46	43	100	na	na
Latvia	27	**35**	31	38	20	32	43	39	34	33	42	32	29	100	na	na
Lithuania	27	**31**	30	32	27	25	39	47	27	17	38	32	25	100	na	na
Luxembourg	na	**20**	19	22	18	20	22	22	22	16	30	18	13	100	na	na
Macedonia	na	**34**	33	35	29	33	41	34	34	37	35	35	32	100	na	na
Malta	na	**35**	30	39	22	37	41	51	31	12	45	33	26	100	na	na
Mexico	25	**25**	25	26	21	26	31	31	20	13	29	26	19	100	na	na
Moldova	na	**46**	44	47	41	46	50	52	47	39	49	50	44	100	na	na
Montenegro	na	**46**	44	49	35	42	58	61	41	28	54	49	42	100	na	na
Morocco	na	**39**	34	43	36	40	43	42	29	14	32	33	38	100	na	na
Netherlands	10	**12**	9	15	11	9	16	21	9	6	17	12	4	100	na	na
New Zealand	na	**9**	10	8	7	10	9	9	11	8	11	7	9	100	na	na
Nigeria	36	**35**	33	38	33	39	33	39	34	33	33	37	37	100	na	na
Northern Ireland	22	**25**	23	28	17	25	29	29	25	14	31	25	18	100	na	na
Norway	29	**14**	12	15	11	10	19	23	11	7	0	0	0	100	na	na
Pakistan	na	**58**	60	55	53	59	64	69	45	44	70	59	38	100	na	na
Peru	na	**21**	20	21	20	21	21	28	22	13	24	21	14	100	na	na
Philippines	na	**39**	38	40	36	39	46	42	40	36	45	36	38	100	na	na
Poland	31	**37**	31	42	35	34	41	44	31	23	42	34	31	100	na	na
Portugal	34	**36**	30	41	21	28	51	42	25	16	52	33	30	100	na	na
Puerto Rico	na	**12**	11	12	10	10	14	21	13	10	14	12	10	100	na	na
Romania	44	**45**	41	50	39	42	52	60	45	22	55	51	35	100	na	na
Russian Fed.	39	**52**	46	57	41	51	60	66	54	40	59	53	45	100	na	na
Serbia	na	**48**	45	51	40	42	56	67	44	26	56	53	37	100	na	na
Singapore	na	**27**	22	31	18	30	49	34	21	32	35	26	23	100	na	na
Slovakia	na	**46**	41	50	38	42	57	60	41	30	58	49	35	100	na	na
Slovenia	28	**17**	16	17	11	16	22	24	15	11	23	12	15	100	na	na
South Africa	35	**37**	35	40	35	36	47	35	41	31	37	35	40	100	na	na
Spain	30	**25**	21	29	13	20	37	32	18	17	28	26	19	100	na	na
Sweden	14	**6**	8	5	7	4	8	10	6	4	8	6	5	100	na	na
Switzerland	14	**14**	12	15	12	14	15	19	14	2	16	16	11	100	na	na
Taiwan	na	**45**	38	52	41	44	50	50	44	41	46	48	46	100	na	na
Tanzania	na	**32**	32	32	30	34	27	32	32	28	36	30	28	100	na	na
Turkey	25	**22**	21	23	18	23	30	26	18	12	23	24	17	100	na	na
Uganda	na	**32**	28	37	30	32	48	37	32	22	27	27	29	100	na	na
Ukraine	na	**46**	41	49	40	43	52	61	47	35	54	41	41	100	na	na
United States	16	**9**	8	11	7	11	9	10	10	9	8	9	10	100	na	na
Uruguay	na	**18**	17	19	10	12	26	24	10	9	31	13	9	100	na	na
Venezuela	na	**25**	24	26	25	24	25	31	26	14	28	26	20	100	na	na
Vietnam	na	**20**	19	21	21	18	22	21	18	24	14	23	20	100	na	na
Zimbabwe	na	**41**	38	44	37	44	45	46	35	0	46	41	32	100	na	na
Total	27	**30**	28	32	26	29	34	36	29	21	34	30	26	100	na	na

RANKING

Country	2000
Azerbaijan	60
Pakistan	58
Russian Fed.	52
Hungary	51
Belarus	50
Bulgaria	49
Serbia	48
Montenegro	46
Georgia	46
Korea, South	46
Slovakia	46
Moldova	46
Ukraine	46
Romania	45
Taiwan	45
Armenia	45
Albania	44
Egypt	43
China	42
Estonia	41
Zimbabwe	41
Jordan	40
Philippines	39
India	39
Bangladesh	39
Morocco	39
Indonesia	38
South Africa	37
Poland	37
Portugal	36
Algeria	35
Nigeria	35
Latvia	35
Malta	35
Macedonia	34
Uganda	32
Tanzania	32
Lithuania	31
Brazil	31
Bosnia and Herz.	30
Germany	28
France	28
Chile	28
Singapore	27
Finland	26
Mexico	25
Northern Ireland	25
Czech Republic	25
Iran	25
Spain	25
Venezuela	25
Belgium	23
Turkey	22
Iceland	22
Peru	21
Luxembourg	20
Ireland	20
Vietnam	20
Greece	19
Dominican Rep.	19
Argentina	18
Uruguay	18
Slovenia	17
Japan	17
Israel	16
Croatia	15
Italy	14
Colombia	14
Switzerland	14
Norway	14
Netherlands	12
Puerto Rico	12
United States	9
New Zealand	9
Denmark	9
Canada	8
Australia	8
Austria	8
Sweden	6
Total	30

Y002) POSTMATERIALIST

MATERIALIST-POSTMATERIALIST VALUES

% Postmaterialist (WVS: V405)

Country	Wave		Gender		Age			Education			Income			Values		
	1990	2000	Male	Female	16-29	30-49	50+	Lower	Middle	Upper	Lower	Middle	Upper	Mat	Mixed	Postm.
Albania	na	**4**	5	3	4	4	3	3	4	6	5	4	3	na	na	100
Algeria	na	**9**	10	9	11	10	5	5	7	15	8	13	12	na	na	100
Argentina	19	**25**	26	25	29	27	20	17	35	47	16	23	38	na	na	100
Armenia	na	**5**	5	6	7	4	4	4	5	7	7	4	5	na	na	100
Australia	na	**35**	34	35	37	36	31	29	33	41	32	34	41	na	na	100
Austria	25	**30**	29	30	38	32	23	23	33	46	24	30	37	na	na	100
Azerbaijan	na	**3**	4	3	3	4	3	2	3	5	3	5	3	na	na	100
Bangladesh	na	**5**	5	5	6	4	4	4	6	5	5	6	4	na	na	100
Belarus	7	**6**	8	5	8	8	3	2	6	13	3	6	11	na	na	100
Belgium	24	**20**	24	17	22	24	16	6	19	33	15	19	27	na	na	100
Bosnia and Herz.	na	**4**	5	4	5	5	3	3	5	5	5	4	5	na	na	100
Brazil	7	**12**	13	10	14	11	9	6	14	23	6	10	20	na	na	100
Bulgaria	9	**3**	4	3	6	4	1	2	4	4	2	4	3	na	na	100
Canada	26	**29**	31	26	34	28	26	23	26	38	24	30	33	na	na	100
Chile	19	**17**	17	17	20	19	9	10	17	28	13	16	24	na	na	100
China	6	**3**	2	4	4	4	2	2	4	9	2	4	5	na	na.	100
Colombia	na	**8**	8	8	11	7	5	6	10	8	8	7	9	na	na	100
Croatia	na	**19**	21	18	27	20	13	13	21	31	14	18	23	na	na	100
Czech Republic	11	**10**	11	9	13	10	8	7	11	19	7	9	14	na	na	100
Denmark	16	**16**	15	17	12	23	12	10	19	26	10	18	27	na	na	100
Dominican Rep.	na	**16**	18	15	17	15	0	6	13	18	16	14	17	na	na	100
Egypt	na	**6**	6	5	9	4	3	3	7	11	5	5	7	na	na	100
El Salvador	na	**na**	na	na	na	na	na	na	na	na	na	na	na	na	na	na
Estonia	6	**3**	3	2	5	2	2	1	3	4	1	2	4	na	na	100
Finland	29	**11**	11	11	14	10	9	9	11	18	13	9	10	na	na	100
France	25	**18**	20	16	24	21	13	11	25	31	16	16	25	na	na	100
Georgia	na	**4**	5	3	4	4	3	2	4	4	4	3	4	na	na	100
Germany	23	**17**	19	16	27	18	12	9	21	36	13	14	23	na	na	100
Great Britain	20	**na**	na	na	na	na	na	na	na	na	na	na	na	na	na	na
Greece	na	**17**	21	14	19	14	17	15	15	18	21	14	15	na	na	100
Hungary	4	**2**	4	1	4	3	1	2	4	4	2	3	2	na	na	100
Iceland	11	**11**	11	10	11	11	10	6	9	23	11	10	11	na	na	100
India	6	**2**	3	2	3	3	1	1	3	4	2	2	3	na	na	100
Indonesia	na	**3**	4	2	3	4	2	2	2	5	1	4	4	na	na	100
Iran	na	**10**	11	9	11	9	8	5	10	15	8	9	12	na	na	100
Ireland	19	**14**	13	15	15	14	13	19	14	11	11	13	17	na	na	100
Israel	na	**4**	4	3	5	3	3	3	4	3	3	4	4	na	na	100
Italy	22	**28**	30	27	37	33	20	17	35	41	24	34	35	na	na	100
Japan	10	**9**	11	8	10	10	9	7	8	15	8	8	13	na	na	100
Jordan	na	**6**	7	6	8	7	3	5	6	10	5	6	7	na	na	100
Korea, South	11	**6**	6	6	14	4	1	0	3	10	6	5	6	na	na	100
Latvia	9	**5**	7	3	10	5	3	3	5	6	4	4	7	na	na	100
Lithuania	13	**6**	8	5	9	8	3	1	7	11	3	5	9	na	na	100
Luxembourg	na	**17**	15	18	16	21	13	11	17	27	14	15	24	na	na	100
Macedonia	na	**5**	5	4	8	5	2	5	5	4	3	6	5	na	na	100
Malta	na	**8**	9	7	9	9	5	4	8	17	5	5	11	na	na	100
Mexico	12	**12**	14	11	15	13	7	8	15	25	8	15	17	na	na	100
Moldova	na	**5**	6	5	7	5	4	4	4	9	2	4	8	na	na	100
Montenegro	na	**6**	6	6	9	8	2	4	7	9	4	5	7	na	na	100
Morocco	na	**6**	8	5	8	5	4	4	11	24	6	10	6	na	na	100
Netherlands	36	**22**	25	19	19	24	22	15	23	29	20	21	26	na	na	100
New Zealand	na	**20**	22	18	19	23	17	13	18	29	17	20	23	na	na	100
Nigeria	7	**9**	9	9	9	8	9	6	9	11	10	8	8	na	na	100
Northern Ireland	15	**17**	19	16	26	20	11	14	20	21	14	14	19	na	na	100
Norway	10	**11**	12	11	12	14	8	6	10	18	0	0	0	na	na	100
Pakistan	na	**1**	1	1	1	1	0	0	1	1	0	0	2	na	na	100
Peru	na	**14**	17	12	17	12	13	8	14	20	13	14	17	na	na	100
Philippines	na	**6**	4	8	8	6	4	5	6	7	5	5	8	na	na	100
Poland	10	**8**	10	6	10	7	7	6	8	13	5	8	13	na	na	100
Portugal	12	**10**	10	10	17	9	7	6	17	20	3	7	14	na	na	100
Puerto Rico	na	**22**	23	21	29	21	19	13	19	25	14	22	29	na	na	100
Romania	7	**7**	9	5	12	8	4	1	7	17	5	3	11	na	na	100
Russian Fed.	6	**2**	3	1	2	2	1	1	1	3	1	2	2	na	na	100
Serbia	na	**6**	7	5	7	7	4	2	5	15	2	5	10	na	na	100
Singapore	na	**7**	8	6	11	4	3	6	7	9	7	7	7	na	na	100
Slovakia	na	**4**	5	3	5	4	3	2	4	12	3	4	5	na	na	100
Slovenia	7	**16**	17	15	21	16	13	15	16	18	14	17	16	na	na	100
South Africa	8	**7**	7	7	10	6	3	8	6	11	7	7	6	na	na	100
Spain	21	**17**	19	15	29	19	8	10	23	28	14	15	22	na	na	100
Sweden	23	**22**	20	25	28	22	19	9	25	30	23	20	24	na	na	100
Switzerland	24	**17**	15	19	24	16	15	10	18	24	16	15	19	na	na	100
Taiwan	na	**5**	5	4	3	5	5	4	5	5	4	6	4	na	na	100
Tanzania	na	**2**	2	2	3	2	2	2	2	2	3	2	2	na	na	100
Turkey	20	**18**	21	15	22	17	12	12	23	36	13	20	26	na	na	100
Uganda	na	**12**	13	10	13	8	19	11	11	22	13	15	13	na	na	100
Ukraine	na	**4**	4	3	6	2	3	0	2	8	2	2	6	na	na	100
United States	23	**25**	28	23	28	24	25	22	23	28	25	25	25	na	na	100
Uruguay	na	**23**	22	24	34	28	14	14	32	47	13	23	35	na	na	100
Venezuela	na	**14**	14	14	16	15	9	9	15	19	11	16	15	na	na	100
Vietnam	na	**8**	9	8	12	7	7	8	8	10	9	9	8	na	na	100
Zimbabwe	na	**6**	6	6	6	5	6	5	6	9	7	6	3	na	na	100
Total	15	**11**	12	10	13	11	9	7	11	17	9	10	13	na	na	100

RANKING	
Country	2000
Australia	35
Austria	30
Canada	29
Italy	28
Argentina	25
United States	25
Uruguay	23
Sweden	22
Netherlands	22
Puerto Rico	22
Belgium	20
New Zealand	20
Croatia	19
Turkey	18
France	18
Switzerland	17
Germany	17
Northern Ireland	17
Spain	17
Chile	17
Greece	17
Luxembourg	17
Denmark	16
Slovenia	16
Dominican Rep.	16
Peru	14
Venezuela	14
Ireland	14
Mexico	12
Brazil	12
Uganda	12
Norway	11
Finland	11
Iceland	11
Portugal	10
Czech Republic	10
Iran	10
Japan	9
Algeria	9
Nigeria	9
Vietnam	8
Colombia	8
Poland	8
Malta	8
South Africa	7
Romania	7
Singapore	7
Jordan	6
Lithuania	6
Philippines	6
Belarus	6
Morocco	6
Serbia	6
Montenegro	6
Korea, South	6
Egypt	6
Zimbabwe	6
Armenia	5
Moldova	5
Bangladesh	5
Latvia	5
Taiwan	5
Macedonia	5
Bosnia and Herz.	4
Slovakia	4
Albania	4
Georgia	4
Israel	4
Ukraine	4
Azerbaijan	3
Bulgaria	3
China	3
Indonesia	3
Estonia	3
Hungary	2
India	2
Tanzania	2
Russian Fed.	2
Pakistan	1
Total	11

Cross-Cultural Comparisons, Survey Methodology and the Values Surveys

Yilmaz Esmer

The Values Surveys, which have produced an enormous and hitherto unmatched database for comparative and longitudinal analyses of the belief and value systems of societies, use the sample survey as its mode of data collection. To gain an understanding of the issues and questions that the Values Surveys aim to address, there is no alternative. If one is interested in finding out what a person thinks or believes one had better ask directly. Trying to infer values from secondary or indirect sources would be a very poor substitute for data collected by survey interviews.

The advantages and pitfalls of the sample survey method are widely known and well documented. A vast literature now exists on survey techniques and numerous methodological experiments have been conducted to help identify potential problem areas. It is not the aim of this chapter to review this literature. Rather, I will limit myself to the issues concerning cross-national and cross-cultural surveys in general and the Values Surveys project in particular.

Questionnaire design, sampling, data collection (in our case, face-to-face interviews) and analysis are the basic stages of a sample survey. These are also the basic sources of error. In a project of the magnitude of the Values Surveys, each one of these stages is more complicated than usual. Additionally, when we consider translation problems and practical problems of all sorts, we can begin to appreciate the enormity and complexity of the task in our hands.

Briefly and succinctly, the sample survey can be defined as "consist[ing] of relatively systematic, standardized approaches to the collection of information on individuals, households, or larger organized entities through the questioning of systematically identified samples of individuals."[1] There are two basic elements in this definition: "systematic" and "standardized." Now let us recall that we are dealing with more than 80 countries, many more languages and hundreds of ethnic groups. Achieving standardization under these circumstances, as anyone who has collected data in a single city alone

[1] Rossi, Peter H. et al, "Sample Surveys: History, Current Practice, and Future Prospects" in Rossi, Peter H., James D. Wright and Andy B. Anderson, eds., *Handbook of Survey Research*, San Diego: Academic Press, Inc., 1983, p. 1.

will testify, will have to be "relative" indeed. It is very easy to criticize such an endeavor from the perspective of a methodological purist. One could without much effort find faults with many aspects of the design, that is, the questions, the sampling, the translations, and the interviewing techniques. It would be foolish to deny the well-known difficulties and errors associated with cross-cultural surveys, and the Values Surveys project is not immune to them. But research, in any field and with any method, is an arduous undertaking. The researcher's job is not to throw up his/her hands in despair but to be as meticulous and demanding as he/she possibly can. The road is full of hurdles of all types and sizes but, then, "Fear not [....] your reward shall be very great."[2]

Questionnaire design, sampling, data collection and analysis are the four basic aspects of sample surveys. Beginning with questionnaires, I will comment on each one of these four topics with reference to the Values Surveys.

A question for all cultures?

Writing survey questions and designing a questionnaire even for homogenous populations requires considerable experience and knowledge. Wording, question order, question type, order and nature of response categories, presence or absence of a no answer category can alter both the responses and the response rates. In addition there are problems related to context effects, social desirability effects, need for approval effects, acquiescence effects, to mention but a few examples. Sensitive topics or questions inquiring about illegal behavior comprise another set of challenges for the survey researcher.

The Detroit Area Studies carried out by the University of Michigan have produced a sizeable literature on these issues. These surveys are based on data collected from not a country, not a state but only the city of greater Detroit, Michigan. It goes without saying that multinational, multicultural, multilingual settings can only increase the magnitude and add to the variety of problems. What is sensitive, legal or socially desirable, for example, varies greatly from one country to another. Marijuana for personal use is legal in Amsterdam and is sold in so-called coffee shops but its possession will result in years of imprisonment in some countries. Fully 61 percent of Czech citizens, 49 percent of the Estonians, 39 percent of both the French and the Dutch say they do not believe in God. Daring to say this in public is no less than a capital offense in some Islamic states. Asking a man about his sexual preferences is not much of a problem in San Francisco but may be a cause for murder in a Turkish village. One could think of numerous other examples but there is no need to belabor the point: cultures differ enormously, in many ways that are directly related to the conduct of surveys and cross-cultural researchers must be keenly aware of this fact.

What is a family?

One of the most frequent criticisms that cross-cultural survey researchers hear refers to the different ways a given question is understood in different places. "How can you," the argument goes, "compare 'religiosity' in Poland and Japan when the concept refers

[2] Genesis, 15:1.

to very different things in these two countries?" We are, at times, even accused of being unaware that God in monotheist cultures has an entirely different meaning than, say, in Buddhist or Confucian societies.

Cross-cultural survey researchers are very much aware that the same question, based on even rather simple concepts, can be understood differently in different countries. But is this really a problem only when the survey covers more than one society? Do all Americans understand a given question in the same way? Or all New Yorkers? Within Sweden, are the political "left" and "right" interpreted in the same way by a university graduate and a person with no formal education? Better yet, do two Swedish PhD's have the same perception of these and other concepts? Pushed to the extreme, do husbands and wives always agree on the meaning of a word or a sentence? Do you and your daughter understand a phrase from a contemporary television show in exactly the same way? This line of reasoning can easily lead us to the position that since no two individuals' cognitive processes are identical, a question cannot be standardized even for two persons in the same household. Clearly, such a conclusion is not of much help for social science researchers who study shared meanings, and coherent and consistent patterns.

Family is a simple concept and is as universal as one can get. Yet, we know that it refers to a nuclear family in Norway --and a very small one at that-- while in Nigeria it can include a whole village and sometimes two or three. But whatever operational meaning they attach to it, family is very important for people and universally so. So much so that, of the 97,237 respondents from 67 societies who answered the question "how important is family in your life?" in the last round of the Values Surveys, 89.4 percent said "very important." Only 1.1 percent said family was "not important" for them and the proportion of those whose response was "not important at all" was negligible - merely 0.3 percent. This is strong evidence that, despite differences in operational definitions, the concept has a common core meaning in all societies. It is difficult to think of another plausible explanation for this extremely low variance in the responses from almost one hundred thousand respondents scattered all over the globe.

Religion, God and culture

The fact that different societies have different understandings of "religion" and "God," is frequently cited to question the validity of data obtained from standardized questions containing these concepts and asked in widely differing cultures. Let us then try to assess the performance of such questions, using Values Surveys data, which, fortunately, allow us to evaluate the "construct validity"[3] of these concepts.

Being skeptics about the comparability of "religiosity" and "belief in God" across cultures and being particularly concerned with the different understanding of these concepts in East Asian civilizations, we should be able to agree on the following proposition:

---

[3] Babbie (Babbie, Earl R., *The Practice of Social Research*, 9th ed., Belmont: Wadsworth/Thomson Learning, 2001, p. 143) explains construct validity as follows: "We can consider how the variable in question ought, theoretically, to relate to other variables. **Construct validity** [author's emphasis] is based on the logical relationship among variables."

An individual's level of religiosity will have a strong positive correlation with how much importance God has in that individual's life in monotheistic (Christian, Islamic, Judaic) cultures. However, no such correlation will be observed outside of this monotheist cultural zone, since the wordings of these questions have entirely different meanings, for example, in Japan, Korea or China. Therefore, they have no validity in these societies and will probably produce random responses.

We now turn to our data to test these hypotheses. The survey instrument used by Values Surveys included the following two questions:

1. How important is God in your life? (Respondents were shown a 10-point scale.)

2. Independently of whether you go to church (mosque, synagogue, temple), would you say you are a religious person, not a religious person or a convinced atheist?

An examination of 87,931 cases reveals that the mean importance of God score for those who described themselves as religious is 8.63 while the mean score for the non-religious sample is 4.81. Taking into account that the overall standard deviation of the importance of God scale is 3.09, this difference of 3.82 between the group means is of considerable magnitude.

Table 1 gives the mean "importance of God" scores broken down by religion and religiosity. We observe that in all cases, respondents who described themselves as religious attach more importance, on the whole, to God than those who said they were not religious. In Hindu, Buddhist, Muslim, Protestant, Catholic and Jewish cultures, being more religious is linked with attaching more importance of God, regardless of how these different cultures understand and define these concepts. An analysis at the country level yields similar results. For example, in Japan, the mean importance of God score for religious respondents is 6.95 while it is only 4.74 for the non-religious sample. The questions do seem to work in Japan as well.

The next question we ask concerns what is referred to in the literature as "criterion-related validity."[4] In other words, can an outside variable unrelated to the survey that should theoretically be related to the construct in question, be predicted by the latter. It has been frequently argued that decreased levels of religiosity and faith are important components of the "modernization syndrome." Better living conditions and higher levels of education are known to correlate negatively with religiosity. "Thus, according to the dominant view, in modern society religion and church leaders are decreasingly able to dictate people's decisions in everyday life. The taken for granted status in consciousness and beliefs has disappeared and in secularized society, religious and moral beliefs and practices are said to be dependent upon personal desires and preferences and constantly open to debate, reformulation and change."[5] According to this "dominant view," then, the Human Development Index (HDI) published annually by the United Nations Development Program should serve as a good "outside criterion" to test the

[4] Babbie, *Ibid*.

[5] Draulans, Veerle and Loek Halman, "Religious and Moral Pluralism in Contemporary Europe" in Arts, Will, Jacques Hagenaars and Loek Halman, eds., *The Cultural Diversity of European Unity*, Leiden-Boston: Brill, 2003, p. 373.

validity of our constructs, since the HDI is a composite index of income, education and life expectancy. Secularization theory implies that as a country's HDI score rises, its level of emphasis on religion should fall significantly. The secularization thesis, as summarized by Draulans and Halman, also suggests that modernization and individualization should decrease people's confidence in organized religion, i.e. the church or its functional equivalent. A number of questions in the instruments used by Values Surveys are appropriate for testing these hypotheses. We will continue to use the "importance of God scale" as an indicator of individual religiosity. If we find that the HDI is a good predictor of how much importance a society attaches to God, and its level of confidence in organized religion, it means that our data from more than 80 societies are behaving according to widely shared theoretical expectations—giving us greater confidence in the cross-cultural validity of our measure.

If we correlate the mean on the importance of God scale, with each country's HDI score[6], we get a Pearson r = 0.64 (N = 60, sig.< .000). This is an impressive correlation coefficient, which translates into an r2 of 0.40, i.e. the HDI scores explain 40 percent of the cross-national variance in the importance of God scale. The corresponding simple regression equation estimates that an increase of one standard deviation in the HDI (0.137 in original units) is expected to produce a decrease of 3 units (for example, from a mean of 9 to a mean of 6 on the ten-point scale) in a country's mean importance of God.

A scatterplot of the mean HDI scores for each country with the Importance of God mean scores reveals two things: (1) the relationship is not linear and a second degree polynomial can improve the fit considerably, and (2) the United States and Vietnam are the two conspicuous outliers (Figure 1). When we modify the equation accordingly, the percentage of explained variance rises to 48 percent. Moreover, if the two outliers, the United States and Vietnam, are omitted from the equation, r^2 increases by another 5 percentage points. When an outside "objective" variable (in our case, the HDI), explains more than half of the cross-national variation in a variable (the importance of God), the argument that the variable lacks criterion-related validity can no longer be entertained.

We repeat the analysis, this time with "confidence in church" as the independent variable. This is important because church organizations are radically different in different countries. The Roman Catholic Church, for example, is a well-defined hierarchical organization. Church membership and church tax are automatic in many Western European countries and a formal petition is required if an individual wishes to rescind his/her membership. In Iran the head of the clergy is also the political authority for all practical purposes while in Turkey, with a 98 percent Muslim population, no clergy, church organization, or formal membership exist. Given such massive contextual variation, can a question like "How much confidence do you have in the church (or functional equivalent)?" have any cross-cultural validity? It turns out that the answer is definitely "yes" and even to a greater degree than with the importance of God question.

A country's score on the HDI explains 51 percent of the cross-national variation in the degree of confidence in the church.[7] Moreover, an examination of the scatterplot

[6] UNDP, *Human Development Report 2002*, New York-Oxford: Oxford University Press, 2002.

[7] Coded from 1 (not at all) to 4 (a great deal); country mean scores are used in the analysis.

(Figure 2) reveals a pattern that is very similar to the one observed with the importance of God variable -a curvilinear relationship with the United States and Vietnam being the outliers again. Including the square of the independent variable (mean confidence in the church) in the equation increases the r^2 to 61 percent. And if the United States and Vietnam are removed, we explain two-thirds of the total variance.

It is fair to conclude that, despite the very real and very serious difficulties that critics of cross-cultural research evoke, these data show a high degree of cross-cultural validity.

Religious institutions and worldviews vary immensely from one society to another. Nevertheless, it is clear that a sufficient degree of shared meanings exist that people from widely different cultures understand and respond to such concepts as "God" or "church" in broadly comparable ways.

Sampling for the Values Surveys

It is beyond the scope of this article to discuss the technical issues related to sampling. However, since surveys in some Values Surveys countries have used quota sampling, we should briefly address the arguments against and in defense this method. It should be made clear that the comparison is not between a full probability sample and crude quota designs that are no longer used except by novices.[8] Rather, the case in point is a combination of probability and quota designs. For instance, some surveys used a probability model (area sampling) down to the household level, but switched to a quota design at this last stage. This design is very similar to what Sudman calls "probability sampling with quotas." As he explains, "these quotas are normally determined for the smallest geographic area for which information is available."[9]

There is hardly any disagreement that probability samples —as opposed to non-probability samples such as quota— have a number of desirable properties. First and foremost, only full probability samples (in which every unit in the population has a known and nonzero probability of selection) allow us to calculate sampling errors and confidence intervals. Furthermore, all significance tests are based on this assumption. But probability sampling is expensive—and often prohibitively expensive. It can multiply the cost of a survey by a factor of three or four.[10] Probability sampling requires repeated callbacks to persons with whom an interview cannot be completed at the first visit for whatever reason. If the mode of data collection is face-to-face interviewing, as is almost exclusively the case with the Values Surveys, this means repeated trips to remote places to complete a single interview. "A researcher must do what a researcher must do" one could say, and this is what the book says should be done. Unfortunately,

[8] By "crude quota samples" we are referring to plans that, at their worst, may involve no more than handing the interviewer the quotas for each category and instructing him/her to fill these quotas (e.g. gender and age) in any way he/she can in a given locality which can be as large as an entire city.

[9] Sudman, *op.cit.* p. 193

[10] "Comparing the total costs of probability callback and quota studies, call-back sample costs per case are typically three times higher than the costs per case of quota samples…" Sudman, Seymour, *Applied Sampling,* New York: Academic Press, 1976, p. 199.

many funding agencies are not swayed by this argument— and in many societies, research funding is very limited.

What does one lose by switching to a combination of probability plus quota design? The methodologist's response to this question will be simple: "Sorry to say, we cannot know." As far as sampling error is concerned, this is true. But one must consider the following points as well:

a. Low response rates have become a serious problem for probability designs. To cite one example, the recent European Social Survey project, which made data from 15 countries available in the fall of 2003, reports that the response rate was 33.5 percent in Switzerland, 43.7 percent in Italy, and 53.2 percent in Spain.[11] With such low response rates, which are fast becoming the norm rather than the exception, especially in industrialized Western countries, it is difficult to contend that a probability design still retains its desirable properties.
b. It is well known that sampling error constitutes only a rather small proportion of the total error in a survey. This should especially be true for large scale cross-cultural studies which exacerbate the problems related to questionnaire design and data collection. When resources are scarce, it is necessary to weigh the small reductions in sampling error that an ideal design can offer, against the astronomical increases in cost. In many instances, the researcher is not even in a position to choose. The options are, use a mixed probability/quota design, or give up hope of carrying out the survey. A purist would choose the latter course—which is why survey data from most low-income countries is scarce or non-existent.
c. It is not an easy task, to put it mildly, to come up with a reasonably acceptable sampling frame in some parts of the globe. There are places where there are no addresses, no lists, no registries and where the size of the relevant population is a mystery: a few huts on top of a hill, tents in the middle of a desert or nomads who take to the mountains in the summer. Often there is no record, official or otherwise, of these groups. Under these circumstances, any kind of sampling, let alone probability sampling, is a major challenge. An added complication is the lack of infrastructure. In some instances, the only mode of transportation can be hours of walking or of riding various kinds of animals.
d. Wars, internal strife, terrorism and violence can present insurmountable obstacles both in terms of the preparation of a sampling frame and, of course, interviewer access.

When one or more of these conditions (and more could easily be added to this list) exist, it would be a folly to pretend that one has an ideal sampling design. Imple-

[11] ESS (European Social Survey) project is uncompromising with respect to methodological rigor and goes to great lengths to ensure the highest standards and maximum adherence to the rules of good survey practice. They are to be commended for openly sharing full methodological information including response rates with the academic community at large. The above figures on response are from "Round 1 Technical Report, Chapter 6." More information is available on "http://www.europeansocialsurvey.org."

menting the survey instrument in all corners of the globe, the WVS policy with respect to sampling can be summarized as follows:

a. Encourage full probability sampling whenever feasible.
b. When this is not feasible or possible, use a combination of probability and refined quota sampling.
c. In any case, provide a full technical report of all sample properties, problems and deviations. Response rates should be reported when probability sample designs are used.

Known population characteristics can provide a benchmark to assess the performance of a sample. If certain sample statistics are within acceptable error margins with respect to population parameters obtained through, say, an official census of the population, this is strong indication that the sample on the whole is satisfactory.[12] With this criterion, the vast majority of Values Surveys samples perform very well. We should not hesitate to add that there are exceptions; there are countries, which have oversampled certain areas (e.g. urban centers) or certain groups (e.g. the highly educated or a given ethnic group). Some of these deviations from probability proportional to size (PPS) sampling can easily be salvaged by weighting. But, obviously, weighting has its limits too. First, it decreases the effective sample size. Second, weighting assumes that population data are available for the given attributes. Third, weighting cannot compensate for the absence or near absence of certain groups in the sample.

The intellectual costs of limiting Values Research to the roughly 30 countries in which almost all previous social science surveys have been carried out are even greater than the difficulties of dealing with reasonably accurate, but less than optimal data. The problem is not merely that the 30-some societies usually surveyed omit most of the world's population; it is that these societies constitute an extremely skewed sample of the world's societies, omitting most of the cultural, economic and social variation found in the world as a whole. If we are to understand how the world is changing, we need to analyze the much more diverse range of societies included in the Values Surveys. At this point in history, there is a trade-off between methodological purism and broad coverage, and we are keenly aware of it. Many of the participants in the Values Surveys network have devoted much of their professional lives to methodological questions. Hopefully, in the future, as more adequate resources become available for cross-national research, such trade-offs will not be necessary. But when it comes to the choice between methodological purism and being able to analyze the much wider range of variation that actually exists in the world as a whole, Values Surveys have come down on the side of "cautious inclusiveness".

---

[12] Of course, the fact that gender, age and educational level distributions in a sample are close to those given by census data is no way a guarantee that we have a perfect sample but it does help to ease the worries of the researcher.

Comparisons over time

The Values Surveys provide a unique opportunity to assess the performances of various country samples. The second, third and fourth waves of these surveys are approximately five years apart. The basic values and demographic structure in a society should remain fairly stable over such a short period of time, unless there is a traumatic event like a war or severe economic crisis. Thus, it is a rather simple exercise. Select certain variables that are relatively stable against short-term fluctuations, and compare their distributions in successive rounds of surveys.[13] Obviously, this requires country-by-country and variable-by-variable comparisons and assumes highly reliable and valid measurements but is a worthwhile challenge for the meticulous analyst. Clearly, not all differences point to sampling problems. After all, if no change were expected, repeated surveys would be unnecessary. Cultural change is a reality and, therefore, the differences between surveys often indicate genuine change. We know that values related to gender equity or sexual tolerance, for example, have gone through rapid changes in most countries in the last decade or so. But under normal circumstances, mass conversions from one religious faith to another, for example, would not be expected to occur in five years and consequently, if we found major changes in the religious affiliations of a given public, it would send a strong warning signal to the analyst.

We conclude this section by presenting an example of this type of analysis, using data from the third (1995-97) and the fourth (1999-2001) waves of WVS. I have argued elsewhere[14] that responses to a question on the individual's health have a strong cultural component that does not change much over time. Thus a Nigerian and a Japanese, with the same health status from a medical point of view, are likely to offer very different subjective evaluations of their health. If this is true and subjective health is a reasonably enduring cultural trait, a comparison of the distributions should give some clues to the adequacy of given samples. Table 2 compares the percentages of respondents who said the state of their health was good or very good in the two waves of surveys, for the 21 WVS countries for which data are available. The results are encouraging. In 16 out of 21 countries in Table 2, the discrepancy is five percentage points or less —well within acceptable sampling error limits. Nigeria and South Africa show larger shifts from one wave to the next.[15] Nevertheless, 19 of the 21 countries show differences of eight points or less between the two waves and the mean shift from one wave to the next is only 3 percentage points.

---

[13] To cite but one example, Turkish second and third wave surveys produced almost identical distributions for life satisfaction and income satisfaction -both 10-point scales. Household income satisfaction distributions for the second and third waves are given below. The probability of obtaining such similar distributions by chance is infinitesimal.

Score	1	2	3	4	5	6	7	8	9	10	mean
1990-91 %	7	6	9	10	36	14	8	5	1	5	5.02
1996-97 %	8	4	9	8	36	12	9	7	1	5	5.09

[14] Esmer, Yilmaz, *Devrim, Evrim, Statuko*, Istanbul: Tesev, 1999.

[15] Of course, there could be substantive explanations for these significant differences.

Analyzing Values Survey Data

The proof of the pudding is in the eating, as the saying goes. We believe that the ultimate litmus test for any data set is its performance. Do the analyses produce meaningful, coherent, consistent and stable results? Do the findings make theoretical sense? Are there plausible explanations for any deviations or anomalies? Overall, the Values Surveys data provide very satisfactory answers to these questions. Without any question, there are imperfections in the data set. In some cases, errors of various types are of greater magnitude than one would be willing to allow. Nevertheless, analyses of the Values Surveys data since 1981 have produced extremely interesting results with great theoretical import. Moreover, the resulting relationships and patterns have been consistent.

Recent decades have witnessed considerable progress in quantitative data analysis methods in the social sciences. Today's statistical packages contain procedures that were unheard of in the 1960s or even 1970s. Furthermore, with the widespread availability of extremely low cost but high speed and high capacity personal computing, these techniques have become household goods. While writing this article at my home computer, I frequently consulted the almost 200,000 case Values Surveys data file occupying only a fraction of the space on my hard disk. This was not possible on the so-called mainframes at the largest universities 25 or 30 years ago.

The advances in techniques for analysis coupled with the enormous increases in computing capacity and speed, however, can easily make us forget that our subject matter is human beings and that we analyze data provided by them. Surveys collect data from men and women whose basic make-up and reactions remain the same. They still yearn for social desirability; they still cannot remember a dozen response categories in a question; they still can be very inconsistent from the perspective of an outside person; and they still have basic fears. The moral of the story is that social science data usually are approximate, and contain a substantial component of measurement error. We, as social scientists, should recognize this fact and not pretend that our data can match the accuracy of a physicist's data.

We would be well advised to heed Dogan's[16] warning:

> "After decades of methodological improvements in comparative research we are today in a situation of imbalance between the level of accurate quantitative data and the technological capacity of statistical treatment. We have arrived at a stage where the available statistical information simply does not match the methodological sophistication achieved.
>
> ....
>
> Measurement and statistical evidence are obviously needed in all social sciences. The limits to quantification appear when there is a gap between the amount and quality of data available and the statistical technique adopted for its treatment. In other words, over quantification consists in the treatment of soft data by very sophisticated techniques."

---

[16] Dogan, Mattei, "Use and Misuse of Statistics in Comparative Research" in Dogan, Mattei and Ali Kazancigil, eds., *Comparing Nations*, Oxford: Blackwell, 1994, p. 37.

Perhaps the two graphs presented in the introductory chapter to this sourcebook can better illustrate what I have called the "litmus test of data." They help us to visually grasp the remarkably coherent patterns that are obtained from analysis of the Values Surveys data.

The highly structured patterns and the strong correlations with objective criterion variables that appear in Figures 1 and 2 would not emerge if these data were heavily contaminated by measurement error. When one asks questions that are meaningless in a given cultural context, one obtains a great deal of non-response or random answers; and when one asks questions that are understood in completely different ways in different cultural settings, one obtains weakly-related or unrelated patterns of cross-national response. Both of these problems tend to produce weakly structured or uncorrelated responses. But the findings shown in Figures 1 and 2 in the Introductory Chapter are just the opposite: both the Traditional/Secular-rational and the Survival/Self-expression dimensions show remarkably strong correlations with a country's level of economic development (in Figure 1) and with a society's historic cultural heritage (in Figure 2). Moreover (as is demonstrated in Inglehart and Welzel, 2004), these dimensions show remarkably strong correlations with other criterion variables, such as a society's human fertility rate, or its score on the UN Gender Equality Measure. If low levels of cross-cultural validity (or massive measurement error) were present, we would not find such crisply structured cross-national patterns. Finally, these same highly structured patterns appear in each successive wave of the surveys, with each society generally falling into a position very close to the same relative position that it occupied in previous surveys. This would not happen unless the results for given societies were reasonably accurate.

Despite the very real difficulties linked with cross-cultural survey research, we have learned, and can continue to learn, a great deal about human values and behavior from survey data.

Conclusion

The Values Surveys project is the largest social science data collection effort undertaken to date. It started out with what in retrospect seems to be a modest number of countries (24) in 1981 and has expanded its coverage to over 80 societies. Social scientists now have at their disposal time series cultural values data from all over the world and can analyze it to help answer a wide range of significant questions. These data, to be sure, contain both random and systematic error. They contain sampling error, interviewer error, respondent error and other types of error. They are prone to all types of effects that may produce bias that are cited in the literature. The Values Surveys project faces all the usual difficulties of survey research, plus the additional difficulties of cross-cultural research. In addition, there are a number of practical difficulties that researchers working in the West need not worry about. But in statistical terms, we have every reason to believe that the error sum of squares is only a small proportion of the total sum of squares.

We have discussed at some length the problems of validity in cross-cultural research. Various methodological remedies, some very ingenious,[17] have been proposed

[17] The "anchoring vignettes" approach is one interesting example. Gary King's website at http://gking.harvard.edu/vign/ contains detailed information on this approach.

to ameliorate cross-cultural measurement efforts. Some of these techniques will probably be incorporated in future waves of these surveys. Nevertheless, using Values Surveys data, we have tried to demonstrate that some of the most difficult concepts for cross-cultural research have high construct validity and criterion-related validity. With carefully designed questionnaires and carefully worded and constructed questions, reliability and validity problems of cross-cultural research can be minimized.

Commenting on the difficulties of doing research in the Arab world, Saad Eddin Ibrahim wrote that "many problems are associated with the conduct of survey research and other kinds of social inquiry in the Arab world. Among them are such meta-sociological problems as (1) the lack of trained researchers, (2) the lack of research funds, and (3) the absence of academic freedom."[18] The lack of research funds is universal. But the lack of trained researchers and the absence of freedoms are serious problems in many parts of the world. The 2000 WVS was the first national sample survey ever carried out in some countries. We are in complete agreement with Ibrahim that lack of academic freedom in particular, and violations of basic human rights in general, are serious obstacles to all social research, but especially to survey research, which depends on answers from ordinary citizens who cannot be expected to speak their minds under the threat of imprisonment or other severe punishment. Fortunately, there are researchers who are making heroic efforts to conduct surveys under these circumstances and the research community owes much to them.

Table 1
Importance of God by Religiosity and Religion
(mean score)

	Respondent is					
	Religious			Not Religious		
	n	Mean	St. Dev.	n	Mean	St. Dev.
Muslim	16,662	9.66	1.15	1,940	8.62	2.50
Roman Catholic	21,526	8.36	2.13	3,614	5.82	3.16
Protestant	7,988	8.22	2.38	2,094	4.12	2.86
Buddhist	422	6.72	2.90	430	4.87	2.37
Hindu	1,286	9.00	1.03	262	7.90	2.53
Jew	218	8.73	2.04	73	5.49	2.80

Note: Table is based on respondents who mentioned these broad religious categories and ignores those who offered finer denominational affiliations.

Table 2
Percent of Respondents Describing their Health as Good or Very Good

	1999-01	1995-97	Difference
Albania	75	73	2
Argentina	65	62	3
Bosnia Herzegovina	64	62	2
Chile	69	61	8
China	61	68	–7
India	63	59	4
Japan	55	56	–1
S Korea	78	76	2
Mexico	61	56	5
Moldova	30	31	–1
Nigeria	90	75	15
Pakistan	66	64	2
Peru	49	50	–1
Philippines	57	52	5
Puerto Rico	73	68	5
S Africa	78	68	10
Spain	76	68	8
Turkey	64	61	3
Macedonia	71	73	–2
USA	84	79	5
Serbia-Montenegro	56	51	5
	mean difference		3.4

Technical Note

Jaime Díez-Medrano and Ruud Luijkx

Questionnaire Development

The 1999-2001 Values Studies build on previous waves of this project that were carried out in 1981-82, 1990-91, and 1995-96. Each successive wave has covered a broader range of societies than the previous one, with the 1981 wave being carried out in 24 countries, the 1990 wave in 43 societies, the 1995 wave in 62 societies and the 2000 wave in 82 societies. Analysis of each successive wave has indicated that certain questions tapped theoretically interesting and substantively important concepts, while others were of little value. This led to the more useful items being replicated in future waves, while the less useful items were dropped, making room to add new items. The current wave added batteries of questions designed to probe into social capital, gender equality, pro-democratic political democracy, feelings of solidarity, and work ethics.

In preparation for the current wave, the WVS group gave special attention to improving our measures of support for gender equality and a democratic political culture, while the EVS group focused on items tapping religion and morality, society and politics, primary relations, and work. Suggestions were solicited from participants throughout the world, and expert groups developed the questionnaires used in the 1999-2001 survey, giving particular attention to issues of comparability between and across countries. An EVS methodology group also developed a methodological questionnaire to be completed by the principal investigators in each country, giving a detailed report on how fieldwork had been carried out in their country. These questionnaires are included in the CD-ROM that accompanies this sourcebook. We will not repeat all of these details here, but will simply give a general description of how fieldwork was conducted.

A final master questionnaire was prepared in English, and it was translated into the various national languages and, in many cases, the translated questionnaire was then independently translated back into English to check the accuracy of the translation. In most countries, the translated questionnaire was then pre-tested to help identify questions or concepts, for which the translation was problematic. In some cases, certain problematic questions were omitted from the national questionnaire.

In many countries, country-specific questions were included; in two-thirds of the countries all core questions were asked and in almost all countries the order of the questions in the master questionnaire was followed.

More details on questionnaire development and fieldwork is available from Halman (2001) and from the methodological questionnaires on the accompanying CD-ROM. The actual questionnaires, in the languages used in the various national surveys, are also available on the accompanying CD-ROM.

Sampling Procedures

In most countries, some form of stratified multistage random sampling was used to obtain representative national samples. In the first stages, a random selection of sampling points was made based on the given society's statistical regions, districts, census units, election sections, electoral registers, or voting stations, and central population registers. In most countries, the population size and/or degree of urbanization of these Primary Sampling Units was taken into account. In some countries, individuals were drawn directly from national registers. When no named individuals were drawn, various methods were used to select respondents, such as the Kish selection grid, the Troldhal and Carter-method, last or next birthday method, quota sampling on the basis of gender and age, and sometimes also on education or profession, and, in a few cases, random routes with age and gender quota. In most countries, substitution of respondents was allowed.

In all countries, samples were drawn from the entire population of 18 years and older. In most countries, no upper age limit was imposed. For a more detailed description of the sampling procedures, see the methodological questionnaires on the accompanying CD-ROM.

Fieldwork

Representative national samples of each country's public were interviewed using uniformly structured questionnaires. Fieldwork for most of the European countries was carried out in 1999; in most of the non-European countries, fieldwork took in 2001, but a few surveys carried over into 2002.

In most countries, the survey was carried out by professional survey organizations, using face-to-face interviews. In Iceland, phone interviews were used for remote areas (constituting 26% of the sample). The response rates varied from a low of 25 percent in Spain to a high of 95 percent in Slovakia.

In most countries, the sample was weighted to correct for deviations from national parameters. This weight factor was not constructed uniformly over countries. The following characteristics were used to construct the weighting factor in various countries: nationality, region, the urban/rural divide, town size, household size, sex, age, occupation, education, marital status, and economic activity.

In Spain, Morocco and Turkey, two surveys were carried out for the fourth wave of the Values Surveys: in Spain, the first was carried out in March-April, 1999 and the second in November, 2000; in Morocco, the first survey was carried out in August, 2001 and the second in February-March, 2002; in Turkey, the first survey was carried out in December 2000 to January 2001 and the second in September-October, 2001.

The tables in this sourcebook show the combined results from the two surveys, since our main interest is in comparing basic values that are relatively stable. But any reader who wishes to compare the results from these two surveys can do so by using the data on the accompanying CD-ROM, using variable S001 to distinguish between the two surveys.

Principal Investigators

Survey organizations, fieldwork dates, sample sizes and the principal investigators for each country are shown below. If not otherwise noted, the investigator is affiliated with the institution that carried out the fieldwork.

ALBANIA — INDEX Albania; February 17 to March 5, 2002. N = 1000. Principal investigator: Kosta Barjaba. A nationally representative multistage random probability sample of the population aged 18 and over.

ALGERIA — University of Algiers; March 1 to May 31, 2002. N = 1282. Principal investigators: Abdallah Bedaida, Mark Tessler. Respondents were selected by quota in each district based on sex and age.

ARGENTINA — Instituto Gallup de Argentina; January 22 to February 9, 1999. N = 1280. Principal investigator: Marita Carballo. A nationally representative sample of the population aged 18 and over. The sample was stratified according to two criteria, using multistage random selection of the sampling units.

ARMENIA — Sociological Research Center, Armenian Academy of Sciences (Yerevan). February, 1997. N = 2000. Principal Investigators, Gevork Pogosian and Hans-Dieter Klingemann, Berlin Science Center for Social Research.

AUSTRALIA — Roy Morgan Research Center (Melbourne); Fall, 1995. N = 2048. Principal investigator, Alan Black, Edith Cowan University.

AUSTRIA — Fessel GfK Austria N = 1522; August-October 1999. Principal investigator, Paul M. Zulehner, Universität Wien, Vienna.

AZERBAIJAN — SIAR (Baku); Nov, 1996. N = 2002. Principal Investigators, Dr. Ali Aliev and Hans-Dieter Klingemann, Berlin Science Center for Social Research.

BANGLADESH — Bangladesh Unnayan Parishad; August 20 to September 15, 2002. N = 1499. Principal investigators: Q. K. Ahmad, Nilufar Banu. Population 18 years old and over, representative of Bangladesh. Stratified random sampling used.

BELARUS — The Centre of Political and Sociological Researches of Belarus State University N = 1000; March-April 2000. Principal investigators, David Rotman and Larissa Titarenko, Belarus State University, Minsk.

BELGIUM — Nationaal Instituut voor Dataverzameling/Dimarso; N = 1912; March-June 1999. Principal investigators, Karel Dobbelaere and Jaak Billiet, Katholieke Universiteit, Leuven, and Bernadette Bawin, Université de Liège.

BOSNIA-HERCEGOVINA — Mareco INDEX Bosnia; December 3 to 10, 2001. N = 1200. Principal investigator: Hans-Dieter Klingemann. The survey interviewed in 16 cantons/regions, ensuring the required ethnic and demographic structure of the sample.

BRAZIL — Instituto Gallup de Opiniao Publico (Sao Paulo); Fall, 1997. N = 1149. Principal investigator, Carlos Matheus.

BULGARIA — Institute of Sociology at the Bulgarian Academy of Sciences N = 1000; June-July 1999. Principal investigators, Georgy Fotev and Mario Marinov, Bulgarian Academy of Sciences, Sofia.

CANADA — Dept. of Political Science, University of Toronto; August 3 to September 24, 2000. N = 1931. Principal investigator: Neil Nevitte. National probability sample of Canadians aged 18 and over.

CHILE — Latinobarómetro / MORI Chile; November 9 to 19, 2000. N = 1791. Principal investigator: Marta Lagos. Modified probabilistic sample, random in the first and second stage, by age and sex quota on the last stage.

CHINA — Research Center for Contemporary China, Peking University. N = 1000. Principal investigator: Shen Mingming. Population 18 years old and over, representative of China.

COLOMBIA — Centro Nacional de Consultoria (Bogota), 1997 and april 1998. n = 6025. Principal Investigators, Dr. Carlos Lemoine, John Sudarsky.

CROATIA — Market Research Agency "Target" N = 1003; March-April 1999. Principal investigator, Josip Baloban, Universitatis Zagrabiensies, Zagreb

CZECH REPUBLIC — SC&C Ltd., Statistical Computations and Computing N = 1908; March-May 1999. Principal investigator, Ladislav Rabušic, Masaryk University, Brno.

DENMARK — SFI, the Danish national institute of social research N = 1023; April-November 1999. Principal investigator, Peter Gundelach, University of Copenhagen, Copenhagen.

DOMINICAN REPUBLIC — Centro POVEDA (Santo Domingo); April, 1996. N = 417. Principal Investigators, Josefina Zaiter, Marcos Villaman and Julio Valeiron.

EL SALVADOR Universidad Centroamericana José Simeón Cañas y FEPADE; September 1999. N = 417. .

ESTONIA — Saar Poll, Ltd. N = 1005; October 1999. Principal investigator, Andrus Saar, Saar Poll, Tallinn.

EGYPT — Emac Research and Training Center in collaboration with Women's College, Ain Shams University; July 1, 2000 to January 1, 2001. N = 3000. Principal investigators: Abdel-Hamid Abdel-Latif, Mansoor Moaddel. A random sample of households in each PSU's was first selected. Eligible individuals who were 16 years old and over with certain educational level were then selected.

FINLAND — Suomen Gallup Oy N = 1038; September-October 2000. Principal investigator, Juhani Pehkonen, Suomen Gallup Oy, Helsinki.

FRANCE — Research International N = 1615; March-April 1999. Principal investigator, Jean-François Tchernia, Tchernia Etudes Conseil, Paris.

GEORGIA — Georgian Institute of Public Opinion, (Tbilisi); December, 1996. N = 2593. Principal Investigator, Merab Pachulia (GIPO) and Hans-Dieter Klingemann, Berlin Science Center for Social Research.

GERMANY — INFASS (Bonn) N = 2036; October-December 1999. Principal investigator, Wolfgang Jagodzinski, Universität zu Köln, Cologne.

GREAT BRITAIN — Quality Fieldwork & Research Services N = 1000; October-November 1999. Principal investigator, Helmut Anheier, London School of Economics and Political Science, London.

GREECE — Department of Psychology, School of Philosophy, the University of Athens N = 1142; March-June 1999. Principal investigators, James Georgas, Kostas Mylonas and Aikaterini Gari, the University of Athens, Athens.

HUNGARY — Szonda-Ipsos Média-, Vélemény- és Piaclutató Intézet (Budapest) N = 1000; November-December 1999. Principal investigator, Miklós Tomka, Hungarian Religious Research Centre, Budapest.

ICELAND — The Institute of Social Research at the University of Iceland N = 968; June-December 1999. Principal investigators, Fridrik H. Jonsson and Stefan Olafsson, University of Iceland, Reykjavik.

INDIA — Political Science Faculty, Bangalore University; August 20 to October 15, 2001. N = 2002. Principal investigators: Sandeep Shastri, Pradeep Chibber. National representative sample of Indians aged 18 and over.

INDONESIA — Institute of Quranic Studies; March 1 to September 30, 2001. N = 1004. Principal investigator: Nadra Muhamad Hosen. Stratified sample.

IRAN — Institute of Social Research and Studies, University of Teheran. N = 2532. Principal investigators: Taghi Azadarmaki, Mansoor Moaddel.

IRELAND — The Survey Unit, The Economic and Social Research Unit (Dublin) N = 1012; October 1999-February 2000. Principal investigators, Tony Fahey, ESRI, Dublin, Bernadette C. Hayes, the Queen's University, Belfast, and Richard Sinnott, Trinity College, Dublin.

ISRAEL — B.I. Cohen Institute for Public Opinion Research; September 1 to November 1, 2001. N = 1199. Principal investigator: Noah Lewin-Epstein. Population 18 years old and over, representative of Israel. Multistage sampling using Kish-grid method.

ITALY — Centro Ricerche Sociali di Moncomo G. e C. SaS (Milan) N = 2000; March-May 1999. Principal investigator, Renzo Gubert, University of Trento, Trento.

JAPAN — Nippon Research Center; July 11 to 26, 2000. N = 1362. Principal investigators: Seiko Yamazaki, Toru Takahashi. Population 17 years old and over, representative of Japan. Stratified multistage sampling.

JORDAN — Center for Strategic Studies, University of Jordan; September 15 to 21, 2001. N = 1223. Principal investigator: Fares al-Braizat, Mustafa Harmaneh. National representative multistage sampling of population 18 years old and over.

LATVIA — Latvia Social Research Centre N = 1013; March 1999. Principal investigator, Brigita Zepa, Baltic Institute of Social Sciences, Riga.

LITHUANIA — Baltic Surveys Ltd. N = 1018; November-December 1999. Principal investigators, Stanislovas Juknevicius, Lithuanian Institute of Culture and Arts, and Rasa Alishauskene, Institute for Social Research, Vilnius.

LUXEMBOURG — ILRES Market Research N = 1211; July-October 1999. Principal investigators, Pol Estgen and Michel Legrand, SeSoPi Centre Intercommunautaire a.s.b.l., Luxembourg.

MALTA — MISCO International N = 1002; March-May 1999. Principal investigator, Anthony M. Abela, University of Malta.

MACEDONIA — BRIMA Skopje; November 28 to December 2, 2001, N = 1055. Principal investigator: Hans-Dieter Klingemann. A nationally representative multistage random probability sample of the population aged 18 and over.

MEXICO — Instituto Tecnológico Autónomo de México; January 28 to February 7, 2000. N = 1535. Principal investigator: Alejandro Moreno. Multistage sampling procedure. Population between 18 and 94 years of age.

MOLDOVA — Institute of Sociology, Moldovan Academy of Sciences (Chisinau), N = 1008. Principal investigators: Ljubov Ishimova, Hans-Dieter Klingemann.

MONTENEGRO — Institute of Social Sciences, Belgrade; November 1 to 17, 2001. N = 1060. Principal investigators: Dragomir Pantic, Hans-Dieter Klingemann, Ronald Inglehart. Three-stage stratified probability sample, 18 years old and over.

MOROCCO 1 — SEREC, Bureau d'études; August 2 to 28, 2001. N = 1247. Principal investigator: Juan Diez-Nicolas (ASEP, Spain). The sampling method is based on sex, age, education level, socio-economic and professional level and place of residence.

MOROCCO 2 — SEREC, Bureau d'études; February 8 to March 7, 2002. N = 1013. Principal investigator: Mansoor Moaddel. The sampling method is based on sex, age, education level, socio-economic and professional level and place of residence.

NETHERLANDS — Survey data (Tilburg) N = 1003; March-August 1999. Principal investigators ,Wil Arts, Jacques Hagenaars, Loek Halman, and Ruud Luijkx, Tilburg University, Tilburg.

NEW ZEALAND — The New Zealand Study of Values Trust in association with The School of Sociology and Women's Studies- Massey University; September, 1998. N = 1201. Principal investigator, Dr. Paul Perry (Massey University), Dr. Alan Webster.

NIGERIA — Research and Marketing Services; October 13 to November 22, 2000. N = 2022. Principal investigators: Bukola Bandele, Kareem Tejumola. Population 18 years old and over, representative of Nigeria. Multi-stage sampling method was observed until the final respondent selection. The final respondent was selected by quota by age and sex in all locations

NORTHERN IRELAND — Research and Evaluation Services (Belfast) N = 1000; July-November 1999. Principal investigators, Bernadette C. Hayes, the Queen's University, Belfast, Tony Fahey, ESRI, Dublin, and Richard Sinnott, Trinity College, Dublin.

NORWAY — Norwegian Central Bureau of Statistics; Fall, 1996. N = 1,127. Principal investigator, Ola Listhaug, University of Trondheim.

PAKISTAN — Faculty of Agricultural, Economics and Rural Sociology, University of Agriculture; August 15, 2001 to February 28, 2002. N = 2000. Principal investigator: Farooq Tanwir. Combination of purposive, random and quota sampling.

PERU — Instituto Bartolomé de las Casas / Datum International; July 19 to 25, 2001. N = 1501. Principal investigator: Catalina Romero. Combination of random and probability sampling method. Kish method used to select final respondent.

PHILIPPINES — Social Weather Stations, July 9 to 27, 2001: N = 1200. Principal investigators: Linda Luz Guerrero, Gerardo Sandoval, Mahar Mangahas. Voting age adults (18 years old and over), representative of Philippines. Multistage probability sampling was used in the selection of sample spots.

POLAND — CBOS- Public Opinion Research Centre N = 1095; February-March 1999. Principal investigators, Aleksandra Jasinska-Kania, Mira Marody and Joanna Konieczna, University of Warsaw, Warsaw.

PORTUGAL — Euroteste-Marketing E Opinião N = 1000; October-December 1999. Principal investigators, Jorge Vala, Alice Ramos and Manuel Villaverde Cabral, Instituto de Cienciais Sociais, Lisbon.

PUERTO RICO — Dept. of Political Science, University of Puerto Rico; April 15 to May 15, 2001. N = 720. Principal investigators: Jorge Benítez-Nazario, Ángel Rivera-Ortiz. National population representative of Puerto Rico, without age cut-offs. Structured random sample.

ROMANIA — The Research Institute for the Quality of Life N = 1146; July 1999. Principal investigators, Malina Voicu, C t lin Zamfir and Lucien Pop, Romanian Academy, Bucharest.

RUSSIA — ROMIR (Moscow) N = 2500; April-June 1999. Principal investigator, Elena Bashkirova, ROMIR Research Group, Moscow.

SERBIA — Institute of Social Sciences, Belgrade; October 29 to November 8, 2001. N = 1200. Principal investigators: Dragomir Pantic, Hans-Dieter Klingemann, Ronald Inglehart. Three-stage stratified probability sample, 18 years old and over.

SINGAPORE — Faculty of Arts and Social Sciences, National University of Singapore with the assistance of Joshua Research Consultants; March 14 to August 7, 2002. N = 1512. Principal investigator: Tan Ern Ser. Stratified, random sample of Singapore citizens.

SLOVAKIA — Agentúra MVK (Bratislava) N = 1331; June-July 1999. Principal investigator, Zuzana Kusá, Slovak Academy of Sciences, Bratislava.

SLOVENIA — Public Opinion and Mass Communications Research Center, Faculty of Social Sciences, University of Ljubljana N = 1006; October 1999. Principal investigators, Niko Tos and Brina Malnar, University of Ljubljana, Ljubljana.

SOUTH AFRICA — Markinor (Stellenbosch); March 1 to May 22, 2001. N = 3000. Principal investigator: Mari Harris, Hennie Kotzé (University of Stellenbosch). National representative sample of South Africa's population aged 16 and over. Random sample according to a selection grid used by Markinor.

SOUTH KOREA — Dpt. of Political Science and Diplomacy, Ewha Women's University; November 10 to 21, 2001. N = 1200. Principal investigator: Soo Young Auh. Population 20 years old and over, representative of the Republic of Korea. Selection of 120 clusters with a sample of 10 chosen from the household of each of the selected clusters.

SPAIN (WVS) — Análisis Sociológicos, Económicos y Políticos, S.A. (ASEP); November 6 to 13, 2000. N = 1209. Principal investigators: Juan Díez-Nicolás, Jose R. Torregrosa, Juan Diez-Medrano. National representative multistage random sample of the Spanish population aged 18 and over. Kish-grid method used.

SPAIN (EVS) — Data SA (Madrid) N = 1200; March-April 1999. Principal investigators, Javier Elzo, Universidad de Deusto, Bilbao, and Francisco Andrés Orizo, DATA, Madrid.

SWEDEN — ARS Research AB, Stockholm; November 15, 1999 to February 13, 2000. N = 1015. Principal investigators: Bi Puranen, Theseus Institute, Sophia Antipolis (France) and Thorleif Pettersson, Uppsala University. A two-stage representative sample of Swedish population aged 18-75 years old.

SWITZERLAND — Gesselleschaft fuer Socialforschung; Fall, 1996. N = 1212. Principal investigators, Simon Hug and Pascal Sciarini, University of Geneva.

TAIWAN — Survey Research Center, Academia Sinica (Taipei); summer, 1994 and summer1995. N = 1452. Principal Investigators, Hei-yuan Chiu, Pi-chao Chen, Jin-yun Liu, Ronald Inglehart.

TANZANIA — University of Dar-es-Salaam, Tanzania; May 30 to November 6, 2001. N = 1171. Principal investigator: Prof. G. K. Munishi. Multistage representative sample of Tanzania's population aged 18 and over.

TURKEY (WVS) — Bogazici University (Istanbul) and Birim Arastirma; December 2000 to January 2001. N = 3401. Principal investigator: Yilmaz Esmer. Multistage representative sample of Turkey's population aged 18 and over.

TURKEY (EVS) — Bogazici University (Istanbul) and Birim Arastirma N = 1206; September-October 2001. Principal investigator, Yilmaz Esmer, Multistage representative sample of Turkey's population aged 18 and over.

UKRAINE — Social Monitoring Centre (NGO) and Ukrainian Institute for Social Research N = 1195; December 1999. Principal investigator, Olga N. Balakireva, Ukrainian Institute for Social Research, Kiev.

UGANDA — Markinor (Stellenbosch, South Africa); March 3 to 18, 2001. N = 1002. Principal investigator: Mari Harris (Stellenbosch). National representative sample of Uganda's population aged 18 and over. Random sample according to a selection grid used by Markinor.

URUGUAY — Equipos Consultores Associados (Montevideo). October, 1996. N = 1000. Principal Investigators, Cesar Aguiar, Jose Arocena, Augustin Canzani, Rafael Mendizabal.

USA — Institute for Social Research, University of Michigan; first phase: November 19 to December 23, 1999; second phase: August 4 to September 25, 2000. N = 1200. Principal investigators: Virginia Hodgkinson, Ronald Inglehart and Miguel Basáñez. A nationally representative multistage random probability sample of the population aged 18 and over.

VENEZUELA — Red Interuniversitaria de Cultura Política, Universidad del Zulia; November 30 to December 20, 2000. N = 1200. Principal investigator: Jose Molina. Random sample stratified by States and Municipalities within locations of 5000 inhabitants and over.

VIETNAM — Institute of Human Studies; August 28 to September 30, 2001. N = 995. Principal investigators: Pham Minh Hac, Pham Thanh Nghi, Russell Dalton and Nhu-Ngoc Ong. . Multistage probability sample.

ZIMBABWE — Markinor (Stellenbosch, South Africa); February 2 to March 28, 2001. N = 1002. Principal investigator: Mari Harris (Stellenbosch). National representative sample of Zimbabwe's population aged 18 and over. Random sample according to the traditional Kish-grid method.

Data cleaning and weighting

After the fieldwork, data cleaning was carried out by the principal investigators. Further cleaning for the European surveys was performed at Tilburg University and the Zentralarchiv in Cologne and by JD Systems in Madrid, for the other countries.

Data validation was carried out, using the documentation, statistical data and survey data cleaning software that makes data cleaning more reliable by providing automatic procedures and tests. Validation involved the following steps:

- Comparing the country questionnaire and the official questionnaire.
- Matching identical questions.

- Finding, documenting and correcting differences in the categories.
- Checking for filter inconsistencies
- Validation of the cleaning procedure by the participant country
- Building a final country file after applying the approved cleaning procedures.

Semantic analysis was done in order to identify inconsistencies, suspicious deviations from other country results or incoherencies between different question answers. Deviations from reasonable patterns were noted and if they seemed significant, the principal investigators from the given country were consulted to determine whether these inconsistencies reflected methodological anomalies or errors in the data validation phase.

Creating the Integrated dataset

To combine the various national datasets into one integrated dataset, a master codebook was created, based on the national data sets, the national questionnaires, and the master questionnaire. For the European datasets, this was done at the Zentralarchiv in Cologne, and Tilburg University (in collaboration with the Netherlands Institute for Scientific Information Services); the country data files were then integrated at Tilburg University. In September 2003, Zentralarchiv, in collaboration with Tilburg University, released the CD-ROM "EVS 1999/2000" containing 33 national data sets, the integrated data set and the relevant documentation required for secondary analyses. (see Luijkx, Brislinger, and Zenk-Moeltgen 2003).

The 47 other surveys were cleaned and combined into one integrated dataset by JD Systems in Madrid, which then combined the European and non-European surveys into the dataset on the accompanying CD-ROM. This CD contains a browsing program developed by JD Systems that provides for:

- Simple and extended searches in a user-friendly manner.
- Analyses and the creation of tables or graphs for frequencies, cross-tabulations and comparative analyses.
- The ability to print codebooks, tables and graphs.

In addition, the user can get direct access to the following information:

- The national data sets and the integrated data set (in SPSS-format).
- The original questionnaires and the methodological questionnaires of all participating countries.
- The Master Questionnaire and the summarized information from the methodological questionnaires.
- The List of Country Codes, which also contains the ZA number to identify the data sets and the corresponding documentation, and the internet abbreviations which were used for the names of the country-specific variables.

All documents are available as PDF-files and can be viewed and printed with Adobe Acrobat Reader included on the CD-ROM. The data files are in SPSS-format for analyses using SPSS software

Construction of the independent variables

In this source book, we cross tabulate each question by the following independent variables: gender, age, education, income, and materialist-postmaterialist values.

For gender, we use the obvious categories "female" (51%) and "male" (49%). For age, the following three age groups are used: 15-29 years: 30% / 30-49 years: 41% / 50+ years 29%. The **education** variable (x025) distinguishes the following categories:

1. inadequately completed elementary education
2. completed (compulsory) elementary education
3. (compulsory) elementary education and basic vocational qualification
4. secondary, intermediate vocational qualification
5. secondary, intermediate general qualification
6. full secondary, maturity level certificate
7. higher education - lower-level tertiary certificate
8. higher education - upper-level tertiary certificate

We construct a category "lower" by collapsing categories 1-3; "medium" by collapsing 4-5-6; and "upper" by combining 7 and 8. The marginals for the constructed variable education are:

Lower	38%
Medium	42%
Upper	20%

For income, we used the national income variables, recoded into three categories: 1=Lower, 2=Middle and 3=Upper. As in Inglehart, Basáñez and Moreno (1998), the sample was recoded so that each category would comprise a third of the sample as closely as possible. In the following table the national codes that fall in each of the three categories are indicated:

	Lower	**Middle**	**Upper**
Albania	1-4	5,6	7-10
Algeria	1,2	3	4-10
Argentina	1-3	4-7	8-10
Armenia	1,2	3,4	5-10
Australia	1-3	4-7	8-10
Austria	1-3	4-6	7-10
Azerbaijan	1,2	3,4	5-7
Bangladesh	1-3	4,5	6-10
Belarus	1-3	4,5	6-9
Belgium	1-3	4-6	7-10
Bosnia and Herzegovina	1-3	4,5	6-10
Brazil	1	2	3-10
Bulgaria	1,2	3-6	7-10
Canada	1-3	4-6	7-10

	Lower	Middle	Upper
Chile	1,2	3-6	7-10
China	1-5	6,7	8-10
Colombia	1-3	4,5	6-10
Croatia	1,2	3,4	5-10
Czech Republic	1,2	3-5	6-10
Denmark	1-3	4-7	8-10
Dominican Republic	1-3	4-6	7-10
Egypt	1-4	5,6	7-10
El Salvador	1-4	5,6	7-10
Estonia	1,2	3,4	5-10
Finland	1-3	4,5	6-10
France	1,2	3-5	6-10
Georgia	1,2	3	4-10
Germany	1-3	4,5	6-10
Great Britain	1-4	5,6	7-10
Greece	1-4	5,6	7-10
Hungary	1,2	3,4	5-10
Iceland	1-3	4-6	7-10
India	1,2	3	4-10
Indonesia	1-5	6,7	8-10
Iran	1-4	5	6-10
Ireland	1-4	5,6	7-10
Israel	1,2	3,4	5-9
Italy	1-3	4-6	7-10
Japan	1-3	4-6	7-10
Jordan	1,2	3,4	5-10
Korea, South	1-4	5	6-10
Latvia	1,2	3	4-10
Lithuania	1,2	3,4	5-10
Luxembourg	1-3	4-7	8-10
Macedonia	1-3	4,5	6-10
Malta	1-3	4,5	6-10
Mexico	1-3	4-6	7-10
Moldavia	1,2	3,4	5-10
Montenegro	1-4	5-7	8-10
Morocco	1-3	4,5	6-10
Netherlands	1-5	6,7	8-10
New Zealand	1-4	5-7	8-10
Nigeria	1-4	5,6	7-10
Northern Ireland	1-4	5,6	7-10
Pakistan	1-3	4,5	6-10
Peru	1,2	3,4	5-9
Philippines	1-3	4,5	6-10
Poland	1-3	4,5	6-10
Portugal	1,2	3,4	5,6
Puerto Rico	1	2,3	4-10

	Lower	Middle	Upper
Romania	1-3	4-6	7-10
Russian Federation	1-4	5-7	8-10
Serbia	1-3	4-6	7-10
Singapore	1,2	3,4	5-10
Slovakia	1-3	4-6	7-10
Slovenia	1-4	5-7	8-10
South Africa	1-3	4,5	6-10
Spain	1-3	4,5	6-10
Sweden	1-4	5-7	8-10
Switzerland	1-3	4-7	8-10
Taiwan	1-3	4-7	8-10
Tanzania	1,2	3,4	5-10
Turkey	1,2	3,4	5-10
Uganda	1,2	3	4-7
Ukraine	1,2	3,4	5-10
United States	1-4	5-7	8-10
Uruguay	1-3	4,5	6-10
Venezuela	1-3	4-6	7-10
Viet Nam	1-4	5	6-10
Zimbabwe	1,2	3,4	5-9

Not all nations used the full ten-point scale in coding income: in some cases, the scale was shortened, or some codes were missing data.

The **Materialist/Postmaterialist Values** variable measures the extent to which the respondent gives top priority to economic and physical security, on one hand; or to autonomy and self-expression. This index is based on the respondent's first and second choices in the original four item Materialist / Postmaterialist values battery, which follows:

> "People sometimes talk about what the aims of this country should be for the next ten years. On this card are listed some of the goals which different people would give top priority. Would you please say which one of these you, yourself, consider the most important? And which would be the second most important?"

	1st CHOICE	2nd CHOICE
1. Maintaining order in the nation	1	1
2. Giving people more say in important government decisions	2	2
3. Fighting rising prices	3	3
4. Protecting freedom of speech	4	4

The first and third options tap Materialist priorities, while the second and fourth options tap Postmaterialist priorities. If both Materialist items are given high priority, the score is "1"; if both Postmaterialist items are given high priority, the score is "3" if one Materialist item and one Postmaterialist item are given high priority, the score is "2." If the respondent makes only one or no choices, the result is missing data.

Most samples contain a **weighting** variable. These weighting variables for the European Values Study are described in more detail in Halman (2001). For the present dataset, we have constructed a new weight variable that incorporates the national weights but also gives each country the same weight to offset the fact that some countries used much larger samples than others, which could distort results when two or more samples are analyzed together. When this weighting factor is used, each country has the same weight, regardless of sample size.

REFERENCES

Halman, Loek. 2001. *The European Values Study: A Third Wave. Source book of the 1999/2000 European Values Study Surveys*. Tilburg: EVS/WORC.

Inglehart, Ronald, Miguel Basáñez, and Alejandro Moreno. 1998. *Human Values and Beliefs. A Cross-Cultural Sourcebook.* Ann Arbor (MI): The University of Michigan Press.

Luijkx, Ruud, E. Brislinger, and W. Zenk-Moeltgen. 2003. „European Values Study 1999/2000- A Third Wave: Data, Documentation and Databases on CD-ROM." *ZA-Information* 52:171-183.

World values survey 2000-2001 questionnaire

INTRODUCTION BY INTERVIEWER:

Hello. I am from the [NAME OF ORGANIZATION]. We are carrying out the [NATION] part of a world-wide study of what people value in life. This study will interview samples representing most of the world's people. Your name has been selected at random as part of a representative sample of the [BRAZILIAN] public. I'd like to ask your views on a number of different subjects. Your help will contribute to a better understanding of what people all over the world believe and want out of life.

SHOW CARD A

For each of the following, indicate how important it is in your life. Would you say it is:

		Very important	Rather important	Not very important	Not at all important	DK
v4	Family	1	2	3	4	9
v5	Friends	1	2	3	4	9
v6	Leisure time	1	2	3	4	9
v7	Politics	1	2	3	4	9
v8	Work	1	2	3	4	9
v9	Religion	1	2	3	4	9
v10	Service to others	1	2	3	4	9

V11. Taking all things together, would you say you are:
[READ OUT]

1. Very happy
2. Quite happy
3. Not very happy
4. Not at all happy
9. Don't know [DO NOT READ OUT]

V12. All in all, how would you describe your state of health these days? Would you say it is... (READ OUT REVERSING ORDER FOR ALTERNATE CONTACTS)

1. Very good
2. Good
3. Fair
4. Poor
9. Don't know [DO NOT READ OUT]

SHOW CARD B

V13. With which of these two statements do you tend to agree? (CODE ONE ANSWER ONLY)

A. Regardless of what the qualities and faults of one's parents are, one must always love and respect them
B. One does not have the duty to respect and love parents who have not earned it by their behavior and attitudes
1. Tend to agree with statement A
2. Tend to agree with statement B
9. Don't know [DO NOT READ OUT]

SHOW CARD C

V14. Which of the following statements best describes your views about parents' responsibilities to their children? (CODE ONE ONLY)

1 Parents' duty is to do their best for their children even at the expense of their own well-being
2 Parents have a life of their own and should not be asked to sacrifice their own well-being for the sake of their children
3 Neither [IF VOLUNTEERED]
9 Don't know [DO NOT READ OUT]

SHOW CARD D

Here is a list of qualities that children can be encouraged to learn at home. Which, if any, do you consider to be especially important? Please choose up to five. (CODE FIVE ONLY)

		Important	Not Mentioned
V15	Independence	1	2
V16	Hard work	1	2
V17	Feeling of responsibility	1	2
V18	Imagination	1	2
V19	Tolerance and respect for other people	1	2

		Important	Not Mentioned
V20	Thrift, saving money and things	1	2
V21	Determination, perseverance	1	2
V22	Religious faith	1	2
V23	Unselfishness	1	2
V24	Obedience	1	2

V25. Generally speaking, would you say that most people can be trusted or that you need to be very careful in dealing with people?

1. Most people can be trusted
2. Need to be very careful
9. Don't know [DO NOT READ OUT]

V26. Do you think most people would try to take advantage of you if they got a chance, or would they try to be fair?

1. Would take advantage
2. Would try to be fair
9. Don't know [DO NOT READ OUT]

I'm going to ask how of often you do various things. For each activity, would you say you do them every week or nearly every week; once or twice a month; only a few times a year; or not at all?

		Weekly/ nearly every week	Once or twice a month	Only a few times a year	Not at all	DK
V27	Spend time with parents or other relatives	1	2	3	4	9
V28	Spend time with friends	1	2	3	4	9
V29	Spend time socially with colleagues from work or your profession	1	2	3	4	9
V30	Spend time with people at your church, mosque or synagogue	1	2	3	4	9
V31	Spend time socially with people at sports clubs or voluntary or service organization	1	2	3	4	9

V32. When you get together with your friends, would you say you discuss political matters frequently, occasionally or never?

1. Frequently
2. Occasionally
3. Never
9. Don't know [DO NOT READ OUT]

SHOW CARD B

I am now going to read out some statements about the environment. For each one read out, can you tell me whether you agree strongly, agree, disagree or strongly disagree? (Read out each statement and code an answer for each)

		Strongly Agree	Agree	Disagree	Strongly Disagree	DK
v33	I would give part of my income if I were certain that the money would be used to prevent environmental pollution	1	2	3	4	9
v34	I would agree to an increase in taxes if the extra money were used to prevent environmental pollution	1	2	3	4	9
v35	The Government should reduce environmental pollution, but it should not cost me any money	1	2	3	4	9

V36. Here are two statements people sometimes make when discussing the environment and economic growth. Which of them comes closer to your own point of view?

1. Protecting the environment should be given priority, even if it causes slower economic growth and some loss of jobs.
2. Economic growth and creating jobs should be the top priority, even if the environment suffers to some extent
3. Other answer (VOLUNTEERED)
9. DK

V37. For each of the following pairs of statements, please tell me which one comes closest to your own views:

1. Human beings should master nature;
   OR
2. Humans should coexist with nature.
9. DK

V38

1. To build good human relationships, it is most important to try to understand others' preferences;
   OR
2. To build good relationships, it is most important to express one's own preferences clearly.
9. DK

SHOW CARD C

Please look carefully at the following list of voluntary organisations and activities and say...

which, if any, do you belong to? (Code all 'yes' answers as 1, if not mentioned code as 2)

		Belong	Not Mentioned
V39	Social welfare services for elderly, handicapped or deprived people	1	2
V40	Religious or church organizations	1	2
V41	Education, arts, music or cultural activities	1	2
V42	Labor unions	1	2
V43	Political parties or groups	1	2
V44	Local community action on issues like poverty, employment, housing, racial equality	1	2
V45	Third world development or human rights	1	2
V46	Conservation, environment, animal rights groups	1	2
V47	Professional associations	1	2
V48	Youth work (e.g. scouts, guides, youth clubs etc.)	1	2
V49	Sports or recreation	1	2
V50	Women's groups	1	2
V51	Peace movement	1	2
V52	Voluntary organizations concerned with health	1	2
V53	Other groups	1	2

B) And for which, if any, are you currently doing unpaid voluntary work?
[Code all 'yes' answers as 1; if not mentioned code as 2]

		Do voluntary work	Not Mentioned
V54	Social welfare services for elderly, handicapped or deprived people	1	2
V55	Religious or church organizations	1	2
V56	Education, arts, music or cultural activities	1	2
V57	Labor unions	1	2
V58	Political parties or groups	1	2

		Do voluntary work	Not Mentioned
V59	Local community action on issues like poverty, employment, housing, racial equality	1	2
V60	Third world development or human rights	1	2
V61	Conservation, environmental, animal rights groups	1	2
V62	Professional associations	1	2
V63	Youth work (scouts, guides, youth clubs, etc.)	1	2
V64	Sports or recreation	1	2
V65	Women's groups	1	2
V66	Peace movement	1	2
V67	Voluntary organizations concerned with health	1	2

SHOW CARD G

On this list are various groups of people. Could you please sort out any that you would not like to have as neighbors? (CODE AN ANSWER FOR EACH)

		Mentioned	Not Mentioned
V68	People with a criminal record	1	2
V69	People of a different race	1	2
V70	Heavy drinkers	1	2
V71	Emotionally unstable people	1	2
V72	Muslims	1	2
V73	Immigrants/foreign workers	1	2
V74	People who have AIDS	1	2
V75	Drug addicts	1	2
V76	Homosexuals	1	2
V77	Jews	1	2

In societies with Islamic majorities, ask about Christians
If Jews are not a salient group in your society, substitute some small but visible minority group

Do you agree or disagree with the following statements?

		Agree	Neither	Disagree	DK
V78	When jobs are scarce, men should have more right to a job than women	1	2	3	4
V79	When jobs are scarce, employers should give priority to [BRITISH] people over immigrants	1	2	3	4

[Substitute your own nationality]

SHOW CARD H

V80. How satisfied are you with the financial situation of your household? If "1" means you are completely dissatisfied on this scale, and "10" means you are completely satisfied, where would you put your satisfaction with your household's financial situation?

Dissatisfied					Satisfied				
1	2	3	4	5	6	7	8	9	10

DK = 99

SHOW CARD H AGAIN

V81. All things considered, how satisfied are you with your life as a whole these days? Please use this card to help with your answer.

Dissatisfied					Satisfied				
1	2	3	4	5	6	7	8	9	10

DK = 99

V82. Some people feel they have completely free choice and control over their lives, while other people feel that what they do has no real effect on what happens to them. Please use this scale where 1 means "none at all" and 10 means "a great deal" to indicate how much freedom of choice and control you feel you have over the way your life turns out.

None at all					A great deal				
1	2	3	4	5	6	7	8	9	10

DK = 99

SHOW CARD I

V83. Which point on this scale most clearly describes how much weight you place on work (including housework and schoolwork), as compared with leisure or recreation?

1. It's leisure that makes life worth living, not work
2.
3.
4.
5. Work is what makes life worth living, not leisure
9. DK

SHOW CARD J

V84. Now I would like to ask you something about the things which would seem to you, personally, most important if you were looking for a job. Here are some of the things many people take into account in relation to their work. Regardless of whether you're actually looking for a job, which one would you, personally, place first if you were looking for a job?

1. A good income so that you do not have any worries about money
2. A safe job with no risk of closing down or unemployment
3. Working with people you like
4. Doing an important job which gives you a feeling of accomplishment
9. DK

V85. And what would be your second choice?

1. A good income so that you do not have any worries about money
2. A safe job with no risk of closing down or unemployment
3. Working with people you like
4. Doing an important job which gives you a feeling of accomplishment
9. DK

SHOW CARD J2

Here are some more aspects of a job that people say are important. Please look at them and tell me which ones you personally think are important in a job? (CODE ALL MENTIONED)

		Mentioned	Not mentioned
V86	Good pay	1	2
V87	Not too much pressure	1	2
V88	Good job security	1	2
V89	A job respected by people in general	1	2
V90	Good hours	1	2
V91	An opportunity to use initiative	1	2
V92	Generous holidays	1	2
V93	A job in which you feel you can achieve something	1	2
V94	A responsible job	1	2
V95	A job that is interesting	1	2
V96	A job that meets one's abilities	1	2

SHOW CARD L

N2. Do you agree or disagree with the following statements?

		Strongly agree	Agree	Neither agree or disagree	Disagree	Strongly disagree	DK
V97	To fully develop your talents, you need to have a job	1	2	3	4	5	9

		Strongly agree	Agree	Neither agree or disagree	Disagree	Strongly disagree	DK
V98	It is humiliating to receive money without having to work for it	1	2	3	4	5	9
V99	People who don't work turn lazy	1	2	3	4	5	9
V100	Work is a duty towards society	1	2	3	4	5	9
V101	People should not have to work if they don't want to	1	2	3	4	5	9
V102	Work should always come first, even if it means less spare time	1	2	3	4	5	9

V103. Imagine two secretaries, of the same age, doing practically the same job. One finds out that the other earns considerably more than she does. The better paid secretary, however, is quicker, more efficient and more reliable at her job. In your opinion, is it fair or not fair that one secretary is paid more than the other?

1 Fair
2 Not fair
9 Don't know [DO NOT READ OUT]

SHOW CARD K

V104. There is a lot of discussion about how business and industry should be managed. Which of these four statements comes closest to your opinion? (CODE ONE ONLY)

1 The owners should run their business or appoint the managers
2 The owners and the employees should participate in the selection of managers
3 The government should be the owner and appoint the managers
4 The employees should own the business and should elect the managers
9 Don't know [DO NOT READ OUT]

V105. People have different ideas about following instructions at work. Some say that one should follow one's superior's instructions even when one does not fully agree with them. Others say that one should follow one's superior's instructions only when one is convinced that they are right. With which of these two opinions do you agree?

1 Should follow instructions
2 Must be convinced first
3 Depends [IF VOLUNTEERED]
9 Don't know [DO NOT READ OUT]

V106. Are you currently ....(READ OUT AND CODE ONE ONLY)

1 Married
2 Living together as married
3 Divorced
4 Separated
5 Widowed
6 Single

V107. Have you had any children? IF YES, how many?

0 No child
1 1 child
2 2 children
3 3 children
4 4 children
5 5 children
6 6 children
7 7 children
8 8 or more children
9 No answer

V108. What do you think is the ideal size of the family — how many children, if any?

0 None
1 1 child
2 2 children
3 3 children
4 4 children
5 5 children
6 6 children
7 7 children
8 8 or more children
9 DK, no answer

V109. If someone says a child needs a home with both a father and a mother to grow up happily, would you tend to agree or disagree?

1 Tend to agree
2 Tend to disagree
9 Don't know [DO NOT READ OUT]

V110. Do you think that a woman has to have children in order to be fulfilled or is this not necessary?

1 Needs children
2 Not necessary
9 Don't know [DO NOT READ OUT]

V111. Do you agree or disagree with the following statement? (READ OUT): "Marriage is an out-dated institution"

1 Agree
2 Disagree
9 Don't know [DO NOT READ OUT]

V112. If a woman wants to have a child as a single parent but she doesn't want to have a stable relationship with a man, do you approve or disapprove?

1 Approve
2 Disapprove
3 Depends [IF VOLUNTEERED]
9 Don't know [DO NOT READ OUT]

For each of the following statements I read out, can you tell me how much you agree with each. Do you agree strongly, agree, disagree, or disagree strongly?

		Agree strongly	Agree	Disagree	Strongly disagree	DK
V113	One of my main goals in life has been to make my parents proud	1	2	3	4	9
V114	I make a lot of effort to live up to what my friends expect	1	2	3	4	9
V115	A working mother can establish just as warm and secure a relationship with her children as a mother who does not work	1	2	3	4	9
V116	Being a housewife is just as fulfilling as working for pay	1	2	3	4	9

		Agree strongly	Agree	Disagree	Strongly disagree	DK
V117	Both the husband and wife should contribute to household income	1	2	3	4	9
V118	On the whole, men make better political leaders than women do	1	2	3	4	9
V119	A university education is more important for a boy than for a girl	1	2	3	4	9

SHOW CARD L

V120. People sometimes talk about what the aims of this country should be for the next ten years. On this card are listed some of the goals which different people would give top priority. Would you please say which one of these you, yourself, consider the most important? CODE ONE ANSWER ONLY UNDER "First Choice."

V121. And which would be the next most important? CODE ONE ANSWER ONLY UNDER "Second Choice."

	1st CHOICE	2nd CHOICE
A high level of economic growth	1	1
Making sure this country has strong defense forces	2	2
Seeing that people have more say about how things are done at their jobs and in their communities	3	3
Trying to make our cities and countryside more beautiful	4	4
Don't know [DO NOT READ OUT]	9	9

SHOW CARD M

V122. If you had to choose, which one of the things on this card would you say is most important? CODE ONE ANSWER ONLY

V123. And which would be the next most important? CODE ONE ANSWER ONLY

	1st CHOICE	2nd CHOICE
Maintaining order in the nation	1	1
Giving people more say in important government decisions	2	2
Fighting rising prices	3	3
Protecting freedom of speech	4	4
Don't know [DO NOT READ OUT]	9	9

SHOW CARD N

V124. Here is another list. In your opinion, which one of these is most important? CODE ONE ANSWER ONLY

V125. And what would be the next most important? CODE ONE ANSWER ONLY

	1st CHOICE	2nd CHOICE
A stable economy	1	1
Progress toward a less impersonal and More humane society	2	2
Progress toward a society in which Ideas count more than money	3	3
The fight against crime	4	4
Don't know [DO NOT READ OUT]	9	9

V126. Of course, we all hope that there will not be another war, but if it were to come to that, would you be willing to fight for your country?

1 Yes
2 No
9 Don't know [DO NOT READ OUT]

I'm going to read out a list of various changes in our way of life that might take place in the near future. Please tell me for each one, if it were to happen, whether you think it would be a good thing, a bad thing, or don't you mind?

		GOOD	Don't Mind	BAD
V127	Less emphasis on money and material possessions	1	2	3
V128	Less importance placed on work in our lives	1	2	3
V129	More emphasis on the development of technology	1	2	3
V130	Greater respect for authority	1	2	3
V131	More emphasis on family life	1	2	3

V132. In the long run, do you think the scientific advances we are making will help or harm mankind?

1 Will help
2 Will harm
3 Some of each
9 Don't know [DO NOT READ OUT]

V133. How interested would you say you are in politics?

1 Very interested
2 Somewhat interested
3 Not very interested
4 Not at all interested
9 Don't know [DO NOT READ OUT]

SHOW CARD O

[WHICH LISTS "HAVE DONE," "MIGHT DO," WOULD NEVER DO]

Now I'd like you to look at this card. I'm going to read out some different forms of political action that people can take, and I'd like you to tell me, for each one, whether you have actually done any of these things, whether you might do it or would never, under any circumstances, do it.

		Have done	Might do	Would never do	DK
V134	Signing a petition	1	2	3	4
V135	Joining in boycotts	1	2	3	4
V136	Attending lawful demonstrations	1	2	3	4
V137	Joining unofficial strikes	1	2	3	4
V138	Occupying buildings or factories	1	2	3	4

SHOW CARD P

V139. In political matters, people talk of "the left" and "the right." How would you place your views on this scale, generally speaking?

Left									Right
1	2	3	4	5	6	7	8	9	10

DK = 99

SHOW CARD Q

V140. On this card are three basic kinds of attitudes concerning the society we live in. Please choose the one which best describes your own opinion. CODE ONE ONLY

1 The entire way our society is organized must be radically changed by revolutionary action
2 Our society must be gradually improved by reforms
3 Our present society must be valiantly defended against all subversive forces
9 Don't know [DO NOT READ OUT]

SHOW CARD R

Now I'd like you to tell me your views on various issues. How would you place your views on this scale? 1 means you agree completely with the statement on the left; 10

means you agree completely with the statement on the right; and if your views fall somewhere in between, you can choose any number in between.

V141

Incomes should be made more equal					We need larger income differences as incentives for individual effort				
1	2	3	4	5	6	7	8	9	10

DK = 99

V142

Private ownership of business and industry should be increased					Government ownership of business and industry should be increased				
1	2	3	4	5	6	7	8	9	10

DK = 99

V143

The government should take more responsibility to ensure that everyone is provided for					People should take more responsibility to provide for themselves				
1	2	3	4	5	6	7	8	9	10

DK = 99

V144

Competition is good. It stimulates people to work hard and develop new ideas					Competition is harmful. It brings out the worst in people				
1	2	3	4	5	6	7	8	9	10

DK = 99

Now I'm going to read you some pairs of contrasting statements. For each pair, do you think that the first statement or the second one best describes the CURRENT SITUATION in this country?

NOTE: The early version of this questionnaire, used in some countries including the U.S., has the following item INSTEAD OF V145A –V145F:

V145

Ideas that have stood the test of time are generally best					New ideas are generally better than old ones				
1	2	3	4	5	6	7	8	9	10

DK = 99

	First alternative	Second alternative
V145A.	An egalitarian society where the gap between rich and poor is small, regardless of achievement	A competitive society, where wealth is distributed according to ones' achievement

closer to first	somewhat closer to first	can't say which	somewhat closer to second	closer to second	NA
1	2	3	4	5	9

	First alternative	Second alternative
V145B.	A society with extensive social welfare, but high taxes	A society where taxes are low and individuals take responsibility for themselves

closer to first	somewhat closer to first	can't say which	somewhat closer to second	closer to second	NA
1	2	3	4	5	9

	First alternative	Second alternative
V145C.	A society that assures safety and stability through appropriate regulations	A deregulated society where people are responsible for their own actions

closer to first	somewhat closer to first	can't say which	somewhat closer to second	closer to second	NA
1	2	3	4	5	9

And now, could you please tell me which type of society this country you think this country SHOULD aim to be in the future. For each pair of statements, would you prefer being closer to the first or to the second alternative?

	First alternative	Second alternative
V145D.	An egalitarian society where the gap between rich and poor is small, regardless of achievement	A competitive society, where wealth is distributed according to ones' achievement

closer to first	somewhat closer to first	can't say which	somewhat closer to second	closer to second	NA
1	2	3	4	5	9

	First alternative	Second alternative
V145E.	A society with extensive social taxes	A society where taxes are low welfare, but high individuals take responsibility for themselves

closer to first	somewhat closer to first	can't say which	somewhat closer to second	closer to second	NA
1	2	3	4	5	9

V145F. A society that assures safety and stability through appropriate regulations — A deregulated society where people are responsible for their own actions

closer to first	somewhat closer to first	can't say which	somewhat closer to second	closer to second	NA
1	2	3	4	5	9

V146. How about people from other countries coming here to work. Which one of the following do you think the government should do?

1. Let anyone come who wants to?
2. Let people come as long as there are jobs available?
3. Place strict limits on the number of foreigners who can come here?
4. Prohibit people coming here from other countries?
9. DK

I am going to name a number of organizations. For each one, could you tell me how much confidence you have in them: is it a great deal of confidence, quite a lot of confidence, not very much confidence or none at all?

		A great deal	Quite a lot	Not very much	None at all	DK
V147	The churches	1	2	3	4	9
V148	The armed forces	1	2	3	4	9
V149	The press	1	2	3	4	9
V150	Television	1	2	3	4	9
V151	Labor unions	1	2	3	4	9
V152	The police	1	2	3	4	9
V153	The government in [WASHINGTON/ YOUR CAPITAL]	1	2	3	4	9
V154	Political parties	1	2	3	4	9
V155	Parliament	1	2	3	4	9
V156	The Civil service	1	2	3	4	9
V157	Major Companies	1	2	3	4	9
V158	The Environmental Protection movement	1	2	3	4	9
V159	The women's movement	1	2	3	4	9
V160	The European Union*	1	2	3	4	9
V161	NATO (North Atlantic Treaty Organization)	1	2	3	4	9
V162	The United Nations	1	2	3	4	9

* *In non-European countries ask about the most important regional organization (e.g., in North America, NAFTA).*

V163. People have different views about the system for governing this country. Here is a scale for rating how well things are going: 1 means very bad; 10 means very good

Where on this scale would you put the political system as it was ....

[*in former communist countries*: under the communist regime]
[*in countries where recently a change of regime has taken place*:
under the xxx regime;]
[*in countries where no regime change has taken place*: ten years ago]?

1	2	3	4	5	6	7	8	9	10	99
Bad								Very good		Dk

I'm going to describe various types of political systems and ask what you think about each as a way of governing this country. For each one, would you say it is a very good, fairly good, fairly bad or very bad way of governing this country?

		Very good	Fairly good	Bad	Very bad	DK
164	Having a strong leader who does not have to bother with parliament and elections	1	2	3	4	9
165	Having experts, not government, make decisions according to what they think is best for the country	1	2	3	4	9
166	Having the army rule	1	2	3	4	9
167	Having a democratic political system	1	2	3	4	9

V168. On the whole are you very satisfied, rather satisfied, not very satisfied or not at all satisfied with the way democracy is developing in our country?

1 Very satisfied
2 Rather satisfied
3 Not very satisfied
4 Not at all satisfied
9 DK

I'm going to read off some things that people sometimes say about a democratic political system. Could you please tell me if you agree strongly, agree, disagree or disagree strongly, after I read each one of them?

		Agree strongly	Agree	Disagree	Strongly disagree	DK
V169	In democracy, the economic system runs badly	1	2	3	4	9

		Agree strongly	Agree	Disagree	Strongly disagree	DK
V170	Democracies are indecisive and have too much quibbling	1	2	3	4	9
V171	Democracies aren't good at maintaining order	1	2	3	4	9
V172	Democracy may have problems but it's better than any other form of government	1	2	3	4	9

V173. How much respect is there for individual human rights nowadays (in our country)?. Do you feel there is (read out):

1 A lot of respect for individual human rights
2 Some respect
3 Not much respect
4 No respect at all
9 Don't know

V174. How satisfied are you with the way the people now in national office are handling the country's affairs? Would you say you are very satisfied, fairly satisfied, fairly dissatisfied or very dissatisfied?

1 Very satisfied
2 Fairly satisfied
3 Fairly dissatisfied
4 Very dissatisfied
9 DK

V175. Generally speaking, would you say that this country is run by a few big interests looking out for themselves, or that it is run for the benefit of all the people?

1 Run by a few big interests
2 Run for all the people
9 Don't know

V176. Some people favor, and others are against, having this country provide economic aid to poorer countries. Do you think that this country should provide more or less economic aid to poorer countries? Would you say we should give…

1. A lot more than we do now
2. Somewhat more than we do now
3. Somewhat less than we do now
4. A lot less than we do now
9. DK

Some people believe that certain kinds of problems could be better handled by the United Nations than by the various national governments. Others think that these problems should be left entirely to the respective national governments; while others think they would be handled best by the national governments working together with coordination by the United Nations.

I'm going to mention some problems. For each one, would you tell me whether you think that policies in this area should be decided by the national governments, by the United Nations, or by the national governments with UN coordination?

		National Governments	United Nations	National governments, with UN coordination
V177	International peacekeeping	1	2	3
V178	Protection of the environment	1	2	3
V179	Aid to developing countries	1	2	3
V180	Refugees	1	2	3
V181	Human Rights	1	2	3

V182. How often, if at all, do you think about the meaning and purpose of life?
(READ OUT IN REVERSE ORDER FOR ALTERNATE CONTACTS)

1 Often
2 Sometimes
3 Rarely
4 Never
9 Don't know [DO NOT READ OUT]

SHOW CARD T

V183. Here are two statements which people sometimes make when discussing good and evil.

Which one comes closest to your own point of view?

A. There are absolutely clear guidelines about what is good and evil. These always apply to everyone, whatever the circumstances.

B. There can never be absolutely clear guidelines about what is good and evil. What is good and evil depends entirely upon the circumstances at the time.

1 Agree with statement A
2 Agree with statement B
3 Disagree with both [IF VOLUNTEERED]
9 Don't know [DO NOT READ OUT]

V184. Do you belong to a religious denomination?
IF YES: Which one?
[IF NO: CODE 0]

RELIGIOUS DENOMINATION

NO, not a member	0
Roman Catholic	1
Protestant	2
Orthodox (Russian/Greek/etc.)	3
Jews	4
Muslim	5
Hindu	6
Buddhist	7
Other (WRITE IN)	8
No answer	9

NOTE: if your own society does not fit into this coding system, please devise an alternative, following this as closely as possible; point out any variations when sending the data.

ASK ALL

SHOW CARD U

V185. Apart from weddings, funerals and christenings, about how often do you attend religious services these days?

1 More than once a week
2 Once a week
3 Once a month
4 Only on special holy days
5 Once a year
6 Less often
7 Never, practically never

V186. Independently of whether you go to church or not, would you say you are... (READ OUT)

1 A religious person
2 Not a religious person
3 A convinced atheist
9 Don't know [DO NOT READ OUT]

Generally speaking, do you think that the churches in your country are giving adequate answers to...

(Read out and code one answer for each)

NB: In non-Christian countries, refer to "the religious authorities in your country" or "the religious leaders in your country," instead of "the churches."

		YES	NO	DK
V187	The moral problems and needs of the individual	1	2	9
V188	The problems of family life	1	2	9
V189	People's spiritual needs	1	2	9
V190	The social problems facing our country today	1	2	9

Which, if any, of the following do you believe in? (READ OUT AND CODE ONE ANSWER FOR EACH)

		YES	NO	DK
V191	Do you believe in God?	1	2	9
V192	Do you believe in life after death?	1	2	9
V193	Do you believe people have a soul?	1	2	9
V194	Do you believe in hell?	1	2	9
V195	Do you believe in heaven?	1	2	9

SHOW CARD V

V196. How important is God in your life? Please use this scale to indicate- 10 means very important and 1 means not at all important.

Not at all									Very
1	2	3	4	5	6	7	8	9	10

DK = 99

V197. Do you find that you get comfort and strength from religion?

1 Yes
2 No
9 Don't know [DO NOT READ OUT]

V198. Do you take some moments of prayer, meditation or contemplation or something like that?

1 Yes
2 No
9 Don't know

V199. How often do you pray to God outside of religious services? Would you say...

1 every day
2 more than once a week
3 once a week
4 at least once a month
5 several times a year
6 less often
7 never
9 Don't know

SHOW CARD

How much do you agree or disagree with each of the following

		Agree Strongly	Agree	Neither agree or disagree	Disagree	Strongly disagree	DK
V200	Politicians who do not believe in God are unfit for public office	1	2	3	4	5	9
V201	Religious leaders should not influence how people vote in elections	1	2	3	4	5	9
V202	It would be better for [this country] if more people with strong religious beliefs held public office	1	2	3	4	5	9
V203	Religious leaders should not influence government decisions	1	2	3	4	5	9

SHOW CARD W

Please tell me for each of the following statements whether you think it can always be justified, never be justified, or something in between, using this card. READ OUT STATEMENTS. CODE ONE ANSWER FOR EACH STATEMENT

V204. Claiming government benefits to which you are not entitled

Never Justifiable									Always Justifiable
1	2	3	4	5	6	7	8	9	10

DK = 99

V205. Avoiding a fare on public transport

Never Justifiable									Always Justifiable
1	2	3	4	5	6	7	8	9	10

DK = 99

V206. Cheating on taxes if you have a chance

Never Justifiable									Always Justifiable
1	2	3	4	5	6	7	8	9	10

DK = 99

V207. Someone accepting a bribe in the course of their duties

Never Justifiable									Always Justifiable
1	2	3	4	5	6	7	8	9	10

DK = 99

V208. Homosexuality

Never Justifiable									Always Justifiable
1	2	3	4	5	6	7	8	9	10

DK = 99

V209. Prostitution

Never Justifiable									Always Justifiable
1	2	3	4	5	6	7	8	9	10

DK = 99

V210. Abortion

Never Justifiable									Always Justifiable
1	2	3	4	5	6	7	8	9	10

DK = 99

V211. Divorce

Never Justifiable									Always Justifiable
1	2	3	4	5	6	7	8	9	10

DK = 99

V212. Euthanasia— ending the life of the incurably sick

Never Justifiable									Always Justifiable
1	2	3	4	5	6	7	8	9	10

DK = 99

V213. Suicide

Never Justifiable									Always Justifiable
1	2	3	4	5	6	7	8	9	10

DK = 99

SHOW CARD X

V214. To which of these geographical groups would you say you belong first of all?

V215. And the next?
[substitute your own nation and continent for these]

	FIRST	NEXT
Locality or town where you live	1	1
State or region of country where you live	2	2
[The U.S.] as a whole	3	3
[North America]	4	4
The world as a whole	5	5
Don't know [DO NOT READ OUT]	9	9

V216. How proud are you to be FRENCH? (substitute your own nationality for 'French')

1 Very proud
2 Quite proud
3 Not very proud
4 Not at all proud
5 [IF VOLUNTEERED]: I am not FRENCH
9 Don't know [DO NOT READ OUT]

SHOW CARD N29

V217. How often do you follow politics in the news on television or on the radio or in the daily papers?

1 Every day
2 Several times a week
3 Once or twice a week

4 Less often
5 Never
9 DK

SHOW CARD Y

V218. Which of the following best describes you? Just call out one of the letters on this card.

1 [A] Above all, I am an Hispanic American
2 [B] Above all, I am a Black American
3 [C] Above all, I am a white American
4 [D] Above all, I am an Asian American
5 [E] I am an American first and a member of some ethnic group second

[modify the ethnic groups in this question to fit your own society]

V219. What language do you normally speak at home?

1. English
2. Spanish
3. French
4. Chinese
5. Japanese

[modify the list of languages to fit your own society]

SHOW CARD Z

V220. If there were a national election tomorrow, for which party on this list would you vote? Just call out the number on this card. If DON'T KNOW: Which party appeals to you most?

1. Party 1
2. Party 2
3. Party 3
4. etc.

[use two-column code to cover all major parties in given society; use "01," "02," for first parties]

V221. And which party would be your second choice?

1. Party 1
2. Party 2
3. Party 3
4. etc.

V222. And is there any party on this list that you would never vote for?

01. Party 1
02. Party 2
03. Party 3
04. etc.

DEMOGRAPHICS

V223. Sex of respondent:

1 Male
2 Female

V224. Can you tell me your year of birth, please? 19____
[ENTER ONLY THE LAST TWO DIGITS OF THE YEAR: "19" IS ASSUMED]

V225. This means you are __ __ years old.
[ALSO A TWO DIGIT VARIABLE]

V226. What is the highest educational level that you have attained? (use functional equivalent of the following, in given society; IF STUDENT, CODE HIGHEST LEVEL HE/SHE EXPECTS TO COMPLETE):

1. No formal education
2. Incomplete primary school
3. Complete primary school
4. Incomplete secondary school: technical/vocational type
5. Complete secondary school: technical/vocational type
6. Incomplete secondary: university-preparatory type
7. Complete secondary: university-preparatory type
8. Some university-level education, without degree
9. University-level education, with degree
0. DK/NA

V227. At what age did you (or will you) complete your full time education, either at school or at an institution of higher education? Please exclude apprenticeships:
[IF STUDENT, CODE AGE AT WHICH HE/SHE EXPECTS TO COMPLETE EDUCATION]
WRITE IN AGE IN YEARS _________
[TWO DIGITS]

V228. Do you live with your parents?

1 Yes
2 No

V229. Are you employed now or not?
IF YES:
About how many hours a week? If more than one job: only for the main job

Has paid employment	
Full Time(30 hours a week or more)	1
Part time (less than 30 hours a week)	2
Self employed	3
If no paid employment:	
Retired/pensioned	4
Housewife not otherwise employed	5
Student	6
Unemployed	7
Other PLEASE SPECIFY	8

V230. In which profession/occupation do you or did you work? If more than one job, the main job?
What is/was your job there? WRITE IN AND CODE V230 BELOW
[THIS IS ASKED SIMPLY IN ORDER TO CODE V230 BELOW]

1 Employer/manager of establishment with 10 or more employees
2 Employer/manager of establishment with less than 10 employees
3 Professional worker lawyer, accountant, teacher, etc
4 Supervisory - office worker: supervises others.
5 non-manual - office worker: non-supervisory
6 Foreman and supervisor
7 Skilled manual worker
8 Semi-skilled manual worker
9 Unskilled manual worker
10 Farmer: has own farm
11 Agricultural worker
12 Member of armed forces, security personnel
13 Never had a job

V231. Are you the chief wage earner in your household?

1 Yes - GO TO V234.
2 No - GO TO V232.

V232. Is the chief wage earner employed now or not?

1 Yes
2 No

V233. In which profession/occupation does he/she work? (or did work) If more than one job, the main job? What is/was his/her job there? WRITE IN AND CODE V233 BELOW

1 Employer/manager of establishment with 10 or more employees
2 Employer/manager of establishment with less than 10 employees
3 Professional worker lawyer, accountant, teacher, etc.
4 Supervisory non-manual - office worker.
5 non-manual - office worker: non-supervisory
6 Foreman and supervisor
7 Skilled manual worker
8 Semi-skilled manual worker
9 Unskilled manual worker
10 Farmer: has own farm
11 Agricultural worker
12 Member of armed forces, security personnel
13 Never had a job

V234. During the past year, did your family:

1. Save money
2. Just get by
3. Spent some savings
4. Spent savings and borrowed money
9. DK, NA

V235. People sometimes describe themselves as belonging to the working class, the middle class, or the upper or lower class. Would you describe yourself as belonging to the:

1. Upper class
2. Upper middle class
3. Lower middle class
4. Working class
5. Lower class
9. Don't know [DO NOT READ OUT]

SHOW INCOME CARD AA

V236. Here is a scale of incomes. We would like to know in what group your household is, counting all wages, salaries, pensions and other incomes that come in. Just give the letter of the group your household falls into, before taxes and other deductions.

1	2	3	4	5	6	7	8	9	10
C	D	E	F	G	H	I	J	k	L

No answer = 99

[CODE INCOME CATEGORIES BY DECILES FOR YOUR SOCIETY, 1=LOWEST DECILE, 10=HIGHEST DECILE]

V237. Do you agree strongly, agree, disagree or disagree strongly with the following statement:

"Television is my most important form of entertainment."

1. Agree strongly
2. Agree
3. Disagree
4. Disagree Strongly
9. DK

V238. Time at the end of the interview: ....

V239. Total length of interview Hours Minute

V240. During the interview the respondent was....

1 Very interested
2 Somewhat interested
3 Not very interested

V241. Size of town:

1 Under 2,000
2 2,000 - 5,000
3 5 - 10,000
4 10 - 20,000
5 20 - 50,000
6 50 - 100,000
7 100 - 500,000
8 500,000 and more

V242. Ethnic group [code by observation]:

1 Caucasian white
2 Negro Black
3 South Asian Indian, Pakistani, etc.
4 East Asian Chinese, Japanese, etc.
5 Arabic, Central Asian
6 Other write in ....

V243. Region where the interview was conducted:

1 New England
2 Middle Atlantic states
3 South Atlantic
4 East South Central
5 West South Central

6 East North Central
7 West North Central
8 Rocky Mountain states
9 Northwest
10 California
[use 2-digit regional code appropriate to your own society]

V244. Language in which interview was conducted

1. English
2. French
[IF RELEVANT; use code appropriate to your own society]

V245. Weight variable.

Provide a 4-digit weight variable here to correct your sample to reflect national distributions of key variables. If no weighting is necessary, simply code each case as "1". It is especially important to correct for education. For example, if your sample contains twice as many university-educated respondents as there are in the adult population as a whole, members of this group should be given a weight of .5 (coded as "50").

European values study
1999 questionnaire (February version)

Variable names: v = master / o = optional / c = country-specific - to be included before demographics - / DK = don't know = code –1 / Na = no answer = code –2 / Not applicable = code –3 / caseno = respondent number / country = country code / intno = interviewer number

SHOW CARD 1

1 Please say, for each of the following, how important it is in your life.

			Very important	Quite important	Not important	Not at all important	Dk	Na
v1	A	Work	1	2	3	4	-1	-2
v2	B	Family	1	2	3	4	-1	-2
v3	C	Friends and acquaintances	1	2	3	4	-1	-2
v4	D	Leisure time	1	2	3	4	-1	-2
v5	E	Politics	1	2	3	4	-1	-2
v6	F	Religion	1	2	3	4	-1	-2

2 When you get together with your friends, would you say you discuss political matters frequently, occasionally or never?

v7	A	Frequently	1
	B	Occasionally	2
	C	Never	3
		Don't know	-1
		No answer	-2

SHOW CARD 3

3 I am now going to read out some statements about the environment. For each one read out, can you tell me whether you agree strongly, agree, disagree or strongly disagree? (Read out each statement and code an answer for each)

			Strongly agree	Agree	Disagree	Strongly disagree	Dk	Na
v8	A	I would give part of my income if I were certain that the money would be used to prevent environmental pollution	1	2	3	4	-1	-2
v9	B	I would agree to an increase in taxes if the extra money is used to prevent environmental pollution	1	2	3	4	-1	-2
v10	C	The Government has to reduce environmental pollution but it should not cost me any money	1	2	3	4	-1	-2

SHOW CARD 4

4 Taking all things together, would you say you are:

v11	A	Very happy	1
	B	Quite happy	2
	C	Not very happy	3
	D	Not at all happy	4
		Don't know	-1
		No answer	-2

SHOW CARD 5

5 Please look carefully at the following list of voluntary organisations and activities and say...

a) which, if any, do you belong to? (Code all mentioned under (a))

b) which, if any, are you currently doing unpaid voluntary work for? (Code all mentioned under (b))

				a		b	
				mentioned	not mentioned	mentioned	not mentioned
v12	v30	A	Social welfare services for elderly, handicapped or deprived people	1	0	1	0
v13	v31	B	Religious or church organisations	1	0	1	0
v14	v32	C	Education, arts, music or cultural activities	1	0	1	0
v15	v33	D	Trade unions	1	0	1	0
v16	v34	E	Political parties or groups	1	0	1	0
v17	v35	F	Local community action on issues like poverty, employment, housing, racial equality	1	0	1	0
v18	v36	G	Third world development or human rights	1	0		
v19	v37	H	Conservation, the environment, ecology, animal rights	1	0	1	0
v20	v38	I	Professional associations				
v21	v39	J	Youth work (e.g. scouts, guides, youth clubs etc.)	1	0	1	0
v22	v40	K	Sports or recreation	1	0	1	0
v23	v41	L	Women's groups	1	0	1	0
v24	v42	M	Peace movement	1	0	1	0
v25	v43	N	Voluntary organisations concerned with health	1	0	1	0
v26	v44	O	Other groups	1	0	1	0
v27	v45		None	1	0	1	0
v28	v46		Don't know	-1	0	-1	0
v29	v47		No answer	-2	0	-2	0

SHOW CARD 6

6 I'm going to ask how often you do certain things. For each activity,would you say you do them every week or nearly every week; once or twice a month; only a few times a year; or not at all? *(Interviewer: Code 'Not applicable' when respondent is not involved in work, church or club)*

			Every Week	Once or twice a month	A few times a year	Not at all	Dk	Na	Nap
v48	A	Spend time with friends	1	2	3	4	-1	-2	
v49	B	Spend time with colleagues from work or your profession outside the workplace	1	2	3	4	-1	-2	-3
v50	C	Spend time with people at your church, mosque or synagogue	1	2	3	4	-1	-2	-3
v51	D	Spend time with people in clubs and voluntary associations (sport, culture, communal)	1	2	3	4	-1	-2	-3

SHOW CARD 7

7 On this list are various groups of people. Could you please sort out any that you would not like to have as neighbours? (Code an answer for each)

			not mentioned	mentioned
v52	A	People with a criminal record	1	0
v53	B	People of a different race	1	0
v54	C	Left wing extremists	1	0
v55	D	Heavy drinkers	1	0
v56	E	Right wing extremists	1	0
v57	F	People with large families	1	0
v58	G	Emotionally unstable people	1	0
v59	H	Muslims	1	0
v60	I	Immigrants/foreign workers	1	0
v61	J	People who have AIDS	1	0
v62	K	Drug addicts	1	0
v63	L	Homosexuals	1	0
v64	M	Jews	1	0
v65	N	Gypsies	1	0
o1	*O*	*Hindus*	*1*	*0*

v66 8 Generally speaking, would you say that most people can be trusted or that you can't be too careful in dealing with people?

A	Most people can be trusted	1
B	Can't be too careful	2
	Don't know	-1
	No answer	-2

SHOW CARD 9

v67 9 Some people feel they have completely free choice and control over their lives, and other people feel that what they do has no real effect on what happens to them. Please use the scale to indicate how much freedom of choice and control you feel you have over the way your life turns out?

1	2	3	4	5	6	7	8	9	10	-1	-2
None at all								A great deal		Dk	Na

SHOW CARD 10

v68 10 All things considered, how satisfied are you with your life as a whole these days? Please use this card to help with your answer.

1	2	3	4	5	6	7	8	9	10	-1	-2
Dissatisfied								Satisfied		Dk	Na

SHOW CARD 11

v69 11 Why are there people in this country who live in need? Here are four possible reasons. Which <u>one</u> reason do you consider to be most important? (Code one under (a) below)

v70 12 And which reason do you consider to be the second most important? (Code one under (b) below)

		Most important	Second most important
A	Because they are unlucky	1	1
B	Because of laziness and lack of willpower	2	2
C	Because of injustice in our society	3	3
D	It's an inevitable part of modern progress	4	4
	None of these	5	5
	Don't know	-1	-1
	No answer	-2	-2

SHOW CARD 13

13 Here are some aspects of a job that people say are important. Please look at them and tell me which ones you personally think are important in a job? (Code all mentioned)

			mentioned	not mentioned
v71	A	Good pay	1	0
v72	B	Pleasant people to work with	1	0
v73	C	Not too much pressure	1	0
v74	D	Good job security	1	0
v75	E	Good chances for promotion	1	0
v76	F	A job respected by people in general	1	0
v77	G	Good hours	1	0
v78	H	An opportunity to use initiative	1	0
v79	I	A useful job for society	1	0
v80	J	Generous holidays	1	0
v81	K	Meeting people	1	0
v82	L	A job in which you feel you can achieve something	1	0
v83	M	A responsible job	1	0
v84	N	A job that is interesting	1	0
v85	O	A job that meets one's abilities	1	0
o2	*P*	*Good physical working conditions*	*1*	*0*
o3	*Q*	*To have time off at the weekends*	*1*	*0*
v86		None of these	1	0

v87 14 Are you yourself employed or not?

A Yes 1 ——➤ go to 15
B No 2 ——➤ go to 17

SHOW CARD 15

v88 15 Overall, how satisfied or dissatisfied are you with your job?

1	2	3	4	5	6	7	8	9	10	-1	-2	-3
Dissatisfied									Satisfied	Dk	Na	Nap

SHOW CARD 16

v89 16 How free are you to make decisions in your job? Please use this card to indicate how much decision-making freedom you feel you have.

1	2	3	4	5	6	7	8	9	10	-1	-2	-3
None at all									A great deal	Dk	Na	Nap

SHOW CARD 16a

o4 *16a And how satisfied or dissatisfied are you with your job security? Please use this card to indicate how satisfied or dissatisfied you are.*

1	*2*	*3*	*4*	*5*	*6*	*7*	*8*	*9*	*10*	*-1*	*-2*	*-3*
Dissatisfied								*Satisfied*		*Dk*	*Na*	*Nap*

ASK ALL
SHOW CARD 17

17 Do you agree or disagree with the following statements?

			Agree strongly	Agree	Neither agree nor disagree	Disagree	Disagree strongly	Dk	Na
v90	A	To fully develop your talents, you need to have a job	1	2	3	4	5	-1	-2
v91	B	It is humiliating to receive money without having to work for it	1	2	3	4	5	-1	-2
v92	C	People who don't work turn lazy	1	2	3	4	5	-1	-2
v93	D	Work is a duty towards society	1	2	3	4	5	-1	-2
v94	E	People should not have to work if they don't want to	1	2	3	4	5	-1	-2
v95	F	Work should always come first, even if it means less spare time	1	2	3	4	5	-1	-2

v96 18 Imagine two secretaries, of the same age, doing practically the same job. One finds out that the other earns £ 30 (**Countries other than UK: Please use own currency**) a week more than she does. The better paid secretary, however, is quicker, more efficient and more reliable at her job.

In your opinion is it fair or not fair that one secretary is paid more than the other?

A	Fair	1
B	Unfair	2
	Don't know	-1
	No answer	-2

SHOW CARD 19

v97 19 People have different ideas about following instruction at work. Some say that one should follow instructions of one's superiors even when one does not fully agree with them. Others say that one should follow one's superior's instructions only when one is convinced that they are right. Which of these two opinions do you agree with?

A	Should follow instructions	1
B	Must be convinced first	2
C	Depends	3
	Don't know	-1
	No answer	-2

20 Do you agree or disagree with the following statements?

			Agree	Disagree	Neither	Dk	Na
v98	A	When jobs are scarce, employers should give priority to British **(Countries other than UK: please substitute your nationality!)** people over immigrants	1	2	3	-1	-2
v99	B	When jobs are scarce, men have more right to a job than women	1	2	3	-1	-2
o5	*C*	*When jobs are scarce, employers should give priority to local people over people from other parts of the country*	*1*	*2*	*3*	*-1*	*-2*

SHOW CARD 20a

o6 *20a How often , if at all, do you think about the meaning and purpose of life? (Read out in reverse order for alternate contacts)*

A	*Often*	*1*
B	*Sometimes*	*2*
C	*Rarely*	*3*
D	*Never*	*4*
	Don't know	*-1*
	No answer	*-2*

SHOW CARD 21

v100 21 Here are two statements which people sometimes make when discussing good and evil. Which one comes closest to your own point of view?

A There are absolutely clear guidelines about what is good and evil. These always apply to everyone, whatever the circumstances.

B There can never be absolutely clear guidelines about what is good and evil. What is good and evil depends entirely upon the circumstances at the time.

A	Agree with statement A	1
B	Agree with statement B	2
C	Disagree with both	3
	Don't know	-1
	No answer	-2

v101 22 Do you belong to a religious denomination?

A Yes 1 ⟶ go to q. 23
B No 2 ⟶ go to q. 24a

SHOW CARD 23

v102 23 Which one?

NB: PRESENT COUNTRY SPECIFIC LIST! RECODE INTO:

Roman Catholic	1
Church of England (Protestant)	2
Free Church/Non-Conformist/Evangelical	3
Jew	4
Muslim	5
Hindu	6
Buddhist	7
Orthodox	8
Other (Write in)	9
Don't know	-1
No answer	-2
Not applicable	-3

v103 24a Were you ever a member of a religious denomination?

A Yes 1 ⟶ go to q. 24b
B No 2 ⟶ go to q. 25

SHOW CARD 24

v104 24b Which one?

Which one?

NB: PRESENT COUNTRY SPECIFIC LIST! RECODE INTO:

	b
Roman Catholic	1
Church of England (Protestant)	2
Free Church/Non-Conformist/ Evangelical	3
Jew	4
Muslim	5
Hindu	6
Buddhist	7
Orthodox	8
Other (Write in)	9
Don't know	-1
No answer	-2
Not applicable	-3

SHOW CARD 25

v105 25 Apart from weddings, funerals and christenings, about how often do you attend religious services these days?

A	More than once a week	1
B	Once a week	2
C	Once a month	3
D	Christmas/Easter day	4
E	Other specific holy days	5
F	Once a year	6
G	Less often	7
H	Never, practically never	8
	Don't know	-1
	No answer	-2

SHOW CARD 26

v106 26 Apart from weddings, funerals and christenings, about how often did you attend religious services when you were 12 years old?

A	More than once a week	1
B	Once a week	2
C	Once a month	3

D	Christmas/Easter day	4
E	Other specific holy days	5
F	Once a year	6
G	Less often	7
H	Never, practically never	8
	Don't know	-1
	No answer	-2

27 Do you personally think it is important to hold a religious service for any of the following events?

			Yes	No	Dk	Na
v107	A	Birth	1	2	-1	-2
v108	B	Marriage	1	2	-1	-2
v109	C	Death	1	2	-1	-2

V110 28 Independently of whether you go to church or not, would you say you are ... (Read out reversing order)

A	A religious person	1
B	Not a religious person	2
C	A convinced atheist	3
	Don't know	-1
	No answer	-2

29 Generally speaking, do you think that your church is/the churches are giving, in your country, adequate answers to ...(Read out and code one answer for each)

NB:For those belonging to a church or a religious community; ask YOUR church/ religious community

For those not belonging to a church or religious community ask: THE churches

			Yes	No	Dk	Na
V111	A	The moral problems and needs of the individual	1	2	-1	-2
V112	B	The problems of family life	1	2	-1	-2
V113	C	People's spiritual needs	1	2	-1	-2
V114	D	The social problems facing our country today	1	2	-1	-2

30 Which, if any, of the following do you believe in? (Read out and code one answer for each)

			Yes	No	Dk	Na
V115	A	God	1	2	-1	-2
V116	B	Life after death	1	2	-1	-2

			Yes	No	Dk	Na
V117	C	Hell	1	2	-1	-2
V118	D	Heaven	1	2	-1	-2
V119	E	Sin	1	2	-1	-2
V120	F	Telepathy	1	2	-1	-2

V121 31 Do you believe in re-incarnation, that is, that we are born into this world again?

A	Yes	1
B	No	2
	Don't know	-1
	No answer	-2

o7 *31a Which is the most important for you?*

1	*2*	*3*	*4*	*5*	*6*	*7*	*8*	*9*	*10*	*-1*	*-2*
to stick to a particular faith						*to explore teachings of different religious traditions*				*DK*	*NA*

o8 *31b Do you believe in angels?*

A	*Yes*	*1*
B	*No*	*2*
	Don't know	*-1*
	No answer	*-2*

SHOW CARD 32

V122 32 Which of these statements comes closest to your beliefs? (Code one answer only)

A	There is a personal God	1
B	There is some sort of spirit or life force	2
C	I don't really know what to think	3
D	I don't really think there is any sort of spirit, God or life force	4
	Don't know	-1
	No answer	-2

SHOW CARD 33

V123 33 And how important is God in your life? Please use this card to indicate - 10 means very important and 1 means not at all important.

1	2	3	4	5	6	7	8	9	10	-1	-2
Not at all									Very	Dk	Na

V124 34 Do you find that you get comfort and strength from religion or not?

A	Yes	1
B	No	2
	Don't know	-1
	No answer	-2

V125 35 Do you take some moments of prayer, meditation or contemplation or something like that?

A	Yes	1
B	No	2
	Don't know	-1
	No answer	-2

SHOW CARD 36

V126 36 How often do you pray to God outside of religious services? Would you say...

A	every day	1
B	more than once a week	2
C	once a week	3
D	at least once a month	4
E	several times a year	5
F	less often	6
G	never	7
	Don't know	-1
	No answer	-2

o9 *36a Do you believe in supernatural forces, which may be expressed in terms like a Life Force, a Mighty Power, God, a Spirit, a Universal Law, a Cosmic Conscience or a Source of all creation?*

A	*Yes, absolutely*	*1*
B	*Yes, somewhat*	*2*
C	*No, not so much*	*3*
D	*No, not at all*	*4*
	Don't know	*-1*
	No answer	*-2*

V127 37 Do you have a lucky charm such as a mascot or a talisman?

A	Yes	1
B	No	2
	Don't know	-1
	No answer	-2

SHOW CARD 38

V128 38 Do you believe that a lucky charm such as a mascot or a talisman can protect or help you?

1	2	3	4	5	6	7	8	9	10	-1	-2
Definitely not									Definitely yes	Dk	Na

o10 *38a How often do you consult your horoscope to know about your future?*

A	*every day*	*1*
B	*at least once a week*	*2*
C	*at least once a month*	*3*
D	*less often*	*4*
E	*never*	*5*
	Don't know	*-1*
	No answer	*-2*

o11 *38b How often do you take this into account in your daily life?*

A	*always*	*1*
B	*most of the time*	*2*
C	*sometimes*	*3*
D	*not very often*	*4*
E	*never*	*5*
	Don't know	*-1*
	No answer	*-2*

SHOW CARD 38

39 How much do you agree or disagree with each of the following:

			Agree strongly	Agree	Neither agree nor disagree	Disagree	Disagree strongly	Dk	Na
v129	A	Politicians who do not believe in God are unfit for public office	1	2	3	4	5	-1	-2
v130	B	Religious leaders should not influence how people vote in elections	1	2	3	4	5	-1	-2

			Agree strongly	Agree	Neither agree nor disagree	Disagree	Disagree strongly	Dk	Na
v131	C	It would be better for **[Britain]** if more people with strong religious beliefs held public office	1	2	3	4	5	-1	-2
v132	D	Religious leaders should not influence government decisions	1	2	3	4	5	-1	-2
o12	*E*	*If a nurse were asked to help perform a legal abortion, she should be allowed to refuse on religious grounds*	*1*	*2*	*3*	*4*	*5*	*-1*	*-2*

SHOW CARD 39a

o13 *39a* *In my opinion, some time should be set aside for prayer, meditation or contemplation in all schools.*

A	*I strongly agree*	*1*
B	*I agree*	*2*
C	*I don't agree nor disagree*	*3*
D	*I strongly disagree*	*4*
	Don't know	*-1*
	No answer	*-2*

SHOW CARD 39b

o14 *39B* *Should books and films that attack religions be prohibited by law or should they be allowed?*

A	*Definitely should be banned*	*1*
B	*Probably should be banned*	*2*
C	*Probably should be allowed*	*3*
D	*Definitely should be allowed*	*4*
E	*Can't choose*	*5*
	Don't know	*-1*
	No answer	*-2*

SHOW CARD 39c

o15 *39c Do you think that the church(es) have an influence on national politics or not?*

A	*yes, absolutely*	*1*
B	*yes, I think so*	*2*
C	*no, I don't think they have*	*3*
D	*no, absolutely not*	*4*
	Don't know	*-1*
	No answer	*-2*

SHOW CARD 40

40 Here is a list of things which some people think make for a successful marriage. Please tell me, for each one, whether you think it is very important, rather important or not very important for a successful marriage? (Read out each item)

			Very	Rather	Not	Dk	Na
v133	A	Faithfulness	1	2	3	-1	-2
v134	B	An adequate income	1	2	3	-1	-2
v135	C	Being of the same social background	1	2	3	-1	-2
v136	D	Mutual respect and appreciation	1	2	3	-1	-2
v137	E	Shared religious beliefs	1	2	3	-1	-2
v138	F	Good housing	1	2	3	-1	-2
v139	G	Agreement on politics	1	2	3	-1	-2
v140	H	Understanding and tolerance	1	2	3	-1	-2
v141	I	Living apart from your in-laws	1	2	3	-1	-2
v142	J	Happy sexual relationship	1	2	3	-1	-2
v143	K	Sharing household chores	1	2	3	-1	-2
v144	L	Children	1	2	3	-1	-2
v145	M	Being willing to discuss the problems that come up between husband and wife	1	2	3	-1	-2
v146	N	Spending as much time together as possible	1	2	3	-1	-2
v147	O	Talking a lot about mutual interests	1	2	3	-1	-2
o16	*P*	*Same etnic background*	*1*	*2*	*3*	*-1*	*-2*

v148 41 If someone says a child needs a home with both a father and a mother to grow up happily, would you tend to agree or disagree?

A	Tend to agree	1
B	Tend to disagree	2
	Don't know	-1
	No answer	-2

v149 42 Do you think that a woman has to have children in order to be fulfilled or is this not necessary?

A	Needs children	1
B	Not necessary	2
	Don't know	-1
	No answer	-2

v150 43 Do you agree or disagree with the following statement? (Read out)

	Agree	Disagree	Dk	Na
Marriage is an outdated institution	1	2	-1	-2

v151 44 If a woman wants to have a child as a single parent, but she doesn't want to have a stable relationship with a man, do you approve or disapprove?

A	Approve	1
B	Disapprove	2
C	Depends	3
	Don't know	-1
	No answer	-2

SHOW CARD 45

45 How would you feel about the following statements? Do you agree or disagree with them?

			Agree strongly	Agree	Neither agree nor disagree	Disagree	Disagree strongly	Dk	Na
v152	A	A man has to have children in order to be fulfilled	1	2	3	4	5	-1	-2
v153	B	A marriage or a long-term stable relationship is necessary to be happy	1	2	3	4	5	-1	-2

SHOW CARD 46

46 People talk about the changing roles of men and women today. For each of the following statements I read out, can you tell me how much you agree with each. Please use the responses on this card.

			Strongly agree	Agree	Disagree	Strongly disagree	Dk	Na
v154	A	A working mother can establish just as warm and secure a relationship with her children as a mother who does not work	1	2	3	4	-1	-2
v155	B	A pre-school child is likely to suffer if his or her mother works	1	2	3	4	-1	-2
v156	C	A job is alright but what most women really want is a home and children	1	2		4	-1	-2
v157	D	Being a housewife is just as fulfilling as working for pay	1	2	3	4	-1	-2
v158	E	Having a job is the best way for a woman to be an independent person	1	2	3	4	-1	-2
v159	F	Both the husband and wife should contribute to household income	1	2	3	4	-1	-2
v160	G	In general, fathers are as well suited to look after their children as mothers	1	2	3	4	-1	-2
V161	H	Men are less able to handle emotions in relationships than women	1	2	3	4	-1	-2

SHOW CARD 47

V162 47 Which of these two statements do you tend to agree with? (Code one answer only)

A Regardless of what the qualities and faults of ones parents are, one must always love and respect them

B One does not have the duty to respect and love parents who have not earned it by their behaviour and attitudes

A	Tend to agree with statement A	1
B	Tend to agree with statement B	2
	Don't know	-1
	No answer	-2

SHOW CARD 48

V163 48 Which of the following statements best describes your views about parents, responsibilities to their children? (Code one only)

A	Parents' duty is to do their best for their children even at the expense of their own well-being	1
B	Parents have a life of their own and should not be asked to sacrifice their own well-being for	2
	the sake of their children	2
C	Neither	3
	Don't know	-1
	No answer	-2

SHOW CARD 49

49 Here is a list of qualities which children can be encouraged to learn at home. Which, if any, do you consider to be especially important? **Please choose up to five? (Code five only)**

			Important	not mentioned
v164	A	Good manners	1	0
v165	B	Independence	1	0
v166	C	Hard work	1	0
v167	D	Feeling of responsibility	1	0
v168	E	Imagination	1	0
v169	F	Tolerance and respect for other people	1	0
v170	G	Thrift, saving money and things	1	0
v171	H	Determination, perseverance	1	0
v172	I	Religious faith	1	0
v173	J	Unselfishness	1	0
v174	K	Obedience	1	0
v175		Don't know	-1	0
v176		No answer	-2	0

SHOW CARD 50

50 Do you approve or disapprove of abortion under the following circumstances?

			Approve	Disapprove	Dk	Na
v177	A	Where the woman is not married	1	2	-1	-2

			Approve	Disapprove	Dk	Na
v178	B	Where a married couple does not want to have any more children	1	2	-1	-2

o17 *51a* *How interested would you say you are in politics?*

A	*Very interested*	*1*
B	*Somewhat interested*	*2*
C	*Not very interested*	*3*
D	*Not at all interested*	*4*
	Don't know	*-1*
	No answer	*-2*

SHOW CARD 51

51 Now I'd like you to look at this card. I'm going to read out some different forms of political action that people can take, and I'd like you to tell me, for each one, whether you have actually done any of these things, whether you might do it or would never, under any circumstances, do it.

			Have Done	Might Do	Would Never do	Dk	Na
v179	A	Signing a petition	1	2	3	-1	-2
v180	B	Joining in boycotts	1	2	3	-1	-2
v181	C	Attending lawful demonstrations	1	2	3	-1	-2
v182	D	Joining unofficial strikes	1	2	3	-1	-2
v183	E	Occupying buildings or factories	1	2	3	-1	-2

SHOW CARD 52

v184 52 Which of these two statements comes closest to your own opinion?

A I find that both freedom and equality are important. But if I were to choose one or the other, I would consider personal freedom more important, that is, everyone can live in freedom and develop without hinderance

B Certainly both freedom and equality are important. But if I were to choose one or the other, I would consider equality more important, that is, that nobody is underprivileged and that social class differences are not so strong

A	Agree with statement A	1
B	Agree with statement B	2
C	Neither	3
	Don't know	-1
	No answer	-2

SHOW CARD 53

v185 53 In political matters, people talk of 'the left' and the 'the right'. How would you place your views on this scale, generally speaking?

1	2	3	4	5	6	7	8	9	10	-1	-2
Left									Right	Dk	Na

SHOW CARD 53

54 Now I'd like you to tell me your views on various issues. How would you place yourviews on this scale?

		1	2	3	4	5	6	7	8	9	10	-1	-2
v186	A	Individuals should take more responsibility for providing for themselves									The state should take more responsibility to ensure that everyone is provided for	Dk	Na
v187	B	People who are unemployed should have to take any job available or lose their unemployment benefits									People who are unemployed should have the right to refuse a job they do not want	Dk	Na
v188	C	Competition is good. It stimulates people to work hard and develop new ideas									Competition is harmful, it brings out the worst in people	Dk	Na
v189	D	The state should give more freedom to firms									The state should control firms more effectively	Dk	Na
o18	*E*	*Incomes should be made more equal*									*There should be greater incentives for individual effort*	*Dk*	*Na*
o19	*F*	*Private ownership of business and industry should be increased*									*Government ownership of business and industry should be increased*	*Dk*	*Na*
o20	*G*	*Each individual should be responsible for arranging his or her own pension*									*The state should be responsible for everyone's pension*	*Dk*	*Na*

		1	*2*	*3*	*4*	*5*	*6*	*7*	*8*	*9*	*10*	*-1*	*-2*
o21	*H*	*Each individual should be responsible for arranging his or her own housing*									*The state should be responsible for everyone's housing*	*Dk*	*Na*

		1	*2*	*3*	*4*	*5*	*6*	*7*	*8*	*9*	*10*	*-1*	*-2*
o22	*I*	*One should be cautious about making major changes in life*									*You will never achieve much unless you act boldly*	*Dk*	*Na*

SHOW CARD 54a

o23 *54a* *On this card are three basic kinds of attitudes vis-à-vis the society we live in. Please choose the one which best describes your own opinion. (Code one only)*

A	*The entire way our society is organised must be radically changed by revolutionary action*	*1*
B	*Our society must be gradually improved by reforms*	*2*
C	*Our present society must be valiantly defended against all subversive forces*	*3*
	Don't know	*-1*
	No answer	*-2*

SHOW CARD 55

v190 55 There is a lot of talk these days about what the aims of this country should be for the next ten years. On this card are listed some of the goals which different people would give top priority. If you had to choose, which of the things on this card would you say is most important? (Code one answer only)

v191 56 And which would be the next most important? (Code one answer only)

		First Choice	Second Choice
A	Maintaining order in the nation	1	1
B	Giving people more say in important government decisions	2	2
C	Fighting rising prices	3	3
D	Protecting freedom of speech	4	4
	Don't know	-1	-1
	No answer	-2	-2

SHOW CARD 56a

o24 *56a Of course we all hope that there will not be another war, but if it were to come to that, would you be willing to fight for your country?*

A	*Yes*	*1*
B	*No*	*2*
	Don't know	*-1*
	No answer	*-2*

SHOW CARD 57

57 Here is a list of various changes in our way of life that might take place in the near future. Please tell me for each one, if it were to happen whether you think it would be a good thing, a bad thing, or don't you mind?

			Good	Bad	Don't mind	Dk	Na
v192	A	Less emphasis on money and material possessions	1	2	3	-1	-2
v193	B	Decrease in the importance of work in our lives	1	2	3	-1	-2
v194	C	More emphasis on the development of technology	1	2	3	-1	-2
v195	D	Greater emphasis on the development of the individual	1	2	3	-1	-2
v196	E	Greater respect for authority	1	2	3	-1	-2
v197	F	More emphasis on family life	1	2	3	-1	-2
v198	G	A simple and more natural lifestyle	1	2	3	-1	-2
v199	H	More power to local authorities	1	2	3	-1	-2

o25 *57a In the long run, do you think the scientific advances we are making will help or harm mankind?*

A	*Will help*	*1*
B	*Will harm*	*2*
C	*Some of each*	*3*
	Don't know	*-1*
	No answer	*-2*

SHOW CARD 58

58 Please look at this card and tell me, for each item listed, how much confidence you have in them, is it a great deal, quite a lot, not very much or none at all?
(Code one answer for each item)

			A great deal	Quite a lot	Not very much	None at all	Dk	Na
v200	A	The church	1	2	3	4	-1	-2
v201	B	The armed forces	1	2	3	4	-1	-2
v202	C	The education system	1	2	3	4	-1	-2
v203	D	The press	1	2	3	4	-1	-2
v204	E	Trade unions	1	2	3	4	-1	-2
v205	F	The police	1	2	3	4	-1	-2
v206	G	Parliament	1	2	3	4	-1	-2
v207	H	Civil service	1	2	3	4	-1	-2
v208	I	The social security system	1	2	3	4	-1	-2
v209	J	The European Union	1	2	3	4	-1	-2
o26	*K*	*NATO*	*1*	*2*	*3*	*4*	*-1*	*-2*
v210	L	United Nations Organization	1	2	3	4	-1	-2
v211	M	Health care system	1	2	3	4	-1	-2
v212	N	The justice system	1	2	3	4	-1	-2
o27	*O*	*Major companies*	*1*	*2*	*3*	*4*	*-1*	*-2*

58a Do you agree or disagree with the following statements on international cooperation?

			Agree strongly	Agree	Disagree	Strongly disagree	Dk	Na
o28	*A*	***[Belgium]** cannot solve its environmental problems by itself, but needs to collaborate with international organisations on environment protection*	*1*	*2*	*3*	*4*	*-1*	*-2*
o29	*B*	***[Belgium]** cannot solve its problem of criminality by itself, but needs to collaborate with international police organisations*	*1*	*2*	*3*	*4*	*-1*	*-2*

			Agree strongly	Agree	Disagree	Strongly disagree	Dk	Na
o30	*C*	***[Belgium]** cannot solve its problems of unemployment by itself, but needs to collaborate with international organisations on economic development*	*1*	*2*	*3*	*4*	*-1*	*-2*

v213 59 On the whole are you very satisfied, rather satisfied, not very satisfied or not at all satisfied with the way democracy is developing in our country?

A	Very satisfied	1
B	Rather satisfied	2
C	Not very satisfied	3
D	Not at all satisfied	4
	Don't know	-1
	No answer	-2

SHOW CARD 60

v214 60 People have different views about the system for governing this country. Here is a scale for rating how well things are going: 1 means very bad; 10 means very good

1	2	3	4	5	6	7	8	9	10	-1	-2
Bad								Very good		Dk	Na

SHOW CARD 60

v215 61 Where on this scale would you put the political system as it was ....
[*in former communist countries*: under communist regime]
[*in countries where recently a change of regime xx has taken place*: under xx regime;]
[*in countries where no regime change has taken place*: ten years ago]?

1	2	3	4	5	6	7	8	9	10	-1	-2
Bad								Very good		Dk	Na

SHOW CARD 60

62 I'm going to describe various types of political systems and ask what you think about each as a way of governing this country. For each one, would you say it is a very good, fairly good, fairly bad or very bad way of governing this country?

			Very good	Fairly good	Fairly bad	Very bad	Dk	Na
v216	A	Having a strong leader who does not have to bother with parliament and elections	1	2	3	4	-1	-2
v217	B	Having experts, not government, make decisions according to what they think is best for the country	1	2	3	4	-1	-2
v218	C	Having the army rule the country	1	2	3	4	-1	-2
v219	D	Having a democratic political system	1	2	3	4	-1	-2

SHOW CARD 60

63 I'm going to read off some things that people sometimes say about a democratic political system. Could you please tell me if you agree strongly, agree, disagree or disagree strongly, after I read each of them?

			Agree strongly	Agree	Disagree	Disagree strongly	Dk	Na
v220	A	Democracy may have problems but it's better than any other form of government	1	2	3	4	-1	-2
v221	B	In democracy, the economic system runs badly	1	2	3	4	-1	-2
v222	C	Democracies are indecisive and have too much squabbling	1	2	3	4	-1	-2
v223	D	Democracies aren't good at maintaining order	1	2	3	4	-1	-2

v224 64 How much respect is there for individual human rights nowadays (in our country)? Do you feel there is (read out):

A	A lot of respect for individual human rights	1
B	Some respect	2
C	Not much respect	3
D	No respect at all	4
	Don't know	-1
	No answer	-2

o31 *64a* *In politics, different parties often hold different views. Which do you think is better?*

A *A party leader should stand firm for what he or she believes, even if others disagree*
or
B *A party leader should be prepared to cooperate with other groups, even if it means compromising some important beliefs*

A	*Agree most with statement A*	*1*
B	*Agree most with statement B*	2
	Don't know	*-1*
	No answer	-2

o32 *64b* *If you had to choose, which would you say is the most important responsibility of government?*

A *To maintain order in society*
or
B *to respect freedom of the individual*

A	*Agree most with statement A*	*1*
B	*Agree most with statement B*	2
	Don't know	*-1*
	No answer	-2

SHOW CARD 65

65 Please tell me for each of the following statements whether you think it can always be justified, never be justified, or something in between, using this card. (Read out statements reversing order for alternate contacts. Code one answer for each statement)

1	2	3	4	5	6	7	8	9	10	-1	-2
Never									Always	Dk	Na

v225 A Claiming state benefits which you are not entitled to
v226 B Cheating on tax if you have the chance
v227 C Taking and driving away a car belonging to someone else (joyriding)
v228 D Taking the drug marijuana or hashish
v229 E Lying in your own interest
v230 F Married men/women having an affair
v231 G Someone accepting a bribe in the course of their duties
v232 H Homosexuality
v233 I Abortion
v234 J Divorce
v235 K Euthanasia (terminating the life of the incurably sick)

v236	L	Suicide
v237	M	Throwing away litter in a public place
v238	N	Driving under the influence of alcohol
v239	O	Paying cash for services to avoid taxes
v240	P	Having casual sex
v241	Q	Smoking in public buildings
v242	R	Speeding over the limit in built-up areas
o33	*S*	*Avoiding a fare on public transport*
o34	*T*	*Sex under the legal age of consent*
o35	*U*	*Prostitution*
o36	*V*	*Political assassinations*
o37	*W*	*Scientific experiments on human embryos*
o38	*X*	*Genetic manipulation of food stuffs*

SHOW CARD 66

66 According to you, how many of your compatriots do the following?

			Almost all	Many	Some	Almost none	Dk	Na
v243	A	Claiming state benefits to which they are not entitled	1	2	3	4	-1	-2
v244	B	Cheating on tax if they have the chance	1	2	3	4	-1	-2
v245	C	Paying cash for services to avoid taxes	1	2	3	4	-1	-2
v246	D	Taking the drug marijuana or hash	1	2	3	4	-1	-2
v247	E	Throwing away litter in a public place	1	2	3	4	-1	-2
v248	F	Speeding over the limit in built-up areas	1	2	3	4	-1	-2
v249	G	Driving under the influence of alcohol	1	2	3	4	-1	-2
v250	H	Having casual sex	1	2	3	4	-1	-2
o39	*I*	*Avoiding a fare on public transport*	*1*	*2*	*3*	*4*	*-1*	-2
o40	*J*	*Lying in their own interest*	*1*	2	*3*	*4*	*-1*	-2
o41	*K*	*Accepting a bribe in the course of their duties*	*1*	2	*3*	*4*	*-1*	-2

SHOW CARD 66a

66a Do you fully agree, agree, disagree, fully disagree with the following statements:
Stealing food in a shop should be punished more severely if:

			Agree strongly	Agree	Agree nor disagree	Disagree	Disagree strongly	Dk	Na
o42	*A*	*the thief is young*	*1*	*2*	*3*	*4*	*5*	*-1*	*-2*
o43	*B*	*the thief is poor*	*1*	*2*	*3*	*4*	*5*	*-1*	*-2*
o44	*C*	*the shop is part of a supermarket chain*	*1*	*2*	*3*	*4*	*5*	*-1*	*-2*

SHOW CARD 67

v251 67 Which of these geographical groups would you say you belong to first of all?

v252 68 And the next?

v253 69 And which do you belong to least of all?

		First	Next	The least
A	Locality or town where you live	1	1	1
B	Region of country where you live	2	2	2
C	Your country as a whole	3	3	3
D	Europe	4	4	4
E	The world as a whole	5	5	5
	Don't know	-1	-1	-1
	No answer	-2	-2	-2

Countries other than UK: Please put in corresponding explanations if necessary)

v254 70 Are you a citizen of Britain? **(Countries other than UK: Please substitute your nation for 'Britain'!)**

A Yes 1 ⟶ go to 71
B No 2 ⟶ go to 72

v255 71 How proud are you to be a British citizen? **(Countries other than UK: Please substitute your nationality for 'British'!)**

A	Very proud	1
B	Quite proud	2
C	Not very proud	3

D	Not at all proud	4
	Don't know	-1
	No answer	-2
	Not applicable	-3

SHOW CARD 71a

o45 *71a Using the responses on this card, could you tell me how much you trust* ***[Britisch]*** *people in general? (Countries other than UK: Please substitute your nationality for 'British')*

A	*Trust them completely*	*1*
B	*Trust them a little*	*2*
C	*Neither trust nor distrust them*	*3*
D	*Do not trust them very much*	*4*
E	*Do not trust them at all*	*5*
	Don't know	*-1*
	No answer	*-2*

SHOW CARD 71b

o46 *71b There is much talk about what the individual member states of the European Community Union have in common and what makes each one distinct. (Interviewer presents illustration with responses and scale from 1 to 7)*

A Some people say: If the European member states were truly to be united, this would mean the end of their national, historical and cultural identities. Their national economic interests would also be sacrificed.

B Others say: Only a truly united Europe can protect its states' national, historical and cultural identities and their national economic interests from the challenges of the superpowers.

Which opinion is closest to your own opinion, the first one or the second one? Please use the scale listed.1 would mean that you agree completely with A and 7 would mean that you agree completely with B. The numbers in between allow you to show which of the opinions you tend to agree with, whether you tend to agree more with the one or with the other.

1	*2*	*3*	*4*	*5*	*6*	*7*	*-1*	*-2*
A						*B*	*Dk*	*Na*

SHOW CARD 72

v256 72 If there was a general election tomorrow, which party would you vote for? (Code one answer under (a) below)

v257 73 If don't know in (a): And which party appeals to you most?(Code one answer under (b) below)

COUNTRY SPECIFIC LIST OF POLITICAL PARTIES!

	a	b
	..	..
I would not vote	96	96
I would cast a blank ballot	97	97
Response refused	-2	-2
Don't know	-1	-1

SHOW CARD 72

v258 74 How about people from less developed countries coming here to work. Which one of the following do you think the government should do?

A	Let anyone come who wants to	1
B	Let people come as long as there are jobs available	2
C	Put strict limits on the number of foreigners who can come here	3
D	Prohibit people coming here from other countries	4
	Don't know	-1
	No answer	-2

o47 *74a Do you tend to agree or disagree with the following statement: The future is so uncertain that it is best to live from day to day*

A	*Tend to agree*	*1*
B	*Tend to disagree*	*2*
	Don't know	*-1*
	No answer	*-2*

SHOW CARD 75

v259 75 Which of these statements is the nearest to your opinion?

A	For the greater good of society it is better if immigrants maintain theirdistinct customs and traditions	1
B	For the greater good of society it is better if immigrants do not maintain their distinct customs and traditions but take over the customs of the country	2
	Don't know	-1
	No answer	-2

SHOW CARD 75

76 In order to be considered "just", what should a society provide? Please tell me for each statement if it is important or unimportant to you. 1 means very important; 5 means not important at all.

			Very important	2	3	4	Not at all important	Dk	Na
v260	A	Eliminating big inequalities in income between citizens	1	2	3	4	5	-1	-2
v261	B	Guaranteeing that basic needs are met for all, in terms of food, housing, cloths, education, health	1	2	3	4	5	-1	-2
v262	C	Recognizing people on their merits	1	2	3	4	5	-1	-2
o48	*D*	*Giving young people equal opportunity to pursue their education irrespective of family income*	*1*	*2*	*3*	*4*	*5*	*-1*	*-2*

SHOW CARD 77

v263 77 How often do you follow politics in the news on television or on the radio or in the daily papers?

A	Every day	1
B	Several times a week	2
C	Once or twice a week	3
D	Less often	4
E	Never	5
	Don't know	-1
	No answer	-2

SHOW CARD 78

78 Can you tell me your opinion on each of the following statements?

			Agree strongly	Agree	Neither agree nor disagree	Disagree	Disagree strongly	Dk	Na
v264	A	If someone has information that may help justice be done, generally he or she should give it to authorities	1	2	3	4	5	-1	-2

			Agree strongly	Agree	Neither agree nor disagree	Disagree	Disagree strongly	Dk	Na
v265	B	People should stick to their own affairs and not show too much interest in what others say or do	1	2	3	4	5	-1	-2

SHOW CARD 79

79 To what extent do you feel concerned about the living conditions of:

			Very much	Much	To a certain extent	Not so much	Not at all	DK	Na
v266	A	Your immediate family	1	2	3	4	5	-1	-2
v267	B	People in your neighbourhood	1	2	3	4	5	-1	-2
v268	C	The people of the region you live in	1	2	3	4	5	-1	-2
v269	D	Your fellow countrymen	1	2	3	4	5	-1	-2
v270	E	Europeans	1	2	3	4	5	-1	-2
v271	F	Human kind	1	2	3	4	5	-1	-2

SHOW CARD 80

80 To what extent do you feel concerned about the living conditions of:

			Very much	Much	To a certain extent	Not so much	Not at all	DK	Na
v272	A	elderly people in your country	1	2	3	4	5	-1	-2
v273	B	unemployed people in your country	1	2	3	4	5	-1	-2
v274	C	immigrants in your country	1	2	3	4	5	-1	-2
v275	D	sick and disabled people in your country	1	2	3	4	5	-1	-2

SHOW CARD 81

81 Would you be prepared to actually do something to improve the conditions of:

			Absolutely yes	Yes	Maybe yes/ maybe no	No	Absolutely no	DK	Na
v276	A	your immediate family	1	2	3	4	5	-1	-2
v277	B	people in your neighbourhood/ community	1	2	3	4	5	-1	-2
v278	C	elderly people in your country	1	2	3	4	5	-1	-2
v279	D	immigrants in your country	1	2	3	4	5	-1	-2
v280	E	sick and disabled people in your country	1	2	3	4	5	-1	-2

INTERVIEWER: ONLY those who have absolutely yes or yes on 81c!

SHOW CARD 82

82 There can be several reasons to do something to help the elderly people your country. Please tell me for each of the reasons I am going to read out, if they apply to you or not. (Code an answer for each reason).

			Very much	Much	To a certain extent	Not so much	Not at all	DK	Na	Nap
v281	A	Because you feel you have a moral duty to help	1	2	3	4	5	-1	-2	-3
v282	B	Because you sympathize with them	1	2	3	4	5	-1	-2	-3
v283	C	Because it is in the interest of society	1	2	3	4	5	-1	-2	-3
v284	D	Because it is in your own interest	1	2	3	4	5	-1	-2	-3
v285	E	To do something in return	1	2	3	4	5	-1	-2	-3

INTERVIEWER: ONLY those who have absolutely yes or yes on 81d!

SHOW CARD 83

83 There can be several reasons to do something to help immigrants in your country. Please tell me for each of the reasons I am going to read out, if they apply to you or not? (Code an answer for each reason)

			Very much	Much	To a certain extent	Not so much	Not at all	DK	Na	Nap
v286	A	Because you feel you have a moral duty to help	1	2	3	4	5	-1	-2	-3
v287	B	Because you sympathize with them	1	2	3	4	5	-1	-2	-3
v288	C	Because it is in the interest of society	1	2	3	4	5	-1	-2	-3
v289	D	Because it is in your own interest	1	2	3	4	5	-1	-2	-3
v290	E	To do something in return	1	2	3	4	5	-1	-2	-3

INCLUDE COUNTRY-SPECIFIC QUESTIONS HERE

ASK ALL
DEMOGRAPHICS

v291 84 Sex of respondent

A male 1
B female 2

v292 85 Can you tell me your year of birth, please 19..

v293 86 Whether you are married or not: Do you live in a stable relationship with a partner?

A Yes 1
B No 2 → go to 88

v294 87 Are you legally married to this partner?

A Yes 1 → go to 90
B No 2 → go to 89
Not applicable -3

v295 88 Did you ever live in a stable relationship before, i.e. without being married?

A	Yes	1
B	No	2
	Not applicable	-3

v296 89 What is your current legal marital status?

A	Married	1	
B	Widowed	2	
C	Divorced	3	⟶ go to 91
D	Separated	4	
E	Never married	5	⟶ go to 91
	Don't know	-1	
	No answer	-2	
	Not applicable	-3	

v297 90 Have you ever been divorced?

A	Yes	1
B	No	2
	Don't know	-1
	No answer	-2
	Not applicable	-3

v298 91 How many children, including deceased children, have you yourself ever had?
.... (write in)

92 How many people, including yourself, are currently living in your household?

v299	A	Aged 18 and over	......
v300	B	Aged between 13 and 17	......
v301	C	Aged between 5 and 12	......
v302	D	Under 5	......

v303 93 At what age did you (or will you) complete your full time education, either at school or at an institution of higher education? Please exclude apprenticeships. (*Interviewer instruction: If respondent is still at school, ask: at what age do you expect you will have completed your education?*) (Write in age) ....

v304 94 What is the highest level you have reached in your education?
To be measured as detailed as possible on national level and to be transformed into this variable:

A	Inadequately completed elementary education	1
B	Completed (compulsory) elementary education	2
C	(Compulsory) elementary education and basic vocational qualification	3
D	Secondary, intermediate vocational qualification	4
E	Secondary, intermediate general qualification	5
F	Full secondary, maturity level certificate	6
G	Higher education – lower-level tertiary certificate	7
H	Higher education – upper-level tertiary certificate	8

v305 95 Do you live with your parents?

A	Yes	1
B	No	2

v306 96 Are you yourself employed now or not? If yes: About how many hours a week? (If more than one job: only for the main job)

Has paid employment		
30 hours a week or more	1	
Less than 30 hours a week	2	
Self employed	3	→ go to 100
If no paid employment		
Retired/pensioned	4	→ go to 101
Housewife not otherwise employed	5	→ go to 105
Student	6	→ go to 105
Unemployed	7	→ go to 104
Other (Please specify)	8	→ go to 105

v307 97 In your present job, do you supervise anyone who is directly responsible to you?

A	Yes	1	
B	No	2	→ go to 101
	Don't know	-1	
	No answer	-2	

v308 98 How many people do you supervise? ...... (write in number)

v309 99 How many other people usually work for the organization? .... (write in number) → go to 101

v310 100 How many employees do you have? ...... (write in number)

101 In which profession/industry do you or did you work? (If more than one job: the main job) (Write in) ....

v311 **Code according to ISCO88**

102 What is/was your job there? (Write in and code below)........................

v312 103
a Employer/manager of establishment with 10 or more employees 1
b Employer/manager of establishment with less then 10 employees 2
c professional worker (lawyer, accountant, teacher etc.) 3
d Middle level non-manual - office worker etc. 4
e Junior level non-manual - office worker etc. 5
f Foreman and supervisor 6
g Skilled manual worker 7
h Semi-skilled manual worker 8
i Unskilled manual worker 9
j Farmer: employer, manager on own account 10
k Agricultural worker 11
l Member of armed forces 12
m Never had a job 13
Don't know -1
No answer -2

v313 **Code according to ISCO88** ....

v314 104 And for how long are you unemployed?

A Less than half a year 1
B Between half a year and one year 2
C One year 3
D Between one and two years 4
E Two years 5
F More than two years 6
Don't know -1
No answer -2
Not applicable -3

v315 105 Are you the chief wage earner?

A Yes 1 ⟶ 110
B No 2

v316 106 Is the chief wage earner employed now or not?

A Yes 1
B No 2
Don't know -1
No answer -2
Not applicable -3

107 In which profession/industry does/did he (she) work? (Write in)

....

v317 **Code according to ISCO88** ....

108 What is/was his/her job? (Write in and code below) ....

v318 109

a	Employer/manager, of establishment with 10 or more employees	1
b	Employer/manager of establishment with less then 10 employees	2
c	Professional worker (lawyer, accountant, teacher etc.)	3
d	Middle level non-manual - office worker etc.	4
e	Junior level non-manual - office worker etc.	5
f	Foreman and supervisor	6
g	Skilled manual worker	7
h	Semi-skilled manual worker	8
i	Unskilled manual worker	9
j	Farmer:employer, manager on own account	10
k	Agricultural worker	11
l	Member of armed forces	12
m	Never had a job	13
	Don't know	-1
	No answer	-2
	Not applicable	-3

v319 **Code according to ISCO88** ....

ASK ALL
SHOW INCOME CARD

v320 110 Here is a scale of incomes and we would like to know in what group your household is, counting all wages, salaries, pensions and other incomes that come in. Just give the letter of the group your household falls into, after taxes and other deductions.

1	2	3	4	5	6	7	8	9	10	-1	-2
										Dk	Na

o49 *110a* *Interviewer code by yourself*
Socio-ecomonic status of respondent

A	*AB (upper, uppr-middle class)*	*1*
B	*C1 (middle, non-manual workers)*	*2*
C	*C2 (manual workers -skilled, semi-skilled)*	*3*
D	*DE (manual workers -unskilled, unemployed)*	*4*

v321 111 Town where the interview was conducted. (Please write in) ....

NB: ZIP code and/or official statistical code for place of living

v322 112 Size of town

Under 2.000	1	5 - 10.000	2
2 - 5.000	3	10 - 20.000	4
20 - 50.000	5	100 - 500.000	7
50 - 100.000	6	500.000 and more	8

v332 113 Region: (Please write in) .... **(code + label)**

o50 *Date of the interview:............(day , month)*

Total length of interview

o51 *...........Hours*

o52 *...........Minutes*

o53 *114 During the interview the respondent was ...*

A	*Very interested*	*1*
B	*Somewhat interested*	*2*
C	*Not very interested*	*3*

Appendix: list of variables on CD-ROM, but not in the Source Book

For reasons of space, we haven't included all the existing variables in the present source book. Doing so would have turned an already large book into an immense book. Variables that were not asked in all, or almost all surveys in a given wave, have been omitted. All variables *are* included in the accompanying CD-ROM, however.

The CD-ROM has an auto run feature that will make the program run upon inserting it. If it doesn't start automatically, you may execute JDSSURVEY.EXE from the root directory. The program allows browsing all included documentation, survey results with a select, and click interface. All included documentation can also be found in the \DATA folder of this CD-ROM.

The additional variables that can be found in the CD-ROM are grouped in three categories:

- IVS variables: This is the set of variables included in a special Islamic Values Survey module, integrated within the WVS wave. The detailed variables are:

LABEL	VARIABLE
Government protects freedom	F108
Government protects religion	F109
Laws: people's wishes	F110
Laws of the shari'a	F111
Justifiable: Drinking alcohol	F124
Aggression from neighboring country.	E184
Exploitation of local resources	E185
Cultural invasion by the west	E186
Where R lived after married	X010
Woman wearing weil	D067
Woman good mother	D068
Woman good wife	D069
Woman religious	D070

LABEL	VARIABLE
Woman educated	D071
More than one wife	D076
Wife must obey	D077
Woman being independent	D072
Woman having work outside home	D073
Woman maintaining her family	D074
Woman being sociable	D075

- Country variations of “Neighbours” question:

LABEL	VARIABLE
Neighbours: Evangelists	A134
Neighbours: People of a different religion	A135
Neighbours: People same religion	A136
Neighbours: Militant minority	A137
Neighbours: Zoroastrians	A138
Neighbours: People not from country of origin	A139
Neighbours: Political extremists	A141
Neighbours: trafficants	A142
Neighbours: Indians or Lebanese	A143
Neighbours: Chinese or Philippino-Chinese	A144
Neighbours: Spiritists	A145
Neighbours: Protestants	A146
Neighbours: Christians	A147
Neighbours: Witchdoctors and related labels	A148

- Country variations of “Confidence in institutions” question:

LABEL	VARIABLE
Confidence: the Arab League	E089
Confidence: the Association of South East Asian nations —ASEAN	E090
Confidence: the Organisation for African Unity-OAU	E091
Confidence: the NAFTA	E092
Confidence: the Andean Pact	E093
Confidence: the Mercosur	E094

LABEL	VARIABLE
Confidence: the SAARC	E095
Confidence: the ECO	E096
Confidence: the APEC	E097
Confidence: the Tratado de Libre Comercio	E098
Confidence: the Organización de Estados Unidos Americanos (OEA)	E099
Confidence: the Movimiento en pro de Vieques (Puerto Rico)	E100
Confidence: local/regional government	E101
Confidence: SADC/SADEC	E102
Confidence: East African Cooperation (EAC)	E103
Confidence: the Presidence	E103B
Confidence: the civil society groups	E103C

- WVS-2000 optional questions:

LABEL	VARIABLE
Egalitarian vs. Competitive society	E063
Extensive welfare vs. Low taxes	E064
Regulated vs. Responsible society	E065
Should: egalitarian vs. Competitive	E066
Should: extensive welfare or low taxes	E067
Should: regulated — responsible	E068
Rate political system in 10 years	E113

- Country specific questions:

LABEL	VARIABLE
Which of the following best describes you	G015
Language at home	G016
Party that would never vote	E182
Education (country specific)	X025CS
Size of town (country specific)	X049CS
Ethnic group	X051

Index

Printed by Programas Educativos, S. A. de C. V.
Calz. Chabacano núm. 65 local A, Col. Asturias
06850, México, D. F.
August 2004

Printing house certificated by
Instituto Mexicano de Normalización y Certificación, A. C.
followin the ISO-9002: 1994 / NMX-CC-004: 1995
(registration number RSC-048)
and ISO 14000: 1996 NMX-SSA-001: 1998 IMNC
(registration number RSSA-003) standards.